Relationship Section

Rotated Alphabetical Terms Section

Alphabetical Term Clusters Section

Margin Index: To use, bend pages of book backward and follow
margin index to pages with black edge markers.

Thesaurus

OF PSYCHOLOGICAL INDEX TERMS

TWENTIETH
ANNIVERSARY
1974-1994

Alvin Walker, Jr., Editor

SEVENTH EDITION

■

Library of Congress Cataloging-in-Publication Data

Thesaurus of psychological index terms. — 7th ed. / Alvin Walker,
Jr., editor.
     p.   cm.
    "Twentieth anniversary 1974–1994."
    ISBN 1-55798-225-2 : $75.00
    1. Subject headings—Psychology.   2. Psychology—Abstracting and
indexing.   I. Walker, Alvin, 1959– .
Z695.1.P7T48   1994
025.4'915—dc20   93-44714
                                                CIP

Printed in the United States of America
ISBN 1-55798-225-2

Table of Contents

History of the *Thesaurus*

Psychology has multiple roots in the older disciplines of philosophy, medicine, education, and physics. As a result, the vocabulary of the psychological literature is characterized by considerable diversity. As the field has grown, each new generation of psychologists has added to the vocabulary in attempting to describe their studies and perceptions of behavioral processes. This uncontrolled evolution of the psychological vocabulary has contributed to complex literature search and retrieval problems.

In response to these problems, the American Psychological Association developed the first edition of the *Thesaurus of Psychological Index Terms* in 1974. This controlled vocabulary was designed to provide a means of structuring the subject matter of psychology and to serve as an efficient indexing and retrieval tool. Since the publication of the first edition, the PsycINFO indexing staff has charted trends and newly emerging areas of interest reflected in the psychological literature as a way of updating and revising the *Thesaurus*. The present edition represents a concerted effort to provide a more valuable tool for researchers, practitioners, students, information science providers, and others interested in the field of psychology.

First Edition (1974)

Term selection was the first step in the development of the 1974 edition. The 800 index terms used by *Psychological Abstracts* (PA) prior to 1973 and a list of the frequencies of the occurrence of single words in titles and abstracts in PA over a 5-year period were taken as the starting points. In addition, phrases and terms were obtained from keyword-in-context (KWIC) lists produced from 10,000 titles of journal articles, books, separates, and dissertations. Inclusion/exclusion rules were developed, with a resulting list of about 3,000 potential terms reviewed by subject matter specialists for final selection. These terms were arranged to express interrelationships, including use, used for, broader, narrower, and related categories.

Second Edition (1977)

The first major revision of the *Thesaurus*, which included 204 new terms, was published in 1977. Some 180 never-used terms from the original *Thesaurus* were deleted, and a rotated alphabetical term section was added to make it faster and easier to find index terms.

Third Edition (1982)

The second major revision of the *Thesaurus*, which included 240 new terms, was published in 1982. The most significant change introduced in the third edition, was the development of scope notes or definitions for over 1,300 terms. In addition superscript dates were added to all terms to indicate the date of inclusion in the *Thesaurus* vocabulary.

Fourth Edition (1985)

The third major revision of the *Thesaurus* included 247 new terms and over 162 new and revised scope notes. Posting notes (PN) were added to each index term to indicate the number of times the terms had been used for indexing. Dates were added to each index term to show in what year it was added to the Thesaurus vocabulary. Also, each postable index term was given a unique five-digit code that can be used in online searching as an alternative to entering the term text.

Fifth Edition (1988)

An important change occurred during the fourth major revision—incorporation of all nonpostable terms into the Rotated Alphabetical Terms Section. These terms appeared in nonbold italic print and marked with a star (★). Over 250 postable terms and 100 nonpostable terms were added to the vocabulary. In addition, over 100 new scope notes were added and over 75 scopes notes were revised. Because the *Thesaurus* had been in use for many years, an extensive hierarchy reconstruction project was begun with the intention of continuing the process for future editions.

Sixth Edition (1991)

The fifth major revision of the *Thesaurus* included the addition of 238 new postable terms and 100 new nonpostable terms. Over 50 scope notes were rewritten and 120 new scope notes were added to the vocabulary. In a continuing effort to make the *Thesaurus* more useful, the Relationship Section was enhanced by the addition of down arrows (↓) in each main term's hierarchy next to narrower and related terms that also have narrower terms. Alphabetical Term Clusters were developed to present a collection of index terms based on conceptual similarity to assist users unfamiliar with the *Thesaurus* vocabulary. As in earlier editions, revision of existing hierarchical relationships continued.

Development of the Seventh Edition (1994)

New Terms

Since the publication of the sixth edition, 219 new postable index terms and 114 nonpostable index terms have been added to the seventh edition. The new terms represent concepts and terminology expressed in the psychological and behavioral literature as well as the literature found in fringe areas of psychology, e.g., social work, education, or sociology. In addition, new terminology was developed for classic psychological concepts requiring appropriate controlled vocabulary. These additions to the vocabulary brings the total number of postable and nonpostable index terms to 7,311.

The criteria for index term inclusion involved: (1) the frequency of the term's occurrence in the psychological literature, (2) the term's potential usefulness in providing access to a concept, (3) the term's relationship to or overlap with existing *Thesaurus* terminology, and (4) user feedback and need. Every term has been researched extensively and integrated into the hierarchies in the Relationship Section. See **Appendix A** for a list of all new postable index terms and **Appendix B** for a list of all new nonpostable index terms added to the Seventh Edition.

New Features

Restructured Rotated Alphabetical Terms Section

In a continuing effort to make the *Thesaurus* a more useful product, nonpostable terms were added to the Rotated Alphabetical Terms Section in 1988, the fifth edition. However, because nonpostable terms are not used during the indexing process and are primarily natural language entry points into the vocabulary, users had to refer to the Relationship Section for the appropriate "**Use**" term. Now, for the first time, nonpostable terms will appear with their appropriate "**Use**" term in the Rotated Section.

New Alphabetical Term Cluster

Clusters were developed for the 1991 Edition primarily for our users who are unfamiliar with the *Thesaurus* vocabulary. This section presents a collection of index terms based on likeness and similarity. For this edition, a new "Neuropsychology and Neurology" cluster with 7 subclusters was added (see User Guide for more detailed information).

Other Changes

Posting Notes

Primarily as an aid to psychologists, researchers, librarians, and students, each postable index term in the Relationship Section appears with a posting note (**PN**) reference indicating how many times that index term has been used in the indexing process at the time of this publication. These posting notes are based on cumulations of term usage through June 1993. Index terms with posting notes (**PN**) = 0 are new 1994 terms that have been added to this edition, have not been used in the indexing process, and have yet to accumulate any postings.

Scope Notes

Approximately 110 new scope notes (**SN**s) have been added to the existing 1,970 scope notes in the sixth edition (1991). These include scope notes for many of the new 1994 terms as well as for old terms that existed prior to publication of this edition. Approximately 20 scope notes have been rewritten or revised to improve clarity, broaden or restrict a term's range of application, or accommodate new 1994 terms.

Term Hierarchies

Extensive revision of hierarchical relationships occurred during the development of this edition. Hierarchies were examined to ensure accuracy, completeness, and consistency. Over 1,190 hierarchies were revised to minimize any misleading and redundant relationships as well as to maintain a coherent and cohesive vocabulary structure.

Array Terms

In past editions, array term status represented conceptually broad areas of subject matter, e.g., education or treatment. There were 45 terms that were easily identified by a slash (/) following each term. With this edition, the slash has been dropped and the hierarchies for these terms reconstructed to include both narrower and related terms. These terms continue to represent conceptual broad areas and are used in the indexing and searching process when a more specific term is not available.

User Guide

General Information

Word Form Conventions

Conventions dealing with singular and plural word forms, direct and indirect entries, abbreviations, acronyms, homographs, and punctuation have been used to ensure standardization of the *Thesaurus* vocabulary. For example, noun forms are preferred entries, with the plural form used when the term is a noun that can be qualified (e.g., **Computers**, **College Students**, or **Employment Tests**) and the singular form when the term refers to processes, properties, or conditions (e.g., **Learning, Grief,** or **Rehabilitation**). Direct entry or natural word order is preferred when a concept is represented by two or more words (e.g., **Mental Health** vs "Health, Mental" or **Artificial Intelligence** vs "Intelligence, Artificial").

Some terms that would exceed the 36 character limit if completely spelled out are abbreviated (e.g., **Minn Multiphasic Personality Inven** and **Rotter Intern Extern Locus Cont Scal**). A selected number of acronyms are also used, such as **DOPA**, **REM Sleep,** and **ROTC Students**. In cases where ambiguity may occur and to clarify the meaning of homographs, qualifying expressions are included in parentheses (e.g., **Culture (Anthropological)**, **Conservation (Ecological Behavior)**, and **Reconstruction (Learning)**).

Term Relationships

The terms in the Relationship Section are displayed to reflect the following relationships:

USE. Directs the user from a term that cannot be used (nonpostable) to a term that can be used (postable) in indexing and searching. The **Use** reference indicates preferred forms of synonyms, abbreviations, spelling, and word sequence:

> Language Handicaps
> **Use** Language Disorders

UF (Used For). Reciprocal of the **Use** Reference. Terms listed as **UF** (used for) references represent some but not all of the most frequently encountered synonyms, abbreviations, alternate spellings, or word sequences:

> **Language Disorders** [82]
> **UF** Language Handicaps

B (Broader Term) and **N (Narrower Term).** Reciprocal designators used to indicate hierarchical relationships:

> **Academic Achievement** [67]
> **B** Achievement [67]
>
> **Achievement** [67]
> **N** Academic Achievement [67]

R (Related Term). Reciprocal designator used to indicate relationships that are semantic or conceptual, but not hierarchical. Related term references indicate to searchers or indexers terms that they may not have considered, but may be related to their topic of interest:

> **Achievement Motivation** [67]
> **R** Fear of Success [78]

Relationship Section

Each *Thesaurus* term is listed alphabetically and, as appropriate, is cross-referenced and displayed with its broader, narrower, and related terms (i.e., subterms). The date of the term's inclusion in the *Thesaurus* appears as a superscript. Each postable subterm in a main term's hierarchy also has its date of inclusion shown. Ten dates can be found: '67, '71, '73, '78, '82, '84, '85, '88, '91, and '94. The subject code (**SC**) gives the unique five-digit code associated with the term, and can be used to retrieve records instead of entering the term text on any online search system.

Each postable index term in the Relationship Section appears with a posting note (**PN**) reference indicating how many times that term has been used in the indexing of PsycINFO/PsycLIT records. Posting notes are based on cumulations of term usage through June 1993. Terms with PN=0 are new 1994 terms that have been added to this edition and have yet to accumulate any postings. These terms will appear in the next edition of the *Thesaurus* with appropriate posting notes.

Many terms that have ambiguous meanings, applications unique to the PsycINFO database, or usage patterns that have changed over time have scope notes (**SN**). In many cases, a scope note provides a definition and/or information on proper use of the term. The scope note always refers to the one term with which it is associated and does not necessarily have implications for the subterms dis-

played in the term's hierarchy. The following are examples of some of the scope notes found in the Relationship Section:

Definition and usage

Social Isolation [67]
SN Voluntary or involuntary absence of contact with others. Used for human or animal populations.

Change in usage

Brain Lesions [67]
SN Not defined prior to 1982. From 1982 limited to experimentally induced lesions and used primarily for animal populations.

Mandatory application

School Age Children [73]
SN Ages 6-12 years. Used in noneducational contexts. Application of terms designating age is mandatory for ages 0-17.

Change in status

Phobic Neurosis
SN Term discontinued in 1988. Use Phobic Neurosis to access references from 73-87.

Nonpostable index terms, those not used in the indexing process, are shown in nonbold print with an appropriate **USE** reference. Nonpostable terms are provided as points of entry into the *Thesaurus* vocabulary.

The following example from the Relationship Section illustrates a nonpostable term entry:

Nonpostable Index Term   Working Memory

Use Term   **USE** Short Term
(postable index term)   Memory [67]

Finally, the Relationship Section has been augmented by the use of down arrows (↓) in front of any narrower (**N**) or related (**R**) terms that have narrower terms themselves. This feature alerts the user to consider another more specific hierarchical level. The PsycINFO database is indexed to the level of specificity in a given document. In using the Relationship Section and in choosing index terms, consider following any main term's subterms (**N** and **R** terms only) to its lowest level of specificity by turning to the page in the *Thesaurus* where the narrower (**N**) or related (**R**) subterm appears as a main entry to determine if more specific terminology is available.

The following example from the Relationship Section illustrates the various components that may be included in the hierarchy of a postable index term:

Postable Index Term   **Multivariate Analysis** [82]
(with date of entry)

Posting Note and Subject Code   **PN**   560   **SC** 32513

Scope Note   **SN**   Any statistical technique designed to measure the influence of many independent variables acting simultaneously on more than one dependent variable.

Used for term   **UF**   Canonical Correlation
(nonpostable term)

Broader Term   **B**   Statistical Analysis [67]

Narrower Terms   **N**   ↓ Factor Analysis [67]
(Down arrow indicates   Multiple Regression [82]
more specific terms)   Path Analysis [91]

Related Terms   **R**   Analysis of Covariance [73]
(Down arrow indicates   Analysis of Variance [67]
more specific terms)   ↓ Statistical Correlation [67]
          ↓ Statistical Regression [85]

Rotated Alphabetical Terms Section

Many terms represent concepts not expressed in a single word, therefore postable and nonpostable *Thesaurus* terms in this section are listed in alphabetical order by each word contained within them. The Rotated Alphabetical Terms Section is useful in finding all *Thesaurus* terms that have a particular word in common. This display groups related terms when they may otherwise be separated in the alphabetical Relationship Section. It is important to note that this section should be used in conjunction with the Relationship Section since hierarchies, scope notes, posting notes, and term dates do not appear. A term containing three words will appear in three locations in the Rotated Alphabetical Terms Section as illustrated below:

> **Academic** Underachievement
> College   **Academic** Achievement
> **Acalculia**

> **Achievement** Potential
> College Academic **Achievement**
> Mathematics **Achievement**

> **Collective** Behavior
> **College** Academic Achievement
> **College** Dropouts

Nonpostable index terms (terms not used for indexing) are represented in nonbold print followed by the appropriate **"Use"** term in italics. Each word of the term, just like the postable terms above, appear in different locations depending on how many words are contained in the index term as illustrated below:

> **Illumination**
> Illumination Therapy *USE Phototherapy*
> Autokinetic **Illusion**

> Hormone **Therapy**
> Illumination Therapy *USE Phototherapy*
> Implosive **Therapy**

Some *Thesaurus* terms have unusual spellings because of a term length limitation of 36 characters, e.g., **Mental Retardation (Attit Toward)** or **Minn Multiphasic Personality Inven**. The shortened word contained in these terms will appear in alphabetical order as if the word were spelled out completely:

> Mental Illness **(Attitudes** Toward)
> Mental Retardation **(Attit** Toward)
> Middle Class **Attitudes**

> **Minks**
> **Minn** Multiphasic Personality Inven
> **Minnesota** Teacher Attitude Inventory

Alphabetical Term Clusters Section

Clusters are collections of index terms that are related to one another conceptually rather than hierarchically, and are displayed together under broad subject categories. This permits all terms in each cluster to be seen collectively.

Clusters provide an entry point into the *Thesaurus* vocabulary by allowing a large group of similar terms to be scanned easily and efficiently, and helping the user translate their search vocabulary into *Thesaurus* vocabulary. In a sense, the clusters present an "index" to the indexing vocabulary. It is important to note the Clusters Section cannot be used by itself. More detailed information regarding particular index terms can be found in the Relationship Section. The Relationship Section should always be consulted for additional term information, e.g., scope notes, posting notes, hierarchies, and dates for term inclusion.

There are approximately 3,000 postable index terms in the Clusters Section. They are arranged under subclusters of nine broad cluster areas. Terms can appear in more than one broad cluster and also more than one subcluster under any broad area, if appropriate. The Alphabetical Term Clusters and Subclusters are listed in the table on the following page:

Alphabetical Clusters and Subclusters

Disorders Cluster
Antisocial Behavior & Behavior Disorders
Diagnosis
Disorder Characteristics
Learning Disorders & Mental Retardation
Physical & Psychosomatic Disorders
Psychological Disorders
Speech & Language Disorders
Symptomatology

Educational Cluster
Academic Learning & Achievement
Curricula
Educational Personnel & Administration
Educational Testing & Counseling
Schools & Institutions
Special Education
Student Characteristics & Academic
    Environment
Student Populations
Teaching & Teaching Methods

Geographic Cluster
Africa
Antarctica
Asia
Central America
Europe
Latin America
North America
Pacific Islands
South America
West Indies

Legal Cluster
Adjudication
Criminal Groups
Criminal Offenses
Criminal Rehabilitation
Laws
Legal Issues
Legal Personnel
Legal Processes

Neuropsychology & Neurology Cluster
Assessment & Diagnosis
Electrophysiology
Neuroanatomy
Neurological Disorders
Neurological Intervention
Neurosciences
Neurotransmitters & Neuroregulators

Occupational & Employment Cluster
Career Areas
Employee, Occupational & Job Characteristics
Management & Professional Personnel Issues
Occupational Groups
Organizations & Organizational Behavior
Personnel Management

Statistical Cluster
Design, Analysis & Interpretation
Statistical Reliability & Validity
Statistical Theory & Experimentation

Tests & Testing Cluster
Academic Achievement & Aptitude Measures
Attitude & Interest Measures
Intelligence Measures
Nonprojective Personality Measures
Perceptual Measures
Projective Personality Measures
Testing
Testing Methods

Treatment Cluster
Alternative Therapies
Behavior Modification
Counseling
Hospitalization & Institutionalization
Medical & Physical Treatment
Psychotherapy
Rehabilitation
Treatment (General)
Treatment Facilities

Searching Using the *Thesaurus*

Introduction

Using the *Thesaurus of Psychological Index Terms* to search PsycINFO, PsycLIT, ClinPSYC, and *Psychological Abstracts* (PA) can enhance the precision of your retrieved references and guide you to closely related topics that you may otherwise have missed. For effective searches and development of comprehensive search strategies, follow the steps outlined below:

1. Select a search topic

   Example: "I'm interested in high schoolers and AIDS."

2. Specifically define the concepts of the topic using single or multiple word phrases and develop a list of synonyms that represent the concepts. This can include independent and/or dependent experimental variables and/or a population. A properly defined concept can result in an efficient search with precise retrieval of highly relevant articles, and will also reduce the need to scan and eliminate irrelevant references. The following example shows a more specific and defined topic.

   Example: "I'm interested in AIDS educational and prevention programs for high school students."

3. Look up your concepts in the *Thesaurus of Psychological Index Terms*. Start in any of the three sections depending on your topic and familiarity with *Thesaurus* vocabulary. The Clusters Section includes clusters of index terms grouped into 9 categories. This section is useful to consult if you are unfamiliar with the vocabulary or need a guide to related concepts in a particular area of psychology. The Rotated Section is helpful in finding terms that include the concept sought, even if the searcher is unsure of the word order. Consulting this section can also reduce key strokes in an electronic search by showing groups of terms with a single word

in common, which can be retrieved by a simple one-word command. The Relationship Section, the heart of the *Thesaurus* includes scope notes to describe how terms are used, as well as posting notes, subject codes, term dates, and the critical *used for, broader, narrower,* and *related* terms. The most important things to look for in the Relationship Section are the narrower terms and the dates for main term entry (for indexing articles received after that date). Also note each entry's posting notes, which is a rough guide to the number of articles you can expect to find under that term. To retrieve articles relevant to terms before their inclusion in the *Thesaurus*, consider their broader concepts as index terms or use free-text strategies to find records added to the database before the starting date.

It is important to remember that all PsycINFO products are indexed to each article's level of specificity. For example, an author who calls an experimental population "high school students" will find this article indexed under "**High School Students**", not the broader and less specific term, "**Students**". Therefore, any applicable narrower terms should be added as synonyms to the list of index terms in your search. Related terms may also closely match a search topic, and should be considered carefully when formulating a strategy.

Examples:

   a. Acquired Immune Deficiency Syndrome (This is the term PsycINFO uses for AIDS)

   b. Educational Programs or Health Education or AIDS Prevention (These terms can be used to describe the concept of educational and prevention programs)

   c. High School Students or High Schools or Secondary Education (These terms form the context of high school education.

Searching in *Psychological Abstracts* (PA)

Look up the previous *Thesaurus* terms in the annual *PA* Subject Volume Indexes from your years of interest—typically the most recent year first—and work backward. Start with the terms you consider most relevant to your search. If all the terms are of equal relevance, begin with the one with the fewest postings. You will find a short key phrase to describe each article indexed with that term. Select the most relevant phrases, then note the volume, which is printed on the spine of the index, and the abstract number, which is listed after each phrase in the index.

A separate Brief Subject Index appears at the back of each monthly issue of *PA* as a guide to that issue's contents only. No phrases are included in this index. The Brief Subject Index allows access to the current literature otherwise available only in the annual Volume Indexes published at the end of each year.

The final step in the search is to look up the abstracts themselves from the individual monthly issues of *PA*, using the volume and abstract numbers as a guide. Read the abstracts, then copy the citations of the ones of interest in order to locate the complete articles. Abstracts should never be used as substitutes for original articles.

Searching on Electronic Systems (Online or CD-ROM)

Each vendor system that carries PsycINFO, PsycLIT, or ClinPSYC operates differently, yet each has the capability to limit a search to the descriptor or index term field. Online and CD-ROM search systems give you the opportunity to manipulate your search statement to provide precision and recall in retrieval. Formulate your topic and refer to the *Thesaurus* for appropriate terminology, then consult **Appendix D**, a quick reference guide to all vendor systems, to determine how to enter index terms as descriptors. Also, refer to **Appendix D** for other specific field names and search examples.

Electronic systems allow the use of Boolean logic in a search, which is difficult or impossible to do in a manual search of *PA*. Use the Boolean logical operators **AND, OR**, and **NOT** to combine terms precisely.

Example of Boolean Logic

(Shaded Areas Indicate Retrieval)

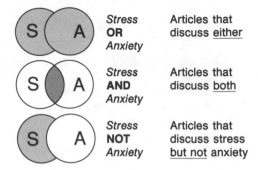

Stress **OR** *Anxiety*	Articles that discuss <u>either</u>
Stress **AND** *Anxiety*	Articles that discuss <u>both</u>
Stress **NOT** *Anxiety*	Articles that discuss stress <u>but not</u> anxiety

Example:

Acquired Immune Deficiency Syndrome

AND (Educational Progams **OR** Health Education **OR** AIDS Prevention)

AND (High School Students **OR** High Schools **OR** Secondary Education)

Once satisfactory sets have been formed, each search system allows customization of the format of the retrieved records to meet special preferences. The search system's documentation describes this procedure in detail.

ELECTRONIC THESAURUS: For added convenience in searching, DIALOG, BRS, and DIMDI offer an electronic thesaurus and the PsycLIT and ClinPSYC systems offer an on-disc thesaurus which can automatically display terms along with their broader, narrower, and related concepts. This feature can help reduce typing and enhance the speed of a search, especially when several narrower terms need to be entered.

SAVED SEARCHES: Saved Searches are stored sets of index terms in popular subject areas that save valuable search time. When a SAVED SEARCH is invoked, the index terms will be searched automatically, and the resulting sets can be manipulated. On DIALOG and Data-Star, SAVED SEARCHES can be executed at any time during a search session; however, on BRS SAVED SEARCHES must be executed as Step 1 and only one SAVED SEARCH can be executed per session. Enter the command exactly as it appears on the next page. Do not substitute your own user number for the "3471" in the DIALOG examples. SAVED SEARCHES for CD-ROM systems are available free from PsycINFO. Please contact PsycINFO's User Services Department for details.

Saved Search Topics

TOPIC	DIALOG	BRS	DATA-STAR
Psychiatric Patients	?EX SBMDIS/USER 3471	..EXEC CP(PSY1)	..EXEC CL=MDIS
Substance Abuse	?EX SBABUSE/USER 3471	..EXEC CP(PSY2)	..EXEC CL=ABUS
Learning Disabilities	?EX SBLDIS/USER 3471	..EXEC CP(PSY3)	..EXEC CL=LDIS
Communication/Language/ Speech Disorders	?EX SBCDIS/USER 3471	..EXEC CP(PSY4)	..EXEC CL=CDIS
Racial and Ethnic Groups	?EX SBRACE/USER 3471	..EXEC CP(PSY5)	..EXEC CL=RACE
Tests and Measurements	?EX SBTEST/USER 3471	..EXEC CP(PSY6)	..EXEC CL=TEST
Mental Health Personnel	?EX SBMHPRS/USER 3471	..EXEC CP(PSY7)	..EXEC CL=MHPR
"Talking" Therapies	?EX SBTHRPY/USER 3471	..EXEC CP(PSY8)	..EXEC CL=THRP
Developing Countries	?EX SBWORLD/USER 3471	..EXEC CP(PSY9)	..EXEC CL=WRLD

Searching using Age Groups

All electronic systems use 4 specific identifying tags for human populations. A record may have more than one age group tag and ELDERLY is a subset of ADULT.

AGE	AGE GROUP TAG (AG)
0-12	CHILD
13-17	ADOLESCENT
18+	ADULT
65+	ELDERLY

Consult **APPENDIX D** for information on how to search the composite age group (AG) field.

If a more specific age range is desired in a search, choose appropriate descriptors from the table below. On the left side of the table, find the age range, then select one or more index terms from the appropriate column for the setting, i.e, nonschool or school related.

Age Descriptors

AGE RANGE	NON-SCHOOL-RELATED	SCHOOL-RELATED
0-1 month	NEONATES [67]	
2-23 months	INFANTS [67]	
0-12 years	CHILDREN [67]	
2-5 years	PRESCHOOL AGE CHILDREN [67]	NURSERY SCHOOL STUDENTS [73] KINDERGARTEN STUDENTS [73] PRESCHOOL STUDENTS [82]
6-12 years	PREDELINQUENT YOUTH [78] SCHOOL AGE CHILDREN [73]	ELEMENTARY SCHOOL STUDENTS [67] INTERMEDIATE SCHOOL STUDENTS [73] PRIMARY SCHOOL STUDENTS [73] MIDDLE SCHOOL STUDENTS [85]
10-12 years	PREADOLESCENTS [88]	
13-17 years	ADOLESCENTS [67] JUVENILE DELINQUENTS [73] MALE DELINQUENTS [73] FEMALE DELINQUENTS [73] ADOLESCENT MOTHERS [85] ADOLESCENT FATHERS [85]	MIDDLE SCHOOL STUDENTS [85] JUNIOR HIGH SCHOOL STUDENTS [71] VOCATIONAL SCHOOL STUDENTS [73] HIGH SCHOOL STUDENTS [67]

Searching using Content Classification Codes

PsycINFO uses a content classification system that divides the field of psychology into 22 major or broad categories and 134 subcategories. Content classification codes can be searched in all systems. Use of the content classification system in searching can shorten online time and screen out undesired references. Content classification codes are particularly useful to retrieve records from a broad subject area in which many different index terms may have been used. Classification codes generally limit a search, since only one or two codes are assigned to each record.

Search classification codes at their broad level. Using the first two digits of a category retrieves the entire category and enables the search to be executed throughout the entire year range of the database. If more specific information is needed, search one or more four-digit subcategories. Four

digit subcategories were added in 1976; therefore, a search on a four digit subcategory will limit retrieval to records added in 1976 and later.

A list of the content classification codes appears in **Appendix C**.

PsycINFO ACTIONLINE (800) 374-2722

Professional indexers and search analysts are available to answer questions and give assistance in search strategy formulation via our toll free 800 line: (800) 374-2722. This free service is available in North America, 9:00 a.m. to 5:00 p.m., U.S. Eastern time, Monday through Friday.

For those who do not have toll free access, our User Services Department can be contacted at (202) 336-5650, FAX (202) 336-5633, or TTY (202) 336-6123. Electronic mail is accepted via Internet at psycinfo@apa.org.

Sample PsycINFO Journal Record

Vendor Record ⟵ 00890543   80-15471 ⟶ *Psychological
Number   Abstracts* **Volume**

Document Title ⟵ Individual and relational predictors of adjustment **and Abstract #**
in first-year college students.

Holmbeck, Grayson N.; Wandrei, Mary L. ⟶ **Author(s)/Editor(s)
(up to 4)**

Affiliation of ⟵ Loyola U, Chicago, IL, US
First Author

Journal of Counseling Psychology ⟶ **Journal Name**

Issue Citation and ⟵ 1993 Jan Vol 40(1) 73-78
Page Number

International ⟵ ISSN: 00220167
Standard Serial   **Journal**
Number   Journal Announcement: 8004 ⟶ **Announcement
(PsycINFO Volume
and Issue #)**

Document ⟵ Language: English
Language

Document Type: JOURNAL ARTICLE ⟶ **Document Type**

Population Age ⟵ Composite Age: ADULT
Tags

        Assessed the differential predictive utility of home-
leaving status, family functioning, separation-individuation
issues, cognitive constructions of the home-leaving
process, and personality variables for adjustment during
the 1st yr of college with a sample of 286 college
freshmen (182 women and 104 men). Findings revealed
that the separation-individuation, family relations, and
personality variables were better predictors of adjustment ⟶ **Document**
than were the cognitive indicators or home-leaving status. **Abstract**
Results also varied as a function of gender; less well-
adjusted men were more disconnected from significant
others, whereas less well-adjusted women exhibited higher
levels of separation anxiety and enmeshment seeking.
Implications for counseling interventions are discussed.
(PsycINFO Database Copyright 1993 American
Psychological Assn, all rights reserved)

Major Descriptors ⟵ Major Descriptors: *FAMILY RELATIONS; *SEPARATION
INDIVIDUATION; *COGNITIVE PROCESSES;
*PERSONALITY TRAITS; *ADJUSTMENT

Minor Descriptors: ADULTHOOD; COLLEGE STUDENTS ⟶ **Minor Descriptors**

Descriptor ⟵ Descriptor Codes: 19250; 46665; 10130; 37860;
Searching Codes 00850; 01150; 10320

Identifiers: home leaving status & family functioning ⟶ **Descriptive Key**
& separation individuation & cognitive processed & **Phrases**
personality, prediction of adjustment, college freshmen

Classification ⟵ Section Headings: 3560-CLASSROOM DYNAMICS &
Heading STUDENT ADJUSTMENT & ATTITUDES

Sample PsycLIT Book/Chapter Record

FIELD NAME	SAMPLE BOOK RECORD
Accession Number	AN: EDITED BOOK 93-148025-000
Book Title	TI: Memory and affect in development
Author	AU: Nelson,-Charles-A. (Ed.)
Author Affiliation	IN: U Minnesota, MN, US
Institutional Sponsor	SP: National Inst of Mental Health, Rockville, MD, US; General Mills Foundation, Minneapolis, MN, US
Publisher	PB: Hillsdale, NJ, US: Lawrence Erlbaum Associates, Inc; x, 278 pp.
Publication Year	PY: 1993
Series Title	SE: The Minnesota Symposia on Child Psychology, Vol. 26.
ISBN(s)	IS: 0-8058-1261-X (hardcover)
Language	LA: English
Chapters Selected/Total	CH: 11 chapters selected from 11
Audience Type	AT: P2 Psychology: Graduate/Professional
Update	UD: 9312
Descriptors	DE: COGNITIVE-DEVELOPMENT; MEMORY-; EMOTIONAL-DEVELOPMENT; CHILDREN-; PROFESSIONAL-MEETINGS-AND-SYMPOSIA
Classification Code	CC: 2800; 28
Population	PO: Human
Content Representation	CR: (from the preface) Of the many changes that have occurred in recent years in developmental psychology, two have been particularly prominent. One has been how diverse this field has become...[*content representation continues*]
Table of Contents	TC: (Abbreviated)
	001- <<SEE CHAPTER>> Events, narratives, memory: What develops?/ Katherine Nelson
	002- <<SEE CHAPTER>> Identifying subsystems of autobiographical memory: Commentary on Nelson/ Patricia J. Bauer...[*table of contents continues*]

FIELD NAME	SAMPLE CHAPTER RECORD
Accession Number	AN: CHAPTER 93-148025-007 <<SEE PREVIOUS CHAPTER>> <<SEE NEXT CHAPTER>>
Chapter Title	TI: Children's memory for other people: An integrative review.
Author	AU: Davies,-Graham-M.
Author Affiliation	IN: U Leicester, Leicester, England
Parent Book	BK: Memory and affect in development. The Minnesota Symposia on Child Psychology, Vol. 26. (Charles A. Nelson, Ed.) pp. 123-157. Lawrence Erlbaum Associates, Inc, Hillsdale, NJ, US, x, 278 pp.<<SEE BOOK>>
Publication Year	PY: 1993
ISBN	IS: 0-8058-1261-x (hardcover)
Language	LA: English
Audience Type	AT: M2; Interdisciplinary: Graduate/Professional
Document Type	DT: 9850: Literature Review
Update	UD: 9312
Descriptors	DE: WITNESSES-; MEMORY-; LEGAL-TESTIMONY; CHILDREN-; LITERATURE-REVIEW
Classification Code	CC: 2820; 28
Population	PO: Human
Age Group	AG: Child
Content Representation	CR: (from the preface) [reviews] research on children as eyewitnesses/ discusses children's eyewitness memory based on both laboratory and field research...[*content representation continues*]
References	RF: References

Appendix A—New Postable Terms

Adjustment Disorders
Adolescent Psychotherapy
Advance Directives
Age Discrimination
AIDS Prevention
Alcohol Withdrawal
Aluminum
Animal Assisted Therapy
Animal Captivity
Anniversary Events
Anosognosia
Antiviral Drugs
Augmentative Communication
Autobiographical Memory
Automated Speech Recognition
Avoidant Personality
Bayley Scales of Infant
    Development
Behavioral Genetics
Benzodiazepine Agonists
Bicuculline
Biological Psychiatry
Blame
Blood Alcohol Concentration
Blood Brain Barrier
Brand Preferences
Bupropion
Cardiovascular Reactivity
Caregiver Burden
Causal Analysis
Cerebral Atrophy
Cerebral Blood Flow
Child Behavior Checklist
Choice Shift
Civil Law
Client Satisfaction
Cochlear Implants
Coercion
College Athletes
Computer Programing
Computer Training
Conjoint Measurement
Connectionism
Constructivism
Consumer Satisfaction
Cooperative Learning
Corticotropin Releasing Factor
Couples Therapy
Court Referrals
Creative Arts Therapy
Creative Writing
Creutzfeldt Jakob Syndrome
Cross Cultural Treatment
Cued Recall
Cultural Sensitivity
Curriculum Based Assessment
Daily Activities
Delayed Alternation
Dependent Personality
Developmental Measures
Diagnostic and Statistical Manual

Dietary Restraint
Disability Laws
Discharge Planning
Disgust
Doxepin
Drug Abstinence
Drug Abuse Liability
Drug Abuse Prevention
Eating Attitudes
Eclectic Psychotherapy
Ecological Psychology
Educational Program
    Accreditation
Elder Care
Employment Discrimination
Environmental Education
Epstein Barr Viral Disorder
Experimental Attrition
Extrapyramidal Symptoms
Fee for Service
Feminist Therapy
Fluvoxamine
Forensic Evaluation
Fragile X Syndrome
Fraud
Free Association
Genetic Engineering
Genetic Linkage
Glucose Metabolism
Grade Level
Grandiosity
Health Care Costs
Health Care Policy
Health Knowledge
Health Personnel
Home Schooling
Homesickness
Homosexual Parents
Hormone Therapy
Hygiene
Hypersomnia
Immunoreactivity
Intake Interview
Interferons
Interleukins
Interracial Adoption
Intravenous Drug Usage
Involuntary Treatment
Jury Selection
Koro
Legal Interrogation
Likert Scales
Living Alone
Long Term Care
Lucid Dreaming
Magnetic Resonance Imaging
Mail Surveys
Mammography
Managed Care
Matching to Sample
Medicaid

Memory Training
Metalinguistics
Metapsychology
Methylphenyltetrahydropyridine
Mini Mental State Examination
Morita Therapy
Munchausen Syndrome
Muscimol
N-Methyl-D-Aspartate
Napping
Nature Nurture
Needle Sharing
Nerve Growth Factor
Neural Plasticity
Never Married
Nortriptyline
Nucleus Basalis Magnocellularis
Omnipotence
Pain Management
Parental Characteristics
Parkinsonism
Paroxetine
Patient Seclusion
Patient Violence
Peer Pressure
Performance Anxiety
Perinatal Period
Physical Mobility
Piperazines
Poetry Therapy
Polydrug Abuse
Posthypnotic Suggestions
Preconditioning
Prefrontal Cortex
Preoptic Area
Professional Client Sexual
    Relations
Professional Examinations
Projective Identification
Prosopagnosia
Psychoeducation
Purkinje Cells
Quinpirole
Race and Ethnic Discrimination
Recurrent Depression
Reference Groups
Relapse Prevention
Research Diagnostic Criteria
Rett Syndrome
Role Satisfaction
Rotational Behavior
Schizoaffective Disorder
Schizophreniform Disorder
School Refusal
School Retention
School to Work Transition
Secrecy
Seduction
Self Analysis
Self Confidence
Self Determination

Appendix B—New Nonpostable Terms

Abstinence (Drugs)
Use Drug Abstinence

Abuse Potential (Drugs)
Use Drug Abuse Liability

Academic Grade Level
Use Grade Level

Accreditation (Educational
Programs)
Use Educational Program
Accreditation

ACTH Releasing Factor
Use Corticotropin Releasing
Factor

Ambulatory Care
Use Outpatient Treatment

Anniversary Reactions
Use Anniversary Events

Anxiety Disorders
Use Anxiety Neurosis

Arachnophobia
Use Phobias

Association (Free)
Use Free Association

Atrophy (Cerebral)
Use Cerebral Atrophy

Automatic Speaker Recognition
Use Automated Speech
Recognition

Autotomy
Use Self Mutilation

Azidothymidine
Use Zidovudine

AZT
Use Zidovudine

Birth Parents
Use Biological Family

Body Rotation
Use Rotational Behavior

Captivity (Animal)
Use Animal Captivity

Certification Examinations
Use Professional
Examinations

Chewing Tobacco
Use Smokeless Tobacco

China
Use Peoples Republic of
China

Chlorophenylpiperazine
Use Piperazines

Chorda Tympani Nerve
Use Facial Nerve

Client Violence
Use Patient Violence

Cognitive Load
Use Human Channel Capacity

Communicable Diseases
Use Infectious Disorders

Confidence (Self)
Use Self Confidence

Confirmatory Factor Analysis
Use Factor Analysis

Constructionism
Use Constructivism

Consumer Fraud
Use Fraud

Control Groups
Use Experiment Controls

Coronary Heart Disease
Use Heart Disorders

Cortical Atrophy
Use Cerebral Atrophy

Court Ordered Treatment
Use Court Referrals

Drug Testing
Use Drug Usage Screening

DSM
Use Diagnostic and Statistical
Manual

Duchennes Disease
Use Muscular Dystrophy

Dyscalculia
Use Acalculia

Dyspraxia
Use Movement Disorders

Estrogen Replacement Therapy
Use Hormone Therapy

Ethnic Discrimination
Use Race and Ethnic
Discrimination

Ethnic Sensitivity
Use Cultural Sensitivity

Facilitated Communication
Use Augmentative
Communication

Family Caregivers
Use Caregivers

Fibromyalgia Syndrome
Use Muscular Disorders

Gay Males
Use Male Homosexuality

Gay Parents
Use Homosexual Parents

Generalized Anxiety Disorder
Use Anxiety Neurosis

Glycoproteins
Use Globulins

Hypercholesterolemia
Use Metabolism Disorders

IV Drug Usage
Use Intravenous Drug Usage

Job Discrimination
Use Employment
Discrimination

Language Alternation
Use Code Switching

Lesbian Parents
Use Homosexual Parents

Licensure Examinations
Use Professional
Examinations

Linkage Analysis
Use Genetic Linkage

Living Wills
Use Advance Directives

Matching Test
Use Matching to Sample

MCPP
Use Piperazines

Medical Care Costs
Use Health Care Costs

Meningomyelocele
Use Spina Bifida

Mental Health Care Costs
Use Health Care Costs

Mental Health Care Policy
Use Health Care Policy

MPTP
Use Methylphenyltetrahydropyridine

MRI
Use Magnetic Resonance
Imaging

Multidrug Abuse
Use Polydrug Abuse

Myelomeningocele
Use Spina Bifida

Nazism
Use Fascism

Nervous System Plasticity
Use Neural Plasticity

Networks (Social)
Use Social Networks

Neuropeptides
Use Peptides

NMDA
Use N-Methyl-D-Aspartate

Office Environment
Use Working Conditions

Pantherine
Use Muscimol

Parasuicide
Use Attempted Suicide

Patient Satisfaction
Use Client Satisfaction

Appendix C—Content Classification System

NOTE: This classification code system was designed to describe the content of the PsycINFO database, not the field of psychology.

2100 General Psychology
2140 History & Systems

2200 Psychometrics & Statistics & Methodology
2220 Tests & Testing
  2221 Sensory & Motor Testing
  2222 Developmental Scales & Schedules
  2223 Personality Scales & Inventories
  2224 Clinical Psychological Testing
  2225 Neuropsychological Assessment
  2226 Health Psychology Testing
  2227 Educational Measurement
  2228 Occupational & Employment Testing
  2229 Consumer Opinion & Attitude Testing
2240 Statistics & Mathematics
2260 Research Methods & Experimental Design

2300 Human Experimental Psychology
2320 Sensory Perception
  2323 Visual Perception
  2326 Auditory & Speech Perception
2330 Motor Processes
2340 Cognitive Processes
  2343 Learning & Memory
  2346 Attention
2360 Motivation & Emotion
2380 Consciousness States
2390 Parapsychology

2400 Animal Experimental & Comparative Psychology
2420 Learning & Motivation
2440 Social & Instinctive Behavior

2500 Physiological Psychology & Neuroscience
2510 Genetics
2520 Neuropsychology & Neurology
2530 Electrophysiology
2540 Physiological Processes
2560 Psychophysiology
2580 Psychopharmacology

2600 Psychology & the Humanities
2610 Literature & Fine Arts
2630 Philosophy

2700 Communication Systems
2720 Linguistics & Language & Speech
2750 Mass Media Communications

2800 Developmental Psychology
2820 Cognitive & Perceptual Development
2840 Psychosocial & Personality Development
2860 Gerontology

2900 Social Processes & Social Issues
2910 Social Structure & Organization
2920 Religion
2930 Culture & Ethnology
2950 Marriage & Family
  2953 Divorce & Remarriage
  2956 Childrearing & Child Care
2960 Political Processes & Political Issues
2970 Sex Roles & Womens Issues

2980 Sexual Behavior & Sexual Orientation
2990 Drug & Alcohol Usage (Legal)

3000 Social Psychology
3020 Group & Interpersonal Processes
3040 Social Perception & Cognition

3100 Personality Psychology
3120 Personality Traits & Processes
3140 Personality Theory
  3143 Psychoanalytic Theory

3200 Psychological & Physical Disorders
3210 Psychological Disorders
  3211 Affective Disorders
  3213 Schizophrenia & Psychotic States
  3215 Neuroses & Anxiety Disorders
  3217 Personality Disorders
3230 Behavior Disorders & Antisocial Behavior
  3233 Substance Abuse & Addiction
  3236 Criminal Behavior & Juvenile Delinquency
3250 Developmental Disorders & Autism
  3253 Learning Disorders
  3256 Mental Retardation
3260 Eating Disorders
3270 Speech & Language Disorders
3280 Environmental Toxins & Health
3290 Physical & Somatoform & Psychogenic Disorders
  3291 Immunological Disorders
  3293 Cancer
  3295 Cardiovascular Disorders
  3297 Neurological Disorders & Brain Damage
  3299 Vision & Hearing & Sensory Disorders

3300 Health & Mental Health Treatment & Prevention
3310 Psychotherapy & Psychotherapeutic Counseling
  3311 Cognitive Therapy
  3312 Behavior Therapy & Behavior Modification
  3313 Group & Family Therapy
  3314 Interpersonal & Client Centered & Humanistic Therapy
  3315 Psychoanalytic Therapy
3340 Clinical Psychopharmacology
3350 Specialized Interventions
  3351 Clinical Hypnosis
  3353 Self Help Groups
  3355 Lay & Paraprofessional & Pastoral Counseling
  3357 Art & Music & Movement Therapy
3360 Health Psychology & Medicine
  3361 Behavioral & Psychological Treatment of Physical Illness
  3363 Medical Treatment of Physical Illness
  3365 Promotion & Maintenance of Health & Wellness
3370 Health & Mental Health Services
  3371 Outpatient Services
  3373 Community & Social Services
  3375 Home Care & Hospice

  3377 Nursing Homes & Residential Care
  3379 Inpatient & Hospital Services
3380 Rehabilitation
  3383 Drug & Alcohol Rehabilitation
  3384 Occupational & Vocational Rehabilitation
  3385 Speech & Language Therapy
  3386 Criminal Rehabilitation & Penology

3400 Professional Psychological & Health Personnel Issues
3410 Professional Education & Training
3430 Professional Personnel Attitudes & Characteristics
3450 Professional Ethics & Standards & Liability
3470 Impaired Professionals

3500 Educational Psychology
3510 Educational Administration & Personnel
3530 Curriculum & Programs & Teaching Methods
3550 Academic Learning & Achievement
3560 Classroom Dynamics & Student Adjustment & Attitudes
3570 Special & Remedial Education
  3575 Gifted & Talented
3580 Educational/Vocational Counseling & Student Services

3600 Industrial & Organizational Psychology
3610 Occupational Interests & Guidance
3620 Personnel Management & Selection & Training
3630 Personnel Evaluation & Job Performance
3640 Management & Management Training
3650 Personnel Attitudes & Job Satisfaction
3660 Organizational Behavior
3670 Working Conditions & Industrial Safety

3700 Sport Psychology & Leisure
3720 Sports
3740 Recreation & Leisure

3800 Military Psychology

3900 Consumer Psychology
3920 Consumer Attitudes & Behavior
3940 Marketing & Advertising

4000 Engineering & Environmental Psychology
4010 Human Factors Engineering
4030 Lifespace & Institutional Design
4050 Community & Environmental Planning
4070 Environmental Issues & Attitudes
4090 Transportation

4100 Intelligent Systems
4120 Artificial Intelligence & Expert Systems
4140 Robotics
4160 Neural Networks

4200 Forensic Psychology & Legal Issues
4210 Civil Rights & Civil Law
4230 Criminal Law & Criminal Adjudication
4250 Mediation & Conflict Resolution
4270 Crime Prevention
4290 Police & Legal Personnel

Appendix D—PsycINFO ONLINE/ PsycLIT on CD-ROM Master Quick Reference Guide

The chart on the following two pages is a guide to the command syntax required to search PsycINFO and PsycLIT record fields on the online and CD-ROM vendor systems available at the time of this edition's publication.

The far-left column of the chart contains PsycINFO and PsycLIT field names. To find a field's corresponding label and search syntax, read across the field's row to the appropriate vendor column.

On PsycLIT, the syntax for subject searching of titles, descriptors, and classification codes is identical for journal articles, book chapters, and books, since these fields are common to the three types of records. Another source of chapter/book subject information is the content representation field, which is unique to chapter and book records, serving the same purpose as the journal-article abstract.

For complete information about searching, users should consult the *PsycINFO User Manual* or contact PsycINFO User Services to obtain vendor-specific documentation or searching information.

PsycINFO/PsycLIT MASTER QUICK REFERENCE GUIDE

PsycINFO/PsycLIT FIELD NAME	BRS LABEL	BRS SEARCH EXAMPLES	DATA-STAR LABEL	DATA-STAR SEARCH EXAMPLES	DIALOG LABEL	DIALOG SEARCH EXAMPLES
Accession Number	.AN.	03185 adj 77-$2.AN.	.AN.	03222 adj 77-$2.an.	AN=	s an=77-03185
Title	.TI.	electrical$2 adj stimulat$4.ti. cultur$2 same change$1.ti.	.TI.	electrical$2 adj stimulat$4.ti. cultur$2 same change$1.ti.	/TI	s hand()preference?/ti s dysfunct?(2n)famil?/ti
Author	.AU. ROOT	baumeister-r$.au. root vandenbos-g	.AU. ROOT	baumeister-r$.au. root vandenbos-g.au.	AU= E AU=	s au=baumeister, r? e au=siever, l
Author Affiliation	.IN.	u adj oregon same eugene.in.	.IN.	u adj oregon same eugene.in.	CS=	s cs=(u()oregon(f)eugene)
Journal Name	.SO.	australian adj psychologist.so.	.SO. ROOT	new-england-journal-of-medicine.so. root social-work.so.	JN= E JN= SO=	s jn=journal of applied social? e jn=topics in early childhood s so=(private()practice)
Book Publisher						
Publication Year	.YR.	..L/1 yr gt 1989 yr1993 1993.yr.	.YR.	yr=93 85.yr. ..L 4 yr>92	PY=	s py=1993 s py=1985:1993 s s1/1990:1993
ISSN	.IS.	0303-8300.is.	.IS.	0095-8964.is.	SN=	s sn=0219029
ISBN						
Update Code	.UP.	up9303 9302.up. ..L 2 up gt 8800	ED=	ed=90 ..L 5 ed>85	UD=	s ud=9103 s ud=9001:9999 s ud=91?
Language	.LG.	..L/3 lg=en russian.lg. lgfr	.LG.	lg=en ge.lg. ..L 6 lg=fr	LA=	s la=french s s3/eng
Publication Type	.PT.	dissertation.pt. '11'.pt. literature adj review.pt.	.PT.	pt=j pt=10 pt=r	DT=	s dt=journal article s dt=dissertation s dt=review
Composite Age	.AG.	child.ag.	.AG.	adolescent.ag.	AG=	s ag=adult
Abstract	.AB.	special adj education.ab. social$2 with perception$1.ab.	.AB.	special adj education.ab. social$2 with perception$1.ab.	/AB	s diazepam/ab s guilt?(f)conscience/ab s wisc()r/ab
Book/Chapter Content Representation						
Descriptors All	.DE.	military.de. defense adj mechanism$1.de. impression-management	.DE.	military.de. concept-formation.de. impression-management	/DE	s schizophrenia/de s achievement motivation s child()relations/de s death "and" dying
Major	.MJ.	professional-ethics.mj. accidents.mj. child adj relations.mj.	.MJ.	professional-ethics.mj. accidents.mj. child adj relations.mj.	/DE*	s memory disorders/de* s phencyclidine/de*
One-Word	SW=	sw=neurosis	.W..DE.	neurosis.w..de.	/DF	s health/df
One-Word Major	.SJ.	personality.sj.	.W..MJ.	personality.w..mj.	/DF*	s personality/df*
Descriptor Code	.SC.	01360.sc.	.SC.	01360.sc.	DC=	s dc=45440
Key Phrase	.ID.	art same education.id.	.ID.	art same education.id.	/ID	corporate()moral?/id s computer(1n)litera?/id
Content Classification	.CC.	3570.cc. '32'.cc. ('32' or '33').cc.	.CC.	3570.cc. 22#.cc. (32# or 33#).cc.	SH=	s sh=3570 s sh=32 s sh=(32 or 33)
Human/Animal	CT=	ct=human ct=animal	H=Y H=N	..L 7 h=y ..L 8 h=n	/HUMAN /ANIMAL	s s1/human s emotion?/animal

Abdomen 73
PN 97   SC 00010
  B   Anatomy 67

Abdominal Wall 73
PN 6   SC 00020
  B   Muscles 67

Abducens Nerve 73
PN 16   SC 00030
  UF   Nerve (Abducens)
  B   Cranial Nerves 73

Ability 67
PN 2555   SC 00070
  SN   Conceptually broad array term referring to
the skills, talents or qualities that enable one to
perform a task. Use a more specific term if pos-
sible.
  UF   Aptitude
       Skills
       Talent
  N   Academic Aptitude 73
       ↓ Cognitive Ability 73
       ↓ Communication Skills 73
       ↓ Employee Skills 73
       Learning Ability 73
       ↓ Nonverbal Ability 88
       ↓ Reading Skills 73
       Self Care Skills 78
       Social Skills 78
  R   Ability Grouping 73
       Ability Level 78
       ↓ Achievement Potential 73
       Competence 82
       Creativity 67
       Gifted 67
       Idiot Savants 73
       Intelligence 67
       ↓ Performance 67

Ability Grouping 73
PN 259   SC 00040
  SN   Grouping or selection of individuals for in-
structional or other purposes based on differ-
ences in ability or achievement.
  R   ↓ Ability 67
       Ability Level 78
       Academic Aptitude 73
       ↓ Education 67
       Educational Placement 78
       Grade Level 94
       Special Education 67

Ability Level 78
PN 652   SC 00050
  SN   Demonstrated level of performance. Used in
academic, cognitive, perceptual, or occupational
contexts.
  R   ↓ Ability 67
       Ability Grouping 73
       Adaptive Testing 85

Ability Tests
  Use   Aptitude Measures

Ablation
  Use   Lesions

Abortion (Induced)
  Use   Induced Abortion

Abortion (Spontaneous)
  Use   Spontaneous Abortion

Abortion Laws 73
PN 51   SC 00110

Abortion Laws — (cont'd)
  B   Laws 67
  R   Induced Abortion 71

Abreaction
  Use   Catharsis

Absenteeism (Employee)
  Use   Employee Absenteeism

Absorption (Physiological) 73
PN 50   SC 00140
  B   Physiology 67
  R   Bioavailability 91
       ↓ Cells (Biology) 73
       Intestines 73
       Skin (Anatomy) 67

Abstinence (Drugs)
  Use   Drug Abstinence

Abstinence (Sexual)
  Use   Sexual Abstinence

Abstraction 67
PN 756   SC 00160
  SN   Process of selecting or isolating a certain
aspect from a concrete whole, as a part of the
process of evaluation or communication.
  B   Thinking 67
  N   ↓ Imagery 67
  R   Divergent Thinking 73

Abuse Potential (Drugs)
  Use   Drug Abuse Liability

Academic Achievement 67
PN 13177   SC 00190
  UF   Gradepoint Average
       Scholastic Achievement
       School Achievement
  B   Achievement 67
  N   Academic Overachievement 67
       Academic Underachievement 67
       College Academic Achievement 67
       Mathematics Achievement 73
       Reading Achievement 73
  R   Academic Achievement Motivation 73
       Academic Achievement Prediction 67
       Academic Aptitude 73
       Academic Failure 78
       ↓ Education 67
       School Graduation 91
       School Learning 67

Academic Achievement Motivation 73
PN 1121   SC 00200
  B   Achievement Motivation 67
  R   ↓ Academic Achievement 67

Academic Achievement Prediction 67
PN 2472   SC 00210
  SN   Prediction of future academic achievement
based on results of tests, inventories, or other
measures.
  B   Prediction 67
  R   ↓ Academic Achievement 67

Academic Aptitude 73
PN 1091   SC 00220
  SN   Potential ability to perform or achieve in
scholastic pursuits.
  UF   Aptitude (Academic)
       Scholastic Aptitude
  B   Ability 67
       Achievement Potential 73
  R   Ability Grouping 73

Academic Aptitude — (cont'd)
  R   ↓ Academic Achievement 67
       ↓ Education 67
       ↓ Nonverbal Ability 88
       Reading Ability 73
       Student Admission Criteria 73
       Verbal Ability 67

Academic Environment 73
PN 203   SC 00230
  SN   Physical setting or emotional climate where
formal instruction takes place.
  B   Social Environments 73
  N   Classroom Environment 73
       ↓ School Environment 73

Academic Failure 78
PN 533   SC 00233
  B   Failure 67
  R   ↓ Academic Achievement 67
       Academic Underachievement 67

Academic Grade Level
  Use   Grade Level

Academic Overachievement 67
PN 451   SC 00240
  SN   Academic achievement greater than that an-
ticipated on basis of one's scholastic aptitude
score or individual intelligence.
  UF   Overachievement (Academic)
  B   Academic Achievement 67

Academic Records
  Use   Student Records

Academic Specialization 73
PN 1407   SC 00250
  SN   Concentration of effort or interest in a spe-
cial area of knowledge or discipline at an institu-
tion of learning.
  UF   College Major
       Specialization (Academic)
  R   Educational Aspirations 73
       Professional Specialization 91

Academic Underachievement 67
PN 1298   SC 00260
  SN   Academic achievement less than that ex-
pected based on one's scholastic aptitude score
or individual intelligence.
  UF   Underachievement (Academic)
  B   Academic Achievement 67
  R   Academic Failure 78
       ↓ Failure 67

Acalculia 73
PN 43   SC 00270
  SN   Form of aphasia involving impaired ability to
perform simple arithmetic calculations.
  UF   Dyscalculia
  B   Aphasia 67
  R   ↓ Learning Disabilities 73

Accelerated Speech
  Use   Speech Rate

Acceleration Effects 73
PN 130   SC 00290
  SN   Behavioral, physiological, or psychological
effects resulting from acceleration onset/offset or
changes in acceleration rate.
  R   ↓ Aviation 67
       Decompression Effects 73
       Flight Simulation 73
       ↓ Gravitational Effects 67
       Physiological Stress 67
       Spaceflight 67

Acceptance (Social)
Use Social Acceptance

Accessory Nerve
Use Cranial Nerves

Accident Prevention [73]
PN 308   SC 00330
B   Prevention [73]
R ↓ Accidents [67]
      ↓ Safety [67]
      ↓ Transportation Accidents [73]

Accident Proneness [73]
PN 136   SC 00340
R ↓ Accidents [67]
      ↓ Safety [67]

Accidents [67]
PN 443   SC 00350
N   Home Accidents [73]
        Industrial Accidents [73]
        Pedestrian Accidents [73]
      ↓ Transportation Accidents [73]
R   Accident Prevention [73]
        Accident Proneness [73]
      ↓ Disasters [73]
        Driving Under The Influence [88]
      ↓ Hazardous Materials [91]
        Hazards [73]
      ↓ Injuries [73]
      ↓ Safety [67]

Acclimatization (Thermal)
Use Thermal Acclimatization

Accomplishment
Use Achievement

Accountability [88]
PN 104   SC 00385
SN Liability and/or responsibility for specified results or outcomes of an activity over which one has authority.
B   Responsibility [73]
R   Blame [94]
        Competence [82]
        Consumer Protection [73]
        Criminal Responsibility [91]
      ↓ Management [67]
        Professional Liability [85]
      ↓ Professional Standards [73]
        Quality Control [88]
        Quality of Care [88]

Accountants [73]
PN 149   SC 00390
UF Certified Public Accountants
B   White Collar Workers [73]

Accreditation (Education Personnel) [73]
PN 59   SC 00400
SN Professional licensing or certification of teachers, school psychologists, or other educational personnel, usually required for employment.
UF Teacher Accreditation
B   Professional Certification [73]
        Professional Licensing [73]
R ↓ Education [67]
        Professional Examinations [94]

Accreditation (Educational Programs)
Use Educational Program Accreditation

Acculturation
SN Term discontinued in 1982. Use ACCULTURATION or CULTURAL ASSIMILATION to access references from 73–81.
Use Cultural Assimilation

Acetaldehyde [82]
PN 50   SC 00415
SN First oxidation product of primary alcohol metabolism. Acetaldehyde has narcotic properties.
UF Acetic Aldehyde
        Ethanal
        Ethylaldehyde
R ↓ Alcohols [67]
      ↓ Carbohydrate Metabolism [73]
      ↓ Dopamine Metabolites [82]

Acetazolamide [73]
PN 15   SC 00420
B   Diuretics [73]
        Enzyme Inhibitors [85]
R ↓ Anticonvulsive Drugs [73]
        Carbonic Anhydrase [73]

Acetic Aldehyde
Use Acetaldehyde

Acetylcholine [73]
PN 487   SC 00430
B   Cholinergic Drugs [73]
        Cholinomimetic Drugs [73]
        Neurotransmitters [85]
R   Acetylcholinesterase [73]
      ↓ Choline [73]
        Cholinergic Nerves [73]

Acetylcholinesterase [73]
PN 169   SC 00440
B   Esterases [73]
R   Acetylcholine [73]
        Cholinesterase [73]

Acetylsalicylic Acid
Use Aspirin

Aches
Use Pain

Achievement [67]
PN 2436   SC 00470
UF Accomplishment
        Attainment (Achievement)
        Success
N ↓ Academic Achievement [67]
        Occupational Success [78]
R ↓ Achievement Measures [67]
        Competence [82]
      ↓ Failure [67]
      ↓ Performance [67]

Achievement Measures [67]
PN 1772   SC 00490
SN Tests designed to measure knowledge and/or skills acquired from learning, experience, or training.
UF Tests (Achievement)
B   Measurement [67]
N   Iowa Tests of Basic Skills [73]
        Stanford Achievement Test [73]
        Wide Range Achievement Test [73]
        Woodcock Johnson Psychoed Battery [94]
R ↓ Achievement [67]
        Criterion Referenced Tests [82]

Achievement Motivation [67]
PN 2845   SC 00500

Achievement Motivation — (cont'd)
SN Need that drives an individual to improve, succeed, or excel.
UF NAch
        Need Achievement
B   Motivation [67]
N   Academic Achievement Motivation [73]
R ↓ Achievement Potential [73]
        Fear of Success [78]
        Needs [67]

Achievement Potential [73]
PN 87   SC 00510
SN One's general ability to achieve in any area, including academic.
UF Potential (Achievement)
N   Academic Aptitude [73]
R ↓ Ability [67]
      ↓ Achievement Motivation [67]

Achilles Tendon Reflex [73]
PN 11   SC 00520
B   Reflexes [71]

Achromatic Color [73]
PN 83   SC 00530
SN Visual quality which lacks hue and saturation, consequently varying only in brilliance. Includes variations from black through gray to white.
B   Color [67]

Acids [73]
PN 407   SC 00550
N ↓ Amino Acids [73]
        Ascorbic Acid [73]
        Aspirin [73]
        Dihydroxyphenylacetic Acid [91]
      ↓ Fatty Acids [73]
        Heparin [73]
        Homovanillic Acid [78]
        Hydroxyindoleacetic Acid (5-) [85]
        Kainic Acid [88]
        Lactic Acid [91]
        Lysergic Acid Diethylamide [67]
        Nicotinic Acid [73]
      ↓ Nucleic Acids [73]
        Taurine [82]
        Uric Acid [73]
R ↓ Drugs [67]
      ↓ Solvents [82]

Acoustic Nerve [73]
PN 58   SC 00570
UF Auditory Nerve
        Nerve (Acoustic)
B   Cranial Nerves [73]

Acoustic Reflex [73]
PN 248   SC 00580
SN Bilateral contraction of stapedius muscles when a loud sound is presented.
UF Intra Aural Muscle Reflex
        Stapedius Reflex
B   Reflexes [71]
R   Startle Reflex [67]

Acoustic Stimuli
Use Auditory Stimulation

Acquaintance Rape [91]
PN 42   SC 00593
SN Rape perpetrated by a person or persons known to the victim.
UF Date Rape
B   Rape [73]

2

Adrenal Gland Secretion [73]
PN 63   SC 01020
 B Endocrine Gland Secretion [73]

Adrenal Glands [73]
PN 339   SC 01030
 B Endocrine Glands [73]
 R ↓ Adrenal Cortex Hormones [73]

Adrenal Medulla Hormones [73]
PN 27   SC 01040
 B Hormones [67]
 N Norepinephrine [73]
 R ↓ Adrenal Cortex Hormones [73]

Adrenalectomy [73]
PN 282   SC 01050
 B Endocrine Gland Surgery [73]

Adrenaline
 Use Epinephrine

Adrenergic Blocking Drugs [73]
PN 732   SC 01070
 UF Beta Blockers
 B Drugs [67]
 N Alpha Methylparatyrosine [78]
   Dihydroergotamine [73]
   Hydroxydopamine (6-) [78]
   Phenoxybenzamine [73]
   Propranolol [73]
   Yohimbine [88]
 R ↓ Adrenolytic Drugs [73]
  ↓ Antihypertensive Drugs [73]
  ↓ Ergot Derivatives [73]
  ↓ Sympathetic Nervous System [73]
  ↓ Sympatholytic Drugs [73]

Adrenergic Drugs [73]
PN 239   SC 01080
 B Drugs [67]
 N ↓ Amphetamine [67]
   Dextroamphetamine [73]
   Ephedrine [73]
   Epinephrine [67]
   Methoxamine [73]
   Tyramine [73]
 R ↓ Catecholamines [73]
   Serotonin [73]
  ↓ Sympathetic Nervous System [73]
  ↓ Sympathomimetic Drugs [73]

Adrenergic Nerves [73]
PN 193   SC 01090
 UF Nerves (Adrenergic)
 B Autonomic Nervous System [67]

Adrenocorticotropin
 Use Corticotropin

Adrenolytic Drugs [73]
PN 8   SC 01120
 B Drugs [67]
 N Chlorpromazine [67]
   Chlorprothixene [73]
 R ↓ Adrenergic Blocking Drugs [73]
   Epinephrine [67]
  ↓ Sympathetic Nervous System [73]
  ↓ Sympatholytic Drugs [73]

Adult Attitudes [88]
PN 2379   SC 01122
 SN Attitudes of, not toward, adults.
 B Attitudes [67]
 R ↓ Adults [67]

Adult Children
 Use Adult Offspring

Adult Development [78]
PN 1554   SC 01127
 SN Process of physical, cognitive, personality, and psychosocial growth occurring from age 18. Use a more specific term if possible.
 B Human Development [67]
 R ↓ Adults [67]
  ↓ Aged [73]
  ↓ Developmental Age Groups [73]
  ↓ Developmental Stages [73]
   Mentor [85]
   Middle Aged [73]
   Physiological Aging [67]
  ↓ Psychogenesis [73]
   Young Adults [73]

Adult Education [73]
PN 1112   SC 01130
 SN Formal or informal education for adults, including but not limited to basic education, high school equivalency, vocational education, correspondence courses, continuing education, non-degree coursework, and lifelong learning programs.
 UF High School Equivalency
 B Education [67]
 N ↓ Continuing Education [85]
 R Reentry Students [85]

Adult Offspring [85]
PN 1164   SC 01135
 SN Ages 18 or older.
 UF Adult Children
   Grown Children
 B Adults [67]
   Family Members [73]
   Offspring [88]
 R Empty Nest [91]

Adultery
 Use Extramarital Intercourse

Adulthood [84]
PN 216643   SC 01150
 SN Mandatory age identifier used for ages 18 or older. Where appropriate, more specific index terms (e.g., MIDDLE AGED) are used in addition to this age identifier. The other two age identifiers are ADOLESCENCE and CHILDHOOD.
 R ↓ Adults [67]

Adults [67]
PN 4113   SC 01160
 SN Ages 18 years or older. Used in noneducational contexts. Applied only if age is important to the research focus.
 B Developmental Age Groups [73]
 N Adult Offspring [85]
  ↓ Aged [73]
   Middle Aged [73]
   Young Adults [73]
 R Adult Attitudes [88]
   Adult Development [78]
   Adulthood [84]

Advance Directives [94]
PN 0   SC 01163
 SN Declaration of personal wishes through legal documents or written instructions pertaining to future medical care if one becomes incapacitated.
 UF Living Wills
 R Client Rights [88]
  ↓ Death and Dying [67]
   Euthanasia [73]
  ↓ Legal Processes [73]
   Palliative Care [91]

Advance Directives — (cont'd)
 R Terminally Ill Patients [73]
   Treatment Refusal [94]
   Treatment Withholding [88]

Advance Organizers [85]
PN 140   SC 01165
 SN Structural overview of material to be taught to facilitate incorporation of new material into that previously learned or known.
 UF Structured Overview
 B Instructional Media [67]
   Teaching Methods [67]

Adventitiously Handicapped [73]
PN 32   SC 01170
 SN Persons with handicaps resulting from illness or injury during developmental or adult years.
 B Handicapped [67]
 R Congenitally Handicapped [73]

Adverbs [73]
PN 45   SC 01180
 B Form Classes (Language) [73]

Advertising [67]
PN 1392   SC 01190
 N Television Advertising [73]
 R Brand Names [78]
   Brand Preferences [94]
  ↓ Consumer Research [73]
   Marketing [73]
  ↓ Mass Media [67]
   Public Relations [73]
   Retailing [91]

Advocacy [85]
PN 264   SC 01195
 SN The process of defending or pleading the cause of another individual or group.
 UF Child Advocacy
 R Child Welfare [88]
  ↓ Civil Rights [78]
   Empowerment [91]
  ↓ Government Policy Making [73]
   Independent Living Programs [91]
   Legislative Processes [73]

Aerobic Exercise [88]
PN 199   SC 01197
 B Exercise [73]
 R Health Behavior [82]
   Physical Fitness [73]
   Weight Control [85]

Aerospace Personnel [73]
PN 231   SC 01200
 UF Aircraft Crew
   Aviation Personnel
   Flight Attendants
   Navigators (Aircraft)
 B Professional Personnel [78]
 N Aircraft Pilots [73]
   Astronauts [73]
 R ↓ Business and Industrial Personnel [67]
   Engineers [67]
   Physicists [73]
   Scientists [67]

Aesthetic Preferences [73]
PN 988   SC 01210
 B Preferences [67]
 R Aesthetics [67]
   Interior Design [82]

Aesthetics [67]
PN 739   SC 01220

Aesthetics — (cont'd)
SN Scientific or philosophical study of beauty or judgments of beauty. Also, the aesthetic qualities themselves.
  R Aesthetic Preferences [73]
    ↓ Arts [73]
      Interior Design [82]

Aetiology
  Use Etiology

Affection [73]
PN 333   **SC** 01250
  UF Liking
  B Emotional States [73]
  R ↓ Interpersonal Interaction [67]
      Intimacy [73]
      Love [73]

Affective Disorders
  Use Affective Disturbances

Affective Disturbances [67]
PN 3048   **SC** 01260
  UF Affective Disorders
  B Neurosis [67]
  N ↓ Major Depression [88]
    ↓ Mania [67]
    ↓ Manic Depression [73]
      Schizoaffective Disorder [94]
      Seasonal Affective Disorder [91]
  R Alexithymia [82]
    ↓ Anxiety Neurosis [73]

Affective Education [82]
PN 369   **SC** 01265
  SN Curriculum aimed at changing emotional and social behavior of students and enhancing their understanding of such behavior.
  UF Humanistic Education
  B Curriculum [67]
  R Self Actualization [73]
    ↓ Self Concept [67]
      Social Skills [78]

Affective Psychosis [73]
PN 254   **SC** 01270
  B Psychosis [67]
  N Involutional Depression [73]
  R ↓ Manic Depression [73]

Afferent Pathways [82]
PN 585   **SC** 01275
  SN Collections of fibers that carry neural impulses toward neural processing areas from sensory mechanisms or other processing areas.
  UF Sensory Pathways
  B Neural Pathways [82]
  N ↓ Lemniscal System [85]
      Spinothalamic Tracts [73]
  R Dorsal Horns [85]
    ↓ Efferent Pathways [82]
    ↓ Receptive Fields [85]
    ↓ Sensory Neurons [73]

Afferent Stimulation [73]
PN 98   **SC** 01280
  SN Sensory stimulation causing nerve impulses to be carried toward the brain, spinal cord, or sensory relay and processing areas.
  UF Afferentation
  B Stimulation [67]
  R ↓ Nervous System [67]
    ↓ Perceptual Stimulation [73]
    ↓ Stereotaxic Techniques [73]
    ↓ Surgery [71]

Afferentation
  Use Afferent Stimulation

Affiliation Motivation [67]
PN 536   **SC** 01300
  SN Need for association with others and formation of friendships.
  UF Need for Affiliation
  B Motivation [67]
  R Needs [67]

Affirmative Action [85]
PN 88   **SC** 01305
  SN Programs or policies designed to actively recruit women and minority group members for employment or higher education, in an effort to correct underrepresentative distributions of these groups relative to the general population.
  R Age Discrimination [94]
    ↓ Civil Rights [78]
      Employment Discrimination [94]
      Minority Groups [67]
    ↓ Personnel [67]
    ↓ Personnel Management [73]
    ↓ Personnel Recruitment [73]
    ↓ Personnel Selection [67]
      Race and Ethnic Discrimination [94]
      Sex Discrimination [78]
    ↓ Social Discrimination [82]
      Social Equality [73]

Afghanistan [88]
PN 6   **SC** 01307
  B Asia [73]

Africa [67]
PN 1661   **SC** 01310
  N Algeria [88]
      Angola [88]
      Benin [91]
      Botswana [88]
      Cameroon [91]
      Congo [91]
      East Africa [88]
      Egypt [82]
      Ethiopia [82]
      Ghana [88]
      Guinea [91]
      Ivory Coast [88]
      Kenya [82]
      Liberia [91]
      Libya [88]
      Malawi [91]
      Mali [91]
      Morocco [88]
      Mozambique [88]
      Niger [91]
      Nigeria [82]
      Rwanda [91]
      Senegal [88]
      Sierra Leone [88]
      Somalia [91]
      South Africa [82]
      Sudan [88]
      Swaziland [91]
      Tanzania [82]
      Tunisia [91]
      Uganda [88]
      West Africa [88]
      Zaire [88]
      Zambia [82]
      Zimbabwe [88]
  R Madagascar [91]
      Mauritius [91]
      Middle East [78]

African Americans
  Use Blacks

Aftercare [73]
PN 472   **SC** 01320
  SN Continuing program of rehabilitation designed to reinforce and maintain the effects of treatment and to help clients adjust to their environment after hospital release.
  B Treatment [67]
  R Discharge Planning [94]
      Outpatient Commitment [91]
    ↓ Outpatient Treatment [67]
      Partial Hospitalization [85]
      Posttreatment Followup [73]

Aftereffect (Perceptual)
  Use Perceptual Aftereffect

Afterimage [67]
PN 225   **SC** 01340
  SN Persistence of sensory excitation, usually visual, after cessation of stimulation. This temporary illusory sensation is due to physiological changes in the receptor cells.
  UF Successive Contrast
  B Perceptual Aftereffect [67]

Age Differences [67]
PN 25107   **SC** 01360
  SN Age comparisons of behavioral, developmental, and cognitive variations between individuals or groups. Used for human or animal subjects. Consider also DEVELOPMENTAL DIFFERENCES to access references prior to 1982.
  UF Developmental Differences
  R Animal Development [78]
      Cohort Analysis [88]
    ↓ Development [67]
    ↓ Developmental Age Groups [73]
      Generation Gap [73]
      Grade Level [94]
    ↓ Human Development [67]
    ↓ Physical Development [73]
    ↓ Psychogenesis [73]

Age Discrimination [94]
PN 0   **SC** 01363
  SN Use SOCIAL DISCRIMINATION to access references from 82-93.
  B Social Discrimination [82]
  R Affirmative Action [85]
      Aged (Attitudes Toward) [78]
      Aging (Attitudes Toward) [85]
    ↓ Civil Rights [78]
      Employment Discrimination [94]
    ↓ Prejudice [67]
      Stereotyped Attitudes [67]

Age Regression (Hypnotic) [88]
PN 33   **SC** 01365
  SN Technique used to recapture early life experiences by inducing amnesia for present dates and events and guiding clients back year by year.
  B Hypnosis [67]
      Hypnotherapy [73]
  R Early Experience [67]
      Early Memories [85]
      Life Experiences [73]
    ↓ Psychotherapeutic Techniques [67]

Aged [73]
PN 23934   **SC** 01370
  SN Ages 65 years or older. Use GERIATRICS or GERONTOLOGY to access references from 67-72.
  UF Old Age
      Senescence
      Senior Citizens
  B Adults [67]
  N Very Old [88]
  R Adult Development [78]

Aged — (cont'd)
R   Aged (Attitudes Toward) [78]
   ↓ Aging [91]
    Elder Abuse [88]
    Elder Care [94]
    Geriatric Patients [73]
    Geriatrics [67]
    Gerontology [67]
    Homebound [88]
    Physiological Aging [67]
   ↓ Senile Dementia [73]

Aged (Attitudes Toward) [78]
PN 747   SC 01372
B   Attitudes [67]
R   Age Discrimination [94]
   ↓ Aged [73]
   ↓ Aging [91]
    Aging (Attitudes Toward) [85]
    Geriatrics [67]
    Gerontology [67]
    Physiological Aging [67]
    Very Old [88]

Agencies (Groups)
Use Organizations

Aggressive Behavior [67]
PN 5707   SC 01390
UF   Agonistic Behavior
    Fighting
B   Social Behavior [67]
N   ↓ Animal Aggressive Behavior [73]
    Attack Behavior [73]
    Coercion [94]
   ↓ Conflict [67]
R   ↓ Behavior Disorders [71]
    Conduct Disorder [91]
    Retaliation [91]
   ↓ Social Interaction [67]

Aggressiveness [73]
PN 1030   SC 01400
B   Personality Traits [67]

Agility (Physical)
Use Physical Agility

Aging [91]
PN 436   SC 01413
N   Physiological Aging [67]
R   ↓ Aged [73]
    Aged (Attitudes Toward) [78]
    Aging (Attitudes Toward) [85]
   ↓ Developmental Age Groups [73]
   ↓ Developmental Stages [73]
    Geriatrics [67]
    Gerontology [67]
   ↓ Human Development [67]
    Life Expectancy [82]
    Middle Aged [73]
    Very Old [88]

Aging (Attitudes Toward) [85]
PN 207   SC 01415
SN Attitudes toward the aging process. Includes attitudes toward one's own physical aging and psychological and social maturation.
B   Attitudes [67]
R   Age Discrimination [94]
    Aged (Attitudes Toward) [78]
   ↓ Aging [91]
   ↓ Physical Development [73]
    Physiological Aging [67]
   ↓ Psychosocial Development [73]
    Self Perception [67]

Aging (Physiological)
Use Physiological Aging

Agitated Depression
SN Use DEPRESSION (EMOTION) to access references from 73-87.
Use Major Depression

Agitation [91]
PN 63   SC 01440
SN State usually characterized by restlessness, anxiety, and anguish.
R   Akathisia [91]
   ↓ Anxiety [67]
    Distress [73]
    Restlessness [73]

Agnosia [73]
PN 166   SC 01450
SN Inability to recognize, understand, or interpret sensory stimuli in the absence of sensory defects. Also, the selective loss of knowledge of specific objects due to emotional disturbance, as seen in schizophrenia, hysteria, or depression.
B   Aphasia [67]
    Perceptual Disturbances [73]
N   Anosognosia [94]
    Prosopagnosia [94]

Agonistic Behavior
Use Aggressive Behavior

Agoraphobia [73]
PN 1129   SC 01480
SN Excessive fear of being alone, or being in public places or situations (e.g., in crowds or elevators) from which there is no easy escape or where help cannot be obtained in the event of an incapacitating reaction or panic.
B   Phobias [67]

Agrammatism
Use Aphasia

Agraphia [73]
PN 109   SC 01490
SN Inability to write (letters, syllables, words, or phrases) due to an injury to a specific cerebral area or occasionally due to emotional factors.
B   Aphasia [67]
R   ↓ Learning Disabilities [73]

Agricultural Extension Workers [73]
PN 55   SC 01500
SN Government employees (usually local, county, or state) who assist with agricultural matters, distribute educational materials, and provide services pertaining to agriculture.
UF   County Agricultural Agents
    Extension Workers (Agricultural)
B   Government Personnel [73]
R   ↓ Agricultural Workers [73]

Agricultural Workers [73]
PN 333   SC 01510
UF   Farmers
    Laborers (Farm)
B   Nonprofessional Personnel [82]
N   Migrant Farm Workers [73]
R   Agricultural Extension Workers [73]
   ↓ Business and Industrial Personnel [67]

AIDS
Use Acquired Immune Deficiency Syndrome

AIDS Prevention [94]
PN 0   SC 01517

AIDS Prevention — (cont'd)
SN Health related programs or services directed toward those at risk for HIV/AIDS. Includes prevention of HIV/AIDS and personal risk through health behavior and lifestyle characteristics.
B   Prevention [73]
R   Acquired Immune Deficiency Syndrome [88]
    Condoms [91]
    Health Behavior [82]
   ↓ Health Education [73]
    Health Promotion [91]
   ↓ Human Immunodeficiency Virus [91]

Air Encephalography
Use Pneumoencephalography

Air Force Personnel [67]
PN 843   SC 01530
B   Military Personnel [67]
R   National Guardsmen [73]

Air Traffic Accidents [73]
PN 124   SC 01540
B   Transportation Accidents [73]
R   Air Traffic Control [73]
    Air Transportation [73]
   ↓ Aviation Safety [73]

Air Traffic Control [73]
PN 179   SC 01550
B   Aviation Safety [73]
R   Air Traffic Accidents [73]
    Air Transportation [73]
   ↓ Transportation Accidents [73]

Air Transportation [73]
PN 111   SC 01560
B   Transportation [73]
R   Air Traffic Accidents [73]
    Air Traffic Control [73]
   ↓ Aircraft [73]
    Public Transportation [73]
    Spacecraft [73]

Aircraft [73]
PN 144   SC 01570
UF   Airplanes
N   Helicopters [73]
R   Air Transportation [73]
    Aircraft Pilots [73]

Aircraft Crew
Use Aerospace Personnel

Aircraft Pilots [73]
PN 1006   SC 01580
UF   Aviators
    Pilots (Aircraft)
B   Aerospace Personnel [73]
R   ↓ Aircraft [73]
    Astronauts [73]
   ↓ Aviation Safety [73]

Airplanes
Use Aircraft

Akathisia [91]
PN 49   SC 01595
SN The inability to remain in a sitting posture or motor restlessness often resulting from heavy doses of tranquilizing drugs.
R   Agitation [91]
    Restlessness [73]
   ↓ Side Effects (Drug) [73]
   ↓ Symptoms [67]

Akinesia
Use Apraxia

Alanines 73
PN 17   SC 01610
B   Amino Acids 73
N   ↓ Phenylalanine 73

Alarm Responses 73
PN 205   SC 01620
SN   Behavioral, emotional, or physiological reactions to actual or perceived physical threat. Used primarily for animal populations.
R   ↓ Animal Defensive Behavior 82
     Animal Distress Calls 73
     Animal Escape Behavior 73
     ↓ Animal Ethology 67
     ↓ Fear 67
     Startle Reflex 67
     Tonic Immobility 78

Alaska 73
PN 98   SC 01630
B   United States 67
R   Arctic Regions 91

Albinism 73
PN 50   SC 01640
B   Genetic Disorders 73
R   ↓ Eye Disorders 73
     ↓ Skin Disorders 73

Albino Rats
Use Rats

Alcohol Abstinence
Use Sobriety

Alcohol Abuse 88
PN 1413   SC 01660
UF   Problem Drinking
B   Alcohol Drinking Patterns 67
     Drug Abuse 73
N   ↓ Alcohol Intoxication 73
     ↓ Alcoholism 67
R   Alcohol Withdrawal 94
     Blood Alcohol Concentration 94
     Codependency 91
     Drug Abuse Liability 94
     Polydrug Abuse 94

Alcohol Dehydrogenases 73
PN 40   SC 01670
B   Dehydrogenases 73
R   ↓ Alcohols 67

Alcohol Drinking Attitudes 73
PN 733   SC 01680
SN   Attitudes toward the use or abuse of alcohol.
UF   Drinking Attitudes
B   Drug Usage Attitudes 73
R   Sobriety 88

Alcohol Drinking Patterns 67
PN 4038   SC 01690
UF   Drinking (Alcohol)
B   Drinking Behavior 78
     Drug Usage 71
N   ↓ Alcohol Abuse 88
     Social Drinking 73
R   ↓ Alcohol Intoxication 73
     ↓ Alcoholism 67
     Blood Alcohol Concentration 94

Alcohol Education
Use Drug Education

Alcohol Intoxication 73
PN 952   SC 01700
UF   Drunkenness
     Intoxication (Alcohol)
B   Alcohol Abuse 88
     Toxic Disorders 73
N   Acute Alcoholic Intoxication 73
     Chronic Alcoholic Intoxication 73
R   ↓ Alcohol Drinking Patterns 67
     ↓ Alcoholism 67
     Blood Alcohol Concentration 94
     Driving Under The Influence 88
     Toxic Psychoses 73

Alcohol Rehabilitation 82
PN 2524   SC 01705
SN   Treatment for alcoholism which may include detoxification, psychotherapy, behavior therapy, Alcoholics Anonymous, and medication. Use DRUG REHABILITATION to access references from 73–81.
B   Drug Rehabilitation 73
N   Alcoholics Anonymous 73
     Detoxification 73
R   Alcohol Withdrawal 94
     Rehabilitation Counseling 78
     Sobriety 88

Alcohol Withdrawal 94
PN 0   SC 01707
SN   Used for human or animal populations.
B   Drug Withdrawal 73
R   ↓ Alcohol Abuse 88
     ↓ Alcohol Rehabilitation 82
     ↓ Alcoholic Psychosis 73
     ↓ Alcoholism 67
     Detoxification 73
     Sobriety 88

Alcoholic Beverages 73
PN 404   SC 01710
UF   Beverages (Alcoholic)
N   Beer 73
     Liquor 73
     Wine 73
R   Beverages (Nonalcoholic) 78
     ↓ Drinking Behavior 78
     Prenatal Exposure 91

Alcoholic Hallucinosis 73
PN 35   SC 01720
B   Alcoholic Psychosis 73
     Hallucinosis 73
N   Delirium Tremens 73
     Korsakoffs Psychosis 73

Alcoholic Psychosis 73
PN 61   SC 01730
B   Organic Brain Syndromes 73
     Psychosis 67
N   ↓ Alcoholic Hallucinosis 73
R   Alcohol Withdrawal 94
     ↓ Nutritional Deficiencies 73
     Toxic Psychoses 73

Alcoholics Anonymous 73
PN 262   SC 01740
SN   A self-supporting, informal, international fellowship whose primary purpose is to help members achieve sobriety.
B   Alcohol Rehabilitation 82
     Support Groups 91
R   ↓ Community Services 67

Alcoholism 67
PN 10397   SC 01750
B   Addiction 73
     Alcohol Abuse 88
N   Korsakoffs Psychosis 73

Alcoholism — (cont'd)
N   Wernickes Syndrome 73
R   ↓ Alcohol Drinking Patterns 67
     ↓ Alcohol Intoxication 73
     Alcohol Withdrawal 94
     Fetal Alcohol Syndrome 85
     ↓ Nutritional Deficiencies 73
     Sobriety 88
     ↓ Toxic Disorders 73

Alcohols 67
PN 1242   SC 01760
B   Drugs 67
N   Ephedrine 73
     Ethanol 73
     Isoproterenol 73
     Mephenesin 73
     Methanol 73
     Methoxamine 73
     Propranolol 73
     Tetrahydrocannabinol 73
     Trihexyphenidyl 73
R   Acetaldehyde 82
     Alcohol Dehydrogenases 73
     Blood Alcohol Concentration 94
     ↓ Solvents 82

Aldolases 73
PN 3   SC 01770
B   Enzymes 73

Aldosterone 73
PN 58   SC 01780
B   Adrenal Cortex Hormones 73
     Corticosteroids 73

Alexia 82
PN 81   SC 01785
SN   Inability to read which may be the result of neurological impairment. In a less severe form, often referred to as dyslexia.
UF   Word Blindness
B   Dysphasia 78
N   Dyslexia 73
R   ↓ Reading Disabilities 67

Alexithymia 82
PN 296   SC 01788
SN   Affective and cognitive disturbances characterized by impaired fantasy life and an inability to verbalize or differentiate emotions. These disturbances overlap diagnostic categories and appear generally in psychosomatic patients.
B   Mental Disorders 67
R   ↓ Affective Disturbances 67

Algebra
Use Mathematics

Algeria 88
PN 23   SC 01795
B   Africa 67

Algorithms 73
PN 693   SC 01800
SN   Set of well-defined rules established for step-by-step solution of problems in a finite number of steps.
B   Mathematics (Concepts) 67
R   Computer Programing 94

Alienation 71
PN 1119   SC 01810
SN   Withdrawal or estrangement from persons, objects, or positions of former attachment; feelings of detachment from self or avoidance of emotional experiences.

Alienation — (cont'd)
B   Emotional States [73]
R   Anomie [78]
     Depersonalization [73]

Alkaloids [73]
PN   158   SC   01820
UF   Opium Alkaloids
B   Drugs [67]
N   Apomorphine [73]
     Atropine [73]
     Bromocriptine [88]
     Caffeine [73]
     Cocaine [73]
     Codeine [73]
     Ephedrine [73]
   ↓ Gamma Aminobutyric Acid Antagonists [85]
     Heroin [73]
     Homatropine [73]
     Mescaline [73]
     Morphine [73]
     Nicotine [73]
     Papaverine [73]
     Peyote [73]
     Physostigmine [73]
     Pilocarpine [73]
     Quinidine [73]
     Quinine [73]
     Reserpine [67]
     Scopolamine [73]
     Strychnine [73]
     Theophylline [73]
     Tubocurarine [73]
R ↓ Anti Inflammatory Drugs [82]
     Curare [73]
   ↓ Ergot Derivatives [73]

Allergens
Use   Antigens

Allergic Disorders [73]
PN   138   SC   01830
B   Immunologic Disorders [73]
N   Allergic Skin Disorders [73]
     Drug Allergies [73]
     Food Allergies [73]
     Hay Fever [73]
R   Anaphylactic Shock [73]

Allergic Skin Disorders [73]
PN   13   SC   01840
B   Allergic Disorders [73]
     Skin Disorders [73]
R ↓ Dermatitis [73]
     Eczema [73]
     Neurodermatitis [73]

Alligators
Use   Crocodilians

Allport Vernon Lindzey Study Values [73]
PN   9   SC   01870
B   Attitude Measures [67]

Alopecia [73]
PN   44   SC   01880
SN   Baldness or the loss of hair.
UF   Hair Loss
B   Skin Disorders [73]
R ↓ Genetic Disorders [73]
     Hair [73]

Alpha Methylparatyrosine [78]
PN   103   SC   01887
UF   Alpha Methyltyrosine
B   Adrenergic Blocking Drugs [73]
     Antihypertensive Drugs [73]
     Tyrosine [73]

Alpha Methyltyrosine
Use   Alpha Methylparatyrosine

Alpha Rhythm [73]
PN   539   SC   01890
SN   Electrically measured impulses or waves of
low amplitude and a frequency of 8-13 cycles per
second usually observable in the electroencephalogram during wakeful rest.
B   Electrical Activity [67]
     Electroencephalography [67]

Alphabets [73]
PN   83   SC   01900
SN   Systems for writing a language.
B   Written Language [67]
N   Initial Teaching Alphabet [73]
   ↓ Letters (Alphabet) [73]
R   Orthography [73]

Alprazolam [88]
PN   259   SC   01903
B   Benzodiazepines [78]
     Minor Tranquilizers [73]
     Sedatives [73]

Alternative Schools
Use   Nontraditional Education

Altitude Effects [73]
PN   128   SC   01910
B   Environmental Effects [73]
R ↓ Aviation [67]
   ↓ Gravitational Effects [67]

Altruism [73]
PN   780   SC   01920
SN   Consideration for well-being of others as op-
posed to self-love or egoism. Used for human or
animal populations.
B   Personality Traits [67]
     Prosocial Behavior [82]
R   Assistance (Social Behavior) [73]
     Charitable Behavior [73]
   ↓ Sharing (Social Behavior) [78]

Aluminum [94]
PN   0   SC   01930
B   Metallic Elements [73]

Alzheimers Disease [73]
PN   3204   SC   01940
B   Organic Brain Syndromes [73]
     Presenile Dementia [73]
R   Picks Disease [73]
   ↓ Senile Dementia [73]

Amantadine [78]
PN   61   SC   01945
UF   Amatadine
B   Antibiotics [73]
     Antitremor Drugs [73]
R   Parkinsons Disease [73]

Amatadine
Use   Amantadine

Amaurotic Familial Idiocy [73]
PN   19   SC   01950
UF   Familial Idiocy (Amaurotic)
     Idiocy (Amaurotic Familial)
     Tay Sachs Disease
B   Genetic Disorders [73]
     Lipid Metabolism Disorders [73]
     Mental Retardation [67]
     Neonatal Disorders [73]

Ambiguity (Stimulus)
Use   Stimulus Ambiguity

Ambiguity (Tolerance)
Use   Tolerance for Ambiguity

Ambition
Use   Aspirations

Ambivalence [73]
PN   124   SC   01990
B   Emotional States [73]

Amblyopia [73]
PN   140   SC   02000
SN   An optically uncorrectable loss of visual acu-
ity without apparent organic change or defect.
B   Eye Disorders [73]
R ↓ Refraction Errors [73]
     Strabismus [73]

Ambulatory Care
Use   Outpatient Treatment

Amenorrhea [73]
PN   83   SC   02010
SN   Absence or abnormal cessation of the men-
ses.
B   Menstrual Disorders [73]

Amentia
Use   Mental Retardation

American Indians [67]
PN   1537   SC   02030
SN   Native populations of North and South
America and the Caribbean Islands, with the ex-
ception of Eskimos.
UF   Indians (American)
     Native Americans
B   Ethnic Groups [73]
R   Minority Groups [67]

American Samoa [91]
PN   5   SC   02035
B   South Pacific [78]

Amine Oxidase Inhibitors [73]
PN   6   SC   02040
B   Enzyme Inhibitors [85]
N ↓ Dopamine Antagonists [82]
     Iproniazid [73]
     Isocarboxazid [73]
     Lysergic Acid Diethylamide [67]
     Nialamide [73]
R ↓ Monoamine Oxidase Inhibitors [73]

Amines [73]
PN   407   SC   02060
B   Drugs [67]
N   Amitriptyline [73]
     Atropine [73]
     Bufotenine [73]
     Chlordiazepoxide [73]
     Chlorimipramine [73]
     Chlorisondamine [73]
     Chlorpromazine [67]
     Chlorprothixene [73]
     Cocaine [73]
     Diphenhydramine [73]
     Galanthamine [73]
     Guanethidine [73]
     Histamine [73]
     Homatropine [73]
     Hydroxylamine [73]
     Imipramine [73]
     Mecamylamine [73]

Amines — (cont'd)
N Meperidine [73]
  Methylphenidate [73]
  Orphenadrine [73]
  Phenethylamines [85]
  Phenoxybenzamine [73]
  Physostigmine [73]
  Puromycin [73]
  Scopolamine [73]
  Serotonin [73]
  ↓ Sympathomimetic Amines [73]
  Thalidomide [73]
  Trihexyphenidyl [73]
  Tryptamine [73]
R ↓ Amino Acids [73]
  Deanol [82]

Amino Acids [73]
PN 587   SC 02070
B Acids [73]
N ↓ Alanines [73]
  ↓ Aspartic Acid [73]
  Cysteine [73]
  DOPA [73]
  Folic Acid [73]
  Gamma Aminobutyric Acid [78]
  Glutamic Acid [73]
  Glutamine [73]
  Glycine [73]
  Histidine [73]
  Leucine [73]
  Methionine [73]
  Proline [82]
  ↓ Tryptophan [73]
  ↓ Tyrosine [73]
R ↓ Amines [73]
  Nerve Growth Factor [94]
  ↓ Neurotransmitters [85]
  ↓ Proteins [73]

Aminotransferases
Use Transaminases

Amitriptyline [73]
PN 780   SC 02090
UF Elavil
B Amines [73]
  Antidepressant Drugs [71]
  Tranquilizing Drugs [67]

Amnesia [67]
PN 1514   SC 02120
SN Systematic and extensive loss of memory caused by organic or psychological factors. The loss may be temporary or permanent, and may involve old or recent memories. Compare FORGETTING and MEMORY DECAY.
B Dissociative Patterns [73]
  Memory Disorders [73]
N Fugue Reaction [73]
R Forgetting [73]

Amniocentesis
Use Prenatal Diagnosis

Amniotic Fluid [73]
PN 22   SC 02130
B Body Fluids [73]

Amobarbital [73]
PN 123   SC 02140
UF Amobarbital Sodium
  Amytal
B Barbiturates [67]
  CNS Depressant Drugs [73]
  Hypnotic Drugs [73]
  Narcoanalytic Drugs [73]
  Sedatives [73]

Amobarbital Sodium
Use Amobarbital

Amphetamine [67]
PN 2119   SC 02160
UF Amphetamine (dl-)
  Amphetamine Sulfate
  Benzedrine
B Adrenergic Drugs [73]
  Appetite Depressing Drugs [73]
  CNS Stimulating Drugs [73]
  Dopamine Agonists [85]
  Sympathomimetic Amines [73]
  Vasoconstrictor Drugs [73]
N Dextroamphetamine [73]
  Methamphetamine [73]
R Phenethylamines [85]

Amphetamine (d-)
Use Dextroamphetamine

Amphetamine (dl-)
Use Amphetamine

Amphetamine Sulfate
Use Amphetamine

Amphibia [73]
PN 51   SC 02200
B Vertebrates [73]
N Frogs [67]
  Salamanders [73]
  Toads [73]

Amplifiers (Apparatus) [73]
PN 37   SC 02210
B Apparatus [67]

Amplitude (Response)
Use Response Amplitude

Amputation [73]
PN 68   SC 02230
B Surgery [71]
N Mastectomy [73]
R Phantom Limbs [73]
  ↓ Prostheses [73]

Amputees [73]
PN 79   SC 02240
B Physically Handicapped [67]

Amygdaloid Body [73]
PN 1018   SC 02250
B Basal Ganglia [73]
  Limbic System [73]
R Medial Forebrain Bundle [82]

Amytal
Use Amobarbital

Anabolism [73]
PN 10   SC 02280
SN Constructive part of metabolism concerned especially with macromolecular synthesis.
B Metabolism [67]

Anabolites
Use Metabolites

Anaclitic Depression [73]
PN 28   SC 02290
SN Syndrome of withdrawal characterizing infants separated from their mothers for a long period of time.
B Major Depression [88]
R Attachment Behavior [85]

Anaclitic Depression — (cont'd)
R Object Relations [82]
  ↓ Parental Absence [73]

Anagram Problem Solving [73]
PN 274   SC 02300
B Problem Solving [67]
R Anagrams [73]

Anagrams [73]
PN 26   SC 02310
SN Words or phrases made by rearranging letters of other words or phrases (e.g., leader from dealer).
B Vocabulary [67]
R Anagram Problem Solving [73]

Analeptic Drugs [73]
PN 51   SC 02320
UF Antagonists (CNS Depressant Drugs)
  CNS Depressant Drug Antagonists
B CNS Stimulating Drugs [73]
N Bemegride [73]
  Bicuculline [94]
  Picrotoxin [73]
  Strychnine [73]
R Barbiturate Poisoning [73]
  Caffeine [73]
  ↓ Cholinomimetic Drugs [73]
  ↓ Heart Rate Affecting Drugs [73]
  Methylphenidate [73]
  Pentylenetetrazol [73]
  Theophylline [73]

Analgesia [82]
PN 1130   SC 02325
SN Pain insensitivity chemically or electrically induced or occurring as a natural phenomenon (e.g., Kiesow's area on the inner cheek).
B Pain Perception [73]
R ↓ Analgesic Drugs [73]
  ↓ Anesthesia (Feeling) [73]
  ↓ Endorphins [82]
  Enkephalins [82]
  Pain Management [94]

Analgesic Drugs [73]
PN 623   SC 02330
UF Anodynes
  Pain Relieving Drugs
B Drugs [67]
N Aspirin [73]
  Atropine [73]
  Carbamazepine [88]
  Codeine [73]
  Dihydroergotamine [73]
  Heroin [73]
  Meperidine [73]
  Methadone [73]
  Morphine [73]
  Papaverine [73]
  Pentazocine [91]
  Phencyclidine [82]
  Procaine [82]
  Quinine [73]
  Scopolamine [73]
R Analgesia [82]
  ↓ Anesthetic Drugs [73]
  ↓ Anti Inflammatory Drugs [82]
  ↓ CNS Depressant Drugs [73]
  ↓ Hypnotic Drugs [73]
  ↓ Narcotic Drugs [73]
  ↓ Pain [67]
  Pain Management [94]
  ↓ Sedatives [73]

Analog Computers [73]
PN 17   SC 02340

Analog Computers — (cont'd)
SN Electronic, mechanical, or electromechanical machines that measure continuous electrical or physical magnitudes (e.g., automobile speedometer) rather than operating on discrete digits.
  B   Computers [67]

Analogy [91]
PN 85   SC 02345
  R   Connotations [73]
      ↓ Figurative Language [85]
      Inference [73]
      Logical Thinking [67]
      Metaphor [82]
      ↓ Reasoning [67]

Analysis [67]
PN 1122   SC 02370
SN Conceptually broad array term referring to the process of examination of a complex problem, its elements, and their relations. Use a more specific term if possible.
  N   Behavioral Assessment [82]
      Causal Analysis [94]
      Cohort Analysis [88]
      Content Analysis [78]
      Content Analysis (Test) [67]
      ↓ Costs and Cost Analysis [73]
      Error Analysis [73]
      Item Analysis (Test) [67]
      Job Analysis [67]
      Risk Analysis [91]
      ↓ Statistical Analysis [67]
      Systems Analysis [73]
      Task Analysis [67]
  R   Analysis of Covariance [73]
      Analysis of Variance [67]
      Multidimensional Scaling [82]

Analysis of Covariance [73]
PN 318   SC 02350
  B   Variability Measurement [73]
  R   ↓ Analysis [67]
      Analysis of Variance [67]
      Multiple Regression [82]
      ↓ Multivariate Analysis [82]

Analysis of Variance [67]
PN 976   SC 02360
  UF ANOVA (Statistics)
  B   Variability Measurement [73]
  R   ↓ Analysis [67]
      Analysis of Covariance [73]
      Multiple Regression [82]
      ↓ Multivariate Analysis [82]
      ↓ Statistical Regression [85]
      Variance Homogeneity [85]

Analysts
  Use Psychoanalysts

Analytic Psychology
  Use Jungian Psychology

Analytical Psychotherapy [73]
PN 347   SC 02390
SN Form of psychotherapy based on work of C. G. Jung. The unconscious, personal and collective, is disclosed through free association and dream analysis. Therapeutic goals include integration of conscious and unconscious for growth and personality development and a life of fuller awareness.
  B   Psychotherapy [67]
  R   Archetypes [91]
      Jung (Carl) [73]
      Jungian Psychology [73]

Anaphylactic Shock [73]
PN 10   SC 02400
SN Immunologic or allergic reaction to antigens such as drugs or foreign proteins to which a hypersensitivity has been established by previous contact.
  UF Protein Sensitization
      Sensitization (Protein)
  B   Immunologic Disorders [73]
  R   ↓ Allergic Disorders [73]
      Shock [67]

Anatomical Systems [73]
PN 14   SC 02410
SN Conceptually broad array term referring to anatomically related structures (e.g., vascular system). Use a more specific term if possible.
  B   Anatomy [67]
      Systems [67]
  N   ↓ Cardiovascular System [67]
      ↓ Digestive System [67]
      ↓ Endocrine System [73]
      ↓ Musculoskeletal System [73]
      ↓ Nervous System [67]
      ↓ Respiratory System [73]
      ↓ Urogenital System [73]

Anatomically Detailed Dolls [91]
PN 16   SC 02415
SN Dolls used in a general play setting or for evaluation and assessment purposes in a therapeutic or legal context.
  B   Toys [73]
  R   ↓ Child Abuse [71]
      Childhood Play Behavior [78]
      Clinical Judgment (Not Diagnosis) [73]
      Doll Play [73]
      ↓ Sexual Abuse [88]

Anatomy [67]
PN 1106   SC 02420
SN Conceptually broad array term referring both to the science of anatomy and the actual structure or morphology of an organism. Use specific anatomical or neuroanatomical terms if possible.
  N   Abdomen [73]
      ↓ Anatomical Systems [73]
      Back (Anatomy) [73]
      ↓ Body Fluids [73]
      Breast [73]
      ↓ Cells (Biology) [73]
      Face (Anatomy) [73]
      Feet (Anatomy) [73]
      Hair [73]
      Hand (Anatomy) [67]
      Head (Anatomy) [73]
      Neck (Anatomy) [73]
      Palm (Anatomy) [73]
      Scalp (Anatomy) [73]
      ↓ Sense Organs [73]
      Thigh [73]
      ↓ Tissues (Body) [73]
  R   Morphology [73]
      Neuroanatomy [67]
      ↓ Physiology [67]

Ancestors [73]
PN 13   SC 02430
  UF Great Grandparents
  B   Family Members [73]
  N   Grandparents [73]
      ↓ Parents [67]

Androgen Antagonists
  Use Antiandrogens

Androgens [73]
PN 396   SC 02440

Androgens — (cont'd)
  B   Sex Hormones [73]
  N   Testosterone [73]
  R   Antiandrogens [82]
      Antiestrogens [82]

Androgyny [82]
PN 576   SC 02445
SN Combination of masculine and feminine personality characteristics in one individual.
  B   Personality Traits [67]
  R   Femininity [67]
      Masculinity [67]
      Sex Roles [67]

Anemia [73]
PN 103   SC 02450
  B   Blood and Lymphatic Disorders [73]
  R   ↓ Genetic Disorders [73]
      Sickle Cell Disease [94]

Anencephaly [73]
PN 8   SC 02460
  B   Brain Disorders [67]
      Mental Retardation [67]
      Neonatal Disorders [73]

Anesthesia (Feeling) [73]
PN 144   SC 02470
  N   Hysterical Anesthesia [73]
  R   Analgesia [82]
      ↓ Disorders [67]
      ↓ Sense Organ Disorders [73]
      ↓ Tactual Perception [67]

Anesthesiology [73]
PN 49   SC 02480
  B   Medical Sciences [67]

Anesthetic Drugs [73]
PN 380   SC 02490
  B   Drugs [67]
  N   ↓ General Anesthetics [73]
      Hexobarbital [73]
      ↓ Local Anesthetics [73]
      Pentobarbital [73]
      Phencyclidine [82]
      Procaine [82]
  R   ↓ Analgesic Drugs [73]
      ↓ Anticonvulsive Drugs [73]
      ↓ Barbiturates [67]
      ↓ CNS Depressant Drugs [73]
      ↓ Hypnotic Drugs [73]
      ↓ Muscle Relaxing Drugs [73]
      ↓ Narcotic Drugs [73]
      ↓ Sedatives [73]

Aneurysms [73]
PN 42   SC 02500
  B   Cardiovascular Disorders [67]

Anger [67]
PN 1248   SC 02510
  UF Rage
  B   Emotional States [73]
  N   Hostility [67]
  R   Jealousy [73]
      Tantrums [73]

Angina Pectoris [73]
PN 80   SC 02530
  B   Heart Disorders [73]
  R   Myocardial Infarctions [73]

Angiography [73]
PN 30   SC 02540
  B   Roentgenography [73]

Angiotensin 73
PN 277   SC 02550
   B   Peptides 73
       Vasoconstrictor Drugs 73
   R   Captopril 91

Anglos 88
PN 202   SC 02553
   B   Ethnic Groups 73
   R   Whites 82

Angola 88
PN 1   SC 02555
   B   Africa 67

Angst
   Use Anxiety

Anguish
   Use Distress

Anhedonia 85
PN 65   SC 02575
SN Loss or absence of ability to experience pleasure.
   B   Symptoms 67
   R   Dysthymic Disorder 88
     ↓ Neurosis 67
       Pleasure 73
     ↓ Schizophrenia 67

Animal Aggressive Behavior 73
PN 3531   SC 02580
   B   Aggressive Behavior 67
       Animal Social Behavior 67
   N   Animal Predatory Behavior 78
       Attack Behavior 73
       Muricide 88
       Threat Postures 73
   R   Animal Dominance 73
       Territoriality 67

Animal Assisted Therapy 94
PN 0   SC 02585
SN A type of therapy based on the human-animal companion bond used in an effort to assist in restoring feelings of hope, self worth, responsibility, and communication.
   UF   Pet Therapy
   B   Psychotherapeutic Techniques 67
   R   ↓ Animals 67
       Geriatric Psychotherapy 73
       Interspecies Interaction 91
       Pets 82
     ↓ Rehabilitation 67

Animal Behavior
   Use Animal Ethology

Animal Biological Rhythms 73
PN 298   SC 02600
SN Rhythmic and periodic variations in behavioral or physiological functions of animals. Use BIOLOGICAL RHYTHMS to access references from 67–72.
   UF   Biological Clocks (Animal)
   B   Animal Ethology 67
       Biological Rhythms 67
   N   Animal Circadian Rhythms 73
   R   Animal Sexual Receptivity 73
       Estrus 73
       Hibernation 73

Animal Breeding 73
PN 1942   SC 02610

Animal Breeding — (cont'd)
SN Propagation (or reproduction) of a species in its natural environment or in captive settings. Includes birth rate and breeding success. Compare ANIMAL DOMESTICATION, EUGENICS, and SELECTIVE BREEDING.
   UF   Breeding (Animal)
   N   Selective Breeding 73
   R   Animal Captivity 94
       Animal Domestication 78
     ↓ Animal Mating Behavior 67
     ↓ Animal Sexual Behavior 85
       Animal Strain Differences 82
     ↓ Animals 67
       Assortative Mating 91
     ↓ Genetics 67
       Litter Size 85
     ↓ Sexual Reproduction 73

Animal Captivity 94
PN 0   SC 02615
   UF   Captivity (Animal)
       Zoo Environment
   B   Animal Environments 67
   R   ↓ Animal Breeding 73
       Animal Domestication 78
       Animal Rearing 91
       Animal Welfare 85

Animal Circadian Rhythms 73
PN 1523   SC 02620
SN Diurnal cyclical variations or patterns of behavioral or physiological functions of animals. Use BIOLOGICAL RHYTHMS to access references from 67–72.
   UF   Circadian Rhythms (Animal)
       Daily Biological Rhythms (Animal)
   B   Animal Biological Rhythms 73
   R   Animal Nocturnal Behavior 73

Animal Coloration 85
PN 144   SC 02625
SN Physical aspect of body color.
   R   Animal Courtship Displays 73
     ↓ Animal Defensive Behavior 82
     ↓ Pigments 73

Animal Communication 67
PN 936   SC 02630
   B   Animal Social Behavior 67
       Communication 67
   N   Animal Distress Calls 73
   R   Animal Scent Marking 85
     ↓ Animal Vocalizations 73
     ↓ Vocalization 67

Animal Courtship Behavior 73
PN 651   SC 02640
   UF   Courtship (Animal)
   B   Animal Sexual Behavior 85
       Animal Social Behavior 67
   N   Animal Courtship Displays 73
   R   Animal Mate Selection 82
     ↓ Animal Mating Behavior 67

Animal Courtship Displays 73
PN 187   SC 02650
   UF   Courtship Displays (Animal)
   B   Animal Courtship Behavior 73
       Animal Social Behavior 67
   R   Animal Coloration 85
     ↓ Animal Mating Behavior 67
       Territoriality 67

Animal Defensive Behavior 82
PN 1107   SC 02652
SN Innate protective responses that occur in presence of predator or other threatening stimulus.

Animal Defensive Behavior — (cont'd)
   UF   Defensive Behavior (Animal)
   B   Animal Ethology 67
   N   Animal Escape Behavior 73
       Threat Postures 73
   R   Alarm Responses 73
       Animal Coloration 85
       Attack Behavior 73
       Instinctive Behavior 82
       Tonic Immobility 78

Animal Development 78
PN 1645   SC 02655
SN Conceptually broad array term. Use a more specific term if possible.
   B   Development 67
   R   Age Differences 67
     ↓ Animals 67
     ↓ Motor Development 73
       Neural Development 85
       Perceptual Motor Development 91
     ↓ Physical Development 73
     ↓ Prenatal Development 73

Animal Distress Calls 73
PN 221   SC 02660
   UF   Distress Calls (Animal)
   B   Animal Communication 67
       Animal Vocalizations 73
   R   Alarm Responses 73

Animal Division of Labor 73
PN 116   SC 02670
   UF   Division of Labor (Animal)
   B   Animal Social Behavior 67
       Division of Labor 88
   R   Animal Dominance 73

Animal Domestication 78
PN 101   SC 02677
SN Adaptation of wild animals to life and breeding in tame conditions according to the interests of human society. Compare ANIMAL BREEDING, EUGENICS, and SELECTIVE BREEDING.
   UF   Domestication (Animal)
   R   ↓ Animal Breeding 73
       Animal Captivity 94
       Selective Breeding 73

Animal Dominance 73
PN 1312   SC 02680
   UF   Dominance (Animal)
       Pecking Order
   B   Animal Social Behavior 67
       Dominance 67
   R   ↓ Animal Aggressive Behavior 73
       Animal Division of Labor 73
       Animal Scent Marking 85
       Dominance Hierarchy 73
       Territoriality 67

Animal Drinking Behavior 73
PN 1635   SC 02690
   UF   Drinking Behavior (Animal)
   B   Animal Ethology 67
       Drinking Behavior 78
   R   Licking 88
       Polydipsia 82
       Sucking 78
       Thirst 67
       Water Intake 67

Animal Emotionality 78
PN 652   SC 02696
   R   Animal Motivation 67
     ↓ Emotional Responses 67

Animal Environments [67]
PN 4250   SC 02700
SN Physical and social conditions of an animal's existence or habitat.
B   Social Environments [73]
N   Animal Captivity [94]
R   Animal Rearing [91]
  ↓ Animals [67]
    Place Conditioning [91]

Animal Escape Behavior [73]
PN 591   SC 02710
UF   Escape Behavior (Animal)
B   Animal Defensive Behavior [82]
R   Alarm Responses [73]

Animal Ethology [67]
PN 2225   SC 02720
SN Study of animal behavior especially in relation to ecology, evolution, neuroanatomy, neurophysiology, and genetics. Used for the discipline or the ethological processes themselves. Use a more specific term if possible.
UF   Animal Behavior
    Ethology (Animal)
B   Behavior [67]
N   ↓ Animal Biological Rhythms [73]
  ↓ Animal Defensive Behavior [82]
    Animal Drinking Behavior [73]
    Animal Exploratory Behavior [73]
    Animal Feeding Behavior [73]
    Animal Foraging Behavior [85]
    Animal Grooming Behavior [78]
    Animal Hoarding Behavior [73]
    Animal Homing [91]
    Animal Nocturnal Behavior [73]
    Animal Open Field Behavior [73]
  ↓ Animal Parental Behavior [82]
    Animal Play [73]
    Animal Sex Differences [67]
  ↓ Animal Sexual Behavior [85]
  ↓ Animal Social Behavior [67]
  ↓ Animal Vocalizations [73]
    Hibernation [73]
    Imprinting [67]
    Licking [88]
    Migratory Behavior (Animal) [73]
    Nest Building [73]
    Species Recognition [85]
    Territoriality [67]
R   Alarm Responses [73]
  ↓ Animals [67]
    Echolocation [73]
    Instinctive Behavior [82]
    Stereotyped Behavior [73]
    Tool Use [91]

Animal Exploratory Behavior [73]
PN 1283   SC 02730
SN Use EXPLORATORY BEHAVIOR to access references from 67–72.
B   Animal Ethology [67]
    Exploratory Behavior [67]
R   Animal Foraging Behavior [85]
    Neophobia [85]
    Spontaneous Alternation [82]

Animal Feeding Behavior [73]
PN 3653   SC 02740
UF   Feeding Behavior (Animal)
B   Animal Ethology [67]
R   Animal Foraging Behavior [85]
    Animal Maternal Behavior [73]
    Animal Paternal Behavior [91]
  ↓ Food Intake [67]
    Hunger [67]
    Sucking [78]

Animal Foraging Behavior [85]
PN 770   SC 02743
UF   Foraging (Animal)
B   Animal Ethology [67]
R   Animal Exploratory Behavior [73]
    Animal Feeding Behavior [73]
    Animal Predatory Behavior [78]

Animal Grooming Behavior [78]
PN 497   SC 02745
UF   Grooming Behavior (Animal)
B   Animal Ethology [67]
R   Licking [88]

Animal Hoarding Behavior [73]
PN 148   SC 02750
UF   Hoarding Behavior (Animal)
B   Animal Ethology [67]

Animal Homing [91]
PN 21   SC 02755
SN Returning accurately to one's home or natal area from a distance.
UF   Homing (Animal)
B   Animal Ethology [67]
R   Instinctive Behavior [82]
    Migratory Behavior (Animal) [73]
    Territoriality [67]

Animal Human Interaction
  Use Interspecies Interaction

Animal Innate Behavior
  SN Term discontinued in 1982. Use ANIMAL INNATE BEHAVIOR or ANIMAL INSTINCTIVE BEHAVIOR to access references from 73–81 and 67–81, respectively.
  Use Instinctive Behavior

Animal Instinctive Behavior
  SN Term discontinued in 1982. Use ANIMAL INSTINCTIVE BEHAVIOR or ANIMAL INNATE BEHAVIOR to access references from 67–81 and 73–81, respectively.
  Use Instinctive Behavior

Animal Licking Behavior
  Use Licking

Animal Locomotion [82]
PN 1215   SC 02775
SN Any form of motor activity resulting in bodily propulsion.
B   Motor Processes [67]

Animal Mate Selection [82]
PN 547   SC 02778
SN Ethological processes surrounding the choice of mate for sexual reproduction.
UF   Mate Selection
R   ↓ Animal Courtship Behavior [73]
  ↓ Animal Mating Behavior [67]
  ↓ Animal Sexual Behavior [85]
    Assortative Mating [91]
  ↓ Genetics [67]
  ↓ Sexual Reproduction [73]

Animal Maternal Behavior [73]
PN 1899   SC 02780
UF   Maternal Behavior (Animal)
B   Animal Parental Behavior [82]
R   Animal Feeding Behavior [73]
    Animal Maternal Deprivation [88]
    Animal Paternal Behavior [91]
    Animal Rearing [91]
    Licking [88]

Animal Maternal Deprivation [88]
PN 70   SC 02785
SN Consider using ANIMAL MATERNAL BEHAVIOR prior to 1988.
R   Animal Maternal Behavior [73]
    Animal Rearing [91]
  ↓ Social Isolation [67]

Animal Mating Behavior [67]
PN 3755   SC 02790
UF   Coitus (Animal)
    Copulation (Animal)
    Mating Behavior (Animal)
B   Animal Sexual Behavior [85]
    Animal Social Behavior [67]
N   Animal Sexual Receptivity [73]
R   ↓ Animal Breeding [73]
  ↓ Animal Courtship Behavior [73]
    Animal Courtship Displays [73]
    Animal Mate Selection [82]
    Assortative Mating [91]
    Nest Building [73]
    Pheromones [73]
  ↓ Sexual Reproduction [73]

Animal Models [88]
PN 1000   SC 02797
SN Experimentally induced simulations of human conditions in animals designed to investigate the etiology and characteristics of diseases, psychological and psychiatric disorders, or learning processes.
B   Models [67]
R   ↓ Animals [67]
  ↓ Experimental Design [67]
  ↓ Experimentation [67]

Animal Motivation [67]
PN 1281   SC 02800
B   Motivation [67]
R   Animal Emotionality [78]
  ↓ Animals [67]
    Instinctive Behavior [82]

Animal Navigation
  Use Migratory Behavior (Animal)

Animal Nocturnal Behavior [73]
PN 100   SC 02820
UF   Nocturnal Behavior (Animal)
B   Animal Ethology [67]
R   Animal Circadian Rhythms [73]

Animal Open Field Behavior [73]
PN 1420   SC 02825
SN Spontaneous animal behavior studied in relatively unrestricted laboratory environments. Prior to 1985 also used for spontaneous animal behavior in natural environments.
UF   Open Field Behavior (Animal)
B   Animal Ethology [67]

Animal Parental Behavior [82]
PN 529   SC 02828
SN Nurturance and care of offspring performed by male and/or female parents.
UF   Parental Behavior (Animal)
B   Animal Ethology [67]
    Animal Social Behavior [67]
N   Animal Maternal Behavior [73]
    Animal Paternal Behavior [91]
R   Animal Rearing [91]

Animal Paternal Behavior [91]
PN 46   SC 02829
B   Animal Parental Behavior [82]
R   Animal Feeding Behavior [73]
    Animal Maternal Behavior [73]
    Animal Rearing [91]

Animal Play [73]
PN 334   SC 02830
  UF   Play (Animal)
  B   Animal Ethology [67]
  R   ↓ Animal Social Behavior [67]

Animal Predatory Behavior [78]
PN 1055   SC 02834
  UF   Predatory Behavior (Animal)
  B   Animal Aggressive Behavior [73]
  R   Animal Foraging Behavior [85]
       Attack Behavior [73]
       Threat Postures [73]

Animal Rearing [91]
PN 139   SC 02836
SN Conditions or environment in which animals are bred, nourished, and raised. Compare ANIMAL PARENTAL BEHAVIOR.
  R   Animal Captivity [94]
      ↓ Animal Environments [67]
       Animal Maternal Behavior [73]
       Animal Maternal Deprivation [88]
      ↓ Animal Parental Behavior [82]
       Animal Paternal Behavior [91]

Animal Scent Marking [85]
PN 168   SC 02837
  UF   Scent Marking (Animal)
  R   ↓ Animal Communication [67]
       Animal Dominance [73]
       Pheromones [73]
       Territoriality [67]

Animal Sex Differences [67]
PN 2184   SC 02840
SN Animal behavioral, developmental, and physiological/anatomical differences between the sexes.
  UF   Sex Differences (Animal)
  B   Animal Ethology [67]
  R   Sex [67]

Animal Sexual Behavior [85]
PN 1000   SC 02845
SN Any form of sexual behavior in animals.
  B   Animal Ethology [67]
  N   ↓ Animal Courtship Behavior [73]
      ↓ Animal Mating Behavior [67]
  R   ↓ Animal Breeding [73]
       Animal Mate Selection [82]
       Sex [67]

Animal Sexual Receptivity [73]
PN 1041   SC 02850
  UF   Lordosis (Animal)
       Sexual Receptivity (Animal)
  B   Animal Mating Behavior [67]
  R   ↓ Animal Biological Rhythms [73]
       Estrus [73]

Animal Social Behavior [67]
PN 4409   SC 02860
  B   Animal Ethology [67]
       Social Behavior [67]
  N   ↓ Animal Aggressive Behavior [73]
      ↓ Animal Communication [67]
      ↓ Animal Courtship Behavior [73]
       Animal Courtship Displays [73]
       Animal Division of Labor [73]
       Animal Dominance [73]
      ↓ Animal Mating Behavior [67]
      ↓ Animal Parental Behavior [82]
  R   Animal Play [73]
       Interspecies Interaction [91]
       Physical Contact [82]

Animal Strain Differences [82]
PN 1382   SC 02863
SN Anatomical, physiological, and/or behavioral variations between members of different subspecies or strains. Use GENETICS and ANIMAL BREEDING together to access references from 73-81. Compare SPECIES DIFFERENCES.
  UF   Strain Differences (Animal)
  R   ↓ Animal Breeding [73]
      ↓ Genetics [67]

Animal Tool Use
  Use Tool Use

Animal Vocalizations [73]
PN 2191   SC 02870
  UF   Vocalizations (Animal)
  B   Animal Ethology [67]
       Vocalization [67]
  N   Animal Distress Calls [73]
  R   ↓ Animal Communication [67]
       Echolocation [73]

Animal Welfare [85]
PN 138   SC 02875
  R   Animal Captivity [94]
       Experimental Ethics [78]

Animals [67]
PN 2732   SC 02880
SN Conceptually broad array term. Use a more specific term if possible (e.g., VERTEBRATES, MAMMALS, DOGS).
  N   Female Animals [73]
       Infants (Animal) [78]
      ↓ Invertebrates [73]
       Male Animals [73]
      ↓ Vertebrates [73]
  R   Animal Assisted Therapy [94]
      ↓ Animal Breeding [73]
       Animal Development [78]
      ↓ Animal Environments [67]
      ↓ Animal Ethology [67]
       Animal Models [88]
       Animal Motivation [67]
       Biological Symbiosis [73]
       Interspecies Interaction [91]
       Pets [82]
       Species Differences [82]

Animism [73]
PN 61   SC 02890
SN Ascribing life to inanimate objects. Also, the Piagetian stage of development in which children ascribe emotional attributes and intentions to inanimate objects.
  B   Philosophies [67]
  R   Ethnology [67]
       Myths [67]
       Taboos [73]

Ankle [73]
PN 14   SC 02900
  B   Joints (Anatomy) [73]
  R   Feet (Anatomy) [73]
       Leg (Anatomy) [73]

Anniversary Events [94]
PN 0   SC 02905
SN Annual occurrence of a specific date that marks a notable event or experience. Includes aspects of both positive or negative reactions to the event or experience.
  UF   Anniversary Reactions
  B   Experiences (Events) [73]
  R   Autobiographical Memory [94]
       Early Experience [67]
       Early Memories [85]
       Life Experiences [73]

Anniversary Events — (cont'd)
  R   Life Review [91]
       Reminiscence [85]

Anniversary Reactions
  Use Anniversary Events

Annual Leave
  Use Employee Leave Benefits

Annual Report [73]
PN 37   SC 02920
SN Mandatory term used as a document type identifier.

Anodynes
  Use Analgesic Drugs

Anomie [78]
PN 152   SC 02940
SN Sense of alienation or despair resulting from the loss or weakening of previously held values. Also, a state of lawlessness or a lack of normative standards within groups or societies.
  B   Social Processes [67]
  R   Alienation [71]
       Personal Values [73]
       Social Values [73]

Anonymity [73]
PN 149   SC 02945
SN Unknown, unacknowledged, or concealed personal identity.
  R   Privileged Communication [73]
       Secrecy [94]
       Self Disclosure [73]
      ↓ Social Perception [67]

Anorexia Nervosa [73]
PN 2224   SC 02950
SN Syndrome in which the primary features include excessive fear of becoming overweight, body image disturbance, significant weight loss, refusal to maintain minimal normal weight, and amenorrhea. This disorder occurs most frequently in adolescent females.
  B   Appetite Disorders [73]
       Underweight [73]
  R   Bulimia [85]
      ↓ Nutritional Deficiencies [73]
      ↓ Psychosomatic Disorders [67]

Anorexigenic Drugs
  Use Appetite Depressing Drugs

Anosmia [73]
PN 118   SC 02970
SN Loss of the sense of smell.
  B   Sense Organ Disorders [73]
  R   ↓ Olfactory Perception [67]

Anosognosia [94]
PN 0   SC 02975
SN Lack of awareness of, or refusal or failure to deal with or recognize that one has a mental or physical disorder.
  B   Agnosia [73]
  R   Coping Behavior [67]
       Denial [73]
       Illness Behavior [82]

ANOVA (Statistics)
  Use Analysis of Variance

Anoxia [73]
PN 301   SC 02990
SN Absence or reduction of oxygen in body tissue.

Anoxia — (cont'd)
UF Asphyxia
     Hypoxia
B   Symptoms [67]
R ↓ Ischemia [73]
    ↓ Respiratory Distress [73]

Antabuse
Use Disulfiram

Antagonism
Use Hostility

Antagonists (CNS Depressant Drugs)
Use Analeptic Drugs

Antarctica [73]
PN 50   SC 03020

Anthropologists [73]
PN 24   SC 03030
B   Professional Personnel [78]
R   Scientists [67]
     Sociologists [73]

Anthropology [67]
PN 541   SC 03040
SN Science dealing with the study of the inter-relations of biological, cultural, geographical, and historical characteristics of the human species. Use a more specific term if possible.
B   Social Sciences [67]
R   Ethnography [73]
     Ethnology [67]

Anti Inflammatory Drugs [82]
PN 67   SC 03041
SN Agents which reduce inflammation by acting on body mechanisms, without directly antagonizing the causative agent.
UF Antipyretic Drugs
B   Drugs [67]
N   Aspirin [73]
    ↓ Glucocorticoids [82]
R ↓ Alkaloids [73]
    ↓ Analgesic Drugs [73]
    ↓ Enzymes [73]
    ↓ Hormones [67]
    Hydrocortisone [73]
    Prostaglandins [82]
    ↓ Steroids [73]

Antiandrogens [82]
PN 65   SC 03042
SN Substances capable of preventing the normal effects of androgenic hormones on responsive tissues by antagonistic effects on tissue or by inhibiting androgenic effects.
UF Androgen Antagonists
B   Drugs [67]
R ↓ Androgens [73]
    ↓ Estrogens [73]
    ↓ Steroids [73]

Antianxiety Drugs
Use Tranquilizing Drugs

Antibiotics [73]
PN 176   SC 03050
B   Drugs [67]
N   Amantadine [78]
    Cycloheximide [73]
    Penicillins [73]
    Puromycin [73]
R   Antineoplastic Drugs [82]

Antibodies [73]
PN 281   SC 03060

Antibodies — (cont'd)
B   Globulins [73]
R   Antigens [82]
    Blood Serum [73]
    ↓ Drugs [67]
    Gamma Globulin [73]
    Immunization [73]
    ↓ Immunoglobulins [73]
    ↓ Neurotoxins [82]

Anticholinergic Drugs
Use Cholinergic Blocking Drugs

Anticholinesterase Drugs
Use Cholinesterase Inhibitors

Anticipation (Serial Learning)
Use Serial Anticipation (Learning)

Anticoagulant Drugs [73]
PN 19   SC 03100
B   Drugs [67]
N   Heparin [73]

Anticonvulsive Drugs [73]
PN 700   SC 03110
SN Use ANTICONVULSIVE DRUGS or ANTIEPI-LEPTIC DRUGS (including DIPHENYLHYDAN-TOIN, or PRIMIDONE) to access references from 73–81.
UF Antiepileptic Drugs
B   Drugs [67]
N   Carbamazepine [88]
    Chloral Hydrate [73]
    Clonazepam [91]
    Diphenylhydantoin [73]
    Nitrazepam [78]
    Oxazepam [78]
    Pentobarbital [73]
    Phenobarbital [73]
    Primidone [73]
    Valproic Acid [91]
R   Acetazolamide [73]
    ↓ Anesthetic Drugs [73]
    ↓ Antispasmodic Drugs [73]
    ↓ Barbiturates [67]
    ↓ Benzodiazepines [78]
    ↓ CNS Depressant Drugs [73]
    ↓ Convulsions [67]
    ↓ Epilepsy [67]
    ↓ Hypnotic Drugs [73]
    ↓ Muscle Relaxing Drugs [73]
    ↓ Narcotic Drugs [73]
    ↓ Sedatives [73]
    ↓ Spasms [73]
    ↓ Tranquilizing Drugs [67]

Antidepressant Drugs [71]
PN 4003   SC 03120
B   Drugs [67]
N   Amitriptyline [73]
    Bupropion [94]
    Chlorimipramine [73]
    Deanol [82]
    Desipramine [73]
    Doxepin [94]
    Fluoxetine [91]
    Fluvoxamine [94]
    Imipramine [73]
    Iproniazid [73]
    Isocarboxazid [73]
    Lithium Carbonate [73]
    Maprotiline [82]
    Methylphenidate [73]
    Mianserin [82]
    Molindone [82]
    Nialamide [73]
    Nomifensine [82]

Antidepressant Drugs — (cont'd)
N   Nortriptyline [94]
    Paroxetine [94]
    Phenelzine [73]
    Pheniprazine [73]
    Pipradrol [73]
    Sulpiride [73]
    Tranylcypromine [73]
    Trazodone [88]
    Zimeldine [88]
R ↓ CNS Stimulating Drugs [73]
    ↓ Lithium [73]
    ↓ Monoamine Oxidase Inhibitors [73]

Antiemetic Drugs [73]
PN 60   SC 03140
UF Antinauseant Drugs
B   Drugs [67]
N   Chlorpromazine [67]
    Chlorprothixene [73]
    Fluphenazine [73]
    Perphenazine [73]
    Piracetam [82]
    Prochlorperazine [73]
    Promethazine [73]
    Sulpiride [73]
R ↓ Cholinergic Blocking Drugs [73]
    ↓ Hypnotic Drugs [73]
    Nausea [73]
    ↓ Sedatives [73]
    ↓ Tranquilizing Drugs [67]
    Vomiting [73]

Antiepileptic Drugs
SN Term discontinued in 1982. Use ANTIEPI-LEPTIC DRUGS (including DIPHENYLHYDAN-TOIN, or PRIMIDONE) or ANTICONVULSIVE DRUGS to access references from 73–81.
Use Anticonvulsive Drugs

Antiestrogens [82]
PN 22   SC 03155
SN Substances capable of preventing the normal effects of estrogenic hormones on responsive tissues by antagonistic effects on tissue or by inhibiting estrogenic effects.
UF Estrogen Antagonists
B   Drugs [67]
R ↓ Androgens [73]
    Antineoplastic Drugs [82]
    ↓ Estrogens [73]
    ↓ Steroids [73]

Antigens [82]
PN 144   SC 03158
SN Substances such as microorganisms or foreign tissues, cells, proteins, toxoids, or exotoxins having the ability to induce antibody formation.
UF Allergens
     Immunogens
R   Antibodies [73]
    Blood Groups [73]
    ↓ Immunoglobulins [73]
    Interleukins [94]

Antihistaminic Drugs [73]
PN 171   SC 03160
B   Drugs [67]
N   Chlorprothixene [73]
    Cimetidine [85]
    Diphenhydramine [73]
    Mianserin [82]
    Orphenadrine [73]
    Promethazine [73]
R   Histamine [73]
    Hydroxyzine [73]
    ↓ Hypnotic Drugs [73]
    ↓ Sedatives [73]

Antihypertensive Drugs 73
PN 168   SC 03170
B   Drugs 67
N   Alpha Methylparatyrosine 78
    Captopril 91
    Chlorisondamine 73
    Chlorpromazine 67
    Clonidine 73
    Guanethidine 73
    Hexamethonium 73
    Hydralazine 73
    Iproniazid 73
    Mecamylamine 73
    Methyldopa 73
    Pargyline 73
    Pheniprazine 73
    Phenoxybenzamine 73
    Quinpirole 94
    Rauwolfia 73
    Reserpine 67
R   ↓ Adrenergic Blocking Drugs 73
    ↓ Diuretics 73
    ↓ Ganglion Blocking Drugs 73
    ↓ Heart Rate Affecting Drugs 73
    ↓ Hypertension 73
    ↓ Hypnotic Drugs 73
    ↓ Muscle Relaxing Drugs 73
    ↓ Sedatives 73
    ↓ Tranquilizing Drugs 67
    ↓ Vasodilator Drugs 73

Antinauseant Drugs
Use Antiemetic Drugs

Antineoplastic Drugs 82
PN 68   SC 03179
SN Drugs used in the prevention of the development, maturation, or spread of neoplastic cells.
B   Drugs 67
R   ↓ Antibiotics 73
    Antiestrogens 82
    ↓ Hormones 67
    Interferons 94
    ↓ Neoplasms 67
    ↓ Steroids 73

Antiparkinsonian Drugs
Use Antitremor Drugs

Antipathy
Use Aversion

Antipsychotic Drugs
SN Term discontinued in 1982. Use ANTIPSYCHOTIC DRUGS (from 73–81) or the specific tranquilizing or neuroleptic drug to access references prior to 1982. From 1982, see the specific tranquilizing drugs, neuroleptic drugs, or other appropriate drug classes.
Use Neuroleptic Drugs

Antipyretic Drugs
Use Anti Inflammatory Drugs

Antischizophrenic Drugs
SN Term discontinued in 1982. Use ANTISCHIZOPHRENIC DRUGS (from 73–81) or the specific tranquilizing or neuroleptic drug to access references prior to 1982. From 1982, see the specific tranquilizing drugs, neuroleptic drugs, or other appropriate drug classes.
Use Neuroleptic Drugs

AntiSemitism 73
PN 221   SC 03220
B   Racial and Ethnic Attitudes 82
    Religious Prejudices 73
R   Holocaust 88

AntiSemitism — (cont'd)
R   Judaism 67
    ↓ Prejudice 67
    Racism 73

Antisocial Behavior 71
PN 1572   SC 03230
UF Deviant Behavior
    Sociopathology
B   Behavior 67
N   Child Neglect 88
    ↓ Crime 67
    Cruelty 73
    Elder Abuse 88
    Emotional Abuse 91
    Juvenile Delinquency 67
    Partner Abuse 91
    Patient Abuse 91
    Persecution 73
    Physical Abuse 91
    Recidivism 73
    Runaway Behavior 73
    ↓ Sexual Abuse 88
    Terrorism 82
    Torture 88
R   Antisocial Personality 73
    ↓ Behavior Disorders 71
    Explosive Personality 73
    ↓ Prosocial Behavior 82
    ↓ Social Behavior 67

Antisocial Personality 73
PN 695   SC 03240
SN Personality disorder characterized by conflict with others, low frustration tolerance, inadequate conscience development, and rejection of authority and discipline.
UF Psychopath
    Sociopath
B   Personality Disorders 67
R   ↓ Antisocial Behavior 71

Antispasmodic Drugs 73
PN 3   SC 03250
SN Drugs that prevent or reduce spasms usually by relaxation of smooth muscle.
B   Drugs 67
N   Atropine 73
    Chlorprothixene 73
    Meperidine 73
    Orphenadrine 73
    Papaverine 73
    Trihexyphenidyl 73
R   ↓ Anticonvulsive Drugs 73
    ↓ Cholinergic Blocking Drugs 73
    ↓ Muscle Relaxing Drugs 73
    ↓ Spasms 73

Antitremor Drugs 73
PN 154   SC 03260
SN Drugs that diminish skeletal muscle tone through action on the central nervous system.
UF Antiparkinsonian Drugs
B   Drugs 67
N   Amantadine 78
    Diphenhydramine 73
    Levodopa 73
    Nomifensine 82
    Orphenadrine 73
    Trihexyphenidyl 73
R   ↓ Decarboxylase Inhibitors 82
    Parkinsons Disease 73
    Tremor 73

Antitubercular Drugs 73
PN 7   SC 03270
B   Drugs 67
N   Iproniazid 73

Antitubercular Drugs — (cont'd)
N   Isoniazid 73
R   ↓ Tuberculosis 73

Antiviral Drugs 94
PN 0   SC 03280
B   Drugs 67
N   Zidovudine 94

Antonyms 73
PN 50   SC 03290
B   Semantics 67
    Vocabulary 67
R   Words (Phonetic Units) 67

Ants 73
PN 273   SC 03300
B   Insects 67
R   Larvae 73

Anxiety 67
PN 13259   SC 03310
SN Apprehension or fear of impending actual or imagined danger, vulnerability, or uncertainty. Prior to 1988, also used for anxiety disorders.
UF Angst
    Anxiousness
    Apprehension
    Worry
B   Emotional States 73
N   Mathematics Anxiety 85
    Performance Anxiety 94
    Social Anxiety 85
    Speech Anxiety 85
    Test Anxiety 67
R   Agitation 91
    ↓ Anxiety Neurosis 73
    ↓ Fear 67
    Fear of Success 78
    Guilt 67
    Jealousy 73
    Panic 73
    Panic Disorder 88
    ↓ Phobias 67
    Shame 94
    ↓ Stress 67

Anxiety Disorders
Use Anxiety Neurosis

Anxiety Neurosis 73
PN 1763   SC 03320
SN Disorders characterized by anxiety or dread without apparent object or cause. Symptoms include irritability, anxious expectation, pangs of conscience, anxiety attacks, or phobias. Prior to 1988, use also ANXIETY.
UF Anxiety Disorders
    Generalized Anxiety Disorder
B   Neurosis 67
N   Castration Anxiety 73
    Death Anxiety 78
    Obsessive Compulsive Neurosis 73
    Panic Disorder 88
    ↓ Phobias 67
    Posttraumatic Stress Disorder 85
    Separation Anxiety 73
R   ↓ Affective Disturbances 67
    ↓ Anxiety 67
    Fear of Success 78
    Guilt 67
    Hypochondriasis 73
    Mathematics Anxiety 85
    Performance Anxiety 94
    Social Anxiety 85
    Speech Anxiety 85
    Test Anxiety 67

Anxiety Reducing Drugs
Use Tranquilizing Drugs

Anxiolytic Drugs
Use Tranquilizing Drugs

Anxiousness
Use Anxiety

Aorta [73]
PN 16　　　　　SC 03360
B Arteries (Anatomy) [73]

Apathy [73]
PN 64　　　　　SC 03380
UF Indifference
B Emotional States [73]

Apes
Use Primates (Nonhuman)

Aphagia [73]
PN 44　　　　　SC 03400
SN Not eating, the refusal to eat, or an inability to swallow foods or fluids.
B Pain [67]
　　Symptoms [67]
R ↓ Appetite Disorders [73]

Aphasia [67]
PN 2252　　　　　SC 03410
SN Partial or complete impairment of language comprehension, formulation, or use due to brain damage.
UF Agrammatism
　　Word Deafness
B Brain Disorders [67]
　　Language Disorders [82]
N Acalculia [73]
　　↓ Agnosia [73]
　　Agraphia [73]
　　↓ Dysphasia [78]
R ↓ Learning Disabilities [73]
　　↓ Perceptual Disturbances [73]

Aphrodisiacs [73]
PN 15　　　　　SC 03420
R ↓ Cannabis [73]

Aplysia
Use Snails

Apnea [73]
PN 152　　　　　SC 03430
SN Temporary absence of breathing or prolonged respiratory failure.
B Respiratory Distress [73]
　　Respiratory Tract Disorders [73]
N Sleep Apnea [91]
R ↓ Neonatal Disorders [73]
　　Sudden Infant Death [82]

Apomorphine [73]
PN 1157　　　　　SC 03440
UF Apomorphine Hydrochloride
B Alkaloids [73]
　　Dopamine Agonists [85]
　　Emetic Drugs [73]
　　Hypnotic Drugs [73]
　　Narcotic Drugs [73]

Apomorphine Hydrochloride
Use Apomorphine

Apoplexy
Use Cerebrovascular Accidents

Appalachia [73]
PN 85　　　　　SC 03470
SN A mountainous eastern North American geographic region.
B United States [67]

Apparatus [67]
PN 3257　　　　　SC 03480
SN Set of materials, instruments, or equipment designed for specific operation. Use a more specific term if possible.
UF Devices (Experimental)
　　Equipment
　　Experimental Apparatus
N Amplifiers (Apparatus) [73]
　　Audiometers [73]
　　Cage Apparatus [73]
　　Cameras [73]
　　↓ Computer Peripheral Devices [85]
　　↓ Computers [67]
　　Electrodes [67]
　　Generators (Apparatus) [73]
　　Incubators (Apparatus) [73]
　　Keyboards [85]
　　↓ Mazes [67]
　　Metronomes [73]
　　Microscopes [73]
　　Oscilloscopes [73]
　　Polygraphs [73]
　　Shuttle Box Hurdles [73]
　　↓ Shuttle Boxes [73]
　　Skinner Boxes [73]
　　Sonar [73]
　　↓ Stimulators (Apparatus) [73]
　　Tachistoscopes [73]
　　↓ Tape Recorders [73]
　　Timers (Apparatus) [73]
　　Transducers [73]
　　Transistors (Apparatus) [73]
　　Vibrators (Apparatus) [73]
　　Volt Meters [73]
R ↓ Augmentative Communication [94]
　　↓ Television [67]

Apparent Distance [73]
PN 91　　　　　SC 03490
SN Subjective perception of distance as opposed to actual distance, based on comparison of retinal and familiar sizes.
B Distance Perception [73]

Apparent Movement [67]
PN 635　　　　　SC 03500
SN Subjective perception of movement in the absence of real physical movement.
UF Stroboscopic Movement
B Motion Perception [67]
N Autokinetic Illusion [67]

Apparent Size [73]
PN 206　　　　　SC 03510
SN Subjective perception of size as opposed to real or actual size.
UF Size (Apparent)
B Size Discrimination [67]

Apperception [73]
PN 21　　　　　SC 03520
SN Process of assimilating new perceptions and relating them to existing body of knowledge.
R ↓ Attention [67]
　　↓ Perception [67]

Appetite [73]
PN 335　　　　　SC 03530
SN Indicates an instinctive or acquired motivation, impulse, or desire stemming from internal physiological conditions. Compare HUNGER.

Appetite — (cont'd)
B Physiology [67]
N Hunger [67]
R ↓ Appetite Depressing Drugs [73]
　　↓ Appetite Disorders [73]
　　Dietary Restraint [94]
　　↓ Eating [67]
　　Eating Attitudes [94]
　　Satiation [67]

Appetite Depressing Drugs [73]
PN 110　　　　　SC 03540
UF Anorexigenic Drugs
B Drugs [67]
N ↓ Amphetamine [67]
　　Dextroamphetamine [73]
　　Fenfluramine [73]
　　Phenmetrazine [73]
R ↓ Appetite [73]

Appetite Disorders [73]
PN 890　　　　　SC 03550
UF Eating Disorders
B Disorders [67]
　　Mental Disorders [67]
　　Symptoms [67]
N Anorexia Nervosa [73]
　　Bulimia [85]
　　Hyperphagia [73]
　　Obesity [73]
R Aphagia [73]
　　↓ Appetite [73]
　　Binge Eating [91]
　　Nausea [73]
　　↓ Nutritional Deficiencies [73]
　　↓ Underweight [73]

Applied Psychology [73]
PN 313　　　　　SC 03560
SN Broad discipline in which psychological principles and theories are used to solve practical problems.
B Psychology [67]
N ↓ Clinical Psychology [67]
　　Community Psychology [73]
　　Consumer Psychology [73]
　　Counseling Psychology [73]
　　↓ Educational Psychology [67]
　　Engineering Psychology [67]
　　Environmental Psychology [82]
　　Industrial Psychology [67]
　　Military Psychology [67]
　　Social Psychology [67]
　　Sport Psychology [82]

Apprehension
Use Anxiety

Apprenticeship [73]
PN 65　　　　　SC 03580
B Personnel Training [67]
R Mentor [85]

Approval (Social)
Use Social Approval

Apraxia [73]
PN 316　　　　　SC 03600
SN Inability to execute complex coordinated movements resulting from lesions in the motor area of the cortex but involving no sensory impairment or paralysis.
UF Akinesia
B Movement Disorders [85]
　　Symptoms [67]
R Parkinsonism [94]
　　↓ Speech Disorders [67]

Aptitude
　Use Ability

Aptitude (Academic)
　Use Academic Aptitude

Aptitude Measures [67]
PN 1980　　　　　　　　　SC 03630
SN Tests designed to assess capacities or potential abilities in performing tasks, skills, or other acts which have not yet been learned.
　UF Ability Tests
　　　Tests (Aptitude)
　B Measurement [67]
　N Army General Classification Test [67]
　　　Coll Ent Exam Bd Scholastic Apt Test [73]
　　　Differential Aptitude Tests [73]
　　　General Aptitude Test Battery [73]
　　　Graduate Record Examination [73]
　　　Modern Language Aptitude Test [73]
　　　School and College Ability Test [73]

Arabs [88]
PN 141　　　　　　　　　　SC 03635
SN Persons of Arabic-speaking descent residing in countries other than the country of their origin.
　UF Palestinians
　B Ethnic Groups [73]
　R Minority Groups [67]

Arachnida [73]
PN 177　　　　　　　　　　SC 03640
　UF Spiders
　B Arthropoda [73]

Arachnophobia
　Use Phobias

Archetypes [91]
PN 43　　　　　　　　　　SC 03650
SN Unconscious representation of inherited collective experience on which the personality is built. Anima, animus, and the shadow are major archetypes. Consider JUNGIAN PSYCHOLOGY to access references from 73-90.
　R Analytical Psychotherapy [73]
　　↓ Imagery [67]
　　　Jung (Carl) [73]
　　　Jungian Psychology [73]
　　　Myths [67]
　　　Unconscious (Personality Factor) [67]

Architects [73]
PN 55　　　　　　　　　　SC 03670
　B Business and Industrial Personnel [67]

Architecture [73]
PN 483　　　　　　　　　　SC 03680
　B Arts [73]
　N Interior Design [82]
　R ↓ Environment [67]
　　↓ Environmental Planning [82]
　　　Religious Buildings [73]
　　　Urban Planning [73]

Arctic Regions [91]
PN 9　　　　　　　　　　SC 03685
　R Alaska [73]

Arecoline [73]
PN 64　　　　　　　　　　SC 03690
　UF Arecoline Hydrobromide
　B Cholinomimetic Drugs [73]
　R ↓ Bromides [73]

Arecoline Hydrobromide
　Use Arecoline

Argentina [82]
PN 87　　　　　　　　　　SC 03706
　B South America [67]

Arguments [73]
PN 192　　　　　　　　　　SC 03710
　B Conflict [67]
　　　Interpersonal Communication [73]

Arithmetic
　Use Mathematics

Arm (Anatomy) [73]
PN 242　　　　　　　　　　SC 03730
　B Musculoskeletal System [73]
　R Elbow (Anatomy) [73]
　　　Hand (Anatomy) [67]
　　　Shoulder (Anatomy) [73]
　　　Wrist [73]

Army General Classification Test [67]
PN 7　　　　　　　　　　SC 03740
　B Aptitude Measures [67]

Army Personnel [67]
PN 824　　　　　　　　　　SC 03750
　B Military Personnel [67]
　R Draftees [73]
　　　National Guardsmen [73]

Arousal (Physiological)
　Use Physiological Arousal

Arousal (Sexual)
　Use Sexual Arousal

Arrest (Law)
　Use Legal Arrest

Arrhythmias (Heart) [73]
PN 138　　　　　　　　　　SC 03790
　B Heart Disorders [73]
　N Bradycardia [73]
　　　Fibrillation (Heart) [73]
　　　Tachycardia [73]

Arson [85]
PN 89　　　　　　　　　　SC 03795
　UF Firesetting
　B Crime [67]

Art [67]
PN 866　　　　　　　　　　SC 03800
SN Products of aesthetic expression. Not used as a document type identifier.
　UF Artwork
　B Arts [73]
　N Crafts [73]
　　　Drawing [67]
　　　Painting (Art) [73]
　　　Photographic Art [73]
　　　Sculpturing [73]

Art Education [73]
PN 422　　　　　　　　　　SC 03810
　B Curriculum [67]

Art Therapy [73]
PN 909　　　　　　　　　　SC 03820
SN Therapy that uses the creative work of clients for emotional expression, sublimation, achievement, and to reveal underlying conflicts.
　B Creative Arts Therapy [94]
　R Recreation Therapy [73]

Arterial Pulse [73]
PN 318　　　　　　　　　　SC 03830

Arterial Pulse — (cont'd)
　UF Pulse (Arterial)
　R Blood Circulation [73]

Arteries (Anatomy) [73]
PN 98　　　　　　　　　　SC 03840
　UF Coronary Vessels
　　　Retinal Vessels
　B Blood Vessels [73]
　N Aorta [73]
　　　Carotid Arteries [73]

Arteriosclerosis [73]
PN 34　　　　　　　　　　SC 03850
　B Cardiovascular Disorders [67]
　N Atherosclerosis [73]
　　　Cerebral Arteriosclerosis [73]
　R ↓ Blood Pressure Disorders [73]

Arthritis [73]
PN 228　　　　　　　　　　SC 03860
　UF Rheumatism
　B Joint Disorders [73]
　N Rheumatoid Arthritis [73]
　R ↓ Infectious Disorders [73]

Arthropoda [73]
PN 26　　　　　　　　　　SC 03870
　B Invertebrates [73]
　N Arachnida [73]
　　↓ Crustacea [73]
　　↓ Insects [67]

Articulation (Speech) [67]
PN 1067　　　　　　　　　SC 03880
SN Production of speech sounds, specifically consonant production.
　B Speech Characteristics [73]
　　　Verbal Communication [67]
　R Phonetics [67]
　　　Pronunciation [73]

Articulation Disorders [73]
PN 354　　　　　　　　　　SC 03890
SN Speech disorders involving the substitution, omission, distortion, and addition of phonemes.
　B Speech Disorders [67]
　N Dysarthria [73]

Artificial Insemination
　Use Reproductive Technology

Artificial Intelligence [82]
PN 823　　　　　　　　　　SC 03895
SN Study and application of computers to simulate and perform functions of human information processing.
　B Computer Applications [73]
　N Expert Systems [91]
　　　Neural Networks [91]
　R Automated Speech Recognition [94]
　　　Automation [67]
　　↓ Cognitive Processes [67]
　　↓ Computers [67]
　　　Cybernetics [67]
　　　Intelligence [67]
　　　Man Machine Systems [73]
　　　Robotics [85]

Artificial Limbs
　Use Prostheses

Artificial Pacemakers [73]
PN 29　　　　　　　　　　SC 03910
　UF Pacemakers (Artificial)
　B Medical Therapeutic Devices [73]

Artificial Respiration [73]
PN 25   SC 03920
UF   Lifesaving
B   Physical Treatment Methods [73]
R   Respiration [67]
     ↓ Respiratory System [73]
     ↓ Respiratory Tract Disorders [73]

Artistic Ability [73]
PN 173   SC 03930
B   Nonverbal Ability [88]
N   Musical Ability [73]
R   Creativity [67]

Artists [73]
PN 791   SC 03940
B   Personnel [67]
N   Musicians [91]
     Writers [91]

Arts [73]
PN 202   SC 03950
SN   Conceptually broad term referring to all
forms of the arts, including the performing arts.
Use a more specific term if possible.
UF   Performing Arts
N   ↓ Architecture [73]
     ↓ Art [67]
     Dance [73]
     ↓ Literature [67]
     ↓ Music [67]
     ↓ Theatre [73]
R   Aesthetics [67]

Artwork
Use Art

Asbestos
Use Hazardous Materials

Asceticism [73]
PN 13   SC 03970
B   Philosophies [67]
     Religious Practices [73]
R   Religion [67]
     ↓ Religious Beliefs [73]

Ascorbic Acid [73]
PN 63   SC 03980
UF   Vitamin C
B   Acids [73]
     Vitamins [73]

Asia [73]
PN 424   SC 04000
N   Afghanistan [88]
     Bangladesh [82]
     Hong Kong [78]
     India [67]
     Iran [73]
     Iraq [88]
     Israel [67]
     Japan [67]
     Jordan [88]
     ↓ Korea [73]
     Lebanon [88]
     Middle East [78]
     Nepal [91]
     Pakistan [82]
     ↓ Peoples Republic of China [73]
     Saudi Arabia [85]
     ↓ Southeast Asia [73]
     Sri Lanka [88]
     Syria [88]
     Taiwan [73]
     Turkey [73]
     Union of Soviet Socialist Republics [67]

Asian Americans
SN   Term discontinued in 1982. Use ASIAN
AMERICANS to access references from 78-81.
Use Asians

Asians [82]
PN 1650   SC 04007
SN   Populations of Asian descent residing in
countries other than the country of their origin.
(For those residing in their own country use the
appropriate country name). Use ASIAN AMERI-
CANS to access references from 78–81.
UF   Asian Americans
     Chinese Americans
     Japanese Americans
     Orientals
B   Ethnic Groups [73]
R   Minority Groups [67]
     Race (Anthropological) [73]

Aspartic Acid [73]
PN 305   SC 04010
B   Amino Acids [73]
     Neurotransmitters [85]
N   N-Methyl-D-Aspartate [94]

Aspergers Syndrome [91]
PN 20   SC 04015
UF   Autistic Psychopathy
B   Personality Disorders [67]
     Syndromes [73]
R   ↓ Autism [67]

Asphyxia
Use Anoxia

Aspiration Level [73]
PN 260   SC 04030
SN   Level of expectations for future achieve-
ment.
R   ↓ Aspirations [67]

Aspirations [67]
PN 582   SC 04040
SN   Individual desires to achieve goals and
ideals. Use a more specific term if possible.
UF   Ambition
N   Educational Aspirations [73]
     Occupational Aspirations [73]
R   Aspiration Level [73]
     ↓ Goals [67]
     ↓ Motivation [67]

Aspirin [73]
PN 70   SC 04050
UF   Acetylsalicylic Acid
B   Acids [73]
     Analgesic Drugs [73]
     Anti Inflammatory Drugs [82]

Assassination (Political)
Use Political Assassination

Assertiveness [73]
PN 1544   SC 04070
B   Personality Traits [67]
R   Assertiveness Training [78]
     Empowerment [91]

Assertiveness Training [78]
PN 858   SC 04072
SN   Training in the social skills required to be
able to refuse requests; to express both positive
and negative feelings; to initiate, engage in, and
terminate conversation; and to make personal requests without suffering from excessive stress.
B   Human Potential Movement [82]
R   Assertiveness [73]

Assertiveness Training — (cont'd)
R   ↓ Behavior Modification [73]
     Communication Skills Training [82]
     Human Relations Training [78]
     Social Skills Training [82]

Assessment
Use Measurement

Assessment Centers [82]
PN 148   SC 04082
SN   Standardized, systematic behavioral evaluation process used to make selection, promotion,
development, counseling, and career planning
personnel decisions.
R   Occupational Guidance [67]
     ↓ Personnel Evaluation [73]
     Personnel Placement [73]
     Personnel Promotion [78]
     ↓ Personnel Selection [67]

Assimilation (Cultural)
Use Cultural Assimilation

Assistance (Social Behavior) [73]
PN 1403   SC 04100
SN   Act of rendering aid or help. Limited to hu-
man populations.
UF   Helping Behavior
B   Interpersonal Interaction [67]
     Prosocial Behavior [82]
R   Altruism [73]
     Charitable Behavior [73]
     Help Seeking Behavior [78]
     Social Support Networks [82]

Assistance Seeking (Professional)
Use Health Care Utilization

Association (Free)
Use Free Association

Associationism [73]
PN 36   SC 04120
SN   Theory which holds that learning and mental
development consist mainly of combinations and
recombinations of irreducible mental elements.
Also, the basis for theories that explain learning
in terms of stimulus and response.
B   History of Psychology [67]

Associations (Contextual)
Use Contextual Associations

Associations (Groups)
Use Organizations

Associations (Word)
Use Word Associations

Associative Processes [67]
PN 1719   SC 04160
SN   Development or maintenance of learned or
cognitive connections (associations) between
events, sensations, ideas, memories, or behavior
as the result of functional relationships, similarity-
contrast, or spatial-temporal contiguity.
B   Cognitive Processes [67]
N   Cognitive Contiguity [73]
     Connotations [73]
     Contextual Associations [67]
     Isolation Effect [73]
R   Cognitive Generalization [67]
     Connectionism [94]
     Cues [67]
     Word Associations [67]
     Word Recognition [88]

Assortative Mating [91]
PN 19   **SC** 04165
SN Nonrandom mating between unrelated individuals with similar characteristics. Used for human or animal populations.
  UF Assortive Mating
  R ↓ Animal Breeding [73]
     Animal Mate Selection [82]
     ↓ Animal Mating Behavior [67]
     Family Resemblance [91]
     ↓ Genetics [67]
     Human Mate Selection [88]
     Phenotypes [73]
     Population Genetics [73]
     ↓ Psychosexual Behavior [67]

Assortive Mating
  Use Assortative Mating

Asthenia [73]
PN 36   **SC** 04170
SN Physical weakness, lack of strength and vitality, or a lack of concentration.
  B Symptoms [67]
  N Myasthenia [73]
  R Asthenic Personality [73]
     Neurasthenic Neurosis [73]

Asthenic Personality [73]
PN 5   **SC** 04180
SN Personality disorder characterized by a lack of energy and enthusiasm, incapacity for pleasure, and susceptibility to physical and emotional stress.
  B Personality Disorders [67]
  R ↓ Asthenia [73]
     Dependent Personality [94]
     Neurasthenic Neurosis [73]

Asthma [67]
PN 755   **SC** 04190
  B Dyspnea [73]
  R ↓ Immunologic Disorders [73]
     ↓ Psychosomatic Disorders [67]

Astrology [73]
PN 74   **SC** 04200
  R ↓ Parapsychology [67]
     Superstitions [73]

Astronauts [73]
PN 52   **SC** 04210
  B Aerospace Personnel [73]
  R Aircraft Pilots [73]
     ↓ Military Personnel [67]
     Spacecraft [73]

Asylums
  Use Psychiatric Hospitals

At Risk Populations [85]
PN 4754   **SC** 04225
SN Groups or individuals considered in danger of developing a physical, mental, emotional, behavioral, or other disorder due to adverse internal or external factors.
  UF High Risk Populations
     Risk Populations
  R Coronary Prone Behavior [82]
     Predisposition [73]
     Premorbidity [78]
     Susceptibility (Disorders) [73]

Ataractic Drugs
  Use Tranquilizing Drugs

Ataraxic Drugs
  Use Tranquilizing Drugs

Ataxia [73]
PN 159   **SC** 04250
SN Loss of coordination of voluntary muscular movement.
  UF Dysmetria
  B Movement Disorders [85]
     Symptoms [67]
  R Hyperkinesis [73]

Atheism [73]
PN 25   **SC** 04260
  B Religious Beliefs [73]

Atherosclerosis [73]
PN 68   **SC** 04270
  B Arteriosclerosis [73]

Athetosis [73]
PN 21   **SC** 04280
SN Nonprogressive, developmentally-evolving disorder arising from basal ganglia damage in the full term brain characterized by postural reflex impairments, involuntary movements, and dysarthria with preservation of sensation, ocular movement, and frequently, intelligence.
  B Brain Disorders [67]
     Movement Disorders [85]
  R Cerebral Palsy [67]

Athletes [73]
PN 1944   **SC** 04287
  N College Athletes [94]
  R Athletic Participation [73]
     Athletic Performance [91]
     Athletic Training [91]
     ↓ Sports [67]

Athletic Participation [73]
PN 804   **SC** 04290
  B Participation [73]
     Recreation [67]
  R ↓ Athletes [73]
     College Athletes [94]
     ↓ Extracurricular Activities [73]
     ↓ Sports [67]

Athletic Performance [91]
PN 204   **SC** 04300
  UF Sport Performance
  B Performance [67]
  R ↓ Athletes [73]
     Athletic Training [91]
     College Athletes [94]
     ↓ Sports [67]
     Teams [88]

Athletic Training [91]
PN 79   **SC** 04305
  UF Sport Training
     Training (Athletic)
  R ↓ Athletes [73]
     Athletic Performance [91]
     Coaches [88]
     College Athletes [94]
     ↓ Education [67]
     ↓ Extracurricular Activities [73]
     ↓ Sports [67]
     Teams [88]

Atmospheric Conditions [73]
PN 270   **SC** 04310
  UF Barometric Pressure
     Climate (Meteorological)
     Weather
  B Environmental Effects [73]
  R Pollution [73]
     ↓ Temperature Effects [67]
     Thermal Acclimatization [73]

Atomism
  Use Reductionism

Atria (Heart)
  Use Heart Auricles

Atrophy (Cerebral)
  Use Cerebral Atrophy

Atrophy (Muscular)
  Use Muscular Atrophy

Atropine [73]
PN 411   **SC** 04350
  UF Hyoscyamine (dl-)
     Methylatropine
  B Alkaloids [73]
     Amines [73]
     Analgesic Drugs [73]
     Antispasmodic Drugs [73]
     Cholinergic Blocking Drugs [73]
     Narcotic Drugs [73]
     Sedatives [73]

Attachment Behavior [85]
PN 1315   **SC** 04355
SN Formation of and investment in significant relationships. Usually refers to the emotional and biological attachment of human or animal infants to caretaking figures.
  UF Bonding (Emotional)
  B Behavior [67]
  R Anaclitic Depression [73]
     Dependency (Personality) [67]
     Emotional Development [73]
     Intimacy [73]
     Love [73]
     Object Relations [82]
     ↓ Parent Child Relations [67]
     Postpartum Depression [73]
     Separation Anxiety [73]
     Separation Individuation [82]
     Stranger Reactions [88]

Attack Behavior [73]
PN 625   **SC** 04360
SN Forceful, assaultive behavior. Used for human or animal populations.
  B Aggressive Behavior [67]
     Animal Aggressive Behavior [73]
  R ↓ Animal Defensive Behavior [82]
     Animal Predatory Behavior [78]
     Retaliation [91]

Attainment (Achievement)
  Use Achievement

Attempted Suicide [73]
PN 1932   **SC** 04380
  UF Parasuicide
     Suicide (Attempted)
  B Behavior Disorders [71]
     Self Destructive Behavior [85]
  R Suicidal Ideation [91]
     Suicide [67]
     Suicide Prevention [73]

Attendance (School)
  Use School Attendance

Attendants (Institutions) [73]
PN 215   **SC** 04400
  UF Hospital Attendants
     Residential Care Attendants
  B Paramedical Personnel [73]
  R Prison Personnel [73]
     ↓ Psychiatric Hospital Staff [73]

Attention [67]
PN 6342   SC 04410
SN Condition of perceptual or cognitive awareness of or focusing on some aspect of one's environment. Compare ATTENTION SPAN and VIGILANCE.
B   Awareness [67]
N   Divided Attention [73]
   ↓ Monitoring [73]
    Selective Attention [73]
    Vigilance [67]
R   Apperception [73]
    Attention Span [73]
    Distraction [78]
    Human Channel Capacity [73]
   ↓ Perception [67]
    Rotary Pursuit [67]
    Signal Detection (Perception) [67]
    Time On Task [88]
   ↓ Tracking [67]

Attention Deficit Disorder [85]
PN 1124   SC 04412
SN Deficit in the ability to sustain attention.
B   Disorders [67]
R   Attention Span [73]
    Distractibility [73]
    Hyperkinesis [73]
    Impulsiveness [73]
    Minimal Brain Disorders [73]

Attention Span [73]
PN 245   SC 04413
SN Temporal duration of concentration or amount of material grasped during exposure to stimuli or information. Compare ATTENTION.
R ↓ Attention [67]
    Attention Deficit Disorder [85]
  ↓ Conceptual Tempo [85]
    Distraction [78]
    Vigilance [67]

Attitude Change [67]
PN 3967   SC 04430
SN Significant alteration in individual or group attitudes or opinions.
UF   Opinion Change
R ↓ Attitudes [67]
    Brainwashing [82]

Attitude Formation [73]
PN 436   SC 04440
SN Process of developing an opinion or attitude, especially as influenced by psychological, emotional, social, and experiential factors.
R ↓ Attitudes [67]

Attitude Measurement [73]
PN 566   SC 04460
SN Projective, physiological, self-report, or other approaches to the assessment of attitudes.
B   Measurement [67]
R ↓ Attitude Measures [67]
  ↓ Attitudes [67]
    Likert Scales [94]

Attitude Measures [67]
PN 2461   SC 04470
SN Instruments or devices used in the assessment of attitudes.
UF   Opinion Questionnaires
    Opinion Surveys
B   Measurement [67]
N   Allport Vernon Lindzey Study Values [73]
    Minnesota Teacher Attitude Inventory [73]
    Opinion Attitude and Interest Survey [73]
    Parent Attitude Research Instrument [73]
    Wilson Patterson Conservatism Scale [73]
R   Attitude Measurement [73]

Attitude Measures — (cont'd)
R ↓ Attitudes [67]
    Likert Scales [94]
    Semantic Differential [67]

Attitude Similarity [73]
PN 879   SC 04480
R ↓ Attitudes [67]

Attitudes [67]
PN 8163   SC 04500
SN Conceptually broad array term referring to a mental position or feeling toward certain ideas, facts, or persons. Use a more specific term if possible.
UF   Beliefs (Nonreligious)
    Opinions
N   Adolescent Attitudes [88]
    Adult Attitudes [88]
    Aged (Attitudes Toward) [78]
    Aging (Attitudes Toward) [85]
    Child Attitudes [88]
    Childrearing Attitudes [73]
  ↓ Client Attitudes [82]
    Community Attitudes [73]
    Computer Attitudes [88]
  ↓ Consumer Attitudes [73]
    Counselor Attitudes [73]
    Death Attitudes [73]
  ↓ Drug Usage Attitudes [73]
    Eating Attitudes [94]
  ↓ Employee Attitudes [67]
    Employer Attitudes [73]
    Environmental Attitudes [78]
    Family Planning Attitudes [73]
  ↓ Handicapped (Attitudes Toward) [73]
    Health Attitudes [85]
  ↓ Health Personnel Attitudes [85]
    Homosexuality (Attitudes Toward) [82]
    Job Applicant Attitudes [73]
    Marriage Attitudes [73]
    Occupational Attitudes [73]
    Parental Attitudes [73]
  ↓ Political Attitudes [73]
    Psychologist Attitudes [91]
    Public Opinion [73]
  ↓ Racial and Ethnic Attitudes [82]
  ↓ Sex Role Attitudes [78]
    Sexual Attitudes [73]
  ↓ Socioeconomic Class Attitudes [73]
    Stereotyped Attitudes [67]
    Student Attitudes [67]
    Teacher Attitudes [67]
    Work (Attitudes Toward) [73]
R   Attitude Change [67]
    Attitude Formation [73]
    Attitude Measurement [73]
  ↓ Attitude Measures [67]
    Attitude Similarity [73]
    Attribution [73]
  ↓ Cognitions [85]
    Hedonism [73]
    Impression Formation [78]
    Irrational Beliefs [82]
    Labeling [78]
  ↓ Prejudice [67]
  ↓ Religious Beliefs [73]
    Stigma [91]
    Superstitions [73]
    World View [88]

Attorneys [73]
PN 492   SC 04510
UF   Lawyers
B   Legal Personnel [85]
R ↓ Law Enforcement Personnel [73]
    Law Students [78]

Attraction (Interpersonal)
   Use Interpersonal Attraction

Attribution [73]
PN 7459   SC 04525
SN Perception of causes of behavior or events or of dispositional properties of an individual or group.
B   Social Perception [67]
R ↓ Attitudes [67]
    Blame [94]
    Causal Analysis [94]
    Impression Formation [78]
    Inference [73]
    Internal External Locus of Control [67]
    Learned Helplessness [78]

Atypical Paranoid Disorder
   Use Paranoia (Psychosis)

Atypical Somatoform Disorder
   Use Dysmorphophobia

Audiences [67]
PN 433   SC 04530
SN Groups of spectators or listeners.
R   Observers [73]

Audiogenic Seizures [78]
PN 67   SC 04536
B   Convulsions [67]
R ↓ Auditory Stimulation [67]

Audiology [73]
PN 84   SC 04540
SN Scientific study of hearing, including: anatomical and functional properties of the ear; hearing disorders and their assessment and treatment; and the rehabilitation of hearing-impaired persons. Consider also AUDIOMETRY and SPEECH AND HEARING MEASURES.
B   Paramedical Sciences [73]

Audiometers [73]
PN 17   SC 04550
B   Apparatus [67]

Audiometry [67]
PN 999   SC 04560
SN Specific procedures or audiometric tests used to measure hearing acuity and range in the diagnosis and evaluation of hearing impairments. Consider also AUDIOLOGY and SPEECH AND HEARING MEASURES.
UF   Bekesy Audiometry
N   Bone Conduction Audiometry [73]
R   Auditory Acuity [88]
  ↓ Auditory Stimulation [67]
  ↓ Perceptual Measures [73]

Audiotapes [73]
PN 309   SC 04570
SN Tape recordings of sound used in both educational and noneducational settings. Not used as a document type identifier.
B   Audiovisual Communications Media [73]

Audiovisual Aids (Educational)
   Use Educational Audiovisual Aids

Audiovisual Communications Media [73]
PN 152   SC 04590
B   Communications Media [73]
N   Audiotapes [73]
  ↓ Educational Audiovisual Aids [73]
    Film Strips [67]
  ↓ Motion Pictures [73]
    Photographs [67]

Audiovisual Communications Media —
(cont'd)
N   Radio [73]
     ↓ Television [67]
     Television Advertising [73]
     Videotapes [73]

Audiovisual Instruction [73]
PN 232   SC 04600
B   Teaching Methods [67]
N   Televised Instruction [73]
     Videotape Instruction [73]
R   ↓ Educational Audiovisual Aids [73]

Audition
Use Auditory Perception

Auditory Acuity [88]
PN 48   SC 04615
SN The ability or capacity of a listener to per-
ceive fine detail. Consider AUDITORY THRESH-
OLDS or AUDITORY DISCRIMINATION to access
references prior to 1988.
UF   Hearing Acuity
B   Auditory Perception [67]
     Perceptual Discrimination [73]
R   ↓ Audiometry [67]
     Auditory Discrimination [67]
     Auditory Localization [73]
     Auditory Thresholds [73]

Auditory Cortex [67]
PN 310   SC 04620
UF   Cortex (Auditory)
B   Temporal Lobe [73]

Auditory Discrimination [67]
PN 2328   SC 04630
SN Distinguishing between sounds of different
intensity, frequency, pattern, or complexity.
B   Auditory Perception [67]
     Perceptual Discrimination [73]
R   Auditory Acuity [88]

Auditory Displays [73]
PN 34   SC 04640
SN Presentations of patterned auditory stimula-
tion.
B   Auditory Stimulation [67]
     Displays [67]

Auditory Evoked Potentials [73]
PN 1820   SC 04650
B   Evoked Potentials [67]
R   ↓ Cortical Evoked Potentials [73]

Auditory Feedback [73]
PN 234   SC 04660
SN Return of information on specified behavioral functions or parameters by means of auditory stimulation. Such stimulation may serve to
regulate or control subsequent behavior, cognition, perception, or performance. Also, the process of hearing one's own vocalizations, especially as pertains to regulating the parameters of
one's speech.
B   Auditory Stimulation [67]
     Sensory Feedback [73]
N   Delayed Auditory Feedback [73]

Auditory Hallucinations [73]
PN 231   SC 04670
B   Hallucinations [67]

Auditory Localization [73]
PN 493   SC 04680

Auditory Localization — (cont'd)
SN Subjective determination of the specific spa-
tial location of a sound source or relative loca-
tions of sound sources.
UF   Localization (Sound)
     Sound Localization
B   Auditory Perception [67]
     Perceptual Localization [67]
R   Auditory Acuity [88]

Auditory Masking [73]
PN 667   SC 04690
SN Change in perceptual sensitivity to an au-
ditory stimulus due to the presence of a second
stimulus in close temporal proximity.
B   Masking [67]
R   ↓ Auditory Stimulation [67]

Auditory Nerve
Use Acoustic Nerve

Auditory Neurons [73]
PN 144   SC 04710
B   Sensory Neurons [73]

Auditory Perception [67]
PN 5813   SC 04720
SN Awareness, detection, or identification of
sounds.
UF   Audition
     Listening
B   Perception [67]
N   Auditory Acuity [88]
     Auditory Discrimination [67]
     Auditory Localization [73]
     ↓ Loudness Perception [73]
     ↓ Pitch Perception [73]
     Speech Perception [67]
R   Auditory Thresholds [73]
     ↓ Ear Disorders [73]
     ↓ Rhythm [91]

Auditory Stimulation [67]
PN 6044   SC 04730
UF   Acoustic Stimuli
     Noise (Sound)
     Sound
B   Perceptual Stimulation [73]
N   Auditory Displays [73]
     ↓ Auditory Feedback [73]
     Dichotic Stimulation [82]
     Filtered Noise [73]
     ↓ Loudness [67]
     ↓ Pitch (Frequency) [67]
     White Noise [73]
R   Audiogenic Seizures [78]
     ↓ Audiometry [67]
     Auditory Masking [73]
     Bone Conduction Audiometry [73]
     ↓ Speech Processing (Mechanical) [73]

Auditory Thresholds [73]
PN 1107   SC 04740
SN The minimal level of auditory stimulation, the
minimal difference between any auditory stimuli,
or the minimal stimulus change that is perceptu-
ally detectable.
B   Thresholds [67]
R   Auditory Acuity [88]
     ↓ Auditory Perception [67]
     ↓ Perceptual Measures [73]

Augmentative Communication [94]
PN 0   SC 04750
SN Communication that is supported by keyboards, typewriters, books, gestural systems, or
other devices to enable individuals with communication or speech disorders to communicate effectively.

Augmentative Communication — (cont'd)
UF   Facilitated Communication
B   Communication [67]
N   ↓ Manual Communication [78]
R   ↓ Apparatus [67]
     ↓ Communication Disorders [82]
     ↓ Medical Therapeutic Devices [73]
     ↓ Speech Disorders [67]
     Speech Therapy [67]

Aura [73]
PN 21   SC 04760
SN Sensations experienced immediately prior to
the onset of a seizure, migraine headache, or
other nervous system disorder symptoms. Also,
the patient's recognition of the beginning of an
epileptic attack. Use PARAPSYCHOLOGY or
PARAPSYCHOLOGICAL PHENOMENA to access
references on psychic auras and halos.
B   Symptoms [67]
R   ↓ Epilepsy [67]

Aurally Handicapped [73]
PN 1043   SC 04770
SN Persons with varying degrees of hearing
loss due to ear disorders or an organic defect of
the sensorineural pathways.
B   Sensorially Handicapped [94]
N   ↓ Deaf [67]
     Partially Hearing Impaired [73]
R   Cochlear Implants [94]
     ↓ Communication Disorders [82]
     ↓ Ear Disorders [73]
     Hearing Disorders [82]
     Sensory Handicaps (Attit Toward) [73]

Auricles (Heart)
Use Heart Auricles

Auricular Fibrillation
Use Fibrillation (Heart)

Australia [73]
PN 1547   SC 04800
R   ↓ South Pacific [78]

Austria [73]
PN 128   SC 04810
B   Europe [73]

Authoritarianism [67]
PN 1708   SC 04820
SN Complex of personality characteristics ex-
pressed as antidemocratic social attitudes, rigid
attachment to traditional values, uncritical accep-
tance of authority, and intolerance of opposing
views.
UF   Domination
B   Personality Traits [67]
R   Dogmatism [78]
     ↓ Dominance [67]
     Egalitarianism [85]
     Openmindedness [78]

Authoritarianism (Parental)
Use Parental Permissiveness

Authoritarianism Rebellion Scale [73]
PN 2   SC 04840
B   Nonprojective Personality Measures [73]

Authority [67]
PN 523   SC 04845
SN Ability or vested power to influence thought,
attitudes, and behavior.
R   Coercion [94]
     ↓ Dominance [67]
     ↓ Leadership [67]

Authority — (cont'd)
R   Omnipotence ⁹⁴
     Power ⁶⁷
     ↓ Social Influences ⁶⁷

Authors
Use Writers

Autism ⁶⁷
PN 1617   SC 04850
B   Mental Disorders ⁶⁷
N   Early Infantile Autism ⁷³
R   Aspergers Syndrome ⁹¹
     Autistic Children ⁷³
     Autistic Thinking ⁷³
     Developmental Disabilities ⁸²

Autistic Children ⁷³
PN 1561   SC 04860
B   Emotionally Disturbed ⁷³
R   ↓ Autism ⁶⁷
     ↓ Childhood Psychosis ⁶⁷
     ↓ Children ⁶⁷
     Early Infantile Autism ⁷³

Autistic Psychopathy
Use Aspergers Syndrome

Autistic Thinking ⁷³
PN 12   SC 04870
B   Thinking ⁶⁷
     Thought Disturbances ⁷³
R   ↓ Autism ⁶⁷

Autobiographical Memory ⁹⁴
PN 0   SC 04875
SN Personal memories of past events that have occurred over the course of one's life. Compare REMINISCENCE and LIFE REVIEW.
B   Memory ⁶⁷
R   Anniversary Events ⁹⁴
     Early Experience ⁶⁷
     Early Memories ⁸⁵
     Life Experiences ⁷³
     Life Review ⁹¹
     Reminiscence ⁸⁵

Autobiography ⁷³
PN 287   SC 04880
SN Recorded account of one's own life. Not used as a document type identifier.
B   Biography ⁶⁷

Autoeroticism
Use Masturbation

Autogenic Training ⁷³
PN 359   SC 04900
SN Physiological form of psychotherapy based on studies of sleep and hypnosis and the application of yoga principles.
B   Psychotherapeutic Techniques ⁶⁷
     Psychotherapy ⁶⁷
R   Biofeedback Training ⁷⁸
     ↓ Relaxation Therapy ⁷⁸

Autohypnosis ⁷³
PN 160   SC 04910
SN Practice, process, or hypnotic state resulting from self-induced hypnosis.
UF Self Hypnosis
B   Hypnosis ⁶⁷
R   Catalepsy ⁷³

Autoimmune Disorders
Use Immunologic Disorders

Autokinetic Illusion ⁶⁷
PN 248   SC 04930
SN Apparent movement of a fixated light in a dark field.
UF Illusion (Autokinetic)
B   Apparent Movement ⁶⁷
     Visual Perception ⁶⁷

Automated Information Coding ⁷³
PN 41   SC 04940
B   Automated Information Processing ⁷³
R   ↓ Computers ⁶⁷

Automated Information Processing ⁷³
PN 388   SC 04950
UF Information Processing (Automated)
N   Automated Information Coding ⁷³
     ↓ Automated Information Retrieval ⁷³
     Automated Information Storage ⁷³
R   ↓ Communication Systems ⁷³
     ↓ Computers ⁶⁷
     ↓ Data Processing ⁶⁷
     Expert Systems ⁹¹
     Information ⁶⁷
     Information Systems ⁹¹

Automated Information Retrieval ⁷³
PN 196   SC 04960
UF Information Retrieval (Automated)
B   Automated Information Processing ⁷³
N   Computer Searching ⁹¹
R   Automated Information Storage ⁷³
     ↓ Computers ⁶⁷
     Databases ⁹¹
     Information Services ⁸⁸
     Information Systems ⁹¹

Automated Information Storage ⁷³
PN 72   SC 04970
B   Automated Information Processing ⁷³
R   ↓ Automated Information Retrieval ⁷³
     ↓ Computers ⁶⁷
     Databases ⁹¹
     Information Systems ⁹¹

Automated Speech Recognition ⁹⁴
PN 0   SC 04975
SN Machine or other apparatus used in the automatic recognition and understanding of human speech.
UF Automatic Speaker Recognition
B   Speech Processing (Mechanical) ⁷³
R   ↓ Artificial Intelligence ⁸²
     ↓ Computer Applications ⁷³
     Expert Systems ⁹¹
     Speech Perception ⁶⁷

Automatic Speaker Recognition
Use Automated Speech Recognition

Automation ⁶⁷
PN 273   SC 04980
SN Use of mechanical and/or electronic devices to automatically control the operation of an apparatus, system, or process.
R   ↓ Artificial Intelligence ⁸²
     ↓ Computers ⁶⁷

Automatism ⁷³
PN 53   SC 04990
SN An act or movement performed without conscious control.
B   Symptoms ⁶⁷

Automobile Accidents
Use Motor Traffic Accidents

Automobile Safety
Use Highway Safety

Automobiles ⁷³
PN 169   SC 05020
B   Motor Vehicles ⁸²
R   Drivers ⁷³

Autonomic Ganglia ⁷³
PN 12   SC 05050
UF Celiac Plexus
     Hypogastric Plexus
     Myenteric Plexus
     Postganglionic Autonomic Fibers
     Preganglionic Autonomic Fibers
     Stellate Ganglion
     Submucous Plexus
B   Autonomic Nervous System ⁶⁷
     Ganglia ⁷³
R   ↓ Peripheral Nervous System ⁷³

Autonomic Nervous System ⁶⁷
PN 866   SC 05060
B   Peripheral Nervous System ⁷³
N   Adrenergic Nerves ⁷³
     Autonomic Ganglia ⁷³
     Cholinergic Nerves ⁷³
     ↓ Parasympathetic Nervous System ⁷³
     ↓ Sympathetic Nervous System ⁷³
R   Autonomic Nervous System Disorders ⁷³

Autonomic Nervous System Disorders ⁷³
PN 39   SC 05070
B   Nervous System Disorders ⁶⁷
R   ↓ Autonomic Nervous System ⁶⁷

Autonomy (Government) ⁷³
PN 33   SC 05080
R   Government ⁶⁷

Autonomy (Personality)
Use Independence (Personality)

Autopsy ⁷³
PN 76   SC 05090
R   ↓ Diagnosis ⁶⁷
     ↓ Medical Diagnosis ⁷³
     Psychological Autopsy ⁸⁸

Autoregulation
Use Homeostasis

Autoshaping ⁷⁸
PN 308   SC 05106
SN Learned behavior or the experimental paradigm involving a Pavlovian pairing of a reinforcer and a stimulus independent of the subject's behavior until the subject makes a response to the stimulus. At that point the reinforcer is made contingent on the acquired response to the stimulus, thereby bringing the response under operant control.
B   Conditioning ⁶⁷
R   Noncontingent Reinforcement ⁸⁸
     ↓ Reinforcement ⁶⁷

Autosome Disorders ⁷³
PN 42   SC 05110
B   Chromosome Disorders ⁷³
N   Crying Cat Syndrome ⁷³
     Downs Syndrome ⁶⁷
     Trisomy 21 ⁷³
R   Autosomes ⁷³

Autosomes ⁷³
PN 17   SC 05120
B   Chromosomes ⁷³
R   ↓ Autosome Disorders ⁷³

Autotomy
Use Self Mutilation

Aversion [67]
PN 578 SC 05130
UF Antipathy
Dislike
B Emotional States [73]
N Hate [73]
R Disgust [94]

Aversion Conditioning [82]
PN 1151 SC 05135
SN Conditioning paradigm in which aversive effects are paired with external stimuli resulting in an aversion to the stimuli. Also, the learned aversion itself.
UF Odor Aversion Conditioning
Taste Aversion Conditioning
B Conditioning [67]
N Covert Sensitization [88]
R Aversive Stimulation [73]

Aversion Therapy [73]
PN 434 SC 05140
SN Form of behavior therapy designed to eliminate undesirable behavior patterns through learned associations with unpleasant or painful stimuli. Also known as aversive conditioning therapy.
B Behavior Therapy [67]
N Covert Sensitization [88]
R Counterconditioning [73]
↓ Shock Therapy [73]

Aversive Stimulation [73]
PN 1219 SC 05150
SN Presentation of a noxious stimulus. Also, any noxious stimuli (i.e., stimuli that an organism attempts to avoid or escape from). Compare PUNISHMENT.
B Stimulation [67]
R ↓ Aversion Conditioning [82]
Covert Sensitization [88]

Aviation [67]
PN 521 SC 05160
N Flight Instrumentation [73]
Spaceflight [67]
R Acceleration Effects [73]
Altitude Effects [73]
↓ Aviation Safety [73]
↓ Gravitational Effects [67]

Aviation Personnel
Use Aerospace Personnel

Aviation Safety [73]
PN 91 SC 05170
B Safety [67]
N Air Traffic Control [73]
R Air Traffic Accidents [73]
Aircraft Pilots [73]
↓ Aviation [67]
↓ Transportation Accidents [73]

Aviators
Use Aircraft Pilots

Avoidance [67]
PN 1653 SC 05190
UF Escape
R Avoidance Conditioning [67]
Neophobia [85]

Avoidance Conditioning [67]
PN 5919 SC 05200

Avoidance Conditioning — (cont'd)
SN Learned behavior or the operant conditioning procedure in which the subject learns a behavior that prevents the occurrence of an aversive stimulus. Compare ESCAPE CONDITIONING.
UF Active Avoidance
Conditioning (Avoidance)
Passive Avoidance
B Operant Conditioning [67]
R Avoidance [67]

Avoidant Personality [94]
PN 0 SC 05205
SN Personality disorder characterized by excessive social discomfort, extreme sensitivity to negative perceptions of oneself, pervasive preoccupation with being criticized or rejected in social situations, and low self esteem.
B Personality Disorders [67]
R Social Anxiety [85]
Social Phobia [85]

Awareness [67]
PN 1465 SC 05210
SN Conscious realization, perception, or knowledge.
B Consciousness States [71]
N ↓ Attention [67]
Body Awareness [82]
R Metacognition [91]
Sensory Gating [91]

Axons [73]
PN 132 SC 05220
B Neurons [73]

Azidothymidine
Use Zidovudine

AZT
Use Zidovudine

Babbling
Use Infant Vocalization

Babies
Use Infants

Babinski Reflex [73]
PN 2 SC 05250
B Reflexes [71]

Baboons [73]
PN 432 SC 05260
B Primates (Nonhuman) [73]

Babysitting
Use Child Care

Back (Anatomy) [73]
PN 97 SC 05270
B Anatomy [67]

Back Pain [82]
PN 502 SC 05275
B Pain [67]
R Chronic Pain [85]
↓ Disorders [67]

Background (Family)
Use Family Background

Backward Masking
Use Masking

Baclofen [91]
PN 33 SC 05293
B Muscle Relaxing Drugs [73]

Bacteria
Use Microorganisms

Bacterial Disorders [73]
PN 41 SC 05300
B Infectious Disorders [73]
N Bacterial Meningitis [73]
Gonorrhea [73]
Pulmonary Tuberculosis [73]
↓ Tuberculosis [73]
R Pneumonia [73]
Rheumatic Fever [73]

Bacterial Meningitis [73]
PN 8 SC 05310
B Bacterial Disorders [73]
Meningitis [73]

Bahama Islands [73]
PN 14 SC 05330
B West Indies [73]

Balance (Motor Processes)
Use Equilibrium

Ballet
Use Dance

Bangladesh [82]
PN 43 SC 05355
B Asia [73]

Bannister Repertory Grid [73]
PN 23 SC 05360
B Nonprojective Personality Measures [73]

Barbados [91]
PN 6 SC 05370
B West Indies [73]

Barbital [73]
PN 53 SC 05380
B Barbiturates [67]
CNS Depressant Drugs [73]
Hypnotic Drugs [73]
Sedatives [73]

Barbiturate Poisoning [73]
PN 4 SC 05390
B Toxic Disorders [73]
R ↓ Analeptic Drugs [73]
↓ Barbiturates [67]

Barbiturates [67]
PN 215 SC 05400
B Drugs [67]
N Amobarbital [73]
Barbital [73]
Hexobarbital [73]
Methohexital [73]
Pentobarbital [73]
Phenobarbital [73]
Secobarbital [73]
Thiopental [73]
R ↓ Anesthetic Drugs [73]
↓ Anticonvulsive Drugs [73]
Barbiturate Poisoning [73]
↓ CNS Depressant Drugs [73]
↓ Hypnotic Drugs [73]
Primidone [73]
↓ Sedatives [73]

Bargaining [73]
PN 457   SC 05410
  B   Negotiation [73]

Barium [73]
PN 6   SC 05420
  B   Metallic Elements [73]

Barometric Pressure
  Use Atmospheric Conditions

Baroreceptors [73]
PN 43   SC 05440
  UF Pressoreceptors
  B   Neural Receptors [73]
       Sensory Neurons [73]
       Sympathetic Nervous System [73]

Barrett Lennard Relationship Invent [73]
PN 9   SC 05450
  B   Nonprojective Personality Measures [73]

Barron Welsh Art Scale [73]
PN 6   SC 05460
  B   Nonprojective Personality Measures [73]

Basal Ganglia [73]
PN 1156   SC 05470
  UF Corpus Striatum
  B   Ganglia [73]
       Telencephalon [73]
  N   Amygdaloid Body [73]
       Caudate Nucleus [73]
       Globus Pallidus [73]
       Putamen [85]
  R   Extrapyramidal Symptoms [94]
       Nucleus Basalis Magnocellularis [94]
       Substantia Nigra [94]

Basal Metabolism [73]
PN 36   SC 05480
SN The amount of heat produced by the body to maintain life processes at the lowest level of cell activity in the waking state.
  B   Metabolism [67]

Basal Readers
  Use Reading Materials

Basal Skin Resistance [73]
PN 12   SC 05500
SN Baseline or minimum electrical current generated or conducted by the body as measured on the skin surface during a resting state.
  B   Skin Resistance [73]

Baseball [73]
PN 132   SC 05510
  B   Recreation [67]
       Sports [67]

Basic Skills Testing
  Use Minimum Competency Tests

Basketball [73]
PN 256   SC 05520
  B   Recreation [67]
       Sports [67]

Bass (Fish) [73]
PN 22   SC 05530
  B   Fishes [67]

Bats [73]
PN 184   SC 05550
  B   Mammals [73]

Battered Child Syndrome [73]
PN 32   SC 05560
SN Behavioral pattern, including inability to relate to others and feelings of rejection, characteristic of infants and children who have been abused.
  B   Child Abuse [71]
       Syndromes [73]
  R   Physical Abuse [91]

Battered Females [88]
PN 402   SC 05561
SN Use FAMILY VIOLENCE to access references from 85-87.
  B   Human Females [73]
  R ↓ Family Violence [82]
       Partner Abuse [91]
       Physical Abuse [91]
       Shelters [91]

Bayes Theorem
  Use Statistical Probability

Bayley Scales of Infant Development [94]
PN 0   SC 05575
  B   Developmental Measures [94]
  R ↓ Intelligence Measures [67]

Beavers [73]
PN 8   SC 05580
  B   Rodents [73]

Beck Depression Inventory [88]
PN 97   SC 05588
  B   Nonprojective Personality Measures [73]

Bedwetting
  Use Urinary Incontinence

Beer [73]
PN 77   SC 05590
  B   Alcoholic Beverages [73]

Bees [73]
PN 328   SC 05600
  B   Insects [67]
  R   Larvae [73]

Beetles [73]
PN 122   SC 05610
  B   Insects [67]
  R   Larvae [73]

Behavior [67]
PN 3731   SC 05670
SN Conceptually broad array term referring to any or all aspects of human or animal behavior. Use a more specific term if possible.
  N   Adaptive Behavior [91]
    ↓ Adjunctive Behavior [82]
    ↓ Animal Ethology [67]
    ↓ Antisocial Behavior [71]
      Attachment Behavior [85]
      Childhood Play Behavior [78]
      Choice Behavior [67]
      Classroom Behavior [73]
      Conservation (Ecological Behavior) [78]
      Consumer Behavior [67]
      Coping Behavior [67]
      Coronary Prone Behavior [82]
    ↓ Drinking Behavior [78]
    ↓ Driving Behavior [67]
    ↓ Exploratory Behavior [67]
      Health Behavior [82]
      Illness Behavior [82]
      Instinctive Behavior [82]
    ↓ Organizational Behavior [78]
    ↓ Psychosexual Behavior [67]

Behavior — (cont'd)
  N   Self Defeating Behavior [88]
    ↓ Self Destructive Behavior [85]
    ↓ Social Behavior [67]
      Stereotyped Behavior [73]
      Voting Behavior [73]
      Wandering Behavior [91]
  R   Behavior Change [73]
    ↓ Behavior Disorders [71]
    ↓ Behavior Modification [73]
    ↓ Behavior Problems [67]
    ↓ Behavior Therapy [67]
      Behavioral Assessment [82]
      Behavioral Contrast [78]
      Behaviorism [67]

Behavior Analysis
  Use Behavioral Assessment

Behavior Change [73]
PN 1736   SC 05620
SN Detectable changes in behavior due to psychotherapeutic, behavioral or other intervention, or spontaneous occurrence.
  R ↓ Behavior [67]
    ↓ Behavior Modification [73]

Behavior Contracting [78]
PN 226   SC 05624
SN Therapeutic technique involving a formal written contract, usually between two parties, which explicitly states the relationship between a particular behavior and its consequences (sanctions). Viewed as a structural means of scheduling reinforcement between the two parties, it is used as a method of controlling contingencies of reinforcement.
  R ↓ Behavior Modification [73]
    ↓ Behavior Therapy [67]

Behavior Disorders [71]
PN 2794   SC 05630
SN Disorders characterized by persistent and repetitive patterns of behavior that violate societal norms or rules or that seriously impair a person's functioning. Compare BEHAVIOR PROBLEMS.
  B   Disorders [67]
  N ↓ Addiction [73]
      Attempted Suicide [73]
    ↓ Crime [67]
    ↓ Drug Abuse [73]
    ↓ Homicide [67]
      Juvenile Delinquency [67]
      Self Mutilation [73]
  R   Acting Out [67]
    ↓ Aggressive Behavior [67]
    ↓ Antisocial Behavior [71]
    ↓ Behavior [67]
    ↓ Behavior Problems [67]
      Body Rocking [73]
      Conduct Disorder [91]
      Faking [73]
      Fecal Incontinence [73]
      Hair Pulling [73]
    ↓ Mental Disorders [67]
      Pathological Gambling [88]
    ↓ Self Destructive Behavior [85]
    ↓ Symptoms [67]
      Thumbsucking [73]
      Urinary Incontinence [73]

Behavior Modification [73]
PN 6186   SC 05640
SN Use of classical conditioning or operant (instrumental) learning techniques to modify behavior.
  B   Treatment [67]
  N ↓ Behavior Therapy [67]

Behavior Modification — (cont'd)
- N   Biofeedback Training [78]
-      Classroom Behavior Modification [73]
-    ↓ Contingency Management [73]
-      Fading (Conditioning) [82]
-      Omission Training [85]
-      Overcorrection [85]
-    ↓ Self Management [85]
-      Time Out [85]
- R   Assertiveness Training [78]
-    ↓ Behavior [67]
-      Behavior Change [73]
-      Behavior Contracting [78]
-      Behavioral Assessment [82]
-      Cognitive Restructuring [85]
-      Cognitive Therapy [82]
-      Communication Skills Training [82]
-      Counterconditioning [73]
-    ↓ Operant Conditioning [67]
-    ↓ Relaxation Therapy [78]
-    ↓ Self Help Techniques [82]
-      Self Monitoring [82]
-      Social Skills Training [82]
-      Stress Management [85]

Behavior Problems [67]
PN 5380   SC 05650
SN Disruptive or improper behaviors that generally fall within societal norms and do not seriously impair a person's functioning. Compare BEHAVIOR DISORDERS.
- UF   Disruptive Behavior
-      Misbehavior
-      Misconduct
- N   Tantrums [73]
- R   ↓ Behavior [67]
-    ↓ Behavior Disorders [71]
-      Conduct Disorder [91]

Behavior Therapy [67]
PN 5826   SC 05660
SN Psychotherapeutic approach which employs classical conditioning and operant learning techniques in an attempt to eliminate or modify problem behavior, addressing itself primarily to the client's overt behavior, as opposed to thoughts, feelings, or other cognitive processes.
- B   Behavior Modification [73]
- N   ↓ Aversion Therapy [73]
-      Implosive Therapy [73]
-      Reciprocal Inhibition Therapy [73]
-      Systematic Desensitization Therapy [73]
- R   ↓ Behavior [67]
-      Behavior Contracting [78]
-      Counterconditioning [73]
-      Paradoxical Techniques [82]
-    ↓ Psychotherapy [67]
-      Rational Emotive Therapy [78]

Behavioral Assessment [82]
PN 1584   SC 05671
SN Objective identification of response units and their controlling environmental and organismic variables for the purpose of understanding, analyzing, or changing behavior. Primarily used for human populations.
- UF   Behavior Analysis
- B   Analysis [67]
- R   ↓ Behavior [67]
-    ↓ Behavior Modification [73]
-      Educational Program Evaluation [73]
-    ↓ Empirical Methods [73]
-      Mental Health Program Evaluation [73]

Behavioral Contrast [78]
PN 223   SC 05674
SN Change in response rate or latency following a change in reinforcement of one component of multiple operant discrimination schedules of reinforcement.

Behavioral Contrast — (cont'd)
- R   ↓ Behavior [67]
-    ↓ Reinforcement [67]
-      Response Frequency [73]
-      Response Latency [67]
-      Stimulus Discrimination [73]

Behavioral Genetics [94]
PN 0   SC 57405
SN Scientific discipline concerned with the role of genes and gene action in the expression of behavior. Includes analysis of whole populations for specific traits, e.g., intelligence. Used for the scientific discipline or the behavioral genetic processes themselves.
- B   Genetics [67]
- R   Biopsychosocial Approach [91]
-    ↓ Genetic Disorders [73]
-      Genetic Dominance [73]
-      Genetic Recessiveness [73]
-      Nature Nurture [94]
-      Population Genetics [73]
-      Psychobiology [82]
-      Sociobiology [82]

Behavioral Health
Use Health Care Psychology

Behavioral Medicine
Use Health Care Psychology

Behavioral Sciences
Use Social Sciences

Behaviorism [67]
PN 1073   SC 05690
- B   History of Psychology [67]
- R   ↓ Behavior [67]
-      Skinner (Burrhus Frederic) [91]
-      Watson (John Broadus) [91]

Bekesy Audiometry
Use Audiometry

Belgium [73]
PN 176   SC 05710
- B   Europe [73]

Beliefs (Nonreligious)
Use Attitudes

Beliefs (Religion)
Use Religious Beliefs

Belize [88]
PN 5   SC 05725
- B   Central America [73]

Bem Sex Role Inventory [88]
PN 40   SC 05727
- B   Nonprojective Personality Measures [73]

Bemegride [73]
PN 19   SC 05730
- B   Analeptic Drugs [73]

Benactyzine [73]
PN 23   SC 05740
- B   Cholinergic Blocking Drugs [73]
-      Tranquilizing Drugs [67]

Benadryl
Use Diphenhydramine

Bender Gestalt Test [67]
PN 345   SC 05770

Bender Gestalt Test — (cont'd)
- B   Projective Personality Measures [73]
- R   ↓ Neuropsychological Assessment [82]

Benign Neoplasms [73]
PN 14   SC 05800
- B   Neoplasms [67]

Benin [91]
PN 4   SC 05805
- B   Africa [67]

Benton Revised Visual Retention Test [73]
PN 30   SC 05810
- B   Intelligence Measures [67]
- R   ↓ Neuropsychological Assessment [82]

Benzedrine
Use Amphetamine

Benzodiazepine Agonists [94]
PN 0   SC 05821
- R   ↓ Benzodiazepines [78]

Benzodiazepine Antagonists [85]
PN 249   SC 05822
- R   ↓ Benzodiazepines [78]

Benzodiazepines [78]
PN 1695   SC 05824
- B   Drugs [67]
- N   Alprazolam [88]
-      Chlordiazepoxide [73]
-      Clonazepam [91]
-      Diazepam [73]
-      Flurazepam [82]
-      Lorazepam [88]
-      Midazolam [91]
-      Nitrazepam [78]
-      Oxazepam [78]
- R   ↓ Anticonvulsive Drugs [73]
-      Benzodiazepine Agonists [94]
-      Benzodiazepine Antagonists [85]
-    ↓ Hypnotic Drugs [73]
-    ↓ Minor Tranquilizers [73]
-    ↓ Muscle Relaxing Drugs [73]
-    ↓ Sedatives [73]
-    ↓ Tranquilizing Drugs [67]

Bereavement
Use Grief

Bermuda [91]
PN 0   SC 05825
- B   West Indies [73]

Beta Blockers
Use Adrenergic Blocking Drugs

Between Groups Design [85]
PN 14   SC 05828
SN Experimental design in which the subjects serve in only one treatment condition. Includes designs of matched or correlated groups and randomized groups.
- B   Experimental Design [67]

Beverages (Alcoholic)
Use Alcoholic Beverages

Beverages (Nonalcoholic) [78]
PN 100   SC 05833
- UF   Coffee
-      Tea
- R   ↓ Alcoholic Beverages [73]
-    ↓ Drinking Behavior [78]
-      Nutrition [73]

Bias (Experimenter)
  Use Experimenter Bias

Bias (Response)
  Use Response Bias

Biased Sampling 73
PN 109   SC 05860
SN Inadequate selection of subject samples resulting in an inaccurate representation of the larger population.
  B Sampling (Experimental) 73
  R Experiment Volunteers 73

Bible 73
PN 209   SC 05870
  B Religious Literature 73
  R ↓ Christianity 73
     Judaism 67
     ↓ Religious Beliefs 73

Bibliography 67
PN 1484   SC 05880
SN Mandatory term used as a document type identifier.
  R Literature Review 67

Bibliotherapy 73
PN 239   SC 05890
SN Use of reading as adjunct to psychotherapy.
  B Treatment 67
  R Poetry Therapy 94

Bicuculline 94
PN 0   SC 05895
SN Use GAMMA AMINOBUTYRIC ACID ANTAGONISTS to access references from 85-93.
  B Analeptic Drugs 73
     Gamma Aminobutyric Acid Antagonists 85

Bile 73
PN 10   SC 05900
  B Body Fluids 73
  R Taurine 82

Bilingual Education 78
PN 354   SC 05907
SN Education in one's native language as well as the majority language of the country in which one is educated or education in two languages.
  B Education 67
  R Bilingualism 73
     Foreign Language Learning 67
     Foreign Languages 73
     Multicultural Education 88
     ↓ Multilingualism 73
     ↓ Teaching 67

Bilingualism 73
PN 1343   SC 05910
  B Multilingualism 73
  R Bilingual Education 78
     Code Switching 88
     ↓ Language 67
     Language Proficiency 88

Binge Eating 91
PN 86   SC 05915
SN Eating excessive quantities of food often after stressful events. Compare BULIMIA.
  B Eating 67
  R ↓ Appetite Disorders 73
     Bulimia 85
     ↓ Symptoms 67

Binocular Vision 67
PN 944   SC 05920
  B Visual Perception 67

Binomial Distribution 73
PN 43   SC 05930
  B Statistical Probability 67
  R Statistical Sample Parameters 73

Bioavailability 91
PN 22   SC 05935
SN The degree and rate at which a drug enters the bloodstream and is circulated to specific organs or tissues, as measured by drug concentrations in body fluids or by pharmacologic or therapeutic response.
  UF Bioequivalence
  R Absorption (Physiological) 73
     ↓ Biochemistry 67
     ↓ Drug Dosages 73
     ↓ Drug Therapy 67
     ↓ Drugs 67
     ↓ Metabolism 67
     ↓ Pharmacology 73

Biochemical Markers
  Use Biological Markers

Biochemistry 67
PN 3494   SC 05940
SN Study of the biological and physiological chemistry of living organisms. Used for the scientific discipline or the biochemical processes themselves.
  B Chemistry 67
  N ↓ Neurochemistry 73
  R Bioavailability 91
     Biological Markers 91
     ↓ Physiology 67

Bioequivalence
  Use Bioavailability

Biofeedback 73
PN 1006   SC 05945
SN Provision of immediate ongoing information regarding one's own physiological processes.
  B Feedback 67
  N Biofeedback Training 78
  R ↓ Conditioning 67
     ↓ Reinforcement 67
     ↓ Stimulation 67

Biofeedback Training 78
PN 1904   SC 05946
SN Self-directed process by which a person uses biofeedback information to gain voluntary control over processes or functions which are primarily under autonomic control. Used in experimental or treatment settings with human subjects.
  B Behavior Modification 73
     Biofeedback 73
  R Autogenic Training 73

Biographical Data 78
PN 586   SC 05948
SN Information identifying an individual's background, life history, or present status. Not used as a document type identifier.
  R Biographical Inventories 73
     Demographic Characteristics 67
     ↓ Educational Background 67
     ↓ Family Background 73
     Life Experiences 73
     Patient History 73

Biographical Inventories 73
PN 93   SC 05950
SN Sets of items listing information on an individual's background. Not used as a document type identifier.

Biographical Inventories — (cont'd)
  B Inventories 67
  R Biographical Data 78

Biography 67
PN 351   SC 05960
SN Recorded account of a person's life. Also used as a document type identifier.
  B Prose 73
  N Autobiography 73
  R Psychohistory 78

Biological Clocks (Animal)
  Use Animal Biological Rhythms

Biological Family 88
PN 104   SC 05975
SN The genetic family members of a person in contrast to adoptive or foster families.
  UF Birth Parents
     Natural Family
  B Family 67
     Family Members 73
  R Family of Origin 91

Biological Markers 91
PN 167   SC 05977
  UF Biochemical Markers
     Clinical Markers
  R ↓ Biochemistry 67
     Interleukins 94
     ↓ Medical Diagnosis 73
     Physiological Correlates 67
     Prognosis 73
     ↓ Screening 82

Biological Psychiatry 94
PN 0   SC 05978
SN A branch of psychiatry focusing on biological, physical, and neurological factors in the etiology and treatment of mental and behavioral disorders.
  B Psychiatry 67
  R Neurobiology 73
     Neuropsychiatry 73
     Psychobiology 82

Biological Rhythms 67
PN 419   SC 05980
SN Rhythmic and periodic variations in physiological and psychological functions. Used for human or animal populations.
  N ↓ Animal Biological Rhythms 73
     Human Biological Rhythms 73
     Sleep Wake Cycle 85
  R Lunar Synodic Cycle 73
     Seasonal Variations 73

Biological Symbiosis 73
PN 115   SC 06000
SN Intimate relationship between organisms of two or more kinds, particularly one in which the symbiont benefits from the host. Includes parasitic behavior. Limited to animal populations.
  UF Parasitism
     Symbiosis (Biological)
  R ↓ Animals 67
     ↓ Biology 67
     Interspecies Interaction 91

Biology 67
PN 1032   SC 06010
SN Branch of science dealing with living organisms. Used for the scientific discipline or the biological processes themselves.
  B Sciences 67
  N Botany 73
     Neurobiology 73
     Sociobiology 82

Biology — (cont'd)
N   Zoology [73]
R   Biological Symbiosis [73]
    Biosynthesis [73]
    Phylogenesis [73]
    Psychobiology [82]

Biopsy [73]
PN 28   SC 06020
B   Medical Diagnosis [73]
R ↓ Surgery [71]

Biopsychosocial Approach [91]
PN 88   SC 06024
SN A systematic integration of biological, psychological, and social approaches to the study, treatment, and understanding of mental health and mental disorders.
UF   Biopsychosocial Model
R   Behavioral Genetics [94]
    Holistic Health [85]
    Interdisciplinary Treatment Approach [73]
    Psychobiology [82]
    Systems Theory [88]

Biopsychosocial Model
Use Biopsychosocial Approach

Biosynthesis [73]
PN 65   SC 06030
SN Formation of chemical compounds of relatively complex structure from nutrients by enzyme-catalyzed reactions in living cells.
B   Metabolism [67]
R ↓ Biology [67]

Bipolar Depression
Use Manic Depression

Birds [67]
PN 3493   SC 06040
UF   Fowl
B   Vertebrates [73]
N   Blackbirds [73]
    Budgerigars [73]
    Canaries [73]
    Chickens [67]
    Doves [73]
    Ducks [73]
    Geese [73]
    Penguins [73]
    Pigeons [67]
    Quails [73]
    Robins [73]
    Sea Gulls [73]

Birth [67]
PN 1418   SC 06050
UF   Childbirth
    Parturition
N   Natural Childbirth [78]
    Premature Birth [73]
R   Birth Injuries [73]
    Birth Rites [73]
    Birth Trauma [73]
    Birth Weight [85]
    Childbirth Training [78]
    Labor (Childbirth) [73]
    Midwifery [85]
    Obstetrical Complications [78]
    Perinatal Period [94]
  ↓ Pregnancy [67]
  ↓ Sexual Reproduction [73]

Birth Control [71]
PN 893   SC 06060
UF   Contraception
    Population Control

Birth Control — (cont'd)
B   Family Planning [73]
N ↓ Contraceptive Devices [73]
    Rhythm Method [73]
    Tubal Ligation [73]
    Vasectomy [73]
R   Condoms [91]
    Induced Abortion [71]
    Overpopulation [73]
    Sexual Abstinence [73]
  ↓ Sterilization (Sex) [73]

Birth Control Attitudes
Use Family Planning Attitudes

Birth Injuries [73]
PN 49   SC 06070
SN Physical injuries (such as brain damage) received during birth, mostly in, but not limited to, breech births, instrument deliveries, neonatal anoxia, or premature births.
UF   Injuries (Birth)
B   Injuries [73]
R ↓ Birth [67]
    Birth Trauma [73]
  ↓ Neonatal Disorders [73]
    Obstetrical Complications [78]

Birth Order [67]
PN 1380   SC 06080
B   Family Structure [73]

Birth Parents
Use Biological Family

Birth Rate [82]
PN 84   SC 06087
SN Ratio of the number of live births to the number of individuals in a human population within a specified time period.
R   Fertility [88]
  ↓ Population [73]

Birth Rites [73]
PN 52   SC 06090
UF   Circumcision
B   Rites of Passage [73]
R ↓ Birth [67]

Birth Trauma [73]
PN 50   SC 06100
SN Stress, as experienced by infants, of being born and bombarded with external stimuli that may have negative influences on subsequent psychological development.
R ↓ Birth [67]
    Birth Injuries [73]

Birth Weight [85]
PN 316   SC 06105
UF   Low Birth Weight
B   Body Weight [67]
R ↓ Birth [67]
    Neonates [67]
    Premature Birth [73]

Bisexuality [73]
PN 275   SC 06110
B   Homosexuality [67]
    Psychosexual Behavior [67]
R   Lesbianism [73]
    Male Homosexuality [73]
    Pedophilia [73]
    Transsexualism [73]
    Transvestism [73]

Bitterness
Use Taste Perception

Black Power Movement [73]
PN 31   SC 06130
B   Social Movements [67]
R ↓ Activist Movements [73]

Blackbirds [73]
PN 142   SC 06140
B   Birds [67]

Blacks [82]
PN 5697   SC 06150
SN Populations of black African descent. May also be used to refer to population groups in Africa when cultural or ethnic comparisons are studied. Use NEGROES to access references from 67–81.
UF   African Americans
    Negroes
R ↓ Ethnic Groups [73]
    Minority Groups [67]
    Race (Anthropological) [73]

Blacky Pictures Test [73]
PN 1   SC 06160
B   Projective Personality Measures [73]

Bladder [73]
PN 36   SC 06170
B   Urogenital System [73]

Blame [94]
PN 0   SC 06175
SN To assign fault or responsibility for an event, state, or behavior, or the condition of fault or responsibility for something believed to deserve censure.
R   Accountability [88]
    Attribution [73]
    Guilt [67]
  ↓ Responsibility [73]
    Shame [94]
  ↓ Social Perception [67]

Blind [67]
PN 2155   SC 06180
B   Visually Handicapped [67]
N   Deaf Blind [91]
R ↓ Vision Disorders [82]

Blink Reflex
Use Eyeblink Reflex

Block Design Test (Kohs)
Use Kohs Block Design Test

Blood [67]
PN 1467   SC 06200
B   Body Fluids [73]
N ↓ Blood Plasma [73]
R   Blood Alcohol Concentration [94]
  ↓ Blood and Lymphatic Disorders [73]
    Blood Groups [73]
    Blood Volume [73]
  ↓ Heart [67]

Blood Alcohol Concentration [94]
PN 0   SC 06205
R ↓ Alcohol Abuse [88]
  ↓ Alcohol Drinking Patterns [67]
  ↓ Alcohol Intoxication [73]
  ↓ Alcohols [67]
  ↓ Blood [67]
    Driving Under The Influence [88]
    Drug Usage Screening [88]

Blood and Lymphatic Disorders [73]
PN 167   SC 06210

Blood and Lymphatic Disorders — (cont'd)
- UF Blood Disorders
  - Hematologic Disorders
  - Lymphatic Disorders
- B Disorders [67]
- N Anemia [73]
  - Hemophilia [73]
  - Leukemias [73]
  - Malaria [73]
  - Porphyria [73]
  - Rh Incompatibility [73]
  - Sickle Cell Disease [94]
- R ↓ Blood [67]

Blood Brain Barrier [94]
PN 0   SC 06215
SN Functional barrier between brain blood vessels and brain tissues.
- R Blood Circulation [73]
  - ↓ Blood Flow [73]
  - ↓ Blood Vessels [73]
  - ↓ Brain [67]
  - ↓ Cardiovascular System [67]
  - Cerebrospinal Fluid [73]
  - ↓ Neurochemistry [73]

Blood Cells [73]
PN 92   SC 06220
- B Cells (Biology) [73]
- N Erythrocytes [73]
  - ↓ Leucocytes [73]

Blood Circulation [73]
PN 132   SC 06230
- UF Circulation (Blood)
- R Arterial Pulse [73]
  - Blood Brain Barrier [94]
  - ↓ Blood Flow [73]
  - Blood Volume [73]
  - Cerebral Blood Flow [94]

Blood Coagulation [73]
PN 16   SC 06240
- UF Coagulation (Blood)

Blood Disorders
Use Blood and Lymphatic Disorders

Blood Donation
Use Tissue Donation

Blood Flow [73]
PN 586   SC 06270
- N Cerebral Blood Flow [94]
- R Blood Brain Barrier [94]
  - Blood Circulation [73]
  - Blood Volume [73]

Blood Glucose
Use Blood Sugar

Blood Groups [73]
PN 65   SC 06300
SN Genetically determined classes of human erythrocytes based on specific antigens for which the groups are named.
- R Antigens [82]
  - ↓ Blood [67]
  - Erythrocytes [73]
  - ↓ Genetics [67]

Blood Plasma [73]
PN 2300   SC 06310
- UF Plasma (Blood)
- B Blood [67]
- N Blood Serum [73]

Blood Platelets [73]
PN 688   SC 06320
- UF Platelets (Blood)

Blood Pressure [67]
PN 1891   SC 06330
- N Diastolic Pressure [73]
  - Systolic Pressure [73]
- R ↓ Blood Pressure Disorders [73]
  - Blood Volume [73]
  - Cardiovascular Reactivity [94]
  - Cerebral Blood Flow [94]
  - ↓ Vasoconstrictor Drugs [73]
  - ↓ Vasodilator Drugs [73]

Blood Pressure Disorders [73]
PN 12   SC 06340
- B Cardiovascular Disorders [67]
- N Hypotension [73]
  - Syncope [73]
- R ↓ Arteriosclerosis [73]
  - ↓ Blood Pressure [67]
  - Vasoconstriction [73]
  - Vasodilation [73]

Blood Proteins [73]
PN 66   SC 06350
- B Proteins [73]
- N Hemoglobin [73]
  - ↓ Immunoglobulins [73]
  - Serum Albumin [73]

Blood Serum [73]
PN 1000   SC 06360
- UF Serum (Blood)
- B Blood Plasma [73]
- R Antibodies [73]

Blood Sugar [73]
PN 253   SC 06370
- UF Blood Glucose
- B Glucose [73]

Blood Transfusion [73]
PN 28   SC 06380
- UF Transfusion (Blood)
- B Physical Treatment Methods [73]
- R Hemodialysis [73]
  - Tissue Donation [91]

Blood Vessels [73]
PN 20   SC 06390
- B Cardiovascular System [67]
- N ↓ Arteries (Anatomy) [73]
  - Capillaries (Anatomy) [73]
  - Veins (Anatomy) [73]
- R Blood Brain Barrier [94]

Blood Volume [73]
PN 93   SC 06400
- R ↓ Blood [67]
  - Blood Circulation [73]
  - ↓ Blood Flow [73]
  - ↓ Blood Pressure [67]

Blue Collar Workers [73]
PN 775   SC 06410
SN Employees whose unskilled, semiskilled, or skilled occupations involve physical labor.
- UF Laborers (Construct and Indust)
- B Business and Industrial Personnel [67]
- N Industrial Foremen [73]
  - Skilled Industrial Workers [73]
  - Unskilled Industrial Workers [73]
- R Technical Service Personnel [73]

Boarding Schools [88]
PN 42   SC 06412

Boarding Schools — (cont'd)
SN Elementary or secondary residential educational institutions for students enrolled in an instructional program. Primarily used for non-disordered populations.
- B Schools [67]
- R Institutional Schools [78]

Boards of Education [78]
PN 77   SC 06416
SN Governing bodies responsible for managing public school systems.
- R ↓ Education [67]
  - Educational Administration [67]
  - ↓ School Administrators [73]

Body Awareness [82]
PN 242   SC 06425
SN Perception of one's physical self or body at any particular time.
- B Awareness [67]
- R ↓ Body Image [67]
  - Self Perception [67]
  - ↓ Somesthetic Perception [67]

Body Fluids [73]
PN 68   SC 06430
- B Anatomy [67]
- N Amniotic Fluid [73]
  - Bile [73]
  - ↓ Blood [67]
  - Cerebrospinal Fluid [73]
  - Mucus [73]
  - Saliva [73]
  - Sweat [73]
  - Urine [73]
- R ↓ Physiology [67]

Body Height [73]
PN 228   SC 06440
- UF Height (Body)
- B Body Size [85]
- R Physique [67]

Body Image [67]
PN 1506   SC 06450
SN Mental representation of one's body according to feedback received from one's body, the environment, and other people.
- N ↓ Body Image Disturbances [73]
- R Body Awareness [82]

Body Image Disturbances [73]
PN 287   SC 06460
SN Distortions in the evaluative picture or mental representation an individual has of his/her body.
- B Body Image [67]
- N Koro [94]
  - Phantom Limbs [73]
- R Castration Anxiety [73]
  - ↓ Surgery [71]

Body Language [73]
PN 237   SC 06470
SN Type of nonverbal communication in which thoughts, feelings, etc., are expressed through bodily movement or posture.
- B Interpersonal Communication [73]
  - Nonverbal Communication [71]
- R Gestures [73]
  - Posture [73]

Body Rocking [73]
PN 45   SC 06480
- UF Rocking (Body)
- B Symptoms [67]
- R ↓ Behavior Disorders [71]

Body Rotation
Use   Rotational Behavior

Body Size [85]
PN   361   SC   06485
SN   Used for human or animal populations. For human populations consider also PHYSIQUE or SOMATOTYPES.
B   Size [73]
N   Body Height [73]
      ↓ Body Weight [67]
R   Physique [67]

Body Sway Testing [73]
PN   32   SC   06490
B   Measurement [67]

Body Temperature [73]
PN   1040   SC   06500
UF   Temperature (Body)
B   Physiology [67]
N   Skin Temperature [73]
      Thermoregulation (Body) [73]
R   Hypothermia [73]

Body Types
Use   Somatotypes

Body Weight [67]
PN   2921   SC   06520
UF   Weight (Body)
B   Body Size [85]
N   Birth Weight [85]
      Obesity [73]
      ↓ Underweight [73]
R   Physique [67]
      Weight Control [85]

Bolivia [88]
PN   8   SC   06522
B   South America [67]

Bombesin [88]
PN   52   SC   06523
B   Peptides [73]

Bonding (Emotional)
Use   Attachment Behavior

Bone Conduction Audiometry [73]
PN   29   SC   06530
B   Audiometry [67]
R   ↓ Auditory Stimulation [67]
      ↓ Perceptual Measures [73]

Bone Disorders [73]
PN   58   SC   06540
B   Musculoskeletal Disorders [73]
N   Osteoporosis [91]

Bone Marrow [73]
PN   65   SC   06550
B   Tissues (Body) [73]
R   Bones [73]

Bones [73]
PN   29   SC   06570
B   Connective Tissues [73]
      Musculoskeletal System [73]
R   Bone Marrow [73]
      Jaw [73]
      Spinal Column [73]

Bonuses [73]
PN   16   SC   06580
B   Employee Benefits [73]
R   Salaries [73]

Book [67]
PN   7191   SC   06590
SN   Mandatory term used as a document type identifier.

Books [73]
PN   418   SC   06600
SN   Refers to books as a means of communication, as distinct from the document type identifier BOOK.
B   Printed Communications Media [73]
N   ↓ Textbooks [78]
R   Reading Materials [73]

Borderline Mental Retardation [73]
PN   67   SC   06610
SN   IQ 71–84.
B   Mental Retardation [67]
R   Psychosocial Mental Retardation [73]

Borderline Mentally Retarded
Use   Slow Learners

Borderline States [78]
PN   2040   SC   06624
SN   Personality disorder characterized by instability of mood, interpersonal behavior, or personal identity and possible transient psychotic episodes; also, state in which individual has not broken with reality but may become psychotic if exposed to unfavorable circumstances (e.g., borderline schizophrenia).
B   Mental Disorders [67]
R   ↓ Neurosis [67]
      ↓ Personality Disorders [67]
      ↓ Psychosis [67]

Boredom [73]
PN   201   SC   06630
B   Emotional States [73]
R   Monotony [78]

Botany [73]
PN   25   SC   06640
B   Biology [67]
R   Phylogenesis [73]

Botswana [88]
PN   18   SC   06645
B   Africa [67]

Bottle Feeding [73]
PN   69   SC   06650
B   Feeding Practices [73]

Bourgeois
Use   Middle Class

Bowel Disorders
Use   Colon Disorders

Boys
Use   Human Males

Brachial Plexus
Use   Spinal Nerves

Bradycardia [73]
PN   77   SC   06730
B   Arrhythmias (Heart) [73]

Braille [78]
PN   101   SC   06737
B   Reading [67]
R   Braille Instruction [73]
      Reading Education [73]
      Reading Materials [73]

Braille — (cont'd)
R   ↓ Tactual Perception [67]
      ↓ Visually Handicapped [67]

Braille Instruction [73]
PN   40   SC   06740
B   Curriculum [67]
R   Braille [78]
      Reading Education [73]
      ↓ Visually Handicapped [67]

Brain [67]
PN   3961   SC   06750
N   ↓ Brain Stem [73]
      ↓ Cerebellum [73]
      ↓ Forebrain [85]
      ↓ Mesencephalon [73]
R   Blood Brain Barrier [94]
      ↓ Brain Disorders [67]
      Brain Size [73]
      Brain Weight [73]
      Cerebral Atrophy [94]
      ↓ Cerebral Dominance [73]
      ↓ Lateral Dominance [67]
      Left Brain [91]
      Ocular Dominance [73]
      Right Brain [91]

Brain Ablation
Use   Brain Lesions

Brain Concussion [73]
PN   54   SC   06770
UF   Concussion (Brain)
B   Brain Damage [67]
      Head Injuries [73]

Brain Damage [67]
PN   3322   SC   06780
SN   Brain injury resulting from accident, surgery, or disease. Used primarily for human populations.
UF   Brain Injuries
B   Brain Disorders [67]
N   Brain Concussion [73]
R   ↓ Brain Damaged [73]
      Cerebral Atrophy [94]
      ↓ Epilepsy [67]
      ↓ Head Injuries [73]
      ↓ Mental Retardation [67]
      ↓ Neuropsychological Assessment [82]

Brain Damaged [73]
PN   2670   SC   06790
B   Handicapped [67]
N   Minimally Brain Damaged [73]
R   ↓ Brain Damage [67]
      Congenitally Handicapped [73]

Brain Disorders [67]
PN   1529   SC   06800
B   Central Nervous System Disorders [73]
N   Acute Alcoholic Intoxication [73]
      Anencephaly [73]
      ↓ Aphasia [67]
      Athetosis [73]
      ↓ Brain Damage [67]
      Brain Neoplasms [73]
      Cerebral Palsy [67]
      Cerebrovascular Accidents [73]
      Chronic Alcoholic Intoxication [73]
      Encephalitis [73]
      ↓ Encephalopathies [82]
      ↓ Epilepsy [67]
      ↓ Epileptic Seizures [73]
      Hydrocephaly [73]
      Microcephaly [73]
      Minimal Brain Disorders [73]

Brain Disorders — (cont'd)
- N ↓ Organic Brain Syndromes [73]
  - Parkinsons Disease [73]
- R ↓ Brain [67]
  - Cerebral Atrophy [94]
  - ↓ Convulsions [67]
  - ↓ Mental Disorders [67]
  - Rett Syndrome [94]

Brain Injuries
- **Use** Brain Damage

Brain Lesions [67]
PN 6746   SC 06830
SN Not defined prior to 1982. From 1982, limited to experimentally induced lesions and used primarily for animal populations.
- UF Brain Ablation
  - Cerebral Lesions
  - Subcortical Lesions
- B Lesions [67]
- N Hypothalamus Lesions [73]
- R Decerebration [73]
  - Decortication (Brain) [73]

Brain Mapping
- **Use** Stereotaxic Atlas

Brain Maps
- **Use** Stereotaxic Atlas

Brain Metabolism
- **Use** Neurochemistry

Brain Neoplasms [73]
PN 257   SC 06860
- B Brain Disorders [67]
  - Nervous System Neoplasms [73]

Brain Self Stimulation [85]
PN 316   SC 06864
- UF Intracranial Self Stimulation
- B Brain Stimulation [67]
  - Self Stimulation [67]

Brain Size [73]
PN 269   SC 06868
- B Size [73]
- R ↓ Brain [67]
  - Brain Weight [73]
  - Cerebral Atrophy [94]

Brain Stem [73]
PN 916   SC 06870
- B Brain [67]
- N Locus Ceruleus [82]
  - Medulla Oblongata [73]
  - ↓ Pons [73]
  - Reticular Formation [67]

Brain Stimulation [67]
PN 1685   SC 06880
- B Stereotaxic Techniques [73]
  - Stimulation [67]
- N Brain Self Stimulation [85]
  - Chemical Brain Stimulation [73]
  - Electrical Brain Stimulation [73]
  - Spreading Depression [67]
- R Physiological Arousal [67]

Brain Weight [73]
PN 107   SC 06882
- R ↓ Brain [67]
  - Brain Size [73]
  - Cerebral Atrophy [94]

Brainstorming [82]
PN 45   SC 06883
SN Group problem-solving technique involving spontaneous contribution of ideas from all group members.
- B Group Problem Solving [73]
- R Choice Shift [94]
  - ↓ Group Dynamics [67]

Brainwashing [82]
PN 22   SC 06884
SN Forcible indoctrination of an individual or group by means of physical or psychological duress in order to alter their political, social, religious, or moral beliefs.
- UF Thought Control
- B Persuasive Communication [67]
- R Attitude Change [67]
  - Coercion [94]
  - Propaganda [73]

Brand Names [78]
PN 384   SC 06885
- B Names [85]
- R ↓ Advertising [67]
  - Brand Preferences [94]
  - Consumer Behavior [67]
  - ↓ Consumer Research [73]
  - Marketing [73]
  - Retailing [91]

Brand Preferences [94]
PN 0   SC 06887
SN Includes loyalty to brand name products or product switching.
- B Consumer Attitudes [73]
  - Preferences [67]
- R ↓ Advertising [67]
  - Brand Names [78]
  - Consumer Behavior [67]
  - ↓ Consumer Research [73]
  - Marketing [73]

Bravery
- **Use** Courage

Brazil [73]
PN 582   SC 06900
- B South America [67]

Breakthrough (Psychotherapeutic)
- **Use** Psychotherapeutic Breakthrough

Breast [73]
PN 148   SC 06920
- B Anatomy [67]

Breast Examination
- **Use** Self Examination (Medical)

Breast Feeding [73]
PN 314   SC 06930
- B Feeding Practices [73]
- R Weaning [73]

Breast Neoplasms [73]
PN 538   SC 06940
- UF Mammary Neoplasms
- B Neoplasms [67]
- R Mammography [94]
  - Mastectomy [73]

Breathing
- **Use** Respiration

Breeding (Animal)
- **Use** Animal Breeding

Brief Psychotherapy [67]
PN 1351   SC 06970
SN Short-term or time-limited methods of interactive psychotherapy.
- UF Short Term Psychotherapy
  - Time Limited Psychotherapy
- B Psychotherapy [67]

Brief Reactive Psychosis
- **Use** Acute Psychosis

Bright Light Therapy
- **Use** Phototherapy

Brightness Constancy [85]
PN 16   SC 06975
SN The tendency to perceive the brightness of stimuli as stable despite objective changes in illumination.
- B Brightness Perception [73]
  - Perceptual Constancy [85]

Brightness Contrast [85]
PN 117   SC 06977
- B Visual Contrast [85]

Brightness Perception [73]
PN 1035   SC 06980
- UF Luminance Threshold
- B Visual Perception [67]
- N Brightness Constancy [85]
- R ↓ Illumination [67]
  - Luminance [82]

Bromides [73]
PN 21   SC 06990
- B Drugs [67]
- N Lithium Bromide [73]
- R Arecoline [73]
  - Homatropine [73]
  - Neostigmine [73]
  - Scopolamine [73]

Bromocriptine [88]
PN 106   SC 06995
- B Alkaloids [73]
  - Enzyme Inhibitors [85]
  - Ergot Derivatives [73]

Bronchi [73]
PN 7   SC 07000
- B Respiratory System [73]

Bronchial Disorders [73]
PN 42   SC 07010
- B Respiratory Tract Disorders [73]

Brothers [73]
PN 101   SC 07020
- B Human Males [73]
  - Siblings [67]

Bruxism [85]
PN 17   SC 07035
SN Use NOCTURNAL TEETH GRINDING to access references from 73–84.
- UF Teeth Grinding
- N Nocturnal Teeth Grinding [73]
- R Myofascial Pain [91]

Buddhism [73]
PN 140   SC 07040
- B Religious Affiliation [73]
- N Zen Buddhism [73]

Budgerigars [73]
PN 40   SC 07050
   B   Birds [67]

Budgets
   Use Costs and Cost Analysis

Bufotenine [73]
PN 12   SC 07060
   B   Amines [73]
       Hallucinogenic Drugs [67]
       Vasoconstrictor Drugs [73]

Bulgaria [82]
PN 34   SC 07075
   B   Europe [73]

Bulimia [85]
PN 1834   SC 07078
SN Disorder characterized primarily by binge eating and often accompanied by self-induced vomiting and/or misuse of laxatives.
   B   Appetite Disorders [73]
   R   Anorexia Nervosa [73]
       Binge Eating [91]
     ↓ Psychosomatic Disorders [67]

Bulls
   Use Cattle

Bupropion [94]
PN 0   SC 07081
   B   Antidepressant Drugs [71]

Burma [91]
PN 2   SC 07083
   B   Southeast Asia [73]

Burnout
   Use Occupational Stress

Burns [73]
PN 198   SC 07090
   B   Injuries [73]
   R   Electrical Injuries [73]
     ↓ Wounds [73]

Buses
   Use Motor Vehicles

Bush Babies
   Use Lemurs

Business [67]
PN 849   SC 07110
   UF   Commerce
       Industry
       Manufacturing
   R   Business Management [73]
       Business Organizations [73]
       Business Students [73]
       Entrepreneurship [91]
     ↓ Management [67]
       Ownership [85]
       Retailing [91]
       Self Employment [94]

Business and Industrial Personnel [67]
PN 3719   SC 07120
   UF   Businessmen
       Industrial Personnel
   N   Architects [73]
     ↓ Blue Collar Workers [73]
       Industrial Psychologists [73]
       Sales Personnel [73]
       Secretarial Personnel [73]
     ↓ Service Personnel [91]

Business and Industrial Personnel —
   (cont'd)
   N   Skilled Industrial Workers [73]
     ↓ Technical Personnel [78]
     ↓ White Collar Workers [73]
   R   ↓ Aerospace Personnel [73]
     ↓ Agricultural Workers [73]
       Engineers [67]
     ↓ Government Personnel [73]
     ↓ Nonprofessional Personnel [82]
     ↓ Professional Personnel [78]
       Scientists [67]
       Technical Service Personnel [73]

Business Education [73]
PN 238   SC 07123
   B   Curriculum [67]
   R   Business Management [73]
       Management Training [73]
     ↓ Personnel Management [73]
     ↓ Personnel Training [67]

Business Management [73]
PN 246   SC 07130
   B   Management [67]
   R   Business [67]
       Business Education [73]
       Entrepreneurship [91]
     ↓ Management Methods [73]
     ↓ Personnel Management [73]

Business Organizations [73]
PN 710   SC 07140
   UF   Companies
       Corporations
   B   Organizations [67]
       Private Sector [85]
   R   Business [67]

Business Students [73]
PN 408   SC 07150
   B   Students [67]
   R   Business [67]

Businessmen
   Use Business and Industrial Personnel

Buspirone [91]
PN 161   SC 07165
   B   Minor Tranquilizers [73]
   R   Serotonin Agonists [88]

Butterflies [73]
PN 73   SC 07170
   B   Insects [67]
   R   Larvae [73]

Butyrylperazine [73]
PN 2   SC 07180
   B   Phenothiazine Derivatives [73]

Buying
   Use Consumer Behavior

Cadres
   Use Social Groups

Caffeine [73]
PN 683   SC 07210
   B   Alkaloids [73]
       CNS Stimulating Drugs [73]
       Diuretics [73]
       Heart Rate Affecting Drugs [73]
       Respiration Stimulating Drugs [73]
   R   ↓ Analeptic Drugs [73]

Cage Apparatus [73]
PN 49   SC 07220
   B   Apparatus [67]

Calcium [73]
PN 250   SC 07240
   B   Chemical Elements [73]
       Metallic Elements [73]
   N   Calcium Ions [73]

Calcium Channel Blockers
   Use Channel Blockers

Calcium Ions [73]
PN 58   SC 07260
   B   Calcium [73]
       Electrolytes [73]

Calculators
   Use Digital Computers

Calculus
   Use Mathematics

California F Scale [73]
PN 29   SC 07290
   B   Nonprojective Personality Measures [73]

California Psychological Inventory [67]
PN 240   SC 07300
   B   Personality Measures [67]

California Test of Mental Maturity [73]
PN 9   SC 07310
   B   Intelligence Measures [67]

California Test of Personality [73]
PN 13   SC 07320
   B   Nonprojective Personality Measures [73]

Calories [73]
PN 220   SC 07330
   R   Energy Expenditure [67]

Cambodia [88]
PN 2   SC 07340
   B   Southeast Asia [73]

Cameras [73]
PN 30   SC 07350
   B   Apparatus [67]

Cameroon [91]
PN 3   SC 07355
   B   Africa [67]

Campaigns (Political)
   Use Political Campaigns

Camping [73]
PN 87   SC 07370
   B   Recreation [67]
   R   Summer Camps (Recreation) [73]
       Vacationing [73]

Camps (Therapeutic)
   Use Therapeutic Camps

Campuses [73]
PN 24   SC 07390
   B   School Facilities [73]

Canada [71]
PN 2337   SC 07400
   B   North America [73]

Canaries [73]
PN 31   SC 07410
  B   Birds [67]

Cancers
  Use Neoplasms

Candidates (Political)
  Use Political Candidates

Cannabinoids [82]
PN 48   SC 07436
  UF   Nabilone
  N   Tetrahydrocannabinol [73]
  R   ↓ Cannabis [73]

Cannabis [73]
PN 244   SC 07440
  UF   Hemp (Cannabis)
  B   Drugs [67]
  N   Hashish [73]
          Marihuana [71]
  R   Aphrodisiacs [73]
        ↓ Cannabinoids [82]
        ↓ Hallucinogenic Drugs [67]
        ↓ Narcotic Drugs [73]
          Tetrahydrocannabinol [73]

Canonical Correlation
  Use Multivariate Analysis

Capgras Syndrome [85]
PN 107   SC 07447
SN Clinical condition in which patient believes an acquaintance, a closely related person, or a close associate has been replaced by a double or an impostor.
  B   Psychosis [67]
          Syndromes [73]
  R   Delusions [67]
        ↓ Symptoms [67]

Capillaries (Anatomy) [73]
PN 12   SC 07450
  B   Blood Vessels [73]

Capital Punishment [73]
PN 201   SC 07460
  UF   Death Penalty
          Punishment (Capital)

Capitalism [73]
PN 93   SC 07470
  B   Political Economic Systems [73]
  R   Entrepreneurship [91]
          Ownership [85]

Capsaicin [91]
PN 20   SC 07475
  B   Fatty Acids [73]

Captivity (Animal)
  Use Animal Captivity

Captopril [91]
PN 12   SC 07477
  B   Antihypertensive Drugs [73]
          Enzyme Inhibitors [85]
  R   Angiotensin [73]

Carbachol [73]
PN 152   SC 07480
  B   Cholinomimetic Drugs [73]

Carbamazepine [88]
PN 336   SC 07483

Carbamazepine — (cont'd)
  B   Analgesic Drugs [73]
          Anticonvulsive Drugs [73]

Carbidopa [88]
PN 14   SC 07485
SN Use DECARBOXYLASES to access references from 82-87.
  B   Decarboxylase Inhibitors [82]
  R   DOPA [73]

Carbohydrate Metabolism [73]
PN 67   SC 07490
  B   Metabolism [67]
  N   Glucose Metabolism [94]
  R   Acetaldehyde [82]
          Guanosine [85]

Carbohydrates [73]
PN 276   SC 07510
  N   Deoxyglucose [91]
        ↓ Sugars [73]

Carbon [73]
PN 9   SC 07520
  B   Nonmetallic Elements [73]

Carbon Dioxide [73]
PN 143   SC 07530
  R   Respiration [67]

Carbon Monoxide [73]
PN 112   SC 07540
  R   ↓ Poisons [73]

Carbon Monoxide Poisoning [73]
PN 33   SC 07550
  UF   Carboxyhemoglobinemia
  B   Toxic Disorders [73]

Carbonic Anhydrase [73]
PN 2   SC 07560
  B   Enzymes [73]
  R   Acetazolamide [73]

Carboxyhemoglobinemia
  Use Carbon Monoxide Poisoning

Carcinogens [73]
PN 12   SC 07580
  R   ↓ Drugs [67]
          Pollution [73]
          Tobacco Smoking [67]

Carcinomas
  Use Neoplasms

Cardiac Disorders
  Use Heart Disorders

Cardiac Rate
  Use Heart Rate

Cardiography [73]
PN 12   SC 07620
  B   Medical Diagnosis [73]
  N   Electrocardiography [67]

Cardiology [73]
PN 22   SC 07630
  B   Medical Sciences [67]
  R   ↓ Cardiovascular System [67]

Cardiotonic Drugs [85]
PN 1   SC 07635

Cardiotonic Drugs — (cont'd)
SN Chemical agents that affect the contractility of heart muscle.
  B   Drugs [67]
  R   Channel Blockers [91]
          Dopamine [73]
          Epinephrine [67]
        ↓ Heart Rate Affecting Drugs [73]
          Isoproterenol [73]
          Norepinephrine [73]
        ↓ Sympathomimetic Drugs [73]

Cardiovascular Disorders [67]
PN 1676   SC 07640
  UF   Circulatory Disorders
          Coronary Disorders
          Raynauds Disease
          Vascular Disorders
  B   Disorders [67]
  N   Aneurysms [73]
        ↓ Arteriosclerosis [73]
        ↓ Blood Pressure Disorders [73]
        ↓ Cerebrovascular Disorders [73]
          Embolisms [73]
        ↓ Heart Disorders [73]
        ↓ Hemorrhage [73]
        ↓ Hypertension [73]
        ↓ Ischemia [73]
        ↓ Thromboses [73]
  R   ↓ Cardiovascular System [67]
          Coronary Prone Behavior [82]
        ↓ Dyspnea [73]
        ↓ Heart Rate Affecting Drugs [73]

Cardiovascular Reactivity [94]
PN 0   SC 07645
SN Cardiovascular system responses to mental, physical, or environmental stress or other states due to intervention or natural occurrence.
  R   ↓ Blood Pressure [67]
        ↓ Cardiovascular System [67]
          Heart Rate [67]
          Physiological Arousal [67]
          Physiological Correlates [67]
        ↓ Psychophysiology [67]
          Stress Reactions [73]

Cardiovascular System [67]
PN 1489   SC 07650
  B   Anatomical Systems [73]
  N   ↓ Blood Vessels [73]
        ↓ Heart [67]
  R   Blood Brain Barrier [94]
          Cardiology [73]
        ↓ Cardiovascular Disorders [67]
          Cardiovascular Reactivity [94]
          Spleen [73]

Career Aspirations
  Use Occupational Aspirations

Career Change [78]
PN 313   SC 07666
  UF   Job Change
  R   Career Development [85]
          Employment History [78]
          Job Satisfaction [67]
          Occupational Adjustment [73]
          Occupational Aspirations [73]
          Occupational Choice [67]
          Occupational Mobility [73]
        ↓ Occupations [67]
          Professional Development [82]

Career Choice
  Use Occupational Choice

Career Counseling
Use Occupational Guidance

Career Development [85]
PN 912   SC 07672
SN Formation of work identity or progression of career decisions and/or events as influenced by life or work experience, education, on-the-job training, or other factors.
UF Career Transitions
    Management Development
B Development [67]
    Personnel Management [73]
R Career Change [78]
    Employment History [78]
  ↓ Management [67]
    Occupational Choice [67]
  ↓ Occupations [67]
    Personnel Placement [73]
    Personnel Promotion [78]
  ↓ Personnel Training [67]
    Professional Development [82]
    Professional Identity [91]
    Professional Specialization [91]

Career Education [78]
PN 585   SC 07675
SN Comprehensive educational programs focusing on individual career development beginning in childhood and continuing through the adult years.
UF Career Exploration
B Curriculum [67]
R Occupational Guidance [67]

Career Exploration
Use Career Education

Career Goals
Use Occupational Aspirations

Career Guidance
Use Occupational Guidance

Career Maturity
Use Vocational Maturity

Career Preference
Use Occupational Preference

Career Transitions
Use Career Development

Careers
Use Occupations

Caregiver Burden [94]
PN 0   SC 07713
SN Used primarily for family or nonprofessional caregivers and the stress or associated emotional responses experienced when caring for the mentally or physically disabled. Consider OCCUPATIONAL STRESS for professional caregivers, e.g., health care personnel.
R Caregivers [88]
    Elder Care [94]
    Home Care [85]
    Homebound [88]
    Respite Care [88]
  ↓ Stress [67]

Caregivers [88]
PN 1222   SC 07715
SN Family members, professionals, or paraprofessionals who provide constant care.
UF Family Caregivers
R Caregiver Burden [94]
    Elder Care [94]
  ↓ Health Care Services [78]

Caregivers — (cont'd)
R Home Care [85]
    Quality of Care [88]
    Respite Care [88]
  ↓ Treatment [67]

Carotid Arteries [73]
PN 80   SC 07720
B Arteries (Anatomy) [73]

Carp [73]
PN 36   SC 07740
B Fishes [67]
N Goldfish [73]

Cartoons (Humor) [73]
PN 173   SC 07780
B Humor [67]

Case History
Use Patient History

Case Law [85]
PN 726   SC 07787
SN Mandatory term applied to descriptions of specific legal cases. Limited to documents that describe or summarize court decisions. Not used for documents that discuss or describe the implications or effects of specific legal decisions. Consider LEGAL DECISIONS for discussions of the effects of specific court decisions.
R ↓ Adjudication [67]
  ↓ Laws [67]
    Legal Decisions [91]
  ↓ Legal Processes [73]

Case Management [91]
PN 176   SC 07788
SN Evaluation of health and social service needs of individuals and development and delivery of service or treatment. Includes attention to justification and length of treatment, costs, and health insurance reimbursement.
B Management [67]
N Discharge Planning [94]
R Cost Containment [91]
    Health Care Costs [94]
  ↓ Health Care Delivery [78]
  ↓ Health Insurance [73]
    Intake Interview [94]
    Long Term Care [94]
  ↓ Managed Care [94]
    Needs Assessment [85]
    Social Casework [67]
  ↓ Treatment [67]
  ↓ Treatment Duration [88]

Case Report [67]
PN 16519   SC 07790
SN Mandatory term applied to exploratory studies of single or multiple clinical cases.

Caseworkers
Use Social Workers

Caste System [73]
PN 184   SC 07810
B Social Structure [67]
    Systems [67]

Castration [67]
PN 173   SC 07820
B Endocrine Gland Surgery [73]
    Sterilization (Sex) [73]
N Male Castration [73]
    Ovariectomy [73]

Castration Anxiety [73]
PN 91   SC 07830
B Anxiety Neurosis [73]
R ↓ Body Image Disturbances [73]

Cat Learning [67]
PN 114   SC 07840
SN Not defined prior to 1982. Use CAT LEARNING or CATS to access references from 67–81. From 1982 used for discussions of hypotheses or theories of learning in cats.
B Learning [67]
R Cats [67]

CAT Scan
Use Tomography

Catabolism [73]
PN 13   SC 07850
SN Destructive metabolism involving release of energy (heat) and resulting in breakdown of complex materials within the organism.
B Metabolism [67]

Catabolites
Use Metabolites

Catalepsy [73]
PN 228   SC 07860
SN Condition of muscular semirigidity and trance-like postures. Cataleptic persons make no voluntary motor movements and may display waxy flexibility.
B Movement Disorders [85]
    Symptoms [67]
R Autohypnosis [73]
  ↓ Hysteria [67]
  ↓ Schizophrenia [67]
    Suggestibility [67]

Catamnesis
Use Posttreatment Followup

Cataplexy [73]
PN 43   SC 07880
SN Temporary loss of muscle tone or weakness following extreme emotion.
B Movement Disorders [85]
    Muscular Disorders [73]
    Neuromuscular Disorders [73]
R Narcolepsy [73]

Cataracts [73]
PN 37   SC 07890
B Eye Disorders [73]

Catatonia [73]
PN 231   SC 07900
SN Reaction characterized by muscular rigidity or stupor sometimes punctuated by sudden violent outbursts, panic, or hallucinations.
B Symptoms [67]
R Catatonic Schizophrenia [73]

Catatonic Schizophrenia [73]
PN 88   SC 07910
B Schizophrenia [67]
R Catatonia [73]

Catecholamines [73]
PN 1299   SC 07920
UF Monoamines (Brain)
B Neurotransmitters [85]
    Sympathomimetic Amines [73]
N Dopamine [73]
    Epinephrine [67]
    Norepinephrine [73]
R ↓ Adrenergic Drugs [73]

Catecholamines — (cont'd)
R ↓ Decarboxylase Inhibitors [82]
    ↓ Dopamine Antagonists [82]
    Methyldopa [73]

Categorizing
Use Classification (Cognitive Process)

Catharsis [73]
PN 153   SC 07940
SN Psychoanalytic term pertaining to the process of recalling and describing painful experiences and attitudes, and the associated emotional responses.
UF Abreaction
B Personality Processes [67]
R ↓ Psychoanalysis [67]

Catheterization [73]
PN 55   SC 07950
B Physical Treatment Methods [73]

Cathexis [73]
PN 82   SC 07960
SN Psychoanalytic term designating the attachment of intense emotions to a particular object, person, or oneself.
B Personality Processes [67]

Cathode Ray Tubes
Use Video Display Units

Catholicism (Roman)
Use Roman Catholicism

Cats [67]
PN 5772   SC 07980
B Mammals [73]
R Cat Learning [67]

Cattell Culture Fair Intell Test
Use Culture Fair Intelligence Test

Cattell Infant Intelligence Scale
Use Infant Intelligence Scale

Cattle [73]
PN 296   SC 08010
UF Bulls
    Cows
B Mammals [73]

Caucasians
SN Term discontinued in 1982. Use CAUCASIANS to access references from 73–81.
Use Whites

Cauda Equina
Use Spinal Nerves

Caudate Nucleus [73]
PN 586   SC 08040
B Basal Ganglia [73]
R Nucleus Accumbens [82]

Causal Analysis [94]
PN 0   SC 08045
SN Systematic analysis of causal relationships among variables.
B Analysis [67]
    Methodology [67]
R Attribution [73]
  ↓ Experimentation [67]
    Path Analysis [91]
  ↓ Statistical Regression [85]
    Structural Equation Modeling [94]

Celiac Plexus
Use Autonomic Ganglia

Celibacy
Use Sexual Abstinence

Cell Nucleus [73]
PN 10   SC 08070
R ↓ Cells (Biology) [73]

Cells (Biology) [73]
PN 259   SC 08080
B Anatomy [67]
N ↓ Blood Cells [73]
  ↓ Chromosomes [73]
    Cones (Eye) [73]
    Connective Tissue Cells [73]
    Epithelial Cells [73]
  ↓ Neurons [73]
    Sperm [73]
R Absorption (Physiological) [73]
    Cell Nucleus [73]
    Cytology [73]
    Cytoplasm [73]
  ↓ Physiology [67]

Censorship [78]
PN 29   SC 08086
R ↓ Civil Rights [78]
  ↓ Communication [67]
  ↓ Communications Media [73]
    Freedom [78]
    Information [67]
  ↓ Laws [67]
  ↓ Social Issues [91]

Centering [91]
PN 1   SC 08088
SN Focusing of attention and concentration on a particular stimulus or on the whole of the present environment and circumstances. Used primarily in, but not limited to, therapeutic settings.
R ↓ Consciousness States [71]
    Meditation [73]
  ↓ Psychotherapeutic Techniques [67]
  ↓ Self Management [85]

Central America [73]
PN 226   SC 08090
N Belize [88]
    Costa Rica [88]
    El Salvador [88]
    Guatemala [82]
    Honduras [88]
    Nicaragua [88]
    Panama [88]
R Latin America [88]

Central Nervous System [67]
PN 1454   SC 08100
B Nervous System [67]
N Extrapyramidal Tracts [73]
    Meninges [73]
    Neural Analyzers [73]
  ↓ Neural Pathways [82]
  ↓ Spinal Cord [73]
R ↓ Central Nervous System Disorders [73]

Central Nervous System Disorders [73]
PN 407   SC 08110
B Nervous System Disorders [67]
N ↓ Brain Disorders [67]
  ↓ Chorea [73]
    Dysarthria [73]
  ↓ Meningitis [73]
  ↓ Myelitis [73]
    Neurosyphilis [73]
R ↓ Central Nervous System [67]

Central Nervous System Disorders — (cont'd)
R Hemiplegia [78]
    Hypothermia [73]
  ↓ Paralysis [73]
    Paraplegia [78]
    Quadriplegia [85]
    Spinal Cord Injuries [73]

Central Nervous System Drugs
Use CNS Affecting Drugs

Central Tendency Measures [73]
PN 16   SC 08130
B Statistical Analysis [67]
    Statistical Measurement [73]
N Mean [73]
    Median [73]
R ↓ Population (Statistics) [73]
    T Test [73]
  ↓ Variability Measurement [73]

Central Vision
Use Foveal Vision

CER (Conditioning)
Use Conditioned Emotional Responses

Cerebellar Cortex
Use Cerebellum

Cerebellar Nuclei
Use Cerebellum

Cerebellopontile Angle
Use Cerebellum

Cerebellum [73]
PN 637   SC 08180
UF Cerebellar Cortex
    Cerebellar Nuclei
    Cerebellopontile Angle
B Brain [67]
N Purkinje Cells [94]

Cerebral Aqueduct
Use Cerebral Ventricles

Cerebral Arteriosclerosis [73]
PN 35   SC 08210
B Arteriosclerosis [73]
    Cerebrovascular Disorders [73]
R Cerebrovascular Accidents [73]
  ↓ Senile Dementia [73]

Cerebral Atrophy [94]
PN 0   SC 08215
UF Atrophy (Cerebral)
    Cortical Atrophy
R ↓ Brain [67]
  ↓ Brain Damage [67]
  ↓ Brain Disorders [67]
    Brain Size [73]
    Brain Weight [73]
  ↓ Cerebral Cortex [67]
  ↓ Cerebral Dominance [73]

Cerebral Blood Flow [94]
PN 0   SC 08217
B Blood Flow [73]
R Blood Circulation [73]
  ↓ Blood Pressure [67]
  ↓ Cerebral Cortex [67]

Cerebral Cortex [67]
PN 3309   SC 08220

Cerebral Cortex — (cont'd)
UF   Cortex (Cerebral)
B   Telencephalon [73]
N   Cerebral Ventricles [73]
      Corpus Callosum [73]
     ↓ Frontal Lobe [73]
      Left Brain [91]
     ↓ Limbic System [73]
     ↓ Occipital Lobe [73]
     ↓ Parietal Lobe [73]
      Right Brain [91]
     ↓ Temporal Lobe [73]
R   Cerebral Atrophy [94]
      Cerebral Blood Flow [94]
      Interhemispheric Interaction [85]

Cerebral Dominance [73]
PN 4162   SC 08230
SN The control of lower brain centers by the cerebrum or cerebral cortex. Compare LATERAL DOMINANCE.
B   Dominance [67]
N ↓ Lateral Dominance [67]
R ↓ Brain [67]
      Cerebral Atrophy [94]
      Interhemispheric Interaction [85]
      Left Brain [91]
      Right Brain [91]

Cerebral Hemorrhage [73]
PN 108   SC 08250
B   Cerebrovascular Disorders [73]
      Hemorrhage [73]
R   Cerebrovascular Accidents [73]

Cerebral Ischemia [73]
PN 133   SC 08260
B   Cerebrovascular Disorders [73]
      Ischemia [73]
R   Cerebrovascular Accidents [73]

Cerebral Lesions
Use Brain Lesions

Cerebral Palsy [67]
PN 687   SC 08280
B   Brain Disorders [67]
      Paralysis [73]
R   Athetosis [73]

Cerebral Vascular Disorders
Use Cerebrovascular Disorders

Cerebral Ventricles [73]
PN 494   SC 08310
UF   Cerebral Aqueduct
      Choroid Plexus
      Ependyma
      Ventricles (Cerebral)
B   Cerebral Cortex [67]

Cerebrospinal Fluid [73]
PN 944   SC 08320
UF   Spinal Fluid
B   Body Fluids [73]
R   Blood Brain Barrier [94]

Cerebrovascular Accidents [73]
PN 1162   SC 08330
UF   Apoplexy
      Stroke (Cerebrum)
B   Brain Disorders [67]
      Cerebrovascular Disorders [73]
R   Cerebral Arteriosclerosis [73]
      Cerebral Hemorrhage [73]
      Cerebral Ischemia [73]
      Coma [73]

Cerebrovascular Disorders [73]
PN 246   SC 08340
UF   Cerebral Vascular Disorders
B   Cardiovascular Disorders [67]
N   Cerebral Arteriosclerosis [73]
      Cerebral Hemorrhage [73]
      Cerebral Ischemia [73]
      Cerebrovascular Accidents [73]
R   Coma [73]
     ↓ Hypertension [73]
      Multi Infarct Dementia [91]
     ↓ Nervous System Disorders [67]

Certification (Professional)
Use Professional Certification

Certification Examinations
Use Professional Examinations

Certified Public Accountants
Use Accountants

Cervical Plexus
Use Spinal Nerves

Cervix [73]
PN 59   SC 08390
B   Uterus [73]

Chance (Fortune) [73]
PN 175   SC 08420
SN The possibility of a favorable or unfavorable outcome in an uncertain situation.
UF   Luck
B   Probability [67]
N ↓ Statistical Probability [67]
R   Uncertainty [91]

Change (Organizational)
Use Organizational Change

Change (Social)
Use Social Change

Channel Blockers [91]
PN 85   SC 08450
UF   Calcium Channel Blockers
B   Drugs [67]
R   Cardiotonic Drugs [85]
     ↓ Vasodilator Drugs [73]
      Verapamil [91]

Chaplains [73]
PN 37   SC 08460
SN Clergymen officially attached to branch of military, hospital, institution, court, or university.
B   Clergy [73]
R   Lay Religious Personnel [73]
     ↓ Military Personnel [67]
      Ministers (Religion) [73]
      Priests [73]
      Rabbis [73]

Character
Use Personality

Character Development
Use Personality Development

Character Disorders
Use Personality Disorders

Character Formation
Use Personality Development

Charisma [88]
PN 47   SC 08515
B   Personality Traits [67]
R   Leadership Style [73]

Charitable Behavior [73]
PN 374   SC 08520
SN Generous or spontaneous goodness as manifested in actions for the benefit of others, especially of the needy, poor, or helpless.
B   Interpersonal Interaction [67]
      Prosocial Behavior [82]
R   Altruism [73]
      Assistance (Social Behavior) [73]
      Sharing (Social Behavior) [78]
      Tissue Donation [91]

Cheating [73]
PN 208   SC 08530
B   Deception [67]
R   Dishonesty [73]
      Fraud [94]
      Test Taking [85]

Chemical Brain Stimulation [73]
PN 920   SC 08540
B   Brain Stimulation [67]
      Stereotaxic Techniques [73]

Chemical Elements [73]
PN 168   SC 08550
B   Chemicals [91]
N ↓ Calcium [73]
     ↓ Nonmetallic Elements [73]
R ↓ Electrolytes [73]
      Food Additives [78]

Chemicals [91]
PN 56   SC 08555
SN May include compounds.
N ↓ Chemical Elements [73]
R ↓ Hazardous Materials [91]

Chemistry [67]
PN 251   SC 08560
SN Study of the atomic composition of substances, elements, and their reactions, and the formation, decomposition, and properties of molecules. Used for the scientific discipline or the chemical processes themselves.
B   Sciences [67]
N ↓ Biochemistry [67]

Chemoreceptors [73]
PN 249   SC 08570
B   Neural Receptors [73]
      Sensory Neurons [73]
R   Olfactory Mucosa [73]
      Taste Buds [73]
      Vomeronasal Sense [82]

Chemotherapy
Use Drug Therapy

Chess [73]
PN 84   SC 08590
B   Games [67]

Chest
Use Thorax

Chewing Tobacco
Use Smokeless Tobacco

Chi Square Test [73]
PN 136   SC 08620

Chi Square Test — (cont'd)
 B   Nonparametric Statistical Tests 67
 R   Statistical Significance 73

Chicanos
 Use Mexican Americans

Chickens 67
PN   1438   SC 08630
 B   Birds 67

Child Abuse 71
PN   4139   SC 08650
SN   Abuse of children or adolescents in a family,
institutional, or other setting.
 B   Crime 67
      Family Violence 82
 N   Battered Child Syndrome 73
 R   Anatomically Detailed Dolls 91
      Child Neglect 88
      Child Welfare 88
      Emotional Abuse 91
      Failure to Thrive 88
      Patient Abuse 91
      Pedophilia 73
      Physical Abuse 91
      ↓ Sexual Abuse 88

Child Advocacy
 Use Advocacy

Child Attitudes 88
PN   643   SC 08658
SN   Attitudes of, not toward, children.
 B   Attitudes 67
 R   ↓ Children 67

Child Behavior Checklist 94
PN   0   SC 08659
 B   Nonprojective Personality Measures 73

Child Care 91
PN   129   SC 08660
SN   Care of children of any age in any setting.
 UF   Babysitting
 N   Child Day Care 73
      Child Self Care 88
 R   ↓ Childrearing Practices 67
      Foster Care 78

Child Care Workers 78
PN   588   SC 08663
SN   Mental health, educational, or social services
personnel providing day care or residential care
for children.
 R   Child Day Care 73
      Day Care Centers 73
      ↓ Nonprofessional Personnel 82
      ↓ Service Personnel 91

Child Custody 82
PN   654   SC 08665
SN   Legal guardianship of a child.
 B   Legal Processes 73
 R   Child Support 88
      Child Visitation 88
      Divorce 73
      Guardianship 88
      Joint Custody 88
      ↓ Living Arrangements 91
      Mediation 88
      ↓ Parental Absence 73

Child Day Care 73
PN   1016   SC 08670

Child Day Care — (cont'd)
SN   Day care that provides for a child's physical
needs and often his/her developmental or educa-
tional needs. Kinds of day care include day care
centers and school-based programs.
 UF   Day Care (Child)
 B   Child Care 91
 R   Child Care Workers 78
      Child Self Care 88
      Child Welfare 88
      Day Care Centers 73
      Quality of Care 88

Child Discipline 73
PN   484   SC 08680
 UF   Discipline (Child)
 B   Childrearing Practices 67
      Family Relations 67
 N   Parental Permissiveness 73
 R   ↓ Parent Child Relations 67
      Parental Role 73

Child Guidance Clinics 73
PN   207   SC 08690
SN   Facilities which exist for the diagnosis and
treatment of behavioral and emotional disorders
in childhood.
 UF   Child Psychiatric Clinics
 B   Clinics 67
 R   ↓ Community Facilities 73
      Community Mental Health Centers 73
      ↓ Mental Health Programs 73
      ↓ Mental Health Services 78
      Psychiatric Clinics 73

Child Neglect 88
PN   344   SC 08695
SN   Failure of parents or caretakers to provide
basic care and emotional support necessary for
normal development.
 B   Antisocial Behavior 71
 R   ↓ Child Abuse 71
      Child Welfare 88
      Emotional Abuse 91
      Failure to Thrive 88

Child Psychiatric Clinics
 Use Child Guidance Clinics

Child Psychiatry 67
PN   1224   SC 08710
SN   Branch of psychiatry devoted to the study
and treatment of behavioral, mental, and emo-
tional disorders of children. Use a more specific
term if possible.
 B   Psychiatry 67
 R   Orthopsychiatry 73

Child Psychology 67
PN   316   SC 08720
SN   Branch of developmental psychology devoted to the study of behavior, adjustment, and
development and the treatment of behavioral,
mental, and emotional disorders of children. Use
a more specific term if possible.
 B   Developmental Psychology 73

Child Psychotherapy 67
PN   1433   SC 08730
 B   Psychotherapy 67
 N   Play Therapy 73
 R   Adolescent Psychotherapy 94
      Reality Therapy 73

Child Self Care 88
PN   48   SC 08733

Child Self Care — (cont'd)
SN   Responsibility for personal care without
adult supervision usually before or after the
school day. Primarily used for children under age
14.
 UF   Latchkey Children
 B   Child Care 91
 R   Child Day Care 73
      Child Welfare 88
      Self Care Skills 78

Child Support 88
PN   24   SC 08735
SN   Legal obligation of parents or guardians to
contribute to the economic maintenance of their
children including provision of education, clothing,
and food.
 R   Child Custody 82
      Divorce 73
      Joint Custody 88
      ↓ Marital Separation 73

Child Visitation 88
PN   66   SC 08737
SN   The right of or court-granted permission to
parents, grandparents, or guardians to visit chil-
dren.
 UF   Visitation Rights
 B   Legal Processes 73
 R   Child Custody 82

Child Welfare 88
PN   225   SC 08738
 R   ↓ Adoption (Child) 67
      Advocacy 85
      ↓ Child Abuse 71
      Child Day Care 73
      Child Neglect 88
      Child Self Care 88
      Foster Care 78
      Social Casework 67
      ↓ Social Services 82

Childbirth
 Use Birth

Childbirth (Natural)
 Use Natural Childbirth

Childbirth Training 78
PN   154   SC 08746
 B   Prenatal Care 91
 R   ↓ Birth 67
      Labor (Childbirth) 73
      Natural Childbirth 78
      ↓ Obstetrics 78
      ↓ Pregnancy 67

Childhood 84
PN   56869   SC 08750
SN   Mandatory age identifier used for ages 0–
12. Where appropriate, more specific index terms
(e.g., INFANTS, PRESCHOOL AGE CHILDREN)
are used in addition to this age identifier. The
other two age identifiers are ADOLESCENCE and
ADULTHOOD.
 R   ↓ Children 67
      ↓ Infants 67
      Neonates 67

Childhood Development 67
PN   5122   SC 08760
SN   Process of physical, cognitive, personality,
and psychosocial growth occurring from birth
through age 12. Use a more specific term if
possible.
 B   Human Development 67
 N   ↓ Early Childhood Development 73
 R   Adolescent Development 73

Childhood Development — (cont'd)
- R ↓ Children [67]
  - ↓ Developmental Age Groups [73]
  - ↓ Developmental Stages [73]
  - ↓ Motor Development [73]
  - Object Relations [82]
  - ↓ Perceptual Development [73]
  - ↓ Physical Development [73]
  - Preschool Age Children [67]
  - ↓ Psychogenesis [73]
  - ↓ Psychomotor Development [73]
  - ↓ School Age Children [73]
  - Separation Individuation [82]
  - Transitional Objects [85]

Childhood Memories
- Use Early Memories

Childhood Neurosis [73]
PN 123   SC 08770
- UF Infantile Neurosis
- B Neurosis [67]

Childhood Play Behavior [78]
PN 1903   SC 08777
- UF Play Behavior (Childhood)
- B Behavior [67]
- R Anatomically Detailed Dolls [91]
  - Childhood Play Development [73]
  - Childrens Recreational Games [73]
  - Doll Play [73]
  - ↓ Games [67]
  - ↓ Recreation [67]
  - Role Playing [67]
  - Toy Selection [73]
  - ↓ Toys [73]

Childhood Play Development [73]
PN 529   SC 08780
- UF Play Development (Childhood)
- B Psychosocial Development [73]
- R Childhood Play Behavior [78]
  - Childrens Recreational Games [73]
  - Emotional Development [73]

Childhood Psychosis [67]
PN 533   SC 08790
- UF Infantile Psychosis
- B Psychosis [67]
- N Childhood Schizophrenia [67]
  - Early Infantile Autism [73]
  - Symbiotic Infantile Psychosis [73]
- R Autistic Children [73]
  - ↓ Emotionally Disturbed [73]

Childhood Schizophrenia [67]
PN 573   SC 08800
- B Childhood Psychosis [67]
  - Schizophrenia [67]
- R Early Infantile Autism [73]
  - Symbiotic Infantile Psychosis [73]

Childlessness [82]
PN 121   SC 08805
- SN State of having no children.
- B Family Structure [73]
  - Parenthood Status [85]
- R Delayed Parenthood [85]
  - Family Planning Attitudes [73]

Childrearing Attitudes [73]
PN 813   SC 08810
- B Attitudes [67]
- R ↓ Family Relations [67]
  - Parental Attitudes [73]

Childrearing Practices [67]
PN 3207   SC 08820

Childrearing Practices — (cont'd)
- SN Limited to human populations.
- B Family Relations [67]
- N ↓ Child Discipline [73]
  - Toilet Training [73]
  - Weaning [73]
- R ↓ Child Care [91]
  - Father Child Relations [73]
  - ↓ Feeding Practices [73]
  - Mother Child Relations [67]
  - ↓ Parent Child Relations [67]
  - Parent Training [78]
  - Parental Attitudes [73]
  - ↓ Parental Characteristics [94]
  - Parental Role [73]
  - ↓ Sociocultural Factors [67]

Children [67]
PN 18484   SC 08830
- SN Ages 0–12 years. Used in noneducational contexts. Application of terms designating age is mandatory for ages 0–17.
- UF Youth (Children)
- B Developmental Age Groups [73]
- N ↓ Infants [67]
  - Only Children [82]
  - Preschool Age Children [67]
  - ↓ School Age Children [73]
- R Adopted Children [73]
  - Autistic Children [73]
  - Child Attitudes [88]
  - Childhood [84]
  - ↓ Childhood Development [67]
  - ↓ Elementary School Students [67]
  - Foster Children [73]
  - Illegitimate Children [73]
  - Intermediate School Students [73]
  - Junior High School Students [71]
  - Kindergarten Students [73]
  - Nursery School Students [73]
  - Predelinquent Youth [78]
  - Primary School Students [73]
  - Stepchildren [73]

Childrens Apperception Test [73]
PN 23   SC 08840
- B Projective Personality Measures [73]

Childrens Manifest Anxiety Scale [73]
PN 24   SC 08850
- B Nonprojective Personality Measures [73]

Childrens Personality Questionnaire [73]
PN 14   SC 08860
- B Nonprojective Personality Measures [73]

Childrens Recreational Games [73]
PN 50   SC 08870
- B Games [67]
  - Recreation [67]
- R Childhood Play Behavior [78]
  - Childhood Play Development [73]
  - ↓ Toys [73]

Chile [82]
PN 102   SC 08878
- B South America [67]

Chimpanzees [73]
PN 464   SC 08890
- B Mammals [73]
  - Primates (Nonhuman) [73]

China
- Use Peoples Republic of China

Chinchillas [73]
PN 59   SC 08900

Chinchillas — (cont'd)
- B Mammals [73]
  - Rodents [73]

Chinese Americans
- Use Asians

Chloral Hydrate [73]
PN 23   SC 08910
- B Anticonvulsive Drugs [73]
  - Hypnotic Drugs [73]
  - Sedatives [73]

Chloralose [73]
PN 9   SC 08920
- B Hypnotic Drugs [73]

Chlordiazepoxide [73]
PN 680   SC 08930
- UF Librium
- B Amines [73]
  - Benzodiazepines [78]
  - Minor Tranquilizers [73]

Chloride Ions [73]
PN 40   SC 08940
- B Electrolytes [73]
  - Nonmetallic Elements [73]

Chlorimipramine [73]
PN 487   SC 08950
- UF Clomipramine
- B Amines [73]
  - Antidepressant Drugs [71]

Chlorisondamine [73]
PN 7   SC 08960
- B Amines [73]
  - Antihypertensive Drugs [73]
  - Ganglion Blocking Drugs [73]

Chloroform [73]
PN 7   SC 08970
- B General Anesthetics [73]

Chlorophenylpiperazine
- Use Piperazines

Chlorpromazine [67]
PN 1275   SC 08990
- UF Thorazine
- B Adrenolytic Drugs [73]
  - Amines [73]
  - Antiemetic Drugs [73]
  - Antihypertensive Drugs [73]
  - CNS Depressant Drugs [73]
  - Phenothiazine Derivatives [73]
  - Sedatives [73]

Chlorprothixene [73]
PN 21   SC 09000
- B Adrenolytic Drugs [73]
  - Amines [73]
  - Antiemetic Drugs [73]
  - Antihistaminic Drugs [73]
  - Antispasmodic Drugs [73]
  - Minor Tranquilizers [73]
  - Phenothiazine Derivatives [73]

Choice Behavior [67]
PN 3817   SC 09010
- SN Motivational or judgmental processes involved in the decision or tendency to select one alternative over another or others. Used for human or animal populations.
- B Behavior [67]
  - Decision Making [67]

Choice Behavior — (cont'd)
R   Classification (Cognitive Process) 67
     Freedom 78
     Human Mate Selection 88
     Psychological Reactance 78
     Therapist Selection 94
     Uncertainty 91
     Volition 88

Choice Shift 94
PN 0   SC 09013
SN In social psychology, the changes or shifts
in choices made by groups during decision mak-
ing processes that may differ from choices made
by each group member acting on their own.
UF   Risky Shift
B   Group Decision Making 78
R   Brainstorming 82
     Group Discussion 67
     ↓ Group Dynamics 67
     ↓ Group Problem Solving 73
     ↓ Risk Taking 67

Cholecystokinin 82
PN 386   SC 09015
SN Hormone secreted by upper intestinal mu-
cosa on contact with gastric contents, it stimu-
lates contraction of the gallbladder. Also, a neu-
rotransmitter.
UF   Pancreozymin
B   Hormones 67
     Neurotransmitters 85
     Peptides 73

Cholesterol 73
PN 195   SC 09020
B   Steroids 73

Choline 73
PN 240   SC 09030
UF   Choline Chloride
B   Vitamins 73
N   Lecithin 91
R   Acetylcholine 73
     Cholinesterase 73
     Succinylcholine 73

Choline Chloride
Use Choline

Cholinergic Blocking Drugs 73
PN 493   SC 09050
UF   Anticholinergic Drugs
     Cholinolytic Drugs
     Parasympatholytic Drugs
B   Drugs 67
N   Atropine 73
     Benactyzine 73
     Homatropine 73
     Levodopa 73
     Nicotine 73
     Orphenadrine 73
     Scopolamine 73
     Trihexyphenidyl 73
R   ↓ Antiemetic Drugs 73
     ↓ Antispasmodic Drugs 73
     Cholinergic Nerves 73
     Cholinesterase 73
     ↓ Cholinomimetic Drugs 73
     ↓ Hallucinogenic Drugs 67
     ↓ Parasympathetic Nervous System 73
     ↓ Phenothiazine Derivatives 73

Cholinergic Drugs 73
PN 289   SC 09060
UF   Muscarinic Drugs
B   Drugs 67
N   Acetylcholine 73

Cholinergic Drugs — (cont'd)
N   Physostigmine 73
     Pilocarpine 73
R   ↓ Cholinomimetic Drugs 73

Cholinergic Nerves 73
PN 374   SC 09070
UF   Nerves (Cholinergic)
B   Autonomic Nervous System 67
R   Acetylcholine 73
     ↓ Cholinergic Blocking Drugs 73
     ↓ Cholinomimetic Drugs 73

Cholinesterase 73
PN 69   SC 09080
B   Esterases 73
R   Acetylcholinesterase 73
     ↓ Choline 73
     ↓ Cholinergic Blocking Drugs 73
     ↓ Cholinesterase Inhibitors 73

Cholinesterase Inhibitors 73
PN 178   SC 09090
UF   Anticholinesterase Drugs
B   Enzyme Inhibitors 85
N   Galanthamine 73
     Neostigmine 73
     Physostigmine 73
R   Cholinesterase 73
     ↓ Cholinomimetic Drugs 73

Cholinolytic Drugs
Use Cholinergic Blocking Drugs

Cholinomimetic Drugs 73
PN 88   SC 09100
UF   Parasympathomimetic Drugs
B   Drugs 67
N   Acetylcholine 73
     Arecoline 73
     Carbachol 73
     Neostigmine 73
     Physostigmine 73
     Pilocarpine 73
R   ↓ Analeptic Drugs 73
     ↓ Cholinergic Blocking Drugs 73
     ↓ Cholinergic Drugs 73
     Cholinergic Nerves 73
     ↓ Cholinesterase Inhibitors 73
     ↓ Parasympathetic Nervous System 73

Chorda Tympani Nerve
Use Facial Nerve

Chorea 73
PN 33   SC 09120
B   Central Nervous System Disorders 73
     Movement Disorders 85
N   Huntingtons Chorea 73
R   ↓ Infectious Disorders 73

Choroid
Use Eye (Anatomy)

Choroid Plexus
Use Cerebral Ventricles

Christianity 73
PN 950   SC 09150
B   Religious Affiliation 73
N   ↓ Protestantism 73
     Roman Catholicism 73
R   Bible 73

Chromosome Disorders 73
PN 203   SC 09160

Chromosome Disorders — (cont'd)
UF   Karyotype Disorders
     Mosaicism
B   Genetic Disorders 73
N   ↓ Autosome Disorders 73
     Deletion (Chromosome) 73
     ↓ Sex Chromosome Disorders 73
     Translocation (Chromosome) 73
     ↓ Trisomy 73
R   ↓ Chromosomes 73

Chromosomes 73
PN 146   SC 09170
B   Cells (Biology) 73
N   Autosomes 73
     Sex Chromosomes 73
R   ↓ Chromosome Disorders 73
     Genes 73
     Genetic Linkage 94
     ↓ Genetics 67
     Mutations 73

Chronic Alcoholic Intoxication 73
PN 38   SC 09180
B   Alcohol Intoxication 73
     Brain Disorders 67
     Chronic Illness 91
R   Toxic Encephalopathies 73

Chronic Illness 91
PN 256   SC 09183
SN An illness or disorder that persists for a
prolonged period of time.
B   Disorders 67
N   Chronic Alcoholic Intoxication 73
     Chronic Pain 85
     Chronic Psychosis 73
R   Chronicity (Disorders) 82
     ↓ Mental Disorders 67
     Severity (Disorders) 82

Chronic Pain 85
PN 1126   SC 09185
B   Chronic Illness 91
     Pain 67
R   Back Pain 82
     Myofascial Pain 91
     Psychogenic Pain 73

Chronic Psychosis 73
PN 100   SC 09190
B   Chronic Illness 91
     Psychosis 67

Chronic Schizophrenia
SN Term discontinued in 1988. Use CHRONIC
SCHIZOPHRENIA to access references from 67-
87.
Use Schizophrenia

Chronicity (Disorders) 82
PN 1190   SC 09203
SN Used only when chronicity itself is a factor,
variable, or major focus of the research.
R   ↓ Chronic Illness 91
     ↓ Disorders 67
     ↓ Mental Disorders 67
     Severity (Disorders) 82

Churches
Use Religious Buildings

Cichlids 73
PN 173   SC 09210
B   Fishes 67

Cigarette Smoking
Use Tobacco Smoking

Cimetidine [85]
PN 30   SC 09225
  B   Antihistaminic Drugs [73]

Circadian Rhythms (Animal)
  Use Animal Circadian Rhythms

Circadian Rhythms (Human)
  Use Human Biological Rhythms

Circulation (Blood)
  Use Blood Circulation

Circulatory Disorders
  Use Cardiovascular Disorders

Circumcision
  Use Birth Rites AND Surgery

Cirrhosis (Liver) [73]
PN 55   SC 09260
  B   Liver Disorders [73]
  R   Jaundice [73]

Cities
  Use Urban Environments

Citizenship [73]
PN 57   SC 09280
SN Formal status or social quality of being a member of a community, country, or some other political designation.
  R   Immigration [73]
    ↓ Laws [67]
    ↓ Political Attitudes [73]

Civil Law [94]
PN 0   SC 09284
  B   Law (Government) [73]
  R ↓ Civil Rights [78]
    Disability Laws [94]
    ↓ Law Enforcement [78]
    ↓ Legal Processes [73]

Civil Rights [78]
PN 926   SC 09288
SN Rights of personal liberty and equality guaranteed to citizens by constitution and legislation.
  B   Human Rights [78]
  N   Equal Education [78]
  R   Advocacy [85]
    Affirmative Action [85]
    Age Discrimination [94]
    Censorship [78]
    Civil Law [94]
    Civil Rights Movement [73]
    Client Rights [88]
    Democracy [73]
    Disability Laws [94]
    Empowerment [91]
    Freedom [78]
    Informed Consent [85]
    ↓ Justice [73]
    ↓ Laws [67]
    ↓ Legal Processes [73]
    Race and Ethnic Discrimination [94]
    Sex Discrimination [78]
    ↓ Social Discrimination [82]
    Social Equality [73]
    ↓ Social Integration [82]
    ↓ Social Issues [91]
    ↓ Social Movements [67]

Civil Rights Movement [73]
PN 101   SC 09290

Civil Rights Movement — (cont'd)
SN Social and political effort to gain the constitutional rights of citizens, especially by minority groups whose rights have been denied. See SOCIAL MOVEMENTS for more specific terms.
  B   Social Movements [67]
  R ↓ Activist Movements [73]
    ↓ Civil Rights [78]

Civil Servants
  Use Government Personnel

Clairvoyance [73]
PN 83   SC 09310
  B   Extrasensory Perception [67]
  N   Precognition [73]

Class Attitudes
  Use Socioeconomic Class Attitudes

Classical Conditioning [67]
PN 2978   SC 09330
SN Learned behavior or the experimental paradigm or procedure used to develop and evoke classically conditioned responses.
  UF Conditioning (Classical)
    Pavlovian Conditioning
    Respondent Conditioning
  B   Conditioning [67]
  N   Conditioned Emotional Responses [67]
    ↓ Conditioned Responses [67]
    Eyelid Conditioning [73]
    Unconditioned Responses [73]
  R   Conditioned Stimulus [73]
    Pavlov (Ivan) [91]
    Unconditioned Stimulus [73]

Classification (Cognitive Process) [67]
PN 4880   SC 09370
  UF Categorizing
    Sorting (Cognition)
  B   Cognitive Processes [67]
  R   Choice Behavior [67]

Classification Systems
  Use Taxonomies

Classmates [73]
PN 31   SC 09400
  B   Students [67]

Classroom Behavior [73]
PN 2920   SC 09405
  B   Behavior [67]
  R   Classroom Behavior Modification [73]
    Classroom Discipline [73]
    Classroom Environment [73]

Classroom Behavior Modification [73]
PN 1784   SC 09410
  B   Behavior Modification [73]
  R   Classroom Behavior [73]
    Classroom Discipline [73]
    ↓ Education [67]

Classroom Discipline [73]
PN 851   SC 09420
  UF Discipline (Classroom)
  R   Classroom Behavior [73]
    Classroom Behavior Modification [73]
    ↓ Education [67]
    School Suspension [73]
    Teacher Student Interaction [73]

Classroom Environment [73]
PN 2000   SC 09430

Classroom Environment — (cont'd)
SN Physical, social, emotional, psychological, or intellectual characteristics of a classroom, especially as they contribute to the learning process. Includes classroom climate and class size.
  B   Academic Environment [73]
  R   Classroom Behavior [73]
    Classrooms [67]
    ↓ School Environment [73]

Classroom Instruction
  Use Teaching

Classroom Teachers
  Use Teachers

Classrooms [67]
PN 553   SC 09460
  B   School Facilities [73]
  R   Classroom Environment [73]

Claustrophobia [73]
PN 43   SC 09470
  B   Phobias [67]

Cleft Palate [67]
PN 90   SC 09480
  B   Congenital Disorders [73]
    Neonatal Disorders [73]
  R ↓ Speech Disorders [67]

Clergy [73]
PN 283   SC 09490
  B   Religious Personnel [73]
  N   Chaplains [73]
    Ministers (Religion) [73]
    Priests [73]
    Rabbis [73]
  R   Evangelists [73]
    Lay Religious Personnel [73]
    Missionaries [73]

Clerical Personnel [73]
PN 411   SC 09500
  UF Keypunch Operators
    Typists
  B   White Collar Workers [73]
  R   Secretarial Personnel [73]

Clerical Secretarial Skills [73]
PN 185   SC 09510
  UF Secretarial Skills
  B   Employee Skills [73]
  R   Proofreading [88]
    Typing [91]
    Word Processing [91]

Client Abuse
  Use Patient Abuse

Client Attitudes [82]
PN 2861   SC 09527
SN Attitudes of clients that may affect compliance with a particular treatment modality, or preferences for a particular type of treatment. May include attitudes toward health care professionals.
  UF Patient Attitudes
  B   Attitudes [67]
    Client Characteristics [73]
  N   Client Satisfaction [94]
  R   Clients [73]
    Therapist Selection [94]
    Treatment Compliance [82]

Client Centered Therapy [67]
PN 519   SC 09530

Client Centered Therapy — (cont'd)
UF   Nondirective Therapy
B   Psychotherapy [67]
R   ↓ Psychotherapeutic Techniques [67]
       Rogers (Carl) [91]

Client Characteristics [73]
PN 6654   SC 09540
SN   Physical, psychological, emotional, and other
traits of individual clients or patients influencing
the outcome of the therapeutic process.
UF   Patient Characteristics
N   ↓ Client Attitudes [82]
       Health Behavior [82]
       Illness Behavior [82]
       Patient Violence [94]
R   Clients [73]
       Cross Cultural Treatment [94]
       Patient History [73]

Client Counselor Interaction
Use   Psychotherapeutic Processes

Client Education [85]
PN 876   SC 09555
SN   Informing or instructing patients or clients on
the specifics of their disorder and/or its treat-
ment. For client educational level use EDUCA-
TIONAL BACKGROUND.
UF   Patient Education
       Pretraining (Therapy)
B   Education [67]
R   ↓ Health Education [73]
       Health Knowledge [94]
       Health Promotion [91]
       Psychoeducation [94]
     ↓ Therapeutic Processes [78]
       Treatment Compliance [82]

Client Rights [88]
PN 363   SC 09557
SN   Right of patient or client to be fully informed
of benefits or risks of treatment procedures and
to make informed decisions to accept or reject
treatment.
UF   Patient Rights
B   Human Rights [78]
R   Advance Directives [94]
     ↓ Civil Rights [78]
       Clients [73]
       Empowerment [91]
       Guardianship [88]
       Informed Consent [85]
       Involuntary Treatment [94]
     ↓ Treatment [67]
       Treatment Compliance [82]
       Treatment Refusal [94]
       Treatment Withholding [88]

Client Satisfaction [94]
PN 0   SC 09558
UF   Patient Satisfaction
B   Client Attitudes [82]
       Satisfaction [73]
R   Clients [73]

Client Violence
Use   Patient Violence

Clients [73]
PN 792   SC 09560
SN   Persons receiving psychotherapy, counsel-
ing, or other mental health or social service. Con-
sider also PATIENTS or one of its narrower
terms.
UF   Counselees
R   ↓ Client Attitudes [82]
     ↓ Client Characteristics [73]

Clients — (cont'd)
R   Client Rights [88]
       Client Satisfaction [94]

Climacteric Depression
Use   Involutional Depression

Climacteric Paranoia
Use   Involutional Paranoid Psychosis

Climate (Meteorological)
Use   Atmospheric Conditions

Climate (Organizational)
Use   Organizational Climate

Climax (Sexual)
Use   Orgasm

Clinical Judgment (Med Diagnosis)
Use   Medical Diagnosis

Clinical Judgment (Not Diagnosis) [73]
PN 1965   SC 09620
SN   Analysis, evaluation, or prediction of disordered behavior. Includes assessing the appro-
priateness of a particular treatment and the degree or likelihood of clinical improvement.
R   Anatomically Detailed Dolls [91]
       Intake Interview [94]
     ↓ Psychodiagnostic Typologies [67]

Clinical Judgment (Psychodiagnosis)
Use   Psychodiagnosis

Clinical Markers
Use   Biological Markers

Clinical Methods Training [73]
PN 1540   SC 09640
SN   Instruction and skills training in methods for
management and treatment of mental and behav-
ior disorders. Includes training of populations
such as parents, teachers, clergy, and admin-
istrators as well as mental health or medical per-
sonnel.
UF   Training (Clinical Methods)
B   Education [67]
N   ↓ Clinical Psychology Grad Training [73]
       Clinical Psychology Internship [73]
     ↓ Community Mental Health Training [73]
       Psychiatric Training [73]
       Psychoanalytic Training [73]
       Psychotherapy Training [73]
R   Counselor Education [73]
       Microcounseling [78]
       Personal Therapy [91]
       Practicum Supervision [78]
       Theoretical Orientation [82]

Clinical Psychologists [73]
PN 740   SC 09650
B   Mental Health Personnel [67]
       Psychologists [67]
R   Clinicians [73]
       Hypnotherapists [73]
     ↓ Psychotherapists [73]

Clinical Psychology [67]
PN 1259   SC 09660
B   Applied Psychology [73]
       Psychology [67]
N   Medical Psychology [73]

Clinical Psychology Grad Training [73]
PN 675   SC 09670

Clinical Psychology Grad Training —
   (cont'd)
UF   Training (Clinical Psychology Grad)
B   Clinical Methods Training [73]
       Graduate Psychology Education [67]
       Postgraduate Training [73]
N   Clinical Psychology Internship [73]
R   Practicum Supervision [78]

Clinical Psychology Internship [73]
PN 193   SC 09680
B   Clinical Methods Training [73]
       Clinical Psychology Grad Training [73]
       Postgraduate Training [73]
R   Practicum Supervision [78]

Clinical Supervision
Use   Professional Supervision

Clinicians [73]
PN 338   SC 09690
B   Professional Personnel [78]
R   Clinical Psychologists [73]
     ↓ Medical Personnel [67]
     ↓ Physicians [67]
       Psychiatrists [67]

Clinics [67]
PN 592   SC 09700
B   Treatment Facilities [73]
N   Child Guidance Clinics [73]
       Psychiatric Clinics [73]
       Walk In Clinics [73]
R   Community Mental Health Centers [73]
     ↓ Crisis Intervention Services [73]
     ↓ Hospitals [67]
     ↓ Treatment [67]

Cliques
Use   Social Groups

Clomipramine
Use   Chlorimipramine

Clonazepam [91]
PN 58   SC 09735
B   Anticonvulsive Drugs [73]
       Benzodiazepines [78]
       Minor Tranquilizers [73]

Clonidine [73]
PN 659   SC 09740
B   Antihypertensive Drugs [73]
       CNS Stimulating Drugs [73]

Closed Circuit Television [73]
PN 54   SC 09750
B   Television [67]

Closedmindedness
Use   Openmindedness

Closure (Perceptual)
Use   Perceptual Closure

Clothing [67]
PN 496   SC 09770
SN   Use CLOTHING FASHIONS to access refer-
ences prior to 1991.
B   Fads and Fashions [73]
R   ↓ Physical Appearance [82]

Clozapine [91]
PN 200   SC 09775
B   Neuroleptic Drugs [73]
       Sedatives [73]

Cloze Testing [73]
PN 236   SC 09780
SN Tests or procedures assessing comprehension (e.g., reading or listening) in which the person being tested is required to provide missing components.
B   Testing Methods [67]
R   Sentence Completion Tests [91]

Clubs (Social Organizations) [73]
PN 58   SC 09790
B   Recreation [67]

Cluster Analysis [73]
PN 718   SC 09800
UF   Clustering
B   Statistical Analysis [67]

Clustering
Use   Cluster Analysis

CNS Affecting Drugs [73]
PN 115   SC 09840
UF   Central Nervous System Drugs
B   Drugs [67]
N   ↓ CNS Depressant Drugs [73]
    ↓ CNS Stimulating Drugs [73]
R   ↓ Heart Rate Affecting Drugs [73]

CNS Depressant Drug Antagonists
Use   Analeptic Drugs

CNS Depressant Drugs [73]
PN 75   SC 09860
B   CNS Affecting Drugs [73]
N   Amobarbital [73]
    Barbital [73]
    Chlorpromazine [67]
    Glutethimide [73]
    Haloperidol [73]
    Lithium Bromide [73]
    Scopolamine [73]
R   ↓ Analgesic Drugs [73]
    ↓ Anesthetic Drugs [73]
    ↓ Anticonvulsive Drugs [73]
    ↓ Barbiturates [67]
    ↓ Dopamine Antagonists [82]
    Flurazepam [82]
    ↓ Hypnotic Drugs [73]
    ↓ Muscle Relaxing Drugs [73]
    ↓ Narcotic Drugs [73]
    ↓ Sedatives [73]

CNS Stimulating Drugs [73]
PN 498   SC 09870
UF   Stimulants of CNS
B   CNS Affecting Drugs [73]
N   ↓ Amphetamine [67]
    ↓ Analeptic Drugs [73]
    Caffeine [73]
    Clonidine [73]
    Dextroamphetamine [73]
    Ephedrine [73]
    Methamphetamine [73]
    Methylphenidate [73]
    Pemoline [78]
    Pentylenetetrazol [73]
    Pipradrol [73]
    Piracetam [82]
R   ↓ Antidepressant Drugs [71]
    ↓ Emetic Drugs [73]
    ↓ Heart Rate Affecting Drugs [73]
    Smokeless Tobacco [94]

Coaches [88]
PN 123   SC 09880

Coaches — (cont'd)
SN Use TEACHERS to access references from 73-87.
R   Athletic Training [91]
    ↓ Sports [67]

Coagulation (Blood)
Use   Blood Coagulation

Coalition Formation [73]
PN 197   SC 09910
SN Temporary alliance of distinct parties, persons, or states for joint action.
B   Social Processes [67]
R   ↓ Social Movements [67]

Coast Guard Personnel [88]
PN 8   SC 00915
B   Military Personnel [67]

Cobalt [73]
PN 15   SC 09920
B   Metallic Elements [73]

Cocaine [73]
PN 1522   SC 09930
B   Alkaloids [73]
    Amines [73]
    Local Anesthetics [73]

Cochlea [73]
PN 391   SC 09940
UF   Organ of Corti
B   Labyrinth (Anatomy) [73]
R   Cochlear Implants [94]

Cochlear Implants [94]
PN 0   SC 09945
B   Hearing Aids [73]
    Prostheses [73]
    Surgery [71]
R   ↓ Aurally Handicapped [73]
    Cochlea [73]
    ↓ Deaf [67]
    Hearing Disorders [82]
    Partially Hearing Impaired [73]

Cochran Q Test [73]
PN 4   SC 09950
UF   Q Test
B   Nonparametric Statistical Tests [67]

Cockroaches [73]
PN 122   SC 09960
B   Insects [67]
R   Larvae [73]

Code Switching [88]
PN 33   SC 09965
SN Alternating use of languages, dialects, or language styles in speech.
UF   Language Alternation
B   Oral Communication [85]
R   Bilingualism [73]
    Sociolinguistics [85]

Codeine [73]
PN 49   SC 09970
UF   Codeine Sulfate
    Methylmorphine
B   Alkaloids [73]
    Analgesic Drugs [73]
    Hypnotic Drugs [73]
    Opiates [73]

Codeine Sulfate
Use   Codeine

Codependency [91]
PN 57   SC 09985
R   ↓ Alcohol Abuse [88]
    ↓ Drug Abuse [73]
    Dysfunctional Family [91]
    ↓ Emotional Adjustment [73]
    ↓ Family [67]
    ↓ Family Relations [67]
    ↓ Interpersonal Interaction [67]
    ↓ Marital Relations [67]
    ↓ Parent Child Relations [67]
    ↓ Personality Traits [67]

Coeds
Use   College Students

Coeducation [73]
PN 84   SC 10000
SN Education of male and female students at the same institution.
R   ↓ Education [67]

Coercion [94]
PN 0   SC 10020
B   Aggressive Behavior [67]
    Social Influences [67]
R   Authority [67]
    Brainwashing [82]
    ↓ Dominance [67]
    Obedience [73]
    ↓ Persuasive Communication [67]
    Power [67]
    Punishment [67]
    Threat [67]
    Torture [88]
    ↓ Violence [73]

Coffee
Use   Beverages (Nonalcoholic)

Cognition [67]
PN 2541   SC 10040
SN Act or process of knowing which includes awareness and judgment, perceiving, reasoning, and conceiving.
R   ↓ Cognitive Development [73]
    ↓ Cognitive Processes [67]
    Intuition [73]
    Metacognition [91]

Cognition Enhancing Drugs
Use   Nootropic Drugs

Cognitions [85]
PN 1090   SC 10045
SN The content of cognitive or thinking processes.
UF   Thought Content
N   ↓ Expectations [67]
    Irrational Beliefs [82]
R   ↓ Attitudes [67]
    Concepts [67]
    Mind [91]

Cognitive Ability [73]
PN 6450   SC 10050
SN Level of functioning in intellectual tasks.
UF   Cognitive Functioning
    Intellectual Functioning
B   Ability [67]
N   Mathematical Ability [73]
    Reading Ability [73]
    Spatial Ability [82]
    Verbal Ability [67]
R   Metacognition [91]

Cognitive Behavior Therapy
Use   Cognitive Therapy

Cognitive Complexity [73]
PN 743   SC 10060
SN Conceptual, behavioral, or perceptual dimensions of thinking style that characterize an individual's differentiation or processing of stimuli.
UF Complexity (Cognitive)
B Cognitive Style [67]

Cognitive Contiguity [73]
PN 34   SC 10070
SN View of memory organization which holds that events that are experienced together tend to become associated with each other in memory.
UF Contiguity (Cognitive)
B Associative Processes [67]

Cognitive Development [73]
PN 9436   SC 10080
SN Acquisition of conscious thought, reasoning, symbol manipulation, and problem solving abilities beginning in infancy and following an orderly sequence.
B Psychogenesis [73]
N ↓ Intellectual Development [73]
   ↓ Language Development [67]
   ↓ Perceptual Development [73]
R Cognition [67]
   ↓ Concept Formation [67]
   Conservation (Concept) [73]
   Constructivism [94]
   Egocentrism [78]
   Object Permanence [85]
   Piaget (Jean) [67]
   ↓ Speech Development [73]

Cognitive Discrimination [73]
PN 890   SC 10090
SN Ability to distinguish between examples vs nonexamples of a concept, based on the presence or absence of its defining attributes.
UF Discrimination (Cognitive)
B Cognitive Processes [67]
   Concept Formation [67]
   Discrimination [67]
R ↓ Lexical Access [88]
   Lexical Decision [88]
   Stroop Effect [88]
   Visual Search [82]

Cognitive Dissonance [67]
PN 1048   SC 10100
SN Psychological conflict resulting from incongruous beliefs or attitudes held simultaneously, or from inconsistency between belief and behavior.
UF Dissonance (Cognitive)
R ↓ Cognitive Processes [67]
   Psychological Reactance [78]

Cognitive Functioning
Use Cognitive Ability

Cognitive Generalization [67]
PN 565   SC 10110
SN Ability to evaluate the equivalence of an example of a concept or object across different contexts or modalities.
UF Generalization (Cognitive)
B Cognitive Processes [67]
   Concept Formation [67]
R ↓ Associative Processes [67]
   Semantic Generalization [73]

Cognitive Hypothesis Testing [82]
PN 225   SC 10112

Cognitive Hypothesis Testing — (cont'd)
SN Problem-solving behavior in which the individual derives a set of rules (hypotheses) that are then sampled and tested until the one rule is discovered that consistently results in correct responding to the problem. Use HYPOTHESIS TESTING or other appropriate terms to access references prior to 1982.
UF Rule Learning
B Learning [67]
   Problem Solving [67]
R ↓ Concept Formation [67]
   ↓ Reasoning [67]

Cognitive Load
Use Human Channel Capacity

Cognitive Maps [82]
PN 521   SC 10117
SN Internal or symbolic representations of social or physical environments, means-end relationships, or spatial relationships.
B Cognitive Processes [67]
R Schema [88]
   Spatial Imagery [82]
   Spatial Memory [88]
   Spatial Organization [73]
   Spatial Orientation (Perception) [73]

Cognitive Mediation [67]
PN 997   SC 10120
SN Intervention of cognitive processes between observable stimuli and responses, resulting in a change in subsequent behavior.
UF Mediation (Cognitive)
B Cognitive Processes [67]
R Naming [88]

Cognitive Processes [67]
PN 15258   SC 10130
SN Mental processes involved in the acquisition, processing, and utilization of knowledge or information.
UF Human Information Processes
   Information Processes (Human)
N ↓ Associative Processes [67]
   Classification (Cognitive Process) [67]
   Cognitive Discrimination [73]
   Cognitive Generalization [67]
   Cognitive Maps [82]
   Cognitive Mediation [67]
   ↓ Comprehension [67]
   Concentration [82]
   ↓ Concept Formation [67]
   ↓ Decision Making [67]
   ↓ Ideation [73]
   Imagination [67]
   Intuition [73]
   Mental Rotation [91]
   Metacognition [91]
   Naming [88]
   ↓ Problem Solving [67]
   Schema [88]
   Semantic Generalization [73]
   Social Cognition [94]
   ↓ Thinking [67]
   Transposition (Cognition) [73]
R ↓ Artificial Intelligence [82]
   Cognition [67]
   Cognitive Dissonance [67]
   Cognitive Psychology [85]
   ↓ Conflict Resolution [82]
   Connectionism [94]
   Generation Effect (Learning) [91]
   Human Information Storage [73]
   ↓ Learning [67]
   ↓ Learning Strategies [91]
   ↓ Memory [67]
   Mind [91]

Cognitive Processes — (cont'd)
R Questioning [82]
   Reality Testing [73]
   Spatial Ability [82]
   ↓ Strategies [67]
   Word Associations [67]

Cognitive Psychology [85]
PN 653   SC 10135
SN Branch of psychology concerned with aspects of behavior as they relate to mental processes.
B Psychology [67]
R ↓ Cognitive Processes [67]
   Connectionism [94]

Cognitive Rehabilitation [85]
PN 296   SC 10136
SN Procedures used to restore or enhance the cognitive functioning level of individuals with mental disability, injury, or disease (e.g., brain damaged stroke patients).
B Rehabilitation [67]
R Memory Training [94]

Cognitive Restructuring [85]
PN 219   SC 10137
SN Cognitive technique for altering self-defeating thought patterns by first identifying and analyzing negative self-statements and then developing adaptive self-statements.
B Cognitive Techniques [85]
R ↓ Behavior Modification [73]
   Cognitive Therapy [82]

Cognitive Style [67]
PN 4186   SC 10140
SN Preferred or habitual style of learning or thinking.
UF Learning Style
B Personality Traits [67]
N Cognitive Complexity [73]
   ↓ Conceptual Tempo [85]
   Field Dependence [73]
   Impulsiveness [73]
R ↓ Learning Strategies [91]
   Neurolinguistic Programing [88]
   Perceptual Style [73]
   ↓ Personality [67]
   Schema [88]

Cognitive Techniques [85]
PN 570   SC 10142
SN Methods directed at producing change in thought patterns that may result in changes in affect and behavior.
B Treatment [67]
N Cognitive Restructuring [85]
   Cognitive Therapy [82]
   Self Instructional Training [85]
R Stress Management [85]

Cognitive Therapy [82]
PN 2185   SC 10144
SN Directive therapy based on the belief that the way one perceives and structures the world determines one's feelings and behavior. Treatment aims at altering cognitive schema and hence permitting the patient to change his/her distorted self-view.
UF Cognitive Behavior Therapy
B Cognitive Techniques [85]
R ↓ Behavior Modification [73]
   Cognitive Restructuring [85]
   ↓ Psychotherapy [67]
   Rational Emotive Therapy [78]
   Self Instructional Training [85]
   ↓ Self Management [85]

Cohabitation [73]
PN 173   SC 10150
SN Primarily, but not exclusively, used for un-married couples living together.
B   Living Arrangements [91]
R   Couples [82]
     ↓ Family [67]
     Living Alone [94]
     Roommates [73]

Cohesion (Group)
Use   Group Cohesion

Cohort Analysis [88]
PN 125   SC 10165
SN Analysis of the effects attributed to being a member of a group sharing a particular characteristic, experience, or event. Use AGE DIFFERENCES for effects attributable to normal biological, cognitive, or psychosocial maturation.
B   Analysis [67]
     Experimental Design [67]
     Methodology [67]
R   Age Differences [67]
     Generation Gap [73]

Coitus
Use   Sexual Intercourse (Human)

Coitus (Animal)
Use   Animal Mating Behavior

Cold Effects [73]
PN 479   SC 10200
B   Temperature Effects [67]

Colitis [73]
PN 30   SC 10220
B   Colon Disorders [73]
N   Ulcerative Colitis [73]
R   Gastrointestinal Ulcers [67]
     Irritable Bowel Syndrome [91]

Coll Ent Exam Bd Scholastic Apt Test [73]
PN 232   SC 10230
UF   Preliminary Scholastic Aptitude Test
     SAT
     Scholastic Aptitude Test
B   Aptitude Measures [67]
     Entrance Examinations [73]

Collaboration
Use   Cooperation

Collective Behavior [67]
PN 1740   SC 10250
SN Behaviors which characterize groups or individuals acting in groups, usually working toward or achieving a specific goal. Used for human or animal populations.
B   Interpersonal Interaction [67]
N   Riots [73]
R   Contagion [88]
     Entrapment Games [73]
     ↓ Group Dynamics [67]
     Group Participation [73]
     Mass Hysteria [73]
     Social Demonstrations [73]
     ↓ Sociometry [91]

College Academic Achievement [67]
PN 4324   SC 10260
B   Academic Achievement [67]

College Athletes [94]
PN 0   SC 10270
B   Athletes [73]
     College Students [67]

College Athletes — (cont'd)
R   Athletic Participation [73]
     Athletic Performance [91]
     Athletic Training [91]
     ↓ Sports [67]
     Teams [88]

College Degrees
Use   Educational Degrees

College Dropouts [73]
PN 383   SC 10290
B   School Dropouts [67]

College Education
Use   Undergraduate Education

College Environment [73]
PN 750   SC 10300
SN Social or emotional climate or physical setting of a college or university.
B   School Environment [73]
R   ↓ Colleges [67]
     Community Colleges [78]

College Graduates [82]
PN 207   SC 10304
R   ↓ College Students [67]
     Educational Degrees [73]
     School Graduation [91]
     School to Work Transition [94]

College Major
Use   Academic Specialization

College Students [67]
PN 20528   SC 10320
SN Students attending an institution of higher education.
UF   Coeds
     Undergraduates
B   Students [67]
N   College Athletes [94]
     Community College Students [73]
     Education Students [82]
     Junior College Students [73]
     Nursing Students [73]
     ROTC Students [73]
R   ↓ Adolescents [67]
     College Graduates [82]
     Graduate Students [67]
     Postgraduate Students [73]
     Preservice Teachers [82]
     Reentry Students [85]
     Young Adults [73]

College Teachers [73]
PN 2595   SC 10330
UF   Professors
B   Teachers [67]

Colleges [67]
PN 1989   SC 10350
UF   Junior Colleges
     Universities
B   Schools [67]
N   Community Colleges [78]
R   College Environment [73]
     ↓ Higher Education [73]
     Military Schools [73]

Colombia [82]
PN 110   SC 10360
B   South America [67]

Colon Disorders [73]
PN 138   SC 10370

Colon Disorders — (cont'd)
UF   Bowel Disorders
B   Gastrointestinal Disorders [73]
N   ↓ Colitis [73]
     Constipation [73]
     Diarrhea [73]
     Fecal Incontinence [73]
     Irritable Bowel Syndrome [91]

Color [67]
PN 1896   SC 10380
SN Property of matter or light sources that corresponds to the relative reflectance or absorption of incident light and the wavelength of the incident light or light source. Color is described perceptually by the dimensions of hue, lightness, brightness, and saturation. Compare HUE.
N   Achromatic Color [73]
     Eye Color [91]
     Hue [73]
R   ↓ Pigments [73]
     ↓ Visual Stimulation [73]

Color Blindness [73]
PN 194   SC 10390
B   Eye Disorders [73]
R   ↓ Color Perception [67]
     ↓ Genetic Disorders [73]

Color Constancy [85]
PN 38   SC 10395
SN The tendency to perceive hue, brightness, and saturation as stable despite objective changes in context and illumination.
B   Color Perception [67]
     Perceptual Constancy [85]

Color Contrast [85]
PN 46   SC 10397
B   Color Perception [67]
     Visual Contrast [85]

Color Perception [67]
PN 2390   SC 10400
UF   Spectral Sensitivity
B   Visual Perception [67]
N   Color Constancy [85]
     Color Contrast [85]
R   Color Blindness [73]
     Prismatic Stimulation [73]

Color Pyramid Test [73]
PN 6   SC 10410
B   Projective Personality Measures [73]
     Projective Techniques [67]

Colostomy [73]
PN 31   SC 10430
B   Surgery [71]

Columbia Mental Maturity Scale [73]
PN 13   SC 10440
B   Intelligence Measures [67]

Coma [73]
PN 169   SC 10450
B   Symptoms [67]
R   Cerebrovascular Accidents [73]
     ↓ Cerebrovascular Disorders [73]
     ↓ Consciousness Disturbances [73]
     ↓ Epileptic Seizures [73]
     ↓ Injuries [73]
     Insulin Shock Therapy [73]

Combat Experience [91]
PN 106   SC 10452
SN Direct participation in war.

Combat Experience — (cont'd)
R ↓ Experiences (Events) [73]
  ↓ Military Personnel [67]
  Posttraumatic Stress Disorder [85]
  ↓ War [67]

Comfort (Physical)
Use Physical Comfort

Commerce
Use Business

Commissioned Officers [73]
PN 170 SC 10470
SN Military officers who have received a formal certificate granting rank and authority and who thereby hold a position of command.
UF Military Officers
  Officers (Commissioned)
B Military Personnel [67]
R ↓ Management Personnel [73]
  Volunteer Military Personnel [73]

Commissurotomy [85]
PN 114 SC 10475
UF Split Brain
B Neurosurgery [73]
R Corpus Callosum [73]

Commitment [85]
PN 530 SC 10478
SN The process or extent of devoting one's efforts or resources to an activity, task, or interpersonal relationship.
N Organizational Commitment [91]
R ↓ Involvement [73]
  ↓ Motivation [67]

Commitment (Outpatient)
Use Outpatient Commitment

Commitment (Psychiatric) [73]
PN 837 SC 10480
B Hospitalization [67]
  Legal Processes [73]
N Outpatient Commitment [91]
R Court Referrals [94]
  Guardianship [88]
  ↓ Institutional Release [78]
  Involuntary Treatment [94]
  ↓ Psychiatric Hospital Admission [73]
  Psychiatric Hospital Discharge [78]
  ↓ Psychiatric Hospitalization [73]
  Self Referral [91]

Communes [73]
PN 84 SC 10510
B Communities [67]
N Kibbutz [73]

Communicable Diseases
Use Infectious Disorders

Communication [67]
PN 2618 SC 10570
SN Conceptually broad array term referring to the transmission of verbal or nonverbal information. Use a more specific term if possible.
N ↓ Animal Communication [67]
  ↓ Augmentative Communication [94]
  ↓ Interpersonal Communication [73]
  ↓ Nonverbal Communication [71]
  ↓ Persuasive Communication [67]
  ↓ Scientific Communication [73]
  ↓ Verbal Communication [67]
R Censorship [78]
  ↓ Communication Skills [73]
  Communication Skills Training [82]

Communication — (cont'd)
R ↓ Communication Systems [73]
  Communication Theory [73]
  ↓ Communications Media [73]
  Content Analysis [78]
  Emotional Content [73]
  Information [67]
  Messages [73]
  Privileged Communication [73]
  Rhetoric [91]
  Symbolism [67]
  ↓ Vocalization [67]
  ↓ Voice [73]

Communication (Privileged)
Use Privileged Communication

Communication (Professional)
Use Scientific Communication

Communication Apprehension
Use Speech Anxiety

Communication Disorders [82]
PN 302 SC 10533
SN Impaired ability to communicate usually due to speech, language, or hearing disorders.
B Disorders [67]
N Hearing Disorders [82]
  ↓ Language Disorders [82]
  ↓ Speech Disorders [67]
R ↓ Augmentative Communication [94]
  ↓ Aurally Handicapped [73]
  ↓ Communication Skills [73]
  Communication Skills Training [82]
  Developmental Disabilities [82]
  Speech Anxiety [85]
  Speech Handicapped [73]
  Speech Therapy [67]

Communication Skills [73]
PN 1910 SC 10540
SN Individual ability or competency in any type of communication. Limited to human populations.
UF Communicative Competence
B Ability [67]
N Language Proficiency [88]
  Rhetoric [91]
  Writing Skills [85]
R ↓ Communication [67]
  ↓ Communication Disorders [82]
  Communication Skills Training [82]
  Pragmatics [85]
  Social Cognition [94]
  ↓ Verbal Communication [67]

Communication Skills Training [82]
PN 811 SC 10542
SN Instruction, usually group oriented, to increase quality and capability of interpersonal communication.
B Education [67]
R Assertiveness Training [78]
  ↓ Behavior Modification [73]
  ↓ Communication [67]
  ↓ Communication Disorders [82]
  ↓ Communication Skills [73]
  Human Relations Training [78]
  Sensitivity Training [73]
  ↓ Skill Learning [73]
  Social Skills Training [82]

Communication Systems [73]
PN 305 SC 10550
SN Organized scheme for transmitting and receiving information.
B Systems [67]
N Telephone Systems [73]

Communication Systems — (cont'd)
R ↓ Automated Information Processing [73]
  ↓ Communication [67]
  Information Systems [91]

Communication Theory [73]
PN 191 SC 10560
B Theories [67]
R ↓ Communication [67]
  Cybernetics [67]
  Information Theory [67]

Communications Media [73]
PN 323 SC 10580
UF Media (Communications)
N ↓ Audiovisual Communications Media [73]
  ↓ Mass Media [67]
  ↓ Telecommunications Media [73]
R Censorship [78]
  ↓ Communication [67]

Communicative Competence
Use Communication Skills

Communism [73]
PN 389 SC 10590
UF Marxism
B Political Economic Systems [73]

Communities [67]
PN 1389 SC 10600
B Social Environments [73]
N ↓ Communes [73]
  Neighborhoods [73]

Community Attitudes [73]
PN 784 SC 10620
SN Attitudes which characterize a group of individuals living in close proximity and organized into a social structure, however tenuous.
B Attitudes [67]
R Public Opinion [73]

Community College Students [73]
PN 951 SC 10627
SN Students attending public postsecondary institutions offering 2-year degree programs and transfer components. Mandatory term in educational contexts.
B College Students [67]
R Junior College Students [73]

Community Colleges [78]
PN 304 SC 10630
B Colleges [67]
R College Environment [73]
  ↓ Community Facilities [73]

Community Facilities [73]
PN 408 SC 10640
N Community Mental Health Centers [73]
  ↓ Housing [73]
  Public Transportation [73]
  Shopping Centers [73]
  Suicide Prevention Centers [73]
R Child Guidance Clinics [73]
  Community Colleges [78]
  ↓ Community Services [67]
  Day Care Centers [73]
  Group Homes [82]
  Halfway Houses [73]
  ↓ Libraries [82]
  ↓ Recreation Areas [73]
  ↓ Rehabilitation Centers [73]
  Religious Buildings [73]
  ↓ Schools [67]
  Sheltered Workshops [67]

Community Facilities — (cont'd)
R   Shelters [91]
      Urban Planning [73]

Community Mental Health [73]
PN 403   SC 10647
SN General psychological well-being or adjust-
ment of persons in a given area.
B   Mental Health [67]
R   Community Mental Health Centers [73]
      Community Mental Health Services [78]
      ↓ Community Mental Health Training [73]
      Community Psychiatry [73]
      Community Psychology [73]
      Deinstitutionalization [82]
      ↓ Mental Health Programs [73]

Community Mental Health Centers [73]
PN 1404   SC 10650
UF Mental Health Centers (Community)
B   Community Facilities [73]
      Treatment Facilities [73]
R   Child Guidance Clinics [73]
      ↓ Clinics [67]
      Community Mental Health [73]
      Community Mental Health Services [78]
      ↓ Crisis Intervention Services [73]
      Day Care Centers [73]
      Hot Line Services [73]
      ↓ Mental Health Programs [73]
      ↓ Mental Health Services [78]
      Psychiatric Clinics [73]
      Suicide Prevention Centers [73]

Community Mental Health Services [78]
PN 1899   SC 10656
B   Community Services [67]
      Mental Health Services [78]
R   Community Mental Health [73]
      Community Mental Health Centers [73]
      Community Psychiatry [73]
      Community Psychology [73]
      Deinstitutionalization [82]
      Group Homes [82]
      ↓ Mental Health [67]
      ↓ Mental Health Programs [73]

Community Mental Health Training [73]
PN 229   SC 10660
UF Mental Health Training (Community)
      Training (Community Mental Health)
B   Clinical Methods Training [73]
N   Mental Health Inservice Training [73]
R   Community Mental Health [73]
      ↓ Mental Health Programs [73]

Community Psychiatry [73]
PN 227   SC 10670
SN Branch of psychiatry concerned with the
provision and delivery of community health care
needs such as diagnosis; treatment; primary,
secondary, and tertiary prevention; rehabilitation;
and aftercare. Such services are usually delivered at community mental health centers.
B   Psychiatry [67]
R   Community Mental Health [73]
      Community Mental Health Services [78]
      Community Psychology [73]
      ↓ Mental Health [67]
      ↓ Mental Health Programs [73]

Community Psychology [73]
PN 461   SC 10680
SN Branch of psychology that emphasizes the
analysis of social processes and interactions and
design of social interventions within groups and
the community.
B   Applied Psychology [73]
R   Community Mental Health [73]

Community Psychology — (cont'd)
R   Community Mental Health Services [78]
      Community Psychiatry [73]
      ↓ Mental Health Programs [73]

Community Services [67]
PN 3656   SC 10690
B   Social Services [82]
N   Community Mental Health Services [78]
      Community Welfare Services [73]
      ↓ Crisis Intervention Services [73]
      Home Visiting Programs [73]
      Public Health Services [73]
R   Alcoholics Anonymous [73]
      ↓ Community Facilities [73]
      ↓ Health Care Services [78]
      Independent Living Programs [91]
      ↓ Mental Health Programs [73]
      ↓ Mental Health Services [78]
      ↓ Self Help Techniques [82]
      Shelters [91]
      ↓ Support Groups [91]

Community Welfare Services [73]
PN 108   SC 10700
UF Public Welfare Services
B   Community Services [67]
R   Welfare Services (Government) [73]

Commuting (Travel) [85]
PN 35   SC 10705
R   Geographical Mobility [78]
      ↓ Transportation [73]
      Traveling [73]

Comorbidity [91]
PN 447   SC 10707
SN Coexistence of two or more physical and/or
mental disorders.
R   ↓ Diagnosis [67]
      Differential Diagnosis [67]
      ↓ Disorders [67]
      Dual Diagnosis [91]
      ↓ Mental Disorders [67]
      Psychopathology [67]

Companies
Use Business Organizations

Comparative Psychiatry
Use Transcultural Psychiatry

Comparative Psychology [67]
PN 873   SC 10720
SN Branch of psychology devoted to the study
of behavioral differences between organisms of
different species. Prior to 1982, also used for
comparative studies. From 1982, limited to the
scientific discipline. Use SPECIES DIFFERENCES
for comparative studies.
B   Psychology [67]

Compatibility (Interpersonal)
Use Interpersonal Compatibility

Compensation (Defense Mechanism) [73]
PN 33   SC 10740
SN Defense mechanism of covering up or mak-
ing up for conscious or unconscious insecurity or
feelings of failure.
B   Defense Mechanisms [67]

Compensatory Education [73]
PN 174   SC 10745

Compensatory Education — (cont'd)
SN Education designed to enhance intellectual
and social skills of disadvantaged students, and
to compensate for environmental, experiential,
cultural, or economic deficits. Compare REME-
DIAL EDUCATION.
B   Curriculum [67]
R   ↓ Educational Programs [73]
      Project Follow Through [73]
      Project Head Start [73]
      ↓ Remedial Education [85]
      Upward Bound [73]

Competence [82]
PN 1626   SC 10747
SN Possession of sufficient skills, knowledge, or
qualities as required in a given situation.
R   ↓ Ability [67]
      Accountability [88]
      ↓ Achievement [67]
      Competency to Stand Trial [85]
      Minimum Competency Tests [85]
      ↓ Performance [67]
      Social Skills [78]

Competence (Social)
Use Social Skills

Competency to Stand Trial [85]
PN 203   SC 10749
B   Legal Processes [73]
R   Competence [82]
      Criminal Responsibility [91]
      Forensic Evaluation [94]
      Mentally Ill Offenders [85]

Competition [67]
PN 2295   SC 10750
SN Use for either human or animal populations.
B   Social Behavior [67]

Complexity (Cognitive)
Use Cognitive Complexity

Complexity (Stimulus)
Use Stimulus Complexity

Complexity (Task)
Use Task Complexity

Compliance [73]
PN 1161   SC 10810
SN Limited to human populations.
B   Social Behavior [67]
N   Treatment Compliance [82]

Comprehension [67]
PN 2173   SC 10820
SN Knowledge or understanding of communica-
tions, objects, events, or situations as relates to
their meaning, significance, relationships, or gen-
eral principles.
UF Understanding
B   Cognitive Processes [67]
N   Number Comprehension [73]
      ↓ Verbal Comprehension [85]
R   Intuition [73]
      ↓ Meaning [67]
      Meaningfulness [67]
      Metacognition [91]

Comprehension Tests [73]
PN 38   SC 10830
B   Measurement [67]

Compressed Speech [73]
PN 136   SC 10840
B   Speech Processing (Mechanical) [73]

Compulsions [73]
PN 310   SC 10850
- N   Compulsive Repetition [73]
- R   Obsessions [67]
  - Obsessive Compulsive Neurosis [73]
  - Obsessive Compulsive Personality [73]
  - Perfectionism [88]

Compulsive Gambling
Use Pathological Gambling

Compulsive Neurosis
Use Obsessive Compulsive Neurosis

Compulsive Personality Disorder
Use Obsessive Compulsive Personality

Compulsive Repetition [73]
PN 70   SC 10890
- UF Repetition (Compulsive)
- B   Compulsions [73]

Computer Applications [73]
PN 3346   SC 10900
SN Application of computers, computer technology, or software to any area.
- N ↓ Artificial Intelligence [82]
  - Computer Assisted Diagnosis [73]
  - Computer Assisted Instruction [73]
  - Computer Assisted Testing [88]
  - ↓ Computer Simulation [73]
- R Automated Speech Recognition [94]
  - Computer Searching [91]
  - ↓ Computers [67]
  - Databases [91]
  - Information Systems [91]
  - Microcomputers [85]
  - Word Processing [91]

Computer Assisted Diagnosis [73]
PN 854   SC 10910
- B   Computer Applications [73]
  - Diagnosis [67]
- R   Magnetic Resonance Imaging [94]
  - ↓ Medical Diagnosis [73]
  - ↓ Psychodiagnosis [67]
  - ↓ Tomography [88]

Computer Assisted Instruction [73]
PN 2747   SC 10920
SN Use of computers to present instructional materials to students and to assess performance. Compare TEACHING MACHINES.
- UF Instruction (Computer Assisted)
- B   Computer Applications [73]
  - Teaching Methods [67]
- R   Individualized Instruction [73]
  - Programed Instruction [67]
  - Teaching Machines [73]

Computer Assisted Testing [88]
PN 360   SC 10921
SN Use of computers in test construction or administration, usually in an educational or employment setting. Not used for diagnosis.
- B   Computer Applications [73]
  - Testing [67]
- R   Adaptive Testing [85]

Computer Attitudes [88]
PN 381   SC 10922
- B   Attitudes [67]
- R   ↓ Computers [67]

Computer Games [88]
PN 145   SC 10923
- UF Video Games
- B   Computers [67]

Computer Games — (cont'd)
- B   Games [67]
- R ↓ Computer Simulation [73]
  - ↓ Recreation [67]
  - Simulation Games [73]
  - ↓ Toys [73]

Computer Literacy [91]
PN 33   SC 10924
- B   Literacy [73]
- R   Computer Searching [91]
  - Computer Training [94]
  - ↓ Computers [67]

Computer Peripheral Devices [85]
PN 73   SC 10925
SN Devices used for entering (e.g., keyboards) or displaying (e.g., printers, CRTs) data and programs in computer memory.
- B   Apparatus [67]
- N   Video Display Units [85]
- R ↓ Computers [67]
  - Keyboards [85]
  - Man Machine Systems [73]
  - ↓ Visual Displays [73]

Computer Programing [94]
PN 0   SC 10928
- UF Programing (Computer)
- R   Algorithms [73]
  - Computer Programing Languages [73]
  - ↓ Computer Software [67]
  - ↓ Computers [67]
  - ↓ Data Processing [67]
  - Systems Analysis [73]

Computer Programing Languages [73]
PN 530   SC 10930
- UF FORTRAN
  - Programing Languages (Computer)
- R   Computer Programing [94]
  - ↓ Computers [67]
  - ↓ Data Processing [67]

Computer Programs
Use Computer Software

Computer Searching [91]
PN 36   SC 10945
SN Use of computerized interactive communication system to access and retrieve information.
- UF Online Searching
- B   Automated Information Retrieval [73]
- R ↓ Computer Applications [73]
  - Computer Literacy [91]
  - ↓ Computers [67]
  - Databases [91]
  - Information [67]
  - Information Exchange [73]
  - Information Seeking [73]
  - Information Services [88]
  - Man Machine Systems [73]

Computer Simulation [73]
PN 1069   SC 10950
- B   Computer Applications [73]
  - Simulation [67]
- N   Neural Networks [91]
- R   Computer Games [88]
  - Simulation Games [73]

Computer Software [67]
PN 2769   SC 10960
- UF Computer Programs
- N   Word Processing [91]
- R   Computer Programing [94]
  - ↓ Computers [67]
  - ↓ Data Processing [67]

Computer Software — (cont'd)
- R   Databases [91]
  - ↓ Systems [67]

Computer Training [94]
PN 0   SC 10963
- B   Curriculum [67]
- R   Computer Literacy [91]

Computerized Databases
Use Databases

Computers [67]
PN 2288   SC 10970
- B   Apparatus [67]
- N   Analog Computers [73]
  - Computer Games [88]
  - Digital Computers [73]
  - Microcomputers [85]
- R ↓ Artificial Intelligence [82]
  - Automated Information Coding [73]
  - ↓ Automated Information Processing [73]
  - ↓ Automated Information Retrieval [73]
  - Automated Information Storage [73]
  - Automation [67]
  - ↓ Computer Applications [73]
  - Computer Attitudes [88]
  - Computer Literacy [91]
  - ↓ Computer Peripheral Devices [85]
  - Computer Programing [94]
  - Computer Programing Languages [73]
  - Computer Searching [91]
  - ↓ Computer Software [67]
  - Cybernetics [67]
  - ↓ Data Processing [67]
  - Databases [91]
  - Expert Systems [91]
  - Robotics [85]
  - ↓ Systems [67]

Concentration [82]
PN 186   SC 10977
SN Cognitive effort directed to one object or area of study.
- B   Cognitive Processes [67]
- R   Selective Attention [73]

Concentration Camps [73]
PN 292   SC 10980
- R   Holocaust [88]
  - Prisons [67]

Concept Formation [67]
PN 2850   SC 11000
SN Developmental or learning process involving identification of common properties of objects, events, or qualities, usually represented by words or symbols, and generalization of those properties to all appropriate objects, events, or qualities. Use CONCEPT FORMATION or CONCEPT LEARNING to access references prior to 1982.
- UF Concept Learning
  - Conceptualization
- B   Cognitive Processes [67]
- N   Cognitive Discrimination [73]
  - Cognitive Generalization [67]
- R ↓ Cognitive Development [73]
  - Cognitive Hypothesis Testing [82]
  - Concepts [67]
  - Conservation (Concept) [73]
  - ↓ Discrimination Learning [82]
  - Egocentrism [78]
  - ↓ Generalization (Learning) [82]
  - ↓ Learning [67]

Concept Learning
SN Term discontinued in 1982. Use CONCEPT LEARNING or CONCEPT FORMATION to access references prior to 1982.
  Use Concept Formation

Concept Validity
  Use Construct Validity

Concepts [67]
PN 1468   **SC** 11030
SN Generic ideas or categories derived from common properties of objects, events, or qualities, usually represented by words or symbols.
  R ↓ Cognitions [85]
     ↓ Concept Formation [67]
     Information [67]
     ↓ Mathematics (Concepts) [67]
     ↓ Terminology [91]

Conceptual Imagery [73]
PN 260   **SC** 11040
SN Mental representation of concepts or conceptual relationships.
  UF Imagery (Conceptual)
  B Imagery [67]
  R Imagination [67]
     Schema [88]

Conceptual Tempo [85]
PN 42   **SC** 11045
SN The dimension of cognitive style often measured by response latency or the time required to solve a problem.
  B Cognitive Style [67]
  N Impulsiveness [73]
  R Attention Span [73]
     Perceptual Style [73]
     Reaction Time [67]

Conceptualization
  Use Concept Formation

Concurrent Reinforcement Schedules [88]
PN 87   **SC** 11057
SN Simultaneous use of two or more reinforcement schedules.
  B Reinforcement Schedules [67]

Concurrent Validity [88]
PN 528   **SC** 11058
SN Internal consistency of different parts of a test battery or the correlation between the results of two or more measures or tests presumably taken at the same time.
  B Statistical Validity [73]
  R Construct Validity [82]
     Predictive Validity [73]
     Test Validity [73]

Concussion (Brain)
  Use Brain Concussion

Conditioned Emotional Responses [67]
PN 466   **SC** 11070
  UF CER (Conditioning)
  B Classical Conditioning [67]
     Conditioned Responses [67]
     Emotional Responses [67]
     Operant Conditioning [67]

Conditioned Inhibition
  Use Conditioned Suppression

Conditioned Place Preference
  Use Place Conditioning

Conditioned Reflex
  Use Conditioned Responses

Conditioned Responses [67]
PN 2610   **SC** 11090
  UF Conditioned Reflex
  B Classical Conditioning [67]
     Operant Conditioning [67]
     Responses [67]
  N Conditioned Emotional Responses [67]
     Conditioned Suppression [73]

Conditioned Stimulus [73]
PN 1657   **SC** 11100
SN In classical conditioning, that stimulus (e.g., a light) that acquires the capacity to elicit a conditioned response (e.g., salivation) as a result of that stimulus having been paired consistently with an unconditioned stimulus (e.g., food). In operant conditioning, those stimuli (S+,S-) which differentially signal the presence or absence of reinforcement. Compare CUES.
  UF Discriminative Stimulus
  B Conditioning [67]
  R ↓ Classical Conditioning [67]
     ↓ Operant Conditioning [67]
     Preconditioning [94]
     Secondary Reinforcement [67]
     ↓ Stimulation [67]

Conditioned Suppression [73]
PN 728   **SC** 11110
SN Learned behavior or the conditioning procedure in which the pairing of a neutral stimulus with an aversive stimulus, presented during the performance of a positively-reinforced behavior, results in a decrease of that behavior.
  UF Conditioned Inhibition
     Suppression (Conditioned)
  B Conditioned Responses [67]

Conditioning [67]
PN 2386   **SC** 11120
  B Learning [67]
  N Autoshaping [78]
     ↓ Aversion Conditioning [82]
     ↓ Classical Conditioning [67]
     Conditioned Stimulus [73]
     Counterconditioning [73]
     ↓ Operant Conditioning [67]
     Place Conditioning [91]
     Preconditioning [94]
     Unconditioned Stimulus [73]
  R ↓ Biofeedback [73]
     Primary Reinforcement [73]
     ↓ Reinforcement [67]
     Spontaneous Recovery (Learning) [73]
     ↓ Stimulation [67]

Conditioning (Avoidance)
  Use Avoidance Conditioning

Conditioning (Classical)
  Use Classical Conditioning

Conditioning (Escape)
  Use Escape Conditioning

Conditioning (Eyelid)
  Use Eyelid Conditioning

Conditioning (Operant)
  Use Operant Conditioning

Conditioning (Verbal)
  Use Verbal Learning

Condoms [91]
PN 121   **SC** 11185
  B Contraceptive Devices [73]
  R AIDS Prevention [94]
     ↓ Birth Control [71]
     ↓ Family Planning [73]
     ↓ Prevention [73]
     ↓ Venereal Diseases [73]

Conduct Disorder [91]
PN 190   **SC** 11187
SN Repetitive and persistent aggressive or non-aggressive behavior in which basic rights of others or social norms are violated. Self esteem is generally low, and an inability to develop social relationships and lack of concern for others may or may not be present. Consider using BEHAVIOR DISORDERS prior to 1991.
  B Disorders [67]
  R ↓ Aggressive Behavior [67]
     ↓ Behavior Disorders [71]
     ↓ Behavior Problems [67]
     Explosive Personality [73]
     ↓ Mental Disorders [67]

Cones (Eye) [73]
PN 366   **SC** 11190
  B Cells (Biology) [73]
     Photoreceptors [73]
     Retina [67]
  R Fovea [82]

Confabulation [73]
PN 23   **SC** 11200
SN Giving untruthful answers to questions about situations or events that are not recalled due to memory impairment. Confabulation is not a conscious attempt to deceive.
  B Deception [67]
     Thought Disturbances [73]
  R Korsakoffs Psychosis [73]

Conference Proceedings
SN Term discontinued in 1982. Prior to 1982 this term was not defined and was used interchangeably with PROFESSIONAL MEETINGS AND SYMPOSIA.
  Use Professional Meetings and Symposia

Confession (Religion) [73]
PN 8   **SC** 11220
  B Religious Practices [73]

Confidence (Self)
  Use Self Confidence

Confidence Limits (Statistics) [73]
PN 112   **SC** 11230
  B Statistical Analysis [67]
  R Effect Size (Statistical) [85]
     ↓ Hypothesis Testing [73]
     Predictability (Measurement) [73]
     ↓ Statistical Measurement [73]
     Statistical Sample Parameters [73]
     Statistical Significance [73]
     ↓ Statistical Tests [73]

Confidentiality of Information
  Use Privileged Communication

Confirmatory Factor Analysis
  Use Factor Analysis

Conflict [67]
PN 2953   **SC** 11250
SN Hostile encounter or antagonistic state or action.

Conflict — (cont'd)
B   Aggressive Behavior [67]
    Interpersonal Interaction [67]
N   Arguments [73]
    Riots [73]
    ↓ Violence [73]
    ↓ War [67]

Conflict Resolution [82]
PN 1082   SC 11255
SN   Process of reducing or removing antagonisms among individuals, groups, organizations, or political entities.
N   Mediation [88]
R   ↓ Cognitive Processes [67]
    Forgiveness [88]
    ↓ Negotiation [73]
    ↓ Social Interaction [67]

Conformity (Personality) [67]
PN 1065   SC 11270
B   Personality Traits [67]
    Social Behavior [67]
R   Nonconformity (Personality) [73]

Confusion (Mental)
Use Mental Confusion

Congenital Disorders [73]
PN 442   SC 11290
B   Disorders [67]
N   Cleft Palate [67]
    ↓ Drug Induced Congenital Disorders [73]
    Hermaphroditism [73]
    Prader Willi Syndrome [91]
    Spina Bifida [78]
R   Congenitally Handicapped [73]
    Cystic Fibrosis [85]
    Deaf Blind [91]
    Developmental Disabilities [82]
    ↓ Genetic Disorders [73]
    Hydrocephaly [73]
    Microcephaly [73]
    Myotonia [73]
    ↓ Neonatal Disorders [73]
    Prenatal Diagnosis [88]
    ↓ Syphilis [73]
    Teratogens [88]

Congenitally Handicapped [73]
PN 120   SC 11300
B   Handicapped [67]
R   Adventitiously Handicapped [73]
    ↓ Brain Damaged [73]
    ↓ Congenital Disorders [73]

Congo [91]
PN 1   SC 11305
B   Africa [67]

Conjoint Measurement [94]
PN 0   SC 11307
SN   Statistical measurement of a variable that is composed of two or more components which affect the variable being measured.
B   Statistical Measurement [73]
R   ↓ Experimental Design [67]
    Psychometrics [67]
    ↓ Statistical Analysis [67]

Conjoint Therapy [73]
PN 286   SC 11310
SN   Type of marriage or family therapy in which partners or family members are seen in joint sessions.
UF   Triadic Therapy
B   Family Therapy [67]
    Marriage Counseling [73]

Conjoint Therapy — (cont'd)
R   Couples Therapy [94]
    ↓ Group Psychotherapy [67]
    ↓ Psychotherapeutic Techniques [67]

Connectionism [94]
PN 0   SC 11315
SN   Theoretical principles that characterize all learning and behavior as connected to the stimulus-response paradigm and that neural linkages, whether inherited or acquired, bond these behaviors.
R   ↓ Associative Processes [67]
    ↓ Cognitive Processes [67]
    Cognitive Psychology [85]
    ↓ Learning [67]
    Learning Theory [67]
    Neural Networks [91]

Connective Tissue Cells [73]
PN 7   SC 11320
B   Cells (Biology) [73]
R   ↓ Connective Tissues [73]

Connective Tissues [73]
PN 10   SC 11330
B   Tissues (Body) [73]
N   Bones [73]
R   Connective Tissue Cells [73]

Connotations [73]
PN 170   SC 11340
B   Associative Processes [67]
R   Analogy [91]
    ↓ Figurative Language [85]
    Semantic Generalization [73]
    Word Meaning [73]

Consanguineous Marriage [73]
PN 26   SC 11350
B   Endogamous Marriage [73]

Conscience [67]
PN 84   SC 11360
SN   Cognitive and affective processes which govern the individual's standards of behavior, performance and morality.
B   Psychoanalytic Personality Factors [73]
    Superego [73]

Conscious (Personality Factor) [73]
PN 163   SC 11370
SN   That portion of personal mental functioning which is known to the individual or is observable by introspection. Use CONSCIOUS (PERSONALITY FACTORS) prior to 1988.
B   Psychoanalytic Personality Factors [73]

Consciousness Disturbances [73]
PN 93   SC 11380
N   Delirium [73]
    ↓ Hypnosis [67]
    Place Disorientation [73]
    ↓ Sleep Disorders [73]
    Sleep Talking [73]
    Suggestibility [67]
    Time Disorientation [73]
R   Coma [73]
    ↓ Consciousness States [71]
    ↓ Mental Disorders [67]
    ↓ Sleep [67]

Consciousness Raising Groups [78]
PN 101   SC 11387
SN   Disciplined interaction of a small group of people whose exchange of feelings and experiences results in an increased awareness of social issues such as discriminatory social practices and stereotyped thinking.

Consciousness Raising Groups — (cont'd)
B   Human Potential Movement [82]
R   ↓ Encounter Group Therapy [73]
    ↓ Group Dynamics [67]
    ↓ Group Psychotherapy [67]
    Sensitivity Training [73]

Consciousness States [71]
PN 1431   SC 11390
SN   Conceptually broad term referring to variations in the degree and type of mental awareness. Use a more specific term if possible.
UF   Deja Vu
N   ↓ Awareness [67]
    Wakefulness [73]
R   Centering [91]
    ↓ Consciousness Disturbances [73]
    Mind [91]
    Physiological Arousal [67]
    ↓ Sleep [67]

Conservation (Concept) [73]
PN 1110   SC 11400
SN   Knowledge of constancy of size, volume, or amount in spite of changed distance or shape; used as measure of cognitive development.
R   ↓ Cognitive Development [73]
    ↓ Concept Formation [67]
    Object Permanence [85]
    ↓ Perceptual Development [73]
    Piaget (Jean) [67]

Conservation (Ecological Behavior) [78]
PN 342   SC 11403
B   Behavior [67]
R   Ecology [73]
    Environmental Attitudes [78]
    Environmental Education [94]

Conservatism [73]
PN 326   SC 11405
UF   Traditionalism
B   Personality Traits [67]
R   Political Conservatism [73]

Conservatism (Political)
Use Political Conservatism

Conservatorship
Use Guardianship

Consistency (Measurement) [73]
PN 163   SC 11420
B   Statistical Analysis [67]
R   Error of Measurement [85]
    ↓ Prediction Errors [73]
    Statistical Reliability [73]
    ↓ Statistical Validity [73]

Consonants [73]
PN 630   SC 11430
B   Letters (Alphabet) [73]
    Phonemes [73]
R   Syllables [73]
    Words (Phonetic Units) [67]

Constipation [73]
PN 39   SC 11440
B   Colon Disorders [73]

Construct Validity [82]
PN 1723   SC 11445
SN   Extent to which a test can be said to measure a theoretical construct or trait.
UF   Concept Validity
R   Concurrent Validity [88]
    Factor Structure [85]
    Factorial Validity [73]

Construct Validity — (cont'd)
R ↓ Hypothesis Testing [73]
  ↓ Measurement [67]
  ↓ Statistical Correlation [67]
  ↓ Statistical Validity [73]
  Test Validity [73]
  ↓ Theories [67]

Constructionism
Use Constructivism

Constructivism [94]
PN 0   SC 11448
SN Theoretical perspective that characterizes perceptual experience and reality as constructed by the mind in the observation of the effects of independent actions on objects.
UF Constructionism
B Theories [67]
R ↓ Cognitive Development [73]
  ↓ Learning [67]
  ↓ Perception [67]
  Phenomenology [67]
  Piaget (Jean) [67]

Consultation (Professional)
Use Professional Consultation

Consultation Liaison Psychiatry [91]
PN 96   SC 11465
B Professional Consultation [73]
  Psychiatry [67]

Consumer Attitudes [73]
PN 1648   SC 11470
SN Attitudes of, not toward, consumers.
B Attitudes [67]
N Brand Preferences [94]
  Consumer Satisfaction [94]
R ↓ Consumer Research [73]
  Consumer Surveys [73]
  Public Relations [73]

Consumer Behavior [67]
PN 2711   SC 11480
UF Buying
  Shopping
B Behavior [67]
R Brand Names [78]
  Brand Preferences [94]
  ↓ Consumer Research [73]
  Consumer Satisfaction [94]
  Consumer Surveys [73]
  Retailing [91]
  Shopping Centers [73]

Consumer Fraud
Use Fraud

Consumer Protection [73]
PN 89   SC 11490
R Accountability [88]
  ↓ Laws [67]
  ↓ Legal Processes [73]

Consumer Psychology [73]
PN 99   SC 11500
SN Subdiscipline in psychology that has as its emphasis the behavioral and psychological aspects of consumer behavior.
B Applied Psychology [73]

Consumer Research [73]
PN 733   SC 11510
SN Marketing and advertising research assessing consumer needs, competition, and methods of sale for a product.

Consumer Research — (cont'd)
B Experimentation [67]
N Consumer Surveys [73]
R ↓ Advertising [67]
  Brand Names [78]
  Brand Preferences [94]
  ↓ Consumer Attitudes [73]
  Consumer Behavior [67]
  Consumer Satisfaction [94]
  Mail Surveys [94]
  Marketing [73]
  Telephone Surveys [94]

Consumer Satisfaction [94]
PN 0   SC 11515
B Consumer Attitudes [73]
  Satisfaction [73]
R Consumer Behavior [67]
  ↓ Consumer Research [73]
  Consumer Surveys [73]

Consumer Surveys [73]
PN 180   SC 11520
SN Surveys assessing consumer needs, product usage, and effectiveness of marketing and advertising.
B Consumer Research [73]
  Surveys [67]
R ↓ Consumer Attitudes [73]
  Consumer Behavior [67]
  Consumer Satisfaction [94]
  Mail Surveys [94]
  Telephone Surveys [94]

Contact Lenses [73]
PN 24   SC 11540
B Optical Aids [73]

Contagion [88]
PN 41   SC 11544
SN Transmission of behavior, attitudes, or emotions to other persons through suggestions, verbal communication, imitation, or gestures. Not used for infectious disorders.
B Social Behavior [67]
R ↓ Collective Behavior [67]
  Mass Hysteria [73]

Content Analysis [78]
PN 1036   SC 11548
SN Systematic, objective, quantitative or qualitative description of the manifest or latent content of communications.
B Analysis [67]
  Methodology [67]
R ↓ Communication [67]

Content Analysis (Test) [67]
PN 159   SC 11550
SN Systematic examination of a test, primarily to determine whether the test items constitute an adequate sample of the domain or subject matter to be tested.
B Analysis [67]
  Test Construction [73]
  Testing [67]

Contextual Associations [67]
PN 2800   SC 11560
SN In learning and memory, associations made to environmental or internal conditions during learning or memorization. In perception and communication, environmental conditions that affect such aspects as perceptual accuracy, comprehension, or meaning.
UF Associations (Contextual)
B Associative Processes [67]
R Place Conditioning [91]
  ↓ Priming [88]

Contextual Associations — (cont'd)
R Semantic Priming [94]
  Word Frequency [73]
  Word Meaning [73]

Contiguity (Cognitive)
Use Cognitive Contiguity

Contingency Management [73]
PN 772   SC 11580
SN Behavior modification technique in which the stimuli and reinforcers that control a given behavior are manipulated to increase the likelihood of occurrence of the desired behavior.
B Behavior Modification [73]
N Token Economy Programs [73]
R Noncontingent Reinforcement [88]

Contingent Negative Variation [82]
PN 159   SC 11583
SN Cortical evoked potential of slow negativity recorded in the period between stimulus-presentation and responses and which is associated with states of attention or expectancy.
B Cortical Evoked Potentials [73]

Continuing Education [85]
PN 199   SC 11590
SN Formal or informal courses, educational programs or services, usually at the postsecondary level, designed to advance or update adult learning for personal, academic, or occupational and professional purposes.
B Adult Education [73]
N ↓ Inservice Training [85]
R ↓ Higher Education [73]
  Individualized Instruction [73]
  Professional Development [82]
  Reentry Students [85]

Continuous Reinforcement
Use Reinforcement Schedules

Contour
Use Form and Shape Perception

Contraception
Use Birth Control

Contraceptive Devices [73]
PN 112   SC 11630
B Birth Control [71]
N Condoms [91]
  Diaphragms (Birth Control) [73]
  Intrauterine Devices [73]
  Oral Contraceptives [73]

Contribution (Professional)
Use Professional Criticism

Control Groups
Use Experiment Controls

Controls (Instrument)
Use Instrument Controls

Convergent Thinking
Use Inductive Deductive Reasoning

Conversation [73]
PN 1552   SC 11710
B Interpersonal Communication [73]
  Verbal Communication [67]

Conversion Hysteria
Use Conversion Neurosis

Conversion Neurosis [73]
PN 305   SC 11730
- UF   Conversion Hysteria
  - Hysterical Neurosis (Conversion)
- B   Psychosomatic Disorders [67]
- N   Hysterical Anesthesia [73]
  - Hysterical Paralysis [73]
  - Hysterical Vision Disturbances [73]
  - Pseudocyesis [73]
- R   ↓ Defense Mechanisms [67]
  - Hypochondriasis [73]
  - ↓ Hysteria [67]
  - Hysterical Personality [73]
  - Psychogenic Pain [73]
  - Somatization [94]

Conviction (Criminal)
- Use   Criminal Conviction

Convulsions [67]
PN 1455   SC 11750
- UF   Seizures
- B   Nervous System Disorders [67]
  - Symptoms [67]
- N   Audiogenic Seizures [78]
- R   ↓ Anticonvulsive Drugs [73]
  - ↓ Brain Disorders [67]
  - ↓ Epileptic Seizures [73]
  - Experimental Epilepsy [78]
  - Hydrocephaly [73]
  - ↓ Spasms [73]

Cooperating Teachers [78]
PN 87   SC 11756
SN   Experienced elementary or secondary teachers employed to supervise student teachers or teacher interns in schools which, although not integral parts of teacher education institutions, provide experiences for the student teachers and teacher interns.
- UF   Supervising Teachers
- B   Teachers [67]
- R   Practicum Supervision [78]
  - Student Teachers [73]
  - Student Teaching [73]
  - ↓ Teacher Education [67]

Cooperation [67]
PN 2468   SC 11760
SN   Used for human or animal populations.
- UF   Collaboration
- B   Interpersonal Interaction [67]
  - Prosocial Behavior [82]
- R   Cooperative Learning [94]

Cooperative Education [82]
PN 66   SC 11765
SN   Combined complementary work and study experience or program coordinated by a teacher and designed by the school and the employer to achieve some occupational goal. Not to be confused with work study programs which serve as means for financial assistance.
- B   Vocational Education [73]
- R   Curricular Field Experience [82]
  - ↓ Educational Programs [73]

Cooperative Learning [94]
PN 0   SC 11766
SN   Learning in small groups where cooperation among group members determines rewards and performance.
- B   Learning [67]
- R   Cooperation [67]
  - Group Instruction [73]
  - Peer Tutoring [73]
  - School Learning [67]
  - ↓ Teaching [67]

Cooperative Learning — (cont'd)
- R   ↓ Teaching Methods [67]
  - Teams [88]

Cooperative Therapy
- Use   Cotherapy

Coordination (Motor)
- Use   Motor Coordination

Coordination (Perceptual Motor)
- Use   Perceptual Motor Coordination

Coping Behavior [67]
PN 7627   SC 11790
SN   Use of conscious or unconscious strategies or mechanisms in adapting to stress, various disorders, or environmental demands.
- B   Behavior [67]
- R   Adaptability (Personality) [73]
  - Adjustment Disorders [94]
  - Anosognosia [94]
  - ↓ Emotional Adjustment [73]
  - Emotional Control [73]
  - Illness Behavior [82]

Copper [73]
PN 63   SC 11800
- B   Metallic Elements [73]

Copulation
- Use   Sexual Intercourse (Human)

Copulation (Animal)
- Use   Animal Mating Behavior

Cornea [73]
PN 35   SC 11830
- B   Eye (Anatomy) [67]

Coronary Disorders
- Use   Cardiovascular Disorders

Coronary Heart Disease
- Use   Heart Disorders

Coronary Prone Behavior [82]
PN 1604   SC 11855
SN   Constellation of behaviors or attitudes constituting a risk factor for coronary heart disease. Traits can include ambition, competitiveness, sense of time urgency, devotion to work over relaxation, positive attitude toward pressure, aggressiveness, impatience, need for recognition, and tendency toward hostility.
- UF   Type A Personality
  - Type B Personality
- B   Behavior [67]
- R   At Risk Populations [85]
  - ↓ Cardiovascular Disorders [67]
  - Illness Behavior [82]
  - ↓ Personality [67]
  - ↓ Personality Traits [67]
  - Predisposition [73]
  - Stress Reactions [73]
  - Susceptibility (Disorders) [73]

Coronary Thromboses [73]
PN 5   SC 11860
- B   Heart Disorders [73]
  - Thromboses [73]
- R   Myocardial Infarctions [73]

Coronary Vessels
- Use   Arteries (Anatomy)

Corporal Punishment
- Use   Punishment

Corporations
- Use   Business Organizations

Corpus Callosum [73]
PN 365   SC 11900
- B   Cerebral Cortex [67]
  - Neural Pathways [82]
- R   Commissurotomy [85]
  - Interhemispheric Interaction [85]
  - Left Brain [91]
  - Right Brain [91]

Corpus Striatum
- Use   Basal Ganglia

Correctional Institutions [73]
PN 764   SC 11910
- UF   Institutions (Correctional)
- N   Prisons [67]
  - Reformatories [73]
- R   Halfway Houses [73]
  - Incarceration [73]
  - Institution Visitation [73]
  - Institutional Schools [78]
  - Maximum Security Facilities [85]
  - Penology [73]

Correlation (Statistical)
- Use   Statistical Correlation

Cortex (Auditory)
- Use   Auditory Cortex

Cortex (Cerebral)
- Use   Cerebral Cortex

Cortex (Motor)
- Use   Motor Cortex

Cortex (Somatosensory)
- Use   Somatosensory Cortex

Cortex (Visual)
- Use   Visual Cortex

Cortical Atrophy
- Use   Cerebral Atrophy

Cortical Evoked Potentials [73]
PN 1094   SC 11980
- B   Electrical Activity [67]
  - Evoked Potentials [67]
- N   Contingent Negative Variation [82]
- R   Auditory Evoked Potentials [73]
  - Olfactory Evoked Potentials [73]
  - Somatosensory Evoked Potentials [73]
  - Visual Evoked Potentials [73]

Corticoids
- Use   Corticosteroids

Corticosteroids [73]
PN 336   SC 12000
- UF   Adrenal Cortex Steroids
  - Corticoids
- B   Steroids [73]
- N   Aldosterone [73]
  - Corticosterone [73]
  - Cortisone [73]
  - Deoxycorticosterone [73]
  - Hydrocortisone [73]
  - Prednisolone [73]
- R   ↓ Adrenal Cortex Hormones [73]

Corticosterone 73
PN 654   SC 12010
  B   Adrenal Cortex Hormones 73
      Corticosteroids 73

Corticotropin 73
PN 932   SC 12020
  UF   ACTH (Hormone)
      Adrenocorticotropin
  B   Pituitary Hormones 73
  R   Corticotropin Releasing Factor 94

Corticotropin Releasing Factor 94
PN 0   SC 12025
  UF   ACTH Releasing Factor
  B   Hormones 67
      Peptides 73
  R   Corticotropin 73

Cortisol
  Use Hydrocortisone

Cortisone 73
PN 22   SC 12040
  B   Adrenal Cortex Hormones 73
      Corticosteroids 73

Cost Containment 91
PN 20   SC 12041
SN Policies or procedures to restrain or control
expenses in any setting.
  R   ↓ Case Management 91
     ↓ Costs and Cost Analysis 73
      Diagnosis Related Groups 88
      Economics 85
      Fee for Service 94
      Health Care Costs 94
     ↓ Health Care Services 78
      Health Maintenance Organizations 82
     ↓ Managed Care 94
      Money 67
     ↓ Professional Fees 78
     ↓ Treatment 67

Cost Effectiveness
  Use Costs and Cost Analysis

Costa Rica 88
PN 20   SC 12043
  B   Central America 73

Costs and Cost Analysis 73
PN 2078   SC 12045
SN Applied to any subject and includes prices,
expenses, or payments; also attachment of dollar
estimates to the costs of an operation and its
alternatives.
  UF   Budgets
      Cost Effectiveness
      Price
  B   Analysis 67
  N   Health Care Costs 94
  R   Cost Containment 91
      Economics 85
      Economy 73
      Funding 88
      Money 67
     ↓ Professional Fees 78

Cotherapy 82
PN 120   SC 12047
SN Psychotherapeutic process in which a client
or a group of clients are treated by more than
one therapist. Use CONJOINT THERAPY to ac-
cess references from 73–81.
  UF   Cooperative Therapy
      Multiple Therapy
  B   Psychotherapeutic Techniques 67

Cotherapy — (cont'd)
  R   Psychiatric Training 73
     ↓ Psychotherapy 67
      Psychotherapy Training 73

Counselees
  Use Clients

Counseling 67
PN 5480   SC 12080
SN Conceptually broad array term referring to a
form of helping process which involves giving
advice and information, in order to assist individuals or groups in coping with their problems. Use
a more specific term if possible.
  N   Educational Counseling 67
      Genetic Counseling 78
      Group Counseling 73
     ↓ Marriage Counseling 73
      Microcounseling 78
      Occupational Guidance 67
      Pastoral Counseling 67
      Peer Counseling 78
      Premarital Counseling 73
     ↓ Psychotherapeutic Counseling 73
      Rehabilitation Counseling 78
      School Counseling 82
  R   Counseling Psychology 73
     ↓ Counselors 67
      Employee Assistance Programs 85
     ↓ Family Therapy 67
      Feminist Therapy 94
     ↓ Health Care Services 78
     ↓ Mental Health Services 78
      Social Casework 67
      Student Personnel Services 78
     ↓ Support Groups 91
     ↓ Treatment 67

Counseling (Group)
  Use Group Counseling

Counseling Psychologists 88
PN 85   SC 12065
  B   Psychologists 67
  R   Counseling Psychology 73

Counseling Psychology 73
PN 569   SC 12070
  B   Applied Psychology 73
  R   ↓ Counseling 67
      Counseling Psychologists 88

Counselor Attitudes 73
PN 806   SC 12090
SN Attitudes of, not toward, counselors.
  B   Attitudes 67
      Counselor Characteristics 73
  R   Counselor Role 73
     ↓ Counselors 67
     ↓ Health Personnel Attitudes 85
      Psychologist Attitudes 91

Counselor Characteristics 73
PN 2196   SC 12100
  UF   Counselor Effectiveness
      Counselor Personality
  N   Counselor Attitudes 73
  R   ↓ Counselors 67

Counselor Client Interaction
  Use Psychotherapeutic Processes

Counselor Education 73
PN 2534   SC 12120
  R   ↓ Clinical Methods Training 73
      Microcounseling 78
      Practicum Supervision 78

Counselor Effectiveness
  Use Counselor Characteristics

Counselor Personality
  Use Counselor Characteristics

Counselor Role 73
PN 814   SC 12150
  UF   Role (Counselor)
  B   Roles 67
  R   Counselor Attitudes 73
     ↓ Counselors 67
      Therapist Role 78

Counselor Trainees 73
PN 1340   SC 12160
  R   ↓ Counselors 67
      Therapist Trainees 73

Counselors 67
PN 2190   SC 12170
  B   Professional Personnel 78
  N   Rehabilitation Counselors 78
      School Counselors 73
      Vocational Counselors 73
  R   ↓ Counseling 67
      Counselor Attitudes 73
     ↓ Counselor Characteristics 73
      Counselor Role 73
      Counselor Trainees 73
     ↓ Health Personnel 94
     ↓ Mental Health Personnel 67
     ↓ Psychologists 67
     ↓ Social Workers 73
      Sociologists 73
     ↓ Therapists 67

Counterconditioning 73
PN 73   SC 12180
SN Technique used to extinguish a response to
a certain stimulus by conditioning an alternative,
often incompatible response to that stimulus.
  B   Conditioning 67
  R   ↓ Aversion Therapy 73
     ↓ Behavior Modification 73
     ↓ Behavior Therapy 67
      Reciprocal Inhibition Therapy 73

Countertransference 73
PN 1182   SC 12190
SN Conscious or unconscious emotional reac-
tion of the therapist to the patient which may
interfere with the treatment.
  B   Psychotherapeutic Processes 67
  R   Professional Client Sexual Relations 94
      Psychotherapeutic Transference 67

Countries 67
PN 1888   SC 12195
SN Applies to cross-national studies when in-
dividual countries are not mentioned or are too
numerous to list.
  N   Developed Countries 85
      Developing Countries 85
  R   Geography 73

County Agricultural Agents
  Use Agricultural Extension Workers

Couples 82
PN 1241   SC 12205
SN Two individuals in an intimate relationship.
  R   Cohabitation 73
      Dyads 73
     ↓ Family 67
      Significant Others 91
      Social Dating 73
     ↓ Spouses 73

Couples Therapy 94
PN 0   SC 12207
SN Used specifically for unmarried couples. Use MARRIAGE COUNSELING for married couples.
  R   Conjoint Therapy 73
    ↓ Marriage Counseling 73
    ↓ Psychotherapy 67
    Sex Therapy 78

Courage 73
PN 37   SC 12210
  UF   Bravery
  B   Personality Traits 67

Course Evaluation 78
PN 328   SC 12215
SN Procedures, materials, or the process involved in the assessment of quality or effectiveness of an academic or vocational course or program by its students or participants. Evaluation may include content, structure, or method of material presentation.
  B   Evaluation 67
  R   ↓ Curriculum 67
    Educational Program Evaluation 73
    Teacher Effectiveness Evaluation 78
    ↓ Teaching 67

Course Objectives
  Use   Educational Objectives

Court Ordered Treatment
  Use   Court Referrals

Court Referrals 94
PN 0   SC 12219
SN Court ordered assessment, treatment, consultation, or other services for defendants, plaintiffs, or criminals.
  UF   Court Ordered Treatment
  B   Adjudication 67
  R   ↓ Commitment (Psychiatric) 73
    ↓ Criminal Justice 91
    ↓ Criminals 67
    Defendants 85
    Forensic Evaluation 94
    Insanity Defense 85
    Involuntary Treatment 94
    Mediation 88
    Mentally Ill Offenders 85
    Probation 73
    Professional Referral 73
    ↓ Treatment 67

Courts
  Use   Adjudication

Courtship (Animal)
  Use   Animal Courtship Behavior

Courtship (Human)
  Use   Human Courtship

Courtship Displays (Animal)
  Use   Animal Courtship Displays

Cousins 73
PN 11   SC 12260
  B   Family Members 73

Covert Sensitization 88
PN 17   SC 12265
SN Form of aversion conditioning in which noxious mental images, thoughts, or feelings are associated with undesirable behavior by verbal cues. Frequently used in therapeutic settings.

Covert Sensitization — (cont'd)
  B   Aversion Conditioning 82
    Aversion Therapy 73
  R   Aversive Stimulation 73

Cows
  Use   Cattle

Crabs 73
PN 194   SC 12300
  B   Crustacea 73

Crafts 73
PN 29   SC 12310
  UF   Handicrafts
  B   Art 67

Cramps (Muscle)
  Use   Muscular Disorders

Cranial Nerves 73
PN 82   SC 12330
  UF   Accessory Nerve
    Glossopharyngeal Nerve
    Hypoglossal Nerve
    Nerve (Accessory)
    Nerves (Cranial)
    Oculomotor Nerve
    Trochlear Nerve
  B   Peripheral Nervous System 73
  N   Abducens Nerve 73
    Acoustic Nerve 73
    Facial Nerve 73
    Olfactory Nerve 73
    Optic Nerve 73
    Trigeminal Nerve 73
    Vagus Nerve 73

Cranial Spinal Cord 73
PN 2   SC 12340
  B   Spinal Cord 73

Crayfish 73
PN 76   SC 12360
  B   Crustacea 73

Creative Arts Therapy 94
PN 0   SC 12365
SN Therapeutic use of the arts in medicine, mental health, or education.
  B   Treatment 67
  N   Art Therapy 73
    Dance Therapy 73
    Music Therapy 73
    Poetry Therapy 94
    Recreation Therapy 73
  R   ↓ Psychotherapeutic Techniques 67

Creative Writing 94
PN 0   SC 12370
SN Use LITERATURE to access references from 73-93.
  UF   Writing (Creative)
  B   Written Communication 85
  R   ↓ Literature 67
    Poetry 73
    ↓ Prose 73
    Rhetoric 91
    Storytelling 88

Creativity 67
PN 5521   SC 12380
SN Ability to perceive new relationships, and to derive new ideas and solve problems by pursuing nontraditional patterns of thinking. Compare DIVERGENT THINKING.
  UF   Innovativeness
    Originality

Creativity — (cont'd)
  B   Personality Traits 67
  R   ↓ Ability 67
    ↓ Artistic Ability 73
    Divergent Thinking 73
    Gifted 67
    Intelligence 67

Creativity Measurement 73
PN 342   SC 12390
  B   Measurement 67

Credibility 73
PN 525   SC 12400
  R   ↓ Interpersonal Communication 73
    ↓ Social Perception 67

Creutzfeldt Jakob Syndrome 94
PN 0   SC 12410
  B   Encephalopathies 82
    Presenile Dementia 73
    Syndromes 73
    Viral Disorders 73

Cri du Chat Syndrome
  Use   Crying Cat Syndrome

Crib Death
  Use   Sudden Infant Death

Crime 67
PN 3175   SC 12430
  UF   Felonies
    Misdemeanors
  B   Antisocial Behavior 71
    Behavior Disorders 71
    Social Issues 91
  N   Arson 85
    ↓ Child Abuse 71
    Driving Under The Influence 88
    Kidnapping 88
    ↓ Sex Offenses 82
    ↓ Theft 73
    Vandalism 78
  R   Crime Prevention 85
    ↓ Crime Victims 82
    ↓ Criminal Justice 91
    Criminal Responsibility 91
    ↓ Criminals 67
    Fraud 94
    Informants 88
    ↓ Perpetrators 88
    Self Defense 85
    Terrorism 82
    Victimization 73

Crime Prevention 85
PN 191   SC 12432
SN Measures aimed at deterring the occurrence of crime or delinquent behavior.
  B   Prevention 73
  R   ↓ Crime 67
    ↓ Criminal Justice 91
    Juvenile Delinquency 67
    ↓ Law Enforcement 78

Crime Victims 82
PN 708   SC 12434
SN Individuals subjected to and adversely affected by criminal activity. Use VICTIMIZATION to access references from 73–81.
  N   Hostages 88
  R   ↓ Crime 67
    Self Defense 85
    Victimization 73

Criminal Conviction 73
PN 271   SC 12440

Criminal Conviction — (cont'd)
SN Declaration made by a court finding a person guilty and responsible for a criminal offense.
UF Conviction (Criminal)
B Criminal Justice [91]
R ↓ Adjudication [67]
  ↓ Criminals [67]
  Legal Decisions [91]

Criminal Justice [91]
PN 96   **SC** 12445
SN Used for the system, discipline, or the actual process itself.
B Justice [73]
  Legal Processes [73]
N Criminal Conviction [73]
R ↓ Adjudication [67]
  Court Referrals [94]
  ↓ Crime [67]
  Crime Prevention [85]
  Criminal Law [73]
  Forensic Psychiatry [73]
  Forensic Psychology [85]
  ↓ Law Enforcement [78]
  Legal Decisions [91]
  Penology [73]

Criminal Law [73]
PN 216   **SC** 12450
B Law (Government) [73]
R ↓ Criminal Justice [91]

Criminal Responsibility [91]
PN 57   **SC** 12453
SN State of mind that permits one to be held accountable for criminal acts.
B Responsibility [73]
R Accountability [88]
  ↓ Adjudication [67]
  Competency to Stand Trial [85]
  ↓ Crime [67]
  ↓ Criminals [67]
  Defendants [85]
  Insanity Defense [85]
  ↓ Perpetrators [88]

Criminally Insane
Use Mentally Ill Offenders

Criminals [67]
PN 2500   **SC** 12460
UF Offenders (Adult)
B Perpetrators [88]
N Female Criminals [73]
  Male Criminals [73]
  Mentally Ill Offenders [85]
R Court Referrals [94]
  ↓ Crime [67]
  Criminal Conviction [73]
  Criminal Responsibility [91]
  Defendants [85]
  Forensic Evaluation [94]
  ↓ Juvenile Delinquents [73]
  ↓ Prisoners [67]
  Recidivism [73]

Criminology [73]
PN 205   **SC** 12470
R Penology [73]

Crippled
Use Physically Handicapped

Crises [71]
PN 636   **SC** 12490
N Family Crises [73]
  Identity Crisis [73]
  Organizational Crises [73]

Crises — (cont'd)
R ↓ Crisis Intervention [73]
  ↓ Crisis Intervention Services [73]
  ↓ Disasters [73]
  ↓ Experiences (Events) [73]
  ↓ Stress [67]

Crisis (Reactions to)
Use Stress Reactions

Crisis Intervention [73]
PN 842   **SC** 12510
SN Brief therapeutic approach which is ameliorative rather than curative of acute psychiatric emergencies. Used in such contexts as emergency rooms of psychiatric or general hospitals, or in the home or place of crisis occurrence, this treatment approach focuses on interpersonal and intrapsychic factors and environmental modification of behavior.
B Treatment [67]
N Suicide Prevention [73]
R ↓ Crises [71]
  ↓ Crisis Intervention Services [73]

Crisis Intervention Services [73]
PN 361   **SC** 12520
SN Community organizations, programs, or mental health personnel which provide crisis care.
B Community Services [67]
  Mental Health Programs [73]
  Treatment [67]
N Hot Line Services [73]
  Suicide Prevention Centers [73]
R ↓ Clinics [67]
  Community Mental Health Centers [73]
  ↓ Crises [71]
  ↓ Crisis Intervention [73]
  Emergency Services [73]
  ↓ Treatment Facilities [73]
  Walk In Clinics [73]

Criterion Referenced Tests [82]
PN 209   **SC** 12525
SN Tests in which scores are measured against explicitly stated objectives rather than a group norm.
UF Mastery Tests
  Objective Referenced Tests
B Measurement [67]
R ↓ Achievement Measures [67]
  Performance Tests [73]

Critical Flicker Fusion Threshold [67]
PN 318   **SC** 12530
UF Flicker Fusion Frequency
B Visual Thresholds [73]
R ↓ Perceptual Measures [73]

Critical Period [88]
PN 26   **SC** 12533
R ↓ Development [67]
  Imprinting [67]

Critical Scores
Use Cutting Scores

Criticism [73]
PN 175   **SC** 12540
B Social Behavior [67]
  Social Influences [67]
R Social Approval [67]

Criticism (Professional)
Use Professional Criticism

Crocodilians [73]
PN 18   **SC** 12570
UF Alligators
B Reptiles [67]

Cross Cultural Differences [67]
PN 7806   **SC** 12590
UF Cultural Differences
B Sociocultural Factors [67]
R Cross Cultural Treatment [94]
  Cultural Sensitivity [94]
  Ethnology [67]
  Racial and Ethnic Differences [82]

Cross Cultural Treatment [94]
PN 0   **SC** 12593
SN Treatment, in any context, where the racial, ethnic, or cultural background of the patient or client is different from that of the health care provider, e.g., therapist, counselor, or physician. Used primarily when the cultural or racial aspects of the treatment paradigm are the major focus.
B Treatment [67]
R ↓ Client Characteristics [73]
  Cross Cultural Differences [67]
  Cultural Sensitivity [94]
  Racial and Ethnic Differences [82]
  ↓ Therapist Characteristics [73]
  Transcultural Psychiatry [73]

Cross Disciplinary Research
Use Interdisciplinary Research

Crossed Eyes
Use Strabismus

Crowding [78]
PN 391   **SC** 12610
SN Conditions of high population density for a given area. Used for animal or human populations.
R Environmental Stress [73]
  Overpopulation [73]
  Personal Space [73]
  Social Density [78]

CRT
Use Video Display Units

Cruelty [73]
PN 30   **SC** 12620
B Antisocial Behavior [71]
  Personality Traits [67]

Crustacea [73]
PN 221   **SC** 12630
B Arthropoda [73]
N Crabs [73]
  Crayfish [73]

Crying [73]
PN 343   **SC** 12640
B Vocalization [67]
  Voice [73]
R Infant Vocalization [73]

Crying Cat Syndrome [73]
PN 16   **SC** 12650
UF Cri du Chat Syndrome
B Autosome Disorders [73]
  Mental Retardation [67]
  Neonatal Disorders [73]
  Syndromes [73]

Cuba [73]
PN 147   **SC** 12670
B West Indies [73]

Cuban Americans
Use Hispanics

Cued Recall [94]
PN 0   **SC** 12678
B   Recall (Learning) [67]
R   Cues [67]
     Forgetting [73]
     Free Recall [73]
     ↓ Memory [67]

Cues [67]
PN 5661   **SC** 12680
SN Internal or external verbal or nonverbal signals which influence learning, performance, or behavior. Cues are often only obscure secondary stimuli which, though not fully detected, serve to facilitate learning, performance, or behavior. Compare CONDITIONED STIMULUS.
R   ↓ Associative Processes [67]
     Cued Recall [94]
     Isolation Effect [73]
     ↓ Memory [67]
     Mnemonic Learning [73]
     ↓ Priming [88]
     Semantic Priming [94]

Cultism [73]
PN 307   **SC** 12690
R   Ethnology [67]
     Myths [67]
     Occultism [78]
     ↓ Religious Beliefs [73]
     Shamanism [73]
     ↓ Sociocultural Factors [67]

Cultural Assimilation [73]
PN 1018   **SC** 12700
SN Contact of at least two autonomous cultural groups resulting in change in one or the other, or both groups. Includes the process of a minority group giving up its own cultural traits and absorbing those of a dominant society. Use CULTURAL ASSIMILATION or ACCULTURATION to access references from 73–81.
UF Acculturation
     Assimilation (Cultural)
B   Culture Change [67]
R   Cultural Sensitivity [94]

Cultural Deprivation [73]
PN 188   **SC** 12710
SN Inability of individuals to participate in their society's cultural achievements because of poverty, social discrimination, or other disadvantage. Consider also SOCIAL DEPRIVATION.
UF Culturally Disadvantaged
B   Deprivation [67]
     Sociocultural Factors [67]
R   Disadvantaged [67]
     Poverty Areas [73]
     ↓ Social Deprivation [73]
     ↓ Social Environments [73]

Cultural Differences
Use Cross Cultural Differences

Cultural Familial Mental Retardation
Use Psychosocial Mental Retardation

Cultural Psychiatry
Use Transcultural Psychiatry

Cultural Sensitivity [94]
PN 0   **SC** 12728
SN Awareness and appreciation of the values, norms, and beliefs unique to a particular cultural, minority, ethnic, or racial group.

Cultural Sensitivity — (cont'd)
UF Ethnic Sensitivity
R   Cross Cultural Differences [67]
     Cross Cultural Treatment [94]
     Cultural Assimilation [73]
     ↓ Culture (Anthropological) [67]
     ↓ Ethnic Groups [73]
     Ethnic Identity [73]
     Ethnic Values [73]
     Minority Groups [67]
     ↓ Racial and Ethnic Attitudes [82]
     Racial and Ethnic Differences [82]
     ↓ Sociocultural Factors [67]

Cultural Test Bias [73]
PN 623   **SC** 12730
SN Any significant differential performance on tests by different populations (e.g., Hispanics vs Blacks) as a result of test characteristics that are sensitive to cultural, subcultural, racial, or ethnic factors but which are irrelevant to the variable or construct being measured.
UF Test Bias (Cultural)
B   Test Bias [85]
R   Response Bias [67]
     Test Interpretation [85]

Culturally Disadvantaged
Use Cultural Deprivation

Culture (Anthropological) [67]
PN 3085   **SC** 12750
N   ↓ Society [67]
     Subculture (Anthropological) [73]
R   Cultural Sensitivity [94]
     Ethnology [67]
     ↓ Family Structure [73]
     ↓ Sociocultural Factors [67]

Culture Change [67]
PN 318   **SC** 12760
SN Modification in behavior, values, customs, or artifacts over time or as the result of migration to a different cultural environment.
B   Sociocultural Factors [67]
N   Cultural Assimilation [73]
R   Culture Shock [73]
     Ethnology [67]

Culture Fair Intelligence Test [73]
PN 29   **SC** 12770
UF Cattell Culture Fair Intell Test
B   Intelligence Measures [67]

Culture Shock [73]
PN 122   **SC** 12780
SN Social, psychological, or emotional difficulties in adapting to a new culture or similar difficulties in adapting to one's own culture as the result of rapid social or cultural changes.
R   ↓ Culture Change [67]
     Ethnology [67]

Curare [73]
PN 25   **SC** 12790
B   Muscle Relaxing Drugs [73]
R   ↓ Alkaloids [73]
     Tubocurarine [73]

Curiosity [67]
PN 243   **SC** 12800
UF Inquisitiveness
B   Personality Traits [67]
R   ↓ Exploratory Behavior [67]
     Questioning [82]

Curricular Field Experience [82]
PN 204   **SC** 12805

Curricular Field Experience — (cont'd)
SN Organizationally or institutionally supervised educational activities, restricted primarily to high school and college, usually undertaken outside the classroom or campus in order to promote practical experience in a specific discipline.
UF Field Instruction
     Field Work (Educational)
B   Teaching Methods [67]
R   Cooperative Education [82]
     ↓ Curriculum [67]
     Educational Field Trips [73]
     ↓ Educational Programs [73]
     ↓ Practice [67]

Curriculum [67]
PN 4950   **SC** 12810
SN Set of courses constituting a framework for education in a given subject area.
B   Education [67]
N   Affective Education [82]
     Art Education [73]
     Braille Instruction [73]
     Business Education [73]
     Career Education [78]
     Compensatory Education [73]
     Computer Training [94]
     Driver Education [73]
     Foreign Language Education [73]
     ↓ Health Education [73]
     Home Economics [85]
     ↓ Language Arts Education [73]
     Mathematics Education [73]
     Music Education [73]
     Physical Education [67]
     ↓ Psychology Education [78]
     Science Education [73]
     Social Studies Education [78]
     ↓ Vocational Education [73]
R   Course Evaluation [78]
     Curricular Field Experience [82]
     Curriculum Based Assessment [94]
     Curriculum Development [73]
     Educational Objectives [78]
     Educational Program Accreditation [94]
     Home Schooling [94]
     ↓ Nontraditional Education [82]

Curriculum Based Assessment [94]
PN 0   **SC** 12815
B   Educational Measurement [67]
R   ↓ Curriculum [67]

Curriculum Development [73]
PN 1593   **SC** 12820
SN Initiating, designing, implementing, and testing of activities designed to create new curricula or to change existing ones.
B   Development [67]
R   ↓ Curriculum [67]
     Educational Program Planning [73]
     ↓ Program Development [91]

Cursive Writing [73]
PN 34   **SC** 12830
UF Writing (Cursive)
B   Handwriting [67]
R   Orthography [73]

Cushings Syndrome [73]
PN 49   **SC** 12840
B   Adrenal Gland Disorders [73]
     Metabolism Disorders [73]
     Syndromes [73]

Cutaneous Receptive Fields [85]
PN 22   **SC** 12845

Cutaneous Receptive Fields — (cont'd)
SN The area of skin being supplied by specific peripheral nerves and localized synaptic distribution in the CNS.
UF Dermatomes
B Receptive Fields [85]

Cutaneous Sense [67]
PN 1092   SC 12850
SN Any of the senses, such as pressure, pain, warmth, cold, and touch, whose receptors lie within or beneath the skin or in the mucous membrane.
UF Haptic Perception
B Somesthetic Perception [67]
N ↓ Tactual Perception [67]

Cutting Scores [85]
PN 49   SC 12855
SN Points at which a continuum of scores may be divided into groups for such purposes as pass/fail decisions or test interpretations.
UF Critical Scores
B Scoring (Testing) [73]
Test Scores [67]
R Score Equating [85]
Test Interpretation [85]

Cybernetics [67]
PN 338   SC 12860
SN Study of control and communication between humans, machines, animals, and organizations and the parallels between information processing machines and human or animal intellectual or brain function.
R ↓ Artificial Intelligence [82]
Communication Theory [73]
↓ Computers [67]
Expert Systems [91]
Man Machine Systems [73]
Robotics [85]

Cyclic Adenosine Monophosphate [78]
PN 156   SC 12875
B Nucleotides [78]
R Guanosine [85]

Cycloheximide [73]
PN 142   SC 12880
B Antibiotics [73]

Cyclothymic Disorder
Use Cyclothymic Personality

Cyclothymic Personality [73]
PN 78   SC 12890
SN Affective disorder characterized by alternating and recurring periods of depression and elation, similar to manic depressive disorder but of a less severe nature.
UF Cyclothymic Disorder
B Manic Depression [73]
R Hypomania [73]

Cynicism [73]
PN 63   SC 12900
B Personality Traits [67]
R Negativism [73]
Pessimism [73]

Cyprus [91]
PN 1   SC 12905
R Middle East [78]

Cysteine [73]
PN 6   SC 12910
B Amino Acids [73]

Cystic Fibrosis [85]
PN 123   SC 12915
B Digestive System Disorders [73]
Lung Disorders [73]
Metabolism Disorders [73]
R ↓ Congenital Disorders [73]

Cytochrome Oxidase [73]
PN 19   SC 12920
B Oxidases [73]

Cytology [73]
PN 48   SC 12930
R ↓ Cells (Biology) [73]

Cytoplasm [73]
PN 14   SC 12940
R ↓ Cells (Biology) [73]

Czechoslovakia [73]
PN 355   SC 12950
B Europe [73]

Daily Activities [94]
PN 0   SC 12955
SN Daily patterns of behavior that are not reflective of functional ability.
R Activities of Daily Living [91]
Activity Level [82]
Hobbies [73]
↓ Interests [67]
Leisure Time [73]
Lifestyle [78]
↓ Recreation [67]
Self Care Skills [78]

Daily Biological Rhythms (Animal)
Use Animal Circadian Rhythms

Dance [73]
PN 176   SC 12970
UF Ballet
B Arts [73]
Recreation [67]
R Dance Therapy [73]

Dance Therapy [73]
PN 169   SC 12980
B Creative Arts Therapy [94]
R Dance [73]
Recreation Therapy [73]

Dangerousness [88]
PN 253   SC 12985
R Patient Violence [94]
↓ Violence [73]

Dark Adaptation [73]
PN 302   SC 12990
UF Adaptation (Dark)
B Sensory Adaptation [67]
Visual Perception [67]
R Light Adaptation [82]
↓ Perceptual Measures [73]
↓ Visual Thresholds [73]

Darwinism [73]
PN 120   SC 13000
SN Biological theory of evolution formulated by C. Darwin, proposing natural selection as the operating principle of organic change.
B Theories [67]
R Theory of Evolution [67]

Data Collection [82]
PN 691   SC 13005

Data Collection — (cont'd)
SN Systematic accumulation, generation, or assembly of information. Compare EXPERIMENTAL METHODS.
B Methodology [67]
R ↓ Data Processing [67]
Information [67]
Medical Records Keeping [78]
↓ Sampling (Experimental) [73]
Statistical Data [82]
↓ Statistical Measurement [73]
↓ Surveys [67]

Data Processing [67]
PN 212   SC 13020
N Word Processing [91]
R ↓ Automated Information Processing [73]
Computer Programing [94]
Computer Programing Languages [73]
↓ Computer Software [67]
↓ Computers [67]
Data Collection [82]
Expert Systems [91]
Information [67]
Information Systems [91]
Medical Records Keeping [78]

Databases [91]
PN 72   SC 13024
SN Collection of computerized data stored in a computer or on magnetic tape or disks from which information can be accessed and retrieved.
UF Computerized Databases
Online Databases
R ↓ Automated Information Retrieval [73]
Automated Information Storage [73]
↓ Computer Applications [73]
Computer Searching [91]
↓ Computer Software [67]
↓ Computers [67]
Expert Systems [91]
Information [67]
Information Exchange [73]
Information Services [88]
Information Systems [91]
Man Machine Systems [73]

Date Rape
Use Acquaintance Rape

Dating (Social)
Use Social Dating

Daughters [73]
PN 809   SC 13040
B Family Members [73]
Human Females [73]
Offspring [88]

Day Camps (Recreation)
Use Summer Camps (Recreation)

Day Care (Child)
Use Child Day Care

Day Care (Treatment)
Use Partial Hospitalization

Day Care Centers [73]
PN 395   SC 13070
SN Facilities for day care of individuals of any age.
R Child Care Workers [78]
Child Day Care [73]
↓ Community Facilities [73]
Community Mental Health Centers [73]

Day Hospital
Use Partial Hospitalization

Daydreaming [73]
PN 214　　　　　SC 13080
　R　Fantasy (Defense Mechanism) [67]

DDT (Insecticide) [73]
PN 4　　　　　SC 13090
　B　Insecticides [73]

Deaf [67]
PN 3466　　　　　SC 13100
SN Profoundly or severely hearing impaired.
Consider also PARTIALLY HEARING IMPAIRED
for severely hearing impaired.
　B　Aurally Handicapped [73]
　N　Deaf Blind [91]
　R　Cochlear Implants [94]
　　　Hearing Disorders [82]
　　　Lipreading [73]
　　　Partially Hearing Impaired [73]

Deaf Blind [91]
PN 19　　　　　SC 13103
　B　Blind [67]
　　　Deaf [67]
　　　Multiply Handicapped [73]
　R　↓ Congenital Disorders [73]
　　　Developmental Disabilities [82]

Deanol [82]
PN 3　　　　　SC 13105
SN Probable precursor of acetylcholine. May be
effective in the treatment of learning or behavior
problems, and learning and/or hyperkinetic dis-
orders.
　UF　Dimethylaminoethanol
　B　Antidepressant Drugs [71]
　R　↓ Amines [73]

Death and Dying [67]
PN 3573　　　　　SC 13110
　UF　Dying
　　　Mortality
　N　Euthanasia [73]
　R　Advance Directives [94]
　　　Death Anxiety [78]
　　　Death Attitudes [73]
　　　Death Education [82]
　　　Death Rites [73]
　　　Grief [73]
　　　Mortality Rate [73]
　　　Near Death Experiences [85]
　　　Palliative Care [91]
　　　Psychological Autopsy [88]
　　　Sudden Infant Death [82]
　　　Suicide [67]
　　　Terminal Cancer [73]
　　　Terminally Ill Patients [73]
　　　Treatment Withholding [88]

Death Anxiety [78]
PN 619　　　　　SC 13115
　B　Anxiety Neurosis [73]
　R　↓ Death and Dying [67]
　　　Death Attitudes [73]

Death Attitudes [73]
PN 1183　　　　　SC 13120
　B　Attitudes [67]
　R　↓ Death and Dying [67]
　　　Death Anxiety [78]
　　　Euthanasia [73]
　　　↓ Religious Beliefs [73]

Death Education [82]
PN 185　　　　　SC 13124

Death Education — (cont'd)
SN Education in the process of death and dying.
Applies to patients or students of any age includ-
ing helping professionals.
　UF　Thanatology
　B　Education [67]
　R　↓ Death and Dying [67]
　　　↓ Treatment [67]

Death Instinct [88]
PN 77　　　　　SC 13127
　UF　Thanatos
　B　Psychoanalytic Personality Factors [73]
　R　Unconscious (Personality Factor) [67]

Death Penalty
Use Capital Punishment

Death Rate
Use Mortality Rate

Death Rites [73]
PN 77　　　　　SC 13150
　UF　Funerals
　B　Rites of Passage [73]
　R　↓ Death and Dying [67]

Debriefing (Experimental) [91]
PN 8　　　　　SC 13154
SN At the conclusion of an experiment, the pro-
cess that removes any deception and discloses
the facts to subjects participating in the research
by giving full details of the research purpose and
procedures.
　UF　Disclosure (Experimental)
　R　↓ Experimental Design [67]
　　　Experimental Ethics [78]
　　　↓ Experimental Subjects [85]
　　　↓ Experimentation [67]
　　　Informed Consent [85]

Decarboxylase Inhibitors [82]
PN 40　　　　　SC 13157
　B　Enzyme Inhibitors [85]
　N　Carbidopa [88]
　R　↓ Antitremor Drugs [73]
　　　↓ Catecholamines [73]
　　　↓ Dopamine Antagonists [82]
　　　↓ Enzymes [73]
　　　↓ Serotonin Antagonists [73]

Decarboxylases [73]
PN 51　　　　　SC 13160
　B　Enzymes [73]

Decentralization [78]
PN 30　　　　　SC 13166
SN Process of distributing or allocating admin-
istrative control over organizational functions to
authorities that are more local.
　R　Educational Administration [67]
　　　Hospital Administration [78]
　　　↓ Organizational Change [73]
　　　Organizational Development [73]
　　　Organizational Objectives [73]
　　　Organizational Structure [67]

Deception [67]
PN 1099　　　　　SC 13170
　UF　Lying
　N　Cheating [73]
　　　Confabulation [73]
　　　Faking [73]
　　　Fraud [94]
　　　Malingering [73]
　R　Dishonesty [73]

Decerebration [73]
PN 87　　　　　SC 13180
SN Elimination of cerebral functioning by tran-
secting the brain stem or by cutting off the cere-
bral blood supply.
　B　Neurosurgery [73]
　R　↓ Brain Lesions [67]

Decision Making [67]
PN 6821　　　　　SC 13190
SN Cognitive process involving evaluation of the
incentives, goals, and outcomes of alternative ac-
tions.
　B　Cognitive Processes [67]
　N　Choice Behavior [67]
　　　↓ Group Decision Making [78]
　　　Management Decision Making [73]
　R　Expert Systems [91]
　　　↓ Problem Solving [67]
　　　Risk Analysis [91]
　　　Uncertainty [91]
　　　Volition [88]

Decoding
Use Human Information Storage

Decompression Effects [73]
PN 23　　　　　SC 13200
　R　Acceleration Effects [73]
　　　↓ Gravitational Effects [67]
　　　Physiological Stress [67]
　　　Spaceflight [67]
　　　Underwater Effects [73]

Decortication (Brain) [73]
PN 110　　　　　SC 13210
SN Functional deactivation or physical removal
of all or portions of the cortical substance of the
brain. Primarily used for experimental contexts.
　B　Neurosurgery [73]
　R　↓ Brain Lesions [67]

Deductive Reasoning
Use Inductive Deductive Reasoning

Deer [73]
PN 125　　　　　SC 13230
　B　Mammals [73]

Defecation [67]
PN 171　　　　　SC 13240
　B　Excretion [67]

Defendants [85]
PN 210　　　　　SC 13245
SN Persons who are being sued or prosecuted
in a court of law.
　R　Court Referrals [94]
　　　Criminal Responsibility [91]
　　　↓ Criminals [67]
　　　↓ Law (Government) [73]

Defense Mechanisms [67]
PN 1936　　　　　SC 13250
SN Any unconscious intrapsychic strategies that
serve to provide relief from emotional conflict and
frustration and from unreasonable or undesirable
thoughts which lead to anxiety.
　B　Personality Processes [67]
　N　Compensation (Defense Mechanism) [73]
　　　Denial [73]
　　　Displacement (Defense Mechanism) [73]
　　　Fantasy (Defense Mechanism) [67]
　　　Grandiosity [94]
　　　Identification (Defense Mechanism) [73]
　　　Intellectualization [73]
　　　Introjection [73]
　　　Isolation (Defense Mechanism) [73]

Defense Mechanisms — (cont'd)
  N   Projection (Defense Mechanism) [67]
      Projective Identification [94]
      Rationalization [73]
      Reaction Formation [73]
      Regression (Defense Mechanism) [67]
      Repression (Defense Mechanism) [67]
      Sublimation [73]
      Suppression (Defense Mechanism) [73]
      Withdrawal (Defense Mechanism) [73]
  R   ↓ Conversion Neurosis [73]
      ↓ Mental Disorders [67]
      ↓ Personality Disorders [67]

Defensive Behavior (Animal)
  Use Animal Defensive Behavior

Defensiveness [67]
PN 336   SC 13260
  B   Personality Traits [67]

Deformity
  Use Physical Disfigurement

Degrees (Educational)
  Use Educational Degrees

Dehydration [88]
PN 24   SC 13285
SN State of excessively reduced body water or water deficit.
  R   Homeostasis [73]
      Water Deprivation [67]
      Water Intake [67]

Dehydrogenases [73]
PN 59   SC 13290
  B   Enzymes [73]
  N   Alcohol Dehydrogenases [73]
      Lactate Dehydrogenase [73]

Deinstitutionalization [82]
PN 899   SC 13293
SN Programs emphasizing out-of-hospital treatment and community residence of clients, usually chronic psychiatric or handicapped patients, including those who may never have been hospitalized or who may or may not have experienced normal community life.
  B   Mental Health Programs [73]
  R   Community Mental Health [73]
      Community Mental Health Services [78]
      Discharge Planning [94]
      Habilitation [91]
      Homeless [88]
      ↓ Institutional Release [78]
      ↓ Mainstreaming [91]
      Partial Hospitalization [85]
      ↓ Rehabilitation [67]

Deja Vu
  Use Consciousness States

Delay of Gratification [78]
PN 181   SC 13297
SN Voluntary postponement of need satisfaction or fulfillment of desires.
  R   ↓ Motivation [67]
      ↓ Reinforcement [67]
      Reinforcement Delay [85]
      ↓ Rewards [67]

Delayed Alternation [94]
PN 0   SC 13298
SN Alternation of rewards, usually in maze learning, with a delay between successive trials, forcing experimental subject to also alternate responses in order to receive the reward.

Delayed Alternation — (cont'd)
  B   Operant Conditioning [67]
  R   ↓ Learning [67]
      Reinforcement Delay [85]
      Response Variability [73]
      ↓ Rewards [67]
      Spontaneous Alternation [82]

Delayed Auditory Feedback [73]
PN 103   SC 13300
  B   Auditory Feedback [73]
      Delayed Feedback [73]

Delayed Development [73]
PN 1191   SC 13310
SN Delays in any or all areas including cognitive, social, language, sensory, and emotional development.
  B   Development [67]
  N   Failure to Thrive [88]
      Language Delay [88]
      Retarded Speech Development [73]
  R   ↓ Developmental Age Groups [73]
      Developmental Disabilities [82]
      ↓ Human Development [67]
      ↓ Physical Development [73]
      ↓ Psychogenesis [73]

Delayed Feedback [73]
PN 110   SC 13320
  B   Feedback [67]
      Perceptual Stimulation [73]
  N   Delayed Auditory Feedback [73]

Delayed Parenthood [85]
PN 24   SC 13325
SN Voluntary decision to postpone parenthood, usually for reasons involving personal development or career interests.
  R   Childlessness [82]
      ↓ Family Planning [73]
      Family Planning Attitudes [73]
      Parental Role [73]

Delayed Reinforcement
  Use Reinforcement Delay

Delayed Speech
  Use Retarded Speech Development

Deletion (Chromosome) [73]
PN 2   SC 13340
  B   Chromosome Disorders [73]

Delinquency (Juvenile)
  Use Juvenile Delinquency

Delirium [73]
PN 379   SC 13360
  B   Consciousness Disturbances [73]
      Symptoms [67]
  R   Hyperthermia [73]

Delirium Tremens [73]
PN 95   SC 13370
SN Acute alcoholic, psychotic condition characterized by intense tremors, anxiety, hallucinations, and delusions.
  B   Alcoholic Hallucinosis [73]
      Syndromes [73]

Delta Rhythm [73]
PN 55   SC 13380
SN Electrically measured impulses or waves of high amplitude and low frequency (1-3 cycles per second) observable in the electroencephalogram during sleep stages 3 and 4 (moderate to deep sleep).

Delta Rhythm — (cont'd)
  B   Electrical Activity [67]
      Electroencephalography [67]

Delusions [67]
PN 1020   SC 13390
SN False personal beliefs held contrary to reality, despite contradictory evidence and common sense.
  B   Thought Disturbances [73]
  R   Capgras Syndrome [85]
      Grandiosity [94]

Dementia [85]
PN 2095   SC 13395
  B   Organic Brain Syndromes [73]
  N   Multi Infarct Dementia [91]
      ↓ Presenile Dementia [73]
      ↓ Senile Dementia [73]
  R   Pseudodementia [85]

Dementia (Multi Infarct)
  Use Multi Infarct Dementia

Dementia (Presenile)
  Use Presenile Dementia

Dementia (Senile)
  Use Senile Dementia

Dementia Paralytica
  Use General Paresis

Dementia Praecox
  Use Schizophrenia

Democracy [73]
PN 88   SC 13440
  B   Political Economic Systems [73]
  R   ↓ Civil Rights [78]

Democratic Party
  Use Political Parties

Demographic Characteristics [67]
PN 9036   SC 13460
  UF Population Characteristics
  R   Biographical Data [78]
      ↓ Population [73]
      Psychosocial Factors [88]

Demonstrations (Social)
  Use Social Demonstrations

Dendrites [73]
PN 129   SC 13490
  B   Neurons [73]

Denial [73]
PN 484   SC 13500
SN Exclusion from conscious awareness of unpleasant realities, which would produce anxiety if acknowledged.
  B   Defense Mechanisms [67]
  R   Anosognosia [94]

Denmark [73]
PN 433   SC 13510
  B   Scandinavia [78]

Density (Social)
  Use Social Density

Dental Education [73]
PN 50   SC 13520
  B   Graduate Education [73]

Dental Students [73]
PN 92   SC 13530
  B Students [67]
  R Graduate Students [67]

Dental Surgery [73]
PN 52   SC 13540
  B Dental Treatment [73]
      Surgery [71]

Dental Treatment [73]
PN 417   SC 13550
  B Physical Treatment Methods [73]
  N Dental Surgery [73]

Dentist Patient Interaction
  Use Therapeutic Processes

Dentistry [73]
PN 73   SC 13560
  B Medical Sciences [67]

Dentists [73]
PN 109   SC 13570
  B Medical Personnel [67]

Deoxycorticosterone [73]
PN 21   SC 13580
  B Adrenal Cortex Hormones [73]
      Corticosteroids [73]

Deoxyglucose [91]
PN 11   SC 13585
  B Carbohydrates [73]

Deoxyribonucleic Acid [73]
PN 133   SC 13590
  UF DNA (Deoxyribonucleic Acid)
  B Nucleic Acids [73]

Dependency (Drug)
  Use Drug Dependency

Dependency (Personality) [67]
PN 1588   SC 13620
SN Lack of self-reliance, reflecting need for security, love, and protection from others.
  B Personality Traits [67]
  R Attachment Behavior [85]
      Dependent Personality [94]

Dependent Personality [94]
PN 0   SC 13625
SN Personality disorder characterized by pervasive patterns of dependent, passive, and submissive behavior.
  B Personality Disorders [67]
  R Asthenic Personality [73]
      Dependency (Personality) [67]

Dependent Variables [73]
PN 65   SC 13630
SN Statistical or experimental parameters whose values change as a consequence of changes in one or more other independent variables.
  B Statistical Variables [73]

Depersonalization [73]
PN 153   SC 13640
SN State in which an individual perceives or experiences a sensation of unreality concerning himself or his environment; seen in disorders such as schizophrenia, affective disorders, organic mental disorders, and personality disorders.

Depersonalization — (cont'd)
  B Symptoms [67]
  R Alienation [71]
    ↓ Dissociative Patterns [73]

Depression (Emotion) [67]
PN 13022   SC 13650
SN Mild depression in normal populations. Prior to 1988, also used for major depression in clinical populations.
  B Emotional States [73]
  R ↓ Major Depression [88]
      Sadness [73]

Depressive Reaction (Neurotic)
  Use Neurotic Depressive Reaction

Deprivation [67]
PN 1019   SC 13680
SN Removal or denial of something needed or desired.
  N Cultural Deprivation [73]
      Food Deprivation [67]
      REM Dream Deprivation [73]
      Sleep Deprivation [67]
    ↓ Stimulus Deprivation [73]
      Water Deprivation [67]
  R Environmental Stress [73]
    ↓ Motivation [67]
      Physiological Stress [67]
      Psychological Stress [73]
    ↓ Stress [67]

Depth Perception [67]
PN 1265   SC 13690
  B Spatial Perception [67]
  N Stereoscopic Vision [73]
  R Eye Convergence [82]
      Linear Perspective [82]
      Ocular Accommodation [82]

Depth Psychology [73]
PN 80   SC 13700
SN Any of the psychological theories which study the unconscious motives of the personality.
  B Psychology [67]

Dermatitis [73]
PN 52   SC 13710
  B Skin Disorders [73]
  N Eczema [73]
      Neurodermatitis [73]
  R Allergic Skin Disorders [73]
    ↓ Infectious Disorders [73]
    ↓ Toxic Disorders [73]

Dermatomes
  Use Cutaneous Receptive Fields

Desegregation
  Use Social Integration

Desensitization (Systematic)
  Use Systematic Desensitization Therapy

Design (Experimental)
  Use Experimental Design

Design (Man Machine Systems)
  Use Man Machine Systems Design

Desipramine [73]
PN 584   SC 13760
  B Antidepressant Drugs [71]

Desirability (Social)
  Use Social Desirability

Desires
  Use Motivation

Detection (Signal)
  Use Signal Detection (Perception)

Detention (Legal)
  Use Legal Detention

Detoxification [73]
PN 410   SC 13820
  B Alcohol Rehabilitation [82]
      Drug Rehabilitation [73]
  R Alcohol Withdrawal [94]
    ↓ Drug Abstinence [94]
    ↓ Drug Therapy [67]
    ↓ Drug Withdrawal [73]
      Sobriety [88]

Developed Countries [85]
PN 84   SC 13823
  B Countries [67]

Developing Countries [85]
PN 362   SC 13825
  UF Third World Countries
      Underdeveloped Countries
  B Countries [67]

Development [67]
PN 1351   SC 13830
  UF Growth
      Ontogeny
  N Animal Development [78]
      Career Development [85]
      Curriculum Development [73]
    ↓ Delayed Development [73]
    ↓ Human Development [67]
      Organizational Development [73]
    ↓ Physical Development [73]
      Precocious Development [73]
      Professional Development [82]
    ↓ Program Development [91]
    ↓ Psychogenesis [73]
  R Age Differences [67]
      Critical Period [88]
    ↓ Developmental Age Groups [73]
    ↓ Developmental Stages [73]
      Sex Linked Developmental Differences [73]

Developmental Age Groups [73]
PN 164   SC 13840
SN Groups defined by a chronological age span, and characterized by certain physical, behavioral, psychological, and social attributes. Use AGE DIFFERENCES for age comparisons within or between groups.
  N ↓ Adolescents [67]
    ↓ Adults [67]
    ↓ Children [67]
  R Adolescent Development [73]
      Adult Development [78]
      Age Differences [67]
    ↓ Aging [91]
    ↓ Childhood Development [67]
    ↓ Delayed Development [73]
    ↓ Development [67]
    ↓ Developmental Stages [73]
      Emotional Development [73]
    ↓ Human Development [67]
      Mental Age [73]
    ↓ Motor Development [73]
    ↓ Physical Development [73]
      Precocious Development [73]
    ↓ Psychogenesis [73]

Developmental Differences
SN Term discontinued in 1982. Use DEVELOP-MENTAL DIFFERENCES or AGE DIFFERENCES to access references from 73–81.
Use Age Differences

Developmental Disabilities [82]
PN 1371   **SC** 13853
SN As encompassed in federal legislation for educational assistance to handicapped children, includes disabilities originating before age 18 that constitute substantial barriers to normal functioning. Use a more specific term if possible.
R ↓ Autism [67]
  ↓ Communication Disorders [82]
  ↓ Congenital Disorders [73]
  Deaf Blind [91]
  ↓ Delayed Development [73]
  ↓ Genetic Disorders [73]
  ↓ Handicapped [67]
  ↓ Human Development [67]
  ↓ Learning Disorders [67]
  ↓ Mental Retardation [67]
  ↓ Nervous System Disorders [67]

Developmental Measures [94]
PN 0   **SC** 13857
N Bayley Scales of Infant Development [94]

Developmental Psychology [73]
PN 663   **SC** 13860
B Psychology [67]
N Adolescent Psychology [73]
  Child Psychology [67]
  Gerontology [67]
R ↓ Human Development [67]

Developmental Stages [73]
PN 1294   **SC** 13870
SN Phases in an individual's development characterized by certain physical, behavioral, mental, or social attributes, e.g., the latency stage of psychosexual development or the sensorimotor intelligence stage of cognitive development.
N Menopause [73]
  ↓ Prenatal Developmental Stages [73]
  Puberty [73]
R Adolescent Development [73]
  Adult Development [78]
  ↓ Aging [91]
  ↓ Childhood Development [67]
  ↓ Development [67]
  ↓ Developmental Age Groups [73]
  Erikson (Erik) [91]
  ↓ Human Development [67]
  Object Permanence [85]
  ↓ Perceptual Development [73]
  ↓ Physical Development [73]
  Piaget (Jean) [67]
  ↓ Psychogenesis [73]

Deviant Behavior
Use Antisocial Behavior

Deviation IQ
Use Standard Scores

Deviations (Sexual)
Use Sexual Deviations

Devices (Experimental)
Use Apparatus

Dexamethasone [85]
PN 580   **SC** 13905
SN A synthetic analogue of cortisol.
B Glucocorticoids [82]
R Dexamethasone Suppression Test [88]

Dexamethasone Suppression Test [88]
PN 500   **SC** 13907
SN Laboratory analysis of hypersecretion of cortisol and the body's failure to suppress cortisol after the administration of dexamethasone. Used primarily for diagnosis of major depressive disorders.
B Medical Diagnosis [73]
R Dexamethasone [85]

Dexamphetamine
Use Dextroamphetamine

Dexedrine
Use Dextroamphetamine

Dexterity (Physical)
Use Physical Dexterity

Dextroamphetamine [73]
PN 1423   **SC** 13940
UF Amphetamine (d-)
  Dexamphetamine
  Dexedrine
B Adrenergic Drugs [73]
  Amphetamine [67]
  Appetite Depressing Drugs [73]
  CNS Stimulating Drugs [73]
  Sympathomimetic Amines [73]

Diabetes [73]
PN 801   **SC** 13950
B Endocrine Disorders [73]
  Metabolism Disorders [73]
N Diabetes Insipidus [73]
  Diabetes Mellitus [73]

Diabetes Insipidus [73]
PN 78   **SC** 13960
B Diabetes [73]
R ↓ Genetic Disorders [73]

Diabetes Mellitus [73]
PN 455   **SC** 13970
B Diabetes [73]

Diacetylmorphine
Use Heroin

Diagnosis [67]
PN 4305   **SC** 13990
N Computer Assisted Diagnosis [73]
  Differential Diagnosis [67]
  Educational Diagnosis [78]
  Galvanic Skin Response [67]
  ↓ Medical Diagnosis [73]
  ↓ Psychodiagnosis [67]
R Autopsy [73]
  Comorbidity [91]
  Diagnosis Related Groups [88]
  Dual Diagnosis [91]
  General Health Questionnaire [91]
  Intake Interview [94]
  Labeling [78]
  ↓ Mental Disorders [67]
  ↓ Neuropsychological Assessment [82]
  Patient History [73]
  Prognosis [73]
  Research Diagnostic Criteria [94]
  ↓ Screening [82]
  Severity (Disorders) [82]
  Symptom Checklists [91]

Diagnosis Related Groups [88]
PN 50   **SC** 13985
UF DRGs
R Cost Containment [91]

Diagnosis Related Groups — (cont'd)
R ↓ Diagnosis [67]
  Health Care Costs [94]
  ↓ Health Insurance [73]
  ↓ Professional Fees [78]

Diagnostic and Statistical Manual [94]
PN 0   **SC** 13988
SN Used when the current Diagnostic and Statistical Manual or its revisions is the primary focus of the reference. Use PSYCHODIAGNOSTIC TYPOLOGIES to access references prior to 1994. Not used for specific psychodiagnostic categories.
UF DSM
B Psychodiagnostic Typologies [67]
R ↓ Mental Disorders [67]
  ↓ Psychodiagnosis [67]
  Research Diagnostic Criteria [94]

Diagnostic Interview Schedule [91]
PN 21   **SC** 13900
B Psychodiagnostic Interview [73]
R ↓ Psychodiagnostic Typologies [67]
  ↓ Screening [82]

Dialect [73]
PN 239   **SC** 14000
SN A variety of language characteristic of a geographical region or ethnic, occupational, socioeconomic, or other group.
B Language [67]
N Nonstandard English [73]
R Ethnolinguistics [73]

Dialectics [73]
PN 188   **SC** 14010
SN Intellectual investigation through deductive reasoning and juxtaposition of opposing or contradictory ideas.
R ↓ Reasoning [67]

Dialysis [73]
PN 146   **SC** 14020
B Physical Treatment Methods [73]
N Hemodialysis [73]

Diaphragm (Anatomy) [73]
PN 13   **SC** 14030
B Muscles [67]
  Respiratory System [73]
R Thorax [73]

Diaphragms (Birth Control) [73]
PN 9   **SC** 14040
B Contraceptive Devices [73]

Diarrhea [73]
PN 41   **SC** 14050
B Colon Disorders [73]
R Fecal Incontinence [73]

Diastolic Pressure [73]
PN 161   **SC** 14060
B Blood Pressure [67]

Diazepam [73]
PN 1397   **SC** 14070
UF Valium
B Benzodiazepines [78]
  Minor Tranquilizers [73]
  Muscle Relaxing Drugs [73]

Dichoptic Stimulation [82]
PN 82   **SC** 14075
SN Simultaneous presentation of different stimuli to each eye independently.
B Visual Stimulation [73]

Dichotic Stimulation [82]
PN 515   SC 14077
SN Simultaneous presentation of different sounds to the two ears.
B   Auditory Stimulation [67]

Dictionary [73]
PN 10   SC 14090
SN Mandatory term used as a document type identifier.
R   Glossary [73]

Dieldrin [73]
PN 7   SC 14100
B   Insecticides [73]

Diencephalon [73]
PN 212   SC 14110
B   Forebrain [85]
N   ↓ Hypothalamus [67]
      Optic Chiasm [73]
      ↓ Thalamus [67]

Dietary Restraint [94]
PN 0   SC 14112
R   ↓ Appetite [73]
      Diets [78]
      ↓ Eating [67]
      ↓ Food Intake [67]

Diets [78]
PN 1800   SC 14114
SN Food and drink regularly consumed or prescribed for a special reason. Used for human or animal populations.
R   Dietary Restraint [94]
      ↓ Drinking Behavior [78]
      ↓ Eating [67]
      Food [78]
      Food Additives [78]
      Food Allergies [73]
      Food Deprivation [67]
      Food Preferences [73]
      Health Behavior [82]
      Nutrition [73]
      ↓ Nutritional Deficiencies [73]
      Obesity [73]
      ↓ Underweight [73]
      Weight Control [85]

Differential Aptitude Tests [73]
PN 31   SC 14150
B   Aptitude Measures [67]

Differential Diagnosis [67]
PN 3359   SC 14160
SN Distinguishing between physical and/or mental disorders of similar character by comparison of symptoms.
B   Diagnosis [67]
R   Comorbidity [91]
      Dual Diagnosis [91]
      Educational Diagnosis [78]
      ↓ Medical Diagnosis [73]
      ↓ Psychodiagnosis [67]

Differential Limen
Use Thresholds

Differential Personality Inventory [73]
PN 8   SC 14180
B   Nonprojective Personality Measures [73]

Differential Reinforcement [73]
PN 692   SC 14190

Differential Reinforcement — (cont'd)
SN Selective reinforcement of one response in a defined category (response class) of responses to the exclusion of any other members (responses) of that category. Has application in treatment as well as in experimental contexts.
B   Reinforcement [67]
R   ↓ Discrimination Learning [82]
      Omission Training [85]

Difficulty Level (Test) [73]
PN 233   SC 14200
UF   Test Difficulty
B   Test Construction [73]
      Testing [67]
R   Item Response Theory [85]

Digestion [73]
PN 65   SC 14210
B   Physiology [67]
R   ↓ Digestive System [67]
      Salivation [73]
      Swallowing [88]

Digestive System [67]
PN 364   SC 14220
B   Anatomical Systems [73]
N   Esophagus [73]
      ↓ Gastrointestinal System [73]
      Liver [73]
      Mouth (Anatomy) [67]
      Pharynx [73]
      Teeth (Anatomy) [73]
      ↓ Tongue [73]
R   Digestion [73]
      ↓ Digestive System Disorders [73]
      Salivary Glands [73]

Digestive System Disorders [73]
PN 67   SC 14230
B   Disorders [67]
N   Cystic Fibrosis [85]
      ↓ Gastrointestinal Disorders [73]
      Jaundice [73]
      ↓ Liver Disorders [73]
R   ↓ Digestive System [67]
      ↓ Infectious Disorders [73]
      ↓ Neoplasms [67]
      ↓ Symptoms [67]
      ↓ Toxic Disorders [73]

Digit Span Testing [73]
PN 180   SC 14240
SN Test of immediate recall involving presentation of a random series of numerals which the subject repeats after the series has been presented.
B   Measurement [67]

Digital Computers [73]
PN 145   SC 14250
SN Electronic or electromechanical machines that operate directly on binary digits when executing programs and manipulating data (e.g., calculators).
UF   Calculators
B   Computers [67]

Digits (Mathematics)
Use Numbers (Numerals)

Dihydroergotamine [73]
PN 14   SC 14270
B   Adrenergic Blocking Drugs [73]
      Analgesic Drugs [73]
      Ergot Derivatives [73]
      Vasoconstrictor Drugs [73]

Dihydroxyphenylacetic Acid [91]
PN 44   SC 14273
UF   DOPAC
B   Acids [73]
      Dopamine Metabolites [82]

Dihydroxytryptamine [91]
PN 16   SC 14275
B   Serotonin Antagonists [73]

Dilantin
Use Diphenylhydantoin

Dilation (Pupil)
Use Pupil Dilation

Dimethylaminoethanol
Use Deanol

Diphenhydramine [73]
PN 32   SC 14310
UF   Benadryl
B   Amines [73]
      Antihistaminic Drugs [73]
      Antitremor Drugs [73]

Diphenylhydantoin [73]
PN 145   SC 14320
UF   Dilantin
      Diphenylhydantoin Sodium
      Phenytoin
B   Anticonvulsive Drugs [73]

Diphenylhydantoin Sodium
Use Diphenylhydantoin

Diptera [73]
PN 172   SC 14350
UF   Flies
B   Insects [67]
N   Drosophila [73]
R   Larvae [73]

Directed Discussion Method [73]
PN 92   SC 14360
B   Teaching Methods [67]
R   Lecture Method [73]

Directed Reverie Therapy [78]
PN 195   SC 14364
SN Waking dream technique in psychotherapy used especially in brief therapy and group therapy.
UF   Guided Daydreams
      Guided Fantasy
B   Psychotherapeutic Techniques [67]
      Psychotherapy [67]

Disability Evaluation [88]
PN 56   SC 14367
SN Evaluation of one's ability to work in order to determine the need for insurance or health benefits.
R   ↓ Employee Benefits [73]
      ↓ Insurance [73]
      Social Security [88]

Disability Laws [94]
PN 0   SC 57410
SN Rules declared by federal or state governments and enacted by legislative bodies that affect populations with mental or physical disabilities or disorders. Used for the laws themselves, or the interpretation or application of the laws.
B   Laws [67]
R   Civil Law [94]

Disability Laws — (cont'd)
R ↓ Civil Rights [78]
  ↓ Handicapped [67]

Disability Management [91]
PN 6   SC 14368
SN Process of returning an impaired or disabled worker to the workplace. Includes evaluation, assessment, early intervention, and rehabilitation.
B   Management [67]
R   Employee Assistance Programs [85]
  ↓ Prevention [73]
  ↓ Rehabilitation [67]
    Vocational Evaluation [91]
  ↓ Vocational Rehabilitation [67]

Disadvantaged [67]
PN 2726   SC 14370
SN Individuals deprived of equal access to society's resources, especially as regards education, culture, and employment.
UF Economically Disadvantaged
    Socially Disadvantaged
    Underprivileged
R   Cultural Deprivation [73]
    Homeless [88]
    Poverty [73]
  ↓ Social Class [67]
  ↓ Social Deprivation [73]
  ↓ Socioeconomic Status [67]

Disappointment [73]
PN 18   SC 14380
B   Emotional States [73]
R   Dissatisfaction [73]

Disasters [73]
PN 315   SC 14390
N   Natural Disasters [73]
R ↓ Accidents [67]
  ↓ Crises [71]
  ↓ Stress [67]

Discharge Planning [94]
PN 0   SC 14395
B   Case Management [91]
R   Aftercare [73]
    Deinstitutionalization [82]
  ↓ Facility Discharge [88]
  ↓ Hospital Discharge [73]
  ↓ Institutional Release [78]
    Posttreatment Followup [73]
    Psychiatric Hospital Discharge [78]
    Treatment Termination [82]

Discipline (Child)
Use Child Discipline

Discipline (Classroom)
Use Classroom Discipline

Disclosure (Experimental)
Use Debriefing (Experimental)

Discovery Teaching Method [73]
PN 112   SC 14430
SN Unstructured or guided instruction which encourages independent exploration or discovery.
B   Teaching Methods [67]
R   Montessori Method [73]
    Nondirected Discussion Method [73]
    Open Classroom Method [73]

Discrimination [67]
PN 2428   SC 14450

Discrimination — (cont'd)
SN Conceptually broad array term referring to the general process of differentiation between qualities, entities, or people. Use a more specific term if possible.
N   Cognitive Discrimination [73]
    Drug Discrimination [85]
  ↓ Perceptual Discrimination [73]
  ↓ Social Discrimination [82]
    Stimulus Discrimination [73]
R ↓ Discrimination Learning [82]
  ↓ Perception [67]

Discrimination (Cognitive)
Use Cognitive Discrimination

Discrimination Learning [82]
PN 1777   SC 14445
SN Learning paradigm in which responses to one stimulus (S+) are reinforced while responses to another stimulus (S-) are either not reinforced or are punished. Also, the learned discriminative responses themselves.
UF Discriminative Learning
B   Learning [67]
    Operant Conditioning [67]
N   Drug Discrimination [85]
    Matching to Sample [94]
    Nonreversal Shift Learning [73]
    Reversal Shift Learning [67]
R ↓ Concept Formation [67]
    Differential Reinforcement [73]
  ↓ Discrimination [67]
    Extinction (Learning) [67]
    Fading (Conditioning) [82]
  ↓ Generalization (Learning) [82]
    Kinship Recognition [88]
    Stimulus Control [67]
    Stimulus Discrimination [73]

Discriminative Learning
Use Discrimination Learning

Discriminative Stimulus
Use Conditioned Stimulus

Discussion (Group)
Use Group Discussion

Disease Course [91]
PN 463   SC 14470
SN Stages or progression of physical or mental disorders. Compare PROGNOSIS.
UF Disorder Course
R ↓ Disorders [67]
  ↓ Mental Disorders [67]
    Prognosis [73]

Diseases
Use Disorders

Diseases (Venereal)
Use Venereal Diseases

Disgust [94]
PN 0   SC 14495
B   Emotional States [73]
R ↓ Aversion [67]

Dishonesty [73]
PN 51   SC 14500
B   Personality Traits [67]
R   Cheating [73]
  ↓ Deception [67]
    Fraud [94]

Dislike
Use Aversion

Disorder Course
Use Disease Course

Disorders [67]
PN 5954   SC 14520
SN Conceptually broad array term referring primarily to physical illness. Also used when particular disorders are not specified. Use a more specific term if possible. For general discussions of health impairment consider also the term HEALTH.
UF Diseases
    Illness (Physical)
    Physical Illness
N ↓ Appetite Disorders [73]
    Attention Deficit Disorder [85]
  ↓ Behavior Disorders [71]
  ↓ Blood and Lymphatic Disorders [73]
  ↓ Cardiovascular Disorders [67]
  ↓ Chronic Illness [91]
  ↓ Communication Disorders [82]
    Conduct Disorder [91]
  ↓ Congenital Disorders [73]
  ↓ Digestive System Disorders [73]
  ↓ Endocrine Disorders [73]
  ↓ Ethnospecific Disorders [73]
  ↓ Genetic Disorders [73]
  ↓ Immunologic Disorders [73]
  ↓ Infectious Disorders [73]
  ↓ Learning Disorders [67]
  ↓ Memory Disorders [73]
  ↓ Mental Disorders [67]
  ↓ Metabolism Disorders [73]
  ↓ Musculoskeletal Disorders [73]
  ↓ Neonatal Disorders [73]
  ↓ Neoplasms [67]
  ↓ Nervous System Disorders [67]
  ↓ Nutritional Deficiencies [73]
  ↓ Respiratory Tract Disorders [73]
    Rett Syndrome [94]
  ↓ Sense Organ Disorders [73]
  ↓ Sexual Function Disturbances [73]
  ↓ Skin Disorders [73]
  ↓ Sleep Disorders [73]
  ↓ Toxic Disorders [73]
  ↓ Urogenital Disorders [73]
  ↓ Vision Disorders [82]
    Work Related Illnesses [94]
R   Adaptive Behavior [91]
  ↓ Anesthesia (Feeling) [73]
    Back Pain [82]
    Chronicity (Disorders) [82]
    Comorbidity [91]
    Disease Course [91]
    Etiology [67]
    Illness Behavior [82]
  ↓ Injuries [73]
    Onset (Disorders) [73]
    Physical Disfigurement [78]
    Predisposition [73]
    Premorbidity [78]
    Prenatal Exposure [91]
    Prognosis [73]
    Recovery (Disorders) [73]
    Relapse (Disorders) [73]
  ↓ Remission (Disorders) [73]
    Research Diagnostic Criteria [94]
    Severity (Disorders) [82]
    Special Needs [94]
    Susceptibility (Disorders) [73]
  ↓ Symptoms [67]
  ↓ Syndromes [73]
  ↓ Treatment Resistant Disorders [94]

Disorientation (Place)
Use Place Disorientation

Disorientation (Time)
 Use Time Disorientation

Displacement (Defense Mechanism) [73]
 PN 40　　　　　　　　　**SC** 14550
 B　Defense Mechanisms [67]

Displays [67]
 PN 314　　　　　　　　**SC** 14560
 SN Physical arrangements of stimuli to form a
desired pattern; temporal, spatial, or otherwise.
 N　Auditory Displays [73]
　　Graphical Displays [85]
　　Tactual Displays [73]
　↓ Visual Displays [73]
 R　↓ Instrument Controls [85]

Disposition
 Use Personality

Disruptive Behavior
 Use Behavior Problems

Dissatisfaction [73]
 PN 76　　　　　　　　　**SC** 14590
 B　Emotional States [73]
 R　Disappointment [73]
　　Frustration [67]

Dissociative Neurosis [73]
 PN 37　　　　　　　　　**SC** 14600
 UF　Hysterical Neurosis (Dissociation)
 B　Neurosis [67]
 R　↓ Hysteria [67]
　　Hysterical Personality [73]

Dissociative Patterns [73]
 PN 309　　　　　　　　**SC** 14610
 SN Neurotic reactions involving repression and
alteration of normal integrative functions of iden-
tity, consciousness, or motor behavior. Aspects
of personality and memory become separate en-
tities and function independently of the rest of
the mental processes.
 B　Mental Disorders [67]
 N　↓ Amnesia [67]
　　Fugue Reaction [73]
　　Multiple Personality [73]
 R　Depersonalization [73]
　↓ Hysteria [67]
　　Hysterical Personality [73]
　↓ Personality Disorders [67]
　　Sleepwalking [73]

Dissonance (Cognitive)
 Use Cognitive Dissonance

Distance Discrimination
 Use Distance Perception

Distance Perception [73]
 PN 606　　　　　　　　**SC** 14640
 UF　Distance Discrimination
 B　Spatial Perception [67]
 N　Apparent Distance [73]
 R　Eye Convergence [82]
　　Linear Perspective [82]

Distortion (Perceptual)
 Use Perceptual Distortion

Distractibility [73]
 PN 270　　　　　　　　**SC** 14660
 B　Symptoms [67]
 R　Attention Deficit Disorder [85]
　　Distraction [78]

Distraction [78]
 PN 664　　　　　　　　**SC** 14663
 SN Process or potential cause of interruption of
attention.
 R　↓ Attention [67]
　　Attention Span [73]
　　Distractibility [73]
　　Divided Attention [73]
　　Selective Attention [73]

Distress [73]
 PN 1655　　　　　　　**SC** 14670
 SN Negative emotional state characterized by
physical and/or emotional discomfort, pain, or an-
guish. Compare STRESS.
 UF　Anguish
 B　Emotional States [73]
 R　Agitation [91]
　↓ Stress [67]
　　Suffering [73]

Distress Calls (Animal)
 Use Animal Distress Calls

Distributed Practice [73]
 PN 131　　　　　　　　**SC** 14690
 SN Practice schedule in which relatively short
periods of practice are spaced with intermittent
rest or periods of activity unrelated to the prac-
ticed task. Compare MASSED PRACTICE.
 B　Learning Schedules [67]
　　Practice [67]

Distribution (Frequency)
 Use Frequency Distribution

Distributive Justice
 Use Justice

Distrust
 Use Suspicion

Disulfiram [78]
 PN 101　　　　　　　　**SC** 14725
 UF　Antabuse
 B　Emetic Drugs [73]

Diuresis [73]
 PN 16　　　　　　　　　**SC** 14730
 B　Physical Treatment Methods [73]

Diuretics [73]
 PN 86　　　　　　　　　**SC** 14740
 B　Drugs [67]
 N　Acetazolamide [73]
　　Caffeine [73]
　　Theophylline [73]
 R　↓ Antihypertensive Drugs [73]
　　Probenecid [82]
　　Urination [67]

Diurnal Variations
 Use Human Biological Rhythms

Divergent Thinking [73]
 PN 468　　　　　　　　**SC** 14760
 SN Component of intelligence which is mani-
fested in the ability to generate a wide variety of
original ideas or solutions to a particular problem.
Compare CREATIVITY.
 B　Thinking [67]
 R　↓ Abstraction [67]
　　Creativity [67]
　↓ Inductive Deductive Reasoning [73]
　　Intelligence [67]

Divided Attention [73]
 PN 343　　　　　　　　**SC** 14765

Divided Attention — (cont'd)
 SN Simultaneous attending to two or more stim-
uli or through two or more perceptual modalities.
Compare SELECTIVE ATTENTION.
 B　Attention [67]
 R　Distraction [78]
　　Selective Attention [73]

Division of Labor [88]
 PN 92　　　　　　　　　**SC** 14767
 N　Animal Division of Labor [73]
 R　Economics [85]
　　Household Management [85]
　↓ Occupations [67]
　　Sex Roles [67]
　　Work Load [82]

Division of Labor (Animal)
 Use Animal Division of Labor

Divorce [73]
 PN 2318　　　　　　　**SC** 14780
 B　Marital Separation [73]
 R　Child Custody [82]
　　Child Support [88]
　　Divorced Persons [73]
　↓ Family [67]
　　Joint Custody [88]
　　Mediation [88]
　　Remarriage [85]

Divorced Persons [73]
 PN 510　　　　　　　　**SC** 14790
 R　Divorce [73]
　↓ Family [67]
　↓ Marital Separation [73]
　↓ Marital Status [73]
　↓ Parental Absence [73]

Dizygotic Twins
 Use Heterozygotic Twins

Dizziness
 Use Vertigo

DNA (Deoxyribonucleic Acid)
 Use Deoxyribonucleic Acid

Doctors
 Use Physicians

Dogmatism [78]
 PN 473　　　　　　　　**SC** 14830
 B　Personality Traits [67]
 R　Authoritarianism [67]
　　Openmindedness [78]

Dogs [67]
 PN 1707　　　　　　　**SC** 14840
 B　Mammals [73]

Doll Play [73]
 PN 77　　　　　　　　　**SC** 14850
 B　Recreation [67]
 R　Anatomically Detailed Dolls [91]
　　Childhood Play Behavior [78]

Dolphins [73]
 PN 68　　　　　　　　　**SC** 14860
 B　Whales [85]
 R　Porpoises [73]

Domestic Service Personnel [73]
 PN 16　　　　　　　　　**SC** 14870
 UF　Maids
 B　Service Personnel [91]
 R　↓ Nonprofessional Personnel [82]

Domestic Violence
Use Family Violence

Domestication (Animal)
Use Animal Domestication

Dominance 67
PN 677   SC 14900
SN Conceptually broad array term referring to relative positions of objects, persons, things, or processes. Use a more specific term if possible.
N Animal Dominance 73
   ↓ Cerebral Dominance 73
   Dominance Hierarchy 73
   Genetic Dominance 73
R Authoritarianism 67
   Authority 67
   Coercion 94
   Emotional Superiority 73
   Power 67

Dominance (Animal)
Use Animal Dominance

Dominance Hierarchy 73
PN 561   SC 14890
SN Social structure of a group as it relates to the relative social rank or dominance status of its members. Used for human or animal populations.
B Dominance 67
R Animal Dominance 73
   ↓ Social Behavior 67
   ↓ Social Structure 67

Domination
Use Authoritarianism

Dominican Republic 73
PN 16   SC 14920
B West Indies 73
R Hispaniola 73

DOPA 73
PN 62   SC 14940
B Amino Acids 73
R Carbidopa 88
   Dopamine 73
   Levodopa 73
   Methyldopa 73

DOPAC
Use Dihydroxyphenylacetic Acid

Dopamine 73
PN 3073   SC 14950
B Catecholamines 73
R Cardiotonic Drugs 85
   DOPA 73
   ↓ Dopamine Metabolites 82
   ↓ Heart Rate Affecting Drugs 73
   Homovanillic Acid 78
   Levodopa 73
   Methyldopa 73
   Methylphenyltetrahydropyridine 94

Dopamine Agonists 85
PN 411   SC 14951
B Drugs 67
N ↓ Amphetamine 67
   Apomorphine 73
   Morphine 73
   Quinpirole 94

Dopamine Antagonists 82
PN 471   SC 14952
B Amine Oxidase Inhibitors 73
N Sulpiride 73

Dopamine Antagonists — (cont'd)
R ↓ Catecholamines 73
   ↓ CNS Depressant Drugs 73
   ↓ Decarboxylase Inhibitors 82
   ↓ Narcotic Drugs 73
   ↓ Tranquilizing Drugs 67

Dopamine Metabolites 82
PN 154   SC 14955
SN Molecules generated from the metabolism of dopamine.
B Metabolites 73
N Dihydroxyphenylacetic Acid 91
   Homovanillic Acid 78
R Acetaldehyde 82
   Dopamine 73
   ↓ Metabolism 67

Dormitories 73
PN 356   SC 14960
UF Residence Halls
B Housing 73
   School Facilities 73

Dorsal Horns 85
PN 32   SC 14965
SN Longitudinal columns of gray matter (i.e., neuronal cell bodies) in the posterior spinal cord mainly serving sensory mechanisms.
B Spinal Cord 73
R ↓ Afferent Pathways 82
   Dorsal Roots 73

Dorsal Roots 73
PN 60   SC 14970
B Spinal Cord 73
R Dorsal Horns 85

Double Bind Interaction 73
PN 84   SC 14990
SN Simultaneous communication of conflicting messages in which the response to either message evokes rejection or disapproval.
B Interpersonal Communication 73
R Dysfunctional Family 91
   Schizophrenogenic Family 67
   Schizophrenogenic Mothers 73

Doubt 73
PN 34   SC 15000
B Emotional States 73
R Mental Confusion 73
   Suspicion 73
   Uncertainty 91

Doves 73
PN 133   SC 15010
B Birds 67

Downs Syndrome 67
PN 1414   SC 15020
UF Mongolism
B Autosome Disorders 73
   Mental Retardation 67
   Neonatal Disorders 73
   Syndromes 73
R Trainable Mentally Retarded 73
   Trisomy 21 73

Doxepin 94
PN 0   SC 15025
SN Use ANTIDEPRESSANT DRUGS or TRANQUILIZING DRUGS to access references from 73-93.
B Antidepressant Drugs 71
   Tranquilizing Drugs 67

Draftees 73
PN 45   SC 15030
SN Military personnel conscripted for service.
B Enlisted Military Personnel 73
R Army Personnel 67
   Navy Personnel 67

Drama 73
PN 531   SC 15040
B Theatre 73
R ↓ Literature 67
   Motion Pictures (Entertainment) 73
   Writers 91

Draw A Man Test
SN Prior to 1988, use Goodenough Harris Draw A Person Test.
Use Human Figures Drawing

Drawing 67
PN 1908   SC 15050
B Art 67

Dream Analysis 73
PN 762   SC 15060
UF Dream Interpretation
B Psychoanalysis 67
   Psychotherapeutic Techniques 67
R ↓ Dreaming 67
   ↓ Parapsychology 67

Dream Content 73
PN 757   SC 15070
R ↓ Dreaming 67
   Nightmares 73
   ↓ Sleep 67

Dream Interpretation
Use Dream Analysis

Dream Recall 73
PN 215   SC 15090
R ↓ Dreaming 67
   Lucid Dreaming 94

Dreaming 67
PN 1109   SC 15100
N Lucid Dreaming 94
   Nightmares 73
   REM Dreams 73
R Dream Analysis 73
   Dream Content 73
   Dream Recall 73
   ↓ Sleep 67

DRGs
Use Diagnosis Related Groups

Drinking (Alcohol)
Use Alcohol Drinking Patterns

Drinking Attitudes
Use Alcohol Drinking Attitudes

Drinking Behavior 78
PN 89   SC 15127
B Behavior 67
N ↓ Alcohol Drinking Patterns 67
   Animal Drinking Behavior 73
   Water Intake 67
R ↓ Alcoholic Beverages 73
   Beverages (Nonalcoholic) 78
   Diets 78
   Driving Under The Influence 88
   ↓ Fluid Intake 85
   Sucking 78
   Thirst 67

Drinking Behavior (Animal)
  Use Animal Drinking Behavior

Drive
  Use Motivation

Driver Education [73]
PN 136   **SC** 15150
  B   Curriculum [67]
  R   Drivers [73]

Driver Safety
  Use Highway Safety

Drivers [73]
PN 635   **SC** 15170
  R   Automobiles [73]
      Driver Education [73]
      ↓ Driving Behavior [67]
      Highway Safety [73]
      Motor Traffic Accidents [73]
      ↓ Motor Vehicles [82]

Driving Behavior [67]
PN 1569   **SC** 15180
SN Manner in which one operates a motor vehicle.
  B   Behavior [67]
  N   Driving Under The Influence [88]
  R   Drivers [73]
      Highway Safety [73]
      Motor Traffic Accidents [73]
      Pedestrian Accidents [73]
      Safety Belts [73]

Driving Under The Influence [88]
PN 372   **SC** 15185
  UF Drunk Driving
  B   Crime [67]
      Driving Behavior [67]
  R   ↓ Accidents [67]
      ↓ Alcohol Intoxication [73]
      Blood Alcohol Concentration [94]
      ↓ Drinking Behavior [78]
      ↓ Drug Usage [71]
      Highway Safety [73]

Dropouts [73]
PN 227   **SC** 15190
  N   Potential Dropouts [73]
      ↓ School Dropouts [67]
      Treatment Dropouts [78]
  R   ↓ Education [67]
      Experimental Attrition [94]
      ↓ School Enrollment [73]

Drosophila [73]
PN 410   **SC** 15200
  UF Fruit Fly
  B   Diptera [73]
  R   Larvae [73]

Drowsiness
  Use Sleep Onset

Drug Abstinence [94]
PN 0   **SC** 15215
SN Voluntary or involuntary abstinence from drugs. For alcohol abstinence, use SOBRIETY.
  UF Abstinence (Drugs)
  N   Sobriety [88]
  R   Detoxification [73]
      ↓ Drug Abuse [73]
      ↓ Drug Rehabilitation [73]
      ↓ Drug Usage [71]
      ↓ Drug Withdrawal [73]

Drug Abstinence — (cont'd)
  R   Recovery (Disorders) [73]
      Smoking Cessation [88]

Drug Abuse [73]
PN 5480   **SC** 15220
  UF Substance Abuse
  B   Behavior Disorders [71]
      Drug Usage [71]
  N   ↓ Alcohol Abuse [88]
      ↓ Drug Dependency [73]
      ↓ Inhalant Abuse [85]
      Polydrug Abuse [94]
  R   ↓ Addiction [73]
      Codependency [91]
      ↓ Drug Abstinence [94]
      Drug Abuse Liability [94]
      Drug Abuse Prevention [94]
      ↓ Drug Addiction [67]
      Drug Overdoses [78]
      Drug Usage Screening [88]
      ↓ Drugs [67]
      Intravenous Drug Usage [94]
      Needle Sharing [94]
      ↓ Social Issues [91]

Drug Abuse Liability [94]
PN 0   **SC** 15225
SN Properties of any psychoactive drug or substance which lead to self administration and potentiality for abuse, dependence, and addiction.
  UF Abuse Potential (Drugs)
  R   ↓ Alcohol Abuse [88]
      ↓ Drug Abuse [73]
      ↓ Drug Addiction [67]
      ↓ Drug Dependency [73]
      ↓ Pharmacology [73]
      Psychopharmacology [67]

Drug Abuse Prevention [94]
PN 0   **SC** 15227
  UF Substance Abuse Prevention
  B   Prevention [73]
  R   ↓ Drug Abuse [73]
      Drug Education [73]
      Early Intervention [82]
      Preventive Medicine [73]
      Primary Mental Health Prevention [73]

Drug Addiction [67]
PN 2900   **SC** 15230
SN Physical and emotional dependence on a chemical substance. Compare DRUG DEPENDENCY.
  B   Addiction [73]
      Drug Dependency [73]
      Side Effects (Drug) [73]
  N   Heroin Addiction [73]
  R   ↓ Drug Abuse [73]
      Drug Abuse Liability [94]
      Drug Overdoses [78]
      ↓ Drug Withdrawal [73]
      Intravenous Drug Usage [94]
      Methadone Maintenance [78]
      Polydrug Abuse [94]

Drug Administration Methods [73]
PN 1102   **SC** 15240
SN Techniques, procedures, and routes (e.g., oral, intravenous) of administration of drugs (in experimental or therapeutic contexts) including dosage forms (e.g., liquids, tablets), frequency, and duration of drug administration. Used only when methodological aspects of administering drugs are discussed.
  N   ↓ Injections [73]
  R   ↓ Drug Dosages [73]
      ↓ Drugs [67]

Drug Adverse Reactions
SN Term discontinued in 1982. Use DRUG ADVERSE REACTIONS or SIDE EFFECTS (DRUG) to access references from 73–81.
  Use Side Effects (Drug)

Drug Allergies [73]
PN 11   **SC** 15260
  B   Allergic Disorders [73]
      Side Effects (Drug) [73]
  R   Drug Sensitivity [73]

Drug Dependency [73]
PN 1846   **SC** 15270
SN Psychological craving for or habituation to the use of a chemical substance which may or may not be accompanied by physical dependency. Used for animal or human populations. Compare DRUG ADDICTION.
  UF Dependency (Drug)
  B   Drug Abuse [73]
      Side Effects (Drug) [73]
  N   ↓ Drug Addiction [67]
  R   Drug Abuse Liability [94]
      Drug Usage Screening [88]
      Polydrug Abuse [94]

Drug Discrimination [85]
PN 528   **SC** 15272
SN A discrimination learning paradigm used to study psychopharmacological and neuropharmacological phenomena. Also, the organism's ability to discriminate the presence, absence, or other qualitative aspects of a chemical substance.
  B   Discrimination [67]
      Discrimination Learning [82]
  R   ↓ Drugs [67]

Drug Dissociation
  Use State Dependent Learning

Drug Dosages [73]
PN 2920   **SC** 15280
  N   Drug Overdoses [78]
  R   Bioavailability [91]
      ↓ Drug Administration Methods [73]
      ↓ Drugs [67]

Drug Education [73]
PN 1083   **SC** 15290
  UF Alcohol Education
  B   Health Education [73]
  R   Drug Abuse Prevention [94]
      ↓ Drugs [67]

Drug Effects
SN Term discontinued in 1982. Prior to 1982, a mandatory term applied to all studies involving any use of chemical substances administered for nontreatment purposes to human or animal subjects. From 1982, use DRUGS, specific drug classes or names, or terms referring to the chemical substance introduced for nontreatment purposes.
  Use Drugs

Drug Induced Congenital Disorders [73]
PN 65   **SC** 15310
  B   Congenital Disorders [73]
      Toxic Disorders [73]
  N   Fetal Alcohol Syndrome [85]
  R   Thalidomide [73]

Drug Induced Hallucinations [73]
PN 35   **SC** 15320
  B   Hallucinations [67]
  R   Psychedelic Experiences [73]

Drug Interactions [82]
PN 2099   SC 15325
SN Chemical and/or pharmacological reactions of drugs in combination, including agonistic and antagonistic interactions. Use DRUG POTENTIATION or DRUG SYNERGISM to access references from 73–81.
UF Drug Potentiation
    Drug Synergism
    Potentiation (Drugs)
R ↓ Drugs [67]
   ↓ Neurotoxins [82]
   Polydrug Abuse [94]

Drug Laws [73]
PN 194   SC 15330
B Laws [67]
N ↓ Marihuana Laws [73]
R ↓ Drugs [67]

Drug Overdoses [78]
PN 210   SC 15335
B Drug Dosages [73]
R ↓ Drug Abuse [73]
   ↓ Drug Addiction [67]
   ↓ Drug Therapy [67]
   ↓ Drug Usage [71]

Drug Potentiation
SN Term discontinued in 1982. Use DRUG POTENTIATION or DRUG SYNERGISM to access references from 73–81.
Use Drug Interactions

Drug Rehabilitation [73]
PN 4940   SC 15350
UF Rehabilitation (Drug)
B Rehabilitation [67]
N ↓ Alcohol Rehabilitation [82]
   Detoxification [73]
R ↓ Drug Abstinence [94]
   Drug Usage Screening [88]
   ↓ Drugs [67]
   Employee Assistance Programs [85]
   Methadone Maintenance [78]
   ↓ Psychosocial Rehabilitation [73]
   Rehabilitation Counseling [78]
   Smoking Cessation [88]
   Sobriety [88]

Drug Sensitivity [73]
PN 722   SC 15360
SN Behavioral or physical sensitivity, resistance, or reactivity to a particular chemical substance.
UF Sensitivity (Drugs)
B Side Effects (Drug) [73]
R Drug Allergies [73]
   Drug Tolerance [73]

Drug Synergism
SN Use DRUG SYNERGISM or DRUG POTENTIATION to access references from 73–81.
Use Drug Interactions

Drug Testing
Use Drug Usage Screening

Drug Therapy [67]
PN 23862   SC 15380
SN Mandatory term applied to studies dealing with any aspect of drug therapy in clinical contexts.
UF Chemotherapy
    Medication
    Pharmacotherapy
    Therapy (Drug)
B Organic Therapies [73]
N Hormone Therapy [94]
   ↓ Narcoanalysis [73]

Drug Therapy — (cont'd)
R Bioavailability [91]
   Detoxification [73]
   Drug Overdoses [78]
   ↓ Drugs [67]
   Neuroleptic Malignant Syndrome [88]
   ↓ Outpatient Treatment [67]
   Prescribing (Drugs) [91]
   Prescription Drugs [91]
   Self Medication [91]
   ↓ Side Effects (Drug) [73]
   Sleep Treatment [73]
   Tardive Dyskinesia [88]
   Treatment Resistant Depression [94]

Drug Tolerance [73]
PN 1348   SC 15390
SN Condition in which, after repeated administration, a drug produces a decreased effect and must be administered in larger doses to produce the effect of the original dose.
UF Tolerance (Drug)
R Drug Sensitivity [73]
   ↓ Drugs [67]
   ↓ Side Effects (Drug) [73]

Drug Usage [71]
PN 3477   SC 15400
SN Act, amount, or mode of using any type of drug. Applies only to humans and should be used when neither abuse nor addiction are the subject matter, regardless of the legality of the particular drug.
N ↓ Alcohol Drinking Patterns [67]
   ↓ Drug Abuse [73]
   Intravenous Drug Usage [94]
   Marihuana Usage [73]
   Tobacco Smoking [67]
R ↓ Addiction [73]
   Driving Under The Influence [88]
   ↓ Drug Abstinence [94]
   Drug Overdoses [78]
   Drug Usage Screening [88]
   ↓ Drugs [67]
   Needle Sharing [94]

Drug Usage Attitudes [73]
PN 840   SC 15410
B Attitudes [67]
N Alcohol Drinking Attitudes [73]
R Health Attitudes [85]
   Marihuana Legalization [73]

Drug Usage Screening [88]
PN 129   SC 15415
SN Procedures used to measure or detect prevalence of drug use through analysis of blood, urine, or other body fluids. Not used for measuring the clinical efficacy of therapeutic drugs.
UF Drug Testing
B Screening [82]
R Blood Alcohol Concentration [94]
   ↓ Drug Abuse [73]
   ↓ Drug Dependency [73]
   ↓ Drug Rehabilitation [73]
   ↓ Drug Usage [71]
   ↓ Drugs [67]
   ↓ Medical Diagnosis [73]
   Physical Examination [88]
   Urinalysis [73]

Drug Withdrawal [73]
PN 1658   SC 15420
SN Processes and symptomatic effects resulting from abstinence from a chemical agent or medication. Used for human or animal populations. Use DRUG WITHDRAWAL or DRUG WITHDRAWAL EFFECTS to access references from 73–81.

Drug Withdrawal — (cont'd)
UF Drug Withdrawal Effects
N Alcohol Withdrawal [94]
R Detoxification [73]
   ↓ Drug Abstinence [94]
   ↓ Drug Addiction [67]

Drug Withdrawal Effects
SN Term discontinued in 1982. Use DRUG WITHDRAWAL EFFECTS or DRUG WITHDRAWAL to access references from 73–81.
Use Drug Withdrawal

Drugs [67]
PN 4088   SC 15440
SN Conceptually broad array term referring to any substance other than food administered for experimental or treatment purposes. Use specific drug classes or names if possible.
UF Drug Effects
    Psychoactive Drugs
    Psychotropic Drugs
N ↓ Adrenergic Blocking Drugs [73]
   ↓ Adrenergic Drugs [73]
   ↓ Adrenolytic Drugs [73]
   ↓ Alcohols [67]
   ↓ Alkaloids [73]
   ↓ Amines [73]
   ↓ Analgesic Drugs [73]
   ↓ Anesthetic Drugs [73]
   ↓ Anti Inflammatory Drugs [82]
   Antiandrogens [82]
   ↓ Antibiotics [73]
   ↓ Anticoagulant Drugs [73]
   ↓ Anticonvulsive Drugs [73]
   ↓ Antidepressant Drugs [71]
   ↓ Antiemetic Drugs [73]
   Antiestrogens [82]
   ↓ Antihistaminic Drugs [73]
   ↓ Antihypertensive Drugs [73]
   Antineoplastic Drugs [82]
   ↓ Antispasmodic Drugs [73]
   ↓ Antitremor Drugs [73]
   ↓ Antitubercular Drugs [73]
   ↓ Antiviral Drugs [94]
   ↓ Appetite Depressing Drugs [73]
   ↓ Barbiturates [67]
   ↓ Benzodiazepines [78]
   ↓ Bromides [73]
   ↓ Cannabis [73]
   Cardiotonic Drugs [85]
   Channel Blockers [91]
   ↓ Cholinergic Blocking Drugs [73]
   ↓ Cholinergic Drugs [73]
   ↓ Cholinomimetic Drugs [73]
   ↓ CNS Affecting Drugs [73]
   ↓ Diuretics [73]
   ↓ Dopamine Agonists [85]
   ↓ Emetic Drugs [73]
   ↓ Enzyme Inhibitors [85]
   ↓ Enzymes [73]
   ↓ Ergot Derivatives [73]
   ↓ Ganglion Blocking Drugs [73]
   ↓ Hallucinogenic Drugs [67]
   ↓ Heart Rate Affecting Drugs [73]
   ↓ Hypnotic Drugs [73]
   ↓ Muscle Relaxing Drugs [73]
   ↓ Narcoanalytic Drugs [73]
   ↓ Narcotic Agonists [88]
   ↓ Narcotic Antagonists [73]
   ↓ Narcotic Drugs [73]
   Nonprescription Drugs [91]
   ↓ Nootropic Drugs [91]
   Prescription Drugs [91]
   ↓ Psychedelic Drugs [73]
   ↓ Psychotomimetic Drugs [73]
   ↓ Respiration Stimulating Drugs [73]
   ↓ Sedatives [73]
   Serotonin Agonists [88]

Drugs — (cont'd)
- N ↓ Serotonin Antagonists [73]
-    ↓ Steroids [73]
-    ↓ Sympatholytic Drugs [73]
-    ↓ Sympathomimetic Drugs [73]
-    ↓ Tranquilizing Drugs [67]
-    ↓ Vasoconstrictor Drugs [73]
-    ↓ Vasodilator Drugs [73]
- R ↓ Acids [73]
-    Antibodies [73]
-    Bioavailability [91]
-    Carcinogens [73]
-    ↓ Drug Abuse [73]
-    ↓ Drug Administration Methods [73]
-    Drug Discrimination [85]
-    ↓ Drug Dosages [73]
-    Drug Education [73]
-    Drug Interactions [82]
-    ↓ Drug Laws [73]
-    ↓ Drug Rehabilitation [73]
-    ↓ Drug Therapy [67]
-    Drug Tolerance [73]
-    ↓ Drug Usage [71]
-    Drug Usage Screening [88]
-    ↓ Hormones [67]
-    ↓ Insecticides [73]
-    ↓ Peptides [73]
-    Placebo [73]
-    Prenatal Exposure [91]
-    Prescribing (Drugs) [91]
-    ↓ Proteins [73]
-    Self Medication [91]
-    ↓ Side Effects (Drug) [73]
-    Teratogens [88]
-    Thyroid Extract [73]
-    Toxicity [73]
-    ↓ Vitamins [73]

Drunk Driving
- Use Driving Under The Influence

Drunkenness
- Use Alcohol Intoxication

DSM
- Use Diagnostic and Statistical Manual

Dual Careers [82]
PN 441   SC 15455
SN Situation in which both partners or spouses in a family pursue careers.
- R ↓ Family [67]
-    ↓ Family Structure [73]
-    Working Women [78]

Dual Diagnosis [91]
PN 123   SC 15457
SN Diagnosis based on the coexistence of two or more DSM-III-R disorders.
- R Comorbidity [91]
-    ↓ Diagnosis [67]
-    Differential Diagnosis [67]
-    ↓ Psychodiagnostic Typologies [67]

Dualism [73]
PN 293   SC 15460
SN Theory viewing mind and body as two separate and irreducible entities.
- UF Mind Body
- B Philosophies [67]
- R Mind [91]

Duchennes Disease
- Use Muscular Disorders

Ducks [73]
PN 261   SC 15480
- B Birds [67]

Duodenum
- Use Intestines

Duration (Response)
- Use Response Duration

Duration (Stimulus)
- Use Stimulus Duration

Dwarfism (Pituitary)
- Use Hypopituitarism

Dyads [73]
PN 1480   SC 15540
- B Social Groups [73]
- R Couples [82]

Dying
- Use Death and Dying

Dying Patients
- Use Terminally Ill Patients

Dynamics (Group)
- Use Group Dynamics

Dynorphins [85]
PN 64   SC 15575
- B Endogenous Opiates [85]
-    Pituitary Hormones [73]

Dysarthria [73]
PN 139   SC 15580
SN Articulation disorder resulting from central nervous system disease, especially brain damage.
- B Articulation Disorders [73]
-    Central Nervous System Disorders [73]
- R Muscular Dystrophy [73]
-    ↓ Paralysis [73]

Dyscalculia
- Use Acalculia

Dysfunctional Family [91]
PN 102   SC 15590
SN A family system in which relationships or communication are impaired.
- R Codependency [91]
-    Double Bind Interaction [73]
-    ↓ Family [67]
-    ↓ Family Relations [67]
-    ↓ Family Structure [73]
-    Marital Conflict [73]
-    Schizophrenogenic Family [67]

Dyskinesia [73]
PN 573   SC 15600
- B Movement Disorders [85]
-    Symptoms [67]
- N Tardive Dyskinesia [88]
- R ↓ Neuromuscular Disorders [73]

Dyslexia [73]
PN 1309   SC 15610
SN Reading disorder involving an inability to understand what is read. Less severe than alexia.
- B Alexia [82]
-    Learning Disabilities [73]
-    Reading Disabilities [67]
- R Educational Diagnosis [78]
-    ↓ Reading [67]

Dysmenorrhea [73]
PN 85   SC 15620
SN Difficult and painful menstruation.
- B Menstrual Disorders [73]

Dysmetria
- Use Ataxia

Dysmorphophobia [73]
PN 54   SC 15640
SN Obsessive fear or delusional conviction that one is physically deformed or otherwise abnormal.
- UF Atypical Somatoform Disorder
- B Psychosomatic Disorders [67]

Dyspareunia [73]
PN 30   SC 15650
- B Sexual Function Disturbances [73]
-    Sexual Intercourse (Human) [73]
- R Frigidity [73]
-    Vaginismus [73]

Dysphasia [78]
PN 117   SC 15655
SN Impairment of language comprehension, formulation, or use due to brain damage. Used only for partial impairments.
- B Aphasia [67]
- N ↓ Alexia [82]

Dysphonia [73]
PN 143   SC 15660
SN Any speech disorder involving problems of voice quality, pitch, or intensity.
- UF Voice Disorders
- B Speech Disorders [67]

Dysphoria
SN Use DEPRESSION (EMOTION) to access references from 73-87.
- Use Major Depression

Dyspnea [73]
PN 33   SC 15680
SN Difficulty in breathing which may or may not have an organic cause.
- B Respiratory Distress [73]
-    Respiratory Tract Disorders [73]
-    Symptoms [67]
- N Asthma [67]
- R ↓ Cardiovascular Disorders [67]
-    ↓ Lung Disorders [73]
-    ↓ Psychosomatic Disorders [67]

Dyspraxia
- Use Movement Disorders

Dysthymia
SN Use DEPRESSION (EMOTION) to access references from 73-87.
- Use Dysthymic Disorder

Dysthymic Disorder [88]
PN 255   SC 15693
SN Chronic affective disorder characterized by either relatively mild depressive symptoms or marked loss of pleasure in usual activities. Consider DEPRESSION (EMOTION) to access references prior to 1988.
- UF Dysthymia
- B Major Depression [88]
- R Anhedonia [85]

Dystonia
- Use Muscular Disorders

Dystrophy (Muscular)
- Use Muscular Dystrophy

Eagerness
- Use Enthusiasm

Ear (Anatomy) [67]
PN 429   SC 15720
- B   Sense Organs [73]
- N   External Ear [73]
- ↓ Labyrinth (Anatomy) [73]
-   Middle Ear [73]
- ↓ Vestibular Apparatus [67]
- R   ↓ Ear Disorders [73]

Ear Canal
Use   External Ear

Ear Disorders [73]
PN 180   SC 15740
SN   Disorders of the external, middle, or inner ear. Use HEARING DISORDERS for pathology involving auditory neural pathways beyond the inner ear.
- B   Sense Organ Disorders [73]
- N   ↓ Labyrinth Disorders [73]
-   Otosclerosis [73]
-   Tinnitus [73]
- R   ↓ Auditory Perception [67]
-   ↓ Aurally Handicapped [73]
-   ↓ Ear (Anatomy) [67]
-   Hearing Disorders [82]
-   ↓ Sensorially Handicapped [94]

Ear Ossicles
Use   Middle Ear

Early Childhood
Use   Preschool Age Children

Early Childhood Development [73]
PN 995   SC 15770
SN   Process of physical, cognitive, personality, and psychosocial growth occurring from birth through age 5. Use a more specific term if possible.
- B   Childhood Development [67]
- N   ↓ Infant Development [73]
- R   Early Experience [67]
-   Early Memories [85]
-   ↓ Physical Development [73]
-   ↓ Psychogenesis [73]

Early Experience [67]
PN 4056   SC 15780
SN   Any occurrences early in an individual's life. Used for human or animal populations.
- B   Experiences (Events) [73]
- R   Age Regression (Hypnotic) [88]
-   Anniversary Events [94]
-   Autobiographical Memory [94]
-   ↓ Early Childhood Development [73]
-   Early Memories [85]
-   Life Review [91]

Early Infantile Autism [73]
PN 404   SC 15790
- B   Autism [67]
-   Childhood Psychosis [67]
- R   Autistic Children [73]
-   Childhood Schizophrenia [67]
-   Symbiotic Infantile Psychosis [73]

Early Intervention [82]
PN 1155   SC 15793
SN   Action taken utilizing medical, family, school, social, or mental health resources and aimed at infants and children at risk for, or in the early stages of mental, physical, learning, or other disorders.
- R   Drug Abuse Prevention [94]
-   ↓ Prenatal Care [91]
-   ↓ Prevention [73]
-   Primary Mental Health Prevention [73]
-   Special Education [67]

Early Intervention — (cont'd)
- R   Special Needs [94]
-   ↓ Treatment [67]

Early Memories [85]
PN 229   SC 15796
SN   Memories of events that occurred early in an individual's life.
- UF   Childhood Memories
- B   Memory [67]
- R   Age Regression (Hypnotic) [88]
-   Anniversary Events [94]
-   Autobiographical Memory [94]
-   ↓ Early Childhood Development [73]
-   Early Experience [67]
-   Life Review [91]
-   Reminiscence [85]

Earthworms [73]
PN 24   SC 15800
- B   Worms [67]

East Africa [88]
PN 7   SC 15805
- B   Africa [67]

East German Democratic Republic
SN   Term discontinued in 1982. Use EAST GERMAN DEMOCRATIC REPUBLIC to access references from 67–81.
Use   East Germany

East Germany [82]
PN 132   SC 15812
SN   Use EAST GERMAN DEMOCRATIC REPUBLIC to access references from 67–81.
- UF   East German Democratic Republic
- B   Germany [88]

Eastern Europe [88]
PN 17   SC 15815
- B   Europe [73]

Eating [67]
PN 1202   SC 15820
SN   Use EATING or EATING PATTERNS to access references prior to 1982.
- UF   Eating Patterns
- B   Food Intake [67]
- N   Binge Eating [91]
- R   ↓ Appetite [73]
-   Dietary Restraint [94]
-   Diets [78]
-   Eating Attitudes [94]
-   Food [78]

Eating Attitudes [94]
PN 0   SC 15823
- B   Attitudes [67]
- R   ↓ Appetite [73]
-   ↓ Eating [67]
-   Food Preferences [73]

Eating Disorders
Use   Appetite Disorders

Eating Patterns
SN   Term discontinued in 1982. Use EATING PATTERNS or EATING to access references prior to 1982.
Use   Eating

Echinodermata [73]
PN 29   SC 15840
- UF   Starfish
- B   Invertebrates [73]

Echoencephalography [73]
PN 8   SC 15850
- B   Encephalography [73]
-   Medical Diagnosis [73]

Echolalia [73]
PN 83   SC 15870
- B   Language Disorders [82]
- R   Gilles de la Tourette Disorder [73]

Echolocation [73]
PN 93   SC 15880
- R   ↓ Animal Ethology [67]
-   ↓ Animal Vocalizations [73]

Eclectic Psychology
Use   Theoretical Orientation

Eclectic Psychotherapy [94]
PN 0   SC 15887
- B   Psychotherapy [67]
- R   Interdisciplinary Treatment Approach [73]
-   Multimodal Treatment Approach [91]

Ecological Factors [73]
PN 538   SC 15890
SN   Elements involved in relations between organisms and their natural environments.
- N   Pollution [73]
-   Topography [73]
- R   Ecological Psychology [94]
-   Ecology [73]
-   ↓ Environmental Effects [73]

Ecological Psychology [94]
PN 0   SC 15895
SN   Branch of psychology that studies the frequency or nature of psychological processes or behavior as they occur in natural settings. Compare ENVIRONMENTAL PSYCHOLOGY.
- B   Psychology [67]
- R   ↓ Ecological Factors [73]
-   Environmental Psychology [82]

Ecology [73]
PN 421   SC 15900
- R   Conservation (Ecological Behavior) [78]
-   ↓ Ecological Factors [73]
-   ↓ Environment [67]
-   Environmental Attitudes [78]
-   Environmental Education [94]
-   Pollution [73]

Economically Disadvantaged
Use   Disadvantaged

Economics [85]
PN 958   SC 15915
SN   Social science dealing with the production, distribution, and consumption of goods and services. Used for the discipline or economic factors themselves.
- B   Social Sciences [67]
- R   Cost Containment [91]
-   ↓ Costs and Cost Analysis [73]
-   ↓ Division of Labor [88]
-   Economy [73]
-   Health Care Costs [94]
-   Money [67]
-   ↓ Political Economic Systems [73]

Economy [73]
PN 592   SC 15920
- R   ↓ Costs and Cost Analysis [73]
-   Economics [85]
-   Money [67]
-   ↓ Political Economic Systems [73]
-   Taxation [85]

ECS Therapy
  Use Electroconvulsive Shock Therapy

Ecstasy (Drug)
  Use Methylenedioxymethamphetamine

ECT (Therapy)
  Use Electroconvulsive Shock Therapy

Ecuador [88]
PN 17   **SC** 15945
  B South America [67]

Eczema [73]
PN 29   **SC** 15950
  B Dermatitis [73]
  R Allergic Skin Disorders [73]

Educable Mentally Retarded [73]
PN 2950   **SC** 15960
SN IQ 50–70.
  UF Mildly Mentally Retarded
  B Mentally Retarded [67]
  R Slow Learners [73]

Education [67]
PN 5391   **SC** 16000
SN Conceptually broad array term referring to the process of imparting or obtaining knowledge, skills, and values. Use a more specific term if possible.
  UF Educational Process
       Training
  N ↓ Adult Education [73]
       Bilingual Education [78]
       Client Education [85]
    ↓ Clinical Methods Training [73]
       Communication Skills Training [82]
    ↓ Curriculum [67]
       Death Education [82]
       Elementary Education [73]
    ↓ Higher Education [73]
       Middle School Education [85]
       Multicultural Education [88]
    ↓ Nontraditional Education [82]
       Nursing Education [73]
       Paraprofessional Education [73]
       Parent Training [78]
    ↓ Personnel Training [67]
       Preschool Education [73]
       Private School Education [73]
       Public School Education [73]
       Religious Education [73]
    ↓ Remedial Education [85]
       Secondary Education [73]
       Social Work Education [73]
       Special Education [67]
    ↓ Teacher Education [67]
  R Ability Grouping [73]
    ↓ Academic Achievement [67]
       Academic Aptitude [73]
       Accreditation (Education Personnel) [73]
       Athletic Training [91]
       Boards of Education [78]
       Classroom Behavior Modification [73]
       Classroom Discipline [73]
       Coeducation [73]
    ↓ Dropouts [73]
       Educational Administration [67]
       Educational Aspirations [73]
    ↓ Educational Background [67]
       Educational Counseling [67]
       Educational Degrees [73]
       Educational Diagnosis [78]
       Educational Financial Assistance [73]
       Educational Incentives [73]
    ↓ Educational Laboratories [73]
    ↓ Educational Measurement [67]

Education — (cont'd)
  R Educational Objectives [78]
    ↓ Educational Personnel [73]
       Educational Placement [78]
       Educational Program Accreditation [94]
    ↓ Educational Programs [73]
    ↓ Educational Psychology [67]
       Educational Television [67]
       Environmental Education [94]
       Equal Education [78]
    ↓ Extracurricular Activities [73]
       Grade Level [94]
       Home Schooling [94]
       Mainstreaming (Educational) [78]
       Psychoeducation [94]
       Questioning [82]
       School Adjustment [67]
       School Attendance [73]
       School Counseling [82]
    ↓ School Dropouts [67]
    ↓ School Enrollment [73]
    ↓ School Environment [73]
    ↓ School Facilities [73]
       School Graduation [91]
       School Integration [82]
       School Learning [67]
       School Readiness [73]
       School to Work Transition [94]
       School Truancy [73]
    ↓ Schools [67]
       Student Admission Criteria [73]
       Student Attitudes [67]
    ↓ Student Characteristics [82]
       Student Personnel Services [78]
       Student Records [78]
    ↓ Students [67]
       Study Habits [73]
    ↓ Teacher Characteristics [73]
       Teacher Student Interaction [73]
       Teacher Tenure [73]
    ↓ Teaching [67]
    ↓ Teaching Methods [67]
       Theories of Education [73]

Education Students [82]
PN 287   **SC** 15995
SN Students enrolled in a school or department of education.
  B College Students [67]
  R Preservice Teachers [82]
       Student Teachers [73]
    ↓ Teacher Education [67]

Educational Administration [67]
PN 1880   **SC** 16010
  UF School Administration
       School Organization
  R Boards of Education [78]
       Decentralization [78]
    ↓ Education [67]

Educational Administrators
  Use School Administrators

Educational Aspirations [73]
PN 766   **SC** 16020
SN Personal desire for achievement in a certain educational field or to a certain level or degree.
  B Aspirations [67]
  R Academic Specialization [73]
    ↓ Education [67]
       Educational Objectives [78]

Educational Audiovisual Aids [73]
PN 215   **SC** 16030
  UF Audiovisual Aids (Educational)
  B Audiovisual Communications Media [73]
       Instructional Media [67]

Educational Audiovisual Aids — (cont'd)
  N Motion Pictures (Educational) [73]
  R ↓ Audiovisual Instruction [73]
       Educational Television [67]
       Film Strips [67]
       Televised Instruction [73]
       Videotape Instruction [73]

Educational Background [67]
PN 3124   **SC** 16040
  N Parent Educational Background [73]
  R Biographical Data [78]
    ↓ Education [67]
       School Leavers [88]

Educational Background (Parents)
  Use Parent Educational Background

Educational Counseling [67]
PN 2413   **SC** 16060
SN Assistance offered to school or college students on school program planning, course selection, or academic specialization. Compare SCHOOL COUNSELING.
  UF Educational Guidance
       Guidance (Educational)
  B Counseling [67]
  R ↓ Education [67]
       Occupational Guidance [67]
       Student Personnel Services [78]

Educational Degrees [73]
PN 527   **SC** 16070
  UF College Degrees
       Degrees (Educational)
       Graduate Degrees
       High School Diplomas
       Undergraduate Degrees
  R College Graduates [82]
    ↓ Education [67]
       Educational Program Accreditation [94]
       High School Graduates [78]
    ↓ Higher Education [73]
       School Graduation [91]

Educational Diagnosis [78]
PN 2295   **SC** 16075
SN Identification of cognitive, perceptual, emotional, and other factors which influence academic performance or school adjustment, usually for such purposes as placement of students in curricula or programs suited to their needs, and referral.
  B Diagnosis [67]
  R Differential Diagnosis [67]
       Dyslexia [73]
    ↓ Education [67]
    ↓ Educational Measurement [67]
       Educational Placement [78]
    ↓ Learning Disabilities [73]
    ↓ Learning Disorders [67]
    ↓ Psychodiagnosis [67]
       Psychological Report [88]
    ↓ Reading Disabilities [67]
       Woodcock Johnson Psychoed Battery [94]

Educational Field Trips [73]
PN 48   **SC** 16080
  UF Field Trips (Educational)
  B Teaching Methods [67]
  R Curricular Field Experience [82]

Educational Financial Assistance [73]
PN 120   **SC** 16090
  UF Financial Assistance (Educational)
       Scholarships
       School Federal Aid
       School Financial Assistance

Educational Financial Assistance — (cont'd)

- UF Stipends
- R   ↓ Education [67]
      Funding [88]
      Student Personnel Services [78]

Educational Guidance
- Use Educational Counseling

Educational Incentives [73]
PN 88   SC 16120
SN Any type of incentive used or experienced in a school, classroom, or other educational context.
- B   Incentives [67]
      Motivation [67]
- R   ↓ Education [67]

Educational Inequality
- Use Equal Education

Educational Laboratories [73]
PN 120   SC 16130
- UF Laboratories (Educational)
- B   School Facilities [73]
- N   Language Laboratories [73]
- R   ↓ Education [67]

Educational Measurement [67]
PN 3689   SC 16140
SN Practices, procedures, methods, and tests used in the assessment of student characteristics or performance, such as academic achievement and school adjustment.
- B   Testing [67]
- N   Curriculum Based Assessment [94]
      ↓ Entrance Examinations [73]
      Grading (Educational) [73]
      Minimum Competency Tests [85]
- R   ↓ Education [67]
      Educational Diagnosis [78]
      ↓ Screening [82]

Educational Objectives [78]
PN 956   SC 16145
SN Specific educational goals toward which one's efforts are directed, or goals proposed or established by educational authorities.
- UF Course Objectives
      Instructional Objectives
- B   Goals [67]
- R   ↓ Curriculum [67]
      ↓ Education [67]
      Educational Aspirations [73]
      Mastery Learning [85]

Educational Personnel [73]
PN 1529   SC 16150
- UF Faculty
- B   Professional Personnel [78]
- N   ↓ School Administrators [73]
      School Counselors [73]
      School Nurses [73]
      Teacher Aides [73]
      ↓ Teachers [67]
- R   ↓ Education [67]
      ↓ Educational Psychologists [73]
      ↓ Mental Health Personnel [67]
      Missionaries [73]
      Professional Supervision [88]
      Speech Therapists [73]
      ↓ Volunteer Personnel [73]

Educational Placement [78]
PN 1307   SC 16155

Educational Placement — (cont'd)
SN Assignment of students to classes, programs, or schools according to their abilities and readiness.
- UF Placement (Educational)
- R   Ability Grouping [73]
      ↓ Education [67]
      Educational Diagnosis [78]
      Grade Level [94]
      ↓ Mainstreaming [91]
      Mainstreaming (Educational) [78]
      Remedial Reading [73]
      ↓ Screening [82]
      Special Education [67]

Educational Process
- Use Education

Educational Program Accreditation [94]
PN 0   SC 16165
SN Recognition and approval of educational programs or institution's maintenance of standards to qualify graduates for professional practice or admission to higher or more specialized educational institutions.
- UF Accreditation (Educational Programs)
      School Accreditation
- R   ↓ Curriculum [67]
      ↓ Education [67]
      Educational Degrees [73]
      ↓ Educational Programs [73]
      ↓ Graduate Psychology Education [67]
      ↓ Higher Education [73]
      ↓ Psychology Education [78]

Educational Program Evaluation [73]
PN 1901   SC 16170
SN Techniques, materials, or process of determining the worth or effectiveness of an educational program in relation to its goals or other criteria.
- UF Program Evaluation (Educational)
- B   Program Evaluation [85]
- R   Behavioral Assessment [82]
      Course Evaluation [78]
      ↓ Educational Programs [73]

Educational Program Planning [73]
PN 822   SC 16180
- UF Program Planning (Educational)
- B   Program Development [91]
- R   Curriculum Development [73]
      ↓ Educational Programs [73]

Educational Programs [73]
PN 4244   SC 16190
SN Specially funded or mandated programs established for a specific purpose.
- UF Work Study Programs
- N   Foreign Study [73]
      Project Follow Through [73]
      Project Head Start [73]
      Special Education [67]
      Upward Bound [73]
- R   Compensatory Education [73]
      Cooperative Education [82]
      Curricular Field Experience [82]
      ↓ Education [67]
      Educational Program Accreditation [94]
      Educational Program Evaluation [73]
      Educational Program Planning [73]
      Multicultural Education [88]
      ↓ Nontraditional Education [82]
      ↓ Program Development [91]

Educational Psychologists [73]
PN 248   SC 16200

Educational Psychologists — (cont'd)
SN Psychologists conducting research and formulating policies in areas of diagnosis and measurement, school adjustment, school learning, and special education.
- B   Psychologists [67]
- N   School Psychologists [73]
- R   ↓ Educational Personnel [73]

Educational Psychology [67]
PN 1075   SC 16210
SN Branch of psychology that emphasizes the application of psychological theories and research findings to educational processes, especially in the areas of learning and motivation.
- B   Applied Psychology [73]
- N   School Psychology [73]
- R   ↓ Education [67]

Educational Supervision
- Use Professional Supervision

Educational Television [67]
PN 144   SC 16220
- B   Television [67]
- R   ↓ Education [67]
      ↓ Educational Audiovisual Aids [73]
      Televised Instruction [73]

Educational Therapy
- Use School Counseling

Educational Toys [73]
PN 20   SC 16230
- B   Toys [73]

Edwards Personal Preference Schedule [67]
PN 105   SC 16240
- B   Nonprojective Personality Measures [73]

Edwards Personality Inventory [73]
PN 6   SC 16250
- B   Nonprojective Personality Measures [73]

Edwards Social Desirability Scale [73]
PN 11   SC 16260
- B   Nonprojective Personality Measures [73]

EEG (Electrophysiology)
- Use Electroencephalography

Effect Size (Statistical) [85]
PN 91   SC 16272
SN A statistical estimate that represents the magnitude of a statistically significant result.
- UF Magnitude of Effect (Statistical)
- B   Statistical Analysis [67]
- R   Confidence Limits (Statistics) [73]
      Statistical Significance [73]

Efferent Pathways [82]
PN 238   SC 16275
SN Collections of fibers that typically carry neural impulses away from central nervous system connections toward muscular and glandular innervations.
- UF Motor Pathways
- B   Neural Pathways [82]
      Parasympathetic Nervous System [73]
- N   Extrapyramidal Tracts [73]
      Pyramidal Tracts [73]
- R   ↓ Afferent Pathways [82]
      Motor Neurons [73]
      ↓ Motor Processes [67]

Efficacy Expectations
- Use Self Efficacy

Efficiency (Employee)
Use Employee Efficiency

Effort
Use Energy Expenditure

Egalitarianism [85]
PN 32   SC 16287
B   Personality Traits [67]
R   Authoritarianism [67]
↓ Equity (Social) [78]

Ego [67]
PN 3012   SC 16290
B   Psychoanalytic Personality Factors [73]
R   ↓ Ego Development [91]
Ego Identity [91]

Ego Development [91]
PN 151   SC 16294
SN Gradual development of part of the id into the ego under the influence of environmental factors. This development goes from a preconscious to a conscious stage in which the ego functions to differentiate the external from the internal world.
B   Personality Development [67]
N   Ego Identity [91]
R   Ego [67]
Psychoanalytic Theory [67]

Ego Identity [91]
PN 64   SC 16297
SN The experience of the self as a recognizable entity resulting from one's ego ideal, behavior and social roles, and adjustments to reality.
B   Ego Development [91]
R   Ego [67]
Erikson (Erik) [91]
↓ Personality Development [67]
↓ Self Concept [67]

Egocentrism [78]
PN 516   SC 16300
SN Self-centered preoccupation or concern regarding one's own needs, wishes, desires, or preferences and usually accompanied by a disregard for the concerns of others. Also, in cognitive development, the inclination to believe that others maintain the same experiential perspective as oneself. Use EGOCENTRISM to access references to role taking or perspective taking from 78–81.
R   ↓ Cognitive Development [73]
↓ Concept Formation [67]
Narcissism [67]
↓ Personality [67]
↓ Personality Traits [67]
Role Taking [82]

Egotism [73]
PN 117   SC 16310
B   Personality Traits [67]

Egypt [82]
PN 133   SC 16315
SN Use UNITED ARAB REPUBLIC to access references from 73–81.
UF United Arab Republic
B   Africa [67]
R   Middle East [78]

Eidetic Imagery [73]
PN 85   SC 16320
SN Clear and detailed memory for objects or events perceived, usually visually.
UF Photographic Memory
B   Memory [67]
R   Episodic Memory [88]

Eidetic Imagery — (cont'd)
R   Spatial Memory [88]
Visual Memory [94]

Ejaculation
Use Male Orgasm

EKG (Electrophysiology)
Use Electrocardiography

El Salvador [88]
PN 20   SC 16345
B   Central America [73]

Elavil
Use Amitriptyline

Elbow (Anatomy) [73]
PN 45   SC 16360
B   Joints (Anatomy) [73]
R   Arm (Anatomy) [73]

Elder Abuse [88]
PN 67   SC 16363
SN Abuse or neglect of elderly persons in a family, institutional, or other setting.
B   Antisocial Behavior [71]
R   ↓ Aged [73]
Emotional Abuse [91]
↓ Family Violence [82]
Patient Abuse [91]
Physical Abuse [91]
↓ Sexual Abuse [88]

Elder Care [94]
PN 0   SC 16364
SN Informal or formal support systems or programs for the care of the elderly or assistance to the families who have responsibilities for their care.
R   ↓ Aged [73]
Caregiver Burden [94]
Caregivers [80]
Employee Assistance Programs [85]
↓ Employee Benefits [73]
Home Care [85]
Home Visiting Programs [73]
Homebound [88]

Elected Government Officials
Use Government Personnel

Elections (Political)
Use Political Elections

Elective Abortion
Use Induced Abortion

Elective Mutism [73]
PN 132   SC 16390
B   Mental Disorders [67]
Mutism [73]

Electra Complex [73]
PN 3   SC 16400
B   Psychoanalytic Personality Factors [73]

Electric Fishes [73]
PN 71   SC 16410
B   Fishes [67]

Electrical Activity [67]
PN 6117   SC 16420

Electrical Activity — (cont'd)
SN Electrically measured responses or response patterns, usually of individual units (i.e., cells) or groups of cells, in any part of the nervous system. Includes neural or neuron impulses; neural depolarization or hyperpolarization; spike, resting, action, generator, graded, presynaptic, or postsynaptic potentials. Compare ELECTROPHYSIOLOGY.
B   Electrophysiology [73]
N   Alpha Rhythm [73]
↓ Cortical Evoked Potentials [73]
Delta Rhythm [73]
↓ Evoked Potentials [67]
Kindling [85]
Postactivation Potentials [85]
Theta Rhythm [73]
R   Electrocardiography [67]
↓ Electroencephalography [67]

Electrical Brain Stimulation [73]
PN 2780   SC 16430
B   Brain Stimulation [67]
Electrical Stimulation [73]
Electrophysiology [73]
Stereotaxic Techniques [73]
R   ↓ Evoked Potentials [67]
Postactivation Potentials [85]
↓ Self Stimulation [67]

Electrical Injuries [73]
PN 12   SC 16440
B   Injuries [73]
R   Burns [73]
Shock [67]
↓ Wounds [73]

Electrical Stimulation [73]
PN 1255   SC 16460
B   Stimulation [67]
N   Electrical Brain Stimulation [73]
↓ Electroconvulsive Shock [67]
R   Experimental Epilepsy [78]
Shock [67]

Electro Oculography [73]
PN 120   SC 16470
UF EOG (Electrophysiology)
B   Electrophysiology [73]
Medical Diagnosis [73]
Ophthalmologic Examination [73]
R   Electroretinography [67]

Electrocardiography [67]
PN 250   SC 16480
UF EKG (Electrophysiology)
B   Cardiography [73]
Electrophysiology [73]
R   ↓ Electrical Activity [67]

Electroconvulsive Shock [67]
PN 741   SC 16490
B   Electrical Stimulation [73]
N   Electroconvulsive Shock Therapy [67]
R   Shock [67]

Electroconvulsive Shock Therapy [67]
PN 1607   SC 16500
UF ECS Therapy
ECT (Therapy)
Electroshock Therapy
B   Electroconvulsive Shock [67]
Shock Therapy [73]

Electrodermal Response
Use Galvanic Skin Response

Electrodes [67]
PN 228   SC 16520
B   Apparatus [67]
R ↓ Stimulators (Apparatus) [73]

Electroencephalography [67]
PN 6488   SC 16530
SN Method of graphically recording the electrical activity (potentials) of the brain by means of intracranial electrodes or electrodes applied to the scalp. Used both for the method as well as the resulting electroencephalogram or the electrophysiological activity itself.
UF   EEG (Electrophysiology)
B   Electrophysiology [73]
    Encephalography [73]
    Medical Diagnosis [73]
N   Alpha Rhythm [73]
    Delta Rhythm [73]
    Theta Rhythm [73]
R ↓ Electrical Activity [67]
    Magnetoencephalography [85]
    Rheoencephalography [73]

Electrolytes [73]
PN 168   SC 16540
UF   Ions
N   Calcium Ions [73]
    Chloride Ions [73]
    Magnesium Ions [73]
    Potassium Ions [73]
    Sodium Ions [73]
    Zinc [85]
R ↓ Chemical Elements [73]

Electromyography [67]
PN 1937   SC 16550
UF   EMG (Electrophysiology)
B   Electrophysiology [73]
    Medical Diagnosis [73]

Electronystagmography [73]
PN 9   SC 16560
B   Electrophysiology [73]
    Medical Diagnosis [73]

Electrophysiology [73]
PN 1195   SC 16570
SN Branch of physiology concerned with the study of electrical phenomena within the living organism (i.e., nerve and muscle tissue). Used for the scientific discipline or the electrophysiological processes themselves. Compare ELECTRICAL ACTIVITY.
B   Physiology [67]
N ↓ Electrical Activity [67]
    Electrical Brain Stimulation [73]
    Electro Oculography [73]
    Electrocardiography [67]
    ↓ Electroencephalography [67]
    Electromyography [67]
    Electronystagmography [73]
    Electroplethysmography [73]
    Electroretinography [67]
    Galvanic Skin Response [67]
    ↓ Skin Electrical Properties [73]
    Skin Potential [73]
R ↓ Medical Diagnosis [73]

Electroplethysmography [73]
PN 4   SC 16580
B   Electrophysiology [73]
    Medical Diagnosis [73]
    Plethysmography [73]

Electroretinography [67]
PN 148   SC 16590
B   Electrophysiology [73]
    Medical Diagnosis [73]

Electroretinography — (cont'd)
B   Ophthalmologic Examination [73]
R   Electro Oculography [73]

Electroshock Therapy
Use Electroconvulsive Shock Therapy

Electrosleep Treatment [78]
PN 15   SC 16605
SN Therapeutic application of a low intensity, intermittent electrical current to the skull, often producing a state of relaxation, but not necessarily sleep.
B   Organic Therapies [73]
R ↓ Shock Therapy [73]
    Sleep Treatment [73]

Elementarism
Use Reductionism

Elementary Education [73]
PN 627   SC 16620
B   Education [67]
R   Elementary Schools [73]

Elementary School Students [67]
PN 22303   SC 16630
SN Students in grades 1–6. Mandatory term in educational contexts.
B   Students [67]
N   Intermediate School Students [73]
    Primary School Students [73]
R ↓ Children [67]
    Grade Level [94]
    Middle School Students [85]
    Preadolescents [88]
    ↓ School Age Children [73]

Elementary School Teachers [73]
PN 3656   SC 16640
B   Teachers [67]

Elementary Schools [73]
PN 590   SC 16650
UF   Grammar Schools
    Primary Schools
B   Schools [67]
R   Elementary Education [73]

Elephants [73]
PN 30   SC 16660
B   Mammals [73]

Elimination (Excretion)
Use Excretion

Ellis (Albert) [91]
PN 3   SC 16680
SN Identifies biographical or autobiographical studies and discussions of Ellis's works.
R ↓ Psychologists [67]
    Rational Emotive Therapy [78]
    Self Talk [88]

Embarrassment [73]
PN 130   SC 16690
B   Emotional States [73]
R   Shame [94]

Embedded Figures Testing [67]
PN 157   SC 16700
B   Nonprojective Personality Measures [73]

Embolisms [73]
PN 18   SC 16710
B   Cardiovascular Disorders [67]
R ↓ Thromboses [73]

Embryo [73]
PN 125   SC 16720
B   Prenatal Developmental Stages [73]

Emergency Services [73]
PN 720   SC 16730
R ↓ Crisis Intervention Services [73]
    Natural Disasters [73]

Emetic Drugs [73]
PN 67   SC 16740
UF   Vomit Inducing Drugs
B   Drugs [67]
N   Apomorphine [73]
    Disulfiram [78]
R ↓ CNS Stimulating Drugs [73]
    ↓ Narcotic Drugs [73]
    Vomiting [73]

EMG (Electrophysiology)
Use Electromyography

Emotional Abuse [91]
PN 67   SC 16755
UF   Psychological Abuse
B   Antisocial Behavior [71]
R ↓ Child Abuse [71]
    Child Neglect [88]
    Elder Abuse [88]
    Partner Abuse [91]
    Patient Abuse [91]
    Physical Abuse [91]

Emotional Adjustment [73]
PN 4904   SC 16760
SN Personal acceptance, adaptation, and relation to one's inner self and environment.
UF   Emotional Maladjustment
    Maladjustment (Emotional)
    Personal Adjustment
    Psychological Adjustment
B   Adjustment [67]
N   Emotional Control [73]
    Identity Crisis [73]
R   Adjustment Disorders [94]
    Codependency [91]
    Coping Behavior [67]
    ↓ Emotionally Disturbed [73]
    ↓ Emotions [67]
    ↓ Personality [67]

Emotional Content [73]
PN 898   SC 16765
SN Emotional themes, substance, form, or characteristics of feelings, especially as they are portrayed in various forms of communication (e.g., reading material, motion pictures) or as manifested in specific situations.
R ↓ Communication [67]
    ↓ Emotions [67]

Emotional Control [73]
PN 130   SC 16770
SN Attempt to direct or govern one's own or another's emotions. Not to be confused with EMOTIONAL MATURITY which involves the exhibition of emotional behavior appropriate to one's age.
UF   Emotional Restraint
B   Emotional Adjustment [73]
R   Coping Behavior [67]
    Tantrums [73]

Emotional Development [73]
PN 1271   SC 16780
B   Psychogenesis [73]
R   Attachment Behavior [85]
    Childhood Play Development [73]

Emotional Development — (cont'd)
R ↓ Developmental Age Groups [73]
   ↓ Emotions [67]
   Object Relations [82]
   ↓ Personality Development [67]
   ↓ Physical Development [73]
   Psychosexual Development [82]
   ↓ Psychosocial Development [73]

Emotional Expressiveness
Use Emotionality (Personality)

Emotional Immaturity [73]
PN 38   SC 16800
SN Tendency to exhibit emotional reactions considered inappropriate for one's age.
UF Immaturity (Emotional)
B Personality Traits [67]
R Emotional Maturity [73]

Emotional Inferiority [73]
PN 37   SC 16810
SN Conscious or unconscious feelings of insecurity, insignificance, and inadequacy and of being unable to cope with life's demands.
UF Inferiority (Emotional)
B Personality Traits [67]

Emotional Insecurity
Use Emotional Security

Emotional Instability [73]
PN 76   SC 16830
SN Tendency to display unpredictable and rapidly changing emotions or moods.
UF Instability (Emotional)
B Personality Traits [67]
R Emotional Stability [73]

Emotional Maladjustment
Use Emotional Adjustment

Emotional Maturity [73]
PN 333   SC 16850
SN Attainment of a level of emotional development and exhibition of emotional patterns commonly associated with persons of a specific age level. Not to be confused with EMOTIONAL CONTROL which involves the suppression or control of direction of one's emotions.
UF Maturity (Emotional)
B Personality Traits [67]
R Emotional Immaturity [73]

Emotional Responses [67]
PN 4163   SC 16860
SN From 1982, limited to human populations. Use ANIMAL EMOTIONALITY for nonhuman subjects.
B Responses [67]
N Conditioned Emotional Responses [67]
R Animal Emotionality [78]
   ↓ Emotions [67]
   Laughter [78]
   Stranger Reactions [88]

Emotional Restraint
Use Emotional Control

Emotional Security [73]
PN 249   SC 16880
SN Possession of inner resources enabling one to cope with unfamiliar or threatening situations, especially as engendered through early nurturance.
UF Emotional Insecurity
   Insecurity (Emotional)

Emotional Security — (cont'd)
UF Security (Emotional)
B Personality Traits [67]

Emotional Stability [73]
PN 254   SC 16890
SN Resistance to affective disruption or tendency toward evenness of feelings.
UF Stability (Emotional)
B Personality Traits [67]
R Emotional Instability [73]

Emotional States [73]
PN 5263   SC 16900
UF Moods
B Emotions [67]
N Affection [73]
   Alienation [71]
   Ambivalence [73]
   ↓ Anger [67]
   ↓ Anxiety [67]
   Apathy [73]
   ↓ Aversion [67]
   Boredom [73]
   Depression (Emotion) [67]
   Disappointment [73]
   Disgust [94]
   Dissatisfaction [73]
   Distress [73]
   Doubt [73]
   Embarrassment [73]
   Emotional Trauma [67]
   Enthusiasm [73]
   Euphoria [73]
   ↓ Fear [67]
   Frustration [67]
   Grief [73]
   Guilt [67]
   Happiness [73]
   Homesickness [94]
   Hope [91]
   Hopelessness [88]
   Jealousy [73]
   Loneliness [73]
   Love [73]
   Mental Confusion [73]
   Optimism [73]
   Pessimism [73]
   Pleasure [73]
   Pride [73]
   Restlessness [73]
   Sadness [73]
   Shame [94]
   Suffering [73]
   Suspicion [73]
   Sympathy [73]
R ↓ Emotionally Disturbed [73]
   Irritability [88]
   Learned Helplessness [78]
   Morale [78]
   ↓ Personality [67]

Emotional Superiority [73]
PN 19   SC 16910
SN Feeling that one is better than others in ability, virtue, or worth.
UF Superiority (Emotional)
B Personality Traits [67]
R ↓ Dominance [67]

Emotional Trauma [67]
PN 1019   SC 16920
UF Trauma (Emotional)
B Emotional States [73]
R Adjustment Disorders [94]
   Posttraumatic Stress Disorder [85]

Emotionality (Personality) [73]
PN 800   SC 16930

Emotionality (Personality) — (cont'd)
SN Degree to which a person tends to react emotionally; characteristic of persons who react strongly or excessively to emotional situations.
UF Emotional Expressiveness
B Personality Traits [67]
R ↓ Emotions [67]

Emotionally Disturbed [73]
PN 3071   SC 16940
B Handicapped [67]
N Autistic Children [73]
R Acting Out [67]
   ↓ Childhood Psychosis [67]
   ↓ Emotional Adjustment [73]
   ↓ Emotional States [73]
   ↓ Emotions [67]

Emotions [67]
PN 4730   SC 16960
SN Conceptually broad array term referring to the affective aspects of human consciousness. Use a more specific term if possible. Use ANIMAL EMOTIONALITY for nonhuman subjects.
UF Feelings
N ↓ Emotional States [73]
R ↓ Emotional Adjustment [73]
   Emotional Content [73]
   Emotional Development [73]
   ↓ Emotional Responses [67]
   Emotionality (Personality) [73]
   ↓ Emotionally Disturbed [73]
   Expressed Emotion [91]
   Morale [78]
   ↓ Personality [67]

Empathy [67]
PN 2481   SC 16970
B Personality Traits [67]

Emphysema (Pulmonary)
Use Pulmonary Emphysema

Empirical Methods [73]
PN 546   SC 16990
SN Scientific methodology based on experimentation, systematic observation, or measurement, rather than theoretical formulation.
B Methodology [67]
N ↓ Experimental Methods [67]
   Observation Methods [67]
R Behavioral Assessment [82]

Employability [73]
PN 388   SC 17000
SN Potential usefulness of an individual as judged on the basis of job skills, functional literacy, emotional or social maturity, intellectual development, or personal values (e.g., personal responsibility).
R ↓ Employee Skills [73]
   ↓ Employment Status [82]
   ↓ Personnel [67]
   Supported Employment [94]
   Vocational Evaluation [91]

Employee Absenteeism [73]
PN 529   SC 17010
UF Absenteeism (Employee)
R ↓ Personnel [67]

Employee Assistance Programs [85]
PN 590   SC 17015
SN Programs or services provided by the employer to help employees with personal or other matters, including retirement planning or alcohol rehabilitation.
B Employee Benefits [73]
R ↓ Counseling [67]

Employee Assistance Programs — (cont'd)
R   Disability Management [91]
   ↓ Drug Rehabilitation [73]
   Elder Care [94]
   ↓ Program Development [91]
   ↓ Support Groups [91]

Employee Attitudes [67]
PN   3039   SC   17020
SN   Attitudes of, not toward, employees.
B   Attitudes [67]
   Employee Characteristics [88]
N   Job Satisfaction [67]
R   Employee Motivation [73]
   Job Involvement [78]
   ↓ Job Performance [67]
   Organizational Commitment [91]
   Work (Attitudes Toward) [73]

Employee Benefits [73]
PN   218   SC   17030
SN   Benefits provided by an employer that may be voluntary or mandated by federal or state law.
N   Bonuses [73]
   Employee Assistance Programs [85]
   ↓ Employee Health Insurance [73]
   Employee Leave Benefits [73]
   Employee Pension Plans [73]
   Workmens Compensation Insurance [73]
R   Disability Evaluation [88]
   Elder Care [94]
   ↓ Personnel [67]
   Salaries [73]

Employee Characteristics [88]
PN   436   SC   17035
N   ↓ Employee Attitudes [67]
   Employee Efficiency [73]
   Employee Motivation [73]
   Employee Productivity [73]
   ↓ Employee Skills [73]
R   Organizational Commitment [91]
   ↓ Personnel [67]
   Professional Identity [91]

Employee Efficiency [73]
PN   112   SC   17040
UF   Efficiency (Employee)
B   Employee Characteristics [88]
   Job Performance [67]

Employee Health Insurance [73]
PN   29   SC   17050
B   Employee Benefits [73]
   Health Insurance [73]
N   Workmens Compensation Insurance [73]

Employee Interaction [88]
PN   541   SC   17055
SN   Dynamics of interpersonal interaction between employees. Also used for supervisor/subordinate relations.
B   Interpersonal Interaction [67]
   Organizational Behavior [78]
R   ↓ Personnel [67]

Employee Leave Benefits [73]
PN   36   SC   17060
UF   Annual Leave
   Sick Leave
   Vacation Benefits
B   Employee Benefits [73]

Employee Motivation [73]
PN   1266   SC   17080
B   Employee Characteristics [88]
   Motivation [67]

Employee Motivation — (cont'd)
R   ↓ Employee Attitudes [67]
   Job Involvement [78]

Employee Pension Plans [73]
PN   14   SC   17090
UF   Pension Plans (Employee)
B   Employee Benefits [73]

Employee Productivity [73]
PN   894   SC   17110
UF   Productivity (Employee)
B   Employee Characteristics [88]
   Job Performance [67]

Employee Selection
Use   Personnel Selection

Employee Skills [73]
PN   325   SC   17130
B   Ability [67]
   Employee Characteristics [88]
N   Clerical Secretarial Skills [73]
R   Employability [73]
   Supported Employment [94]
   Vocational Evaluation [91]

Employee Termination
Use   Personnel Termination

Employee Turnover [73]
PN   767   SC   17140
UF   Turnover
R   Employment History [78]
   Job Security [78]
   ↓ Occupational Tenure [73]
   ↓ Personnel [67]

Employees
Use   Personnel

Employer Attitudes [73]
PN   307   SC   17160
SN   Attitudes of, not toward, employers.
B   Attitudes [67]
R   Organizational Commitment [91]
   ↓ Personnel [67]
   Work (Attitudes Toward) [73]

Employment
Use   Employment Status

Employment Discrimination [94]
PN   0   SC   17173
SN   Prejudiced and differential treatment of employees or job applicants based on factors other than performance or qualifications.
UF   Job Discrimination
B   Social Discrimination [82]
R   Affirmative Action [85]
   Age Discrimination [94]
   Job Applicant Screening [73]
   ↓ Personnel Evaluation [73]
   ↓ Personnel Management [73]
   ↓ Personnel Selection [67]
   ↓ Prejudice [67]
   Race and Ethnic Discrimination [94]
   Racism [73]
   Sex Discrimination [78]
   Sexism [88]

Employment History [78]
PN   309   SC   17174
SN   Past record of an individual's working life, including periods of unemployment.
R   Career Change [78]
   Career Development [85]

Employment History — (cont'd)
R   Employee Turnover [73]
   ↓ Employment Status [82]
   Job Experience Level [73]
   Occupational Mobility [73]
   Occupational Success [78]
   ↓ Occupational Tenure [73]
   ↓ Occupations [67]
   ↓ Personnel [67]
   Personnel Promotion [78]
   Personnel Termination [73]
   Professional Development [82]
   Retirement [73]
   Unemployment [67]

Employment Interviews
Use   Job Applicant Interviews

Employment Processes
Use   Personnel Recruitment

Employment Status [82]
PN   1733   SC   17196
SN   Condition of employment including full- or part-time, temporary or permanent, and unemployment. Use OCCUPATIONS to access references from 67N81.
UF   Employment
N   Self Employment [94]
   Unemployment [67]
R   Employability [73]
   Employment History [78]
   Job Applicants [85]
   ↓ Occupational Tenure [73]
   Reemployment [91]
   Retirement [73]
   Supported Employment [94]
   Working Women [78]

Employment Tests [73]
PN   263   SC   17200
SN   Tests used in personnel selection to measure the suitability of an applicant for a given occupation.
B   Measurement [67]
R   Job Applicant Screening [73]

Empowerment [91]
PN   137   SC   17203
SN   Promotion or attainment of autonomy and freedom of choice for individuals or groups.
R   Advocacy [85]
   Assertiveness [73]
   ↓ Civil Rights [78]
   Client Rights [88]
   Independence (Personality) [73]
   ↓ Involvement [73]
   Power [67]
   Self Determination [94]

Empty Nest [91]
PN   7   SC   17205
SN   Home environment after children have reached maturity and left home. Also, includes the concept of adult children returning to the home.
UF   Return to Home
R   Adult Offspring [85]
   ↓ Family [67]
   ↓ Family Relations [67]
   Family Size [73]
   ↓ Family Structure [73]
   Home Environment [73]
   Intergenerational Relations [88]
   ↓ Living Arrangements [91]
   ↓ Parent Child Relations [67]

Encephalitis [73]
PN   162   SC   17210

Encephalitis — (cont'd)
B   Brain Disorders [67]
     Viral Disorders [73]
R   Encephalomyelitis [73]
     ↓ Infectious Disorders [73]

Encephalography [73]
PN   9   SC   17220
B   Medical Diagnosis [73]
N   Echoencephalography [73]
     ↓ Electroencephalography [67]
     Pneumoencephalography [73]
     Rheoencephalography [73]
R   ↓ Roentgenography [73]

Encephalography (Air)
Use Pneumoencephalography

Encephalomyelitis [73]
PN   18   SC   17240
B   Myelitis [73]
R   Encephalitis [73]
     ↓ Infectious Disorders [73]

Encephalopathies [82]
PN   165   SC   17247
SN   Degenerative diseases of the brain.
B   Brain Disorders [67]
N   Creutzfeldt Jakob Syndrome [94]
     Toxic Encephalopathies [73]
     Wernickes Syndrome [73]
R   Thyrotoxicosis [73]

Encoding
Use Human Information Storage

Encopresis
Use Fecal Incontinence

Encounter Group Therapy [73]
PN   236   SC   17270
SN   Goal-oriented unstructured groups whose
members seek heightened self-awareness and
fulfillment of their human potential. The group
leader (not necessarily a clinically trained thera-
pist) participates freely in the group activity.
Techniques used include role playing, sensory
awareness, and physical contact.
B   Group Psychotherapy [67]
     Human Potential Movement [82]
N   Marathon Group Therapy [73]
R   Consciousness Raising Groups [78]
     Human Relations Training [78]
     Sensitivity Training [73]

Encouragement [73]
PN   92   SC   17290
B   Social Interaction [67]
R   ↓ Social Reinforcement [67]

Endocrine Disorders [73]
PN   110   SC   17300
B   Disorders [67]
N   ↓ Adrenal Gland Disorders [73]
     ↓ Diabetes [73]
     Endocrine Neoplasms [73]
     ↓ Endocrine Sexual Disorders [73]
     Parathyroid Disorders [73]
     ↓ Pituitary Disorders [73]
     ↓ Thyroid Disorders [73]
R   ↓ Endocrine System [73]
     Hypothermia [73]
     Migraine Headache [73]
     ↓ Psychosomatic Disorders [67]
     ↓ Secretion (Gland) [73]

Endocrine Gland Secretion [73]
PN   78   SC   17310

Endocrine Gland Secretion — (cont'd)
B   Secretion (Gland) [73]
N   Adrenal Gland Secretion [73]
R   ↓ Endocrine Glands [73]

Endocrine Gland Surgery [73]
PN   5   SC   17320
B   Surgery [71]
N   Adrenalectomy [73]
     ↓ Castration [67]
     Hypophysectomy [73]
     Pinealectomy [73]
     Thyroidectomy [73]

Endocrine Glands [73]
PN   30   SC   17330
B   Endocrine System [73]
     Glands [67]
N   Adrenal Glands [73]
     ↓ Gonads [73]
     Parathyroid Glands [73]
     Pineal Body [73]
     ↓ Pituitary Gland [73]
     Thyroid Gland [73]
R   ↓ Endocrine Gland Secretion [73]
     ↓ Hormones [67]
     Pancreas [73]

Endocrine Neoplasms [73]
PN   12   SC   17340
B   Endocrine Disorders [73]
     Neoplasms [67]

Endocrine Sexual Disorders [73]
PN   33   SC   17350
UF   Ovary Disorders
     Testes Disorders
B   Endocrine Disorders [73]
     Genital Disorders [67]
N   ↓ Hypogonadism [73]
     Testicular Feminization Syndrome [73]
R   ↓ Adrenal Gland Disorders [73]
     ↓ Gynecological Disorders [73]
     Hermaphroditism [73]
     ↓ Infertility [73]
     ↓ Male Genital Disorders [73]
     ↓ Pituitary Disorders [73]
     ↓ Thyroid Disorders [73]

Endocrine System [73]
PN   155   SC   17360
B   Anatomical Systems [73]
N   ↓ Endocrine Glands [73]
R   ↓ Endocrine Disorders [73]
     Pancreas [73]

Endocrinology [73]
PN   106   SC   17370
SN   Scientific discipline dealing with the study of
endocrine glands and internal secretions.
B   Medical Sciences [67]
N   Neuroendocrinology [85]
R   Psychoneuroimmunology [91]

Endogamous Marriage [73]
PN   16   SC   17380
B   Marriage [67]
N   Consanguineous Marriage [73]

Endogenous Depression [78]
PN   1022   SC   17384
B   Major Depression [88]

Endogenous Opiates [85]
PN   245   SC   17385
UF   Opioids (Endogenous)
B   Opiates [73]
     Peptides [73]

Endogenous Opiates — (cont'd)
N   Dynorphins [85]
     ↓ Endorphins [82]

Endorphins [82]
PN   608   SC   17386
SN   Endogenous morphine-like brain polypep-
tides that can bind to opiate receptors.
B   Endogenous Opiates [85]
     Neurotransmitters [85]
     Proteins [73]
N   Enkephalins [82]
R   Analgesia [82]

Endurance [73]
PN   65   SC   17390
SN   Ability to withstand hardship, adversity, or
stress. Used for human or animal populations.
N   Physical Endurance [73]
     Psychological Endurance [73]
R   ↓ Stress [67]

Energy Expenditure [67]
PN   957   SC   17400
SN   Expenditure of mental or physical effort.
UF   Effort
R   Calories [73]
     Metabolic Rates [73]

Engineering Psychology [67]
PN   471   SC   17410
SN   Branch of applied psychology that emphasizes the study of machine design, the relationship between humans and machines, and the
effects of machines on human behavior. Use a
more specific term if possible.
B   Applied Psychology [73]
R   Human Factors Engineering [73]

Engineers [67]
PN   498   SC   17420
B   Professional Personnel [78]
R   ↓ Aerospace Personnel [73]
     ↓ Business and Industrial Personnel [67]
     Scientists [67]

England [73]
PN   1265   SC   17430
B   Great Britain [71]

Enjoyment
Use Pleasure

Enkephalins [82]
PN   330   SC   17475
SN   Endogenous morphine-like brain polypep-
tides closely related to endorphins.
B   Endorphins [82]
R   Analgesia [82]
     ↓ Peptides [73]

Enlisted Military Personnel [73]
PN   192   SC   17480
SN   Military personnel ranking below commis-
sioned officers.
B   Military Personnel [67]
N   Draftees [73]
     Noncommissioned Officers [73]
R   Volunteer Military Personnel [73]

Enlistment (Military)
Use Military Enlistment

Enrollment (School)
Use School Enrollment

Enteropeptidase
Use Kinases

Enthusiasm 73
PN 31   SC 17530
UF   Eagerness
B   Emotional States 73
R   Morale 78
     ↓ Motivation 67

Entrance Examinations 73
PN 94   SC 17540
B   Educational Measurement 67
N   Coll Ent Exam Bd Scholastic Apt Test 73
R   Student Admission Criteria 73

Entrapment Games 73
PN 14   SC 17550
B   Games 67
R   ↓ Collective Behavior 67
     Game Theory 67
     Non Zero Sum Games 73
     Prisoners Dilemma Game 73

Entrepreneurship 91
PN 52   SC 17555
SN   Initiation, organization, management, and assumption of the attendant risks of a business or enterprise.
R   Business 67
     Business Management 73
     Capitalism 73
     ↓ Leadership 67
     ↓ Management 67
     Ownership 85
     ↓ Private Sector 85
     Self Employment 94

Enuresis
Use   Urinary Incontinence

Environment 67
PN 4107   SC 17570
SN   Totality of physical, social, psychological, or cultural conditions surrounding an organism.
N   ↓ Facility Environment 88
     ↓ Social Environments 73
R   ↓ Architecture 73
     Ecology 73
     Environmental Adaptation 73
     Environmental Attitudes 78
     Environmental Education 94
     ↓ Environmental Planning 82
     Environmental Stress 73
     Geography 73
     ↓ Hazardous Materials 91
     Nature Nurture 94
     Person Environment Fit 91
     Physical Comfort 82
     Urban Planning 73

Environmental Adaptation 73
PN 343   SC 17590
SN   Physiological or biological adaptation to conditions in the physical environment. For psychological, social, or emotional adaptation use ADJUSTMENT or one of its related terms.
UF   Adaptation (Environmental)
B   Adaptation 67
R   ↓ Environment 67
     Person Environment Fit 91

Environmental Attitudes 78
PN 676   SC 17594
SN   Perceptions of or beliefs regarding the physical environment, including factors affecting its quality (e.g., overpopulation, pollution).
B   Attitudes 67
R   Conservation (Ecological Behavior) 78
     Ecology 73
     ↓ Environment 67
     Environmental Education 94

Environmental Design
Use   Environmental Planning

Environmental Education 94
PN 0   SC 17598
SN   Used for educational and noneducational settings.
R   Conservation (Ecological Behavior) 78
     Ecology 73
     ↓ Education 67
     ↓ Environment 67
     Environmental Attitudes 78
     Pollution 73

Environmental Effects 73
PN 744   SC 17600
N   Altitude Effects 73
     Atmospheric Conditions 73
     ↓ Gravitational Effects 67
     Noise Effects 73
     Seasonal Variations 73
     ↓ Temperature Effects 67
     Underwater Effects 73
R   ↓ Ecological Factors 73
     Environmental Stress 73
     Lunar Synodic Cycle 73
     Physiological Stress 67

Environmental Planning 82
PN 268   SC 17607
SN   Planning and design of environment with goals of efficient human-environment interaction and minimal ecological disruption.
UF   Environmental Design
N   Interior Design 82
     Urban Planning 73
R   ↓ Architecture 73
     ↓ Environment 67
     Person Environment Fit 91
     ↓ Recreation Areas 73

Environmental Psychology 82
PN 245   SC 17609
SN   Branch of psychology that studies the relationship between environmental variables and behavior, including manipulation of one by the other.
B   Applied Psychology 73
R   Ecological Psychology 94

Environmental Stress 73
PN 482   SC 17610
SN   Naturally occurring or experimentally manipulated qualities of the physical environment which result in strain or disequilibrium. Consider also other specific terms (e.g., CROWDING, NOISE EFFECTS).
B   Stress 67
R   Crowding 78
     ↓ Deprivation 67
     ↓ Environment 67
     ↓ Environmental Effects 73
     Overpopulation 73
     Physiological Stress 67
     Thermal Acclimatization 73

Environmental Therapy
Use   Milieu Therapy

Envy
Use   Jealousy

Enzyme Inhibitors 85
PN 101   SC 17625
SN   Any agent that slows or otherwise disrupts the activity of an enzyme, such as antienzymes or enzyme antibodies.
B   Drugs 67
N   Acetazolamide 73

Enzyme Inhibitors — (cont'd)
N   ↓ Amine Oxidase Inhibitors 73
     Bromocriptine 88
     Captopril 91
     ↓ Cholinesterase Inhibitors 73
     ↓ Decarboxylase Inhibitors 82
     Hydroxylase Inhibitors 85
     ↓ Monoamine Oxidase Inhibitors 73
     Theophylline 73
R   ↓ Enzymes 73

Enzymes 73
PN 542   SC 17630
B   Drugs 67
N   Aldolases 73
     Carbonic Anhydrase 73
     Decarboxylases 73
     ↓ Dehydrogenases 73
     ↓ Esterases 73
     Hydroxylases 73
     Isozymes 73
     Kinases 82
     ↓ Oxidases 73
     Phosphatases 73
     Phosphorylases 73
     Proteinases 73
     ↓ Transferases 73
R   ↓ Anti Inflammatory Drugs 82
     ↓ Decarboxylase Inhibitors 82
     ↓ Enzyme Inhibitors 85
     ↓ Proteins 73

EOG (Electrophysiology)
Use   Electro Oculography

Ependyma
Use   Cerebral Ventricles

Ephedrine 73
PN 22   SC 17660
B   Adrenergic Drugs 73
     Alcohols 67
     Alkaloids 73
     CNS Stimulating Drugs 73
     Sympathomimetic Amines 73
     Vasoconstrictor Drugs 73
R   ↓ Local Anesthetics 73

Epidemiology 73
PN 4547   SC 17670
SN   Study of the occurrence, distribution, and containment of disease or mental disorders. Used for the scientific discipline as a whole or for specific epidemiological factors or findings (e.g., disease incidence or prevalence statistics).
B   Medical Sciences 67

Epilepsy 67
PN 2819   SC 17680
B   Brain Disorders 67
N   ↓ Epileptic Seizures 73
     Experimental Epilepsy 78
     Grand Mal Epilepsy 73
     Petit Mal Epilepsy 73
R   ↓ Anticonvulsive Drugs 73
     Aura 73
     ↓ Brain Damage 67
     Fugue Reaction 73

Epileptic Seizures 73
PN 495   SC 17690
B   Brain Disorders 67
     Epilepsy 67
N   Experimental Epilepsy 78
R   Coma 73
     ↓ Convulsions 67

Epinephrine [67]
PN 684   SC 17700
- UF Adrenaline
- B   Adrenergic Drugs [73]
      Catecholamines [73]
      Heart Rate Affecting Drugs [73]
      Hormones [67]
- R ↓ Adrenolytic Drugs [73]
      Cardiotonic Drugs [85]
      Vasoconstriction [73]
      Vasodilation [73]

Episodic Memory [88]
PN 97   SC 17705
- B   Memory [67]
- R   Eidetic Imagery [73]

Epistemology [73]
PN 633   SC 17710
- SN Philosophical study of knowledge, including its origin, nature, and limits.
- B   Philosophies [67]
- R   Hermeneutics [91]

Epithelial Cells [73]
PN 10   SC 17720
- B   Cells (Biology) [73]
- R   Skin (Anatomy) [67]

Epithelium
- Use Skin (Anatomy)

Epstein Barr Viral Disorder [94]
PN 0   SC 17740
- B   Infectious Disorders [73]
      Viral Disorders [73]

Equal Education [78]
PN 102   SC 17745
- SN Provision of comparable educational opportunities to all individuals irrespective of race, national origin, religion, sex, socioeconomic status, or ability.
- UF Educational Inequality
- B   Civil Rights [78]
- R ↓ Education [67]
      School Integration [82]
      Social Equality [73]

Equality (Social)
- Use Social Equality

Equilibrium [73]
PN 249   SC 17760
- SN Maintenance of postural balance. For physiological equilibrium consider HOMEOSTASIS.
- UF Balance (Motor Processes)
- R ↓ Perceptual Motor Processes [67]
      Spatial Orientation (Perception) [73]

Equimax Rotation [73]
PN 2   SC 17770
- B   Orthogonal Rotation [73]

Equipment
- Use Apparatus

Equity (Payment) [78]
PN 443   SC 17784
- SN In society, group, or other interpersonal situations, the process of equal allocation of economic resources, rewards, or payoffs.
- B   Equity (Social) [78]
- R ↓ Justice [73]
      Money [67]
      Salaries [73]
   ↓ Social Behavior [67]
   ↓ Social Processes [67]

Equity (Social) [78]
PN 410   SC 17786
- SN In society, group, or other interpersonal situations, the maintenance of relationships in which the proportions of each member's societal and cultural contributions or benefits are approximately equal.
- N   Equity (Payment) [78]
- R   Egalitarianism [85]
   ↓ Justice [73]
   ↓ Social Behavior [67]
   ↓ Social Processes [67]

Erection (Penis) [73]
PN 331   SC 17790
- B   Psychosexual Behavior [67]
- R   Impotence [73]

Ergonomics
- Use Human Factors Engineering

Ergot Derivatives [73]
PN 122   SC 17810
- B   Drugs [67]
- N   Bromocriptine [88]
      Dihydroergotamine [73]
- R ↓ Adrenergic Blocking Drugs [73]
   ↓ Alkaloids [73]
      Lysergic Acid Diethylamide [67]
      Tyramine [73]

Erikson (Erik) [91]
PN 10   SC 17815
- SN Identifies biographical or autobiographical studies and discussions of Erikson's works.
- R ↓ Developmental Stages [73]
      Ego Identity [91]
   ↓ Neopsychoanalytic School [73]
   ↓ Psychoanalysis [67]
      Psychoanalytic Theory [67]
   ↓ Psychologists [67]
   ↓ Psychosocial Development [73]

Eroticism [73]
PN 322   SC 17820
- B   Sexual Arousal [78]

Errata [91]
PN 294   SC 17825
- SN Mandatory term applied to corrections of errors in the text, abstract, or data of previously published material. Also used as a document type identifier.
- R ↓ Errors [67]
      Retraction of Publication [91]
   ↓ Scientific Communication [73]

Error Analysis [73]
PN 493   SC 17830
- SN Collection, classification and/or analysis of mistakes, especially in task or test performance.
- B   Analysis [67]
- R ↓ Errors [67]
      Man Machine Systems [73]

Error of Measurement [85]
PN 163   SC 17835
- SN Observed differences in obtained scores or measures due to chance variance.
- UF Error Variance
      Standard Error of Measurement
- B   Errors [67]
      Statistical Analysis [67]
- R   Consistency (Measurement) [73]
      Least Squares [85]
   ↓ Scoring (Testing) [73]
      Standard Deviation [73]
   ↓ Statistical Measurement [73]
   ↓ Test Bias [85]

Error of Measurement — (cont'd)
- R   Test Reliability [73]
   ↓ Test Scores [67]

Error Variance
- Use Error of Measurement

Errors [67]
PN 1826   SC 17840
- SN Inappropriate, inaccurate, or incorrect responses or performance. Also, factual errors or other informational inaccuracies and performance errors on the part of others to which a subject reacts.
- UF Mistakes
- N   Error of Measurement [85]
   ↓ Prediction Errors [73]
   ↓ Refraction Errors [73]
- R   Errata [91]
      Error Analysis [73]
      Halo Effect [82]
      Proofreading [88]

Erythroblastosis Fetalis
- Use Rh Incompatibility

Erythrocytes [73]
PN 269   SC 17860
- UF Red Blood Cells
- B   Blood Cells [73]
- R   Blood Groups [73]

Escape
- Use Avoidance

Escape Behavior (Animal)
- Use Animal Escape Behavior

Escape Conditioning [73]
PN 392   SC 17890
- SN Learned behavior or the operant conditioning procedure in which the subject learns a specific behavior that results in the termination of an ongoing aversive stimulus. Consider also NEGATIVE REINFORCEMENT. Compare AVOIDANCE CONDITIONING.
- UF Conditioning (Escape)
- B   Operant Conditioning [67]

Eserine
- Use Physostigmine

Eskimos [73]
PN 163   SC 17910
- SN Native populations of northern Canada, Greenland, Alaska, and eastern Siberia.
- B   Ethnic Groups [73]
- R   Minority Groups [67]

Esophagus [73]
PN 84   SC 17920
- B   Digestive System [67]

ESP (Parapsychology)
- Use Extrasensory Perception

Essay Testing [73]
PN 53   SC 17940
- B   Testing Methods [67]

Essential Hypertension [73]
PN 277   SC 17950
- B   Hypertension [73]

Esterases [73]
PN 29   SC 17970

Esterases — (cont'd)
- **B** Enzymes [73]
- **N** Acetylcholinesterase [73]
  - Cholinesterase [73]
- **R** Hydroxylases [73]
  - Phosphatases [73]

Estimation [67]
PN 1204   SC 17980
SN Subjective judgment or inference about the character, quality, or nature of a person, process, or thing which may or may not involve the inspection or availability of data or pertinent information.
- **N** ↓ Statistical Estimation [85]
  - Time Estimation [67]

Estradiol [73]
PN 875   SC 18000
- **B** Estrogens [73]

Estrogen Antagonists
Use Antiestrogens

Estrogen Replacement Therapy
Use Hormone Therapy

Estrogens [73]
PN 587   SC 18010
- **B** Sex Hormones [73]
- **N** Estradiol [73]
  - Estrone [73]
- **R** Antiandrogens [82]
  - Antiestrogens [82]

Estrone [73]
PN 8   SC 18020
- **B** Estrogens [73]

Estrus [73]
PN 471   SC 18030
- **R** ↓ Animal Biological Rhythms [73]
  - Animal Sexual Receptivity [73]
  - ↓ Menstrual Cycle [73]
  - ↓ Menstruation [73]

Ethanal
Use Acetaldehyde

Ethanol [73]
PN 2865   SC 18040
- **UF** Ethyl Alcohol
- **B** Alcohols [67]
- **R** Fetal Alcohol Syndrome [85]

Ether (Anesthetic) [73]
PN 40   SC 18050
- **UF** Ethyl Ether (Anesthetic)
- **B** General Anesthetics [73]

Ethics [67]
PN 866   SC 18060
- **N** Experimental Ethics [78]
  - Professional Ethics [73]
  - ↓ Values [67]
- **R** Euthanasia [73]
  - Morality [67]
  - ↓ Religious Beliefs [73]
  - ↓ Social Influences [67]

Ethiopia [82]
PN 45   SC 18064
- **B** Africa [67]

Ethnic Differences
Use Racial and Ethnic Differences

Ethnic Discrimination
Use Race and Ethnic Discrimination

Ethnic Disorders
Use Ethnospecific Disorders

Ethnic Groups [73]
PN 2656   SC 18080
- **N** American Indians [67]
  - Anglos [88]
  - Arabs [88]
  - Asians [82]
  - Eskimos [73]
  - Gypsies [73]
  - ↓ Hispanics [82]
- **R** Blacks [82]
  - Cultural Sensitivity [94]
  - Ethnic Values [73]
  - Ethnology [67]
  - ↓ Ethnospecific Disorders [73]
  - Minority Groups [67]
  - ↓ Racial and Ethnic Attitudes [82]
  - Racial and Ethnic Differences [82]
  - Tribes [73]
  - Whites [82]

Ethnic Identity [73]
PN 1138   SC 18090
SN Feelings, ties, or associations that an individual experiences as a member of a particular ethnic group.
- **B** Sociocultural Factors [67]
- **R** Cultural Sensitivity [94]
  - Reference Groups [94]
  - ↓ Social Identity [88]

Ethnic Sensitivity
Use Cultural Sensitivity

Ethnic Values [73]
PN 237   SC 18100
- **B** Social Influences [67]
  - Sociocultural Factors [67]
  - Values [67]
- **R** Cultural Sensitivity [94]
  - ↓ Ethnic Groups [73]

Ethnocentrism [73]
PN 162   SC 18110
SN Exaggerated tendency to identify with one's own ethnic group, or the inclination to judge others in terms of standards and values of one's own group.
- **B** Racial and Ethnic Attitudes [82]
- **R** ↓ Social Identity [88]

Ethnography [73]
PN 348   SC 18120
SN Descriptive study of cultures and societies. Used for the scientific discipline or the descriptive analyses themselves. Consider also ETHNOLOGY.
- **R** Anthropology [67]
  - Ethnology [67]
  - Kinship Structure [73]
  - Race (Anthropological) [73]
  - ↓ Rites of Passage [73]
  - ↓ Sociocultural Factors [67]

Ethnolinguistics [73]
PN 152   SC 18130
SN A part of anthropological linguistics concerned with the interrelation between a language and the cultural behavior of those who speak it.
- **B** Linguistics [73]
- **R** ↓ Dialect [73]
  - Ethnology [67]
  - Metalinguistics [94]

Ethnolinguistics — (cont'd)
- **R** Psycholinguistics [67]
  - Slang [73]
  - Sociolinguistics [85]

Ethnology [67]
PN 1517   SC 18140
SN Conceptually broad array term referring to the study of the origin, distribution, characteristics, and relations of the cultures or ethnic groups of the world. Also, a branch of anthropology dealing with the comparative or analytical study of human culture or societies. Use a more specific term if possible. Consider also ETHNOGRAPHY.
- **R** Animism [73]
  - Anthropology [67]
  - Cross Cultural Differences [67]
  - Cultism [73]
  - ↓ Culture (Anthropological) [67]
  - ↓ Culture Change [67]
  - Culture Shock [73]
  - ↓ Ethnic Groups [73]
  - Ethnography [73]
  - Ethnolinguistics [73]
  - ↓ Ethnospecific Disorders [73]
  - Folk Medicine [73]
  - Folklore [91]
  - Kinship [85]
  - Kinship Structure [73]
  - Myths [67]
  - Race (Anthropological) [73]
  - ↓ Racial and Ethnic Attitudes [82]
  - Racial and Ethnic Differences [82]
  - Racial and Ethnic Relations [82]
  - Shamanism [73]
  - ↓ Sociocultural Factors [67]
  - Taboos [73]
  - Transcultural Psychiatry [73]
  - Witchcraft [73]

Ethnospecific Disorders [73]
PN 22   SC 18150
- **UF** Ethnic Disorders
- **B** Disorders [67]
- **N** Koro [94]
  - Sickle Cell Disease [94]
- **R** ↓ Ethnic Groups [73]
  - Ethnology [67]
  - ↓ Mental Disorders [67]
  - ↓ Personality Disorders [67]
  - Transcultural Psychiatry [73]

Ethology (Animal)
Use Animal Ethology

Ethyl Alcohol
Use Ethanol

Ethyl Ether (Anesthetic)
Use Ether (Anesthetic)

Ethylaldehyde
Use Acetaldehyde

Etiology [67]
PN 6697   SC 18190
SN Study of the causes and origins of disorders. Used for the science itself or the specific etiological findings and processes.
- **UF** Aetiology
  - Pathogenesis
- **R** ↓ Disorders [67]
  - Patient History [73]

Etymology [73]
PN 52   SC 18200

Etymology — (cont'd)
SN Branch of linguistic science which traces the origin of words and morphemes to their earliest determinable base in a given language group and describes historical changes in words. Used for the discipline or specific etymological aspects of given words.
UF Word Origins
B Linguistics [73]
R Words (Phonetic Units) [67]

Eugenics [73]
PN 27   SC 18210
SN Applied science or the biosocial movement which advocates the use of practices aimed at improving the genetic composition of a population. Usually refers to human populations. Compare ANIMAL BREEDING, ANIMAL DOMESTICATION, and SELECTIVE BREEDING.
B Genetic Engineering [94]
Genetics [67]
Sciences [67]
R ↓ Family Planning [73]
Genetic Counseling [78]
Reproductive Technology [88]
Selective Breeding [73]
↓ Sterilization (Sex) [73]

Euphoria [73]
PN 93   SC 18230
B Emotional States [73]
R Happiness [73]
Pleasure [73]

Europe [73]
PN 532   SC 18240
N Austria [73]
Belgium [73]
Bulgaria [82]
Czechoslovakia [73]
Eastern Europe [88]
Finland [73]
France [67]
↓ Germany [88]
Greece [73]
Hungary [73]
Iceland [82]
↓ Ireland [73]
Italy [67]
Liechtenstein [91]
Netherlands [73]
Poland [73]
Portugal [82]
Romania [82]
↓ Scandinavia [78]
Spain [73]
Switzerland [73]
Union of Soviet Socialist Republics [67]
↓ United Kingdom [73]
Western Europe [88]
Yugoslavia [73]

Eustachian Tube
Use Middle Ear

Euthanasia [73]
PN 165   SC 18255
UF Mercy Killing
B Death and Dying [67]
R Advance Directives [94]
Death Attitudes [73]
↓ Ethics [67]
Professional Ethics [73]
↓ Treatment [67]
Treatment Withholding [88]

Evaluation [67]
PN 3222   SC 18260

Evaluation — (cont'd)
SN Conceptually broad term referring to the appraisal of the characteristics, significance, importance, or relative value of a person, organization, or thing.
N Course Evaluation [78]
Forensic Evaluation [94]
Needs Assessment [85]
Peer Evaluation [82]
↓ Personnel Evaluation [73]
↓ Program Evaluation [85]
Self Evaluation [67]
Treatment Effectiveness Evaluation [73]
Vocational Evaluation [91]
R Intake Interview [94]
Psychological Report [88]

Evaluation (Treatment Effectiveness)
Use Treatment Effectiveness Evaluation

Evangelists [73]
PN 42   SC 18320
B Religious Personnel [73]
R ↓ Clergy [73]
Lay Religious Personnel [73]
Missionaries [73]

Evidence (Legal)
Use Legal Evidence

Evoked Potentials [67]
PN 2162   SC 18330
B Electrical Activity [67]
N Auditory Evoked Potentials [73]
↓ Cortical Evoked Potentials [73]
Olfactory Evoked Potentials [73]
Somatosensory Evoked Potentials [73]
Visual Evoked Potentials [73]
R Electrical Brain Stimulation [73]
Sensory Gating [91]

Evolution (Theory of)
Use Theory of Evolution

Exceptional Children (Gifted)
Use Gifted

Exceptional Children (Handicapped)
Use Handicapped

Excretion [67]
PN 574   SC 18370
UF Elimination (Excretion)
B Physiology [67]
N Defecation [67]
Urination [67]

Executives
Use Top Level Managers

Exercise [73]
PN 1976   SC 18390
UF Physical Exercise
B Motor Processes [67]
N Aerobic Exercise [88]
Weightlifting [94]
Yoga [73]
R Health Behavior [82]
Physical Fitness [73]
Weight Control [85]

Exhaustion
Use Fatigue

Exhibitionism [73]
PN 154   SC 18420

Exhibitionism — (cont'd)
B Sexual Deviations [67]
R Voyeurism [73]

Existential Therapy [73]
PN 118   SC 18430
SN Form of psychotherapy that deals with the here and now of the patient's total situation rather than with his/her past; it emphasizes emotional experiences rather than rational thinking, and stresses a person's responsibility for his/her own existence.
B Psychotherapy [67]

Existentialism [67]
PN 663   SC 18440
SN Philosophy based on the analysis of the individual's existence in the world which holds that human existence cannot be completely described in scientific terms. Existentialism also stresses the freedom and responsibility of the individual as well as the uniqueness of religious and ethical experiences and the analysis of subjective phenomena such as anxiety, guilt, and suffering.
B Philosophies [67]
R ↓ Religious Beliefs [73]

Exogamous Marriage [73]
PN 59   SC 18450
UF Interethnic Marriage
Intermarriage
B Marriage [67]
N Interfaith Marriage [73]
Interracial Marriage [73]

Expectant Fathers [85]
PN 66   SC 18455
B Expectant Parents [85]
R ↓ Fathers [67]

Expectant Mothers [85]
PN 154   SC 18456
B Expectant Parents [85]
R ↓ Mothers [67]

Expectant Parents [85]
PN 55   SC 18457
N Expectant Fathers [85]
Expectant Mothers [85]
R ↓ Parents [67]

Expectations [67]
PN 7269   SC 18460
SN Anticipation of future behavior or events. Also refers to investigations of the effects of that anticipation on behavior.
B Cognitions [85]
N Experimenter Expectations [73]
Role Expectations [73]
Teacher Expectations [78]
R Future [91]
Halo Effect [82]
Hope [91]
Self Efficacy [85]

Experience (Practice)
Use Practice

Experience Level [88]
PN 1003   SC 18495
SN Amount of practical knowledge, skill, or practice as a result of direct participation in a particular activity.
UF Expertise
N Job Experience Level [73]
R ↓ Knowledge Level [78]

Experience Level (Job)
Use Job Experience Level

Experiences (Events) [73]
PN 1543　　　　　　SC 18510
SN Perceptual, emotional, and/or cognitive consequences associated with specific events or contexts. Compare LIFE EXPERIENCES.
N Anniversary Events [94]
　　Early Experience [67]
　　Life Experiences [73]
　　Vicarious Experiences [73]
R Combat Experience [91]
　↓ Crises [71]
　　Familiarity [67]
　　Homesickness [94]
　　Near Death Experiences [85]
　↓ Practice [67]

Experiences (Life)
Use Life Experiences

Experiential Psychotherapy [73]
PN 94　　　　　　SC 18520
SN Psychotherapeutic approach, having some roots in existentialism, that emphasizes the concrete, lived, and felt experience of the client.
B Psychotherapy [67]

Experiment Controls [73]
PN 191　　　　　　SC 18530
UF Control Groups
R ↓ Experimental Design [67]
　↓ Experimental Subjects [85]
　↓ Experimentation [67]
　↓ Methodology [67]

Experiment Volunteers [73]
PN 295　　　　　　SC 18540
UF Volunteers (Experiment)
B Experimental Subjects [85]
R Biased Sampling [73]
　↓ Experimental Design [67]
　　Informed Consent [85]
　　Random Sampling [73]

Experimental Apparatus
Use Apparatus

Experimental Attrition [94]
PN 0　　　　　　SC 18555
SN Reduction in the number of experimental subjects over time as a result of resignation or other factors.
UF Research Dropouts
R ↓ Dropouts [73]
　↓ Experimental Subjects [85]
　↓ Experimentation [67]

Experimental Design [67]
PN 2865　　　　　　SC 18560
SN General procedural plan for conducting an experiment in view of the specific data desired. This may include identification of the independent and dependent variables; selection of subjects and their assignment to specific experimental conditions/treatments; the sequence of experimental conditions/treatments; and a method of analysis. Consider also EXPERIMENTAL METHODS.
UF Design (Experimental)
　　Research Design
N Between Groups Design [85]
　　Cohort Analysis [88]
　　Followup Studies [73]
　↓ Hypothesis Testing [73]
　　Longitudinal Studies [73]
　　Repeated Measures [85]
R Animal Models [88]

Experimental Design — (cont'd)
R Conjoint Measurement [94]
　　Debriefing (Experimental) [91]
　　Experiment Controls [73]
　　Experiment Volunteers [73]
　↓ Experimental Methods [67]
　↓ Experimentation [67]
　↓ Methodology [67]
　↓ Population (Statistics) [73]
　　Psychometrics [67]
　↓ Sampling (Experimental) [73]
　↓ Statistical Analysis [67]
　↓ Statistical Variables [73]
　↓ Test Construction [73]

Experimental Epilepsy [78]
PN 145　　　　　　SC 18564
SN Paroxysmal transient disruption of normal electrical activity in the brain induced by chemical, electrical, or physical stimulation of the brain or by repetitive sensory stimulation.
B Epilepsy [67]
　　Epileptic Seizures [73]
R ↓ Convulsions [67]
　↓ Electrical Stimulation [73]
　　Kindling [85]

Experimental Ethics [78]
PN 462　　　　　　SC 18566
B Ethics [67]
R Animal Welfare [85]
　　Debriefing (Experimental) [91]
　↓ Experimentation [67]
　　Fraud [94]
　　Informed Consent [85]
　　Professional Ethics [73]

Experimental Instructions [67]
PN 2509　　　　　　SC 18570
SN Directions given to a subject participating in an experiment.
UF Instructions (Experimental)
R ↓ Experimentation [67]
　↓ Methodology [67]

Experimental Laboratories [73]
PN 241　　　　　　SC 18580
UF Laboratories (Experimental)
R ↓ Experimentation [67]
　↓ Methodology [67]

Experimental Methods [67]
PN 3554　　　　　　SC 18590
SN System of scientific investigation, usually based on a design and carried out under controlled conditions with the aim of testing a hypothesis.
UF Scientific Methods
B Empirical Methods [73]
N ↓ Stimulus Presentation Methods [73]
R ↓ Experimental Design [67]

Experimental Neurosis [73]
PN 52　　　　　　SC 18600
SN Acute neurotic-like state produced experimentally by requiring discrimination or problem solving responses which are beyond the subject's ability or level of learning. Such states are induced by the repeated delivery of aversive stimulation following failure.
B Neurosis [67]
R Experimental Psychosis [73]
　　Learned Helplessness [78]

Experimental Psychologists [73]
PN 33　　　　　　SC 18610
B Psychologists [67]

Experimental Psychology [67]
PN 496　　　　　　SC 18620
B Psychology [67]
R ↓ Experimentation [67]

Experimental Psychosis [73]
PN 12　　　　　　SC 18630
SN Experimentally induced psychotic-like state or condition usually achieved through drug administration. Not to be confused with inadvertent induction of psychotic conditions resulting from toxic side effects in drug therapy. Compare TOXIC PSYCHOSES.
B Psychosis [67]
R Experimental Neurosis [73]
　↓ Hallucinogenic Drugs [67]
　↓ Psychotomimetic Drugs [73]

Experimental Replication [73]
PN 2568　　　　　　SC 18640
SN Mandatory term applied to replications of original findings with same or different subjects or with variations in procedure and instrumentation.
UF Replication (Experimental)
R ↓ Experimentation [67]
　↓ Methodology [67]

Experimental Subjects [85]
PN 327　　　　　　SC 18645
SN Any individual who is, knowingly or unknowingly, a member of an experiment or research population. Used only when methodological or procedural aspects are discussed regarding research subjects. Used primarily for human populations.
UF Research Subjects
N Experiment Volunteers [73]
R Debriefing (Experimental) [91]
　　Experiment Controls [73]
　　Experimental Attrition [94]
　↓ Experimentation [67]

Experimentation [67]
PN 10566　　　　　　SC 18650
SN Conceptually broad array term referring to any or all aspects of scientific research. Use a more specific term if possible.
UF Investigation
　　Research
N ↓ Consumer Research [73]
　　Interdisciplinary Research [85]
R Animal Models [88]
　　Causal Analysis [94]
　　Debriefing (Experimental) [91]
　　Experiment Controls [73]
　　Experimental Attrition [94]
　↓ Experimental Design [67]
　　Experimental Ethics [78]
　　Experimental Instructions [67]
　　Experimental Laboratories [73]
　　Experimental Psychology [67]
　　Experimental Replication [73]
　↓ Experimental Subjects [85]
　　Experimenters [73]
　↓ Measurement [67]
　↓ Methodology [67]
　↓ Population (Statistics) [73]
　　Privileged Communication [73]
　　Psychometrics [67]
　　Psychophysics [67]
　↓ Sampling (Experimental) [73]
　↓ Statistical Analysis [67]
　↓ Statistical Correlation [67]
　　Statistical Reliability [73]
　↓ Statistical Validity [73]
　↓ Statistical Variables [73]
　↓ Theories [67]

Experimenter Bias [67]
PN 404   SC 18660
SN Potential and unintentional influence on experimental outcomes caused by the experimenter.
UF Bias (Experimenter)
R   Experimenter Expectations [73]
     Experimenters [73]
     Halo Effect [82]

Experimenter Expectations [73]
PN 130   SC 18670
SN Results from experimentation which are anticipated or desired by the researcher in order to confirm a hypothesis and which may serve as a potential factor in experimenter bias.
B   Expectations [67]
R   Experimenter Bias [67]
     Experimenters [73]

Experimenters [73]
PN 276   SC 18680
R   ↓ Experimentation [67]
     Experimenter Bias [67]
     Experimenter Expectations [73]

Expert Systems [91]
PN 185   SC 18685
UF Knowledge Based Systems
B   Artificial Intelligence [82]
     Systems [67]
R   ↓ Automated Information Processing [73]
     Automated Speech Recognition [94]
     ↓ Computers [67]
     Cybernetics [67]
     ↓ Data Processing [67]
     Databases [91]
     ↓ Decision Making [67]
     Information Systems [91]
     Man Machine Systems [73]
     ↓ Problem Solving [67]
     Robotics [85]

Expert Testimony [73]
PN 665   SC 18690
SN Legal testimony by persons who by virtue of their training, skills, or expertise are qualified to give evidence concerning some scientific, technical, or professional matter.
UF Testimony (Expert)
B   Legal Testimony [82]
R   Forensic Evaluation [94]
     Forensic Psychiatry [73]
     Forensic Psychology [85]

Expertise
   Use Experience Level

Exploratory Behavior [67]
PN 555   SC 18700
SN Locomotor activity or perceptual processes involved in investigating and/or orienting oneself to an environment. From 1973, limited to human populations. From 1973, use ANIMAL EXPLORATORY BEHAVIOR to access references to nonhumans.
B   Behavior [67]
N   Animal Exploratory Behavior [73]
R   Curiosity [67]
     Information Seeking [73]
     ↓ Motivation [67]

Explosive Personality [73]
PN 19   SC 18710
SN Disorder characterized by discrete episodes of loss of control of aggressive impulses that may result in serious assault or destruction of property.

Explosive Personality — (cont'd)
UF Intermittent Explosive Personality
B   Mental Disorders [67]
R   ↓ Antisocial Behavior [71]
     Conduct Disorder [91]
     ↓ Personality Disorders [67]

Exposure Time (Stimulus)
   Use Stimulus Duration

Expressed Emotion [91]
PN 91   SC 18725
SN Frequency and quality of negative emotions, e.g., anger or hostility, expressed by family members or significant others, that often lead to a high relapse rate, especially in schizophrenic patients.
R   ↓ Emotions [67]
     Relapse (Disorders) [73]
     ↓ Schizophrenia [67]

Expressions (Facial)
   Use Facial Expressions

Expressive Psychotherapy [73]
PN 33   SC 18740
SN Psychotherapeutic method used to promote more effective personality functioning through uninhibited expression of feelings and open discussion of personal problems.
B   Psychotherapy [67]

Expulsion (School)
   Use School Expulsion

Extended Family [73]
PN 129   SC 18760
B   Family [67]
     Family Structure [73]

Extension Workers (Agricultural)
   Use Agricultural Extension Workers

External Ear [73]
PN 42   SC 18780
UF Ear Canal
B   Ear (Anatomy) [67]

External Rewards [73]
PN 276   SC 18790
SN Tangible or overtly identifiable rewards given in return for service or attainment which may act as reinforcement for the activity rewarded. Compare PRIMARY REINFORCEMENT.
UF Extrinsic Rewards
B   Rewards [67]
R   Extrinsic Motivation [73]
     Internal External Locus of Control [67]

Externalization [73]
PN 55   SC 18800
B   Personality Processes [67]

Extinction (Learning) [67]
PN 2973   SC 18810
SN Learned behavior or the experimental paradigm involving withholding reinforcement for a conditioned response and resulting in a gradual reduction and eventual elimination of responding or a return to a rate of responding comparable to levels prior to conditioning. Term may be used in either classical (Pavlovian) or operant (instrumental) conditioning contexts.
B   Learning [67]
R   ↓ Discrimination Learning [82]
     ↓ Reinforcement [67]

Extracurricular Activities [73]
PN 340   SC 18820
N   Fraternity Membership [73]
     School Club Membership [73]
     Sorority Membership [73]
R   Athletic Participation [73]
     Athletic Training [91]
     ↓ Education [67]

Extradimensional Shift Learning
   Use Nonreversal Shift Learning

Extramarital Intercourse [73]
PN 144   SC 18830
UF Adultery
     Mate Swapping
B   Sexual Intercourse (Human) [73]
R   Promiscuity [73]

Extrapyramidal Symptoms [94]
PN 0   SC 18835
B   Symptoms [67]
R   ↓ Basal Ganglia [73]
     Extrapyramidal Tracts [73]
     ↓ Nervous System Disorders [67]

Extrapyramidal Tracts [73]
PN 95   SC 18840
B   Central Nervous System [67]
     Efferent Pathways [82]
     Spinal Cord [73]
R   Extrapyramidal Symptoms [94]

Extrasensory Perception [67]
PN 506   SC 18850
UF ESP (Parapsychology)
B   Parapsychological Phenomena [73]
     Perception [67]
N   ↓ Clairvoyance [73]
     Psychokinesis [73]
R   Telepathy [73]

Extraversion [67]
PN 2047   SC 18854
B   Personality Traits [67]

Extrinsic Motivation [73]
PN 296   SC 18860
SN Need or desire arising from outside the individual which causes action toward some goal.
B   Motivation [67]
R   External Rewards [73]
     ↓ Goals [67]
     Internal External Locus of Control [67]
     Needs [67]

Extrinsic Rewards
   Use External Rewards

Eye (Anatomy) [67]
PN 930   SC 18890
UF Choroid
     Sclera
B   Sense Organs [73]
N   Cornea [73]
     Eye Color [91]
     Fovea [82]
     Iris (Eye) [73]
     Lens (Eye) [73]
     Pupil (Eye) [73]
     ↓ Retina [67]
R   ↓ Eye Disorders [73]
     ↓ Eye Movements [67]
     Ocular Dominance [73]
     Pupil Dilation [73]
     Retinal Image [73]
     ↓ Visual Perception [67]

Eye Color [91]
PN 7   SC 18895
B   Color [67]
    Eye (Anatomy) [67]
R   Iris (Eye) [73]
    ↓ Pigments [73]

Eye Contact [73]
PN 525   SC 18900
SN Form of nonverbal communication in which two individuals meet each other's glance.
B   Interpersonal Communication [73]
    Nonverbal Communication [71]
R   ↓ Social Reinforcement [67]

Eye Convergence [82]
PN 113   SC 18902
SN Turning the eyes toward or away from each other when fixating on distal objects.
UF Vergence Movements
B   Eye Movements [67]
R   ↓ Depth Perception [67]
    ↓ Distance Perception [73]
    Strabismus [73]

Eye Disorders [73]
PN 227   SC 18910
SN Diseases or defects of the eye. Use VISION DISORDERS for other pathology involving visual neural pathways.
B   Vision Disorders [82]
N   Amblyopia [73]
    Cataracts [73]
    Color Blindness [73]
    Glaucoma [73]
    Hemianopia [73]
    Nystagmus [73]
    ↓ Refraction Errors [73]
    Strabismus [73]
    Tunnel Vision [73]
R   Albinism [73]
    ↓ Eye (Anatomy) [67]
    Hysterical Vision Disturbances [73]
    Ocular Dominance [73]
    ↓ Sensorially Handicapped [94]
    ↓ Visual Perception [67]

Eye Dominance
Use Ocular Dominance

Eye Examination
Use Ophthalmologic Examination

Eye Fixation [82]
PN 579   SC 18924
SN Orienting one's eye(s) toward and stabilizing one's gaze on a specified visual stimulus.
UF Gazing
    Ocular Fixation
    Visual Fixation
B   Visual Perception [67]
R   Visual Field [67]

Eye Movements [67]
PN 3680   SC 18930
UF Oculomotor Response
    Saccadic Eye Movements
N   Eye Convergence [82]
    Nystagmus [73]
    Rapid Eye Movement [71]
R   ↓ Eye (Anatomy) [67]
    REM Dreams [73]
    REM Sleep [73]
    Visual Search [82]

Eyeblink Reflex [73]
PN 319   SC 18940

Eyeblink Reflex — (cont'd)
UF Blink Reflex
B   Reflexes [71]
R   Startle Reflex [67]

Eyelid Conditioning [73]
PN 444   SC 18950
SN Conditioned eye blinking or the classical conditioning paradigm resulting in conditioned eye blinking.
UF Conditioning (Eyelid)
B   Classical Conditioning [67]

Eyewitnesses
Use Witnesses

Eysenck Personality Inventory [73]
PN 352   SC 18960
B   Nonprojective Personality Measures [73]

F Test [73]
PN 65   SC 18970
B   Parametric Statistical Tests [73]
R   ↓ Variability Measurement [73]

Face (Anatomy) [73]
PN 339   SC 18980
B   Anatomy [67]
R   Facial Features [73]
    Head (Anatomy) [73]

Face Perception [85]
PN 834   SC 18985
SN Used for human or animal populations.
UF Face Recognition
B   Visual Perception [67]
R   ↓ Facial Expressions [67]
    Facial Features [73]
    Prosopagnosia [94]
    ↓ Social Perception [67]

Face Recognition
Use Face Perception

Facial Expressions [67]
PN 1306   SC 18990
UF Expressions (Facial)
B   Nonverbal Communication [71]
N   Grimaces [73]
    Smiles [73]
R   Face Perception [85]
    Facial Features [73]

Facial Features [73]
PN 505   SC 18993
R   Face (Anatomy) [73]
    Face Perception [85]
    ↓ Facial Expressions [67]
    ↓ Physical Appearance [82]
    Physical Attractiveness [73]

Facial Muscles [73]
PN 189   SC 19000
B   Muscles [67]

Facial Nerve [73]
PN 68   SC 19010
UF Chorda Tympani Nerve
    Nerve (Facial)
B   Cranial Nerves [73]

Facilitated Communication
Use Augmentative Communication

Facilitation (Social)
Use Social Facilitation

Facility Admission [88]
PN 50   SC 19024
UF Facility Readmission
N   ↓ Hospital Admission [73]
R   ↓ Facility Discharge [88]
    ↓ Institutionalization [67]
    ↓ Treatment Facilities [73]

Facility Discharge [88]
PN 30   SC 19026
N   ↓ Hospital Discharge [73]
R   Discharge Planning [94]
    ↓ Facility Admission [88]
    ↓ Institutionalization [67]
    ↓ Treatment Facilities [73]

Facility Environment [88]
PN 189   SC 19028
B   Environment [67]
N   Hospital Environment [82]
R   ↓ Treatment Facilities [73]

Facility Readmission
Use Facility Admission

Factitious Disorders [88]
PN 133   SC 19035
UF Ganser Syndrome
B   Mental Disorders [67]
N   Munchausen Syndrome [94]
R   Malingering [73]
    Pseudodementia [85]

Factor Analysis [67]
PN 4044   SC 19040
SN Use FACTOR ANALYSIS to access references to the factor structure of psychometric measures from 67-84.
UF Confirmatory Factor Analysis
B   Multivariate Analysis [82]
N   Item Analysis (Statistical) [73]
    ↓ Statistical Rotation [73]
R   Factor Structure [85]
    Goodness of Fit [88]
    Path Analysis [91]
    ↓ Statistical Correlation [67]
    Statistical Significance [73]
    Structural Equation Modeling [94]

Factor Structure [85]
PN 1752   SC 19045
SN The internal correlational structure of a set of variables said to measure a given construct. Use FACTOR ANALYSIS to access references prior to 1985.
R   Construct Validity [82]
    ↓ Factor Analysis [67]
    Factorial Validity [73]
    ↓ Statistical Rotation [73]
    Structural Equation Modeling [94]

Factorial Validity [73]
PN 349   SC 19050
SN Degree of correlation of an assessment instrument or its individual items with the factors derived from factor analysis of another instrument or group of instruments. The proportion of total variance in the test scores that are accounted for by a specific factor can be used as an index of the construct validity of the instrument for that particular factor.
B   Statistical Validity [73]
R   Construct Validity [82]
    Factor Structure [85]
    Test Validity [73]

Factory Environments
Use Working Conditions

Faculty
Use Educational Personnel

Fading (Conditioning) 82
PN 96   SC 19087
SN Gradual attenuation of dissimilarity of stimuli dimensions contingent on the subject's mastery of difference between those stimuli. The fading technique is used to facilitate errorless discrimination learning.
  B   Behavior Modification 73
      Operant Conditioning 67
  R ↓ Discrimination Learning 82
      Stimulus Attenuation 73
      Stimulus Discrimination 73

Fads and Fashions 73
PN 48   SC 19090
  N   Clothing 67
  R   Social Change 67
      Trends 91

Failure 67
PN 1298   SC 19100
  N   Academic Failure 78
  R   Academic Underachievement 67
     ↓ Achievement 67

Failure to Thrive 88
PN 73   SC 19105
SN Growth disorder of infants and children due to nutritional and/or emotional deprivation and resulting in loss of weight and delayed physical, emotional and social development.
  UF   Reactive Attachment Disorder
  B   Delayed Development 73
  R ↓ Child Abuse 71
      Child Neglect 88
     ↓ Nutritional Deficiencies 73

Fainting
Use Syncope

Fairy Tales
Use Folklore

Faith Healing 73
PN 219   SC 19120
  B   Religious Practices 73
  R   Folk Medicine 73
      Shamanism 73
      Witchcraft 73

Faking 73
PN 297   SC 19130
  B   Deception 67
  R ↓ Behavior Disorders 71

False Pregnancy
Use Pseudocyesis

Fame 85
PN 33   SC 19145
  R ↓ Social Perception 67
     ↓ Status 67

Familial Idiocy (Amaurotic)
Use Amaurotic Familial Idiocy

Familiarity 67
PN 2764   SC 19160
SN Knowledge of, or close acquaintance with an object, stimulus, person, environment, situation or act to be performed.
  R ↓ Experiences (Events) 73
     ↓ Practice 67
      Stranger Reactions 88

Family 67
PN 3415   SC 19300
SN Conceptually broad array term. Use a more specific term if possible.
  N   Biological Family 88
      Extended Family 73
      Family of Origin 91
      Interethnic Family 88
      Interracial Family 88
      Nuclear Family 73
      Schizophrenogenic Family 67
      Stepfamily 91
  R   Codependency 91
      Cohabitation 73
      Couples 82
      Divorce 73
      Divorced Persons 73
      Dual Careers 82
      Dysfunctional Family 91
      Empty Nest 91
     ↓ Family Background 73
      Family Crises 73
     ↓ Family Members 73
     ↓ Family Planning 73
     ↓ Family Relations 67
      Family Resemblance 91
     ↓ Family Structure 73
      Kinship 85
     ↓ Living Arrangements 91
     ↓ Marital Separation 73
     ↓ Marital Status 73
     ↓ Marriage 67
      Transgenerational Patterns 91
      Widowers 73
      Widows 73
      Working Women 78

Family Background 73
PN 2394   SC 19170
  UF   Background (Family)
  N   Family Socioeconomic Level 73
      Parent Educational Background 73
      Parental Occupation 73
  R   Biographical Data 78
     ↓ Family 67
      Family of Origin 91
     ↓ Marital Status 73

Family Caregivers
Use Caregivers

Family Counseling
Use Family Therapy

Family Crises 73
PN 303   SC 19190
  B   Crises 71
  R ↓ Family 67
     ↓ Stress 67

Family Life
Use Family Relations

Family Medicine 88
PN 126   SC 19205
  B   Medical Sciences 67

Family Members 73
PN 3740   SC 19210
  N   Adopted Children 73
      Adult Offspring 85
     ↓ Ancestors 73
      Biological Family 88
      Cousins 73
      Daughters 73
      Foster Children 73
      Grandchildren 73
      Grandparents 73

Family Members — (cont'd)
  N   Illegitimate Children 73
      Orphans 73
     ↓ Parents 67
     ↓ Siblings 67
      Sons 73
     ↓ Spouses 73
      Stepchildren 73
  R ↓ Family 67
      Family of Origin 91
      Family Resemblance 91
     ↓ Offspring 88
      Only Children 82
      Significant Others 91

Family of Origin 91
PN 98   SC 19215
SN Family in which an individual was raised. Compare BIOLOGICAL FAMILY.
  B   Family 67
  R   Biological Family 88
     ↓ Family Background 73
     ↓ Family Members 73
     ↓ Family Structure 73
      Stepfamily 91

Family Physicians 73
PN 522   SC 19220
  B   Physicians 67
  R   General Practitioners 73

Family Planning 73
PN 401   SC 19230
  N ↓ Birth Control 71
  R   Condoms 91
      Delayed Parenthood 85
      Eugenics 73
     ↓ Family 67
      Fertility Enhancement 73
      Induced Abortion 71
     ↓ Sterilization (Sex) 73

Family Planning Attitudes 73
PN 676   SC 19240
  UF   Birth Control Attitudes
  B   Attitudes 67
  R   Childlessness 82
      Delayed Parenthood 85
     ↓ Family Relations 67

Family Relations 67
PN 10497   SC 19250
SN Dynamics of interpersonal interaction and developmental processes taking place between and among members of a biological or socially defined family unit. See FAMILY MEMBERS for references to biological relatives in a family.
  UF   Family Life
  N ↓ Child Discipline 73
     ↓ Childrearing Practices 67
     ↓ Marital Relations 67
     ↓ Parent Child Relations 67
      Parental Role 73
      Sibling Relations 73
  R   Childrearing Attitudes 73
      Codependency 91
      Dysfunctional Family 91
      Empty Nest 91
     ↓ Family 67
      Family Planning Attitudes 73
     ↓ Family Violence 82
      Intergenerational Relations 88
      Marriage Attitudes 73
      Social Support Networks 82
      Transgenerational Patterns 91

Family Resemblance 91
PN 5   SC 19255

Family Resemblance — (cont'd)
- R   Assortative Mating [91]
- ↓ Family [67]
- ↓ Family Members [73]
- ↓ Genetics [67]
-   Transgenerational Patterns [91]
- ↓ Twins [67]

Family Size [73]
PN 687   SC 19260
- B   Family Structure [73]
-   Size [73]
- R   Empty Nest [91]
- ↓ Parenthood Status [85]

Family Socioeconomic Level [73]
PN 524   SC 19270
- B   Family Background [73]
-   Socioeconomic Status [67]
- R   Parent Educational Background [73]
-   Parental Occupation [73]

Family Structure [73]
PN 1805   SC 19280
- N   Birth Order [67]
-   Childlessness [82]
-   Extended Family [73]
-   Family Size [73]
-   Matriarchy [73]
-   Nuclear Family [73]
- ↓ Parental Absence [73]
-   Patriarchy [73]
-   Polygamy [73]
-   Schizophrenogenic Family [67]
-   Stepfamily [91]
- R ↓ Culture (Anthropological) [67]
-   Dual Careers [82]
-   Dysfunctional Family [91]
-   Empty Nest [91]
- ↓ Family [67]
-   Family of Origin [91]
-   Homosexual Parents [94]
-   Kinship Structure [73]
-   Living Alone [94]
- ↓ Living Arrangements [91]
-   Only Children [82]
- ↓ Parenthood Status [85]
- ↓ Single Parents [78]
- ↓ Sociocultural Factors [67]
-   Stepchildren [73]
-   Stepparents [73]

Family Therapy [67]
PN 6319   SC 19290
- UF   Family Counseling
- B   Psychotherapeutic Counseling [73]
- N   Conjoint Therapy [73]
- R ↓ Counseling [67]
-   Social Casework [67]

Family Violence [82]
PN 1130   SC 19294
SN   Injurious or abusive behavior in family or other domestic interpersonal situations.
- UF   Domestic Violence
- B   Violence [73]
- N ↓ Child Abuse [71]
- R   Battered Females [88]
-   Elder Abuse [88]
- ↓ Family Relations [67]
-   Marital Conflict [73]
-   Partner Abuse [91]
-   Physical Abuse [91]
- ↓ Sexual Abuse [88]
-   Shelters [91]

Fantasies (Thought Disturbances) [67]
PN 430   SC 19310

Fantasies (Thought Disturbances) —
(cont'd)
SN   Thinking that severely distorts reality.
- B   Thought Disturbances [73]
- R   Magical Thinking [73]

Fantasy
Use   Imagination

Fantasy (Defense Mechanism) [67]
PN 601   SC 19320
SN   Daydreaming dominated by unconscious material and primary processes for the purpose of wish fulfillment or to alleviate social isolation.
- B   Defense Mechanisms [67]
- R   Daydreaming [73]

Farmers
Use   Agricultural Workers

Fascism [73]
PN 188   SC 19342
- UF   Nazism
- B   Political Economic Systems [73]
- R   Holocaust [88]

Fat Metabolism
Use   Lipid Metabolism

Fatalism [73]
PN 39   SC 19360
- B   Philosophies [67]

Father Absence [73]
PN 435   SC 19370
SN   From 1982, limited to human populations. For animals consider ANIMAL PARENTAL BEHAVIOR.
- B   Parental Absence [73]
- R   Matriarchy [73]

Father Child Communication [85]
PN 39   SC 19375
SN   Verbal or nonverbal communication between father and child.
- B   Parent Child Communication [73]
- R   Father Child Relations [73]

Father Child Relations [73]
PN 1251   SC 19380
SN   From 1982, limited to human populations. For animals consider ANIMAL PARENTAL BEHAVIOR.
- B   Parent Child Relations [67]
- R ↓ Childrearing Practices [67]
-   Father Child Communication [85]
-   Parental Attitudes [73]
-   Parental Permissiveness [73]
-   Parental Role [73]

Fathers [67]
PN 1962   SC 19390
SN   From 1982, limited to human populations. For animals consider ANIMAL PARENTAL BEHAVIOR.
- B   Human Males [73]
-   Parents [67]
- N   Adolescent Fathers [85]
-   Single Fathers [94]
- R   Expectant Fathers [85]

Fatigue [67]
PN 870   SC 19400
- UF   Exhaustion
-   Tiredness
- B   Symptoms [67]
- R   Hypersomnia [94]

Fatty Acids [73]
PN 216   SC 19410
- B   Acids [73]
-   Lipids [73]
- N   Capsaicin [91]
- ↓ Phosphatides [73]
- R   Prostaglandins [82]

Fear [67]
PN 3146   SC 19420
- B   Emotional States [73]
- N   Fear of Success [78]
-   Panic [73]
- R   Alarm Responses [73]
- ↓ Anxiety [67]
-   Neophobia [85]
- ↓ Phobias [67]
-   Shame [94]
-   Social Anxiety [85]
-   Stranger Reactions [88]

Fear of Public Speaking
Use   Speech Anxiety

Fear of Strangers
Use   Stranger Reactions

Fear of Success [78]
PN 336   SC 19424
SN   Need to inhibit maximum utilization of one's abilities in achievement situations due to expected negative consequences.
- B   Fear [67]
-   Motivation [67]
- R ↓ Achievement Motivation [67]
- ↓ Anxiety [67]
- ↓ Anxiety Neurosis [73]
-   Self Handicapping Strategy [88]

Fear Survey Schedule [73]
PN 38   SC 19430
- B   Nonprojective Personality Measures [73]

Fecal Incontinence [73]
PN 228   SC 19440
- UF   Encopresis
-   Incontinence (Fecal)
- B   Colon Disorders [73]
- R ↓ Behavior Disorders [71]
-   Diarrhea [73]
- ↓ Symptoms [67]

Fee for Service [94]
PN 0   SC 19450
SN   Payment for health related services in which the health care provider is reimbursed for services by the client or health insurance carrier.
- B   Health Insurance [73]
-   Professional Fees [78]
- R   Cost Containment [91]
- ↓ Health Care Delivery [78]
- ↓ Health Care Services [78]
-   Health Maintenance Organizations [82]
- ↓ Managed Care [94]

Feedback [67]
PN 4862   SC 19460
SN   General concept denoting the return of information that may regulate or control subsequent behavior, cognition, perception, or performance. Use a more specific term if possible.
- N ↓ Biofeedback [73]
- ↓ Delayed Feedback [73]
-   Knowledge of Results [67]
- ↓ Sensory Feedback [73]
- R ↓ Learning [67]
- ↓ Reinforcement [67]
- ↓ Stimulation [67]

Feeding Behavior (Animal)
Use Animal Feeding Behavior

Feeding Practices 73
PN 185   SC 19480
SN Limited to human populations.
UF Mealtimes
N Bottle Feeding 73
    Breast Feeding 73
    Weaning 73
R ↓ Childrearing Practices 67

Feelings
Use Emotions

Feet (Anatomy) 73
PN 99   SC 19500
UF Heels (Anatomy)
    Toes (Anatomy)
B Anatomy 67
    Musculoskeletal System 73
R Ankle 73
    Leg (Anatomy) 73

Felonies
Use Crime

Female Animals 73
PN 2519   SC 19520
B Animals 67

Female Criminals 73
PN 228   SC 19530
B Criminals 67
    Human Females 73

Female Delinquents 73
PN 249   SC 19540
B Human Females 73
    Juvenile Delinquents 73
R Male Delinquents 73

Female Genitalia 73
PN 151   SC 19550
SN Used for both human and animal populations.
UF Genitalia (Female)
B Urogenital System 73
N Ovaries 73
    ↓ Uterus 73
    Vagina 73

Female Orgasm 73
PN 231   SC 19560
SN Used for both human and animal populations.
B Orgasm 73
R Frigidity 73
    Masturbation 73
    ↓ Sexual Intercourse (Human) 73

Females (Human)
Use Human Females

Femininity 67
PN 1435   SC 19580
B Personality Traits 67
R Androgyny 82
    Masculinity 67
    Sex Roles 67

Feminism 78
PN 1081   SC 19585
R Feminist Therapy 94
    ↓ Sex Role Attitudes 78
    Womens Liberation Movement 73

Feminist Therapy 94
PN 0   SC 19587
SN An approach to psychotherapy, counseling, or consultation based on the assumptions and tenets of feminism.
B Psychotherapy 67
R ↓ Counseling 67
    Feminism 78

Feminization Syndrome (Testicular)
Use Testicular Feminization Syndrome

Femoral Nerve
Use Spinal Nerves

Fenfluramine 73
PN 304   SC 19610
B Appetite Depressing Drugs 73
    Sympathomimetic Drugs 73

Fentanyl 85
PN 48   SC 19613
SN Synthetic opiate frequently used illicitly.
B Opiates 73

Fertility 88
PN 94   SC 19618
SN The quality or state of being capable of breeding or reproducing. Used for human and animal populations.
B Sexual Reproduction 73
R Birth Rate 82
    Fertility Enhancement 73
    ↓ Infertility 73

Fertility Enhancement 73
PN 19   SC 19620
R ↓ Family Planning 73
    Fertility 88
    ↓ Hormones 67
    Oral Contraceptives 73

Fertilization 73
PN 65   SC 19630
R ↓ Pregnancy 67
    Reproductive Technology 88
    ↓ Sexual Reproduction 73

Fetal Alcohol Syndrome 85
PN 129   SC 19635
B Drug Induced Congenital Disorders 73
    Syndromes 73
R ↓ Alcoholism 67
    Ethanol 73
    ↓ Mental Retardation 67
    ↓ Prenatal Development 73

Fetishism 73
PN 130   SC 19640
UF Sexual Fetishism
B Sexual Deviations 67
R Sexual Masochism 73
    Sexual Sadism 73
    Transvestism 73

Fetus 67
PN 418   SC 19650
B Prenatal Developmental Stages 73

Fever
Use Hyperthermia

Fibrillation (Heart) 73
PN 14   SC 19680
UF Auricular Fibrillation
    Ventricular Fibrillation
B Arrhythmias (Heart) 73

Fibromyalgia Syndrome
Use Muscular Disorders

Fiction
Use Literature

Field Dependence 73
PN 1788   SC 19710
SN Aspect of cognitive style as seen in relative lack of autonomy from external referents, the inability to overcome embedding contexts, or the reliance on visual rather than gravitational cues in perception of the upright. Used also for reciprocal concept of field independence.
B Cognitive Style 67
R ↓ Personality Traits 67

Field Instruction
Use Curricular Field Experience

Field Trips (Educational)
Use Educational Field Trips

Field Work (Educational)
Use Curricular Field Experience

Fighting
Use Aggressive Behavior

Figurative Language 85
PN 128   SC 19736
SN Verbal expressions that signify one concept by using words that would normally be used to signify some other concept as a result of a conceptual analogy or qualitative similarity between the concepts.
UF Figures of Speech
    Simile
B Language 67
N Metaphor 82
R Analogy 91
    Connotations 73
    Symbolism 67
    ↓ Verbal Meaning 73

Figure Ground Discrimination 73
PN 544   SC 19740
SN Discrimination of a portion of a visual configuration as a coherent figure distinct from the background.
B Perceptual Discrimination 73
R Form and Shape Perception 67
    Pattern Discrimination 67
    ↓ Spatial Perception 67

Figures of Speech
Use Figurative Language

Fiji 91
PN 2   SC 19747
B South Pacific 78

Film Strips 67
PN 525   SC 19750
SN Strips of film for still projection. Not used as a document type identifier.
B Audiovisual Communications Media 73
R ↓ Educational Audiovisual Aids 73

Filtered Noise 73
PN 27   SC 19760
B Auditory Stimulation 67

Filtered Speech 73
PN 30   SC 19770
B Speech Processing (Mechanical) 73

Financial Assistance (Educational)
  Use Educational Financial Assistance

Fine Motor Skill Learning 73
PN 106   SC 19790
  B   Perceptual Motor Learning 67
       Skill Learning 73

Finger Tapping 73
PN 209   SC 19800
  B   Motor Performance 73

Fingers (Anatomy) 73
PN 283   SC 19820
  B   Musculoskeletal System 73
  N   Thumb 73
  R   Hand (Anatomy) 67

Fingerspelling 73
PN 60   SC 19830
  B   Manual Communication 78
  R   Sign Language 73

Finland 73
PN 463   SC 19840
  B   Europe 73
  R ↓ Scandinavia 78

Fire Fighters 91
PN 26   SC 19845
  R   Fire Prevention 73
     ↓ Government Personnel 73
     ↓ Paramedical Personnel 73
     ↓ Volunteer Personnel 73

Fire Prevention 73
PN 33   SC 19850
  B   Prevention 73
  R   Fire Fighters 91
     ↓ Safety 67

Firearms
  Use Weapons

Firesetting
  Use Arson

FIRO-B
  Use Fund Interper Rela Orientat Beh Ques

Fishes 67
PN 1497   SC 19870
  B   Vertebrates 73
  N   Bass (Fish) 73
     ↓ Carp 73
       Cichlids 73
       Electric Fishes 73
       Salmon 73
       Sticklebacks 73
  R   Larvae 73

Fixed Interval Reinforcement 73
PN 623   SC 19880
  UF   Interval Reinforcement
  B   Reinforcement Schedules 67

Fixed Ratio Reinforcement 73
PN 612   SC 19890
  UF   Ratio Reinforcement
  B   Reinforcement Schedules 67

Flashbacks
  Use Hallucinations

Flexibility (Personality)
  Use Adaptability (Personality)

Flexion Reflex 73
PN 97   SC 19910
  B   Reflexes 71

Flextime
  Use Work Scheduling

Flicker Fusion Frequency
  Use Critical Flicker Fusion Threshold

Flies
  Use Diptera

Flight Attendants
  Use Aerospace Personnel

Flight Instrumentation 73
PN 96   SC 19930
  UF   Instrumentation (Flight)
  B   Aviation 67
       Instrument Controls 85

Flight Simulation 73
PN 389   SC 19940
  B   Simulation 67
  R   Acceleration Effects 73
     ↓ Gravitational Effects 67

Flooding Therapy
  Use Implosive Therapy

Fluency
  Use Verbal Fluency

Fluid Intake 85
PN 519   SC 19965
  SN   Ingestion of liquids or solutions. Frequently
  used as an objective measure of physiological or
  motivational state or learning. Used for human or
  animal populations.
  N   Water Intake 67
  R ↓ Drinking Behavior 78
       Thirst 67

Fluoxetine 91
PN 379   SC 19967
  UF   Prozac
  B   Antidepressant Drugs 71

Fluphenazine 73
PN 380   SC 19970
  UF   Prolixin
  B   Antiemetic Drugs 73
       Phenothiazine Derivatives 73

Flurazepam 82
PN 84   SC 19974
  SN   Organic heterocyclic compound, used as a
  benzodiazepine tranquilizer and a nonbarbiturate
  sedative.
  B   Benzodiazepines 78
       Hypnotic Drugs 73
       Sedatives 73
  R ↓ CNS Depressant Drugs 73

Fluvoxamine 94
PN 0   SC 19975
  B   Antidepressant Drugs 71
       Serotonin Antagonists 73

Focusing (Visual)
  Use Ocular Accommodation

Folic Acid 73
PN 59   SC 19980
  B   Amino Acids 73

Folie A Deux 73
PN 67   SC 19990
  UF   Shared Paranoid Disorder
  B   Paranoia (Psychosis) 67
  R   Involutional Paranoid Psychosis 73
       Paranoid Schizophrenia 67

Folk Medicine 73
PN 319   SC 20000
  R   Ethnology 67
       Faith Healing 73
     ↓ Medical Sciences 67
       Shamanism 73
       Transcultural Psychiatry 73

Folklore 91
PN 61   SC 20010
  SN   Use MYTHS to access references from 73-
  90.
  UF   Fairy Tales
       Folktales
  R   Ethnology 67
     ↓ Literature 67
       Myths 67
       Storytelling 88

Folktales
  SN   Use MYTHS to access references from 73-
  90.
  Use Folklore

Follicle Stimulating Hormone 91
PN 6   SC 20025
  B   Gonadotropic Hormones 73

Followup (Posttreatment)
  Use Posttreatment Followup

Followup Studies 73
PN 7461   SC 20040
  SN   Mandatory term applied to reexaminations
  of an individual or group comparing the present
  findings with the original observations or mea-
  surements. Differentiate from POSTTREATMENT
  FOLLOWUP which is used in the context of after-
  care.
  UF   Studies (Followup)
  B   Experimental Design 67

Food 78
PN 682   SC 20045
  R   Diets 78
     ↓ Eating 67
       Food Additives 78
       Food Allergies 73
     ↓ Food Intake 67
       Food Preferences 73
       Nutrition 73

Food Additives 78
PN 97   SC 20047
  R ↓ Chemical Elements 73
       Diets 78
       Food 78
       Nutrition 73

Food Allergies 73
PN 42   SC 20050
  B   Allergic Disorders 73
  R   Diets 78
       Food 78

Food Deprivation 67
PN 1578   SC 20060
  SN   Absence of ad libitum food access. In experimental settings, food deprivation is used to
  achieve a definable level of motivation within the
  organism.

Food Deprivation — (cont'd)
B   Deprivation [67]
     Stimulus Deprivation [73]
R   Diets [78]
     Hunger [67]
     ↓ Nutritional Deficiencies [73]
     Starvation [73]

Food Intake [67]
PN   4580   SC   20070
SN   Ingestion of food. Frequently used as an objective measure of physiological or motivational state or learning. Used for human or animal populations.
N   ↓ Eating [67]
R   Animal Feeding Behavior [73]
     Dietary Restraint [94]
     Food [78]
     Sucking [78]
     Weight Control [85]

Food Preferences [73]
PN   1166   SC   20080
B   Preferences [67]
R   Diets [78]
     Eating Attitudes [94]
     Food [78]

Football [73]
PN   148   SC   20090
B   Recreation [67]
     Sports [67]

Foraging (Animal)
Use   Animal Foraging Behavior

Forced Choice (Testing Method) [67]
PN   154   SC   20100
SN   Assessment method requiring a choice between equally unlikely or undesirable alternatives, designed to reduce the effects of social desirability on the selection of test answers.
B   Testing Methods [67]

Forebrain [85]
PN   271   SC   20105
UF   Prosencephalon
B   Brain [67]
N   ↓ Diencephalon [73]
     Nucleus Basalis Magnocellularis [94]
     ↓ Telencephalon [73]

Foreign Language Education [73]
PN   593   SC   20110
SN   Curriculum, teaching methods, and educational programs used in the instruction of a language that is not native to the learner.
UF   Immersion Programs
     Second Language Education
B   Curriculum [67]

Foreign Language Learning [67]
PN   1207   SC   20120
B   Learning [67]
R   Bilingual Education [78]
     Foreign Languages [73]
     ↓ Language Development [67]
     Language Laboratories [73]
     Language Proficiency [88]

Foreign Language Translation [73]
PN   1229   SC   20130
SN   Rendering from one language to another. Use with foreign language test translations. Not used as a document type identifier.
R   Foreign Languages [73]

Foreign Languages [73]
PN   889   SC   20140
SN   Second or nonnative languages.
B   Language [67]
R   Bilingual Education [78]
     Foreign Language Learning [67]
     Foreign Language Translation [73]

Foreign Nationals [85]
PN   52   SC   20145
SN   Persons living in a country other than their own, generally with intent to return to their home country.
N   Foreign Students [73]
     Foreign Workers [85]
R   Immigration [73]

Foreign Organizations [73]
PN   14   SC   20150
SN   Organizations located in or originating from a foreign country.
B   Organizations [67]
R   International Organizations [73]

Foreign Policy Making [73]
PN   106   SC   20160
UF   Policy Making (Foreign)
B   Government Policy Making [73]
R   Government [67]
     International Relations [67]
     Peace [88]
     ↓ War [67]

Foreign Students [73]
PN   574   SC   20168
SN   Persons attending school or a training program in a country other than their own, generally with intent to return to their home country.
B   Foreign Nationals [85]
     Students [67]
R   Foreign Study [73]

Foreign Study [73]
PN   79   SC   20170
SN   Pursuit of an educational program in a country other than one's own, generally with intent to return to the home country.
B   Educational Programs [73]
R   Foreign Students [73]

Foreign Workers [85]
PN   69   SC   20175
SN   Persons employed in a country other than their own, generally with intent to return to their home country.
UF   Guest Workers
B   Foreign Nationals [85]
R   Migrant Farm Workers [73]

Foremen (Industrial)
Use   Industrial Foremen

Forensic Evaluation [94]
PN   0   SC   20185
B   Evaluation [67]
     Legal Processes [73]
R   Competency to Stand Trial [85]
     Court Referrals [94]
     ↓ Criminals [67]
     Expert Testimony [73]
     Forensic Psychiatry [73]
     Forensic Psychology [85]
     Insanity Defense [85]
     Mentally Ill Offenders [85]
     ↓ Psychodiagnosis [67]
     Psychological Report [88]

Forensic Psychiatry [73]
PN   608   SC   20190
SN   Branch of psychiatry devoted to legal issues relating to disordered behavior and mental disorders, including legal responsibility, competency to stand trial, and commitment issues.
B   Psychiatry [67]
R   ↓ Criminal Justice [91]
     Expert Testimony [73]
     Forensic Evaluation [94]
     Forensic Psychology [85]
     Insanity Defense [85]

Forensic Psychology [85]
PN   272   SC   20195
UF   Legal Psychology
B   Psychology [67]
R   ↓ Criminal Justice [91]
     Expert Testimony [73]
     Forensic Evaluation [94]
     Forensic Psychiatry [73]
     Psychological Autopsy [88]

Forgetting [73]
PN   484   SC   20200
SN   Inability to recall, recollect, or reproduce previously learned material, behavior, or experience. Compare AMNESIA and MEMORY DECAY.
R   ↓ Amnesia [67]
     Cued Recall [94]
     Free Recall [73]
     Fugue Reaction [73]
     ↓ Interference (Learning) [67]
     ↓ Learning [67]
     ↓ Memory [67]
     Memory Decay [73]
     Memory Training [94]
     Reminiscence [85]
     ↓ Retention [67]
     Serial Recall [94]
     Suppression (Defense Mechanism) [73]

Forgiveness [88]
PN   48   SC   20205
R   ↓ Conflict Resolution [82]
     ↓ Religious Beliefs [73]
     ↓ Social Interaction [67]

Form and Shape Perception [67]
PN   2908   SC   20210
SN   Perception of the physical form or shape of objects through any of the senses, usually haptic or visual.
UF   Contour
     Form Perception
     Shape Perception
B   Perception [67]
R   Figure Ground Discrimination [73]
     Pattern Discrimination [67]

Form Classes (Language) [73]
PN   270   SC   20220
UF   Words (Form Classes)
B   Language [67]
     Syntax [71]
N   Adjectives [73]
     Adverbs [73]
     Nouns [73]
     Pronouns [73]
     Verbs [73]

Form Perception
Use   Form and Shape Perception

Fornix [82]
PN   101   SC   20234
SN   Arched white fiber tract extending from the hippocampal formation to the septum, anterior nucleus of the thalamus, and mammillary body.

Fornix — (cont'd)
- **UF** Hippocampal Commissure
  Trigonum Cerebrale
- **B** Limbic System [73]
  Neural Pathways [82]
- **R** Medial Forebrain Bundle [82]
  Septal Nuclei [82]

FORTRAN
- **Use** Computer Programing Languages

Forward Masking
- **Use** Masking

Foster Care [78]
PN 675   SC 20245
- **SN** Family care provided by persons other than the natural or adoptive parents.
- **UF** Foster Homes
- **R** ↓ Child Care [91]
  Child Welfare [88]
  Foster Children [73]
  Foster Parents [73]

Foster Children [73]
PN 230   SC 20250
- **B** Family Members [73]
- **R** ↓ Children [67]
  Foster Care [78]

Foster Homes
- **Use** Foster Care

Foster Parents [73]
PN 217   SC 20260
- **B** Parents [67]
- **R** Foster Care [78]
  Surrogate Parents (Humans) [73]

Fovea [82]
PN 124   SC 20265
- **SN** Centrally located and depressed portion of the retina containing only cone photoreceptors.
- **B** Eye (Anatomy) [67]
- **R** Cones (Eye) [73]
  Foveal Vision [88]
  Visual Field [67]

Foveal Vision [88]
PN 122   SC 20267
- **UF** Central Vision
- **B** Visual Perception [67]
- **R** Fovea [82]

Fowl
- **Use** Birds

Foxes [73]
PN 39   SC 20290
- **B** Mammals [73]

Fragile X Syndrome [94]
PN 0   SC 20295
- **B** Sex Linked Hereditary Disorders [73]
  Syndromes [73]
- **R** ↓ Mental Retardation [67]
  ↓ Sex Chromosome Disorders [73]

Fragmentation (Schizophrenia) [73]
PN 6   SC 20300
- **UF** Loosening of Associations
- **B** Thought Disturbances [73]
- **R** ↓ Schizophrenia [67]

Frail
- **Use** Health Impaired

France [67]
PN 1436   SC 20310
- **B** Europe [73]

Franck Drawing Completion Test [73]
PN 4   SC 20320
- **B** Projective Personality Measures [73]
  Projective Techniques [67]

Frankness
- **Use** Honesty

Fraternity Membership [73]
PN 76   SC 20340
- **SN** Belonging to a club traditionally restricted to males. Used also for fraternity organizations.
- **B** Extracurricular Activities [73]

Fraud [94]
PN 0   SC 20345
- **UF** Consumer Fraud
- **B** Deception [67]
- **R** Cheating [73]
  ↓ Crime [67]
  Dishonesty [73]
  Experimental Ethics [78]
  Retraction of Publication [91]

Free Association [94]
PN 0   SC 20347
- **SN** Spontaneous association of ideas or mental images restricted by consciousness. Primarily used in, but not restricted to, psychoanalysis or Jungian analysis as a method to gain access to the organization and content of a patient's mind.
- **UF** Association (Free)
- **R** Jungian Psychology [73]
  ↓ Psychoanalysis [67]
  Psychoanalytic Theory [67]
  ↓ Psychotherapeutic Techniques [67]
  Unconscious (Personality Factor) [67]

Free Recall [73]
PN 1514   SC 20350
- **SN** Method of measuring the retention of learned material in which a subject is asked to recall as much of the material as possible, in any order, without the aid of external cues. Compare SERIAL ANTICIPATION (LEARNING) and RECONSTRUCTION (LEARNING).
- **B** Recall (Learning) [67]
- **R** Cued Recall [94]
  Forgetting [73]
  ↓ Memory [67]
  Serial Recall [94]

Free Will
- **Use** Volition

Freedom [78]
PN 270   SC 20354
- **R** Censorship [78]
  Choice Behavior [67]
  ↓ Civil Rights [78]
  ↓ Justice [73]
  ↓ Political Processes [73]
  Psychological Reactance [78]
  Volition [88]

Frequency (Pitch)
- **Use** Pitch (Frequency)

Frequency (Response)
- **Use** Response Frequency

Frequency (Stimulus)
- **Use** Stimulus Frequency

Frequency Distribution [73]
PN 237   SC 20380
- **UF** Distribution (Frequency)
- **B** Statistical Analysis [67]
  Statistical Measurement [73]
- **N** Normal Distribution [73]
  Skewed Distribution [73]
- **R** Standard Deviation [73]

Freud (Sigmund) [67]
PN 1796   SC 20390
- **SN** Identifies biographical or autobiographical studies and discussions of Freud's works.
- **R** Freudian Psychoanalytic School [73]
  ↓ Neopsychoanalytic School [73]
  ↓ Psychoanalysis [67]
  Psychoanalytic Theory [67]
  ↓ Psychologists [67]

Freudian Psychoanalytic School [73]
PN 324   SC 20400
- **UF** Psychoanalytic School (Freudian)
- **B** History of Psychology [67]
- **R** Freud (Sigmund) [67]
  Metapsychology [94]
  Psychoanalytic Interpretation [67]
  Psychoanalytic Theory [67]

Friendship [67]
PN 1529   SC 20410
- **B** Interpersonal Interaction [67]
- **R** Interpersonal Compatibility [73]
  Peer Pressure [94]
  ↓ Peer Relations [67]
  Significant Others [91]
  Social Dating [73]
  Social Support Networks [82]

Frigidity [73]
PN 44   SC 20420
- **B** Sexual Function Disturbances [73]
- **R** Dyspareunia [73]
  Female Orgasm [73]
  Impotence [73]
  ↓ Orgasm [73]
  ↓ Symptoms [67]
  Vaginismus [73]

Frogs [67]
PN 668   SC 20430
- **B** Amphibia [73]
- **R** Larvae [73]

Frontal Lobe [73]
PN 1406   SC 20440
- **B** Cerebral Cortex [67]
- **N** Gyrus Cinguli [73]
  Motor Cortex [73]
  Prefrontal Cortex [94]

Frostig Development Test Vis Percept [73]
PN 34   SC 20450
- **B** Intelligence Measures [67]

Fruit Fly
- **Use** Drosophila

Frustration [67]
PN 1087   SC 20470
- **B** Emotional States [73]
- **R** Dissatisfaction [73]
  Mental Confusion [73]

Fugue Reaction [73]
PN 15   SC 20480

Fugue Reaction — (cont'd)
SN Dissociative reaction characterized by extensive amnesia and a sudden change in one's lifestyle. Upon recovery, prefugue events are remembered but those that occurred during the fugue are forgotten.
B Amnesia [67]
Dissociative Patterns [73]
R ↓ Epilepsy [67]
Forgetting [73]

Fulfillment
Use Satisfaction

Functionalism [73]
PN 70   **SC** 20500
SN Doctrine or system of psychology which holds (contrary to structural psychology) that mental processes are the proper subject matter of psychology and that an essential feature of all psychological processes is the part they play in the adaptive functions of an organism.
B History of Psychology [67]
R James (William) [91]

Fund Interper Rela Orientat Beh Ques [73]
PN 51   **SC** 20510
UF FIRO-B
B Nonprojective Personality Measures [73]

Fundamentalism [73]
PN 89   **SC** 20520
B Protestantism [73]

Funding [88]
PN 212   **SC** 20524
R ↓ Costs and Cost Analysis [73]
Educational Financial Assistance [73]
↓ Government Policy Making [73]
↓ Government Programs [73]
Money [67]

Funerals
Use Death Rites

Furniture [85]
PN 17   **SC** 20527
R Human Factors Engineering [73]
Interior Design [82]
Physical Comfort [82]

Future [91]
PN 94   **SC** 20528
R ↓ Expectations [67]
↓ History [73]
↓ Prediction [67]
Social Change [67]
↓ Time [67]
Trends [91]

Fuzzy Set Theory [91]
PN 40   **SC** 20529
B Statistical Analysis [67]
Theories [67]
R ↓ Mathematical Modeling [73]
↓ Psychophysical Measurement [67]
↓ Statistical Probability [67]

Galanthamine [73]
PN 8   **SC** 20530
B Amines [73]
Cholinesterase Inhibitors [73]

Galvanic Skin Response [67]
PN 1640   **SC** 20550
SN Means of assessing sympathetic nervous system activity (i.e., arousal) by measuring onset of palmar sweat gland response.

Galvanic Skin Response — (cont'd)
UF Electrodermal Response
GSR (Electrophysiology)
B Diagnosis [67]
Electrophysiology [73]
Medical Diagnosis [73]
R Skin Potential [73]
↓ Skin Resistance [73]

Gambling [73]
PN 361   **SC** 20560
B Recreation [67]
Risk Taking [67]
Social Behavior [67]
N Pathological Gambling [88]
R ↓ Games [67]
Risk Analysis [91]

Game Theory [67]
PN 275   **SC** 20570
SN Mathematical theory which attempts to analyze and model the decision making process involved in gain-loss situations.
B Theories [67]
R Entrapment Games [73]
↓ Games [67]
Non Zero Sum Games [73]
Prisoners Dilemma Game [73]
Risk Analysis [91]
↓ Simulation [67]

Games [67]
PN 1505   **SC** 20580
N Chess [73]
Childrens Recreational Games [73]
Computer Games [88]
Entrapment Games [73]
Non Zero Sum Games [73]
Prisoners Dilemma Game [73]
Simulation Games [73]
R Childhood Play Behavior [78]
↓ Gambling [73]
Game Theory [67]
↓ Recreation [67]
↓ Toys [73]

Gamma Aminobutyric Acid [78]
PN 625   **SC** 20585
B Amino Acids [73]
Neurotransmitters [85]
R ↓ Gamma Aminobutyric Acid Agonists [85]
↓ Gamma Aminobutyric Acid Antagonists [85]

Gamma Aminobutyric Acid Agonists [85]
PN 211   **SC** 20587
N Muscimol [94]
R Gamma Aminobutyric Acid [78]

Gamma Aminobutyric Acid Antagonists [85]
PN 158   **SC** 20589
B Alkaloids [73]
N Bicuculline [94]
Picrotoxin [73]
R Gamma Aminobutyric Acid [78]

Gamma Globulin [73]
PN 7   **SC** 20590
B Immunoglobulins [73]
R Antibodies [73]

Ganglia [73]
PN 162   **SC** 20600
B Nervous System [67]
N Autonomic Ganglia [73]
↓ Basal Ganglia [73]
Spinal Ganglia [73]

Ganglion Blocking Drugs [73]
PN 11   **SC** 20610
B Drugs [67]
N Chlorisondamine [73]
Hexamethonium [73]
Mecamylamine [73]
Nicotine [73]
R ↓ Antihypertensive Drugs [73]

Ganglion Cells (Retina) [85]
PN 81   **SC** 20615
UF Retinal Ganglion Cells
B Neurons [73]
Retina [67]

Gangs (Juvenile)
Use Juvenile Gangs

Ganser Syndrome
Use Factitious Disorders

Gastrointestinal Disorders [73]
PN 311   **SC** 20630
B Digestive System Disorders [70]
N ↓ Colon Disorders [73]
Gastrointestinal Ulcers [67]
Vomiting [73]
R Influenza [73]
↓ Neoplasms [67]
↓ Psychosomatic Disorders [67]
↓ Toxic Disorders [73]

Gastrointestinal System [73]
PN 179   **SC** 20640
B Digestive System [67]
N Intestines [73]
Stomach [73]
R Pancreas [73]

Gastrointestinal Ulcers [67]
PN 439   **SC** 20650
UF Peptic Ulcers
Ulcers (Gastrointestinal)
B Gastrointestinal Disorders [73]
R ↓ Colitis [73]

Gastropods
Use Mollusca

Gates MacGinitie Reading Tests [73]
PN 13   **SC** 20670
UF Gates Reading Readiness Tests
Gates Reading Test
B Reading Measures [73]

Gates Reading Readiness Tests
Use Gates MacGinitie Reading Tests

Gates Reading Test
Use Gates MacGinitie Reading Tests

Gating (Sensory)
Use Sensory Gating

Gay Liberation Movement
Use Homosexual Liberation Movement

Gay Males
Use Male Homosexuality

Gay Parents
Use Homosexual Parents

Gazing
Use Eye Fixation

Geese [73]
PN 74   SC 20710
  B   Birds [67]

Gender Differences
  Use   Human Sex Differences

Gender Identity [85]
PN 382   SC 20717
SN   Inner conviction that one is male or female.
  R   ↓ Personality [67]
      Psychosexual Development [82]
      ↓ Self Concept [67]
      Sex Roles [67]
      Transsexualism [73]

General Anesthetics [73]
PN 49   SC 20720
  B   Anesthetic Drugs [73]
  N   Chloroform [73]
      Ether (Anesthetic) [73]
      Methohexital [73]
      Thiopental [73]

General Aptitude Test Battery [73]
PN 44   SC 20730
  B   Aptitude Measures [67]

General Health Questionnaire [91]
PN 33   SC 20740
  B   Personality Measures [67]
      Questionnaires [67]
  R   ↓ Diagnosis [67]
      ↓ Health [73]
      ↓ Screening Tests [82]

General Paresis [73]
PN 26   SC 20750
  UF   Dementia Paralytica
      Paresis (General)
  B   Paralysis [73]
  R   Neurosyphilis [73]
      ↓ Syphilis [73]

General Practitioners [73]
PN 378   SC 20760
  B   Physicians [67]
  R   Family Physicians [73]

Generalization (Cognitive)
  Use   Cognitive Generalization

Generalization (Learning) [82]
PN 942   SC 20775
SN   Responding in a similar manner to different
stimuli that have some common property as the
result of a conditioned or learned similarity. Also
known as secondary generalization. Also includes
generalization of any learned behavior to a new
context or setting. Compare TRANSFER (LEARN-
ING) or STIMULUS GENERALIZATION.
  B   Learning [67]
  N   Response Generalization [73]
      Stimulus Generalization [67]
  R   ↓ Concept Formation [67]
      ↓ Discrimination Learning [82]
      ↓ Transfer (Learning) [67]

Generalization (Response)
  Use   Response Generalization

Generalization (Semantic)
  Use   Semantic Generalization

Generalization (Stimulus)
  Use   Stimulus Generalization

Generalized Anxiety Disorder
  Use   Anxiety Neurosis

Generation Effect (Learning) [91]
PN 20   SC 20802
SN   In learning or memory contexts, the effect of
generating a stimuli oneself rather than having it
presented by external sources.
  B   Learning [67]
  R   ↓ Cognitive Processes [67]
      ↓ Memory [67]

Generation Gap [73]
PN 145   SC 20805
SN   Differences in values, morals, attitudes, and
behavior of young adults and older adults in con-
temporary society.
  R   Age Differences [67]
      Cohort Analysis [88]
      Intergenerational Relations [88]
      ↓ Parent Child Relations [67]
      Transgenerational Patterns [91]

Generators (Apparatus) [73]
PN 29   SC 20810
  B   Apparatus [67]

Genes [73]
PN 176   SC 20820
  R   ↓ Chromosomes [73]
      Genetic Linkage [94]
      ↓ Genetics [67]

Genetic Counseling [78]
PN 118   SC 20826
SN   Presentation and discussion, usually with
prospective parents, of factors involved in poten-
tial inheritance of disorders.
  B   Counseling [67]
  R   Eugenics [73]
      ↓ Genetic Disorders [73]
      ↓ Genetic Engineering [94]
      ↓ Genetics [67]

Genetic Disorders [73]
PN 343   SC 20830
  UF   Hereditary Disorders
  B   Disorders [67]
  N   Albinism [73]
      Amaurotic Familial Idiocy [73]
      ↓ Chromosome Disorders [73]
      Huntingtons Chorea [73]
      Phenylketonuria [73]
      Porphyria [73]
      Rh Incompatibility [73]
      ↓ Sex Linked Hereditary Disorders [73]
      Sickle Cell Disease [94]
  R   Alopecia [73]
      Anemia [73]
      Behavioral Genetics [94]
      Color Blindness [73]
      ↓ Congenital Disorders [73]
      Developmental Disabilities [82]
      Diabetes Insipidus [73]
      Genetic Counseling [78]
      ↓ Genetic Engineering [94]
      ↓ Genetics [67]
      Hypopituitarism [73]
      Mutations [73]
      Picks Disease [73]
      Prenatal Diagnosis [88]
      ↓ Refraction Errors [73]

Genetic Dominance [73]
PN 37   SC 20840
  B   Dominance [67]
  R   Behavioral Genetics [94]

Genetic Dominance — (cont'd)
  R   Genetic Recessiveness [73]
      ↓ Genetics [67]

Genetic Engineering [94]
PN 0   SC 20845
  N   Eugenics [73]
  R   Genetic Counseling [78]
      ↓ Genetic Disorders [73]
      Genetic Linkage [94]
      ↓ Genetics [67]
      Population Genetics [73]
      Reproductive Technology [88]
      Selective Breeding [73]

Genetic Linkage [94]
PN 0   SC 20847
SN   Linkage of genes at different loci on the
same chromosome and analysis of how genes
are inherited together.
  UF   Linkage Analysis
  R   ↓ Chromosomes [73]
      Genes [73]
      ↓ Genetic Engineering [94]
      ↓ Genetics [67]
      Genotypes [73]

Genetic Recessiveness [73]
PN 23   SC 20850
  UF   Recessiveness (Genetic)
  R   Behavioral Genetics [94]
      Genetic Dominance [73]
      ↓ Genetics [67]

Genetics [67]
PN 6999   SC 20860
SN   Conceptually broad array term referring both
to the science of heredity and the biological pro-
cess of transmission of characteristics from pro-
genitor to offspring.
  UF   Heredity
  N   Behavioral Genetics [94]
      Eugenics [73]
      Population Genetics [73]
  R   ↓ Animal Breeding [73]
      Animal Mate Selection [82]
      Animal Strain Differences [82]
      Assortative Mating [91]
      Blood Groups [73]
      ↓ Chromosomes [73]
      Family Resemblance [91]
      Genes [73]
      Genetic Counseling [78]
      ↓ Genetic Disorders [73]
      Genetic Dominance [73]
      ↓ Genetic Engineering [94]
      Genetic Linkage [94]
      Genetic Recessiveness [73]
      Genotypes [73]
      Hybrids (Biology) [73]
      Instinctive Behavior [82]
      Mutations [73]
      Nature Nurture [94]
      ↓ Nucleic Acids [73]
      Phenotypes [73]
      Predisposition [73]
      Reproductive Technology [88]
      Selective Breeding [73]
      ↓ Sexual Reproduction [73]
      Species Differences [82]
      Translocation (Chromosome) [73]
      ↓ Twins [67]

Geniculate Bodies (Thalamus) [73]
PN 342   SC 20870
  B   Thalamus [67]
  R   Visual Receptive Fields [82]

Genital Disorders [67]
PN 141   SC 20880
UF   Sex Differentiation Disorders
      Sexual Disorders (Physiological)
B   Urogenital Disorders [73]
N ↓ Endocrine Sexual Disorders [73]
   ↓ Gynecological Disorders [73]
     Hermaphroditism [73]
   ↓ Infertility [73]
   ↓ Male Genital Disorders [73]
R   Sex [67]

Genital Herpes
Use   Herpes Genitalis

Genitalia (Female)
Use   Female Genitalia

Genitalia (Male)
Use   Male Genitalia

Geniuses
Use   Gifted

Genocide [88]
PN 11   SC 20915
SN   Deliberate and systematic destruction of a racial, political, or cultural group.
B   Homicide [67]
N   Holocaust [88]

Genotypes [73]
PN 286   SC 20920
R   Genetic Linkage [94]
   ↓ Genetics [67]
     Phenotypes [73]

Genuineness
Use   Sincerity

Geographic Regions
Use   Geography

Geographical Mobility [78]
PN 290   SC 20924
SN   Capacity or facility of individuals to move from one geographic region to another. Includes job- or study-related commuting.
UF   Mobility (Geographical)
R   Commuting (Travel) [85]
   ↓ Human Migration [73]

Geography [73]
PN 468   SC 20925
SN   Science dealing with the description of the topographical features of the earth and the distribution of life on earth. Also, geographic areas or their features.
UF   Geographic Regions
     Physical Divisions (Geographic)
     Physical Geography
     Political Divisions (Geographic)
B   Sciences [67]
R ↓ Countries [67]
   ↓ Environment [67]

Geomagnetism
Use   Magnetism

Geometry
Use   Mathematics

Gerbils [73]
PN 506   SC 20940
B   Rodents [73]

Geriatric Patients [73]
PN 2285   SC 20950
SN   Older persons suffering from mental or physical diseases and disabilities and under some form of treatment.
B   Patients [67]
R ↓ Aged [73]

Geriatric Psychotherapy [73]
PN 139   SC 20960
B   Psychotherapy [67]
R   Animal Assisted Therapy [94]
     Geriatrics [67]
     Physiological Aging [67]

Geriatrics [67]
PN 985   SC 20970
SN   Medical subdiscipline which deals with the problems of old age and aging. Use GERIATRICS or GERONTOLOGY to access references on the aged (elderly) from 67–72.
B   Medical Sciences [67]
R ↓ Aged [73]
     Aged (Attitudes Toward) [78]
   ↓ Aging [91]
     Geriatric Psychotherapy [73]
     Gerontology [67]
     Physiological Aging [67]

German Measles
Use   Rubella

Germany [88]
PN 245   SC 20995
SN   Used for articles about Germany prior to 1945 or when East Germany or West Germany is not specified. Use a more specific term if possible.
B   Europe [73]
N   East Germany [82]
     West Germany [82]

Gerontology [67]
PN 816   SC 21000
SN   Scientific study of old age and the phenomena associated with old age. Use GERONTOLOGY or GERIATRICS to access references to the aged (elderly) from 67–72.
B   Developmental Psychology [73]
R ↓ Aged [73]
     Aged (Attitudes Toward) [78]
   ↓ Aging [91]
     Geriatrics [67]
     Life Review [91]

Gestalt Psychology [67]
PN 453   SC 21010
SN   School of psychology concerned with the study of the individual's perception of and response to configurational wholes.
B   History of Psychology [67]

Gestalt Therapy [73]
PN 514   SC 21020
SN   Type of psychotherapy which emphasizes treatment of the individual as a whole and focuses on sensory awareness of present experience.
B   Human Potential Movement [82]
     Psychotherapy [67]

Gestation
Use   Pregnancy

Gestures [73]
PN 442   SC 21040
B   Nonverbal Communication [71]
R   Body Language [73]

Ghana [88]
PN 17   SC 21045
B   Africa [67]

Ghettoes [73]
PN 88   SC 21050
UF   Urban Ghettoes
B   Urban Environments [67]
R   Poverty Areas [73]

Gifted [67]
PN 3212   SC 21060
UF   Exceptional Children (Gifted)
     Geniuses
     Intellectually Gifted
     Talented
R ↓ Ability [67]
     Creativity [67]
     Intelligence [67]

Gilles de la Tourette Disorder [73]
PN 518   SC 21070
UF   Tourette Syndrome
B   Neuromuscular Disorders [73]
R   Echolalia [73]

Girls
Use   Human Females

Glands [67]
PN 633   SC 21080
N ↓ Endocrine Glands [73]
     Mammary Glands [73]
     Pancreas [73]
     Salivary Glands [73]
R   Pheromones [73]

Glaucoma [73]
PN 25   SC 21090
B   Eye Disorders [73]

Globulins [73]
PN 22   SC 21100
UF   Glycoproteins
B   Proteins [73]
N   Antibodies [73]
   ↓ Immunoglobulins [73]

Globus Pallidus [73]
PN 137   SC 21110
B   Basal Ganglia [73]

Glossary [73]
PN 12   SC 21120
SN   Mandatory term used as a document type identifier. Compare PSYCHOLOGICAL TERMINOLOGY.
R   Dictionary [73]

Glossolalia [73]
PN 33   SC 21130
SN   Unintelligible speech occurring in hypnotic or mediumistic trances, religious ecstasies, or some mental disorders.
R ↓ Mental Disorders [67]
   ↓ Religious Practices [73]

Glossopharyngeal Nerve
Use   Cranial Nerves

Glucagon [73]
PN 50   SC 21150
B   Hormones [67]

Glucocorticoids [82]
PN 186   SC 21155

Glucocorticoids — (cont'd)
SN Any steroid-like compound capable of significantly influencing intermediary metabolism. Glucocorticoids are also clinically useful anti-inflammatory agents.
B   Adrenal Cortex Hormones [73]
     Anti Inflammatory Drugs [82]
N   Dexamethasone [85]

Glucose [73]
PN 830   SC 21160
B   Sugars [73]
N   Blood Sugar [73]
R   Glucose Metabolism [94]
     Glycogen [73]

Glucose Metabolism [94]
PN 0   SC 21165
B   Carbohydrate Metabolism [73]
R   ↓ Glucose [73]
     ↓ Neurochemistry [73]

Glue Sniffing [73]
PN 54   SC 21170
B   Inhalant Abuse [85]

Glutamic Acid [73]
PN 209   SC 21180
B   Amino Acids [73]
     Neurotransmitters [85]
R   Kainic Acid [88]

Glutamine [73]
PN 38   SC 21190
B   Amino Acids [73]

Glutethimide [73]
PN 14   SC 21210
B   CNS Depressant Drugs [73]
     Hypnotic Drugs [73]
     Sedatives [73]

Glycine [73]
PN 67   SC 21220
B   Amino Acids [73]
     Neurotransmitters [85]

Glycogen [73]
PN 29   SC 21230
R   ↓ Glucose [73]

Glycoproteins
Use Globulins

Goals [67]
PN 2272   SC 21240
SN Aims toward which an individual or a group aspire or toward which effort is directed. Use a more specific term if possible.
UF Objectives
N   Educational Objectives [78]
     Organizational Objectives [73]
R   ↓ Aspirations [67]
     Extrinsic Motivation [73]
     ↓ Incentives [67]
     Intention [88]
     Intrinsic Motivation [73]
     ↓ Motivation [67]
     Needs [67]

Goats [73]
PN 90   SC 21250
B   Mammals [73]

God Concepts [73]
PN 179   SC 21260
B   Religious Beliefs [73]

Goiters [73]
PN 12   SC 21270
B   Thyroid Disorders [73]
R   Hyperthyroidism [73]
     Hypothyroidism [73]

Goldfish [73]
PN 408   SC 21280
B   Carp [73]

Goldstein Scheerer Object Sort Test [73]
PN 4   SC 21290
B   Nonprojective Personality Measures [73]

Gonadotropic Hormones [73]
PN 214   SC 21300
UF Gonadotropin
B   Hormones [67]
N   Follicle Stimulating Hormone [91]
     Luteinizing Hormone [78]
     Prolactin [73]
R   ↓ Pituitary Hormones [73]
     ↓ Sex Hormones [73]

Gonadotropin
Use Gonadotropic Hormones

Gonads [73]
PN 77   SC 21320
B   Endocrine Glands [73]
     Urogenital System [73]
N   Ovaries [73]
     Testes [73]

Gonorrhea [73]
PN 17   SC 21330
B   Bacterial Disorders [73]
     Venereal Diseases [73]

Goodenough Harris Draw A Person Test [67]
PN 116   SC 21340
B   Intelligence Measures [67]
R   Human Figures Drawing [73]

Goodness of Fit [88]
PN 76   SC 21350
B   Statistical Analysis [67]
R   ↓ Factor Analysis [67]
     ↓ Mathematical Modeling [73]
     Maximum Likelihood [85]
     Statistical Significance [73]

Gorillas [73]
PN 127   SC 21370
B   Primates (Nonhuman) [73]

Gossip [82]
PN 32   SC 21375
SN Idle personal talk or communication of unsubstantiated information.
UF Rumors
B   Interpersonal Communication [73]
R   Messages [73]

Gough Adjective Check List [73]
PN 21   SC 21380
B   Nonprojective Personality Measures [73]

Government [67]
PN 568   SC 21390
UF Government Bureaucracy
B   Public Sector [85]
R   Autonomy (Government) [73]
     Foreign Policy Making [73]
     Government Agencies [73]
     ↓ Government Personnel [73]

Government — (cont'd)
R   ↓ Government Policy Making [73]
     ↓ Government Programs [73]
     Gun Control Laws [73]
     Job Corps [73]
     ↓ Law (Government) [73]
     ↓ Law Enforcement [78]
     ↓ Laws [67]
     ↓ Legal Processes [73]
     Legislative Processes [73]
     ↓ Marihuana Laws [73]
     Marihuana Legalization [73]
     Peace Corps [73]
     ↓ Political Economic Systems [73]
     ↓ Politics [67]
     Project Follow Through [73]
     Project Head Start [73]
     Taxation [85]
     Upward Bound [73]
     Volunteers in Service to America [73]
     Welfare Services (Government) [73]

Government Agencies [73]
PN 326   SC 21400
B   Organizations [67]
     Public Sector [85]
R   Government [67]

Government Bureaucracy
Use Government

Government Personnel [73]
PN 894   SC 21420
UF Civil Servants
     Elected Government Officials
B   Personnel [67]
N   Agricultural Extension Workers [73]
     ↓ Law Enforcement Personnel [73]
     ↓ Military Personnel [67]
     Police Personnel [73]
     Public Health Service Nurses [73]
R   ↓ Business and Industrial Personnel [67]
     Fire Fighters [91]
     Government [67]

Government Policy Making [73]
PN 1832   SC 21430
UF Policy Making (Government)
     Public Policy
B   Policy Making [88]
N   Foreign Policy Making [73]
     ↓ Laws [67]
     Legislative Processes [73]
R   Advocacy [85]
     Funding [88]
     Government [67]
     Health Care Policy [94]
     ↓ Legal Processes [73]
     ↓ War [67]

Government Programs [73]
PN 722   SC 21440
UF Programs (Government)
N   Job Corps [73]
     Medicaid [94]
     Medicare [88]
     Peace Corps [73]
     Project Follow Through [73]
     Project Head Start [73]
     Social Security [88]
     Upward Bound [73]
     Volunteers in Service to America [73]
     Welfare Services (Government) [73]
R   Funding [88]
     Government [67]
     ↓ Program Development [91]
     Shelters [91]
     ↓ Social Services [82]

Grade Level [94]
PN 0   SC 21445
  UF Academic Grade Level
  R   Ability Grouping [73]
      Age Differences [67]
      ↓ Education [67]
      Educational Placement [78]
      ↓ Elementary School Students [67]
      High School Students [67]
      Junior High School Students [71]
      Kindergarten Students [73]
      Special Education Students [73]
      Transfer Students [73]

Gradepoint Average
  Use Academic Achievement

Grading (Educational) [73]
PN 461   SC 21460
  SN Rating of achievement level by means of
  established scales or standards. Consider also
  SCORING (TESTING) or TEST SCORES.
  B   Educational Measurement [67]
  R   ↓ Scoring (Testing) [73]

Graduate Degrees
  Use Educational Degrees

Graduate Education [73]
PN 367   SC 21480
  B   Higher Education [73]
  N   Dental Education [73]
      ↓ Graduate Psychology Education [67]
      ↓ Medical Education [73]

Graduate Psychology Education [67]
PN 2044   SC 21490
  UF Training (Graduate Psychology)
  B   Graduate Education [73]
      Psychology Education [78]
  N   ↓ Clinical Psychology Grad Training [73]
  R   Educational Program Accreditation [94]

Graduate Record Examination [73]
PN 85   SC 21500
  B   Aptitude Measures [67]

Graduate Schools [73]
PN 44   SC 21510
  B   Schools [67]
  R   ↓ Higher Education [73]
      School Graduation [91]

Graduate Students [67]
PN 2331   SC 21520
  SN Students pursuing academic studies past
  the college level. Mandatory term in educational
  contexts.
  B   Students [67]
  R   ↓ College Students [67]
      Dental Students [73]
      Law Students [78]
      Medical Students [67]
      Postgraduate Students [73]
      Young Adults [73]

Graduation (School)
  Use School Graduation

Grammar [67]
PN 1420   SC 21530
  SN Science of the structure of language including universal grammar, descriptive and prescrip-
  tive grammar, and the rules and principles of
  syntax, phonology, and semantics applied in verbal communication. Compare SYNTAX.
  B   Linguistics [73]
  N   Morphology (Language) [73]

Grammar — (cont'd)
  N   ↓ Phonology [73]
      ↓ Semantics [67]
      ↓ Syntax [71]
      Transformational Generative Grammar [73]
  R   ↓ Language [67]
      ↓ Verbal Communication [67]
      Words (Phonetic Units) [67]

Grammar Schools
  Use Elementary Schools

Grand Mal Epilepsy [73]
PN 23   SC 21550
  B   Epilepsy [67]

Grandchildren [73]
PN 107   SC 21560
  B   Family Members [73]

Grandiosity [94]
PN 0   SC 21565
  B   Defense Mechanisms [67]
  R   Delusions [67]
      Narcissism [67]
      Omnipotence [94]

Grandparents [73]
PN 293   SC 21570
  B   Ancestors [73]
      Family Members [73]

Graphical Displays [85]
PN 367   SC 21575
  SN Pictorial rendering of data (e.g., bar graphs,
  continuous line graphs, and data plots). Consider
  VISUAL DISPLAYS to access references from
  73-84.
  B   Displays [67]
  R   Statistical Data [82]
      ↓ Statistical Measurement [73]

Graphology
  Use Handwriting

Grasshoppers [73]
PN 54   SC 21590
  B   Insects [67]
  R   Larvae [73]

Gravitational Effects [67]
PN 114   SC 21600
  B   Environmental Effects [73]
  N   Weightlessness [67]
  R   Acceleration Effects [73]
      Altitude Effects [73]
      ↓ Aviation [67]
      Decompression Effects [73]
      Flight Simulation [73]
      Spaceflight [67]
      Underwater Effects [73]

Great Britain [71]
PN 1077   SC 21620
  B   United Kingdom [73]
  N   England [73]
      Scotland [73]
      Wales [73]
  R   Northern Ireland [73]

Great Grandparents
  Use Ancestors

Greece [73]
PN 226   SC 21650
  B   Europe [73]
  R   Middle East [78]

Gregariousness [73]
PN 16   SC 21660
  B   Personality Traits [67]
  R   Sociability [73]

Grid (Shuttle Box)
  Use Shuttle Box Grids

Grief [73]
PN 2089   SC 21680
  UF Bereavement
      Mourning
  B   Emotional States [73]
  R   ↓ Death and Dying [67]
      Suffering [73]

Grimaces [73]
PN 7   SC 21690
  B   Facial Expressions [67]

Grooming Behavior (Animal)
  Use Animal Grooming Behavior

Gross Motor Skill Learning [73]
PN 138   SC 21700
  B   Perceptual Motor Learning [67]
      Skill Learning [73]

Ground Transportation [73]
PN 72   SC 21710
  B   Transportation [73]
  N   ↓ Motor Vehicles [82]
      Railroad Trains [73]
  R   Highway Safety [73]

Group Cohesion [73]
PN 628   SC 21730
  SN Mutual bonds formed among the members
  of a group as a consequence of their combined
  efforts toward a common goal or purpose.
  UF Cohesion (Group)
  B   Group Dynamics [67]

Group Counseling [73]
PN 2476   SC 21740
  UF Counseling (Group)
  B   Counseling [67]
  R   ↓ Self Help Techniques [82]
      ↓ Support Groups [91]

Group Decision Making [78]
PN 810   SC 21745
  SN Process of arriving at a decision or judg-
  ment by a group.
  B   Decision Making [67]
  N   Choice Shift [94]
  R   Management Decision Making [73]

Group Discussion [67]
PN 1532   SC 21750
  UF Discussion (Group)
  B   Group Dynamics [67]
      Interpersonal Communication [73]
  R   Choice Shift [94]

Group Dynamics [67]
PN 4689   SC 21760
  UF Dynamics (Group)
  N   Group Cohesion [73]
      Group Discussion [67]
      Group Participation [73]
      Group Performance [67]
      Group Size [67]
      Group Structure [67]
      Intergroup Dynamics [73]
  R   Brainstorming [82]
      Choice Shift [94]

Group Dynamics — (cont'd)
R ↓ Collective Behavior [67]
     Consciousness Raising Groups [78]
     Group Instruction [73]
     ↓ Group Problem Solving [73]
     ↓ Group Psychotherapy [67]
     Human Relations Training [78]
     ↓ Organizational Behavior [78]
     Peer Pressure [94]
     Reference Groups [94]
     Sensitivity Training [73]
     ↓ Sociometry [91]
     Teams [88]

Group Health Plans
Use Health Maintenance Organizations

Group Homes [82]
PN 412   SC 21767
SN Housing for groups of patients, children, or others who need or desire emotional and physical support.
B   Housing [73]
R ↓ Community Facilities [73]
     Community Mental Health Services [78]
     ↓ Residential Care Institutions [73]
     Shelters [91]

Group Instruction [73]
PN 615   SC 21770
B   Teaching Methods [67]
R   Cooperative Learning [94]
     ↓ Group Dynamics [67]

Group Participation [73]
PN 1086   SC 21780
SN Involvement in a group's purpose or activities.
B   Group Dynamics [67]
     Interpersonal Interaction [67]
     Participation [73]
R ↓ Collective Behavior [67]

Group Performance [67]
PN 992   SC 21790
SN Process and effectiveness of a group in accomplishing an intended goal.
B   Group Dynamics [67]
     Interpersonal Interaction [67]
     Performance [67]

Group Problem Solving [73]
PN 956   SC 21800
SN Dynamics of group interaction during the process of analyzing, defining, and attaining the solution to a problem.
B   Problem Solving [67]
N   Brainstorming [82]
R   Choice Shift [94]
     ↓ Group Dynamics [67]

Group Psychotherapy [67]
PN 6227   SC 21810
UF Group Therapy
B   Psychotherapy [67]
N ↓ Encounter Group Therapy [73]
     Therapeutic Community [67]
R   Conjoint Therapy [73]
     Consciousness Raising Groups [78]
     ↓ Group Dynamics [67]
     ↓ Human Potential Movement [82]
     Psychodrama [67]
     Sensitivity Training [73]
     ↓ Support Groups [91]

Group Size [67]
PN 1081   SC 21820

Group Size — (cont'd)
UF Size (Group)
B   Group Dynamics [67]
     Size [73]

Group Structure [67]
PN 767   SC 21830
SN Patterns of organization, behavior, and communication of a group that determine the interpersonal relations of its members.
B   Group Dynamics [67]

Group Testing [73]
PN 180   SC 21840
B   Measurement [67]
R   Test Administration [73]

Group Therapy
Use Group Psychotherapy

Groups (Organizations)
Use Organizations

Groups (Social)
Use Social Groups

Grown Children
Use Adult Offspring

Growth
Use Development

Growth Centers
Use Human Potential Movement

Growth Hormone
Use Somatotropin

Growth Hormone Inhibitor
Use Somatostatin

GSR (Electrophysiology)
Use Galvanic Skin Response

Guanethidine [73]
PN 29   SC 21930
B   Amines [73]
     Antihypertensive Drugs [73]
R   Norepinephrine [73]

Guanosine [85]
PN 29   SC 21929
R ↓ Carbohydrate Metabolism [73]
     Cyclic Adenosine Monophosphate [78]
     ↓ Nucleic Acids [73]

Guardianship [88]
PN 49   SC 21932
SN Court appointment of an individual to act as a guardian or conservator and to legally act and speak in the interest of a minor or a physically or mentally disabled adult.
UF Conservatorship
B   Legal Processes [73]
R   Child Custody [82]
     Client Rights [88]
     ↓ Commitment (Psychiatric) [73]
     Informed Consent [85]

Guatemala [82]
PN 40   SC 21931
B   Central America [73]

Guessing [73]
PN 162   SC 21933

Guessing — (cont'd)
SN Responding to questions or test items on the basis of little or no knowledge of the correct answer.
R   Intuition [73]
     Questioning [82]
     ↓ Strategies [67]
     Test Taking [85]

Guest Workers
Use Foreign Workers

Guidance (Educational)
Use Educational Counseling

Guidance (Occupational)
Use Occupational Guidance

Guidance Counseling
Use School Counseling

Guided Daydreams
Use Directed Reverie Therapy

Guided Fantasy
Use Directed Reverie Therapy

Guilford Zimmerman Temperament Surv [73]
PN 18   SC 21960
B   Nonprojective Personality Measures [73]

Guilt [67]
PN 1192   SC 21970
B   Emotional States [73]
R ↓ Anxiety [67]
     ↓ Anxiety Neurosis [73]
     Blame [94]
     Shame [94]

Guinea [91]
PN 0   SC 21975
B   Africa [67]

Guinea Pigs [67]
PN 642   SC 21980
B   Rodents [73]

Gulls
Use Sea Gulls

Gun Control Laws [73]
PN 37   SC 22000
B   Laws [67]
R   Government [67]
     Weapons [78]

Gustatory Perception
Use Taste Perception

Guyana [88]
PN 7   SC 22020
B   South America [67]

Gymnastic Therapy
Use Recreation Therapy

Gynecological Disorders [73]
PN 91   SC 22040
B   Genital Disorders [67]
     Urogenital Disorders [73]
N ↓ Menstrual Disorders [73]
R ↓ Endocrine Sexual Disorders [73]
     Hermaphroditism [73]
     ↓ Hypogonadism [73]
     ↓ Infertility [73]

Gynecological Disorders — (cont'd)
R   Pseudocyesis [73]
    Sterility [73]

Gynecologists [73]
PN 31   SC 22050
B   Physicians [67]
R   Obstetricians [78]
    Surgeons [73]

Gynecology [78]
PN 86   SC 22053
SN Medical specialty dealing with the female endocrine system, reproductive physiology, and diseases of the genital tract. Used for the medical specialty or the specific gynecological issues or findings.
B   Medical Sciences [67]
R   ↓ Obstetrics [78]

Gypsies [73]
PN 25   SC 22055
SN Nomadic populations of Indian descent living chiefly in Europe and the U.S.
B   Ethnic Groups [73]
R   ↓ Human Migration [73]
    Minority Groups [67]

Gyrus Cinguli [73]
PN 97   SC 22060
B   Frontal Lobe [73]
    Limbic System [73]

Habilitation [91]
PN 30   SC 22065
SN Establishment, not restoration, of fundamental capabilities, knowledge, experiences, and attitudes before or along with the usual rehabilitation procedures as a means of increasing patient awareness and developing their potential . Used primarily for physically or mentally disabled populations. Compare REHABILITATION.
R   Activities of Daily Living [91]
    Deinstitutionalization [82]
    Independent Living Programs [91]
    ↓ Mainstreaming [91]
    ↓ Rehabilitation [67]
    ↓ Skill Learning [73]

Habitat Selection
Use Territoriality

Habits [67]
PN 225   SC 22080
UF Mannerisms
N   Hair Pulling [73]
    Nail Biting [73]
    Thumbsucking [73]
    Tobacco Smoking [67]
R   ↓ Learning [67]

Habituation [67]
PN 1769   SC 22090
SN Progressive attenuation of a response elicited by repetitive stimulation.
R   ↓ Sensory Adaptation [67]

Hair [73]
PN 138   SC 22100
B   Anatomy [67]
R   Alopecia [73]
    Scalp (Anatomy) [73]
    Skin (Anatomy) [67]

Hair Loss
Use Alopecia

Hair Pulling [73]
PN 132   SC 22120
UF Trichotillomania
B   Habits [67]
R   ↓ Behavior Disorders [71]
    ↓ Self Destructive Behavior [85]

Haiti [73]
PN 17   SC 22130
B   West Indies [73]
R   Hispaniola [73]

Halfway Houses [73]
PN 199   SC 22140
SN Facilities for psychiatric, drug, or alcohol rehabilitation patients or mentally retarded individuals who no longer need hospitalization or institutionalization, but who are not yet fully prepared to return to their communities.
B   Residential Care Institutions [73]
    Treatment Facilities [73]
R   ↓ Community Facilities [73]
    ↓ Correctional Institutions [73]
    ↓ Psychiatric Hospital Programs [67]
    Psychiatric Hospitals [67]

Hallucinations [67]
PN 666   SC 22150
SN Perceptions through any sense modality in the absence of an appropriate stimulus. (Usually indicative of abnormality but may be experienced occasionally by normal persons).
UF Flashbacks
B   Perceptual Disturbances [73]
N   Auditory Hallucinations [73]
    Drug Induced Hallucinations [73]
    Hypnagogic Hallucinations [73]
    Visual Hallucinations [73]
R   ↓ Hallucinogenic Drugs [67]
    ↓ Hallucinosis [73]
    Near Death Experiences [85]

Hallucinogenic Drugs [67]
PN 332   SC 22160
B   Drugs [67]
N   Bufotenine [73]
    Lysergic Acid Diethylamide [67]
    Mescaline [73]
    Peyote [73]
    Phencyclidine [82]
    Psilocybin [73]
R   ↓ Cannabis [73]
    ↓ Cholinergic Blocking Drugs [73]
    Experimental Psychosis [73]
    ↓ Hallucinations [67]
    ↓ Psychedelic Drugs [73]
    ↓ Psychotomimetic Drugs [73]
    Tetrahydrocannabinol [73]

Hallucinosis [73]
PN 22   SC 22170
SN Mental disorder characterized by hallucinations occurring in a normal state of consciousness and attributable to specific organic factors.
B   Psychosis [67]
N   ↓ Alcoholic Hallucinosis [73]
R   ↓ Hallucinations [67]

Halo Effect [82]
PN 101   SC 22177
SN Tendency to rate individuals too high or too low on the basis of one outstanding trait or an erroneous overall impression. Often the source of error in rating scales.
R   ↓ Errors [67]
    ↓ Expectations [67]
    Experimenter Bias [67]
    Rating [67]
    ↓ Social Perception [67]

Haloperidol [73]
PN 1895   SC 22180
B   CNS Depressant Drugs [73]
    Sedatives [73]
    Tranquilizing Drugs [67]

Halstead Reitan Neuropsych Battery [91]
PN 29   SC 22184
SN Use NEUROPSYCHOLOGICAL ASSESSMENT to access references from 82-90.
B   Neuropsychological Assessment [82]

Hamsters [73]
PN 949   SC 22190
B   Rodents [73]

Hand (Anatomy) [67]
PN 564   SC 22200
B   Anatomy [67]
    Musculoskeletal System [73]
R   Arm (Anatomy) [73]
    ↓ Fingers (Anatomy) [73]
    Palm (Anatomy) [73]
    Wrist [73]

Handedness [78]
PN 1537   SC 22210
SN Learned or spontaneous differential dexterity with and tendency to use one hand rather than the other.
B   Lateral Dominance [67]

Handicapped [67]
PN 5031   SC 22220
UF Exceptional Children (Handicapped)
N   Adventitiously Handicapped [73]
    ↓ Brain Damaged [73]
    Congenitally Handicapped [73]
    ↓ Emotionally Disturbed [73]
    ↓ Mentally Retarded [67]
    ↓ Multiply Handicapped [73]
    ↓ Physically Handicapped [67]
    ↓ Sensorially Handicapped [94]
    Slow Learners [73]
    Speech Handicapped [73]
R   Adaptive Behavior [91]
    Developmental Disabilities [82]
    Disability Laws [94]
    Homebound [88]
    ↓ Learning Disabilities [73]
    Physical Mobility [94]
    Special Needs [94]

Handicapped (Attitudes Toward) [73]
PN 1009   SC 22230
B   Attitudes [67]
N   Mental Illness (Attitudes Toward) [67]
    Mental Retardation (Attit Toward) [73]
    Physical Handicaps (Attit Toward) [73]
    Sensory Handicaps (Attit Toward) [73]
R   Physical Illness (Attitudes Toward) [85]

Handicrafts
Use Crafts

Handwriting [67]
PN 662   SC 22250
UF Graphology
    Writing (Handwriting)
B   Verbal Communication [67]
    Written Language [67]
N   Cursive Writing [73]
    Handwriting Legibility [73]
    Printing (Handwriting) [73]

Handwriting Legibility [73]
PN 41   SC 22260

Handwriting Legibility — (cont'd)
- UF   Legibility (Handwriting)
- B   Handwriting [67]
-       Legibility [78]

Happiness [73]
PN 522   SC 22270
- UF   Joy
- B   Emotional States [73]
- R   Euphoria [73]
-       Pleasure [73]

Haptic Perception
- **Use** Cutaneous Sense

Hardiness
- **Use** Psychological Endurance

Hashish [73]
PN 60   SC 22290
- B   Cannabis [73]
- R   Marihuana [71]
-       Tetrahydrocannabinol [73]

Hate [73]
PN 62   SC 22300
- B   Aversion [67]
- R   Hostility [67]

Hawaii [73]
PN 154   SC 22310
- B   United States [67]

Hay Fever [73]
PN 10   SC 22320
- B   Allergic Disorders [73]
-       Respiratory Tract Disorders [73]
- R ↓ Psychosomatic Disorders [67]

Hazardous Materials [91]
PN 45   SC 22325
- UF   Asbestos
-       Toxic Waste
- N ↓ Insecticides [73]
-   ↓ Poisons [73]
-       Teratogens [88]
- R ↓ Accidents [67]
-   ↓ Chemicals [91]
-   ↓ Environment [67]
-       Occupational Exposure [88]
-       Pollution [73]
-   ↓ Safety [67]
-       Toxicity [73]

Hazards [73]
PN 117   SC 22330
- R ↓ Accidents [67]
-   ↓ Safety [67]
-   ↓ Safety Devices [73]

Head (Anatomy) [73]
PN 294   SC 22340
- B   Anatomy [67]
- R   Face (Anatomy) [73]
-       Scalp (Anatomy) [73]
-       Skin (Anatomy) [67]

Head Banging [73]
PN 42   SC 22350
- B   Self Destructive Behavior [85]

Head Injuries [73]
PN 1370   SC 22360
- B   Injuries [73]
- N   Brain Concussion [73]
- R ↓ Brain Damage [67]
-   ↓ Wounds [73]

Head Start
- **Use** Project Head Start

Headache [73]
PN 568   SC 22380
- B   Pain [67]
-       Symptoms [67]
- N   Migraine Headache [73]
-       Muscle Contraction Headache [73]
- R ↓ Psychosomatic Disorders [67]

Health [73]
PN 3930   SC 22390
- UF   Wellness
- N   Holistic Health [85]
-   ↓ Mental Health [67]
-       Public Health [88]
- R   General Health Questionnaire [91]
-       Health Attitudes [85]
-       Health Behavior [82]
-       Health Knowledge [94]
-       Hygiene [94]
-       Preventive Medicine [73]
-       Public Health Services [73]
-       Well Being [94]

Health Attitudes [85]
PN 1251   SC 22391
- UF   Health Locus of Control
- B   Attitudes [67]
- R ↓ Drug Usage Attitudes [73]
-   ↓ Health [73]
-       Health Behavior [82]
-       Health Knowledge [94]
-       Health Promotion [91]
-       Physical Illness (Attitudes Toward) [85]

Health Behavior [82]
PN 1829   SC 22392
- SN   Individual lifestyle and behavior aimed at enhancing and maintaining good health.
- B   Behavior [67]
-       Client Characteristics [73]
- R   Aerobic Exercise [88]
-       AIDS Prevention [94]
-       Diets [78]
-   ↓ Exercise [73]
-   ↓ Health [73]
-       Health Attitudes [85]
-       Health Knowledge [94]
-       Health Promotion [91]
-       Holistic Health [85]
-       Hygiene [94]
-       Lifestyle [78]
-   ↓ Prenatal Care [91]
-       Preventive Medicine [73]
-       Self Examination (Medical) [88]
-       Self Referral [91]
-       Weight Control [85]

Health Care Costs [94]
PN 0   SC 22393
- UF   Medical Care Costs
-       Mental Health Care Costs
- B   Costs and Cost Analysis [73]
- R ↓ Case Management [91]
-       Cost Containment [91]
-       Diagnosis Related Groups [88]
-       Economics [85]
-   ↓ Health Care Delivery [78]
-   ↓ Health Care Services [78]
-       Health Care Utilization [85]
-   ↓ Health Insurance [73]
-       Health Maintenance Organizations [82]
-   ↓ Managed Care [94]
-   ↓ Mental Health Services [78]
-   ↓ Professional Fees [78]
-   ↓ Treatment [67]

Health Care Delivery [78]
PN 2950   SC 22394
- SN   Practices, policies, or referral processes that contribute to making mental and/or medical health care personnel, services, or facilities available to persons in need of such care.
- N   Home Care [85]
-       Hospice [82]
-   ↓ Managed Care [94]
- R ↓ Case Management [91]
-       Fee for Service [94]
-       Health Care Costs [94]
-       Health Care Policy [94]
-   ↓ Health Care Services [78]
-       Health Care Utilization [85]
-       Health Maintenance Organizations [82]
-   ↓ Mental Health Programs [73]
-   ↓ Mental Health Services [78]
-       Needs Assessment [85]
-       Palliative Care [91]
-   ↓ Prevention [73]
-       Primary Health Care [88]
-       Private Practice [78]
-       Quality of Care [88]
-   ↓ Treatment [67]

Health Care Policy [94]
PN 0   SC 57415
- UF   Mental Health Care Policy
- B   Policy Making [88]
- R ↓ Government Policy Making [73]
-   ↓ Health Care Delivery [78]
-   ↓ Health Care Services [78]
-   ↓ Health Insurance [73]
-       Medicaid [94]
-       Medicare [88]
-   ↓ Mental Health Services [78]

Health Care Professionals
- SN   Use MEDICAL PERSONNEL or MENTAL HEALTH PERSONNEL to access references prior to 1994.
- **Use** Health Personnel

Health Care Psychology [85]
PN 252   SC 22398
- UF   Behavioral Health
-       Behavioral Medicine
-       Health Psychology
- N   Medical Psychology [73]
- R   Interdisciplinary Treatment Approach [73]
-       Psychosomatic Medicine [78]

Health Care Services [78]
PN 1778   SC 22396
- B   Treatment [67]
- N   Long Term Care [94]
-   ↓ Mental Health Services [78]
-       Palliative Care [91]
-       Primary Health Care [88]
- R   Caregivers [88]
-   ↓ Community Services [67]
-       Cost Containment [91]
-   ↓ Counseling [67]
-       Fee for Service [94]
-       Health Care Costs [94]
-   ↓ Health Care Delivery [78]
-       Health Care Policy [94]
-       Health Care Utilization [85]
-       Health Maintenance Organizations [82]
-   ↓ Managed Care [94]
-   ↓ Mental Health Programs [73]
-   ↓ Prenatal Care [91]
-   ↓ Prevention [73]
-   ↓ Rehabilitation [67]
-       Self Referral [91]
-       Social Casework [67]
-   ↓ Social Services [82]

Health Care Utilization [85]
PN 1684   SC 22397
SN Processes involved in or factors affecting usage of professional or nonprofessional health services or programs. Use HELP SEEKING BEHAVIOR to access references from 78-84.
  UF Assistance Seeking (Professional)
      Health Service Utilization
      Utilization (Health Care)
  R   Health Care Costs [94]
    ↓ Health Care Delivery [78]
    ↓ Health Care Services [78]
      Help Seeking Behavior [78]
      Self Referral [91]

Health Education [73]
PN 1924   SC 22400
SN Instruction or programs in school, institutional, or community settings which present material about factors affecting health behavior and attitudes.
  B   Curriculum [67]
  N   Drug Education [73]
      Sex Education [73]
  R   AIDS Prevention [94]
      Client Education [85]
      Health Knowledge [94]
      Health Promotion [91]
    ↓ Prenatal Care [91]
    ↓ Prevention [73]
      Psychoeducation [94]

Health Impaired [73]
PN 259   SC 22410
  UF Frail
  B   Physically Handicapped [67]
  R   Homebound [88]

Health Insurance [73]
PN 448   SC 22420
  B   Insurance [73]
  N ↓ Employee Health Insurance [73]
      Fee for Service [94]
      Health Maintenance Organizations [82]
      Medicaid [94]
      Medicare [88]
  R ↓ Case Management [91]
      Diagnosis Related Groups [88]
      Health Care Costs [94]
      Health Care Policy [94]
    ↓ Hospitalization [67]
    ↓ Managed Care [94]

Health Knowledge [94]
PN 0   SC 22421
SN Knowledge or understanding of illness, health, or mental health and health related issues.
  B   Knowledge Level [78]
  R   Client Education [85]
    ↓ Health [73]
      Health Attitudes [85]
      Health Behavior [82]
    ↓ Health Education [73]
      Health Promotion [91]
      Mental Illness (Attitudes Toward) [67]
      Physical Illness (Attitudes Toward) [85]

Health Locus of Control
  Use Health Attitudes

Health Maintenance Organizations [82]
PN 180   SC 22425
SN Organizations providing comprehensive, coordinated medical services to voluntarily enrolled members on a prepaid basis.
  UF Group Health Plans
      HMO
  B   Health Insurance [73]

Health Maintenance Organizations —
  (cont'd)
  B   Managed Care [94]
      Organizations [67]
  R   Cost Containment [91]
      Fee for Service [94]
      Health Care Costs [94]
    ↓ Health Care Delivery [78]
    ↓ Health Care Services [78]
      Health Promotion [91]
      Preventive Medicine [73]

Health Personnel [94]
PN 0   SC 57420
SN Personnel working in a medical or mental health profession. Used for unspecified health care professionals or when both medical and mental health professionals are discussed. Use a more specific term if possible. Consider MEDICAL PERSONNEL OR MENTAL HEALTH PERSONNEL to access references prior to 1994.
  UF Health Care Professionals
  B   Professional Personnel [78]
  N ↓ Medical Personnel [67]
    ↓ Mental Health Personnel [67]
  R ↓ Counselors [67]
    ↓ Social Workers [73]
    ↓ Therapists [67]

Health Personnel Attitudes [85]
PN 1762   SC 22426
SN Attitudes of persons working in health or medical professions.
  B   Attitudes [67]
  N ↓ Therapist Attitudes [78]
  R   Counselor Attitudes [73]
      Psychologist Attitudes [91]

Health Promotion [91]
PN 241   SC 22423
SN Consider using HEALTH EDUCATION to access references from 73-90.
  R   AIDS Prevention [94]
      Client Education [85]
      Health Attitudes [95]
      Health Behavior [82]
    ↓ Health Education [73]
      Health Knowledge [94]
      Health Maintenance Organizations [82]
    ↓ Prevention [73]
      Preventive Medicine [73]
      Public Health [88]
    ↓ Screening [82]

Health Psychology
  Use Health Care Psychology

Health Screening
  Use Physical Examination

Health Service Utilization
  Use Health Care Utilization

Hearing Acuity
  Use Auditory Acuity

Hearing Aids [73]
PN 341   SC 22430
  B   Medical Therapeutic Devices [73]
  N   Cochlear Implants [94]

Hearing Disorders [82]
PN 651   SC 22435
SN Disorders involving the hearing mechanisms, specifically the sensorineural pathways.
  UF Sensorineural Hearing Loss
  B   Communication Disorders [82]
  R ↓ Aurally Handicapped [73]

Hearing Disorders — (cont'd)
  R   Cochlear Implants [94]
    ↓ Deaf [67]
    ↓ Ear Disorders [73]
    ↓ Sensorially Handicapped [94]

Hearing Impaired (Partially)
  Use Partially Hearing Impaired

Hearing Measures
  Use Speech and Hearing Measures

Heart [67]
PN 370   SC 22460
  B   Cardiovascular System [67]
  N   Heart Auricles [73]
      Heart Valves [73]
      Heart Ventricles [73]
      Myocardium [73]
  R ↓ Blood [67]
      Vagus Nerve [73]

Heart Attacks
  Use Heart Disorders

Heart Auricles [73]
PN 7   SC 22470
  UF Atria (Heart)
      Auricles (Heart)
  B   Heart [67]

Heart Disorders [73]
PN 819   SC 22480
  UF Cardiac Disorders
      Coronary Heart Disease
      Heart Attacks
  B   Cardiovascular Disorders [67]
  N   Angina Pectoris [73]
    ↓ Arrhythmias (Heart) [73]
      Coronary Thromboses [73]
      Myocardial Infarctions [73]
  R   Rheumatic Fever [73]

Heart Rate [67]
PN 4634   SC 22490
  UF Cardiac Rate
      Heartbeat
  R   Cardiovascular Reactivity [94]

Heart Rate Affecting Drugs [73]
PN 47   SC 22500
  B   Drugs [67]
  N   Caffeine [73]
      Epinephrine [67]
      Quinidine [73]
      Theophylline [73]
      Verapamil [91]
  R ↓ Analeptic Drugs [73]
    ↓ Antihypertensive Drugs [73]
      Cardiotonic Drugs [85]
    ↓ Cardiovascular Disorders [67]
    ↓ CNS Affecting Drugs [73]
    ↓ CNS Stimulating Drugs [73]
      Dopamine [73]
    ↓ Muscle Relaxing Drugs [73]
    ↓ Vasoconstrictor Drugs [73]
    ↓ Vasodilator Drugs [73]

Heart Surgery [73]
PN 270   SC 22510
  B   Surgery [71]
  R   Organ Transplantation [73]

Heart Transplants
  Use Organ Transplantation

Heart Valves [73]
PN 37   SC 22530
  UF   Valves (Heart)
  B   Heart [67]

Heart Ventricles [73]
PN 26   SC 22540
  UF   Ventricles (Heart)
  B   Heart [67]

Heartbeat
  Use   Heart Rate

Heat Effects [73]
PN 395   SC 22560
  B   Temperature Effects [67]

Hebephrenic Schizophrenia [73]
PN 100   SC 22570
  UF   Schizophrenia (Disorganized Type)
  B   Schizophrenia [67]

Hedonism [73]
PN 55   SC 22580
  R   ↓ Attitudes [67]
       ↓ Philosophies [67]

Heels (Anatomy)
  Use   Feet (Anatomy)

Height (Body)
  Use   Body Height

Helicopters [73]
PN 44   SC 22610
  B   Aircraft [73]

Helium [73]
PN 24   SC 22620
  B   Nonmetallic Elements [73]

Help Seeking Behavior [78]
PN 1022   SC 22624
SN   Searching for or requesting help from others through formal or informal mechanisms. From 78-84 used primarily for the seeking or utilization of professional care or services. From 1985, use HEALTH CARE UTILIZATION for the latter concept.
  B   Social Behavior [67]
  R   Assistance (Social Behavior) [73]
       Health Care Utilization [85]
       Self Referral [91]

Helping Behavior
  Use   Assistance (Social Behavior)

Helplessness (Learned)
  Use   Learned Helplessness

Hematologic Disorders
  Use   Blood and Lymphatic Disorders

Hematoma [73]
PN 33   SC 22640
  B   Hemorrhage [73]
       Symptoms [67]
  R   ↓ Injuries [73]

Hemianopia [73]
PN 64   SC 22650
  UF   Hemiopia
  B   Eye Disorders [73]
  R   ↓ Nervous System Disorders [67]

Hemiopia
  Use   Hemianopia

Hemiplegia [78]
PN 137   SC 22675
SN   Paralysis of one side of the body resulting from disease or injury to the brain or spinal cord.
  B   Paralysis [73]
  R   ↓ Central Nervous System Disorders [73]
       ↓ Injuries [73]
       ↓ Musculoskeletal Disorders [73]
       Paraplegia [78]
       ↓ Physically Handicapped [67]
       Quadriplegia [85]
       Spinal Cord Injuries [73]

Hemispherectomy [73]
PN 80   SC 22680
  B   Neurosurgery [73]

Hemispheric Specialization
SN   Use CEREBRAL DOMINANCE to access references from 73-90.
  Use   Lateral Dominance

Hemodialysis [73]
PN 404   SC 22690
  B   Dialysis [73]
  R   Blood Transfusion [73]

Hemoglobin [73]
PN 53   SC 22700
  B   Blood Proteins [73]
       Pigments [73]

Hemophilia [73]
PN 132   SC 22710
  B   Blood and Lymphatic Disorders [73]
       Sex Linked Hereditary Disorders [73]

Hemorrhage [73]
PN 37   SC 22720
  B   Cardiovascular Disorders [67]
       Symptoms [67]
  N   Cerebral Hemorrhage [73]
       Hematoma [73]

Hemp (Cannabis)
  Use   Cannabis

Henmon Nelson Tests Mental Ability [73]
PN 3   SC 22740
  B   Intelligence Measures [67]

Heparin [73]
PN 9   SC 22750
  B   Acids [73]
       Anticoagulant Drugs [73]

Hepatic Disorders
  Use   Liver Disorders

Hepatitis [73]
PN 47   SC 22770
  B   Liver Disorders [73]
  N   Toxic Hepatitis [73]
  R   ↓ Infectious Disorders [73]
       Jaundice [73]

Hereditary Disorders
  Use   Genetic Disorders

Heredity
  Use   Genetics

Hermaphroditism [73]
PN 53   SC 22800
  B   Congenital Disorders [73]
       Genital Disorders [67]
  R   ↓ Endocrine Sexual Disorders [73]
       ↓ Gynecological Disorders [73]
       ↓ Male Genital Disorders [73]
       Sterility [73]
       Testicular Feminization Syndrome [73]

Hermeneutics [91]
PN 67   SC 22805
  B   Philosophies [67]
  R   Epistemology [73]
       Metaphysics [73]
       Phenomenology [67]
       Rhetoric [91]
       ↓ Semiotics [85]

Heroin [73]
PN 270   SC 22810
  UF   Diacetylmorphine
  B   Alkaloids [73]
       Analgesic Drugs [73]
       Opiates [73]
       Sedatives [73]
  R   Heroin Addiction [73]

Heroin Addiction [73]
PN 968   SC 22820
  B   Drug Addiction [67]
  R   Heroin [73]
       Methadone Maintenance [78]

Herpes Genitalis [88]
PN 39   SC 22825
  UF   Genital Herpes
  B   Venereal Diseases [73]
       Viral Disorders [73]

Herpes Simplex [73]
PN 110   SC 22830
  B   Skin Disorders [73]
       Viral Disorders [73]

Heterogeneity of Variance
  Use   Variance Homogeneity

Heterosexual Interaction
  Use   Male Female Relations

Heterosexuality [73]
PN 551   SC 22840
  B   Psychosexual Behavior [67]
  R   Lesbianism [73]
       Male Homosexuality [73]
       Sex Linked Developmental Differences [73]
       Sexual Development [73]

Heterozygotic Twins [73]
PN 415   SC 22850
  UF   Dizygotic Twins
  B   Twins [67]

Heuristic Modeling [73]
PN 166   SC 22860
  B   Simulation [67]
  R   ↓ Mathematical Modeling [73]

Hexamethonium [73]
PN 22   SC 22870
  B   Antihypertensive Drugs [73]
       Ganglion Blocking Drugs [73]

Hexobarbital [73]
PN 25   SC 22880

Hexobarbital — (cont'd)
B   Anesthetic Drugs [73]
     Barbiturates [67]
     Hypnotic Drugs [73]
     Sedatives [73]

Hibernation [73]
PN 57   SC 22890
B   Animal Ethology [67]
R   ↓ Animal Biological Rhythms [73]

Hidden Figures Test [73]
PN 14   SC 22900
B   Intelligence Measures [67]

High Risk Populations
Use At Risk Populations

High Sch Personality Questionnaire [73]
PN 29   SC 22910
B   Nonprojective Personality Measures [73]

High School Diplomas
Use Educational Degrees

High School Equivalency
Use Adult Education

High School Graduates [78]
PN 181   SC 22924
R   ↓ Adolescents [67]
     Educational Degrees [73]
     High School Students [67]
     School Graduation [91]
     School to Work Transition [94]

High School Students [67]
PN 12495   SC 22930
SN   Students in grades 9–12. Mandatory term in
educational contexts.
B   Students [67]
R   ↓ Adolescents [67]
     Grade Level [94]
     High School Graduates [78]
     Reentry Students [85]

High School Teachers [73]
PN 1768   SC 22940
B   Teachers [67]

High Schools [73]
PN 563   SC 22950
B   Schools [67]
R   Military Schools [73]
     Secondary Education [73]

Higher Education [73]
PN 822   SC 22960
SN   College or university education, also called
tertiary education, requiring for entrance the suc-
cessful completion of high school, grammar
school, or another type of secondary school, or
the attainment of an approved equivalent.
B   Education [67]
N   ↓ Graduate Education [73]
     ↓ Postgraduate Training [73]
     Undergraduate Education [78]
R   ↓ Colleges [67]
     ↓ Continuing Education [85]
     Educational Degrees [73]
     Educational Program Accreditation [94]
     Graduate Schools [73]
     Professional Specialization [91]
     School Graduation [91]

Highway Safety [73]
PN 504   SC 22980

Highway Safety — (cont'd)
UF   Automobile Safety
     Driver Safety
B   Safety [67]
R   Drivers [73]
     ↓ Driving Behavior [67]
     Driving Under The Influence [88]
     ↓ Ground Transportation [73]
     Motor Traffic Accidents [73]
     ↓ Transportation Accidents [73]

Hinduism [73]
PN 189   SC 22990
B   Religious Affiliation [73]

Hippies
Use Subculture (Anthropological)

Hippocampal Commissure
Use Fornix

Hippocampus [67]
PN 2832   SC 23010
B   Limbic System [73]
R   Medial Forebrain Bundle [82]
     Septal Nuclei [82]

Hips [73]
PN 43   SC 23020
B   Musculoskeletal System [73]

Hiring
Use Personnel Selection

Hispanics [82]
PN 2108   SC 23035
SN   Populations of Spanish, Portuguese, or Latin
American descent residing in countries other than
the country of their origin. (For those residing in
their own country use the appropriate country
name). Use SPANISH AMERICANS to access
references from 78–81.
UF   Cuban Americans
     Latinos
     Puerto Rican Americans
     Spanish Americans
B   Ethnic Groups [73]
N   Mexican Americans [73]
R   Minority Groups [67]

Hispaniola [73]
PN 3   SC 23040
B   West Indies [73]
R   Dominican Republic [73]
     Haiti [73]

Histamine [73]
PN 116   SC 23050
B   Amines [73]
     Neurotransmitters [85]
R   ↓ Antihistaminic Drugs [73]
     Histidine [73]

Histidine [73]
PN 25   SC 23060
B   Amino Acids [73]
R   Histamine [73]

Histology [73]
PN 77   SC 23070
SN   Branch of anatomy dealing with the structure of cells, tissues, and organs in relation to
their functions. Used for the scientific discipline
or the organic structure itself.
R   Morphology [73]
     ↓ Physiology [67]
     ↓ Tissues (Body) [73]

History [73]
PN 3696   SC 23075
SN   Recording and/or explanation of previous
events, experiences, trends, and treatments.
N   ↓ History of Psychology [67]
R   Future [91]
     Psychohistory [78]
     Trends [91]

History of Psychology [67]
PN 4306   SC 23080
B   History [73]
N   Associationism [73]
     Behaviorism [67]
     Freudian Psychoanalytic School [73]
     Functionalism [73]
     Gestalt Psychology [67]
     ↓ Neopsychoanalytic School [73]
     Structuralism [73]
R   Phenomenology [67]
     ↓ Psychology [67]
     ↓ Theories [67]

Histrionic Personality Disorder
Use Hysterical Personality

HIV
Use Human Immunodeficiency Virus

HMO
Use Health Maintenance Organizations

Hoarding Behavior (Animal)
Use Animal Hoarding Behavior

Hobbies [73]
PN 23   SC 23100
SN   Use RECREATION to access references
from 73-88.
R   Daily Activities [94]
     ↓ Interests [67]
     Leisure Time [73]
     ↓ Recreation [67]

Hoffmanns Reflex [73]
PN 33   SC 23110
SN   Flexing of the thumb and some other finger
resulting from a sudden tapping of the nail of the
index, middle, or ring finger. Also known as digital reflex, finger flexion reflex, snapping reflex, H
reflex, or Hoffmann's (H) response.
B   Reflexes [71]

Holidays [88]
PN 30   SC 23113
SN   Days marked by general suspension of work
in commemoration or celebration of an event.
R   Leisure Time [73]
     ↓ Recreation [67]
     Vacationing [73]

Holistic Health [85]
PN 245   SC 23115
SN   Personal practices or medical or psychological diagnosis and treatment based on the concept that humans are composed of body, mind,
and spirit. An observed disorder or dysfunction in
one component implies the need for treatment of
the whole organism to restore health.
UF   Wholistic Health
B   Health [73]
R   Biopsychosocial Approach [91]
     Health Behavior [82]
     Lifestyle [78]
     Meditation [73]
     ↓ Physical Treatment Methods [73]
     Preventive Medicine [73]
     ↓ Psychotherapy [67]

Holocaust [88]
PN 75　　　　　　　　　　SC 23117
SN Nazi persecution and genocide of Jews and others in Europe between 1933 and 1945.
B　Genocide [88]
R　AntiSemitism [73]
　　Concentration Camps [73]
　　Fascism [73]
　　Holocaust Survivors [88]
　　Judaism [67]

Holocaust Survivors [88]
PN 123　　　　　　　　　SC 23118
B　Survivors [94]
R　Holocaust [88]

Holtzman Inkblot Technique [67]
PN 132　　　　　　　　　SC 23120
B　Projective Personality Measures [73]
　　Projective Techniques [67]

Homatropine [73]
PN 7　　　　　　　　　　SC 23130
B　Alkaloids [73]
　　Amines [73]
　　Cholinergic Blocking Drugs [73]
R　↓ Bromides [73]

Home Accidents [73]
PN 23　　　　　　　　　SC 23140
B　Accidents [67]

Home Birth
Use Midwifery

Home Care [85]
PN 611　　　　　　　　　SC 23145
SN Health and personal care provided in the home environment, usually by family members.
B　Health Care Delivery [78]
R　Caregiver Burden [94]
　　Caregivers [88]
　　Elder Care [94]
　　Home Visiting Programs [73]
　　Homebound [88]
　　Hospice [82]
　　Long Term Care [94]
　　↓ Outpatient Treatment [67]
　　Quality of Care [88]
　　Respite Care [88]

Home Economics [85]
PN 40　　　　　　　　　SC 23147
B　Curriculum [67]
R　Household Management [85]

Home Environment [73]
PN 2831　　　　　　　　SC 23150
B　Social Environments [73]
R　Empty Nest [91]
　　Living Alone [94]
　　↓ Living Arrangements [91]

Home Reared Mentally Retarded [73]
PN 39　　　　　　　　　SC 23160
B　Mentally Retarded [67]
R　Institutionalized Mentally Retarded [73]

Home Schooling [94]
PN 0　　　　　　　　　SC 23165
SN Provision of compulsory education in the home.
B　Nontraditional Education [82]
R　↓ Curriculum [67]
　　↓ Education [67]
　　↓ Teaching Methods [67]

Home Visiting Programs [73]
PN 366　　　　　　　　SC 23170
SN Planned educational, health, or counseling procedures or activities that take place in the home.
B　Community Services [67]
　　Mental Health Programs [73]
R　Elder Care [94]
　　Home Care [85]
　　Homebound [88]
　　↓ Program Development [91]

Homebound [88]
PN 15　　　　　　　　　SC 23173
SN Individuals restricted to place of residence for health or disability reasons.
R　↓ Aged [73]
　　Caregiver Burden [94]
　　Elder Care [94]
　　↓ Handicapped [67]
　　Health Impaired [73]
　　Home Care [85]
　　Home Visiting Programs [73]

Homeless [88]
PN 566　　　　　　　　SC 23174
B　Social Issues [91]
R　Deinstitutionalization [82]
　　Disadvantaged [67]
　　Poverty [73]
　　Shelters [91]
　　↓ Social Deprivation [73]

Homemaking
Use Household Management

Homeostasis [73]
PN 181　　　　　　　　SC 23180
SN Tendency of an organism to maintain a state of physiological equilibrium and the processes by which such a stable internal environment is maintained.
UF　Autoregulation
B　Physiology [67]
R　Dehydration [88]
　　Instinctive Behavior [82]

Homesickness [94]
PN 0　　　　　　　　　SC 23183
B　Emotional States [73]
R　↓ Experiences (Events) [73]
　　Life Experiences [73]
　　Loneliness [73]
　　Reminiscence [85]
　　Sadness [73]

Homework [88]
PN 65　　　　　　　　　SC 23185
SN Assignment given to students or clients to be completed outside regular classroom period or therapeutic setting.
R　Note Taking [91]
　　↓ Psychotherapeutic Techniques [67]
　　Study Habits [73]

Homicide [67]
PN 1039　　　　　　　　SC 23190
UF　Murder
B　Behavior Disorders [71]
N　↓ Genocide [88]
　　Infanticide [78]

Homing (Animal)
Use Animal Homing

Homographs [73]
PN 52　　　　　　　　　SC 23200

Homographs — (cont'd)
SN Words identical in spelling but different in derivation, pronunciation, and meaning.
B　Vocabulary [67]
R　Homonyms [73]
　　Orthography [73]
　　Words (Phonetic Units) [67]

Homonyms [73]
PN 53　　　　　　　　　SC 23210
B　Semantics [67]
　　Vocabulary [67]
R　Homographs [73]
　　Words (Phonetic Units) [67]

Homophobia
Use Homosexuality (Attitudes Toward)

Homosexual Liberation Movement [73]
PN 31　　　　　　　　　SC 23220
UF　Gay Liberation Movement
B　Social Movements [67]
R　↓ Activist Movements [73]

Homosexual Parents [94]
PN 0　　　　　　　　　SC 23225
UF　Gay Parents
　　Lesbian Parents
B　Parents [67]
R　↓ Family Structure [73]
　　Lesbianism [73]
　　Male Homosexuality [73]
　　Significant Others [91]

Homosexuality [67]
PN 1134　　　　　　　　SC 23230
B　Psychosexual Behavior [67]
N　Bisexuality [73]
　　Lesbianism [73]
　　Male Homosexuality [73]
R　Homosexuality (Attitudes Toward) [82]
　　Transsexualism [73]
　　Transvestism [73]

Homosexuality (Attitudes Toward) [82]
PN 435　　　　　　　　SC 23233
SN Attitudes regarding sexual contact between persons of the same sex.
UF　Homophobia
B　Attitudes [67]
R　↓ Homosexuality [67]

Homovanillic Acid [78]
PN 380　　　　　　　　SC 23235
SN Excretion product of dopamine metabolism.
B　Acids [73]
　　Dopamine Metabolites [82]
R　Dopamine [73]

Honduras [88]
PN 3　　　　　　　　　SC 23237
B　Central America [73]

Honesty [73]
PN 183　　　　　　　　SC 23240
UF　Frankness
B　Personality Traits [67]

Hong Kong [78]
PN 389　　　　　　　　SC 23245
B　Asia [73]

Hope [91]
PN 41　　　　　　　　　SC 23247
B　Emotional States [73]
R　↓ Expectations [67]
　　Hopelessness [88]

Hope — (cont'd)
R   Optimism [73]
     Positivism [73]
     Trust (Social Behavior) [67]

Hopelessness [88]
PN 182   SC 23250
SN Feeling that one's physical, emotional, or social state is beyond improvement.
B   Emotional States [73]
R   Hope [91]

Hormone Therapy [94]
PN 0   SC 23255
UF   Estrogen Replacement Therapy
B   Drug Therapy [67]
R   ↓ Hormones [67]

Hormones [67]
PN 2099   SC 23260
N   ↓ Adrenal Cortex Hormones [73]
     ↓ Adrenal Medulla Hormones [73]
     Cholecystokinin [82]
     Corticotropin Releasing Factor [94]
     Epinephrine [67]
     Glucagon [73]
     ↓ Gonadotropic Hormones [73]
     Insulin [73]
     Melatonin [73]
     Parathyroid Hormone [73]
     ↓ Pituitary Hormones [73]
     ↓ Progestational Hormones [85]
     ↓ Sex Hormones [73]
     ↓ Thyroid Hormones [73]
R   ↓ Anti Inflammatory Drugs [82]
     Antineoplastic Drugs [82]
     ↓ Drugs [67]
     ↓ Endocrine Glands [73]
     Fertility Enhancement [73]
     Hormone Therapy [94]
     Pheromones [73]
     Prostaglandins [82]
     ↓ Steroids [73]

Horses [73]
PN 139   SC 23270
B   Mammals [73]

Hospice [82]
PN 340   SC 23275
SN Supportive palliative care of terminally ill patients usually in their own home by a treatment team and family members; sometimes involves residential care.
B   Health Care Delivery [78]
R   Home Care [85]
     Palliative Care [91]
     Terminally Ill Patients [73]

Hospital Accreditation [73]
PN 14   SC 23280
SN Recognition of a hospital as maintaining standards set by a government agency.
R   ↓ Hospitals [67]

Hospital Administration [78]
PN 210   SC 23286
B   Management [67]
R   Decentralization [78]
     ↓ Hospitals [67]
     Medical Records Keeping [78]

Hospital Admission [73]
PN 261   SC 23290
UF   Admission (Hospital)
     Readmission (Hospital)
B   Facility Admission [88]
     Hospitalization [67]

Hospital Admission — (cont'd)
N   ↓ Psychiatric Hospital Admission [73]
R   ↓ Hospital Discharge [73]
     ↓ Institutional Release [78]
     ↓ Psychiatric Hospitalization [73]

Hospital Attendants
Use Attendants (Institutions)

Hospital Discharge [73]
PN 315   SC 23303
B   Facility Discharge [88]
     Hospitalization [67]
     Institutional Release [78]
N   Psychiatric Hospital Discharge [78]
R   Discharge Planning [94]
     ↓ Hospital Admission [73]
     ↓ Psychiatric Hospital Admission [73]
     Psychiatric Hospital Readmission [73]
     ↓ Psychiatric Hospitalization [73]
     Treatment Termination [82]

Hospital Environment [82]
PN 553   SC 23304
SN Physical, organizational, or psychological characteristics of a hospital, and their potential impact on hospital staff and patients.
B   Facility Environment [88]
R   ↓ Hospitals [67]
     Intensive Care [88]

Hospital Programs [78]
PN 1147   SC 23306
SN Organized plans for care, including psychiatric treatment, or training in general medical hospital settings.
N   ↓ Psychiatric Hospital Programs [67]
R   Intensive Care [88]
     Partial Hospitalization [85]
     ↓ Program Development [91]
     Psychiatric Units [91]

Hospital Psychiatric Units
Use Psychiatric Units

Hospital Staff
Use Medical Personnel

Hospitalization [67]
PN 1109   SC 23320
B   Institutionalization [67]
N   ↓ Commitment (Psychiatric) [73]
     ↓ Hospital Admission [73]
     ↓ Hospital Discharge [73]
     ↓ Psychiatric Hospitalization [73]
R   ↓ Health Insurance [73]
     Long Term Care [94]
     Patient Seclusion [94]
     Psychiatric Units [91]

Hospitalized Patients [73]
PN 3614   SC 23330
B   Patients [67]

Hospitals [67]
PN 1403   SC 23340
UF   Infirmaries
B   Residential Care Institutions [73]
     Treatment Facilities [73]
N   Psychiatric Hospitals [67]
     Sanatoriums [73]
R   ↓ Clinics [67]
     Hospital Accreditation [73]
     Hospital Administration [78]
     Hospital Environment [82]
     Intensive Care [88]
     Maximum Security Facilities [85]
     Nursing Homes [73]

Hospitals — (cont'd)
R   Psychiatric Clinics [73]
     Psychiatric Units [91]

Hostages [88]
PN 27   SC 23347
SN Use CRIME VICTIMS to access references from 82-87.
B   Crime Victims [82]
R   Kidnapping [88]
     Prisoners of War [73]
     Terrorism [82]

Hostility [67]
PN 1553   SC 23350
UF   Antagonism
     Resentment
B   Anger [67]
R   Hate [73]
     Retaliation [91]

Hot Line Services [73]
PN 272   SC 23360
SN Telephone information, counseling, and crisis intervention services.
UF   Telephone Hot Lines
B   Crisis Intervention Services [73]
     Mental Health Programs [73]
R   Community Mental Health Centers [73]
     Information Services [88]
     Suicide Prevention Centers [73]

Household Management [85]
PN 275   SC 23365
SN Activities carried out for the regular maintenance of home and personal belongings.
UF   Homemaking
     Housework
B   Management [67]
R   ↓ Division of Labor [88]
     Home Economics [85]
     Housewives [73]

Household Structure
Use Living Arrangements

Housewives [73]
PN 344   SC 23370
B   Wives [73]
R   Household Management [85]

Housework
Use Household Management

Housing [73]
PN 827   SC 23380
B   Community Facilities [73]
N   Dormitories [73]
     Group Homes [82]
     Shelters [91]
R   ↓ Living Arrangements [91]
     Social Programs [73]

Hue [73]
PN 224   SC 23390
SN One of the perceived dimensions of color corresponding to the wavelength of the light. Compare COLOR.
B   Color [67]

Human Animal Interaction
Use Interspecies Interaction

Human Biological Rhythms [73]
PN 1466   SC 23400
SN Periodic variations in human physiological and psychological functions. Use BIOLOGICAL RHYTHMS to access references from 67-72.

Human Biological Rhythms — (cont'd)
UF   Circadian Rhythms (Human)
        Diurnal Variations
B   Biological Rhythms [67]

Human Channel Capacity [73]
PN 628   SC 23410
SN Number of signals or information volume which can be processed simultaneously.
UF   Cognitive Load
        Mental Load
R   ↓ Attention [67]
        Human Information Storage [73]
        Work Load [82]

Human Courtship [73]
PN 159   SC 23420
UF   Courtship (Human)
B   Psychosexual Behavior [67]
N   Social Dating [73]
R   Human Mate Selection [88]
        Male Female Relations [88]

Human Development [67]
PN 931   SC 23430
SN Conceptually broad array term. Use a more specific term if possible.
UF   Maturation
B   Development [67]
N   Adolescent Development [73]
        Adult Development [78]
        ↓ Childhood Development [67]
R   Age Differences [67]
        ↓ Aging [91]
        ↓ Delayed Development [73]
        ↓ Developmental Age Groups [73]
        Developmental Disabilities [82]
        ↓ Developmental Psychology [73]
        ↓ Developmental Stages [73]
        Life Expectancy [82]
        Nature Nurture [94]
        ↓ Physical Development [73]
        ↓ Psychogenesis [73]

Human Factors Engineering [73]
PN 1286   SC 23440
UF   Ergonomics
R   Engineering Psychology [67]
        Furniture [85]
        ↓ Instrument Controls [85]
        Man Machine Systems [73]
        Quality Control [88]
        ↓ Working Conditions [73]

Human Females [73]
PN 15469   SC 23450
SN Used for all-female populations when sex is pertinent to the focus of the study. For comparison of sexes use HUMAN SEX DIFFERENCES.
UF   Females (Human)
        Girls
        Women
N   Battered Females [88]
        Daughters [73]
        Female Criminals [73]
        Female Delinquents [73]
        ↓ Mothers [67]
        Sisters [73]
        Widows [73]
        ↓ Wives [73]
        Working Women [78]
R   ↓ Human Sex Differences [67]
        Sex Linked Developmental Differences [73]

Human Figures Drawing [73]
PN 467   SC 23460

Human Figures Drawing — (cont'd)
SN Projective measures or techniques designed to yield information from drawings of human figures and responses to questions about the drawings.
UF   Draw A Man Test
B   Projective Personality Measures [73]
R   Goodenough Harris Draw A Person Test [67]
        Mirror Image [91]

Human Immunodeficiency Virus [91]
PN 1035   SC 23465
UF   HIV
B   Immunologic Disorders [73]
        Viral Disorders [73]
N   Acquired Immune Deficiency Syndrome [88]
R   AIDS Prevention [94]
        ↓ Venereal Diseases [73]
        Zidovudine [94]

Human Information Processes
Use Cognitive Processes

Human Information Storage [73]
PN 4853   SC 23480
SN Process of information perception, encoding, or storage, and retrieval of material from memory.
UF   Decoding
        Encoding
        Information Storage (Human)
R   ↓ Cognitive Processes [67]
        Human Channel Capacity [73]
        Information [67]
        ↓ Lexical Access [88]
        Lexical Decision [88]
        ↓ Memory [67]
        Word Recognition [88]

Human Males [73]
PN 5230   SC 23490
SN Used for all-male populations when sex is pertinent to the focus of the study. For comparison of sexes use HUMAN SEX DIFFERENCES.
UF   Boys
        Males (Human)
        Men
N   Brothers [73]
        ↓ Fathers [67]
        Male Criminals [73]
        Male Delinquents [73]
        Sons [73]
        Widowers [73]
R   ↓ Human Sex Differences [67]
        Sex Linked Developmental Differences [73]

Human Mate Selection [88]
PN 100   SC 23495
UF   Mate Selection
R   Assortative Mating [91]
        Choice Behavior [67]
        ↓ Human Courtship [73]
        Interpersonal Attraction [67]
        ↓ Psychosexual Behavior [67]

Human Migration [73]
PN 712   SC 23500
SN Movement of residence from one place to another. Includes nomadism; labor or seasonal migration; patterns of rural, urban, or suburban migration; or voluntary or forced relocation.
UF   Migration (Human)
B   Social Processes [73]
N   Refugees [88]
R   Geographical Mobility [78]
        Gypsies [73]

Human Migration — (cont'd)
R   Immigration [73]
        Migrant Farm Workers [73]

Human Potential Movement [82]
PN 163   SC 23504
SN Movement aimed at the enhancement of personal psychological growth. Formats used include Gestalt therapy, sensory awakening, sensory awareness, meditation, encounter, transactional analysis, assertiveness training, and humanistic psychology.
UF   Growth Centers
        Personal Growth Techniques
N   Assertiveness Training [78]
        Consciousness Raising Groups [78]
        ↓ Encounter Group Therapy [73]
        Gestalt Therapy [73]
        Human Relations Training [78]
        Sensitivity Training [73]
        Transactional Analysis [73]
R   ↓ Group Psychotherapy [67]
        Humanism [73]
        ↓ Humanistic Psychology [85]
        Maslow (Abraham Harold) [91]
        Meditation [73]
        Self Actualization [73]

Human Relations Training [78]
PN 439   SC 23506
SN Techniques aimed at promoting awareness of feelings and needs of others in order to facilitate positive interpersonal interactions.
UF   T Groups
B   Human Potential Movement [82]
R   Assertiveness Training [78]
        Communication Skills Training [82]
        ↓ Encounter Group Therapy [73]
        ↓ Group Dynamics [67]
        Marathon Group Therapy [73]
        Parent Training [78]
        ↓ Personnel Training [67]
        Sensitivity Training [73]
        Social Skills Training [82]

Human Resources
Use Personnel Management

Human Rights [78]
PN 275   SC 23508
SN Fundamental rights of every human being to life, freedom, and equality. Often used for freedom from arbitrary governmental interference.
B   Social Issues [91]
N   ↓ Civil Rights [78]
        Client Rights [88]
R   Social Equality [73]
        ↓ Social Movements [67]
        ↓ Social Processes [67]
        Treatment Withholding [88]

Human Sex Differences [67]
PN 28776   SC 23510
UF   Gender Differences
        Sex Differences (Human)
N   Sex Linked Developmental Differences [73]
R   ↓ Human Females [73]
        ↓ Human Males [73]
        Sex [67]

Humanism [73]
PN 543   SC 23520
SN Philosophy that asserts an individual's capacity for self-realization through reason and often rejects the supernatural.
B   Philosophies [67]
R   ↓ Human Potential Movement [82]
        ↓ Humanistic Psychology [85]

102

Humanistic Education
  Use Affective Education

Humanistic Psychology 85
PN 243   SC 23527
SN School of psychology emphasizing the holis-
tic approach, self-actualization, creativity, and
free choice.
  B   Psychology 67
  N   Transpersonal Psychology 88
  R ↓ Human Potential Movement 82
       Humanism 73
       Maslow (Abraham Harold) 91
       Neurolinguistic Programing 88

Humor 67
PN 1041   SC 23540
  N   Cartoons (Humor) 73
       Jokes 73
  R   Laughter 78

Hungary 73
PN 179   SC 23550
  B   Europe 73

Hunger 67
PN 346   SC 23560
SN Need or desire for food. May also be defined operationally in experimental settings as the
duration of food deprivation or the organism's
percentage of normal body weight following food
deprivation. Compare APPETITE.
  B   Appetite 73
       Motivation 67
  R   Animal Feeding Behavior 73
       Food Deprivation 67
       Starvation 73

Huntingtons Chorea 73
PN 401   SC 23570
  B   Chorea 73
       Genetic Disorders 73

Hurdle (Shuttle Box)
  Use Shuttle Box Hurdles

Husbands 73
PN 889   SC 23590
  B   Spouses 73

Hybrids (Biology) 73
PN 69   SC 23600
  R ↓ Genetics 67

Hydralazine 73
PN 8   SC 23620
  B   Antihypertensive Drugs 73
       Sympatholytic Drugs 73

Hydrocephaly 73
PN 176   SC 23630
  B   Brain Disorders 67
  R ↓ Congenital Disorders 73
     ↓ Convulsions 67
     ↓ Infectious Disorders 73
     ↓ Mental Retardation 67
     ↓ Neonatal Disorders 73

Hydrocortisone 73
PN 1251   SC 23640
  UF   Cortisol
  B   Adrenal Cortex Hormones 73
       Corticosteroids 73
  R ↓ Anti Inflammatory Drugs 82

Hydrogen 73
PN 10   SC 23650
  B   Nonmetallic Elements 73

Hydroxydopamine (6-) 78
PN 517   SC 23656
  B   Adrenergic Blocking Drugs 73

Hydroxyindoleacetic Acid (5-) 85
PN 239   SC 23658
SN Major metabolic product of serotonin.
  B   Acids 73
       Serotonin Metabolites 78

Hydroxylamine 73
PN 1   SC 23660
  B   Amines 73

Hydroxylase Inhibitors 85
PN 12   SC 23665
  B   Enzyme Inhibitors 85
  R   Hydroxylases 73

Hydroxylases 73
PN 201   SC 23670
  B   Enzymes 73
  R ↓ Esterases 73
       Hydroxylase Inhibitors 85
       Phosphatases 73

Hydroxytryptamine (5-)
  Use Serotonin

Hydroxytryptophan (5-) 91
PN 17   SC 23685
  B   Tryptophan 73

Hydroxyzine 73
PN 19   SC 23690
  B   Minor Tranquilizers 73
  R ↓ Antihistaminic Drugs 73

Hygiene 94
PN 0   SC 23700
SN Use HEALTH to access references from 73-
93.
  R   Activities of Daily Living 91
     ↓ Health 73
       Health Behavior 82
       Self Care Skills 78

Hyoscine
  Use Scopolamine

Hyoscyamine (dl-)
  Use Atropine

Hyperactivity
  Use Hyperkinesis

Hypercholesterolemia
  Use Metabolism Disorders

Hyperglycemia 85
PN 27   SC 23745
  B   Symptoms 67
  R ↓ Metabolism Disorders 73

Hyperkinesis 73
PN 2694   SC 23760
  UF   Hyperactivity
  B   Nervous System Disorders 67
       Symptoms 67
  R   Ataxia 73
       Attention Deficit Disorder 85
       Minimal Brain Disorders 73

Hyperkinesis — (cont'd)
  R ↓ Neuromuscular Disorders 73
       Restlessness 73

Hyperparathyroidism
  Use Parathyroid Disorders

Hyperphagia 73
PN 222   SC 23800
  B   Appetite Disorders 73
       Symptoms 67
  R   Obesity 73
     ↓ Psychosomatic Disorders 67

Hypersensitivity (Immunologic)
  Use Immunologic Disorders

Hypersexuality 73
PN 33   SC 23820
  UF   Nymphomania
  B   Psychosexual Behavior 67
  R   Promiscuity 73

Hypersomnia 94
PN 0   SC 23825
SN Excessive sleepiness.
  B   Sleep Disorders 73
  R   Fatigue 67
       Narcolepsy 73
     ↓ Symptoms 67

Hypertension 73
PN 1255   SC 23830
  B   Cardiovascular Disorders 67
  N   Essential Hypertension 73
  R ↓ Antihypertensive Drugs 73
     ↓ Cerebrovascular Disorders 73

Hyperthermia 73
PN 169   SC 23840
  UF   Fever
  B   Symptoms 67
  R   Delirium 73
       Thermoregulation (Body) 73

Hyperthyroidism 73
PN 95   SC 23850
  B   Thyroid Disorders 73
  R   Goiters 73
       Tachycardia 73
       Thyrotoxicosis 73
     ↓ Underweight 73

Hyperventilation 73
PN 168   SC 23860
  B   Respiratory Distress 73
       Respiratory Tract Disorders 73
       Symptoms 67
  R ↓ Psychosomatic Disorders 67

Hypnagogic Hallucinations 73
PN 21   SC 23870
SN False sensory perceptions without actual ap-
propriate stimuli, occurring while falling asleep.
  B   Hallucinations 67
  R ↓ Sleep Disorders 73

Hypnoanalysis
  Use Hypnotherapy

Hypnosis 67
PN 2652   SC 23890
SN Trance-like state induced by effective sug-
gestion and characterized by increased suggest-
ibility to the hypnotist.
  B   Consciousness Disturbances 73
  N   Age Regression (Hypnotic) 88

Hypnosis — (cont'd)
N　Autohypnosis [73]
R　↓ Hypnotherapy [73]
　　Posthypnotic Suggestions [94]

Hypnotherapists [73]
PN　22　　　　　　　　　　　SC　23900
SN　Persons conducting treatment by means of hypnosis.
B　Hypnotists [73]
　　Psychotherapists [73]
R　Clinical Psychologists [73]
　　Psychiatrists [67]
　　Psychoanalysts [73]

Hypnotherapy [73]
PN　1821　　　　　　　　　　SC　23910
SN　Use of hypnosis in treatment.
UF　Hypnoanalysis
B　Psychotherapy [67]
N　Age Regression (Hypnotic) [88]
R　↓ Hypnosis [67]
　　Posthypnotic Suggestions [94]
　　Progressive Relaxation Therapy [78]
　　↓ Psychoanalysis [67]
　　↓ Relaxation Therapy [78]

Hypnotic Drugs [73]
PN　415　　　　　　　　　　SC　23920
UF　Sleep Inducing Drugs
B　Drugs [67]
N　Amobarbital [73]
　　Apomorphine [73]
　　Barbital [73]
　　Chloral Hydrate [73]
　　Chloralose [73]
　　Codeine [73]
　　Flurazepam [82]
　　Glutethimide [73]
　　Hexobarbital [73]
　　Lithium Bromide [73]
　　Meprobamate [73]
　　Methaqualone [73]
　　Nitrazepam [78]
　　Paraldehyde [82]
　　Pentobarbital [73]
　　Phenobarbital [73]
　　Secobarbital [73]
　　Thalidomide [73]
　　Thiopental [73]
　　Triazolam [88]
R　↓ Analgesic Drugs [73]
　　↓ Anesthetic Drugs [73]
　　↓ Anticonvulsive Drugs [73]
　　↓ Antiemetic Drugs [73]
　　↓ Antihistaminic Drugs [73]
　　↓ Antihypertensive Drugs [73]
　　↓ Barbiturates [67]
　　↓ Benzodiazepines [78]
　　↓ CNS Depressant Drugs [73]
　　↓ Narcotic Drugs [73]
　　↓ Sedatives [73]

Hypnotic Susceptibility [73]
PN　1098　　　　　　　　　　SC　23930
SN　Personal characteristic or state of being receptive to hypnosis.
UF　Susceptibility (Hypnotic)
B　Personality Traits [67]
R　Posthypnotic Suggestions [94]

Hypnotists [73]
PN　27　　　　　　　　　　　SC　23940
SN　Persons conducting scientific experiments by means of hypnosis.
B　Personnel [67]
N　Hypnotherapists [73]

Hypochondriasis [73]
PN　357　　　　　　　　　　SC　23950
B　Psychosomatic Disorders [67]
R　↓ Anxiety Neurosis [73]
　　↓ Conversion Neurosis [73]
　　Psychogenic Pain [73]
　　Somatization [94]

Hypogastric Plexus
Use　Autonomic Ganglia

Hypoglossal Nerve
Use　Cranial Nerves

Hypoglycemia [73]
PN　149　　　　　　　　　　SC　23980
B　Symptoms [67]
R　↓ Metabolism Disorders [73]

Hypogonadism [73]
PN　25　　　　　　　　　　　SC　24000
B　Endocrine Sexual Disorders [73]
N　Klinefelters Syndrome [73]
　　Turners Syndrome [73]
R　↓ Gynecological Disorders [73]
　　Hypopituitarism [73]
　　↓ Male Genital Disorders [73]
　　Sterility [73]

Hypomania [73]
PN　119　　　　　　　　　　SC　24010
B　Mania [67]
R　Cyclothymic Personality [73]

Hypoparathyroidism
Use　Parathyroid Disorders

Hypophysectomy [73]
PN　111　　　　　　　　　　SC　24030
UF　Pituitary Gland Surgery
B　Endocrine Gland Surgery [73]

Hypophysis Disorders
Use　Pituitary Disorders

Hypopituitarism [73]
PN　53　　　　　　　　　　　SC　24050
UF　Dwarfism (Pituitary)
　　Pituitary Dwarfism
B　Pituitary Disorders [73]
R　↓ Genetic Disorders [73]
　　↓ Hypogonadism [73]

Hypotension [73]
PN　81　　　　　　　　　　　SC　24060
B　Blood Pressure Disorders [73]

Hypothalamo Hypophyseal System [73]
PN　219　　　　　　　　　　SC　24070
B　Hypothalamus [67]
　　Pituitary Gland [73]

Hypothalamus [67]
PN　3239　　　　　　　　　　SC　24080
UF　Mammillary Bodies (Hypothalamic)
B　Diencephalon [73]
N　Hypothalamo Hypophyseal System [73]
　　Preoptic Area [94]
R　Medial Forebrain Bundle [82]

Hypothalamus Lesions [73]
PN　819　　　　　　　　　　SC　24090
SN　Not defined prior to 1982. From 1982, limited to experimentally induced lesions and used primarily for animal populations.
B　Brain Lesions [67]

Hypothermia [73]
PN　313　　　　　　　　　　SC　24100
B　Symptoms [67]
R　↓ Body Temperature [73]
　　↓ Central Nervous System Disorders [73]
　　↓ Endocrine Disorders [73]
　　Thermoregulation (Body) [73]

Hypothesis Testing [73]
PN　557　　　　　　　　　　SC　24110
SN　Application of statistical tests to determine whether a research hypothesis should be accepted or rejected. From 1982, limited to discussions of statistical procedures. Use HYPOTHESIS TESTING or other appropriate terms to access references to COGNITIVE HYPOTHESIS TESTING prior to 1982.
B　Experimental Design [67]
N　Null Hypothesis Testing [73]
R　Confidence Limits (Statistics) [73]
　　Construct Validity [82]
　　Predictability (Measurement) [73]
　　↓ Prediction Errors [73]
　　↓ Probability [67]
　　↓ Statistical Analysis [67]
　　Statistical Power [91]
　　Statistical Significance [73]
　　↓ Theories [67]
　　Theory Formulation [73]
　　Theory Verification [73]

Hypothyroidism [73]
PN　147　　　　　　　　　　SC　24120
UF　Myxedema
B　Thyroid Disorders [73]
R　Goiters [73]
　　↓ Infertility [73]
　　↓ Metabolism Disorders [73]
　　Thyroid Extract [73]
　　Thyrotropin [73]
　　Thyroxine [73]

Hypoxia
Use　Anoxia

Hysterectomy [73]
PN　136　　　　　　　　　　SC　24150
B　Sterilization (Sex) [73]
　　Surgery [71]
R　Ovariectomy [73]

Hysteria [67]
PN　722　　　　　　　　　　SC　24160
B　Mental Disorders [67]
N　Mass Hysteria [73]
R　Catalepsy [73]
　　↓ Conversion Neurosis [73]
　　Dissociative Neurosis [73]
　　↓ Dissociative Patterns [73]
　　Hysterical Personality [73]
　　Suggestibility [67]

Hysterical Anesthesia [73]
PN　2　　　　　　　　　　　SC　24170
B　Anesthesia (Feeling) [73]
　　Conversion Neurosis [73]

Hysterical Blindness
Use　Hysterical Vision Disturbances

Hysterical Neurosis (Conversion)
Use　Conversion Neurosis

Hysterical Neurosis (Dissociation)
Use　Dissociative Neurosis

Hysterical Paralysis [73]
PN　20　　　　　　　　　　　SC　24220

Hysterical Paralysis — (cont'd)
  UF   Paralysis (Hysterical)
  B   Conversion Neurosis [73]

Hysterical Personality [73]
PN 205   SC 24230
SN Personality disorder characterized by emotional instability, excitability, overreaction, self-dramatization, self-centeredness, and over-dependence on others.
  UF   Histrionic Personality Disorder
  B   Personality Disorders [67]
  R ↓ Conversion Neurosis [73]
       Dissociative Neurosis [73]
    ↓ Dissociative Patterns [73]
    ↓ Hysteria [67]

Hysterical Vision Disturbances [73]
PN 21   SC 24240
  UF   Hysterical Blindness
       Vision Disturbances (Hysterical)
  B   Conversion Neurosis [73]
  R ↓ Eye Disorders [73]

Iatrogenic Effects
  Use Side Effects (Treatment)

Ibotenic Acid [91]
PN 23   SC 24245
  B   Insecticides [73]
       Neurotoxins [82]
  N   Muscimol [94]

Iceland [82]
PN 45   SC 24247
  B   Europe [73]
  R ↓ Scandinavia [78]

Iconic Memory [85]
PN 59   SC 24248
SN Brief sensory memory, usually lasting only fractions of a second.
  B   Short Term Memory [67]

Id [73]
PN 52   SC 24250
  B   Psychoanalytic Personality Factors [73]
  R   Unconscious (Personality Factor) [67]

Ideal Self
  Use Self Concept

Idealism [73]
PN 78   SC 24260
  B   Personality Traits [67]
       Philosophies [67]

Ideation [73]
PN 223   SC 24270
SN Process of idea or image formation.
  B   Cognitive Processes [67]
  N   Imagination [67]
       Suicidal Ideation [91]

Identical Twins
  Use Monozygotic Twins

Identification (Defense Mechanism) [73]
PN 541   SC 24290
  B   Defense Mechanisms [67]
  R   Introjection [73]
       Projective Identification [94]

Identity (Personal)
  Use Self Concept

Identity (Professional)
  Use Professional Identity

Identity Crisis [73]
PN 231   SC 24320
  B   Crises [71]
       Emotional Adjustment [73]
  R ↓ Personality Development [67]
    ↓ Stress [67]

Idiocy (Amaurotic Familial)
  Use Amaurotic Familial Idiocy

Idiot Savants [73]
PN 50   SC 24350
  B   Mentally Retarded [67]
  R ↓ Ability [67]

Ileum
  Use Intestines

Illegitimate Children [73]
PN 27   SC 24380
  B   Family Members [73]
  R ↓ Children [67]

Illinois Test Psycholinguist Abil [73]
PN 169   SC 24390
  B   Intelligence Measures [67]

Illiteracy
  Use Literacy

Illness (Physical)
  Use Disorders

Illness Behavior [82]
PN 725   SC 24415
SN Adaptive or nonadaptive behaviors exhibited by an individual during the course of an illness or dysfunction.
  B   Behavior [67]
       Client Characteristics [73]
  R   Anosognosia [94]
       Coping Behavior [67]
       Coronary Prone Behavior [82]
    ↓ Disorders [67]
       Physical Illness (Attitudes Toward) [85]
    ↓ Psychosomatic Disorders [67]
       Recovery (Disorders) [73]
       Somatization [94]
       Treatment Compliance [82]

Illumination [67]
PN 3687   SC 24420
SN Visible portion of the electromagnetic radiation spectrum but may include ultraviolet and infrared light. May also refer more generally to ambient light. Compare LUMINANCE.
  UF   Light
       Photic Threshold
  B   Visual Stimulation [73]
  N   Photopic Stimulation [73]
       Scotopic Stimulation [73]
  R ↓ Brightness Perception [73]
       Light Adaptation [82]
    ↓ Light Refraction [82]
       Luminance [82]

Illumination Therapy
  Use Phototherapy

Illusion (Autokinetic)
  Use Autokinetic Illusion

Illusions (Perception) [67]
PN 2021   SC 24440

Illusions (Perception) — (cont'd)
SN Misperception or alteration of reality in subjective perception.
  UF   Optical Illusions
  B   Perception [67]
  N   Mueller Lyer Illusion [88]
    ↓ Perceptual Aftereffect [67]
       Spatial Distortion [73]
  R ↓ Perceptual Distortion [82]
    ↓ Perceptual Disturbances [73]

Image (Retinal)
  Use Retinal Image

Imagery [67]
PN 4452   SC 24470
  UF   Visualization
  B   Abstraction [67]
  N   Conceptual Imagery [73]
       Spatial Imagery [82]
  R   Archetypes [91]
       Imagination [67]

Imagery (Conceptual)
  Use Conceptual Imagery

Imagination [67]
PN 1375   SC 24490
SN Process of forming mental images of objects, qualities, situations, or relationships, which are not immediately apparent to the senses.
  UF   Fantasy
  B   Cognitive Processes [67]
       Ideation [73]
  R   Conceptual Imagery [73]
    ↓ Imagery [67]
       Magical Thinking [73]
       Vicarious Experiences [73]

Imipramine [73]
PN 1326   SC 24520
  UF   Tofranil
  B   Amines [73]
       Antidepressant Drugs [71]

Imitation (Learning) [67]
PN 3066   SC 24530
SN Mimicking by human or animal subjects to learn a model's behavior or responses.
  UF   Modeling Behavior
  B   Social Learning [73]
  R   Observational Learning [73]
       Role Models [82]

Immaturity (Emotional)
  Use Emotional Immaturity

Immersion Programs
  Use Foreign Language Education

Immigrants
  Use Immigration

Immigration [73]
PN 1213   SC 24560
SN Permanent resettlement in a country other than the country of one's origin.
  UF   Immigrants
  B   Social Processes [67]
  R   Citizenship [73]
    ↓ Foreign Nationals [85]
    ↓ Human Migration [73]
       Refugees [88]

Immunization [73]
PN 89   SC 24570

Immunization — (cont'd)
UF   Vaccination
B   Physical Treatment Methods [73]
R   Antibodies [73]

Immunogens
Use Antigens

Immunoglobulins [73]
PN 139   SC 24580
B   Blood Proteins [73]
     Globulins [73]
N   Gamma Globulin [73]
R   Antibodies [73]
     Antigens [82]
     ↓ Immunologic Disorders [73]
     Immunoreactivity [94]
     Interferons [94]

Immunologic Disorders [73]
PN 298   SC 24590
UF   Autoimmune Disorders
     Hypersensitivity (Immunologic)
B   Disorders [67]
N   ↓ Allergic Disorders [73]
     Anaphylactic Shock [73]
     ↓ Human Immunodeficiency Virus [91]
     Rh Incompatibility [73]
R   Asthma [67]
     ↓ Immunoglobulins [73]

Immunology [73]
PN 962   SC 24600
SN   Medical science dealing with the study of immunity. Used for the scientific discipline or the immunological processes themselves.
UF   Immunopathology
B   Medical Sciences [67]
N   Psychoneuroimmunology [91]
R   Immunoreactivity [94]

Immunopathology
Use Immunology

Immunoreactivity [94]
PN 0   SC 24613
SN   Use IMMUNOLOGY to access references from 73-93.
R   ↓ Immunoglobulins [73]
     ↓ Immunology [73]
     Interleukins [94]

Impaired Professionals [85]
PN 152   SC 24615
SN   Professional personnel who are physically or psychologically disordered to the extent that such disorders interfere with the performance of professional duties or conflict with professional standards. Does not include handicaps that do not interfere with professional performance.
R   ↓ Medical Personnel [67]
     ↓ Mental Health Personnel [67]
     Personal Therapy [91]
     Professional Ethics [73]
     Professional Liability [85]
     ↓ Professional Personnel [78]
     ↓ Professional Standards [73]

Implosive Therapy [73]
PN 317   SC 24620
SN   Behavioral therapy involving flooding the client with anxiety through intense or prolonged real-life or imagined exposure to feared objects or situations, thereby demonstrating that they cause no harm. The aim is gradual extinction of anxiety or phobic responses.
UF   Flooding Therapy
B   Behavior Therapy [67]

Impotence [73]
PN 343   SC 24630
B   Sexual Function Disturbances [73]
R   Erection (Penis) [73]
     Frigidity [73]
     ↓ Male Orgasm [73]
     ↓ Orgasm [73]
     Premature Ejaculation [73]

Impression Formation [78]
PN 832   SC 24634
SN   Process by which an individual transforms various perceptions and observations about another person or group into an overall impression or set of attitudes toward or about that person or group.
B   Social Perception [67]
R   ↓ Attitudes [67]
     Attribution [73]
     Impression Management [78]

Impression Management [78]
PN 332   SC 24636
SN   Techniques of image cultivation or impression formation designed to obtain good evaluations of one's self and to win approval from others.
UF   Ingratiation
R   Impression Formation [78]
     Self Monitoring (Personality) [85]
     ↓ Social Behavior [67]
     ↓ Social Perception [67]
     Uncertainty [91]

Imprinting [67]
PN 329   SC 24640
SN   Rapid learning process that takes place during early critical periods of development in social animals. Establishes the basis for patterns of social behavior.
B   Animal Ethology [67]
     Social Learning [73]
R   Critical Period [88]
     Species Recognition [85]

Impulsiveness [73]
PN 1312   SC 24650
UF   Reflectiveness
B   Cognitive Style [67]
     Conceptual Tempo [85]
R   Attention Deficit Disorder [85]
     Kleptomania [73]
     Pathological Gambling [88]
     Pyromania [73]

In Vitro Fertilization
Use Reproductive Technology

Inadequate Personality [73]
PN 3   SC 24660
SN   Inadequate responses to physical, social, and emotional demands; general ineptness and instability, despite absence of actual physical or mental deficit.
B   Personality Disorders [67]

Incarceration [73]
PN 513   SC 24670
B   Institutionalization [67]
     Law Enforcement [78]
R   ↓ Correctional Institutions [73]
     Institution Visitation [73]
     ↓ Institutional Release [78]

Incentives [67]
PN 902   SC 24680

Incentives — (cont'd)
SN   Events or objects which increase or induce drives or determination. Popularly described as one's expectation of reward. May be used for human or animal populations. Compare REWARDS and REINFORCEMENT.
B   Motivation [67]
N   Educational Incentives [73]
     Monetary Incentives [73]
R   ↓ Goals [67]
     Needs [67]
     ↓ Rewards [67]
     Temptation [73]

Incest [73]
PN 1063   SC 24690
B   Sexual Abuse [88]
     Sexual Deviations [67]
     Sexual Intercourse (Human) [73]
R   Pedophilia [73]
     ↓ Perpetrators [88]
     ↓ Sex Offenses [82]

Incidental Learning [67]
PN 621   SC 24700
SN   Learning which takes place without the intent to learn or in the absence of formal instructions. From 1982, limited to human populations. Use LATENT LEARNING for animal populations.
B   Learning [67]
N   Latent Learning [73]

Income (Economic) [73]
PN 288   SC 24710
SN   Monetary gain (such as wages, interest, dividends, profits) received by individuals or nations within a given period for labor or services rendered or from capital resources.
R   ↓ Income Level [73]
     Poverty [73]
     Salaries [73]
     ↓ Socioeconomic Status [67]
     Taxation [85]

Income Level [73]
PN 662   SC 24720
SN   Total amount of monetary gain received within a given period that is associated with socioeconomic status.
B   Socioeconomic Status [67]
N   Lower Income Level [73]
     Middle Income Level [73]
     Upper Income Level [73]
R   Income (Economic) [73]
     Salaries [73]
     ↓ Social Class [67]

Incompatibility (Rh)
Use Rh Incompatibility

Incomplete Man Test [73]
PN 2   SC 24750
B   Projective Techniques [67]

Incontinence (Fecal)
Use Fecal Incontinence

Incontinence (Urinary)
Use Urinary Incontinence

Incubators (Apparatus) [73]
PN 6   SC 24780
B   Apparatus [67]

Independence (Personality) [73]
PN 1068   SC 24790
UF   Autonomy (Personality)
B   Personality Traits [67]

Independence (Personality) — (cont'd)
R   Empowerment [91]
    Self Determination [94]

Independent Living
Use   Self Care Skills

Independent Living Programs [91]
PN 43   SC 24798
SN   Community based programs or services to assist disabled individuals to perform all or most of their daily functions, thus increasing self sufficiency and self determination and eliminating a need to depend on others.
R   Activities of Daily Living [91]
    Advocacy [85]
    ↓ Community Services [67]
    Habilitation [91]
    ↓ Mainstreaming [91]
    ↓ Program Development [91]
    ↓ Rehabilitation [67]
    Self Care Skills [78]

Independent Party (Political)
Use   Political Parties

Independent Study
Use   Individualized Instruction

Independent Variables [73]
PN 71   SC 24810
SN   Statistical or experimental parameters that are manipulated in an attempt to analyze their relative effect on specified dependent variables.
B   Statistical Variables [73]

India [67]
PN 2717   SC 24820
B   Asia [73]

Indians (American)
Use   American Indians

Indifference
Use   Apathy

Individual Counseling
Use   Individual Psychotherapy

Individual Differences [67]
PN 3889   SC 24860
SN   Any specific characteristic or quantitative difference in a quality or trait that can serve to distinguish one individual from another. Used for human or animal populations.
R   ↓ Personality [67]

Individual Problem Solving
Use   Problem Solving

Individual Psychology [73]
PN 631   SC 24880
SN   Theory and practice of Adlerian psychology, stressing the unique wholeness of the individual and viewing the striving to overcome and master obstacles as the primary motivating force.
B   Neopsychoanalytic School [73]
R   Adler (Alfred) [67]

Individual Psychotherapy [73]
PN 932   SC 24890
UF   Adlerian Psychotherapy
    Individual Counseling
    Individual Therapy
B   Psychotherapy [67]

Individual Testing [73]
PN 71   SC 24900
B   Measurement [67]
R   Test Administration [73]

Individual Therapy
Use   Individual Psychotherapy

Individualism
Use   Individuality

Individuality [73]
PN 402   SC 24930
UF   Individualism
B   Personality Traits [67]
R   Nonconformity (Personality) [73]
    Self Determination [94]

Individualized Instruction [73]
PN 1592   SC 24940
SN   Instruction adapted to individual needs or instruction in which a student works alone or only with a teacher. Also, self-initiated study with or without formal academic guidance or involvement.
UF   Independent Study
    Instruction (Individualized)
    Self Directed Learning
    Self Instruction
B   Teaching Methods [67]
R   Computer Assisted Instruction [73]
    ↓ Continuing Education [85]
    ↓ Learning [67]
    Open Classroom Method [73]
    Programed Instruction [67]
    ↓ Tutoring [73]

Indonesia [82]
PN 115   SC 24945
B   Southeast Asia [73]

Induced Abortion [71]
PN 737   SC 24950
UF   Abortion (Induced)
    Elective Abortion
    Therapeutic Abortion
B   Surgery [71]
R   Abortion Laws [73]
    ↓ Birth Control [71]
    ↓ Family Planning [73]
    Spontaneous Abortion [71]

Inductive Deductive Reasoning [73]
PN 664   SC 24960
UF   Convergent Thinking
    Deductive Reasoning
    Syllogistic Reasoning
B   Reasoning [67]
N   Inference [73]
R   Divergent Thinking [73]
    Logical Thinking [67]
    ↓ Problem Solving [67]

Industrial Accidents [73]
PN 336   SC 24970
B   Accidents [67]
R   Occupational Exposure [88]
    Occupational Safety [73]
    Work Related Illnesses [94]

Industrial Arts Education
Use   Vocational Education

Industrial Foremen [73]
PN 51   SC 24980
UF   Foremen (Industrial)
B   Blue Collar Workers [73]
R   ↓ Management Personnel [73]

Industrial Personnel
Use   Business and Industrial Personnel

Industrial Psychologists [73]
PN 77   SC 25000
B   Business and Industrial Personnel [67]
    Psychologists [67]
R   Social Psychologists [73]

Industrial Psychology [67]
PN 810   SC 25010
UF   Organizational Psychology
B   Applied Psychology [73]

Industrial Safety
Use   Occupational Safety

Industrialization [73]
PN 342   SC 25030
B   Social Processes [67]
R   ↓ Technology [73]
    Urbanization [73]

Industry
Use   Business

Infancy
Use   Infants

Infant Development [73]
PN 1782   SC 25060
B   Early Childhood Development [73]
N   Neonatal Development [73]
R   ↓ Physical Development [73]
    ↓ Psychogenesis [73]

Infant Intelligence Scale [73]
PN 3   SC 25070
UF   Cattell Infant Intelligence Scale
B   Intelligence Measures [67]

Infant Vocalization [73]
PN 438   SC 25080
UF   Babbling
    Vocalization (Infant)
B   Voice [73]
R   Crying [73]

Infanticide [78]
PN 182   SC 25085
UF   Neonaticide
B   Homicide [67]

Infantile Neurosis
Use   Childhood Neurosis

Infantile Paralysis
Use   Poliomyelitis

Infantile Psychosis
Use   Childhood Psychosis

Infantilism [73]
PN 12   SC 25120
R   ↓ Mental Disorders [67]

Infants [67]
PN 10922   SC 25130
SN   Ages 2–23 months. Application of terms designating age is mandatory for ages 0–17 years.
UF   Babies
    Infancy
B   Children [67]
N   Neonates [67]
R   Childhood [84]

Infants (Animal) [78]
PN 3638   SC 25134
  UF   Neonates (Animal)
  B   Animals [67]

Infarctions (Myocardial)
  Use Myocardial Infarctions

Infections
  Use Infectious Disorders

Infectious Disorders [73]
PN 180   SC 25160
  UF   Communicable Diseases
        Infections
        Neuroinfections
  B   Disorders [67]
  N   ↓ Bacterial Disorders [73]
        Epstein Barr Viral Disorder [94]
      ↓ Parasitic Disorders [73]
      ↓ Venereal Diseases [73]
      ↓ Viral Disorders [73]
  R   ↓ Arthritis [73]
      ↓ Chorea [73]
      ↓ Dermatitis [73]
      ↓ Digestive System Disorders [73]
        Encephalitis [73]
        Encephalomyelitis [73]
      ↓ Hepatitis [73]
        Hydrocephaly [73]
        Jaundice [73]
      ↓ Liver Disorders [73]
      ↓ Myelitis [73]

Inference [73]
PN 1406   SC 25180
  B   Inductive Deductive Reasoning [73]
  R   Analogy [91]
        Attribution [73]

Inferior Colliculus [73]
PN 120   SC 25190
  B   Mesencephalon [73]

Inferiority (Emotional)
  Use Emotional Inferiority

Infertility [73]
PN 287   SC 25210
  B   Genital Disorders [67]
  N   Sterility [73]
  R   ↓ Endocrine Sexual Disorders [73]
        Fertility [88]
      ↓ Gynecological Disorders [73]
        Hypothyroidism [73]
        Klinefelters Syndrome [73]
      ↓ Male Genital Disorders [73]
      ↓ Venereal Diseases [73]

Infirmaries
  Use Hospitals

Inflection [73]
PN 305   SC 25230
SN A grammatically functional change in the
pitch or loudness of the voice. Also, the syntactic
change in words to designate such factors as
case, gender, or tense.
  B   Prosody [91]
  R   ↓ Phonology [73]
      ↓ Speech Characteristics [73]
      ↓ Syntax [71]

Influence (Interpersonal)
  Use Interpersonal Influences

Influences (Social)
  Use Social Influences

Influenza [73]
PN 40   SC 25260
  B   Viral Disorders [73]
  R   ↓ Gastrointestinal Disorders [73]
      ↓ Nervous System Disorders [67]
      ↓ Respiratory Tract Disorders [73]

Informants [88]
PN 15   SC 25270
SN Persons who provide information against an-
other person who is suspected of committing a
violation.
  UF   Whistleblowing
  R   ↓ Crime [67]
        Labor Management Relations [67]
      ↓ Organizational Behavior [78]
      ↓ Social Behavior [67]

Information [67]
PN 3405   SC 25360
SN Conceptually broad array term referring to a
body of knowledge. Use a more specific term if
possible. Differentiate from KNOWLEDGE LEVEL
which is the amount of information acquired or
received by an individual or group.
  R   ↓ Automated Information Processing [73]
        Censorship [78]
      ↓ Communication [67]
        Computer Searching [91]
        Concepts [67]
        Data Collection [82]
      ↓ Data Processing [67]
        Databases [91]
        Human Information Storage [73]
        Information Exchange [73]
        Information Seeking [73]
        Information Services [88]
      ↓ Information Specialists [88]
        Information Systems [91]
        Information Theory [67]
      ↓ Knowledge Level [78]
      ↓ Libraries [82]
        Messages [73]
        Privileged Communication [73]

Information (Messages)
  Use Messages

Information Exchange [73]
PN 471   SC 25290
SN Interchange of information between humans
or humans and machines.
  R   Computer Searching [91]
        Databases [91]
        Information [67]
        Information Seeking [73]
      ↓ Scientific Communication [73]

Information Processes (Human)
  Use Cognitive Processes

Information Processing (Automated)
  Use Automated Information Processing

Information Retrieval (Automated)
  Use Automated Information Retrieval

Information Seeking [73]
PN 818   SC 25330
  R   Computer Searching [91]
      ↓ Exploratory Behavior [67]
        Information [67]
        Information Exchange [73]
        Questioning [82]

Information Services [88]
PN 59   SC 25335
  R   ↓ Automated Information Retrieval [73]
        Computer Searching [91]
        Databases [91]
        Hot Line Services [73]
        Information [67]
        Information Systems [91]
      ↓ Libraries [82]

Information Specialists [88]
PN 4   SC 25338
  B   Professional Personnel [78]
  N   Librarians [88]
  R   Information [67]

Information Storage (Human)
  Use Human Information Storage

Information Systems [91]
PN 92   SC 25345
SN Collection, organization, and storage of data
or the operational functions used to process in-
formation.
  UF   Management Information Systems
  B   Systems [67]
  R   ↓ Automated Information Processing [73]
      ↓ Automated Information Retrieval [73]
        Automated Information Storage [73]
      ↓ Communication Systems [73]
      ↓ Computer Applications [73]
      ↓ Data Processing [67]
        Databases [91]
        Expert Systems [91]
        Information [67]
        Information Services [88]
        Word Processing [91]

Information Theory [67]
PN 445   SC 25350
SN Branch of science which deals statistically
with the transmission of information and its mea-
surable characteristics. Used for the scientific
discipline or for application of information theory
to specific areas of investigation.
  B   Theories [67]
  R   Communication Theory [73]
        Information [67]
      ↓ Stochastic Modeling [73]

Informed Consent [85]
PN 371   SC 25363
SN Process of making rational decisions regard-
ing one's treatment or participation in experimen-
tal procedures.
  R   ↓ Civil Rights [78]
        Client Rights [88]
        Debriefing (Experimental) [91]
        Experiment Volunteers [73]
        Experimental Ethics [78]
        Guardianship [88]
        Involuntary Treatment [94]
      ↓ Legal Processes [73]
        Professional Ethics [73]
        Treatment Compliance [82]
        Treatment Refusal [94]
        Treatment Withholding [88]

Ingratiation
  Use Impression Management

Inhalant Abuse [85]
PN 123   SC 25367
SN Inhalation of vapors from volatile chemical
substances (such as aerosol sprays, solvents,
and anesthetics) in order to produce mind-alter-
ing effects.
  UF   Solvent Abuse
  B   Drug Abuse [73]

Inhalant Abuse — (cont'd)
N   Glue Sniffing [73]
R ↓ Solvents [82]

Inhibition (Personality) [73]
PN 400   SC 25380
B   Personality Processes [67]

Inhibition (Proactive)
Use Proactive Inhibition

Inhibition (Retroactive)
Use Retroactive Inhibition

Initial Teaching Alphabet [73]
PN 15   SC 25410
B   Alphabets [73]
R ↓ Language Arts Education [73]
    ↓ Reading [67]
    Reading Education [73]
    ↓ Teaching Methods [67]

Initiation Rites [73]
PN 41   SC 25420
B   Rites of Passage [73]

Initiative [73]
PN 58   SC 25430
B   Personality Traits [67]

Injections [73]
PN 118   SC 25440
B   Drug Administration Methods [73]
N   Intramuscular Injections [73]
    Intraperitoneal Injections [73]
    Intravenous Injections [73]
    Subcutaneous Injections [73]

Injuries [73]
PN 795   SC 25450
UF Physical Trauma
    Trauma (Physical)
N   Birth Injuries [73]
    Burns [73]
    Electrical Injuries [73]
   ↓ Head Injuries [73]
    Spinal Cord Injuries [73]
   ↓ Wounds [73]
R ↓ Accidents [67]
    Coma [73]
   ↓ Disorders [67]
    Hematoma [73]
    Hemiplegia [78]
    Paraplegia [78]
    Physical Disfigurement [78]
    Quadriplegia [85]
   ↓ Safety [67]
    Shock [67]

Injuries (Birth)
Use Birth Injuries

Inmates (Prison)
Use Prisoners

Innate Behavior (Animal)
Use Instinctive Behavior

Inner City
Use Urban Environments

Inner Ear
Use Labyrinth (Anatomy)

Inner Speech
Use Self Talk

Innovativeness
Use Creativity

Inquisitiveness
Use Curiosity

Insanity
Use Mental Disorders

Insanity Defense [85]
PN 376   SC 25525
SN Legal defense designed to invoke an exemption from criminal responsibility on the basis of a mental disorder at the time of the alleged criminal offense.
B   Legal Processes [73]
R   Court Referrals [94]
    Criminal Responsibility [91]
    Forensic Evaluation [94]
    Forensic Psychiatry [73]
   ↓ Mental Disorders [67]
    Mentally Ill Offenders [85]

Insecticides [73]
PN 113   SC 25530
UF Pesticides
B   Hazardous Materials [91]
N   DDT (Insecticide) [73]
    Dieldrin [73]
   ↓ Ibotenic Acid [91]
    Parathion [73]
R ↓ Drugs [67]
   ↓ Insects [67]
   ↓ Neurotoxins [82]
    Nicotine [73]
   ↓ Poisons [73]

Insects [67]
PN 940   SC 25540
B   Arthropoda [73]
N   Ants [73]
    Bees [73]
    Beetles [73]
    Butterflies [73]
    Cockroaches [73]
   ↓ Diptera [73]
    Grasshoppers [73]
    Larvae [73]
    Mantis [73]
    Moths [73]
    Wasps [82]
R ↓ Insecticides [73]

Insecurity (Emotional)
Use Emotional Security

Insensitivity (Personality)
Use Sensitivity (Personality)

Inservice Teacher Education [73]
PN 1289   SC 25570
SN Course or program designed to provide teachers with growth in job-related competencies or skills. Usually school sponsored.
B   Inservice Training [85]
    Teacher Education [67]
R   On the Job Training [73]
    Professional Development [82]

Inservice Training [85]
PN 226   SC 25575
B   Continuing Education [85]
    Personnel Training [67]
N   Inservice Teacher Education [73]
    Mental Health Inservice Training [73]
R   On the Job Training [73]
    Professional Development [82]

Inservice Training (Mental Health)
Use Mental Health Inservice Training

Insight [73]
PN 190   SC 25590
B   Personality Traits [67]
R   Intuition [73]
    Perceptiveness (Personality) [73]

Insight (Psychotherapeutic Process) [73]
PN 144   SC 25600
B   Psychotherapeutic Processes [67]

Insight Therapy [73]
PN 141   SC 25610
SN Psychotherapeutic method which seeks to uncover the causes of the client's conflicts through conscious awareness (i.e., insight) of the current dynamics of feelings, responses, and behavior, primarily in relations with others.
B   Psychotherapy [67]

Insomnia [73]
PN 706   SC 25620
B   Sleep Disorders [73]
    Symptoms [67]

Instability (Emotional)
Use Emotional Instability

Instinctive Behavior [82]
PN 234   SC 25638
SN Stereotyped, unlearned, largely stimulus-bound, adaptive behavior limited in its expression by the inherent properties of the nervous system and genetic factors. Used for human or animal populations. Use ANIMAL INSTINCTIVE BEHAVIOR or ANIMAL INNATE BEHAVIOR to access references to nonhuman populations from 67–81 and 73–81, respectively.
UF Animal Innate Behavior
    Animal Instinctive Behavior
    Innate Behavior (Animal)
B   Behavior [67]
R ↓ Animal Defensive Behavior [82]
   ↓ Animal Ethology [67]
    Animal Homing [91]
    Animal Motivation [67]
   ↓ Genetics [67]
    Homeostasis [73]
   ↓ Motivation [67]
    Neophobia [85]
   ↓ Nervous System [67]
   ↓ Physiology [67]
    Species Recognition [85]
    Spontaneous Alternation [82]
    Stereotyped Behavior [73]

Institution Visitation [73]
PN 85   SC 25650
SN Visiting a patient or convict in an institution (e.g., hospital, prison, or nursing home) by someone from outside the institution (e.g., friends or family).
UF Visitation (Institution)
R ↓ Correctional Institutions [73]
    Incarceration [73]
   ↓ Residential Care Institutions [73]

Institutional Release [78]
PN 127   SC 25664
SN Discharge or release of an individual from any type of correctional or therapeutic residential facility.
B   Institutionalization [67]
N ↓ Hospital Discharge [73]
R ↓ Commitment (Psychiatric) [73]
    Deinstitutionalization [82]
    Discharge Planning [94]

Institutional Release — (cont'd)
R ↓ Hospital Admission [73]
    Incarceration [73]
  ↓ Psychiatric Hospital Admission [73]
  ↓ Psychiatric Hospitalization [73]

Institutional Schools [78]
PN 195   SC 25666
SN Schools that are part of larger residential institutions such as hospitals or prisons.
B Schools [67]
R Boarding Schools [88]
  ↓ Correctional Institutions [73]
  ↓ Residential Care Institutions [73]
  ↓ Treatment Facilities [73]

Institutionalization [67]
PN 1541   SC 25670
N ↓ Hospitalization [67]
    Incarceration [73]
  ↓ Institutional Release [78]
R ↓ Facility Admission [88]
  ↓ Facility Discharge [88]
    Orphanages [73]

Institutionalized Mentally Retarded [73]
PN 1217   SC 25680
B Mentally Retarded [67]
R Home Reared Mentally Retarded [73]
  ↓ Residential Care Institutions [73]

Institutions (Correctional)
Use Correctional Institutions

Institutions (Residential Care)
Use Residential Care Institutions

Instruction
Use Teaching

Instruction (Computer Assisted)
Use Computer Assisted Instruction

Instruction (Individualized)
Use Individualized Instruction

Instruction (Programed)
Use Programed Instruction

Instructional Media [67]
PN 997   SC 25740
SN Formats or technologies for conveyance of didactic content, including print, film, computers, phonographic records and magnetic tape.
B Teaching [67]
N Advance Organizers [85]
  ↓ Educational Audiovisual Aids [73]
    Reading Materials [73]
    Teaching Machines [73]
  ↓ Textbooks [78]

Instructional Objectives
Use Educational Objectives

Instructions (Experimental)
Use Experimental Instructions

Instructors
Use Teachers

Instrument Controls [85]
PN 37   SC 25765
SN May include knobs, handles, levers, latches, dials, switches, buttons, and any other mechanism used to control the operation of machines and instruments. Consider VISUAL DISPLAYS to access references from 73-84.

Instrument Controls — (cont'd)
UF Controls (Instrument)
N Flight Instrumentation [73]
R ↓ Displays [67]
    Human Factors Engineering [73]
    Keyboards [85]
    Man Machine Systems Design [73]

Instrumental Conditioning
Use Operant Conditioning

Instrumental Learning
Use Operant Conditioning

Instrumentality [91]
PN 28   SC 25785
R ↓ Motivation [67]
  ↓ Personality Traits [67]
    Self Efficacy [85]

Instrumentation (Flight)
Use Flight Instrumentation

Insulin [73]
PN 463   SC 25800
B Hormones [67]
R Insulin Shock Therapy [73]

Insulin Shock Therapy [73]
PN 28   SC 25820
B Shock Therapy [73]
R Coma [73]
  Insulin [73]

Insurance [73]
PN 93   SC 25830
N ↓ Health Insurance [73]
    Life Insurance [73]
    Social Security [88]
R Disability Evaluation [88]

Insurance Agents
Use Sales Personnel

Intake Interview [94]
PN 0   SC 25845
SN Initial evaluation, assessment, or screening of clients or patients to determine needs and appropriate health, mental health, rehabilitation, or other services.
B Interviews [67]
R ↓ Case Management [91]
    Clinical Judgment (Not Diagnosis) [73]
  ↓ Diagnosis [67]
  ↓ Evaluation [67]
    Needs Assessment [85]
  ↓ Psychodiagnostic Interview [73]
  ↓ Screening [82]

Integration (Racial)
Use Social Integration

Intellectual Development [73]
PN 1074   SC 25860
SN Acquisition of factual knowledge. For acquisition of reasoning, thought, and problem solving abilities, use COGNITIVE DEVELOPMENT.
B Cognitive Development [73]
N ↓ Language Development [67]
R Intelligence [67]

Intellectual Functioning
Use Cognitive Ability

Intellectualism [73]
PN 12   SC 25870

Intellectualism — (cont'd)
SN Doctrine which attempts to explain emotion and volition in terms of cognitive processes.
B Philosophies [67]

Intellectualization [73]
PN 12   SC 25880
SN Defense mechanism in which emotional content of a painful situation is avoided by construction of logic-tight arguments.
B Defense Mechanisms [67]
R Isolation (Defense Mechanism) [73]

Intellectually Gifted
Use Gifted

Intelligence [67]
PN 5677   SC 25900
SN General ability to learn, to apply knowledge, or to deal effectively with the environment. Consider also INTELLIGENCE QUOTIENT.
R ↓ Ability [67]
  ↓ Artificial Intelligence [82]
    Creativity [67]
    Divergent Thinking [73]
    Gifted [67]
  ↓ Intellectual Development [73]
    Intelligence Quotient [67]
    Mental Age [73]
    Wisdom [94]

Intelligence Age
Use Mental Age

Intelligence Measures [67]
PN 3402   SC 25910
UF Tests (Intelligence)
B Measurement [67]
N Benton Revised Visual Retention Test [73]
  California Test of Mental Maturity [73]
  Columbia Mental Maturity Scale [73]
  Culture Fair Intelligence Test [73]
  Frostig Development Test Vis Percept [73]
  Goodenough Harris Draw A Person Test [67]
  Henmon Nelson Tests Mental Ability [73]
  Hidden Figures Test [73]
  Illinois Test Psycholinguist Abil [73]
  Infant Intelligence Scale [73]
  Kaufman Assessment Battery Children [88]
  Kohs Block Design Test [73]
  Leiter Adult Intelligence Scale [73]
  Lorge Thorndike Intelligence Test [73]
  Lowenfeld Mosaic Test [73]
  Miller Analogies Test [73]
  Peabody Picture Vocabulary Test [73]
  Porteus Maze Test [73]
  Raven Coloured Progressive Matrices [73]
  Raven Progressive Matrices [78]
  Remote Associates Test [73]
  Slosson Intelligence Test for Child [73]
  Stanford Binet Intelligence Scale [67]
  Temporal Spatial Concept Scale [73]
  Vane Kindergarten Test [73]
  Wechsler Adult Intelligence Scale [67]
  Wechsler Bellevue Intelligence Scale [67]
  Wechsler Intelligence Scale Children [67]
  Wechsler Preschool Primary Scale [88]
R Bayley Scales of Infant Development [94]

Intelligence Quotient [67]
PN 2684   SC 25920
SN Relative intelligence of an individual expressed as a score on a standardized test of intelligence. Consider also INTELLIGENCE.
B Test Scores [67]
R Intelligence [67]
  Mental Age [73]

Intensity (Stimulus)
  Use Stimulus Intensity

Intensive Care [88]
PN 116   SC 25942
  R Hospital Environment [82]
    ↓ Hospital Programs [78]
    ↓ Hospitals [67]

Intention [88]
PN 633   SC 25945
  SN Determination to act in a certain manner.
  R ↓ Goals [67]
    ↓ Motivation [67]

Intentional Learning [73]
PN 246   SC 25950
  SN Purposive or motivated learning.
  B Learning [67]

Interaction (Interpersonal)
  Use Interpersonal Interaction

Interaction (Social)
  Use Social Interaction

Interaction Analysis (Statistics) [73]
PN 86   SC 25990
  B Statistical Analysis [67]
  R Interaction Variance [73]

Interaction Variance [73]
PN 10   SC 26000
  B Variability Measurement [73]
  R Interaction Analysis (Statistics) [73]

Intercourse (Sexual)
  Use Sexual Intercourse (Human)

Interdisciplinary Research [85]
PN 156   SC 26025
  SN Any research effort coordinated or executed by members of two or more specialties, disciplines, or theoretical orientations.
  UF Cross Disciplinary Research
    Multidisciplinary Research
  B Experimentation [67]
  R Interdisciplinary Treatment Approach [73]

Interdisciplinary Treatment Approach [73]
PN 1683   SC 26030
  SN Combination of two or more disciplines in the prevention, diagnosis, treatment, or rehabilitation of mental or physical disorders.
  UF Multidisciplinary Treatment Approach
  B Treatment [67]
  R Biopsychosocial Approach [91]
    Eclectic Psychotherapy [94]
    ↓ Health Care Psychology [85]
    Interdisciplinary Research [85]
    Multimodal Treatment Approach [91]
    Partial Hospitalization [85]
    Teams [88]

Interest Inventories [73]
PN 434   SC 26040
  B Inventories [67]

Interest Patterns
  SN Term discontinued in 1982. Use INTEREST PATTERNS or INTERESTS to access references prior to 1982.
  Use Interests

Interests [67]
PN 940   SC 26080

Interests — (cont'd)
  SN Use INTERESTS or INTEREST PATTERNS to access references prior to 1982.
  UF Interest Patterns
  N Occupational Interests [67]
  R Daily Activities [94]
    Hobbies [73]

Interethnic Family [88]
PN 11   SC 26070
  B Family [67]
  R Interracial Adoption [94]
    Interracial Family [88]
    Racial and Ethnic Differences [82]

Interethnic Marriage
  Use Exogamous Marriage

Interfaith Marriage [73]
PN 21   SC 26090
  B Exogamous Marriage [73]

Interference (Learning) [67]
PN 2645   SC 26100
  SN Inhibition of learning due to negative transfer effects of competing memories, thoughts, or learned behavior. Effects include slower learning and poorer memory.
  B Learning [67]
  N Proactive Inhibition [73]
    Retroactive Inhibition [73]
  R Forgetting [73]
    ↓ Retention [67]
    Stroop Effect [88]

Interferons [94]
PN 0   SC 26103
  B Proteins [73]
  R Antineoplastic Drugs [82]
    ↓ Immunoglobulins [73]

Intergenerational Relations [88]
PN 382   SC 26105
  SN Contact between related or nonrelated persons of different generational age groups.
  R Empty Nest [91]
    ↓ Family Relations [67]
    Generation Gap [73]
    Transgenerational Patterns [91]

Intergroup Dynamics [73]
PN 549   SC 26110
  B Group Dynamics [67]

Interhemispheric Interaction [85]
PN 274   SC 26112
  SN Any neurophysiological, electrophysiological, or neurochemical exchange occurring between the cerebral hemispheres.
  UF Interhemispheric Transfer
  R ↓ Cerebral Cortex [67]
    ↓ Cerebral Dominance [73]
    Corpus Callosum [73]
    Left Brain [91]
    Right Brain [91]

Interhemispheric Transfer
  Use Interhemispheric Interaction

Interior Design [82]
PN 165   SC 26115
  SN Practice or resultant product of planning and implementing the design of architectural interiors and furnishings.
  B Architecture [73]
    Environmental Planning [82]
  R Aesthetic Preferences [73]

Interior Design — (cont'd)
  R Aesthetics [67]
    Furniture [85]

Interleukins [94]
PN 0   SC 26117
  SN Compounds produced by lymphocytes that regulate immune system functioning and individual cell mediated immunity.
  R Antigens [82]
    Biological Markers [91]
    Immunoreactivity [94]
    Lymphocytes [73]

Intermarriage
  Use Exogamous Marriage

Intermediate School Students [73]
PN 48   SC 26130
  SN Includes the middle and/or upper elementary school grades, usually grades 4, 5, and 6. Use ELEMENTARY SCHOOL STUDENTS unless specific reference is made to population as intermediate school students. Use of a student term is mandatory in educational contexts.
  B Elementary School Students [67]
  R ↓ Children [67]
    Preadolescents [88]
    ↓ School Age Children [73]

Intermittent Explosive Personality
  Use Explosive Personality

Intermittent Reinforcement
  Use Reinforcement Schedules

Internal Consistency
  Use Test Reliability

Internal External Locus of Control [67]
PN 7688   SC 26150
  UF Locus of Control
  B Personality Traits [67]
  R Attribution [73]
    External Rewards [73]
    Extrinsic Motivation [73]
    Internal Rewards [73]
    Intrinsic Motivation [73]
    Self Determination [94]

Internal Rewards [73]
PN 98   SC 26160
  SN Satisfaction of a personal value or intrinsic criteria of behavior through action or attainment. Compare SECONDARY REINFORCEMENT.
  UF Intrinsic Rewards
  B Rewards [67]
  R Internal External Locus of Control [67]
    Intrinsic Motivation [73]

International Organizations [73]
PN 130   SC 26170
  B Organizations [67]
  R Foreign Organizations [73]

International Relations [67]
PN 591   SC 26180
  R Foreign Policy Making [73]
    Peace [88]

Internists [73]
PN 79   SC 26190
  B Physicians [67]

Internship (Medical)
  Use Medical Internship

Interobserver Reliability
  Use Interrater Reliability

Interocular Transfer 85
PN 52   SC 26207
SN Any neurophysiological, electrophysiological, or perceptual interaction between the two eyes.
  B Visual Perception 67
  R Ocular Dominance 73
  ↓ Perceptual Aftereffect 67
  ↓ Sensory Adaptation 67

Interpersonal Attraction 67
PN 2402   SC 26210
  UF Attraction (Interpersonal)
  B Interpersonal Interaction 67
  R Human Mate Selection 88
   Likability 88
   Physical Attractiveness 73

Interpersonal Communication 73
PN 4425   SC 26220
  B Communication 67
   Interpersonal Interaction 67
  N Arguments 73
   Body Language 73
   Conversation 73
   Double Bind Interaction 73
   Eye Contact 73
   Gossip 82
   Group Discussion 67
   Interviewing 73
  ↓ Interviews 67
   Job Applicant Interviews 73
  ↓ Negotiation 73
  ↓ Parent Child Communication 73
  R Credibility 73
   Neurolinguistic Programing 88
   Pragmatics 85
  ↓ Scientific Communication 73
   Self Disclosure 73
   Self Reference 94
   Speech Anxiety 85

Interpersonal Compatibility 73
PN 332   SC 26230
  UF Compatibility (Interpersonal)
  B Interpersonal Interaction 67
  R Friendship 67

Interpersonal Distance
  Use Personal Space

Interpersonal Influences 67
PN 2830   SC 26240
SN Effect one individual has on another with or without apparent intention or direct exercise of command.
  UF Influence (Interpersonal)
  B Interpersonal Interaction 67
  N Peer Pressure 94
  R Reference Groups 94
  ↓ Social Influences 67

Interpersonal Interaction 67
PN 10918   SC 26250
  UF Interaction (Interpersonal)
   Rapport
  B Social Interaction 67
  N Assistance (Social Behavior) 73
   Charitable Behavior 73
  ↓ Collective Behavior 67
  ↓ Conflict 67
   Cooperation 67
   Employee Interaction 88
   Friendship 67
   Group Participation 73
   Group Performance 67

Interpersonal Interaction — (cont'd)
  N Interpersonal Attraction 67
  ↓ Interpersonal Communication 73
   Interpersonal Compatibility 73
  ↓ Interpersonal Influences 67
   Male Female Relations 88
  ↓ Participation 73
  ↓ Peer Relations 67
   Persecution 73
   Rivalry 73
   Social Dating 73
   Stranger Reactions 88
  R Affection 73
   Codependency 91
   Intimacy 73
   Mentor 85
   Popularity 88
   Retaliation 91
   Social Cognition 94
  ↓ Social Networks 94

Interpersonal Perception
  Use Social Perception

Interracial Adoption 94
PN 0   SC 26265
  UF Transracial Adoption
  B Adoption (Child) 67
  R Adopted Children 73
  ↓ Adoptees 85
   Adoptive Parents 73
   Interethnic Family 88
   Interracial Family 88

Interracial Family 88
PN 16   SC 26270
  B Family 67
  R Interethnic Family 88
   Interracial Adoption 94
   Interracial Marriage 73
   Interracial Offspring 88
   Racial and Ethnic Differences 82
   Racial and Ethnic Relations 82

Interracial Marriage 73
PN 75   SC 26280
  UF Miscegenous Marriage
  B Exogamous Marriage 73
  R Interracial Family 88
   Interracial Offspring 88
   Racial and Ethnic Relations 82

Interracial Offspring 88
PN 19   SC 26282
  B Offspring 88
  R Interracial Family 88
   Interracial Marriage 73
   Racial and Ethnic Differences 82
   Racial and Ethnic Relations 82

Interrater Reliability 82
PN 910   SC 26284
SN Statistically measured correspondence between judgments by observers of a common event.
  UF Interobserver Reliability
  R Observation Methods 67
   Rating 67
   Statistical Reliability 73

Interresponse Time 73
PN 230   SC 26290
SN Interval between successive responses.
  B Response Parameters 73
   Time 67
  R Response Frequency 73

Intersensory Integration
  Use Sensory Integration

Intersensory Processes 78
PN 724   SC 26295
  B Perception 67
  N Sensory Integration 91
  R Perceptual Motor Development 91
  ↓ Perceptual Motor Processes 67

Interspecies Interaction 91
PN 134   SC 26297
SN Social behavior involving members of two or more animal species including humans and animals.
  UF Animal Human Interaction
   Human Animal Interaction
  B Social Behavior 67
  R Animal Assisted Therapy 94
  ↓ Animal Social Behavior 67
  ↓ Animals 67
   Biological Symbiosis 73
   Pets 82
   Species Differences 82

Interstimulus Interval 67
PN 1923   SC 26300
SN In conditioning contexts, the temporal interval separating the conditioned stimulus and unconditioned stimulus or the temporal interval between the elements of a multiple component (i.e., compound) stimulus.
  B Stimulus Intervals 73
  R Reinforcement Delay 85

Intertrial Interval 73
PN 865   SC 26310
SN Temporal interval between successive discrete trials in conditioning or learning contexts.
  B Stimulus Intervals 73

Interval Reinforcement
  Use Fixed Interval Reinforcement OR Variable Interval Reinforcement

Interviewers 88
PN 59   SC 26330
  R Interviewing 73
  ↓ Interviews 67

Interviewing 73
PN 854   SC 26340
  B Interpersonal Communication 73
  R Interviewers 88
  ↓ Interviews 67
   Legal Interrogation 94
   Microcounseling 78

Interviews 67
PN 1679   SC 26350
  B Interpersonal Communication 73
  N Intake Interview 94
   Job Applicant Interviews 73
  ↓ Psychodiagnostic Interview 73
  R Interviewers 88
   Interviewing 73
  ↓ Measurement 67

Intestines 73
PN 110   SC 26360
  UF Duodenum
   Ileum
  B Gastrointestinal System 73
  R Absorption (Physiological) 73

Intimacy 73
PN 1372   SC 26370

Intimacy — (cont'd)
R   Affection [73]
     Attachment Behavior [85]
     ↓ Interpersonal Interaction [67]
     Love [73]
     Physical Contact [82]

Intoxication
Use Toxic Disorders

Intoxication (Alcohol)
Use Alcohol Intoxication

Intra Aural Muscle Reflex
Use Acoustic Reflex

Intracranial Self Stimulation
Use Brain Self Stimulation

Intramuscular Injections [73]
PN 26   SC 26400
B   Injections [73]

Intraperitoneal Injections [73]
PN 38   SC 26410
B   Injections [73]

Intrauterine Devices [73]
PN 20   SC 26420
B   Contraceptive Devices [73]

Intravenous Drug Usage [94]
PN 0   SC 26425
UF   IV Drug Usage
B   Drug Usage [71]
R   ↓ Drug Abuse [73]
     ↓ Drug Addiction [67]
     Intravenous Injections [73]
     Needle Sharing [94]

Intravenous Injections [73]
PN 335   SC 26430
B   Injections [73]
R   Intravenous Drug Usage [94]
     Needle Sharing [94]

Intrinsic Motivation [73]
PN 856   SC 26440
SN   Need or desire which arises from within the
individual and causes action toward some goal.
B   Motivation [67]
R   ↓ Goals [67]
     Internal External Locus of Control [67]
     Internal Rewards [73]
     Needs [67]

Intrinsic Rewards
Use Internal Rewards

Introjection [73]
PN 68   SC 26460
B   Defense Mechanisms [67]
R   Identification (Defense Mechanism) [73]

Introspection [73]
PN 136   SC 26470
B   Personality Processes [67]

Introversion [67]
PN 968   SC 26480
B   Personality Traits [67]

Intuition [73]
PN 289   SC 26485
B   Cognitive Processes [67]
R   Cognition [67]

Intuition — (cont'd)
R   ↓ Comprehension [67]
     Guessing [73]
     Insight [73]

Inventories [67]
PN 2318   SC 26490
B   Measurement [67]
N   Biographical Inventories [73]
     Interest Inventories [73]

Invertebrates [73]
PN 131   SC 26540
B   Animals [67]
N   ↓ Arthropoda [73]
     Echinodermata [73]
     ↓ Mollusca [73]
     ↓ Worms [67]
R   ↓ Vertebrates [73]

Investigation
Use Experimentation

Involuntary Treatment [94]
PN 0   SC 26555
B   Treatment [67]
R   Client Rights [88]
     ↓ Commitment (Psychiatric) [73]
     Court Referrals [94]
     Informed Consent [85]
     Treatment Compliance [82]
     Treatment Dropouts [78]
     Treatment Refusal [94]

Involutional Depression [73]
PN 59   SC 26560
UF   Climacteric Depression
B   Affective Psychosis [73]
     Major Depression [88]

Involutional Paranoid Psychosis [73]
PN 7   SC 26570
UF   Climacteric Paranoia
B   Paranoia (Psychosis) [67]
R   Folie A Deux [73]
     Paranoid Schizophrenia [67]

Involvement [73]
PN 1151   SC 26575
B   Social Behavior [67]
N   Job Involvement [78]
R   ↓ Commitment [85]
     Empowerment [91]
     ↓ Participation [73]

Ions
Use Electrolytes

Iowa Tests of Basic Skills [73]
PN 40   SC 26590
B   Achievement Measures [67]

Iproniazid [73]
PN 16   SC 26600
B   Amine Oxidase Inhibitors [73]
     Antidepressant Drugs [71]
     Antihypertensive Drugs [73]
     Antitubercular Drugs [73]
     Monoamine Oxidase Inhibitors [73]

Iran [73]
PN 221   SC 26610
B   Asia [73]
R   Middle East [78]

Iraq [88]
PN 12   SC 26615

Iraq — (cont'd)
B   Asia [73]
R   Middle East [78]

Ireland [73]
PN 255   SC 26620
B   Europe [73]
N   Northern Ireland [73]

Iris (Eye) [73]
PN 49   SC 26630
B   Eye (Anatomy) [67]
R   Eye Color [91]

Iron [73]
PN 56   SC 26640
B   Metallic Elements [73]

Irradiation
Use Radiation

Irrational Beliefs [82]
PN 395   SC 26654
SN   Erroneous or distorted convictions or ideas
firmly held despite objective and obvious con-
tradictory proof or evidence.
B   Cognitions [85]
R   ↓ Attitudes [67]
     Superstitions [73]

Irritability [88]
PN 67   SC 26658
SN   Used for human or animal populations.
B   Personality Traits [67]
R   ↓ Emotional States [73]

Irritable Bowel Syndrome [91]
PN 33   SC 26659
SN   Functional disorder of the colon that is gen-
erally psychosomatic.
B   Colon Disorders [73]
R   ↓ Colitis [73]
     ↓ Psychosomatic Disorders [67]
     ↓ Syndromes [73]

Ischemia [73]
PN 130   SC 26660
B   Cardiovascular Disorders [67]
N   Cerebral Ischemia [73]
R   Anoxia [73]

Islam [73]
PN 222   SC 26670
UF   Moslems
     Muslims
B   Religious Affiliation [73]

Isocarboxazid [73]
PN 28   SC 26680
B   Amine Oxidase Inhibitors [73]
     Antidepressant Drugs [71]
     Monoamine Oxidase Inhibitors [73]

Isoenzymes
Use Isozymes

Isolation (Defense Mechanism) [73]
PN 130   SC 26700
SN   Unconscious separation of an unacceptable
impulse, idea, or act from its original memory
source, removing the emotional charge associ-
ated with the original memory.
B   Defense Mechanisms [67]
R   Intellectualization [73]

Isolation (Social)
Use Social Isolation

Isolation Effect [73]
PN 203   SC 26720
SN Facilitating effect of isolation of distinctive features of an item (e.g., type face, color) in learning. Prior to 1982 the term was not defined and was used inconsistently.
B   Associative Processes [67]
R   Cues [67]
    Stimulus Salience [73]
    ↓ Verbal Learning [67]

Isoniazid [73]
PN 14   SC 26730
B   Antitubercular Drugs [73]

Isoproterenol [73]
PN 103   SC 26740
B   Alcohols [67]
    Sympathomimetic Drugs [73]
R   Cardiotonic Drugs [85]

Isozymes [73]
PN 17   SC 26750
UF Isoenzymes
B   Enzymes [73]

Israel [67]
PN 1715   SC 26760
B   Asia [73]
R   Middle East [78]

Italy [67]
PN 842   SC 26780
B   Europe [73]

Itching
Use Pruritus

Item Analysis (Statistical) [73]
PN 573   SC 26800
SN Quantitative analysis of a test item, especially regarding its difficulty level and validity.
B   Factor Analysis [67]
R   Adaptive Testing [85]
    Item Response Theory [85]
    Statistical Weighting [85]
    Test Items [73]

Item Analysis (Test) [67]
PN 1084   SC 26810
SN Qualitative analysis of a test item, especially regarding its content and form.
B   Analysis [67]
    Test Construction [73]
    Testing [67]
R   Item Content (Test) [73]
    Test Items [73]

Item Bias
Use Test Bias

Item Content (Test) [73]
PN 328   SC 26820
SN Topics or subject matter covered in test questions, units, or tasks.
B   Test Construction [73]
    Testing [67]
R   Item Analysis (Test) [67]
    Test Forms [88]
    Test Items [73]

Item Response Theory [85]
PN 479   SC 26825
SN A statistical approach in psychological measurement. Also known as item characteristic curve theory.
UF Latent Trait Theory
    Logistic Models

Item Response Theory — (cont'd)
UF Rasch Model
B   Testing [67]
    Theories [67]
R   Difficulty Level (Test) [73]
    Item Analysis (Statistical) [73]
    Psychometrics [67]
    ↓ Test Scores [67]

IV Drug Usage
Use Intravenous Drug Usage

Ivory Coast [88]
PN 9   SC 26830
B   Africa [67]

Jails
Use Prisons

Jamaica [73]
PN 106   SC 26850
B   West Indies [73]

James (William) [91]
PN 43   SC 26855
SN Identifies biographical or autobiographical studies and discussions of James's works.
R   Functionalism [73]
    ↓ Psychologists [67]

Japan [67]
PN 2015   SC 26860
B   Asia [73]

Japanese Americans
Use Asians

Jaundice [73]
PN 21   SC 26870
B   Digestive System Disorders [73]
    Liver Disorders [73]
R   Cirrhosis (Liver) [73]
    ↓ Hepatitis [73]
    ↓ Infectious Disorders [73]

Jaw [73]
PN 141   SC 26880
UF Mandibula
    Maxilla
B   Musculoskeletal System [73]
R   Bones [73]

Jealousy [73]
PN 273   SC 26890
UF Envy
B   Emotional States [73]
R   ↓ Anger [67]
    ↓ Anxiety [67]

Jews
Use Judaism

Job Analysis [67]
PN 1313   SC 26910
SN Analysis specifying job duties, responsibilities, and technical components.
B   Analysis [67]
    Personnel Management [73]
R   ↓ Job Characteristics [85]
    Task Analysis [67]
    Work Load [82]

Job Applicant Attitudes [73]
PN 115   SC 26920
SN Attitudes of, not toward, job applicants.
B   Attitudes [67]
R   Job Applicants [85]

Job Applicant Attitudes — (cont'd)
R   Job Search [85]
    Occupational Attitudes [73]
    ↓ Personnel [67]

Job Applicant Interviews [73]
PN 487   SC 26930
UF Employment Interviews
B   Interpersonal Communication [73]
    Interviews [67]
    Personnel Selection [67]
R   Job Search [85]
    ↓ Personnel Evaluation [73]

Job Applicant Screening [73]
PN 429   SC 26940
UF Testing (Job Applicants)
B   Personnel Selection [67]
    Screening [82]
R   Employment Discrimination [94]
    Employment Tests [73]
    Job Search [85]
    ↓ Personnel Evaluation [73]

Job Applicants [85]
PN 223   SC 26953
SN Persons seeking employment.
R   ↓ Employment Status [82]
    Job Applicant Attitudes [73]
    Job Search [85]
    ↓ Personnel [67]

Job Change
Use Career Change

Job Characteristics [85]
PN 1102   SC 26957
SN Responsibilities or tasks that characterize a specific job.
N   Work Load [82]
R   Job Analysis [67]
    ↓ Occupations [67]
    Quality of Work Life [88]

Job Corps [73]
PN 28   SC 26960
SN U.S. Government program of vocational and psychosocial training and counseling for disadvantaged adolescents and adults.
B   Government Programs [73]
R   Government [67]

Job Discrimination
Use Employment Discrimination

Job Enrichment [73]
PN 88   SC 26980
SN Programs or techniques used to enhance the quality of a job or to further challenge the employee.
B   Working Conditions [73]

Job Experience Level [73]
PN 1364   SC 26990
UF Experience Level (Job)
B   Experience Level [88]
R   Employment History [78]
    Occupational Status [78]

Job Involvement [78]
PN 810   SC 26994
B   Involvement [73]
R   ↓ Employee Attitudes [67]
    Employee Motivation [73]
    ↓ Job Performance [67]
    Job Satisfaction [67]
    Organizational Commitment [91]

114

Job Involvement — (cont'd)
R   Participative Management [88]
       Work (Attitudes Toward) [73]

Job Mobility
Use Occupational Mobility

Job Performance [67]
PN 5414   SC 27010
B   Performance [67]
N   Employee Efficiency [73]
       Employee Productivity [73]
R ↓ Employee Attitudes [67]
       Job Involvement [78]
       Organizational Commitment [91]
     ↓ Personnel [67]
     ↓ Personnel Evaluation [73]
       Personnel Promotion [78]
       Work Load [82]

Job Promotion
Use Personnel Promotion

Job Reentry
Use Reemployment

Job Satisfaction [67]
PN 5952   SC 27040
SN Positive attitudes toward one's work when
tangible and/or intangible rewards fulfill expecta-
tions.
B   Employee Attitudes [67]
       Satisfaction [73]
R   Career Change [78]
       Job Involvement [78]
       Organizational Commitment [91]
       Quality of Work Life [88]
       Role Satisfaction [94]

Job Search [85]
PN 183   SC 27043
SN Process of seeking employment. For consid-
eration of career alternatives use CAREER EDU-
CATION.
R   Job Applicant Attitudes [73]
       Job Applicant Interviews [73]
       Job Applicant Screening [73]
       Job Applicants [85]
       Reemployment [91]
       Unemployment [67]

Job Security [78]
PN 75   SC 27045
SN Probable assurance of continued employ-
ment.
R   Employee Turnover [73]
     ↓ Occupational Tenure [73]
       Personnel Termination [73]
       Retirement [73]
       Unemployment [67]

Job Selection
Use Occupational Choice

Job Status
Use Occupational Status

Job Training
Use Personnel Training

Jobs
Use Occupations

Joint Custody [88]
PN 45   SC 27065

Joint Custody — (cont'd)
R   Child Custody [82]
       Child Support [88]
       Divorce [73]

Joint Disorders [73]
PN 42   SC 27070
B   Musculoskeletal Disorders [73]
N ↓ Arthritis [73]
R ↓ Joints (Anatomy) [73]

Joints (Anatomy) [73]
PN 75   SC 27080
B   Musculoskeletal System [73]
N   Ankle [73]
       Elbow (Anatomy) [73]
       Knee [73]
       Shoulder (Anatomy) [73]
       Wrist [73]
R ↓ Joint Disorders [73]

Jokes [73]
PN 141   SC 27090
B   Humor [67]

Jordan [88]
PN 44   SC 27095
B   Asia [73]
R   Middle East [78]

Journalists [73]
PN 47   SC 27100
B   Professional Personnel [78]

Joy
Use Happiness

Judaism [67]
PN 1016   SC 27130
UF   Jews
B   Religious Affiliation [73]
R   AntiSemitism [73]
       Bible [73]
       Holocaust [88]
       Rabbis [73]

Judges [85]
PN 140   SC 27135
B   Legal Personnel [85]

Judgment [67]
PN 3256   SC 27140
SN Mental act of comparing or evaluating
choices within a given set of values frequently
with the purpose of choosing a course of action.
N   Probability Judgment [78]
R   Judgment Disturbances [73]
       Uncertainty [91]
       Wisdom [94]

Judgment Disturbances [73]
PN 6   SC 27150
SN Maladaptive judgment resulting from wish-
fulfilling, impulsive decisions based on need for
immediate infantile gratification.
B   Thought Disturbances [73]
R ↓ Judgment [67]

Judo [73]
PN 27   SC 27160
B   Recreation [67]
       Sports [67]
R   Martial Arts [85]

Jumping [73]
PN 74   SC 27170

Jumping — (cont'd)
B   Motor Performance [73]
       Motor Processes [67]

Jung (Carl) [73]
PN 309   SC 27180
SN Identifies biographical or autobiographical
studies and discussions of Jung's works.
R   Analytical Psychotherapy [73]
       Archetypes [91]
       Jungian Psychology [73]
     ↓ Psychologists [67]

Jungian Psychology [73]
PN 1068   SC 27190
SN Analytical psychology characterized by theo-
ries of the collective unconscious, the archetype,
the complex, and psychological types.
UF   Analytic Psychology
B   Neopsychoanalytic School [73]
R   Analytical Psychotherapy [73]
       Archetypes [91]
       Free Association [94]
       Jung (Carl) [73]

Junior College Students [73]
PN 179   SC 27200
SN Students in 2-year colleges. Mandatory term
in educational contexts.
B   College Students [67]
R   Community College Students [73]

Junior Colleges
Use Colleges

Junior High School Students [71]
PN 7331   SC 27220
SN Students in grades 7 and 8. Mandatory term
in educational contexts.
B   Students [67]
R ↓ Adolescents [67]
     ↓ Children [67]
       Grade Level [94]
       Middle School Students [85]

Junior High School Teachers [73]
PN 1033   SC 27230
B   Teachers [67]

Junior High Schools [73]
PN 230   SC 27240
B   Schools [67]
R   Secondary Education [73]

Juries [85]
PN 392   SC 27245
SN Bodies of persons sworn to give a verdict in
a court of law. Also used for mock and simulated
juries. Use ADJUDICATION to access references
from 73-84.
R ↓ Adjudication [67]
       Jury Selection [94]
     ↓ Legal Personnel [85]

Jury Selection [94]
PN 0   SC 27252
SN Use JURIES to access references from 85-
93.
R ↓ Adjudication [67]
       Juries [85]

Justice [73]
PN 594   SC 27260
SN Used for the impartial and fair settlement of
conflict and differences, or the designation of
rewards or punishment.
UF   Distributive Justice
N ↓ Criminal Justice [91]

115

Justice — (cont'd)
R ↓ Civil Rights [78]
    Equity (Payment) [78]
    ↓ Equity (Social) [78]
    Freedom [78]
    ↓ Law (Government) [73]
    ↓ Law Enforcement [78]
    Morality [67]
    Reward Allocation [88]
    Social Equality [73]
    ↓ Social Issues [91]

Juvenile Court
Use Adjudication

Juvenile Delinquency [67]
PN 2235   SC 27280
UF Delinquency (Juvenile)
B Antisocial Behavior [71]
   Behavior Disorders [71]
R Crime Prevention [85]
   ↓ Juvenile Delinquents [73]
   Predelinquent Youth [78]

Juvenile Delinquents [73]
PN 2132   SC 27290
SN Youths characterized by antisocial behavior which is subject to legal sanctions.
UF Offenders (Juvenile)
N Female Delinquents [73]
   Male Delinquents [73]
R ↓ Adolescents [67]
   ↓ Criminals [67]
   Juvenile Delinquency [67]
   Juvenile Gangs [73]
   Preadolescents [88]
   Predelinquent Youth [78]

Juvenile Gangs [73]
PN 91   SC 27300
UF Gangs (Juvenile)
R ↓ Juvenile Delinquents [73]

Kainic Acid [88]
PN 61   SC 27305
B Acids [73]
R Glutamic Acid [73]
   ↓ Neurotoxins [82]

Kangaroos [73]
PN 11   SC 27310
B Marsupials [73]

Karate
Use Martial Arts

Karyotype Disorders
Use Chromosome Disorders

Kaufman Assessment Battery Children [88]
PN 114   SC 27324
B Intelligence Measures [67]

Kenya [82]
PN 118   SC 27326
B Africa [67]

Keyboards [85]
PN 46   SC 27328
B Apparatus [67]
R ↓ Computer Peripheral Devices [85]
   ↓ Instrument Controls [85]
   Typing [91]

Keypunch Operators
Use Clerical Personnel

Kibbutz [73]
PN 244   SC 27340
B Communes [73]

Kidnapping [88]
PN 22   SC 27345
B Crime [67]
R Hostages [88]

Kidney Diseases [88]
PN 166   SC 27347
B Urogenital Disorders [73]

Kidney Transplants
Use Organ Transplantation

Kidneys [73]
PN 194   SC 27360
B Urogenital System [73]

Kinases [82]
PN 38   SC 27366
SN Enzymes that catalyze the conversion of proenzymes to active enzymes or the transfer of phosphate groups to form triphosphates (ATP).
UF Enteropeptidase
B Enzymes [73]

Kindergarten Students [73]
PN 2342   SC 27370
SN Students in kindergarten. Mandatory term in educational contexts.
B Students [67]
R ↓ Children [67]
   Grade Level [94]
   Preschool Age Children [67]
   ↓ Preschool Students [82]

Kindergartens [73]
PN 159   SC 27380
B Schools [67]

Kindling [85]
PN 136   SC 27385
SN Afterdischarges and generalized convulsions produced by repeated brain stimulation, usually electrical. Often used as an experimental model of epilepsy.
B Electrical Activity [67]
R Experimental Epilepsy [78]

Kinesthetic Perception [67]
PN 826   SC 27390
SN Sensory modality involving awareness of body movement, position, and posture, and movement of body parts, such as muscles, tendons, and joints.
B Somesthetic Perception [67]
R Spatial Orientation (Perception) [73]

Kinship [85]
PN 238   SC 27395
SN The state of being related such as by birth, common ancestry, or marriage. Used for human or animal populations.
R Ethnology [67]
   ↓ Family [67]
   Kinship Recognition [88]
   Kinship Structure [73]

Kinship Recognition [88]
PN 150   SC 27399
R ↓ Discrimination Learning [82]
   Kinship [85]
   Species Recognition [85]

Kinship Structure [73]
PN 143   SC 27400

Kinship Structure — (cont'd)
R Ethnography [73]
   Ethnology [67]
   ↓ Family Structure [73]
   Kinship [85]
   ↓ Sociocultural Factors [67]

Kleptomania [73]
PN 29   SC 27420
R Impulsiveness [73]
   ↓ Personality Disorders [67]

Klinefelters Syndrome [73]
PN 54   SC 27430
B Hypogonadism [73]
   Male Genital Disorders [73]
   Neonatal Disorders [73]
   Sex Chromosome Disorders [73]
   Syndromes [73]
R ↓ Infertility [73]
   ↓ Mental Retardation [67]

Knee [73]
PN 30   SC 27440
B Joints (Anatomy) [73]
R Leg (Anatomy) [73]

Knowledge Based Systems
Use Expert Systems

Knowledge Level [78]
PN 4905   SC 27446
SN Range of received or acquired information, understanding, or awareness. Limited to human populations.
N Health Knowledge [94]
R ↓ Experience Level [88]
   Information [67]
   Wisdom [94]

Knowledge of Results [67]
PN 449   SC 27450
B Feedback [67]

Kohlberg (Lawrence) [91]
PN 7   SC 27455
SN Identifies biographical or autobiographical studies and discussions of Kohlberg's works.
R Moral Development [73]
   ↓ Psychologists [67]

Kohs Block Design Test [73]
PN 21   SC 27460
UF Block Design Test (Kohs)
B Intelligence Measures [67]

Kolmogorov Smirnov Test [73]
PN 3   SC 27470
B Nonparametric Statistical Tests [67]

Korea [73]
PN 148   SC 27480
SN Used for historical articles or when North Korea or South Korea is not specified. Term discontinued from 82-87, use North Korea or South Korea for that period.
B Asia [73]
N North Korea [82]
   South Korea [82]

Koro [94]
PN 0   SC 27485
SN A mental disorder characterized by fear or delusions of the shrinkage of the penis, labia, or breasts into the abdomen or chest. Observed primarily in Southern Chinese and some African cultures.

Koro — (cont'd)
B   Body Image Disturbances [73]
    Ethnospecific Disorders [73]
    Mental Disorders [67]

Korsakoffs Psychosis [73]
PN 330   SC 27490
B   Alcoholic Hallucinosis [73]
    Alcoholism [67]
R   Confabulation [73]

Kuder Occupational Interest Survey [73]
PN 37   SC 27510
B   Occupational Interest Measures [73]

Kuder Preference Record [73]
PN 17   SC 27520
B   Preference Measures [73]

Kupfer Detre Self Rating Scale [73]
PN 1   SC 27540
B   Nonprojective Personality Measures [73]

Kuwait [91]
PN 22   SC 27545
R   Middle East [78]

Kwashiorkor [73]
PN 8   SC 27550
B   Protein Deficiency Disorders [73]

L Dopa
   Use Levodopa

Labeling [78]
PN 918   SC 27565
SN In social or therapeutic settings, designating the condition of an individual or group by a simplistic word or phrase which may serve to indicate status, stigma, or other characteristics.
R   ↓ Attitudes [67]
    ↓ Diagnosis [67]
    ↓ Names [85]
    ↓ Psychodiagnostic Typologies [67]
    ↓ Social Perception [67]
    Stigma [91]

Labor (Childbirth) [73]
PN 251   SC 27570
R   ↓ Birth [67]
    Childbirth Training [78]
    Midwifery [85]
    Obstetrical Complications [78]

Labor Management Relations [67]
PN 424   SC 27580
UF Labor Relations
B   Personnel Management [73]
R   Informants [88]
    Labor Unions [73]
    ↓ Management [67]
    Mediation [88]
    Strikes [73]

Labor Relations
   Use Labor Management Relations

Labor Union Members [73]
PN 135   SC 27600
R   ↓ Personnel [67]

Labor Unions [73]
PN 256   SC 27610
B   Organizations [67]
R   Labor Management Relations [67]

Laboratories (Educational)
   Use Educational Laboratories

Laboratories (Experimental)
   Use Experimental Laboratories

Laborers (Construct and Indust)
   Use Blue Collar Workers

Laborers (Farm)
   Use Agricultural Workers

Labyrinth (Anatomy) [73]
PN 70   SC 27660
SN The bony structure of the inner ear that houses the membranous labyrinth (i.e., the cochlea, vestibule, semicircular canals, utricle, and saccule). May also refer to these latter membranous structures.
UF Inner Ear
B   Ear (Anatomy) [67]
N   Cochlea [73]
R   ↓ Vestibular Apparatus [67]

Labyrinth (Apparatus)
   Use Mazes

Labyrinth Disorders [73]
PN 18   SC 27680
B   Ear Disorders [73]
N   Menieres Disease [73]
    Motion Sickness [73]
R   ↓ Somesthetic Perception [67]
    Vertigo [73]

Lactate Dehydrogenase [73]
PN 11   SC 27690
B   Dehydrogenases [73]

Lactation [73]
PN 382   SC 27700
B   Secretion (Gland) [73]
R   Postnatal Period [73]

Lactic Acid [91]
PN 15   SC 27720
UF Sodium Lactate
B   Acids [73]

Landscapes
   Use Topography

Language [67]
PN 4399   SC 27740
N   ↓ Dialect [73]
    ↓ Figurative Language [85]
    Foreign Languages [73]
    ↓ Form Classes (Language) [73]
    Phrases [73]
    Profanity [91]
    Rhetoric [91]
    Sentences [67]
    Sign Language [73]
    Spelling [73]
    ↓ Vocabulary [67]
    ↓ Written Language [67]
R   Bilingualism [73]
    ↓ Grammar [67]
    ↓ Language Development [67]
    ↓ Linguistics [73]
    ↓ Literacy [73]
    Metalinguistics [94]
    Monolingualism [73]
    ↓ Multilingualism [73]
    Neurolinguistics [91]
    Symbolism [67]
    ↓ Verbal Communication [67]

Language Alternation
   Use Code Switching

Language Arts Education [73]
PN 1356   SC 27750
SN Education in subjects aimed at development of comprehension and use of written and oral language.
B   Curriculum [67]
N   Phonics [73]
    Reading Education [73]
    Spelling [73]
R   Initial Teaching Alphabet [73]

Language Delay [88]
PN 110   SC 27755
B   Delayed Development [73]
    Language Development [67]
R   ↓ Language Disorders [82]
    Retarded Speech Development [73]

Language Development [67]
PN 6553   SC 27760
SN Acquisition of the rules governing the structure of language (e.g., syntax) and meaning. Use SPEECH DEVELOPMENT for acquisition of speech sound production. Compare VERBAL LEARNING.
B   Cognitive Development [73]
    Intellectual Development [73]
N   Language Delay [88]
R   Foreign Language Learning [67]
    ↓ Language [67]
    ↓ Language Disorders [82]
    Metalinguistics [94]
    ↓ Speech Development [73]
    ↓ Verbal Communication [67]
    Vygotsky (Lev) [91]

Language Disorders [82]
PN 1251   SC 27763
SN Disorders, usually due to cognitive or neurological dysfunction, resulting in problems in symbolization or in delays in language and speech development.
UF Language Handicaps
B   Communication Disorders [82]
N   ↓ Aphasia [67]
    Echolalia [73]
    ↓ Mutism [73]
R   Language Delay [88]
    ↓ Language Development [67]
    Neurolinguistics [91]
    ↓ Speech Disorders [67]
    Speech Handicapped [73]

Language Handicaps
   Use Language Disorders

Language Laboratories [73]
PN 6   SC 27770
B   Educational Laboratories [73]
R   Foreign Language Learning [67]
    Learning Centers (Educational) [73]

Language Proficiency [88]
PN 252   SC 27773
SN Accuracy and fluency of verbal communication in a second language learning or bilingual context. Includes concept of Limited English Proficiency, which is knowledge of English without sufficient proficiency to communicate or participate in an English-speaking society. Consider VERBAL FLUENCY for other contexts.
UF Limited English Proficiency
B   Communication Skills [73]
    Verbal Communication [67]
R   Bilingualism [73]
    Foreign Language Learning [67]

Language Proficiency — (cont'd)
R   Verbal Ability [67]
     Verbal Fluency [73]

Laos [88]
PN 2   SC 27775
B   Southeast Asia [73]

Larvae [73]
PN 169   SC 27780
B   Insects [67]
R   Ants [73]
     Bees [73]
     Beetles [73]
     Butterflies [73]
     Cockroaches [73]
    ↓ Diptera [73]
     Drosophila [73]
    ↓ Fishes [67]
     Frogs [67]
     Grasshoppers [73]
     Mantis [73]
     Moths [73]
     Salamanders [73]
     Toads [73]
     Wasps [82]

Laryngeal Disorders [73]
PN 76   SC 27790
B   Respiratory Tract Disorders [73]

Larynx [73]
PN 104   SC 27800
B   Respiratory System [73]
N   Vocal Cords [73]

Laser Irradiation [73]
PN 13   SC 27810
B   Radiation [67]

Latchkey Children
Use Child Self Care

Latent Learning [73]
PN 80   SC 27830
SN Learning that is not immediately manifested in performance but which remains dormant until activated by some contingency. From 1982, limited to animal populations. Use INCIDENTAL LEARNING for human populations.
B   Incidental Learning [67]

Latent Trait Theory
Use Item Response Theory

Lateral Dominance [67]
PN 3794   SC 27840
SN The tendency for the right or left hemisphere to be dominant over the other for most functions, leading to a differential primacy, functional asymmetry, or preference for one side of the body. Compare CEREBRAL DOMINANCE.
UF Hemispheric Specialization
B   Cerebral Dominance [73]
N   Handedness [78]
     Ocular Dominance [73]
R ↓ Brain [67]
     Left Brain [91]
     Right Brain [91]

Latin America [88]
PN 83   SC 27843
R ↓ Central America [73]
     Mexico [73]
    ↓ South America [67]
    ↓ West Indies [73]

Latinos
Use Hispanics

Laughter [78]
PN 143   SC 27855
B   Vocalization [67]
R ↓ Emotional Responses [67]
    ↓ Humor [67]
    ↓ Nonverbal Communication [71]
     Smiles [73]

Law (Government) [73]
PN 102   SC 27860
SN Science and philosophy of law as sanctioned by governmental authority. For specific laws or statutes, use LAWS.
N   Civil Law [94]
     Criminal Law [73]
R   Defendants [85]
     Government [67]
    ↓ Justice [73]
    ↓ Law Enforcement [78]
    ↓ Laws [67]

Law Enforcement [78]
PN 327   SC 27865
B   Legal Processes [73]
N ↓ Adjudication [67]
     Incarceration [73]
     Legal Arrest [73]
     Legal Detention [73]
R   Civil Law [94]
     Crime Prevention [85]
    ↓ Criminal Justice [91]
     Government [67]
    ↓ Justice [73]
    ↓ Law (Government) [73]
    ↓ Laws [67]
    ↓ Legal Evidence [91]
     Legal Interrogation [94]
     Parole [73]
     Probation [73]

Law Enforcement Personnel [73]
PN 241   SC 27870
B   Government Personnel [73]
     Legal Personnel [85]
N   Parole Officers [73]
     Police Personnel [73]
     Prison Personnel [73]
     Probation Officers [73]
R   Attorneys [73]
    ↓ Social Workers [73]

Law Students [78]
PN 121   SC 27875
B   Students [67]
R   Attorneys [73]
     Graduate Students [67]

Laws [67]
PN 2853   SC 27880
SN Rules of conduct made obligatory by some legal or controlling authority; includes statutes enacted by a legislative body.
B   Government Policy Making [73]
N   Abortion Laws [73]
     Disability Laws [94]
    ↓ Drug Laws [73]
     Gun Control Laws [73]
R   Case Law [85]
     Censorship [78]
     Citizenship [73]
    ↓ Civil Rights [78]
     Consumer Protection [73]
     Government [67]
    ↓ Law (Government) [73]
    ↓ Law Enforcement [78]

Laws — (cont'd)
R   Legal Decisions [91]
    ↓ Legal Processes [73]
     Legislative Processes [73]

Lawyers
Use Attorneys

Lay Religious Personnel [73]
PN 51   SC 27900
SN Participants or members of a religious group or organization who perform various functional and ceremonial tasks not requiring a member of the clergy.
B   Religious Personnel [73]
R   Chaplains [73]
    ↓ Clergy [73]
     Evangelists [73]
     Missionaries [73]

Lead (Metal) [73]
PN 115   SC 27910
B   Metallic Elements [73]

Lead Poisoning [73]
PN 215   SC 27920
B   Toxic Disorders [73]
R   Pica [73]

Leadership [67]
PN 3368   SC 27930
B   Social Behavior [67]
N   Leadership Style [73]
R   Authority [67]
     Entrepreneurship [91]
    ↓ Management [67]

Leadership Style [73]
PN 1813   SC 27940
B   Leadership [67]
     Personality Traits [67]
     Social Behavior [67]
R   Charisma [88]

Learned Helplessness [78]
PN 1159   SC 27945
SN Learned expectation that one's responses are independent of reward and, hence, do not predict or control the occurrence of rewards. Learned helplessness derives from a history, experimentally induced or naturally occurring, of having received punishment/aversive stimulation regardless of responses made. Such circumstances result in an impaired ability to learn. Used for human or animal populations.
UF Helplessness (Learned)
R   Attribution [73]
    ↓ Emotional States [73]
     Experimental Neurosis [73]

Learning [67]
PN 8559   SC 28030
SN Conceptually broad array term referring to the process of acquiring knowledge, skills, or behaviors by instruction, study, or experience. Use a more specific term if possible.
N   Cat Learning [67]
     Cognitive Hypothesis Testing [82]
    ↓ Conditioning [67]
     Cooperative Learning [94]
    ↓ Discrimination Learning [82]
     Extinction (Learning) [67]
     Foreign Language Learning [67]
    ↓ Generalization (Learning) [82]
     Generation Effect (Learning) [91]
    ↓ Incidental Learning [67]
     Intentional Learning [73]
    ↓ Interference (Learning) [67]
     Mastery Learning [85]

Learning — (cont'd)
- N   Maze Learning [67]
  - Mnemonic Learning [73]
  - Nonverbal Learning [73]
  - Observational Learning [73]
  - Overlearning [67]
  - ↓ Perceptual Motor Learning [67]
  - Probability Learning [67]
  - Rat Learning [67]
  - Relearning [73]
  - School Learning [67]
  - Sequential Learning [73]
  - ↓ Serial Learning [67]
  - ↓ Skill Learning [73]
  - ↓ Social Learning [73]
  - Spatial Learning [94]
  - Spontaneous Recovery (Learning) [73]
  - State Dependent Learning [82]
  - ↓ Transfer (Learning) [67]
  - Trial and Error Learning [73]
  - ↓ Verbal Learning [67]
- R   ↓ Cognitive Processes [67]
  - ↓ Concept Formation [67]
  - Connectionism [94]
  - Constructivism [94]
  - Delayed Alternation [94]
  - ↓ Feedback [67]
  - Forgetting [73]
  - ↓ Habits [67]
  - Individualized Instruction [73]
  - Learning Ability [73]
  - ↓ Learning Disorders [67]
  - Learning Rate [73]
  - ↓ Learning Schedules [67]
  - ↓ Learning Strategies [91]
  - Learning Theory [67]
  - ↓ Memory [67]
  - Metacognition [91]
  - Primacy Effect [73]
  - Recency Effect [73]
  - ↓ Reinforcement [67]
  - ↓ Retention [67]
  - ↓ Serial Position Effect [82]
  - Spontaneous Alternation [82]
  - ↓ Strategies [67]
  - Time On Task [88]

Learning Ability [73]
PN 644   SC 27960
SN Capacity to acquire a behavior, skill, or knowledge from experience, formal instruction, or conditioning. Used for animal or human populations.
- B   Ability [67]
- R   ↓ Learning [67]

Learning Centers (Educational) [73]
PN 54   SC 27970
- B   School Facilities [73]
- R   Language Laboratories [73]

Learning Disabilities [73]
PN 8299   SC 27980
SN According to U.S. federal legislation, disorders involved in understanding or using language, manifested in impaired listening, thinking, talking, reading, writing, or arithmetic skills. Includes perceptual handicaps, brain injury, minimal brain dysfunction, and developmental aphasia. Compare LEARNING DISORDERS.
- B   · Learning Disorders [67]
- N   Dyslexia [73]
- R   Acalculia [73]
  - Agraphia [73]
  - ↓ Aphasia [67]
  - Educational Diagnosis [78]
  - ↓ Handicapped [67]
  - Minimally Brain Damaged [73]
  - ↓ Perceptual Disturbances [73]

Learning Disorders [67]
PN 1031   SC 27990
SN According to U.S. federal legislation, learning problems that are due to visual, hearing, or motor handicaps, mental retardation, emotional disturbance or environmental, cultural, or economic disadvantage. Compare LEARNING DISABILITIES.
- B   Disorders [67]
- N   ↓ Learning Disabilities [73]
  - ↓ Reading Disabilities [67]
- R   Developmental Disabilities [82]
  - Educational Diagnosis [78]
  - ↓ Learning [67]
  - ↓ Mental Disorders [67]

Learning Rate [73]
PN 487   SC 28000
- R   ↓ Learning [67]
  - ↓ Serial Position Effect [82]

Learning Schedules [67]
PN 85   SC 28010
- UF   Schedules (Learning)
- N   Distributed Practice [73]
  - Massed Practice [73]
- R   ↓ Learning [67]

Learning Strategies [91]
PN 320   SC 28013
SN Techniques, methods, or tactics used for learning.
- UF   Strategies (Learning)
- B   Strategies [67]
- N   Mnemonic Learning [73]
  - Observational Learning [73]
  - ↓ Social Learning [73]
  - Trial and Error Learning [73]
- R   ↓ Cognitive Processes [67]
  - ↓ Cognitive Style [67]
  - ↓ Learning [67]
  - Memory Training [94]
  - Metacognition [91]
  - Note Taking [91]
  - Study Habits [73]
  - Time Management [94]

Learning Style
Use Cognitive Style

Learning Theory [67]
PN 1259   SC 28020
- B   Theories [67]
- R   Connectionism [94]
  - ↓ Learning [67]

Learys Interpersonal Check List [73]
PN 8   SC 28040
SN Use LEARYS INTERPERSONAL CHECK LIST or LEARY INTERPERSONAL CHECK LIST to access references from 73–77.
- B   Nonprojective Personality Measures [73]

Least Preferred Coworker Scale [73]
PN 58   SC 28050
- B   Preference Measures [73]

Least Squares [85]
PN 101   SC 28055
SN Method of estimating the curve-of-best-fit or regression line of a set of points representing statistical data.
- B   Statistical Estimation [85]
- R   Error of Measurement [85]
  - ↓ Statistical Regression [85]

Lebanon [88]
PN 32   SC 28057

Lebanon — (cont'd)
- B   Asia [73]
- R   Middle East [78]

Lecithin [91]
PN 5   SC 28058
- B   Choline [73]
  - Phosphatides [73]

Lecture Method [73]
PN 526   SC 28060
- B   Teaching Methods [67]
- R   Directed Discussion Method [73]

Left Brain [91]
PN 36   SC 28070
SN Used only when the left hemisphere of the brain is the focus of the document.
- B   Cerebral Cortex [67]
- R   ↓ Brain [67]
  - ↓ Cerebral Dominance [73]
  - Corpus Callosum [73]
  - Interhemispheric Interaction [85]
  - ↓ Lateral Dominance [67]
  - Ocular Dominance [73]
  - Right Brain [91]

Leg (Anatomy) [73]
PN 118   SC 28080
- B   Musculoskeletal System [73]
- R   Ankle [73]
  - Feet (Anatomy) [73]
  - Knee [73]
  - Thigh [73]

Legal Arrest [73]
PN 260   SC 28090
SN Taking custody, under legal authority, of a person for the purpose of holding or detaining him/her to answer criminal charges or civil demands.
- UF   Arrest (Law)
- B   Law Enforcement [78]

Legal Decisions [91]
PN 62   SC 28095
SN Used for discussions of the implications or the effects of specific judicial decisions. Not used for the actual process of judicial decision making. Consider CASE LAW for descriptions, not discussions, of laws resulting from court decisions.
- R   ↓ Adjudication [67]
  - Case Law [85]
  - Criminal Conviction [73]
  - ↓ Criminal Justice [91]
  - ↓ Laws [67]
  - ↓ Legal Processes [73]
  - Legislative Processes [73]

Legal Detention [73]
PN 60   SC 28100
SN Being detained (e.g., in jail) by law enforcers for having committed or for being suspected of having committed a crime, especially immediately prior to a legal court disposition.
- UF   Detention (Legal)
- B   Law Enforcement [78]
- R   Legal Interrogation [94]

Legal Evidence [91]
PN 45   SC 28103
SN Testimony, records, documents, objects, and diagrams submitted to a court during a hearing or trial.
- UF   Evidence (Legal)
- B   Legal Processes [73]
- N   ↓ Legal Testimony [82]
- R   ↓ Adjudication [67]
  - ↓ Law Enforcement [78]

Legal Evidence — (cont'd)
R   Legal Interrogation [94]
      Witnesses [85]

Legal Interrogation [94]
PN 0   SC 28104
UF   Police Interrogation
B   Legal Processes [73]
R   Interviewing [73]
      ↓ Law Enforcement [78]
      Legal Detention [73]
      ↓ Legal Evidence [91]
      ↓ Legal Testimony [82]
      Polygraphs [73]
      Questioning [82]
      Witnesses [85]

Legal Liability (Professional)
Use   Professional Liability

Legal Personnel [85]
PN 71   SC 28107
UF   Paralegal Personnel
B   Professional Personnel [78]
N   Attorneys [73]
      Judges [85]
      ↓ Law Enforcement Personnel [73]
R   Juries [85]

Legal Processes [73]
PN 2947   SC 28110
SN Broad concept encompassing psychological
and behavioral aspects of the law—its formation,
enforcement, impact, and implications. Also includes reference to the legal justice system and
legislative processes as they relate to psychology.
N   ↓ Adoption (Child) [67]
      Child Custody [82]
      Child Visitation [88]
      ↓ Commitment (Psychiatric) [73]
      Competency to Stand Trial [85]
      ↓ Criminal Justice [91]
      Forensic Evaluation [94]
      Guardianship [88]
      Insanity Defense [85]
      ↓ Law Enforcement [78]
      ↓ Legal Evidence [91]
      Legal Interrogation [94]
      ↓ Legal Testimony [82]
      Legislative Processes [73]
      Parole [73]
      Probation [73]
R   Advance Directives [94]
      Case Law [85]
      Civil Law [94]
      ↓ Civil Rights [78]
      Consumer Protection [73]
      Government [67]
      ↓ Government Policy Making [73]
      Informed Consent [85]
      ↓ Laws [67]
      Legal Decisions [91]
      Professional Liability [85]
      ↓ Social Issues [91]

Legal Psychology
Use   Forensic Psychology

Legal Testimony [82]
PN 322   SC 28115
SN Evidence presented by a witness under oath
or affirmation (as distinguished from evidence de-
rived from other sources) either orally or written
as deposition or affidavit.
B   Legal Evidence [91]
      Legal Processes [73]
N   Expert Testimony [73]

Legal Testimony — (cont'd)
R   Legal Interrogation [94]
      Witnesses [85]

Legalization (Marihuana)
Use   Marihuana Legalization

Legibility [78]
PN 39   SC 28127
N   Handwriting Legibility [73]
R   Readability [78]
      ↓ Written Language [67]

Legibility (Handwriting)
Use   Handwriting Legibility

Legislative Processes [73]
PN 365   SC 28140
B   Government Policy Making [73]
      Legal Processes [73]
R   Advocacy [85]
      Government [67]
      ↓ Laws [67]
      Legal Decisions [91]

Leisure Time [73]
PN 1110   SC 28150
R   Daily Activities [94]
      Hobbies [73]
      Holidays [88]
      ↓ Recreation [67]
      Relaxation [73]

Leiter Adult Intelligence Scale [73]
PN 4   SC 28160
B   Intelligence Measures [67]

Lemniscal System [85]
PN 7   SC 28165
SN Long ascending sensory neural pathways
projecting to the diencephalon. This system in-
cludes the medial lemniscus, lateral lemniscus,
spinothalamic tracts, and secondary trigeminal
projections.
B   Afferent Pathways [82]
N   Spinothalamic Tracts [73]
R   Reticular Formation [67]

Lemurs [73]
PN 161   SC 28170
UF   Bush Babies
B   Mammals [73]

Lens (Eye) [73]
PN 46   SC 28180
B   Eye (Anatomy) [67]
R   ↓ Light Refraction [82]
      Ocular Accommodation [82]

Lesbian Parents
Use   Homosexual Parents

Lesbianism [73]
PN 797   SC 28190
B   Homosexuality [67]
R   Bisexuality [73]
      Heterosexuality [73]
      Homosexual Parents [94]
      Male Homosexuality [73]

Lesions [67]
PN 2049   SC 28200
SN Not defined prior to 1982. From 1982, limit-
ed to experimentally induced lesions and used
primarily for animal populations.
UF   Ablation
      Sectioning (Lesion)

Lesions — (cont'd)
N   ↓ Brain Lesions [67]
      Neural Lesions [73]
R   ↓ Surgery [71]

Lesson Plans [73]
PN 97   SC 28220
B   Teaching Methods [67]

Letters (Alphabet) [73]
PN 1323   SC 28230
B   Alphabets [73]
N   Consonants [73]
      Vowels [73]

Leucine [73]
PN 45   SC 28240
B   Amino Acids [73]

Leucocytes [73]
PN 166   SC 28250
UF   Leukocytes
      White Blood Cells
B   Blood Cells [73]
N   Lymphocytes [73]

Leukemias [73]
PN 215   SC 28260
B   Blood and Lymphatic Disorders [73]
      Neoplasms [67]

Leukocytes
Use   Leucocytes

Leukotomy
Use   Psychosurgery

Levodopa [73]
PN 484   SC 28290
UF   L Dopa
B   Antitremor Drugs [73]
      Cholinergic Blocking Drugs [73]
R   DOPA [73]
      Dopamine [73]

Lexical Access [88]
PN 313   SC 29293
N   Lexical Decision [88]
R   Cognitive Discrimination [73]
      Human Information Storage [73]
      Semantic Memory [88]
      ↓ Verbal Memory [94]
      Word Meaning [73]
      Words (Phonetic Units) [67]

Lexical Decision [88]
PN 487   SC 29296
B   Lexical Access [88]
R   Cognitive Discrimination [73]
      Human Information Storage [73]
      Semantic Memory [88]
      ↓ Verbal Memory [94]
      Word Meaning [73]
      Words (Phonetic Units) [67]

Liberalism [73]
PN 104   SC 28298
B   Personality Traits [67]
R   Political Liberalism [73]

Liberalism (Political)
Use   Political Liberalism

Liberia [91]
PN 0   SC 28305
B   Africa [67]

Libido [73]
PN 115   SC 28310
B   Psychoanalytic Personality Factors [73]
R   Sex Drive [73]

Librarians [88]
PN 17   SC 28314
B   Information Specialists [88]
R   ↓ Professional Personnel [78]

Libraries [82]
PN 61   SC 28317
N   School Libraries [73]
R   ↓ Community Facilities [73]
     Information [67]
     Information Services [88]

Libraries (School)
Use School Libraries

Librium
Use Chlordiazepoxide

Libya [88]
PN 10   SC 28335
B   Africa [67]
R   Middle East [78]

Licensing (Professional)
Use Professional Licensing

Licensure Examinations
Use Professional Examinations

Licking [88]
PN 71   SC 28345
SN   Used for human or animal populations.
UF   Animal Licking Behavior
B   Animal Ethology [67]
     Motor Processes [67]
R   Animal Drinking Behavior [73]
     Animal Grooming Behavior [78]
     Animal Maternal Behavior [73]

Lidocaine [73]
PN 82   SC 28350
UF   Xylocaine
B   Local Anesthetics [73]

Liechtenstein [91]
PN 0   SC 28353
B   Europe [73]

Life Change
Use Life Experiences

Life Expectancy [82]
PN 160   SC 28352
SN   Anticipated number of years of life for an
individual, based on statistical probability. Use
AGED and PHYSIOLOGICAL AGING together to
access references from 73–81.
UF   Life Span
     Longevity
R   ↓ Aging [91]
     ↓ Human Development [67]
     Physiological Aging [67]

Life Experiences [73]
PN 3855   SC 28355
SN   Specific events which are commonly considered noteworthy or memorable (e.g., college
graduation, wedding) or are considered unusual
or otherwise significant (e.g., life change due to
illness). Compare EXPERIENCES (EVENTS).
UF   Experiences (Life)
     Life Change

Life Experiences — (cont'd)
B   Experiences (Events) [73]
R   Age Regression (Hypnotic) [88]
     Anniversary Events [94]
     Autobiographical Memory [94]
     Biographical Data [78]
     Homesickness [94]
     Life Review [91]
     Life Satisfaction [85]

Life Insurance [73]
PN 16   SC 28360
B   Insurance [73]

Life Review [91]
PN 37   SC 28361
SN   Reflection on and return to past life experiences in order to think about and reintegrate
them into present life circumstances. Usually performed in a treatment or intervention setting. Not
limited to elderly populations. Consider using
REMINISCENCE to access references from 85-
90.
R   Anniversary Events [94]
     Autobiographical Memory [94]
     Early Experience [67]
     Early Memories [85]
     Gerontology [67]
     Life Experiences [73]
     Reminiscence [85]
     ↓ Treatment [67]

Life Satisfaction [85]
PN 1063   SC 28362
B   Satisfaction [73]
R   Life Experiences [73]
     ↓ Quality of Life [85]
     Role Satisfaction [94]
     Well Being [94]

Life Span
Use Life Expectancy

Lifesaving
Use Artificial Respiration

Lifestyle [78]
PN 1378   SC 28375
SN   Typical way of life or manner of living char-
acteristic of an individual or groups.
R   Daily Activities [94]
     Health Behavior [82]
     Holistic Health [85]
     ↓ Personality [67]
     ↓ Personality Processes [67]
     ↓ Quality of Life [85]

Light
Use Illumination

Light Adaptation [82]
PN 122   SC 28393
SN   Change in the general level of sensitivity of
the photoreceptors as a result of exposure to
light.
UF   Adaptation (Light)
B   Sensory Adaptation [67]
R   Dark Adaptation [73]
     ↓ Illumination [67]
     ↓ Visual Thresholds [73]

Light Refraction [82]
PN 22   SC 28395
SN   Deflection of light from a straight path when
passing obliquely through the interface of two
media that have different densities.

Light Refraction — (cont'd)
N   ↓ Refraction Errors [73]
R   ↓ Illumination [67]
     Lens (Eye) [73]

Likability [88]
PN 61   SC 28387
B   Personality Traits [67]
R   Interpersonal Attraction [67]
     Peer Pressure [94]
     Social Approval [67]
     ↓ Social Perception [67]

Likert Scales [94]
PN 0   SC 28388
B   Rating Scales [67]
R   Attitude Measurement [73]
     ↓ Attitude Measures [67]
     Self Report [82]
     Semantic Differential [67]
     ↓ Surveys [67]

Liking
Use Affection

Limbic System [73]
PN 689   SC 28410
B   Cerebral Cortex [67]
     Neural Pathways [82]
N   Amygdaloid Body [73]
     Fornix [82]
     Gyrus Cinguli [73]
     Hippocampus [67]
     Medial Forebrain Bundle [82]
     Olfactory Bulb [73]
     Septal Nuclei [82]
R   Nucleus Accumbens [82]
     Raphe Nuclei [82]

Limen
Use Thresholds

Limited English Proficiency
Use Language Proficiency

Linear Perspective [82]
PN 71   SC 28427
SN   Apparent convergence of parallel contours
that are projected into the plane of sight of the
observer.
UF   Visual Perspective
B   Vision [67]
R   ↓ Depth Perception [67]
     ↓ Distance Perception [73]
     ↓ Size Discrimination [67]
     ↓ Visual Stimulation [73]

Linear Regression [73]
PN 210   SC 28430
B   Statistical Correlation [67]
     Statistical Regression [85]
R   Multiple Regression [82]

Linguistics [73]
PN 1287   SC 28450
N   Ethnolinguistics [73]
     Etymology [73]
     ↓ Grammar [67]
     Metalinguistics [94]
     Neurolinguistics [91]
     Orthography [73]
     Psycholinguistics [67]
     Sociolinguistics [85]
R   ↓ Language [67]
     Pragmatics [85]
     ↓ Prosody [91]
     Semiotics [85]
     ↓ Verbal Communication [67]

Linkage Analysis
Use Genetic Linkage

Lipid Metabolism [73]
PN 83   SC 28460
UF Fat Metabolism
B Metabolism [67]
R ↓ Lipids [73]

Lipid Metabolism Disorders [73]
PN 20   SC 28470
B Metabolism Disorders [73]
N Amaurotic Familial Idiocy [73]

Lipids [73]
PN 311   SC 28480
N ↓ Fatty Acids [73]
R Lipid Metabolism [73]
↓ Steroids [73]

Lipoproteins [73]
PN 40   SC 28490
R ↓ Proteins [73]

Lipreading [73]
PN 211   SC 28500
UF Speechreading
R ↓ Deaf [67]
Speech Perception [67]
↓ Visual Perception [67]

Lips (Face) [73]
PN 72   SC 28510
R Mouth (Anatomy) [67]

Liquor [73]
PN 24   SC 28520
B Alcoholic Beverages [73]

Listening
Use Auditory Perception

Listening Comprehension [73]
PN 1112   SC 28540
B Verbal Comprehension [85]

Literacy [73]
PN 602   SC 28550
UF Illiteracy
N Computer Literacy [91]
R ↓ Language [67]
↓ Reading Skills [73]
Writing Skills [85]

Literature [67]
PN 3307   SC 28560
UF Fiction
B Arts [73]
N Poetry [73]
↓ Prose [73]
R Creative Writing [94]
Drama [73]
Folklore [91]
Metaphor [82]
Myths [67]
↓ Religious Literature [73]
Writers [91]

Literature Review [67]
PN 15987   SC 28580
SN Mandatory term applied to surveys of pre-viously published material. Limited to documents that are entirely or primarily literature reviews. Also used as a document type identifier.
UF Review (of Literature)
R Bibliography [67]
Meta Analysis [85]

Lithium [73]
PN 2040   SC 28590
SN Used for documents that do not specify the type of lithium used, e.g., carbonate or bromide. Use a more specific term if possible.
B Metallic Elements [73]
N Lithium Bromide [73]
Lithium Carbonate [73]
R ↓ Antidepressant Drugs [71]

Lithium Bromide [73]
PN 5   SC 28600
B Bromides [73]
CNS Depressant Drugs [73]
Hypnotic Drugs [73]
Lithium [73]
Sedatives [73]

Lithium Carbonate [73]
PN 624   SC 28610
B Antidepressant Drugs [71]
Lithium [73]

Litter Size [85]
PN 64   SC 28615
SN Used for animal populations only.
B Size [73]
R ↓ Animal Breeding [73]

Liver [73]
PN 198   SC 28620
B Digestive System [67]

Liver Disorders [73]
PN 108   SC 28630
UF Hepatic Disorders
B Digestive System Disorders [73]
N Cirrhosis (Liver) [73]
↓ Hepatitis [73]
Jaundice [73]
R ↓ Infectious Disorders [73]
↓ Neoplasms [67]
↓ Toxic Disorders [73]

Living Alone [94]
PN 0   SC 28633
SN Use LIVING ARRANGEMENTS to access references from 91-93.
B Living Arrangements [91]
R Cohabitation [73]
↓ Family Structure [73]
Home Environment [73]
↓ Marital Status [73]
Single Persons [73]

Living Arrangements [91]
PN 143   SC 28635
UF Household Structure
N Cohabitation [73]
Living Alone [94]
R Child Custody [82]
Empty Nest [91]
↓ Family [67]
↓ Family Structure [73]
Home Environment [73]
↓ Housing [73]
↓ Marital Status [73]
Roommates [73]
Shelters [91]

Living Wills
Use Advance Directives

Lizards [73]
PN 258   SC 28640
B Reptiles [67]

Lobotomy
Use Psychosurgery

Local Anesthetics [73]
PN 43   SC 28660
B Anesthetic Drugs [73]
N Cocaine [73]
Lidocaine [73]
Quinine [73]
R Ephedrine [73]
Methoxamine [73]

Localization (Perceptual)
Use Perceptual Localization

Localization (Sound)
Use Auditory Localization

Locus Ceruleus [82]
PN 224   SC 28687
SN Pigmented nucleus in the brain stem that synthesizes norepinephrine.
B Brain Stem [73]
R Reticular Formation [67]

Locus of Control
Use Internal External Locus of Control

Logic (Philosophy) [73]
PN 171   SC 28700
B Philosophies [67]

Logical Thinking [67]
PN 1047   SC 28710
UF Ratiocination
B Thinking [67]
R Analogy [91]
↓ Inductive Deductive Reasoning [73]

Logistic Models
Use Item Response Theory

Logotherapy [73]
PN 180   SC 28720
SN Existential analysis based on spiritual values and emphasizing search for the meaning of hu-man existence.
B Psychotherapy [67]

Loneliness [73]
PN 771   SC 28730
B Emotional States [73]
R Homesickness [94]

Long Term Care [94]
PN 0   SC 28735
SN Delivery of health or mental health services over a prolonged or extended period. Care can be in an institutional setting or in the community, e.g., at home, and delivered by health care pro-fessionals, family, or friends.
B Health Care Services [78]
Treatment Duration [88]
R ↓ Case Management [91]
Home Care [85]
↓ Hospitalization [67]
↓ Mental Health Services [78]
Nursing Homes [73]
Palliative Care [91]

Long Term Memory [73]
PN 1086   SC 28740
SN Retention of events or learned material for relatively long periods, presumed to be based on permanent storage of information transferred from short term memory. Consider also RETEN-TION.
B Memory [67]

Long Term Potentiation
　Use Postactivation Potentials

Longevity
　Use Life Expectancy

Longitudinal Studies [73]
PN 7022　　　　　　　　　SC 28760
SN Mandatory term applied to observations or measurements of the same individual or group over an extended period.
　UF Studies (Longitudinal)
　B Experimental Design [67]

Loosening of Associations
　Use Fragmentation (Schizophrenia)

Lorazepam [88]
PN 147　　　　　　　　　SC 28765
　B Benzodiazepines [78]
　　Minor Tranquilizers [73]

Lordosis (Animal)
　Use Animal Sexual Receptivity

Lorge Thorndike Intelligence Test [73]
PN 14　　　　　　　　　SC 28770
　B Intelligence Measures [67]

Loudness [67]
PN 285　　　　　　　　　SC 28780
　UF Sound Pressure Level
　B Auditory Stimulation [67]
　N Noise Levels (Work Areas) [73]

Loudness Discrimination [73]
PN 136　　　　　　　　　SC 28790
　B Loudness Perception [73]

Loudness Perception [73]
PN 227　　　　　　　　　SC 28800
　B Auditory Perception [67]
　N Loudness Discrimination [73]

Love [73]
PN 773　　　　　　　　　SC 28830
　B Emotional States [73]
　R Affection [73]
　　Attachment Behavior [85]
　　Intimacy [73]

Low Birth Weight
　Use Birth Weight

Lowenfeld Mosaic Test [73]
PN 8　　　　　　　　　SC 28840
　B Intelligence Measures [67]

Lower Class [73]
PN 718　　　　　　　　　SC 28850
　B Social Class [67]
　　Socioeconomic Status [67]

Lower Class Attitudes [73]
PN 45　　　　　　　　　SC 28860
SN Attitudes of, not toward, the lower class.
　B Socioeconomic Class Attitudes [73]

Lower Income Level [73]
PN 842　　　　　　　　　SC 28870
　B Income Level [73]
　R Poverty [73]

Loxapine [82]
PN 31　　　　　　　　　SC 28875

Loxapine — (cont'd)
SN Organic heterocyclic compound used as a tranquilizing agent.
　UF Oxilapine
　B Minor Tranquilizers [73]

Loyalty [73]
PN 100　　　　　　　　　SC 28880
　B Personality Traits [67]

LSD (Drug)
　Use Lysergic Acid Diethylamide

Lucid Dreaming [94]
PN 0　　　　　　　　　SC 28893
　B Dreaming [67]
　R Dream Recall [73]
　　REM Dreams [73]
　　REM Sleep [73]
　　↓ Sleep [67]

Luck
　Use Chance (Fortune)

Lumbar Spinal Cord [73]
PN 66　　　　　　　　　SC 28900
　B Spinal Cord [73]

Lumbrosacral Plexus
　Use Spinal Nerves

Luminance [82]
PN 600　　　　　　　　　SC 28930
SN Product of multiplying the physical intensity of a light wave by the spectral sensitivity of the typical observer's visual system for that specific wavelength. Compare ILLUMINATION.
　R ↓ Brightness Perception [73]
　　↓ Illumination [67]
　　Stimulus Intensity [67]
　　↓ Visual Thresholds [73]

Luminance Threshold
　Use Brightness Perception AND Visual Thresholds

Lunar Synodic Cycle [73]
PN 83　　　　　　　　　SC 28950
SN Successive phases of the moon reflecting its motion around the earth.
　R ↓ Biological Rhythms [67]
　　↓ Environmental Effects [73]

Lung [73]
PN 32　　　　　　　　　SC 28960
　B Respiratory System [73]

Lung Disorders [73]
PN 149　　　　　　　　　SC 28970
　B Respiratory Tract Disorders [73]
　N Cystic Fibrosis [85]
　　Pneumonia [73]
　　Pulmonary Emphysema [73]
　　Pulmonary Tuberculosis [73]
　R ↓ Dyspnea [73]

Lupus [73]
PN 109　　　　　　　　　SC 28980
　B Skin Disorders [73]
　R ↓ Tuberculosis [73]

Luria Nebraska Neuropsych Battery [91]
PN 29　　　　　　　　　SC 28982
SN Use NEUROPSYCHOLOGICAL ASSESSMENT to access references from 82-90.
　B Neuropsychological Assessment [82]

Luteinizing Hormone [78]
PN 325　　　　　　　　　SC 28985
　B Gonadotropic Hormones [73]
　R ↓ Pituitary Hormones [73]
　　↓ Sex Hormones [73]

Lying
　Use Deception

Lymphatic Disorders
　Use Blood and Lymphatic Disorders

Lymphocytes [73]
PN 315　　　　　　　　　SC 29060
　B Leucocytes [73]
　R Interleukins [94]

Lysergic Acid Diethylamide [67]
PN 731　　　　　　　　　SC 29070
　UF LSD (Drug)
　B Acids [73]
　　Amine Oxidase Inhibitors [73]
　　Hallucinogenic Drugs [67]
　　Psychedelic Drugs [73]
　　Psychotomimetic Drugs [73]
　　Serotonin Antagonists [73]
　R ↓ Ergot Derivatives [73]

Machiavellianism [73]
PN 297　　　　　　　　　SC 29087
SN Extent to which an individual feels that any means, however unscrupulous, can justifiably be used to achieve power.
　B Personality Traits [67]

Madagascar [91]
PN 1　　　　　　　　　SC 29088
　R ↓ Africa [67]

Magazines [73]
PN 212　　　　　　　　　SC 29090
　B Printed Communications Media [73]

Magical Thinking [73]
PN 66　　　　　　　　　SC 29100
SN Belief that one's utterances, thoughts, or behavior can have a controlling influence on specific events or prevent their occurrence by means that operate beyond the normal laws of cause and effect.
　B Thinking [67]
　　Thought Disturbances [73]
　R Fantasies (Thought Disturbances) [67]
　　Imagination [67]
　　Omnipotence [94]

Magnesium [73]
PN 105　　　　　　　　　SC 29110
　B Metallic Elements [73]
　N Magnesium Ions [73]

Magnesium Ions [73]
PN 9　　　　　　　　　SC 29120
　B Electrolytes [73]
　　Magnesium [73]

Magnet Schools
　Use Nontraditional Education

Magnetic Resonance Imaging [94]
PN 0　　　　　　　　　SC 29133
　UF MRI
　B Tomography [88]
　R Computer Assisted Diagnosis [73]
　　Magnetoencephalography [85]

Magnetism [85]
PN 125   SC 29135
  UF   Geomagnetism
  R   Magnetoencephalography [85]
       Physics [73]

Magnetoencephalography [85]
PN 34   SC 29136
  R   ↓ Electroencephalography [67]
       Magnetic Resonance Imaging [94]
       Magnetism [85]

Magnitude Estimation [91]
PN 41   SC 29138
  SN   Unidimensional scaling method in statistics
  and psychophysics for quantitative judgment and
  ratio estimation.
  B   Psychophysical Measurement [67]
       Statistical Estimation [85]
  R   Scaling (Testing) [67]

Magnitude of Effect (Statistical)
  Use Effect Size (Statistical)

Maids
  Use Domestic Service Personnel

Mail Surveys [94]
PN 0   SC 29141
  B   Surveys [67]
  R   ↓ Consumer Research [73]
       Consumer Surveys [73]
       ↓ Methodology [67]
       ↓ Questionnaires [67]
       Telephone Surveys [94]

Mainstreaming [91]
PN 24   SC 29144
  SN   Integration or transition into society of individuals who have been considered for institutionalization or other type of isolation but are now
  considered able to learn from education or community involvement.
  N   Mainstreaming (Educational) [78]
  R   Deinstitutionalization [82]
       Educational Placement [78]
       Habilitation [91]
       Independent Living Programs [91]
       ↓ Rehabilitation [67]
       School to Work Transition [94]
       ↓ Social Integration [82]
       Special Education [67]
       Special Needs [94]

Mainstreaming (Educational) [78]
PN 1771   SC 29145
  SN   Integration of children with special education
  needs into classes or schools with regular stu-
  dents.
  B   Mainstreaming [91]
  R   ↓ Education [67]
       Educational Placement [78]
       Special Education [67]

Major Depression [88]
PN 9810   SC 29143
  SN   Affective disorder marked by dysphoric
  mood, inactivity, and self depreciation. Consider
  DEPRESSION (EMOTION) to access references
  prior to 1988.
  UF   Agitated Depression
       Dysphoria
       Melancholia
       Psychotic Depressive Reaction
       Unipolar Depression
  B   Affective Disturbances [67]
  N   Anaclitic Depression [73]
       Dysthymic Disorder [88]
       Endogenous Depression [78]

Major Depression — (cont'd)
  N   Involutional Depression [73]
       Neurotic Depressive Reaction [73]
       Postpartum Depression [73]
       Reactive Depression [73]
       Recurrent Depression [94]
       Treatment Resistant Depression [94]
  R   Depression (Emotion) [67]
       ↓ Manic Depression [73]
       Pseudodementia [85]
       Seasonal Affective Disorder [91]

Major Tranquilizers
  Use Neuroleptic Drugs

Maladjustment (Emotional)
  Use Emotional Adjustment

Maladjustment (Social)
  Use Social Adjustment

Malaria [73]
PN 17   SC 29180
  B   Blood and Lymphatic Disorders [73]
       Parasitic Disorders [73]
  R   ↓ Nervous System Disorders [67]

Malawi [91]
PN 4   SC 29183
  B   Africa [67]

Malaysia [82]
PN 105   SC 29184
  B   Southeast Asia [73]

Male Animals [73]
PN 2512   SC 29190
  B   Animals [67]

Male Castration [73]
PN 596   SC 29200
  SN   Used for both human and animal popula-
  tions.
  B   Castration [67]

Male Criminals [73]
PN 588   SC 29210
  B   Criminals [67]
       Human Males [73]

Male Delinquents [73]
PN 838   SC 29220
  B   Human Males [73]
       Juvenile Delinquents [73]
  R   Female Delinquents [73]

Male Female Relations [88]
PN 443   SC 29225
  SN   Relationships or interactions between the
  sexes. Limited to human populations.
  UF   Heterosexual Interaction
  B   Interpersonal Interaction [67]
  R   ↓ Human Courtship [73]
       ↓ Marital Relations [67]
       Social Dating [73]
       Social Skills [78]

Male Genital Disorders [73]
PN 26   SC 29230
  B   Genital Disorders [67]
  N   Klinefelters Syndrome [73]
       Testicular Feminization Syndrome [73]
  R   ↓ Endocrine Sexual Disorders [73]
       Hermaphroditism [73]
       ↓ Hypogonadism [73]
       ↓ Infertility [73]
       Sterility [73]

Male Genitalia [73]
PN 104   SC 29240
  SN   Used for both human and animal popula-
  tions.
  UF   Genitalia (Male)
  B   Urogenital System [73]
  N   Penis [73]
       Prostate [73]
       Testes [73]

Male Homosexuality [73]
PN 1495   SC 29250
  UF   Gay Males
  B   Homosexuality [67]
  R   Bisexuality [73]
       Heterosexuality [73]
       Homosexual Parents [94]
       Lesbianism [73]

Male Orgasm [73]
PN 205   SC 29260
  SN   Used for both human and animal popula-
  tions.
  UF   Ejaculation
  B   Orgasm [73]
  N   Nocturnal Emission [73]
       Premature Ejaculation [73]
  R   Impotence [73]
       Masturbation [73]
       ↓ Sexual Intercourse (Human) [73]

Males (Human)
  Use Human Males

Mali [91]
PN 2   SC 29275
  B   Africa [67]

Malignant Neoplasms
  Use Neoplasms

Malingering [73]
PN 217   SC 29290
  SN   Feigning or exaggerating illness or symp-
  toms usually in order to escape work, evoke
  sympathy, or gain compensation.
  B   Deception [67]
  R   ↓ Factitious Disorders [88]
       ↓ Mental Disorders [67]
       Munchausen Syndrome [94]
       ↓ Psychosomatic Disorders [67]

Malnutrition
  Use Nutritional Deficiencies

Malpractice
  Use Professional Liability

Mammals [73]
PN 881   SC 29310
  B   Vertebrates [73]
  N   Bats [73]
       Cats [67]
       Cattle [73]
       Chimpanzees [73]
       Chinchillas [73]
       Deer [73]
       Dogs [67]
       Elephants [73]
       Foxes [73]
       Goats [73]
       Horses [73]
       Lemurs [73]
       ↓ Marsupials [73]
       ↓ Primates (Nonhuman) [73]
       Rabbits [67]
       ↓ Rodents [73]
       Seals (Animal) [73]

Mammals — (cont'd)
N   Sheep [73]
     ↓ Whales [85]
     Wolves [73]

Mammary Glands [73]
PN   13   SC   29320
B   Glands [67]

Mammary Neoplasms
Use Breast Neoplasms

Mammillary Bodies (Hypothalamic)
Use Hypothalamus

Mammography [94]
PN   0   SC   29345
B   Roentgenography [73]
R   Breast Neoplasms [73]
     ↓ Medical Diagnosis [73]
     Physical Examination [88]
     Preventive Medicine [73]

Man Machine Systems [73]
PN   931   SC   29350
SN   Systems based on the human engineering
concept that views human operators and the ma-
chines they operate as functionally integrated
parts of a larger goal-oriented system.
B   Systems [67]
R   ↓ Artificial Intelligence [82]
     ↓ Computer Peripheral Devices [85]
     Computer Searching [91]
     Cybernetics [67]
     Databases [91]
     Error Analysis [73]
     Expert Systems [91]
     Human Factors Engineering [73]
     Man Machine Systems Design [73]
     Systems Analysis [73]

Man Machine Systems Design [73]
PN   792   SC   29360
UF   Design (Man Machine Systems)
R   ↓ Instrument Controls [85]
     Man Machine Systems [73]
     ↓ Systems [67]

Managed Care [94]
PN   0   SC   29365
SN   Competitive prepaid plan of health care de-
livery to contain costs and provide access to
quality health care. Use CASE MANAGEMENT to
access references from 91-93.
B   Health Care Delivery [78]
N   Health Maintenance Organizations [82]
R   ↓ Case Management [91]
     Cost Containment [91]
     Fee for Service [94]
     Health Care Costs [94]
     ↓ Health Care Services [78]
     ↓ Health Insurance [73]
     Quality of Care [88]

Management [67]
PN   1311   SC   29420
SN   Conceptually broad array term referring to
the process of manipulation of human or material
resources to accomplish given goals. Use a more
specific term if possible.
N   Business Management [73]
     ↓ Case Management [91]
     Disability Management [91]
     Hospital Administration [78]
     Household Management [85]
     ↓ Personnel Management [73]
     ↓ Self Management [85]
     Stress Management [85]

Management — (cont'd)
N   Time Management [94]
R   Accountability [88]
     Business [67]
     Career Development [85]
     Entrepreneurship [91]
     Labor Management Relations [67]
     ↓ Leadership [67]
     Management Decision Making [73]
     ↓ Management Methods [73]
     ↓ Management Personnel [73]
     Management Planning [73]
     Management Training [73]

Management Decision Making [73]
PN   961   SC   29370
B   Decision Making [67]
R   ↓ Group Decision Making [78]
     ↓ Management [67]
     ↓ Management Methods [73]
     Management Planning [73]
     Participative Management [88]

Management Development
Use Career Development

Management Information Systems
Use Information Systems

Management Methods [73]
PN   2065   SC   29380
N   Participative Management [88]
R   Business Management [73]
     ↓ Management [67]
     Management Decision Making [73]
     Management Planning [73]
     Teams [88]
     Work Scheduling [73]

Management Personnel [73]
PN   4905   SC   29390
UF   Administrators
     Supervisors
B   White Collar Workers [73]
N   Middle Level Managers [73]
     Top Level Managers [73]
R   Commissioned Officers [73]
     Industrial Foremen [73]
     ↓ Management [67]
     ↓ School Administrators [73]

Management Planning [73]
PN   243   SC   29400
UF   Planning (Management)
R   ↓ Management [67]
     Management Decision Making [73]
     ↓ Management Methods [73]
     Marketing [73]

Management Training [73]
PN   946   SC   29410
B   Personnel Training [67]
R   Business Education [73]
     ↓ Management [67]
     Wilderness Experience [91]

Mandibula
Use Jaw

Mania [67]
PN   1155   SC   29450
B   Affective Disturbances [67]
N   Hypomania [73]
R   ↓ Manic Depression [73]

Manic Depression [73]
PN   2550   SC   29457

Manic Depression — (cont'd)
UF   Bipolar Depression
     Manic Depressive Psychosis
B   Affective Disturbances [67]
N   Cyclothymic Personality [73]
R   ↓ Affective Psychosis [73]
     ↓ Major Depression [88]
     ↓ Mania [67]

Manic Depressive Psychosis
SN   Term discontinued in 1988. Use MANIC DE-
PRESSIVE PSYCHOSIS to access references
from 67-87.
Use Manic Depression

Mann Whitney U Test [73]
PN   15   SC   29470
B   Nonparametric Statistical Tests [67]

Mannerisms
Use Habits

Manpower
SN   Use PERSONNEL to access references from
67N81.
Use Personnel Supply

Mantis [73]
PN   16   SC   29500
UF   Praying Mantis
B   Insects [67]
R   Larvae [73]

Manual Communication [78]
PN   110   SC   29505
SN   Form of communication used by the deaf in
which sign language and finger spelling are sub-
stituted for speech. Also, an unsystematic or in-
formal method of communication with gestures.
B   Augmentative Communication [94]
     Nonverbal Communication [71]
     Verbal Communication [67]
N   Fingerspelling [73]
     Sign Language [73]

Manufacturing
Use Business

Maprotiline [82]
PN   153   SC   29527
SN   Polycyclic hydrocarbon used as an antide-
pressant agent.
B   Antidepressant Drugs [71]

Marathon Group Therapy [73]
PN   132   SC   29540
SN   Encounter group that meets for extended
sessions and that aims to develop the ability to
express oneself emotionally and to initiate in-
timate interpersonal interactions.
B   Encounter Group Therapy [73]
R   Human Relations Training [78]
     Sensitivity Training [73]

Marihuana [71]
PN   542   SC   29550
UF   Marijuana
B   Cannabis [73]
R   Hashish [73]
     ↓ Marihuana Laws [73]
     Marihuana Usage [73]
     Tetrahydrocannabinol [73]

Marihuana Laws [73]
PN   20   SC   29560
B   Drug Laws [73]
N   Marihuana Legalization [73]
R   Government [67]

Marihuana Laws — (cont'd)
R   Marihuana [71]
       Marihuana Usage [73]

Marihuana Legalization [73]
PN 27   SC 29570
UF   Legalization (Marihuana)
B   Marihuana Laws [73]
R   ↓ Drug Usage Attitudes [73]
       Government [67]

Marihuana Usage [73]
PN 833   SC 29580
B   Drug Usage [71]
R   Marihuana [71]
      ↓ Marihuana Laws [73]

Marijuana
Use Marihuana

Marine Personnel [73]
PN 151   SC 29600
B   Military Personnel [67]

Marital Adjustment
Use Marital Relations

Marital Conflict [73]
PN 806   SC 29620
B   Marital Relations [67]
R   Dysfunctional Family [91]
      ↓ Family Violence [82]

Marital Relations [67]
PN 4999   SC 29640
UF   Marital Adjustment
B   Family Relations [67]
N   Marital Conflict [73]
       Marital Satisfaction [88]
R   Codependency [91]
       Male Female Relations [88]
       Postpartum Depression [73]

Marital Satisfaction [88]
PN 542   SC 29645
B   Marital Relations [67]
       Satisfaction [73]
R   Role Satisfaction [94]

Marital Separation [73]
PN 542   SC 29650
UF   Separation (Marital)
N   Divorce [73]
R   Child Support [88]
       Divorced Persons [73]
      ↓ Family [67]
      ↓ Marital Status [73]
      ↓ Parental Absence [73]

Marital Status [73]
PN 1245   SC 29660
N   Never Married [94]
R   Divorced Persons [73]
      ↓ Family [67]
      ↓ Family Background [73]
       Living Alone [94]
      ↓ Living Arrangements [91]
      ↓ Marital Separation [73]
       Remarriage [85]
      ↓ Single Parents [78]
       Single Persons [73]
       Widowers [73]
       Widows [73]

Marital Therapy
Use Marriage Counseling

Marketing [73]
PN 1135   SC 29670
R   ↓ Advertising [67]
       Brand Names [78]
       Brand Preferences [94]
      ↓ Consumer Research [73]
       Management Planning [73]
       Retailing [91]

Markov Chains [73]
PN 146   SC 29680
SN Statistical model representing conditional and sequential probabilities to determine the future values of a random variable.
B   Simulation [67]
       Stochastic Modeling [73]

Marlowe Crowne Soc Desirabil Scale [73]
PN 42   SC 29690
B   Nonprojective Personality Measures [73]

Marriage [67]
PN 1178   SC 29700
N   ↓ Endogamous Marriage [73]
      ↓ Exogamous Marriage [73]
       Polygamy [73]
       Remarriage [85]
R   ↓ Family [67]
       Marriage Rites [73]

Marriage Attitudes [73]
PN 494   SC 29710
SN General attitudes toward marriage and divorce, or attitudes toward a specific marital relationship.
B   Attitudes [67]
R   ↓ Family Relations [67]

Marriage Counseling [73]
PN 1882   SC 29720
UF   Marital Therapy
       Marriage Therapy
B   Counseling [67]
N   Conjoint Therapy [73]
R   Couples Therapy [94]
      ↓ Psychotherapeutic Counseling [73]
      ↓ Psychotherapy [67]
       Sex Therapy [78]

Marriage Rites [73]
PN 30   SC 29730
B   Rites of Passage [73]
R   ↓ Marriage [67]

Marriage Therapy
Use Marriage Counseling

Married Couples
Use Spouses

Marsupials [73]
PN 25   SC 29760
B   Mammals [73]
N   Kangaroos [73]
       Opossums [73]

Martial Arts [85]
PN 48   SC 29765
UF   Karate
B   Recreation [67]
       Sports [67]
R   Judo [73]
       Meditation [73]
       Self Defense [85]

Marxism
Use Communism

Masculinity [67]
PN 1366   SC 29780
B   Personality Traits [67]
R   Androgyny [82]
       Femininity [67]
       Sex Roles [67]

Masking [67]
PN 515   SC 29790
SN Changes in perceptual sensitivity to a stimulus due to the presence of a second stimulus in close temporal proximity.
UF   Backward Masking
       Forward Masking
N   Auditory Masking [73]
       Visual Masking [73]
R   ↓ Perceptual Stimulation [73]

Maslow (Abraham Harold) [91]
PN 16   SC 29795
SN Identifies biographical or autobiographical studies and discussions of Maslow's works.
R   ↓ Human Potential Movement [82]
      ↓ Humanistic Psychology [85]
      ↓ Psychologists [67]
       Self Actualization [73]

Masochism [73]
PN 152   SC 29800
SN Pleasure derived from being physically or psychologically abused.
B   Sadomasochism [73]
N   Sexual Masochism [73]
R   Masochistic Personality [73]
      ↓ Sadism [73]
      ↓ Self Destructive Behavior [85]

Masochistic Personality [73]
PN 41   SC 29810
SN Borderline personality marked by self-destructiveness and an enjoyment of suffering and tendency to seek opportunity for pain.
B   Sadomasochistic Personality [73]
R   ↓ Masochism [73]
      ↓ Self Destructive Behavior [85]
       Sexual Masochism [73]

Mass Hysteria [73]
PN 40   SC 29820
B   Hysteria [67]
R   ↓ Collective Behavior [67]
       Contagion [88]

Mass Media [67]
PN 941   SC 29830
B   Communications Media [73]
N   ↓ Motion Pictures [73]
      ↓ Printed Communications Media [73]
       Radio [73]
      ↓ Television [67]
R   ↓ Advertising [67]

Massed Practice [73]
PN 141   SC 29840
SN Practice schedule with trials that are closely spaced and continuous over a long period. Compare DISTRIBUTED PRACTICE.
B   Learning Schedules [67]
       Practice [67]

Mastectomy [73]
PN 178   SC 29850
B   Amputation [73]
R   Breast Neoplasms [73]

Mastery Learning [85]
PN 118   SC 29855

Mastery Learning — (cont'd)
SN Educational approach involving specification of educational objectives and success criteria and individual pacing in attaining them.
B Learning [67]
R Educational Objectives [78]
School Learning [67]
Sequential Learning [73]
↓ Teaching Methods [67]

Mastery Tests
Use Criterion Referenced Tests

Masticatory Muscles [73]
PN 29   **SC** 29860
B Muscles [67]

Masturbation [73]
PN 238   **SC** 29870
UF Autoeroticism
B Psychosexual Behavior [67]
R Female Orgasm [73]
↓ Male Orgasm [73]

Matching Test
Use Matching to Sample

Matching to Sample [94]
PN 0   **SC** 29873
UF Matching Test
B Discrimination Learning [82]
R ↓ Memory [67]
Recognition (Learning) [67]

Mate Selection
Use Animal Mate Selection OR Human Mate Selection

Mate Swapping
Use Extramarital Intercourse

Materialism [73]
PN 89   **SC** 29890
B Philosophies [67]

Maternal Behavior (Animal)
Use Animal Maternal Behavior

Maternal Behavior (Human)
Use Mother Child Relations

Mates (Humans)
Use Spouses

Mathematical Ability [73]
PN 1110   **SC** 29930
UF Numerical Ability
B Cognitive Ability [73]
Nonverbal Ability [88]
R ↓ Mathematics (Concepts) [67]
Mathematics Anxiety [85]

Mathematical Modeling [73]
PN 2649   **SC** 29940
SN Use of mathematical formulas or equations to analyze or systematize data for description in quantitative terms.
B Simulation [67]
N Structural Equation Modeling [94]
R Fuzzy Set Theory [91]
Goodness of Fit [88]
Heuristic Modeling [73]
↓ Stochastic Modeling [73]

Mathematical Psychology [73]
PN 52   **SC** 29950

Mathematical Psychology — (cont'd)
SN Discipline that attempts to systematize the data of psychology by means of mathematical and statistical models and applications.
B Psychology [67]

Mathematicians [73]
PN 19   **SC** 29960
B Professional Personnel [78]
R Physicists [73]
Scientists [67]

Mathematics [82]
PN 455   **SC** 29965
SN Science of numbers and the operations performed on them. Compare MATHEMATICS (CONCEPTS).
UF Algebra
Arithmetic
Calculus
Geometry
B Sciences [67]
N Statistics [82]
R Mathematics Anxiety [85]

Mathematics (Concepts) [67]
PN 1840   **SC** 29970
SN Specific principles that are cognitively internalized or are to be learned concerning numbers, their relations, and mathematical operations performed on them. Compare MATHEMATICS.
N Algorithms [73]
Number Systems [73]
Numbers (Numerals) [67]
R Concepts [67]
Mathematical Ability [73]
Mathematics Achievement [73]
Mathematics Education [73]
↓ Statistical Analysis [67]

Mathematics Achievement [73]
PN 2774   **SC** 29980
B Academic Achievement [67]
R ↓ Mathematics (Concepts) [67]
Mathematics Anxiety [85]

Mathematics Anxiety [85]
PN 149   **SC** 29985
SN Fear or tension associated with the study or performance of arithmetic and mathematical tasks.
B Anxiety [67]
R ↓ Anxiety Neurosis [73]
Mathematical Ability [73]
↓ Mathematics [82]
Mathematics Achievement [73]

Mathematics Education [73]
PN 2194   **SC** 29990
B Curriculum [67]
R ↓ Mathematics (Concepts) [67]

Mating Behavior (Animal)
Use Animal Mating Behavior

Matriarchy [73]
PN 16   **SC** 30010
B Family Structure [73]
R Father Absence [73]

Matriculation
Use School Enrollment

Maturation
Use Human Development

Maturity (Emotional)
Use Emotional Maturity

Maturity (Physical)
Use Physical Maturity

Maturity (Vocational)
Use Vocational Maturity

Maudsley Personality Inventory [73]
PN 13   **SC** 30060
B Nonprojective Personality Measures [73]

Mauritius [91]
PN 1   **SC** 30065
R ↓ Africa [67]

Maxilla
Use Jaw

Maximum Likelihood [85]
PN 148   **SC** 30075
SN Method of estimating population parameters from sample data by selecting parameter values that maximize the likelihood of the occurrence of the observed sample results.
B Statistical Estimation [85]
R Goodness of Fit [88]

Maximum Security Facilities [85]
PN 54   **SC** 30077
R ↓ Correctional Institutions [73]
↓ Hospitals [67]

Maze Learning [67]
PN 1675   **SC** 30080
SN Learning the correct route through a maze to obtain reinforcement. Used for human or animal populations.
B Learning [67]

Maze Pathways [73]
PN 93   **SC** 30090
SN Use when specifically referring to pathway choice, discrimination, or spatial organization of pathway. Used for human or animal populations. When comparing types of mazes, use MAZES.
UF Runways (Maze)
B Mazes [67]

Mazes [67]
PN 117   **SC** 30110
SN System of pathways consisting of a number of blind alleys and one or more correct paths leading to a goal/reinforcement. Used to study learning and motivation in humans and animals.
UF Labyrinth (Apparatus)
B Apparatus [67]
N Maze Pathways [73]
T Mazes [73]

MCPP
Use Piperazines

MDMA
Use Methylenedioxymethamphetamine

Mealtimes
Use Feeding Practices

Mean [73]
PN 161   **SC** 30160
B Central Tendency Measures [73]
R Standard Scores [85]

Meaning [67]
PN 1433   **SC** 30170
SN Generally refers to the significance, sense, connotation, or denotation conveyed by any form of information.

Meaning — (cont'd)
- **N** Nonverbal Meaning [73]
- ↓ Verbal Meaning [73]
- **R** ↓ Comprehension [67]
- Meaningfulness [67]

Meaningfulness [67]
PN 1036   SC 30180
- **R** ↓ Comprehension [67]
- ↓ Meaning [67]

Measles [73]
PN 7   SC 30190
- **B** Viral Disorders [73]
- **R** Rubella [73]

Measurement [67]
PN 10548   SC 30200
- **SN** Conceptually broad array term referring to the process and tools used in psychological assessment of human subjects. Use specific test names or procedures if possible. For other types of measurement that do not involve psychological tests, consider METHODOLOGY, EVALUATION, or other appropriate terms.
- **UF** Assessment
- Tests
- **N** ↓ Achievement Measures [67]
- ↓ Aptitude Measures [67]
- Attitude Measurement [73]
- ↓ Attitude Measures [67]
- Body Sway Testing [73]
- Comprehension Tests [73]
- Creativity Measurement [73]
- Criterion Referenced Tests [82]
- Digit Span Testing [73]
- Employment Tests [73]
- Group Testing [73]
- Individual Testing [73]
- ↓ Intelligence Measures [67]
- ↓ Inventories [67]
- Multidimensional Scaling [82]
- Needs Assessment [85]
- ↓ Neuropsychological Assessment [82]
- ↓ Occupational Interest Measures [73]
- ↓ Perceptual Measures [73]
- Performance Tests [73]
- ↓ Personality Measures [67]
- Posttesting [73]
- ↓ Preference Measures [73]
- Pretesting [73]
- Professional Examinations [94]
- Profiles (Measurement) [73]
- Projective Testing Technique [73]
- Psychometrics [67]
- ↓ Questionnaires [67]
- ↓ Rating Scales [67]
- ↓ Reading Measures [73]
- ↓ Retention Measures [73]
- ↓ Screening [82]
- ↓ Screening Tests [82]
- ↓ Selection Tests [73]
- ↓ Sensorimotor Measures [73]
- Sociometric Tests [67]
- ↓ Speech and Hearing Measures [73]
- Standardized Tests [85]
- ↓ Statistical Measurement [73]
- Subtests [73]
- ↓ Surveys [67]
- Symptom Checklists [91]
- ↓ Testing [67]
- Verbal Tests [73]
- **R** Construct Validity [82]
- ↓ Experimentation [67]
- ↓ Interviews [67]
- Piagetian Tasks [73]
- ↓ Prediction Errors [73]
- Response Bias [67]
- Semantic Differential [67]

Measurement — (cont'd)
- **R** Sociograms [73]
- ↓ Statistical Analysis [67]
- ↓ Test Construction [73]
- Test Norms [73]
- ↓ Test Scores [67]
- ↓ Testing Methods [67]
- Testwiseness [78]

Mecamylamine [73]
PN 59   SC 30220
- **B** Amines [73]
- Antihypertensive Drugs [73]
- Ganglion Blocking Drugs [73]

Mechanical Aptitude [73]
PN 56   SC 30230
- **B** Nonverbal Ability [88]

Mechanoreceptors [73]
PN 111   SC 30250
- **B** Neural Receptors [73]
- Sensory Neurons [73]

Media (Communications)
- **Use** Communications Media

Medial Forebrain Bundle [82]
PN 104   SC 30286
- **SN** Complex group of nerve fibers arising from basal olfactory regions, the periamygdaloid region, and the septal nuclei passing to, and through, the lateral preoptic and hypothalamic regions. This bundle provides the chief pathway for reciprocal connections between the hypothalamus and the biogenic amine systems of the brain stem.
- **B** Limbic System [73]
- **R** Amygdaloid Body [73]
- Fornix [82]
- Hippocampus [67]
- ↓ Hypothalamus [67]
- Septal Nuclei [82]

Median [73]
PN 12   SC 30290
- **B** Central Tendency Measures [73]

Median Nerve
- **Use** Spinal Nerves

Mediated Responses [67]
PN 52   SC 30310
- **SN** Intervening or anticipatory responses aroused by stimuli and subsequently responsible for the initiation of behavior.
- **B** Responses [67]

Mediation [88]
PN 348   SC 30315
- **SN** Intervention by independent and impartial third party or parties to promote reconciliation, settlement, or compromise between conflicting parties.
- **B** Conflict Resolution [82]
- **R** Child Custody [82]
- Court Referrals [94]
- Divorce [73]
- Labor Management Relations [67]
- ↓ Negotiation [73]

Mediation (Cognitive)
- **Use** Cognitive Mediation

Medicaid [94]
PN 0   SC 30323

Medicaid — (cont'd)
- **SN** Government health care program for impoverished citizens administered by most local public assistance offices. Compare MEDICARE.
- **B** Government Programs [73]
- Health Insurance [73]
- **R** Health Care Policy [94]
- Medicare [88]
- Social Security [88]
- Welfare Services (Government) [73]

Medical Care Costs
- **Use** Health Care Costs

Medical Diagnosis [73]
PN 2072   SC 30330
- **SN** Diagnosis of mental or physical disorders through use of medical methods or tests. Compare PSYCHODIAGNOSIS.
- **UF** Clinical Judgment (Med Diagnosis)
- **B** Diagnosis [67]
- **N** Biopsy [73]
- ↓ Cardiography [73]
- Dexamethasone Suppression Test [88]
- Echoencephalography [73]
- Electro Oculography [73]
- ↓ Electroencephalography [67]
- Electromyography [67]
- Electronystagmography [73]
- Electroplethysmography [73]
- Electroretinography [67]
- ↓ Encephalography [73]
- Galvanic Skin Response [67]
- ↓ Ophthalmologic Examination [73]
- ↓ Plethysmography [73]
- Pneumoencephalography [73]
- Prenatal Diagnosis [88]
- Rheoencephalography [73]
- ↓ Roentgenography [73]
- ↓ Tomography [88]
- Urinalysis [73]
- **R** Autopsy [73]
- Biological Markers [91]
- Computer Assisted Diagnosis [73]
- Differential Diagnosis [67]
- Drug Usage Screening [88]
- ↓ Electrophysiology [73]
- Mammography [94]
- Patient History [73]
- Physical Examination [88]
- Prognosis [73]
- Psychological Report [88]

Medical Education [73]
PN 1681   SC 30340
- **B** Graduate Education [73]
- **N** Medical Internship [73]
- Medical Residency [73]
- Psychiatric Training [73]
- **R** Nursing Education [73]

Medical History
- **Use** Patient History

Medical Internship [73]
PN 81   SC 30350
- **UF** Internship (Medical)
- **B** Medical Education [73]
- Postgraduate Training [73]

Medical Model [78]
PN 351   SC 30355
- **SN** Conceptual approach to disorders originally applied to the study and treatment of physical illness. Also known as the disease or faulty mechanism model.
- **B** Models [67]

Medical Patients [73]
PN 2200   SC 30360
B   Patients [67]

Medical Personnel [67]
PN 1790   SC 30370
UF   Hospital Staff
B   Health Personnel [94]
N   Dentists [73]
    Military Medical Personnel [73]
    ↓ Nurses [67]
    Optometrists [73]
    ↓ Paramedical Personnel [73]
    Pharmacists [91]
    Physical Therapists [73]
    ↓ Physicians [67]
    ↓ Psychiatric Hospital Staff [73]
R   Clinicians [73]
    Impaired Professionals [85]
    ↓ Medical Sciences [67]
    ↓ Mental Health Personnel [67]
    Scientists [67]

Medical Personnel Supply [73]
PN 19   SC 30380
SN   Manpower needs and availability of medical personnel.
B   Personnel Supply [73]

Medical Psychology [73]
PN 163   SC 30390
SN   Subspecialty of clinical psychology concerned with physical health and illness.
B   Clinical Psychology [67]
    Health Care Psychology [85]
R   ↓ Medical Sciences [67]

Medical Records Keeping [78]
PN 305   SC 30395
R   Data Collection [82]
    ↓ Data Processing [67]
    Hospital Administration [78]
    Patient History [73]
    ↓ Treatment [67]

Medical Regimen Compliance
Use   Treatment Compliance

Medical Residency [73]
PN 895   SC 30400
SN   Required hospital training in a medical specialty for a graduate and licensed physician.
UF   Psychiatric Residency
    Residency (Medical)
B   Medical Education [73]
    Postgraduate Training [73]

Medical Sciences [67]
PN 1333   SC 30410
UF   Medicine (Science of)
B   Sciences [67]
N   Anesthesiology [73]
    Cardiology [73]
    Dentistry [73]
    ↓ Endocrinology [73]
    Epidemiology [73]
    Family Medicine [88]
    Geriatrics [67]
    Gynecology [78]
    ↓ Immunology [73]
    Neurology [67]
    ↓ Obstetrics [78]
    Ophthalmology [73]
    ↓ Pathology [73]
    Pediatrics [73]
    ↓ Psychiatry [67]
    Psychosomatic Medicine [78]
    Radiology [73]

Medical Sciences — (cont'd)
N   ↓ Surgery [71]
    Veterinary Medicine [73]
R   Folk Medicine [73]
    ↓ Medical Personnel [67]
    Medical Psychology [73]
    ↓ Neurosciences [73]
    ↓ Paramedical Sciences [73]

Medical Students [67]
PN 1906   SC 30420
B   Students [67]
R   Graduate Students [67]

Medical Therapeutic Devices [73]
PN 253   SC 30430
SN   Equipment designed for rehabilitation or treatment of abnormal or undesirable conditions.
UF   Therapeutic Devices (Medical)
N   Artificial Pacemakers [73]
    ↓ Hearing Aids [73]
    ↓ Optical Aids [73]
    ↓ Prostheses [73]
R   ↓ Augmentative Communication [94]
    Mobility Aids [78]

Medical Treatment (General) [73]
PN 1020   SC 30440
SN   Use for medical treatment as a broad topic.
B   Treatment [67]
R   ↓ Physical Treatment Methods [73]

Medicare [88]
PN 61   SC 30445
SN   Government health care program for the aged administered through the Social Security Administration or the US Health Care Financing Administration. Compare MEDICAID.
B   Government Programs [73]
    Health Insurance [73]
R   Health Care Policy [94]
    Medicaid [94]
    Social Security [88]

Medication
Use   Drug Therapy

Medicine (Science of)
Use   Medical Sciences

Medics [73]
PN 7   SC 30470
B   Paramedical Personnel [73]
R   Military Medical Personnel [73]

Meditation [73]
PN 855   SC 30480
SN   Family of contemplative techniques all of which involve a conscious attempt to focus one's attention in a nonanalytical way and to refrain from ruminating, discursive thought. Frequently, a spiritual or religious practice.
B   Religious Practices [73]
R   Centering [91]
    Holistic Health [85]
    ↓ Human Potential Movement [82]
    Martial Arts [85]
    Prayer [73]

Medulla Oblongata [73]
PN 253   SC 30490
B   Brain Stem [73]

Melancholia
SN   Use DEPRESSION (EMOTION) to access references from 73-87.
Use   Major Depression

Melancholy
Use   Sadness

Melanin [73]
PN 23   SC 30530
B   Pigments [73]
R   Melanocyte Stimulating Hormone [85]
    Melatonin [73]
    ↓ Tyrosine [73]

Melanocyte Stimulating Hormone [85]
PN 54   SC 30535
UF   Melanotropin
B   Peptides [73]
    Pituitary Hormones [73]
R   Melanin [73]
    Melatonin [73]

Melanotropin
Use   Melanocyte Stimulating Hormone

Melatonin [73]
PN 285   SC 30540
B   Hormones [67]
R   Melanin [73]
    Melanocyte Stimulating Hormone [85]
    Pineal Body [73]

Mellaril
Use   Thioridazine

Membranes [73]
PN 125   SC 30560
B   Tissues (Body) [73]
N   Meninges [73]
    ↓ Nasal Mucosa [73]
    Nictitating Membrane [73]

Memory [67]
PN 13471   SC 30570
N   Autobiographical Memory [94]
    Early Memories [85]
    Eidetic Imagery [73]
    Episodic Memory [88]
    Long Term Memory [73]
    Memory Decay [73]
    Memory Trace [73]
    Reminiscence [85]
    ↓ Short Term Memory [67]
    Spatial Memory [88]
    Spontaneous Recovery (Learning) [73]
    ↓ Verbal Memory [94]
    Visual Memory [94]
R   ↓ Cognitive Processes [67]
    Cued Recall [94]
    Cues [67]
    Forgetting [73]
    Free Recall [73]
    Generation Effect (Learning) [91]
    Human Information Storage [73]
    ↓ Learning [67]
    Matching to Sample [94]
    ↓ Memory Disorders [73]
    Memory Training [94]
    Metacognition [91]
    Note Taking [91]
    ↓ Recall (Learning) [67]
    Relearning [73]
    ↓ Retention [67]
    Rote Learning [73]
    Serial Recall [94]

Memory Decay [73]
PN 117   SC 30580
SN   Fading of memory traces over time. Compare FORGETTING and AMNESIA.

Memory Decay — (cont'd)
- **B** Memory [67]
- **R** Forgetting [73]
  Memory Training [94]

Memory Disorders [73]
PN 553   SC 30590
- **B** Disorders [67]
  Thought Disturbances [73]
- **N** ↓ Amnesia [67]
- **R** ↓ Memory [67]
  Memory Training [94]
  ↓ Mental Disorders [67]

Memory Enhancing Drugs
- **Use** Nootropic Drugs

Memory for Designs Test [73]
PN 28   SC 30610
- **B** Nonprojective Personality Measures [73]
- **R** ↓ Neuropsychological Assessment [82]

Memory Trace [73]
PN 265   SC 30620
- **SN** Hypothetical change in nerve cells or brain activity that accompanies the storage of information.
- **B** Memory [67]

Memory Training [94]
PN 0   SC 30623
- **R** Cognitive Rehabilitation [85]
  Forgetting [73]
  ↓ Learning Strategies [91]
  ↓ Memory [67]
  Memory Decay [73]
  ↓ Memory Disorders [73]
  Mnemonic Learning [73]
  ↓ Practice [67]
  ↓ Recall (Learning) [67]
  Recognition (Learning) [67]
  ↓ Retention [67]

Men
- **Use** Human Males

Menarche [73]
PN 108   SC 30630
- **B** Menstruation [73]
- **R** Puberty [73]

Menieres Disease [73]
PN 34   SC 30640
- **B** Labyrinth Disorders [73]
  Syndromes [73]
- **R** Vertigo [73]

Meninges [73]
PN 13   SC 30650
- **B** Central Nervous System [67]
  Membranes [73]

Meningitis [73]
PN 27   SC 30660
- **B** Central Nervous System Disorders [73]
- **N** Bacterial Meningitis [73]

Meningomyelocele
- **Use** Spina Bifida

Menopause [73]
PN 243   SC 30670
- **B** Developmental Stages [73]
- **R** ↓ Menstrual Cycle [73]

Menstrual Cycle [73]
PN 669   SC 30680

Menstrual Cycle — (cont'd)
- **N** ↓ Menstruation [73]
  Ovulation [73]
  Premenstrual Tension [73]
- **R** Estrus [73]
  Menopause [73]

Menstrual Disorders [73]
PN 107   SC 30690
- **B** Gynecological Disorders [73]
- **N** Amenorrhea [73]
  Dysmenorrhea [73]
- **R** Premenstrual Tension [73]

Menstruation [73]
PN 186   SC 30700
- **B** Menstrual Cycle [73]
- **N** Menarche [73]
- **R** Estrus [73]

Mental Age [73]
PN 209   SC 30710
- **SN** Intelligence level expressed in units of chronological age and determined by comparison with other individuals of the same age using intelligence test scores.
- **UF** Intelligence Age
- **R** ↓ Developmental Age Groups [73]
  Intelligence [67]
  Intelligence Quotient [67]

Mental Confusion [73]
PN 237   SC 30720
- **UF** Confusion (Mental)
- **B** Emotional States [73]
- **R** Doubt [73]
  Frustration [67]
  ↓ Thought Disturbances [73]

Mental Deficiency
- **Use** Mental Retardation

Mental Disorders [67]
PN 13279   SC 30740
- **SN** Conceptually broad array term referring to all forms of psychopathological behavior. Use a more specific term if possible.
- **UF** Insanity
  Mental Illness
  Nervous Breakdown
  Psychiatric Disorders
- **B** Disorders [67]
- **N** Adjustment Disorders [94]
  Alexithymia [82]
  ↓ Appetite Disorders [73]
  ↓ Autism [67]
  Borderline States [78]
  ↓ Dissociative Patterns [73]
  Elective Mutism [73]
  Explosive Personality [73]
  ↓ Factitious Disorders [88]
  ↓ Hysteria [67]
  Koro [94]
  ↓ Neurosis [67]
  ↓ Personality Disorders [67]
  Pseudodementia [85]
  Psychopathy [73]
  ↓ Psychosis [67]
  ↓ Sexual Deviations [67]
- **R** ↓ Behavior Disorders [71]
  ↓ Brain Disorders [67]
  ↓ Chronic Illness [91]
  Chronicity (Disorders) [82]
  Comorbidity [91]
  Conduct Disorder [91]
  ↓ Consciousness Disturbances [73]
  ↓ Defense Mechanisms [67]
  ↓ Diagnosis [67]

Mental Disorders — (cont'd)
- **R** Diagnostic and Statistical Manual [94]
  Disease Course [91]
  ↓ Ethnospecific Disorders [73]
  Glossolalia [73]
  Infantilism [73]
  Insanity Defense [85]
  ↓ Learning Disorders [67]
  Malingering [73]
  ↓ Memory Disorders [73]
  Mental Illness (Attitudes Toward) [67]
  ↓ Mental Retardation [67]
  Mentally Ill Offenders [85]
  Microcephaly [73]
  Narcissism [67]
  Onset (Disorders) [73]
  ↓ Organic Brain Syndromes [73]
  ↓ Perceptual Disturbances [73]
  ↓ Personality Processes [67]
  Porphyria [73]
  Predisposition [73]
  Premorbidity [78]
  Prognosis [73]
  Psychopathology [67]
  Recovery (Disorders) [73]
  Relapse (Disorders) [73]
  ↓ Remission (Disorders) [73]
  Research Diagnostic Criteria [94]
  ↓ Sadomasochism [73]
  Schizophrenogenic Family [67]
  Severity (Disorders) [82]
  Special Needs [94]
  Suicide [67]
  Susceptibility (Disorders) [73]
  ↓ Symptoms [67]
  ↓ Thought Disturbances [73]
  ↓ Toxic Disorders [73]
  ↓ Treatment Resistant Disorders [94]

Mental Health [67]
PN 5189   SC 30750
- **B** Health [73]
- **N** Community Mental Health [73]
- **R** Community Mental Health Services [78]
  Community Psychiatry [73]
  ↓ Mental Health Personnel [67]
  ↓ Mental Health Programs [73]
  ↓ Mental Health Services [78]
  Primary Mental Health Prevention [73]
  Well Being [94]

Mental Health Care Costs
- **Use** Health Care Costs

Mental Health Care Policy
- **Use** Health Care Policy

Mental Health Centers (Community)
- **Use** Community Mental Health Centers

Mental Health Consultation
- **SN** Term discontinued in 1982. Use MENTAL HEALTH CONSULTATION or PROFESSIONAL CONSULTATION to access references prior to 1982.
- **Use** Professional Consultation

Mental Health Inservice Training [73]
PN 355   SC 30780
- **UF** Inservice Training (Mental Health)
  Training (Mental Health Inservice)
- **B** Community Mental Health Training [73]
  Inservice Training [85]
- **R** ↓ Mental Health Programs [73]
  Professional Development [82]

Mental Health Personnel [67]
PN 3548   SC 30790

Mental Health Personnel — (cont'd)

- B   Health Personnel [94]
- N   Clinical Psychologists [73]
- ↓ Psychiatric Hospital Staff [73]
-     Psychiatric Nurses [73]
-     Psychiatric Social Workers [73]
-     Psychiatrists [67]
- ↓ Psychotherapists [73]
-     School Psychologists [73]
- R ↓ Counselors [67]
- ↓ Educational Personnel [73]
-     Impaired Professionals [85]
- ↓ Medical Personnel [67]
- ↓ Mental Health [67]
-     Mental Health Personnel Supply [73]
-     Occupational Therapists [73]
- ↓ Paraprofessional Personnel [73]
-     Personal Therapy [91]
-     Professional Supervision [88]
- ↓ Psychologists [67]
- ↓ Social Workers [73]
- ↓ Therapists [67]

Mental Health Personnel Supply [73]
PN 82   SC 30800
- B   Personnel Supply [73]
- R ↓ Mental Health Personnel [67]

Mental Health Program Evaluation [73]
PN 815   SC 30810
SN Methodology or procedures for assessment of any mental health program in relation to previously established goals or other criteria. Also used for the formal evaluations themselves. For effectiveness of particular treatment modes, use the specific type of treatment (e.g., DRUG THERAPY). For efficacy of treatment for a particular disorder, use the specific disorder (e.g., MANIA).
- UF Program Evaluation (Mental Health)
- B   Program Evaluation [85]
- R   Behavioral Assessment [82]
- ↓ Mental Health Programs [73]
-     Psychotherapeutic Outcomes [73]
- ↓ Treatment [67]
-     Treatment Effectiveness Evaluation [73]
- ↓ Treatment Outcomes [82]

Mental Health Programs [73]
PN 1376   SC 30820
SN Plans or systems for maintenance of mental health.
- UF Programs (Mental Health)
- N ↓ Crisis Intervention Services [73]
-     Deinstitutionalization [82]
-     Home Visiting Programs [73]
-     Hot Line Services [73]
-     Suicide Prevention Centers [73]
- R   Child Guidance Clinics [73]
-     Community Mental Health [73]
-     Community Mental Health Centers [73]
-     Community Mental Health Services [78]
- ↓ Community Mental Health Training [73]
-     Community Psychiatry [73]
-     Community Psychology [73]
- ↓ Community Services [67]
- ↓ Health Care Delivery [78]
- ↓ Health Care Services [78]
- ↓ Mental Health [67]
-     Mental Health Inservice Training [73]
-     Mental Health Program Evaluation [73]
- ↓ Mental Health Services [78]
-     Partial Hospitalization [85]
-     Primary Mental Health Prevention [73]
- ↓ Program Development [91]
-     Psychiatric Clinics [73]
-     Public Health Services [73]

Mental Health Services [78]
PN 3133   SC 30825

Mental Health Services — (cont'd)
SN Services available for maintenance of mental health and treatment of mental disorders.
- B   Health Care Services [78]
- N   Community Mental Health Services [78]
- R   Child Guidance Clinics [73]
-     Community Mental Health Centers [73]
- ↓ Community Services [67]
- ↓ Counseling [67]
-     Health Care Costs [94]
- ↓ Health Care Delivery [78]
-     Health Care Policy [94]
-     Long Term Care [94]
- ↓ Mental Health [67]
- ↓ Mental Health Programs [73]
- ↓ Prevention [73]
- ↓ Psychiatric Hospital Programs [67]
-     School Counseling [82]
-     Social Casework [67]
- ↓ Social Services [82]
-     Student Personnel Services [78]
- ↓ Support Groups [91]

Mental Health Training (Community)
Use Community Mental Health Training

Mental Hospitals
Use Psychiatric Hospitals

Mental Illness
Use Mental Disorders

Mental Illness (Attitudes Toward) [67]
PN 1068   SC 30860
- B   Handicapped (Attitudes Toward) [73]
- R   Health Knowledge [94]
- ↓ Mental Disorders [67]

Mental Load
Use Human Channel Capacity

Mental Retardation [67]
PN 4691   SC 30870
SN Impaired intellectual (IQ below 70) and adaptive functioning manifested during the developmental period. Use for the concept or disorder itself, and use MENTALLY RETARDED, or a more specific term, for mentally retarded populations.
- UF Amentia
-     Mental Deficiency
-     Oligophrenia
-     Retardation (Mental)
- N   Amaurotic Familial Idiocy [73]
-     Anencephaly [73]
-     Borderline Mental Retardation [73]
-     Crying Cat Syndrome [73]
-     Downs Syndrome [67]
-     Microcephaly [73]
-     Psychosocial Mental Retardation [73]
- R   Adaptive Behavior [91]
- ↓ Brain Damage [67]
-     Developmental Disabilities [82]
-     Fetal Alcohol Syndrome [85]
-     Fragile X Syndrome [94]
-     Hydrocephaly [73]
-     Klinefelters Syndrome [73]
- ↓ Mental Disorders [67]
-     Mental Retardation (Attit Toward) [73]
- ↓ Mentally Retarded [67]
-     Phenylketonuria [73]
-     Prader Willi Syndrome [91]
-     Rett Syndrome [94]

Mental Retardation (Attit Toward) [73]
PN 500   SC 30880
- B   Handicapped (Attitudes Toward) [73]
- R ↓ Mental Retardation [67]

Mental Rotation [91]
PN 52   SC 30883
- B   Cognitive Processes [67]
- R   Mirror Image [91]
-     Spatial Ability [82]
-     Spatial Imagery [82]
-     Spatial Organization [73]
- ↓ Spatial Perception [67]

Mentally Ill Offenders [85]
PN 589   SC 30885
- UF Criminally Insane
- B   Criminals [67]
- R   Competency to Stand Trial [85]
-     Court Referrals [94]
-     Forensic Evaluation [94]
-     Insanity Defense [85]
- ↓ Mental Disorders [67]

Mentally Retarded [67]
PN 7236   SC 30890
SN Persons exhibiting impaired intellectual (IQ below 70) and adaptive functioning manifested during the developmental period. Use for populations of mentally retarded persons. Use a more specific term if possible. Use MENTAL RETARDATION for discussions of the concept or the disorder itself.
- UF Retarded (Mentally)
- B   Handicapped [67]
- N   Educable Mentally Retarded [73]
-     Home Reared Mentally Retarded [73]
-     Idiot Savants [73]
-     Institutionalized Mentally Retarded [73]
-     Profoundly Mentally Retarded [73]
-     Severely Mentally Retarded [73]
-     Trainable Mentally Retarded [73]
- R   Adaptive Behavior [91]
- ↓ Mental Retardation [67]
-     Slow Learners [73]

Mentor [85]
PN 235   SC 30895
SN An individual who befriends and facilitates the development of a less experienced individual, especially within a profession, business, trade, or academic environment.
- R   Adult Development [78]
-     Apprenticeship [73]
- ↓ Interpersonal Interaction [67]
-     Occupational Aspirations [73]
-     Occupational Guidance [67]
-     Peer Counseling [78]
-     Professional Development [82]
-     Significant Others [91]
- ↓ Social Influences [67]
-     Vocational Counselors [73]

Meperidine [73]
PN 47   SC 30900
- B   Amines [73]
-     Analgesic Drugs [73]
-     Antispasmodic Drugs [73]
-     Narcotic Drugs [73]
-     Sedatives [73]

Mephenesin [73]
PN 3   SC 30910
- B   Alcohols [67]
-     Muscle Relaxing Drugs [73]

Meprobamate [73]
PN 53   SC 30920
- B   Hypnotic Drugs [73]
-     Muscle Relaxing Drugs [73]
-     Sedatives [73]
-     Tranquilizing Drugs [67]

Mercury (Metal) [73]
PN 39   SC 30930
  B   Metallic Elements [73]

Mercury Poisoning [73]
PN 64   SC 30940
  B   Toxic Disorders [73]

Mercy Killing
  Use Euthanasia

Mescaline [73]
PN 106   SC 30950
  B   Alkaloids [73]
       Hallucinogenic Drugs [67]
       Psychotomimetic Drugs [73]
  R   Peyote [73]

Mesencephalon [73]
PN 1338   SC 30960
  UF   Midbrain
       Red Nucleus
  B   Brain [67]
  N   Inferior Colliculus [73]
       Optic Lobe [73]
       Substantia Nigra [94]
       Superior Colliculus [73]
       ↓ Tegmentum [91]

Mesoridazine [73]
PN 34   SC 30970
  B   Phenothiazine Derivatives [73]

Messages [73]
PN 822   SC 30980
SN Informational content of communications transmitted between persons or systems.
  UF   Information (Messages)
  R   ↓ Communication [67]
       Gossip [82]
       Information [67]

Meta Analysis [85]
PN 1042   SC 30985
SN Statistical analysis of a large collection of results from individual studies for the purpose of integrating findings. Also used as a document type identifier.
  B   Methodology [67]
       Statistical Analysis [67]
  R   Literature Review [67]

Metabolic Rates [73]
PN 116   SC 30990
  R   Energy Expenditure [67]
       ↓ Metabolism [67]
       ↓ Physiology [67]

Metabolism [67]
PN 1848   SC 31000
SN Biochemical changes in the cells, digestive system, and body tissues by which energy is provided, new material is incorporated, and substances, such as drugs, are disposed.
  B   Physiology [67]
  N   Anabolism [73]
       Basal Metabolism [73]
       Biosynthesis [73]
       ↓ Carbohydrate Metabolism [73]
       Catabolism [73]
       Lipid Metabolism [73]
       ↓ Metabolites [73]
       Protein Metabolism [73]
  R   Bioavailability [91]
       ↓ Dopamine Metabolites [82]
       Metabolic Rates [73]
       ↓ Metabolism Disorders [73]

Metabolism — (cont'd)
  R   ↓ Norepinephrine Metabolites [82]
       Thermoregulation (Body) [73]

Metabolism Disorders [73]
PN 258   SC 31020
  UF   Hypercholesterolemia
  B   Disorders [67]
  N   Cushings Syndrome [73]
       Cystic Fibrosis [85]
       ↓ Diabetes [73]
       ↓ Lipid Metabolism Disorders [73]
       Phenylketonuria [73]
       Porphyria [73]
  R   Hyperglycemia [85]
       Hypoglycemia [73]
       Hypothyroidism [73]
       ↓ Metabolism [67]
       ↓ Nutritional Deficiencies [73]

Metabolites [73]
PN 576   SC 31030
SN Biochemical products of metabolism.
  UF   Anabolites
       Catabolites
  B   Metabolism [67]
  N   ↓ Dopamine Metabolites [82]
       ↓ Norepinephrine Metabolites [82]
       ↓ Serotonin Metabolites [78]

Metacognition [91]
PN 235   SC 31040
SN Awareness, monitoring, and knowledge of one's own cognitive processes and activities including memory and comprehension.
  UF   Metamemory
  B   Cognitive Processes [67]
  R   ↓ Awareness [67]
       Cognition [67]
       ↓ Cognitive Ability [73]
       ↓ Comprehension [67]
       ↓ Learning [67]
       ↓ Learning Strategies [91]
       ↓ Memory [67]
       Metalinguistics [94]
       School Learning [67]

Metalinguistics [94]
PN 0   SC 31045
SN Branch of linguistics concerned with how language is used, the role of language in culture, and the use of particular linguistic forms.
  B   Linguistics [73]
  R   Ethnolinguistics [73]
       ↓ Language [67]
       ↓ Language Development [67]
       Metacognition [91]
       Pragmatics [85]
       Psycholinguistics [67]
       Sociolinguistics [85]
       Verbal Ability [67]
       ↓ Verbal Communication [67]

Metallic Elements [73]
PN 262   SC 31050
  B   Metals [91]
  N   Aluminum [94]
       Barium [73]
       ↓ Calcium [73]
       Cobalt [73]
       Copper [73]
       Iron [73]
       Lead (Metal) [73]
       ↓ Lithium [73]
       ↓ Magnesium [73]
       Mercury (Metal) [73]
       ↓ Potassium [73]
       ↓ Sodium [73]
       Zinc [85]

Metals [91]
PN 10   SC 31052
SN May include alloys.
  N   ↓ Metallic Elements [73]

Metamemory
  Use Metacognition

Metaphor [82]
PN 774   SC 31057
SN Figures of speech used to suggest an analogy between one kind of object or idea and another.
  B   Figurative Language [85]
  R   Analogy [91]
       ↓ Literature [67]
       Myths [67]
       ↓ Semantics [67]
       Symbolism [67]

Metaphysics [73]
PN 108   SC 31060
  B   Philosophies [67]
  R   Hermeneutics [91]

Metapsychology [94]
PN 0   SC 31070
  B   Psychology [67]
  R   Freudian Psychoanalytic School [73]
       Psychoanalytic Theory [67]

Methadone [73]
PN 507   SC 31080
  B   Analgesic Drugs [73]
       Narcotic Drugs [73]
  R   Methadone Maintenance [78]

Methadone Maintenance [78]
PN 715   SC 31083
SN Rehabilitation of heroin addicts by substituting methadone for heroin, enabling the addict to lead a relatively normal life. Methadone maintenance does not actually treat the addiction.
  R   ↓ Drug Addiction [67]
       ↓ Drug Rehabilitation [73]
       Heroin Addiction [73]
       Methadone [73]

Methamphetamine [73]
PN 269   SC 31090
  UF   Methedrine
  B   Amphetamine [67]
       CNS Stimulating Drugs [73]
       Vasoconstrictor Drugs [73]
  R   Methylenedioxymethamphetamine [91]

Methanol [73]
PN 21   SC 31100
  UF   Methyl Alcohol
  B   Alcohols [67]

Methaqualone [73]
PN 43   SC 31110
  B   Hypnotic Drugs [73]
       Sedatives [73]

Methedrine
  Use Methamphetamine

Methionine [73]
PN 80   SC 31130
  B   Amino Acids [73]

Methodology [67]
PN 8965   SC 31140

Methodology — (cont'd)
SN Conceptually broad array term that refers generally to strategies, techniques, or procedures used in applied, descriptive, or experimental studies. Compare EXPERIMENTAL METHODS.
UF Research Methods
N Causal Analysis [94]
　　Cohort Analysis [88]
　　Content Analysis [78]
　　Data Collection [82]
　　↓ Empirical Methods [73]
　　Meta Analysis [85]
　　Self Report [82]
R Experiment Controls [73]
　　↓ Experimental Design [67]
　　Experimental Instructions [67]
　　Experimental Laboratories [73]
　　Experimental Replication [73]
　　↓ Experimentation [67]
　　Mail Surveys [94]
　　↓ Surveys [67]
　　Telephone Surveys [94]
　　Theory Formulation [73]
　　Theory Verification [73]

Methohexital [73]
PN 31   **SC** 31150
B Barbiturates [67]
　　General Anesthetics [73]

Methoxamine [73]
PN 18   **SC** 31160
B Adrenergic Drugs [73]
　　Alcohols [67]
　　Sympathomimetic Amines [73]
　　Vasoconstrictor Drugs [73]
R ↓ Local Anesthetics [73]

Methoxyhydroxyphenylglycol (3,4) [91]
PN 32   **SC** 31165
UF MHPG
B Norepinephrine Metabolites [82]

Methyl Alcohol
Use Methanol

Methylatropine
Use Atropine

Methyldopa [73]
PN 48   **SC** 31190
B Antihypertensive Drugs [73]
R ↓ Catecholamines [73]
　　DOPA [73]
　　Dopamine [73]

Methylenedioxymethamphetamine [91]
PN 32   **SC** 31195
UF Ecstasy (Drug)
　　MDMA
R Methamphetamine [73]

Methylmorphine
Use Codeine

Methylphenidate [73]
PN 790   **SC** 31210
UF Ritalin
B Amines [73]
　　Antidepressant Drugs [71]
　　CNS Stimulating Drugs [73]
R ↓ Analeptic Drugs [73]

Methylphenyltetrahydropyridine [94]
PN 0   **SC** 31213

Methylphenyltetrahydropyridine — (cont'd)
UF MPTP
B Neurotoxins [82]
R Dopamine [73]

Methysergide
Use Serotonin Antagonists

Metrazole
Use Pentylenetetrazol

Metronomes [73]
PN 16   **SC** 31230
B Apparatus [67]

Metropolitan Readiness Tests [78]
PN 24   **SC** 31240
SN Use METROPOLITAN READING READINESS TEST to access references from 73–77.
B Reading Measures [73]

Mexican Americans [73]
PN 2101   **SC** 31250
SN Populations of Mexican descent residing permanently in the U.S.
UF Chicanos
B Hispanics [82]

Mexico [73]
PN 692   **SC** 31260
B North America [73]
R Latin America [88]

MHPG
Use Methoxyhydroxyphenylglycol (3,4)

Mianserin [82]
PN 196   **SC** 31266
SN Organic heterocyclic compound having antiserotonin properties and used as an antihistamine.
B Antidepressant Drugs [71]
　　Antihistaminic Drugs [73]
　　Serotonin Antagonists [73]

Mice [73]
PN 7519   **SC** 31270
B Rodents [73]

Microcephaly [73]
PN 36   **SC** 31280
B Brain Disorders [67]
　　Mental Retardation [67]
R ↓ Congenital Disorders [73]
　　↓ Mental Disorders [67]
　　↓ Neonatal Disorders [73]

Microcomputers [85]
PN 762   **SC** 31282
UF Personal Computers
B Computers [67]
R ↓ Computer Applications [73]

Microcounseling [78]
PN 88   **SC** 31284
SN Short-term technique for teaching basic interviewing skills using role playing, videotape analysis, and feedback in prepracticum training.
B Counseling [67]
R ↓ Clinical Methods Training [73]
　　Counselor Education [73]
　　Interviewing [73]
　　Paraprofessional Education [73]

Microorganisms [85]
PN 19   **SC** 31287

Microorganisms — (cont'd)
SN Single-celled microscopic or ultramicroscopic organisms.
UF Bacteria
　　Single Cell Organisms
N Protozoa [73]

Microscopes [73]
PN 5   **SC** 31290
B Apparatus [67]

Micturition
Use Urination

Midazolam [91]
PN 49   **SC** 31303
B Benzodiazepines [78]
　　Minor Tranquilizers [73]

Midbrain
Use Mesencephalon

Middle Aged [73]
PN 1905   **SC** 31310
SN Ages 40–59. Applied only if age is important to the research focus.
B Adults [67]
R Adult Development [78]
　　↓ Aging [91]

Middle Class [73]
PN 590   **SC** 31320
UF Bourgeois
B Social Class [67]

Middle Class Attitudes [73]
PN 41   **SC** 31330
SN Attitudes of, not toward, the middle class.
B Socioeconomic Class Attitudes [73]

Middle Ear [73]
PN 104   **SC** 31340
UF Ear Ossicles
　　Eustachian Tube
　　Tympanic Membrane
B Ear (Anatomy) [67]

Middle East [78]
PN 326   **SC** 31344
B Asia [73]
R ↓ Africa [67]
　　Cyprus [91]
　　Egypt [82]
　　Greece [73]
　　Iran [73]
　　Iraq [88]
　　Israel [67]
　　Jordan [88]
　　Kuwait [91]
　　Lebanon [88]
　　Libya [88]
　　Saudi Arabia [85]
　　Syria [88]
　　Turkey [73]
　　Yemen [91]

Middle Income Level [73]
PN 70   **SC** 31350
B Income Level [73]

Middle Level Managers [73]
PN 414   **SC** 31360
SN Second-line managers or supervisors primarily responsible for daily work flow and production in a business or industrial organization.
B Management Personnel [73]
R Top Level Managers [73]

Middle School Education [85]
PN 90   SC 31364
SN Education for grades six through eight (sometimes five through eight) using methods and materials specifically focusing on the needs and characteristics of early adolescents.
B   Education [67]

Middle School Students [85]
PN 499   SC 31367
SN Students in grades six through eight. Sometimes may include 5th graders. Use ELEMENTARY SCHOOL STUDENTS or JUNIOR HIGH SCHOOL STUDENTS, as appropriate, unless specific reference is made to the population as middle school students. Application of a student term is mandatory in educational contexts.
R ↓ Elementary School Students [67]
        Junior High School Students [71]
        Preadolescents [88]

Midwifery [85]
PN 30   SC 31368
UF   Home Birth
B   Obstetrics [78]
R ↓ Birth [67]
        Labor (Childbirth) [73]

Migraine Headache [73]
PN 667   SC 31370
B   Headache [73]
R ↓ Endocrine Disorders [73]
        Nausea [73]
     ↓ Psychosomatic Disorders [67]

Migrant Farm Workers [73]
PN 65   SC 31380
B   Agricultural Workers [73]
R   Foreign Workers [85]
     ↓ Human Migration [73]

Migration (Human)
Use Human Migration

Migratory Behavior (Animal) [73]
PN 401   SC 31400
UF   Animal Navigation
B   Animal Ethology [67]
R   Animal Homing [91]

Mildly Mentally Retarded
Use Educable Mentally Retarded

Milieu Therapy [88]
PN 83   SC 31420
SN Modification or manipulation of patient's personal life circumstances or environment through controlled and stimulatory environments. Treatment setting can be a hospital, therapeutic community or home. Use THERAPEUTIC COMMUNITY to access references from 73-87.
UF   Environmental Therapy
        Socioenvironmental Therapy
B   Treatment [67]
R   Sociotherapy [73]
        Therapeutic Community [67]

Militancy [73]
PN 47   SC 31430
B   Social Behavior [67]

Military Enlistment [73]
PN 211   SC 31440
UF   Enlistment (Military)
R   Military Recruitment [73]

Military Medical Personnel [73]
PN 100   SC 31450

Military Medical Personnel — (cont'd)
B   Medical Personnel [67]
        Military Personnel [67]
R   Medics [73]

Military Officers
Use Commissioned Officers

Military Personnel [67]
PN 1970   SC 31470
UF   Servicemen
B   Government Personnel [73]
N   Air Force Personnel [67]
        Army Personnel [67]
        Coast Guard Personnel [88]
        Commissioned Officers [73]
     ↓ Enlisted Military Personnel [73]
        Marine Personnel [73]
        Military Medical Personnel [73]
        National Guardsmen [73]
        Navy Personnel [67]
        ROTC Students [73]
        Volunteer Military Personnel [73]
R   Astronauts [73]
        Chaplains [73]
        Combat Experience [91]
        Military Veterans [73]

Military Psychology [67]
PN 377   SC 31480
B   Applied Psychology [73]

Military Recruitment [73]
PN 190   SC 31490
UF   Recruitment (Military)
B   Personnel Recruitment [73]
R   Military Enlistment [73]

Military Schools [73]
PN 133   SC 31500
B   Schools [67]
R ↓ Colleges [67]
        High Schools [73]

Military Training [73]
PN 1053   SC 31510
B   Personnel Training [67]

Military Veterans [73]
PN 1361   SC 31520
UF   Veterans (Military)
R ↓ Military Personnel [67]
     ↓ Personnel [67]

Miller Analogies Test [73]
PN 11   SC 31530
B   Intelligence Measures [67]

Millon Clinical Multiaxial Inventory [88]
PN 154   SC 31540
B   Nonprojective Personality Measures [73]

Mind [91]
PN 133   SC 31550
SN Conceptually broad term referring to the organized totality of conscious and unconscious mental processes or psychic activities of an individual.
R ↓ Cognitions [85]
     ↓ Cognitive Processes [67]
     ↓ Consciousness States [71]
        Dualism [73]
     ↓ Perception [67]
        Unconscious (Personality Factor) [67]

Mind Body
Use Dualism

Mini Mental State Examination [94]
PN 0   SC 31548
B   Neuropsychological Assessment [82]

Minimal Brain Disorders [73]
PN 376   SC 31560
B   Brain Disorders [67]
R   Attention Deficit Disorder [85]
        Hyperkinesis [73]
        Minimally Brain Damaged [73]

Minimally Brain Damaged [73]
PN 92   SC 31580
B   Brain Damaged [73]
R ↓ Learning Disabilities [73]
        Minimal Brain Disorders [73]

Minimum Competency Tests [85]
PN 79   SC 31585
UF   Basic Skills Testing
B   Educational Measurement [67]
R   Competence [82]

Ministers (Religion) [73]
PN 348   SC 31590
UF   Pastors
B   Clergy [73]
R   Chaplains [73]
        Missionaries [73]

Minks [73]
PN 24   SC 31600
B   Rodents [73]

Minn Multiphasic Personality Inven [67]
PN 3055   SC 31610
B   Nonprojective Personality Measures [73]

Minnesota Teacher Attitude Inventory [73]
PN 7   SC 31620
B   Attitude Measures [67]

Minor Tranquilizers [73]
PN 165   SC 31630
B   Tranquilizing Drugs [67]
N   Alprazolam [88]
        Buspirone [91]
        Chlordiazepoxide [73]
        Chlorprothixene [73]
        Clonazepam [91]
        Diazepam [73]
        Hydroxyzine [73]
        Lorazepam [88]
        Loxapine [82]
        Midazolam [91]
        Oxazepam [78]
R ↓ Benzodiazepines [78]
     ↓ Neurosis [67]

Minority Group Discrimination
SN Term discontinued in 1982. Use RACIAL DISCRIMINATION to access references from 73-81 and MINORITY GROUP DISCRIMINATION to access references from 78-81. Use SOCIAL DISCRIMINATION to access references from 82-93.
Use Race and Ethnic Discrimination

Minority Groups [67]
PN 1426   SC 31640
SN Includes ethnic and linguistic minority groups and in/out social groups.
B   Social Groups [73]
R   Affirmative Action [85]
        American Indians [67]
        Arabs [88]
        Asians [82]
        Blacks [82]
        Cultural Sensitivity [94]

Minority Groups — (cont'd)
R   Eskimos [73]
  ↓ Ethnic Groups [73]
    Gypsies [73]
  ↓ Hispanics [82]
    Race and Ethnic Discrimination [94]
  ↓ Social Identity [88]

Mirror Image [91]
PN 47   SC 31645
R   Human Figures Drawing [73]
    Mental Rotation [91]
  ↓ Perceptual Discrimination [73]
    Self Perception [67]
  ↓ Visual Perception [67]

Misanthropy [73]
PN 13   SC 31650
UF   Misogyny
B   Personality Traits [67]

Misbehavior
Use Behavior Problems

Miscarriage
Use Spontaneous Abortion

Miscegenous Marriage
Use Interracial Marriage

Misconduct
Use Behavior Problems

Misdemeanors
Use Crime

Misogyny
Use Misanthropy

Missionaries [73]
PN 85   SC 31720
B   Religious Personnel [73]
R ↓ Clergy [73]
  ↓ Educational Personnel [73]
    Evangelists [73]
    Lay Religious Personnel [73]
    Ministers (Religion) [73]
    Nuns [73]
    Priests [73]

Mistakes
Use Errors

Mnemonic Learning [73]
PN 635   SC 31750
SN   Use of artificial ways (e.g., imagery) to facilitate learning, memory, recognition, and recall of material learned.
B   Learning [67]
    Learning Strategies [91]
R   Cues [67]
    Memory Training [94]
    Note Taking [91]

Mobility (Geographical)
Use Geographical Mobility

Mobility (Occupational)
Use Occupational Mobility

Mobility (Social)
Use Social Mobility

Mobility Aids [78]
PN 112   SC 31774

Mobility Aids — (cont'd)
UF   Seeing Eye Dogs
    Tactual Maps
    Wheelchairs
R ↓ Medical Therapeutic Devices [73]
    Physical Mobility [94]

Modeling
Use Simulation

Modeling Behavior
Use Imitation (Learning)

Models [67]
PN 13003   SC 31805
SN   Quantitative or descriptive representations of how systems function, or criteria used for comparison purposes. Not to be used for role models.
N   Animal Models [88]
    Medical Model [78]

Moderately Mentally Retarded
Use Trainable Mentally Retarded

Modern Language Aptitude Test [73]
PN 4   SC 31820
B   Aptitude Measures [67]

Molindone [82]
PN 25   SC 31833
SN   Organic heterocyclic indole having antiserotonin properties and used as an antidepressant, sedative, and tranquilizer.
B   Antidepressant Drugs [71]
    Neuroleptic Drugs [73]
    Sedatives [73]
    Serotonin Antagonists [73]

Mollusca [73]
PN 247   SC 31840
UF   Gastropods
B   Invertebrates [73]
N   Octopus [73]
    Snails [73]

Monetary Incentives [73]
PN 385   SC 31850
SN   Money expected or promised in return for service or attainment which may encourage the continued occurrence of the activity being rewarded.
B   Incentives [67]
    Motivation [67]
R   Monetary Rewards [73]
    Needs [67]

Monetary Rewards [73]
PN 350   SC 31860
SN   Money given in return for service or attainment which may act as reinforcement for the activity being rewarded.
B   Rewards [67]
R   Monetary Incentives [73]

Money [67]
PN 901   SC 31870
R   Cost Containment [91]
  ↓ Costs and Cost Analysis [73]
    Economics [85]
    Economy [73]
    Equity (Payment) [78]
    Funding [88]
  ↓ Professional Fees [78]

Mongolism
Use Downs Syndrome

Monitoring [73]
PN 443   SC 31890
SN   Systematic observation or recording of events, processes, or individuals.
B   Attention [67]
N   Self Monitoring [82]
    Vigilance [67]
R   Selective Attention [73]
  ↓ Tracking [67]

Monkeys [67]
PN 7202   SC 31900
B   Primates (Nonhuman) [73]

Monoamine Oxidase Inhibitors [73]
PN 536   SC 31920
B   Enzyme Inhibitors [85]
N   Iproniazid [73]
    Isocarboxazid [73]
    Nialamide [73]
    Pargyline [73]
    Phenelzine [73]
    Pheniprazine [73]
    Tranylcypromine [73]
R ↓ Amine Oxidase Inhibitors [73]
  ↓ Antidepressant Drugs [71]
    Monoamine Oxidases [73]

Monoamine Oxidases [73]
PN 460   SC 31930
B   Oxidases [73]
R ↓ Monoamine Oxidase Inhibitors [73]

Monoamines (Brain)
Use Catecholamines

Monocular Vision [73]
PN 533   SC 31940
B   Visual Perception [67]

Monolingualism [73]
PN 95   SC 31950
R ↓ Language [67]

Monotony [78]
PN 45   SC 31955
SN   Quality of task or stimulation characterized by tedious or wearisome sameness and uniformity.
R   Boredom [73]

Monozygotic Twins [73]
PN 641   SC 31960
UF   Identical Twins
B   Twins [67]

Montessori Method [73]
PN 61   SC 31970
SN   Method of early childhood education developed by M. Montessori, stressing individual instruction and guidance and emphasizing practical life activities.
B   Teaching Methods [67]
R   Discovery Teaching Method [73]
    Open Classroom Method [73]

Moodiness [73]
PN 6   SC 31980
B   Personality Traits [67]

Moods
Use Emotional States

Mooney Problem Check List [73]
PN 10   SC 32000
B   Nonprojective Personality Measures [73]

Moral Development [73]
PN 2339   SC 32006
SN Process of acquiring ethical judgment.
B   Psychogenesis [73]
R   Kohlberg (Lawrence) [91]
    Morality [67]
    ↓ Personality Development [67]
    ↓ Psychosocial Development [73]

Morale [78]
PN 447   SC 32008
SN Prevailing spirit or attitude of an individual or group characterized by self confidence and motivation and sense of purpose.
R   ↓ Emotional States [73]
    ↓ Emotions [67]
    Enthusiasm [73]

Morality [67]
PN 1598   SC 32010
SN Subjective or objective standards of right or wrong, based on societal norms or ethical principles. Use MORALITY or MORALS to access references prior to 1982.
UF   Morals
R   ↓ Ethics [67]
    ↓ Justice [73]
    Moral Development [73]
    Personal Values [73]
    ↓ Religious Beliefs [73]
    Shame [94]
    Social Values [73]
    ↓ Values [67]

Morals
SN Term discontinued in 1982. Use MORALS or MORALITY to access references prior to 1982.
Use   Morality

Mores
Use   Values

Morita Therapy [94]
PN 0   SC 32035
B   Psychotherapeutic Techniques [67]

Morocco [88]
PN 17   SC 32040
B   Africa [67]

Morphemes [73]
PN 136   SC 32050
SN Minimum meaningful linguistic units that contain no smaller meaningful units.
R   Morphology (Language) [73]
    Phonetics [67]

Morphine [73]
PN 2299   SC 32060
B   Alkaloids [73]
    Analgesic Drugs [73]
    Dopamine Agonists [85]
    Opiates [73]

Morphology [73]
PN 456   SC 32070
SN Branch of biology that deals with the structure and form of plants and animals. Used for the scientific discipline or the morphological structure itself.
R   ↓ Anatomy [67]
    Histology [73]
    ↓ Physiology [67]

Morphology (Language) [73]
PN 214   SC 32080

Morphology (Language) — (cont'd)
SN Study of morphemes, including both their phonology and semantics. Used for the linguistic discipline or the specific morphological principles or characteristics of words. Compare MORPHEMES.
B   Grammar [67]
R   Morphemes [73]
    ↓ Phonology [73]
    ↓ Prosody [91]
    ↓ Semantics [67]
    ↓ Syntax [71]
    Words (Phonetic Units) [67]

Mortality
Use   Death and Dying

Mortality Rate [73]
PN 936   SC 32100
UF   Death Rate
R   ↓ Death and Dying [67]
    ↓ Population [73]

Mosaicism
Use   Chromosome Disorders

Moslems
Use   Islam

Mother Absence [73]
PN 214   SC 32120
SN From 1982, limited to human populations. For animals use ANIMAL MATERNAL DEPRIVATION.
B   Parental Absence [73]
R   Patriarchy [73]

Mother Child Communication [85]
PN 487   SC 32125
SN Verbal or nonverbal communication between mother and child.
B   Parent Child Communication [73]
R   Mother Child Relations [67]

Mother Child Relations [67]
PN 5820   SC 32130
SN From 1982, limited to human populations. For animals consider ANIMAL MATERNAL BEHAVIOR.
UF   Maternal Behavior (Human)
B   Parent Child Relations [67]
R   ↓ Childrearing Practices [67]
    Mother Child Communication [85]
    Parental Attitudes [73]
    Parental Permissiveness [73]
    Parental Role [73]
    Postpartum Depression [73]
    Schizophrenogenic Mothers [73]
    Separation Individuation [82]
    Symbiotic Infantile Psychosis [73]

Mothers [67]
PN 7838   SC 32140
SN From 1982, limited to human populations. For animals consider ANIMAL MATERNAL BEHAVIOR.
B   Human Females [73]
    Parents [67]
N   Adolescent Mothers [85]
    Schizophrenogenic Mothers [73]
    Single Mothers [94]
    Unwed Mothers [73]
R   Expectant Mothers [85]

Moths [73]
PN 82   SC 32150
B   Insects [67]
R   Larvae [73]

Motion Perception [67]
PN 2695   SC 32160
UF   Movement Perception
B   Spatial Perception [67]
N   ↓ Apparent Movement [67]

Motion Pictures [73]
PN 248   SC 32170
SN Use a more specific term if possible. Not used as a document type identifier.
B   Audiovisual Communications Media [73]
    Mass Media [67]
N   Motion Pictures (Educational) [73]
    Motion Pictures (Entertainment) [73]

Motion Pictures (Educational) [73]
PN 134   SC 32180
SN Films produced for educational purposes. Not used as a document type identifier.
B   Educational Audiovisual Aids [73]
    Motion Pictures [73]

Motion Pictures (Entertainment) [73]
PN 416   SC 32190
SN Not used as a document type identifier.
UF   Movies
B   Motion Pictures [73]
R   Drama [73]
    Photographic Art [73]

Motion Sickness [73]
PN 230   SC 32200
B   Labyrinth Disorders [73]

Motivation [67]
PN 7936   SC 32210
UF   Desires
    Drive
N   ↓ Achievement Motivation [67]
    Affiliation Motivation [67]
    Animal Motivation [67]
    Educational Incentives [73]
    Employee Motivation [73]
    Extrinsic Motivation [73]
    Fear of Success [78]
    Hunger [67]
    ↓ Incentives [67]
    Intrinsic Motivation [73]
    Monetary Incentives [73]
    Procrastination [85]
    Sex Drive [73]
    Temptation [73]
    Thirst [67]
R   Activity Level [82]
    ↓ Aspirations [67]
    ↓ Commitment [85]
    Delay of Gratification [78]
    ↓ Deprivation [67]
    Enthusiasm [73]
    ↓ Exploratory Behavior [67]
    ↓ Goals [67]
    Instinctive Behavior [82]
    Instrumentality [91]
    Intention [88]
    Motivation Training [73]
    Needs [67]
    Persistence [73]
    ↓ Reinforcement [67]
    Satiation [67]

Motivation Training [73]
PN 86   SC 32220
UF   Training (Motivation)
R   ↓ Motivation [67]

Motor Coordination [73]
PN 614   SC 32230

Motor Coordination — (cont'd)
- UF   Coordination (Motor)
- B   Motor Processes [67]
- R   ↓ Motor Performance [73]
-      Motor Skills [73]
-    ↓ Perceptual Motor Coordination [73]
-    ↓ Physical Agility [73]

Motor Cortex [73]
PN 397   SC 32240
- UF   Cortex (Motor)
- B   Frontal Lobe [73]

Motor Development [73]
PN 1171   SC 32250
- B   Physical Development [73]
- N   Perceptual Motor Development [91]
-    ↓ Psychomotor Development [73]
- R   Animal Development [78]
-    ↓ Childhood Development [67]
-    ↓ Developmental Age Groups [73]
-    ↓ Motor Processes [67]
-      Physical Mobility [94]

Motor Disorders
- Use   Nervous System Disorders

Motor Evoked Potentials
- Use   Somatosensory Evoked Potentials

Motor Neurons [73]
PN 384   SC 32290
- B   Neurons [73]
- R   ↓ Efferent Pathways [82]

Motor Pathways
- Use   Efferent Pathways

Motor Performance [73]
PN 3874   SC 32300
- B   Motor Processes [67]
-      Performance [67]
- N   Finger Tapping [73]
-      Jumping [73]
-      Running [73]
-      Walking [73]
- R   Motor Coordination [73]

Motor Processes [67]
PN 7335   SC 32310
- N   Activity Level [82]
-      Animal Locomotion [82]
-    ↓ Exercise [73]
-      Jumping [73]
-      Licking [88]
-      Motor Coordination [73]
-    ↓ Motor Performance [73]
-      Motor Skills [73]
-    ↓ Physical Agility [73]
-      Physical Mobility [94]
-      Rotational Behavior [94]
-      Sucking [78]
-      Swallowing [88]
-      Swimming [73]
-      Tonic Immobility [78]
-      Tool Use [91]
-      Wandering Behavior [91]
- R   ↓ Efferent Pathways [82]
-    ↓ Motor Development [73]
-      Muscle Tone [85]
-    ↓ Perceptual Motor Processes [67]
-      Physical Restraint [82]
-      Posture [73]

Motor Skill Learning
- Use   Perceptual Motor Learning

Motor Skills [73]
PN 816   SC 32330
- B   Motor Processes [67]
-      Nonverbal Ability [88]
- R   Motor Coordination [73]
-    ↓ Tracking [67]

Motor Traffic Accidents [73]
PN 750   SC 32340
- UF   Automobile Accidents
-      Traffic Accidents (Motor)
- B   Transportation Accidents [73]
- R   Drivers [73]
-    ↓ Driving Behavior [67]
-      Highway Safety [73]
-      Pedestrian Accidents [73]

Motor Vehicles [82]
PN 95   SC 32350
- SN   Automotive vehicles not operated on rails.
- UF   Buses
-      Motorcycles
-      Trucks
- B   Ground Transportation [73]
- N   Automobiles [73]
- R   Drivers [73]

Motorcycles
- Use   Motor Vehicles

Mourning
- Use   Grief

Mouse Killing
- Use   Muricide

Mouth (Anatomy) [67]
PN 258   SC 32370
- B   Digestive System [67]
- R   Lips (Face) [73]
-      Salivary Glands [73]
-      Teeth (Anatomy) [73]
-    ↓ Tongue [73]

Movement Disorders [85]
PN 180   SC 32375
- SN   Physically- or psychologically-based abnormalities in motor processes relating primarily to posture, coordination, or locomotion.
- UF   Dyspraxia
- B   Nervous System Disorders [67]
- N   Apraxia [73]
-      Ataxia [73]
-      Athetosis [73]
-      Catalepsy [73]
-      Cataplexy [73]
-    ↓ Chorea [73]
-    ↓ Dyskinesia [73]
-      Myasthenia Gravis [73]
-      Myoclonia [73]
-    ↓ Paralysis [73]
-    ↓ Spasms [73]
-      Tics [73]
-      Torticollis [73]
-      Tremor [73]
- R   ↓ Muscular Disorders [73]
-    ↓ Musculoskeletal Disorders [73]
-    ↓ Neuromuscular Disorders [73]
-    ↓ Symptoms [67]

Movement Perception
- Use   Motion Perception

Movies
- Use   Motion Pictures (Entertainment)

Mozambique [88]
PN 3   SC 32430
- B   Africa [67]

MPTP
- Use   Methylphenyltetrahydropyridine

MRI
- Use   Magnetic Resonance Imaging

Mucus [73]
PN 17   SC 32440
- B   Body Fluids [73]

Mueller Lyer Illusion [88]
PN 36   SC 32439
- B   Illusions (Perception) [67]

Multi Infarct Dementia [91]
PN 97   SC 32442
- UF   Dementia (Multi Infarct)
- B   Dementia [85]
- R   ↓ Cerebrovascular Disorders [73]

Multicultural Education [88]
PN 60   SC 32441
- SN   Educational program involving two or more ethnic or cultural groups designed to help participants define their own ethnic or cultural identity and to appreciate that of others. The primary purposes are to reduce prejudice and stereotyping, and to promote cultural pluralism.
- B   Education [67]
- R   Bilingual Education [78]
-    ↓ Educational Programs [73]

Multidimensional Scaling [82]
PN 412   SC 32443
- SN   Set of psychological data analysis techniques that represent perceived stimuli in multidimensional spatial or pictorial configurations.
- B   Measurement [67]
- R   ↓ Analysis [67]
-    ↓ Rating Scales [67]
-      Scaling (Testing) [67]

Multidisciplinary Research
- Use   Interdisciplinary Research

Multidisciplinary Treatment Approach
- Use   Interdisciplinary Treatment Approach

Multidrug Abuse
- Use   Polydrug Abuse

Multilingualism [73]
PN 54   SC 32450
- N   Bilingualism [73]
- R   Bilingual Education [78]
-    ↓ Language [67]

Multimodal Treatment Approach [91]
PN 103   SC 32455
- SN   Use of different therapeutic techniques based on the theoretical principles from one medical or psychological specialty or discipline. Compare INTERDISCIPLINARY TREATMENT APPROACH.
- B   Treatment [67]
- R   Eclectic Psychotherapy [94]
-      Interdisciplinary Treatment Approach [73]

Multiple Births [73]
PN 21   SC 32460
- SN   Birth of more than one child at the same time to the same parents. Also used to refer to the children themselves. Use a more specific term if possible.

Multiple Births — (cont'd)
B   Siblings [67]
N   Triplets [73]
↓ Twins [67]

Multiple Choice (Testing Method) [73]
PN 491   SC 32470
B   Testing Methods [67]

Multiple Personality [73]
PN 478   SC 32480
UF   Split Personality
B   Dissociative Patterns [73]

Multiple Regression [82]
PN 182   SC 32485
SN   Method of analyzing the collective and sepa-
rate influences of two or more independent vari-
ables on the variation of a criterion variable.
B   Multivariate Analysis [82]
Statistical Regression [85]
R   Analysis of Covariance [73]
Analysis of Variance [67]
Linear Regression [73]
Nonlinear Regression [73]
Path Analysis [91]
↓ Statistical Correlation [67]

Multiple Sclerosis [73]
PN 517   SC 32490
B   Sclerosis (Nervous System) [73]
R   ↓ Myelitis [73]

Multiple Therapy
Use Cotherapy

Multiply Handicapped [73]
PN 643   SC 32510
B   Handicapped [67]
N   Deaf Blind [91]

Multivariate Analysis [82]
PN 560   SC 32513
SN   Any statistical technique designed to mea-
sure the influence of many independent variables
acting simultaneously on more than one depend-
ent variable.
UF   Canonical Correlation
B   Statistical Analysis [67]
N   ↓ Factor Analysis [67]
Multiple Regression [82]
Path Analysis [91]
R   Analysis of Covariance [73]
Analysis of Variance [67]
↓ Statistical Correlation [67]
↓ Statistical Regression [85]

Munchausen Syndrome [94]
PN 0   SC 32517
SN   Use FACTITIOUS DISORDERS to access
references from 88-93.
B   Factitious Disorders [88]
R   Malingering [73]
↓ Psychosomatic Disorders [67]

Murder
Use Homicide

Muricide [88]
PN 31   SC 32523
UF   Mouse Killing
B   Animal Aggressive Behavior [73]

Muscarinic Drugs
Use Cholinergic Drugs

Muscimol [94]
PN 0   SC 32525
SN   Use GAMMA AMINOBUTYRIC ACID AGO-
NISTS to access references from 85-93.
UF   Pantherine
B   Gamma Aminobutyric Acid Agonists [85]
Ibotenic Acid [91]

Muscle Contraction Headache [73]
PN 329   SC 32530
UF   Tension Headache
B   Headache [73]

Muscle Contractions [73]
PN 440   SC 32540
UF   Rigidity (Muscles)
R   Muscle Relaxation [73]
Muscle Tone [85]
↓ Muscles [67]
Parkinsonism [94]
↓ Reflexes [71]

Muscle Cramps
Use Muscular Disorders

Muscle Relaxation [73]
PN 378   SC 32557
R   Muscle Contractions [73]
↓ Muscles [67]
Progressive Relaxation Therapy [78]
Relaxation [73]
↓ Relaxation Therapy [78]

Muscle Relaxation Therapy
Use Relaxation Therapy

Muscle Relaxing Drugs [73]
PN 128   SC 32560
UF   Neuromuscular Blocking Drugs
B   Drugs [67]
N   Baclofen [91]
Curare [73]
Diazepam [73]
Mephenesin [73]
Meprobamate [73]
Orphenadrine [73]
Papaverine [73]
Succinylcholine [73]
Theophylline [73]
Tubocurarine [73]
R   ↓ Anesthetic Drugs [73]
↓ Anticonvulsive Drugs [73]
↓ Antihypertensive Drugs [73]
↓ Antispasmodic Drugs [73]
↓ Benzodiazepines [78]
↓ CNS Depressant Drugs [73]
↓ Heart Rate Affecting Drugs [73]
↓ Tranquilizing Drugs [67]
Vasodilation [73]

Muscle Spasms [73]
PN 50   SC 32570
B   Spasms [73]
R   ↓ Muscles [67]

Muscle Tone [85]
PN 35   SC 32575
R   ↓ Motor Processes [67]
Muscle Contractions [73]
↓ Reflexes [71]

Muscles [67]
PN 1283   SC 32580
B   Musculoskeletal System [73]
N   Abdominal Wall [73]
Diaphragm (Anatomy) [73]
Facial Muscles [73]
Masticatory Muscles [73]

Muscles — (cont'd)
N   Oculomotor Muscles [73]
R   Muscle Contractions [73]
Muscle Relaxation [73]
Muscle Spasms [73]
↓ Tissues (Body) [73]

Muscular Atrophy [73]
PN 18   SC 32590
UF   Atrophy (Muscular)
B   Muscular Disorders [73]

Muscular Disorders [73]
PN 291   SC 32600
UF   Cramps (Muscle)
Duchennes Disease
Dystonia
Fibromyalgia Syndrome
Muscle Cramps
B   Musculoskeletal Disorders [73]
N   Cataplexy [73]
Muscular Atrophy [73]
Muscular Dystrophy [73]
Myasthenia Gravis [73]
Myoclonia [73]
Myofascial Pain [91]
Myotonia [73]
Torticollis [73]
R   ↓ Movement Disorders [85]
↓ Neuromuscular Disorders [73]

Muscular Dystrophy [73]
PN 91   SC 32610
UF   Dystrophy (Muscular)
B   Muscular Disorders [73]
Neuromuscular Disorders [73]
R   Dysarthria [73]
↓ Peripheral Nerve Disorders [73]

Musculocutaneous Nerve
Use Spinal Nerves

Musculoskeletal Disorders [73]
PN 159   SC 32630
UF   Skeletomuscular Disorders
Temporomandibular Joint Syndrome
B   Disorders [67]
N   ↓ Bone Disorders [73]
↓ Joint Disorders [73]
↓ Muscular Disorders [73]
R   Hemiplegia [78]
↓ Movement Disorders [85]
↓ Musculoskeletal System [73]
↓ Neuromuscular Disorders [73]
↓ Paralysis [73]
Paraplegia [78]
Poliomyelitis [73]
Quadriplegia [85]
↓ Tuberculosis [73]

Musculoskeletal System [73]
PN 38   SC 32640
B   Anatomical Systems [73]
N   Arm (Anatomy) [73]
Bones [73]
Feet (Anatomy) [73]
↓ Fingers (Anatomy) [73]
Hand (Anatomy) [67]
Hips [73]
Jaw [73]
↓ Joints (Anatomy) [73]
Leg (Anatomy) [73]
↓ Muscles [67]
Skull [73]
Spinal Column [73]
Tendons [73]
Thorax [73]

Musculoskeletal System — (cont'd)
R ↓ Musculoskeletal Disorders [73]
   ↓ Nose [73]

Music [67]
PN 2657   SC 32650
B   Arts [73]
N   Musical Instruments [73]
     Rock Music [91]
R   Musicians [91]
   ↓ Rhythm [91]

Music Education [73]
PN 714   SC 32660
B   Curriculum [67]

Music Therapy [73]
PN 601   SC 32670
B   Creative Arts Therapy [94]
R   Recreation Therapy [73]

Musical Ability [73]
PN 524   SC 32680
B   Artistic Ability [73]

Musical Instruments [73]
PN 120   SC 32690
UF   Piano
B   Music [67]

Musicians [91]
PN 76   SC 32695
B   Artists [73]
R ↓ Music [67]

Muslims
Use   Islam

Mutations [73]
PN 155   SC 32710
SN   Individual, strain, or species genetic variation resulting from an abrupt or unusual change in gene structure. Also, an externally induced or naturally occurring change in gene characteristics that is propagated in subsequent divisions of the cell.
R ↓ Chromosomes [73]
   ↓ Genetic Disorders [73]
   ↓ Genetics [67]
     Translocation (Chromosome) [73]

Mutilation (Self)
Use   Self Mutilation

Mutism [73]
PN 161   SC 32730
B   Language Disorders [82]
N   Elective Mutism [73]

Mutual Storytelling Technique [73]
PN 35   SC 32740
UF   Storytelling Technique
B   Psychotherapeutic Techniques [67]

Myasthenia [73]
PN 8   SC 32750
SN   Anomaly of the muscles, resulting in muscular debility, weakness, lack of tone, fatigue, or exhaustion.
B   Asthenia [73]

Myasthenia Gravis [73]
PN 36   SC 32760
B   Movement Disorders [85]
     Muscular Disorders [73]
     Neuromuscular Disorders [73]
     Peripheral Nerve Disorders [73]

Myelin Sheath [73]
PN 46   SC 32780
B   Nerve Tissues [73]

Myelitis [73]
PN 6   SC 32790
B   Central Nervous System Disorders [73]
N   Encephalomyelitis [73]
     Poliomyelitis [73]
R ↓ Infectious Disorders [73]
     Multiple Sclerosis [73]

Myelomeningocele
Use   Spina Bifida

Myenteric Plexus
Use   Autonomic Ganglia

Myers Briggs Type Indicator [73]
PN 149   SC 32810
B   Nonprojective Personality Measures [73]

Myocardial Infarctions [73]
PN 598   SC 32820
UF   Infarctions (Myocardial)
B   Heart Disorders [73]
R   Angina Pectoris [73]
     Coronary Thromboses [73]

Myocardium [73]
PN 12   SC 32830
B   Heart [67]

Myoclonia [73]
PN 105   SC 32840
B   Movement Disorders [85]
     Muscular Disorders [73]

Myofascial Pain [91]
PN 10   SC 32845
B   Muscular Disorders [73]
     Pain [67]
R ↓ Bruxism [85]
     Chronic Pain [85]
   ↓ Psychosomatic Disorders [67]
   ↓ Syndromes [73]

Myopia [73]
PN 91   SC 32850
UF   Nearsightedness
B   Refraction Errors [73]

Myotonia [73]
PN 18   SC 32860
B   Muscular Disorders [73]
R ↓ Congenital Disorders [73]

Mysticism [67]
PN 256   SC 32870
UF   Visions (Mysticism)
B   Philosophies [67]
R   Occultism [78]
   ↓ Religious Beliefs [73]
   ↓ Religious Practices [73]

Myths [67]
PN 748   SC 32890
R   Animism [73]
     Archetypes [91]
     Cultism [73]
     Ethnology [67]
     Folklore [91]
   ↓ Literature [67]
     Metaphor [82]
     Storytelling [88]
     Transcultural Psychiatry [73]

Myxedema
Use   Hypothyroidism

N-Methyl-D-Aspartate [94]
PN 0   SC 32905
UF   NMDA
B   Aspartic Acid [73]

Nabilone
Use   Cannabinoids

NAch
Use   Achievement Motivation

Nail Biting [73]
PN 59   SC 32920
B   Habits [67]

Nalorphine [73]
PN 41   SC 32940
B   Narcotic Antagonists [73]

Naloxone [78]
PN 1365   SC 32944
B   Narcotic Antagonists [73]

Naltrexone [88]
PN 227   SC 32945
B   Narcotic Antagonists [73]

Names [85]
PN 199   SC 32947
N   Brand Names [78]
R   Labeling [78]
     Nouns [73]

Naming [88]
PN 418   SC 32948
SN   Process of identifying an object or concept with a word or phrase.
B   Cognitive Processes [67]
R   Cognitive Mediation [67]

Napping [94]
PN 0   SC 32949
B   Sleep [67]
R   Sleep Onset [73]
     Sleep Wake Cycle [85]

Narcissism [67]
PN 957   SC 32950
SN   Self-love in which all sources of pleasure are unrealistically believed to emanate from within oneself, resulting in a false sense of omnipotence, and in which the libido is no longer attached to external love objects, but is redirected to one's self.
B   Personality Traits [67]
R   Egocentrism [78]
     Grandiosity [94]
   ↓ Mental Disorders [67]
     Narcissistic Personality [73]

Narcissistic Personality [73]
PN 502   SC 32960
SN   Personality disorder characterized by excessive self-love and egocentrism.
B   Personality Disorders [67]
R   Narcissism [67]

Narcoanalysis [73]
PN 18   SC 32970
SN   Sleep-like state induced by medication or hypnosis and used in the treatment of mental disorders.
B   Drug Therapy [67]
     Organic Therapies [73]

Narcoanalysis — (cont'd)
N   Sleep Treatment [73]
R ↓ Narcoanalytic Drugs [73]

Narcoanalytic Drugs [73]
PN 5   SC 32980
B   Drugs [67]
N   Amobarbital [73]
     Thiopental [73]
R ↓ Narcoanalysis [73]

Narcolepsy [73]
PN 210   SC 32990
B   Sleep Disorders [73]
R   Cataplexy [73]
     Hypersomnia [94]

Narcosis [73]
PN 61   SC 33000
B   Toxic Disorders [73]
R ↓ Narcotic Drugs [73]

Narcotic Agonists [88]
PN 218   SC 32995
UF Opiate Agonists
B   Drugs [67]
N   Pentazocine [91]
R ↓ Narcotic Drugs [73]

Narcotic Antagonists [73]
PN 575   SC 33010
UF Opiate Antagonists
B   Drugs [67]
N   Nalorphine [73]
     Naloxone [78]
     Naltrexone [88]
R ↓ Narcotic Drugs [73]

Narcotic Drugs [73]
PN 392   SC 33020
B   Drugs [67]
N   Apomorphine [73]
     Atropine [73]
     Meperidine [73]
     Methadone [73]
   ↓ Opiates [73]
R ↓ Analgesic Drugs [73]
   ↓ Anesthetic Drugs [73]
   ↓ Anticonvulsive Drugs [73]
   ↓ Cannabis [73]
   ↓ CNS Depressant Drugs [73]
   ↓ Dopamine Antagonists [82]
   ↓ Emetic Drugs [73]
   ↓ Hypnotic Drugs [73]
     Narcosis [73]
   ↓ Narcotic Agonists [88]
   ↓ Narcotic Antagonists [73]
   ↓ Tranquilizing Drugs [67]

Nasal Mucosa [73]
PN 28   SC 33030
B   Membranes [73]
     Nose [73]
N   Olfactory Mucosa [73]

National Guardsmen [73]
PN 29   SC 33040
B   Military Personnel [67]
R   Air Force Personnel [67]
     Army Personnel [67]
     Volunteer Military Personnel [73]
   ↓ Volunteer Personnel [73]

Nationalism [67]
PN 108   SC 33050
B   Political Attitudes [73]

Native Americans
Use American Indians

Natural Childbirth [78]
PN 34   SC 33056
UF Childbirth (Natural)
B   Birth [67]
R   Childbirth Training [78]

Natural Disasters [73]
PN 303   SC 33060
SN Calamity caused by natural forces resulting in substantial damage, loss, and distress.
B   Disasters [73]
R   Emergency Services [73]
   ↓ Stress [67]

Natural Family
Use Biological Family

Nature Nurture [94]
PN 0   SC 33075
SN Debatable issue concerning the controversial role of genetics or heredity versus environment or experience in normal or abnormal developmental processes.
R   Behavioral Genetics [94]
   ↓ Environment [67]
   ↓ Genetics [67]
   ↓ Human Development [67]
     Predisposition [73]
   ↓ Psychogenesis [73]

Nausea [73]
PN 149   SC 33080
B   Symptoms [67]
R ↓ Antiemetic Drugs [73]
   ↓ Appetite Disorders [73]
     Migraine Headache [73]
     Vomiting [73]

Navigators (Aircraft)
Use Aerospace Personnel

Navy Personnel [67]
PN 839   SC 33100
B   Military Personnel [67]
R   Draftees [73]

Nazism
Use Fascism

Near Death Experiences [85]
PN 146   SC 33105
SN Psychological and sensory phenomena reported by persons who were near clinical death.
B   Parapsychological Phenomena [73]
R ↓ Death and Dying [67]
   ↓ Experiences (Events) [73]
   ↓ Hallucinations [67]
     Out of Body Experiences [88]

Nearsightedness
Use Myopia

Neck (Anatomy) [73]
PN 81   SC 33120
B   Anatomy [67]

Need Achievement
Use Achievement Motivation

Need for Affiliation
Use Affiliation Motivation

Need Satisfaction [73]
PN 493   SC 33170

Need Satisfaction — (cont'd)
B   Satisfaction [73]
R   Needs [67]

Needle Sharing [94]
PN 0   SC 33175
R ↓ Drug Abuse [73]
   ↓ Drug Usage [71]
     Intravenous Drug Usage [94]
     Intravenous Injections [73]
     Sharing (Social Behavior) [78]

Needs [67]
PN 2730   SC 33180
R ↓ Achievement Motivation [67]
     Affiliation Motivation [67]
     Extrinsic Motivation [73]
   ↓ Goals [67]
   ↓ Incentives [67]
     Intrinsic Motivation [73]
     Monetary Incentives [73]
   ↓ Motivation [67]
     Need Satisfaction [73]
     Needs Assessment [85]
     Nurturance [85]
     Special Needs [94]

Needs Assessment [85]
PN 633   SC 33185
SN Systematic identification of needs of an individual or a group.
B   Evaluation [67]
     Measurement [67]
R ↓ Case Management [91]
   ↓ Health Care Delivery [78]
     Intake Interview [94]
     Needs [67]
     Special Needs [94]
   ↓ Surveys [67]

Negative Reinforcement [73]
PN 301   SC 33200
SN A stimulus or stimulus situation that, when withdrawn or discontinued following a response, increases the probability of occurrence of that response. Consider also ESCAPE CONDITIONING.
B   Reinforcement [67]

Negative Transfer [73]
PN 178   SC 33210
SN Previous learning or practice that hinders the acquisition of new material or skills as the result of dissimilar characteristics of the prior and current learning situation.
B   Transfer (Learning) [67]

Negativism [73]
PN 124   SC 33220
SN State of mind or behavior characterized by extreme skepticism and persistent opposition or resistance to outside suggestions or advice.
B   Personality Traits [67]
R   Cynicism [73]
     Pessimism [73]

Negotiation [73]
PN 598   SC 33230
B   Interpersonal Communication [73]
N   Bargaining [73]
R ↓ Conflict Resolution [82]
     Mediation [88]

Negroes
SN Term discontinued in 1982. Use NEGROES to access references from 67–81.
Use Blacks

Neighborhoods [73]
PN 441   SC 33260
B   Communities [67]

Nembutal
Use   Pentobarbital

NeoFreudian School
Use   Neopsychoanalytic School

Neologisms [73]
PN 22   SC 33290
B   Vocabulary [67]
R   Words (Phonetic Units) [67]

Neonatal Development [73]
PN 444   SC 33320
SN   Process of physical, cognitive, personality, and psychosocial growth occurring during the first month of life. Use a more specific term if possible.
B   Infant Development [73]
R   ↓ Physical Development [73]
    ↓ Psychogenesis [73]

Neonatal Disorders [73]
PN 84   SC 33330
B   Disorders [67]
N   Amaurotic Familial Idiocy [73]
    Anencephaly [73]
    Cleft Palate [67]
    Crying Cat Syndrome [73]
    Downs Syndrome [67]
    Klinefelters Syndrome [73]
    Phenylketonuria [73]
    Turners Syndrome [73]
R   ↓ Apnea [73]
    Birth Injuries [73]
    ↓ Congenital Disorders [73]
    Hydrocephaly [73]
    Microcephaly [73]
    Rh Incompatibility [73]
    Sleep Apnea [91]

Neonates [67]
PN 2559   SC 33360
SN   Ages 0 through 1 month. Application of terms designating age is mandatory for ages 0–17 years.
UF   Newborn Infants
B   Infants [67]
R   Birth Weight [85]
    Childhood [84]

Neonates (Animal)
Use   Infants (Animal)

Neonaticide
Use   Infanticide

Neophobia [85]
PN 78   SC 33368
SN   Fearful or cautious exploration or reaction to novel objects, situations, or stimuli. Usually examined in subhuman species.
R   Animal Exploratory Behavior [73]
    Avoidance [67]
    ↓ Fear [67]
    Instinctive Behavior [82]
    Stimulus Novelty [73]

Neoplasms [67]
PN 2650   SC 33370
UF   Cancers
    Carcinomas
    Malignant Neoplasms
    Sarcomas
    Tumors

Neoplasms — (cont'd)
B   Disorders [67]
N   Benign Neoplasms [73]
    Breast Neoplasms [73]
    Endocrine Neoplasms [73]
    Leukemias [73]
    ↓ Nervous System Neoplasms [73]
    Terminal Cancer [73]
R   Antineoplastic Drugs [82]
    ↓ Digestive System Disorders [73]
    ↓ Gastrointestinal Disorders [73]
    ↓ Liver Disorders [73]

Neopsychoanalytic School [73]
PN 28   SC 33380
SN   School of psychoanalysis originating with Jung and Adler which differs from Freudian orthodoxy in emphasizing the importance of social and cultural factors in development of an individual's personality.
UF   NeoFreudian School
B   History of Psychology [67]
N   Individual Psychology [73]
    Jungian Psychology [73]
R   Erikson (Erik) [91]
    Freud (Sigmund) [67]

Neostigmine [73]
PN 34   SC 33390
UF   Proserine
B   Cholinesterase Inhibitors [73]
    Cholinomimetic Drugs [73]
R   ↓ Bromides [73]

Nepal [91]
PN 19   SC 33395
B   Asia [73]

Nerve (Abducens)
Use   Abducens Nerve

Nerve (Accessory)
Use   Cranial Nerves

Nerve (Acoustic)
Use   Acoustic Nerve

Nerve (Facial)
Use   Facial Nerve

Nerve Cells
Use   Neurons

Nerve Endings [73]
PN 27   SC 33450
B   Nervous System [67]
N   ↓ Neural Receptors [73]
    Proprioceptors [73]
    Synapses [73]
    Thermoreceptors [73]

Nerve Growth Factor [94]
PN 0   SC 33455
SN   Polypeptide proteins that stimulate growth and development of peripheral, sympathetic, and sensory neurons.
B   Peptides [73]
R   ↓ Amino Acids [73]
    ↓ Nervous System [67]
    Neural Development [85]
    ↓ Neurons [73]

Nerve Tissues [73]
PN 60   SC 33460
B   Nervous System [67]
    Tissues (Body) [73]

Nerve Tissues — (cont'd)
N   Myelin Sheath [73]
R   ↓ Neurons [73]

Nerves (Adrenergic)
Use   Adrenergic Nerves

Nerves (Cholinergic)
Use   Cholinergic Nerves

Nerves (Cranial)
Use   Cranial Nerves

Nerves (Peripheral)
Use   Peripheral Nervous System

Nerves (Spinal)
Use   Spinal Nerves

Nervous Breakdown
Use   Mental Disorders

Nervous System [67]
PN 486   SC 33530
B   Anatomical Systems [73]
N   ↓ Central Nervous System [67]
    ↓ Ganglia [73]
    ↓ Nerve Endings [73]
    ↓ Nerve Tissues [73]
    ↓ Neurons [73]
    ↓ Peripheral Nervous System [73]
    ↓ Receptive Fields [85]
R   Afferent Stimulation [73]
    Instinctive Behavior [82]
    Nerve Growth Factor [94]
    ↓ Nervous System Disorders [67]
    Neural Development [85]
    Neural Networks [91]
    Neural Plasticity [94]
    ↓ Stereotaxic Techniques [73]

Nervous System Disorders [67]
PN 3366   SC 33540
UF   Motor Disorders
    Neuroinfections
    Neurological Disorders
    Neuropathy
B   Disorders [67]
N   Autonomic Nervous System Disorders [73]
    ↓ Central Nervous System Disorders [73]
    ↓ Convulsions [67]
    Hyperkinesis [73]
    ↓ Movement Disorders [85]
    ↓ Nervous System Neoplasms [73]
    ↓ Neuromuscular Disorders [73]
    ↓ Peripheral Nerve Disorders [73]
    ↓ Sclerosis (Nervous System) [73]
R   ↓ Cerebrovascular Disorders [73]
    Developmental Disabilities [82]
    Extrapyramidal Symptoms [94]
    Hemianopia [73]
    Influenza [73]
    Malaria [73]
    ↓ Nervous System [67]
    Nystagmus [73]
    Parkinsonism [94]
    ↓ Symptoms [67]
    ↓ Tuberculosis [73]

Nervous System Neoplasms [73]
PN 11   SC 33550
B   Neoplasms [67]
    Nervous System Disorders [67]
N   Brain Neoplasms [73]

Nervous System Plasticity
Use   Neural Plasticity

Nervousness [73]
PN 45   SC 33560
  B   Personality Traits [67]

Nest Building [73]
PN 403   SC 33570
  B   Animal Ethology [67]
  R ↓ Animal Mating Behavior [67]

Netherlands [73]
PN 743   SC 33580
  B   Europe [73]

Netherlands Antilles [88]
PN 2   SC 33590
  B   West Indies [73]

Networks (Social)
  Use Social Networks

Neural Analyzers [73]
PN 19   SC 33600
SN The peripheral sensory receptors or nerve endings (e.g., visual analyzer, acoustic analyzer) that select and transform stimuli and their associated projections and terminations in the central nervous system where synthesis of the transformations occurs.
  B   Central Nervous System [67]

Neural Development [85]
PN 682   SC 33605
SN Functional and morphological development of central and peripheral nervous systems and supportive tissue.
  UF Neural Regeneration
        Reinnervation
  B   Physical Development [73]
  R   Animal Development [78]
        Nerve Growth Factor [94]
      ↓ Nervous System [67]
        Neural Plasticity [94]
        Neural Transplantation [85]

Neural Lesions [73]
PN 598   SC 33610
SN Not defined prior to 1982. From 1982, limited to experimentally induced neural lesions and used primarily for animal populations.
  B   Lesions [67]

Neural Networks [91]
PN 458   SC 33612
SN Computer simulation that duplicates the neural structure and cognitive processes of the human or animal brain.
  B   Artificial Intelligence [82]
        Computer Simulation [73]
  R   Connectionism [94]
      ↓ Nervous System [67]
        Neuroanatomy [67]

Neural Pathways [82]
PN 548   SC 33615
SN Collections of central or peripheral neural fibers having a common neurological function and serving to connect neuroanatomical systems such as sensory or motor mechanisms or central nervous system nuclei.
  B   Central Nervous System [67]
        Peripheral Nervous System [73]
  N ↓ Afferent Pathways [82]
        Corpus Callosum [73]
      ↓ Efferent Pathways [82]
        Fornix [82]
      ↓ Limbic System [73]
        Optic Chiasm [73]
        Optic Tract [82]
        Reticular Formation [67]

Neural Plasticity [94]
PN 0   SC 33617
SN Change in reactivity of the nervous system and its components as a result of constant successive activations.
  UF Nervous System Plasticity
  R ↓ Nervous System [67]
        Neural Development [85]
        Postactivation Potentials [85]
      ↓ Receptive Fields [85]

Neural Receptors [73]
PN 2133   SC 33620
  UF Receptors (Neural)
  B   Nerve Endings [73]
  N   Baroreceptors [73]
        Chemoreceptors [73]
        Mechanoreceptors [73]
        Nociceptors [85]
      ↓ Photoreceptors [73]
        Proprioceptors [73]
        Thermoreceptors [73]
  R   Receptor Binding [85]

Neural Regeneration
  Use Neural Development

Neural Transplantation [85]
PN 152   SC 33628
  R   Neural Development [85]
        Organ Transplantation [73]
        Tissue Donation [91]

Neuralgia [73]
PN 22   SC 33630
  B   Pain [67]
        Peripheral Nerve Disorders [73]
  N   Trigeminal Neuralgia [73]

Neurasthenic Neurosis [73]
PN 81   SC 33640
  B   Neurosis [67]
  R ↓ Asthenia [73]
        Asthenic Personality [73]

Neuroanatomy [67]
PN 1607   SC 33660
SN Branch of neurology concerned with the anatomy of the nervous system. Used for the scientific discipline or the anatomical structures themselves.
  B   Neurosciences [73]
  R ↓ Anatomy [67]
        Neural Networks [91]

Neurobiology [73]
PN 372   SC 33670
SN Biology of the nervous system. Used for the scientific discipline or the neurobiological processes themselves.
  B   Biology [67]
        Neurosciences [73]
  R   Biological Psychiatry [94]

Neurochemistry [73]
PN 5595   SC 33680
SN Chemical makeup and metabolism of nervous tissue. Used for the scientific discipline or the neurochemical processes themselves.
  UF Brain Metabolism
  B   Biochemistry [67]
        Neurosciences [73]
  N   Neuroendocrinology [85]
        Receptor Binding [85]
  R   Blood Brain Barrier [94]
        Glucose Metabolism [94]

Neurodermatitis [73]
PN 22   SC 33690
  B   Dermatitis [73]
        Psychosomatic Disorders [67]
  R   Allergic Skin Disorders [73]

Neuroendocrinology [85]
PN 417   SC 33695
SN Study of the biological, chemical, and physical relations between the nervous system and endocrine glands. Used for the scientific discipline or neuroendocrinological processes themselves.
  B   Endocrinology [73]
        Neurochemistry [73]
        Neurophysiology [73]

Neuroinfections
  Use Infectious Disorders AND Nervous System Disorders

Neuroleptic Drugs [73]
PN 3156   SC 33710
SN Use NEUROLEPTIC DRUGS, ANTIPSYCHOTIC DRUGS, ANTISCHIZOPHRENIC DRUGS, or the specific tranquilizing drugs, neuroleptic drugs, or other appropriate drug classes to access references from 73–81.
  UF Antipsychotic Drugs
        Antischizophrenic Drugs
        Major Tranquilizers
  B   Tranquilizing Drugs [67]
  N   Clozapine [91]
        Molindone [82]
        Nialamide [73]
        Reserpine [67]
        Spiroperidol [91]
        Sulpiride [73]
        Tetrabenazine [73]
  R   Neuroleptic Malignant Syndrome [88]
        Prostaglandins [82]
        Tardive Dyskinesia [88]

Neuroleptic Malignant Syndrome [88]
PN 194   SC 33715
  B   Syndromes [73]
        Toxic Disorders [73]
  R ↓ Drug Therapy [67]
      ↓ Neuroleptic Drugs [73]
      ↓ Side Effects (Drug) [73]

Neurolinguistic Programing [88]
PN 55   SC 33718
SN R. Bandler's model of techniques and strategies for interpersonal communication based on elements of transformational grammar and preferred sensory representations for learning and self expression. Also, self intervention method in humanistic psychology aimed at personal growth and human potential.
  R ↓ Cognitive Style [67]
      ↓ Humanistic Psychology [85]
      ↓ Interpersonal Communication [73]
        Neurolinguistics [91]
        Perceptual Style [73]

Neurolinguistics [91]
PN 15   SC 33719
SN Study of the neurological mechanisms involved in the development, acquisition, and use of language. Used for the scientific discipline or the neurolinguistic processes themselves.
  B   Linguistics [73]
  R ↓ Language [67]
      ↓ Language Disorders [82]
        Neurolinguistic Programing [88]
        Psycholinguistics [67]
      ↓ Verbal Communication [67]

Neurological Disorders
Use Nervous System Disorders

Neurologists [73]
PN 40   SC 33730
UF Neuropathologists
B Physicians [67]
R Surgeons [73]

Neurology [67]
PN 4791   SC 33740
SN Scientific discipline dealing with the anatomy, physiology, and organic diseases of the nervous system. Used for the scientific discipline or the neurological findings themselves.
B Medical Sciences [67]
     Neurosciences [73]
R Neuropathology [73]

Neuromuscular Blocking Drugs
Use Muscle Relaxing Drugs

Neuromuscular Disorders [73]
PN 130   SC 33760
B Nervous System Disorders [67]
N Cataplexy [73]
     Gilles de la Tourette Disorder [73]
     Muscular Dystrophy [73]
     Myasthenia Gravis [73]
     ↓ Paralysis [73]
     Parkinsons Disease [73]
R ↓ Dyskinesia [73]
     Hyperkinesis [73]
     ↓ Movement Disorders [85]
     ↓ Muscular Disorders [73]
     ↓ Musculoskeletal Disorders [73]
     ↓ Sclerosis (Nervous System) [73]
     Spinal Cord Injuries [73]

Neurons [73]
PN 2063   SC 33770
UF Nerve Cells
B Cells (Biology) [73]
     Nervous System [67]
N Axons [73]
     Dendrites [73]
     Ganglion Cells (Retina) [85]
     Motor Neurons [73]
     Purkinje Cells [94]
     ↓ Sensory Neurons [73]
R Nerve Growth Factor [94]
     ↓ Nerve Tissues [73]
     Visual Receptive Fields [82]

Neuropathologists
Use Neurologists

Neuropathology [73]
PN 938   SC 33790
SN Branch of medicine dealing with morphological and other aspects of nervous system disorders. Used for the scientific discipline or the neuropathological findings themselves.
B Neurosciences [73]
     Pathology [73]
R Neurology [67]

Neuropathy
Use Nervous System Disorders

Neuropeptides
Use Peptides

Neurophysiology [73]
PN 2560   SC 33810
SN Physiology of the nervous system. Used for the scientific discipline or the neurophysiological processes themselves.

Neurophysiology — (cont'd)
B Neurosciences [73]
     Physiology [67]
N Neuroendocrinology [85]
     Receptor Binding [85]

Neuropsychiatrists
Use Psychiatrists

Neuropsychiatry [73]
PN 334   SC 33830
SN Medical specialty that combines psychiatry and neurology. Used for the scientific discipline or the neuropsychiatric findings themselves.
B Neurosciences [73]
     Psychiatry [67]
R Biological Psychiatry [94]

Neuropsychological Assessment [82]
PN 2040   SC 33835
SN Use of tests, including intelligence, motor, and lateralization measures, to diagnose brain damage or other neurological dysfunction.
B Measurement [67]
N Halstead Reitan Neuropsych Battery [91]
     Luria Nebraska Neuropsych Battery [91]
     Mini Mental State Examination [94]
     Wechsler Memory Scale [88]
     Wisconsin Card Sorting Test [94]
R Bender Gestalt Test [67]
     Benton Revised Visual Retention Test [73]
     ↓ Brain Damage [67]
     ↓ Diagnosis [67]
     Memory for Designs Test [73]
     ↓ Testing [67]

Neuropsychology [73]
PN 2343   SC 33840
SN Branch of clinical psychology emphasizing the relationship between brain and behavior, including the diagnosis of brain pathology using psychological tests. Used for the discipline or the neuropsychological functions themselves.
B Neurosciences [73]
     Physiological Psychology [67]
R Psychoneuroimmunology [91]

Neurosciences [73]
PN 127   SC 33850
SN Scientific disciplines concerned with the development, structure, function, chemistry, and pathology of the nervous system.
B Sciences [67]
N Neuroanatomy [67]
     Neurobiology [73]
     ↓ Neurochemistry [73]
     Neurology [67]
     Neuropathology [73]
     ↓ Neurophysiology [73]
     Neuropsychiatry [73]
     Neuropsychology [73]
R ↓ Medical Sciences [67]

Neurosis [67]
PN 4096   SC 33860
UF Psychoneurosis
B Mental Disorders [67]
N ↓ Affective Disturbances [67]
     ↓ Anxiety Neurosis [73]
     Childhood Neurosis [73]
     Dissociative Neurosis [73]
     Experimental Neurosis [73]
     Neurasthenic Neurosis [73]
     Neurotic Depressive Reaction [73]
     Occupational Neurosis [73]
     ↓ Psychosomatic Disorders [67]
     Traumatic Neurosis [73]
R Anhedonia [85]

Neurosis — (cont'd)
R Borderline States [78]
     ↓ Minor Tranquilizers [73]

Neurosurgeons
Use Surgeons

Neurosurgery [73]
PN 371   SC 33890
B Surgery [71]
N Commissurotomy [85]
     Decerebration [73]
     Decortication (Brain) [73]
     Hemispherectomy [73]
     ↓ Psychosurgery [73]
     Pyramidotomy [73]
     Sympathectomy [73]
     Tractotomy [73]
     Vagotomy [73]

Neurosyphilis [73]
PN 25   SC 33900
B Central Nervous System Disorders [73]
     Syphilis [73]
R General Paresis [73]

Neurotensin [85]
PN 87   SC 33905
B Neurotransmitters [85]
     Peptides [73]

Neurotic Depressive Reaction [73]
PN 303   SC 33910
SN Major depressive episode including some interference in social and occupational functioning.
UF Depressive Reaction (Neurotic)
B Major Depression [88]
     Neurosis [67]
R Reactive Depression [73]

Neuroticism [73]
PN 1259   SC 33915
B Personality Traits [67]

Neurotoxins [82]
PN 640   SC 33920
SN Bacterial, chemical, or pharmacological substances that are destructive to nerve tissue.
B Poisons [73]
N ↓ Ibotenic Acid [91]
     Methylphenyltetrahydropyridine [94]
R Antibodies [73]
     Drug Interactions [82]
     ↓ Insecticides [73]
     Kainic Acid [88]
     ↓ Toxic Disorders [73]
     Toxicity [73]

Neurotransmitters [85]
PN 369   SC 33924
SN Chemical substances, synthesized and released by nerve cells, or glandular hormones that excite or inhibit other nerve, muscle, or gland cells. Use a more specific term if possible.
N Acetylcholine [73]
     ↓ Aspartic Acid [73]
     ↓ Catecholamines [73]
     Cholecystokinin [82]
     ↓ Endorphins [82]
     Gamma Aminobutyric Acid [78]
     Glutamic Acid [73]
     Glycine [73]
     Histamine [73]
     Neurotensin [85]
     Serotonin [73]
     Substance P [85]
R ↓ Amino Acids [73]
     ↓ Peptides [73]

Never Married [94]
PN 0   SC 33926
  B   Marital Status [73]
  R ↓ Single Parents [78]
       Single Persons [73]
       Unwed Mothers [73]

New Guinea
  SN Term discontinued in 1982. Use NEW GUIN-
  EA to access references from 73–81.
  Use Papua New Guinea

New Zealand [73]
PN 547   SC 33930
  R ↓ South Pacific [78]

Newborn Infants
  Use Neonates

Newsletters (Professional)
  Use Scientific Communication

Newspapers [73]
PN 277   SC 33960
  B   Printed Communications Media [73]

Niacin
  Use Nicotinic Acid

Niacinamide
  Use Nicotinamide

Nialamide [73]
PN 39   SC 33990
  B   Amine Oxidase Inhibitors [73]
       Antidepressant Drugs [71]
       Monoamine Oxidase Inhibitors [73]
       Neuroleptic Drugs [73]

Nicaragua [88]
PN 13   SC 33995
  B   Central America [73]

Nicotinamide [73]
PN 25   SC 34000
  UF   Niacinamide
       Nicotinic Acid Amide
  B   Vitamins [73]
  R   Nicotinic Acid [73]
       Pellagra [73]

Nicotine [73]
PN 957   SC 34010
  UF   Tobacco (Drug)
  B   Alkaloids [73]
       Cholinergic Blocking Drugs [73]
       Ganglion Blocking Drugs [73]
  R ↓ Insecticides [73]
       Smokeless Tobacco [94]
       Tobacco Smoking [67]

Nicotinic Acid [73]
PN 55   SC 34020
  UF   Niacin
  B   Acids [73]
       Vasodilator Drugs [73]
       Vitamins [73]
  R   Nicotinamide [73]

Nicotinic Acid Amide
  Use Nicotinamide

Nictitating Membrane [73]
PN 249   SC 34040

Nictitating Membrane — (cont'd)
  SN Fold of transparent or semitransparent mucous membrane present in many vertebrates that
  can be drawn over the eye like a third eyelid.
  This membrane cleans and moistens the cornea
  without occluding light.
  B   Membranes [73]

Niger [91]
PN 3   SC 34043
  B   Africa [67]

Nigeria [82]
PN 607   SC 34045
  B   Africa [67]

Night Terrors
  Use Sleep Disorders

Nightmares [73]
PN 191   SC 34050
  B   Dreaming [67]
  R   Dream Content [73]

Nihilism [73]
PN 9   SC 34060
  B   Philosophies [67]

Nitrazepam [78]
PN 48   SC 34066
  B   Anticonvulsive Drugs [73]
       Benzodiazepines [78]
       Hypnotic Drugs [73]
       Sedatives [73]

Nitrogen [73]
PN 59   SC 34070
  B   Nonmetallic Elements [73]

NMDA
  Use N-Methyl-D-Aspartate

Nociception
  Use Pain Perception

Nociceptors [85]
PN 61   SC 34080
  UF   Pain Receptors
  B   Neural Receptors [73]
       Sensory Neurons [73]

Nocturnal Behavior (Animal)
  Use Animal Nocturnal Behavior

Nocturnal Emission [73]
PN 6   SC 34100
  B   Male Orgasm [73]

Nocturnal Teeth Grinding [73]
PN 40   SC 34110
  SN Use NOCTURNAL TEETH GRINDING to ac-
  cess references to BRUXISM from 73–84.
  B   Bruxism [85]
  R ↓ Sleep [67]

Noise (Sound)
  Use Auditory Stimulation

Noise Effects [73]
PN 1157   SC 34150
  SN Behavioral, physiological, or psychological
  effects of environmental or experimentally ma-
  nipulated noise on an organism.
  B   Environmental Effects [73]
  R   Pollution [73]

Noise Levels (Work Areas) [73]
PN 222   SC 34160
  B   Loudness [67]
       Working Conditions [73]

Nomenclature (Psychological)
  Use Psychological Terminology

Nomifensine [82]
PN 118   SC 34175
  SN Organic heterocyclic compound used as an
  antiparkinson agent and antidepressive agent.
  B   Antidepressant Drugs [71]
       Antitremor Drugs [73]

Non Zero Sum Games [73]
PN 31   SC 34180
  SN Quantitative games in which all players may
  win points as opposed to zero sum games in
  which points won by one player must be lost by
  another or others.
  B   Games [67]
  R   Entrapment Games [73]
       Game Theory [67]
       Prisoners Dilemma Game [73]

Noncommissioned Officers [73]
PN 35   SC 34200
  SN Subordinate military officers (e.g., sergeants)
  appointed from enlisted personnel.
  UF   Officers (Noncommissioned)
  B   Enlisted Military Personnel [73]

Nonconformity (Personality) [73]
PN 53   SC 34210
  B   Personality Traits [67]
  R   Conformity (Personality) [67]
       Individuality [73]

Noncontingent Reinforcement [88]
PN 21   SC 34215
  SN Presentation of reinforcement (punishment
  or positive rewards) independently of behavior.
  B   Reinforcement [67]
  R   Autoshaping [78]
     ↓ Contingency Management [73]

Nondirected Discussion Method [73]
PN 13   SC 34220
  SN Teaching method which encourages stu-
  dents' spontaneity and restricts the leader's role
  to that of a moderator.
  B   Teaching Methods [67]
  R   Discovery Teaching Method [73]

Nondirective Therapy
  Use Client Centered Therapy

Nongraded Schools [73]
PN 11   SC 34250
  SN Schools that group students according to
  such characteristics as academic achievement,
  mental and physical ability, or emotional development, rather than by age or grade level.
  B   Schools [67]

Nonlinear Regression [73]
PN 45   SC 34260
  B   Statistical Correlation [67]
       Statistical Regression [85]
  R   Multiple Regression [82]

Nonmetallic Elements [73]
PN 4   SC 34270
  B   Chemical Elements [73]
  N   Carbon [73]
       Chloride Ions [73]
       Helium [73]

Nonmetallic Elements — (cont'd)
- N   Hydrogen [73]
-     Nitrogen [73]
-     Oxygen [73]
-     Phosphorus [73]

Nonparametric Statistical Tests [67]
PN 255   SC 34280
- B   Statistical Tests [73]
- N   Chi Square Test [73]
-     Cochran Q Test [73]
-     Kolmogorov Smirnov Test [73]
-     Mann Whitney U Test [73]
-     Sign Test [73]
-     Wilcoxon Sign Rank Test [73]

Nonprescription Drugs [91]
PN 20   SC 34285
SN Drugs or medication sold legally without prescription.
- UF   Over The Counter Drugs
- B   Drugs [67]
- R   Prescription Drugs [91]
-     Self Medication [91]

Nonprofessional Personnel [82]
PN 86   SC 34290
SN Conceptually broad array term. Use a more specific term if possible. Use PARAPROFESSIONAL PERSONNEL to access references from 73–81.
- B   Personnel [67]
- N   ↓ Agricultural Workers [73]
- R   ↓ Business and Industrial Personnel [67]
-     Child Care Workers [78]
-     Domestic Service Personnel [73]
-     ↓ Paraprofessional Personnel [73]
-     ↓ Professional Personnel [78]
-     ↓ Service Personnel [91]
-     Technical Service Personnel [73]

Nonprofit Organizations [73]
PN 87   SC 34300
- B   Organizations [67]

Nonprojective Personality Measures [73]
PN 1109   SC 34304
SN Direct assessment of personality traits through scoring of a subject's responses to questions on structured, standardized tests. Use a more specific term if possible.
- B   Personality Measures [67]
- N   Authoritarianism Rebellion Scale [73]
-     Bannister Repertory Grid [73]
-     Barrett Lennard Relationship Invent [73]
-     Barron Welsh Art Scale [73]
-     Beck Depression Inventory [88]
-     Bem Sex Role Inventory [88]
-     California F Scale [73]
-     California Test of Personality [73]
-     Child Behavior Checklist [94]
-     Childrens Manifest Anxiety Scale [73]
-     Childrens Personality Questionnaire [73]
-     Differential Personality Inventory [73]
-     Edwards Personal Preference Schedule [67]
-     Edwards Personality Inventory [73]
-     Edwards Social Desirability Scale [73]
-     Embedded Figures Testing [67]
-     Eysenck Personality Inventory [73]
-     Fear Survey Schedule [73]
-     Fund Interper Rela Orientat Beh Ques [73]
-     Goldstein Scheerer Object Sort Test [73]
-     Gough Adjective Check List [73]
-     Guilford Zimmerman Temperament Surv [73]
-     High Sch Personality Questionnaire [73]
-     Kupfer Detre Self Rating Scale [73]
-     Learys Interpersonal Check List [73]

Nonprojective Personality Measures — (cont'd)
- N   Marlowe Crowne Soc Desirabil Scale [73]
-     Maudsley Personality Inventory [73]
-     Memory for Designs Test [73]
-     Millon Clinical Multiaxial Inventory [88]
-     Minn Multiphasic Personality Inven [67]
-     Mooney Problem Check List [73]
-     Myers Briggs Type Indicator [73]
-     Omnibus Personality Inventory [73]
-     Personal Orientation Inventory [73]
-     Psychological Screening Inventory [73]
-     Repression Sensitization Scale [73]
-     Rod and Frame Test [73]
-     Rokeach Dogmatism Scale [73]
-     Rotter Intern Extern Locus Cont Scal [73]
-     Sixteen Personality Factors Question [73]
-     State Trait Anxiety Inventory [73]
-     Taylor Manifest Anxiety Scale [73]
-     Tennessee Self Concept Scale [73]
-     Vineland Social Maturity Scale [73]
-     Welsh Figure Preference Test [73]
-     White Betz A B Scale [73]
-     Zungs Self Rating Depression Scale [73]

Nonrapid Eye Movement Sleep
   Use NREM Sleep

NonREM Sleep
   Use NREM Sleep

Nonreversal Shift Learning [73]
PN 37   SC 34330
SN Experimental technique used for the demonstration of mediating processes in concept formation that assesses the ability to shift dimensions in stimulus discrimination tasks, as, for example, from size to color.
- UF   Extradimensional Shift Learning
- B   Discrimination Learning [82]

Nonsense Syllable Learning [67]
PN 152   SC 34340
SN Verbal learning paradigm in which collections or lists of letters, which have no obvious meaning (e.g., XAB, GZL), are used as stimulus items. Also, the actual acquisition, retention, and retrieval of such stimulus items.
- B   Verbal Learning [67]

Nonstandard English [73]
PN 235   SC 34350
- B   Dialect [73]
- R   Slang [73]

Nontraditional Careers [85]
PN 244   SC 34352
SN Occupations in which certain groups (usually males or females) have traditionally been underrepresented.
- B   Occupations [67]
- R   Occupational Choice [67]
-     Sex Roles [67]

Nontraditional Education [82]
PN 265   SC 34355
SN Alternative educational programs within or without the formal educational system that provide flexible and innovative teaching, curriculum, grading, or degree requirements.
- UF   Alternative Schools
-     Magnet Schools
-     Open Universities
- B   Education [67]
- N   Home Schooling [94]
- R   ↓ Curriculum [67]
-     ↓ Educational Programs [73]
-     ↓ Teaching Methods [67]

Nonverbal Ability [88]
PN 109   SC 34357
SN Ability in nonlanguage areas such as spatial relations, mathematics, or music.
- B   Ability [67]
- N   ↓ Artistic Ability [73]
-     Mathematical Ability [73]
-     Mechanical Aptitude [73]
-     Motor Skills [73]
-     Spatial Ability [82]
- R   Academic Aptitude [73]
-     ↓ Nonverbal Communication [71]

Nonverbal Communication [71]
PN 2494   SC 34360
- B   Communication [67]
- N   Body Language [73]
-     Eye Contact [73]
-     ↓ Facial Expressions [67]
-     Gestures [73]
-     ↓ Manual Communication [78]
- R   Laughter [78]
-     ↓ Nonverbal Ability [88]

Nonverbal Learning [73]
PN 109   SC 34370
SN Acquisition, retention, and retrieval of knowledge or skills that do not involve verbally presented information or language, such as perceptual responses or motor activities.
- B   Learning [67]

Nonverbal Meaning [73]
PN 43   SC 34380
- B   Meaning [67]

Nonverbal Reinforcement [73]
PN 30   SC 34390
- B   Social Reinforcement [67]

Nonviolence [91]
PN 3   SC 34393
- B   Social Interaction [67]
- R   Pacifism [73]
-     ↓ Political Attitudes [73]
-     ↓ Violence [73]

Nootropic Drugs [91]
PN 74   SC 34395
- UF   Cognition Enhancing Drugs
-     Memory Enhancing Drugs
- B   Drugs [67]
- N   Piracetam [82]

Noradrenaline
   Use Norepinephrine

Norepinephrine [73]
PN 2153   SC 34410
- UF   Noradrenaline
- B   Adrenal Medulla Hormones [73]
-     Catecholamines [73]
-     Vasoconstrictor Drugs [73]
- R   Cardiotonic Drugs [85]
-     Guanethidine [73]
-     ↓ Norepinephrine Metabolites [82]

Norepinephrine Metabolites [82]
PN 278   SC 34413
SN Molecules generated from the metabolism of norepinephrine.
- B   Metabolites [73]
- N   Methoxyhydroxyphenylglycol (3,4) [91]
- R   ↓ Metabolism [67]
-     Norepinephrine [73]

Normal Distribution [73]
PN 97   SC 34420

Normal Distribution — (cont'd)
B   Frequency Distribution [73]
R   Statistical Sample Parameters [73]

Normalization (Test)
Use   Test Standardization

Norms (Social)
Use   Social Norms

Norms (Statistical)
Use   Statistical Norms

Norms (Test)
Use   Test Norms

North America [73]
PN   114   SC   34460
N   Canada [71]
    Mexico [73]
    ↓ United States [67]

North Korea [82]
PN   9   SC   34465
SN   Use KOREA to access references from 73–81.
B   Korea [73]

North Vietnam
SN   Term discontinued in 1982. Use NORTH VIETNAM to access references from 73–81.
Use   Vietnam

Northern Ireland [73]
PN   127   SC   34480
B   Ireland [73]
R   ↓ Great Britain [71]

Nortriptyline [94]
PN   0   SC   34485
SN   Use ANTIDEPRESSANT DRUGS to access references from 78-93.
B   Antidepressant Drugs [71]

Norway [73]
PN   377   SC   34490
B   Scandinavia [78]

Norway Rats [73]
PN   106   SC   34500
B   Rats [67]

Nose [73]
PN   44   SC   34510
B   Respiratory System [73]
N   ↓ Nasal Mucosa [73]
R   ↓ Musculoskeletal System [73]

Note Taking [91]
PN   26   SC   34515
R   Homework [88]
    ↓ Learning Strategies [91]
    ↓ Memory [67]
    Mnemonic Learning [73]
    ↓ Strategies [67]
    Study Habits [73]
    ↓ Written Communication [85]

Nouns [73]
PN   432   SC   34520
B   Form Classes (Language) [73]
R   ↓ Names [85]

Novel Stimuli
Use   Stimulus Novelty

Novelty Seeking
Use   Sensation Seeking

Novocaine
SN   Term discontinued in 1982. Use NOVOCAINE to access references from 73–81.
Use   Procaine

NREM Sleep [73]
PN   469   SC   34550
UF   Nonrapid Eye Movement Sleep
    NonREM Sleep
    Slow Wave Sleep
B   Sleep [67]

Nuclear Family [73]
PN   126   SC   34560
B   Family [67]
    Family Structure [73]

Nuclear Technology [85]
PN   235   SC   34565
B   Technology [73]

Nuclear War [85]
PN   411   SC   34567
B   War [67]

Nucleic Acids [73]
PN   55   SC   34570
B   Acids [73]
N   Adenosine [73]
    Deoxyribonucleic Acid [73]
    ↓ Nucleotides [78]
    Ribonucleic Acid [73]
R   ↓ Genetics [67]
    Guanosine [85]

Nucleotides [78]
PN   76   SC   34573
B   Nucleic Acids [73]
N   Cyclic Adenosine Monophosphate [78]

Nucleus Accumbens [82]
PN   511   SC   34574
SN   One of the largest nuclei in the septal region lying anteriorly and medially to the junction of the caudate nucleus and putamen and laterally to the septal nuclei.
R   Caudate Nucleus [73]
    ↓ Limbic System [73]
    Septal Nuclei [82]

Nucleus Basalis Magnocellularis [94]
PN   0   SC   57425
B   Forebrain [85]
R   ↓ Basal Ganglia [73]

Nudity [73]
PN   30   SC   34575
R   Obscenity [78]
    ↓ Physical Appearance [82]
    Pornography [73]

Null Hypothesis Testing [73]
PN   94   SC   34580
SN   Application of statistical tests to determine whether a null hypothesis should be accepted or rejected. Limited to discussions of statistical procedures.
B   Hypothesis Testing [73]

Number Comprehension [73]
PN   222   SC   34590
SN   Knowledge or understanding of the meaning, significance, and relationships symbolized by numerals.
B   Comprehension [67]

Number Systems [73]
PN   29   SC   34600
B   Mathematics (Concepts) [67]
    Systems [67]
R   Numbers (Numerals) [67]

Numbers (Numerals) [67]
PN   756   SC   34610
SN   Symbol of a member of an abstract mathematical system which is subject to rules of succession, addition, and multiplication.
UF   Digits (Mathematics)
B   Mathematics (Concepts) [67]
    Written Language [67]
R   Number Systems [73]
    Numerosity Perception [67]

Numerical Ability
Use   Mathematical Ability

Numerosity Perception [67]
PN   260   SC   34630
SN   Perception of quantities in stimulus sets in visual, auditory, or other perceptual modes.
B   Perception [67]
R   Numbers (Numerals) [67]

Nuns [73]
PN   93   SC   34640
B   Religious Personnel [73]
R   Missionaries [73]

Nurse Patient Interaction
Use   Therapeutic Processes

Nursery School Students [73]
PN   336   SC   34650
SN   Students attending a nursery school, usually ages 2, 3, and 4. Mandatory term in educational contexts.
B   Preschool Students [82]
R   ↓ Children [67]
    Preschool Age Children [67]

Nursery Schools [73]
PN   95   SC   34660
B   Schools [67]

Nurses [67]
PN   3282   SC   34670
B   Medical Personnel [67]
N   Psychiatric Nurses [73]
    Public Health Service Nurses [73]
    School Nurses [73]

Nursing [73]
PN   1270   SC   34680
B   Paramedical Sciences [73]

Nursing Education [73]
PN   806   SC   34690
B   Education [67]
R   ↓ Medical Education [73]

Nursing Homes [73]
PN   1504   SC   34700
SN   Establishments where maintenance and personal or nursing care are provided for persons (as the aged or chronically ill) who are unable to care for themselves.
B   Residential Care Institutions [73]
    Treatment Facilities [73]
R   ↓ Hospitals [67]
    Long Term Care [94]
    Psychiatric Units [91]
    Sanatoriums [73]

Nursing Students [73]
PN 1090   SC 34710
B   College Students [67]

Nurturance [85]
PN 110   SC 34714
SN Need, tendency, or process of providing care and support to others. For animal populations, use ANIMAL MATERNAL BEHAVIOR or ANIMAL PARENTAL BEHAVIOR.
B   Personality Traits [67]
      Social Behavior [67]
R   Needs [67]
      ↓ Parent Child Relations [67]

Nutrition [73]
PN 925   SC 34720
R   Beverages (Nonalcoholic) [78]
      Diets [78]
      Food [78]
      Food Additives [78]
      ↓ Nutritional Deficiencies [73]
      ↓ Physiology [67]

Nutritional Deficiencies [73]
PN 682   SC 34730
UF   Malnutrition
B   Disorders [67]
N   ↓ Protein Deficiency Disorders [73]
      Starvation [73]
      ↓ Vitamin Deficiency Disorders [73]
R   ↓ Alcoholic Psychosis [73]
      ↓ Alcoholism [67]
      Anorexia Nervosa [73]
      ↓ Appetite Disorders [73]
      Diets [78]
      Failure to Thrive [88]
      Food Deprivation [67]
      ↓ Metabolism Disorders [73]
      Nutrition [73]
      ↓ Underweight [73]

Nymphomania
Use Hypersexuality

Nystagmus [73]
PN 452   SC 34760
SN Eye movement reflex stabilizing the retinal image of a visual stimulus to compensate for head or stimulus movement. Also, eye movement defects resulting from neurological, muscular, or genetic disorders.
UF   Optokinetic Nystagmus
      Vestibular Nystagmus
B   Eye Disorders [73]
      Eye Movements [67]
      Reflexes [71]
R   ↓ Nervous System Disorders [67]

Obedience [73]
PN 191   SC 34770
SN Limited to human populations.
UF   Submissiveness
B   Personality Traits [67]
R   Coercion [94]

Obesity [73]
PN 2540   SC 34780
UF   Overweight
B   Appetite Disorders [73]
      Body Weight [67]
      Symptoms [67]
R   Diets [78]
      Hyperphagia [73]
      ↓ Psychosomatic Disorders [67]

Obituary [67]
PN 162   SC 34785

Obituary — (cont'd)
SN Mandatory term used as a document type identifier.

Object Permanence [85]
PN 108   SC 34788
SN Knowledge of the continued existence of an object even when it is not directly perceived.
R   ↓ Cognitive Development [73]
      Conservation (Concept) [73]
      ↓ Developmental Stages [73]
      ↓ Perceptual Constancy [85]

Object Relations [82]
PN 1390   SC 34786
SN Psychoanalytic description of emotional attachments formed between one person and another, as opposed to interest and love for oneself; individual's mode of relation to the outside world.
R   Anaclitic Depression [73]
      Attachment Behavior [85]
      ↓ Childhood Development [67]
      Emotional Development [73]
      Psychoanalytic Theory [67]
      ↓ Psychosocial Development [73]
      Separation Individuation [82]
      Transitional Objects [85]

Objective Referenced Tests
Use Criterion Referenced Tests

Objectives
Use Goals

Objectives (Organizational)
Use Organizational Objectives

Objectivity [73]
PN 317   SC 34810
B   Personality Traits [67]
R   Subjectivity [94]

Oblique Rotation [71]
PN 51   SC 34820
B   Statistical Rotation [73]

Obscenity [78]
PN 59   SC 34826
R   Nudity [73]
      Pornography [73]
      Profanity [91]

Observation Methods [67]
PN 1951   SC 34830
SN In research, any techniques used in the intentional examination of persons or processes in natural or manipulated settings for the purpose of obtaining facts or reporting conclusions.
B   Empirical Methods [73]
R   Interrater Reliability [82]
      Self Monitoring [82]

Observational Learning [73]
PN 606   SC 34840
SN Learning by observation of others by human or animal subjects or learning by visualization of behavior without actually performing an act and experiencing its consequences.
B   Learning [67]
      Learning Strategies [91]
R   Imitation (Learning) [67]
      ↓ Social Learning [73]

Observers [73]
PN 413   SC 34850

Observers — (cont'd)
SN Individuals who examine, record, or rate specified events, behaviors, or processes in experimental, social, or therapeutic situations.
R   Audiences [67]

Obsessions [67]
PN 434   SC 34860
B   Thought Disturbances [73]
R   ↓ Compulsions [73]
      Obsessive Compulsive Neurosis [73]
      Obsessive Compulsive Personality [73]

Obsessive Compulsive Disorder
Use Obsessive Compulsive Neurosis

Obsessive Compulsive Neurosis [73]
PN 1379   SC 34870
SN Disorder characterized by recurrent obsessions or compulsions that may interfere with the individual's daily functioning or serve as a source of distress.
UF   Compulsive Neurosis
      Obsessive Compulsive Disorder
      Obsessive Neurosis
B   Anxiety Neurosis [73]
R   ↓ Compulsions [73]
      Obsessions [67]
      Obsessive Compulsive Personality [73]

Obsessive Compulsive Personality [73]
PN 168   SC 34880
SN Personality disorder characterized by perfectionism, indecisiveness, excessive devotion to work, inability to express warm emotions, and insistence that things be done in accord with one's own preferences.
UF   Compulsive Personality Disorder
B   Personality Disorders [67]
R   ↓ Compulsions [73]
      Obsessions [67]
      Obsessive Compulsive Neurosis [73]

Obsessive Neurosis
Use Obsessive Compulsive Neurosis

Obstetrical Complications [78]
PN 310   SC 34895
R   ↓ Birth [67]
      Birth Injuries [73]
      Labor (Childbirth) [73]
      ↓ Obstetrics [78]
      Postsurgical Complications [73]
      ↓ Pregnancy [67]
      Premature Birth [73]

Obstetricians [78]
PN 28   SC 34900
B   Physicians [67]
R   Gynecologists [73]
      Surgeons [73]

Obstetrics [78]
PN 106   SC 34910
SN Use OBSTETRICS GYNECOLOGY to access references from 73–77.
B   Medical Sciences [67]
N   Midwifery [85]
R   Childbirth Training [78]
      Gynecology [78]
      Obstetrical Complications [78]
      ↓ Prenatal Care [91]

Obturator Nerve
Use Spinal Nerves

Occipital Lobe [73]
PN 283   SC 34930

Occipital Lobe — (cont'd)
B   Cerebral Cortex [67]
N   Visual Cortex [67]

Occultism [78]
PN 75   SC 34935
R   Cultism [73]
     Mysticism [67]
     ↓ Parapsychology [67]
     ↓ Religious Beliefs [73]

Occupation (Parental)
Use Parental Occupation

Occupational Adjustment [73]
PN 865   SC 34950
SN Personal adaptation to one's vocation.
UF   Vocational Adjustment
B   Adjustment [67]
R   Adjustment Disorders [94]
     Career Change [78]
     Occupational Neurosis [73]
     ↓ Occupations [67]
     School to Work Transition [94]
     Work Adjustment Training [91]

Occupational Aspirations [73]
PN 1609   SC 34960
UF   Career Aspirations
     Career Goals
     Vocational Aspirations
B   Aspirations [67]
R   Career Change [78]
     Mentor [85]
     ↓ Occupations [67]
     Professional Development [82]

Occupational Attitudes [73]
PN 1495   SC 34970
SN Attitudes toward specific occupations or careers.
B   Attitudes [67]
R   Job Applicant Attitudes [73]
     ↓ Occupations [67]
     Vocational Maturity [78]
     Work (Attitudes Toward) [73]

Occupational Choice [67]
PN 2896   SC 34980
UF   Career Choice
     Job Selection
     Vocational Choice
R   Career Change [78]
     Career Development [85]
     Nontraditional Careers [85]
     Occupational Preference [73]
     ↓ Occupations [67]
     Professional Specialization [91]
     Reemployment [91]
     Vocational Maturity [78]

Occupational Exposure [88]
PN 176   SC 34985
SN Exposure to conditions, substances, or apparatus in the workplace that may be harmful to health.
R   ↓ Hazardous Materials [91]
     Industrial Accidents [73]
     Occupational Safety [73]
     ↓ Occupations [67]
     Work Related Illnesses [94]
     ↓ Working Conditions [73]

Occupational Guidance [67]
PN 3274   SC 34990

Occupational Guidance — (cont'd)
SN Assistance in career selection or development; assessment of interests, abilities, or aptitude; compilation of occupational and economic information; and referral to placement services.
UF   Career Counseling
     Career Guidance
     Guidance (Occupational)
     Vocational Counseling
     Vocational Guidance
B   Counseling [67]
R   Assessment Centers [82]
     Career Education [78]
     Educational Counseling [67]
     Mentor [85]
     Occupational Success Prediction [73]
     ↓ Occupations [67]
     Student Personnel Services [78]
     Vocational Counselors [73]

Occupational Interest Measures [73]
PN 534   SC 35000
B   Measurement [67]
N   Kuder Occupational Interest Survey [73]
     Strong Vocational Interest Blank [67]

Occupational Interests [67]
PN 1412   SC 35010
UF   Vocational Interests
B   Interests [67]
R   ↓ Occupations [67]
     Vocational Maturity [78]

Occupational Mobility [73]
PN 408   SC 35020
SN The capacity or actual tendency toward upward progression in occupational status or occupational attainment.
UF   Job Mobility
     Mobility (Occupational)
     Vocational Mobility
R   Career Change [78]
     Employment History [78]
     ↓ Occupational Tenure [73]
     ↓ Occupations [67]

Occupational Neurosis [73]
PN 16   SC 35030
SN Neurotic disorder developed as a consequence of occupational stress, inappropriate occupational choice, overwork, job dissatisfaction, or other job-related stress.
B   Neurosis [67]
R   Occupational Adjustment [73]
     Occupational Stress [73]

Occupational Preference [73]
PN 839   SC 35040
UF   Career Preference
     Vocational Preference
B   Preferences [67]
R   Occupational Choice [67]
     ↓ Occupations [67]
     Professional Specialization [91]
     Vocational Maturity [78]

Occupational Safety [73]
PN 349   SC 35050
UF   Industrial Safety
B   Safety [67]
     Working Conditions [73]
R   Industrial Accidents [73]
     Occupational Exposure [88]
     ↓ Occupations [67]
     Work Related Illnesses [94]

Occupational Status [78]
PN 1207   SC 35056

Occupational Status — (cont'd)
SN Occupational rank or position achieved by employee, usually based on abilities or competence. Also, social prestige attributed to specific occupations.
UF   Job Status
     Prestige (Occupational)
B   Status [67]
R   Job Experience Level [73]
     ↓ Occupational Tenure [73]
     ↓ Occupations [67]
     Personnel Promotion [78]

Occupational Stress [73]
PN 3777   SC 35060
UF   Burnout
B   Stress [67]
R   Occupational Neurosis [73]
     ↓ Occupations [67]
     Quality of Work Life [88]
     Work Related Illnesses [94]

Occupational Success [78]
PN 627   SC 35067
B   Achievement [67]
R   Employment History [78]
     Occupational Success Prediction [73]
     ↓ Occupations [67]
     Personnel Promotion [78]

Occupational Success Prediction [73]
PN 604   SC 35070
B   Personnel Evaluation [73]
     Prediction [67]
R   Occupational Guidance [67]
     Occupational Success [78]

Occupational Tenure [73]
PN 281   SC 35080
UF   Tenure (Occupational)
N   Teacher Tenure [73]
R   Employee Turnover [73]
     Employment History [78]
     ↓ Employment Status [82]
     Job Security [78]
     Occupational Mobility [73]
     Occupational Status [78]
     ↓ Occupations [67]
     Personnel Termination [73]

Occupational Therapists [73]
PN 305   SC 35090
B   Therapists [67]
R   ↓ Mental Health Personnel [67]
     ↓ Paraprofessional Personnel [73]
     ↓ Psychiatric Hospital Staff [73]

Occupational Therapy [67]
PN 1224   SC 35100
SN Method of treatment for physical or mental disorders that involves engagement of patients in useful or creative activities or work as a means of improving functional skills in the areas of work, daily living, or vocational activities.
B   Rehabilitation [67]
R   Physical Therapy [73]

Occupations [67]
PN 3342   SC 35110
SN Conceptually broad array term referring to work specialties as defined by duties and required skills. Use OCCUPATIONS to access references on employment status from 67N81. Use a more specific term if possible.
UF   Careers
     Jobs
     Vocations
N   Nontraditional Careers [85]
R   Career Change [78]

Occupations — (cont'd)
R   Career Development [85]
  ↓ Division of Labor [88]
    Employment History [78]
  ↓ Job Characteristics [85]
    Occupational Adjustment [73]
    Occupational Aspirations [73]
    Occupational Attitudes [73]
    Occupational Choice [67]
    Occupational Exposure [88]
    Occupational Guidance [67]
    Occupational Interests [67]
    Occupational Mobility [73]
    Occupational Preference [73]
    Occupational Safety [73]
    Occupational Status [78]
    Occupational Stress [73]
    Occupational Success [78]
  ↓ Occupational Tenure [73]
  ↓ Personnel [67]
  ↓ Professional Personnel [78]
  ↓ Vocational Education [73]
    Vocational Maturity [78]
    Working Women [78]

Octopus [73]
PN 31   SC 35120
B   Mollusca [73]

Ocular Accommodation [82]
PN 168   SC 35127
SN Process of focusing an image on the retina by means of a flattening or bulging of the lens.
UF Focusing (Visual)
B   Reflexes [71]
R ↓ Depth Perception [67]
    Lens (Eye) [73]
  ↓ Refraction Errors [73]

Ocular Dominance [73]
PN 204   SC 35130
UF Eye Dominance
B   Lateral Dominance [67]
R ↓ Brain [67]
  ↓ Eye (Anatomy) [67]
  ↓ Eye Disorders [73]
    Interocular Transfer [85]
    Left Brain [91]
    Right Brain [91]

Ocular Fixation
Use Eye Fixation

Oculomotor Muscles [73]
PN 85   SC 35140
B   Muscles [67]

Oculomotor Nerve
Use Cranial Nerves

Oculomotor Response
Use Eye Movements

Odor Aversion Conditioning
Use Aversion Conditioning

Odor Discrimination [73]
PN 527   SC 35170
B   Olfactory Perception [67]
    Perceptual Discrimination [73]
R   Olfactory Thresholds [73]

Oedipal Complex [73]
PN 534   SC 35180
B   Psychoanalytic Personality Factors [73]

Offenders (Adult)
Use Criminals

Offenders (Juvenile)
Use Juvenile Delinquents

Office Environment
Use Working Conditions

Officers (Commissioned)
Use Commissioned Officers

Officers (Noncommissioned)
Use Noncommissioned Officers

Offspring [88]
PN 610   SC 35230
SN Used specifically for children, regardless of age, whose parents had significant experiences or conditions, e.g., alcoholism, fame, or political persecution. Not used as an age identifier.
N   Adult Offspring [85]
    Daughters [73]
    Interracial Offspring [88]
    Sons [73]
R ↓ Family Members [73]

Old Age
Use Aged

Olfactory Bulb [73]
PN 447   SC 35247
B   Limbic System [73]

Olfactory Evoked Potentials [73]
PN 36   SC 35250
B   Evoked Potentials [67]
R ↓ Cortical Evoked Potentials [73]

Olfactory Mucosa [73]
PN 45   SC 35260
B   Nasal Mucosa [73]
R   Chemoreceptors [73]

Olfactory Nerve [73]
PN 94   SC 35270
B   Cranial Nerves [73]

Olfactory Perception [67]
PN 1468   SC 35280
UF Smell Perception
B   Perception [67]
N   Odor Discrimination [73]
    Olfactory Thresholds [73]
R   Anosmia [73]
    Taste Perception [67]
    Vomeronasal Sense [82]

Olfactory Stimulation [78]
PN 575   SC 35285
B   Perceptual Stimulation [73]

Olfactory Thresholds [73]
PN 95   SC 35290
B   Olfactory Perception [67]
    Thresholds [67]
R   Odor Discrimination [73]
  ↓ Perceptual Measures [73]

Oligophrenia
Use Mental Retardation

Oligophrenia (Phenylpyruvic)
Use Phenylketonuria

Omission Training [85]
PN 8   SC 35315
SN Removal of positive reinforcement upon occurrence of undesirable behavior. Has applications in both therapeutic and experimental contexts.
B   Behavior Modification [73]
    Operant Conditioning [67]
R   Differential Reinforcement [73]
    Time Out [85]

Omnibus Personality Inventory [73]
PN 11   SC 35320
B   Nonprojective Personality Measures [73]

Omnipotence [94]
PN 0   SC 35325
B   Personality Traits [67]
R   Authority [67]
    Grandiosity [94]
    Magical Thinking [73]
    Power [67]

On the Job Training [73]
PN 137   SC 35330
B   Personnel Training [67]
R   Inservice Teacher Education [73]
  ↓ Inservice Training [85]

Online Databases
Use Databases

Online Searching
Use Computer Searching

Only Children [82]
PN 51   SC 35335
SN Children having no siblings.
B   Children [67]
R ↓ Family Members [73]
  ↓ Family Structure [73]

Onomatopoeia and Images Test [73]
PN 7   SC 35340
B   Projective Personality Measures [73]

Onset (Disorders) [73]
PN 1328   SC 35350
SN Beginning or first appearance of a mental or physical disorder.
R ↓ Disorders [67]
  ↓ Mental Disorders [67]
    Premorbidity [78]

Ontogeny
Use Development

Open Classroom Method [73]
PN 357   SC 35370
SN Approach to teaching and learning emphasizing the student's right to make decisions and viewing the teacher as a facilitator of learning rather than a transmitter of knowledge. May include grouping of students across grades, independent study, individualized rates of progression, open-plan schools without interior walls, or unstructured time and curricula.
B   Teaching Methods [67]
R   Discovery Teaching Method [73]
    Individualized Instruction [73]
    Montessori Method [73]
    Team Teaching Method [73]

Open Field Behavior (Animal)
Use Animal Open Field Behavior

Open Universities
Use Nontraditional Education

Openmindedness [78]
PN 115   SC 35376
   UF   Closedmindedness
   B   Personality Traits [67]
   R   Authoritarianism [67]
       Dogmatism [78]

Operant Conditioning [67]
PN 5781   SC 35380
SN   Learned behavior or the experimental paradigm in which reinforcers (positive or negative) or
punishers immediately and contingently follow the
performance of some behavior, the frequency of
which changes as a direct consequence of such
contingent reinforcement.
   UF   Conditioning (Operant)
       Instrumental Conditioning
       Instrumental Learning
   B   Conditioning [67]
   N   Avoidance Conditioning [67]
       Conditioned Emotional Responses [67]
     ↓ Conditioned Responses [67]
       Delayed Alternation [94]
     ↓ Discrimination Learning [82]
       Escape Conditioning [73]
       Fading (Conditioning) [82]
       Omission Training [85]
       Time Out [85]
   R   ↓ Adjunctive Behavior [82]
     ↓ Behavior Modification [73]
       Conditioned Stimulus [73]
       Polydipsia [82]
     ↓ Reinforcement [67]
     ↓ Self Stimulation [67]
       Skinner (Burrhus Frederic) [91]
       Unconditioned Stimulus [73]

Operation (Surgery)
   Use   Surgery

Ophidiophobia [73]
PN 240   SC 35400
SN   Fear of snakes.
   UF   Snake Phobia
   B   Phobias [67]

Ophthalmologic Examination [73]
PN 52   SC 35410
   UF   Eye Examination
   B   Medical Diagnosis [73]
   N   Electro Oculography [73]
       Electroretinography [67]

Ophthalmology [73]
PN 27   SC 35420
   B   Medical Sciences [67]
   R   Optometry [73]

Opiate Agonists
   Use   Narcotic Agonists

Opiate Antagonists
   Use   Narcotic Antagonists

Opiates [73]
PN 1307   SC 35430
   UF   Opioids
       Opium Alkaloids
       Opium Derivatives
   B   Narcotic Drugs [73]
   N   Codeine [73]
     ↓ Endogenous Opiates [85]
       Fentanyl [85]
       Heroin [73]
       Morphine [73]
       Papaverine [73]

Opinion (Public)
   Use   Public Opinion

Opinion Attitude and Interest Survey [73]
PN 4   SC 35450
   B   Attitude Measures [67]

Opinion Change
   Use   Attitude Change

Opinion Questionnaires
   Use   Attitude Measures

Opinion Surveys
   Use   Attitude Measures

Opinions
   Use   Attitudes

Opioids
   Use   Opiates

Opioids (Endogenous)
   Use   Endogenous Opiates

Opium Alkaloids
   Use   Alkaloids AND Opiates

Opium Derivatives
   Use   Opiates

Opossums [73]
PN 53   SC 35530
   B   Marsupials [73]

Optic Chiasm [73]
PN 56   SC 35540
   B   Diencephalon [73]
       Neural Pathways [82]
   R   Optic Nerve [73]

Optic Lobe [73]
PN 98   SC 35550
   B   Mesencephalon [73]

Optic Nerve [73]
PN 179   SC 35560
   B   Cranial Nerves [73]
   R   Optic Chiasm [73]

Optic Tract [82]
PN 62   SC 35563
SN   Portion of the optic pathway that extends
posteriorly from the optic chiasm in two nerve
fiber bundles to synapse near the superior col-
liculi and in the lateral geniculate body of the
thalamus.
   B   Neural Pathways [82]

Optical Aids [73]
PN 106   SC 35565
   B   Medical Therapeutic Devices [73]
   N   Contact Lenses [73]

Optical Illusions
   Use   Illusions (Perception)

Optimism [73]
PN 246   SC 35580
SN   Attitude characterized by a positive and
cheerful disposition and inclination to anticipate
the most favorable outcome of events or actions.
   B   Emotional States [73]
       Personality Traits [67]
   R   Hope [91]
       Positivism [73]

Optokinetic Nystagmus
   Use   Nystagmus

Optometrists [73]
PN 22   SC 35590
   B   Medical Personnel [67]

Optometry [73]
PN 83   SC 35600
   B   Paramedical Sciences [73]
   R   Ophthalmology [73]

Oral Communication [85]
PN 1820   SC 35610
SN   Expression of information in oral form. Use
VERBAL COMMUNICATION to access refer-
ences from 67-84.
   UF   Speech
       Verbalization
   B   Verbal Communication [67]
   N   Code Switching [88]
       Oral Reading [73]
       Public Speaking [73]
       Self Talk [88]
     ↓ Speech Characteristics [73]
   R   Rhetoric [91]
       Verbal Ability [67]
       Verbal Fluency [73]
     ↓ Vocalization [67]
     ↓ Voice [73]

Oral Contraceptives [73]
PN 196   SC 35620
   B   Contraceptive Devices [73]
   R   Fertility Enhancement [73]

Oral Reading [73]
PN 805   SC 35630
SN   Reading aloud by individuals or groups or
the condition of being read to by others.
   B   Oral Communication [85]
       Reading [67]

Organ Donation
   Use   Tissue Donation

Organ of Corti
   Use   Cochlea

Organ Transplantation [73]
PN 383   SC 35660
   UF   Heart Transplants
       Kidney Transplants
       Transplants (Organ)
   B   Surgery [71]
   R   Heart Surgery [73]
       Neural Transplantation [85]
       Tissue Donation [91]

Organic Brain Syndromes [73]
PN 564   SC 35670
   B   Brain Disorders [67]
       Syndromes [73]
   N   ↓ Alcoholic Psychosis [73]
       Alzheimers Disease [73]
     ↓ Dementia [85]
       Toxic Psychoses [73]
   R   ↓ Mental Disorders [67]
       Postpartum Depression [73]

Organic Therapies [73]
PN 62   SC 35680
SN   Somatic treatment methods used in psychi-
atry. Compare PHYSICAL TREATMENT METH-
ODS.
   B   Treatment [67]
   N   ↓ Drug Therapy [67]
       Electrosleep Treatment [78]

Organic Therapies — (cont'd)
  N ↓ Narcoanalysis ⁷³
    Phototherapy ⁹¹
   ↓ Psychosurgery ⁷³
   ↓ Shock Therapy ⁷³
    Vitamin Therapy ⁷⁸
  R ↓ Psychotherapy ⁶⁷

Organizational Behavior ⁷⁸
PN 2715 SC 35695
SN Behavior of organizations and of individuals within organizational settings.
  B Behavior ⁶⁷
  N Employee Interaction ⁸⁸
    Organizational Effectiveness ⁸⁵
  R ↓ Group Dynamics ⁶⁷
    Informants ⁸⁸
    Organizational Commitment ⁹¹
    Organizational Structure ⁶⁷
   ↓ Organizations ⁶⁷
   ↓ Sociometry ⁹¹

Organizational Change ⁷³
PN 1131 SC 35700
  UF Change (Organizational)
  N Organizational Merger ⁷³
  R Decentralization ⁷⁸
    Organizational Climate ⁷³
    Organizational Crises ⁷³
    Organizational Development ⁷³

Organizational Climate ⁷³
PN 1884 SC 35710
SN Environmental characteristics of an organization which affect the behavior or performance of its members.
  UF Climate (Organizational)
  R ↓ Organizational Change ⁷³
    Organizational Crises ⁷³
    Quality of Work Life ⁸⁸
   ↓ Working Conditions ⁷³

Organizational Commitment ⁹¹
PN 214 SC 35715
SN Commitment of organizations and of individuals within organizational settings.
  B Commitment ⁸⁵
  R ↓ Employee Attitudes ⁶⁷
   ↓ Employee Characteristics ⁸⁸
    Employer Attitudes ⁷³
    Job Involvement ⁷⁸
   ↓ Job Performance ⁶⁷
    Job Satisfaction ⁶⁷
   ↓ Organizational Behavior ⁷⁸
    Organizational Effectiveness ⁸⁵
    Organizational Objectives ⁷³

Organizational Crises ⁷³
PN 91 SC 35720
  B Crises ⁷¹
  R ↓ Organizational Change ⁷³
    Organizational Climate ⁷³
   ↓ Stress ⁶⁷

Organizational Development ⁷³
PN 1100 SC 35730
SN Application of behavioral, management, or other techniques to organizations in order to integrate individuals' or members' needs with organizational goals and objectives.
  B Development ⁶⁷
  R Decentralization ⁷⁸
   ↓ Organizational Change ⁷³
    Organizational Objectives ⁷³
    Organizational Structure ⁶⁷

Organizational Effectiveness ⁸⁵
PN 358 SC 35735

Organizational Effectiveness — (cont'd)
SN Measure of the ability of an organization to meet the needs of its environment, including personnel needs.
  UF Organizational Performance
  B Organizational Behavior ⁷⁸
  R Organizational Commitment ⁹¹
    Organizational Objectives ⁷³
    Quality Control ⁸⁸

Organizational Goals
  Use Organizational Objectives

Organizational Merger ⁷³
PN 53 SC 35750
  B Organizational Change ⁷³
  R Organizational Structure ⁶⁷

Organizational Objectives ⁷³
PN 416 SC 35760
  UF Objectives (Organizational)
    Organizational Goals
  B Goals ⁶⁷
  R Decentralization ⁷⁸
    Organizational Commitment ⁹¹
    Organizational Development ⁷³
    Organizational Effectiveness ⁸⁵
    Quality Control ⁸⁸

Organizational Performance
  Use Organizational Effectiveness

Organizational Psychology
  Use Industrial Psychology

Organizational Structure ⁶⁷
PN 2434 SC 35770
  R Decentralization ⁷⁸
   ↓ Organizational Behavior ⁷⁸
    Organizational Development ⁷³
    Organizational Merger ⁷³
   ↓ Organizations ⁶⁷

Organizations ⁶⁷
PN 1192 SC 35780
  UF Agencies (Groups)
    Associations (Groups)
    Groups (Organizations)
  N Business Organizations ⁷³
    Foreign Organizations ⁷³
    Government Agencies ⁷³
    Health Maintenance Organizations ⁸²
    International Organizations ⁷³
    Labor Unions ⁷³
    Nonprofit Organizations ⁷³
    Professional Organizations ⁷³
    Religious Organizations ⁹¹
  R ↓ Organizational Behavior ⁷⁸
    Organizational Structure ⁶⁷

Orgasm ⁷³
PN 50 SC 35790
  UF Climax (Sexual)
  B Psychosexual Behavior ⁶⁷
  N Female Orgasm ⁷³
   ↓ Male Orgasm ⁷³
  R Frigidity ⁷³
    Impotence ⁷³
    Sexual Satisfaction ⁹⁴

Orientals
  Use Asians

Orientation (Perceptual)
  Use Perceptual Orientation

Orientation (Spatial)
  Use Spatial Orientation (Perception)

Orienting Reflex ⁶⁷
PN 878 SC 35820
SN Innate physiological responses, such as pupil dilation, galvanic skin response, and EEG activity, to novel stimuli.
  B Reflexes ⁷¹
    Sensory Adaptation ⁶⁷

Orienting Responses ⁶⁷
PN 899 SC 35830
SN Behavioral reactions in an organism, such as arrest of movement or head turning, to novel stimuli; behavioral correlate of orienting reflex.
  B Responses ⁶⁷
    Sensory Adaptation ⁶⁷

Originality
  Use Creativity

Orphanages ⁷³
PN 34 SC 35850
  B Residential Care Institutions ⁷³
  R ↓ Institutionalization ⁶⁷
    Orphans ⁷³

Orphans ⁷³
PN 69 SC 35860
  B Family Members ⁷³
  R Orphanages ⁷³

Orphenadrine ⁷³
PN 11 SC 35870
  B Amines ⁷³
    Antihistaminic Drugs ⁷³
    Antispasmodic Drugs ⁷³
    Antitremor Drugs ⁷³
    Cholinergic Blocking Drugs ⁷³
    Muscle Relaxing Drugs ⁷³

Orthogonal Rotation ⁷³
PN 77 SC 35880
  B Statistical Rotation ⁷³
  N Equimax Rotation ⁷³
    Quartimax Rotation ⁷³
    Varimax Rotation ⁷³

Orthography ⁷³
PN 467 SC 35890
SN Art and formal rules of writing and spelling according to accepted usage. Also used to refer to the representation of the sounds of a language by written symbols.
  B Linguistics ⁷³
  R ↓ Alphabets ⁷³
    Cursive Writing ⁷³
    Homographs ⁷³
    Proofreading ⁸⁸
    Spelling ⁷³
   ↓ Written Language ⁶⁷

Orthopedically Handicapped
  Use Physically Handicapped

Orthopsychiatry ⁷³
PN 15 SC 35910
SN Interdisciplinary approach combining psychiatry, psychology, pediatrics, and other related fields for prevention and early treatment of mental disorders, particularly in children and adolescents.
  B Psychiatry ⁶⁷
  R Child Psychiatry ⁶⁷

Oscilloscopes [73]
PN 20　　　　　　　　　　SC 35920
　B　　Apparatus [67]

Osteoporosis [91]
PN 7　　　　　　　　　　SC 35930
　B　　Bone Disorders [73]

Otosclerosis [73]
PN 8　　　　　　　　　　SC 35940
　B　　Ear Disorders [73]

Out of Body Experiences [88]
PN 22　　　　　　　　　　SC 35945
　B　　Parapsychological Phenomena [73]
　R　　Near Death Experiences [85]

Outcomes (Psychotherapeutic)
　Use Psychotherapeutic Outcomes

Outcomes (Treatment)
　Use Treatment Outcomes

Outpatient Commitment [91]
PN 11　　　　　　　　　　SC 35957
SN Legally mandated psychiatric or psychological treatment on an outpatient basis.
　UF　Commitment (Outpatient)
　B　　Commitment (Psychiatric) [73]
　　　　Outpatient Treatment [67]
　R　　Aftercare [73]
　　　　Partial Hospitalization [85]

Outpatient Psychiatric Clinics
　Use Psychiatric Clinics

Outpatient Treatment [67]
PN 1782　　　　　　　　　　SC 35970
SN Treatment in private practice, clinic, or hospital for ambulatory, non-hospitalized patients. Compare PARTIAL HOSPITALIZATION.
　UF　Ambulatory Care
　B　　Treatment [67]
　N　　Outpatient Commitment [91]
　R　　Aftercare [73]
　　　↓ Drug Therapy [67]
　　　　Home Care [85]
　　　　Outpatients [73]
　　　　Psychiatric Clinics [73]

Outpatients [73]
PN 995　　　　　　　　　　SC 35980
　B　　Patients [67]
　R　↓ Outpatient Treatment [67]

Outward Bound
　Use Wilderness Experience

Ovariectomy [73]
PN 711　　　　　　　　　　SC 35990
　B　　Castration [67]
　R　　Hysterectomy [73]

Ovaries [73]
PN 72　　　　　　　　　　SC 36000
　B　　Female Genitalia [73]
　　　　Gonads [73]

Ovary Disorders
　Use Endocrine Sexual Disorders

Over The Counter Drugs
　Use Nonprescription Drugs

Overachievement (Academic)
　Use Academic Overachievement

Overcorrection [85]
PN 39　　　　　　　　　　SC 36025
SN Therapeutic technique involving restitution and/or intensive practice of appropriate behavior following the occurrence of disruptive or inappropriate behavior.
　B　　Behavior Modification [73]
　R　　Overlearning [67]
　　　↓ Practice [67]

Overlearning [67]
PN 202　　　　　　　　　　SC 36030
SN Learning in which practice continues beyond the point of mastery of the material or task.
　B　　Learning [67]
　R　　Overcorrection [85]

Overpopulation [73]
PN 171　　　　　　　　　　SC 36040
　B　　Population [73]
　R　↓ Birth Control [71]
　　　　Crowding [78]
　　　　Environmental Stress [73]
　　　　Social Density [78]

Overweight
　Use Obesity

Ovulation [73]
PN 92　　　　　　　　　　SC 36060
　B　　Menstrual Cycle [73]

Ownership [85]
PN 164　　　　　　　　　　SC 36065
　UF　Possession
　　　　Property
　R　　Business [67]
　　　　Capitalism [73]
　　　　Entrepreneurship [91]
　　　↓ Private Sector [85]
　　　　Self Employment [94]

Oxazepam [78]
PN 85　　　　　　　　　　SC 36075
　B　　Anticonvulsive Drugs [73]
　　　　Benzodiazepines [78]
　　　　Minor Tranquilizers [73]

Oxidases [73]
PN 19　　　　　　　　　　SC 36080
　B　　Enzymes [73]
　N　　Cytochrome Oxidase [73]
　　　　Monoamine Oxidases [73]

Oxilapine
　Use Loxapine

Oxygen [73]
PN 169　　　　　　　　　　SC 36090
　B　　Nonmetallic Elements [73]

Oxygenation [73]
PN 38　　　　　　　　　　SC 36100
　B　　Physiology [67]

Oxytocin [73]
PN 176　　　　　　　　　　SC 36120
　B　　Pituitary Hormones [73]

Pacemakers (Artificial)
　Use Artificial Pacemakers

Pacific Islands [88]
PN 27　　　　　　　　　　SC 36135
　N　↓ South Pacific [78]

Pacifism [73]
PN 18　　　　　　　　　　SC 36140
　B　　Philosophies [67]
　R　　Nonviolence [91]

Pain [67]
PN 2581　　　　　　　　　　SC 36150
　UF　Aches
　B　　Symptoms [67]
　N　　Aphagia [73]
　　　　Back Pain [82]
　　　　Chronic Pain [85]
　　　↓ Headache [73]
　　　　Myofascial Pain [91]
　　　↓ Neuralgia [73]
　　　　Psychogenic Pain [73]
　R　↓ Analgesic Drugs [73]
　　　　Pain Management [94]
　　　↓ Pain Perception [73]
　　　　Pain Thresholds [73]
　　　↓ Spasms [73]
　　　　Suffering [73]

Pain (Psychogenic)
　Use Psychogenic Pain

Pain Management [94]
PN 0　　　　　　　　　　SC 36165
　B　　Treatment [67]
　R　　Analgesia [82]
　　　↓ Analgesic Drugs [73]
　　　↓ Pain [67]
　　　↓ Pain Perception [73]
　　　　Pain Thresholds [73]
　　　　Palliative Care [91]
　　　↓ Physical Treatment Methods [73]

Pain Perception [73]
PN 1645　　　　　　　　　　SC 36170
　UF　Nociception
　B　　Somesthetic Perception [67]
　N　　Analgesia [82]
　　　　Pain Thresholds [73]
　R　↓ Pain [67]
　　　　Pain Management [94]

Pain Receptors
　Use Nociceptors

Pain Relieving Drugs
　Use Analgesic Drugs

Pain Thresholds [73]
PN 599　　　　　　　　　　SC 36190
　B　　Pain Perception [73]
　　　　Thresholds [67]
　R　↓ Pain [67]
　　　　Pain Management [94]
　　　↓ Perceptual Measures [73]

Painting (Art) [73]
PN 350　　　　　　　　　　SC 36200
　B　　Art [67]

Paired Associate Learning [67]
PN 2649　　　　　　　　　　SC 36210
　B　　Verbal Learning [67]
　R　　Word Associations [67]

Pakistan [82]
PN 79　　　　　　　　　　SC 36215
SN Use WEST PAKISTAN to access references from 73–81.
　B　　Asia [73]

Palestinians
　Use Arabs

Palliative Care [91]
PN 60   SC 36219
B   Health Care Services [78]
R   Advance Directives [94]
     ↓ Death and Dying [67]
     ↓ Health Care Delivery [78]
     Hospice [82]
     Long Term Care [94]
     Pain Management [94]
     Terminally Ill Patients [73]

Palm (Anatomy) [73]
PN 28   SC 36220
B   Anatomy [67]
R   Hand (Anatomy) [67]

Palsy
Use Paralysis

Panama [88]
PN 5   SC 36235
B   Central America [73]

Pancreas [73]
PN 60   SC 36240
B   Glands [67]
R   ↓ Endocrine Glands [73]
     ↓ Endocrine System [73]
     ↓ Gastrointestinal System [73]

Pancreozymin
Use Cholecystokinin

Panic [73]
PN 633   SC 36260
SN Prior to 1988, also used for PANIC DIS-
ORDER.
B   Fear [67]
R   ↓ Anxiety [67]
     Panic Disorder [88]

Panic Disorder [88]
PN 1441   SC 36265
SN Consider PANIC to access references from
73–87.
B   Anxiety Neurosis [73]
R   ↓ Anxiety [67]
     Panic [73]

Pantherine
Use Muscimol

Papaverine [73]
PN 31   SC 36270
B   Alkaloids [73]
     Analgesic Drugs [73]
     Antispasmodic Drugs [73]
     Muscle Relaxing Drugs [73]
     Opiates [73]

Papua New Guinea [82]
PN 137   SC 36273
SN Use NEW GUINEA to access references
from 73–81.
UF New Guinea

Parachlorophenylalanine [78]
PN 155   SC 36275
B   Phenylalanine [73]
     Serotonin Antagonists [73]

Paradigmatic Techniques
Use Paradoxical Techniques

Paradoxical Sleep
Use REM Sleep

Paradoxical Techniques [82]
PN 310   SC 36282
SN Techniques designed to disrupt dysfunctional behavior patterns through systematically encouraging them, thus allaying anticipatory anxiety, creating resistance to the symptomatic behavior, or enabling clients to achieve voluntary
control over this behavior.
UF Paradigmatic Techniques
     Reframing
     Symptom Prescription
B   Psychotherapeutic Techniques [67]
R   ↓ Behavior Therapy [67]
     ↓ Psychotherapy [67]

Paragraphs [73]
PN 58   SC 36300
B   Written Language [67]

Paraguay [88]
PN 5   SC 36303
B   South America [67]

Paraldehyde [82]
PN 2   SC 36305
SN Corrected for misspelling. Use PARALYDE-
HYDE to access references from 73–81.
UF Paralydehyde
B   Hypnotic Drugs [73]
     Sedatives [73]

Paralegal Personnel
Use Legal Personnel

Paralydehyde
SN Corrected for misspelling. Use PARALYDE-
HYDE to access references from 73–81.
Use Paraldehyde

Paralysis [73]
PN 203   SC 36320
UF Palsy
B   Movement Disorders [85]
     Neuromuscular Disorders [73]
N   Cerebral Palsy [67]
     General Paresis [73]
     Hemiplegia [78]
     Paraplegia [78]
     Parkinsons Disease [73]
     Quadriplegia [85]
R   ↓ Central Nervous System Disorders [73]
     Dysarthria [73]
     ↓ Musculoskeletal Disorders [73]
     ↓ Peripheral Nerve Disorders [73]
     Poliomyelitis [73]
     ↓ Sclerosis (Nervous System) [73]
     Spinal Cord Injuries [73]

Paralysis (Hysterical)
Use Hysterical Paralysis

Paralysis (Infantile)
Use Poliomyelitis

Paralysis Agitans
Use Parkinsons Disease

Paramedical Personnel [73]
PN 181   SC 36360
B   Medical Personnel [67]
     Paraprofessional Personnel [73]
N   Attendants (Institutions) [73]
     Medics [73]
     Psychiatric Aides [73]
R   Fire Fighters [91]
     ↓ Paramedical Sciences [73]
     ↓ Psychiatric Hospital Staff [73]

Paramedical Sciences [73]
PN 5   SC 36370
N   Audiology [73]
     Nursing [73]
     Optometry [73]
     ↓ Pharmacology [73]
     Physical Therapy [73]
R   ↓ Medical Sciences [67]
     ↓ Paramedical Personnel [73]

Parameter Estimation
Use Statistical Estimation

Parameters (Response)
Use Response Parameters

Parameters (Stimulus)
Use Stimulus Parameters

Parametric Statistical Tests [73]
PN 71   SC 36400
B   Statistical Tests [73]
N   F Test [73]
     T Test [73]

Paranoia [88]
PN 56   SC 36410
SN Mild paranoia in normal populations.
B   Personality Traits [67]
R   Paranoid Personality [73]

Paranoia (Psychosis) [67]
PN 680   SC 36420
SN Gradual development of an elaborate and
complex delusional system, usually involving per-
secutory or grandiose delusions with few other
signs of personality or thought disturbance.
UF Acute Paranoid Disorder
     Atypical Paranoid Disorder
     Paranoid Disorder
B   Psychosis [67]
N   Folie A Deux [73]
     Involutional Paranoid Psychosis [73]
R   Paranoid Personality [73]
     Paranoid Schizophrenia [67]

Paranoid Disorder
Use Paranoia (Psychosis)

Paranoid Personality [73]
PN 112   SC 36430
SN Nonpsychotic personality disorder marked
by hypersensitivity, jealousy, and unwarranted
suspicion with tendency to blame others for
one's shortcomings.
UF Paranoid Personality Disorder
B   Personality Disorders [67]
R   Paranoia [88]
     ↓ Paranoia (Psychosis) [67]
     Paranoid Schizophrenia [67]

Paranoid Personality Disorder
Use Paranoid Personality

Paranoid Schizophrenia [67]
PN 898   SC 36440
SN Type of schizophrenia characterized by
grandiosity, suspiciousness, and delusions of
persecution, often with hallucinations.
B   Schizophrenia [67]
R   Folie A Deux [73]
     Involutional Paranoid Psychosis [73]
     ↓ Paranoia (Psychosis) [67]
     Paranoid Personality [73]
     ↓ Psychosis [67]

Paraphilias
Use Sexual Deviations

Paraplegia [78]
PN 108   SC 36446
SN Paralysis of the lower limbs and trunk.
B   Paralysis [73]
R ↓ Central Nervous System Disorders [73]
     Hemiplegia [78]
   ↓ Injuries [73]
   ↓ Musculoskeletal Disorders [73]
   ↓ Physically Handicapped [67]
     Quadriplegia [85]
     Spinal Cord Injuries [73]

Paraprofessional Education [73]
PN 565   SC 36450
SN Training or education of aides, such as par-
amedical and paralegal personnel, who assist
professional persons.
B   Education [67]
R   Microcounseling [78]

Paraprofessional Personnel [73]
PN 1000   SC 36460
SN Persons with minimal or special training in a
profession working as aides or assistants to pro-
fessionals. Use PARAPROFESSIONAL PERSON-
NEL to access references to nonprofessional
personnel from 73–81.
B   Personnel [67]
N ↓ Paramedical Personnel [73]
     Teacher Aides [73]
R ↓ Mental Health Personnel [67]
   ↓ Nonprofessional Personnel [82]
     Occupational Therapists [73]
   ↓ Professional Personnel [78]
     Volunteer Civilian Personnel [73]
   ↓ Volunteer Personnel [73]

Parapsychological Phenomena [73]
PN 797   SC 36470
B   Parapsychology [67]
N ↓ Extrasensory Perception [67]
     Near Death Experiences [85]
     Out of Body Experiences [88]
     Telepathy [73]

Parapsychology [67]
PN 808   SC 36480
N ↓ Parapsychological Phenomena [73]
R   Astrology [73]
     Dream Analysis [73]
     Occultism [78]
     Witchcraft [73]

Parasitic Disorders [73]
PN 53   SC 36490
B   Infectious Disorders [73]
N   Malaria [73]

Parasitism
Use Biological Symbiosis

Parasuicide
Use Attempted Suicide

Parasympathetic Nervous System [73]
PN 35   SC 36500
B   Autonomic Nervous System [67]
N ↓ Efferent Pathways [82]
     Vagus Nerve [73]
R ↓ Cholinergic Blocking Drugs [73]
   ↓ Cholinomimetic Drugs [73]

Parasympatholytic Drugs
Use Cholinergic Blocking Drugs

Parasympathomimetic Drugs
Use Cholinomimetic Drugs

Parathion [73]
PN 7   SC 36530
B   Insecticides [73]

Parathyroid Disorders [73]
PN 36   SC 36540
UF   Hyperparathyroidism
     Hypoparathyroidism
B   Endocrine Disorders [73]

Parathyroid Glands [73]
PN 6   SC 36550
B   Endocrine Glands [73]
R   Parathyroid Hormone [73]

Parathyroid Hormone [73]
PN 10   SC 36560
B   Hormones [67]
R   Parathyroid Glands [73]

Parent Attitude Research Instrument [73]
PN 5   SC 36570
B   Attitude Measures [67]

Parent Child Communication [73]
PN 1115   SC 36580
SN From 1982, limited to human populations.
For animals consider ANIMAL PARENTAL BE-
HAVIOR or ANIMAL MATERNAL BEHAVIOR.
B   Interpersonal Communication [73]
N   Father Child Communication [85]
     Mother Child Communication [85]
R ↓ Parent Child Relations [67]
   ↓ Parental Characteristics [94]

Parent Child Relations [67]
PN 6452   SC 36590
SN From 1982, limited to human populations.
For animals consider ANIMAL PARENTAL BE-
HAVIOR or ANIMAL MATERNAL BEHAVIOR.
UF   Parental Influence
B   Family Relations [67]
N   Father Child Relations [73]
     Mother Child Relations [67]
     Parental Attitudes [73]
     Parental Permissiveness [73]
R   Attachment Behavior [85]
   ↓ Child Discipline [73]
   ↓ Childrearing Practices [67]
     Codependency [91]
     Empty Nest [91]
     Generation Gap [73]
     Nurturance [85]
   ↓ Parent Child Communication [73]
     Parent School Relationship [82]
     Parent Training [78]
   ↓ Parental Characteristics [94]
     Parental Role [73]
     Transgenerational Patterns [91]

Parent Educational Background [73]
PN 542   SC 36600
UF   Educational Background (Parents)
B   Educational Background [67]
     Family Background [73]
     Parental Characteristics [94]
R   Family Socioeconomic Level [73]
     Parental Occupation [73]

Parent Effectiveness Training
Use Parent Training

Parent School Relationship [82]
PN 608   SC 36605
SN Interaction between parents and school and/
or educational personnel, such as parent-teacher
conferences.

Parent School Relationship — (cont'd)
UF   PTA
R ↓ Parent Child Relations [67]
     Parent Training [78]
     Teacher Attitudes [67]

Parent Training [78]
PN 2089   SC 36606
SN Educational materials, information, or in-
struction for parents.
UF   Parent Effectiveness Training
B   Education [67]
R ↓ Childrearing Practices [67]
     Human Relations Training [78]
   ↓ Parent Child Relations [67]
     Parent School Relationship [82]
     Parental Role [73]

Parental Absence [73]
PN 354   SC 36610
SN From 1982, limited to human populations.
For animals consider ANIMAL PARENTAL BE-
HAVIOR or ANIMAL MATERNAL BEHAVIOR.
B   Family Structure [73]
N   Father Absence [73]
     Mother Absence [73]
R   Anaclitic Depression [73]
     Child Custody [82]
     Divorced Persons [73]
   ↓ Marital Separation [73]
   ↓ Parental Characteristics [94]
   ↓ Single Parents [78]
     Widowers [73]
     Widows [73]

Parental Attitudes [73]
PN 4739   SC 36620
SN Attitudes of, not toward, parents.
B   Attitudes [67]
     Parent Child Relations [67]
     Parental Characteristics [94]
R   Childrearing Attitudes [73]
   ↓ Childrearing Practices [67]
     Father Child Relations [73]
     Mother Child Relations [67]
     Parental Permissiveness [73]
     Parental Role [73]

Parental Authoritarianism
Use Parental Permissiveness

Parental Behavior (Animal)
Use Animal Parental Behavior

Parental Characteristics [94]
PN 0   SC 36637
N   Parent Educational Background [73]
     Parental Attitudes [73]
     Parental Occupation [73]
     Parental Permissiveness [73]
     Parental Role [73]
R ↓ Childrearing Practices [67]
   ↓ Parent Child Communication [73]
   ↓ Parent Child Relations [67]
   ↓ Parental Absence [73]
   ↓ Parents [67]

Parental Influence
Use Parent Child Relations

Parental Occupation [73]
PN 306   SC 36650
UF   Occupation (Parental)
B   Family Background [73]
     Parental Characteristics [94]
R   Family Socioeconomic Level [73]
     Parent Educational Background [73]

Parental Permissiveness [73]
PN 209   SC 36660
UF   Authoritarianism (Parental)
     Parental Authoritarianism
     Permissiveness (Parental)
B   Child Discipline [73]
     Parent Child Relations [67]
     Parental Characteristics [94]
R   Father Child Relations [73]
     Mother Child Relations [67]
     Parental Attitudes [73]
     Parental Role [73]

Parental Role [73]
PN 1466   SC 36670
SN Descriptions, perceptions, and attitudes about the social, psychological, behavioral, or emotional role of parents.
B   Family Relations [67]
     Parental Characteristics [94]
     Roles [67]
R   ↓ Child Discipline [73]
     ↓ Childrearing Practices [67]
     Delayed Parenthood [85]
     Father Child Relations [73]
     Mother Child Relations [67]
     ↓ Parent Child Relations [67]
     Parent Training [78]
     Parental Attitudes [73]
     Parental Permissiveness [73]

Parenthood Status [85]
PN 372   SC 36675
SN State of having or not having children, or, the number of children one has.
N   Childlessness [82]
R   Family Size [73]
     ↓ Family Structure [73]

Parents [67]
PN 6886   SC 36680
SN From 1982, limited to human populations. For animals consider ANIMAL PARENTAL BEHAVIOR or ANIMAL MATERNAL BEHAVIOR.
B   Ancestors [73]
     Family Members [73]
N   Adoptive Parents [73]
     ↓ Fathers [67]
     Foster Parents [73]
     Homosexual Parents [94]
     ↓ Mothers [67]
     ↓ Single Parents [78]
     Stepparents [73]
     Surrogate Parents (Humans) [73]
R   ↓ Expectant Parents [85]
     ↓ Parental Characteristics [94]
     ↓ Spouses [73]

Paresis (General)
Use General Paresis

Pargyline [73]
PN 75   SC 36700
B   Antihypertensive Drugs [73]
     Monoamine Oxidase Inhibitors [73]

Parietal Lobe [73]
PN 411   SC 36710
B   Cerebral Cortex [67]
N   Somatosensory Cortex [73]

Parkinsonism [94]
PN 0   SC 36715
SN Clinical state, usually drug induced, characterized by tremors, muscle rigidity, postural reflex dysfunction, and akinesia. Compare PARKINSONS DISEASE.
R   Apraxia [73]
     Muscle Contractions [73]

Parkinsonism — (cont'd)
R   ↓ Nervous System Disorders [67]
     Parkinsons Disease [73]
     ↓ Reflexes [71]
     ↓ Symptoms [67]
     Tremor [73]

Parkinsons Disease [73]
PN 1297   SC 36720
SN A disease characterized as a progressive motor disability manifested by tremors, shaking, muscular rigidity, and lack of postural reflexes.
UF   Paralysis Agitans
B   Brain Disorders [67]
     Neuromuscular Disorders [73]
     Paralysis [73]
R   Amantadine [78]
     ↓ Antitremor Drugs [73]
     Parkinsonism [94]
     Tremor [73]

Parks (Recreational)
Use Recreation Areas

Parochial School Education
Use Private School Education

Parole [73]
PN 197   SC 36750
SN Conditional release of a prisoner serving an indeterminate or unexpired sentence.
UF   Parolees
B   Legal Processes [73]
R   ↓ Law Enforcement [78]
     Probation [73]

Parole Officers [73]
PN 39   SC 36760
B   Law Enforcement Personnel [73]
R   Probation Officers [73]

Parolees
Use Parole

Paroxetine [94]
PN 0   SC 36770
B   Antidepressant Drugs [71]

Partial Hospitalization [85]
PN 648   SC 36775
SN Ambulatory treatment program of intensive, multidisciplinary care. Involves stabilization, rehabilitation, and/or maintenance of patients through more comprehensive treatment than is possible in an outpatient setting. Compare OUTPATIENT TREATMENT.
UF   Day Care (Treatment)
     Day Hospital
B   Treatment [67]
R   Aftercare [73]
     Deinstitutionalization [82]
     ↓ Hospital Programs [78]
     Interdisciplinary Treatment Approach [73]
     ↓ Mental Health Programs [73]
     Outpatient Commitment [91]
     ↓ Rehabilitation [67]

Partial Reinforcement
Use Reinforcement Schedules

Partially Hearing Impaired [73]
PN 2000   SC 36790
UF   Hearing Impaired (Partially)
B   Aurally Handicapped [73]
R   Cochlear Implants [94]
     ↓ Deaf [67]

Partially Sighted [73]
PN 95   SC 36800
B   Visually Handicapped [67]

Participation [73]
PN 1349   SC 36810
SN Taking part in an activity. Use a more specific term if possible.
B   Interpersonal Interaction [67]
N   Athletic Participation [73]
     Group Participation [73]
     Participative Management [88]
R   ↓ Involvement [73]

Participative Management [88]
PN 175   SC 36820
SN Management technique permitting nonmanagement personnel to be involved in the governance, management, or policy-making processes of an institution or organization.
UF   Quality Circles
B   Management Methods [73]
     Participation [73]
R   Job Involvement [78]
     Management Decision Making [73]
     Quality Control [88]

Partner Abuse [91]
PN 154   SC 36825
SN Includes married and unmarried persons.
UF   Spouse Abuse
B   Antisocial Behavior [71]
R   Battered Females [88]
     Emotional Abuse [91]
     ↓ Family Violence [82]
     Physical Abuse [91]
     ↓ Sexual Abuse [88]
     ↓ Violence [73]

Parturition
Use Birth

Passive Aggressive Personality [73]
PN 22   SC 36850
B   Personality Disorders [67]

Passive Avoidance
Use Avoidance Conditioning

Passiveness [73]
PN 169   SC 36870
B   Personality Traits [67]

Pastoral Counseling [67]
PN 821   SC 36880
SN Provision of counseling by religious personnel.
B   Counseling [67]
R   ↓ Psychotherapy [67]

Pastors
Use Ministers (Religion)

Path Analysis [91]
PN 14   SC 36895
SN Quantification of the causal relationships that exists among variables.
B   Multivariate Analysis [82]
R   Causal Analysis [94]
     ↓ Factor Analysis [67]
     Multiple Regression [82]

Pathogenesis
Use Etiology

Pathological Gambling [88]
PN 196   SC 36905

Pathological Gambling — (cont'd)
  UF Compulsive Gambling
  B   Gambling [73]
  R ↓ Addiction [73]
      ↓ Behavior Disorders [71]
      Impulsiveness [73]

Pathologists [73]
PN 7   SC 36920
  B   Physicians [67]
  R   Surgeons [73]

Pathology [73]
PN 188   SC 36930
  B   Medical Sciences [67]
  N   Neuropathology [73]
      Psychopathology [67]

Patient Abuse [91]
PN 17   SC 36935
  UF Client Abuse
  B   Antisocial Behavior [71]
  R ↓ Child Abuse [71]
      Elder Abuse [88]
      Emotional Abuse [91]
      Patient Violence [94]
      ↓ Patients [67]
      Physical Abuse [91]
      Professional Client Sexual Relations [94]
      Professional Liability [85]
      ↓ Professional Standards [73]
      ↓ Sexual Abuse [88]
      ↓ Therapeutic Processes [78]
      ↓ Treatment [67]

Patient Attitudes
  Use Client Attitudes

Patient Characteristics
  Use Client Characteristics

Patient Education
  Use Client Education

Patient History [73]
PN 1493   SC 36955
  UF Case History
      Medical History
      Psychiatric History
  R   Biographical Data [78]
      ↓ Client Characteristics [73]
      ↓ Diagnosis [67]
      Etiology [67]
      ↓ Medical Diagnosis [73]
      Medical Records Keeping [78]
      Premorbidity [78]
      Prognosis [73]
      ↓ Psychodiagnosis [67]
      ↓ Treatment [67]

Patient Rights
  Use Client Rights

Patient Satisfaction
  Use Client Satisfaction

Patient Seclusion [94]
PN 0   SC 36959
  UF Seclusion (Patient)
  B   Social Isolation [67]
  R ↓ Hospitalization [67]
      Patient Violence [94]
      ↓ Patients [67]
      ↓ Psychiatric Hospitalization [73]
      Psychiatric Hospitals [67]
      Psychiatric Units [91]

Patient Therapist Interaction
  Use Psychotherapeutic Processes

Patient Therapist Sexual Relations
  Use Professional Client Sexual Relations

Patient Violence [94]
PN 0   SC 36965
SN Violence of psychiatric or medical patients directed toward other patients, institutional staff, or themselves.
  UF Client Violence
  B   Client Characteristics [73]
      Violence [73]
  R   Dangerousness [88]
      Patient Abuse [91]
      Patient Seclusion [94]
      ↓ Patients [67]
      Physical Restraint [82]
      ↓ Therapeutic Processes [78]

Patients [67]
PN 1067   SC 36970
SN Persons under medical care. Use a more specific term if possible. Consider also CLIENTS.
  N   Geriatric Patients [73]
      Hospitalized Patients [73]
      Medical Patients [73]
      Outpatients [73]
      Psychiatric Patients [67]
      Surgical Patients [73]
      Terminally Ill Patients [73]
  R   Patient Abuse [91]
      Patient Seclusion [94]
      Patient Violence [94]

Patriarchy [73]
PN 52   SC 36980
  B   Family Structure [73]
  R   Mother Absence [73]

Pattern Discrimination [67]
PN 2414   SC 37000
SN Distinguishing temporal, spatial, or pictorial/symbolic regularities (patterns) of visual, auditory, or other types of stimuli. Includes the concept of pattern perception.
  B   Perceptual Discrimination [73]
  R   Figure Ground Discrimination [73]
      Form and Shape Perception [67]
      Perceptual Closure [73]
      ↓ Rhythm [91]
      Texture Perception [82]
      Visual Acuity [82]
      Visual Search [82]

Pavlov (Ivan) [91]
PN 13   SC 37005
SN Identifies biographical or autobiographical studies and discussions of Pavlov's works.
  R ↓ Classical Conditioning [67]
      ↓ Psychologists [67]

Pavlovian Conditioning
  Use Classical Conditioning

Pay
  Use Salaries

PCP
  Use Phencyclidine

Peabody Picture Vocabulary Test [73]
PN 253   SC 37030
  B   Intelligence Measures [67]

Peace [88]
PN 119   SC 37038

Peace — (cont'd)
  B   Social Interaction [67]
      Social Issues [91]
  R   Foreign Policy Making [73]
      International Relations [67]
      ↓ Social Movements [67]
      ↓ War [67]

Peace Corps [73]
PN 17   SC 37040
  B   Government Programs [73]
  R   Government [67]

Pearson Prod Moment Correl Coeff
  Use Statistical Correlation

Pecking Order
  Use Animal Dominance

Pederasty
  Use Pedophilia

Pedestrian Accidents [73]
PN 45   SC 37090
  B   Accidents [67]
  R ↓ Driving Behavior [67]
      Motor Traffic Accidents [73]
      Pedestrians [73]

Pedestrians [73]
PN 102   SC 37100
  R   Pedestrian Accidents [73]

Pediatricians [73]
PN 275   SC 37110
  B   Physicians [67]

Pediatrics [73]
PN 595   SC 37120
  B   Medical Sciences [67]

Pedophilia [73]
PN 263   SC 37130
  UF Pederasty
  B   Sexual Deviations [67]
  R   Bisexuality [73]
      ↓ Child Abuse [71]
      Incest [73]
      ↓ Sexual Abuse [88]

Peer Counseling [78]
PN 417   SC 37135
SN Supervised performance of limited counselor functions by a person of approximately the same age or status as the counselee.
  B   Counseling [67]
  R   Mentor [85]
      ↓ Peer Relations [67]
      Peer Tutoring [73]
      Peers [78]

Peer Evaluation [82]
PN 507   SC 37137
SN Appraisal by one's peers.
  UF Peer Review
  B   Evaluation [67]
  R ↓ Peer Relations [67]
      ↓ Personnel Evaluation [73]
      ↓ Professional Fees [78]
      ↓ Professional Standards [73]

Peer Pressure [94]
PN 0   SC 37138
  B   Interpersonal Influences [67]
      Peer Relations [67]
  R   Friendship [67]
      ↓ Group Dynamics [67]

Peer Pressure — (cont'd)
R   Likability [88]
     Peers [78]
     ↓ Persuasive Communication [67]
     Social Acceptance [67]
     Social Approval [67]

Peer Relations [67]
PN 4367   SC 37140
B   Interpersonal Interaction [67]
N   Peer Pressure [94]
R   Friendship [67]
     Peer Counseling [78]
     Peer Evaluation [82]
     Peers [78]
     Reference Groups [94]
     ↓ Sociometry [91]

Peer Review
Use Peer Evaluation

Peer Tutoring [73]
PN 524   SC 37150
SN Teaching method in which students provide individual instruction for other students, not necessarily of the same age or grade level.
B   Tutoring [73]
R   Cooperative Learning [94]
     Peer Counseling [78]
     Peers [78]

Peers [78]
PN 827   SC 37154
R   Peer Counseling [78]
     Peer Pressure [94]
     ↓ Peer Relations [67]
     Peer Tutoring [73]
     Significant Others [91]

Pellagra [73]
PN 9   SC 37160
B   Vitamin Deficiency Disorders [73]
R   Nicotinamide [73]

Pemoline [78]
PN 49   SC 37175
B   CNS Stimulating Drugs [73]

Penguins [73]
PN 35   SC 37180
B   Birds [67]

Penicillins [73]
PN 56   SC 37190
B   Antibiotics [73]

Penis [73]
PN 195   SC 37200
B   Male Genitalia [73]

Penis Envy [73]
PN 49   SC 37210
R   ↓ Psychoanalytic Personality Factors [73]

Penitentiaries
Use Prisons

Penology [73]
PN 140   SC 37230
R   ↓ Correctional Institutions [73]
     ↓ Criminal Justice [91]
     Criminology [73]

Pension Plans (Employee)
Use Employee Pension Plans

Pentazocine [91]
PN 12   SC 37245
B   Analgesic Drugs [73]
     Narcotic Agonists [88]

Pentobarbital [73]
PN 580   SC 37250
UF Nembutal
     Sodium Pentobarbital
B   Anesthetic Drugs [73]
     Anticonvulsive Drugs [73]
     Barbiturates [67]
     Hypnotic Drugs [73]
     Sedatives [73]

Pentothal
Use Thiopental

Pentylenetetrazol [73]
PN 191   SC 37270
UF Metrazole
     Pentylenetetrazole
B   CNS Stimulating Drugs [73]
R   ↓ Analeptic Drugs [73]

Pentylenetetrazole
Use Pentylenetetrazol

Peoples Republic of China [73]
PN 690   SC 37290
UF China
B   Asia [73]
N   Tibet [91]

Peptic Ulcers
Use Gastrointestinal Ulcers

Peptides [73]
PN 1340   SC 37330
UF Neuropeptides
N   Angiotensin [73]
     Bombesin [88]
     Cholecystokinin [82]
     Corticotropin Releasing Factor [94]
     ↓ Endogenous Opiates [85]
     Melanocyte Stimulating Hormone [85]
     Nerve Growth Factor [94]
     Neurotensin [85]
     Somatostatin [91]
     Substance P [85]
R   ↓ Drugs [67]
     Enkephalins [82]
     ↓ Neurotransmitters [85]
     ↓ Proteins [73]

Perception [67]
PN 3558   SC 37350
SN Conceptually broad array term referring to the process of obtaining cognitive or sensory information about the environment. Use a more specific term if possible.
UF Sensation
N   ↓ Auditory Perception [67]
     ↓ Extrasensory Perception [67]
     Form and Shape Perception [67]
     ↓ Illusions (Perception) [67]
     ↓ Intersensory Processes [78]
     Numerosity Perception [67]
     ↓ Olfactory Perception [67]
     Perceptual Closure [73]
     ↓ Perceptual Constancy [85]
     ↓ Perceptual Discrimination [73]
     ↓ Perceptual Distortion [82]
     ↓ Perceptual Localization [67]
     ↓ Perceptual Motor Learning [67]
     ↓ Perceptual Motor Processes [67]
     ↓ Perceptual Orientation [73]
     Perceptual Style [73]

Perception — (cont'd)
N   Role Perception [73]
     Self Perception [67]
     Sensory Gating [91]
     ↓ Social Perception [67]
     ↓ Somesthetic Perception [67]
     ↓ Spatial Perception [67]
     Subliminal Perception [73]
     Taste Perception [67]
     ↓ Time Perception [67]
     ↓ Visual Perception [67]
R   Apperception [73]
     ↓ Attention [67]
     Constructivism [94]
     ↓ Discrimination [67]
     Mind [91]
     ↓ Perceptual Development [73]
     ↓ Perceptual Disturbances [73]
     ↓ Perceptual Measures [73]
     ↓ Perceptual Stimulation [73]
     ↓ Priming [88]
     ↓ Rhythm [91]
     Sensory Neglect [94]
     Signal Detection (Perception) [67]

Perceptiveness (Personality) [73]
PN 12   SC 37360
SN Demonstrating insight or sympathetic understanding or keen powers of observation.
B   Personality Traits [67]
R   Insight [73]

Perceptual Aftereffect [67]
PN 929   SC 37370
SN Subjective perceptual alterations resulting from prolonged exposure to preceding sensory stimulation.
UF Aftereffect (Perceptual)
B   Illusions (Perception) [67]
N   Afterimage [67]
R   Interocular Transfer [85]

Perceptual Closure [73]
PN 91   SC 37380
SN Perception of units which together form a closed unit or whole, being organized together and perceived as a whole.
UF Closure (Perceptual)
     Perceptual Fill
B   Perception [67]
R   Pattern Discrimination [67]

Perceptual Constancy [85]
PN 39   SC 37385
SN Stable perception of a stimulus in any sensory modality despite changes in its objective properties.
B   Perception [67]
N   Brightness Constancy [85]
     Color Constancy [85]
     Size Constancy [85]
R   Object Permanence [85]

Perceptual Development [73]
PN 2248   SC 37390
SN The acquisition of sensory skills or abilities in the natural course of physical and psychological maturation.
B   Cognitive Development [73]
N   Perceptual Motor Development [91]
R   ↓ Childhood Development [67]
     Conservation (Concept) [73]
     ↓ Developmental Stages [73]
     ↓ Perception [67]
     ↓ Physical Development [73]
     ↓ Psychomotor Development [73]

Perceptual Discrimination [73]
PN 652   SC 37400

Perceptual Discrimination — (cont'd)
- B Discrimination [67]
  Perception [67]
- N Auditory Acuity [88]
  Auditory Discrimination [67]
  Figure Ground Discrimination [73]
  Odor Discrimination [73]
  Pattern Discrimination [67]
  Visual Discrimination [67]
- R Mirror Image [91]
  Stroop Effect [88]

Perceptual Distortion [82]
PN 85   SC 37410
SN Lack of correspondence between the common perception of a stimulus and the perception by an individual. Perceptual distortion does not involve hallucinatory or illusory components, but rather is a function of individual differences.
- UF Distortion (Perceptual)
- B Perception [67]
- N Spatial Distortion [73]
- R ↓ Illusions (Perception) [67]
  ↓ Perceptual Disturbances [73]
  Sensory Neglect [94]

Perceptual Disturbances [73]
PN 339   SC 37420
- N ↓ Agnosia [73]
  ↓ Hallucinations [67]
- R ↓ Aphasia [67]
  ↓ Illusions (Perception) [67]
  ↓ Learning Disabilities [73]
  ↓ Mental Disorders [67]
  ↓ Perception [67]
  ↓ Perceptual Distortion [82]
  Sensory Neglect [94]

Perceptual Fill
Use Perceptual Closure

Perceptual Localization [67]
PN 539   SC 37440
SN Discrimination of the physical displacement or spatial location of a stimulus in any sensory modality.
- UF Localization (Perceptual)
- B Perception [67]
- N Auditory Localization [73]
- R ↓ Tracking [67]

Perceptual Measures [73]
PN 533   SC 37450
- B Measurement [67]
- N Rod and Frame Test [73]
  Stroop Color Word Test [73]
- R ↓ Audiometry [67]
  Auditory Thresholds [73]
  Bone Conduction Audiometry [73]
  Critical Flicker Fusion Threshold [67]
  Dark Adaptation [73]
  Olfactory Thresholds [73]
  Pain Thresholds [73]
  ↓ Perception [67]
  ↓ Psychophysical Measurement [67]
  ↓ Sensorimotor Measures [73]
  ↓ Thresholds [67]
  Vibrotactile Thresholds [73]
  ↓ Visual Thresholds [73]

Perceptual Motor Coordination [73]
PN 667   SC 37460
- UF Coordination (Perceptual Motor)
- B Perceptual Motor Processes [67]
- N Physical Dexterity [73]
- R Motor Coordination [73]
  Perceptual Motor Development [91]

Perceptual Motor Development [91]
PN 42   SC 37470
SN Use MOTOR DEVELOPMENT and PERCEPTUAL DEVELOPMENT to access references from 73-90.
- UF Sensorimotor Development
- B Motor Development [73]
  Perceptual Development [73]
- R Animal Development [78]
  ↓ Intersensory Processes [78]
  ↓ Perceptual Motor Coordination [73]
  ↓ Perceptual Motor Learning [67]
  ↓ Perceptual Motor Processes [67]
  ↓ Psychomotor Development [73]

Perceptual Motor Learning [67]
PN 1216   SC 37480
- UF Motor Skill Learning
- B Learning [67]
  Perception [67]
- N Fine Motor Skill Learning [73]
  Gross Motor Skill Learning [73]
- R Perceptual Motor Development [91]
  ↓ Skill Learning [73]
  ↓ Tracking [67]

Perceptual Motor Measures
Use Sensorimotor Measures

Perceptual Motor Processes [67]
PN 3624   SC 37490
- UF Psychomotor Processes
  Sensorimotor Processes
- B Perception [67]
- N ↓ Perceptual Motor Coordination [73]
  Sensory Integration [91]
  ↓ Tracking [67]
- R Equilibrium [73]
  ↓ Intersensory Processes [78]
  ↓ Motor Processes [67]
  Perceptual Motor Development [91]

Perceptual Neglect
Use Sensory Neglect

Perceptual Orientation [73]
PN 743   SC 37500
SN Awareness of one's position in time and space.
- UF Orientation (Perceptual)
- B Perception [67]
- N Spatial Orientation (Perception) [73]
- R Time Perspective [78]

Perceptual Stimulation [73]
PN 316   SC 37510
- B Stimulation [67]
- N ↓ Auditory Stimulation [67]
  ↓ Delayed Feedback [73]
  Olfactory Stimulation [78]
  ↓ Sensory Feedback [73]
  ↓ Somesthetic Stimulation [73]
  Taste Stimulation [67]
  ↓ Visual Stimulation [73]
- R Afferent Stimulation [73]
  ↓ Masking [67]
  ↓ Perception [67]
  Sensory Gating [91]

Perceptual Style [73]
PN 443   SC 37520
SN Manner in which sensory information or stimuli are organized meaningfully by an individual.
- B Perception [67]
- R ↓ Cognitive Style [67]
  ↓ Conceptual Tempo [85]

Perceptual Style — (cont'd)
- R Neurolinguistic Programing [88]
  Schema [88]

Perfectionism [88]
PN 53   SC 37523
- B Personality Traits [67]
- R ↓ Compulsions [73]

Performance [67]
PN 3330   SC 37525
SN Conceptually broad term, having application across broad disciplines and subject matter contexts in which execution or accomplishment of a specified task or objective is of concern. Use terms describing specific activity or performance when possible.
- N Athletic Performance [91]
  Group Performance [67]
  ↓ Job Performance [67]
  ↓ Motor Performance [73]
- R ↓ Ability [67]
  ↓ Achievement [67]
  Competence [82]
  Performance Anxiety [94]

Performance Anxiety [94]
PN 0   SC 37527
- B Anxiety [67]
- R ↓ Anxiety Neurosis [73]
  ↓ Performance [67]

Performance Tests [73]
PN 508   SC 37530
SN Tests requiring nonverbal responses, for example, the manipulation of objects or the performance of motor skills.
- B Measurement [67]
- R Criterion Referenced Tests [82]

Performing Arts
Use Arts

Periaqueductal Gray [85]
PN 135   SC 37550
SN Mesencephalic cells in the gray area surrounding the cerebral aqueduct important for visceral and limbic mechanisms.
- B Tegmentum [91]

Perinatal Period [94]
PN 0   SC 37555
SN Used for human or animal populations.
- R ↓ Birth [67]
  Postnatal Period [73]
  ↓ Pregnancy [67]
  ↓ Prenatal Development [73]

Peripheral Nerve Disorders [73]
PN 40   SC 37560
- B Nervous System Disorders [67]
- N Myasthenia Gravis [73]
  ↓ Neuralgia [73]
- R Muscular Dystrophy [73]
  ↓ Paralysis [73]
  ↓ Peripheral Nervous System [73]

Peripheral Nervous System [73]
PN 201   SC 37570
SN Use PERIPHERAL NERVES to access references from 73-93.
- UF Nerves (Peripheral)
- B Nervous System [67]
- N ↓ Autonomic Nervous System [67]
  ↓ Cranial Nerves [73]
  ↓ Neural Pathways [82]
  Spinal Nerves [73]

Peripheral Nervous System — (cont'd)
R   Autonomic Ganglia [73]
↓ Peripheral Nerve Disorders [73]

Peripheral Vision [88]
PN 150   SC 37580
B   Visual Perception [67]
R   Visual Field [67]

Permissiveness (Parental)
Use Parental Permissiveness

Perpetrators [88]
PN 715   SC 37595
N   ↓ Criminals [67]
R   ↓ Crime [67]
Criminal Responsibility [91]
Incest [73]
Victimization [73]

Perphenazine [73]
PN 98   SC 37600
B   Antiemetic Drugs [73]
Phenothiazine Derivatives [73]

Persecution [73]
PN 68   SC 37610
B   Antisocial Behavior [71]
Interpersonal Interaction [67]
R   Torture [88]
Victimization [73]

Perseverance
Use Persistence

Perseveration [67]
PN 129   SC 37630
SN Persistent repetition of a response to different and perhaps inappropriate stimuli which may be due to a refusal or an inability to interrupt one's behavior or to change from one task to another. Also, pathological repetition of thoughts, acts, or verbalizations.
B   Thought Disturbances [73]

Persistence [73]
PN 698   SC 37640
SN Maintenance of particular behavior despite effort, opposition, or cessation of initiating stimulus. Used for human or animal populations.
UF Perseverance
B   Personality Traits [67]
R   ↓ Motivation [67]

Person Environment Fit [91]
PN 76   SC 37645
SN Compatibility between individuals and their surroundings.
R   ↓ Adjustment [67]
↓ Environment [67]
Environmental Adaptation [73]
↓ Environmental Planning [82]
↓ Personality [67]
↓ Systems [67]
↓ Working Conditions [73]

Personal Adjustment
Use Emotional Adjustment

Personal Computers
Use Microcomputers

Personal Construct Theory
Use Personality Theory

Personal Defense
Use Self Defense

Personal Growth Techniques
Use Human Potential Movement

Personal Orientation Inventory [73]
PN 113   SC 37670
B   Nonprojective Personality Measures [73]

Personal Space [73]
PN 1004   SC 37680
SN Minimal spatial distance preferred by an individual in his/her relations with others.
UF Interpersonal Distance
R   Crowding [78]
Physical Contact [82]
↓ Social Behavior [67]
Social Density [78]

Personal Therapy [91]
PN 25   SC 37685
SN Therapy for professionals working in the mental health field, for example, psychologists, psychiatrists, or social workers.
B   Treatment [67]
R   ↓ Clinical Methods Training [73]
Impaired Professionals [85]
↓ Mental Health Personnel [67]
↓ Professional Consultation [73]
Professional Supervision [88]

Personal Values [73]
PN 1760   SC 37690
SN Set of ideals that an individual deems worthwhile and that govern his/her behavior.
B   Values [67]
R   Anomie [78]
Morality [67]

Personality [67]
PN 6692   SC 37870
SN Conceptually broad array term referring to the totality of an individual's behavioral or emotional characteristics. Use a more specific term if possible.
UF Character
Disposition
Temperament
N   ↓ Personality Traits [67]
↓ Psychoanalytic Personality Factors [73]
R   ↓ Cognitive Style [67]
Coronary Prone Behavior [82]
Egocentrism [78]
↓ Emotional Adjustment [73]
↓ Emotional States [73]
↓ Emotions [67]
Gender Identity [85]
Individual Differences [67]
Lifestyle [78]
Person Environment Fit [91]
Personality Change [67]
Personality Correlates [67]
↓ Personality Development [67]
↓ Personality Disorders [67]
↓ Personality Processes [67]
Personality Theory [67]
Predisposition [73]
Psychodynamics [73]
Self Actualization [73]
↓ Self Concept [67]
Self Disclosure [73]
Self Evaluation [67]
Self Monitoring (Personality) [85]
Self Perception [67]
Somatotypes [73]
Teacher Personality [73]

Personality Assessment
Use Personality Measures

Personality Change [67]
PN 973   SC 37720
SN Process or fact of change associated either with development and maturity, or as the result of stress, illness, treatment, or other factors.
R   ↓ Personality [67]

Personality Characteristics
Use Personality Traits

Personality Correlates [67]
PN 3822   SC 37740
SN Description of numerous or unspecified personality traits which bear a mutual or reciprocal relationship to a particular phenomenon.
R   ↓ Personality [67]

Personality Development [67]
PN 3756   SC 37750
UF Character Development
Character Formation
B   Psychosocial Development [73]
N   ↓ Ego Development [91]
Separation Individuation [82]
R   Ego Identity [91]
Emotional Development [73]
Identity Crisis [73]
Moral Development [73]
↓ Personality [67]
Personality Theory [67]

Personality Disorders [67]
PN 1806   SC 37760
UF Character Disorders
B   Mental Disorders [67]
N   Antisocial Personality [73]
Aspergers Syndrome [91]
Asthenic Personality [73]
Avoidant Personality [94]
Dependent Personality [94]
Hysterical Personality [73]
Inadequate Personality [73]
Narcissistic Personality [73]
Obsessive Compulsive Personality [73]
Paranoid Personality [73]
Passive Aggressive Personality [73]
↓ Sadomasochistic Personality [73]
Schizoid Personality [73]
Schizotypal Personality [91]
R   Borderline States [78]
↓ Defense Mechanisms [67]
↓ Dissociative Patterns [73]
↓ Ethnospecific Disorders [73]
Explosive Personality [73]
Kleptomania [73]
↓ Personality [67]
↓ Personality Processes [67]
Personality Theory [67]
↓ Personality Traits [67]
Pyromania [73]

Personality Factors
Use Personality Traits

Personality Factors (Psychoanalytic)
Use Psychoanalytic Personality Factors

Personality Measures [67]
PN 6418   SC 37790
UF Personality Assessment
Personality Tests
Tests (Personality)
B   Measurement [67]
N   California Psychological Inventory [67]
General Health Questionnaire [91]
↓ Nonprojective Personality Measures [73]
↓ Projective Personality Measures [73]
Rokeach Dogmatism Scale [73]

Personality Measures — (cont'd)
N   Sensation Seeking Scale [73]
    Sentence Completion Tests [91]

Personality Processes [67]
PN 1126   SC 37800
SN Conceptually broad array term referring to the interaction among personality structures (e.g., ego, id) or pattern of characteristic tendencies, often but not exclusively from a psychoanalytic perspective. Use a more specific term if possible.
N   Catharsis [73]
    Cathexis [73]
    ↓ Defense Mechanisms [67]
    Externalization [73]
    Inhibition (Personality) [73]
    Introspection [73]
R   Lifestyle [78]
    ↓ Mental Disorders [67]
    ↓ Personality [67]
    ↓ Personality Disorders [67]
    ↓ Psychoanalytic Personality Factors [73]
    Psychoanalytic Theory [67]
    Reality Testing [73]

Personality Tests
Use   Personality Measures

Personality Theory [67]
PN 1719   SC 37850
UF   Personal Construct Theory
B   Theories [67]
R   ↓ Personality [67]
    ↓ Personality Development [67]
    ↓ Personality Disorders [67]
    ↓ Personality Traits [67]
    Self Perception [67]
    Self Psychology [88]

Personality Traits [67]
PN 14073   SC 37860
UF   Personality Characteristics
    Personality Factors
B   Personality [67]
N   Adaptability (Personality) [73]
    Aggressiveness [73]
    Altruism [73]
    Androgyny [82]
    Assertiveness [73]
    Authoritarianism [67]
    Charisma [88]
    ↓ Cognitive Style [67]
    Conformity (Personality) [67]
    Conservatism [73]
    Courage [73]
    Creativity [67]
    Cruelty [73]
    Curiosity [67]
    Cynicism [73]
    Defensiveness [67]
    Dependency (Personality) [67]
    Dishonesty [73]
    Dogmatism [78]
    Egalitarianism [85]
    Egotism [73]
    Emotional Immaturity [73]
    Emotional Inferiority [73]
    Emotional Instability [73]
    Emotional Maturity [73]
    Emotional Security [73]
    Emotional Stability [73]
    Emotional Superiority [73]
    Emotionality (Personality) [73]
    Empathy [67]
    Extraversion [67]
    Femininity [67]
    Gregariousness [73]
    Honesty [73]
    Hypnotic Susceptibility [73]

Personality Traits — (cont'd)
N   Idealism [73]
    Independence (Personality) [73]
    Individuality [73]
    Initiative [73]
    Insight [73]
    Internal External Locus of Control [67]
    Introversion [67]
    Irritability [88]
    Leadership Style [73]
    Liberalism [73]
    Likability [88]
    Loyalty [73]
    Machiavellianism [73]
    Masculinity [67]
    Misanthropy [73]
    Moodiness [73]
    Narcissism [67]
    Negativism [73]
    Nervousness [73]
    Neuroticism [73]
    Nonconformity (Personality) [73]
    Nurturance [85]
    Obedience [73]
    Objectivity [73]
    Omnipotence [94]
    Openmindedness [78]
    Optimism [73]
    Paranoia [88]
    Passiveness [73]
    Perceptiveness (Personality) [73]
    Perfectionism [88]
    Persistence [73]
    Pessimism [73]
    Positivism [73]
    Psychoticism [78]
    Repression Sensitization [73]
    Rigidity (Personality) [67]
    ↓ Risk Taking [67]
    Self Control [73]
    Selfishness [73]
    Sensation Seeking [78]
    Sensitivity (Personality) [67]
    Seriousness [73]
    Sexuality [73]
    Sincerity [73]
    Sociability [73]
    Subjectivity [94]
    Suggestibility [67]
    Timidity [73]
    ↓ Tolerance [73]
R   Codependency [91]
    Coronary Prone Behavior [82]
    Egocentrism [78]
    Field Dependence [73]
    Instrumentality [91]
    ↓ Personality Disorders [67]
    Personality Theory [67]
    Self Monitoring (Personality) [85]
    Spirituality [88]
    Wisdom [94]

Personnel [67]
PN 2303   SC 37980
SN Conceptually broad array term referring to the body of persons employed by a given organization or associated with a particular occupation. Use a more specific term if possible.
UF   Employees
    Workers
N   Artists [73]
    ↓ Government Personnel [73]
    ↓ Hypnotists [73]
    ↓ Nonprofessional Personnel [82]
    ↓ Paraprofessional Personnel [73]
    ↓ Professional Personnel [78]
    ↓ Religious Personnel [73]
    ↓ Social Workers [73]
    ↓ Volunteer Personnel [73]

Personnel — (cont'd)
R   Affirmative Action [85]
    Employability [73]
    Employee Absenteeism [73]
    ↓ Employee Benefits [73]
    ↓ Employee Characteristics [88]
    Employee Interaction [88]
    Employee Turnover [73]
    Employer Attitudes [73]
    Employment History [78]
    Job Applicant Attitudes [73]
    Job Applicants [85]
    ↓ Job Performance [67]
    Labor Union Members [73]
    Military Veterans [73]
    ↓ Occupations [67]
    ↓ Personnel Management [73]
    ↓ Personnel Supply [73]
    ↓ Personnel Training [67]
    Reemployment [91]
    Retirement [73]
    Teams [88]
    Unemployment [67]
    Work (Attitudes Toward) [73]
    ↓ Working Conditions [73]
    Working Women [78]

Personnel Development
Use   Personnel Training

Personnel Evaluation [73]
PN 1982   SC 37900
B   Evaluation [67]
    Personnel Management [73]
N   Occupational Success Prediction [73]
    Teacher Effectiveness Evaluation [78]
R   Assessment Centers [82]
    Employment Discrimination [94]
    Job Applicant Interviews [73]
    Job Applicant Screening [73]
    ↓ Job Performance [67]
    Peer Evaluation [82]
    Personnel Promotion [78]
    ↓ Personnel Selection [67]

Personnel Management [73]
PN 687   SC 37910
UF   Human Resources
B   Management [67]
N   Career Development [85]
    Job Analysis [67]
    Labor Management Relations [67]
    ↓ Personnel Evaluation [73]
    Personnel Placement [73]
    Personnel Promotion [78]
    ↓ Personnel Recruitment [73]
    ↓ Personnel Selection [67]
    Personnel Termination [73]
R   Affirmative Action [85]
    Business Education [73]
    Business Management [73]
    Employment Discrimination [94]
    ↓ Personnel [67]
    Supported Employment [94]

Personnel Placement [73]
PN 232   SC 37920
UF   Placement (Personnel)
B   Personnel Management [73]
R   Assessment Centers [82]
    Career Development [85]

Personnel Promotion [78]
PN 245   SC 37925
UF   Job Promotion
B   Personnel Management [73]
R   Assessment Centers [82]
    Career Development [85]

Personnel Promotion — (cont'd)
R   Employment History [78]
↓   Job Performance [67]
     Occupational Status [78]
     Occupational Success [78]
↓   Personnel Evaluation [73]

Personnel Recruitment [73]
PN 257   SC 37930
UF   Employment Processes
     Recruitment (Personnel)
B   Personnel Management [73]
N   Military Recruitment [73]
     Teacher Recruitment [73]
R   Affirmative Action [85]

Personnel Selection [67]
PN 2295   SC 37940
UF   Employee Selection
     Hiring
     Selection (Personnel)
B   Personnel Management [73]
N   Job Applicant Interviews [73]
     Job Applicant Screening [73]
R   Affirmative Action [85]
     Assessment Centers [82]
     Employment Discrimination [94]
↓   Personnel Evaluation [73]
↓   Screening [82]

Personnel Supply [73]
PN 90   SC 37950
SN Availability of manpower or human resources required for an occupation or service in order to meet demands.
UF   Manpower
N   Medical Personnel Supply [73]
     Mental Health Personnel Supply [73]
R   ↓ Personnel [67]

Personnel Termination [73]
PN 231   SC 37960
UF   Employee Termination
B   Personnel Management [73]
R   Employment History [78]
     Job Security [78]
↓   Occupational Tenure [73]
     Retirement [73]
     Unemployment [67]

Personnel Training [67]
PN 2422   SC 37970
UF   Job Training
     Personnel Development
     Training (Personnel)
B   Education [67]
N   Apprenticeship [73]
↓   Inservice Training [85]
     Management Training [73]
     Military Training [73]
     On the Job Training [73]
R   Business Education [73]
     Career Development [85]
     Human Relations Training [78]
↓   Personnel [67]
     Sensitivity Training [73]

Perspective Taking
Use Role Taking

Perspiration
Use Sweat

Persuasion Therapy [73]
PN 9   SC 38000

Persuasion Therapy — (cont'd)
SN Limited directive therapy in which the client is encouraged to follow the therapist's advice to deal with current crisis.
B   Psychotherapy [67]

Persuasive Communication [67]
PN 1720   SC 38010
SN Communication aimed at influencing others to accept a position, belief, or course of action.
B   Communication [67]
N   Brainwashing [82]
R   Coercion [94]
     Peer Pressure [94]
     Propaganda [73]
     Rhetoric [91]

Peru [88]
PN 44   SC 38015
B   South America [67]

Pessimism [73]
PN 190   SC 38020
SN Attitude characterized by a gloomy and desperate temperament and inclination to emphasize and expect the worst possible outcome of events and actions.
B   Emotional States [73]
     Personality Traits [67]
R   Cynicism [73]
     Negativism [73]

Pesticides
Use Insecticides

Pet Therapy
Use Animal Assisted Therapy

Petit Mal Epilepsy [73]
PN 38   SC 38030
B   Epilepsy [67]

Pets [82]
PN 263   SC 38035
SN Domesticated animals kept primarily for pleasure rather than utility.
R   Animal Assisted Therapy [94]
↓   Animals [67]
     Interspecies Interaction [91]

Petting [73]
PN 8   SC 38040
B   Psychosexual Behavior [67]
R   ↓ Sexual Intercourse (Human) [73]
     Social Dating [73]

Peyote [73]
PN 5   SC 38050
B   Alkaloids [73]
     Hallucinogenic Drugs [67]
     Psychotomimetic Drugs [73]
R   Mescaline [73]

Phantom Limbs [73]
PN 63   SC 38060
B   Body Image Disturbances [73]
R   ↓ Amputation [73]

Pharmacists [91]
PN 11   SC 38065
B   Medical Personnel [67]

Pharmacology [73]
PN 573   SC 38070
B   Paramedical Sciences [73]
N   Psychopharmacology [67]
R   Bioavailability [91]
     Drug Abuse Liability [94]

Pharmacotherapy
Use Drug Therapy

Pharyngeal Disorders [73]
PN 13   SC 38090
B   Respiratory Tract Disorders [73]

Pharynx [73]
PN 30   SC 38100
B   Digestive System [67]
     Respiratory System [73]

Phenaglycodol [73]
PN 2   SC 38120
B   Sedatives [73]
     Tranquilizing Drugs [67]

Phencyclidine [82]
PN 433   SC 38125
SN Piperadine having hallucinogenic, anesthetic, and analgesic properties.
UF   PCP
B   Analgesic Drugs [73]
     Anesthetic Drugs [73]
     Hallucinogenic Drugs [67]

Phenelzine [73]
PN 225   SC 38130
B   Antidepressant Drugs [71]
     Monoamine Oxidase Inhibitors [73]

Phenethylamines [85]
PN 82   SC 38135
UF   Phenylethylamines
B   Amines [73]
R   ↓ Amphetamine [67]

Pheniprazine [73]
PN 6   SC 38140
B   Antidepressant Drugs [71]
     Antihypertensive Drugs [73]
     Monoamine Oxidase Inhibitors [73]

Phenmetrazine [73]
PN 14   SC 38150
B   Appetite Depressing Drugs [73]
     Sympathomimetic Amines [73]

Phenobarbital [73]
PN 261   SC 38160
B   Anticonvulsive Drugs [73]
     Barbiturates [67]
     Hypnotic Drugs [73]
     Sedatives [73]

Phenomenology [67]
PN 1088   SC 38180
B   Philosophies [67]
R   Constructivism [94]
     Hermeneutics [91]
↓   History of Psychology [67]

Phenothiazine Derivatives [73]
PN 200   SC 38190
B   Tranquilizing Drugs [67]
N   Butyrylperazine [73]
     Chlorpromazine [67]
     Chlorprothixene [73]
     Fluphenazine [73]
     Mesoridazine [73]
     Perphenazine [73]
     Prochlorperazine [73]
     Promazine [73]
     Thioridazine [73]
     Trifluoperazine [73]
     Triflupromazine [73]
R   ↓ Cholinergic Blocking Drugs [73]

Phenotypes 73
PN 208   SC 38200
  R   Assortative Mating 91
     ↓ Genetics 67
     Genotypes 73

Phenoxybenzamine 73
PN 65   SC 38210
  B   Adrenergic Blocking Drugs 73
     Amines 73
     Antihypertensive Drugs 73

Phenylalanine 73
PN 118   SC 38220
  B   Alanines 73
  N   Parachlorophenylalanine 78

Phenylethylamines
  Use Phenethylamines

Phenylketonuria 73
PN 131   SC 38230
  UF Oligophrenia (Phenylpyruvic)
     PKU (Hereditary Disorder)
  B   Genetic Disorders 73
     Metabolism Disorders 73
     Neonatal Disorders 73
  R   ↓ Mental Retardation 67

Phenytoin
  Use Diphenylhydantoin

Pheromones 73
PN 598   SC 38240
SN Chemical substances released by an organism that may influence the behavior of other organisms of the same species in characteristic ways.
  R   ↓ Animal Mating Behavior 67
     Animal Scent Marking 85
     ↓ Glands 67
     ↓ Hormones 67

Phi Coefficient 73
PN 17   SC 38250
  B   Statistical Correlation 67

Philippines 73
PN 306   SC 38260
  B   Southeast Asia 73

Philosophies 67
PN 2783   SC 38270
  N   Animism 73
     Asceticism 73
     Dualism 73
     Epistemology 73
     Existentialism 67
     Fatalism 73
     Hermeneutics 91
     Humanism 73
     Idealism 73
     Intellectualism 73
     Logic (Philosophy) 73
     Materialism 73
     Metaphysics 73
     Mysticism 67
     Nihilism 73
     Pacifism 73
     Phenomenology 67
     Pragmatism 73
     Realism (Philosophy) 73
     Reductionism 73
  R   Hedonism 73

Philosophy of Life
  Use World View

Phobias 67
PN 1806   SC 38280
SN Disorders characterized by persistent, unrealistic, intense fear of an object, activity, or situation.
  UF Arachnophobia
     Phobic Neurosis
     Spider Phobia
  B   Anxiety Neurosis 73
  N   Acrophobia 73
     Agoraphobia 73
     Claustrophobia 73
     Ophidiophobia 73
     School Phobia 73
     Social Phobia 85
  R   ↓ Anxiety 67
     ↓ Fear 67

Phobic Neurosis
SN Term discontinued in 1988. Use PHOBIC NEUROSIS to access references from 73-87.
  Use Phobias

Phonemes 73
PN 737   SC 38300
SN Members of the set of the smallest units of speech that serve to distinguish one utterance from another, as the p of pat and the f of fat. Used both for the concept of phonemes as well as the discipline of phonemics. Compare PHONOLOGY.
  B   Phonology 73
  N   Consonants 73
  R   Phonetics 67
     ↓ Prosody 91
     Vowels 73

Phonetics 67
PN 809   SC 38310
SN Science, study, analysis, and classification of sounds including their production in speech, transmission and perception. Used for the linguistic discipline or the specific phonetic characteristics of utterances themselves.
  B   Phonology 73
  R   Articulation (Speech) 67
     Morphemes 73
     ↓ Phonemes 73
     Syllables 73

Phonics 73
PN 151   SC 38320
SN Science of sound. Also, a method of teaching beginners to read and pronounce words by hearing the phonetic value of letters, letter groups, and especially syllables.
  B   Language Arts Education 73
  R   Reading Education 73

Phonology 73
PN 978   SC 38330
SN Study of the ways in which speech sounds (phonemes) and phonetic features form systems and patterns at a given point in time or from a historical perspective. Used for the linguistic discipline or the specific phonological processes or factors themselves. Compare PHONEMES.
  B   Grammar 67
  N   ↓ Phonemes 73
     Phonetics 67
     ↓ Prosody 91
     Syllables 73
     Vowels 73
  R   Inflection
     Morphology (Language) 73
     ↓ Semantics 67
     ↓ Syntax 71

Phosphatases 73
PN 70   SC 38340

Phosphatases — (cont'd)
  B   Enzymes 73
  R   ↓ Esterases 73
     Hydroxylases 73

Phosphatides 73
PN 132   SC 38350
  UF Phospholipids
  B   Fatty Acids 73
  N   Lecithin 91

Phospholipids
  Use Phosphatides

Phosphorus 73
PN 29   SC 38370
  B   Nonmetallic Elements 73

Phosphorylases 73
PN 12   SC 38380
  B   Enzymes 73

Photic Threshold
  Use Illumination AND Visual Thresholds

Photographic Art 73
PN 28   SC 38400
  B   Art 67
  R   Motion Pictures (Entertainment) 73

Photographic Memory
  Use Eidetic Imagery

Photographs 67
PN 588   SC 38410
SN Use for photographs as stimuli. Not used as a document type identifier.
  B   Audiovisual Communications Media 73
  R   Pictorial Stimuli 78

Photopic Stimulation 73
PN 172   SC 38420
SN Presentation of light at intensity levels characteristic of daylight illumination, activating cone photoreceptors in the retina.
  B   Illumination 67
  R   Scotopic Stimulation 73

Photoreceptors 73
PN 274   SC 38430
  B   Neural Receptors 73
     Sensory Neurons 73
  N   Cones (Eye) 73
     Rods (Eye) 73
  R   Visual Receptive Fields 82

Phototherapy 91
PN 83   SC 38435
  UF Bright Light Therapy
     Illumination Therapy
  B   Organic Therapies 73
  R   ↓ Psychotherapy 67
     Seasonal Affective Disorder 91

Phrases 73
PN 104   SC 38440
SN Groups of words that function as an element in grammatical structure.
  B   Language 67
  R   ↓ Syntax 71

Phrenic Nerve
  Use Spinal Nerves

Phylogenesis 73
PN 118   SC 38460

Phylogenesis — (cont'd)
R ↓ Biology [67]
    Botany [73]

Physical Abuse [91]
PN 255   SC 38465
B   Antisocial Behavior [71]
R   Battered Child Syndrome [73]
    Battered Females [88]
   ↓ Child Abuse [71]
    Elder Abuse [88]
    Emotional Abuse [91]
   ↓ Family Violence [82]
    Partner Abuse [91]
    Patient Abuse [91]
   ↓ Sexual Abuse [88]
   ↓ Violence [73]

Physical Agility [73]
PN 52   SC 38470
UF Agility (Physical)
B   Motor Processes [67]
N   Physical Dexterity [73]
R   Motor Coordination [73]
    Physical Mobility [94]

Physical Appearance [82]
PN 282   SC 38473
SN Externally visible characteristics or features
of a person.
N   Physique [67]
R   Clothing [67]
    Facial Features [73]
    Nudity [73]
    Physical Attractiveness [73]
    Somatotypes [73]

Physical Attractiveness [73]
PN 1150   SC 38475
R   Facial Features [73]
    Interpersonal Attraction [67]
   ↓ Physical Appearance [82]

Physical Comfort [82]
PN 89   SC 38477
SN Perceived degree of physical well-being in
response to internal or environmental conditions.
UF Comfort (Physical)
R ↓ Environment [67]
    Furniture [85]
   ↓ Satisfaction [73]

Physical Contact [82]
PN 480   SC 38478
SN Bodily contact. Used for human or animal
populations.
UF Touching
B   Social Interaction [67]
R ↓ Animal Social Behavior [67]
    Intimacy [73]
    Personal Space [73]

Physical Development [73]
PN 1270   SC 38480
UF Physical Growth
B   Development [67]
N ↓ Motor Development [73]
    Neural Development [85]
   ↓ Prenatal Development [73]
    Sexual Development [73]
R   Adolescent Development [73]
    Age Differences [67]
    Aging (Attitudes Toward) [85]
    Animal Development [78]
   ↓ Childhood Development [67]
   ↓ Delayed Development [73]
   ↓ Developmental Age Groups [73]
   ↓ Developmental Stages [73]

Physical Development — (cont'd)
R ↓ Early Childhood Development [73]
    Emotional Development [73]
   ↓ Human Development [67]
   ↓ Infant Development [73]
    Neonatal Development [73]
   ↓ Perceptual Development [73]
    Physical Maturity [73]
    Precocious Development [73]
   ↓ Psychogenesis [73]
    Sex Linked Developmental Differences [73]

Physical Dexterity [73]
PN 123   SC 38490
UF Dexterity (Physical)
B   Perceptual Motor Coordination [73]
    Physical Agility [73]
R   Physical Mobility [94]

Physical Disfigurement [78]
PN 109   SC 38492
UF Deformity
R ↓ Disorders [67]
   ↓ Injuries [73]
   ↓ Physically Handicapped [67]

Physical Divisions (Geographic)
Use Geography

Physical Education [67]
PN 1144   SC 38500
B   Curriculum [67]

Physical Endurance [73]
PN 193   SC 38510
B   Endurance [73]
R   Physical Fitness [73]
    Physical Strength [73]
    Physiological Stress [67]

Physical Examination [88]
PN 117   SC 38515
SN Examination or screening of an individual's
overall physical health.
UF Health Screening
R   Drug Usage Screening [88]
    Mammography [94]
   ↓ Medical Diagnosis [73]
    Preventive Medicine [73]
    Self Examination (Medical) [88]

Physical Exercise
Use Exercise

Physical Fitness [73]
PN 742   SC 38530
R   Aerobic Exercise [88]
   ↓ Exercise [73]
    Physical Endurance [73]
    Physical Strength [73]

Physical Geography
Use Geography

Physical Growth
Use Physical Development

Physical Handicaps (Attit Toward) [73]
PN 471   SC 38550
B   Handicapped (Attitudes Toward) [73]
R ↓ Physically Handicapped [67]

Physical Illness
Use Disorders

Physical Illness (Attitudes Toward) [85]
PN 591   SC 38557

Physical Illness (Attitudes Toward) —
    (cont'd)
SN Attitudes toward one's own or other's phys-
ical illness.
R ↓ Handicapped (Attitudes Toward) [73]
    Health Attitudes [85]
    Health Knowledge [94]
    Illness Behavior [82]

Physical Maturity [73]
PN 77   SC 38560
SN Attainment of a stage of physical develop-
ment commonly associated with persons of a
given age level.
UF Maturity (Physical)
R ↓ Physical Development [73]

Physical Mobility [94]
PN 0   SC 38563
SN Ability to move within one's environment.
May be used for mobility problems associated
with aging or handicapping conditions. Used for
human populations only.
B   Motor Processes [67]
R   Activities of Daily Living [91]
    Activity Level [82]
   ↓ Handicapped [67]
    Mobility Aids [78]
   ↓ Motor Development [73]
   ↓ Physical Agility [73]
    Physical Dexterity [73]

Physical Restraint [82]
PN 471   SC 38566
SN Use of any physical means to restrict the
movement of a client or subject, human or ani-
mal.
UF Restraint (Physical)
R ↓ Motor Processes [67]
    Patient Violence [94]
   ↓ Physical Treatment Methods [73]
   ↓ Treatment [67]

Physical Strength [73]
PN 265   SC 38570
UF Strength (Physical)
R   Physical Endurance [73]
    Physical Fitness [73]

Physical Therapists [73]
PN 66   SC 38580
B   Medical Personnel [67]
    Therapists [67]

Physical Therapy [73]
PN 258   SC 38590
SN Treatment of disorder or injury by physical
means, such as light, heat, cold, water, elec-
tricity, or by mechanical apparatus or
kinesitherapy.
UF Physiotherapy
B   Paramedical Sciences [73]
    Rehabilitation [67]
R   Occupational Therapy [67]

Physical Trauma
Use Injuries

Physical Treatment Methods [73]
PN 337   SC 38610
SN Medical, dental, and surgical methods for
treatment of disorder or injury. Use a more spe-
cific term if possible. Compare ORGANIC THER-
APIES.
UF Treatment Methods (Physical)
B   Treatment [67]
N   Acupuncture [73]
    Artificial Respiration [73]
    Blood Transfusion [73]

Physical Treatment Methods — (cont'd)
- N   Catheterization [73]
- ↓   Dental Treatment [73]
- ↓   Dialysis [73]
-     Diuresis [73]
-     Immunization [73]
-     Radiation Therapy [73]
- ↓   Surgery [71]
- R   Holistic Health [85]
-     Medical Treatment (General) [73]
-     Pain Management [94]
-     Physical Restraint [82]

Physically Handicapped [67]
PN 1918   SC 38620
- UF   Crippled
-     Orthopedically Handicapped
- B   Handicapped [67]
- N   Amputees [73]
-     Health Impaired [73]
- R   Hemiplegia [78]
-     Paraplegia [78]
-     Physical Disfigurement [78]
-     Physical Handicaps (Attit Toward) [73]
-     Quadriplegia [85]

Physician Patient Interaction
  Use Therapeutic Processes

Physicians [67]
PN 2954   SC 38640
- UF   Doctors
- B   Medical Personnel [67]
- N   Family Physicians [73]
-     General Practitioners [73]
-     Gynecologists [73]
-     Internists [73]
-     Neurologists [73]
-     Obstetricians [78]
-     Pathologists [73]
-     Pediatricians [73]
-     Psychiatrists [67]
-     Surgeons [73]
- R   Clinicians [73]

Physicists [73]
PN 12   SC 38650
- B   Professional Personnel [78]
- R ↓   Aerospace Personnel [73]
-     Mathematicians [73]
-     Scientists [67]

Physics [73]
PN 368   SC 38660
- B   Sciences [67]
- R   Magnetism [85]

Physiological Aging [67]
PN 2494   SC 38670
SN Biological changes which occur in an organism with the passage of time.
- UF   Aging (Physiological)
- B   Aging [91]
- R   Adult Development [78]
- ↓   Aged [73]
-     Aged (Attitudes Toward) [78]
-     Aging (Attitudes Toward) [85]
-     Geriatric Psychotherapy [73]
-     Geriatrics [67]
-     Life Expectancy [82]
- ↓   Physiology [67]
- ↓   Senile Dementia [73]

Physiological Arousal [67]
PN 2948   SC 38680
SN Condition of alertness and readiness to respond as evidenced by physiological signs such as heart rate or blood pressure.

Physiological Arousal — (cont'd)
- UF   Arousal (Physiological)
- R ↓   Brain Stimulation [67]
-     Cardiovascular Reactivity [94]
- ↓   Consciousness States [71]
-     Physiological Stress [67]
- ↓   Physiology [67]
- ↓   Sexual Arousal [78]

Physiological Correlates [67]
PN 4859   SC 38690
SN Numerous or unspecified physiological processes which accompany a particular psychological or physical action, state, or characteristic.
- R   Biological Markers [91]
-     Cardiovascular Reactivity [94]
-     Physiological Stress [67]
- ↓   Physiology [67]
- ↓   Symptoms [67]

Physiological Psychology [67]
PN 449   SC 38700
SN Study of the physiological correlates of mental, somatic, and behavioral processes. Use PHYSIOLOGY or a more specific term for the specific physiological processes themselves.
- B   Psychology [67]
- N   Neuropsychology [73]

Physiological Stress [67]
PN 1279   SC 38710
- B   Stress [67]
- R   Acceleration Effects [73]
-     Decompression Effects [73]
- ↓   Deprivation [67]
- ↓   Environmental Effects [73]
-     Environmental Stress [73]
-     Physical Endurance [73]
-     Physiological Arousal [67]
-     Physiological Correlates [67]
- ↓   Physiology [67]
-     Pollution [73]
-     Thermal Acclimatization [73]

Physiology [67]
PN 1232   SC 38720
SN Conceptually broad array term referring both to a branch of biological science and the functions and processes of living organisms. Use a more specific term if possible.
- N   Absorption (Physiological) [73]
- ↓   Appetite [73]
- ↓   Body Temperature [73]
-     Digestion [73]
- ↓   Electrophysiology [73]
- ↓   Excretion [67]
-     Homeostasis [73]
- ↓   Metabolism [67]
- ↓   Neurophysiology [73]
-     Oxygenation [73]
- ↓   Psychophysiology [67]
- ↓   Reflexes [71]
- ↓   Secretion (Gland) [73]
- ↓   Sexual Reproduction [73]
-     Thermal Acclimatization [73]
- R ↓   Anatomy [67]
- ↓   Biochemistry [67]
- ↓   Body Fluids [73]
- ↓   Cells (Biology) [73]
-     Histology [73]
-     Instinctive Behavior [82]
-     Metabolic Rates [73]
-     Morphology [73]
-     Nutrition [73]
-     Physiological Aging [67]
-     Physiological Arousal [67]
-     Physiological Correlates [67]
-     Physiological Stress [67]

Physiotherapy
  Use Physical Therapy

Physique [67]
PN 406   SC 38740
SN Overall body structure and appearance, including size, musculature, and posture. Limited primarily to human populations. Consider also BODY SIZE or SOMATOTYPES.
- B   Physical Appearance [82]
- R   Body Height [73]
- ↓   Body Size [85]
- ↓   Body Weight [67]
-     Posture [73]
-     Somatotypes [73]

Physostigmine [73]
PN 428   SC 38750
- UF   Eserine
- B   Alkaloids [73]
-     Amines [73]
-     Cholinergic Drugs [73]
-     Cholinesterase Inhibitors [73]
-     Cholinomimetic Drugs [73]

Piaget (Jean) [67]
PN 803   SC 38755
SN Identifies biographical or autobiographical studies and discussions of Piaget's works.
- R ↓   Cognitive Development [73]
-     Conservation (Concept) [73]
-     Constructivism [94]
- ↓   Developmental Stages [73]
-     Piagetian Tasks [73]
- ↓   Psychologists [67]

Piagetian Tasks [73]
PN 678   SC 38757
SN In measurement context, tasks used to assess children's cognitive abilities, based on Piaget's theory of cognitive development.
- R ↓   Measurement [67]
-     Piaget (Jean) [67]

Piano
  Use Musical Instruments

Pica [73]
PN 70   SC 38770
- R ↓   Adjunctive Behavior [82]
-     Lead Poisoning [73]
-     Toxicomania [73]

Picketing
  Use Social Demonstrations

Picks Disease [73]
PN 53   SC 38790
- B   Presenile Dementia [73]
- R   Alzheimers Disease [73]
- ↓   Genetic Disorders [73]

Picrotoxin [73]
PN 156   SC 38800
- B   Analeptic Drugs [73]
-     Gamma Aminobutyric Acid Antagonists [85]

Pictorial Stimuli [78]
PN 2407   SC 38805
SN Drawings, pictures, or other visual stimuli not composed of letters or digits.
- R   Photographs [67]
- ↓   Stimulus Presentation Methods [73]
- ↓   Visual Displays [73]
- ↓   Visual Stimulation [73]

Pigeons [67]
PN 3920   SC 38810
  B   Birds [67]

Pigments [73]
PN 210   SC 38820
  N   Hemoglobin [73]
       Melanin [73]
       Rhodopsin [85]
  R   Animal Coloration [85]
    ↓ Color [67]
       Eye Color [91]

Pigs [73]
PN 346   SC 38830
  B   Vertebrates [73]

Pilocarpine [73]
PN 104   SC 38840
  B   Alkaloids [73]
       Cholinergic Drugs [73]
       Cholinomimetic Drugs [73]

Pilots (Aircraft)
  Use Aircraft Pilots

Pimozide [73]
PN 377   SC 38860
  B   Tranquilizing Drugs [67]

Pineal Body [73]
PN 159   SC 38870
  B   Endocrine Glands [73]
  R   Melatonin [73]

Pinealectomy [73]
PN 54   SC 38880
  B   Endocrine Gland Surgery [73]

Piperazines [94]
PN 0   SC 38885
  UF Chlorophenylpiperazine
       MCPP
  N   Trazodone [88]

Pipradrol [73]
PN 14   SC 38890
  B   Antidepressant Drugs [71]
       CNS Stimulating Drugs [73]

Piracetam [82]
PN 116   SC 38900
  B   Antiemetic Drugs [73]
       CNS Stimulating Drugs [73]
       Nootropic Drugs [91]

Pitch (Frequency) [67]
PN 1397   SC 38910
SN Perceived changes in auditory stimuli that
are a function of the sound's frequency.
  UF Frequency (Pitch)
       Tone (Frequency)
  B   Auditory Stimulation [67]
  N   Speech Pitch [73]
       Ultrasound [73]

Pitch Discrimination [73]
PN 395   SC 38920
  B   Pitch Perception [73]

Pitch Perception [73]
PN 242   SC 38930
  B   Auditory Perception [67]
  N   Pitch Discrimination [73]

Pituitary Disorders [73]
PN 30   SC 38940

Pituitary Disorders — (cont'd)
  UF Hypophysis Disorders
  B   Endocrine Disorders [73]
  N   Hypopituitarism [73]
  R ↓ Adrenal Gland Disorders [73]
    ↓ Endocrine Sexual Disorders [73]
    ↓ Thyroid Disorders [73]

Pituitary Dwarfism
  Use Hypopituitarism

Pituitary Gland [73]
PN 263   SC 38960
  B   Endocrine Glands [73]
  N   Hypothalamo Hypophyseal System [73]

Pituitary Gland Surgery
  Use Hypophysectomy

Pituitary Hormones [73]
PN 204   SC 38980
  B   Hormones [67]
  N   Corticotropin [73]
       Dynorphins [85]
       Melanocyte Stimulating Hormone [85]
       Oxytocin [73]
       Somatotropin [73]
       Thyrotropin [73]
       Vasopressin [73]
  R ↓ Gonadotropic Hormones [73]
       Luteinizing Hormone [78]

PKU (Hereditary Disorder)
  Use Phenylketonuria

Place Conditioning [91]
PN 100   SC 39005
SN Learned behavior or the conditioning proce-
dure in which a stimulus is paired with an envi-
ronment, location, or physical position.
  UF Conditioned Place Preference
  B   Conditioning [67]
  R ↓ Animal Environments [67]
       Contextual Associations [67]

Place Disorientation [73]
PN 35   SC 39010
SN Impaired awareness of place, often char-
acteristic of organic mental disorders.
  UF Disorientation (Place)
  B   Consciousness Disturbances [73]
  R   Wandering Behavior [91]

Placebo [73]
PN 579   SC 39020
SN Any effect of therapeutic intervention that
cannot be attributed to the specific action of a
drug or the treatment. Also, the specific substance used as a control in experiments testing
the effect of a particular drug. Term is used
selectively for studies of the placebo effect or
other methodological issues.
  R ↓ Drugs [67]

Placement (Educational)
  Use Educational Placement

Placement (Personnel)
  Use Personnel Placement

Placenta [73]
PN 34   SC 39040
  R ↓ Pregnancy [67]
    ↓ Uterus [73]

Planarians [73]
PN 26   SC 39060
  B   Worms [67]

Planning (Management)
  Use Management Planning

Plasma (Blood)
  Use Blood Plasma

Plastic Surgery [73]
PN 75   SC 39090
  B   Surgery [71]

Platelets (Blood)
  Use Blood Platelets

Play
  Use Recreation

Play (Animal)
  Use Animal Play

Play Behavior (Childhood)
  Use Childhood Play Behavior

Play Development (Childhood)
  Use Childhood Play Development

Play Therapy [73]
PN 446   SC 39150
  B   Child Psychotherapy [67]

Playgrounds [73]
PN 72   SC 39160
  B   Recreation Areas [73]
  R ↓ School Facilities [73]

Pleasure [73]
PN 393   SC 39170
  UF Enjoyment
  B   Emotional States [73]
  R   Anhedonia [85]
       Euphoria [73]
       Happiness [73]

Plethysmography [73]
PN 46   SC 39180
  B   Medical Diagnosis [73]
  N   Electroplethysmography [73]

PMS
  Use Premenstrual Tension

Pneumoencephalography [73]
PN 27   SC 39190
  UF Air Encephalography
       Encephalography (Air)
  B   Encephalography [73]
       Medical Diagnosis [73]
       Roentgenography [73]

Pneumonia [73]
PN 18   SC 39200
  B   Lung Disorders [73]
  R ↓ Bacterial Disorders [73]
    ↓ Viral Disorders [73]

Poetry [73]
PN 584   SC 39210
  B   Literature [67]
  R   Creative Writing [94]

Poetry Therapy [94]
PN 0   SC 39215

Poetry Therapy — (cont'd)
B   Creative Arts Therapy [94]
R   Bibliotherapy [73]
   ↓ Psychotherapeutic Techniques [67]

Point Biserial Correlation [73]
PN 17   SC 39220
B   Statistical Correlation [67]

Poisoning
Use   Toxic Disorders

Poisons [73]
PN 261   SC 39240
UF   Toxins
B   Hazardous Materials [91]
N   ↓ Neurotoxins [82]
R   Carbon Monoxide [73]
   ↓ Insecticides [73]
   Prenatal Exposure [91]
   Teratogens [88]

Poisson Distribution
Use   Skewed Distribution

Poland [73]
PN 397   SC 39260
B   Europe [73]

Police Interrogation
Use   Legal Interrogation

Police Personnel [73]
PN 1520   SC 39270
B   Government Personnel [73]
   Law Enforcement Personnel [73]

Policy Making [88]
PN 536   SC 39278
N   ↓ Government Policy Making [73]
   Health Care Policy [94]

Policy Making (Foreign)
Use   Foreign Policy Making

Policy Making (Government)
Use   Government Policy Making

Poliomyelitis [73]
PN 25   SC 39300
UF   Infantile Paralysis
   Paralysis (Infantile)
B   Myelitis [73]
   Viral Disorders [73]
R   ↓ Musculoskeletal Disorders [73]
   ↓ Paralysis [73]
   ↓ Respiratory Tract Disorders [73]

Political Assassination [73]
PN 44   SC 39320
UF   Assassination (Political)

Political Attitudes [73]
PN 1669   SC 39330
B   Attitudes [67]
   Politics [67]
N   Nationalism [67]
   Political Conservatism [73]
   Political Liberalism [73]
   Political Radicalism [73]
R   Citizenship [73]
   Nonviolence [91]
   Political Socialization [88]
   Voting Behavior [73]

Political Campaigns [73]
PN 113   SC 39340
UF   Campaigns (Political)
B   Political Processes [73]
R   Political Candidates [73]
   Political Elections [73]
   Political Issues [73]
   Political Parties [73]
   Politicians [78]

Political Candidates [73]
PN 246   SC 39350
UF   Candidates (Political)
B   Politics [67]
R   Political Campaigns [73]
   Political Elections [73]
   Politicians [78]

Political Conservatism [73]
PN 195   SC 39360
UF   Conservatism (Political)
B   Political Attitudes [73]
R   Conservatism [73]

Political Divisions (Geographic)
Use   Geography

Political Economic Systems [73]
PN 187   SC 39370
B   Systems [67]
N   Capitalism [73]
   Communism [73]
   Democracy [73]
   Fascism [73]
   Socialism [73]
   Totalitarianism [73]
R   Economics [85]
   Economy [73]
   Government [67]

Political Elections [73]
PN 199   SC 39380
UF   Elections (Political)
B   Political Processes [73]
R   Political Campaigns [73]
   Political Candidates [73]
   Political Parties [73]
   Politicians [78]
   Voting Behavior [73]

Political Issues [73]
PN 241   SC 39390
B   Politics [67]
R   Political Campaigns [73]
   ↓ Social Issues [91]
   Voting Behavior [73]

Political Liberalism [73]
PN 149   SC 39400
UF   Liberalism (Political)
B   Political Attitudes [73]
R   Liberalism [73]

Political Participation [88]
PN 113   SC 39405
B   Politics [67]
N   Voting Behavior [73]
R   Social Demonstrations [73]
   ↓ Social Movements [67]

Political Parties [73]
PN 190   SC 39410
UF   Democratic Party
   Independent Party (Political)
   Republican Party
B   Politics [67]
R   Political Campaigns [73]
   Political Elections [73]

Political Processes [73]
PN 526   SC 39420
B   Politics [67]
N   Political Campaigns [73]
   Political Elections [73]
   Voting Behavior [73]
R   Freedom [78]
   Political Revolution [73]
   ↓ Social Processes [67]

Political Radicalism [73]
PN 113   SC 39430
UF   Radicalism (Political)
B   Political Attitudes [73]

Political Refugees
Use   Refugees

Political Revolution [73]
PN 87   SC 39440
UF   Revolutions (Political)
B   Radical Movements [73]
R   ↓ Political Processes [73]
   Terrorism [82]

Political Socialization [88]
PN 37   SC 39443
SN   Transmission of political norms through social agents, e.g., school, parents, peers, or mass media.
B   Socialization [67]
R   ↓ Political Attitudes [73]

Politicians [78]
PN 405   SC 39445
R   Political Campaigns [73]
   Political Candidates [73]
   Political Elections [73]
   ↓ Politics [67]

Politics [67]
PN 1219   SC 39450
N   ↓ Political Attitudes [73]
   Political Candidates [73]
   Political Issues [73]
   ↓ Political Participation [88]
   Political Parties [73]
   ↓ Political Processes [73]
R   Government [67]
   Politicians [78]

Pollution [73]
PN 209   SC 39460
B   Ecological Factors [73]
R   Atmospheric Conditions [73]
   Carcinogens [73]
   Ecology [73]
   Environmental Education [94]
   ↓ Hazardous Materials [91]
   Noise Effects [73]
   Physiological Stress [67]
   ↓ Temperature Effects [67]

Polydipsia [82]
PN 241   SC 39465
SN   Noncontingent excessive drinking behavior usually produced and maintained by operant schedules of reinforcement involving food as a reinforcer. Also used for disordered human populations.
B   Adjunctive Behavior [82]
R   Animal Drinking Behavior [73]
   ↓ Operant Conditioning [67]

Polydrug Abuse [94]
PN 0   SC 39467
UF   Multidrug Abuse
B   Drug Abuse [73]

Polydrug Abuse — (cont'd)
R ↓ Alcohol Abuse [88]
  ↓ Drug Addiction [67]
  ↓ Drug Dependency [73]
  Drug Interactions [82]

Polygamy [73]
PN 51   SC 39470
B Family Structure [73]
  Marriage [67]

Polygraphs [73]
PN 171   SC 39480
B Apparatus [67]
R Legal Interrogation [94]

Pons [73]
PN 368   SC 39510
B Brain Stem [73]
N Raphe Nuclei [82]

Popularity [88]
PN 142   SC 39520
SN Use SOCIAL APPROVAL to access references from 73-87.
R ↓ Interpersonal Interaction [67]
  Social Acceptance [67]
  Social Approval [67]
  ↓ Social Influences [67]
  ↓ Social Perception [67]

Population [73]
PN 269   SC 39530
SN Total number of organisms (human or animal) inhabiting a given locality.
N Overpopulation [73]
  ↓ Population (Statistics) [73]
R Birth Rate [82]
  Demographic Characteristics [67]
  Mortality Rate [73]
  Social Density [78]

Population (Statistics) [73]
PN 624   SC 39540
SN All the objects or people of a given class.
B Population [73]
N ↓ Statistical Samples [73]
R ↓ Central Tendency Measures [73]
  ↓ Experimental Design [67]
  ↓ Experimentation [67]
  ↓ Sampling (Experimental) [73]
  ↓ Statistical Analysis [67]
  Statistical Reliability [73]
  ↓ Statistical Variables [73]

Population Characteristics
Use Demographic Characteristics

Population Control
Use Birth Control

Population Genetics [73]
PN 83   SC 39570
SN Study of the genetic composition of human or animal populations; gene interactions and alterations that promote population changes and evolution.
B Genetics [67]
R Assortative Mating [91]
  Behavioral Genetics [94]
  ↓ Genetic Engineering [94]

Pornography [73]
PN 256   SC 39580
R Nudity [73]
  Obscenity [78]
  ↓ Psychosexual Behavior [67]
  Sex [67]

Pornography — (cont'd)
R ↓ Sex Offenses [82]
  ↓ Sexual Deviations [67]

Porphyria [73]
PN 22   SC 39590
B Blood and Lymphatic Disorders [73]
  Genetic Disorders [73]
  Metabolism Disorders [73]
R ↓ Mental Disorders [67]

Porpoises [73]
PN 7   SC 39600
B Whales [85]
R Dolphins [73]

Porteus Maze Test [73]
PN 18   SC 39610
B Intelligence Measures [67]

Portugal [82]
PN 85   SC 39613
B Europe [73]

Positive Reinforcement [73]
PN 740   SC 39620
SN Presentation of a positive reinforcer contingent on the performance of some behavior. Also, the positively reinforcing object or event itself which, when made to follow the performance of some behavior, results in an increase in the frequency of occurrence of that behavior. Compare REWARDS.
B Reinforcement [67]
N Praise [73]

Positive Transfer [73]
PN 162   SC 39630
SN Previous learning or practice which aids the acquisition of new material or skills as the result of common characteristics shared by the prior and current learning situation.
B Transfer (Learning) [67]

Positivism [73]
PN 91   SC 39640
SN Personal quality or state of being positive or confident.
B Personality Traits [67]
R Hope [91]
  Optimism [73]

Positron Emission Tomography
Use Tomography

Possession
Use Ownership

Postactivation Potentials [85]
PN 103   SC 39650
SN Enhancement of synaptic and cellular responses induced by brief high frequency electrical stimulation.
UF Long Term Potentiation
  Short Term Potentiation
B Electrical Activity [67]
R Electrical Brain Stimulation [73]
  Neural Plasticity [94]

Postganglionic Autonomic Fibers
Use Autonomic Ganglia

Postgraduate Students [73]
PN 83   SC 39684
SN Students involved in study or research after having completed a master's or doctoral degree. Such students are not necessarily pursuing a degree. Mandatory term in educational contexts.

Postgraduate Students — (cont'd)
B Students [67]
R ↓ College Students [67]
  Graduate Students [67]
  Young Adults [73]

Postgraduate Training [73]
PN 140   SC 39685
SN Studies or research beyond master's or doctoral degree.
B Higher Education [73]
N ↓ Clinical Psychology Grad Training [73]
  Clinical Psychology Internship [73]
  Medical Internship [73]
  Medical Residency [73]
R Professional Specialization [91]

Posthypnotic Suggestions [94]
PN 0   SC 39687
R ↓ Hypnosis [67]
  ↓ Hypnotherapy [73]
  Hypnotic Susceptibility [73]
  ↓ Relaxation Therapy [78]
  Suggestibility [67]

Postnatal Dysphoria
Use Postpartum Depression

Postnatal Period [73]
PN 971   SC 39690
R Lactation [73]
  Perinatal Period [94]
  Postpartum Depression [73]
  ↓ Pregnancy [67]

Postpartum Depression [73]
PN 386   SC 39700
UF Postnatal Dysphoria
  Postpartum Psychosis
B Major Depression [88]
R ↓ Acute Psychosis [73]
  Acute Schizophrenia [73]
  Attachment Behavior [85]
  ↓ Marital Relations [67]
  Mother Child Relations [67]
  ↓ Organic Brain Syndromes [73]
  Postnatal Period [73]

Postpartum Psychosis
Use Postpartum Depression

Postsurgical Complications [73]
PN 107   SC 39710
UF Surgical Complications
R Obstetrical Complications [78]
  Recovery (Disorders) [73]
  Relapse (Disorders) [73]
  ↓ Surgery [71]
  ↓ Treatment Outcomes [82]

Posttesting [73]
PN 78   SC 39720
SN Measurement performed after experimental manipulation, treatment, or program intervention. Comparison of pretest and posttest scores gives a measure of effectiveness of independent variables such as treatments or programs.
B Measurement [67]
R Repeated Measures [85]
  ↓ Testing Methods [67]

Posttraumatic Stress Disorder [85]
PN 1325   SC 39727
SN Acute, chronic, or delayed reactions to traumatic events such as military combat, assault, or natural disaster. Use TRAUMATIC NEUROSIS or STRESS REACTIONS to access references from 1973–1984.

Posttraumatic Stress Disorder — (cont'd)
B Anxiety Neurosis [73]
R Adjustment Disorders [94]
    Combat Experience [91]
    Emotional Trauma [67]
    Stress Reactions [73]
    Traumatic Neurosis [73]

Posttreatment Followup [73]
PN 678   SC 39730
SN Periodic check-ups of patients. Usually part of a comprehensive aftercare treatment. Differentiate from FOLLOWUP STUDIES which is a mandatory term identifying a type of methodology used in research.
UF Catamnesis
    Followup (Posttreatment)
R Aftercare [73]
    Discharge Planning [94]
  ↓ Treatment [67]

Posture [73]
PN 773   SC 39740
R Body Language [73]
  ↓ Motor Processes [67]
    Physique [67]

Potassium [73]
PN 129   SC 39750
B Metallic Elements [73]
N Potassium Ions [73]

Potassium Ions [73]
PN 40   SC 39770
B Electrolytes [73]
    Potassium [73]

Potential (Achievement)
Use Achievement Potential

Potential Dropouts [73]
PN 83   SC 39790
B Dropouts [73]

Potentiation (Drugs)
Use Drug Interactions

Poverty [73]
PN 451   SC 39820
B Social Issues [91]
R Disadvantaged [67]
    Homeless [88]
    Income (Economic) [73]
    Lower Income Level [73]
  ↓ Socioeconomic Status [67]

Poverty Areas [73]
PN 73   SC 39830
UF Slums
B Social Environments [73]
R Cultural Deprivation [73]
    Ghettoes [73]

Power [67]
PN 2192   SC 39840
SN Social control an individual has over others.
B Social Influences [67]
R Authority [67]
    Coercion [94]
  ↓ Dominance [67]
    Empowerment [91]
    Omnipotence [94]

Practice [67]
PN 3289   SC 39850
SN Use PRACTICE or PRACTICE EFFECTS to access references prior to 1982.

Practice — (cont'd)
UF Experience (Practice)
    Practice Effects
    Rehearsal
N Distributed Practice [73]
    Massed Practice [73]
R Curricular Field Experience [82]
  ↓ Experiences (Events) [73]
    Familiarity [67]
    Memory Training [94]
    Overcorrection [85]

Practice Effects
SN Term discontinued in 1982. Use PRACTICE EFFECTS or PRACTICE to access references prior to 1982.
Use Practice

Practicum Supervision [78]
PN 648   SC 39865
SN Supervision of students involved in practical application of learned material.
R ↓ Clinical Methods Training [73]
  ↓ Clinical Psychology Grad Training [73]
    Clinical Psychology Internship [73]
    Cooperating Teachers [78]
    Counselor Education [73]
  ↓ Teacher Education [67]

Prader Willi Syndrome [91]
PN 15   SC 39867
B Congenital Disorders [73]
    Syndromes [73]
R ↓ Mental Retardation [67]

Pragmatics [85]
PN 294   SC 39868
SN Study of the rules governing the use of language in context. Also used for the actual social interaction aspects of communication.
B Semiotics [85]
    Verbal Communication [67]
R ↓ Communication Skills [73]
  ↓ Interpersonal Communication [73]
  ↓ Linguistics [73]
    Metalinguistics [94]

Pragmatism [73]
PN 25   SC 39870
B Philosophies [67]

Praise [73]
PN 437   SC 39880
B Positive Reinforcement [73]
    Verbal Reinforcement [73]

Prayer [73]
PN 69   SC 39890
B Religious Practices [73]
R Meditation [73]

Praying Mantis
Use Mantis

Preadolescents [88]
PN 119   SC 39905
SN Ages 10-12 years. Use SCHOOL AGE CHILDREN or ADOLESCENTS, as appropriate, unless specific reference is made to the population as preadolescents. Used in noneducational contexts. Application of terms designating age is mandatory for ages 0-17.
B School Age Children [73]
R Adolescence [84]
  ↓ Adolescents [67]
  ↓ Elementary School Students [67]
    Intermediate School Students [73]
  ↓ Juvenile Delinquents [73]

Preadolescents — (cont'd)
R Middle School Students [85]
    Predelinquent Youth [78]

Precocious Development [73]
PN 57   SC 39910
B Development [67]
R ↓ Developmental Age Groups [73]
  ↓ Physical Development [73]
  ↓ Psychogenesis [73]

Precognition [73]
PN 94   SC 39920
B Clairvoyance [73]

Preconditioning [94]
PN 0   SC 39923
SN Presentation of two stimuli in a consecutive manner without reinforcement to determine if subject will respond to both stimuli in a conditioning paradigm.
UF Sensory Preconditioning
B Conditioning [67]
R Conditioned Stimulus [73]

Predatory Behavior (Animal)
Use Animal Predatory Behavior

Predelinquent Youth [78]
PN 62   SC 39927
SN Children considered at risk for developing delinquent behavior because their sociocultural and family backgrounds and early behavior patterns parallel those of juvenile delinquents.
R ↓ Adolescents [67]
  ↓ Children [67]
    Juvenile Delinquency [67]
  ↓ Juvenile Delinquents [73]
    Preadolescents [88]
  ↓ School Age Children [73]

Predictability (Measurement) [73]
PN 126   SC 39930
SN Statistical procedures used to forecast the value of the criterion variables (such as behavior, performance, or outcomes) on the basis of selected predictor variables.
B Statistical Analysis [67]
    Statistical Measurement [73]
R Confidence Limits (Statistics) [73]
  ↓ Hypothesis Testing [73]
  ↓ Prediction [67]
  ↓ Prediction Errors [73]
  ↓ Probability [67]

Prediction [67]
PN 5681   SC 39940
N Academic Achievement Prediction [67]
    Occupational Success Prediction [73]
R Future [91]
    Predictability (Measurement) [73]
  ↓ Prediction Errors [73]
    Predictive Validity [73]
    Prognosis [73]

Prediction Errors [73]
PN 52   SC 39950
B Errors [67]
N Type I Errors [73]
    Type II Errors [73]
R Consistency (Measurement) [73]
  ↓ Hypothesis Testing [73]
  ↓ Measurement [67]
    Predictability (Measurement) [73]
  ↓ Prediction [67]
  ↓ Statistical Analysis [67]
    Statistical Power [91]
    Statistical Reliability [73]

Prediction Errors — (cont'd)
R   ↓ Statistical Validity [73]
     ↓ Statistical Variables [73]

Predictive Validity [73]
PN 2330   SC 39960
SN   Usually expressed as a correlation coeffi-
cient, predictive validity is the extent to which
test scores, grades, assessment methods, scor-
ing techniques, and other variables can be used
to reliably predict future behavior or performance.
B   Statistical Validity [73]
R   Concurrent Validity [88]
   ↓ Prediction [67]
     Test Validity [73]

Predisposition [73]
PN 1887   SC 39970
SN   Proneness toward disorders or propensity
toward certain behaviors due to physical, psy-
chological, social, or situational factors. Consider
also SUSCEPTIBILITY (DISORDERS).
R   At Risk Populations [85]
     Coronary Prone Behavior [82]
   ↓ Disorders [67]
   ↓ Genetics [67]
   ↓ Mental Disorders [67]
     Nature Nurture [94]
   ↓ Personality [67]
     Premorbidity [78]
     Response Bias [67]
     Susceptibility (Disorders) [73]

Prednisolone [73]
PN 24   SC 39980
B   Adrenal Cortex Hormones [73]
     Corticosteroids [73]

Preference Measures [73]
PN 639   SC 39990
B   Measurement [67]
N   Kuder Preference Record [73]
     Least Preferred Coworker Scale [73]
R   ↓ Preferences [67]

Preferences [67]
PN 4634   SC 39995
N   Aesthetic Preferences [73]
     Brand Preferences [94]
     Food Preferences [73]
     Occupational Preference [73]
R   ↓ Preference Measures [73]
     Preferred Rewards [73]

Preferred Rewards [73]
PN 127   SC 40030
B   Rewards [67]
R   ↓ Preferences [67]

Prefrontal Cortex [94]
PN 0   SC 40035
B   Frontal Lobe [73]

Preganglionic Autonomic Fibers
   Use   Autonomic Ganglia

Pregnancy [67]
PN 3146   SC 40050
UF   Gestation
N   Adolescent Pregnancy [88]
R   ↓ Birth [67]
     Childbirth Training [78]
     Fertilization [73]
     Obstetrical Complications [78]
     Perinatal Period [94]
     Placenta [73]
     Postnatal Period [73]
   ↓ Prenatal Care [91]

Pregnancy — (cont'd)
R   Reproductive Technology [88]
   ↓ Sexual Reproduction [73]

Pregnancy (False)
   Use   Pseudocyesis

Prejudice [67]
PN 1054   SC 40070
B   Social Influences [67]
N   ↓ Religious Prejudices [73]
R   Age Discrimination [94]
     AntiSemitism [73]
   ↓ Attitudes [67]
     Employment Discrimination [94]
     Race and Ethnic Discrimination [94]
   ↓ Racial and Ethnic Attitudes [82]
     Racial and Ethnic Relations [82]
     Racism [73]
     Sex Discrimination [78]
     Sexism [88]
     Stigma [91]

Preliminary Scholastic Aptitude Test
   Use   Coll Ent Exam Bd Scholastic Apt Test

Premarital Counseling [73]
PN 115   SC 40090
B   Counseling [67]
R   ↓ Psychotherapeutic Counseling [73]

Premarital Intercourse [73]
PN 225   SC 40100
B   Sexual Intercourse (Human) [73]
R   Promiscuity [73]
     Social Dating [73]
     Virginity [73]

Premature Birth [73]
PN 887   SC 40110
B   Birth [67]
R   Birth Weight [85]
     Obstetrical Complications [78]

Premature Ejaculation [73]
PN 90   SC 40120
B   Male Orgasm [73]
     Sexual Function Disturbances [73]
R   Impotence [73]

Premenstrual Syndrome
   Use   Premenstrual Tension

Premenstrual Tension [73]
PN 572   SC 40130
SN   Physiological, emotional, and mental stress
related to the period of time immediately preced-
ing menstruation.
UF   PMS
     Premenstrual Syndrome
B   Menstrual Cycle [73]
R   ↓ Menstrual Disorders [73]
   ↓ Psychosomatic Disorders [67]

Premorbidity [78]
PN 403   SC 40135
SN   Condition of an individual before onset of
illness or disorder.
R   At Risk Populations [85]
   ↓ Disorders [67]
   ↓ Mental Disorders [67]
     Onset (Disorders) [73]
     Patient History [73]
     Predisposition [73]
     Susceptibility (Disorders) [73]

Prenatal Care [91]
PN 51   SC 40137
SN   Medical, health, and educational services
provided or obtained during pregnancy. Includes
maternal health behavior affecting prenatal devel-
opment.
N   Childbirth Training [78]
R   Early Intervention [82]
     Health Behavior [82]
   ↓ Health Care Services [78]
   ↓ Health Education [73]
   ↓ Obstetrics [78]
   ↓ Pregnancy [67]
   ↓ Prenatal Development [73]
     Prenatal Diagnosis [88]
   ↓ Prevention [73]
     Preventive Medicine [73]

Prenatal Development [73]
PN 1609   SC 40140
SN   Development of an organism prior to birth.
Used for human or animal populations.
B   Physical Development [73]
N   ↓ Prenatal Developmental Stages [73]
R   Animal Development [78]
     Fetal Alcohol Syndrome [85]
     Perinatal Period [94]
   ↓ Prenatal Care [91]
     Prenatal Diagnosis [88]
     Prenatal Exposure [91]
   ↓ Psychogenesis [73]
     Teratogens [88]

Prenatal Developmental Stages [73]
PN 26   SC 40150
B   Developmental Stages [73]
     Prenatal Development [73]
N   Embryo [73]
     Fetus [67]

Prenatal Diagnosis [88]
PN 56   SC 40152
SN   Techniques or procedures used to detect or
identify specific abnormalities or characteristics
of the fetus.
UF   Amniocentesis
B   Medical Diagnosis [73]
R   ↓ Congenital Disorders [73]
   ↓ Genetic Disorders [73]
   ↓ Prenatal Care [91]
   ↓ Prenatal Development [73]
     Reproductive Technology [88]

Prenatal Exposure [91]
PN 344   SC 40156
SN   Exposure to chemicals or other environmen-
tal factors prior to birth. Used for human and
animal populations.
R   ↓ Alcoholic Beverages [73]
   ↓ Disorders [67]
   ↓ Drugs [67]
   ↓ Poisons [73]
   ↓ Prenatal Development [73]
     Teratogens [88]
     Thalidomide [73]
     Tobacco Smoking [67]

Preoptic Area [94]
PN 0   SC 40158
SN   Consider HYPOTHALAMUS to access refer-
ences prior to 1994.
B   Hypothalamus [67]

Preschool Age Children [67]
PN 26031   SC 40160
SN   Ages 2–5 years. Used in noneducational
contexts. Application of terms designating age is
mandatory for ages 0–17.

Preschool Age Children — (cont'd)
- UF   Early Childhood
- B   Children [67]
- R   ↓ Childhood Development [67]
       Kindergarten Students [73]
       Nursery School Students [73]
       ↓ Preschool Students [82]

Preschool Education [73]
PN 1101   SC 40170
- B   Education [67]
- R   Project Head Start [73]

Preschool Students [82]
PN 1418   SC 40173
SN   Students from infancy to entrance in kindergarten or 1st grade. Mandatory term in educational contexts.
- B   Students [67]
- N   Nursery School Students [73]
- R   Kindergarten Students [73]
       Preschool Age Children [67]

Preschool Teachers [85]
PN 237   SC 40176
- B   Teachers [67]

Prescribing (Drugs) [91]
PN 101   SC 40177
- R   ↓ Drug Therapy [67]
       ↓ Drugs [67]
       ↓ Treatment [67]

Prescription Drugs [91]
PN 27   SC 40178
- B   Drugs [67]
- R   ↓ Drug Therapy [67]
       Nonprescription Drugs [91]
       Self Medication [91]

Presenile Dementia [73]
PN 159   SC 40180
- UF   Dementia (Presenile)
- B   Dementia [85]
- N   Alzheimers Disease [73]
       Creutzfeldt Jakob Syndrome [94]
       Picks Disease [73]
- R   ↓ Senile Dementia [73]

Preservice Teachers [82]
PN 385   SC 40205
SN   Education students or graduates prior to employment as teachers.
- B   Teachers [67]
- R   ↓ College Students [67]
       Education Students [82]
       Student Teachers [73]
       ↓ Teacher Education [67]

Pressoreceptors
Use   Baroreceptors

Pressors (Drugs)
Use   Vasoconstrictor Drugs

Pressure Sensation [73]
PN 41   SC 40270
- R   ↓ Somesthetic Perception [67]

Prestige (Occupational)
Use   Occupational Status

Pretesting [73]
PN 121   SC 40280

Pretesting — (cont'd)
SN   Running preliminary trials to establish a baseline. Comparison of pretest and posttest scores gives a measure of effectiveness of independent variables such as treatments or programs.
- B   Measurement [67]
- R   Repeated Measures [85]
       ↓ Testing Methods [67]

Pretraining (Therapy)
Use   Client Education

Prevention [73]
PN 3703   SC 40290
SN   Conceptually broad array term referring to any process that acts to deter undesirable occurrences. Use a more specific term if possible.
- N   Accident Prevention [73]
       AIDS Prevention [94]
       Crime Prevention [85]
       Drug Abuse Prevention [94]
       Fire Prevention [73]
       Preventive Medicine [73]
       Primary Mental Health Prevention [73]
       Relapse Prevention [94]
       Suicide Prevention [73]
- R   Condoms [91]
       Disability Management [91]
       Early Intervention [82]
       ↓ Health Care Delivery [78]
       ↓ Health Care Services [78]
       ↓ Health Education [73]
       Health Promotion [91]
       ↓ Mental Health Services [78]
       ↓ Prenatal Care [91]
       ↓ Safety [67]
       Suicide Prevention Centers [73]
       ↓ Treatment [67]

Preventive Medicine [73]
PN 280   SC 40300
- B   Prevention [73]
       Treatment [67]
- R   Drug Abuse Prevention [94]
       ↓ Health [73]
       Health Behavior [82]
       Health Maintenance Organizations [82]
       Health Promotion [91]
       Holistic Health [85]
       Mammography [94]
       Physical Examination [88]
       ↓ Prenatal Care [91]
       Relapse Prevention [94]

Price
Use   Costs and Cost Analysis

Pride [73]
PN 57   SC 40310
- B   Emotional States [73]

Priests [73]
PN 149   SC 40320
- B   Clergy [73]
- R   Chaplains [73]
       Missionaries [73]

Primacy Effect [73]
PN 174   SC 40328
SN   Component of the serial position effect which is manifested by a greater ease in learning items that occur at the beginning of a series rather than those toward the middle.
- B   Serial Position Effect [82]
- R   ↓ Learning [67]
       Recency Effect [73]

Primal Therapy [78]
PN 45   SC 40329
SN   Combination of intensive individual therapy and group psychotherapy with emphasis on experiencing and expression of blocked traumatic events or feelings (primals) and their integration into total life functioning.
- B   Psychotherapy [67]
- R   ↓ Psychotherapeutic Techniques [67]

Primary Health Care [88]
PN 288   SC 40331
SN   Health care provided by a medical professional with whom a patient has initial contact when entering the health care system and by whom a patient may be referred to a specialist.
- B   Health Care Services [78]
- R   ↓ Health Care Delivery [78]

Primary Mental Health Prevention [73]
PN 964   SC 40330
SN   Mental health programs designed to prevent onset or occurrence of mental illness in high risk or target populations.
- B   Prevention [73]
- R   Drug Abuse Prevention [94]
       Early Intervention [82]
       ↓ Mental Health [67]
       ↓ Mental Health Programs [73]
       Relapse Prevention [94]

Primary Reinforcement [73]
PN 47   SC 40340
SN   Presentation of a primary reinforcer. Also, objects or events which do not require prior pairing with other reinforcers in order to maintain reinforcing properties. Also known as unconditioned reinforcers or unconditioned stimuli. Compare EXTERNAL REWARDS.
- B   Reinforcement [67]
- R   ↓ Conditioning [67]
       Unconditioned Stimulus [73]

Primary School Students [73]
PN 183   SC 40350
SN   Students in kindergarten through 3rd grade. Use ELEMENTARY SCHOOL STUDENTS or KINDERGARTEN STUDENTS unless specific reference is made to population as primary school students. Use of a student term is mandatory in educational contexts.
- B   Elementary School Students [67]
- R   ↓ Children [67]
       ↓ School Age Children [73]

Primary Schools
Use   Elementary Schools

Primates (Nonhuman) [73]
PN 656   SC 40370
- UF   Apes
- B   Mammals [73]
- N   Baboons [73]
       Chimpanzees [73]
       Gorillas [73]
       Monkeys [67]

Primidone [73]
PN 13   SC 40380
- B   Anticonvulsive Drugs [73]
- R   ↓ Barbiturates [67]

Priming [88]
PN 643   SC 40385
- N   Semantic Priming [94]
- R   Contextual Associations [67]
       Cues [67]
       ↓ Perception [67]
       ↓ Semantics [67]

Printed Communications Media [73]
PN 258   SC 40390
- B   Mass Media [67]
- N ↓ Books [73]
      Magazines [73]
      Newspapers [73]

Printing (Handwriting) [73]
PN 37   SC 40400
- B   Handwriting [67]

Prismatic Stimulation [73]
PN 163   SC 40410
- SN   Visual stimulation technique in which special lenses are used to spatially distort or invert visual images or the visual field. Also includes prisms that differentially refract light of different wavelengths to produce an array or spectrum of colors.
- B   Visual Stimulation [73]
- R ↓ Color Perception [67]
      Spatial Distortion [73]

Prison Personnel [73]
PN 335   SC 40420
- B   Law Enforcement Personnel [73]
- R   Attendants (Institutions) [73]

Prisoners [67]
PN 2421   SC 40430
- UF   Inmates (Prison)
- N   Prisoners of War [73]
- R ↓ Criminals [67]

Prisoners Dilemma Game [73]
PN 268   SC 40440
- SN   Nonzero-sum game in which individual outcomes are determined by joint actions of two players. Incentives for both cooperation and competition exist, and no communication is permitted between the two players.
- B   Games [67]
- R   Entrapment Games [73]
      Game Theory [67]
      Non Zero Sum Games [73]

Prisoners of War [73]
PN 100   SC 40450
- B   Prisoners [67]
- R   Hostages [88]

Prisons [67]
PN 780   SC 40460
- UF   Jails
      Penitentiaries
- B   Correctional Institutions [73]
- R   Concentration Camps [73]
      Reformatories [73]

Privacy [73]
PN 298   SC 40467
- R   Privileged Communication [73]
      Secrecy [94]
    ↓ Social Behavior [67]

Private Practice [78]
PN 306   SC 40469
- SN   Employment of professional personnel in independent for-profit practices (as opposed to public offices or nonprofit settings) in which there is direct contact with clients and payment for services rendered. Private practitioners may function in individual practices, partnerships, or incorporated business settings.
- R ↓ Health Care Delivery [78]

Private School Education [73]
PN 379   SC 40470

Private School Education — (cont'd)
- SN   Schools or formal education in schools supported and administered by organizations not affiliated with the government.
- UF   Parochial School Education
- B   Education [67]
- R   Religious Education [73]

Private Sector [85]
PN 167   SC 40475
- SN   Any type of non-government organization, service, or sphere of involvement.
- N   Business Organizations [73]
- R   Entrepreneurship [91]
      Ownership [85]

Privileged Communication [73]
PN 512   SC 40480
- SN   Confidential communication between doctors, lawyers, or therapists and their clients which, by legal sanction, may not be revealed to others. Also, any documents or recorded statements of such communication which can be legally withheld from public inspection.
- UF   Communication (Privileged)
      Confidentiality of Information
- R   Anonymity [73]
    ↓ Communication [67]
    ↓ Experimentation [67]
      Information [67]
      Privacy [73]

Proactive Inhibition [73]
PN 641   SC 40490
- SN   The theory that previous learning of material can interfere with the retention of newly-learned material. Also, the actual proactive interference itself.
- UF   Inhibition (Proactive)
- B   Interference (Learning) [67]

Probability [67]
PN 1373   SC 40500
- SN   The likelihood of the chance occurrence of specific events. May include the mathematical study of probability theory.
- N ↓ Chance (Fortune) [73]
      Response Probability [73]
    ↓ Statistical Probability [67]
- R ↓ Hypothesis Testing [73]
      Predictability (Measurement) [73]
      Probability Judgment [78]
      Probability Learning [67]

Probability Judgment [78]
PN 539   SC 40505
- SN   Process of ascertaining or estimating the degree of likelihood that certain specified conditions or events have, can, or will occur.
- B   Judgment [67]
- R ↓ Probability [67]
      Probability Learning [67]

Probability Learning [67]
PN 544   SC 40510
- SN   Experimental paradigm in which subjects are asked to guess or estimate whether an experimentally controlled event will occur or choose which of various alternative events will occur. As learning occurs, the proportion of correct responses tends to approach the actual probability proportion of event occurrences. Used for the experimental paradigm or task as well as the learned behavior itself.
- B   Learning [67]
- R ↓ Probability [67]
      Probability Judgment [78]

Probation [73]
PN 286   SC 40520

Probation — (cont'd)
- SN   Period of suspended sentence of a convicted offender following good behavior and during which the offender is not incarcerated but is under the supervision of a probation officer.
- B   Legal Processes [73]
- R   Court Referrals [94]
    ↓ Law Enforcement [78]
      Parole [73]

Probation Officers [73]
PN 150   SC 40530
- B   Law Enforcement Personnel [73]
- R   Parole Officers [73]

Probenecid [82]
PN 15   SC 40535
- SN   Agent that promotes the urinary excretion of uric acid.
- R ↓ Diuretics [73]

Problem Drinking
- SN   Term discontinued in 1988. Use PROBLEM DRINKING to access references from 73-87.
- Use Alcohol Abuse

Problem Solving [67]
PN 7226   SC 40550
- SN   Process of determining a correct sequence of alternatives leading to a desired goal or to successful completion or performance of a task.
- UF   Individual Problem Solving
- B   Cognitive Processes [67]
- N   Anagram Problem Solving [73]
      Cognitive Hypothesis Testing [82]
    ↓ Group Problem Solving [73]
- R ↓ Decision Making [67]
      Expert Systems [91]
    ↓ Inductive Deductive Reasoning [73]
    ↓ Reasoning [67]

Procaine [82]
PN 39   SC 40560
- SN   Use NOVOCAINE to access references from 73-81.
- UF   Novocaine
- B   Analgesic Drugs [73]
      Anesthetic Drugs [73]

Process Psychosis [73]
PN 65   SC 40570
- UF   Process Schizophrenia
- B   Psychosis [67]

Process Schizophrenia
- Use Process Psychosis AND Schizophrenia

Prochlorperazine [73]
PN 13   SC 40640
- B   Antiemetic Drugs [73]
      Phenothiazine Derivatives [73]

Procrastination [85]
PN 74   SC 40645
- SN   Habitual, often counterproductive postponing. Use STUDY HABITS to access references in educational contexts from 73-84.
- B   Motivation [67]

Productivity (Employee)
- Use Employee Productivity

Profanity [91]
PN 8   SC 40655
- B   Language [67]
- R   Obscenity [78]

Professional Certification [73]
PN 441   SC 40660
SN In general, certification constitutes permission to use a particular professional title contingent on fulfilling requisite educational and training programs.
UF Certification (Professional)
N Accreditation (Education Personnel) [73]
R Professional Development [82]
   Professional Examinations [94]
↓ Professional Licensing [73]
↓ Professional Personnel [78]

Professional Client Sexual Relations [94]
PN 0   SC 40665
SN Sexual relations, intimacy, or affectionate behavior between a professional (e.g., therapist, lawyer, religious personnel, or educator) and their clients or patients.
UF Patient Therapist Sexual Relations
   Sexual Boundary Violations
   Therapist Patient Sexual Relations
R Countertransference [73]
   Patient Abuse [91]
   Professional Ethics [73]
↓ Professional Standards [73]
↓ Psychosexual Behavior [67]
↓ Psychotherapeutic Processes [67]
   Psychotherapeutic Transference [67]
↓ Sexual Abuse [88]
   Sexual Harassment [85]
↓ Therapeutic Processes [78]

Professional Communication
Use Scientific Communication

Professional Consultation [73]
PN 2244   SC 40680
SN Advisory services offered by specialists in a particular field which may be client or colleague oriented or focus on policy setting, planning, and programs of an organization. Use PROFESSIONAL CONSULTATION or MENTAL HEALTH CONSULTATION to access references prior to 1982.
UF Consultation (Professional)
   Mental Health Consultation
N Consultation Liaison Psychiatry [91]
R Personal Therapy [91]
↓ Professional Personnel [78]
   Professional Supervision [88]

Professional Contribution
SN Prior to 1982 this term was not defined and was used inconsistently.
Use Professional Criticism

Professional Criticism [67]
PN 14133   SC 40700
SN Mandatory term applied to evaluative comments on previously published work.
UF Contribution (Professional)
   Criticism (Professional)
   Professional Contribution

Professional Criticism Reply [73]
PN 4726   SC 40710
SN Mandatory term applied to replies to comments on previously published work.
UF Rebuttal
   Reply (to Professional Criticism)

Professional Development [82]
PN 1006   SC 40715
SN Participation in activities which promote professional career development.
B Development [67]
R Career Change [78]
   Career Development [85]
↓ Continuing Education [85]

Professional Development — (cont'd)
R Employment History [78]
   Inservice Teacher Education [73]
↓ Inservice Training [85]
   Mental Health Inservice Training [73]
   Mentor [85]
   Occupational Aspirations [73]
↓ Professional Certification [73]
   Professional Identity [91]
↓ Professional Personnel [78]
   Professional Specialization [91]
↓ Professional Standards [73]

Professional Ethics [73]
PN 2649   SC 40720
SN Moral principles of conducting professional research or practices.
B Ethics [67]
R Euthanasia [73]
   Experimental Ethics [78]
   Impaired Professionals [85]
   Informed Consent [85]
   Professional Client Sexual Relations [94]
   Professional Liability [85]
↓ Professional Personnel [78]
↓ Professional Standards [73]

Professional Examinations [94]
PN 0   SC 40723
SN Required examinations for licensure or certification in order to practice a profession.
UF Certification Examinations
   Licensure Examinations
   State Board Examinations
B Measurement [67]
R Accreditation (Education Personnel) [73]
↓ Professional Certification [73]
↓ Professional Licensing [73]

Professional Fees [78]
PN 246   SC 40724
N Fee for Service [94]
R Cost Containment [91]
↓ Costs and Cost Analysis [73]
   Diagnosis Related Groups [88]
   Health Care Costs [94]
   Money [67]
   Peer Evaluation [82]
↓ Professional Personnel [78]
   Salaries [73]

Professional Identity [91]
PN 107   SC 40725
SN Concept of self and role within a professional domain.
UF Identity (Professional)
B Social Identity [88]
R Career Development [85]
↓ Employee Characteristics [88]
   Professional Development [82]
↓ Professional Personnel [78]
   Role Perception [73]
↓ Self Concept [67]

Professional Liability [85]
PN 405   SC 40727
SN Legal liabilities relating to the conduct of one's profession.
UF Legal Liability (Professional)
   Malpractice
B Professional Standards [73]
R Accountability [88]
   Impaired Professionals [85]
↓ Legal Processes [73]
   Patient Abuse [91]
   Professional Ethics [73]
↓ Responsibility [73]

Professional Licensing [73]
PN 328   SC 40730
SN Permission from an authority (e.g., government review board) to use a particular professional title as well as to practice the profession. Professional licensing laws also specify what activities constitute the legal or legitimate practice of the profession. One does not necessarily need to be certified (professionally) in order to be licensed.
UF Licensing (Professional)
N Accreditation (Education Personnel) [73]
R ↓ Professional Certification [73]
   Professional Examinations [94]
↓ Professional Personnel [78]

Professional Meetings and Symposia [67]
PN 15060   SC 40740
SN Mandatory term applied to documents relating information presented at a meeting or convention. Consider also CONFERENCE PROCEEDINGS to access references prior to 1982. For behavioral aspects of meetings (attendance, communication, or participation) consider PROFESSIONAL DEVELOPMENT or SCIENTIFIC COMMUNICATION.
UF Conference Proceedings
   Symposia
B Scientific Communication [73]

Professional Newsletters
Use Scientific Communication

Professional Organizations [73]
PN 1172   SC 40760
B Organizations [67]
R ↓ Professional Personnel [78]

Professional Orientation
Use Theoretical Orientation

Professional Personnel [78]
PN 1137   SC 40765
SN Conceptually broad array term referring to members of professions requiring prolonged and specialized training. Use a more specific term if possible.
B Personnel [67]
N ↓ Aerospace Personnel [73]
   Anthropologists [73]
   Clinicians [73]
↓ Counselors [67]
↓ Educational Personnel [73]
   Engineers [67]
↓ Health Personnel [94]
↓ Information Specialists [88]
   Journalists [73]
↓ Legal Personnel [85]
   Mathematicians [73]
   Physicists [73]
↓ Psychologists [67]
   Scientists [67]
   Sociologists [73]
↓ Therapists [67]
R ↓ Business and Industrial Personnel [67]
   Impaired Professionals [85]
   Librarians [88]
↓ Nonprofessional Personnel [82]
↓ Occupations [67]
↓ Paraprofessional Personnel [73]
↓ Professional Certification [73]
↓ Professional Consultation [73]
   Professional Development [82]
   Professional Ethics [73]
↓ Professional Fees [78]
   Professional Identity [91]
↓ Professional Licensing [73]
   Professional Organizations [73]
   Professional Referral [73]

Professional Personnel — (cont'd)
R   Professional Specialization [91]
↓ Professional Standards [73]
    Professional Supervision [88]
↓ Religious Personnel [73]

Professional Referral [73]
PN 1086   SC 40770
SN Act of directing a client to a professional or agency for assessment, treatment, or consultation.
UF Referral (Professional)
R   Court Referrals [94]
↓ Professional Personnel [78]
    Self Referral [91]

Professional Specialization [91]
PN 106   SC 40775
SN Training in or choice of a speciality within a profession.
UF Specialization (Professional)
R   Academic Specialization [73]
    Career Development [85]
↓ Higher Education [73]
    Occupational Choice [67]
    Occupational Preference [73]
↓ Postgraduate Training [73]
    Professional Development [82]
↓ Professional Personnel [78]

Professional Standards [73]
PN 1474   SC 40780
SN Minimally acceptable levels of quality professional care or services maintained in order to promote the welfare of those who make use of such services.
UF Standards (Professional)
N   Professional Liability [85]
R   Accountability [88]
    Impaired Professionals [85]
    Patient Abuse [91]
    Peer Evaluation [82]
    Professional Client Sexual Relations [94]
    Professional Development [82]
    Professional Ethics [73]
↓ Professional Personnel [78]

Professional Supervision [88]
PN 583   SC 40785
SN Processes or techniques of supervision of fully trained educational or mental health personnel.
UF Clinical Supervision
    Educational Supervision
    Supervision (Professional)
R ↓ Educational Personnel [73]
↓ Mental Health Personnel [67]
    Personal Therapy [91]
↓ Professional Consultation [73]
↓ Professional Personnel [78]

Professors
Use College Teachers

Profiles (Measurement) [73]
PN 994   SC 40800
SN Usually a composite of scores obtained through psychological testing utilizing instruments which yield separate measures and which comprises a picture or profile of the individual's characteristics across several areas.
B   Measurement [67]

Profoundly Mentally Retarded [73]
PN 1071   SC 40810
SN IQ below 20.
B   Mentally Retarded [67]

Progestational Hormones [85]
PN 39   SC 40815
UF Progestins
B   Hormones [67]
N   Progesterone [73]

Progesterone [73]
PN 685   SC 40820
B   Progestational Hormones [85]
    Sex Hormones [73]
    Steroids [73]

Progestins
Use Progestational Hormones

Prognosis [73]
PN 1788   SC 40830
SN Prediction of the course, duration, and outcome of a disorder. Compare DISEASE COURSE.
R   Biological Markers [91]
↓ Diagnosis [67]
    Disease Course [91]
↓ Disorders [67]
↓ Medical Diagnosis [73]
↓ Mental Disorders [67]
    Patient History [73]
↓ Prediction [67]
↓ Psychodiagnosis [67]
    Severity (Disorders) [82]
↓ Treatment [67]

Program Development [91]
PN 212   SC 40832
SN Formulation and/or implementation of programs in any setting.
UF Program Planning
B   Development [67]
N   Educational Program Planning [73]
R   Curriculum Development [73]
↓ Educational Programs [73]
    Employee Assistance Programs [85]
↓ Government Programs [73]
    Home Visiting Programs [73]
↓ Hospital Programs [78]
    Independent Living Programs [91]
↓ Mental Health Programs [73]
↓ Program Evaluation [85]
↓ Psychiatric Hospital Programs [67]
    Social Programs [73]

Program Evaluation [85]
PN 651   SC 40835
SN Assessment of programs in any setting.
B   Evaluation [67]
N   Educational Program Evaluation [73]
    Mental Health Program Evaluation [73]
R ↓ Program Development [91]

Program Evaluation (Educational)
Use Educational Program Evaluation

Program Evaluation (Mental Health)
Use Mental Health Program Evaluation

Program Planning
Use Program Development

Program Planning (Educational)
Use Educational Program Planning

Programed Instruction [67]
PN 936   SC 40870
UF Instruction (Programed)
B   Teaching Methods [67]
R   Computer Assisted Instruction [73]
    Individualized Instruction [73]

Programed Instruction — (cont'd)
R   Programed Textbooks [73]
    Teaching Machines [73]

Programed Textbooks [73]
PN 39   SC 40900
SN Textbooks prepared for use with programed instruction. Not used as a document type identifier.
B   Textbooks [78]
R   Programed Instruction [67]

Programing (Computer)
SN Use COMPUTER SOFTWARE to access references from 73-93.
Use Computer Programing

Programing Languages (Computer)
Use Computer Programing Languages

Programs (Government)
Use Government Programs

Programs (Mental Health)
Use Mental Health Programs

Progressive Relaxation Therapy [78]
PN 484   SC 40945
SN Therapeutic procedures which teach clients to tense and relax muscle groups, focusing on the sensations involved in relaxation. This method provides clients with practice in recognizing the sensation of tension which will serve as a cue to produce a state of muscle relaxation.
B   Relaxation Therapy [78]
R ↓ Hypnotherapy [73]
    Muscle Relaxation [73]
    Systematic Desensitization Therapy [73]

Project Follow Through [73]
PN 33   SC 40950
SN U.S. Government educational program for disadvantaged elementary school students to supplement Project Head Start and encourage academic and psychosocial growth.
B   Educational Programs [73]
    Government Programs [73]
R   Compensatory Education [73]
    Government [67]

Project Head Start [73]
PN 279   SC 40960
SN U.S. Government program for disadvantaged 3-5 yr olds aimed at improving children's educational potential by encouraging their psychosocial development and by providing economic assistance to their families.
UF Head Start
B   Educational Programs [73]
    Government Programs [73]
R   Compensatory Education [73]
    Government [67]
    Preschool Education [73]
    School Readiness [73]

Projection (Defense Mechanism) [67]
PN 330   SC 40970
B   Defense Mechanisms [67]
R   Projective Identification [94]

Projective Identification [94]
PN 0   SC 40975
B   Defense Mechanisms [67]
R   Identification (Defense Mechanism) [73]
    Projection (Defense Mechanism) [67]

Projective Personality Measures [73]
PN 707   SC 40980

Projective Personality Measures — (cont'd)
SN Tests which derive an indirect and global assessment of personality through the analysis of meaning or structure freely imposed by the subject upon unstructured or ambiguous materials. Use a more specific term if possible. (Compare NONPROJECTIVE PERSONALITY MEASURES.).
B   Personality Measures [67]
      Projective Techniques [67]
N   Bender Gestalt Test [67]
      Blacky Pictures Test [73]
      Childrens Apperception Test [73]
      Color Pyramid Test [73]
      Franck Drawing Completion Test [73]
      Holtzman Inkblot Technique [67]
      Human Figures Drawing [73]
      Onomatopoeia and Images Test [73]
      Rorschach Test [67]
      Rosenzweig Picture Frustration Study [67]
      Rotter Incomplete Sentences Blank [73]
      Sentence Completion Tests [91]
      Szondi Test [73]
      Thematic Apperception Test [67]
      Zulliger Z Test [73]

Projective Techniques [67]
PN 1425   **SC** 40990
SN Utilization of ambiguous or unstructured stimuli designed to elicit responses which are believed to reveal an individual's attitudes, defense modes or motivations, and personality structure. Also, the specific tests or techniques themselves. Use a more specific term if possible.
UF   Projective Tests
N   Color Pyramid Test [73]
      Franck Drawing Completion Test [73]
      Holtzman Inkblot Technique [67]
      Incomplete Man Test [73]
      ↓ Projective Personality Measures [73]

Projective Testing Technique [73]
PN 318   **SC** 41000
SN Administration, construction, scoring, and interpretation of projective tests.
B   Measurement [67]

Projective Tests
   Use Projective Techniques

Prolactin [73]
PN 951   **SC** 41020
B   Gonadotropic Hormones [73]

Proline [82]
PN 15   **SC** 41027
B   Amino Acids [73]

Prolixin
   Use Fluphenazine

Promazine [73]
PN 21   **SC** 41040
B   Phenothiazine Derivatives [73]

Promethazine [73]
PN 24   **SC** 41050
B   Antiemetic Drugs [73]
      Antihistaminic Drugs [73]
      Sedatives [73]

Promiscuity [73]
PN 52   **SC** 41060
UF   Sexual Delinquency
B   Psychosexual Behavior [67]
R   Extramarital Intercourse [73]
      Hypersexuality [73]

Promiscuity — (cont'd)
R   Premarital Intercourse [73]
      Prostitution [73]

Pronouns [73]
PN 199   **SC** 41070
B   Form Classes (Language) [73]

Pronunciation [73]
PN 343   **SC** 41080
B   Speech Characteristics [73]
R   Articulation (Speech) [67]

Proofreading [88]
PN 26   **SC** 41085
R   Clerical Secretarial Skills [73]
      ↓ Errors [67]
      Orthography [73]
      ↓ Reading [67]
      Verbal Ability [67]
      ↓ Written Communication [85]

Propaganda [73]
PN 49   **SC** 41090
B   Social Influences [67]
R   Brainwashing [82]
      ↓ Persuasive Communication [67]

Property
   Use Ownership

Propranolol [73]
PN 460   **SC** 41100
B   Adrenergic Blocking Drugs [73]
      Alcohols [67]

Proprioceptors [73]
PN 94   **SC** 41110
B   Nerve Endings [73]
      Neural Receptors [73]
      Sensory Neurons [73]

Prose [73]
PN 805   **SC** 41120
B   Literature [67]
N   ↓ Biography [67]
R   Creative Writing [94]
      Text Structure [82]

Prosencephalon
   Use Forebrain

Proserine
   Use Neostigmine

Prosocial Behavior [82]
PN 563   **SC** 41133
SN Positive social behavior generally concerned with promotion of the welfare of others.
B   Social Behavior [67]
N   Altruism [73]
      Assistance (Social Behavior) [73]
      Charitable Behavior [73]
      Cooperation [67]
      Sharing (Social Behavior) [78]
      Trust (Social Behavior) [67]
R   ↓ Antisocial Behavior [71]

Prosody [91]
PN 52   **SC** 41134
SN Use INFLECTION to access references from 88-90.
B   Phonology [73]
N   Inflection [73]
R   ↓ Linguistics [73]
      Morphology (Language) [73]
      ↓ Phonemes [73]

Prosody — (cont'd)
R   Sentence Structure [73]
      ↓ Speech Characteristics [73]

Prosopagnosia [94]
PN 0   **SC** 41135
SN A visual agnosia usually due to brain damage and characterized by an inability to recognize familiar faces, and in some cases, one's own face.
B   Agnosia [73]
R   Face Perception [85]

Prostaglandins [82]
PN 120   **SC** 41136
SN Physiologically potent compounds of ubiquitous occurrence formed from essential fatty acids and affecting the nervous system, female reproductive organs, and metabolism.
R   ↓ Anti Inflammatory Drugs [82]
      ↓ Fatty Acids [73]
      ↓ Hormones [67]
      ↓ Neuroleptic Drugs [73]
      ↓ Sympathomimetic Drugs [73]

Prostate [73]
PN 24   **SC** 41140
B   Male Genitalia [73]

Prostheses [73]
PN 187   **SC** 41150
UF   Artificial Limbs
B   Medical Therapeutic Devices [73]
N   Cochlear Implants [94]
R   ↓ Amputation [73]

Prostitution [73]
PN 235   **SC** 41160
B   Psychosexual Behavior [67]
R   Promiscuity [73]

Protein Deficiency Disorders [73]
PN 37   **SC** 41180
B   Nutritional Deficiencies [73]
N   Kwashiorkor [73]

Protein Metabolism [73]
PN 136   **SC** 41190
B   Metabolism [67]

Protein Sensitization
   Use Anaphylactic Shock

Proteinases [73]
PN 11   **SC** 41210
B   Enzymes [73]

Proteins [73]
PN 792   **SC** 41220
N   ↓ Blood Proteins [73]
      ↓ Endorphins [82]
      ↓ Globulins [73]
      Interferons [94]
R   ↓ Amino Acids [73]
      ↓ Drugs [67]
      ↓ Enzymes [73]
      Lipoproteins [73]
      ↓ Peptides [73]

Protest (Student)
   Use Student Activism

Protestantism [73]
PN 340   **SC** 41250
B   Christianity [73]
N   Fundamentalism [73]

Protozoa [73]
PN 18   SC 41255
  B   Microorganisms [85]

Prozac
  Use Fluoxetine

Pruritus [73]
PN 27   SC 41260
  UF Itching
  B   Skin Disorders [73]
      Symptoms [67]
  R   Scratching [73]

Pseudocyesis [73]
PN 55   SC 41270
  UF False Pregnancy
      Pregnancy (False)
      Pseudopregnancy
  B   Conversion Neurosis [73]
  R ↓ Gynecological Disorders [73]

Pseudodementia [85]
PN 65   SC 41280
SN Dementia-like disorder in the absence of organic brain disease.
  B   Mental Disorders [67]
  R ↓ Dementia [85]
     ↓ Factitious Disorders [88]
     ↓ Major Depression [88]

Pseudopregnancy
  Use Pseudocyesis

Pseudopsychopathic Schizophrenia
SN Term discontinued in 1988. Use PSEUDOPSYCHOPATHIC SCHIZOPHRENIA to access references from 73-87.
  Use Schizophrenia

Psilocybin [73]
PN 28   SC 41310
  B   Hallucinogenic Drugs [67]

Psychedelic Drugs [73]
PN 76   SC 41320
  B   Drugs [67]
  N   Lysergic Acid Diethylamide [67]
  R ↓ Hallucinogenic Drugs [67]
     ↓ Psychotomimetic Drugs [73]

Psychedelic Experiences [73]
PN 34   SC 41330
  R   Drug Induced Hallucinations [73]

Psychiatric Aides [73]
PN 79   SC 41340
  B   Paramedical Personnel [73]
      Psychiatric Hospital Staff [73]
  R   Psychiatric Social Workers [73]

Psychiatric Classifications (Taxon)
  Use Psychodiagnostic Typologies

Psychiatric Clinics [73]
PN 400   SC 41370
  UF Outpatient Psychiatric Clinics
  B   Clinics [67]
  R   Child Guidance Clinics [73]
      Community Mental Health Centers [73]
     ↓ Hospitals [67]
     ↓ Mental Health Programs [73]
     ↓ Outpatient Treatment [67]
      Walk In Clinics [73]

Psychiatric Disorders
  Use Mental Disorders

Psychiatric History
  Use Patient History

Psychiatric Hospital Admission [73]
PN 708   SC 41390
  UF Admission (Psychiatric Hospital)
  B   Hospital Admission [73]
      Psychiatric Hospitalization [73]
  N   Psychiatric Hospital Readmission [73]
  R ↓ Commitment (Psychiatric) [73]
     ↓ Hospital Discharge [73]
     ↓ Institutional Release [78]
      Psychiatric Hospital Discharge [78]

Psychiatric Hospital Discharge [78]
PN 503   SC 41395
  B   Hospital Discharge [73]
      Psychiatric Hospitalization [73]
  R ↓ Commitment (Psychiatric) [73]
      Discharge Planning [94]
     ↓ Psychiatric Hospital Admission [73]
      Psychiatric Hospital Readmission [73]
      Treatment Termination [82]

Psychiatric Hospital Programs [67]
PN 1493   SC 41400
SN Organized plans for care or training in psychiatric hospitals.
  B   Hospital Programs [78]
  N   Therapeutic Community [67]
  R   Halfway Houses [73]
     ↓ Mental Health Services [78]
     ↓ Program Development [91]
      Token Economy Programs [73]

Psychiatric Hospital Readmission [73]
PN 447   SC 41410
  UF Readmission (Psychiatric Hospital)
  B   Psychiatric Hospital Admission [73]
      Psychiatric Hospitalization [73]
  R ↓ Hospital Discharge [73]
      Psychiatric Hospital Discharge [78]

Psychiatric Hospital Staff [73]
PN 572   SC 41420
  B   Medical Personnel [67]
      Mental Health Personnel [67]
  N   Psychiatric Aides [73]
  R   Attendants (Institutions) [73]
      Occupational Therapists [73]
     ↓ Paramedical Personnel [73]
      Psychiatric Nurses [73]
      Psychiatrists [67]

Psychiatric Hospitalization [73]
PN 2862   SC 41430
  B   Hospitalization [67]
  N ↓ Psychiatric Hospital Admission [73]
      Psychiatric Hospital Discharge [78]
      Psychiatric Hospital Readmission [73]
  R ↓ Commitment (Psychiatric) [73]
     ↓ Hospital Admission [73]
     ↓ Hospital Discharge [73]
     ↓ Institutional Release [78]
      Patient Seclusion [94]

Psychiatric Hospitals [67]
PN 2832   SC 41440
  UF Asylums
      Mental Hospitals
      State Hospitals
  B   Hospitals [67]
  R   Halfway Houses [73]
      Patient Seclusion [94]
      Psychiatric Units [91]
      Sanatoriums [73]

Psychiatric Nurses [73]
PN 496   SC 41450
  B   Mental Health Personnel [67]
      Nurses [67]
  R ↓ Psychiatric Hospital Staff [73]

Psychiatric Patients [67]
PN 14595   SC 41460
  B   Patients [67]

Psychiatric Report
  Use Psychological Report

Psychiatric Residency
  Use Medical Residency AND Psychiatric Training

Psychiatric Social Workers [73]
PN 46   SC 41470
  B   Mental Health Personnel [67]
      Social Workers [73]
  R   Psychiatric Aides [73]

Psychiatric Training [73]
PN 1218   SC 41480
  UF Psychiatric Residency
      Training (Psychiatric)
  B   Clinical Methods Training [73]
      Medical Education [73]
  R   Cotherapy [82]
      Psychoanalytic Training [73]
      Psychotherapy Training [73]

Psychiatric Units [91]
PN 138   SC 41485
SN Units in a general hospital or inpatient care facility specializing in psychiatric care of acutely disturbed patients.
  UF Hospital Psychiatric Units
  R ↓ Hospital Programs [78]
     ↓ Hospitalization [67]
     ↓ Hospitals [67]
      Nursing Homes [73]
      Patient Seclusion [94]
      Psychiatric Hospitals [67]
     ↓ Residential Care Institutions [73]

Psychiatrists [67]
PN 2881   SC 41490
  UF Neuropsychiatrists
  B   Mental Health Personnel [67]
      Physicians [67]
  R   Clinicians [73]
      Hypnotherapists [73]
     ↓ Psychiatric Hospital Staff [73]
      Psychoanalysts [73]
     ↓ Psychologists [67]
     ↓ Psychotherapists [73]

Psychiatry [67]
PN 4676   SC 41500
  B   Medical Sciences [67]
  N   Adolescent Psychiatry [85]
      Biological Psychiatry [94]
      Child Psychiatry [67]
      Community Psychiatry [73]
      Consultation Liaison Psychiatry [91]
      Forensic Psychiatry [73]
      Neuropsychiatry [73]
      Orthopsychiatry [73]
      Social Psychiatry [67]
      Transcultural Psychiatry [73]
  R ↓ Treatment [67]

Psychoactive Drugs
  Use Drugs

Psychoanalysis [67]
PN 8870   SC 41520
UF Psychoanalytic Therapy
B   Psychotherapy [67]
N   Dream Analysis [73]
    Self Analysis [94]
R   Catharsis [73]
    Erikson (Erik) [91]
    Free Association [94]
    Freud (Sigmund) [67]
    ↓ Hypnotherapy [73]
    ↓ Psychotherapeutic Processes [67]

Psychoanalysts [73]
PN 906   SC 41530
UF Analysts
B   Psychotherapists [73]
R   Hypnotherapists [73]
    Psychiatrists [67]

Psychoanalytic Interpretation [67]
PN 3820   SC 41540
SN Description or formulation of the meaning or
significance of any particular event, condition, or
process (e.g., patient's productions, art, literature, or historical biographies) from a psychoanalytic perspective.
B   Theoretical Interpretation [88]
R   Freudian Psychoanalytic School [73]
    Psychoanalytic Theory [67]
    Psychohistory [78]

Psychoanalytic Personality Factors [73]
PN 294   SC 41550
UF Personality Factors (Psychoanalytic)
B   Personality [67]
N   Conscience [67]
    Conscious (Personality Factor) [73]
    Death Instinct [88]
    Ego [67]
    Electra Complex [73]
    Id [73]
    Libido [73]
    Oedipal Complex [73]
    Subconscious [73]
    ↓ Superego [73]
    Unconscious (Personality Factor) [67]
R   Penis Envy [73]
    ↓ Personality Processes [67]

Psychoanalytic School (Freudian)
Use Freudian Psychoanalytic School

Psychoanalytic Theory [67]
PN 5971   SC 41570
B   Theories [67]
R   ↓ Ego Development [91]
    Erikson (Erik) [91]
    Free Association [94]
    Freud (Sigmund) [67]
    Freudian Psychoanalytic School [73]
    Metapsychology [94]
    Object Relations [82]
    ↓ Personality Processes [67]
    Psychoanalytic Interpretation [67]
    Self Psychology [88]

Psychoanalytic Therapy
Use Psychoanalysis

Psychoanalytic Training [73]
PN 334   SC 41590
UF Training (Psychoanalytic)
B   Clinical Methods Training [73]
R   Psychiatric Training [73]
    Self Analysis [94]

Psychobiology [82]
PN 265   SC 41595
SN Scientific discipline emphasizing the holistic
functioning of the individual in the environment in
relation to normal or abnormal behavior.
B   Sciences [67]
R   Behavioral Genetics [94]
    Biological Psychiatry [94]
    ↓ Biology [67]
    Biopsychosocial Approach [91]
    ↓ Psychology [67]

Psychodiagnosis [67]
PN 10647   SC 41600
SN Diagnosis of mental disorders through the
use of psychological methods or tests. Compare
MEDICAL DIAGNOSIS.
UF Clinical Judgment (Psychodiagnosis)
B   Diagnosis [67]
N   ↓ Psychodiagnostic Interview [73]
R   Computer Assisted Diagnosis [73]
    Diagnostic and Statistical Manual [94]
    Differential Diagnosis [67]
    Educational Diagnosis [78]
    Forensic Evaluation [94]
    Patient History [73]
    Prognosis [73]
    ↓ Psychodiagnostic Typologies [67]
    Psychological Report [88]
    Research Diagnostic Criteria [94]

Psychodiagnostic Interview [73]
PN 1069   SC 41630
B   Interviews [67]
    Psychodiagnosis [67]
N   Diagnostic Interview Schedule [91]
R   Intake Interview [94]

Psychodiagnostic Typologies [67]
PN 3891   SC 41640
SN Systematic classification of mental, cogni-
tive, emotional, or behavioral disorders.
UF Psychiatric Classifications (Taxon)
    Typologies (Psychodiagnostic)
N   Diagnostic and Statistical Manual [94]
    Research Diagnostic Criteria [94]
R   Clinical Judgment (Not Diagnosis) [73]
    Diagnostic Interview Schedule [91]
    Dual Diagnosis [91]
    Labeling [78]
    ↓ Psychodiagnosis [67]

Psychodrama [67]
PN 577   SC 41650
SN Projective technique and method of group
psychotherapy in which personality make-up, interpersonal relations, conflicts, and emotional
problems are explored through dramatization of
meaningful situations.
B   Psychotherapeutic Techniques [67]
    Psychotherapy [67]
R   ↓ Group Psychotherapy [67]
    Role Playing [67]

Psychodynamics [73]
PN 3811   SC 41660
SN Human behavior and emotions in terms of
conscious and unconscious motivations.
UF Psychological Correlates
R   ↓ Personality [67]
    Psychosocial Factors [88]
    ↓ Social Behavior [67]
    ↓ Social Interaction [67]

Psychoeducation [94]
PN 0   SC 41665
R   Client Education [85]
    ↓ Education [67]
    ↓ Health Education [73]
    ↓ Treatment [67]

Psychogenesis [73]
PN 510   SC 41670
SN Development of mental functions, traits, or
states.
UF Psychological Development
B   Development [67]
N   ↓ Cognitive Development [73]
    Emotional Development [73]
    Moral Development [73]
    ↓ Psychosocial Development [73]
R   Adolescent Development [73]
    Adult Development [78]
    Age Differences [67]
    ↓ Childhood Development [67]
    ↓ Delayed Development [73]
    ↓ Developmental Age Groups [73]
    ↓ Developmental Stages [73]
    ↓ Early Childhood Development [73]
    ↓ Human Development [67]
    ↓ Infant Development [73]
    Nature Nurture [94]
    Neonatal Development [73]
    ↓ Physical Development [73]
    Precocious Development [73]
    ↓ Prenatal Development [73]
    Sex Linked Developmental Differences [73]
    Sexual Development [73]

Psychogenic Pain [73]
PN 146   SC 41680
SN Pain having a psychological rather than a
physical basis.
UF Pain (Psychogenic)
B   Pain [67]
    Psychosomatic Disorders [67]
R   Chronic Pain [85]
    ↓ Conversion Neurosis [73]
    Hypochondriasis [73]
    Somatization [94]

Psychohistory [78]
PN 653   SC 41685
SN Psychological, often psychoanalytical, interpretation of historical events and personalities.
Includes psychobiographies, historical group fantasies and processes, studies of childhood from
an historical perspective and historical psychodynamics.
R   ↓ Biography [67]
    ↓ History [73]
    Psychoanalytic Interpretation [67]

Psychoimmunology
Use Psychoneuroimmunology

Psychokinesis [73]
PN 156   SC 41690
UF Telekinesis
B   Extrasensory Perception [67]

Psycholinguistics [67]
PN 1326   SC 41700
SN Discipline that combines the techniques of
linguistics and psychology in the study of the
relationship of language and behavior and cognitive processes. Used for the discipline as well
as specific psycholinguistic processes themselves.
B   Linguistics [73]
R   Ethnolinguistics [73]
    Metalinguistics [94]

Psycholinguistics — (cont'd)
R Neurolinguistics [91]
    Vygotsky (Lev) [91]

Psychological Abuse
Use Emotional Abuse

Psychological Adjustment
Use Emotional Adjustment

Psychological Autopsy [88]
PN 24   SC 41705
SN Study of possible reasons for an individual's death by examination of personal letters or by interviewing acquaintances and relatives.
R Autopsy [73]
  ↓ Death and Dying [67]
    Forensic Psychology [85]
    Suicide [67]

Psychological Correlates
Use Psychodynamics

Psychological Development
Use Psychogenesis

Psychological Endurance [73]
PN 156   SC 41710
UF Hardiness
B Endurance [73]
R Psychological Stress [73]
    Stress Reactions [73]

Psychological Interpretation
Use Theoretical Interpretation

Psychological Reactance [78]
PN 174   SC 41716
SN Decrease in the attractiveness of an activity, behavior, or attitude as a result of having been forced or induced by external sources to engage in the activity or behavior, or to maintain the attitude. Such reactions may appear as emotional dissatisfaction, involvement and performance decrements, or negative attitude.
UF Reactance
R Choice Behavior [67]
    Cognitive Dissonance [67]
    Freedom [78]

Psychological Report [88]
PN 33   SC 41718
UF Psychiatric Report
R Educational Diagnosis [78]
  ↓ Evaluation [67]
    Forensic Evaluation [94]
  ↓ Medical Diagnosis [73]
  ↓ Psychodiagnosis [67]

Psychological Screening Inventory [73]
PN 28   SC 41720
B Nonprojective Personality Measures [73]
    Screening Tests [82]
    Selection Tests [73]

Psychological Stress [73]
PN 2283   SC 41730
B Stress [67]
R ↓ Deprivation [67]
    Psychological Endurance [73]

Psychological Terminology [73]
PN 921   SC 41740
SN Definitions, analysis, evaluation, or review of individual terms or nomenclature in the field of psychology. Compare GLOSSARY.

Psychological Terminology — (cont'd)
UF Nomenclature (Psychological)
    Terminology (Psychological)
B Terminology [91]
R ↓ Scientific Communication [73]

Psychological Testing
Use Psychometrics

Psychologist Attitudes [91]
PN 96   SC 41747
SN Attitudes of, not toward, psychologists.
B Attitudes [67]
R Counselor Attitudes [73]
  ↓ Health Personnel Attitudes [85]
  ↓ Psychologists [67]
  ↓ Therapist Attitudes [78]

Psychologists [67]
PN 3829   SC 41750
B Professional Personnel [78]
N Clinical Psychologists [73]
    Counseling Psychologists [88]
  ↓ Educational Psychologists [73]
    Experimental Psychologists [73]
    Industrial Psychologists [73]
    Social Psychologists [73]
R Adler (Alfred) [67]
  ↓ Counselors [67]
    Ellis (Albert) [91]
    Erikson (Erik) [91]
    Freud (Sigmund) [67]
    James (William) [91]
    Jung (Carl) [73]
    Kohlberg (Lawrence) [91]
    Maslow (Abraham Harold) [91]
  ↓ Mental Health Personnel [67]
    Pavlov (Ivan) [91]
    Piaget (Jean) [67]
    Psychiatrists [67]
    Psychologist Attitudes [91]
  ↓ Psychotherapists [73]
    Rogers (Carl) [91]
    Scientists [67]
    Skinner (Burrhus Frederic) [91]
  ↓ Social Workers [73]
    Vygotsky (Lev) [91]
    Watson (John Broadus) [91]

Psychology [67]
PN 5295   SC 41760
B Social Sciences [67]
N ↓ Applied Psychology [73]
  ↓ Clinical Psychology [67]
    Cognitive Psychology [85]
    Comparative Psychology [67]
    Depth Psychology [73]
  ↓ Developmental Psychology [73]
    Ecological Psychology [94]
    Experimental Psychology [67]
    Forensic Psychology [85]
  ↓ Humanistic Psychology [85]
    Mathematical Psychology [73]
    Metapsychology [94]
  ↓ Physiological Psychology [67]
    Self Psychology [88]
R ↓ History of Psychology [67]
    Psychobiology [82]
  ↓ Psychophysiology [67]

Psychology Education [78]
PN 1609   SC 41765
B Curriculum [67]
N ↓ Graduate Psychology Education [67]
R Educational Program Accreditation [94]
    Theoretical Orientation [82]

Psychometrics [67]
PN 1557   SC 41770
SN Subdiscipline within psychology dealing with the development and application of statistical techniques to the analysis of psychological data. Also, psychological measurement in which numerical estimates are obtained of a specific aspect of performance.
UF Psychological Testing
B Measurement [67]
R Conjoint Measurement [94]
  ↓ Experimental Design [67]
  ↓ Experimentation [67]
    Item Response Theory [85]
    Psychophysics [67]
  ↓ Statistical Analysis [67]
    Test Interpretation [85]
  ↓ Testing [67]

Psychomotor Development [73]
PN 266   SC 41780
B Motor Development [73]
N ↓ Speech Development [73]
R ↓ Childhood Development [67]
  ↓ Perceptual Development [73]
    Perceptual Motor Development [91]

Psychomotor Processes
Use Perceptual Motor Processes

Psychoneuroimmunology [91]
PN 51   SC 41795
SN Study of the interrelationship among immune responses, psychological processes, and the nervous system. Used for the scientific discipline or the psychoneuroimmunologic processes themselves.
UF Psychoimmunology
B Immunology [73]
    Psychophysiology [67]
R ↓ Endocrinology [73]
    Neuropsychology [73]

Psychoneurosis
Use Neurosis

Psychopath
Use Antisocial Personality

Psychopathology [67]
PN 5566   SC 41820
SN Study, assessment, and treatment of mental disorders or maladaptive behaviors. Used for the scientific discipline or the dysfunction itself.
B Pathology [73]
R Comorbidity [91]
  ↓ Mental Disorders [67]

Psychopathy [73]
PN 292   SC 41830
SN General term for unspecified mental disease or disorder. For psychopathic personality, use the term ANTISOCIAL PERSONALITY.
B Mental Disorders [67]

Psychopharmacology [67]
PN 1015   SC 41840
B Pharmacology [73]
R Drug Abuse Liability [94]

Psychophysical Measurement [67]
PN 1332   SC 41850
SN Techniques or methodology used to assess perceptual sensitivities and functions of any sensory modality as related to the parameters of stimulation.
N Magnitude Estimation [91]
R Fuzzy Set Theory [91]
  ↓ Perceptual Measures [73]

Psychophysical Measurement — (cont'd)
R   Signal Detection (Perception) [67]
     Threshold Determination [73]

Psychophysics [67]
PN 651   SC 41860
R ↓ Experimentation [67]
     Psychometrics [67]

Psychophysiologic Disorders
  Use Psychosomatic Disorders

Psychophysiology [67]
PN 1571   SC 41880
SN Branch of psychology concerned with the physiological correlates of cognitive, emotional, and behavioral processes. Used for the scientific discipline or the psychophysiological processes themselves.
B   Physiology [67]
N   Psychoneuroimmunology [91]
R   Cardiovascular Reactivity [94]
    ↓ Psychology [67]

Psychosexual Behavior [67]
PN 5009   SC 41890
SN Human sexual behavior which includes both mental and somatic aspects of sexuality.
UF Sexual Behavior
B   Behavior [67]
N   Bisexuality [73]
    Erection (Penis) [73]
    Heterosexuality [73]
    ↓ Homosexuality [67]
    ↓ Human Courtship [73]
    Hypersexuality [73]
    Masturbation [73]
    ↓ Orgasm [73]
    Petting [73]
    Promiscuity [73]
    Prostitution [73]
    Seduction [94]
    Sex Roles [67]
    Sexual Abstinence [73]
    ↓ Sexual Arousal [78]
    ↓ Sexual Deviations [67]
    ↓ Sexual Function Disturbances [73]
    ↓ Sexual Intercourse (Human) [73]
    Transsexualism [73]
    Transvestism [73]
    Virginity [73]
R   Assortative Mating [91]
    Human Mate Selection [88]
    Pornography [73]
    Professional Client Sexual Relations [94]
    Psychosexual Development [82]
    Sex [67]
    Sex Linked Developmental Differences [73]
    Sexual Attitudes [73]
    Sexual Development [73]
    Sexual Satisfaction [94]

Psychosexual Development [82]
PN 739   SC 41895
SN Psychological maturation and development of sexual identity, beliefs, and attitudes throughout the life cycle.
B   Psychosocial Development [73]
R   Emotional Development [73]
    Gender Identity [85]
    ↓ Psychosexual Behavior [67]
    Sex [67]
    Sexual Attitudes [73]
    Sexual Development [73]
    Sexuality [73]

Psychosis [67]
PN 5284   SC 41910

Psychosis — (cont'd)
B   Mental Disorders [67]
N ↓ Acute Psychosis [73]
    ↓ Affective Psychosis [73]
    ↓ Alcoholic Psychosis [73]
    Capgras Syndrome [85]
    ↓ Childhood Psychosis [67]
    Chronic Psychosis [73]
    Experimental Psychosis [73]
    ↓ Hallucinosis [73]
    ↓ Paranoia (Psychosis) [67]
    Process Psychosis [73]
    Reactive Psychosis [73]
    ↓ Schizophrenia [67]
    Senile Psychosis [73]
    Toxic Psychoses [73]
R   Borderline States [78]
    Paranoid Schizophrenia [67]

Psychosocial Development [73]
PN 3859   SC 41920
SN Process of psychological and social maturation occurring at any time during the life cycle.
UF Social Development
B   Psychogenesis [73]
N   Childhood Play Development [73]
    ↓ Personality Development [67]
    Psychosexual Development [82]
R   Aging (Attitudes Toward) [85]
    Emotional Development [73]
    Erikson (Erik) [91]
    Moral Development [73]
    Object Relations [82]

Psychosocial Factors [88]
PN 2902   SC 41925
R   Demographic Characteristics [67]
    Psychodynamics [73]
    ↓ Social Influences [67]
    ↓ Sociocultural Factors [67]

Psychosocial Mental Retardation [73]
PN 43   SC 41930
SN Reversible mental retardation due to environmental and/or social factors with no organic etiological component.
UF Cultural Familial Mental Retardation
B   Mental Retardation [67]
R   Borderline Mental Retardation [73]

Psychosocial Readjustment [73]
PN 767   SC 41940
SN Attainment of attitudes and skills which will facilitate an individual's reintegration or functioning in society, especially following traumatic or unusual personal experiences. Use also PSYCHOSOCIAL RESOCIALIZATION to access references from 73–81.
UF Psychosocial Resocialization
    Readjustment (Psychosocial)
    Resocialization (Psychosocial)
R ↓ Psychosocial Rehabilitation [73]
    ↓ Treatment [67]

Psychosocial Rehabilitation [73]
PN 1109   SC 41950
SN Programs, techniques, or processes of treatment by which individuals, institutionalized or otherwise removed from normal community life (e.g., prisoners), acquire psychological and social skills and attitudes which facilitate community reentry.
UF Rehabilitation (Psychosocial)
B   Rehabilitation [67]
N   Therapeutic Social Clubs [73]
    ↓ Vocational Rehabilitation [67]
R ↓ Drug Rehabilitation [73]
    Psychosocial Readjustment [73]
    Rehabilitation Counseling [78]

Psychosocial Resocialization
SN Term discontinued in 1982. Use PSYCHOSOCIAL RESOCIALIZATION or PSYCHOSOCIAL READJUSTMENT to access references from 73–81.
  Use Psychosocial Readjustment

Psychosomatic Disorders [67]
PN 3390   SC 41970
SN Disorders characterized by bodily symptoms caused by psychological factors.
UF Psychophysiologic Disorders
    Somatization Disorder
B   Neurosis [67]
N ↓ Conversion Neurosis [73]
    Dysmorphophobia [73]
    Hypochondriasis [73]
    Neurodermatitis [73]
    Psychogenic Pain [73]
R   Anorexia Nervosa [73]
    Asthma [67]
    Bulimia [85]
    ↓ Dyspnea [73]
    ↓ Endocrine Disorders [73]
    ↓ Gastrointestinal Disorders [73]
    Hay Fever [73]
    ↓ Headache [73]
    Hyperphagia [73]
    Hyperventilation [73]
    Illness Behavior [82]
    Irritable Bowel Syndrome [91]
    Malingering [73]
    Migraine Headache [73]
    Munchausen Syndrome [94]
    Myofascial Pain [91]
    Obesity [73]
    Premenstrual Tension [73]
    Psychosomatic Medicine [78]
    ↓ Sexual Function Disturbances [73]
    ↓ Skin Disorders [73]
    Somatization [94]
    ↓ Symptoms [67]
    ↓ Urinary Function Disorders [73]
    ↓ Urogenital Disorders [73]

Psychosomatic Medicine [78]
PN 323   SC 41975
SN Medical specialty dealing with the diagnosis and treatment of psychosomatic disorders.
B   Medical Sciences [67]
R ↓ Health Care Psychology [85]
    ↓ Psychosomatic Disorders [67]

Psychosurgery [73]
PN 168   SC 41980
UF Leukotomy
    Lobotomy
B   Neurosurgery [73]
    Organic Therapies [73]
N   Thalamotomy [73]
R   Sympathectomy [73]
    Tractotomy [73]

Psychotherapeutic Breakthrough [73]
PN 8   SC 41990
UF Breakthrough (Psychotherapeutic)
B   Psychotherapeutic Processes [67]

Psychotherapeutic Counseling [73]
PN 519   SC 42000
B   Counseling [67]
    Psychotherapy [67]
N ↓ Family Therapy [67]
R ↓ Marriage Counseling [73]
    Premarital Counseling [73]

Psychotherapeutic Methods
  Use Psychotherapeutic Techniques

Psychotherapeutic Outcomes [73]
PN 1882   SC 42030
SN Limited to treatment results that are a direct function of specific characteristics of clients or therapists or a function of unique or specifically-described circumstances of the treatment itself.
UF Outcomes (Psychotherapeutic)
B Treatment Outcomes [82]
R Mental Health Program Evaluation [73]
Treatment Dropouts [78]
Treatment Effectiveness Evaluation [73]

Psychotherapeutic Processes [67]
PN 9466   SC 42040
SN Experiential, attitudinal, emotional, or behavioral phenomena occurring during the course of psychotherapy. Applies to the client or psychotherapist individually or to their interaction.
UF Client Counselor Interaction
Counselor Client Interaction
Patient Therapist Interaction
Therapist Patient Interaction
B Therapeutic Processes [78]
N Countertransference [73]
Insight (Psychotherapeutic Process) [73]
Psychotherapeutic Breakthrough [73]
Psychotherapeutic Resistance [73]
Psychotherapeutic Transference [67]
Therapeutic Alliance [94]
R Professional Client Sexual Relations [94]
↓ Psychoanalysis [67]
↓ Psychotherapy [67]
↓ Treatment Outcomes [82]

Psychotherapeutic Resistance [73]
PN 493   SC 42050
SN Conscious or unconscious defensive attempts by the client to prevent repressed material from coming to consciousness.
UF Resistance (Psychotherapeutic)
B Psychotherapeutic Processes [67]

Psychotherapeutic Techniques [67]
PN 6940   SC 42060
UF Psychotherapeutic Methods
Therapeutic Techniques (Psychother)
B Treatment [67]
N Animal Assisted Therapy [94]
Autogenic Training [73]
Cotherapy [82]
Directed Reverie Therapy [78]
Dream Analysis [73]
Morita Therapy [94]
Mutual Storytelling Technique [73]
Paradoxical Techniques [82]
Psychodrama [67]
R Age Regression (Hypnotic) [88]
Centering [91]
Client Centered Therapy [67]
Conjoint Therapy [73]
↓ Creative Arts Therapy [94]
Free Association [94]
Homework [88]
Poetry Therapy [94]
Primal Therapy [78]
↓ Psychotherapy [67]
Rational Emotive Therapy [78]
Reality Therapy [73]
↓ Relaxation Therapy [78]
Role Playing [67]
↓ Self Help Techniques [82]
Self Talk [88]
Wilderness Experience [91]

Psychotherapeutic Transference [67]
PN 1571   SC 42070

Psychotherapeutic Transference — (cont'd)
SN Unconscious projection of feelings, thoughts, and wishes to the therapist that were originally associated with important figures from the client's past.
UF Transference (Psychotherapeutic)
B Psychotherapeutic Processes [67]
R Countertransference [73]
Professional Client Sexual Relations [94]
Therapeutic Alliance [94]

Psychotherapist Attitudes [73]
PN 428   SC 42080
SN Attitudes of, not toward, psychotherapists.
B Therapist Attitudes [78]
R ↓ Psychotherapists [73]
Therapist Role [78]

Psychotherapist Trainees
Use Therapist Trainees

Psychotherapists [73]
PN 1899   SC 42100
B Mental Health Personnel [67]
Therapists [67]
N Hypnotherapists [73]
Psychoanalysts [73]
R Clinical Psychologists [73]
Psychiatrists [67]
↓ Psychologists [67]
Psychotherapist Attitudes [73]

Psychotherapy [67]
PN 10104   SC 42110
UF Reconstructive Psychotherapy
Supportive Psychotherapy
B Treatment [67]
N Adolescent Psychotherapy [94]
Analytical Psychotherapy [73]
Autogenic Training [73]
Brief Psychotherapy [67]
↓ Child Psychotherapy [67]
Client Centered Therapy [67]
Directed Reverie Therapy [78]
Eclectic Psychotherapy [94]
Existential Therapy [73]
Experiential Psychotherapy [73]
Expressive Psychotherapy [73]
Feminist Therapy [94]
Geriatric Psychotherapy [73]
Gestalt Therapy [73]
↓ Group Psychotherapy [67]
↓ Hypnotherapy [73]
Individual Psychotherapy [73]
Insight Therapy [73]
Logotherapy [73]
Persuasion Therapy [73]
Primal Therapy [78]
↓ Psychoanalysis [67]
Psychodrama [67]
↓ Psychotherapeutic Counseling [73]
Rational Emotive Therapy [78]
Reality Therapy [73]
Relationship Therapy [73]
Transactional Analysis [73]
R ↓ Behavior Therapy [67]
Cognitive Therapy [82]
Cotherapy [82]
Couples Therapy [94]
Holistic Health [85]
↓ Marriage Counseling [73]
↓ Organic Therapies [73]
Paradoxical Techniques [82]
Pastoral Counseling [67]
Phototherapy [91]
↓ Psychotherapeutic Processes [67]
↓ Psychotherapeutic Techniques [67]
Recreation Therapy [73]

Psychotherapy — (cont'd)
R Spontaneous Remission [73]
Theoretical Orientation [82]

Psychotherapy Training [73]
PN 841   SC 42120
UF Training (Psychotherapy)
B Clinical Methods Training [73]
R Cotherapy [82]
Psychiatric Training [73]

Psychotic Depressive Reaction
SN Term discontinued in 1988. Use PSYCHOTIC DEPRESSIVE REACTION to access references from 73-87.
Use Major Depression

Psychotic Episode (Acute)
Use Acute Psychosis

Psychoticism [78]
PN 283   SC 42145
B Personality Traits [67]

Psychotomimetic Drugs [73]
PN 42   SC 42150
B Drugs [67]
N Lysergic Acid Diethylamide [67]
Mescaline [73]
Peyote [73]
R Experimental Psychosis [73]
↓ Hallucinogenic Drugs [67]
↓ Psychedelic Drugs [73]

Psychotropic Drugs
Use Drugs

PTA
Use Parent School Relationship

Puberty [73]
PN 313   SC 42160
B Developmental Stages [73]
R Menarche [73]

Pubescence
Use Sexual Development

Public Attitudes
Use Public Opinion

Public Health [88]
PN 121   SC 42185
B Health [73]
R Health Promotion [91]
Public Health Services [73]

Public Health Service Nurses [73]
PN 46   SC 42190
B Government Personnel [73]
Nurses [67]
R Public Health Services [73]

Public Health Services [73]
PN 359   SC 42200
B Community Services [67]
R ↓ Health [73]
↓ Mental Health Programs [73]
Public Health [88]
Public Health Service Nurses [73]

Public Opinion [73]
PN 1012   SC 42210
UF Opinion (Public)
Public Attitudes
B Attitudes [67]

Public Opinion — (cont'd)
R Community Attitudes [73]
    Public Relations [73]

Public Policy
Use Government Policy Making

Public Relations [73]
PN 81   SC 42220
SN The business of attempting to influence or persuade individuals or the public to have an understanding or concern for, or positive disposition toward a particular person, organization, idea, policy, practice, or activity.
R ↓ Advertising [67]
    ↓ Consumer Attitudes [73]
    Public Opinion [73]

Public School Education [73]
PN 736   SC 42230
SN Education in free tax-supported schools controlled by a local governmental authority.
B Education [67]

Public Sector [85]
PN 238   SC 42235
SN Any type of government-related or public organization, service, or sphere of involvement.
N Government [67]
    Government Agencies [73]

Public Speaking [73]
PN 391   SC 42240
SN Formal or informal speech in a group or public setting.
B Oral Communication [85]
R Speech Anxiety [85]

Public Transportation [73]
PN 71   SC 42250
B Community Facilities [73]
    Transportation [73]
R Air Transportation [73]
    Railroad Trains [73]

Public Welfare Services
Use Community Welfare Services

Puerto Rican Americans
Use Hispanics

Puerto Rico [73]
PN 255   SC 42270
B West Indies [73]

Pulmonary Emphysema [73]
PN 22   SC 42290
UF Emphysema (Pulmonary)
B Lung Disorders [73]

Pulmonary Tuberculosis [73]
PN 12   SC 42300
B Bacterial Disorders [73]
    Lung Disorders [73]
    Tuberculosis [73]

Pulse (Arterial)
Use Arterial Pulse

Punishment [67]
PN 2151   SC 42320
SN Presentation of a punisher contingent on the performance of some behavior. Also, the punishing event or object itself which, when following the performance of some behavior, results in a reduction in the occurrence or frequency of that behavior. Compare AVERSIVE STIMULATION.

Punishment — (cont'd)
UF Corporal Punishment
B Reinforcement [67]
R Coercion [94]
    Threat [67]

Punishment (Capital)
Use Capital Punishment

Pupil (Eye) [73]
PN 90   SC 42340
B Eye (Anatomy) [67]

Pupil Dilation [73]
PN 228   SC 42360
UF Dilation (Pupil)
R ↓ Eye (Anatomy) [67]

Purdue Perceptual Motor Survey [73]
PN 7   SC 42380
B Sensorimotor Measures [73]

Purkinje Cells [94]
PN 0   SC 42385
B Cerebellum [73]
    Neurons [73]

Puromycin [73]
PN 34   SC 42390
B Amines [73]
    Antibiotics [73]

Putamen [85]
PN 68   SC 42405
SN The largest and most lateral part of the basal ganglia which, together with the caudate nucleus and globus pallidus, forms the corpus striatum.
B Basal Ganglia [73]

Pyramidal Tracts [73]
PN 72   SC 42410
B Efferent Pathways [82]
    Spinal Cord [73]

Pyramidotomy [73]
PN 9   SC 42420
B Neurosurgery [73]
R Tractotomy [73]

Pyromania [73]
PN 22   SC 42430
R Impulsiveness [73]
    ↓ Personality Disorders [67]

Q Sort Testing Technique [67]
PN 114   SC 42440
B Testing Methods [67]

Q Test
Use Cochran Q Test

Quadriplegia [85]
PN 66   SC 42470
SN Paralysis of both arms and both legs.
B Paralysis [73]
R ↓ Central Nervous System Disorders [73]
    Hemiplegia [78]
    ↓ Injuries [73]
    ↓ Musculoskeletal Disorders [73]
    Paraplegia [78]
    ↓ Physically Handicapped [67]
    Spinal Cord Injuries [73]

Quails [73]
PN 231   SC 42480
B Birds [67]

Quality Circles
Use Participative Management

Quality Control [88]
PN 74   SC 42483
SN Efforts or techniques directed at the detection of imperfections or shortcomings in products or services.
R Accountability [88]
    Human Factors Engineering [73]
    Organizational Effectiveness [85]
    Organizational Objectives [73]
    Participative Management [88]

Quality of Care [88]
PN 398   SC 42484
R Accountability [88]
    Caregivers [88]
    Child Day Care [73]
    ↓ Health Care Delivery [78]
    Home Care [85]
    ↓ Managed Care [94]
    ↓ Treatment [67]

Quality of Life [85]
PN 952   SC 42485
N Quality of Work Life [88]
R Life Satisfaction [85]
    Lifestyle [78]
    Well Being [94]

Quality of Work Life [88]
PN 109   SC 42487
SN Includes aspects such as salary, benefits, safety, and efficiency, as well as variety and challenge, responsibility, contribution, and recognition.
B Quality of Life [85]
R ↓ Job Characteristics [85]
    Job Satisfaction [67]
    Occupational Stress [73]
    Organizational Climate [73]
    ↓ Working Conditions [73]

Quartimax Rotation [73]
PN 3   SC 42490
B Orthogonal Rotation [73]

Questioning [82]
PN 840   SC 42495
R ↓ Cognitive Processes [67]
    Curiosity [67]
    ↓ Education [67]
    Guessing [73]
    Information Seeking [73]
    Legal Interrogation [94]
    ↓ Teaching [67]

Questionnaires [67]
PN 3042   SC 42500
B Measurement [67]
N General Health Questionnaire [91]
R Mail Surveys [94]
    ↓ Surveys [67]
    Telephone Surveys [94]

Quinidine [73]
PN 6   SC 42540
UF Quinidine Sulfate
B Alkaloids [73]
    Heart Rate Affecting Drugs [73]
R Quinine [73]

Quinidine Sulfate
Use Quinidine

Quinine [73]
PN 103   SC 42560

Quinine — (cont'd)
B   Alkaloids [73]
     Analgesic Drugs [73]
     Local Anesthetics [73]
R   Quinidine [73]

Quinpirole [94]
PN 0   SC 42570
B   Antihypertensive Drugs [73]
     Dopamine Agonists [85]

Rabbis [73]
PN 28   SC 42580
B   Clergy [73]
R   Chaplains [73]
     Judaism [67]

Rabbits [67]
PN 2328   SC 42590
B   Mammals [73]

Race (Anthropological) [73]
PN 162   SC 42600
R   Asians [82]
     Blacks [82]
     Ethnography [73]
     Ethnology [67]
     ↓ Racial and Ethnic Attitudes [82]
     Racial and Ethnic Differences [82]
     ↓ Sociocultural Factors [67]
     Whites [82]

Race and Ethnic Discrimination [94]
PN 0   SC 42605
SN   Use SOCIAL DISCRIMINATION to access
references from 82-93. Use MINORITY GROUP
DISCRIMINATION to access references from 78-
81 and RACIAL DISCRIMINATION to access ref-
erences from 73-81.
UF   Ethnic Discrimination
     Minority Group Discrimination
     Racial Discrimination
B   Social Discrimination [82]
R   Affirmative Action [85]
     ↓ Civil Rights [78]
     Employment Discrimination [94]
     Minority Groups [67]
     ↓ Prejudice [67]
     ↓ Racial and Ethnic Attitudes [82]
     Racial and Ethnic Differences [82]
     Racism [73]
     Stereotyped Attitudes [67]

Race Attitudes
SN   Term discontinued in 1982. Use RACE AT-
TITUDES to access references from 73–81.
     Use Racial and Ethnic Attitudes

Race Relations
SN   Term discontinued in 1982. Use RACE RE-
LATIONS to access references from 78–81.
     Use Racial and Ethnic Relations

Racial and Ethnic Attitudes [82]
PN 844   SC 42617
SN   Attitudes about race or ethnicity or toward
members of a given racial or ethnic group. Use
RACE ATTITUDES to access references from
73–81.
UF   Race Attitudes
B   Attitudes [67]
N   AntiSemitism [73]
     Ethnocentrism [73]
     Racism [73]
R   Cultural Sensitivity [94]
     ↓ Ethnic Groups [73]
     Ethnology [67]
     ↓ Prejudice [67]

Racial and Ethnic Attitudes — (cont'd)
R   Race (Anthropological) [73]
     Race and Ethnic Discrimination [94]
     Racial and Ethnic Relations [82]
     Stereotyped Attitudes [67]

Racial and Ethnic Differences [82]
PN 4591   SC 42618
SN   Differences between two or more racial or
ethnic groups. Use RACIAL DIFFERENCES to
access references from 73–81. Use CROSS
CULTURAL DIFFERENCES for cultural compari-
sons.
UF   Ethnic Differences
     Racial Differences
R   Cross Cultural Differences [67]
     Cross Cultural Treatment [94]
     Cultural Sensitivity [94]
     ↓ Ethnic Groups [73]
     Ethnology [67]
     Interethnic Family [88]
     Interracial Family [88]
     Interracial Offspring [88]
     Race (Anthropological) [73]
     Race and Ethnic Discrimination [94]
     Racism [73]

Racial and Ethnic Relations [82]
PN 362   SC 42619
SN   Contact and interaction between and among
different racial and ethnic groups. Use RACE RE-
LATIONS to access references from 78–81.
UF   Race Relations
B   Social Behavior [67]
R   Ethnology [67]
     Interracial Family [88]
     Interracial Marriage [73]
     Interracial Offspring [88]
     ↓ Prejudice [67]
     ↓ Racial and Ethnic Attitudes [82]
     School Integration [82]
     ↓ Social Discrimination [82]
     Social Equality [73]
     ↓ Social Integration [82]

Racial Differences
SN   Term discontinued in 1982. Use RACIAL
DIFFERENCES to access references from 73–81.
     Use Racial and Ethnic Differences

Racial Discrimination
SN   Term discontinued in 1982. Use RACIAL
DISCRIMINATION to access references from 73-
81 and MINORITY GROUP DISCRIMINATION to
access references from 78-81. Use SOCIAL DIS-
CRIMINATION to access references from 82-93.
     Use Race and Ethnic Discrimination

Racial Integration
SN   Term discontinued in 1982. Use RACIAL IN-
TEGRATION to access references from 67–81.
     Use Social Integration

Racial Segregation (Schools)
     Use School Integration

Racism [73]
PN 350   SC 42660
SN   Belief that racial differences produce inher-
ent superiority of a particular race.
B   Racial and Ethnic Attitudes [82]
R   AntiSemitism [73]
     Employment Discrimination [94]
     ↓ Prejudice [67]
     Race and Ethnic Discrimination [94]
     Racial and Ethnic Differences [82]
     ↓ Social Discrimination [82]
     ↓ Social Issues [91]

Radial Nerve
     Use Spinal Nerves

Radiation [67]
PN 466   SC 42680
UF   Irradiation
N   Laser Irradiation [73]
R   Radiation Therapy [73]
     ↓ Roentgenography [73]

Radiation Therapy [73]
PN 113   SC ·42690
UF   X Ray Therapy
B   Physical Treatment Methods [73]
R   ↓ Radiation [67]

Radical Movements [73]
PN 58   SC 42700
N   Political Revolution [73]
R   ↓ Social Movements [67]
     Terrorism [82]

Radicalism (Political)
     Use Political Radicalism

Radio [73]
PN 201   SC 42730
B   Audiovisual Communications Media [73]
     Mass Media [67]
     Telecommunications Media [73]

Radiography
     Use Roentgenography

Radiology [73]
PN 31   SC 42740
B   Medical Sciences [67]

Rage
     Use Anger

Railroad Trains [73]
PN 73   SC 42760
UF   Trains (Railroad)
B   Ground Transportation [73]
R   Public Transportation [73]

Random Sampling [73]
PN 111   SC 42780
B   Sampling (Experimental) [73]
R   Experiment Volunteers [73]

Rank Difference Correlation [73]
PN 19   SC 42790
UF   Spearman Rho
B   Statistical Correlation [67]

Rank Order Correlation [73]
PN 79   SC 42800
B   Statistical Correlation [67]

Rape [73]
PN 1256   SC 42810
B   Sexual Abuse [88]
     Sexual Intercourse (Human) [73]
N   Acquaintance Rape [91]

Raphe Nuclei [82]
PN 230   SC 42815
SN   Serotonin synthesizing neurons in and near
the median plane of the brain stem lying dorsally
in the pons. These nuclei are sometimes grouped
with the reticular formation and are thought to
function as part of the limbic system.
B   Pons [73]
R   ↓ Limbic System [73]
     Reticular Formation [67]

Rapid Eye Movement [71]
PN 271   SC 42820
UF   REM
B   Eye Movements [67]
R   REM Dream Deprivation [73]
      REM Dreams [73]
      REM Sleep [73]

Rapid Eye Movement Dreams
   Use   REM Dreams

Rapid Eye Movement Sleep
   Use   REM Sleep

Rapport
SN   Use INTERPERSONAL ATTRACTION to access references from 73-90.
   Use   Interpersonal Interaction

Rasch Model
   Use   Item Response Theory

Rat Learning [67]
PN 1841   SC 42860
SN   Not defined prior to 1982. Use RAT LEARNING or RATS to access references from 67-81. From 1982 used for discussions of hypotheses or theories of learning in rats.
B   Learning [67]

Rating [67]
PN 1446   SC 42880
SN   Measurement technique involving relative evaluation or estimate of characteristics or qualities of a person, process, or thing. Used when rating as a technique is the object of interest.
B   Testing [67]
R   Halo Effect [82]
      Interrater Reliability [82]

Rating Scales [67]
PN 4943   SC 42890
B   Measurement [67]
N   Likert Scales [94]
R   Multidimensional Scaling [82]

Ratio Reinforcement
   Use   Fixed Ratio Reinforcement OR Variable Ratio Reinforcement

Ratiocination
   Use   Logical Thinking

Rational Emotive Therapy [78]
PN 606   SC 42915
SN   Stresses cognitive, philosophic, and value-oriented aspects of personality and views the goal of treatment as the client's development of rational as opposed to irrational beliefs about his/her problem.
B   Psychotherapy [67]
R   ↓ Behavior Therapy [67]
      Cognitive Therapy [82]
      Ellis (Albert) [91]
      ↓ Psychotherapeutic Techniques [67]

Rationalization [73]
PN 50   SC 42920
B   Defense Mechanisms [67]

Rats [67]
PN 41350   SC 42930
UF   Albino Rats
      White Rats
B   Rodents [73]
N   Norway Rats [73]

Rauwolfia [73]
PN 5   SC 42940
B   Antihypertensive Drugs [73]
      Sedatives [73]
R   Reserpine [67]

Raven Coloured Progressive Matrices [73]
PN 89   SC 42950
B   Intelligence Measures [67]

Raven Progressive Matrices [78]
PN 133   SC 42960
SN   Use RAVENS PROGRESSIVE MATRICES to access references from 73-77.
B   Intelligence Measures [67]

Raynauds Disease
   Use   Cardiovascular Disorders

RDC
   Use   Research Diagnostic Criteria

Reactance
   Use   Psychological Reactance

Reaction Formation [73]
PN 17   SC 42990
SN   Defense mechanism which leads to the formation of behaviors and attitudes opposite to the repressed anxiety-inducing behavior or feelings.
B   Defense Mechanisms [67]

Reaction Time [67]
PN 6069   SC 43000
SN   Minimal time interval between the onset of a stimulus and the beginning of a subject's response to that stimulus. Compare RESPONSE LATENCY.
UF   Response Lag
      Response Speed
      Response Time
      RT (Response)
      Speed (Response)
B   Response Parameters [73]
R   ↓ Conceptual Tempo [85]

Reactive Attachment Disorder
   Use   Failure to Thrive

Reactive Depression [73]
PN 230   SC 43020
B   Major Depression [88]
R   Neurotic Depressive Reaction [73]

Reactive Psychosis [73]
PN 172   SC 43030
UF   Reactive Schizophrenia
      Traumatic Psychosis
B   Psychosis [67]

Reactive Schizophrenia
   Use   Reactive Psychosis AND Schizophrenia

Readability [78]
PN 332   SC 43045
SN   Textual difficulty or other qualitative aspects of reading material which facilitate comprehension. May include clarity of graphic displays.
B   Written Language [67]
R   ↓ Legibility [78]
      ↓ Reading [67]
      Reading Comprehension [73]
      Reading Materials [73]

Readaptation
   Use   Adaptation

Reading [67]
PN 2413   SC 43080
N   Braille [78]
      Oral Reading [73]
      Remedial Reading [73]
      Silent Reading [73]
R   Dyslexia [73]
      Initial Teaching Alphabet [73]
      Proofreading [88]
      Readability [78]
      Reading Ability [73]
      Reading Achievement [73]
      Reading Comprehension [73]
      ↓ Reading Disabilities [67]
      Reading Education [73]
      Reading Materials [73]
      Reading Readiness [73]
      ↓ Reading Skills [73]
      Reading Speed [73]
      Sight Vocabulary [73]

Reading Ability [73]
PN 2450   SC 43090
SN   Perceptual and intellectual capacity or efficiency in reading.
B   Cognitive Ability [73]
R   Academic Aptitude [73]
      ↓ Reading [67]
      ↓ Reading Skills [73]

Reading Achievement [73]
PN 2997   SC 43100
B   Academic Achievement [67]
R   ↓ Reading [67]

Reading Comprehension [73]
PN 3807   SC 43110
B   Reading Skills [73]
      Verbal Comprehension [85]
R   Readability [78]
      ↓ Reading [67]

Reading Disabilities [67]
PN 2189   SC 43120
B   Learning Disorders [67]
N   Dyslexia [73]
R   ↓ Alexia [82]
      Educational Diagnosis [78]
      ↓ Reading [67]

Reading Education [73]
PN 2863   SC 43130
B   Language Arts Education [73]
R   Braille [78]
      Braille Instruction [73]
      Initial Teaching Alphabet [73]
      Phonics [73]
      ↓ Reading [67]
      Remedial Reading [73]

Reading Materials [73]
PN 983   SC 43140
UF   Basal Readers
B   Instructional Media [67]
R   ↓ Books [73]
      Braille [78]
      Readability [78]
      ↓ Reading [67]
      Text Structure [82]
      ↓ Textbooks [78]

Reading Measures [73]
PN 573   SC 43150
B   Measurement [67]
N   Gates MacGinitie Reading Tests [73]
      Metropolitan Readiness Tests [78]

Reading Readiness 73
PN 371　　　　　　　SC 43160
SN Developmental level at which language skills, cognitive, perceptual and motor abilities, experience and interest combine to enable a child to profit from specific reading activities. Compare SCHOOL READINESS.
R ↓ Reading 67

Reading Skills 73
PN 1241　　　　　　SC 43170
SN Proficiency in reading developed through practice and influenced by ability. Includes word recognition, pronunciation, and comprehension.
B Ability 67
N Reading Comprehension 73
　Reading Speed 73
R ↓ Literacy 73
　↓ Reading 67
　Reading Ability 73
　Sight Vocabulary 73
　Word Recognition 88

Reading Speed 73
PN 505　　　　　　　SC 43180
B Reading Skills 73
R ↓ Reading 67

Readjustment (Psychosocial)
Use Psychosocial Readjustment

Readmission (Hospital)
Use Hospital Admission

Readmission (Psychiatric Hospital)
Use Psychiatric Hospital Readmission

Realism (Philosophy) 73
PN 52　　　　　　　SC 43220
B Philosophies 67

Reality 73
PN 525　　　　　　　SC 43230
R Reality Testing 73
　Reality Therapy 73

Reality Testing 73
PN 123　　　　　　　SC 43240
SN Cognitive process of evaluation and judgment for differentiation between objective perceptions originating outside of the self and subjective stimuli or fantasies.
R ↓ Cognitive Processes 67
　↓ Personality Processes 67
　Reality 73

Reality Therapy 73
PN 283　　　　　　　SC 43250
SN Method of psychotherapeutic treatment based on assumption of client's personal responsibility for his/her behavior. Therapist actively guides client to accurate self-perception for fulfillment of needs of self-worth and respect for others.
B Psychotherapy 67
R ↓ Child Psychotherapy 67
　↓ Psychotherapeutic Techniques 67
　Reality 73

Reasoning 67
PN 2154　　　　　　SC 43260
B Thinking 67
N ↓ Inductive Deductive Reasoning 73
R Analogy 91
　Cognitive Hypothesis Testing 82
　Dialectics 73
　↓ Problem Solving 67

Rebuttal
Use Professional Criticism Reply

Recall (Learning) 67
PN 8110　　　　　　SC 43290
B Retention 67
N Cued Recall 94
　Free Recall 73
　Serial Recall 94
R ↓ Memory 67
　Memory Training 94
　Reminiscence 85

Recency Effect 73
PN 263　　　　　　　SC 43298
SN Component of the serial position effect which is manifested by a greater ease in learning items which occur at the end of a series rather than those toward the middle.
B Serial Position Effect 82
R ↓ Learning 67
　Primacy Effect 73

Receptive Fields 85
PN 46　　　　　　　SC 43299
SN Spatially discrete patterns of peripheral and central neuronal innervation of sensory mechanisms.
B Nervous System 67
N Cutaneous Receptive Fields 85
　Visual Receptive Fields 82
R ↓ Afferent Pathways 82
　Neural Plasticity 94
　Sensory Neglect 94
　↓ Sensory Neurons 73

Receptor Binding 85
PN 1307　　　　　　SC 43297
SN Affinity processes occurring between chemical substances and specific cellular sites in the body (e.g., blood platelet or neural receptor binding of an adrenergic drug.) Consider also NEURAL RECEPTORS.
B Neurochemistry 73
　Neurophysiology 73
R ↓ Neural Receptors 73

Receptors (Neural)
Use Neural Receptors

Recessiveness (Genetic)
Use Genetic Recessiveness

Recidivism 73
PN 847　　　　　　　SC 43320
SN Repetition or recurrence of previous condition or behavior pattern (e.g., behavior disorder or criminal or delinquent behavior), especially when recurrence leads to recommitment or a second conviction.
B Antisocial Behavior 71
R ↓ Criminals 67

Reciprocal Inhibition Therapy 73
PN 63　　　　　　　SC 43330
SN Form of behavior therapy which seeks to evoke one response in order to bring about a suppression or decrease in the strength of a simultaneous response. Used to weaken unadaptive habits, particularly anxiety responses.
B Behavior Therapy 67
R Counterconditioning 73
　Systematic Desensitization Therapy 73

Reciprocity 73
PN 608　　　　　　　SC 43340
B Social Behavior 67
R Retaliation 91

Recognition (Learning) 67
PN 5501　　　　　　SC 43350
B Retention 67
R Matching to Sample 94
　Memory Training 94
　Word Recognition 88

Reconstruction (Learning) 73
PN 121　　　　　　　SC 43360
SN Recalling memorized items in the order in which they were originally presented. Compare FREE RECALL.
B Retention 67

Reconstructive Psychotherapy
Use Psychotherapy

Recorders (Tape)
Use Tape Recorders

Recovery (Disorders) 73
PN 1373　　　　　　SC 43390
R ↓ Disorders 67
　↓ Drug Abstinence 94
　Illness Behavior 82
　↓ Mental Disorders 67
　Postsurgical Complications 73
　Relapse Prevention 94
　↓ Remission (Disorders) 73
　Sobriety 88
　↓ Treatment Outcomes 82

Recreation 67
PN 1441　　　　　　SC 43400
UF Play
N Athletic Participation 73
　Baseball 73
　Basketball 73
　Camping 73
　Childrens Recreational Games 73
　Clubs (Social Organizations) 73
　Dance 73
　Doll Play 73
　Football 73
　↓ Gambling 73
　Judo 73
　Martial Arts 85
　Soccer 94
　Summer Camps (Recreation) 73
　Swimming 73
　Television Viewing 73
　Tennis 73
　Traveling 73
　Vacationing 73
　Weightlifting 94
R Childhood Play Behavior 78
　Computer Games 88
　Daily Activities 94
　↓ Games 67
　Hobbies 73
　Holidays 88
　Leisure Time 73
　Relaxation 73
　↓ Sports 67
　↓ Toys 73
　Wilderness Experience 91

Recreation Areas 73
PN 196　　　　　　　SC 43410
UF Parks (Recreational)
N Playgrounds 73
R ↓ Community Facilities 73
　↓ Environmental Planning 82
　Urban Planning 73

Recreation Therapy 73
PN 235　　　　　　　SC 43420

Recreation Therapy — (cont'd)
UF Activity Therapy
     Gymnastic Therapy
B   Creative Arts Therapy 94
R   Art Therapy 73
     Dance Therapy 73
     Music Therapy 73
     ↓ Psychotherapy 67
     Therapeutic Camps 78

Recreational Day Camps
Use Summer Camps (Recreation)

Recruitment (Military)
Use Military Recruitment

Recruitment (Personnel)
Use Personnel Recruitment

Recruitment (Teachers)
Use Teacher Recruitment

Recurrent Depression 94
PN 0   SC 43465
B   Major Depression 88
R   Relapse (Disorders) 73
     Seasonal Affective Disorder 91

Red Blood Cells
Use Erythrocytes

Red Nucleus
Use Mesencephalon

Reductionism 73
PN 73   SC 43480
UF Atomism
     Elementarism
B   Philosophies 67

Reemployment 91
PN 38   SC 43485
SN Returning to work following a period of absence, e.g., unemployment or retirement.
UF Job Reentry
     Return to Work
R   ↓ Employment Status 82
     Job Search 85
     Occupational Choice 67
     ↓ Personnel 67
     Retirement 73
     Unemployment 67

Reentry Students 85
PN 228   SC 43495
SN Persons reentering school or an educational program after an extended absence; for example, middle-aged adults enrolled in undergraduate programs.
B   Students 67
R   ↓ Adult Education 73
     ↓ College Students 67
     ↓ Continuing Education 85
     High School Students 67
     ↓ School Dropouts 67

Reference Groups 94
PN 0   SC 43497
SN Social groups used as sources for personal and behavioral identification, motivation, and evaluation of one's own status.
B   Social Groups 73
R   Ethnic Identity 73
     ↓ Group Dynamics 67
     ↓ Interpersonal Influences 67
     ↓ Peer Relations 67
     ↓ Self Concept 67

Reference Groups — (cont'd)
R   ↓ Social Identity 88
     ↓ Social Influences 67
     Social Support Networks 82
     ↓ Socialization 67

Referral (Professional)
Use Professional Referral

Referral (Self)
Use Self Referral

Reflectiveness
Use Impulsiveness

Reflexes 71
PN 1110   SC 43530
SN Automatic involuntary neuromuscular responses to stimuli.
B   Physiology 67
N   Achilles Tendon Reflex 73
     Acoustic Reflex 73
     Babinski Reflex 73
     Eyeblink Reflex 73
     Flexion Reflex 73
     Hoffmanns Reflex 73
     Nystagmus 73
     Ocular Accommodation 82
     Orienting Reflex 67
     Startle Reflex 67
     Yawning 88
R   Muscle Contractions 73
     Muscle Tone 85
     Parkinsonism 94

Reformatories 73
PN 46   SC 43540
SN Specific type of correctional institution to which young or first offenders are committed for training and reformation.
B   Correctional Institutions 73
R   Prisons 67

Refraction Errors 73
PN 71   SC 43550
B   Errors 67
     Eye Disorders 73
     Light Refraction 82
N   Myopia 73
R   Amblyopia 73
     ↓ Genetic Disorders 73
     Ocular Accommodation 82

Reframing
Use Paradoxical Techniques

Refugees 88
PN 261   SC 43555
SN Uprooted, homeless, voluntary or involuntary migrants who flee their native country, usually to escape danger or persecution because of their race, religion, or political views, and who no longer possess protection of their former government. Use HUMAN MIGRATION to access references from 82-87.
UF Political Refugees
B   Human Migration 73
R   Immigration 73
     ↓ Social Processes 67

Refusal (Treatment)
Use Treatment Refusal

Regression (Defense Mechanism) 67
PN 355   SC 43560
B   Defense Mechanisms 67

Regression Analysis
Use Statistical Regression

Regression Artifact
Use Statistical Regression

Rehabilitation 67
PN 3490   SC 43580
SN Treatment designed to restore or bring a client to a condition of health or useful and constructive activity. Used for populations including sensory handicapped, retarded, delinquent, criminal, or disordered. Use a more specific term if possible.
B   Treatment 67
N   Cognitive Rehabilitation 85
     ↓ Drug Rehabilitation 73
     Occupational Therapy 67
     Physical Therapy 73
     ↓ Psychosocial Rehabilitation 73
R   Activities of Daily Living 91
     Adaptive Behavior 91
     Animal Assisted Therapy 94
     Deinstitutionalization 82
     Disability Management 91
     Habilitation 91
     ↓ Health Care Services 78
     Independent Living Programs 91
     ↓ Mainstreaming 91
     Partial Hospitalization 85
     ↓ Rehabilitation Centers 73
     Rehabilitation Counseling 78
     Self Care Skills 78
     ↓ Support Groups 91
     Wilderness Experience 91

Rehabilitation (Drug)
Use Drug Rehabilitation

Rehabilitation (Psychosocial)
Use Psychosocial Rehabilitation

Rehabilitation (Vocational)
Use Vocational Rehabilitation

Rehabilitation Centers 73
PN 194   SC 43620
N   Sheltered Workshops 67
R   ↓ Community Facilities 73
     ↓ Rehabilitation 67

Rehabilitation Counseling 78
PN 368   SC 43624
B   Counseling 67
R   ↓ Alcohol Rehabilitation 82
     ↓ Drug Rehabilitation 73
     ↓ Psychosocial Rehabilitation 73
     ↓ Rehabilitation 67
     ↓ Vocational Rehabilitation 67
     Work Adjustment Training 91

Rehabilitation Counselors 78
PN 443   SC 43626
B   Counselors 67
R   ↓ Social Workers 73

Rehearsal
Use Practice

Reinforcement 67
PN 5512   SC 43630
SN Presentation of a reinforcer contingent on the performance of some behavior. Also, the reinforcing event or object itself (i.e., the reinforcer) which, when made to follow the performance of some behavior, results in a change in the frequency of occurrence of that behavior. Compare REWARDS and INCENTIVES.

Reinforcement — (cont'd)
- N Differential Reinforcement [73]
- Negative Reinforcement [73]
- Noncontingent Reinforcement [88]
- ↓ Positive Reinforcement [73]
- Primary Reinforcement [73]
- Punishment [67]
- Reinforcement Amounts [73]
- ↓ Reinforcement Schedules [67]
- ↓ Rewards [67]
- Secondary Reinforcement [67]
- Self Reinforcement [73]
- ↓ Social Reinforcement [67]
- R Autoshaping [78]
- Behavioral Contrast [78]
- ↓ Biofeedback [73]
- ↓ Conditioning [67]
- Delay of Gratification [78]
- Extinction (Learning) [67]
- ↓ Feedback [67]
- ↓ Learning [67]
- ↓ Motivation [67]
- ↓ Operant Conditioning [67]
- ↓ Self Stimulation [67]
- Vicarious Experiences [73]

Reinforcement (Vicarious)
Use Vicarious Experiences

Reinforcement Amounts [73]
PN 880   SC 43640
- B Reinforcement [67]
- R Reinforcement Delay [85]

Reinforcement Delay [85]
PN 168   SC 43645
SN Time delay between the occurrence of a conditioned response and the administration of reinforcement in an operant conditioning paradigm. Consider INTERSTIMULUS INTERVAL for classical conditioning studies.
- UF Delayed Reinforcement
- B Reinforcement Schedules [67]
- R Delay of Gratification [78]
- Delayed Alternation [94]
- Interstimulus Interval [67]
- Reinforcement Amounts [73]
- ↓ Stimulus Intervals [73]

Reinforcement Schedules [67]
PN 4445   SC 43650
- UF Continuous Reinforcement
- Intermittent Reinforcement
- Partial Reinforcement
- Schedules (Reinforcement)
- B Reinforcement [67]
- N Concurrent Reinforcement Schedules [88]
- Fixed Interval Reinforcement [73]
- Fixed Ratio Reinforcement [73]
- Reinforcement Delay [85]
- Variable Interval Reinforcement [73]
- Variable Ratio Reinforcement [73]

Reinnervation
Use Neural Development

Rejection (Social)
Use Social Acceptance

Relapse (Disorders) [73]
PN 1142   SC 43660
SN Recurrence of symptoms after apparent cure or period of improvement.
- R ↓ Disorders [67]
- Expressed Emotion [91]
- ↓ Mental Disorders [67]
- Postsurgical Complications [73]
- Recurrent Depression [94]

Relapse (Disorders) — (cont'd)
- R Relapse Prevention [94]
- ↓ Treatment Outcomes [82]

Relapse Prevention [94]
PN 0   SC 43670
- B Prevention [73]
- R Preventive Medicine [73]
- Primary Mental Health Prevention [73]
- Recovery (Disorders) [73]
- Relapse (Disorders) [73]
- ↓ Remission (Disorders) [73]
- ↓ Treatment [67]
- ↓ Treatment Outcomes [82]

Relationship Therapy [73]
PN 19   SC 43690
SN Psychotherapeutic approach in which the relationship between the therapist and client serves as the basis for the therapy. The therapist provides a supportive setting in which the client can grow and develop and gradually reach differentiation from the therapist and come to perceive his/her own self as separate and distinct.
- B Psychotherapy [67]

Relaxation [73]
PN 710   SC 43697
SN Recreative and restful state, activity, or past-time of lessened muscle tension, stress, or attention.
- R Leisure Time [73]
- Muscle Relaxation [73]
- ↓ Recreation [67]
- Yoga [73]

Relaxation Therapy [78]
PN 1752   SC 43700
SN Therapy emphasizing relaxation and teaching the patient how to relax in order to reduce psychological tensions.
- UF Muscle Relaxation Therapy
- B Treatment [67]
- N Progressive Relaxation Therapy [78]
- R Autogenic Training [73]
- ↓ Behavior Modification [73]
- ↓ Hypnotherapy [73]
- Muscle Relaxation [73]
- Posthypnotic Suggestions [94]
- ↓ Psychotherapeutic Techniques [67]
- Systematic Desensitization Therapy [73]

Relearning [73]
PN 92   SC 43710
- B Learning [67]
- R ↓ Memory [67]

Reliability (Statistical)
SN Term discontinued in 1973. Use RELIABILITY (STATISTICAL) to access references from 67–72.
Use Statistical Reliability

Reliability (Test)
Use Test Reliability

Religion [67]
PN 2213   SC 43740
SN Conceptually broad array term. Use a more specific term if possible.
- UF Theology
- R Asceticism [73]
- ↓ Religious Beliefs [73]
- Religious Buildings [73]
- Religious Education [73]
- ↓ Religious Literature [73]
- Religious Organizations [91]
- ↓ Religious Personnel [73]
- ↓ Religious Practices [73]

Religion — (cont'd)
- R ↓ Religious Prejudices [73]
- Spirituality [88]

Religiosity [73]
PN 1025   SC 43750
SN Degree of one's religious involvement, devotion to religious beliefs, or adherence to religious observances.
- B Religious Beliefs [73]
- R Spirituality [88]

Religious Affiliation [73]
PN 836   SC 43760
- B Religious Beliefs [73]
- N ↓ Buddhism [73]
- ↓ Christianity [73]
- Hinduism [73]
- Islam [73]
- Judaism [67]
- Shamanism [73]
- R ↓ Religious Practices [73]

Religious Beliefs [73]
PN 2219   SC 43770
- UF Beliefs (Religion)
- N Atheism [73]
- God Concepts [73]
- Religiosity [73]
- ↓ Religious Affiliation [73]
- Sin [73]
- R Asceticism [73]
- ↓ Attitudes [67]
- Bible [73]
- Cultism [73]
- Death Attitudes [73]
- ↓ Ethics [67]
- Existentialism [67]
- Forgiveness [88]
- Morality [67]
- Mysticism [67]
- Occultism [78]
- Religion [67]
- Religious Education [73]
- ↓ Religious Literature [73]
- ↓ Religious Practices [73]
- ↓ Religious Prejudices [73]
- Spirituality [88]
- Superstitions [73]

Religious Buildings [73]
PN 26   SC 43780
- UF Churches
- R ↓ Architecture [73]
- ↓ Community Facilities [73]
- Religion [67]

Religious Education [73]
PN 423   SC 43790
- B Education [67]
- R Private School Education [73]
- Religion [67]
- ↓ Religious Beliefs [73]
- ↓ Religious Personnel [73]
- Seminaries [73]

Religious Literature [73]
PN 72   SC 43800
- N Bible [73]
- R ↓ Literature [67]
- Religion [67]
- ↓ Religious Beliefs [73]

Religious Occupations
Use Religious Personnel

Religious Organizations [91]
PN 38   SC 43815

Religious Organizations — (cont'd)
SN Any type of agency, organization, or institution operated by religious groups or persons. Includes, but not limited to, social service, educational, fraternal, recreational, missionary, or rehabilitation organizations.
B   Organizations [67]
R   Religion [67]

Religious Personnel [73]
PN 195   SC 43820
UF   Religious Occupations
B   Personnel [67]
N ↓ Clergy [73]
     Evangelists [73]
     Lay Religious Personnel [73]
     Missionaries [73]
     Nuns [73]
     Seminarians [73]
R ↓ Professional Personnel [78]
     Religion [67]
     Religious Education [73]
   ↓ Volunteer Personnel [73]

Religious Practices [73]
PN 667   SC 43830
UF   Rites (Religion)
     Rituals (Religion)
     Worship
N   Asceticism [73]
     Confession (Religion) [73]
     Faith Healing [73]
     Meditation [73]
     Prayer [73]
     Yoga [73]
R   Glossolalia [73]
     Mysticism [67]
     Religion [67]
   ↓ Religious Affiliation [73]
   ↓ Religious Beliefs [73]

Religious Prejudices [73]
PN 27   SC 43840
B   Prejudice [67]
N   AntiSemitism [73]
R   Religion [67]
   ↓ Religious Beliefs [73]

REM
Use Rapid Eye Movement

REM Dream Deprivation [73]
PN 18   SC 43860
B   Deprivation [67]
R   Rapid Eye Movement [71]

REM Dreams [73]
PN 68   SC 43870
UF   Rapid Eye Movement Dreams
B   Dreaming [67]
R ↓ Eye Movements [67]
     Lucid Dreaming [94]
     Rapid Eye Movement [71]
     REM Sleep [73]

REM Sleep [73]
PN 1384   SC 43880
UF   Paradoxical Sleep
     Rapid Eye Movement Sleep
B   Sleep [67]
R ↓ Eye Movements [67]
     Lucid Dreaming [94]
     Rapid Eye Movement [71]
     REM Dreams [73]

Remarriage [85]
PN 196   SC 43885

Remarriage — (cont'd)
B   Marriage [67]
R   Divorce [73]
   ↓ Marital Status [73]
     Stepfamily [91]

Remedial Education [85]
PN 367   SC 43887
SN Specialized instruction designed to raise academic competence of students with below-normal achievement or learning difficulties. Compare COMPENSATORY EDUCATION.
B   Education [67]
N   Remedial Reading [73]
R   Compensatory Education [73]
     Special Education [67]

Remedial Reading [73]
PN 643   SC 43890
SN Specialized instruction designed to correct faulty reading habits or to improve imperfectly learned reading skills.
B   Reading [67]
     Remedial Education [85]
R   Educational Placement [78]
     Reading Education [73]

Remembering
Use Retention

Reminiscence [85]
PN 302   SC 43905
SN Process of recalling past experiences.
B   Memory [67]
R   Anniversary Events [94]
     Autobiographical Memory [94]
     Early Memories [85]
     Forgetting [73]
     Homesickness [94]
     Life Review [91]
   ↓ Recall (Learning) [67]
   ↓ Retention [67]

Remission (Disorders) [73]
PN 330   SC 43910
SN Diminution or disappearance of symptoms.
N   Spontaneous Remission [73]
     Symptom Remission [73]
R ↓ Disorders [67]
   ↓ Mental Disorders [67]
     Recovery (Disorders) [73]
     Relapse Prevention [94]
   ↓ Treatment Outcomes [82]

Remote Associates Test [73]
PN 16   SC 43920
B   Intelligence Measures [67]

Repairmen
Use Technical Service Personnel

Repeated Measures [85]
PN 76   SC 43935
SN Experimental design in which the subjects serve in all the treatment conditions.
UF   Within Subjects Design
B   Experimental Design [67]
     Testing [67]
R   Posttesting [73]
     Pretesting [73]

Repetition (Compulsive)
Use Compulsive Repetition

Replication (Experimental)
Use Experimental Replication

Reply (to Professional Criticism)
Use Professional Criticism Reply

Repression (Defense Mechanism) [67]
PN 459   SC 43960
B   Defense Mechanisms [67]
R   Suppression (Defense Mechanism) [73]

Repression Sensitization [73]
PN 248   SC 43968
SN Personality continuum which characterizes individual's defensive response to threat, with avoidance (repression or denial) at one extreme and approach (worry or intellectualization) at the other.
UF   Sensitization Repression
B   Personality Traits [67]

Repression Sensitization Scale [73]
PN 28   SC 43970
B   Nonprojective Personality Measures [73]

Reproductive Technology [88]
PN 109   SC 43975
UF   Artificial Insemination
     In Vitro Fertilization
     Test Tube Babies
R   Eugenics [73]
     Fertilization [73]
   ↓ Genetic Engineering [94]
   ↓ Genetics [67]
   ↓ Pregnancy [67]
     Prenatal Diagnosis [88]
     Selective Breeding [73]
   ↓ Sexual Reproduction [73]

Reptiles [67]
PN 37   SC 43980
B   Vertebrates [73]
N   Crocodilians [73]
     Lizards [73]
     Snakes [73]
     Turtles [73]

Republican Party
Use Political Parties

Research
Use Experimentation

Research Design
Use Experimental Design

Research Diagnostic Criteria [94]
PN 0   SC 44013
SN Used when the Research Diagnostic Criteria or its revisions are the focus of the reference. Use PSYCHODIAGNOSTIC TYPOLOGIES to access references prior to 1994. Not used for specific psychodiagnostic categories.
UF   RDC
B   Psychodiagnostic Typologies [67]
R ↓ Diagnosis [67]
     Diagnostic and Statistical Manual [94]
   ↓ Disorders [67]
   ↓ Mental Disorders [67]
   ↓ Psychodiagnosis [67]

Research Dropouts
Use Experimental Attrition

Research Methods
Use Methodology

Research Subjects
Use Experimental Subjects

Resentment
Use Hostility

Reserpine [67]
PN 277   SC 44040
UF Serpasil
B Alkaloids [73]
Antihypertensive Drugs [73]
Neuroleptic Drugs [73]
Sedatives [73]
Sympatholytic Drugs [73]
R Rauwolfia [73]

Residence Halls
Use Dormitories

Residency (Medical)
Use Medical Residency

Residential Care Attendants
Use Attendants (Institutions)

Residential Care Institutions [73]
PN 2857   SC 44080
SN Facilities where individuals or patients live
and receive appropriate treatment or care.
UF Institutions (Residential Care)
N Halfway Houses [73]
↓ Hospitals [67]
Nursing Homes [73]
Orphanages [73]
R Group Homes [82]
Institution Visitation [73]
Institutional Schools [78]
Institutionalized Mentally Retarded [73]
Psychiatric Units [91]
↓ Treatment Facilities [73]

Resistance (Psychotherapeutic)
Use Psychotherapeutic Resistance

Resocialization (Psychosocial)
Use Psychosocial Readjustment

Resonance
Use Vibration

Resource Teachers [73]
PN 91   SC 44130
SN Teachers with special competencies who
supplement regular curricula or programs or who
assist other teachers in specified areas.
B Teachers [67]
R Special Education Teachers [73]

Respiration [67]
PN 1853   SC 44140
UF Breathing
R Artificial Respiration [73]
Carbon Dioxide [73]
↓ Respiration Stimulating Drugs [73]
↓ Respiratory Distress [73]
↓ Respiratory System [73]
↓ Respiratory Tract Disorders [73]
Yawning [88]

Respiration Stimulating Drugs [73]
PN 5   SC 44160
B Drugs [67]
N Caffeine [73]
R Respiration [67]

Respiratory Distress [73]
PN 65   SC 44170
B Symptoms [67]
N ↓ Apnea [73]
↓ Dyspnea [73]

Respiratory Distress — (cont'd)
N Hyperventilation [73]
R Anoxia [73]
Respiration [67]

Respiratory System [73]
PN 49   SC 44180
B Anatomical Systems [73]
N Bronchi [73]
Diaphragm (Anatomy) [73]
↓ Larynx [73]
Lung [73]
↓ Nose [73]
Pharynx [73]
Thorax [73]
Trachea [73]
R Artificial Respiration [73]
Respiration [67]

Respiratory Tract Disorders [73]
PN 229   SC 44190
B Disorders [67]
N ↓ Apnea [73]
Bronchial Disorders [73]
↓ Dyspnea [73]
Hay Fever [73]
Hyperventilation [73]
Laryngeal Disorders [73]
↓ Lung Disorders [73]
Pharyngeal Disorders [73]
R Artificial Respiration [73]
Influenza [73]
Poliomyelitis [73]
Respiration [67]

Respite Care [88]
PN 74   SC 44195
SN Provision of care, relief, or support to care-
givers of physically or mentally disabled persons.
R Caregiver Burden [94]
Caregivers [88]
Home Care [85]

Respondent Conditioning
Use Classical Conditioning

Response Amplitude [73]
PN 496   SC 44210
UF Amplitude (Response)
B Response Parameters [73]

Response Bias [67]
PN 1171   SC 44220
SN Tendency to respond with different styles or
criteria as a result of motivational or physical
influences. Response bias frequently serves as a
source of measurement error in psychophysical,
personality, and other types of measurement.
UF Bias (Response)
R Cultural Test Bias [73]
↓ Measurement [67]
Predisposition [73]
↓ Test Bias [85]
Test Taking [85]

Response Consistency
Use Response Variability

Response Duration [73]
PN 308   SC 44230
UF Duration (Response)
B Response Parameters [73]

Response Frequency [73]
PN 1455   SC 44240
SN Number of responses measured during a
fixed time period.

Response Frequency — (cont'd)
UF Frequency (Response)
Response Rate
B Response Parameters [73]
R Behavioral Contrast [78]
Interresponse Time [73]

Response Generalization [73]
PN 379   SC 44250
SN Learning phenomenon in which an emitted
response is functionally identical to the originally-
conditioned response but which, unlike the con-
ditioned response, was never specifically con-
ditioned.
UF Generalization (Response)
B Generalization (Learning) [82]
Response Parameters [73]

Response Lag
Use Reaction Time

Response Latency [67]
PN 1598   SC 44270
SN Duration of the interval between a stimulus
and the onset of the elicited response. Compare
REACTION TIME.
B Response Parameters [73]
R Behavioral Contrast [78]

Response Parameters [73]
PN 809   SC 44280
UF Parameters (Response)
N Interresponse Time [73]
Reaction Time [67]
Response Amplitude [73]
Response Duration [73]
Response Frequency [73]
Response Generalization [73]
Response Latency [67]
Response Probability [73]
Response Set [67]
Response Variability [73]
R ↓ Responses [67]

Response Probability [73]
PN 100   SC 44290
B Probability [67]
Response Parameters [73]

Response Rate
Use Response Frequency

Response Set [67]
PN 557   SC 44300
SN Cognitive state of concentration or behavioral readiness to respond. Also, deliberate or
inadvertent style or tendency to respond to test
items in characteristic ways (e.g., with socially
desirable answers) that detract from the validity
of the obtained measures.
B Response Parameters [73]

Response Speed
Use Reaction Time

Response Time
Use Reaction Time

Response Variability [73]
PN 397   SC 44330
UF Response Consistency
Variability (Response)
B Response Parameters [73]
R Delayed Alternation [94]
Spontaneous Alternation [82]

Responses [67]
PN 1819   SC 44340

Responses — (cont'd)
- N ↓ Conditioned Responses [67]
- ↓ Emotional Responses [67]
- Mediated Responses [67]
- Orienting Responses [67]
- Unconditioned Responses [73]
- R ↓ Response Parameters [73]

Responsibility [73]
PN 1588   SC 44345
- B Social Behavior [67]
- N Accountability [88]
- Criminal Responsibility [91]
- R Blame [94]
- Professional Liability [85]

Restlessness [73]
PN 126   SC 44350
- B Emotional States [73]
- Symptoms [67]
- R Agitation [91]
- Akathisia [91]
- Hyperkinesis [73]

Restraint (Physical)
- Use Physical Restraint

Restricted Environmental Stimulation
- Use Stimulus Deprivation

Retail Stores
SN Use SHOPPING CENTERS to access references from 73-90.
- Use Retailing

Retailing [91]
PN 75   SC 44362
- UF Retail Stores
- R ↓ Advertising [67]
- Brand Names [78]
- Business [67]
- Consumer Behavior [67]
- Marketing [73]
- Sales Personnel [73]
- Self Employment [94]
- Shopping Centers [73]

Retaliation [91]
PN 13   SC 44364
SN Use RECIPROCITY to access references from 73-90.
- UF Revenge
- B Social Behavior [67]
- R ↓ Aggressive Behavior [67]
- Attack Behavior [73]
- Hostility [67]
- ↓ Interpersonal Interaction [67]
- Reciprocity [73]

Retardation (Mental)
- Use Mental Retardation

Retarded (Mentally)
- Use Mentally Retarded

Retarded Speech Development [73]
PN 107   SC 44390
SN Speech development which is below normal for a specific age level.
- UF Delayed Speech
- B Delayed Development [73]
- Speech Development [73]
- R Language Delay [88]
- ↓ Speech Disorders [67]

Retention [67]
PN 3829   SC 44400

Retention — (cont'd)
SN Persistence of a learned act, information, or experience as measured by reproduction, recall, recognition, or relearning. Consider also LONG TERM MEMORY or SHORT TERM MEMORY.
- UF Remembering
- N ↓ Recall (Learning) [67]
- Recognition (Learning) [67]
- Reconstruction (Learning) [73]
- R Forgetting [73]
- ↓ Interference (Learning) [67]
- ↓ Learning [67]
- ↓ Memory [67]
- Memory Training [94]
- Reminiscence [85]
- ↓ Retention Measures [73]

Retention (School)
- Use School Retention

Retention Measures [73]
PN 102   SC 44410
- B Measurement [67]
- N Wechsler Memory Scale [88]
- R ↓ Retention [67]

Reticular Formation [67]
PN 438   SC 44420
- B Brain Stem [73]
- Neural Pathways [82]
- R ↓ Lemniscal System [85]
- Locus Ceruleus [82]
- Raphe Nuclei [82]

Retina [67]
PN 1159   SC 44430
- B Eye (Anatomy) [67]
- N Cones (Eye) [73]
- Ganglion Cells (Retina) [85]
- Rods (Eye) [73]
- R Retinal Eccentricity [91]

Retinal Eccentricity [91]
PN 31   SC 44435
- R ↓ Retina [67]
- Retinal Image [73]
- Spatial Organization [73]
- ↓ Visual Perception [67]
- Visual Receptive Fields [82]
- ↓ Visual Thresholds [73]

Retinal Ganglion Cells
- Use Ganglion Cells (Retina)

Retinal Image [73]
PN 417   SC 44450
- UF Image (Retinal)
- R ↓ Eye (Anatomy) [67]
- Retinal Eccentricity [91]

Retinal Vessels
- Use Arteries (Anatomy)

Retirement [73]
PN 839   SC 44470
- R Employment History [78]
- ↓ Employment Status [82]
- Job Security [78]
- ↓ Personnel [67]
- Personnel Termination [73]
- Reemployment [91]
- Unemployment [67]

Retraction of Publication [91]
PN 1   SC 44475

Retraction of Publication — (cont'd)
SN Mandatory term applied to notices from journals or authors that retract or recant previously published material because of scientific misconduct, error, unsubstantiated or fabricated data, or other reasons.
- R Errata [91]
- Fraud [94]
- ↓ Scientific Communication [73]

Retroactive Inhibition [73]
PN 479   SC 44480
SN The theory that learning new material can interfere with the retention of previously learned material. Also, the actual retroactive interference itself.
- UF Inhibition (Retroactive)
- B Interference (Learning) [67]

Rett Syndrome [94]
PN 0   SC 44482
- B Disorders [67]
- Syndromes [73]
- R ↓ Brain Disorders [67]
- ↓ Mental Retardation [67]

Return to Home
- Use Empty Nest

Return to Work
- Use Reemployment

Revenge
- Use Retaliation

Reversal Shift Learning [67]
PN 608   SC 44490
SN Experimental technique for demonstration of mediating processes in concept formation which assesses ability to learn to reverse responses in stimulus discrimination task, so that the subject is required to respond to a formerly negative stimulus and not to respond to the formerly positive discriminative stimulus.
- B Discrimination Learning [82]

Review (of Literature)
SN Term discontinued in 1973. Use REVIEW (OF LITERATURE) to access references from 67–72.
- Use Literature Review

Revolutions (Political)
- Use Political Revolution

Reward Allocation [88]
PN 82   SC 44515
- R ↓ Justice [73]
- ↓ Rewards [67]
- ↓ Social Perception [67]

Rewards [67]
PN 2269   SC 44520
SN Events or objects subjectively deemed to be pleasant to a recipient. Compare INCENTIVES, REINFORCEMENT, and POSITIVE REINFORCEMENT.
- B Reinforcement [67]
- N External Rewards [73]
- Internal Rewards [73]
- Monetary Rewards [73]
- Preferred Rewards [73]
- R Delay of Gratification [78]
- Delayed Alternation [94]
- ↓ Incentives [67]
- Reward Allocation [88]

Rh Incompatibility 73
PN 3   SC 44530
UF Erythroblastosis Fetalis
     Incompatibility (Rh)
B   Blood and Lymphatic Disorders 73
     Genetic Disorders 73
     Immunologic Disorders 73
R ↓ Neonatal Disorders 73

Rheoencephalography 73
PN 17   SC 44540
B   Encephalography 73
     Medical Diagnosis 73
R ↓ Electroencephalography 67

Rhetoric 91
PN 54   SC 44545
B   Communication Skills 73
     Language 67
R ↓ Communication 67
     Creative Writing 94
     Hermeneutics 91
   ↓ Oral Communication 85
   ↓ Persuasive Communication 67
   ↓ Written Communication 85

Rheumatic Fever 73
PN 12   SC 44550
R ↓ Bacterial Disorders 73
   ↓ Heart Disorders 73
     Rheumatoid Arthritis 73

Rheumatism
Use Arthritis

Rheumatoid Arthritis 73
PN 386   SC 44570
B   Arthritis 73
R   Rheumatic Fever 73

Rhodopsin 85
PN 7   SC 44575
SN A red pigment localized in the outer segments of rod cells in the retina.
B   Pigments 73
R   Rods (Eye) 73

Rhythm 91
PN 71   SC 44577
N   Speech Rhythm 73
R ↓ Auditory Perception 67
   ↓ Music 67
     Pattern Discrimination 67
   ↓ Perception 67
     Speech Perception 67

Rhythm Method 73
PN 4   SC 44580
B   Birth Control 71

Ribonucleic Acid 73
PN 158   SC 44600
UF RNA (Ribonucleic Acid)
B   Nucleic Acids 73

Right Brain 91
PN 68   SC 44610
SN Used only when the right hemisphere of the brain is the focus of the document.
B   Cerebral Cortex 67
R ↓ Brain 67
   ↓ Cerebral Dominance 73
     Corpus Callosum 73
     Interhemispheric Interaction 85
   ↓ Lateral Dominance 67
     Left Brain 91
     Ocular Dominance 73

Rigidity (Muscles)
Use Muscle Contractions

Rigidity (Personality) 67
PN 204   SC 44620
B   Personality Traits 67

Riots 73
PN 73   SC 44640
B   Collective Behavior 67
     Conflict 67

Risk Analysis 91
PN 137   SC 44643
B   Analysis 67
R ↓ Decision Making 67
   ↓ Gambling 73
     Game Theory 67
   ↓ Risk Taking 67
   ↓ Statistical Probability 67

Risk Populations
Use At Risk Populations

Risk Taking 67
PN 2233   SC 44650
B   Personality Traits 67
     Social Behavior 67
N ↓ Gambling 73
R   Choice Shift 94
     Risk Analysis 91

Risky Shift
Use Choice Shift

Ritalin
Use Methylphenidate

Rites (Nonreligious) 73
PN 317   SC 44670
UF Rituals (Nonreligious)
R ↓ Rites of Passage 73

Rites (Religion)
Use Religious Practices

Rites of Passage 73
PN 69   SC 44690
B   Sociocultural Factors 67
N   Birth Rites 73
     Death Rites 73
     Initiation Rites 73
     Marriage Rites 73
R   Ethnography 73
     Rites (Nonreligious) 73
     Taboos 73

Rituals (Nonreligious)
Use Rites (Nonreligious)

Rituals (Religion)
Use Religious Practices

Rivalry 73
PN 26   SC 44720
B   Interpersonal Interaction 67

RNA (Ribonucleic Acid)
Use Ribonucleic Acid

Robbery
Use Theft

Robins 73
PN 39   SC 44750
B   Birds 67

Robotics 85
PN 122   SC 44755
R ↓ Artificial Intelligence 82
   ↓ Computers 67
     Cybernetics 67
     Expert Systems 91

Rock Music 91
PN 28   SC 44757
B   Music 67

Rocking (Body)
Use Body Rocking

Rod and Frame Test 73
PN 114   SC 44770
B   Nonprojective Personality Measures 73
     Perceptual Measures 73

Rodents 73
PN 543   SC 44780
UF Voles
B   Mammals 73
N   Beavers 73
     Chinchillas 73
     Gerbils 73
     Guinea Pigs 67
     Hamsters 73
     Mice 73
     Minks 73
   ↓ Rats 67
     Squirrels 73

Rods (Eye) 73
PN 205   SC 44790
B   Photoreceptors 73
     Retina 67
R   Rhodopsin 85

Roentgenography 73
PN 106   SC 44800
UF Radiography
     X Ray Diagnosis
B   Medical Diagnosis 73
N   Angiography 73
     Mammography 94
     Pneumoencephalography 73
R ↓ Encephalography 73
   ↓ Radiation 67
   ↓ Tomography 88

Rogers (Carl) 91
PN 24   SC 44805
SN Identifies biographical or autobiographical studies and discussions of Rogers's works.
R   Client Centered Therapy 67
   ↓ Psychologists 67

Rokeach Dogmatism Scale 73
PN 31   SC 44810
B   Nonprojective Personality Measures 73
     Personality Measures 67

Role (Counselor)
Use Counselor Role

Role Conflicts 73
PN 1405   SC 44830
UF Role Strain
R   Role Satisfaction 94
   ↓ Roles 67

Role Expectations 73
PN 698   SC 44840
SN Functional patterns or types of behavior expected from an individual in a specific social or professional position or situation.

Role Expectations — (cont'd)
B   Expectations [67]
R   Role Satisfaction [94]
↓ Roles [67]

Role Models [82]
PN 265   SC 44845
SN Real or theoretical persons consciously or
unconsciously perceived as being a standard for
emulation in one or more of their roles.
R   Imitation (Learning) [67]
Role Perception [73]
↓ Roles [67]
Significant Others [91]
↓ Social Influences [67]

Role Perception [73]
PN 1713   SC 44850
SN Views or understanding of one's own or oth-
ers' function or behavior in particular situations.
B   Perception [67]
R   Professional Identity [91]
Role Models [82]
Role Satisfaction [94]
Role Taking [82]
↓ Roles [67]

Role Playing [67]
PN 1169   SC 44860
SN Psychological or behavioral enactment of
social roles other than one's own, typically seen
in child's play, or used as an experimental, in-
structional, or psychotherapeutic technique. Com-
pare ROLE TAKING.
R   Childhood Play Behavior [78]
Psychodrama [67]
↓ Psychotherapeutic Techniques [67]
Role Taking [82]
↓ Roles [67]

Role Satisfaction [94]
PN 0   SC 44863
B   Satisfaction [73]
R   Job Satisfaction [67]
Life Satisfaction [85]
Marital Satisfaction [88]
Role Conflicts [73]
Role Expectations [73]
Role Perception [73]
↓ Roles [67]
↓ Self Concept [67]

Role Strain
Use Role Conflicts

Role Taking [82]
PN 398   SC 44865
SN Perceiving, understanding, or experiencing
the social, emotional or physical aspects of a
situation from a standpoint of another person or
persons. Use EGOCENTRISM to access refer-
ences from 78–81. Compare ROLE PLAYING.
UF Perspective Taking
R   Egocentrism [78]
Role Perception [73]
Role Playing [67]
↓ Roles [67]
Symbolic Interactionism [88]

Roles [67]
PN 3393   SC 44870
N   Counselor Role [73]
Parental Role [73]
Sex Roles [67]
Therapist Role [78]
R   Role Conflicts [73]
Role Expectations [73]
Role Models [82]
Role Perception [73]

Roles — (cont'd)
R   Role Playing [67]
Role Satisfaction [94]
Role Taking [82]

Roman Catholicism [73]
PN 554   SC 44880
UF Catholicism (Roman)
B   Christianity [73]

Romania [82]
PN 86   SC 44885
B   Europe [73]

Roommates [73]
PN 90   SC 44890
SN Individuals residing in common abodes.
R   Cohabitation [73]
↓ Living Arrangements [91]

Rorschach Test [67]
PN 1833   SC 44900
B   Projective Personality Measures [73]

Rosenzweig Picture Frustration Study [67]
PN 49   SC 44910
B   Projective Personality Measures [73]

Rotary Pursuit [67]
PN 179   SC 44920
B   Tracking [67]
R   ↓ Attention [67]

Rotation Methods (Statistical)
Use Statistical Rotation

Rotational Behavior [94]
PN 0   SC 44935
SN Used primarily for animal populations.
UF Body Rotation
B   Motor Processes [67]
R   Activity Level [82]
Stereotyped Behavior [73]

ROTC Students [73]
PN 61   SC 44940
B   College Students [67]
Military Personnel [67]
R   Volunteer Military Personnel [73]
↓ Volunteer Personnel [73]

Rote Learning [73]
PN 103   SC 44950
SN Verbatim memorization of information which
requires no understanding.
R   ↓ Memory [67]

Rotter Incomplete Sentences Blank [73]
PN 13   SC 44960
B   Projective Personality Measures [73]

Rotter Intern Extern Locus Cont Scal [73]
PN 139   SC 44970
B   Nonprojective Personality Measures [73]

RT (Response)
Use Reaction Time

Rubella [73]
PN 28   SC 45000
UF German Measles
B   Viral Disorders [73]
R   Measles [73]

Rule Learning
Use Cognitive Hypothesis Testing

Rumors
Use Gossip

Runaway Behavior [73]
PN 221   SC 45015
B   Antisocial Behavior [71]
R   Shelters [91]

Running [73]
PN 478   SC 45020
B   Motor Performance [73]

Runways (Maze)
Use Maze Pathways

Rural Environments [67]
PN 2999   SC 45040
B   Social Environments [73]

Rwanda [91]
PN 3   SC 45045
B   Africa [67]

Saccadic Eye Movements
Use Eye Movements

Saccharin [73]
PN 312   SC 45050
R   ↓ Sugars [73]

SAD
Use Seasonal Affective Disorder

Sadism [73]
PN 40   SC 45070
B   Sadomasochism [73]
N   Sexual Sadism [73]
R   ↓ Masochism [73]

Sadness [73]
PN 198   SC 45090
UF Melancholy
B   Emotional States [73]
R   Depression (Emotion) [67]
Homesickness [94]

Sadomasochism [73]
PN 59   SC 45100
SN Derivation of pleasure from infliction of
physical or mental pain on others and oneself,
with presence of high degree of destructiveness.
N   ↓ Masochism [73]
↓ Sadism [73]
R   ↓ Mental Disorders [67]
↓ Sadomasochistic Personality [73]

Sadomasochistic Personality [73]
PN 4   SC 45110
B   Personality Disorders [67]
N   Masochistic Personality [73]
R   ↓ Sadomasochism [73]

Safety [67]
PN 550   SC 45120
N   ↓ Aviation Safety [73]
Highway Safety [73]
Occupational Safety [73]
Water Safety [73]
R   Accident Prevention [73]
Accident Proneness [73]
↓ Accidents [67]
Fire Prevention [73]
↓ Hazardous Materials [91]
Hazards [73]
↓ Injuries [73]
↓ Prevention [73]
↓ Safety Devices [73]

Safety Belts [73]
PN 176   SC 45130
UF   Seat Belts
B   Safety Devices [73]
R   ↓ Driving Behavior [67]
     ↓ Transportation Accidents [73]

Safety Devices [73]
PN 90   SC 45140
N   Safety Belts [73]
R   Hazards [73]
     ↓ Safety [67]

Saint Lucia [91]
PN 1   SC 45145
B   West Indies [73]

Saint Vincent [91]
PN 1   SC 45147
B   West Indies [73]

Salamanders [73]
PN 149   SC 45150
B   Amphibia [73]
R   Larvae [73]

Salaries [73]
PN 830   SC 45160
UF   Pay
     Wages
R   Bonuses [73]
     ↓ Employee Benefits [73]
     Equity (Payment) [78]
     Income (Economic) [73]
     ↓ Income Level [73]
     ↓ Professional Fees [78]

Sales Personnel [73]
PN 553   SC 45170
UF   Insurance Agents
B   Business and Industrial Personnel [67]
     White Collar Workers [73]
R   Retailing [91]
     ↓ Service Personnel [91]

Salience (Stimulus)
Use   Stimulus Salience

Saliva [73]
PN 181   SC 45200
B   Body Fluids [73]
R   Salivation [73]

Salivary Glands [73]
PN 29   SC 45210
B   Glands [67]
R   ↓ Digestive System [67]
     Mouth (Anatomy) [67]

Salivation [73]
PN 156   SC 45220
B   Secretion (Gland) [73]
R   Digestion [73]
     Saliva [73]

Salmon [73]
PN 45   SC 45230
B   Fishes [67]

Saltiness
Use   Taste Perception

Sampling (Experimental) [73]
PN 461   SC 45250

Sampling (Experimental) — (cont'd)
SN   Systematic selection of part of a larger population of individual responses, individuals, or groups for use in experimentation. Results about the entire population are then generalized from this smaller sample.
N   Biased Sampling [73]
     Random Sampling [73]
R   Data Collection [82]
     ↓ Experimental Design [67]
     ↓ Experimentation [67]
     ↓ Population (Statistics) [73]
     ↓ Statistical Analysis [67]
     Statistical Power [91]
     Statistical Reliability [73]
     ↓ Statistical Samples [73]
     ↓ Statistical Variables [73]

Sanatoriums [73]
PN 12   SC 45260
B   Hospitals [67]
R   Nursing Homes [73]
     Psychiatric Hospitals [67]

Sarcomas
Use   Neoplasms

SAT
Use   Coll Ent Exam Bd Scholastic Apt Test

Satiation [67]
PN 632   SC 45280
SN   Primarily limited to gratification or satisfaction of a physiologically-based motivation (e.g., need for food and water) but may also refer to gratification of a psychic goal or motivation. Consider also SATISFACTION or NEED SATISFACTION for the latter concept.
R   ↓ Appetite [73]
     ↓ Motivation [67]

Satisfaction [73]
PN 3109   SC 45290
UF   Fulfillment
N   Client Satisfaction [94]
     Consumer Satisfaction [94]
     Job Satisfaction [67]
     Life Satisfaction [85]
     Marital Satisfaction [88]
     Need Satisfaction [73]
     Role Satisfaction [94]
     Sexual Satisfaction [94]
R   Physical Comfort [82]

Saudi Arabia [85]
PN 128   SC 45295
B   Asia [73]
R   Middle East [78]

Scaling (Testing) [67]
PN 1124   SC 45360
B   Testing [67]
     Testing Methods [67]
R   Magnitude Estimation [91]
     Multidimensional Scaling [82]

Scalp (Anatomy) [73]
PN 40   SC 45370
B   Anatomy [67]
R   Hair [73]
     Head (Anatomy) [73]
     Skin (Anatomy) [67]

Scalp Disorders
Use   Skin Disorders

Scandinavia [78]
PN 79   SC 45385

Scandinavia — (cont'd)
B   Europe [73]
N   Denmark [73]
     Norway [73]
     Sweden [73]
R   Finland [73]
     Iceland [82]

Scent Marking (Animal)
Use   Animal Scent Marking

Schedules (Learning)
Use   Learning Schedules

Schedules (Reinforcement)
Use   Reinforcement Schedules

Scheduling (Work)
Use   Work Scheduling

Schema [88]
PN 696   SC 45425
SN   Cognitive structure used for comprehension, perception, and interpretation of stimuli.
UF   Scripts
B   Cognitive Processes [67]
R   Cognitive Maps [82]
     ↓ Cognitive Style [67]
     Conceptual Imagery [73]
     Perceptual Style [73]
     Social Cognition [94]

Schizoaffective Disorder [94]
PN 0   SC 45427
SN   Presence of an affective disorder accompanied by schizophrenia-like symptomatology.
B   Affective Disturbances [67]
R   ↓ Schizophrenia [67]

Schizoid Personality [73]
PN 306   SC 45430
SN   Personality disorder characterized by alienation, shyness, oversensitivity, seclusiveness, egocentricity, avoidance of intimate relationships, autistic thinking, and withdrawal from and lack of response to the environment.
B   Personality Disorders [67]
R   ↓ Schizophrenia [67]
     Schizotypal Personality [91]

Schizophrenia [67]
PN 16934   SC 45440
UF   Chronic Schizophrenia
     Dementia Praecox
     Process Schizophrenia
     Pseudopsychopathic Schizophrenia
     Reactive Schizophrenia
     Schizophrenia (Residual Type)
     Simple Schizophrenia
B   Psychosis [67]
N   Acute Schizophrenia [73]
     Catatonic Schizophrenia [73]
     Childhood Schizophrenia [67]
     Hebephrenic Schizophrenia [73]
     Paranoid Schizophrenia [67]
     Schizophreniform Disorder [94]
     Undifferentiated Schizophrenia [73]
R   Anhedonia [85]
     Catalepsy [73]
     Expressed Emotion [91]
     Fragmentation (Schizophrenia) [73]
     Schizoaffective Disorder [94]
     Schizoid Personality [73]
     Schizotypal Personality [91]

Schizophrenia (Disorganized Type)
Use   Hebephrenic Schizophrenia

Schizophrenia (Residual Type)
Use Schizophrenia

Schizophreniform Disorder [94]
PN 0   **SC** 45447
SN Use ACUTE SCHIZOPHRENIA to access references from 88-93.
B   Schizophrenia [67]

Schizophrenogenic Family [67]
PN 267   **SC** 45450
B   Family [67]
     Family Structure [73]
R   Double Bind Interaction [73]
     Dysfunctional Family [91]
     ↓ Mental Disorders [67]
     Schizophrenogenic Mothers [73]

Schizophrenogenic Mothers [73]
PN 30   **SC** 45460
B   Mothers [67]
R   Double Bind Interaction [73]
     Mother Child Relations [67]
     Schizophrenogenic Family [67]

Schizotypal Personality [91]
PN 68   **SC** 45465
SN Personality disorder characterized by eccentric thoughts and appearance, inappropriate affect and behavior, extreme social anxiety, and limited interpersonal interaction. Consider using SCHIZOID PERSONALITY to access references from 73-90.
B   Personality Disorders [67]
R   Schizoid Personality [73]
     ↓ Schizophrenia [67]

Scholarships
Use Educational Financial Assistance

Scholastic Achievement
Use Academic Achievement

Scholastic Aptitude
Use Academic Aptitude

Scholastic Aptitude Test
Use Coll Ent Exam Bd Scholastic Apt Test

School Accreditation
Use Educational Program Accreditation

School Achievement
Use Academic Achievement

School Adjustment [67]
PN 2665   **SC** 45510
SN Process of adjusting to school environment and to the role of a student.
B   Adjustment [67]
R   Adjustment Disorders [94]
     ↓ Education [67]

School Administration
Use Educational Administration

School Administrators [73]
PN 1886   **SC** 45530
UF Administrators (School)
     Educational Administrators
B   Educational Personnel [73]
N   School Principals [73]
     School Superintendents [73]
R   Boards of Education [78]
     ↓ Management Personnel [73]

School Age Children [73]
PN 44584   **SC** 45540
SN Ages 6–12 years. Used in noneducational contexts. Application of terms designating age is mandatory for ages 0–17.
B   Children [67]
N   Preadolescents [88]
R   ↓ Childhood Development [67]
     ↓ Elementary School Students [67]
     Intermediate School Students [73]
     Predelinquent Youth [78]
     Primary School Students [73]

School and College Ability Test [73]
PN 5   **SC** 45550
B   Aptitude Measures [67]

School Attendance [73]
PN 840   **SC** 45560
SN Regular presence of students in school or classes or absenteeism due to factors other than truancy. Compare SCHOOL ENROLLMENT.
UF Attendance (School)
R   ↓ Education [67]
     ↓ School Enrollment [73]
     School Refusal [94]
     School Retention [94]
     Student Attrition [91]

School Club Membership [73]
PN 18   **SC** 45570
B   Extracurricular Activities [73]

School Counseling [82]
PN 1837   **SC** 45579
SN Counseling services provided by counselors or teacher counselors in order to help school, college, or university students cope with adjustment problems. Compare EDUCATIONAL COUNSELING.
UF Educational Therapy
     Guidance Counseling
     School Guidance
B   Counseling [67]
R   ↓ Education [67]
     ↓ Mental Health Services [78]
     School Counselors [73]
     Student Personnel Services [78]

School Counselors [73]
PN 1309   **SC** 45580
B   Counselors [67]
     Educational Personnel [73]
R   School Counseling [82]
     School Psychologists [73]
     Vocational Counselors [73]

School Dropouts [67]
PN 917   **SC** 45590
B   Dropouts [73]
N   College Dropouts [73]
R   ↓ Education [67]
     Reentry Students [85]
     School Refusal [94]
     School Retention [94]
     Student Attrition [91]

School Enrollment [73]
PN 326   **SC** 45600
SN Number of students registered to attend school, college or university. Also, the act of enrolling in school. Compare SCHOOL ATTENDANCE.
UF Enrollment (School)
     Matriculation
N   School Expulsion [73]
     School Suspension [73]
     Student Attrition [91]
R   ↓ Dropouts [73]

School Enrollment — (cont'd)
R   ↓ Education [67]
     School Attendance [73]
     School Retention [94]
     School Truancy [73]

School Environment [73]
PN 2230   **SC** 45610
SN School characteristics, including overall social and physical atmosphere or school climate.
B   Academic Environment [73]
N   College Environment [73]
R   Classroom Environment [73]
     ↓ Education [67]
     ↓ School Facilities [73]
     ↓ Schools [67]

School Expulsion [73]
PN 30   **SC** 45620
UF Expulsion (School)
B   School Enrollment [73]
R   School Suspension [73]
     Student Attrition [91]

School Facilities [73]
PN 93   **SC** 45630
N   Campuses [73]
     Classrooms [67]
     Dormitories [73]
     ↓ Educational Laboratories [73]
     Learning Centers (Educational) [73]
     School Libraries [73]
R   ↓ Education [67]
     Playgrounds [73]
     ↓ School Environment [73]
     ↓ Schools [67]

School Federal Aid
Use Educational Financial Assistance

School Financial Assistance
Use Educational Financial Assistance

School Graduation [91]
PN 30   **SC** 45653
SN Completion of a course of study resulting in the award or acceptance of a diploma or degree.
UF Graduation (School)
R   ↓ Academic Achievement [67]
     College Graduates [82]
     ↓ Education [67]
     Educational Degrees [73]
     Graduate Schools [73]
     High School Graduates [78]
     ↓ Higher Education [73]
     School to Work Transition [94]

School Guidance
Use School Counseling

School Integration [82]
PN 181   **SC** 45658
SN Incorporation of students of different racial or ethnic groups into the same school. Use SCHOOL INTEGRATION (RACIAL) to access references from 73–81.
UF Racial Segregation (Schools)
     School Integration (Racial)
B   Social Integration [82]
R   ↓ Activist Movements [73]
     ↓ Education [67]
     Equal Education [78]
     Racial and Ethnic Relations [82]

School Integration (Racial)
SN Term discontinued in 1982. Use SCHOOL INTEGRATION (RACIAL) to access references from 73–81.
  Use School Integration

School Learning [67]
PN 2932   SC 45670
SN Learning in an academic environment. For educational performance use ACADEMIC ACHIEVEMENT or one of its narrower terms.
  B   Learning [67]
  R ↓ Academic Achievement [67]
      Cooperative Learning [94]
     ↓ Education [67]
      Mastery Learning [85]
      Metacognition [91]

School Leavers [88]
PN 38   SC 45675
SN British term referring to persons who have recently left school, generally after the completion of a basic education program and satisfaction of government requirements.
  R ↓ Educational Background [67]
      School Retention [94]
      Student Attrition [91]

School Libraries [73]
PN 77   SC 45680
  UF Libraries (School)
  B   Libraries [82]
      School Facilities [73]

School Nurses [73]
PN 50   SC 45690
  B   Educational Personnel [73]
      Nurses [67]

School Organization
  Use Educational Administration

School Phobia [73]
PN 205   SC 45710
  B   Phobias [67]
  R   School Refusal [94]
      Separation Anxiety [73]
      Student Attitudes [67]

School Principals [73]
PN 1899   SC 45720
  B   School Administrators [73]

School Psychologists [73]
PN 1306   SC 45730
SN Psychologists usually associated with elementary or secondary schools who provide counseling, testing, or diagnostic services to students, teachers, or parents.
  B   Educational Psychologists [73]
      Mental Health Personnel [67]
  R   School Counselors [73]

School Psychology [73]
PN 787   SC 45740
SN Branch of psychology that emphasizes training and certification of school psychologists.
  B   Educational Psychology [67]

School Readiness [73]
PN 420   SC 45750
SN Developmental level at which a child is prepared to adjust to school and the student role. Compare READING READINESS.
  R ↓ Education [67]
      Project Head Start [73]

School Refusal [94]
PN 0   SC 45755
SN Unwillingness of students to attend school or classes.
  R   School Attendance [73]
     ↓ School Dropouts [67]
      School Phobia [73]
      School Truancy [73]
      Separation Anxiety [73]
      Student Attitudes [67]

School Retention [94]
PN 0   SC 45757
SN Retention of students in school or educational programs.
  UF Retention (School)
  R   School Attendance [73]
     ↓ School Dropouts [67]
     ↓ School Enrollment [73]
      School Leavers [88]
      School Truancy [73]
      Student Attrition [91]
     ↓ Students [67]

School Superintendents [73]
PN 337   SC 45760
SN Administrators who coordinate and direct the operations and activities of a school system at the district, city, or state level.
  UF Superintendents (School)
  B   School Administrators [73]

School Suspension [73]
PN 110   SC 45770
SN Temporary, forced withdrawal of a student from school, usually for disciplinary reasons.
  UF Suspension (School)
  B   School Enrollment [73]
  R   Classroom Discipline [73]
      School Expulsion [73]

School to Work Transition [94]
PN 0   SC 45775
SN Transition following school graduation or termination and entry into the work force. Used for normal and disordered populations.
  R   College Graduates [82]
     ↓ Education [67]
      High School Graduates [78]
     ↓ Mainstreaming [91]
      Occupational Adjustment [73]
      School Graduation [91]
     ↓ Vocational Rehabilitation [67]

School Truancy [73]
PN 158   SC 45780
SN Student's deliberate, often chronic absence from school without an accepted medical or other justifiable reason.
  B   Truancy [73]
  R ↓ Education [67]
     ↓ School Enrollment [73]
      School Refusal [94]
      School Retention [94]

Schools [67]
PN 1233   SC 45790
  N   Boarding Schools [88]
     ↓ Colleges [67]
      Elementary Schools [73]
      Graduate Schools [73]
      High Schools [73]
      Institutional Schools [78]
      Junior High Schools [73]
      Kindergartens [73]
      Military Schools [73]
      Nongraded Schools [73]
      Nursery Schools [73]
      Seminaries [73]

Schools — (cont'd)
  N   Technical Schools [73]
  R ↓ Community Facilities [73]
     ↓ Education [67]
     ↓ School Environment [73]
     ↓ School Facilities [73]

Sciatic Nerve
  Use Spinal Nerves

Science Education [73]
PN 2157   SC 45820
  B   Curriculum [67]

Sciences [67]
PN 1237   SC 45825
  N ↓ Biology [67]
     ↓ Chemistry [67]
      Eugenics [73]
      Geography [73]
     ↓ Mathematics [82]
     ↓ Medical Sciences [67]
     ↓ Neurosciences [73]
      Physics [73]
      Psychobiology [82]
     ↓ Social Sciences [67]
  R ↓ Technology [73]

Scientific Communication [73]
PN 2245   SC 45830
SN Formal or informal communication among professionals.
  UF Communication (Professional)
      Newsletters (Professional)
      Professional Communication
      Professional Newsletters
  B   Communication [67]
  N   Professional Meetings and Symposia [67]
  R   Errata [91]
      Information Exchange [73]
     ↓ Interpersonal Communication [73]
      Psychological Terminology [73]
      Retraction of Publication [91]
     ↓ Terminology [91]

Scientific Methods
  Use Experimental Methods

Scientists [67]
PN 862   SC 45850
SN Conceptually broad array term. Use a more specific term if possible.
  B   Professional Personnel [78]
  R ↓ Aerospace Personnel [73]
      Anthropologists [73]
     ↓ Business and Industrial Personnel [67]
      Engineers [67]
      Mathematicians [73]
     ↓ Medical Personnel [67]
      Physicists [73]
     ↓ Psychologists [67]
      Sociologists [73]

Sclera
  Use Eye (Anatomy)

Sclerosis (Nervous System) [73]
PN 90   SC 45870
  B   Nervous System Disorders [67]
  N   Multiple Sclerosis [73]
  R ↓ Neuromuscular Disorders [73]
     ↓ Paralysis [73]

Scopolamine [73]
PN 722   SC 45880
  UF Hyoscine
      Scopolamine Hydrobromide
  B   Alkaloids [73]

Scopolamine — (cont'd)
B   Amines [73]
     Analgesic Drugs [73]
     Cholinergic Blocking Drugs [73]
     CNS Depressant Drugs [73]
     Sedatives [73]
R ↓ Bromides [73]

Scopolamine Hydrobromide
Use Scopolamine

Score Equating [85]
PN 90   SC 45895
SN Techniques, procedures, or methods used to allow scores obtained from various editions of the same test or from different tests measuring the same trait to be compared.
UF   Test Equating
R   Cutting Scores [85]
   ↓ Scoring (Testing) [73]
     Standard Scores [85]

Scores (Test)
Use Test Scores

Scoring (Testing) [73]
PN 1416   SC 45910
SN Assignment of numerical values or other types of codes, or the application of comments to test results in order to evaluate a test performance in reference to some established standard or other criterion. Compare GRADING (EDUCATIONAL) or TEST SCORES.
B   Testing [67]
N   Cutting Scores [85]
R   Error of Measurement [85]
     Grading (Educational) [73]
     Score Equating [85]
     Standard Scores [85]
     Statistical Weighting [85]
     Test Interpretation [85]
   ↓ Test Scores [67]

Scotland [73]
PN 333   SC 45920
B   Great Britain [71]

Scotopic Stimulation [73]
PN 109   SC 45940
SN Presentation of light at intensity levels characteristic of nighttime illumination, activating rod photoreceptors in the retina.
B   Illumination [67]
R   Photopic Stimulation [73]

Scratching [73]
PN 44   SC 45950
B   Symptoms [67]
R   Pruritus [73]

Screening [82]
PN 791   SC 45960
SN Preliminary use of testing procedures or instruments to identify individuals at risk for a particular problem, or in need of a more thorough evaluation, or to determine an individual's suitability for a specific treatment, education, or occupation.
B   Measurement [67]
N   Drug Usage Screening [88]
     Job Applicant Screening [73]
R   Biological Markers [91]
   ↓ Diagnosis [67]
     Diagnostic Interview Schedule [91]
   ↓ Educational Measurement [67]
     Educational Placement [78]
     Health Promotion [91]
     Intake Interview [94]
   ↓ Personnel Selection [67]

Screening — (cont'd)
R ↓ Screening Tests [82]
     Symptom Checklists [91]

Screening Tests [82]
PN 1013   SC 45980
B   Measurement [67]
N   Psychological Screening Inventory [73]
R   General Health Questionnaire [91]
   ↓ Screening [82]

Scripts
Use Schema

Sculpturing [73]
PN 38   SC 45990
B   Art [67]

Sea Gulls [73]
PN 167   SC 46010
UF   Gulls
B   Birds [67]

Seals (Animal) [73]
PN 85   SC 46020
B   Mammals [73]

Seasonal Affective Disorder [91]
PN 120   SC 46025
UF   SAD
     Winter Depression
B   Affective Disturbances [67]
R ↓ Major Depression [88]
     Phototherapy [91]
     Recurrent Depression [94]

Seasonal Variations [73]
PN 897   SC 46030
SN Periodic changes in behavioral, psychological, or physiological responses in relation to seasonal changes. Used for human or animal populations.
B   Environmental Effects [73]
R ↓ Biological Rhythms [67]
   ↓ Temperature Effects [67]

Seat Belts
Use Safety Belts

Seclusion (Patient)
Use Patient Seclusion

Secobarbital [73]
PN 48   SC 46040
UF   Seconal
B   Barbiturates [67]
     Hypnotic Drugs [73]
     Sedatives [73]

Seconal
Use Secobarbital

Second Language Education
Use Foreign Language Education

Secondary Education [73]
PN 704   SC 46060
SN Education provided by comprehensive schools, grammar schools, junior high or high schools, typically for grades 7–12.
B   Education [67]
R   High Schools [73]
     Junior High Schools [73]

Secondary Reinforcement [67]
PN 338   SC 46070

Secondary Reinforcement — (cont'd)
SN Presentation of a secondary reinforcer. Also, objects or events which acquire reinforcing properties only through having been consistently paired or associated with other reinforcers. Also known as conditioned reinforcers or conditioned stimuli. Compare INTERNAL REWARDS.
UF   Token Reinforcement
B   Reinforcement [67]
R   Conditioned Stimulus [73]

Secrecy [94]
PN 0   SC 46075
R   Anonymity [73]
     Privacy [73]
     Self Disclosure [73]

Secretarial Personnel [73]
PN 118   SC 46080
B   Business and Industrial Personnel [67]
     White Collar Workers [73]
R   Clerical Personnel [73]

Secretarial Skills
Use Clerical Secretarial Skills

Secretion (Gland) [73]
PN 96   SC 46100
B   Physiology [67]
N ↓ Endocrine Gland Secretion [73]
     Lactation [73]
     Salivation [73]
     Sweating [73]
R ↓ Endocrine Disorders [73]

Sectioning (Lesion)
Use Lesions

Security (Emotional)
Use Emotional Security

Sedatives [73]
PN 332   SC 46130
B   Drugs [67]
N   Alprazolam [88]
     Amobarbital [73]
     Atropine [73]
     Barbital [73]
     Chloral Hydrate [73]
     Chlorpromazine [67]
     Clozapine [91]
     Flurazepam [82]
     Glutethimide [73]
     Haloperidol [73]
     Heroin [73]
     Hexobarbital [73]
     Lithium Bromide [73]
     Meperidine [73]
     Meprobamate [73]
     Methaqualone [73]
     Molindone [82]
     Nitrazepam [78]
     Paraldehyde [82]
     Pentobarbital [73]
     Phenaglycodol [73]
     Phenobarbital [73]
     Promethazine [73]
     Rauwolfia [73]
     Reserpine [67]
     Scopolamine [73]
     Secobarbital [73]
     Thalidomide [73]
     Thiopental [73]
     Triazolam [88]
R ↓ Analgesic Drugs [73]
   ↓ Anesthetic Drugs [73]
   ↓ Anticonvulsive Drugs [73]
   ↓ Antiemetic Drugs [73]

Sedatives — (cont'd)
R ↓ Antihistaminic Drugs [73]
  ↓ Antihypertensive Drugs [73]
  ↓ Barbiturates [67]
  ↓ Benzodiazepines [78]
  ↓ CNS Depressant Drugs [73]
  ↓ Hypnotic Drugs [73]
  ↓ Tranquilizing Drugs [67]

Seduction [94]
PN 0   SC 46133
B   Psychosexual Behavior [67]

Seeing Eye Dogs
  Use Mobility Aids

Segregation (Racial)
  Use Social Integration

Seizures
  Use Convulsions

Selected Readings [73]
PN 546   SC 46150
SN Mandatory term applied to collections of previously published material.

Selection (Personnel)
  Use Personnel Selection

Selection (Therapist)
  Use Therapist Selection

Selection Tests [73]
PN 397   SC 46170
SN Tests developed to assess specific traits or skills with the purpose of screening or selecting individuals for occupational or educational placement.
B   Measurement [67]
N   Psychological Screening Inventory [73]

Selective Attention [73]
PN 1353   SC 46175
SN Focusing of awareness on a limited range of stimuli. Compare DIVIDED ATTENTION.
B   Attention [67]
R   Concentration [82]
   Distraction [78]
   Divided Attention [73]
  ↓ Monitoring [73]
   Sensory Gating [91]
   Vigilance [67]

Selective Breeding [73]
PN 198   SC 46180
SN Systematic approach to the development of genotype-dependent differences in a physical or behavioral trait. Compare ANIMAL BREEDING, ANIMAL DOMESTICATION, and EUGENICS.
B   Animal Breeding [73]
R   Animal Domestication [78]
   Eugenics [73]
  ↓ Genetic Engineering [94]
  ↓ Genetics [67]
   Reproductive Technology [88]

Self Acceptance
  Use Self Perception

Self Actualization [73]
PN 1883   SC 46190
SN According to A. Maslow's theory, the process of striving to fulfill one's talents, capacities, and potentialities for maximum self realization, ideally with integration of physical, social, intellectual, and emotional needs.

Self Actualization — (cont'd)
UF Actualization (Self)
   Self Realization
R   Affective Education [82]
  ↓ Human Potential Movement [82]
   Maslow (Abraham Harold) [91]
  ↓ Personality [67]
   Self Determination [94]
  ↓ Self Help Techniques [82]

Self Analysis [94]
PN 0   SC 46195
SN In psychoanalytic training, self application of psychoanalytic principles to the psychoanalytic trainee's personal feelings, drives, and behaviors.
B   Psychoanalysis [67]
R   Psychoanalytic Training [73]

Self Assessment
  Use Self Evaluation

Self Care Skills [78]
PN 1131   SC 46215
SN Skills such as personal hygiene, feeding, independent housekeeping, public transportation use, which are often taught in rehabilitation programs for persons with mental, physical, or emotional handicaps.
UF Independent Living
B   Ability [67]
R   Activities of Daily Living [91]
   Adaptive Behavior [91]
   Child Self Care [88]
   Daily Activities [94]
   Hygiene [94]
   Independent Living Programs [91]
  ↓ Rehabilitation [67]
  ↓ Skill Learning [73]
   Special Education [67]

Self Concept [67]
PN 12564   SC 46220
UF Ideal Self
   Identity (Personal)
   Self Image
N   Self Confidence [94]
   Self Esteem [73]
R   Affective Education [82]
   Ego Identity [91]
   Gender Identity [85]
  ↓ Personality [67]
   Professional Identity [91]
   Reference Groups [94]
   Role Satisfaction [94]
   Self Congruence [78]
   Self Perception [67]
  ↓ Social Identity [88]
   Symbolic Interactionism [88]

Self Confidence [94]
PN 0   SC 46230
SN Use SELF ESTEEM to access references from 73-93.
UF Confidence (Self)
B   Self Concept [67]
R   Self Efficacy [85]
   Self Esteem [73]
   Self Perception [67]

Self Congruence [78]
PN 170   SC 46235
SN State of harmony between actual and ideal selves, or congruence between experience and self-concept.
R ↓ Self Concept [67]

Self Consciousness
  Use Self Perception

Self Control [73]
PN 2385   SC 46240
SN The ability to repress or the practice of repressing one's behavior, impulsive reactions, emotions, or desires.
UF Willpower
B   Personality Traits [67]

Self Defeating Behavior [88]
PN 56   SC 46243
SN Behavior that blocks one's own goals and wishes, e.g., the tendency to compete so aggressively that one cannot hold a job.
B   Behavior [67]
R   Self Handicapping Strategy [88]

Self Defense [85]
PN 45   SC 46245
SN Protecting one's self or property against crime.
UF Personal Defense
R ↓ Crime [67]
  ↓ Crime Victims [82]
   Martial Arts [85]
  ↓ Violence [73]

Self Destructive Behavior [85]
PN 446   SC 46244
SN Deliberately or indirectly self-harmful behavior or cognitions.
B   Behavior [67]
N   Attempted Suicide [73]
   Head Banging [73]
   Self Inflicted Wounds [73]
   Self Mutilation [73]
   Suicide [67]
R ↓ Behavior Disorders [71]
   Hair Pulling [73]
  ↓ Masochism [73]
   Masochistic Personality [73]

Self Determination [94]
PN 0   SC 46246
SN The power of individuals to determine their own destiny or actions.
R   Empowerment [91]
   Independence (Personality) [73]
   Individuality [73]
   Internal External Locus of Control [67]
   Self Actualization [73]
  ↓ Self Management [85]
   Volition [88]
   World View [88]

Self Directed Learning
  Use Individualized Instruction

Self Disclosure [73]
PN 2138   SC 46250
R   Anonymity [73]
  ↓ Interpersonal Communication [73]
  ↓ Personality [67]
   Secrecy [94]

Self Efficacy [85]
PN 1410   SC 46255
SN Cognitive mechanism based on expectations or beliefs about one's ability to perform actions necessary to produce a given effect. Also, a theoretical component of behavior change in various therapeutic treatments.
UF Efficacy Expectations
R ↓ Expectations [67]
   Instrumentality [91]
   Self Confidence [94]
   Self Evaluation [67]
   Self Perception [67]

Self Employment [94]
PN 0   SC 46257
  B   Employment Status [82]
  R   Business [67]
       Entrepreneurship [91]
       Ownership [85]
       Retailing [91]

Self Esteem [73]
PN 6966   SC 46260
  UF Self Respect
  B   Self Concept [67]
  R   Self Confidence [94]
       Self Perception [67]

Self Evaluation [67]
PN 3286   SC 46270
  UF Self Assessment
  B   Evaluation [67]
  R   ↓ Personality [67]
       Self Efficacy [85]
       ↓ Self Management [85]
       Self Monitoring [82]
       Self Report [82]
       Social Comparison [85]

Self Examination (Medical) [88]
PN 112   SC 46273
SN Regular self examination for detection of medical conditions or disorders, e.g., breast or testicular cancer. Also used for self administration of medical diagnostic procedures.
  UF Breast Examination
  R   Health Behavior [82]
       Physical Examination [88]

Self Handicapping Strategy [88]
PN 45   SC 46274
SN Psychological ploy that lessens one's chances of performing well at a task in which one is ego-involved and fears failure so that poor performance or lack of ability may be attributed to circumstance.
  R   Fear of Success [78]
       Self Defeating Behavior [88]

Self Help Techniques [82]
PN 858   SC 46275
SN Techniques, materials, or processes designed to assist individuals in solving their own problems.
  N   ↓ Self Management [85]
  R   ↓ Behavior Modification [73]
       ↓ Community Services [67]
       Group Counseling [73]
       ↓ Psychotherapeutic Techniques [67]
       Self Actualization [73]
       Self Monitoring [82]
       Self Referral [91]
       Social Support Networks [82]
       ↓ Support Groups [91]
       ↓ Treatment [67]

Self Hypnosis
  Use Autohypnosis

Self Image
  Use Self Concept

Self Inflicted Wounds [73]
PN 274   SC 46290
SN Any injury to body tissue (including bones) resulting from self directed mechanical violence. Compare SELF MUTILATION.
  B   Self Destructive Behavior [85]
       Wounds [73]
  R   Self Mutilation [73]

Self Instruction
  Use Individualized Instruction

Self Instructional Training [85]
PN 147   SC 46294
SN Cognitive technique for overcoming cognitive deficits in areas such as problem solving, verbal mediation, and information seeking. Overt verbalizations of thought processes are modeled for and imitated by the client. Covert self-verbalizations follow which result in the client gaining verbal control over behavior.
  B   Cognitive Techniques [85]
       Self Management [85]
  R   Cognitive Therapy [82]

Self Management [85]
PN 580   SC 46295
SN Self-regulated modification and/or maintenance of behavior by self-governing of behavioral consequences. Used with disordered or normal populations of all ages.
  B   Behavior Modification [73]
       Management [67]
       Self Help Techniques [82]
  N   Self Instructional Training [85]
  R   Centering [91]
       Cognitive Therapy [82]
       Self Determination [94]
       Self Evaluation [67]
       Self Monitoring [82]
       Self Reinforcement [73]
       Time Management [94]

Self Medication [91]
PN 29   SC 46298
  R   ↓ Drug Therapy [67]
       ↓ Drugs [67]
       Nonprescription Drugs [91]
       Prescription Drugs [91]

Self Monitoring [82]
PN 698   SC 46296
SN Systematic observation and recording of one's own behavior usually for the purpose of changing the behavior by means of behavior modification techniques.
  UF Self Observation
  B   Monitoring [73]
  R   ↓ Behavior Modification [73]
       Observation Methods [67]
       Self Evaluation [67]
       ↓ Self Help Techniques [82]
       ↓ Self Management [85]
       Self Report [82]

Self Monitoring (Personality) [85]
PN 244   SC 46297
SN The process of subjectively observing and comparing one's own behaviors and expressions with those of others in social interactions for the purpose of regulating and controlling one's own verbal and nonverbal behaviors.
  R   Impression Management [78]
       ↓ Personality [67]
       ↓ Personality Traits [67]
       Self Perception [67]
       Social Comparison [85]
       ↓ Social Interaction [67]

Self Mutilation [73]
PN 442   SC 46300
SN Act of inflicting permanent physical damage to oneself, such as cutting off or destroying a limb or other part of the body. Compare SELF INFLICTED WOUNDS.
  UF Autotomy
       Mutilation (Self)
  B   Behavior Disorders [71]

Self Mutilation — (cont'd)
  B   Self Destructive Behavior [85]
  R   Self Inflicted Wounds [73]

Self Observation
  Use Self Monitoring

Self Perception [67]
PN 7284   SC 46310
SN Physical and social awareness and perceptions of oneself.
  UF Self Acceptance
       Self Consciousness
  B   Perception [67]
  R   Aging (Attitudes Toward) [85]
       Body Awareness [82]
       Mirror Image [91]
       ↓ Personality [67]
       Personality Theory [67]
       ↓ Self Concept [67]
       Self Confidence [94]
       Self Efficacy [85]
       Self Esteem [73]
       Self Monitoring (Personality) [85]
       Self Reference [94]
       Self Report [82]

Self Psychology [88]
PN 300   SC 46315
SN Psychological theory focusing on interpretation of behavior in reference to self.
  B   Psychology [67]
  R   Personality Theory [67]
       Psychoanalytic Theory [67]

Self Realization
  Use Self Actualization

Self Reference [94]
PN 0   SC 46323
  R   ↓ Interpersonal Communication [73]
       Self Perception [67]
       ↓ Social Perception [67]

Self Referral [91]
PN 15   SC 46325
SN Act of directing oneself to an agency, service, or professional for assessment, diagnosis, treatment, or consultation.
  UF Referral (Self)
  R   ↓ Commitment (Psychiatric) [73]
       Health Behavior [82]
       ↓ Health Care Services [78]
       Health Care Utilization [85]
       Help Seeking Behavior [78]
       Professional Referral [73]
       ↓ Self Help Techniques [82]

Self Reinforcement [73]
PN 1068   SC 46330
  B   Reinforcement [67]
  R   ↓ Self Management [85]
       ↓ Self Stimulation [67]

Self Report [82]
PN 1793   SC 46335
SN Method for obtaining information through the elicitation of overt verbal responses, oral or written, from the subject/client by the use of questions or directives. Used only when self-report is discussed in reference to methodological considerations.
  B   Methodology [67]
  R   Likert Scales [94]
       Self Evaluation [67]
       Self Monitoring [82]
       Self Perception [67]

Self Respect
Use Self Esteem

Self Stimulation 67
PN 1624   SC 46350
B Stimulation 67
N Brain Self Stimulation 85
R Electrical Brain Stimulation 73
↓ Operant Conditioning 67
↓ Reinforcement 67
Self Reinforcement 73

Self Talk 88
PN 116   SC 46355
SN Vocalized or unvocalized speech that is directed to oneself or an imaginary recipient.
UF Inner Speech
B Oral Communication 85
R Ellis (Albert) 91
↓ Psychotherapeutic Techniques 67
Subvocalization 73

Selfishness 73
PN 40   SC 46360
B Personality Traits 67

Semantic Differential 67
PN 806   SC 46370
SN Technique or test which uses subjective ratings of an idea, concept, or object by means of scaling opposite adjectives in order to study connotative meaning. Also used to assess interactions between people and situations and for attitude assessment.
R ↓ Attitude Measures 67
Likert Scales 94
↓ Measurement 67

Semantic Generalization 73
PN 142   SC 46380
SN Conditioning of a reaction to a nonverbal stimulus and subsequent generalization of the response to verbal signs representative of the original stimulus. The types include generalization from object to sign, from sign to sign, and from sign to object.
UF Generalization (Semantic)
B Cognitive Processes 67
R Cognitive Generalization 67
Connotations 73

Semantic Memory 88
PN 319   SC 46385
SN Organized knowledge about words, their meanings, and their relations.
B Verbal Memory 94
R ↓ Lexical Access 88
Lexical Decision 88
Semantic Priming 94
↓ Semantics 67

Semantic Priming 94
PN 0   SC 46387
B Priming 88
R Contextual Associations 67
Cues 67
Semantic Memory 88
↓ Semantics 67

Semantics 67
PN 3227   SC 46390
SN Linguistic science dealing with the relations between language symbols (words, expressions, phrases) and the objects or concepts to which they refer. Also includes the study of changes in the meanings of words. Used for the discipline or the specific semantic characteristics of linguistic symbols.

Semantics — (cont'd)
B Grammar 67
N Antonyms 73
Homonyms 73
Synonyms 73
R Metaphor 82
Morphology (Language) 73
↓ Phonology 73
↓ Priming 88
Semantic Memory 88
Semantic Priming 94
↓ Syntax 71
↓ Verbal Meaning 73
↓ Vocabulary 67
Words (Phonetic Units) 67

Semicircular Canals 73
PN 33   SC 46400
B Vestibular Apparatus 67

Seminarians 73
PN 160   SC 46410
B Religious Personnel 73
Students 67

Seminaries 73
PN 22   SC 46420
SN Institutions for training for ministry, priesthood, or rabbinate.
B Schools 67
R Religious Education 73

Semiotics 85
PN 108   SC 46425
SN Analysis of signs and symbols, especially their syntactic, semantic, and pragmatic functions in language.
N Pragmatics 85
R Hermeneutics 91
↓ Linguistics 73
Symbolism 67

Senegal 88
PN 13   SC 46427
B Africa 67

Senescence
Use Aged

Senile Dementia 73
PN 707   SC 46440
UF Dementia (Senile)
B Dementia 85
Syndromes 73
N Senile Psychosis 73
R ↓ Aged 73
Alzheimers Disease 73
Cerebral Arteriosclerosis 73
Physiological Aging 67
↓ Presenile Dementia 73

Senile Psychosis 73
PN 15   SC 46450
B Psychosis 67
Senile Dementia 73

Senior Citizens
Use Aged

Sensation
Use Perception

Sensation Seeking 78
PN 462   SC 46477
SN Need for novel experience or stimulation in order to reach optimal levels of arousal. Limited to human populations.

Sensation Seeking — (cont'd)
UF Novelty Seeking
Stimulation Seeking (Personality)
B Personality Traits 67

Sensation Seeking Scale 73
PN 62   SC 46480
B Personality Measures 67

Sense Organ Disorders 73
PN 17   SC 46490
B Disorders 67
N Anosmia 73
↓ Ear Disorders 73
R ↓ Anesthesia (Feeling) 73
↓ Sense Organs 73
↓ Sensorially Handicapped 94

Sense Organs 73
PN 54   SC 46500
B Anatomy 67
N ↓ Ear (Anatomy) 67
↓ Eye (Anatomy) 67
Taste Buds 73
R ↓ Sense Organ Disorders 73

Sensitivity (Drugs)
Use Drug Sensitivity

Sensitivity (Personality) 67
PN 1040   SC 46520
UF Insensitivity (Personality)
B Personality Traits 67

Sensitivity Training 73
PN 1047   SC 46530
SN Group therapy that focuses on interpersonal relations within the group and enhancement of self-confidence, self-perception, behavioral skills, and role flexibility.
B Human Potential Movement 82
R Communication Skills Training 82
Consciousness Raising Groups 78
↓ Encounter Group Therapy 73
↓ Group Dynamics 67
↓ Group Psychotherapy 67
Human Relations Training 78
Marathon Group Therapy 73
↓ Personnel Training 67
Social Skills Training 82

Sensitization (Protein)
Use Anaphylactic Shock

Sensitization Repression
Use Repression Sensitization

Sensorially Handicapped 94
PN 0   SC 46545
SN Used for unspecified sensory handicaps. Use a more specific term if possible.
B Handicapped 67
N ↓ Aurally Handicapped 73
↓ Visually Handicapped 67
R ↓ Ear Disorders 73
↓ Eye Disorders 73
Hearing Disorders 82
↓ Sense Organ Disorders 73
Sensory Handicaps (Attit Toward) 73
↓ Vision Disorders 82

Sensorimotor Development
Use Perceptual Motor Development

Sensorimotor Measures 73
PN 181   SC 46550

Sensorimotor Measures — (cont'd)
UF   Perceptual Motor Measures
B   Measurement [67]
N   Purdue Perceptual Motor Survey [73]
R   ↓ Perceptual Measures [73]

Sensorimotor Processes
Use Perceptual Motor Processes

Sensorineural Hearing Loss
Use Hearing Disorders

Sensory Adaptation [67]
PN 1620   SC 46560
SN Change in sensitivity of sensory systems or components as a result of ongoing or prolonged stimulation.
UF   Adaptation (Sensory)
B   Adaptation [67]
      Thresholds [67]
N   Dark Adaptation [73]
      Light Adaptation [82]
      Orienting Reflex [67]
      Orienting Responses [67]
R   Habituation [67]
      Interocular Transfer [85]
      Sensory Integration [91]

Sensory Deprivation [67]
PN 1002   SC 46570
SN Restriction of sensory or environmental stimulation through surgical or other techniques. Used primarily for animal populations. Consider STIMULUS DEPRIVATION for human populations.
B   Stimulus Deprivation [73]

Sensory Feedback [73]
PN 268   SC 46580
SN Return of afferent neural signals or information from sensory receptors. Sensory feedback may function in the regulation of behavior in general but is especially important in the control of bodily movement. Use a more specific term if possible.
B   Feedback [67]
      Perceptual Stimulation [73]
N   ↓ Auditory Feedback [73]
      Visual Feedback [73]

Sensory Gating [91]
PN 33   SC 46585
SN The internal process of blocking one or more sensory stimuli while attention is focused on another sensory stimuli or sensory channel.
UF   Gating (Sensory)
B   Perception [67]
R   ↓ Awareness [67]
      ↓ Evoked Potentials [67]
      ↓ Perceptual Stimulation [73]
      Selective Attention [73]

Sensory Handicaps (Attit Toward) [73]
PN 90   SC 46590
B   Handicapped (Attitudes Toward) [73]
R   ↓ Aurally Handicapped [73]
      ↓ Sensorially Handicapped [94]
      ↓ Visually Handicapped [67]

Sensory Integration [91]
PN 51   SC 46595
SN Neural processes of organizing sensory inputs from the environment and producing an adaptive response. In treatment, the environment's sensory input is manipulated to facilitate environmental interaction.
UF   Intersensory Integration
B   Intersensory Processes [78]
      Perceptual Motor Processes [67]

Sensory Integration — (cont'd)
R   ↓ Sensory Adaptation [67]
      ↓ Treatment [67]

Sensory Neglect [94]
PN 0   SC 46597
UF   Perceptual Neglect
      Spatial Neglect
      Visual Neglect
R   ↓ Perception [67]
      ↓ Perceptual Distortion [82]
      ↓ Perceptual Disturbances [73]
      ↓ Receptive Fields [85]

Sensory Neurons [73]
PN 456   SC 46610
B   Neurons [73]
N   Auditory Neurons [73]
      Baroreceptors [73]
      Chemoreceptors [73]
      Mechanoreceptors [73]
      Nociceptors [85]
      ↓ Photoreceptors [73]
      Proprioceptors [73]
      Taste Buds [73]
      Thermoreceptors [73]
R   ↓ Afferent Pathways [82]
      ↓ Receptive Fields [85]

Sensory Pathways
Use Afferent Pathways

Sensory Preconditioning
Use Preconditioning

Sentence Completion Tests [91]
PN 8   SC 46617
B   Personality Measures [67]
      Projective Personality Measures [73]
R   Cloze Testing [73]

Sentence Comprehension [73]
PN 1317   SC 46620
B   Verbal Comprehension [85]

Sentence Structure [73]
PN 1292   SC 46630
SN Specific characteristics of a sentence's construction, including such aspects as its syntax, length, and complexity. Compare SYNTAX.
R   ↓ Prosody [91]
      ↓ Syntax [71]
      Text Structure [82]

Sentences [67]
PN 1366   SC 46640
SN Grammatically and syntactically arranged words that constitute a grammatically complete and meaningful unit.
B   Language [67]

Sentencing
Use Adjudication

Separation (Marital)
Use Marital Separation

Separation Anxiety [73]
PN 491   SC 46660
B   Anxiety Neurosis [73]
R   Attachment Behavior [85]
      School Phobia [73]
      School Refusal [94]
      Stranger Reactions [88]

Separation Individuation [82]
PN 792   SC 46665

Separation Individuation — (cont'd)
SN Normal process begun in infancy of disengagement from one's mother and development of a healthy, integrated personality.
B   Personality Development [67]
R   Attachment Behavior [85]
      ↓ Childhood Development [67]
      Mother Child Relations [67]
      Object Relations [82]
      Transitional Objects [85]

Septal Nuclei [82]
PN 332   SC 46676
SN Subcallosal nuclei that form an integral part of the limbic system. These nuclei contribute to the medial forebrain bundle and have processes synapsing in the hippocampus.
UF   Septum
B   Limbic System [73]
R   Fornix [82]
      Hippocampus [67]
      Medial Forebrain Bundle [82]
      Nucleus Accumbens [82]

Septum
Use Septal Nuclei

Sequential Learning [73]
PN 238   SC 46690
SN Type of learning in which a particular task is completed before the next task is given. The learning of each subsequent task is dependent on the previous task completed.
B   Learning [67]
R   Mastery Learning [85]

Serial Anticipation (Learning) [73]
PN 97   SC 46700
SN Learning paradigm which involves the initial presentation of a list of items or a series of events with a short interval between the items or elements in the series. Upon subsequent presentation of the list/series, the subject attempts to guess or anticipate the next item/element in the sequence. Thus, each item/element serves as a cue for the recall of the next. Compare FREE RECALL.
UF   Anticipation (Serial Learning)
B   Serial Learning [67]
R   ↓ Verbal Learning [67]

Serial Learning [67]
PN 1175   SC 46720
SN Learning, usually memorization, of items in a list according to a prescribed order.
B   Learning [67]
N   Serial Anticipation (Learning) [73]
R   ↓ Serial Position Effect [82]
      Serial Recall [94]
      ↓ Verbal Learning [67]

Serial Position Effect [82]
PN 147   SC 46724
SN Effect of the relative position of an item in a series on the rate of learning that item.
N   Primacy Effect [73]
      Recency Effect [73]
R   ↓ Learning [67]
      Learning Rate [73]
      ↓ Serial Learning [67]
      Serial Recall [94]

Serial Recall [94]
PN 0   SC 46727
B   Recall (Learning) [67]
R   Forgetting [73]
      Free Recall [73]
      ↓ Memory [67]

Serial Recall — (cont'd)
R   ↓ Serial Learning [67]
     ↓ Serial Position Effect [82]

Seriousness [73]
PN 12   SC 46730
B   Personality Traits [67]

Serotonin [73]
PN 2656   SC 46740
UF   Hydroxytryptamine (5-)
B   Amines [73]
     Neurotransmitters [85]
     Vasoconstrictor Drugs [73]
R   ↓ Adrenergic Drugs [73]
     Serotonin Agonists [88]
    ↓ Serotonin Antagonists [73]
    ↓ Serotonin Metabolites [78]
    ↓ Serotonin Precursors [78]

Serotonin Agonists [88]
PN 378   SC 46745
B   Drugs [67]
R   Buspirone [91]
     Serotonin [73]
    ↓ Serotonin Antagonists [73]

Serotonin Antagonists [73]
PN 1056   SC 46750
UF   Methysergide
B   Drugs [67]
N   Dihydroxytryptamine [91]
     Fluvoxamine [94]
     Lysergic Acid Diethylamide [67]
     Mianserin [82]
     Molindone [82]
     Parachlorophenylalanine [78]
     Tetrabenazine [73]
R   ↓ Decarboxylase Inhibitors [82]
     Serotonin [73]
     Serotonin Agonists [88]
    ↓ Serotonin Precursors [78]

Serotonin Metabolites [78]
PN 118   SC 46754
B   Metabolites [73]
N   Hydroxyindoleacetic Acid (5-) [85]
R   Serotonin [73]
    ↓ Serotonin Precursors [78]

Serotonin Precursors [78]
PN 90   SC 46756
N   ↓ Tryptophan [73]
R   Serotonin [73]
    ↓ Serotonin Antagonists [73]
    ↓ Serotonin Metabolites [78]

Serpasil
Use   Reserpine

Serum (Blood)
Use   Blood Serum

Serum Albumin [73]
PN 22   SC 46780
B   Blood Proteins [73]

Service Personnel [91]
PN 60   SC 46785
SN Employees who have direct contact with the public; generally nonprofessional and nonsales personnel. Includes hotel, airline, and restaurant personnel, but does not include health care personnel.
B   Business and Industrial Personnel [67]
N   Domestic Service Personnel [73]
     Technical Service Personnel [73]
R   Child Care Workers [78]

Service Personnel — (cont'd)
R   ↓ Nonprofessional Personnel [82]
     Sales Personnel [73]
    ↓ Technical Personnel [78]

Servicemen
Use   Military Personnel

Severely Mentally Retarded [73]
PN 1712   SC 46820
SN IQ 20–34.
B   Mentally Retarded [67]

Severity (Disorders) [82]
PN 1476   SC 46824
SN Degree of severity of mental or physical disorder.
R   ↓ Chronic Illness [91]
     Chronicity (Disorders) [82]
    ↓ Diagnosis [67]
    ↓ Disorders [67]
    ↓ Mental Disorders [67]
     Prognosis [73]

Sex [67]
PN 609   SC 46950
SN Conceptually broad array term referring to the structural, functional, or behavioral characteristics of males and females of a given species. Use a more specific term if possible. For comparisons of the sexes use HUMAN SEX DIFFERENCES or ANIMAL SEX DIFFERENCES.
R   Animal Sex Differences [67]
    ↓ Animal Sexual Behavior [85]
    ↓ Genital Disorders [67]
    ↓ Human Sex Differences [67]
     Pornography [73]
    ↓ Psychosexual Behavior [67]
     Psychosexual Development [82]
     Sex Change [88]
     Sex Chromosomes [73]
     Sex Discrimination [78]
     Sex Drive [73]
     Sex Education [73]
    ↓ Sex Hormones [73]
    ↓ Sex Offenses [82]
    ↓ Sex Role Attitudes [78]
     Sex Therapy [78]
     Sexual Attitudes [73]
     Sexual Development [73]
     Sexual Harassment [85]
    ↓ Sexual Reproduction [73]
     Sexuality [73]

Sex Change [88]
PN 35   SC 46828
UF   Sexual Reassignment
B   Surgery [71]
R   Sex [67]
     Transsexualism [73]

Sex Chromosome Disorders [73]
PN 139   SC 46830
B   Chromosome Disorders [73]
N   Klinefelters Syndrome [73]
R   Fragile X Syndrome [94]
    ↓ Sex Linked Hereditary Disorders [73]

Sex Chromosomes [73]
PN 56   SC 46840
B   Chromosomes [73]
R   Sex [67]

Sex Differences (Animal)
Use   Animal Sex Differences

Sex Differences (Human)
Use   Human Sex Differences

Sex Differentiation Disorders
Use   Genital Disorders

Sex Discrimination [78]
PN 624   SC 46875
SN Prejudiced and differential treatment on the basis of sex rather than on the basis of merit.
B   Social Discrimination [82]
R   Affirmative Action [85]
    ↓ Civil Rights [78]
     Employment Discrimination [94]
    ↓ Prejudice [67]
     Sex [67]
     Sexism [88]
     Stereotyped Attitudes [67]

Sex Drive [73]
PN 148   SC 46880
B   Motivation [67]
R   Libido [73]
     Sex [67]
    ↓ Sexual Arousal [78]

Sex Education [73]
PN 862   SC 46890
B   Health Education [73]
R   Sex [67]

Sex Hormones [73]
PN 336   SC 46900
B   Hormones [67]
N   ↓ Androgens [73]
    ↓ Estrogens [73]
     Progesterone [73]
R   ↓ Gonadotropic Hormones [73]
     Luteinizing Hormone [78]
     Sex [67]

Sex Linked Developmental Differences [73]
PN 1330   SC 46920
SN Differential variation between males and females in specified areas of development.
B   Human Sex Differences [67]
R   Adolescent Development [73]
    ↓ Development [67]
     Heterosexuality [73]
    ↓ Human Females [73]
    ↓ Human Males [73]
    ↓ Physical Development [73]
    ↓ Psychogenesis [73]
    ↓ Psychosexual Behavior [67]
     Sexual Development [73]

Sex Linked Hereditary Disorders [73]
PN 104   SC 46930
SN Disorders occurring in either sex and which are transmitted by genes located on either the X or Y chromosomes.
B   Genetic Disorders [73]
N   Fragile X Syndrome [94]
     Hemophilia [73]
     Testicular Feminization Syndrome [73]
     Turners Syndrome [73]
R   ↓ Sex Chromosome Disorders [73]

Sex Offenses [82]
PN 867   SC 46933
B   Crime [67]
N   ↓ Sexual Abuse [88]
R   Incest [73]
     Pornography [73]
     Sex [67]
    ↓ Sexual Deviations [67]
     Sexual Harassment [85]

Sex Role Attitudes [78]
PN 4233   SC 46935

Sex Role Attitudes — (cont'd)
SN Attitudes toward culturally- or socially-pre-
scribed patterns of behavior for males and fe-
males.
B   Attitudes [67]
N   Sexism [88]
R   Feminism [78]
     Sex [67]
     Sex Roles [67]
     Stereotyped Attitudes [67]

Sex Roles [67]
PN 6839   SC 46940
SN Behavioral patterns in a given society which
are deemed appropriate to one sex or the other.
B   Psychosexual Behavior [67]
     Roles [67]
R   Androgyny [82]
     ↓ Division of Labor [88]
     Femininity [67]
     Gender Identity [85]
     Masculinity [67]
     Nontraditional Careers [85]
     ↓ Sex Role Attitudes [78]
     Social Norms [85]
     Stereotyped Behavior [73]

Sex Therapy [78]
PN 636   SC 46945
SN Treatment of specific sexual function distur-
bances or therapy aimed at improving sexual
relationships.
B   Treatment [67]
R   Couples Therapy [94]
     ↓ Marriage Counseling [73]
     Sex [67]

Sexism [88]
PN 122   SC 46955
B   Sex Role Attitudes [78]
R   Employment Discrimination [94]
     ↓ Prejudice [67]
     Sex Discrimination [78]

Sexual Abstinence [73]
PN 47   SC 46960
UF   Abstinence (Sexual)
     Celibacy
B   Psychosexual Behavior [67]
R   ↓ Birth Control [71]

Sexual Abuse [88]
PN 1742   SC 46965
B   Antisocial Behavior [71]
     Sex Offenses [82]
N   Incest [73]
     ↓ Rape [73]
R   Anatomically Detailed Dolls [91]
     ↓ Child Abuse [71]
     Elder Abuse [88]
     ↓ Family Violence [82]
     Partner Abuse [91]
     Patient Abuse [91]
     Pedophilia [73]
     Physical Abuse [91]
     Professional Client Sexual Relations [94]
     ↓ Sexual Deviations [67]
     Sexual Harassment [85]

Sexual Arousal [78]
PN 675   SC 46970
SN Physiological and/or emotional state of sex-
ual excitation.
UF   Arousal (Sexual)
B   Psychosexual Behavior [67]
N   Eroticism [73]
R   Physiological Arousal [67]
     Sex Drive [73]
     Sexual Satisfaction [94]

Sexual Attitudes [73]
PN 1921   SC 46980
SN Opinions or beliefs about sexual develop-
ment and behavior.
B   Attitudes [67]
R   ↓ Psychosexual Behavior [67]
     Psychosexual Development [82]
     Sex [67]
     Sexual Satisfaction [94]

Sexual Behavior
Use Psychosexual Behavior

Sexual Boundary Violations
Use Professional Client Sexual Relations

Sexual Delinquency
Use Promiscuity

Sexual Development [73]
PN 489   SC 47010
SN Prior to 1982 used for maturation of cog-
nitive, emotional, and physical aspects of sexual-
ity in humans or animals. From 1982 consider
PSYCHOSEXUAL DEVELOPMENT for references
on cognitive and emotional aspects.
UF   Pubescence
B   Physical Development [73]
R   Adolescent Development [73]
     Heterosexuality [73]
     ↓ Psychogenesis [73]
     ↓ Psychosexual Behavior [67]
     Psychosexual Development [82]
     Sex [67]
     Sex Linked Developmental Differences [73]

Sexual Deviations [67]
PN 923   SC 47020
SN Any type of sexual behavior which differs
from social standards for such behavior in any
given culture.
UF   Deviations (Sexual)
     Paraphilias
B   Mental Disorders [67]
     Psychosexual Behavior [67]
N   Exhibitionism [73]
     Fetishism [73]
     Incest [73]
     Pedophilia [73]
     Sexual Masochism [73]
     Sexual Sadism [73]
     Voyeurism [73]
R   Pornography [73]
     ↓ Sex Offenses [82]
     ↓ Sexual Abuse [88]

Sexual Disorders (Physiological)
Use Genital Disorders

Sexual Fetishism
Use Fetishism

Sexual Function Disturbances [73]
PN 1182   SC 47050
B   Disorders [67]
     Psychosexual Behavior [67]
N   Dyspareunia [73]
     Frigidity [73]
     Impotence [73]
     Premature Ejaculation [73]
     Vaginismus [73]
R   ↓ Psychosomatic Disorders [67]
     ↓ Urogenital Disorders [73]

Sexual Harassment [85]
PN 193   SC 47055

Sexual Harassment — (cont'd)
SN Physical or psychological sexual threats or
attempts to willfully subject a person to involuntary sexual activity usually for the purpose of
social control.
R   Professional Client Sexual Relations [94]
     Sex [67]
     ↓ Sex Offenses [82]
     ↓ Sexual Abuse [88]
     Victimization [73]

Sexual Intercourse (Human) [73]
PN 445   SC 47060
UF   Coitus
     Copulation
     Intercourse (Sexual)
B   Psychosexual Behavior [67]
N   Dyspareunia [73]
     Extramarital Intercourse [73]
     Incest [73]
     Premarital Intercourse [73]
     ↓ Rape [73]
R   Female Orgasm [73]
     ↓ Male Orgasm [73]
     Petting [73]
     ↓ Sexual Reproduction [73]
     Sexual Satisfaction [94]

Sexual Masochism [73]
PN 22   SC 47070
B   Masochism [73]
     Sexual Deviations [67]
R   Fetishism [73]
     Masochistic Personality [73]
     Sexual Sadism [73]

Sexual Reassignment
Use Sex Change

Sexual Receptivity (Animal)
Use Animal Sexual Receptivity

Sexual Reproduction [73]
PN 601   SC 47090
B   Physiology [67]
N   Fertility [88]
R   ↓ Animal Breeding [73]
     Animal Mate Selection [82]
     ↓ Animal Mating Behavior [67]
     ↓ Birth [67]
     Fertilization [73]
     ↓ Genetics [67]
     ↓ Pregnancy [67]
     Reproductive Technology [88]
     Sex [67]
     ↓ Sexual Intercourse (Human) [73]
     Sperm [73]

Sexual Sadism [73]
PN 23   SC 47100
B   Sadism [73]
     Sexual Deviations [67]
R   Fetishism [73]
     Sexual Masochism [73]

Sexual Satisfaction [94]
PN 0   SC 47110
B   Satisfaction [73]
R   ↓ Orgasm [73]
     ↓ Psychosexual Behavior [67]
     ↓ Sexual Arousal [78]
     Sexual Attitudes [73]
     ↓ Sexual Intercourse (Human) [73]
     Sexuality [73]

Sexuality [73]
PN 1147   SC 47120

Sexuality — (cont'd)
B   Personality Traits [67]
R   Psychosexual Development [82]
     Sex [67]
     Sexual Satisfaction [94]

Sexually Transmitted Diseases
Use   Venereal Diseases

Shamanism [73]
PN   144   SC   47130
B   Religious Affiliation [73]
R   Cultism [73]
     Ethnology [67]
     Faith Healing [73]
     Folk Medicine [73]
     Transcultural Psychiatry [73]
     ↓ Treatment [67]

Shame [94]
PN   0   SC   47140
SN   Use GUILT to access references from 73-93.
B   Emotional States [73]
R   ↓ Anxiety [67]
     Blame [94]
     Embarrassment [73]
     ↓ Fear [67]
     Guilt [67]
     Morality [67]

Shape Perception
Use   Form and Shape Perception

Shared Paranoid Disorder
Use   Folie A Deux

Sharing (Social Behavior) [78]
PN   267   SC   47155
B   Prosocial Behavior [82]
R   Altruism [73]
     Charitable Behavior [73]
     Needle Sharing [94]

Sheep [73]
PN   411   SC   47170
B   Mammals [73]

Sheltered Workshops [67]
PN   301   SC   47180
SN   Places which provide handicapped individuals with job training and work experience.
B   Rehabilitation Centers [73]
R   ↓ Community Facilities [73]
     Supported Employment [94]

Shelters [91]
PN   62   SC   47185
B   Housing [73]
R   Battered Females [88]
     ↓ Community Facilities [73]
     ↓ Community Services [67]
     ↓ Family Violence [82]
     ↓ Government Programs [73]
     Group Homes [82]
     Homeless [88]
     ↓ Living Arrangements [91]
     Runaway Behavior [73]
     ↓ Social Services [82]

Shifts (Workday)
Use   Workday Shifts

Shock [67]
PN   2921   SC   47200
B   Symptoms [67]
R   Anaphylactic Shock [73]

Shock — (cont'd)
R   Electrical Injuries [73]
     ↓ Electrical Stimulation [73]
     ↓ Electroconvulsive Shock [67]
     ↓ Injuries [73]
     ↓ Shock Therapy [73]
     Shock Units [73]
     Syncope [73]

Shock Therapy [73]
PN   32   SC   47210
B   Organic Therapies [73]
N   Electroconvulsive Shock Therapy [67]
     Insulin Shock Therapy [73]
R   ↓ Aversion Therapy [73]
     Electrosleep Treatment [78]
     Shock [67]

Shock Units [73]
PN   20   SC   47220
B   Stimulators (Apparatus) [73]
R   Shock [67]
     Shuttle Box Grids [73]
     Volt Meters [73]

Shoplifting [73]
PN   98   SC   47230
B   Theft [73]

Shopping
Use   Consumer Behavior

Shopping Centers [73]
PN   104   SC   47250
B   Community Facilities [73]
R   Consumer Behavior [67]
     Retailing [91]

Short Term Memory [67]
PN   3805   SC   47260
SN   Retention of information for very brief periods, usually seconds; also referred to as working memory. Consider also RETENTION.
UF   Working Memory
B   Memory [67]
N   Iconic Memory [85]

Short Term Potentiation
Use   Postactivation Potentials

Short Term Psychotherapy
Use   Brief Psychotherapy

Shoulder (Anatomy) [73]
PN   31   SC   47290
B   Joints (Anatomy) [73]
R   Arm (Anatomy) [73]

Shuttle Box Grids [73]
PN   3   SC   47300
UF   Grid (Shuttle Box)
B   Shuttle Boxes [73]
R   Shock Units [73]

Shuttle Box Hurdles [73]
PN   1   SC   47310
UF   Hurdle (Shuttle Box)
B   Apparatus [67]
R   ↓ Shuttle Boxes [73]

Shuttle Boxes [73]
PN   67   SC   47320
B   Apparatus [67]
N   Shuttle Box Grids [73]
R   Shuttle Box Hurdles [73]

Shyness
Use   Timidity

Siamese Twins [73]
PN   2   SC   47340
B   Twins [67]

Sibling Relations [73]
PN   593   SC   47350
B   Family Relations [67]

Siblings [67]
PN   1163   SC   47360
B   Family Members [73]
N   Brothers [73]
     ↓ Multiple Births [73]
     Sisters [73]

Sick Leave
Use   Employee Leave Benefits

Sickle Cell Disease [94]
PN   0   SC   47380
B   Blood and Lymphatic Disorders [73]
     Ethnospecific Disorders [73]
     Genetic Disorders [73]
R   Anemia [73]

Side Effects (Drug) [73]
PN   4242   SC   47390
SN   Acute or chronic and often undesirable effects of drugs occurring in addition to the intended or therapeutic objective. Use DRUG ADVERSE REACTIONS or SIDE EFFECTS (DRUG) to access references from 73–81.
UF   Drug Adverse Reactions
B   Side Effects (Treatment) [88]
N   ↓ Drug Addiction [67]
     Drug Allergies [73]
     ↓ Drug Dependency [73]
     Drug Sensitivity [73]
R   Akathisia [91]
     ↓ Drug Therapy [67]
     Drug Tolerance [73]
     ↓ Drugs [67]
     Neuroleptic Malignant Syndrome [88]
     Tardive Dyskinesia [88]

Side Effects (Treatment) [88]
PN   285   SC   47392
SN   Acute or chronic and often undesirable effects of treatment other than drug therapy occurring in addition to the intended or therapeutic objective. For side effects of drug therapy use SIDE EFFECTS (DRUG).
UF   Iatrogenic Effects
N   ↓ Side Effects (Drug) [73]
R   ↓ Treatment [67]
     ↓ Treatment Outcomes [82]

Sierra Leone [88]
PN   2   SC   47395
B   Africa [67]

Sight Vocabulary [73]
PN   107   SC   47400
SN   Words that one recognizes immediately while reading.
B   Vocabulary [67]
R   ↓ Reading [67]
     ↓ Reading Skills [73]
     Word Recognition [88]

Sign Language [73]
PN   722   SC   47410
SN   System of hand gestures for communication in which the gestures function as words.

Sign Language — (cont'd)
B   Language [67]
         Manual Communication [78]
R   Fingerspelling [73]

Sign Rank Test
Use Wilcoxon Sign Rank Test

Sign Test [73]
PN 5   **SC** 47430
B   Nonparametric Statistical Tests [67]
R   Statistical Significance [73]

Signal Detection (Perception) [67]
PN 2252   **SC** 47440
SN   Psychophysical technique that permits the
estimation of the bias of the observer as well as
the detectability of the signal (i.e., stimulus) in
any sensory modality. Compare THRESHOLDS.
UF   Detection (Signal)
R ↓ Attention [67]
       ↓ Perception [67]
       ↓ Psychophysical Measurement [67]
         Threshold Determination [73]
         Visual Search [82]

Signal Intensity
Use Stimulus Intensity

Significance (Statistical)
Use Statistical Significance

Significant Others [91]
PN 90   **SC** 47465
SN   Includes teachers, peers, family members,
friends, and unmarried couples.
R   Couples [82]
       ↓ Family Members [73]
         Friendship [67]
         Homosexual Parents [94]
         Mentor [85]
         Peers [78]
         Role Models [82]
         Social Support Networks [82]
       ↓ Spouses [73]

Silent Reading [73]
PN 205   **SC** 47470
B   Reading [67]

Similarity (Stimulus)
Use Stimulus Similarity

Simile
Use Figurative Language

Simple Schizophrenia
SN   Term discontinued in 1988. Use SIMPLE
SCHIZOPHRENIA to access references from 73-
87.
Use Schizophrenia

Simulation [67]
PN 1796   **SC** 47510
UF   Modeling
         Simulators
N ↓ Computer Simulation [73]
         Flight Simulation [73]
         Heuristic Modeling [73]
         Markov Chains [73]
       ↓ Mathematical Modeling [73]
         Simulation Games [73]
       ↓ Stochastic Modeling [73]
R   Game Theory [67]

Simulation Games [73]
PN 362   **SC** 47520

Simulation Games — (cont'd)
B   Games [67]
         Simulation [67]
R   Computer Games [88]
       ↓ Computer Simulation [73]

Simulators
Use Simulation

Sin [73]
PN 46   **SC** 47540
B   Religious Beliefs [73]

Sincerity [73]
PN 27   **SC** 47550
UF   Genuineness
B   Personality Traits [67]

Singapore [91]
PN 32   **SC** 47551
B   Southeast Asia [73]

Single Cell Organisms
Use Microorganisms

Single Fathers [94]
PN 0   **SC** 47554
SN   Use SINGLE PARENTS to access refer-
ences from 78-93.
B   Fathers [67]
         Single Parents [78]
R   Single Persons [73]

Single Mothers [94]
PN 0   **SC** 47555
SN   Use SINGLE PARENTS to access refer-
ences from 78-93.
B   Mothers [67]
         Single Parents [78]
R   Single Persons [73]
         Unwed Mothers [73]
         Working Women [78]

Single Parents [78]
PN 681   **SC** 47556
SN   Parents rearing children alone.
B   Parents [67]
N   Single Fathers [94]
         Single Mothers [94]
R ↓ Family Structure [73]
       ↓ Marital Status [73]
         Never Married [94]
       ↓ Parental Absence [73]
         Single Persons [73]
         Unwed Mothers [73]

Single Persons [73]
PN 295   **SC** 47560
SN   Persons who are not married.
R   Living Alone [94]
       ↓ Marital Status [73]
         Never Married [94]
         Single Fathers [94]
         Single Mothers [94]
       ↓ Single Parents [78]

Sisters [73]
PN 78   **SC** 47570
B   Human Females [73]
         Siblings [67]

Sixteen Personality Factors Question [73]
PN 337   **SC** 47590
B   Nonprojective Personality Measures [73]

Size [73]
PN 533   **SC** 47610

Size — (cont'd)
SN   Relative physical dimensions of objects or
stimuli.
B   Stimulus Parameters [67]
N ↓ Body Size [85]
         Brain Size [73]
         Family Size [73]
         Group Size [67]
         Litter Size [85]
         Size Constancy [85]
       ↓ Size Discrimination [67]

Size (Apparent)
Use Apparent Size

Size (Group)
Use Group Size

Size Constancy [85]
PN 19   **SC** 47635
SN   The tendency for the perceived size of stim-
uli to remain constant despite objective changes
in context and stimulus parameters.
B   Perceptual Constancy [85]
         Size [73]
R ↓ Size Discrimination [67]

Size Discrimination [67]
PN 795   **SC** 47640
B   Size [73]
         Spatial Perception [67]
N   Apparent Size [73]
R   Linear Perspective [82]
         Size Constancy [85]

Skeletomuscular Disorders
Use Musculoskeletal Disorders

Skewed Distribution [73]
PN 49   **SC** 47680
UF   Poisson Distribution
B   Frequency Distribution [73]

Skill Learning [73]
PN 1299   **SC** 47690
B   Learning [67]
N   Fine Motor Skill Learning [73]
         Gross Motor Skill Learning [73]
R   Communication Skills Training [82]
         Habilitation [91]
       ↓ Perceptual Motor Learning [67]
         Self Care Skills [78]
         Social Skills Training [82]

Skilled Industrial Workers [73]
PN 180   **SC** 47700
SN   Blue collar workers who perform skilled la-
bor in an industrial setting.
B   Blue Collar Workers [73]
         Business and Industrial Personnel [67]

Skills
Use Ability

Skin (Anatomy) [67]
PN 638   **SC** 47720
UF   Epithelium
B   Tissues (Body) [73]
R   Absorption (Physiological) [73]
         Epithelial Cells [73]
         Hair [73]
         Head (Anatomy) [73]
         Scalp (Anatomy) [73]

Skin Conduction
Use Skin Resistance

Skin Disorders [73]
PN 265   SC 47740
- UF   Scalp Disorders
- B   Disorders [67]
- N   Allergic Skin Disorders [73]
  - Alopecia [73]
  - ↓ Dermatitis [73]
  - Herpes Simplex [73]
  - Lupus [73]
  - Pruritus [73]
- R   Albinism [73]
  - ↓ Psychosomatic Disorders [67]
  - Sweating [73]
  - ↓ Tuberculosis [73]

Skin Electrical Properties [73]
PN 65   SC 47750
SN General electrodermal characteristics and responses as measured on the skin surface. Use a more specific term if possible.
- B   Electrophysiology [73]
- N   Skin Potential [73]
  - ↓ Skin Resistance [73]

Skin Potential [73]
PN 85   SC 47760
SN Degree of electrical charge of the skin.
- B   Electrophysiology [73]
  - Skin Electrical Properties [73]
- R   Galvanic Skin Response [67]
  - ↓ Skin Resistance [73]

Skin Resistance [73]
PN 1086   SC 47770
SN Resistance of the skin to the flow of electric current; reciprocal of skin conductance.
- UF   Skin Conduction
- B   Skin Electrical Properties [73]
- N   Basal Skin Resistance [73]
- R   Galvanic Skin Response [67]
  - Skin Potential [73]

Skin Temperature [73]
PN 524   SC 47780
- B   Body Temperature [73]

Skinner (Burrhus Frederic) [91]
PN 56   SC 47785
SN Identifies biographical or autobiographical studies and discussions of Skinner's works.
- R   Behaviorism [67]
  - ↓ Operant Conditioning [67]
  - ↓ Psychologists [67]
  - Skinner Boxes [73]

Skinner Boxes [73]
PN 14   SC 47790
- B   Apparatus [67]
- R   Skinner (Burrhus Frederic) [91]

Skull [73]
PN 17   SC 47800
- B   Musculoskeletal System [73]

Slang [73]
PN 40   SC 47810
- B   Vocabulary [67]
- R   Ethnolinguistics [73]
  - Nonstandard English [73]

Sleep [67]
PN 4159   SC 47820
- N   Napping [94]
  - NREM Sleep [73]
  - REM Sleep [73]
- R   ↓ Consciousness Disturbances [73]
  - ↓ Consciousness States [71]
  - Dream Content [73]

Sleep — (cont'd)
- R   ↓ Dreaming [67]
  - Lucid Dreaming [94]
  - Nocturnal Teeth Grinding [73]
  - Sleep Apnea [91]
  - Sleep Deprivation [67]
  - ↓ Sleep Disorders [73]
  - Sleep Onset [73]
  - Sleep Talking [73]
  - Sleep Treatment [73]
  - Sleep Wake Cycle [85]

Sleep Apnea [91]
PN 31   SC 47825
SN Temporary absence of breathing or prolonged respiratory failure occurring during sleep.
- B   Apnea [73]
- R   ↓ Neonatal Disorders [73]
  - ↓ Sleep [67]
  - Sudden Infant Death [82]

Sleep Deprivation [67]
PN 810   SC 47830
- B   Deprivation [67]
- R   ↓ Sleep [67]
  - ↓ Sleep Disorders [73]

Sleep Disorders [73]
PN 822   SC 47840
- UF   Night Terrors
- B   Consciousness Disturbances [73]
  - Disorders [67]
- N   Hypersomnia [94]
  - Insomnia [73]
  - Narcolepsy [73]
  - Sleepwalking [73]
- R   Hypnagogic Hallucinations [73]
  - ↓ Sleep [67]
  - Sleep Deprivation [67]

Sleep Inducing Drugs
- Use   Hypnotic Drugs

Sleep Onset [73]
PN 431   SC 47860
- UF   Drowsiness
- R   Napping [94]
  - ↓ Sleep [67]

Sleep Talking [73]
PN 10   SC 47870
- B   Consciousness Disturbances [73]
- R   ↓ Sleep [67]

Sleep Treatment [73]
PN 27   SC 47880
SN Prolonged sleep or rest used in the treatment of mental disorders. Such sleep may be induced by drugs, hypnosis, or other means. For sleep withdrawal therapy, which is the deprivation of sleep for therapeutic purposes, use SLEEP DEPRIVATION.
- B   Narcoanalysis [73]
- R   ↓ Drug Therapy [67]
  - Electrosleep Treatment [78]
  - ↓ Sleep [67]

Sleep Wake Cycle [85]
PN 528   SC 47885
- B   Biological Rhythms [67]
- R   Napping [94]
  - ↓ Sleep [67]
  - Wakefulness [73]

Sleepwalking [73]
PN 80   SC 47890
SN Use SLEEPWALKING or SOMNAMBULISM to access references from 73–81.

Sleepwalking — (cont'd)
- UF   Somnambulism
- B   Sleep Disorders [73]
- R   ↓ Dissociative Patterns [73]

Slosson Intelligence Test for Child [73]
PN 62   SC 47900
- B   Intelligence Measures [67]

Slow Learners [73]
PN 167   SC 47910
- UF   Borderline Mentally Retarded
- B   Handicapped [67]
- R   Educable Mentally Retarded [73]
  - ↓ Mentally Retarded [67]

Slow Wave Sleep
- Use   NREM Sleep

Slums
- Use   Poverty Areas

Smell Perception
- Use   Olfactory Perception

Smiles [73]
PN 207   SC 47950
- B   Facial Expressions [67]
- R   Laughter [78]

Smokeless Tobacco [94]
PN 0   SC 47960
- UF   Chewing Tobacco
  - Snuff
  - Tobacco (Smokeless)
- R   ↓ CNS Stimulating Drugs [73]
  - Nicotine [73]
  - Tobacco Smoking [67]

Smoking (Tobacco)
- Use   Tobacco Smoking

Smoking Cessation [88]
PN 645   SC 47980
SN Used for cigarette smoking rehabilitation programs or stopping the habit of smoking. Use DRUG REHABILITATION and TOBACCO SMOKING to access references prior to 1988.
- R   ↓ Drug Abstinence [94]
  - ↓ Drug Rehabilitation [73]
  - Tobacco Smoking [67]

Snails [73]
PN 243   SC 47990
- UF   Aplysia
- B   Mollusca [73]

Snake Phobia
- Use   Ophidiophobia

Snakes [73]
PN 207   SC 48010
- B   Reptiles [67]

Snuff
- Use   Smokeless Tobacco

Sobriety [88]
PN 191   SC 48020
- UF   Alcohol Abstinence
- B   Drug Abstinence [94]
- R   Alcohol Drinking Attitudes [73]
  - ↓ Alcohol Rehabilitation [82]
  - Alcohol Withdrawal [94]
  - ↓ Alcoholism [67]
  - Detoxification [73]

Sobriety — (cont'd)
R   ↓ Drug Rehabilitation [73]
     Recovery (Disorders) [73]

Soccer [94]
PN 0   SC 48025
B   Recreation [67]
     Sports [67]

Sociability [73]
PN 261   SC 48030
B   Personality Traits [67]
R   Gregariousness [73]

Social Acceptance [67]
PN 1177   SC 48040
SN   Degree to which an individual is incorporated by others in their activities or is permitted to interact with others informally.
UF   Acceptance (Social)
     Rejection (Social)
     Social Rejection
B   Social Behavior [67]
R   Peer Pressure [94]
     Popularity [88]
     Social Approval [67]
     Stigma [91]

Social Adaptation
Use   Social Adjustment

Social Adjustment [73]
PN 3838   SC 48060
UF   Adaptation (Social)
     Maladjustment (Social)
     Social Adaptation
     Social Maladjustment
B   Adjustment [67]
     Social Behavior [67]
R   Adjustment Disorders [94]

Social Anxiety [85]
PN 303   SC 48065
SN   Apprehension or fear of social interaction or social situations in general. Compare SOCIAL PHOBIA.
B   Anxiety [67]
R   ↓ Anxiety Neurosis [73]
     Avoidant Personality [94]
     ↓ Fear [67]
     ↓ Social Interaction [67]
     ↓ Social Isolation [67]
     Speech Anxiety [85]

Social Approval [67]
PN 1548   SC 48070
SN   Favorable direct or indirect judgment by member or members of a given social group of another member or members, based on conduct, physical makeup, or other characteristics.
UF   Approval (Social)
B   Social Behavior [67]
     Social Influences [67]
R   Criticism [73]
     Likability [88]
     Peer Pressure [94]
     Popularity [88]
     Social Acceptance [67]
     ↓ Social Reinforcement [67]
     Stigma [91]

Social Behavior [67]
PN 3770   SC 48080
B   Behavior [67]
N   ↓ Aggressive Behavior [67]
     ↓ Animal Social Behavior [67]
     Competition [67]
     ↓ Compliance [73]

Social Behavior — (cont'd)
N   Conformity (Personality) [67]
     Contagion [88]
     Criticism [73]
     ↓ Gambling [73]
     Help Seeking Behavior [78]
     Interspecies Interaction [91]
     ↓ Involvement [73]
     ↓ Leadership [67]
     Leadership Style [73]
     Militancy [73]
     Nurturance [85]
     ↓ Prosocial Behavior [82]
     Racial and Ethnic Relations [82]
     Reciprocity [73]
     ↓ Responsibility [73]
     Retaliation [91]
     ↓ Risk Taking [67]
     Social Acceptance [67]
     Social Adjustment [73]
     Social Approval [67]
     Social Cognition [94]
     Social Demonstrations [73]
     Social Drinking [73]
     Social Facilitation [73]
     ↓ Social Interaction [67]
     ↓ Social Perception [67]
     ↓ Social Reinforcement [67]
     Social Skills [78]
R   ↓ Antisocial Behavior [71]
     Dominance Hierarchy [73]
     Equity (Payment) [78]
     ↓ Equity (Social) [78]
     Impression Management [78]
     Informants [88]
     Personal Space [73]
     Privacy [73]
     Psychodynamics [73]
     Social Change [67]
     ↓ Social Influences [67]

Social Casework [67]
PN 2764   SC 48090
UF   Social Work
B   Treatment [67]
R   ↓ Case Management [91]
     Child Welfare [88]
     ↓ Counseling [67]
     ↓ Family Therapy [67]
     ↓ Health Care Services [78]
     ↓ Mental Health Services [78]
     ↓ Social Services [82]

Social Caseworkers
Use   Social Workers

Social Change [67]
PN 2548   SC 48110
UF   Change (Social)
R   ↓ Fads and Fashions [73]
     Future [91]
     ↓ Social Behavior [67]
     ↓ Social Influences [67]
     ↓ Social Movements [67]
     ↓ Social Processes [67]
     Social Programs [73]
     Trends [91]

Social Class [67]
PN 1797   SC 48120
B   Social Structure [67]
     Socioeconomic Status [67]
N   Lower Class [73]
     Middle Class [73]
     Upper Class [73]
R   Disadvantaged [67]
     ↓ Income Level [73]
     ↓ Socioeconomic Class Attitudes [73]

Social Class Attitudes
Use   Socioeconomic Class Attitudes

Social Clubs (Therapeutic)
Use   Therapeutic Social Clubs

Social Cognition [94]
PN 0   SC 48143
SN   Cognitive processes and activity that accompany and mediate social interaction.
B   Cognitive Processes [67]
     Social Behavior [67]
R   ↓ Communication Skills [73]
     ↓ Interpersonal Interaction [67]
     Schema [88]
     ↓ Social Interaction [67]
     ↓ Social Perception [67]
     Social Skills Training [82]

Social Comparison [85]
PN 365   SC 48145
SN   Subjective evaluation of personal characteristics (e.g., ability level, personality traits, accomplishments) in relation to the perceived characteristics of others.
B   Social Perception [67]
R   Self Evaluation [67]
     Self Monitoring (Personality) [85]
     ↓ Social Influences [67]

Social Control [88]
PN 146   SC 48148
SN   Power of institutions, organizations, or laws of society to influence or regulate behavior or attitudes of groups or individuals.
B   Social Processes [67]
R   ↓ Social Influences [67]

Social Dating [73]
PN 666   SC 48150
UF   Dating (Social)
B   Human Courtship [73]
     Interpersonal Interaction [67]
R   Couples [82]
     Friendship [67]
     Male Female Relations [88]
     Petting [73]
     Premarital Intercourse [73]

Social Demonstrations [73]
PN 55   SC 48160
UF   Demonstrations (Social)
     Picketing
B   Social Behavior [67]
R   ↓ Collective Behavior [67]
     ↓ Political Participation [88]
     ↓ Social Movements [67]
     Student Activism [73]

Social Density [78]
PN 358   SC 48165
SN   Number of animals or humans per given space unit. For specifically high density conditions use CROWDING.
UF   Density (Social)
R   Crowding [78]
     Overpopulation [73]
     Personal Space [73]
     ↓ Population [73]
     ↓ Social Environments [73]

Social Deprivation [73]
PN 208   SC 48170
SN   Limited access to society's resources due to poverty, neglect, social discrimination, or other disadvantage. For a lack of social contact use SOCIAL ISOLATION. Consider also CULTURAL DEPRIVATION.

Social Deprivation — (cont'd)
- **B**   Social Processes [67]
      Stimulus Deprivation [73]
- **N**   ↓ Social Isolation [67]
- **R**   Cultural Deprivation [73]
      Disadvantaged [67]
      Homeless [88]

Social Desirability [67]
PN 1081   SC 48180
- **UF**   Desirability (Social)
- **B**   Social Influences [67]

Social Development
   Use Psychosocial Development

Social Discrimination [82]
PN 485   SC 48185
SN   Prejudiced and differential treatment on the basis of religion, sex, racial, ethnic, or other group (e.g., disabled) membership rather than on the basis of merit. Use RACIAL DISCRIMINA-TION to access references from 73-81 and MI-NORITY GROUP DISCRIMINATION to access references from 78-81. Use a more specific term if possible.
- **B**   Discrimination [67]
      Social Issues [91]
- **N**   Age Discrimination [94]
      Employment Discrimination [94]
      Race and Ethnic Discrimination [94]
      Sex Discrimination [78]
- **R**   Affirmative Action [85]
      ↓ Civil Rights [78]
      Racial and Ethnic Relations [82]
      Racism [73]
      ↓ Social Integration [82]
      Stigma [91]

Social Drinking [73]
PN 325   SC 48190
SN   Consumption of alcoholic beverages in so-cial settings.
- **B**   Alcohol Drinking Patterns [67]
      Social Behavior [67]

Social Environments [73]
PN 1389   SC 48200
- **B**   Environment [67]
- **N**   ↓ Academic Environment [73]
      ↓ Animal Environments [67]
      ↓ Communities [67]
      Home Environment [73]
      Poverty Areas [73]
      Rural Environments [67]
      Suburban Environments [67]
      Towns [73]
      ↓ Urban Environments [67]
      ↓ Working Conditions [73]
- **R**   Cultural Deprivation [73]
      Social Density [78]

Social Equality [73]
PN 451   SC 48210
- **UF**   Equality (Social)
- **B**   Social Issues [91]
- **R**   Affirmative Action [85]
      ↓ Civil Rights [78]
      Equal Education [78]
      ↓ Human Rights [78]
      ↓ Justice [73]
      Racial and Ethnic Relations [82]
      ↓ Social Integration [82]

Social Facilitation [73]
PN 340   SC 48220

Social Facilitation — (cont'd)
- **UF**   Facilitation (Social)
- **B**   Social Behavior [67]
- **R**   ↓ Social Influences [67]

Social Groups [73]
PN 654   SC 48230
- **UF**   Cadres
      Cliques
      Groups (Social)
- **N**   Dyads [73]
      Minority Groups [67]
      Reference Groups [94]
- **R**   ↓ Social Networks [94]

Social Identity [88]
PN 301   SC 48235
SN   An aspect of self image based on in-group preference or ethnocentrism and a perception of belonging to a social or cultural group.
- **N**   Professional Identity [91]
- **R**   Ethnic Identity [73]
      Ethnocentrism [73]
      Minority Groups [67]
      Reference Groups [94]
      ↓ Self Concept [67]

Social Immobility
   Use Social Mobility

Social Influences [67]
PN 3439   SC 48250
- **UF**   Influences (Social)
- **N**   Coercion [94]
      Criticism [73]
      Ethnic Values [73]
      Power [67]
      ↓ Prejudice [67]
      Propaganda [73]
      Social Approval [67]
      Social Desirability [67]
      Social Norms [85]
      Social Values [73]
      Superstitions [73]
      Taboos [73]
- **R**   Authority [67]
      ↓ Ethics [67]
      ↓ Interpersonal Influences [67]
      Mentor [85]
      Popularity [88]
      Psychosocial Factors [88]
      Reference Groups [94]
      Role Models [82]
      ↓ Social Behavior [67]
      Social Change [67]
      Social Comparison [85]
      Social Control [88]
      Social Facilitation [73]
      ↓ Social Movements [67]
      ↓ Social Reinforcement [67]

Social Integration [82]
PN 334   SC 48258
SN   Process of uniting diverse groups (racial, ethnic, religious, or handicapped) of a society or organization into a cohesive whole. Use RACIAL INTEGRATION to access references from 67-81.
- **UF**   Desegregation
      Integration (Racial)
      Racial Integration
      Segregation (Racial)
- **B**   Social Issues [91]
      Social Processes [67]
- **N**   School Integration [82]
- **R**   ↓ Activist Movements [73]
      ↓ Civil Rights [78]
      ↓ Mainstreaming [91]
      Racial and Ethnic Relations [82]

Social Integration — (cont'd)
- **R**   ↓ Social Discrimination [82]
      Social Equality [73]

Social Interaction [67]
PN 4391   SC 48260
- **UF**   Interaction (Social)
- **B**   Social Behavior [67]
- **N**   Encouragement [73]
      ↓ Interpersonal Interaction [67]
      Nonviolence [91]
      Peace [88]
      Physical Contact [82]
      Victimization [73]
- **R**   ↓ Aggressive Behavior [67]
      ↓ Conflict Resolution [82]
      Forgiveness [88]
      Psychodynamics [73]
      Self Monitoring (Personality) [85]
      Social Anxiety [85]
      Social Cognition [94]
      ↓ Social Networks [94]
      Social Support Networks [82]
      Symbolic Interactionism [88]

Social Isolation [67]
PN 2262   SC 48270
SN   Voluntary or involuntary absence of contact with others. Used for human or animal popula-tions.
- **UF**   Isolation (Social)
- **B**   Social Deprivation [73]
      Stimulus Deprivation [73]
- **N**   Patient Seclusion [94]
- **R**   Animal Maternal Deprivation [88]
      Social Anxiety [85]

Social Issues [91]
PN 113   SC 48275
SN   Social concerns, including but not limited to problems or conditions perceived to have social causes, definitions, consequences or possible so-lutions.
- **UF**   Social Problems
- **N**   ↓ Crime [67]
      Homeless [88]
      ↓ Human Rights [78]
      Peace [88]
      Poverty [73]
      ↓ Social Discrimination [82]
      Social Equality [73]
      ↓ Social Integration [82]
      Unemployment [67]
      ↓ War [67]
- **R**   Adolescent Pregnancy [88]
      Censorship [78]
      ↓ Civil Rights [78]
      ↓ Drug Abuse [73]
      ↓ Justice [73]
      ↓ Legal Processes [73]
      Political Issues [73]
      Racism [73]
      ↓ Social Movements [67]
      ↓ Social Processes [67]
      Social Programs [73]

Social Learning [73]
PN 901   SC 48280
- **B**   Learning [67]
      Learning Strategies [91]
- **N**   Imitation (Learning) [67]
      Imprinting [67]
- **R**   Observational Learning [73]
      ↓ Social Reinforcement [67]

Social Maladjustment
   Use Social Adjustment

Social Mobility [67]
PN 289   SC 48300
SN Change in social status by an individual or a group.
UF Mobility (Social)
     Social Immobility
B   Social Processes [67]

Social Movements [67]
PN 692   SC 48310
N ↓ Activist Movements [73]
     Black Power Movement [73]
     Civil Rights Movement [73]
     Homosexual Liberation Movement [73]
     Womens Liberation Movement [73]
R ↓ Civil Rights [78]
     Coalition Formation [73]
   ↓ Human Rights [78]
     Peace [88]
   ↓ Political Participation [88]
   ↓ Radical Movements [73]
     Social Change [67]
     Social Demonstrations [73]
   ↓ Social Influences [67]
   ↓ Social Issues [91]
     Social Programs [73]

Social Networks [94]
PN 0   SC 48313
SN A formal or informal linkage, association, or network of individuals or groups that share common interests, contacts, knowledge, or resources. Compare SOCIAL SUPPORT NETWORKS and SUPPORT GROUPS.
UF Networks (Social)
N   Social Support Networks [82]
R ↓ Interpersonal Interaction [67]
   ↓ Social Groups [73]
   ↓ Social Interaction [67]
     Sociograms [73]
   ↓ Sociometry [91]
   ↓ Support Groups [91]

Social Norms [85]
PN 486   SC 48315
SN Rules for social conduct, or standards which comprise a cultural definition of desirable or acceptable behavior. Also, patterns or traits seen as typical in the behavior of a social group.
UF Norms (Social)
B   Social Influences [67]
R   Sex Roles [67]
     Social Values [73]
     Stereotyped Behavior [73]

Social Perception [67]
PN 12300   SC 48320
SN Awareness of social phenomena, including attitudes or behaviors of persons or groups, especially as they relate to one's self.
UF Interpersonal Perception
B   Perception [67]
     Social Behavior [67]
N   Attribution [73]
     Impression Formation [78]
     Social Comparison [85]
R   Anonymity [73]
     Blame [94]
     Credibility [73]
     Face Perception [85]
     Fame [85]
     Halo Effect [82]
     Impression Management [78]
     Labeling [78]
     Likability [88]
     Popularity [88]
     Reward Allocation [88]
     Self Reference [94]
     Social Cognition [94]

Social Perception — (cont'd)
R   Stigma [91]
     Stranger Reactions [88]

Social Phobia [85]
PN 252   SC 48325
SN Extreme apprehension or fear of social interaction or social situations in general. Compare SOCIAL ANXIETY.
B   Phobias [67]
R   Avoidant Personality [94]

Social Problems
Use Social Issues

Social Processes [67]
PN 1925   SC 48330
N   Anomie [78]
     Coalition Formation [73]
   ↓ Human Migration [73]
     Immigration [73]
     Industrialization [73]
     Social Control [88]
   ↓ Social Deprivation [73]
   ↓ Social Integration [82]
     Social Mobility [67]
   ↓ Socialization [67]
   ↓ Status [67]
     Urbanization [73]
R   Equity (Payment) [78]
   ↓ Equity (Social) [78]
   ↓ Human Rights [78]
   ↓ Political Processes [73]
     Refugees [88]
     Social Change [67]
   ↓ Social Issues [91]
   ↓ Sociocultural Factors [67]
     Trends [91]

Social Programs [73]
PN 288   SC 48340
R ↓ Housing [73]
   ↓ Program Development [91]
     Social Change [67]
   ↓ Social Issues [91]
   ↓ Social Movements [67]
   ↓ Social Services [82]

Social Psychiatry [67]
PN 173   SC 48350
SN Branch of psychiatry concerned with the role of ecological, social, cultural, and economic factors in the etiology, incidence, and manifestations of mental disorders. Differentiate from COMMUNITY PSYCHIATRY, which emphasizes the practical and clinical applications of social psychiatry.
B   Psychiatry [67]
R   Social Psychology [67]

Social Psychologists [73]
PN 59   SC 48360
B   Psychologists [67]
R   Industrial Psychologists [73]
     Sociologists [73]

Social Psychology [67]
PN 1920   SC 48370
SN Branch of psychology concerned with the study of individuals in groups and the interpersonal interactions within and between groups.
B   Applied Psychology [73]
R   Social Psychiatry [67]

Social Reinforcement [67]
PN 1284   SC 48380
B   Reinforcement [67]
     Social Behavior [67]
N   Nonverbal Reinforcement [73]

Social Reinforcement — (cont'd)
N ↓ Verbal Reinforcement [73]
R   Encouragement [73]
     Eye Contact [73]
     Social Approval [67]
   ↓ Social Influences [67]
   ↓ Social Learning [73]

Social Rejection
Use Social Acceptance

Social Sciences [67]
PN 1234   SC 48390
SN Group of scientific disciplines which study the behavior of individuals or groups in society.
UF Behavioral Sciences
B   Sciences [67]
N   Anthropology [67]
     Economics [85]
   ↓ Psychology [67]
   ↓ Sociology [67]
R   Theoretical Orientation [82]

Social Security [88]
PN 38   SC 48392
SN Government program providing for economic security and social welfare of individuals or families upon retirement, death, or disability. Used for US and non-US programs.
B   Government Programs [73]
     Insurance [73]
R   Disability Evaluation [88]
     Medicaid [94]
     Medicare [88]

Social Services [82]
PN 1230   SC 48393
SN Activities designed to promote social welfare, usually associated with government or a helping organization (e.g., a church).
N ↓ Community Services [67]
R   Child Welfare [88]
   ↓ Government Programs [73]
   ↓ Health Care Services [78]
   ↓ Mental Health Services [78]
     Shelters [91]
     Social Casework [67]
     Social Programs [73]
   ↓ Support Groups [91]

Social Skills [78]
PN 2997   SC 48395
UF Competence (Social)
B   Ability [67]
     Social Behavior [67]
R   Adaptive Behavior [91]
     Affective Education [82]
     Competence [82]
     Male Female Relations [88]
     Social Skills Training [82]

Social Skills Training [82]
PN 1380   SC 48397
SN Instruction, usually group oriented, to increase quality and capability of interpersonal interaction.
R   Assertiveness Training [78]
   ↓ Behavior Modification [73]
     Communication Skills Training [82]
     Human Relations Training [78]
     Sensitivity Training [73]
   ↓ Skill Learning [73]
     Social Cognition [94]
     Social Skills [78]

Social Stigma
Use Stigma

206

Social Stress [73]
PN 436   SC 48400
 B Stress [67]

Social Structure [67]
PN 1332   SC 48410
 B Society [67]
 N Caste System [73]
  ↓ Social Class [67]
 R Dominance Hierarchy [73]
  ↓ Status [67]

Social Studies Education [78]
PN 393   SC 48415
SN Social sciences education in elementary, junior high, and high schools. Includes history, current events, and political science.
 B Curriculum [67]

Social Support Networks [82]
PN 5615   SC 48417
SN Family members or friends who provide social, emotional, or psychological support or comfort to an individual. Consider also SUPPORT GROUPS.
 B Social Networks [94]
 R Assistance (Social Behavior) [73]
  ↓ Family Relations [67]
  Friendship [67]
  Reference Groups [94]
  ↓ Self Help Techniques [82]
  Significant Others [91]
  ↓ Social Interaction [67]
  ↓ Support Groups [91]

Social Values [73]
PN 1280   SC 48420
 B Social Influences [67]
  Values [67]
 R Anomie [78]
  Morality [67]
  Social Norms [85]
  ↓ Society [67]

Social Work
 Use Social Casework

Social Work Education [73]
PN 751   SC 48440
 B Education [67]

Social Workers [73]
PN 2018   SC 48450
 UF Caseworkers
  Social Caseworkers
 B Personnel [67]
 N Psychiatric Social Workers [73]
 R ↓ Counselors [67]
  ↓ Health Personnel [94]
  ↓ Law Enforcement Personnel [73]
  ↓ Mental Health Personnel [67]
  ↓ Psychologists [67]
  Rehabilitation Counselors [78]
  Sociologists [73]
  ↓ Therapists [67]
  Vocational Counselors [73]

Socialism [73]
PN 188   SC 48460
 B Political Economic Systems [73]

Socialization [67]
PN 2231   SC 48470
SN Process by which individuals acquire characteristics necessary to function effectively in society or in a particular group.

Socialization — (cont'd)
 B Social Processes [67]
 N Political Socialization [88]
 R Reference Groups [94]

Socially Disadvantaged
 Use Disadvantaged

Society [67]
PN 678   SC 48490
 B Culture (Anthropological) [67]
 N ↓ Social Structure [67]
  ↓ Socioeconomic Status [67]
 R Social Values [73]

Sociobiology [82]
PN 280   SC 48495
SN Systematic study of the biological basis of all aspects of social behavior.
 B Biology [67]
  Sociology [67]
 R Behavioral Genetics [94]

Sociocultural Factors [67]
PN 4663   SC 48500
 N Cross Cultural Differences [67]
  Cultural Deprivation [73]
  ↓ Culture Change [67]
  Ethnic Identity [73]
  Ethnic Values [73]
  ↓ Rites of Passage [73]
 R ↓ Childrearing Practices [67]
  Cultism [73]
  Cultural Sensitivity [94]
  ↓ Culture (Anthropological) [67]
  Ethnography [73]
  Ethnology [67]
  ↓ Family Structure [73]
  Kinship Structure [73]
  Psychosocial Factors [88]
  Race (Anthropological) [73]
  ↓ Social Processes [67]

Socioeconomic Class Attitudes [73]
PN 162   SC 48510
SN Attitudes of, not toward, members of a particular socioeconomic class.
 UF Class Attitudes
  Social Class Attitudes
 B Attitudes [67]
 N Lower Class Attitudes [73]
  Middle Class Attitudes [73]
  Upper Class Attitudes [73]
 R ↓ Social Class [67]
  ↓ Socioeconomic Status [67]

Socioeconomic Status [67]
PN 6122   SC 48520
SN The combination of one's social class and income level. Includes socioeconomic differences between individuals or groups.
 B Society [67]
  Status [67]
 N Family Socioeconomic Level [73]
  ↓ Income Level [73]
  Lower Class [73]
  ↓ Social Class [67]
 R Disadvantaged [67]
  Income (Economic) [73]
  Poverty [73]
  ↓ Socioeconomic Class Attitudes [73]

Socioenvironmental Therapy
 Use Milieu Therapy

Sociograms [73]
PN 47   SC 48530

Sociograms — (cont'd)
SN Diagrams in which interactions between group members are analyzed on the basis of mutual attractions or antipathies.
 B Sociometry [91]
 R ↓ Measurement [67]
  ↓ Social Networks [94]

Sociolinguistics [85]
PN 171   SC 48535
SN The study of the sociological aspects of language, concerned with the part language plays in maintaining the social roles in a community.
 B Linguistics [73]
 R Code Switching [88]
  Ethnolinguistics [73]
  Metalinguistics [94]
  ↓ Sociology [67]
  Symbolic Interactionism [88]

Sociologists [73]
PN 56   SC 48540
 B Professional Personnel [78]
 R Anthropologists [73]
  ↓ Counselors [67]
  Scientists [67]
  Social Psychologists [73]
  ↓ Social Workers [73]

Sociology [67]
PN 1096   SC 48550
 B Social Sciences [67]
 N Sociobiology [82]
 R Sociolinguistics [85]
  Symbolic Interactionism [88]

Sociometric Tests [67]
PN 374   SC 48560
SN Tests or techniques used to identify preferences, likes, or dislikes of group members with respect to each other, as well as to identify various patterns of group structure or interaction.
 B Measurement [67]
  Sociometry [91]

Sociometry [91]
PN 59   SC 48565
SN Used for the scientific discipline or the sociometric processes and properties themselves.
 N Sociograms [73]
  Sociometric Tests [67]
 R ↓ Collective Behavior [67]
  ↓ Group Dynamics [67]
  ↓ Organizational Behavior [78]
  ↓ Peer Relations [67]
  ↓ Social Networks [94]

Sociopath
 Use Antisocial Personality

Sociopathology
 Use Antisocial Behavior

Sociotherapy [73]
PN 82   SC 48580
SN Any therapy in which the main emphasis is on socioenvironmental and interpersonal factors. Sometimes used to refer to a therapeutic community.
 B Treatment [67]
 R Milieu Therapy [88]
  Therapeutic Community [67]

Sodium [73]
PN 642   SC 48590
 B Metallic Elements [73]
 N Sodium Ions [73]

Sodium Ions [73]
PN 59   SC 48610
B   Electrolytes [73]
     Sodium [73]

Sodium Lactate
Use Lactic Acid

Sodium Pentobarbital
Use Pentobarbital

Solvent Abuse
Use Inhalant Abuse

Solvents [82]
PN 215   SC 48625
SN Substances that react chemically with a sol-
id to bring it into solution. Also, liquids that dis-
solve another substance (solute) without any
change in chemical composition.
N   Toluene [91]
R ↓ Acids [73]
   ↓ Alcohols [67]
   ↓ Inhalant Abuse [85]

Somalia [91]
PN 3   SC 48626
B   Africa [67]

Somatization [94]
PN 0   SC 57430
SN Process of organically manifesting and ex-
pressing cognitive and emotional disturbances
through bodily symptoms.
R ↓ Conversion Neurosis [73]
     Hypochondriasis [73]
     Illness Behavior [82]
     Psychogenic Pain [73]
   ↓ Psychosomatic Disorders [67]
   ↓ Symptoms [67]

Somatization Disorder
Use Psychosomatic Disorders

Somatosensory Cortex [73]
PN 326   SC 48630
UF   Cortex (Somatosensory)
B   Parietal Lobe [73]

Somatosensory Evoked Potentials [73]
PN 465   SC 48640
UF   Motor Evoked Potentials
B   Evoked Potentials [67]
R ↓ Cortical Evoked Potentials [73]

Somatostatin [91]
PN 49   SC 48645
UF   Growth Hormone Inhibitor
B   Peptides [73]
R   Somatotropin [73]

Somatotropin [73]
PN 504   SC 48650
UF   Growth Hormone
B   Pituitary Hormones [73]
R   Somatostatin [91]

Somatotypes [73]
PN 128   SC 48660
SN Body types as derived from any of various
classifications of body build and which usually
imply a correlation with personality characteris-
tics.
UF   Body Types
R ↓ Personality [67]
   ↓ Physical Appearance [82]
     Physique [67]

Somesthetic Perception [67]
PN 604   SC 48670
SN Awareness of bodily condition or stimuli, in-
cluding kinesthetic and cutaneous perception.
B   Perception [67]
N ↓ Cutaneous Sense [67]
     Kinesthetic Perception [67]
   ↓ Pain Perception [73]
     Temperature Perception [73]
     Weight Perception [67]
R   Body Awareness [82]
   ↓ Labyrinth Disorders [73]
     Pressure Sensation [73]

Somesthetic Stimulation [73]
PN 451   SC 48680
UF   Vestibular Stimulation
B   Perceptual Stimulation [73]
N ↓ Tactual Stimulation [73]
R   Weightlessness [67]

Somnambulism
SN Term discontinued in 1982. Use SOMNAM-
BULISM or SLEEPWALKING to access refer-
ences from 73–81.
Use Sleepwalking

Sonar [73]
PN 25   SC 48700
B   Apparatus [67]

Sons [73]
PN 577   SC 48710
B   Family Members [73]
     Human Males [73]
     Offspring [88]

Sorority Membership [73]
PN 55   SC 48720
SN Belonging to a club traditionally restricted to
females. Used also for sorority organizations.
B   Extracurricular Activities [73]

Sorting (Cognition)
Use Classification (Cognitive Process)

Sound
Use Auditory Stimulation

Sound Localization
Use Auditory Localization

Sound Pressure Level
Use Loudness

Sourness
Use Taste Perception

South Africa [82]
PN 570   SC 48775
SN Use UNION OF SOUTH AFRICA to access
references from 73–81.
UF   Union of South Africa
B   Africa [67]

South America [67]
PN 676   SC 48780
N   Argentina [82]
     Bolivia [88]
     Brazil [73]
     Chile [82]
     Colombia [82]
     Ecuador [88]
     Guyana [88]
     Paraguay [88]
     Peru [88]
     Surinam [91]

South America — (cont'd)
N   Uruguay [88]
     Venezuela [73]
R   Latin America [88]

South Korea [82]
PN 111   SC 48782
SN Use KOREA to access references from 73–
81.
B   Korea [73]

South Pacific [78]
PN 108   SC 48785
B   Pacific Islands [88]
N   American Samoa [91]
     Fiji [91]
     Tonga [91]
     Western Samoa [91]
R   Australia [73]
     New Zealand [73]

South Vietnam
SN Term discontinued in 1982. Use SOUTH
VIETNAM to access references from 73–81.
Use Vietnam

Southeast Asia [73]
PN 190   SC 48800
B   Asia [73]
N   Burma [91]
     Cambodia [88]
     Indonesia [82]
     Laos [88]
     Malaysia [82]
     Philippines [73]
     Singapore [91]
     Thailand [73]
     Vietnam [82]

Spacecraft [73]
PN 26   SC 48820
R   Air Transportation [73]
     Astronauts [73]

Spaceflight [67]
PN 146   SC 48830
B   Aviation [67]
R   Acceleration Effects [73]
     Decompression Effects [73]
   ↓ Gravitational Effects [67]
     Weightlessness [67]

Spain [73]
PN 589   SC 48840
B   Europe [73]

Spanish Americans
SN Term discontinued in 1982. Use SPANISH
AMERICANS to access references from 78–81.
Use Hispanics

Spasms [73]
PN 84   SC 48850
B   Movement Disorders [85]
     Symptoms [67]
N   Muscle Spasms [73]
R ↓ Anticonvulsive Drugs [73]
   ↓ Antispasmodic Drugs [73]
   ↓ Convulsions [67]
   ↓ Pain [67]

Spatial Ability [82]
PN 1144   SC 48855
SN Potential or actual performance on tasks involving mental manipulation of objects or judgments of spatial relationships with respect to actual or imagined bodily orientation.

Spatial Ability — (cont'd)
- **B** Cognitive Ability [73]
- Nonverbal Ability [88]
- **R** ↓ Cognitive Processes [67]
- Mental Rotation [91]
- Spatial Imagery [82]
- Spatial Learning [94]
- Spatial Orientation (Perception) [73]

Spatial Discrimination
- **Use** Spatial Perception

Spatial Distortion [73]
PN 121   SC 48870
SN Alterations of an organism's normal spatial perception in any sensory modality. Distortions may be induced by such means as optical lenses, prisms, mirror displays or images, and left-right inversion of sound stimuli.
- **B** Illusions (Perception) [67]
- Perceptual Distortion [82]
- Spatial Perception [67]
- **R** Prismatic Stimulation [73]

Spatial Frequency [82]
PN 895   SC 48872
SN Number of alternating cycles (e.g., patterns of vertical stripes of light and dark light) occurring in a specified visual angle as, for example, in sine wave or square wave displays.
- **B** Stimulus Parameters [67]
- **R** Temporal Frequency [85]
- ↓ Visual Displays [73]
- ↓ Visual Stimulation [73]

Spatial Imagery [82]
PN 220   SC 48875
SN Mental representation of spatial relationships.
- **B** Imagery [67]
- **R** Cognitive Maps [82]
- Mental Rotation [91]
- Spatial Ability [82]
- Spatial Memory [88]
- Spatial Organization [73]
- Spatial Orientation (Perception) [73]

Spatial Learning [94]
PN 0   SC 48876
- **B** Learning [67]
- **R** Spatial Ability [82]
- Spatial Memory [88]
- ↓ Spatial Perception [67]

Spatial Memory [88]
PN 384   SC 48877
- **B** Memory [67]
- **R** Cognitive Maps [82]
- Eidetic Imagery [73]
- Spatial Imagery [82]
- Spatial Learning [94]
- Visual Memory [94]

Spatial Neglect
- **Use** Sensory Neglect

Spatial Organization [73]
PN 1506   SC 48880
SN Perception of spatial relationships. Also, the actual pattern or physical arrangement of objects or stimuli, including the dimensions of proximity, continuation, and relative position.
- **B** Spatial Perception [67]
- **R** Cognitive Maps [82]
- Mental Rotation [91]
- Retinal Eccentricity [91]
- Spatial Imagery [82]

Spatial Orientation (Perception) [73]
PN 2182   SC 48890
SN Ability to perceive or orient oneself or external stimuli in space with respect to environmentally or egocentrically defined reference points.
- **UF** Orientation (Spatial)
- **B** Perceptual Orientation [73]
- Spatial Perception [67]
- **R** Cognitive Maps [82]
- Equilibrium [73]
- Kinesthetic Perception [67]
- Spatial Ability [82]
- Spatial Imagery [82]

Spatial Perception [67]
PN 2877   SC 48900
- **UF** Spatial Discrimination
- **B** Perception [67]
- **N** ↓ Depth Perception [67]
- ↓ Distance Perception [73]
- ↓ Motion Perception [67]
- ↓ Size Discrimination [67]
- Spatial Distortion [73]
- Spatial Organization [73]
- Spatial Orientation (Perception) [73]
- **R** Figure Ground Discrimination [73]
- Mental Rotation [91]
- Spatial Learning [94]
- Visual Acuity [82]

Spearman Brown Test [73]
PN 8   SC 48910
- **B** Statistical Tests [73]
- **R** Statistical Reliability [73]

Spearman Rho
- **Use** Rank Difference Correlation

Special Education [67]
PN 10001   SC 48930
SN Educational programs and services for handicapped and gifted students whose characteristics and educational needs differ from those who can be taught through normal methods and materials.
- **B** Education [67]
- Educational Programs [73]
- **R** Ability Grouping [73]
- Adaptive Behavior [91]
- Early Intervention [82]
- Educational Placement [78]
- ↓ Mainstreaming [91]
- Mainstreaming (Educational) [78]
- ↓ Remedial Education [85]
- Self Care Skills [78]
- Special Needs [94]

Special Education Students [73]
PN 2326   SC 49010
- **B** Students [67]
- **R** Grade Level [94]

Special Education Teachers [73]
PN 1545   SC 49020
- **B** Teachers [67]
- **R** Resource Teachers [73]

Special Needs [94]
PN 0   SC 49025
SN Unspecified disorder, disability, handicap, or other problem that requires special services or intervention practices. Use a more specific term if possible.
- **R** ↓ Disorders [67]
- Early Intervention [82]
- ↓ Handicapped [67]
- ↓ Mainstreaming [91]
- ↓ Mental Disorders [67]
- Needs [67]

Special Needs — (cont'd)
- **R** Needs Assessment [85]
- Special Education [67]

Specialization (Academic)
- **Use** Academic Specialization

Specialization (Professional)
- **Use** Professional Specialization

Species Differences [82]
PN 994   SC 49035
SN Anatomical, physiological, and/or behavioral variations between members of different species. May be used for comparisons between human and animal populations. Consider COMPARATIVE PSYCHOLOGY to access references from 67–81. Compare ANIMAL STRAIN DIFFERENCES.
- **R** ↓ Animals [67]
- ↓ Genetics [67]
- Interspecies Interaction [91]

Species Recognition [85]
PN 184   SC 49037
SN Ability of members of a given species to identify and recognize other members of the same species.
- **B** Animal Ethology [67]
- **R** Imprinting [67]
- Instinctive Behavior [82]
- Kinship Recognition [88]

Spectral Sensitivity
- **Use** Color Perception

Speech
- **Use** Oral Communication

Speech and Hearing Measures [73]
PN 448   SC 49060
SN Consider also AUDIOLOGY and AUDIOMETRY.
- **UF** Hearing Measures
- Speech Measures
- **B** Measurement [67]
- **N** Wepman Test of Auditory Discrim [73]

Speech Anxiety [85]
PN 213   SC 49065
SN Anxiety or fear associated with actual or anticipated oral communication with others.
- **UF** Communication Apprehension
- Fear of Public Speaking
- **B** Anxiety [67]
- **R** ↓ Anxiety Neurosis [73]
- ↓ Communication Disorders [82]
- ↓ Interpersonal Communication [73]
- Public Speaking [73]
- Social Anxiety [85]

Speech Characteristics [73]
PN 2693   SC 49070
- **B** Oral Communication [85]
- **N** Articulation (Speech) [67]
- Pronunciation [73]
- Speech Pauses [73]
- Speech Pitch [73]
- Speech Rate [73]
- Speech Rhythm [73]
- **R** Inflection [73]
- ↓ Prosody [91]

Speech Development [73]
PN 1165   SC 49080
- **B** Psychomotor Development [73]
- **N** Retarded Speech Development [73]

Speech Development — (cont'd)
R   ↓ Cognitive Development   73
     ↓ Language Development   67

Speech Disorders   67
PN   1551   SC   49090
B   Communication Disorders   82
N   ↓ Articulation Disorders   73
     Dysphonia   73
     Stuttering   67
R   Apraxia   73
     ↓ Augmentative Communication   94
     Cleft Palate   67
     ↓ Language Disorders   82
     Retarded Speech Development   73
     Speech Handicapped   73

Speech Handicapped   73
PN   226   SC   49100
B   Handicapped   67
R   ↓ Communication Disorders   82
     ↓ Language Disorders   82
     ↓ Speech Disorders   67

Speech Measures
Use   Speech and Hearing Measures

Speech Pauses   73
PN   217   SC   49120
B   Speech Characteristics   73

Speech Perception   67
PN   3248   SC   49130
B   Auditory Perception   67
R   Automated Speech Recognition   94
     Lipreading   73
     ↓ Rhythm   91
     Word Recognition   88

Speech Pitch   73
PN   194   SC   49140
B   Pitch (Frequency)   67
     Speech Characteristics   73

Speech Processing (Mechanical)   73
PN   135   SC   49150
N   Automated Speech Recognition   94
     Compressed Speech   73
     Filtered Speech   73
     Synthetic Speech   73
R   ↓ Auditory Stimulation   67
     ↓ Verbal Communication   67

Speech Rate   73
PN   440   SC   49160
UF   Accelerated Speech
B   Speech Characteristics   73
R   Verbal Fluency   73

Speech Rhythm   73
PN   137   SC   49170
B   Rhythm   91
     Speech Characteristics   73

Speech Therapists   73
PN   232   SC   49180
B   Therapists   67
R   ↓ Educational Personnel   73

Speech Therapy   67
PN   1460   SC   49190
B   Treatment   67
R   ↓ Augmentative Communication   94
     ↓ Communication Disorders   82

Speechreading
Use   Lipreading

Speed
Use   Velocity

Speed (Response)
Use   Reaction Time

Spelling   73
PN   1056   SC   49220
SN   Instruction, ability, or performance in the formation of words from letters according to accepted orthographic standards.
B   Language   67
     Language Arts Education   73
R   Orthography   73

Sperm   73
PN   73   SC   49230
B   Cells (Biology)   73
R   ↓ Sexual Reproduction   73

Sperm Donation
Use   Tissue Donation

Spider Phobia
Use   Phobias

Spiders
Use   Arachnida

Spina Bifida   78
PN   185   SC   49245
SN   Birth defect involving inadequate closure of the bony casement of the spinal cord, through which the spinal membranes, with or without spinal cord tissue, may protrude.
UF   Meningomyelocele
     Myelomeningocele
B   Congenital Disorders   73

Spinal Column   73
PN   33   SC   49250
B   Musculoskeletal System   73
R   Bones   73
     ↓ Spinal Cord   73

Spinal Cord   73
PN   537   SC   49260
B   Central Nervous System   67
N   Cranial Spinal Cord   73
     Dorsal Horns   85
     Dorsal Roots   73
     Extrapyramidal Tracts   73
     Lumbar Spinal Cord   73
     Pyramidal Tracts   73
     Spinothalamic Tracts   73
     Ventral Roots   73
R   Spinal Column   73

Spinal Cord Injuries   73
PN   382   SC   49270
B   Injuries   73
R   ↓ Central Nervous System Disorders   73
     Hemiplegia   78
     ↓ Neuromuscular Disorders   73
     ↓ Paralysis   73
     Paraplegia   78
     Quadriplegia   85

Spinal Fluid
Use   Cerebrospinal Fluid

Spinal Ganglia   73
PN   28   SC   49290
B   Ganglia   73

Spinal Nerves   73
PN   181   SC   49300

Spinal Nerves — (cont'd)
UF   Brachial Plexus
     Cauda Equina
     Cervical Plexus
     Femoral Nerve
     Lumbrosacral Plexus
     Median Nerve
     Musculocutaneous Nerve
     Nerves (Spinal)
     Obturator Nerve
     Phrenic Nerve
     Radial Nerve
     Sciatic Nerve
     Thoracic Nerves
     Ulnar Nerve
B   Peripheral Nervous System   73

Spinothalamic Tracts   73
PN   32   SC   49310
B   Afferent Pathways   82
     Lemniscal System   85
     Spinal Cord   73

Spiperone
Use   Spiroperidol

Spirituality   88
PN   339   SC   49315
SN   Degree of involvement or state of awareness or devotion to a higher being or life philosophy. Not always related to conventional religious beliefs.
R   ↓ Personality Traits   67
     Religion   67
     Religiosity   73
     ↓ Religious Beliefs   73

Spiroperidol   91
PN   21   SC   49317
UF   Spiperone
B   Neuroleptic Drugs   73

Spleen   73
PN   32   SC   49320
R   ↓ Cardiovascular System   67

Split Brain
Use   Commissurotomy

Split Personality
Use   Multiple Personality

Spontaneous Abortion   71
PN   163   SC   49350
UF   Abortion (Spontaneous)
     Miscarriage
R   Induced Abortion   71

Spontaneous Alternation   82
PN   111   SC   49352
SN   Instinctive successive alternation of responses between alternatives in a situation involving discrete choices or exploration.
R   Animal Exploratory Behavior   73
     Delayed Alternation   94
     Instinctive Behavior   82
     ↓ Learning   67
     Response Variability   73

Spontaneous Recovery (Learning)   73
PN   56   SC   49357
SN   Recurrence of a conditioned response following experimental extinction. The response is weaker than when originally conditioned and will extinguish rapidly if not reinforced.
B   Learning   67
     Memory   67
R   ↓ Conditioning   67

Spontaneous Remission [73]
PN 54   SC 49360
  B   Remission (Disorders) [73]
  R ↓ Psychotherapy [67]
     ↓ Treatment [67]

Sport Performance
  Use Athletic Performance

Sport Psychology [82]
PN 281   SC 49365
SN Branch of psychology that investigates and
applies psychological and physiological principles
relating to athletic activity. Also used for psychological processes and their manifestations in
such activity.
  B   Applied Psychology [73]

Sport Training
  Use Athletic Training

Sports [67]
PN 1535   SC 49370
  N   Baseball [73]
       Basketball [73]
       Football [73]
       Judo [73]
       Martial Arts [85]
       Soccer [94]
       Swimming [73]
       Tennis [73]
       Weightlifting [94]
  R ↓ Athletes [73]
       Athletic Participation [73]
       Athletic Performance [91]
       Athletic Training [91]
       Coaches [88]
       College Athletes [94]
     ↓ Recreation [67]
       Teams [88]
       Wilderness Experience [91]

Spouse Abuse
  Use Partner Abuse

Spouses [73]
PN 4372   SC 49380
SN Married persons.
  UF   Married Couples
       Mates (Humans)
  B   Family Members [73]
  N   Husbands [73]
     ↓ Wives [73]
  R   Couples [82]
     ↓ Parents [67]
       Significant Others [91]

Spreading Depression [67]
PN 116   SC 49390
SN Cerebral cortex cellular depolarization and a
depressed electrical activity in depolarized cortical areas resulting from application of intense
localized electrical stimulation or local application
of a chemical or localized trauma to the cerebral
cortex.
  B   Brain Stimulation [67]

Squirrels [73]
PN 226   SC 49400
  B   Rodents [73]

Sri Lanka [88]
PN 37   SC 49410
  B   Asia [73]

Stability (Emotional)
  Use Emotional Stability

Stage Plays
  Use Theatre

Stammering
SN Term discontinued in 1982. Use STAMMER-
ING or STUTTERING to access references from
73–81 and 67–81, respectively.
  Use Stuttering

Standard Deviation [73]
PN 102   SC 49450
  B   Variability Measurement [73]
  R   Error of Measurement [85]
     ↓ Frequency Distribution [73]
       Standard Scores [85]
       Variance Homogeneity [85]

Standard Error of Measurement
  Use Error of Measurement

Standard Scores [85]
PN 45   SC 49455
SN Test scores measuring the distance of in-
dividual scores from the mean of the normative
group, expressed in terms of the standard de-
viation.
  UF   Deviation IQ
       Stanines
       Z Scores
  B   Test Scores [67]
  R   Mean [73]
       Score Equating [85]
     ↓ Scoring (Testing) [73]
       Standard Deviation [73]

Standardization (Test)
  Use Test Standardization

Standardized Tests [85]
PN 242   SC 49465
SN Tests with established norms, administration
and scoring procedures, and validity and reliabil-
ity data.
  B   Measurement [67]
  R   Test Norms [73]
       Test Standardization [73]

Standards (Professional)
  Use Professional Standards

Stanford Achievement Test [73]
PN 50   SC 49480
  B   Achievement Measures [67]

Stanford Binet Intelligence Scale [67]
PN 289   SC 49490
  B   Intelligence Measures [67]

Stanines
  Use Standard Scores

Stapedius Reflex
  Use Acoustic Reflex

Starfish
  Use Echinodermata

Startle Reflex [67]
PN 496   SC 49510
  B   Reflexes [71]
  R   Acoustic Reflex [73]
       Alarm Responses [73]
       Eyeblink Reflex [73]

Starvation [73]
PN 60   SC 49520

Starvation — (cont'd)
  B   Nutritional Deficiencies [73]
  R   Food Deprivation [67]
       Hunger [67]

State Board Examinations
  Use Professional Examinations

State Dependent Learning [82]
PN 80   SC 49525
SN Learning phenomenon wherein the transfer
of a response that was learned in the context of
specific internal or external cues is dependent on
the constancy of the stimulus complex in the new
situation to which the behavior is to transfer.
  UF   Drug Dissociation
  B   Learning [67]

State Hospitals
  Use Psychiatric Hospitals

State Trait Anxiety Inventory [73]
PN 128   SC 49540
  B   Nonprojective Personality Measures [73]

Statistical Analysis [67]
PN 5356   SC 49550
SN Application of statistical procedures to the
interpretation of numerical data.
  B   Analysis [67]
  N ↓ Central Tendency Measures [73]
       Cluster Analysis [73]
       Confidence Limits (Statistics) [73]
       Consistency (Measurement) [73]
       Effect Size (Statistical) [85]
       Error of Measurement [85]
     ↓ Frequency Distribution [73]
       Fuzzy Set Theory [91]
       Goodness of Fit [88]
       Interaction Analysis (Statistics) [73]
       Meta Analysis [85]
     ↓ Multivariate Analysis [82]
       Predictability (Measurement) [73]
     ↓ Statistical Correlation [67]
       Statistical Data [82]
     ↓ Statistical Estimation [85]
       Statistical Norms [71]
     ↓ Statistical Probability [67]
     ↓ Statistical Regression [85]
       Statistical Reliability [73]
       Statistical Significance [73]
     ↓ Statistical Tests [73]
     ↓ Statistical Validity [73]
       Statistical Weighting [85]
       Time Series [85]
     ↓ Variability Measurement [73]
  R   Conjoint Measurement [94]
     ↓ Experimental Design [67]
     ↓ Experimentation [67]
     ↓ Hypothesis Testing [73]
     ↓ Mathematics (Concepts) [67]
     ↓ Measurement [67]
     ↓ Population (Statistics) [73]
     ↓ Prediction Errors [73]
       Psychometrics [67]
     ↓ Sampling (Experimental) [73]
     ↓ Statistical Measurement [73]
     ↓ Statistical Variables [73]
       Uncertainty [91]

Statistical Correlation [67]
PN 2611   SC 49560
  UF   Correlation (Statistical)
       Pearson Prod Moment Correl Coeff
  B   Statistical Analysis [67]
  N   Linear Regression [73]
       Nonlinear Regression [73]
       Phi Coefficient [73]

Statistical Correlation — (cont'd)
N   Point Biserial Correlation [73]
     Rank Difference Correlation [73]
     Rank Order Correlation [73]
     Tetrachoric Correlation [73]
R   Construct Validity [82]
    ↓ Experimentation [67]
    ↓ Factor Analysis [67]
    Multiple Regression [82]
    ↓ Multivariate Analysis [82]
    Statistical Data [82]
    ↓ Statistical Regression [85]
    Statistical Significance [73]
    ↓ Statistical Validity [73]
    ↓ Statistical Variables [73]
    ↓ Variability Measurement [73]

Statistical Data [82]
PN 246   SC 49564
SN Sets of quantitative values that summarize, through mathematical operation, or express the parameters that represent a population or some other sample (e.g., response frequency).
B   Statistical Analysis [67]
R   Data Collection [82]
    Graphical Displays [85]
    ↓ Statistical Correlation [67]
    ↓ Statistical Measurement [73]
    Statistical Tables [82]
    ↓ Statistical Variables [73]
    Time Series [85]

Statistical Estimation [85]
PN 467   SC 49567
SN Any inferential mathematical derivation of an estimate of a parameter from one or more samples. Includes interval estimation.
UF Parameter Estimation
B   Estimation [67]
    Statistical Analysis [67]
N   Least Squares [85]
    Magnitude Estimation [91]
    Maximum Likelihood [85]

Statistical Measurement [73]
PN 453   SC 49570
SN Process of or products derived from the collection or manipulation of statistical data in order to derive basic summarizing quantitative values which describe a set of measurements.
B   Measurement [67]
N   ↓ Central Tendency Measures [73]
    Conjoint Measurement [94]
    ↓ Frequency Distribution [73]
    Predictability (Measurement) [73]
    Statistical Norms [71]
    ↓ Statistical Probability [67]
    ↓ Variability Measurement [73]
    Variance Homogeneity [85]
R   Confidence Limits (Statistics) [73]
    Data Collection [82]
    Error of Measurement [85]
    Graphical Displays [85]
    ↓ Statistical Analysis [67]
    Statistical Data [82]
    Statistical Significance [73]
    ↓ Statistical Tests [73]

Statistical Norms [71]
PN 214   SC 49580
UF Norms (Statistical)
B   Statistical Analysis [67]
    Statistical Measurement [73]
R   Statistical Sample Parameters [73]

Statistical Power [91]
PN 28   SC 49585
SN The ability of a statistic to reject a false hypothesis.

Statistical Power — (cont'd)
B   Statistical Probability [67]
R   ↓ Hypothesis Testing [73]
    ↓ Prediction Errors [73]
    ↓ Sampling (Experimental) [73]
    Statistical Significance [73]
    ↓ Statistical Tests [73]
    Type I Errors [73]
    Type II Errors [73]

Statistical Probability [67]
PN 665   SC 49590
UF Bayes Theorem
B   Chance (Fortune) [73]
    Probability [67]
    Statistical Analysis [67]
    Statistical Measurement [73]
N   Binomial Distribution [73]
    Statistical Power [91]
R   Fuzzy Set Theory [91]
    Risk Analysis [91]

Statistical Regression [85]
PN 207   SC 49595
SN Statistical comparison of the frequency distributions of one variable while the other(s) are held constant for the purpose of discovering predictive and functional relationships between variables. Use ANALYSIS OF VARIANCE or more specific terms prior to 1985.
UF Regression Analysis
    Regression Artifact
B   Statistical Analysis [67]
N   Linear Regression [73]
    Multiple Regression [82]
    Nonlinear Regression [73]
R   Analysis of Variance [67]
    Causal Analysis [94]
    Least Squares [85]
    ↓ Multivariate Analysis [82]
    ↓ Statistical Correlation [67]

Statistical Reliability [73]
PN 1535   SC 49600
SN Use RELIABILITY (STATISTICAL) to access references from 67–72.
UF Reliability (Statistical)
B   Statistical Analysis [67]
R   Consistency (Measurement) [73]
    ↓ Experimentation [67]
    Interrater Reliability [82]
    ↓ Population (Statistics) [73]
    ↓ Prediction Errors [73]
    ↓ Sampling (Experimental) [73]
    Spearman Brown Test [73]
    ↓ Statistical Validity [73]

Statistical Rotation [73]
PN 58   SC 49610
UF Rotation Methods (Statistical)
B   Factor Analysis [67]
N   Oblique Rotation [73]
    ↓ Orthogonal Rotation [73]
R   Factor Structure [85]

Statistical Sample Parameters [73]
PN 284   SC 49620
SN Quantities and qualities describing a statistical population.
B   Statistical Samples [73]
R   Binomial Distribution [73]
    Confidence Limits (Statistics) [73]
    Normal Distribution [73]
    Statistical Norms [71]

Statistical Samples [73]
PN 188   SC 49630
SN Portion of a population taken as representative of the whole population.

Statistical Samples — (cont'd)
B   Population (Statistics) [73]
N   Statistical Sample Parameters [73]
R   ↓ Sampling (Experimental) [73]

Statistical Significance [73]
PN 482   SC 49640
UF Significance (Statistical)
B   Statistical Analysis [67]
R   Chi Square Test [73]
    Confidence Limits (Statistics) [73]
    Effect Size (Statistical) [85]
    ↓ Factor Analysis [67]
    Goodness of Fit [88]
    ↓ Hypothesis Testing [73]
    Sign Test [73]
    ↓ Statistical Correlation [67]
    ↓ Statistical Measurement [73]
    Statistical Power [91]
    ↓ Statistical Tests [73]
    T Test [73]

Statistical Tables [82]
PN 84   SC 49647
SN Systematically organized displays of statistical values or distributions or summary data derived from statistical calculation. The table of critical values of the F distribution is an example of the first category, and a contingency table showing test score means as related to the variables of sex and age is an example of the second category.
R   Statistical Data [82]
    ↓ Statistical Variables [73]

Statistical Tests [73]
PN 409   SC 49650
SN Specific mathematical techniques used to analyze data in order to assess the probability that a set of results could have occurred by chance and hence to test for the probable correctness of experimental hypotheses.
UF Tests (Statistical)
B   Statistical Analysis [67]
N   ↓ Nonparametric Statistical Tests [67]
    ↓ Parametric Statistical Tests [73]
    Spearman Brown Test [73]
R   Confidence Limits (Statistics) [73]
    ↓ Statistical Measurement [73]
    Statistical Power [91]
    Statistical Significance [73]

Statistical Validity [73]
PN 1980   SC 49660
SN Use VALIDITY (STATISTICAL) to access references from 67–72.
UF Validity (Statistical)
B   Statistical Analysis [67]
N   Concurrent Validity [88]
    Factorial Validity [73]
    Predictive Validity [73]
R   Consistency (Measurement) [73]
    Construct Validity [82]
    ↓ Experimentation [67]
    ↓ Prediction Errors [73]
    ↓ Statistical Correlation [67]
    Statistical Reliability [73]
    ↓ Statistical Variables [73]

Statistical Variables [73]
PN 617   SC 49670
N   Dependent Variables [73]
    Independent Variables [73]
R   ↓ Experimental Design [67]
    ↓ Experimentation [67]
    ↓ Population (Statistics) [73]
    ↓ Prediction Errors [73]
    ↓ Sampling (Experimental) [73]
    ↓ Statistical Analysis [67]

Statistical Variables — (cont'd)
R ↓ Statistical Correlation 67
      Statistical Data 82
      Statistical Tables 82
   ↓ Statistical Validity 73

Statistical Weighting 85
PN 98   SC 49671
SN A coefficient or mathematical constant that determines the relative contribution of a statistic to a total numeric value. Also, the process of assigning such statistical weights.
UF Weight (Statistics)
B   Statistical Analysis 67
R   Item Analysis (Statistical) 73
   ↓ Scoring (Testing) 73
      Test Interpretation 85
   ↓ Test Scores 67

Statistics 82
PN 216   SC 49672
SN Subdiscipline of mathematics that deals with the gathering and evaluation of numerical data for making inferences from the data. Also used as a document type identifier.
B   Mathematics 82

Status 67
PN 1330   SC 49675
SN General term used to indicate relative social position or rank.
B   Social Processes 67
N   Occupational Status 78
   ↓ Socioeconomic Status 67
R   Fame 85
   ↓ Social Structure 67

Stealing
Use Theft

Stelazine
Use Trifluoperazine

Stellate Ganglion
Use Autonomic Ganglia

Stepchildren 73
PN 150   SC 49720
B   Family Members 73
R ↓ Children 67
   ↓ Family Structure 73
      Stepfamily 91

Stepfamily 91
PN 46   SC 49725
B   Family 67
      Family Structure 73
R   Family of Origin 91
      Remarriage 85
      Stepchildren 73
      Stepparents 73

Stepparents 73
PN 295   SC 49730
B   Parents 67
R ↓ Family Structure 73
      Stepfamily 91

Stereopsis
Use Stereoscopic Vision

Stereoscopic Presentation 73
PN 92   SC 49750
SN Simultaneous presentation of separate two-dimensional pictures (taken from slightly different angles) to each eye of one subject, resulting in a perception of depth.

Stereoscopic Presentation — (cont'd)
B   Stimulus Presentation Methods 73
    Visual Stimulation 73

Stereoscopic Vision 73
PN 427   SC 49760
UF Stereopsis
B   Depth Perception 67
    Visual Perception 67

Stereotaxic Atlas 73
PN 192   SC 49770
UF Brain Mapping
    Brain Maps
R ↓ Stereotaxic Techniques 73

Stereotaxic Techniques 73
PN 117   SC 49780
SN Methods, procedures, or apparatus which permit precise spatial positioning of electrodes or other probes into the brain for experimental or surgical purposes.
B   Surgery 71
N ↓ Brain Stimulation 67
      Chemical Brain Stimulation 73
      Electrical Brain Stimulation 73
R   Afferent Stimulation 73
   ↓ Nervous System 67
      Stereotaxic Atlas 73

Stereotyped Attitudes 67
PN 3256   SC 49790
B   Attitudes 67
R   Age Discrimination 94
    Race and Ethnic Discrimination 94
   ↓ Racial and Ethnic Attitudes 82
    Sex Discrimination 78
   ↓ Sex Role Attitudes 78

Stereotyped Behavior 73
PN 1471   SC 49795
SN Behavior or response that is consistently elicited or determined by a particular situation or motive. The behavior varies little in its topography and is little altered by its outcome. Also used for behavioral patterns in a given society deemed appropriate for one group or another. Used for animal or human populations.
B   Behavior 67
R ↓ Animal Ethology 67
      Instinctive Behavior 82
      Rotational Behavior 94
      Sex Roles 67
      Social Norms 85
   ↓ Symptoms 67

Sterility 73
PN 38   SC 49810
B   Infertility 73
R ↓ Gynecological Disorders 73
      Hermaphroditism 73
   ↓ Hypogonadism 73
   ↓ Male Genital Disorders 73
      Testicular Feminization Syndrome 73
      Turners Syndrome 73
   ↓ Venereal Diseases 73

Sterilization (Sex) 73
PN 85   SC 49820
N ↓ Castration 67
      Hysterectomy 73
      Tubal Ligation 73
      Vasectomy 73
R ↓ Birth Control 71
      Eugenics 73
   ↓ Family Planning 73

Steroids 73
PN 325   SC 49830
B   Drugs 67
N   Cholesterol 73
   ↓ Corticosteroids 73
      Progesterone 73
R ↓ Anti Inflammatory Drugs 82
      Antiandrogens 82
      Antiestrogens 82
      Antineoplastic Drugs 82
   ↓ Hormones 67
   ↓ Lipids 73

Sticklebacks 73
PN 116   SC 49840
B   Fishes 67

Stigma 91
PN 111   SC 49843
SN Perception of a distinguishing personal characteristic or condition, e.g., a physical or psychological disorder, race, or religion, which carries or is believed to carry a physical, psychological, or social disadvantage.
UF Social Stigma
R ↓ Attitudes 67
      Labeling 78
   ↓ Prejudice 67
      Social Acceptance 67
      Social Approval 67
   ↓ Social Discrimination 82
   ↓ Social Perception 67

Stimulants of CNS
Use CNS Stimulating Drugs

Stimulation 67
PN 1063   SC 49850
N   Afferent Stimulation 73
    Aversive Stimulation 73
   ↓ Brain Stimulation 67
   ↓ Electrical Stimulation 73
   ↓ Perceptual Stimulation 73
   ↓ Self Stimulation 67
      Subliminal Stimulation 85
      Verbal Stimuli 82
R ↓ Biofeedback 73
      Conditioned Stimulus 73
   ↓ Conditioning 67
   ↓ Feedback 67
      Stimulus Ambiguity 67
      Stimulus Change 73
      Stimulus Control 67
   ↓ Stimulus Deprivation 73
      Stimulus Discrimination 73
      Stimulus Generalization 67
   ↓ Stimulus Parameters 67
   ↓ Stimulus Presentation Methods 73
      Unconditioned Stimulus 73

Stimulation Seeking (Personality)
Use Sensation Seeking

Stimulators (Apparatus) 73
PN 52   SC 49860
B   Apparatus 67
N   Shock Units 73
R   Electrodes 67
    Vibrators (Apparatus) 73

Stimulus (Unconditioned)
Use Unconditioned Stimulus

Stimulus Ambiguity 67
PN 588   SC 49890
UF Ambiguity (Stimulus)
R ↓ Stimulation 67

Stimulus Ambiguity — (cont'd)
R   Stimulus Generalization [67]
       Stroop Effect [88]

Stimulus Attenuation [73]
PN 65   SC 49900
SN Controlled, progressive, or otherwise manipulated reduction in the intensity, clarity, salience, or other such distinguishing qualities of a stimulus.
B   Stimulus Parameters [67]
R   Fading (Conditioning) [82]

Stimulus Change [73]
PN 321   SC 49910
R   ↓ Stimulation [67]

Stimulus Complexity [71]
PN 1365   SC 49920
UF Complexity (Stimulus)
B   Stimulus Parameters [67]

Stimulus Control [67]
PN 1216   SC 49930
SN Change in the probability of occurrence of a conditioned response as a direct function of the onset, offset, or changes in a conditioned stimulus.
R   ↓ Discrimination Learning [82]
    ↓ Stimulation [67]
    Stimulus Generalization [67]

Stimulus Deprivation [73]
PN 104   SC 49940
UF Restricted Environmental Stimulation
B   Deprivation [67]
N   Food Deprivation [67]
    Sensory Deprivation [67]
    ↓ Social Deprivation [73]
    ↓ Social Isolation [67]
    Water Deprivation [67]
R   ↓ Stimulation [67]

Stimulus Discrimination [73]
PN 1637   SC 49950
B   Discrimination [67]
R   Behavioral Contrast [78]
    ↓ Discrimination Learning [82]
    Fading (Conditioning) [82]
    ↓ Stimulation [67]
    Stimulus Generalization [67]

Stimulus Duration [73]
PN 1913   SC 49960
UF Duration (Stimulus)
    Exposure Time (Stimulus)
B   Stimulus Parameters [67]

Stimulus Frequency [73]
PN 912   SC 49980
SN Number of stimulus presentations within a given trial.
UF Frequency (Stimulus)
B   Stimulus Parameters [67]
R   Temporal Frequency [85]

Stimulus Generalization [67]
PN 663   SC 49990
SN Responding in a similar manner to different stimuli which have some common physical property. Also known as primary generalization. Compare GENERALIZATION (LEARNING).
UF Generalization (Stimulus)
B   Generalization (Learning) [82]
R   ↓ Stimulation [67]
    Stimulus Ambiguity [67]
    Stimulus Control [67]
    Stimulus Discrimination [73]

Stimulus Intensity [67]
PN 2565   SC 50000
UF Intensity (Stimulus)
    Signal Intensity
B   Stimulus Parameters [67]
R   Luminance [82]

Stimulus Intervals [73]
PN 946   SC 50010
SN Temporal intervals between stimuli presented in any sensory modality. Use INTERSTIMULUS INTERVAL in conditioning contexts.
B   Stimulus Parameters [67]
N   Interstimulus Interval [67]
    Intertrial Interval [73]
R   Reinforcement Delay [85]

Stimulus Novelty [73]
PN 1282   SC 50020
SN New, unexpected, or unfamiliar quality of a stimulus.
UF Novel Stimuli
B   Stimulus Parameters [67]
R   Neophobia [85]

Stimulus Offset [85]
PN 32   SC 50023
B   Stimulus Parameters [67]

Stimulus Onset [82]
PN 232   SC 50025
B   Stimulus Parameters [67]

Stimulus Parameters [67]
PN 4077   SC 50030
SN Applied when quantifiable or descriptive characteristics of stimuli in a study are emphasized. Use a more specific term if possible.
UF Parameters (Stimulus)
N   ↓ Size [73]
    Spatial Frequency [82]
    Stimulus Attenuation [73]
    Stimulus Complexity [71]
    Stimulus Duration [73]
    Stimulus Frequency [73]
    Stimulus Intensity [67]
    ↓ Stimulus Intervals [73]
    Stimulus Novelty [73]
    Stimulus Offset [85]
    Stimulus Onset [82]
    Stimulus Salience [73]
    Stimulus Similarity [67]
    Stimulus Variability [73]
    Temporal Frequency [85]
R   ↓ Stimulation [67]

Stimulus Pattern
Use Stimulus Variability

Stimulus Presentation Methods [73]
PN 2049   SC 50050
SN Methodological, procedural, or technical aspects of stimulus presentation. Use a more specific term if possible, e.g., VISUAL STIMULATION for visual stimulus presentation.
B   Experimental Methods [67]
N   Stereoscopic Presentation [73]
    Tachistoscopic Presentation [73]
R   Pictorial Stimuli [78]
    ↓ Stimulation [67]
    Verbal Stimuli [82]

Stimulus Salience [73]
PN 582   SC 50060
SN Relative prominence or distinctiveness of a stimulus.
UF Salience (Stimulus)
B   Stimulus Parameters [67]
R   Isolation Effect [73]

Stimulus Similarity [67]
PN 1722   SC 50070
SN Conceptual or physical resemblance of two or more stimuli.
UF Similarity (Stimulus)
B   Stimulus Parameters [67]

Stimulus Variability [73]
PN 1163   SC 50080
UF Stimulus Pattern
    Variability (Stimulus)
B   Stimulus Parameters [67]

Stipends
Use Educational Financial Assistance

Stochastic Modeling [73]
PN 325   SC 50100
SN Statistical modeling for sequences of events whose probabilities are constantly changing.
B   Simulation [67]
N   Markov Chains [73]
R   Information Theory [67]
    ↓ Mathematical Modeling [73]
    Time Series [85]

Stomach [73]
PN 112   SC 50120
B   Gastrointestinal System [73]

Storytelling [88]
PN 336   SC 50125
B   Verbal Communication [67]
R   Creative Writing [94]
    Folklore [91]
    Myths [67]

Storytelling Technique
Use Mutual Storytelling Technique

Strabismus [73]
PN 114   SC 50140
UF Crossed Eyes
B   Eye Disorders [73]
R   Amblyopia [73]
    Eye Convergence [82]

Strain Differences (Animal)
Use Animal Strain Differences

Stranger Reactions [88]
PN 112   SC 50148
SN Emotional or behavioral responses to unfamiliar persons. Used for all age groups.
UF Fear of Strangers
B   Interpersonal Interaction [67]
R   Attachment Behavior [85]
    ↓ Emotional Responses [67]
    Familiarity [67]
    ↓ Fear [67]
    Separation Anxiety [73]
    ↓ Social Perception [67]

Strategies [67]
PN 3463   SC 50150
SN Methods, techniques, or tactics used in accomplishing a given goal or task.
N   ↓ Learning Strategies [91]
R   ↓ Cognitive Processes [67]
    Guessing [73]
    ↓ Learning [67]
    Note Taking [91]

Strategies (Learning)
Use Learning Strategies

Strength (Physical)
　Use　Physical Strength

Stress [67]
PN　9950　　　　　　　　　　　　SC　50170
SN　Refers to the emotional, psychological, or physical effects as well as the sources of agitation, constraint, or annoyance. Compare DISTRESS.
　N　Environmental Stress [73]
　　　Occupational Stress [73]
　　　Physiological Stress [67]
　　　Psychological Stress [73]
　　　Social Stress [73]
　　　Stress Reactions [73]
　R　Adjustment Disorders [94]
　　　↓ Adrenal Cortex Hormones [73]
　　　↓ Anxiety [67]
　　　Caregiver Burden [94]
　　　↓ Crises [71]
　　　↓ Deprivation [67]
　　　↓ Disasters [73]
　　　Distress [73]
　　　↓ Endurance [73]
　　　Family Crises [73]
　　　Identity Crisis [73]
　　　Natural Disasters [73]
　　　Organizational Crises [73]
　　　Stress Management [85]

Stress Management [85]
PN　774　　　　　　　　　　　　SC　50175
SN　Techniques or services designed to alleviate the effects and/or causes of stress.
　B　Management [67]
　R　↓ Behavior Modification [73]
　　　↓ Cognitive Techniques [85]
　　　↓ Stress [67]
　　　↓ Treatment [67]

Stress Reactions [73]
PN　2937　　　　　　　　　　　　SC　50180
SN　Reactions to stressful events in everyday life or in experimental settings. Differentiate from POSTTRAUMATIC STRESS DISORDER which refers to reactions that seriously impair a person's functioning.
　UF　Crisis (Reactions to)
　B　Stress [67]
　R　Adjustment Disorders [94]
　　　Cardiovascular Reactivity [94]
　　　Coronary Prone Behavior [82]
　　　Posttraumatic Stress Disorder [85]
　　　Psychological Endurance [73]

Striate Cortex
　Use　Visual Cortex

Strikes [73]
PN　94　　　　　　　　　　　　SC　50190
　R　Labor Management Relations [67]

Stroboscopic Movement
　Use　Apparent Movement

Stroke (Cerebrum)
　Use　Cerebrovascular Accidents

Strong Vocational Interest Blank [67]
PN　206　　　　　　　　　　　　SC　50220
　B　Occupational Interest Measures [73]

Stroop Color Word Test [73]
PN　198　　　　　　　　　　　　SC　50250
　B　Perceptual Measures [73]
　R　Stroop Effect [88]

Stroop Effect [88]
PN　117　　　　　　　　　　　　SC　50255
SN　Interference in information or perceptual processing due to presentation of stimuli that are contradictory in different dimensions as a measure of cognitive control, e.g., stimulus word "red" printed in the color green.
　R　Cognitive Discrimination [73]
　　　↓ Interference (Learning) [67]
　　　↓ Perceptual Discrimination [73]
　　　Stimulus Ambiguity [67]
　　　Stroop Color Word Test [73]

Structural Equation Modeling [94]
PN　0　　　　　　　　　　　　SC　50257
　B　Mathematical Modeling [73]
　R　Causal Analysis [94]
　　　↓ Factor Analysis [67]
　　　Factor Structure [85]

Structuralism [73]
PN　105　　　　　　　　　　　　SC　50260
　B　History of Psychology [67]

Structured Overview
　Use　Advance Organizers

Strychnine [73]
PN　87　　　　　　　　　　　　SC　50270
　B　Alkaloids [73]
　　　Analeptic Drugs [73]

Student Activism [73] ^
PN　201　　　　　　　　　　　　SC　50280
　UF　Activism (Student)
　　　Protest (Student)
　　　Student Protest
　B　Activist Movements [73]
　R　Social Demonstrations [73]

Student Admission Criteria [73]
PN　562　　　　　　　　　　　　SC　50290
　UF　Admission Criteria (Student)
　R　Academic Aptitude [73]
　　　↓ Education [67]
　　　↓ Entrance Examinations [73]

Student Attitudes [67]
PN　10767　　　　　　　　　　　SC　50300
SN　Attitudes of, not toward, students.
　B　Attitudes [67]
　　　Student Characteristics [82]
　R　↓ Education [67]
　　　School Phobia [73]
　　　School Refusal [94]

Student Attrition [91]
PN　26　　　　　　　　　　　　SC　50301
SN　Reduction in students enrolled in school as a result of transfers or dropouts.
　B　School Enrollment [73]
　R　School Attendance [73]
　　　↓ School Dropouts [67]
　　　School Expulsion [73]
　　　School Leavers [88]
　　　School Retention [94]
　　　↓ Students [67]

Student Characteristics [82]
PN　2233　　　　　　　　　　　SC　50303
SN　Distinguishing traits or qualities of a student.
　N　Student Attitudes [67]
　R　↓ Education [67]
　　　↓ Students [67]

Student Personnel Services [78]
PN　988　　　　　　　　　　　　SC　50305

Student Personnel Services — (cont'd)
SN　Services offered by schools, colleges, or universities related to health, housing, employment, or other student concerns.
　R　↓ Counseling [67]
　　　↓ Education [67]
　　　Educational Counseling [67]
　　　Educational Financial Assistance [73]
　　　↓ Mental Health Services [78]
　　　Occupational Guidance [67]
　　　School Counseling [82]

Student Protest
　Use　Student Activism

Student Records [78]
PN　55　　　　　　　　　　　　SC　50315
　UF　Academic Records
　R　↓ Education [67]

Student Teachers [73]
PN　1062　　　　　　　　　　　SC　50320
SN　Students engaged in practice teaching under the supervision of a cooperating master teacher as partial fulfillment of an education degree.
　B　Teachers [67]
　R　Cooperating Teachers [78]
　　　Education Students [82]
　　　Preservice Teachers [82]

Student Teaching [73]
PN　210　　　　　　　　　　　　SC　50330
SN　College students teaching under the supervision of a regular teacher in a real school situation. Part of the graduation requirement for education majors.
　UF　Teaching Internship
　B　Teacher Education [67]
　R　Cooperating Teachers [78]

Students [67]
PN　4065　　　　　　　　　　　SC　50340
SN　Persons attending school. Application of a student term is mandatory in educational contexts. Use a more specific term if possible.
　N　Business Students [73]
　　　Classmates [73]
　　　↓ College Students [67]
　　　Dental Students [73]
　　　↓ Elementary School Students [67]
　　　Foreign Students [73]
　　　Graduate Students [67]
　　　High School Students [67]
　　　Junior High School Students [71]
　　　Kindergarten Students [73]
　　　Law Students [78]
　　　Medical Students [67]
　　　Postgraduate Students [73]
　　　↓ Preschool Students [82]
　　　Reentry Students [85]
　　　Seminarians [73]
　　　Special Education Students [73]
　　　Transfer Students [73]
　　　Vocational School Students [73]
　R　↓ Education [67]
　　　School Retention [94]
　　　Student Attrition [91]
　　　↓ Student Characteristics [82]

Students T Test
　Use　T Test

Studies (Followup)
　Use　Followup Studies

Studies (Longitudinal)
　Use　Longitudinal Studies

Study Habits [73]
PN 1286   SC 50380
   UF   Study Skills
   R   ↓ Education [67]
       Homework [88]
       ↓ Learning Strategies [91]
       Note Taking [91]
       Time Management [94]

Study Skills
   Use   Study Habits

Stuttering [67]
PN 1658   SC 50390
SN   Use STUTTERING or STAMMERING to access references from 67–81 and 73–81, respectively.
   UF   Stammering
   B   Speech Disorders [67]

Subconscious [73]
PN 62   SC 50410
   B   Psychoanalytic Personality Factors [73]

Subcortical Lesions
   Use   Brain Lesions

Subculture (Anthropological) [73]
PN 343   SC 50430
   UF   Hippies
   B   Culture (Anthropological) [67]

Subcutaneous Injections [73]
PN 24   SC 50440
   B   Injections [73]

Subjectivity [94]
PN 0   SC 50450
SN   Use OBJECTIVITY to access references from 73-93.
   B   Personality Traits [67]
   R   Objectivity [73]

Sublimation [73]
PN 47   SC 50460
   B   Defense Mechanisms [67]

Subliminal Perception [73]
PN 238   SC 50470
SN   Perceptual response to a stimulus that is below the threshold for conscious detection.
   B   Perception [67]
   R   Subliminal Stimulation [85]

Subliminal Stimulation [85]
PN 169   SC 50475
SN   Below-threshold stimulation.
   B   Stimulation [67]
   R   Subliminal Perception [73]

Submarines [73]
PN 18   SC 50480
   B   Water Transportation [73]

Submissiveness
   Use   Obedience

Submucous Plexus
   Use   Autonomic Ganglia

Substance Abuse
   Use   Drug Abuse

Substance Abuse Prevention
   Use   Drug Abuse Prevention

Substance P [85]
PN 131   SC 50527
   B   Neurotransmitters [85]
       Peptides [73]

Substantia Nigra [94]
PN 0   SC 50530
SN   Use MESENCEPHALON to access references from 73-93.
   B   Mesencephalon [73]
   R   ↓ Basal Ganglia [73]

Subtests [73]
PN 910   SC 50540
   B   Measurement [67]
   R   ↓ Testing Methods [67]

Suburban Environments [67]
PN 457   SC 50550
   B   Social Environments [73]

Subvocalization [73]
PN 81   SC 50555
SN   Covert speech behavior which involves movement of the tongue, mouth, and larynx without producing audible sounds.
   B   Vocalization [67]
   R   Self Talk [88]

Success
   Use   Achievement

Successive Contrast
   Use   Afterimage

Succinylcholine [73]
PN 11   SC 50580
   B   Muscle Relaxing Drugs [73]
   R   ↓ Choline [73]

Sucking [78]
PN 267   SC 50585
   B   Motor Processes [67]
   R   Animal Drinking Behavior [73]
       Animal Feeding Behavior [73]
       ↓ Drinking Behavior [78]
       ↓ Food Intake [67]
       Weaning [73]

Sudan [88]
PN 18   SC 50586
   B   Africa [67]

Sudden Infant Death [82]
PN 74   SC 50587
SN   Unexpected death of an apparently healthy infant during sleep.
   UF   Crib Death
   R   ↓ Apnea [73]
       ↓ Death and Dying [67]
       Sleep Apnea [91]
       ↓ Syndromes [73]

Suffering [73]
PN 177   SC 50590
   B   Emotional States [73]
   R   Distress [73]
       Grief [73]
       ↓ Pain [67]
       Torture [88]

Sugars [73]
PN 545   SC 50600
   B   Carbohydrates [73]
   N   ↓ Glucose [73]
   R   Saccharin [73]

Suggestibility [67]
PN 367   SC 50610
   B   Consciousness Disturbances [73]
       Personality Traits [67]
   R   Catalepsy [73]
       ↓ Hysteria [67]
       Posthypnotic Suggestions [94]

Suicidal Ideation [91]
PN 237   SC 50605
SN   Thoughts of or an unusual preoccupation with suicide.
   B   Ideation [73]
   R   Attempted Suicide [73]
       Suicide [67]

Suicide [67]
PN 4505   SC 50620
   B   Self Destructive Behavior [85]
   R   Attempted Suicide [73]
       ↓ Death and Dying [67]
       ↓ Mental Disorders [67]
       Psychological Autopsy [88]
       Suicidal Ideation [91]
       Suicide Prevention [73]

Suicide (Attempted)
   Use   Attempted Suicide

Suicide Prevention [73]
PN 533   SC 50640
   B   Crisis Intervention [73]
       Prevention [73]
   R   Attempted Suicide [73]
       Suicide [67]
       Suicide Prevention Centers [73]

Suicide Prevention Centers [73]
PN 70   SC 50650
   B   Community Facilities [73]
       Crisis Intervention Services [73]
       Mental Health Programs [73]
   R   Community Mental Health Centers [73]
       Hot Line Services [73]
       ↓ Prevention [73]
       Suicide Prevention [73]

Sulpiride [73]
PN 254   SC 50660
   B   Antidepressant Drugs [71]
       Antiemetic Drugs [73]
       Dopamine Antagonists [82]
       Neuroleptic Drugs [73]

Summer Camps (Recreation) [73]
PN 102   SC 50670
   UF   Day Camps (Recreation)
       Recreational Day Camps
   B   Recreation [67]
   R   Camping [73]
       Vacationing [73]

Superego [73]
PN 206   SC 50690
   B   Psychoanalytic Personality Factors [73]
   N   Conscience [67]

Superintendents (School)
   Use   School Superintendents

Superior Colliculus [73]
PN 426   SC 50700
   B   Mesencephalon [73]

Superiority (Emotional)
   Use   Emotional Superiority

Superstitions [73]
PN 113   SC 50720
  B   Social Influences [67]
  R   Astrology [73]
     ↓ Attitudes [67]
       Irrational Beliefs [82]
     ↓ Religious Beliefs [73]
       Taboos [73]

Supervising Teachers
  Use   Cooperating Teachers

Supervision (Professional)
  Use   Professional Supervision

Supervisors
  Use   Management Personnel

Support Groups [91]
PN 250   SC 50740
SN   Groups, organizations, or institutions providing social and emotional support to an individual. Consider SOCIAL SUPPORT NETWORKS to access references from 82-90. Compare SOCIAL NETWORKS.
  N   Alcoholics Anonymous [73]
  R   ↓ Community Services [67]
     ↓ Counseling [67]
       Employee Assistance Programs [85]
       Group Counseling [73]
     ↓ Group Psychotherapy [67]
     ↓ Mental Health Services [78]
     ↓ Rehabilitation [67]
     ↓ Self Help Techniques [82]
     ↓ Social Networks [94]
     ↓ Social Services [82]
       Social Support Networks [82]

Supported Employment [94]
PN 0   SC 50745
SN   Competitive employment in an integrated setting for persons with disabilities who require ongoing support to perform their jobs.
  B   Vocational Rehabilitation [67]
  R   Employability [73]
     ↓ Employee Skills [73]
     ↓ Employment Status [82]
     ↓ Personnel Management [73]
       Sheltered Workshops [67]
       Work Adjustment Training [91]

Supportive Psychotherapy
  Use   Psychotherapy

Suppression (Conditioned)
  Use   Conditioned Suppression

Suppression (Defense Mechanism) [73]
PN 32   SC 50770
  B   Defense Mechanisms [67]
  R   Forgetting [73]
       Repression (Defense Mechanism) [67]

Surgeons [73]
PN 71   SC 50780
  UF   Neurosurgeons
  B   Physicians [67]
  R   Gynecologists [73]
       Neurologists [73]
       Obstetricians [78]
       Pathologists [73]

Surgery [71]
PN 1233   SC 50790
  UF   Circumcision
       Operation (Surgery)
  B   Medical Sciences [67]
       Physical Treatment Methods [73]

Surgery — (cont'd)
  N   ↓ Amputation [73]
       Cochlear Implants [94]
       Colostomy [73]
       Dental Surgery [73]
     ↓ Endocrine Gland Surgery [73]
       Heart Surgery [73]
       Hysterectomy [73]
       Induced Abortion [71]
     ↓ Neurosurgery [73]
       Organ Transplantation [73]
       Plastic Surgery [73]
       Sex Change [88]
     ↓ Stereotaxic Techniques [73]
       Vasectomy [73]
  R   Afferent Stimulation [73]
       Biopsy [73]
     ↓ Body Image Disturbances [73]
     ↓ Lesions [67]
       Postsurgical Complications [73]

Surgical Complications
  Use   Postsurgical Complications

Surgical Patients [73]
PN 1009   SC 50810
  B   Patients [67]

Surinam [91]
PN 1   SC 50815
  B   South America [67]

Surrogate Parents (Humans) [73]
PN 77   SC 50820
  B   Parents [67]
  R   Foster Parents [73]

Surveys [67]
PN 1471   SC 50830
  B   Measurement [67]
  N   Consumer Surveys [73]
       Mail Surveys [94]
       Telephone Surveys [94]
  R   Data Collection [82]
       Likert Scales [94]
     ↓ Methodology [67]
       Needs Assessment [85]
     ↓ Questionnaires [67]

Survivors [94]
PN 0   SC 50850
SN   Family members, significant others, or individuals surviving traumatic life events. Not used as a general population type identifier.
  N   Holocaust Survivors [88]

Susceptibility (Disorders) [73]
PN 565   SC 50880
SN   Vulnerability to mental or physical disorders due to genetic, immunologic, or other characteristics. Consider also PREDISPOSITION.
  R   At Risk Populations [85]
       Coronary Prone Behavior [82]
     ↓ Disorders [67]
     ↓ Mental Disorders [67]
       Predisposition [73]
       Premorbidity [78]

Susceptibility (Hypnotic)
  Use   Hypnotic Susceptibility

Suspension (School)
  Use   School Suspension

Suspicion [73]
PN 71   SC 50910
  UF   Distrust
  B   Emotional States [73]

Suspicion — (cont'd)
  R   Doubt [73]
       Uncertainty [91]

Swallowing [88]
PN 39   SC 50920
  B   Motor Processes [67]
  R   Digestion [73]

Swaziland [91]
PN 2   SC 50925
  B   Africa [67]

Sweat [73]
PN 26   SC 50930
  UF   Perspiration
  B   Body Fluids [73]
  R   Sweating [73]

Sweating [73]
PN 46   SC 50940
  B   Secretion (Gland) [73]
  R   ↓ Skin Disorders [73]
       Sweat [73]

Sweden [73]
PN 897   SC 50950
  B   Scandinavia [78]

Sweetness
  Use   Taste Perception

Swimming [73]
PN 429   SC 50970
  B   Motor Processes [67]
       Recreation [67]
       Sports [67]

Switzerland [73]
PN 223   SC 50980
  B   Europe [73]

Syllables [73]
PN 502   SC 50990
  B   Phonology [73]
  R   Consonants [73]
       Phonetics [67]
       Vowels [73]

Syllogistic Reasoning
  Use   Inductive Deductive Reasoning

Symbiosis (Biological)
  Use   Biological Symbiosis

Symbiotic Infantile Psychosis [73]
PN 16   SC 51020
  B   Childhood Psychosis [67]
  R   Childhood Schizophrenia [67]
       Early Infantile Autism [73]
       Mother Child Relations [67]

Symbolic Interactionism [88]
PN 55   SC 51025
SN   Sociological theory that assumes that self concept is created through interpretation of symbolic gestures, words, actions, and appearances expressed by others during social interaction.
  R   Role Taking [82]
     ↓ Self Concept [67]
     ↓ Social Interaction [67]
       Sociolinguistics [85]
     ↓ Sociology [67]

Symbolism [67]
PN 1506   SC 51030

Symbolism — (cont'd)
R   ↓ Communication ⁶⁷
    ↓ Figurative Language ⁸⁵
    ↓ Language ⁶⁷
    Metaphor ⁸²
    ↓ Semiotics ⁸⁵

Sympathectomy ⁷³
PN 34   SC 51050
B   Neurosurgery ⁷³
R   ↓ Psychosurgery ⁷³

Sympathetic Nervous System ⁷³
PN 186   SC 51060
B   Autonomic Nervous System ⁶⁷
N   Baroreceptors ⁷³
R   ↓ Adrenergic Blocking Drugs ⁷³
    ↓ Adrenergic Drugs ⁷³
    ↓ Adrenolytic Drugs ⁷³
    ↓ Sympatholytic Drugs ⁷³
    ↓ Sympathomimetic Drugs ⁷³

Sympatholytic Drugs ⁷³
PN 21   SC 51080
B   Drugs ⁶⁷
N   Hydralazine ⁷³
    Reserpine ⁶⁷
R   ↓ Adrenergic Blocking Drugs ⁷³
    ↓ Adrenolytic Drugs ⁷³
    ↓ Sympathetic Nervous System ⁷³
    ↓ Sympathomimetic Drugs ⁷³

Sympathomimetic Amines ⁷³
PN 9   SC 51090
B   Amines ⁷³
    Sympathomimetic Drugs ⁷³
N   ↓ Amphetamine ⁶⁷
    ↓ Catecholamines ⁷³
    Dextroamphetamine ⁷³
    Ephedrine ⁷³
    Methoxamine ⁷³
    Phenmetrazine ⁷³
    Tyramine ⁷³

Sympathomimetic Drugs ⁷³
PN 85   SC 51100
B   Drugs ⁶⁷
N   Fenfluramine ⁷³
    Isoproterenol ⁷³
    ↓ Sympathomimetic Amines ⁷³
R   ↓ Adrenergic Drugs ⁷³
    Cardiotonic Drugs ⁸⁵
    Prostaglandins ⁸²
    ↓ Sympathetic Nervous System ⁷³
    ↓ Sympatholytic Drugs ⁷³

Sympathy ⁷³
PN 62   SC 51110
B   Emotional States ⁷³

Symposia
Use Professional Meetings and Symposia

Symptom Checklists ⁹¹
PN 53   SC 51124
B   Measurement ⁶⁷
R   ↓ Diagnosis ⁶⁷
    ↓ Screening ⁸²
    ↓ Symptoms ⁶⁷

Symptom Prescription
Use Paradoxical Techniques

Symptom Remission ⁷³
PN 48   SC 51130
B   Remission (Disorders) ⁷³
R   ↓ Symptoms ⁶⁷

Symptoms ⁶⁷
PN 8095   SC 51140
N   Acting Out ⁶⁷
    Anhedonia ⁸⁵
    Anoxia ⁷³
    Aphagia ⁷³
    ↓ Appetite Disorders ⁷³
    Apraxia ⁷³
    ↓ Asthenia ⁷³
    Ataxia ⁷³
    Aura ⁷³
    Automatism ⁷³
    Body Rocking ⁷³
    Catalepsy ⁷³
    Catatonia ⁷³
    Coma ⁷³
    ↓ Convulsions ⁶⁷
    Delirium ⁷³
    Depersonalization ⁷³
    Distractibility ⁷³
    ↓ Dyskinesia ⁷³
    ↓ Dyspnea ⁷³
    Extrapyramidal Symptoms ⁹⁴
    Fatigue ⁶⁷
    ↓ Headache ⁷³
    Hematoma ⁷³
    ↓ Hemorrhage ⁷³
    Hyperglycemia ⁸⁵
    Hyperkinesis ⁷³
    Hyperphagia ⁷³
    Hyperthermia ⁷³
    Hyperventilation ⁷³
    Hypoglycemia ⁷³
    Hypothermia ⁷³
    Insomnia ⁷³
    Nausea ⁷³
    Obesity ⁷³
    ↓ Pain ⁶⁷
    Pruritus ⁷³
    ↓ Respiratory Distress ⁷³
    Restlessness ⁷³
    Scratching ⁷³
    Shock ⁶⁷
    ↓ Spasms ⁷³
    Syncope ⁷³
    Tics ⁷³
    Tremor ⁷³
    ↓ Underweight ⁷³
    Vertigo ⁷³
    Vomiting ⁷³
R   Akathisia ⁹¹
    ↓ Behavior Disorders ⁷¹
    Binge Eating ⁹¹
    Capgras Syndrome ⁸⁵
    ↓ Digestive System Disorders ⁷³
    ↓ Disorders ⁶⁷
    Fecal Incontinence ⁷³
    Frigidity ⁷³
    Hypersomnia ⁹⁴
    ↓ Mental Disorders ⁶⁷
    ↓ Movement Disorders ⁸⁵
    ↓ Nervous System Disorders ⁶⁷
    Parkinsonism ⁹⁴
    Physiological Correlates ⁶⁷
    ↓ Psychosomatic Disorders ⁶⁷
    Somatization ⁹⁴
    Stereotyped Behavior ⁷³
    Symptom Checklists ⁹¹
    Symptom Remission ⁷³
    Urinary Incontinence ⁷³
    Wandering Behavior ⁹¹

Synapses ⁷³
PN 558   SC 51150
B   Nerve Endings ⁷³

Syncope ⁷³
PN 48   SC 51160

Syncope — (cont'd)
UF   Fainting
B   Blood Pressure Disorders ⁷³
    Symptoms ⁶⁷
R   Shock ⁶⁷
    Vertigo ⁷³

Syndromes ⁷³
PN 1631   SC 51170
N   Acquired Immune Deficiency
       Syndrome ⁸⁸
    Addisons Disease ⁷³
    Aspergers Syndrome ⁹¹
    Battered Child Syndrome ⁷³
    Capgras Syndrome ⁸⁵
    Creutzfeldt Jakob Syndrome ⁹⁴
    Crying Cat Syndrome ⁷³
    Cushings Syndrome ⁷³
    Delirium Tremens ⁷³
    Downs Syndrome ⁶⁷
    Fetal Alcohol Syndrome ⁸⁵
    Fragile X Syndrome ⁹⁴
    Klinefelters Syndrome ⁷³
    Menieres Disease ⁷³
    Neuroleptic Malignant Syndrome ⁸⁸
    ↓ Organic Brain Syndromes ⁷³
    Prader Willi Syndrome ⁹¹
    Rett Syndrome ⁹⁴
    ↓ Senile Dementia ⁷³
    Testicular Feminization Syndrome ⁷³
    Turners Syndrome ⁷³
    Wernickes Syndrome ⁷³
R   ↓ Disorders ⁶⁷
    Irritable Bowel Syndrome ⁹¹
    Myofascial Pain ⁹¹
    Sudden Infant Death ⁸²

Synonyms ⁷³
PN 90   SC 51190
B   Semantics ⁶⁷
    Vocabulary ⁶⁷
R   Words (Phonetic Units) ⁶⁷

Syntax ⁷¹
PN 1820   SC 51220
SN   Study and rules of the relation of mor-
phemes to one another as expressions of ideas
and as structural components of sentences; the
study and science of sentence construction; and,
the actual grouping and specific combination and
relationship of words in a sentence. Compare
GRAMMAR and SENTENCE STRUCTURE.
B   Grammar ⁶⁷
N   ↓ Form Classes (Language) ⁷³
R   Inflection ⁷³
    Morphology (Language) ⁷³
    ↓ Phonology ⁷³
    Phrases ⁷³
    ↓ Semantics ⁶⁷
    Sentence Structure ⁷³
    Transformational Generative Grammar ⁷³

Synthetic Speech ⁷³
PN 240   SC 51230
SN   Sounds having similar characteristics and
functional properties of natural speech but which
are made by means other than natural vocalization mechanisms (e.g., computer-generated
speech sounds).
B   Speech Processing (Mechanical) ⁷³

Syphilis ⁷³
PN 29   SC 51240
B   Venereal Diseases ⁷³
N   Neurosyphilis ⁷³
R   ↓ Congenital Disorders ⁷³
    General Paresis ⁷³

Syria [88]
PN 2　　　　　　　　　　　　　　SC 51245
　B　Asia [73]
　R　Middle East [78]

Systematic Desensitization Therapy [73]
PN 1439　　　　　　　　　　　　SC 51250
　UF　Desensitization (Systematic)
　B　Behavior Therapy [67]
　R　Progressive Relaxation Therapy [78]
　　Reciprocal Inhibition Therapy [73]
　　↓ Relaxation Therapy [78]

Systems [67]
PN 546　　　　　　　　　　　　SC 51270
SN　Conceptually broad array term referring to interrelated elements acting as or constituting a unified whole. Use a more specific term if possible.
　N　↓ Anatomical Systems [73]
　　Caste System [73]
　　↓ Communication Systems [73]
　　Expert Systems [91]
　　Information Systems [91]
　　Man Machine Systems [73]
　　Number Systems [73]
　　↓ Political Economic Systems [73]
　R　↓ Computer Software [67]
　　↓ Computers [67]
　　Man Machine Systems Design [73]
　　Person Environment Fit [91]
　　Systems Analysis [73]
　　Systems Theory [88]

Systems Analysis [73]
PN 426　　　　　　　　　　　　SC 51260
　B　Analysis [67]
　R　Computer Programing [94]
　　Man Machine Systems [73]
　　↓ Systems [67]
　　Systems Theory [88]
　　Task Analysis [67]

Systems Theory [88]
PN 998　　　　　　　　　　　　SC 51265
SN　Examination of organizations, structures, or procedures from a macroscopic perspective that integrates constituent parts into a whole.
　B　Theories [67]
　R　Biopsychosocial Approach [91]
　　↓ Systems [67]
　　Systems Analysis [73]

Systolic Pressure [73]
PN 219　　　　　　　　　　　　SC 51280
　B　Blood Pressure [67]

Szondi Test [73]
PN 29　　　　　　　　　　　　SC 51290
　B　Projective Personality Measures [73]

T Groups
　Use　Human Relations Training

T Mazes [73]
PN 40　　　　　　　　　　　　SC 51310
　B　Mazes [67]

T Test [73]
PN 72　　　　　　　　　　　　SC 51320
　UF　Students T Test
　B　Parametric Statistical Tests [73]
　R　↓ Central Tendency Measures [73]
　　Statistical Significance [73]

Taboos [73]
PN 96　　　　　　　　　　　　SC 51330

Taboos — (cont'd)
　B　Social Influences [67]
　R　Animism [73]
　　Ethnology [67]
　　↓ Rites of Passage [73]
　　Superstitions [73]
　　Transcultural Psychiatry [73]

Tachistoscopes [73]
PN 39　　　　　　　　　　　　SC 51340
SN　Apparatus used in experimental studies for presentation of visual stimuli for controlled stimulus intervals, intensities, and durations.
　B　Apparatus [67]

Tachistoscopic Presentation [73]
PN 406　　　　　　　　　　　　SC 51350
　B　Stimulus Presentation Methods [73]
　　Visual Stimulation [73]

Tachycardia [73]
PN 56　　　　　　　　　　　　SC 51360
　B　Arrhythmias (Heart) [73]
　R　Hyperthyroidism [73]

Tactual Discrimination
　Use　Tactual Perception

Tactual Displays [73]
PN 76　　　　　　　　　　　　SC 51380
SN　Materials or apparatus designed to present information or patterns by means of touch or manipulation. Also, any information or patterns conveyed by such means.
　B　Displays [67]
　　Tactual Stimulation [73]

Tactual Maps
　Use　Mobility Aids

Tactual Perception [67]
PN 1396　　　　　　　　　　　SC 51390
SN　Awareness of the qualities or characteristics of objects, substances, or surfaces by means of touch.
　UF　Tactual Discrimination
　　Touch
　B　Cutaneous Sense [67]
　N　Texture Perception [82]
　　Vibrotactile Thresholds [73]
　R　↓ Anesthesia (Feeling) [73]
　　Braille [78]

Tactual Stimulation [73]
PN 899　　　　　　　　　　　　SC 51400
SN　Perceptual arousal or excitation of an organism by means of touch.
　B　Somesthetic Stimulation [73]
　N　Tactual Displays [73]

Tailored Testing
　Use　Adaptive Testing

Taiwan [73]
PN 414　　　　　　　　　　　　SC 51410
　B　Asia [73]

Talent
　Use　Ability

Talented
　Use　Gifted

Tantrums [73]
PN 41　　　　　　　　　　　　SC 51440

Tantrums — (cont'd)
　B　Behavior Problems [67]
　R　↓ Anger [67]
　　Emotional Control [73]

Tanzania [82]
PN 28　　　　　　　　　　　　SC 51445
　B　Africa [67]

Tape Recorders [73]
PN 73　　　　　　　　　　　　SC 51450
　UF　Recorders (Tape)
　B　Apparatus [67]
　N　Videotape Recorders [73]

Tardive Dyskinesia [88]
PN 407　　　　　　　　　　　　SC 51460
　B　Dyskinesia [73]
　R　↓ Drug Therapy [67]
　　↓ Neuroleptic Drugs [73]
　　↓ Side Effects (Drug) [73]

Task Analysis [67]
PN 1054　　　　　　　　　　　SC 51470
　B　Analysis [67]
　R　Job Analysis [67]
　　Systems Analysis [73]
　　Task Complexity [73]

Task Complexity [73]
PN 2715　　　　　　　　　　　SC 51480
　UF　Complexity (Task)
　　Task Difficulty
　R　Task Analysis [67]

Task Difficulty
　Use　Task Complexity

Taste Aversion Conditioning
　Use　Aversion Conditioning

Taste Buds [73]
PN 139　　　　　　　　　　　　SC 51500
　B　Sense Organs [73]
　　Sensory Neurons [73]
　　Tongue [73]
　R　Chemoreceptors [73]

Taste Discrimination
　Use　Taste Perception

Taste Perception [67]
PN 2250　　　　　　　　　　　SC 51520
　UF　Bitterness
　　Gustatory Perception
　　Saltiness
　　Sourness
　　Sweetness
　　Taste Discrimination
　B　Perception [67]
　R　↓ Olfactory Perception [67]

Taste Stimulation [67]
PN 664　　　　　　　　　　　　SC 51530
　B　Perceptual Stimulation [73]

Taurine [82]
PN 25　　　　　　　　　　　　SC 51545
SN　Suspected neurotransmitter or membrane stabilizer located in the posterior pituitary gland as well as other mammalian tissue.
　B　Acids [73]
　R　Bile [73]

Taxation [85]
PN 67　　　　　　　　　　　　SC 51547

Taxation — (cont'd)
R   Economy [73]
     Government [67]
     Income (Economic) [73]

Taxonomies [73]
PN   1839   SC   51550
UF   Classification Systems
     Typologies (General)

Tay Sachs Disease
Use   Amaurotic Familial Idiocy

Taylor Manifest Anxiety Scale [73]
PN   20   SC   51570
SN   Use MA SCALE (TEST) to access refer-
ences from 67–72.
B   Nonprojective Personality Measures [73]

Tea
Use   Beverages (Nonalcoholic)

Teacher Accreditation
Use   Accreditation (Education Personnel)

Teacher Aides [73]
PN   104   SC   51600
SN   Paraprofessional school personnel who as-
sist teachers in the instructional process or other
classroom duties.
B   Educational Personnel [73]
     Paraprofessional Personnel [73]

Teacher Attitudes [67]
PN   6912   SC   51610
SN   Attitudes of, not toward, teachers.
B   Attitudes [67]
     Teacher Characteristics [73]
R   Parent School Relationship [82]
     Teacher Expectations [78]
     Teacher Personality [73]
     Teacher Student Interaction [73]

Teacher Characteristics [73]
PN   3426   SC   51615
UF   Teacher Effectiveness
N   Teacher Attitudes [67]
     Teacher Personality [73]
R   ↓ Education [67]
     Teacher Effectiveness Evaluation [78]
     Teacher Expectations [78]
     Teacher Student Interaction [73]
     ↓ Teachers [67]
     ↓ Teaching [67]

Teacher Education [67]
PN   3014   SC   51620
UF   Teacher Training
B   Education [67]
N   Inservice Teacher Education [73]
     Student Teaching [73]
R   Cooperating Teachers [78]
     Education Students [82]
     Practicum Supervision [78]
     Preservice Teachers [82]

Teacher Effectiveness
Use   Teacher Characteristics

Teacher Effectiveness Evaluation [78]
PN   1086   SC   51625
SN   Techniques, materials, or the procedural as-
pects of judging teachers' performance by peers,
students, or others based on stated criteria. Use
PERSONNEL EVALUATION and TEACHERS (or
a more specific term, e.g., COLLEGE TEACH-
ERS) to access references from 73–77.

Teacher Effectiveness Evaluation —
     (cont'd)
B   Personnel Evaluation [73]
R   Course Evaluation [78]
     ↓ Teacher Characteristics [73]

Teacher Expectations [78]
PN   590   SC   51627
B   Expectations [67]
R   Teacher Attitudes [67]
     ↓ Teacher Characteristics [73]
     Teacher Student Interaction [73]

Teacher Personality [73]
PN   458   SC   51630
B   Teacher Characteristics [73]
R   ↓ Personality [67]
     Teacher Attitudes [67]
     Teacher Student Interaction [73]

Teacher Recruitment [73]
PN   23   SC   51640
SN   Process of attracting candidates to the
teaching profession or finding teachers to fill va-
cancies.
UF   Recruitment (Teachers)
B   Personnel Recruitment [73]

Teacher Student Interaction [73]
PN   3245   SC   51650
R   Classroom Discipline [73]
     ↓ Education [67]
     Teacher Attitudes [67]
     ↓ Teacher Characteristics [73]
     Teacher Expectations [78]
     Teacher Personality [73]

Teacher Tenure [73]
PN   82   SC   51670
UF   Tenure (Teacher)
B   Occupational Tenure [73]
R   ↓ Education [67]

Teacher Training
Use   Teacher Education

Teachers [67]
PN   5489   SC   51690
UF   Classroom Teachers
     Instructors
     Tutors
B   Educational Personnel [73]
N   College Teachers [73]
     Cooperating Teachers [78]
     Elementary School Teachers [73]
     High School Teachers [73]
     Junior High School Teachers [73]
     Preschool Teachers [85]
     Preservice Teachers [82]
     Resource Teachers [73]
     Special Education Teachers [73]
     Student Teachers [73]
     Vocational Education Teachers [88]
R   ↓ Teacher Characteristics [73]

Teaching [67]
PN   2522   SC   51700
UF   Classroom Instruction
     Instruction
N   ↓ Instructional Media [67]
     ↓ Teaching Methods [67]
R   Bilingual Education [78]
     Cooperative Learning [94]
     Course Evaluation [78]
     ↓ Education [67]
     Questioning [82]
     ↓ Teacher Characteristics [73]

Teaching Internship
Use   Student Teaching

Teaching Machines [73]
PN   40   SC   51730
SN   Mechanical, electronic, or electrically con-
trolled apparatus for the presentation of pro-
gramed instructional material or texts for inde-
pendent, self-paced education. Compare COM-
PUTER ASSISTED INSTRUCTION.
B   Instructional Media [67]
R   Computer Assisted Instruction [73]
     Programed Instruction [67]

Teaching Methods [67]
PN   12845   SC   51740
B   Teaching [67]
N   Advance Organizers [85]
     ↓ Audiovisual Instruction [73]
     Computer Assisted Instruction [73]
     Curricular Field Experience [82]
     Directed Discussion Method [73]
     Discovery Teaching Method [73]
     Educational Field Trips [73]
     Group Instruction [73]
     Individualized Instruction [73]
     Lecture Method [73]
     Lesson Plans [73]
     Montessori Method [73]
     Nondirected Discussion Method [73]
     Open Classroom Method [73]
     Programed Instruction [67]
     Team Teaching Method [73]
     ↓ Tutoring [73]
R   Cooperative Learning [94]
     ↓ Education [67]
     Home Schooling [94]
     Initial Teaching Alphabet [73]
     Mastery Learning [85]
     ↓ Nontraditional Education [82]

Team Teaching Method [73]
PN   87   SC   51750
B   Teaching Methods [67]
R   Open Classroom Method [73]
     Teams [88]

Teams [88]
PN   349   SC   51751
R   Athletic Performance [91]
     Athletic Training [91]
     College Athletes [94]
     Cooperative Learning [94]
     ↓ Group Dynamics [67]
     Interdisciplinary Treatment Approach [73]
     ↓ Management Methods [73]
     ↓ Personnel [67]
     ↓ Sports [67]
     Team Teaching Method [73]

Technical Education Teachers
Use   Vocational Education Teachers

Technical Personnel [78]
PN   281   SC   51755
B   Business and Industrial Personnel [67]
N   Technical Service Personnel [73]
R   ↓ Service Personnel [91]

Technical Schools [73]
PN   137   SC   51760
SN   Schools that teach specific job skills, usually
at the postsecondary level, often emphasizing
underlying sciences and supporting mathematics
as well as skills, methods, materials, and processes of a specialized field of technology.
UF   Vocational Schools
B   Schools [67]

Technical Service Personnel [73]
PN 108   SC 51770
- UF Repairmen
- B Service Personnel [91]
     Technical Personnel [78]
- R ↓ Blue Collar Workers [73]
   ↓ Business and Industrial Personnel [67]
   ↓ Nonprofessional Personnel [82]

Technology [73]
PN 1097   SC 51805
- N Nuclear Technology [85]
- R Industrialization [73]
   ↓ Sciences [67]

Teenage Fathers
Use Adolescent Fathers

Teenage Mothers
Use Adolescent Mothers

Teenage Pregnancy
Use Adolescent Pregnancy

Teenagers
Use Adolescents

Teeth (Anatomy) [73]
PN 151   SC 51820
- B Digestive System [67]
- R Mouth (Anatomy) [67]

Teeth Grinding
Use Bruxism

Tegmentum [91]
PN 52   SC 51835
- UF Ventral Tegmental Area
- B Mesencephalon [73]
- N Periaqueductal Gray [85]

Telecommunications Media [73]
PN 121   SC 51840
- B Communications Media [73]
- N Radio [73]
     Telephone Systems [73]
   ↓ Television [67]
     Television Advertising [73]
- R Telemetry [73]

Telekinesis
Use Psychokinesis

Telemetry [73]
PN 37   SC 51860
SN Process of measuring and transmitting quantitative information and recording at a remote location.
- R ↓ Telecommunications Media [73]

Telencephalon [73]
PN 284   SC 51870
- B Forebrain [85]
- N ↓ Basal Ganglia [73]
   ↓ Cerebral Cortex [67]

Telepathy [73]
PN 83   SC 51880
- B Parapsychological Phenomena [73]
- R ↓ Extrasensory Perception [67]

Telephone Hot Lines
Use Hot Line Services

Telephone Surveys [94]
PN 0   SC 51895

Telephone Surveys — (cont'd)
- B Surveys [67]
- R ↓ Consumer Research [73]
     Consumer Surveys [73]
     Mail Surveys [94]
   ↓ Methodology [67]
   ↓ Questionnaires [67]
     Telephone Systems [73]

Telephone Systems [73]
PN 410   SC 51900
- B Communication Systems [73]
     Telecommunications Media [73]
- R Telephone Surveys [94]

Televised Instruction [73]
PN 151   SC 51910
- B Audiovisual Instruction [73]
- R ↓ Educational Audiovisual Aids [73]
     Educational Television [67]

Television [67]
PN 1184   SC 51920
- B Audiovisual Communications Media [73]
     Mass Media [67]
     Telecommunications Media [73]
- N Closed Circuit Television [73]
     Educational Television [67]
     Television Advertising [73]
- R ↓ Apparatus [67]
     Video Display Units [85]

Television Advertising [73]
PN 459   SC 51930
- B Advertising [67]
     Audiovisual Communications Media [73]
     Telecommunications Media [73]
     Television [67]

Television Viewing [73]
PN 1278   SC 51940
- B Recreation [67]

Temperament
Use Personality

Temperature (Body)
Use Body Temperature

Temperature Effects [67]
PN 1059   SC 51990
- UF Thermal Factors
- B Environmental Effects [73]
- N Cold Effects [73]
     Heat Effects [73]
- R Atmospheric Conditions [73]
     Pollution [73]
     Seasonal Variations [73]
     Thermal Acclimatization [73]

Temperature Perception [73]
PN 272   SC 52000
- B Somesthetic Perception [67]

Temporal Frequency [85]
PN 240   SC 52015
SN Number of alternating cycles (e.g., patterns of vertical stripes of light and dark light) occurring during a specified time interval. Usually expressed in terms of cycles per second (Hz) as, for example, in sine or square wave visual displays.
- B Stimulus Parameters [67]
- R Spatial Frequency [82]
     Stimulus Frequency [73]
   ↓ Visual Displays [73]
   ↓ Visual Stimulation [73]

Temporal Lobe [73]
PN 862   SC 52010
- B Cerebral Cortex [67]
- N Auditory Cortex [67]

Temporal Spatial Concept Scale [73]
PN 1   SC 52020
- B Intelligence Measures [67]

Temporomandibular Joint Syndrome
Use Musculoskeletal Disorders

Temptation [73]
PN 89   SC 52030
- B Motivation [67]
- R ↓ Incentives [67]

Tendons [73]
PN 6   SC 52050
- B Musculoskeletal System [73]

Tennessee Self Concept Scale [73]
PN 44   SC 52060
- B Nonprojective Personality Measures [73]

Tennis [73]
PN 120   SC 52070
- B Recreation [67]
     Sports [67]

Tension Headache
Use Muscle Contraction Headache

Tenure (Occupational)
Use Occupational Tenure

Tenure (Teacher)
Use Teacher Tenure

Teratogens [88]
PN 147   SC 52105
SN Drugs or other agents that cause developmental malformations.
- B Hazardous Materials [91]
- R ↓ Congenital Disorders [73]
   ↓ Drugs [67]
   ↓ Poisons [73]
   ↓ Prenatal Development [73]
     Prenatal Exposure [91]
     Thalidomide [73]
     Toxicity [73]

Terminal Cancer [73]
PN 228   SC 52110
- B Neoplasms [67]
- R ↓ Death and Dying [67]
     Terminally Ill Patients [73]

Terminally Ill Patients [73]
PN 915   SC 52120
- UF Dying Patients
- B Patients [67]
- R Advance Directives [94]
   ↓ Death and Dying [67]
     Hospice [82]
     Palliative Care [91]
     Terminal Cancer [73]

Terminology [91]
PN 91   SC 52125
SN Definitions, analysis, evaluation, or review of individual terms or nomenclature in any field.
- N Psychological Terminology [73]
- R Concepts [67]
   ↓ Scientific Communication [73]

Terminology (Psychological)
  Use Psychological Terminology

Territoriality [67]
PN 1299   SC 52140
SN Behavioral patterns characteristic of defense or occupation of a territory.
  UF Habitat Selection
  B Animal Ethology [67]
  R ↓ Animal Aggressive Behavior [73]
     Animal Courtship Displays [73]
     Animal Dominance [73]
     Animal Homing [91]
     Animal Scent Marking [85]

Terrorism [82]
PN 126   SC 52150
SN Violence or threats of violence in order to achieve political, economic, or social goals.
  B Antisocial Behavior [71]
  R ↓ Crime [67]
     Hostages [88]
     Political Revolution [73]
     ↓ Radical Movements [73]
     ↓ Violence [73]

Test Administration [73]
PN 1349   SC 52180
SN Instructions, timing, preparation of test materials, testing conditions, mode of presentation, and other factors involved in the administration of tests.
  UF Administration (Test)
  B Testing [67]
  R Group Testing [73]
     Individual Testing [73]
     ↓ Testing Methods [67]

Test Anxiety [67]
PN 1606   SC 52190
SN Fear or tension in anticipation of formal examination frequently resulting in performance decrement and contributing to measurement error.
  B Anxiety [67]
  R ↓ Anxiety Neurosis [73]
     Test Taking [85]

Test Bias [85]
PN 221   SC 52196
SN Any significant differential performance on tests by different populations (e.g., males versus females) as a result of test characteristics which are irrelevant to the variable or construct being measured.
  UF Item Bias
  B Test Construction [73]
     Testing [67]
  N Cultural Test Bias [73]
  R Error of Measurement [85]
     Response Bias [67]

Test Bias (Cultural)
  Use Cultural Test Bias

Test Construction [73]
PN 6709   SC 52210
SN Planning, selection, writing, editing, and statistical analysis of test items, and design of instructions for test administration and scoring.
  N Content Analysis (Test) [67]
     Difficulty Level (Test) [73]
     Item Analysis (Test) [67]
     Item Content (Test) [73]
     ↓ Test Bias [85]
     Test Forms [88]
     Test Items [73]
     Test Reliability [73]
     Test Standardization [73]
     Test Validity [73]

Test Construction — (cont'd)
  R Adaptive Testing [85]
     ↓ Experimental Design [67]
     ↓ Measurement [67]

Test Difficulty
  Use Difficulty Level (Test)

Test Equating
  Use Score Equating

Test Forms [88]
PN 761   SC 52214
SN Includes different versions or schedules of a test.
  B Test Construction [73]
     Testing [67]
  R Item Content (Test) [73]

Test Interpretation [85]
PN 409   SC 52215
SN Judgment and explanation of the significance, meaning, application, or limitation of an assessment instrument and an obtained score or scores.
  B Testing [67]
  R Cultural Test Bias [73]
     Cutting Scores [85]
     Psychometrics [67]
     ↓ Scoring (Testing) [73]
     Statistical Weighting [85]
     ↓ Test Scores [67]
     Test Validity [73]

Test Items [73]
PN 794   SC 52220
  B Test Construction [73]
     Testing [67]
  R Item Analysis (Statistical) [73]
     Item Analysis (Test) [67]
     Item Content (Test) [73]

Test Normalization
  Use Test Standardization

Test Norms [73]
PN 884   SC 52240
  UF Norms (Test)
  R ↓ Measurement [67]
     Standardized Tests [85]

Test Reliability [73]
PN 7237   SC 52250
SN Consistency, dependability, and reproducibility of test scores, expressed as a reliability coefficient.
  UF Internal Consistency
     Reliability (Test)
  B Test Construction [73]
     Testing [67]
  R Error of Measurement [85]
     Test Standardization [73]

Test Scores [67]
PN 3096   SC 52260
SN Quantitative values or evaluations assigned to describe test performance of individuals. Compare SCORING (TESTING) and GRADING (EDUCATIONAL).
  UF Scores (Test)
  N Cutting Scores [85]
     Intelligence Quotient [67]
     Standard Scores [85]
  R Error of Measurement [85]
     Item Response Theory [85]
     ↓ Measurement [67]
     ↓ Scoring (Testing) [73]

Test Scores — (cont'd)
  R Statistical Weighting [85]
     Test Interpretation [85]

Test Standardization [73]
PN 584   SC 52270
  UF Normalization (Test)
     Standardization (Test)
     Test Normalization
  B Test Construction [73]
     Testing [67]
  R Standardized Tests [85]
     Test Reliability [73]
     Test Validity [73]

Test Taking [85]
PN 295   SC 52275
SN Strategies, attitudes, behaviors, or other factors associated with taking any type of test.
  R Cheating [73]
     Guessing [73]
     Response Bias [67]
     Test Anxiety [67]
     ↓ Testing [67]
     Testwiseness [78]

Test Tube Babies
  Use Reproductive Technology

Test Validity [73]
PN 12058   SC 52280
SN Extent to which a test measures what it was designed to measure. Includes criterion-oriented and content validity.
  UF Validity (Test)
  B Test Construction [73]
     Testing [67]
  R Concurrent Validity [88]
     Construct Validity [82]
     Factorial Validity [73]
     Predictive Validity [73]
     Test Interpretation [85]
     Test Standardization [73]

Testes [73]
PN 118   SC 52290
  B Gonads [73]
     Male Genitalia [73]

Testes Disorders
  Use Endocrine Sexual Disorders

Testicular Feminization Syndrome [73]
PN 4   SC 52310
  UF Feminization Syndrome (Testicular)
  B Endocrine Sexual Disorders [73]
     Male Genital Disorders [73]
     Sex Linked Hereditary Disorders [73]
     Syndromes [73]
  R Hermaphroditism [73]
     Sterility [73]

Testimony (Expert)
  Use Expert Testimony

Testing [67]
PN 2844   SC 52330
SN Administration of tests, and analysis and interpretation of test scores in order to measure differences between individuals or between test performances of the same individual on different occasions.
  B Measurement [67]
  N Computer Assisted Testing [88]
     Content Analysis (Test) [67]
     Difficulty Level (Test) [73]
     ↓ Educational Measurement [67]
     Item Analysis (Test) [67]

Testing — (cont'd)
- **N** Item Content (Test) [73]
  - Item Response Theory [85]
  - Rating [67]
  - Repeated Measures [85]
  - Scaling (Testing) [67]
  - ↓ Scoring (Testing) [73]
  - Test Administration [73]
  - ↓ Test Bias [85]
  - Test Forms [88]
  - Test Interpretation [85]
  - Test Items [73]
  - Test Reliability [73]
  - Test Standardization [73]
  - Test Validity [73]
- **R** ↓ Neuropsychological Assessment [82]
  - Psychometrics [67]
  - Test Taking [85]
  - Testwiseness [78]

Testing (Job Applicants)
- **Use** Job Applicant Screening

Testing Methods [67]
PN 980   SC 52370
- **N** Adaptive Testing [85]
  - Cloze Testing [73]
  - Essay Testing [73]
  - Forced Choice (Testing Method) [67]
  - Multiple Choice (Testing Method) [73]
  - Q Sort Testing Technique [67]
  - Scaling (Testing) [67]
- **R** ↓ Measurement [67]
  - Posttesting [73]
  - Pretesting [73]
  - Subtests [73]
  - Test Administration [73]

Testosterone [73]
PN 1429   SC 52380
- **B** Androgens [73]

Tests
- **Use** Measurement

Tests (Achievement)
- **Use** Achievement Measures

Tests (Aptitude)
- **Use** Aptitude Measures

Tests (Intelligence)
- **Use** Intelligence Measures

Tests (Personality)
- **Use** Personality Measures

Tests (Statistical)
- **Use** Statistical Tests

Testwiseness [78]
PN 98   SC 52415
SN High degree of sophistication in test-taking skills resulting in advantage over others with same knowledge or ability.
- **R** ↓ Measurement [67]
  - Test Taking [85]
  - ↓ Testing [67]

Tetrabenazine [73]
PN 32   SC 52430
- **B** Neuroleptic Drugs [73]
  - Serotonin Antagonists [73]

Tetrachoric Correlation [73]
PN 8   SC 52450
- **B** Statistical Correlation [67]

Tetrahydrocannabinol [73]
PN 530   SC 52470
- **B** Alcohols [67]
  - Cannabinoids [82]
- **R** ↓ Cannabis [73]
  - ↓ Hallucinogenic Drugs [67]
  - Hashish [73]
  - Marihuana [71]

Text Structure [82]
PN 1212   SC 52473
SN Arrangement of sentence or paragraph segments, concepts, or physical format of reading material.
- **R** ↓ Prose [73]
  - Reading Materials [73]
  - Sentence Structure [73]
  - ↓ Verbal Communication [67]

Textbooks [78]
PN 588   SC 52475
SN Books focusing on principles of a specific subject and used as basis of instruction. Not used as a document type identifier. Use BOOK to access references that are in themselves textbooks. Use TEXTBOOKS when textbooks are the object of discussion or study (e.g., analyses of best format for textbook chapters).
- **B** Books [73]
  - Instructional Media [67]
- **N** Programed Textbooks [73]
- **R** Reading Materials [73]

Texture Perception [82]
PN 208   SC 52485
SN Perception of the surface characteristics (frequently patterned) or appearance of objects or substances, usually through the visual or haptic senses.
- **B** Tactual Perception [67]
  - Visual Perception [67]
- **R** Pattern Discrimination [67]

Thailand [73]
PN 264   SC 52490
- **B** Southeast Asia [73]

Thalamic Nuclei [73]
PN 254   SC 52500
- **B** Thalamus [67]

Thalamotomy [73]
PN 17   SC 52510
- **B** Psychosurgery [73]

Thalamus [67]
PN 706   SC 52520
- **B** Diencephalon [73]
- **N** Geniculate Bodies (Thalamus) [73]
  - Thalamic Nuclei [73]

Thalidomide [73]
PN 10   SC 52530
- **B** Amines [73]
  - Hypnotic Drugs [73]
  - Sedatives [73]
- **R** ↓ Drug Induced Congenital Disorders [73]
  - Prenatal Exposure [91]
  - Teratogens [88]

Thanatology
- **Use** Death Education

Thanatos
- **Use** Death Instinct

Theatre [73]
PN 140   SC 52540

Theatre — (cont'd)
- **UF** Stage Plays
- **B** Arts [73]
- **N** Drama [73]

Theft [73]
PN 291   SC 52550
- **UF** Robbery
  - Stealing
- **B** Crime [67]
- **N** Shoplifting [73]

Thematic Apperception Test [67]
PN 399   SC 52560
- **B** Projective Personality Measures [73]

Theology
- **Use** Religion

Theophylline [73]
PN 68   SC 52580
- **B** Alkaloids [73]
  - Diuretics [73]
  - Enzyme Inhibitors [85]
  - Heart Rate Affecting Drugs [73]
  - Muscle Relaxing Drugs [73]
- **R** ↓ Analeptic Drugs [73]
  - Vasodilation [73]

Theoretical Interpretation [88]
PN 303   SC 52582
SN Description or analysis of any particular event, condition, or process from a specific psychological perspective. Usually used in conjunction with other index terms, e.g., humanistic psychology.
- **UF** Psychological Interpretation
- **N** Psychoanalytic Interpretation [67]
- **R** ↓ Theories [67]

Theoretical Orientation [82]
PN 1970   SC 52584
SN Adherence to a particular school of thought, theoretical movement, or practice in a scientific or other area of knowledge.
- **UF** Eclectic Psychology
  - Professional Orientation
- **R** ↓ Clinical Methods Training [73]
  - ↓ Psychology Education [78]
  - ↓ Psychotherapy [67]
  - ↓ Social Sciences [67]
  - ↓ Theories [67]
  - ↓ Therapist Characteristics [73]

Theories [67]
PN 11973   SC 52590
SN Conceptually broad array term referring to the systematic deductive derivation of secondary principles explaining observed phenomena. Use a more specific term if possible.
- **N** Communication Theory [73]
  - Constructivism [94]
  - Darwinism [73]
  - Fuzzy Set Theory [91]
  - Game Theory [67]
  - Information Theory [67]
  - Item Response Theory [85]
  - Learning Theory [67]
  - Personality Theory [67]
  - Psychoanalytic Theory [67]
  - Systems Theory [88]
  - Theories of Education [73]
  - Theory of Evolution [67]
- **R** Construct Validity [82]
  - ↓ Experimentation [67]
  - ↓ History of Psychology [67]
  - ↓ Hypothesis Testing [73]
  - ↓ Theoretical Interpretation [88]
  - Theoretical Orientation [82]

Theories — (cont'd)
R   Theory Formulation [73]
     Theory Verification [73]

Theories of Education [73]
PN 451   **SC** 52587
SN Principles and supporting data concerning the educational process, with application for educational practice.
B   Theories [67]
R   ↓ Education [67]

Theory Formulation [73]
PN 738   **SC** 52600
SN Advancement of propositions and formulation of hypotheses concerning description, explanation, or interpretation of facts. Applies both to principles of theory formulation and presentation of new theories.
R   ↓ Hypothesis Testing [73]
     ↓ Methodology [67]
     ↓ Theories [67]
     Theory Verification [73]

Theory of Evolution [67]
PN 931   **SC** 52610
SN Theories explaining the origins of living organisms and the process by which they evolved into their present forms. For C. Darwin's theory of evolution, use DARWINISM.
UF   Evolution (Theory of)
B   Theories [67]
R   Darwinism [73]

Theory Verification [73]
PN 1113   **SC** 52620
SN Process of proving or disproving theoretical assumptions using empirical data. Applies both to principles of theory testing and their applications.
UF   Verification (of Theories)
R   ↓ Hypothesis Testing [73]
     ↓ Methodology [67]
     ↓ Theories [67]
     Theory Formulation [73]

Therapeutic Abortion
Use Induced Abortion

Therapeutic Alliance [94]
PN 0   **SC** 52633
UF   Working Alliance
B   Psychotherapeutic Processes [67]
R   Psychotherapeutic Transference [67]
     ↓ Treatment [67]

Therapeutic Camps [78]
PN 106   **SC** 52635
SN Camps, usually for children, staffed by mental health personnel and offering treatment programs as well as outdoor activities fostering personal growth and accomplishment.
UF   Camps (Therapeutic)
B   Treatment Facilities [73]
R   Recreation Therapy [73]
     Wilderness Experience [91]

Therapeutic Community [67]
PN 1013   **SC** 52640
SN Institutional or residential treatment setting emphasizing social and environmental factors in therapy and management and rehabilitation, usually of psychiatric or drug rehabilitation patients.
B   Group Psychotherapy [67]
     Psychiatric Hospital Programs [67]
R   Milieu Therapy [88]
     Sociotherapy [73]

Therapeutic Devices (Medical)
Use Medical Therapeutic Devices

Therapeutic Outcomes
Use Treatment Outcomes

Therapeutic Processes [78]
PN 2623   **SC** 52655
SN Experiential, attitudinal, emotional, or behavioral phenomena occurring during the course of treatment. Applies to the patient or therapist (i.e., nurse, doctor, etc.) individually or to their interaction.
UF   Dentist Patient Interaction
     Nurse Patient Interaction
     Physician Patient Interaction
N   ↓ Psychotherapeutic Processes [67]
R   Client Education [85]
     Patient Abuse [91]
     Patient Violence [94]
     Professional Client Sexual Relations [94]
     Therapist Selection [94]
     ↓ Treatment [67]
     ↓ Treatment Outcomes [82]
     Treatment Termination [82]

Therapeutic Social Clubs [73]
PN 54   **SC** 52660
SN Associations of persons, usually patients or former patients, who engage in regular social activities stressing self-help and psychosocial rehabilitation.
UF   Social Clubs (Therapeutic)
B   Psychosocial Rehabilitation [73]
R   ↓ Treatment [67]

Therapeutic Techniques (Psychother)
Use Psychotherapeutic Techniques

Therapist Attitudes [78]
PN 720   **SC** 52680
SN Attitudes of, not toward, therapists.
B   Health Personnel Attitudes [85]
     Therapist Characteristics [73]
N   Psychotherapist Attitudes [73]
R   Psychologist Attitudes [91]
     Therapist Role [78]

Therapist Characteristics [73]
PN 2290   **SC** 52690
SN Traits or qualities of therapists, including but not limited to effectiveness, experience level, and personality.
UF   Therapist Effectiveness
     Therapist Experience
     Therapist Personality
N   ↓ Therapist Attitudes [78]
R   Cross Cultural Treatment [94]
     Theoretical Orientation [82]
     Therapist Selection [94]
     ↓ Therapists [67]

Therapist Effectiveness
Use Therapist Characteristics

Therapist Experience
Use Therapist Characteristics

Therapist Patient Interaction
Use Psychotherapeutic Processes

Therapist Patient Sexual Relations
Use Professional Client Sexual Relations

Therapist Personality
Use Therapist Characteristics

Therapist Role [78]
PN 583   **SC** 52735
B   Roles [67]
R   Counselor Role [73]
     Psychotherapist Attitudes [73]
     ↓ Therapist Attitudes [78]

Therapist Selection [94]
PN 0   **SC** 52737
SN Motivational and judgmental processes involved in the decision to choose a particular therapist or counselor.
UF   Selection (Therapist)
R   Choice Behavior [67]
     ↓ Client Attitudes [82]
     ↓ Therapeutic Processes [78]
     ↓ Therapist Characteristics [73]
     ↓ Therapists [67]
     ↓ Treatment [67]

Therapist Trainees [73]
PN 568   **SC** 52740
UF   Psychotherapist Trainees
R   Counselor Trainees [73]
     ↓ Therapists [67]

Therapists [67]
PN 1140   **SC** 52750
SN Conceptually broad array term referring to persons trained in the treatment of problems including mental disorders and behavior disorders. Use a more specific term if possible.
B   Professional Personnel [78]
N   Occupational Therapists [73]
     Physical Therapists [73]
     ↓ Psychotherapists [73]
     Speech Therapists [73]
R   ↓ Counselors [67]
     ↓ Health Personnel [94]
     ↓ Mental Health Personnel [67]
     ↓ Social Workers [73]
     ↓ Therapist Characteristics [73]
     Therapist Selection [94]
     Therapist Trainees [73]

Therapy
Use Treatment

Therapy (Drug)
Use Drug Therapy

Thermal Acclimatization [73]
PN 42   **SC** 52830
SN Adjustment to ambient temperature ranges that may be different from the organism's typical experience or that may be typical but cyclical in nature (e.g., seasonal changes in temperature). Compare THERMOREGULATION (BODY).
UF   Acclimatization (Thermal)
B   Adaptation [67]
     Physiology [67]
R   Atmospheric Conditions [73]
     Environmental Stress [73]
     Physiological Stress [67]
     ↓ Temperature Effects [67]
     Thermoregulation (Body) [73]

Thermal Factors
Use Temperature Effects

Thermoreceptors [73]
PN 25   **SC** 52840
B   Nerve Endings [73]
     Neural Receptors [73]
     Sensory Neurons [73]

Thermoregulation (Body) [73]
PN 431   **SC** 52850

Thermoregulation (Body) — (cont'd)
SN Homeostatic behavioral or physiological responses that maintain body temperature within a viable range. Compare THERMAL ACCLIMATIZATION.
　B　　Body Temperature ⁷³
　R　　Hyperthermia ⁷³
　　　　　Hypothermia ⁷³
　　　　↓ Metabolism ⁶⁷
　　　　　Thermal Acclimatization ⁷³

Theta Rhythm ⁷³
PN 186　　　　　　　　　**SC** 52860
SN Electrically measured impulses or waves of low amplitude and a frequency of 4-7 cycles per second observable in the electroencephalogram during stage 1 sleep.
　B　　Electrical Activity ⁶⁷
　　　　　Electroencephalography ⁶⁷

Thigh ⁷³
PN 3　　　　　　　　　　**SC** 52870
　B　　Anatomy ⁶⁷
　R　　Leg (Anatomy) ⁷³

Thinking ⁶⁷
PN 2692　　　　　　　　　**SC** 52880
SN Cognitive process involving use of symbols in the manipulation of concepts and ideas.
　B　　Cognitive Processes ⁶⁷
　N　↓ Abstraction ⁶⁷
　　　　　Autistic Thinking ⁷³
　　　　　Divergent Thinking ⁷³
　　　　　Logical Thinking ⁶⁷
　　　　　Magical Thinking ⁷³
　　　　↓ Reasoning ⁶⁷

Thiopental ⁷³
PN 22　　　　　　　　　　**SC** 52890
　UF　Pentothal
　B　　Barbiturates ⁶⁷
　　　　　General Anesthetics ⁷³
　　　　　Hypnotic Drugs ⁷³
　　　　　Narcoanalytic Drugs ⁷³
　　　　　Sedatives ⁷³

Thioridazine ⁷³
PN 270　　　　　　　　　**SC** 52900
　UF　Mellaril
　B　　Phenothiazine Derivatives ⁷³

Thiothixene ⁷³
PN 95　　　　　　　　　　**SC** 52910
　B　　Tranquilizing Drugs ⁶⁷

Third World Countries
　Use Developing Countries

Thirst ⁶⁷
PN 228　　　　　　　　　**SC** 52920
　B　　Motivation ⁶⁷
　R　　Animal Drinking Behavior ⁷³
　　　　↓ Drinking Behavior ⁷⁸
　　　　↓ Fluid Intake ⁸⁵
　　　　　Water Deprivation ⁶⁷

Thoracic Nerves
　Use Spinal Nerves

Thorax ⁷³
PN 61　　　　　　　　　　**SC** 52960
　UF　Chest
　B　　Musculoskeletal System ⁷³
　　　　　Respiratory System ⁷³
　R　　Diaphragm (Anatomy) ⁷³

Thorazine
　Use Chlorpromazine

Thought Content
　Use Cognitions

Thought Control
　Use Brainwashing

Thought Disturbances ⁷³
PN 678　　　　　　　　　**SC** 52980
SN Disturbances of thinking that affect thought content, language, and/or communication marked by delusions, incoherence, and profound loosening of associations.
　N　　Autistic Thinking ⁷³
　　　　　Confabulation ⁷³
　　　　　Delusions ⁶⁷
　　　　　Fantasies (Thought Disturbances) ⁶⁷
　　　　　Fragmentation (Schizophrenia) ⁷³
　　　　　Judgment Disturbances ⁷³
　　　　　Magical Thinking ⁷³
　　　　↓ Memory Disorders ⁷³
　　　　　Obsessions ⁶⁷
　　　　　Perseveration ⁶⁷
　R　　Mental Confusion ⁷³
　　　　↓ Mental Disorders ⁶⁷

Threat ⁶⁷
PN 1076　　　　　　　　　**SC** 52990
　R　　Coercion ⁹⁴
　　　　　Punishment ⁶⁷
　　　　　Threat Postures ⁷³

Threat Postures ⁷³
PN 77　　　　　　　　　　**SC** 53000
　B　　Animal Aggressive Behavior ⁷³
　　　　　Animal Defensive Behavior ⁸²
　R　　Animal Predatory Behavior ⁷⁸
　　　　　Threat ⁶⁷

Threshold Determination ⁷³
PN 312　　　　　　　　　**SC** 53010
SN Methods and apparatus used in the measurement of both absolute and difference thresholds for any sensory modality.
　R　↓ Psychophysical Measurement ⁶⁷
　　　　　Signal Detection (Perception) ⁶⁷
　　　　↓ Thresholds ⁶⁷

Thresholds ⁶⁷
PN 1180　　　　　　　　　**SC** 53020
SN The minimal level (e.g., intensity) of stimulation, the minimal difference between any stimuli, or the minimal stimulus change that is perceptually detectable or to which a sensory receptor or other neuron will respond. Compare SIGNAL DETECTION (PERCEPTION).
　UF　Differential Limen
　　　　　Limen
　N　　Auditory Thresholds ⁷³
　　　　　Olfactory Thresholds ⁷³
　　　　　Pain Thresholds ⁷³
　　　　↓ Sensory Adaptation ⁶⁷
　　　　　Vibrotactile Thresholds ⁷³
　　　　↓ Visual Thresholds ⁷³
　R　↓ Perceptual Measures ⁷³
　　　　　Threshold Determination ⁷³

Thromboses ⁷³
PN 18　　　　　　　　　　**SC** 53040
　B　　Cardiovascular Disorders ⁶⁷
　N　　Coronary Thromboses ⁷³
　R　　Embolisms ⁷³

Thumb ⁷³
PN 17　　　　　　　　　　**SC** 53050
　B　　Fingers (Anatomy) ⁷³

Thumbsucking ⁷³
PN 55　　　　　　　　　　**SC** 53060

Thumbsucking — (cont'd)
　B　　Habits ⁶⁷
　R　↓ Behavior Disorders ⁷¹

Thymoleptic Drugs
　Use Tranquilizing Drugs

Thyroid Disorders ⁷³
PN 93　　　　　　　　　　**SC** 53090
　B　　Endocrine Disorders ⁷³
　N　　Goiters ⁷³
　　　　　Hyperthyroidism ⁷³
　　　　　Hypothyroidism ⁷³
　　　　　Thyrotoxicosis ⁷³
　R　↓ Endocrine Sexual Disorders ⁷³
　　　　↓ Pituitary Disorders ⁷³

Thyroid Extract ⁷³
PN 1　　　　　　　　　　**SC** 53100
　R　↓ Drugs ⁶⁷
　　　　　Hypothyroidism ⁷³
　　　　↓ Thyroid Hormones ⁷³

Thyroid Gland ⁷³
PN 69　　　　　　　　　　**SC** 53110
　B　　Endocrine Glands ⁷³

Thyroid Hormones ⁷³
PN 162　　　　　　　　　**SC** 53120
　B　　Hormones ⁶⁷
　N　　Thyroxine ⁷³
　　　　　Triiodothyronine ⁷³
　R　　Thyroid Extract ⁷³

Thyroid Stimulating Hormone
　Use Thyrotropin

Thyroidectomy ⁷³
PN 28　　　　　　　　　　**SC** 53140
　B　　Endocrine Gland Surgery ⁷³

Thyrotoxicosis ⁷³
PN 23　　　　　　　　　　**SC** 53150
　B　　Thyroid Disorders ⁷³
　　　　　Toxic Disorders ⁷³
　R　↓ Encephalopathies ⁸²
　　　　　Hyperthyroidism ⁷³
　　　　　Toxic Psychoses ⁷³

Thyrotropic Hormone
　Use Thyrotropin

Thyrotropin ⁷³
PN 601　　　　　　　　　**SC** 53170
　UF　Thyroid Stimulating Hormone
　　　　　Thyrotropic Hormone
　B　　Pituitary Hormones ⁷³
　R　　Hypothyroidism ⁷³

Thyroxine ⁷³
PN 152　　　　　　　　　**SC** 53180
　B　　Thyroid Hormones ⁷³
　R　　Hypothyroidism ⁷³

Tibet ⁹¹
PN 1　　　　　　　　　　**SC** 53185
　B　　Peoples Republic of China ⁷³

Tic Douloureux
　Use Trigeminal Neuralgia

Tics ⁷³
PN 190　　　　　　　　　**SC** 53200
　B　　Movement Disorders ⁸⁵
　　　　　Symptoms ⁶⁷

Time [67]
PN 3241   SC 53210
SN Continuum in which events or experiences are expressed in terms of the past, the present, and the future. For effects of time-of-day or season consider also SEASONAL VARIATIONS and BIOLOGICAL RHYTHMS or their associated terms.
N   Interresponse Time [73]
R   Future [91]
     Time Disorientation [73]
     Time Management [94]
     ↓ Time Perception [67]
     Time Perspective [78]
     Trends [91]

Time Disorientation [73]
PN 68   SC 53230
UF   Disorientation (Time)
B   Consciousness Disturbances [73]
R   ↓ Time [67]

Time Estimation [67]
PN 729   SC 53240
SN Estimation of duration or passage of time.
B   Estimation [67]
     Time Perception [67]
R   Time Management [94]

Time Limited Psychotherapy
Use Brief Psychotherapy

Time Management [94]
PN 0   SC 51435
B   Management [67]
R   ↓ Learning Strategies [91]
     ↓ Self Management [85]
     Study Habits [73]
     ↓ Time [67]
     Time Estimation [67]
     Time On Task [88]
     ↓ Time Perception [67]
     Time Perspective [78]

Time On Task [88]
PN 213   SC 53244
SN Period of active involvement in a learning or production activity.
R   ↓ Attention [67]
     ↓ Learning [67]
     Time Management [94]

Time Out [85]
PN 92   SC 53245
SN Removal of the availability of reinforcement or punishment for any behavior following the occurrence of an undesired response. Has application in therapeutic and experimental contexts.
B   Behavior Modification [73]
     Operant Conditioning [67]
R   Omission Training [85]

Time Perception [67]
PN 1290   SC 53250
SN Perception of duration, simultaneity, or succession in the passage of time. Prior to the introduction of TIME PERSPECTIVE in 1978, TIME PERCEPTION was used for this concept also.
B   Perception [67]
N   Time Estimation [67]
R   ↓ Time [67]
     Time Management [94]
     Time Perspective [78]

Time Perspective [78]
PN 508   SC 53255

Time Perspective — (cont'd)
SN Mental representation of temporal relationships or the capacity to remember events in their actual chronology. Also, one's outlook on the past, present, and/or future in relation to subjective qualities of time passage. To access references prior to 1978 use TIME PERCEPTION.
R   ↓ Perceptual Orientation [73]
     ↓ Time [67]
     Time Management [94]
     ↓ Time Perception [67]

Time Series [85]
PN 167   SC 53257
SN A set of observational data ordered in time, typically with observations made at regular intervals.
B   Statistical Analysis [67]
R   Statistical Data [82]
     ↓ Stochastic Modeling [73]

Timers (Apparatus) [73]
PN 43   SC 53260
B   Apparatus [67]

Timidity [73]
PN 279   SC 53270
UF   Shyness
B   Personality Traits [67]

Tinnitus [73]
PN 93   SC 53280
B   Ear Disorders [73]

Tiredness
Use Fatigue

Tissue Donation [91]
PN 44   SC 53295
SN Donation of organs, blood, sperm, or other tissues for medical use.
UF   Blood Donation
     Organ Donation
     Sperm Donation
R   Blood Transfusion [73]
     Charitable Behavior [73]
     Neural Transplantation [85]
     Organ Transplantation [73]

Tissues (Body) [73]
PN 71   SC 53300
B   Anatomy [67]
N   Bone Marrow [73]
     ↓ Connective Tissues [73]
     ↓ Membranes [73]
     ↓ Nerve Tissues [73]
     Skin (Anatomy) [67]
R   Histology [73]
     ↓ Muscles [67]

Toads [73]
PN 122   SC 53320
B   Amphibia [73]
R   Larvae [73]

Tobacco (Drug)
Use Nicotine

Tobacco (Smokeless)
Use Smokeless Tobacco

Tobacco Smoking [67]
PN 3726   SC 53340
UF   Cigarette Smoking
     Smoking (Tobacco)
B   Drug Usage [71]
     Habits [67]
R   Carcinogens [73]

Tobacco Smoking — (cont'd)
R   Nicotine [73]
     Prenatal Exposure [91]
     Smokeless Tobacco [94]
     Smoking Cessation [88]

Tobago
SN Term discontinued in 1982. Use TRINIDAD or TOBAGO to access references from 73–81.
Use Trinidad and Tobago

Toes (Anatomy)
Use Feet (Anatomy)

Tofranil
Use Imipramine

Toilet Training [73]
PN 85   SC 53400
B   Childrearing Practices [67]

Token Economy Programs [73]
PN 615   SC 53410
SN Group treatment based on operant conditioning in which elements in a patient's environment are arranged so that reinforcement is made contingent on the patient's behavior. When the desired behavior occurs, a token is given which may be exchanged for a reinforcing agent (e.g., goods or services).
B   Contingency Management [73]
R   ↓ Psychiatric Hospital Programs [67]

Token Reinforcement
Use Secondary Reinforcement

Tolerance [73]
PN 241   SC 53440
B   Personality Traits [67]
N   Tolerance for Ambiguity [67]

Tolerance (Drug)
Use Drug Tolerance

Tolerance for Ambiguity [67]
PN 292   SC 53460
SN Willingness to accept situations having conflicting or different interpretations or outcomes.
UF   Ambiguity (Tolerance)
B   Tolerance [73]

Toluene [91]
PN 14   SC 53465
B   Solvents [82]

Tomography [88]
PN 562   SC 53470
UF   CAT Scan
     Positron Emission Tomography
B   Medical Diagnosis [73]
N   Magnetic Resonance Imaging [94]
R   Computer Assisted Diagnosis [73]
     ↓ Roentgenography [73]

Tone (Frequency)
Use Pitch (Frequency)

Tonga [91]
PN 0   SC 53485
B   South Pacific [78]

Tongue [73]
PN 266   SC 53490
B   Digestive System [67]
N   Taste Buds [73]
R   Mouth (Anatomy) [67]

Tonic Immobility [78]
PN 237   SC 53495
SN Adaptive escape or alarm response in certain species in which the animal adopts a motionless posture as if feigning death.
B   Motor Processes [67]
R   Alarm Responses [73]
  ↓ Animal Defensive Behavior [82]

Tool Use [91]
PN 23   SC 53497
SN Used for human or animal populations.
UF   Animal Tool Use
B   Motor Processes [67]
R ↓ Animal Ethology [67]

Top Level Managers [73]
PN 643   SC 53500
SN Executives in business or industry who are responsible for the major strategic and policy decisions.
UF   Executives
B   Management Personnel [73]
R   Middle Level Managers [73]

Topography [73]
PN 62   SC 53510
UF   Landscapes
B   Ecological Factors [73]

Torticollis [73]
PN 59   SC 53520
UF   Wryneck
B   Movement Disorders [85]
     Muscular Disorders [73]

Tortoises
Use   Turtles

Torture [88]
PN 78   SC 53535
B   Antisocial Behavior [71]
R   Coercion [94]
     Persecution [73]
     Suffering [73]
     Victimization [73]
  ↓ Violence [73]

Totalitarianism [73]
PN 22   SC 53540
B   Political Economic Systems [73]

Touch
Use   Tactual Perception

Touching
Use   Physical Contact

Tourette Syndrome
Use   Gilles de la Tourette Disorder

Towns [73]
PN 50   SC 53560
B   Social Environments [73]

Toxic Disorders [73]
PN 315   SC 53570
UF   Intoxication
     Poisoning
B   Disorders [67]
N   Acute Alcoholic Intoxication [73]
  ↓ Alcohol Intoxication [73]
     Barbiturate Poisoning [73]
     Carbon Monoxide Poisoning [73]
  ↓ Drug Induced Congenital Disorders [73]
     Lead Poisoning [73]
     Mercury Poisoning [73]

Toxic Disorders — (cont'd)
N   Narcosis [73]
     Neuroleptic Malignant Syndrome [88]
     Thyrotoxicosis [73]
     Toxic Encephalopathies [73]
     Toxic Hepatitis [73]
     Toxic Psychoses [73]
R ↓ Alcoholism [67]
  ↓ Dermatitis [73]
  ↓ Digestive System Disorders [73]
  ↓ Gastrointestinal Disorders [73]
  ↓ Liver Disorders [73]
  ↓ Mental Disorders [67]
  ↓ Neurotoxins [82]
     Toxicity [73]
     Toxicomania [73]

Toxic Encephalopathies [73]
PN 65   SC 53580
B   Encephalopathies [82]
     Toxic Disorders [73]
R   Acute Alcoholic Intoxication [73]
     Chronic Alcoholic Intoxication [73]
     Toxic Psychoses [73]

Toxic Hepatitis [73]
PN 4   SC 53590
B   Hepatitis [73]
     Toxic Disorders [73]

Toxic Psychoses [73]
PN 124   SC 53600
SN Psychotic states or conditions resulting from ingestion of toxic agents or by the presence of toxins within the body. Compare EXPERIMENTAL PSYCHOSIS.
B   Organic Brain Syndromes [73]
     Psychosis [67]
     Toxic Disorders [73]
R ↓ Alcohol Intoxication [73]
  ↓ Alcoholic Psychosis [73]
     Thyrotoxicosis [73]
     Toxic Encephalopathies [73]

Toxic Waste
Use   Hazardous Materials

Toxicity [73]
PN 606   SC 53610
R ↓ Drugs [67]
  ↓ Hazardous Materials [91]
  ↓ Neurotoxins [82]
     Teratogens [88]
  ↓ Toxic Disorders [73]

Toxicomania [73]
PN 16   SC 53620
R   Pica [73]
  ↓ Toxic Disorders [73]

Toxins
Use   Poisons

Toy Selection [73]
PN 167   SC 53650
R   Childhood Play Behavior [78]
  ↓ Toys [73]

Toys [73]
PN 299   SC 53660
N   Anatomically Detailed Dolls [91]
     Educational Toys [73]
R   Childhood Play Behavior [78]
     Childrens Recreational Games [73]
     Computer Games [88]
  ↓ Games [67]
  ↓ Recreation [67]
     Toy Selection [73]

Trachea [73]
PN 26   SC 53680
B   Respiratory System [73]

Tracking [67]
PN 392   SC 53700
SN Following the movement of a moving stimulus or the contours (or shape) of a stationary target by means of direct physical contact or through any sensory modality. Used for human or animal populations.
B   Perceptual Motor Processes [67]
N   Rotary Pursuit [67]
     Visual Tracking [73]
R ↓ Attention [67]
  ↓ Monitoring [73]
     Motor Skills [73]
  ↓ Perceptual Localization [67]
  ↓ Perceptual Motor Learning [67]

Tractotomy [73]
PN 11   SC 53710
B   Neurosurgery [73]
R ↓ Psychosurgery [73]
     Pyramidotomy [73]

Traditionalism
Use   Conservatism

Traffic Accidents (Motor)
Use   Motor Traffic Accidents

Trainable Mentally Retarded [73]
PN 1434   SC 53760
SN IQ 35–49.
UF   Moderately Mentally Retarded
B   Mentally Retarded [67]
R   Downs Syndrome [67]

Training
Use   Education

Training (Athletic)
Use   Athletic Training

Training (Clinical Methods)
Use   Clinical Methods Training

Training (Clinical Psychology Grad)
Use   Clinical Psychology Grad Training

Training (Community Mental Health)
Use   Community Mental Health Training

Training (Graduate Psychology)
Use   Graduate Psychology Education

Training (Mental Health Inservice)
Use   Mental Health Inservice Training

Training (Motivation)
Use   Motivation Training

Training (Personnel)
Use   Personnel Training

Training (Psychiatric)
Use   Psychiatric Training

Training (Psychoanalytic)
Use   Psychoanalytic Training

Training (Psychotherapy)
Use   Psychotherapy Training

Trains (Railroad)
Use Railroad Trains

Tranquilizing Drugs [67]
PN 1693   **SC** 53900
  UF Antianxiety Drugs
      Anxiety Reducing Drugs
      Anxiolytic Drugs
      Ataractic Drugs
      Ataraxic Drugs
      Thymoleptic Drugs
  B Drugs [67]
  N Amitriptyline [73]
      Benactyzine [73]
      Doxepin [94]
      Haloperidol [73]
      Meprobamate [73]
      ↓ Minor Tranquilizers [73]
      ↓ Neuroleptic Drugs [73]
      Phenaglycodol [73]
      ↓ Phenothiazine Derivatives [73]
      Pimozide [73]
      Thiothixene [73]
  R ↓ Anticonvulsive Drugs [73]
      ↓ Antiemetic Drugs [73]
      ↓ Antihypertensive Drugs [73]
      ↓ Benzodiazepines [78]
      ↓ Dopamine Antagonists [82]
      ↓ Muscle Relaxing Drugs [73]
      ↓ Narcotic Drugs [73]
      ↓ Sedatives [73]

Transactional Analysis [73]
PN 714   **SC** 53910
SN Type of psychotherapy based on the theory that all interactions between individuals reflect the inner relationships of the Parent, Adult, and Child ego states.
  B Human Potential Movement [82]
      Psychotherapy [67]

Transaminases [73]
PN 20   **SC** 53920
  UF Aminotransferases
  B Transferases [73]

Transcultural Psychiatry [73]
PN 265   **SC** 53930
SN Comparative study of mental illness and mental health among various societies or cultures, including epidemiology and symptomatology.
  UF Comparative Psychiatry
      Cultural Psychiatry
  B Psychiatry [67]
  R Cross Cultural Treatment [94]
      Ethnology [67]
      ↓ Ethnospecific Disorders [73]
      Folk Medicine [73]
      Myths [67]
      Shamanism [73]
      Taboos [73]

Transducers [73]
PN 21   **SC** 53940
  B Apparatus [67]

Transfer (Learning) [67]
PN 2311   **SC** 53950
SN Effect of previous learning on the acquisition of new material or skills as a function of the relative similarity between the prior and current learning situations. Compare GENERALIZATION (LEARNING).
  B Learning [67]
  N Negative Transfer [73]
      Positive Transfer [73]
  R ↓ Generalization (Learning) [82]

Transfer Students [73]
PN 112   **SC** 53955
SN Students transferring from one school or educational program to another.
  B Students [67]
  R Grade Level [94]

Transferases [73]
PN 186   **SC** 53960
  B Enzymes [73]
  N Transaminases [73]

Transference (Psychotherapeutic)
Use Psychotherapeutic Transference

Transformational Generative Grammar [73]
PN 92   **SC** 53980
SN Transformational grammar relates the deep syntactic structures of a language to the surface structures by means of transformational rules. Generative grammar represents, through abstract formulas, all and only the grammatical utterances of a language.
  B Grammar [67]
  R ↓ Syntax [71]

Transfusion (Blood)
Use Blood Transfusion

Transgenerational Patterns [91]
PN 66   **SC** 54005
SN Patterns of behavior, for example, pregnancy in adolescence, drug abuse, or child abuse, that appear in successive generations.
  R ↓ Family [67]
      ↓ Family Relations [67]
      Family Resemblance [91]
      Generation Gap [73]
      Intergenerational Relations [88]
      ↓ Parent Child Relations [67]
      Trends [91]

Transistors (Apparatus) [73]
PN 7   **SC** 54010
  B Apparatus [67]

Transitional Objects [85]
PN 110   **SC** 54015
SN Psychoanalytic concept referring to any material object having a special value that serves an anxiety-reducing function. Such attachment is a normal phenomenon in separation-individuation.
  R ↓ Childhood Development [67]
      Object Relations [82]
      Separation Individuation [82]

Translocation (Chromosome) [73]
PN 17   **SC** 54020
  B Chromosome Disorders [73]
  R ↓ Genetics [67]
      Mutations [73]

Transpersonal Psychology [88]
PN 68   **SC** 54025
SN Subdiscipline of humanistic psychology which studies higher states of consciousness and transcendental experiences.
  B Humanistic Psychology [85]

Transplants (Organ)
Use Organ Transplantation

Transportation [73]
PN 94   **SC** 54040
  N Air Transportation [73]
      ↓ Ground Transportation [73]
      Public Transportation [73]
      ↓ Water Transportation [73]

Transportation — (cont'd)
  R Commuting (Travel) [85]
      ↓ Transportation Accidents [73]

Transportation Accidents [73]
PN 54   **SC** 54050
  B Accidents [67]
  N Air Traffic Accidents [73]
      Motor Traffic Accidents [73]
  R Accident Prevention [73]
      Air Traffic Control [73]
      ↓ Aviation Safety [73]
      Highway Safety [73]
      Safety Belts [73]
      ↓ Transportation [73]

Transposition (Cognition) [73]
PN 42   **SC** 54060
SN Condition in learning in which subjects react to relationships between stimuli rather than to each stimulus itself.
  B Cognitive Processes [67]

Transracial Adoption
Use Interracial Adoption

Transsexualism [73]
PN 457   **SC** 54070
  B Psychosexual Behavior [67]
  R Bisexuality [73]
      Gender Identity [85]
      ↓ Homosexuality [67]
      Sex Change [88]
      Transvestism [73]

Transvestism [73]
PN 133   **SC** 54080
  B Psychosexual Behavior [67]
  R Bisexuality [73]
      Fetishism [73]
      ↓ Homosexuality [67]
      Transsexualism [73]

Tranylcypromine [73]
PN 132   **SC** 54090
  B Antidepressant Drugs [71]
      Monoamine Oxidase Inhibitors [73]

Trauma (Emotional)
Use Emotional Trauma

Trauma (Physical)
Use Injuries

Traumatic Neurosis [73]
PN 120   **SC** 54130
SN Use TRAUMATIC NEUROSIS or STRESS REACTIONS to access references from POST-TRAUMATIC STRESS DISORDER from 73-84.
  B Neurosis [67]
  R Posttraumatic Stress Disorder [85]

Traumatic Psychosis
Use Reactive Psychosis

Traveling [73]
PN 159   **SC** 54150
  B Recreation [67]
  R Commuting (Travel) [85]
      Vacationing [73]

Trazodone [88]
PN 113   **SC** 54152
  B Antidepressant Drugs [71]
      Piperazines [94]

Treatment [67]
PN 11484   SC 54190
SN Conceptually broad array term referring to psychological or physical measures designed to ameliorate or cure an abnormal or undesirable condition. Use a more specific term if possible.
UF Therapy
N ↓ Behavior Modification [73]
    Bibliotherapy [73]
   ↓ Cognitive Techniques [85]
   ↓ Creative Arts Therapy [94]
   ↓ Crisis Intervention [73]
   ↓ Crisis Intervention Services [73]
    Cross Cultural Treatment [94]
   ↓ Health Care Services [78]
    Interdisciplinary Treatment Approach [73]
    Involuntary Treatment [94]
    Medical Treatment (General) [73]
    Milieu Therapy [88]
    Multimodal Treatment Approach [91]
   ↓ Organic Therapies [73]
   ↓ Outpatient Treatment [67]
    Pain Management [94]
    Partial Hospitalization [85]
    Personal Therapy [91]
   ↓ Physical Treatment Methods [73]
    Preventive Medicine [73]
   ↓ Psychotherapeutic Techniques [67]
   ↓ Psychotherapy [67]
   ↓ Rehabilitation [67]
   ↓ Relaxation Therapy [78]
    Sex Therapy [78]
    Social Casework [67]
    Sociotherapy [73]
    Speech Therapy [67]
R   Caregivers [88]
   ↓ Case Management [91]
    Client Rights [88]
   ↓ Clinics [67]
    Cost Containment [91]
   ↓ Counseling [67]
    Court Referrals [94]
    Death Education [82]
    Early Intervention [82]
    Euthanasia [73]
    Health Care Costs [94]
   ↓ Health Care Delivery [78]
    Life Review [91]
    Medical Records Keeping [78]
    Mental Health Program Evaluation [73]
    Patient Abuse [91]
    Patient History [73]
    Physical Restraint [82]
    Posttreatment Followup [73]
    Prescribing (Drugs) [91]
   ↓ Prevention [73]
    Prognosis [73]
   ↓ Psychiatry [67]
    Psychoeducation [94]
    Psychosocial Readjustment [73]
    Quality of Care [88]
    Relapse Prevention [94]
   ↓ Self Help Techniques [82]
    Sensory Integration [91]
    Shamanism [73]
   ↓ Side Effects (Treatment) [88]
    Spontaneous Remission [73]
    Stress Management [85]
    Therapeutic Alliance [94]
   ↓ Therapeutic Processes [78]
    Therapeutic Social Clubs [73]
    Therapist Selection [94]
    Treatment Compliance [82]
   ↓ Treatment Duration [88]
    Treatment Effectiveness Evaluation [73]
   ↓ Treatment Facilities [73]
   ↓ Treatment Outcomes [82]
   ↓ Treatment Resistant Disorders [94]

Treatment — (cont'd)
R   Treatment Termination [82]
    Treatment Withholding [88]

Treatment Compliance [82]
PN 1942   SC 54153
SN Adherence by a patient or client to professional advice or a systematic plan of treatment.
UF Medical Regimen Compliance
B   Compliance [73]
R   ↓ Client Attitudes [82]
    Client Education [85]
    Client Rights [88]
    Illness Behavior [82]
    Informed Consent [85]
    Involuntary Treatment [94]
   ↓ Treatment [67]
    Treatment Dropouts [78]
   ↓ Treatment Duration [88]
    Treatment Refusal [94]
    Treatment Withholding [88]

Treatment Dropouts [78]
PN 758   SC 54155
SN Persons who drop out of treatment, or discontinuation of treatment without the consent of the person in charge of treatment or before scheduled termination.
B   Dropouts [73]
R   Involuntary Treatment [94]
    Psychotherapeutic Outcomes [73]
    Treatment Compliance [82]
   ↓ Treatment Duration [88]
   ↓ Treatment Outcomes [82]
    Treatment Refusal [94]
    Treatment Termination [82]

Treatment Duration [88]
PN 692   SC 54157
SN Length of hospital or institutional stay and length or number of treatment or therapy sessions. Used for any treatment modality.
N   Long Term Care [94]
R   ↓ Case Management [91]
   ↓ Treatment [67]
    Treatment Compliance [82]
    Treatment Dropouts [78]
   ↓ Treatment Outcomes [82]
    Treatment Termination [82]

Treatment Effectiveness Evaluation [73]
PN 2613   SC 54160
SN Methodology or procedures for assessment of treatment success in relation to previously established goals or other criteria. Also used for formal evaluations themselves. For effectiveness of particular treatment modes, use the specific type of treatment (e.g., DRUG THERAPY). For efficacy of treatment for a particular disorder, use the specific disorder (e.g., MANIA) and the specific type of treatment.
UF Evaluation (Treatment Effectiveness)
B   Evaluation [67]
R   Mental Health Program Evaluation [73]
    Psychotherapeutic Outcomes [73]
   ↓ Treatment [67]
   ↓ Treatment Outcomes [82]

Treatment Facilities [73]
PN 268   SC 54170
N   ↓ Clinics [67]
    Community Mental Health Centers [73]
    Halfway Houses [73]
   ↓ Hospitals [67]
    Nursing Homes [73]
    Therapeutic Camps [78]
R   ↓ Crisis Intervention Services [73]
   ↓ Facility Admission [88]
   ↓ Facility Discharge [88]

Treatment Facilities — (cont'd)
R   ↓ Facility Environment [88]
    Institutional Schools [78]
   ↓ Residential Care Institutions [73]
   ↓ Treatment [67]

Treatment Methods (Physical)
Use Physical Treatment Methods

Treatment Outcomes [82]
PN 2530   SC 54185
SN Limited to treatment results that are a function of unique or specifically-described circumstances or characteristics (e.g., race) of the clients/patients, the treatment provider, or the treatment itself. For effectiveness of particular treatment modes, use the specific type of treatment (e.g., DRUG THERAPY). For efficacy of treatment for a particular disorder, use the specific disorder (e.g., MANIA) and the specific type of treatment.
UF Outcomes (Treatment)
    Therapeutic Outcomes
N   Psychotherapeutic Outcomes [73]
R   Mental Health Program Evaluation [73]
    Postsurgical Complications [73]
   ↓ Psychotherapeutic Processes [67]
    Recovery (Disorders) [73]
    Relapse (Disorders) [73]
    Relapse Prevention [94]
   ↓ Remission (Disorders) [73]
   ↓ Side Effects (Treatment) [88]
   ↓ Therapeutic Processes [78]
   ↓ Treatment [67]
    Treatment Dropouts [78]
   ↓ Treatment Duration [88]
    Treatment Effectiveness Evaluation [73]
    Treatment Termination [82]

Treatment Refusal [94]
PN 0   SC 54186
SN Patient or client refusal of or resistance to medical, psychological, or psychiatric treatment. Consider TREATMENT WITHHOLDING for life sustaining contexts.
UF Refusal (Treatment)
R   Advance Directives [94]
    Client Rights [88]
    Informed Consent [85]
    Involuntary Treatment [94]
    Treatment Compliance [82]
    Treatment Dropouts [78]
    Treatment Termination [82]
    Treatment Withholding [88]

Treatment Resistant Depression [94]
PN 0   SC 57440
UF Tricyclic Resistant Depression
B   Major Depression [88]
    Treatment Resistant Disorders [94]
R   ↓ Drug Therapy [67]

Treatment Resistant Disorders [94]
PN 0   SC 57445
SN Used for any disorder that is resistant to any type of psychological or medical treatment.
N   Treatment Resistant Depression [94]
R   ↓ Disorders [67]
   ↓ Mental Disorders [67]
   ↓ Treatment [67]

Treatment Termination [82]
PN 428   SC 54187
SN Completion of medical or psychological/behavioral treatment programs.
R   Discharge Planning [94]
   ↓ Hospital Discharge [73]
    Psychiatric Hospital Discharge [78]
   ↓ Therapeutic Processes [78]
   ↓ Treatment [67]

Treatment Termination — (cont'd)
R   Treatment Dropouts [78]
  ↓ Treatment Duration [88]
  ↓ Treatment Outcomes [82]
   Treatment Refusal [94]
   Treatment Withholding [88]

Treatment Withholding [88]
PN 87   SC 54188
SN Issues involved in making decisions to provide, continue, or limit medical treatment for seriously ill persons. Includes do-not-resuscitate orders. Compare TREATMENT TERMINATION.
R   Advance Directives [94]
   Client Rights [88]
  ↓ Death and Dying [67]
   Euthanasia [73]
  ↓ Human Rights [78]
   Informed Consent [85]
  ↓ Treatment [67]
   Treatment Compliance [82]
   Treatment Refusal [94]
   Treatment Termination [82]

Tremor [73]
PN 167   SC 54200
B   Movement Disorders [85]
   Symptoms [67]
R ↓ Antitremor Drugs [73]
   Parkinsonism [94]
   Parkinsons Disease [73]

Trends [91]
PN 132   SC 54204
SN Used specifically for analysis of past, present, or future patterns in technology, economics, and social or developmental processes.
R ↓ Fads and Fashions [73]
   Future [91]
  ↓ History [73]
   Social Change [67]
  ↓ Social Processes [67]
  ↓ Time [67]
   Transgenerational Patterns [91]

Triadic Therapy
Use Conjoint Therapy

Trial and Error Learning [73]
PN 52   SC 54210
B   Learning [67]
   Learning Strategies [91]

Triazolam [88]
PN 92   SC 54215
B   Hypnotic Drugs [73]
   Sedatives [73]

Tribes [73]
PN 395   SC 54220
R ↓ Ethnic Groups [73]

Trichotillomania
Use Hair Pulling

Tricyclic Resistant Depression
Use Treatment Resistant Depression

Trifluoperazine [73]
PN 106   SC 54230
UF Stelazine
B   Phenothiazine Derivatives [73]

Triflupromazine [73]
PN 3   SC 54240
B   Phenothiazine Derivatives [73]

Trigeminal Nerve [73]
PN 132   SC 54250
B   Cranial Nerves [73]

Trigeminal Neuralgia [73]
PN 25   SC 54260
UF Tic Douloureux
B   Neuralgia [73]

Trigonum Cerebrale
Use Fornix

Trihexyphenidyl [73]
PN 39   SC 54270
B   Alcohols [67]
   Amines [73]
   Antispasmodic Drugs [73]
   Antitremor Drugs [73]
   Cholinergic Blocking Drugs [73]

Triiodothyronine [73]
PN 90   SC 54280
B   Thyroid Hormones [73]

Trinidad
SN Term discontinued in 1982. Use TRINIDAD or TOBAGO to access references from 73–81.
Use Trinidad and Tobago

Trinidad and Tobago [82]
PN 24   SC 54300
SN Use TRINIDAD or TOBAGO to access references from 73–81.
UF Tobago
   Trinidad
B   West Indies [73]

Triplets [73]
PN 21   SC 54310
B   Multiple Births [73]

Trisomy [73]
PN 40   SC 54320
B   Chromosome Disorders [73]
N   Trisomy 21 [73]

Trisomy 21 [73]
PN 44   SC 54340
B   Autosome Disorders [73]
   Trisomy [73]
R   Downs Syndrome [67]

Trochlear Nerve
Use Cranial Nerves

Truancy [73]
PN 77   SC 54360
N   School Truancy [73]

Trucks
Use Motor Vehicles

Trust (Social Behavior) [67]
PN 728   SC 54370
B   Prosocial Behavior [82]
R   Hope [91]

Tryptamine [73]
PN 98   SC 54380
B   Amines [73]
   Vasoconstrictor Drugs [73]

Tryptophan [73]
PN 689   SC 54390

Tryptophan — (cont'd)
B   Amino Acids [73]
   Serotonin Precursors [78]
N   Hydroxytryptophan (5-) [91]

Tubal Ligation [73]
PN 41   SC 54400
B   Birth Control [71]
   Sterilization (Sex) [73]

Tuberculosis [73]
PN 57   SC 54410
B   Bacterial Disorders [73]
N   Pulmonary Tuberculosis [73]
R   Addisons Disease [73]
  ↓ Antitubercular Drugs [73]
   Lupus [73]
  ↓ Musculoskeletal Disorders [73]
  ↓ Nervous System Disorders [67]
  ↓ Skin Disorders [73]

Tubocurarine [73]
PN 14   SC 54420
B   Alkaloids [73]
   Muscle Relaxing Drugs [73]
R   Curare [73]

Tumors
Use Neoplasms

Tunisia [91]
PN 0   SC 54435
B   Africa [67]

Tunnel Vision [73]
PN 8   SC 54440
SN Disorder characterized by severe limitation or total lack of peripheral vision.
B   Eye Disorders [73]
R ↓ Vision [67]

Turkey [73]
PN 160   SC 54450
B   Asia [73]
R   Middle East [78]

Turners Syndrome [73]
PN 80   SC 54460
B   Hypogonadism [73]
   Neonatal Disorders [73]
   Sex Linked Hereditary Disorders [73]
   Syndromes [73]
R   Sterility [73]

Turnover
Use Employee Turnover

Turtles [73]
PN 145   SC 54480
UF Tortoises
B   Reptiles [67]

Tutoring [73]
PN 422   SC 54490
B   Teaching Methods [67]
N   Peer Tutoring [73]
R   Individualized Instruction [73]

Tutors
Use Teachers

Twins [67]
PN 775   SC 54510
B   Multiple Births [73]
N   Heterozygotic Twins [73]
   Monozygotic Twins [73]
   Siamese Twins [73]

Twins — (cont'd)
R   Family Resemblance [91]
↓ Genetics [67]

Tympanic Membrane
Use Middle Ear

Type A Personality
Use Coronary Prone Behavior

Type B Personality
Use Coronary Prone Behavior

Type I Errors [73]
PN 175   SC 54530
B   Prediction Errors [73]
R   Statistical Power [91]

Type II Errors [73]
PN 53   SC 54540
B   Prediction Errors [73]
R   Statistical Power [91]

Typing [91]
PN 22   SC 54550
SN Use CLERICAL SECRETARIAL SKILLS to access references from 73-90.
R   Clerical Secretarial Skills [73]
Keyboards [85]
Word Processing [91]

Typists
Use Clerical Personnel

Typologies (General)
Use Taxonomies

Typologies (Psychodiagnostic)
Use Psychodiagnostic Typologies

Tyramine [73]
PN 64   SC 54580
B   Adrenergic Drugs [73]
Sympathomimetic Amines [73]
Vasoconstrictor Drugs [73]
R   ↓ Ergot Derivatives [73]

Tyrosine [73]
PN 219   SC 54590
B   Amino Acids [73]
N   Alpha Methylparatyrosine [78]
R   Melanin [73]

Uganda [88]
PN 11   SC 54600
B   Africa [67]

Ulcerative Colitis [73]
PN 130   SC 54620
B   Colitis [73]

Ulcers (Gastrointestinal)
Use Gastrointestinal Ulcers

Ulnar Nerve
Use Spinal Nerves

Ultrasound [73]
PN 215   SC 54650
SN Sound waves with frequencies above the range of human hearing.
B   Pitch (Frequency) [67]

Uncertainty [91]
PN 137   SC 54655

Uncertainty — (cont'd)
SN May be used for uncertainty reduction processes; uncertainty in decision making, choice, or judgment; or in statistical contexts.
R   ↓ Chance (Fortune) [73]
Choice Behavior [67]
↓ Decision Making [67]
Doubt [73]
Impression Management [78]
↓ Judgment [67]
↓ Statistical Analysis [67]
Suspicion [73]

Unconditioned Reflex
Use Unconditioned Responses

Unconditioned Responses [73]
PN 84   SC 54680
UF Unconditioned Reflex
B   Classical Conditioning [67]
Responses [67]

Unconditioned Stimulus [73]
PN 1042   SC 54690
UF Stimulus (Unconditioned)
B   Conditioning [67]
R   ↓ Classical Conditioning [67]
↓ Operant Conditioning [67]
Primary Reinforcement [73]
↓ Stimulation [67]

Unconscious (Personality Factor) [67]
PN 731   SC 54700
B   Psychoanalytic Personality Factors [73]
R   Archetypes [91]
Death Instinct [88]
Free Association [94]
Id [73]
Mind [91]

Underachievement (Academic)
Use Academic Underachievement

Underdeveloped Countries
Use Developing Countries

Undergraduate Degrees
Use Educational Degrees

Undergraduate Education [78]
PN 581   SC 54725
UF College Education
B   Higher Education [73]

Undergraduates
Use College Students

Underprivileged
Use Disadvantaged

Understanding
Use Comprehension

Underwater Effects [73]
PN 167   SC 54760
B   Environmental Effects [73]
R   Decompression Effects [73]
↓ Gravitational Effects [67]

Underweight [73]
PN 38   SC 54770
B   Body Weight [67]
Symptoms [67]
N   Anorexia Nervosa [73]
R   ↓ Appetite Disorders [73]
Diets [78]

Underweight — (cont'd)
R   Hyperthyroidism [73]
↓ Nutritional Deficiencies [73]

Undifferentiated Schizophrenia [73]
PN 59   SC 54780
B   Schizophrenia [67]

Unemployment [67]
PN 910   SC 54790
B   Employment Status [82]
Social Issues [91]
R   Employment History [78]
Job Search [85]
Job Security [78]
↓ Personnel [67]
Personnel Termination [73]
Reemployment [91]
Retirement [73]

Union of South Africa
SN Term discontinued in 1982. Use UNION OF SOUTH AFRICA to access references from 73–81.
Use South Africa

Union of Soviet Socialist Republics [67]
PN 2605   SC 54820
B   Asia [73]
Europe [73]

Unipolar Depression
SN Use DEPRESSION (EMOTION) to access references from 82-87.
Use Major Depression

United Arab Republic
SN Term discontinued in 1982. Use UNITED ARAB REPUBLIC to access references from 73–81.
Use Egypt

United Kingdom [73]
PN 773   SC 54840
B   Europe [73]
N   ↓ Great Britain [71]

United States [67]
PN 4614   SC 54850
B   North America [73]
N   Alaska [73]
Appalachia [73]
Hawaii [73]

Universities
Use Colleges

Unskilled Industrial Workers [73]
PN 57   SC 54880
SN Blue collar workers who perform unskilled labor in an industrial setting.
B   Blue Collar Workers [73]

Unwed Mothers [73]
PN 188   SC 54890
SN Consider also ADOLESCENT MOTHERS.
B   Mothers [67]
R   Never Married [94]
Single Mothers [94]
↓ Single Parents [78]

Upper Class [73]
PN 109   SC 54900
B   Social Class [67]

Upper Class Attitudes [73]
PN 8   SC 54910

Upper Class Attitudes — (cont'd)
SN Attitudes of, not toward, the upper class.
B   Socioeconomic Class Attitudes [73]

Upper Income Level [73]
PN 46   SC 54920
B   Income Level [73]

Upward Bound [73]
PN 37   SC 54930
SN U.S. Government educational and counseling program for disadvantaged high school and college students.
B   Educational Programs [73]
       Government Programs [73]
R   Compensatory Education [73]
       Government [67]

Urban Environments [67]
PN 4105   SC 54940
UF   Cities
       Inner City
B   Social Environments [73]
N   Ghettoes [73]
R   Urban Planning [73]

Urban Ghettoes
Use Ghettoes

Urban Planning [73]
PN 130   SC 54960
B   Environmental Planning [82]
R   ↓ Architecture [73]
      ↓ Community Facilities [73]
      ↓ Environment [67]
      ↓ Recreation Areas [73]
      ↓ Urban Environments [67]

Urbanization [73]
PN 128   SC 54970
B   Social Processes [67]
R   Industrialization [73]

Uric Acid [73]
PN 55   SC 55010
B   Acids [73]

Urinalysis [73]
PN 148   SC 55020
B   Medical Diagnosis [73]
R   Drug Usage Screening [88]

Urinary Function Disorders [73]
PN 90   SC 55040
B   Urogenital Disorders [73]
N   Urinary Incontinence [73]
R   ↓ Psychosomatic Disorders [67]

Urinary Incontinence [73]
PN 591   SC 55050
UF   Bedwetting
       Enuresis
       Incontinence (Urinary)
B   Urinary Function Disorders [73]
R   ↓ Behavior Disorders [71]
      ↓ Symptoms [67]

Urination [67]
PN 220   SC 55070
UF   Micturition
B   Excretion [67]
R   ↓ Diuretics [73]

Urine [73]
PN 639   SC 55080
B   Body Fluids [73]

Urogenital Disorders [73]
PN 207   SC 55090
B   Disorders [67]
N   ↓ Genital Disorders [67]
      ↓ Gynecological Disorders [73]
       Kidney Diseases [88]
      ↓ Urinary Function Disorders [73]
R   ↓ Psychosomatic Disorders [67]
      ↓ Sexual Function Disturbances [73]
      ↓ Urogenital System [73]
      ↓ Venereal Diseases [73]

Urogenital System [73]
PN 33   SC 55100
B   Anatomical Systems [73]
N   Bladder [73]
      ↓ Female Genitalia [73]
      ↓ Gonads [73]
       Kidneys [73]
      ↓ Male Genitalia [73]
R   ↓ Urogenital Disorders [73]

Uruguay [88]
PN 6   SC 55105
B   South America [67]

Uterus [73]
PN 44   SC 55110
B   Female Genitalia [73]
N   Cervix [73]
R   Placenta [73]

Utilization (Health Care)
Use Health Care Utilization

Vacation Benefits
Use Employee Leave Benefits

Vacationing [73]
PN 75   SC 55130
B   Recreation [67]
R   Camping [73]
       Holidays [88]
       Summer Camps (Recreation) [73]
       Traveling [73]

Vaccination
Use Immunization

Vagina [73]
PN 147   SC 55150
B   Female Genitalia [73]

Vaginismus [73]
PN 47   SC 55160
B   Sexual Function Disturbances [73]
R   Dyspareunia [73]
       Frigidity [73]

Vagotomy [73]
PN 119   SC 55170
B   Neurosurgery [73]

Vagus Nerve [73]
PN 114   SC 55180
B   Cranial Nerves [73]
       Parasympathetic Nervous System [73]
R   ↓ Heart [67]

Validity (Statistical)
SN Use VALIDITY (STATISTICAL) to access references from 67–72.
Use Statistical Validity

Validity (Test)
Use Test Validity

Valium
Use Diazepam

Valproic Acid [91]
PN 62   SC 55215
B   Anticonvulsive Drugs [73]

Values [67]
PN 4098   SC 55220
SN Qualities, principles or behaviors considered to be morally or intrinsically valuable or desirable. Use a more specific term if possible.
UF   Mores
B   Ethics [67]
N   Ethnic Values [73]
       Personal Values [73]
       Social Values [73]
R   Morality [67]
       World View [88]

Valves (Heart)
Use Heart Valves

Vandalism [78]
PN 75   SC 55235
SN Willful or malicious destruction or defacement of public or private property.
B   Crime [67]

Vane Kindergarten Test [73]
PN 7   SC 55240
B   Intelligence Measures [67]

Variability (Response)
Use Response Variability

Variability (Stimulus)
Use Stimulus Variability

Variability Measurement [73]
PN 188   SC 55270
B   Statistical Analysis [67]
       Statistical Measurement [73]
N   Analysis of Covariance [73]
       Analysis of Variance [67]
       Interaction Variance [73]
       Standard Deviation [73]
R   ↓ Central Tendency Measures [73]
       F Test [73]
      ↓ Statistical Correlation [67]

Variable Interval Reinforcement [73]
PN 545   SC 55280
UF   Interval Reinforcement
B   Reinforcement Schedules [67]

Variable Ratio Reinforcement [73]
PN 133   SC 55290
UF   Ratio Reinforcement
B   Reinforcement Schedules [67]

Variance Homogeneity [85]
PN 31   SC 55295
SN Extent to which the variance in two or more statistical samples is similar or different.
UF   Heterogeneity of Variance
B   Statistical Measurement [73]
R   Analysis of Variance [67]
       Standard Deviation [73]

Varimax Rotation [73]
PN 44   SC 55330
B   Orthogonal Rotation [73]

Vascular Disorders
Use Cardiovascular Disorders

Vasectomy [73]
PN 71 SC 55350
  B Birth Control [71]
    Sterilization (Sex) [73]
    Surgery [71]

Vasoconstriction [73]
PN 79 SC 55360
  R ↓ Blood Pressure Disorders [73]
    Epinephrine [67]

Vasoconstrictor Drugs [73]
PN 21 SC 55370
  UF Pressors (Drugs)
    Vasopressor Drugs
  B Drugs [67]
  N ↓ Amphetamine [67]
    Angiotensin [73]
    Bufotenine [73]
    Dihydroergotamine [73]
    Ephedrine [73]
    Methamphetamine [73]
    Methoxamine [73]
    Norepinephrine [73]
    Serotonin [73]
    Tryptamine [73]
    Tyramine [73]
  R ↓ Blood Pressure [67]
    ↓ Heart Rate Affecting Drugs [73]
    ↓ Vasodilator Drugs [73]
    Vasopressin [73]

Vasodilation [73]
PN 57 SC 55380
  R ↓ Blood Pressure Disorders [73]
    Epinephrine [67]
    ↓ Muscle Relaxing Drugs [73]
    Theophylline [73]

Vasodilator Drugs [73]
PN 150 SC 55390
  B Drugs [67]
  N Nicotinic Acid [73]
    Verapamil [91]
  R ↓ Antihypertensive Drugs [73]
    ↓ Blood Pressure [67]
    Channel Blockers [91]
    ↓ Heart Rate Affecting Drugs [73]
    ↓ Vasoconstrictor Drugs [73]

Vasopressin [73]
PN 565 SC 55400
  B Pituitary Hormones [73]
  R ↓ Vasoconstrictor Drugs [73]

Vasopressor Drugs
  Use Vasoconstrictor Drugs

Veins (Anatomy) [73]
PN 24 SC 55420
  B Blood Vessels [73]

Velocity [73]
PN 619 SC 55430
  UF Speed
  R Vibration [67]

Venereal Diseases [73]
PN 156 SC 55440
  UF Diseases (Venereal)
    Sexually Transmitted Diseases
  B Infectious Disorders [73]
  N Gonorrhea [73]
    Herpes Genitalis [88]
    ↓ Syphilis [73]
  R Acquired Immune Deficiency
    Syndrome [88]

Venereal Diseases — (cont'd)
  R Condoms [91]
    ↓ Human Immunodeficiency Virus [91]
    ↓ Infertility [73]
    Sterility [73]
    ↓ Urogenital Disorders [73]

Venezuela [73]
PN 87 SC 55450
  B South America [67]

Ventral Roots [73]
PN 15 SC 55460
  B Spinal Cord [73]

Ventral Tegmental Area
  Use Tegmentum

Ventricles (Cerebral)
  Use Cerebral Ventricles

Ventricles (Heart)
  Use Heart Ventricles

Ventricular Fibrillation
  Use Fibrillation (Heart)

Verapamil [91]
PN 27 SC 55495
  B Heart Rate Affecting Drugs [73]
    Vasodilator Drugs [73]
  R Channel Blockers [91]

Verbal Ability [67]
PN 2127 SC 55500
  B Cognitive Ability [73]
  R Academic Aptitude [73]
    Language Proficiency [88]
    Metalinguistics [94]
    ↓ Oral Communication [85]
    Proofreading [88]
    ↓ Verbal Communication [67]
    ↓ Verbal Memory [94]
    Writing Skills [85]
    ↓ Written Communication [85]

Verbal Communication [67]
PN 8258 SC 55520
  SN Communication through spoken or written language. Use narrower terms if possible.
  B Communication [67]
  N Articulation (Speech) [67]
    Conversation [73]
    ↓ Handwriting [67]
    Language Proficiency [88]
    ↓ Manual Communication [78]
    ↓ Oral Communication [85]
    Pragmatics [85]
    Storytelling [88]
    ↓ Written Communication [85]
  R ↓ Communication Skills [73]
    ↓ Grammar [67]
    ↓ Language [67]
    ↓ Language Development [67]
    ↓ Linguistics [73]
    Metalinguistics [94]
    Neurolinguistics [91]
    ↓ Speech Processing (Mechanical) [73]
    Text Structure [82]
    Verbal Ability [67]
    ↓ Vocabulary [67]
    ↓ Vocalization [67]

Verbal Comprehension [85]
PN 613 SC 55525
  B Comprehension [67]
  N Listening Comprehension [73]

Verbal Comprehension — (cont'd)
  N Reading Comprehension [73]
    Sentence Comprehension [73]

Verbal Conditioning
  Use Verbal Learning

Verbal Fluency [73]
PN 1074 SC 55540
  SN Ability to produce and manipulate words in thought or speech.
  UF Fluency
  R Language Proficiency [88]
    ↓ Oral Communication [85]
    Speech Rate [73]

Verbal Learning [67]
PN 3164 SC 55550
  SN Acquisition, retention, and retrieval of verbal stimulus materials such as nonsense syllables, words, or sentences. Compare LANGUAGE DEVELOPMENT.
  UF Conditioning (Verbal)
    Verbal Conditioning
  B Learning [67]
  N Nonsense Syllable Learning [67]
    Paired Associate Learning [67]
  R Isolation Effect [73]
    Serial Anticipation (Learning) [73]
    ↓ Serial Learning [67]
    ↓ Verbal Memory [94]

Verbal Meaning [73]
PN 567 SC 55560
  SN Connotative or denotative meaning associated with any verbally informative unit (e.g., morpheme, word, sentence, or phrase).
  B Meaning [67]
  N Word Meaning [73]
  R ↓ Figurative Language [85]
    ↓ Semantics [67]

Verbal Memory [94]
PN 0 SC 55565
  B Memory [67]
  N Semantic Memory [88]
  R ↓ Lexical Access [88]
    Lexical Decision [88]
    Verbal Ability [67]
    ↓ Verbal Learning [67]

Verbal Reinforcement [73]
PN 695 SC 55570
  B Social Reinforcement [67]
  N Praise [73]

Verbal Stimuli [82]
PN 796 SC 55575
  SN Aural or visual presentation of syllables or words or nonword letter combinations.
  B Stimulation [67]
  R ↓ Stimulus Presentation Methods [73]

Verbal Tests [73]
PN 115 SC 55580
  SN Tests designed to assess verbal ability or in which performance depends upon verbal ability.
  B Measurement [67]

Verbalization
  Use Oral Communication

Verbs [73]
PN 457 SC 55600
  B Form Classes (Language) [73]

Verdict Determination
  Use Adjudication

Vergence Movements
  Use Eye Convergence

Verification (of Theories)
  Use Theory Verification

Vernier Acuity
  Use Visual Acuity

Vertebrates [73]
PN 133   SC 55620
  B Animals [67]
  N ↓ Amphibia [73]
    ↓ Birds [67]
    ↓ Fishes [67]
    ↓ Mammals [73]
    Pigs [73]
    ↓ Reptiles [67]
  R ↓ Invertebrates [73]

Vertigo [73]
PN 62   SC 55630
  UF Dizziness
  B Symptoms [67]
  R ↓ Labyrinth Disorders [73]
    Menieres Disease [73]
    Syncope [73]

Very Old [88]
PN 2829   SC 55650
  SN Ages 85 years or older.
  B Aged [73]
  R Aged (Attitudes Toward) [78]
    ↓ Aging [91]

Vestibular Apparatus [67]
PN 363   SC 55660
  SN Major organ of equilibrium which acts as a sensory receptor that detects the position and changes in the position of the head in space.
  B Ear (Anatomy) [67]
  N Semicircular Canals [73]
  R ↓ Labyrinth (Anatomy) [73]

Vestibular Nystagmus
  Use Nystagmus

Vestibular Stimulation
  Use Somesthetic Stimulation

Veterans (Military)
  Use Military Veterans

Veterinary Medicine [73]
PN 30   SC 55680
  B Medical Sciences [67]

Vibration [67]
PN 315   SC 55690
  UF Resonance
  R Velocity [73]

Vibrators (Apparatus) [73]
PN 14   SC 55700
  B Apparatus [67]
  R ↓ Stimulators (Apparatus) [73]

Vibrotactile Thresholds [73]
PN 235   SC 55710
  SN The minimal level of vibratory stimulation, the minimal difference between any such stimuli, or the minimal vibratory stimulus change that is tactually perceptible.
  B Tactual Perception [67]
    Thresholds [67]
  R ↓ Perceptual Measures [73]

Vicarious Experiences [73]
PN 211   SC 55713
  UF Reinforcement (Vicarious)
    Vicarious Reinforcement
  B Experiences (Events) [73]
  R Imagination [67]
    ↓ Reinforcement [67]

Vicarious Reinforcement
  Use Vicarious Experiences

Victimization [73]
PN 2084   SC 55716
  SN Process or state of having been personally subjected to crime, deception, fraud, or other detrimental circumstances as a result of the deeds of others.
  B Social Interaction [67]
  R ↓ Crime [67]
    ↓ Crime Victims [82]
    ↓ Perpetrators [88]
    Persecution [73]
    Sexual Harassment [85]
    Torture [88]

Video Display Terminals
  Use Video Display Units

Video Display Units [85]
PN 313   SC 55718
  SN Electronic devices used to present information or stimulation through visual means. Use VISUAL DISPLAYS to access references from 73-84.
  UF Cathode Ray Tubes
    CRT
    Video Display Terminals
  B Computer Peripheral Devices [85]
    Visual Displays [73]
  R ↓ Television [67]
    ↓ Visual Stimulation [73]

Video Games
  Use Computer Games

Videotape Instruction [73]
PN 423   SC 55720
  SN Audiovisual teaching method which employs presentation of feedback as an aid to learning.
  B Audiovisual Instruction [73]
  R ↓ Educational Audiovisual Aids [73]

Videotape Recorders [73]
PN 62   SC 55730
  SN Device for recording on magnetic tape and having varied applications (e.g., teaching aid, analysis of research data).
  B Tape Recorders [73]

Videotapes [73]
PN 1046   SC 55740
  SN Audiovisual tape recordings used in both noneducational and educational settings. Not used as a document type identifier.
  B Audiovisual Communications Media [73]

Vietnam [82]
PN 31   SC 55745
  SN Use SOUTH VIETNAM or NORTH VIETNAM to access references from 73-81.
  UF North Vietnam
    South Vietnam
  B Southeast Asia [73]

Vigilance [67]
PN 992   SC 55750
  SN State of extended attention characterized by readiness to respond to environmental changes. Compare ATTENTION.

Vigilance — (cont'd)
  B Attention [67]
    Monitoring [73]
  R Attention Span [73]
    Selective Attention [73]

Vineland Social Maturity Scale [73]
PN 21   SC 55760
  B Nonprojective Personality Measures [73]

Violence [73]
PN 2838   SC 55770
  B Conflict [67]
  N ↓ Family Violence [82]
    Patient Violence [94]
  R Coercion [94]
    Dangerousness [88]
    Nonviolence [91]
    Partner Abuse [91]
    Physical Abuse [91]
    Self Defense [85]
    Terrorism [82]
    Torture [88]

Viral Disorders [73]
PN 210   SC 55780
  B Infectious Disorders [73]
  N Creutzfeldt Jakob Syndrome [94]
    Encephalitis [73]
    Epstein Barr Viral Disorder [94]
    Herpes Genitalis [88]
    Herpes Simplex [73]
    ↓ Human Immunodeficiency Virus [91]
    Influenza [73]
    Measles [73]
    Poliomyelitis [73]
    Rubella [73]
  R Pneumonia [73]

Virgin Islands [73]
PN 23   SC 55800
  B West Indies [73]

Virginity [73]
PN 48   SC 55810
  B Psychosexual Behavior [67]
  R Premarital Intercourse [73]

Vision [67]
PN 2883   SC 55820
  N Linear Perspective [82]
    ↓ Visual Perception [67]
  R Tunnel Vision [73]
    Visual Cortex [67]
    Visual Evoked Potentials [73]
    Visual Hallucinations [73]
    Visual Tracking [73]
    ↓ Visually Handicapped [67]

Vision Disorders [82]
PN 389   SC 55825
  SN Disorders involving the visual system, including visual neural pathways.
  B Disorders [67]
  N ↓ Eye Disorders [73]
  R ↓ Blind [67]
    ↓ Sensorially Handicapped [94]
    ↓ Visually Handicapped [67]

Vision Disturbances (Hysterical)
  Use Hysterical Vision Disturbances

Visions (Mysticism)
  Use Mysticism

Visitation (Institution)
  Use Institution Visitation

Visitation Rights
Use Child Visitation

VISTA Volunteers
Use Volunteers in Service to America

Visual Acuity [82]
PN 544   **SC** 55897
SN The ability or capacity of an observer to perceive fine detail. Consider VISUAL THRESHOLDS or VISUAL DISCRIMINATION to access references prior to 1982.
UF Vernier Acuity
B Visual Perception [67]
R Pattern Discrimination [67]
    ↓ Spatial Perception [67]

Visual Contrast [85]
PN 466   **SC** 55898
SN Perceived difference in color, brightness, or other qualities of two or more simultaneously or successively presented visual stimuli despite a lack of objective differences.
B Visual Perception [67]
N Brightness Contrast [85]
    Color Contrast [85]

Visual Cortex [67]
PN 1544   **SC** 55900
UF Cortex (Visual)
    Striate Cortex
B Occipital Lobe [73]
R ↓ Vision [67]
    Visual Receptive Fields [82]

Visual Discrimination [67]
PN 4706   **SC** 55910
SN Ability to recognize quantitative or qualitative differences between visual shapes, forms, and patterns. Use VISUAL DISCRIMINATION or VISUAL THRESHOLDS to access references on visual acuity prior to 1982.
B Perceptual Discrimination [73]
    Visual Perception [67]
R Visual Search [82]
    Visual Tracking [73]

Visual Displays [73]
PN 1838   **SC** 55920
SN Presentation of visual information in the form of charts, graphs, maps, signs, symbols, or patterns. Prior to 1985, used for visual devices such as cathode-ray tubes or instrument panels. From 1985, consider also VIDEO DISPLAY UNITS, INSTRUMENT CONTROLS, or GRAPHICAL DISPLAYS.
B Displays [67]
    Visual Stimulation [73]
N Video Display Units [85]
R ↓ Computer Peripheral Devices [85]
    Pictorial Stimuli [78]
    Spatial Frequency [82]
    Temporal Frequency [85]

Visual Evoked Potentials [73]
PN 1760   **SC** 55930
B Evoked Potentials [67]
R ↓ Cortical Evoked Potentials [73]
    ↓ Vision [67]

Visual Feedback [73]
PN 298   **SC** 55940
SN Return of information on specified behavioral functions or parameters by means of visual stimulation. Such stimulation may serve to regulate or control subsequent behavior, cognition, perception, or performance.
B Sensory Feedback [73]
    Visual Stimulation [73]

Visual Field [67]
PN 2362   **SC** 55950
B Visual Perception [67]
R Eye Fixation [82]
    Fovea [82]
    Peripheral Vision [88]

Visual Fixation
Use Eye Fixation

Visual Hallucinations [73]
PN 147   **SC** 55960
B Hallucinations [67]
R ↓ Vision [67]

Visual Masking [73]
PN 701   **SC** 55970
SN Changes in perceptual sensitivity to a visual stimulus due to the presence of a second stimulus in close temporal proximity.
B Masking [67]
R ↓ Visual Stimulation [73]

Visual Memory [94]
PN 0   **SC** 55973
B Memory [67]
R Eidetic Imagery [73]
    Spatial Memory [88]
    ↓ Visual Perception [67]

Visual Neglect
Use Sensory Neglect

Visual Perception [67]
PN 10841   **SC** 55980
B Perception [67]
    Vision [67]
N Autokinetic Illusion [67]
    Binocular Vision [67]
    ↓ Brightness Perception [73]
    ↓ Color Perception [67]
    Dark Adaptation [73]
    Eye Fixation [82]
    Face Perception [85]
    Foveal Vision [88]
    Interocular Transfer [85]
    Monocular Vision [73]
    Peripheral Vision [88]
    Stereoscopic Vision [73]
    Texture Perception [82]
    Visual Acuity [82]
    ↓ Visual Contrast [85]
    Visual Discrimination [67]
    Visual Field [67]
    ↓ Visual Thresholds [73]
R ↓ Eye (Anatomy) [67]
    ↓ Eye Disorders [73]
    Lipreading [73]
    Mirror Image [91]
    Retinal Eccentricity [91]
    Visual Memory [94]
    Visual Receptive Fields [82]
    Visual Tracking [73]

Visual Perspective
Use Linear Perspective

Visual Receptive Fields [82]
PN 387   **SC** 55985
SN Area of the retina which, when stimulated, affects a specific ganglion cell or lateral geniculate body cell, with zones in each field responding in a complementary way to various properties of visual stimuli such as color or onset/offset. Also, those zones in visual cortex which respond in a complementary way to straight-edge orientation-specific stimuli.

Visual Receptive Fields — (cont'd)
B Receptive Fields [85]
R Geniculate Bodies (Thalamus) [73]
    ↓ Neurons [73]
    ↓ Photoreceptors [73]
    Retinal Eccentricity [91]
    Visual Cortex [67]
    ↓ Visual Perception [67]

Visual Search [82]
PN 652   **SC** 55987
SN Perceptual processes associated with detecting and/or locating specified visual targets which are usually not continuously visible. Compare VISUAL TRACKING.
R Cognitive Discrimination [73]
    ↓ Eye Movements [67]
    Pattern Discrimination [67]
    Signal Detection (Perception) [67]
    Visual Discrimination [67]
    ↓ Visual Thresholds [73]

Visual Stimulation [73]
PN 5020   **SC** 55990
B Perceptual Stimulation [73]
N Dichoptic Stimulation [82]
    ↓ Illumination [67]
    Prismatic Stimulation [73]
    Stereoscopic Presentation [73]
    Tachistoscopic Presentation [73]
    ↓ Visual Displays [73]
    Visual Feedback [73]
R ↓ Color [67]
    Linear Perspective [82]
    Pictorial Stimuli [78]
    Spatial Frequency [82]
    Temporal Frequency [85]
    Video Display Units [85]
    Visual Masking [73]

Visual Thresholds [73]
PN 1628   **SC** 56000
SN The minimal level of stimulation, the minimal difference between any stimuli, or the minimal stimulus change that is visually detectable.
UF Luminance Threshold
    Photic Threshold
B Thresholds [67]
    Visual Perception [67]
N Critical Flicker Fusion Threshold [67]
R Dark Adaptation [73]
    Light Adaptation [82]
    Luminance [82]
    ↓ Perceptual Measures [73]
    Retinal Eccentricity [91]
    Visual Search [82]

Visual Tracking [73]
PN 743   **SC** 56010
SN Perceptual processes associated with following a specified visual target with the eyes along its path of movement. Usually involves a continuously visible target. Compare VISUAL SEARCH.
B Tracking [67]
R ↓ Vision [67]
    Visual Discrimination [67]
    ↓ Visual Perception [67]

Visualization
Use Imagery

Visually Handicapped [67]
PN 1360   **SC** 56020
SN Persons with varying degrees of vision loss, due to eye disorders or an organic defect of the sensorineural pathways.
B Sensorially Handicapped [94]
N ↓ Blind [67]

Visually Handicapped — (cont'd)
- **N** Partially Sighted [73]
- **R** Braille [78]
  - Braille Instruction [73]
  - Sensory Handicaps (Attit Toward) [73]
  - ↓ Vision [67]
  - ↓ Vision Disorders [82]

Vitamin C
- **Use** Ascorbic Acid

Vitamin Deficiency Disorders [73]
PN 102   SC 56040
- **B** Nutritional Deficiencies [73]
- **N** Pellagra [73]
  - Wernickes Syndrome [73]
- **R** ↓ Vitamins [73]

Vitamin Therapy [78]
PN 164   SC 56045
- **B** Organic Therapies [73]
- **R** ↓ Vitamins [73]

Vitamins [73]
PN 271   SC 56050
- **N** Ascorbic Acid [73]
  - ↓ Choline [73]
  - Nicotinamide [73]
  - Nicotinic Acid [73]
- **R** ↓ Drugs [67]
  - ↓ Vitamin Deficiency Disorders [73]
  - Vitamin Therapy [78]

Vocabulary [67]
PN 1467   SC 56060
- **UF** Words (Vocabulary)
- **B** Language [67]
- **N** Anagrams [73]
  - Antonyms [73]
  - Homographs [73]
  - Homonyms [73]
  - Neologisms [73]
  - Sight Vocabulary [73]
  - Slang [73]
  - Synonyms [73]
- **R** ↓ Semantics [67]
  - ↓ Verbal Communication [67]

Vocal Cords [73]
PN 31   SC 56070
- **B** Larynx [73]

Vocalization [67]
PN 604   SC 56075
SN Production of sounds by means of vocal cord vibrations.
- **N** ↓ Animal Vocalizations [73]
  - Crying [73]
  - Laughter [78]
  - Subvocalization [73]
  - ↓ Voice [73]
- **R** ↓ Animal Communication [67]
  - ↓ Communication [67]
  - ↓ Oral Communication [85]
  - ↓ Verbal Communication [67]

Vocalization (Infant)
- **Use** Infant Vocalization

Vocalizations (Animal)
- **Use** Animal Vocalizations

Vocational Adjustment
- **Use** Occupational Adjustment

Vocational Aspirations
- **Use** Occupational Aspirations

Vocational Choice
- **Use** Occupational Choice

Vocational Counseling
- **Use** Occupational Guidance

Vocational Counselors [73]
PN 177   SC 56140
SN Persons engaged in career guidance, usually in social service, school, government agency, industrial, or employment center settings.
- **B** Counselors [67]
- **R** Mentor [85]
  - Occupational Guidance [67]
  - School Counselors [73]
  - ↓ Social Workers [73]

Vocational Education [73]
PN 1268   SC 56150
SN Formal training in or out of school, designed to teach skills and knowledge required for occupational proficiency, especially for paraprofessional, trade, or clerical occupations.
- **UF** Industrial Arts Education
- **B** Curriculum [67]
- **N** Cooperative Education [82]
- **R** ↓ Occupations [67]

Vocational Education Teachers [88]
PN 28   SC 56155
- **UF** Technical Education Teachers
- **B** Teachers [67]

Vocational Evaluation [91]
PN 37   SC 56157
SN Assessment of vocational aptitude, job skills, and performance potential using simulated or real work experiences and measures. Used for disabled or disordered populations.
- **B** Evaluation [67]
  - Vocational Rehabilitation [67]
- **R** Disability Management [91]
  - Employability [73]
  - ↓ Employee Skills [73]
  - Work Adjustment Training [91]

Vocational Guidance
- **Use** Occupational Guidance

Vocational Interests
- **Use** Occupational Interests

Vocational Maturity [78]
PN 798   SC 56175
SN Ability to make age-appropriate vocational decisions and choices, usually predictive of good vocational adjustment.
- **UF** Career Maturity
  - Maturity (Vocational)
- **R** Occupational Attitudes [73]
  - Occupational Choice [67]
  - Occupational Interests [67]
  - Occupational Preference [73]
  - ↓ Occupations [67]

Vocational Mobility
- **Use** Occupational Mobility

Vocational Preference
- **Use** Occupational Preference

Vocational Rehabilitation [67]
PN 2424   SC 56210
SN Planning and providing necessary services required for successful job placement and subsequent vocational adjustment of handicapped clients.

Vocational Rehabilitation — (cont'd)
- **UF** Rehabilitation (Vocational)
- **B** Psychosocial Rehabilitation [73]
- **N** Supported Employment [94]
  - Vocational Evaluation [91]
  - Work Adjustment Training [91]
- **R** Disability Management [91]
  - Rehabilitation Counseling [78]
  - School to Work Transition [94]

Vocational School Students [73]
PN 287   SC 56220
- **B** Students [67]
- **R** ↓ Adolescents [67]

Vocational Schools
- **Use** Technical Schools

Vocations
- **Use** Occupations

Voice [73]
PN 509   SC 56250
- **B** Vocalization [67]
- **N** Crying [73]
  - Infant Vocalization [73]
- **R** ↓ Communication [67]
  - ↓ Oral Communication [85]

Voice Disorders
- **Use** Dysphonia

Voles
- **Use** Rodents

Volition [88]
PN 157   SC 56257
SN Process of deciding on a course of action voluntarily or without direct external influence.
- **UF** Free Will
- **R** Choice Behavior [67]
  - ↓ Decision Making [67]
  - Freedom [78]
  - Self Determination [94]

Volt Meters [73]
PN 3   SC 56260
- **B** Apparatus [67]
- **R** Shock Units [73]

Volunteer Civilian Personnel [73]
PN 101   SC 56280
SN Civilians rendering services free of charge on behalf of various social causes (e.g., mental health, community services, politics).
- **B** Volunteer Personnel [73]
- **R** ↓ Paraprofessional Personnel [73]

Volunteer Military Personnel [73]
PN 27   SC 56290
- **B** Military Personnel [67]
  - Volunteer Personnel [73]
- **R** Commissioned Officers [73]
  - ↓ Enlisted Military Personnel [73]
  - National Guardsmen [73]
  - ROTC Students [73]

Volunteer Personnel [73]
PN 637   SC 56300
- **B** Personnel [67]
- **N** Volunteer Civilian Personnel [73]
  - Volunteer Military Personnel [73]
- **R** ↓ Educational Personnel [73]
  - Fire Fighters [91]
  - National Guardsmen [73]
  - ↓ Paraprofessional Personnel [73]

Volunteer Personnel — (cont'd)
R ↓ Religious Personnel [73]
    ROTC Students [73]

Volunteers (Experiment)
Use Experiment Volunteers

Volunteers in Service to America [73]
PN 1   SC 56320
SN National corps of volunteers whose mission is to address poverty and poverty-related human, social, and environmental problems in the USA. Part of ACTION, a U.S. Government agency.
UF VISTA Volunteers
B Government Programs [73]
R Government [67]

Vomeronasal Sense [82]
PN 68   SC 56327
SN Perceptual system activated by chemical stimuli which trigger vomeronasal nerve activity.
R Chemoreceptors [73]
  ↓ Olfactory Perception [67]

Vomit Inducing Drugs
Use Emetic Drugs

Vomiting [73]
PN 303   SC 56340
B Gastrointestinal Disorders [73]
    Symptoms [67]
R ↓ Antiemetic Drugs [73]
  ↓ Emetic Drugs [73]
    Nausea [73]

Voting Behavior [73]
PN 525   SC 56350
B Behavior [67]
    Political Participation [88]
    Political Processes [73]
R ↓ Political Attitudes [73]
    Political Elections [73]
    Political Issues [73]

Vowels [73]
PN 624   SC 56360
B Letters (Alphabet) [73]
    Phonology [73]
R ↓ Phonemes [73]
    Syllables [73]
    Words (Phonetic Units) [67]

Voyeurism [73]
PN 34   SC 56370
B Sexual Deviations [67]
R Exhibitionism [73]

Vygotsky (Lev) [91]
PN 28   SC 56375
SN Identifies biographical or autobiographical studies and discussions of Vygotsky's works. Sometimes spelled Vigotsky or Vygotski.
R ↓ Language Development [67]
    Psycholinguistics [67]
  ↓ Psychologists [67]

Wages
Use Salaries

Wakefulness [73]
PN 793   SC 56410
B Consciousness States [71]
R Sleep Wake Cycle [85]

Wales [73]
PN 206   SC 56420
B Great Britain [71]

Walk In Clinics [73]
PN 43   SC 56430
SN Facilities in hospitals or other community locations which typically provide immediate access to counseling and referral; are often staffed by volunteers and nondegreed counselors and focus on minority, indigent, or youthful populations.
B Clinics [67]
R ↓ Crisis Intervention Services [73]
    Psychiatric Clinics [73]

Walking [73]
PN 318   SC 56440
B Motor Performance [73]

Wandering Behavior [91]
PN 13   SC 56450
SN Aimless activity usually resulting from a confused mental state.
B Behavior [67]
    Motor Processes [67]
R Place Disorientation [73]
  ↓ Symptoms [67]

War [67]
PN 1270   SC 56460
B Conflict [67]
    Social Issues [91]
N Nuclear War [85]
R Combat Experience [91]
    Foreign Policy Making [73]
  ↓ Government Policy Making [73]
    Peace [88]

Wasps [82]
PN 122   SC 56475
SN Any of numerous social or solitary winged hymenopterous insects.
B Insects [67]
R Larvae [73]

Water Deprivation [67]
PN 634   SC 56480
SN Absence of ad libitum water access. In experimental settings, water deprivation is used to achieve a definable level of motivation within the organism.
B Deprivation [67]
    Stimulus Deprivation [73]
R Dehydration [88]
    Thirst [67]

Water Intake [67]
PN 1755   SC 56490
SN Ingestion of water. Frequently used as an objective measure of physiological or motivational state or learning. Used for human or animal populations.
B Drinking Behavior [78]
    Fluid Intake [85]
R Animal Drinking Behavior [73]
    Dehydration [88]

Water Safety [73]
PN 123   SC 56500
SN Programs or activities for accident prevention in aquatic environments.
B Safety [67]

Water Transportation [73]
PN 143   SC 56510
B Transportation [73]
N Submarines [73]

Watson (John Broadus) [91]
PN 2   SC 56515

Watson (John Broadus) — (cont'd)
SN Identifies biographical or autobiographical studies and discussions of Watson's works.
R Behaviorism [67]
  ↓ Psychologists [67]

Weaning [73]
PN 154   SC 56520
SN Process of acclimating an infant or child to a substitute for the mother's milk. Used for human or animal populations.
B Childrearing Practices [67]
    Feeding Practices [73]
R Breast Feeding [73]
    Sucking [78]

Weapons [78]
PN 210   SC 56525
UF Firearms
R Gun Control Laws [73]

Weather
Use Atmospheric Conditions

Wechsler Adult Intelligence Scale [67]
PN 1281   SC 56530
B Intelligence Measures [67]

Wechsler Bellevue Intelligence Scale [67]
PN 38   SC 56540
B Intelligence Measures [67]

Wechsler Intelligence Scale Children [67]
PN 1810   SC 56550
B Intelligence Measures [67]

Wechsler Memory Scale [88]
PN 66   SC 56553
B Neuropsychological Assessment [82]
    Retention Measures [73]

Wechsler Preschool Primary Scale [88]
PN 55   SC 56555
B Intelligence Measures [67]

Weight (Body)
Use Body Weight

Weight (Statistics)
Use Statistical Weighting

Weight Control [85]
PN 686   SC 56565
SN Deliberate regulation of one's weight through diet, exercise, or other means. Also, the relative weight change resulting from such regulation practices. Used for human populations only.
R Aerobic Exercise [88]
  ↓ Body Weight [67]
    Diets [78]
  ↓ Exercise [73]
  ↓ Food Intake [67]
    Health Behavior [82]

Weight Perception [67]
PN 172   SC 56570
SN Awareness of mass or weight.
B Somesthetic Perception [67]

Weightlessness [67]
PN 37   SC 56580
B Gravitational Effects [67]
R ↓ Somesthetic Stimulation [73]
    Spaceflight [67]

Weightlifting [94]
PN 0   SC 56585
B   Exercise [73]
     Recreation [67]
     Sports [67]

Welfare Services (Government) [73]
PN 399   SC 56600
B   Government Programs [73]
R   Community Welfare Services [73]
     Government [67]
     Medicaid [94]

Well Being [94]
PN 0   SC 56603
R   ↓ Adjustment [67]
     ↓ Health [73]
     Life Satisfaction [85]
     ↓ Mental Health [67]
     ↓ Quality of Life [85]

Wellness
    Use Health

Welsh Figure Preference Test [73]
PN 5   SC 56610
B   Nonprojective Personality Measures [73]

Wepman Test of Auditory Discrim [73]
PN 7   SC 56620
B   Speech and Hearing Measures [73]

Wernickes Syndrome [73]
PN 63   SC 56630
SN   Use APHASIA for Wernicke's aphasia.
B   Alcoholism [67]
     Encephalopathies [82]
     Syndromes [73]
     Vitamin Deficiency Disorders [73]

West Africa [88]
PN 15   SC 56635
B   Africa [67]

West German Federal Republic
SN   Term discontinued in 1982. Use WEST GER-
MAN FEDERAL REPUBLIC to access references
from 67–81.
    Use West Germany

West Germany [82]
PN 897   SC 56642
SN   Use WEST GERMAN FEDERAL REPUBLIC
to access references from 67–81.
UF   West German Federal Republic
B   Germany [88]

West Indies [73]
PN 131   SC 56650
N   Bahama Islands [73]
     Barbados [91]
     Bermuda [91]
     Cuba [73]
     Dominican Republic [73]
     Haiti [73]
     Hispaniola [73]
     Jamaica [73]
     Netherlands Antilles [88]
     Puerto Rico [73]
     Saint Lucia [91]
     Saint Vincent [91]
     Trinidad and Tobago [82]
     Virgin Islands [73]
R   Latin America [88]

Western Europe [88]
PN 34   SC 56663
B   Europe [73]

Western Samoa [91]
PN 3   SC 56664
B   South Pacific [78]

Whales [85]
PN 24   SC 56665
B   Mammals [73]
N   Dolphins [73]
     Porpoises [73]

Wheelchairs
    Use Mobility Aids

Whistleblowing
    Use Informants

White Betz A B Scale [73]
PN 3   SC 56670
B   Nonprojective Personality Measures [73]

White Blood Cells
    Use Leucocytes

White Collar Workers [73]
PN 300   SC 56690
SN   Individuals employed in technical, profes-
sional, sales, administrative, or clerical positions.
B   Business and Industrial Personnel [67]
N   Accountants [73]
     Clerical Personnel [73]
     ↓ Management Personnel [73]
     Sales Personnel [73]
     Secretarial Personnel [73]

White Noise [73]
PN 281   SC 56700
SN   Noise composed of random mixture of
sounds of different wavelengths.
B   Auditory Stimulation [67]

White Rats
    Use Rats

Whites [82]
PN 3306   SC 56720
SN   Populations of European, North African, or
Southwest Asian descent. May also be used to
refer to population groups in these areas when
cultural or ethnic comparisons are studied. Use
CAUCASIANS to access references from 73–81.
UF   Caucasians
R   Anglos [88]
     ↓ Ethnic Groups [73]
     Race (Anthropological) [73]

Wholistic Health
    Use Holistic Health

Wide Range Achievement Test [73]
PN 147   SC 56730
B   Achievement Measures [67]

Widowers [73]
PN 219   SC 56740
B   Human Males [73]
R   ↓ Family [67]
     ↓ Marital Status [73]
     ↓ Parental Absence [73]

Widows [73]
PN 549   SC 56750
B   Human Females [73]
R   ↓ Family [67]

Widows — (cont'd)
R   ↓ Marital Status [73]
     ↓ Parental Absence [73]

Wilcoxon Sign Rank Test [73]
PN 13   SC 56760
UF   Sign Rank Test
B   Nonparametric Statistical Tests [67]

Wilderness Experience [91]
PN 28   SC 56763
SN   Outdoor environment and activities used to
promote experiential learning or to treat and re-
habilitate individuals with physical, emotional, or
behavioral problems.
UF   Outward Bound
R   Management Training [73]
     ↓ Psychotherapeutic Techniques [67]
     ↓ Recreation [67]
     ↓ Rehabilitation [67]
     ↓ Sports [67]
     Therapeutic Camps [78]

Willpower
    Use Self Control

Wilson Patterson Conservatism Scale [73]
PN 15   SC 56780
B   Attitude Measures [67]

Wine [73]
PN 35   SC 56810
B   Alcoholic Beverages [73]

Winter Depression
    Use Seasonal Affective Disorder

Wisconsin Card Sorting Test [94]
PN 0   SC 56835
B   Neuropsychological Assessment [82]

Wisdom [94]
PN 0   SC 56837
R   Intelligence [67]
     ↓ Judgment [67]
     ↓ Knowledge Level [78]
     ↓ Personality Traits [67]

Witchcraft [73]
PN 101   SC 56840
R   Ethnology [67]
     Faith Healing [73]
     ↓ Parapsychology [67]

Withdrawal (Defense Mechanism) [73]
PN 115   SC 56860
SN   Psychoanalytic term describing the escape
from or avoidance of emotionally or psychologi-
cally painful situations.
B   Defense Mechanisms [67]

Within Subjects Design
    Use Repeated Measures

Witnesses [85]
PN 451   SC 56885
SN   Persons giving evidence in a court of law or
observing traumatic events in a nonlegal context.
Also used for analog studies of eyewitness iden-
tification performance, perception of witness
credibility, and other studies of witness charac-
teristics having legal implications.
UF   Eyewitnesses
R   ↓ Legal Evidence [91]
     Legal Interrogation [94]
     ↓ Legal Testimony [82]

Wives [73]
PN 1548   SC 56900
   B   Human Females [73]
       Spouses [73]
   N   Housewives [73]

Wolves [73]
PN 95   SC 56910
   B   Mammals [73]

Women
   Use   Human Females

Womens Liberation Movement [73]
PN 369   SC 56920
   B   Social Movements [67]
   R   ↓ Activist Movements [73]
       Feminism [78]

Woodcock Johnson Psychoed Battery [94]
PN 0   SC 56925
   B   Achievement Measures [67]
   R   Educational Diagnosis [78]

Word Associations [67]
PN 1635   SC 56930
   UF   Associations (Word)
   R   ↓ Associative Processes [67]
       ↓ Cognitive Processes [67]
       Paired Associate Learning [67]

Word Blindness
   Use   Alexia

Word Deafness
   Use   Aphasia

Word Frequency [73]
PN 598   SC 56970
   SN   Statistical probability of the occurrence of a given word in a given natural language.
   R   Contextual Associations [67]

Word Meaning [73]
PN 1846   SC 56980
   SN   Connotative or denotative significance of a word.
   B   Verbal Meaning [73]
   R   Connotations [73]
       Contextual Associations [67]
       ↓ Lexical Access [88]
       Lexical Decision [88]

Word Origins
   Use   Etymology

Word Processing [91]
PN 48   SC 56993
   SN   Use of computer software to compose, edit, and produce text.
   B   Computer Software [67]
       Data Processing [67]
   R   Clerical Secretarial Skills [73]
       ↓ Computer Applications [73]
       Information Systems [91]
       Typing [91]

Word Recognition [88]
PN 885   SC 56995
   R   ↓ Associative Processes [67]
       Human Information Storage [73]
       ↓ Reading Skills [73]
       Recognition (Learning) [67]
       Sight Vocabulary [73]
       Speech Perception [67]
       Words (Phonetic Units) [67]

Words (Form Classes)
   Use   Form Classes (Language)

Words (Phonetic Units) [67]
PN 4556   SC 57020
   SN   Spoken or written symbolic representation of an idea, frequently viewed as the smallest grammatically independent unit.
   R   Antonyms [73]
       Consonants [73]
       Etymology [73]
       ↓ Grammar [67]
       Homographs [73]
       Homonyms [73]
       ↓ Lexical Access [88]
       Lexical Decision [88]
       Morphology (Language) [73]
       Neologisms [73]
       ↓ Semantics [67]
       Synonyms [73]
       Vowels [73]
       Word Recognition [88]

Words (Vocabulary)
   Use   Vocabulary

Work (Attitudes Toward) [73]
PN 1763   SC 57037
   SN   General work values. Use EMPLOYEE ATTITUDES for specific job situations and OCCUPATIONAL ATTITUDES for specific careers.
   UF   Work Ethic
   B   Attitudes [67]
   R   ↓ Employee Attitudes [67]
       Employer Attitudes [73]
       Job Involvement [78]
       Occupational Attitudes [73]
       ↓ Personnel [67]

Work Adjustment Training [91]
PN 14   SC 57045
   SN   Training or programs to help disabled individuals increase work productivity, handle day to day demands of competitive employment, develop work tolerance, and to encourage interpersonal work relationships.
   B   Vocational Rehabilitation [67]
   R   ↓ Adjustment [67]
       Occupational Adjustment [73]
       Rehabilitation Counseling [78]
       Supported Employment [94]
       Vocational Evaluation [91]

Work Environments
   Use   Working Conditions

Work Ethic
   Use   Work (Attitudes Toward)

Work Load [82]
PN 394   SC 57055
   SN   Amount of work or working time expected from, assigned to, or performed by an individual.
   B   Job Characteristics [85]
   R   ↓ Division of Labor [88]
       Human Channel Capacity [73]
       Job Analysis [67]
       ↓ Job Performance [67]
       Work Scheduling [73]
       ↓ Working Conditions [73]

Work Related Illnesses [94]
PN 0   SC 57057
   SN   Includes both physical and mental illnesses, injuries, or disorders. Consider OCCUPATIONAL STRESS for work related stress.
   B   Disorders [67]
   R   Industrial Accidents [73]
       Occupational Exposure [88]

Work Related Illnesses — (cont'd)
   R   Occupational Safety [73]
       Occupational Stress [73]
       ↓ Working Conditions [73]
       Workmens Compensation Insurance [73]

Work Rest Cycles [73]
PN 88   SC 57060
   SN   Strictly scheduled periods of working and resting based on observations that any increase in number of working hours beyond an optimal point diminishes production and efficiency.
   B   Working Conditions [73]
   R   Work Scheduling [73]

Work Scheduling [73]
PN 260   SC 57070
   SN   Individual or organizational distribution of workload or work hours. Consider also WORKDAY SHIFTS.
   UF   Flextime
       Scheduling (Work)
   R   ↓ Management Methods [73]
       Work Load [82]
       Work Rest Cycles [73]

Work Study Programs
   Use   Educational Programs

Work Week Length [73]
PN 58   SC 57080
   SN   Actual number of hours or workdays an employee is required to work during a consecutive 7-day period.
   B   Working Conditions [73]

Workday Shifts [73]
PN 363   SC 57090
   SN   Regularly scheduled daily working hours or scheduled working shifts with core hours being in morning, evening, or late night/predawn. Consider also WORK SCHEDULING.
   UF   Shifts (Workday)
   B   Working Conditions [73]

Workers
   Use   Personnel

Working Alliance
   Use   Therapeutic Alliance

Working Conditions [73]
PN 2557   SC 57120
   SN   Factors which contribute to the global milieu of the workplace. Includes physical environment characteristics, job content and work load, and psychosocial factors such as personnel composition, norms, attitudes, motivation, and employee services.
   UF   Factory Environments
       Office Environment
       Work Environments
   B   Social Environments [73]
   N   Job Enrichment [73]
       Noise Levels (Work Areas) [73]
       Occupational Safety [73]
       Work Rest Cycles [73]
       Work Week Length [73]
       Workday Shifts [73]
       Working Space [73]
   R   Human Factors Engineering [73]
       Occupational Exposure [88]
       Organizational Climate [73]
       Person Environment Fit [91]
       ↓ Personnel [67]
       Quality of Work Life [88]
       Work Load [82]
       Work Related Illnesses [94]

Working Memory
  Use Short Term Memory

Working Space 73
PN 58   SC 57130
SN Physical characteristics of job setting, including such factors as amount of space, noise level, or lighting conditions.
  B Working Conditions 73

Working Women 78
PN 1626   SC 57135
  B Human Females 73
  R Dual Careers 82
    ↓ Employment Status 82
    ↓ Family 67
    ↓ Occupations 67
    ↓ Personnel 67
    Single Mothers 94

Workmens Compensation Insurance 73
PN 112   SC 57140
SN Insurance that provides medical benefits for employees who are injured in work-related accidents and provides continued income during disability.
  B Employee Benefits 73
    Employee Health Insurance 73
  R Work Related Illnesses 94

World View 88
PN 396   SC 57150
  UF Philosophy of Life
  R ↓ Attitudes 67
    Self Determination 94
    ↓ Values 67

Worms 67
PN 77   SC 57160
  B Invertebrates 73
  N Earthworms 73
    Planarians 73

Worry
  Use Anxiety

Worship
  Use Religious Practices

Wounds 73
PN 15   SC 57180
  B Injuries 73
  N Self Inflicted Wounds 73
  R Burns 73
    Electrical Injuries 73
    ↓ Head Injuries 73

Wrist 73
PN 63   SC 57190
  B Joints (Anatomy) 73
  R Arm (Anatomy) 73
    Hand (Anatomy) 67

Writers 91
PN 107   SC 57195
  UF Authors
  B Artists 73
  R Drama 73
    ↓ Literature 67

Writing (Creative)
SN Use LITERATURE to access references from 73-93.
  Use Creative Writing

Writing (Cursive)
  Use Cursive Writing

Writing (Handwriting)
  Use Handwriting

Writing Skills 85
PN 949   SC 57225
SN Proficiency in writing as developed through practice and influenced by ability.
  B Communication Skills 73
  R ↓ Literacy 73
    Verbal Ability 67
    ↓ Written Communication 85

Written Communication 85
PN 1451   SC 57227
SN Expression of information in written form.
  B Verbal Communication 67
  N Creative Writing 94
  R Note Taking 91
    Proofreading 88
    Rhetoric 91
    Verbal Ability 67
    Writing Skills 85

Written Language 67
PN 1259   SC 57230
SN System of signs and symbols used to convey information.
  B Language 67
  N ↓ Alphabets 73
    ↓ Handwriting 67
    Numbers (Numerals) 67
    Paragraphs 73
    Readability 78
  R ↓ Legibility 78
    Orthography 73

Wryneck
  Use Torticollis

X Ray Diagnosis
  Use Roentgenography

X Ray Therapy
  Use Radiation Therapy

Xylocaine
  Use Lidocaine

Yawning 88
PN 71   SC 57300
  B Reflexes 71
  R Respiration 67

Yemen 91
PN 1   SC 57305
  R Middle East 78

Yoga 73
PN 177   SC 57310
  B Exercise 73
    Religious Practices 73
  R Relaxation 73

Yohimbine 88
PN 108   SC 57315
  B Adrenergic Blocking Drugs 73

Young Adults 73
PN 3948   SC 57320
SN Ages 18-29. Used in noneducational contexts. Applied only if age is important to the research focus.
  UF Youth (Adults)
  B Adults 67
  R ↓ Adolescents 67
    Adult Development 78
    ↓ College Students 67

Young Adults — (cont'd)
  R Graduate Students 67
    Postgraduate Students 73

Youth (Adolescents)
  Use Adolescents

Youth (Adults)
  Use Young Adults

Youth (Children)
  Use Children

Yugoslavia 73
PN 235   SC 57360
  B Europe 73

Z Scores
  Use Standard Scores

Zaire 88
PN 31   SC 57364
  B Africa 67

Zambia 82
PN 40   SC 57365
  B Africa 67

Zen Buddhism 73
PN 81   SC 57370
  B Buddhism 73

Zidovudine 94
PN 0   SC 57371
  UF Azidothymidine
    AZT
  B Antiviral Drugs 94
  R Acquired Immune Deficiency
    Syndrome 88
    ↓ Human Immunodeficiency Virus 91

Zimbabwe 88
PN 59   SC 57372
  B Africa 67

Zimeldine 88
PN 38   SC 57373
  B Antidepressant Drugs 71

Zinc 85
PN 71   SC 57375
  B Electrolytes 73
    Metallic Elements 73

Zoo Environment
  Use Animal Captivity

Zoology 73
PN 14   SC 57380
  B Biology 67

Zulliger Z Test 73
PN 11   SC 57390
  B Projective Personality Measures 73

Zungs Self Rating Depression Scale 73
PN 53   SC 57400
  B Nonprojective Personality Measures 73

Abdomen
Abdominal Wall
Abducens Nerve
Ability
Ability Grouping
Ability Level
Ability Tests *USE Aptitude Measures*
Artistic **Ability**
Cognitive **Ability**
Henmon Nelson Tests Mental **Ability**
Illinois Test Psycholinguist **Abil**
Learning **Ability**
Mathematical **Ability**
Musical **Ability**
Nonverbal **Ability**
Numerical Ability *USE Mathematical Ability*
Reading **Ability**
School and College **Ability** Test
Spatial **Ability**
Verbal **Ability**
Ablation *USE Lesions*
Abortion Laws
Elective Abortion *USE Induced Abortion*
Induced **Abortion**
Spontaneous **Abortion**
Therapeutic Abortion *USE Induced Abortion*
Maslow **(Abraham** Harold)
Abreaction *USE Catharsis*
Father **Absence**
Mother **Absence**
Parental **Absence**
Employee **Absenteeism**
Absorption (Physiological)
Abstinence (Drugs) *USE Drug Abstinence*
Alcohol Abstinence *USE Sobriety*
Drug **Abstinence**
Sexual **Abstinence**
Abstraction
Abuse Potential (Drugs)
    USE Drug Abuse Liability
Alcohol **Abuse**
Child **Abuse**
Client Abuse *USE Patient Abuse*
Drug **Abuse**
Drug **Abuse** Liability
Drug **Abuse** Prevention
Elder **Abuse**
Emotional **Abuse**
Inhalant **Abuse**
Multidrug Abuse *USE Polydrug Abuse*
Partner **Abuse**
Patient **Abuse**
Physical **Abuse**
Polydrug **Abuse**
Psychological Abuse *USE Emotional Abuse*
Sexual **Abuse**
Solvent Abuse *USE Inhalant Abuse*
Spouse Abuse *USE Partner Abuse*
Substance Abuse *USE Drug Abuse*
Substance Abuse Prevention
    USE Drug Abuse Prevention
Academic Achievement
Academic Achievement Motivation
Academic Achievement Prediction
Academic Aptitude
Academic Environment
Academic Failure
Academic Grade Level *USE Grade Level*
Academic Overachievement
Academic Records *USE Student Records*
Academic Specialization
Academic Underachievement
College **Academic** Achievement
Acalculia
Accelerated Speech *USE Speech Rate*
Acceleration Effects
Self Acceptance *USE Self Perception*
Social **Acceptance**
Lexical **Access**

Accessory Nerve *USE Cranial Nerves*
Accident Prevention
Accident Proneness
Accidents
Air Traffic **Accidents**
Automobile Accidents *USE Motor Traffic Accidents*
Cerebrovascular **Accidents**
Home **Accidents**
Industrial **Accidents**
Motor Traffic **Accidents**
Pedestrian **Accidents**
Transportation **Accidents**
Thermal **Acclimatization**
Ocular **Accommodation**
Accomplishment *USE Achievement*
Accountability
Accountants
Accreditation (Education Personnel)
Accreditation (Educational Programs)
    USE Educational Program Accreditation
Educational Program **Accreditation**
Hospital **Accreditation**
School Accreditation
    USE Educational Program Accreditation
Teacher Accreditation
    USE Accreditation (Education Personnel)
Acculturation *USE Cultural Assimilation*
Nucleus **Accumbens**
Acetaldehyde
Acetazolamide
Acetic Aldehyde *USE Acetaldehyde*
Acetylcholine
Acetylcholinesterase
Acetylsalicylic Acid *USE Aspirin*
Aches *USE Pain*
Achievement
Achievement Measures
Achievement Motivation
Achievement Potential
Academic **Achievement**
Academic **Achievement** Motivation
Academic **Achievement** Prediction
Attainment (Achievement) *USE Achievement*
College Academic **Achievement**
Mathematics **Achievement**
Need Achievement *USE Achievement Motivation*
Reading **Achievement**
Scholastic Achievement *USE Academic Achievement*
School Achievement *USE Academic Achievement*
Stanford **Achievement** Test
Wide Range **Achievement** Test
Achilles Tendon Reflex
Achromatic Color
Acetylsalicylic Acid *USE Aspirin*
Ascorbic **Acid**
Aspartic **Acid**
Deoxyribonucleic **Acid**
Dihydroxyphenylacetic **Acid**
DNA (Deoxyribonucleic Acid) *USE Deoxyribonucleic Acid*
Folic **Acid**
Gamma Aminobutyric **Acid**
Gamma Aminobutyric **Acid** Agonists
Gamma Aminobutyric **Acid** Antagonists
Glutamic **Acid**
Homovanillic **Acid**
Hydroxyindoleacetic **Acid** (5-)
Ibotenic **Acid**
Kainic **Acid**
Lactic **Acid**
Lysergic **Acid** Diethylamide
Nicotinic **Acid**
Nicotinic Acid Amide *USE Nicotinamide*
Ribonucleic **Acid**
RNA (Ribonucleic Acid) *USE Ribonucleic Acid*
Uric **Acid**
Valproic **Acid**
Acids
Amino **Acids**
Fatty **Acids**

Nucleic **Acids**
Acoustic Nerve
Acoustic Reflex
Acoustic Stimuli *USE Auditory Stimulation*
Acquaintance Rape
Acquired Immune Deficiency Syndrome
Acrophobia
ACTH (Hormone) *USE Corticotropin*
ACTH Releasing Factor
   USE Corticotropin Releasing Factor
Acting Out
Affirmative **Action**
Active Avoidance
   USE Avoidance Conditioning
Student **Activism**
Activist Movements
Activities of Daily Living
Daily **Activities**
Extracurricular **Activities**
Activity Level
Activity Therapy *USE Recreation Therapy*
Electrical **Activity**
Self **Actualization**
Auditory **Acuity**
Hearing Acuity *USE Auditory Acuity*
Vernier Acuity *USE Visual Acuity*
Visual **Acuity**
Acupuncture
Acute Alcoholic Intoxication
Acute Paranoid Disorder
   USE Paranoia (Psychosis)
Acute Psychosis
Acute Psychotic Episode
   USE Acute Psychosis
Acute Schizophrenia
Psychotic Episode (Acute) *USE Acute Psychosis*
Adaptability (Personality)
Adaptation
Dark **Adaptation**
Environmental **Adaptation**
Light **Adaptation**
Sensory **Adaptation**
Social Adaptation *USE Social Adjustment*
Adaptive Behavior
Adaptive Testing
Addiction
Drug **Addiction**
Heroin **Addiction**
Addisons Disease
Food **Additives**
Adenosine
Cyclic **Adenosine** Monophosphate
Gough **Adjective** Check List
Adjectives
Adjudication
Adjunctive Behavior
Adjustment
Adjustment Disorders
Emotional **Adjustment**
Marital Adjustment *USE Marital Relations*
Occupational **Adjustment**
Personal Adjustment *USE Emotional Adjustment*
Psychological Adjustment *USE Emotional Adjustment*
School **Adjustment**
Social **Adjustment**
Vocational Adjustment *USE Occupational Adjustment*
Work **Adjustment** Training
Adler (Alfred)
Adlerian Psychotherapy
   USE Individual Psychotherapy
Drug **Administration** Methods
Educational **Administration**
Hospital **Administration**
School Administration
   USE Educational Administration
Test **Administration**
Administrators
   USE Management Personnel
Educational Administrators *USE School Administrators*

School **Administrators**
Facility **Admission**
Hospital **Admission**
Psychiatric Hospital **Admission**
Student **Admission** Criteria
Adolescence
Adolescent Attitudes
Adolescent Development
Adolescent Fathers
Adolescent Mothers
Adolescent Pregnancy
Adolescent Psychiatry
Adolescent Psychology
Adolescent Psychotherapy
Adolescents
Adopted Children
Adoptees
Adoption (Child)
Interracial **Adoption**
Transracial Adoption *USE Interracial Adoption*
Adoptive Parents
Adrenal Cortex Hormones
Adrenal Cortex Steroids
   USE Corticosteroids
Adrenal Gland Disorders
Adrenal Gland Secretion
Adrenal Glands
Adrenal Medulla Hormones
Adrenalectomy
Adrenaline *USE Epinephrine*
Adrenergic Blocking Drugs
Adrenergic Drugs
Adrenergic Nerves
Adrenocorticotropin *USE Corticotropin*
Adrenolytic Drugs
Adult Attitudes
Adult Children *USE Adult Offspring*
Adult Development
Adult Education
Adult Offspring
Leiter **Adult** Intelligence Scale
Offenders (Adult) *USE Criminals*
Wechsler **Adult** Intelligence Scale
Adultery *USE Extramarital Intercourse*
Adulthood
Adults
Young **Adults**
Advance Directives
Advance Organizers
Adventitiously Handicapped
Adverbs
Drug **Adverse** Reactions
   USE Side Effects (Drug)
Advertising
Television **Advertising**
Advocacy
Child Advocacy *USE Advocacy*
Aerobic Exercise
Aerospace Personnel
Aesthetic Preferences
Aesthetics
CNS **Affecting** Drugs
Heart Rate **Affecting** Drugs
Affection
Affective Disorders
   USE Affective Disturbances
Affective Disturbances
Affective Education
Affective Psychosis
Seasonal **Affective** Disorder
Afferent Pathways
Afferent Stimulation
Afferentation *USE Afferent Stimulation*
Affiliation Motivation
Need for Affiliation *USE Affiliation Motivation*
Religious **Affiliation**
Affirmative Action
Afghanistan
Africa

242

East **Africa**
South **Africa**
West **Africa**
African Americans *USE Blacks*
Aftercare
Perceptual **Aftereffect**
Afterimage
Age Differences
Age Discrimination
Age Regression (Hypnotic)
Developmental **Age** Groups
Intelligence **Age** *USE Mental Age*
Mental **Age**
Old Age *USE Aged*
Preschool **Age** Children
School **Age** Children
Aged
Aged (Attitudes Toward)
Middle **Aged**
Agencies (Groups) *USE Organizations*
Government **Agencies**
Insurance Agents *USE Sales Personnel*
Aggressive Behavior
Animal **Aggressive** Behavior
Passive **Aggressive** Personality
Aggressiveness
Physical **Agility**
Aging
Aging (Attitudes Toward)
Physiological **Aging**
Paralysis Agitans *USE Parkinsons Disease*
Agitated Depression
USE Major Depression
Agitation
Agnosia
Agonistic Behavior
USE Aggressive Behavior
Benzodiazepine **Agonists**
Dopamine **Agonists**
Gamma Aminobutyric Acid **Agonists**
Narcotic **Agonists**
Opiate Agonists *USE Narcotic Agonists*
Serotonin **Agonists**
Agoraphobia
Agrammatism *USE Aphasia*
Agraphia
Agricultural Extension Workers
Agricultural Workers
School Federal Aid *USE Educational Financial Assistance*
Psychiatric **Aides**
Teacher **Aides**
AIDS
USE Acquired Immune Deficiency Syndrome
AIDS Prevention
Educational Audiovisual **Aids**
Hearing **Aids**
Mobility **Aids**
Optical **Aids**
Air Encephalography
USE Pneumoencephalography
Air Force Personnel
Air Traffic Accidents
Air Traffic Control
Air Transportation
Encephalography (Air) *USE Pneumoencephalography*
Aircraft
Aircraft Crew *USE Aerospace Personnel*
Aircraft Pilots
Navigators (Aircraft) *USE Aerospace Personnel*
Airplanes *USE Aircraft*
Akathisia
Akinesia *USE Apraxia*
Alanines
Alarm Responses
Alaska
Ellis **(Albert)**
Albinism
Serum **Albumin**

Alcohol Abstinence *USE Sobriety*
Alcohol Abuse
Alcohol Dehydrogenases
Alcohol Drinking Attitudes
Alcohol Drinking Patterns
Alcohol Education *USE Drug Education*
Alcohol Intoxication
Alcohol Rehabilitation
Alcohol Withdrawal
Blood **Alcohol** Concentration
Ethyl Alcohol *USE Ethanol*
Fetal **Alcohol** Syndrome
Methyl Alcohol *USE Methanol*
Alcoholic Beverages
Alcoholic Hallucinosis
Alcoholic Psychosis
Acute **Alcoholic** Intoxication
Chronic **Alcoholic** Intoxication
Alcoholics Anonymous
Alcoholism
Alcohols
Acetic Aldehyde *USE Acetaldehyde*
Aldolases
Aldosterone
Alexia
Alexithymia
Adler **(Alfred)**
Algebra *USE Mathematics*
Algeria
Algorithms
Alienation
Alkaloids
Opium Alkaloids *USE Alkaloids AND Opiates*
Allergens *USE Antigens*
Allergic Disorders
Allergic Skin Disorders
Drug **Allergies**
Food **Allergies**
Therapeutic **Alliance**
Working Alliance *USE Therapeutic Alliance*
Alligators *USE Crocodilians*
Reward **Allocation**
Allport Vernon Lindzey Study Values
Living **Alone**
Alopecia
Alpha Methylparatyrosine
Alpha Rhythm
Initial Teaching **Alphabet**
Letters **(Alphabet)**
Alphabets
Alprazolam
Delayed **Alternation**
Language Alternation *USE Code Switching*
Spontaneous **Alternation**
Alternative Schools
USE Nontraditional Education
Altitude Effects
Altruism
Aluminum
Alzheimers Disease
Amantadine
Amaurotic Familial Idiocy
Stimulus **Ambiguity**
Tolerance for **Ambiguity**
Ambition *USE Aspirations*
Ambivalence
Amblyopia
Ambulatory Care
USE Outpatient Treatment
Amenorrhea
Amentia *USE Mental Retardation*
Central **America**
Latin **America**
North **America**
South **America**
Volunteers in Service to **America**
American Indians
American Samoa
African Americans *USE Blacks*

Chinese Americans *USE Asians*
Cuban Americans *USE Hispanics*
Japanese Americans *USE Asians*
Mexican **Americans**
Native Americans *USE American Indians*
Puerto Rican Americans *USE Hispanics*
Spanish Americans *USE Hispanics*
Nicotinic Acid Amide *USE Nicotinamide*
Amine Oxidase Inhibitors
Amines
Sympathomimetic **Amines**
Amino Acids
Gamma **Aminobutyric** Acid
Gamma **Aminobutyric** Acid Agonists
Gamma **Aminobutyric** Acid Antagonists
Aminotransferases *USE Transaminases*
Amitriptyline
Amnesia
Amniocentesis *USE Prenatal Diagnosis*
Amniotic Fluid
Amobarbital
Reinforcement **Amounts**
Amphetamine
Amphibia
Amplifiers (Apparatus)
Response **Amplitude**
Amputation
Amputees
Amygdaloid Body
Amytal *USE Amobarbital*
Anabolism
Anabolites *USE Metabolites*
Anaclitic Depression
Anagram Problem Solving
Anagrams
Analeptic Drugs
Analgesia
Analgesic Drugs
Analog Computers
Miller **Analogies** Test
Analogy
Analysis
Analysis of Covariance
Analysis of Variance
Behavior Analysis *USE Behavioral Assessment*
Causal **Analysis**
Cluster **Analysis**
Cohort **Analysis**
Confirmatory Factor Analysis *USE Factor Analysis*
Content **Analysis**
Content **Analysis** (Test)
Costs and Cost **Analysis**
Dream **Analysis**
Error **Analysis**
Factor **Analysis**
Interaction **Analysis** (Statistics)
Item **Analysis** (Statistical)
Item **Analysis** (Test)
Job **Analysis**
Linkage Analysis *USE Genetic Linkage*
Meta **Analysis**
Multivariate **Analysis**
Path **Analysis**
Regression Analysis *USE Statistical Regression*
Risk **Analysis**
Self **Analysis**
Statistical **Analysis**
Systems **Analysis**
Task **Analysis**
Transactional **Analysis**
Analysts *USE Psychoanalysts*
Analytic Psychology
USE Jungian Psychology
Analytical Psychotherapy
Neural **Analyzers**
Anaphylactic Shock
Anatomical Systems
Anatomically Detailed Dolls
Anatomy

Arm **(Anatomy)**
Arteries **(Anatomy)**
Back **(Anatomy)**
Capillaries **(Anatomy)**
Diaphragm **(Anatomy)**
Ear **(Anatomy)**
Elbow **(Anatomy)**
Eye **(Anatomy)**
Face **(Anatomy)**
Feet **(Anatomy)**
Fingers **(Anatomy)**
Hand **(Anatomy)**
Head **(Anatomy)**
Heels (Anatomy) *USE Feet (Anatomy)*
Joints **(Anatomy)**
Labyrinth **(Anatomy)**
Leg **(Anatomy)**
Mouth **(Anatomy)**
Neck **(Anatomy)**
Palm **(Anatomy)**
Scalp **(Anatomy)**
Shoulder **(Anatomy)**
Skin **(Anatomy)**
Teeth **(Anatomy)**
Toes (Anatomy) *USE Feet (Anatomy)*
Veins **(Anatomy)**
Ancestors
Androgen Antagonists
USE Antiandrogens
Androgens
Androgyny
Anemia
Anencephaly
Anesthesia (Feeling)
Hysterical **Anesthesia**
Anesthesiology
Anesthetic Drugs
Ether **(Anesthetic)**
General **Anesthetics**
Local **Anesthetics**
Aneurysms
Anger
Angina Pectoris
Angiography
Angiotensin
Cerebellopontine Angle *USE Cerebellum*
Anglos
Angola
Angst *USE Anxiety*
Anguish *USE Distress*
Anhedonia
Carbonic **Anhydrase**
Animal Aggressive Behavior
Animal Assisted Therapy
Animal Behavior *USE Animal Ethology*
Animal Biological Rhythms
Animal Breeding
Animal Captivity
Animal Circadian Rhythms
Animal Coloration
Animal Communication
Animal Courtship Behavior
Animal Courtship Displays
Animal Defensive Behavior
Animal Development
Animal Distress Calls
Animal Division of Labor
Animal Domestication
Animal Dominance
Animal Drinking Behavior
Animal Emotionality
Animal Environments
Animal Escape Behavior
Animal Ethology
Animal Exploratory Behavior
Animal Feeding Behavior
Animal Foraging Behavior
Animal Grooming Behavior
Animal Hoarding Behavior

Animal Homing
Animal Human Interaction
   USE Interspecies Interaction
Animal Innate Behavior
   USE Instinctive Behavior
Animal Licking Behavior *USE Licking*
Animal Locomotion
Animal Mate Selection
Animal Maternal Behavior
Animal Maternal Deprivation
Animal Mating Behavior
Animal Models
Animal Motivation
Animal Navigation
   USE Migratory Behavior (Animal)
Animal Nocturnal Behavior
Animal Open Field Behavior
Animal Parental Behavior
Animal Paternal Behavior
Animal Play
Animal Predatory Behavior
Animal Rearing
Animal Scent Marking
Animal Sex Differences
Animal Sexual Behavior
Animal Sexual Receptivity
Animal Social Behavior
Animal Strain Differences
Animal Tool Use *USE Tool Use*
Animal Vocalizations
Animal Welfare
Captivity (Animal) *USE Animal Captivity*
Coitus (Animal) *USE Animal Mating Behavior*
Copulation (Animal) *USE Animal Mating Behavior*
Daily Biological Rhythms (Animal) *USE Animal Circadian Rhythms*
Homing (Animal) *USE Animal Homing*
Human Animal Interaction
   USE Interspecies Interaction
Infants **(Animal)**
Lordosis (Animal) *USE Animal Sexual Receptivity*
Migratory Behavior **(Animal)**
Neonates (Animal) *USE Infants (Animal)*
Seals **(Animal)**
Animals
Female **Animals**
Male **Animals**
Animism
Ankle
Anniversary Events
Anniversary Reactions
   USE Anniversary Events
Annual Leave
   USE Employee Leave Benefits
Annual Report
Anodynes *USE Analgesic Drugs*
Anomie
Anonymity
Alcoholics **Anonymous**
Anorexia Nervosa
Anorexigenic Drugs
   USE Appetite Depressing Drugs
Anosmia
Anosognosia
ANOVA (Statistics)
   USE Analysis of Variance
Anoxia
Antabuse *USE Disulfiram*
Antagonism *USE Hostility*
Androgen Antagonists *USE Antiandrogens*
Benzodiazepine **Antagonists**
Dopamine **Antagonists**
Estrogen Antagonists *USE Antiestrogens*
Gamma Aminobutyric Acid **Antagonists**
Narcotic **Antagonists**
Opiate Antagonists *USE Narcotic Antagonists*
Serotonin **Antagonists**
Antarctica
Culture **(Anthropological)**
Race **(Anthropological)**

Subculture **(Anthropological)**
Anthropologists
Anthropology
Anti Inflammatory Drugs
Antiandrogens
Antianxiety Drugs
   USE Tranquilizing Drugs
Antibiotics
Antibodies
Anticholinergic Drugs
   USE Cholinergic Blocking Drugs
Anticholinesterase Drugs
   USE Cholinesterase Inhibitors
Serial **Anticipation** (Learning)
Anticoagulant Drugs
Anticonvulsive Drugs
Antidepressant Drugs
Antiemetic Drugs
Antiepileptic Drugs
   USE Anticonvulsive Drugs
Antiestrogens
Antigens
Antihistaminic Drugs
Antihypertensive Drugs
Netherlands **Antilles**
Antinauseant Drugs
   USE Antiemetic Drugs
Antineoplastic Drugs
Antiparkinsonian Drugs
   USE Antitremor Drugs
Antipathy *USE Aversion*
Antipsychotic Drugs
   USE Neuroleptic Drugs
Antipyretic Drugs
   USE Anti Inflammatory Drugs
Antischizophrenic Drugs
   USE Neuroleptic Drugs
AntiSemitism
Antisocial Behavior
Antisocial Personality
Antispasmodic Drugs
Antitremor Drugs
Antitubercular Drugs
Antiviral Drugs
Antonyms
Ants
Anxiety
Anxiety Disorders *USE Anxiety Neurosis*
Anxiety Neurosis
Anxiety Reducing Drugs
   USE Tranquilizing Drugs
Castration **Anxiety**
Childrens Manifest **Anxiety** Scale
Death **Anxiety**
Generalized Anxiety Disorder *USE Anxiety Neurosis*
Mathematics **Anxiety**
Performance **Anxiety**
Separation **Anxiety**
Social **Anxiety**
Speech **Anxiety**
State Trait **Anxiety** Inventory
Taylor Manifest **Anxiety** Scale
Test **Anxiety**
Anxiolytic Drugs *USE Tranquilizing Drugs*
Anxiousness *USE Anxiety*
Aorta
Apathy
Apes *USE Primates (Nonhuman)*
Aphagia
Aphasia
Aphrodisiacs
Aplysia *USE Snails*
Apnea
Sleep **Apnea**
Apomorphine
Apoplexy *USE Cerebrovascular Accidents*
Appalachia
Apparatus
Amplifiers **(Apparatus)**

245

Cage **Apparatus**
Experimental Apparatus *USE Apparatus*
Generators **(Apparatus)**
Incubators **(Apparatus)**
Labyrinth (Apparatus) *USE Mazes*
Stimulators **(Apparatus)**
Timers **(Apparatus)**
Transistors **(Apparatus)**
Vestibular **Apparatus**
Vibrators **(Apparatus)**
Apparent Distance
Apparent Movement
Apparent Size
Physical **Appearance**
Apperception
Childrens **Apperception** Test
Thematic **Apperception** Test
Appetite
Appetite Depressing Drugs
Appetite Disorders
Job **Applicant** Attitudes
Job **Applicant** Interviews
Job **Applicant** Screening
Job **Applicants**
Computer **Applications**
Applied Psychology
Apprehension *USE Anxiety*
Communication Apprehension *USE Speech Anxiety*
Apprenticeship
Biopsychosocial **Approach**
Interdisciplinary Treatment **Approach**
Multidisciplinary Treatment Approach
USE Interdisciplinary Treatment Approach
Multimodal Treatment **Approach**
Social **Approval**
Apraxia
Aptitude *USE Ability*
Aptitude Measures
Academic **Aptitude**
Coll Ent Exam Bd Scholastic **Apt** Test
Differential **Aptitude** Tests
General **Aptitude** Test Battery
Mechanical **Aptitude**
Modern Language **Aptitude** Test
Preliminary Scholastic Aptitude Test
USE Coll Ent Exam Bd Scholastic Apt Test
Scholastic Aptitude *USE Academic Aptitude*
Scholastic Aptitude Test
USE Coll Ent Exam Bd Scholastic Apt Test
Cerebral Aqueduct *USE Cerebral Ventricles*
United Arab Republic *USE Egypt*
Saudi **Arabia**
Arabs
Arachnida
Arachnophobia *USE Phobias*
Archetypes
Architects
Architecture
Arctic Regions
Preoptic **Area**
Ventral Tegmental Area *USE Tegmentum*
Noise Levels (Work **Areas)**
Poverty **Areas**
Recreation **Areas**
Arecoline
Argentina
Arguments
Arithmetic *USE Mathematics*
Arm (Anatomy)
Army General Classification Test
Army Personnel
Physiological **Arousal**
Sexual **Arousal**
Living **Arrangements**
Legal **Arrest**
Arrhythmias (Heart)

Arson
Art
Art Education
Art Therapy
Barron Welsh **Art** Scale
Painting **(Art)**
Photographic **Art**
Arterial Pulse
Arteries (Anatomy)
Carotid **Arteries**
Arteriosclerosis
Cerebral **Arteriosclerosis**
Arthritis
Rheumatoid **Arthritis**
Arthropoda
Articulation Disorders
Articulation (Speech)
Artificial Insemination
USE Reproductive Technology
Artificial Intelligence
Artificial Limbs *USE Prostheses*
Artificial Pacemakers
Artificial Respiration
Artistic Ability
Artists
Arts
Creative **Arts** Therapy
Industrial Arts Education *USE Vocational Education*
Language **Arts** Education
Martial **Arts**
Performing Arts *USE Arts*
Asbestos *USE Hazardous Materials*
Asceticism
Ascorbic Acid
Asia
Southeast **Asia**
Asians
Aspartic Acid
Aspergers Syndrome
Asphyxia *USE Anoxia*
Aspiration Level
Aspirations
Career Aspirations *USE Occupational Aspirations*
Educational **Aspirations**
Occupational **Aspirations**
Vocational Aspirations *USE Occupational Aspirations*
Aspirin
Political **Assassination**
Assertiveness
Assertiveness Training
Assessment *USE Measurement*
Assessment Centers
Behavioral **Assessment**
Curriculum Based **Assessment**
Kaufman **Assessment** Battery Children
Needs **Assessment**
Neuropsychological **Assessment**
Personality Assessment *USE Personality Measures*
Self Assessment *USE Self Evaluation*
Cultural **Assimilation**
Assistance Seeking (Professional)
USE Health Care Utilization
Assistance (Social Behavior)
Educational Financial **Assistance**
Employee **Assistance** Programs
Animal **Assisted** Therapy
Computer **Assisted** Diagnosis
Computer **Assisted** Instruction
Computer **Assisted** Testing
Paired **Associate** Learning
Remote **Associates** Test
Association (Free) *USE Free Association*
Free **Association**
Associationism
Contextual **Associations**
Loosening of Associations
USE Fragmentation (Schizophrenia)
Word **Associations**
Associative Processes

Assortative Mating
Assortive Mating *USE Assortative Mating*
Asthenia
Asthenic Personality
Asthma
Astrology
Astronauts
Asylums *USE Psychiatric Hospitals*
Ataractic Drugs *USE Tranquilizing Drugs*
Ataraxic Drugs *USE Tranquilizing Drugs*
Ataxia
Atheism
Atherosclerosis
Athetosis
Athletes
College Athletes
Athletic Participation
Athletic Performance
Athletic Training
Training (Athletic) *USE Athletic Training*
Stereotaxic Atlas
Atmospheric Conditions
Atomism *USE Reductionism*
Atria (Heart) *USE Heart Auricles*
Atrophy (Cerebral) *USE Cerebral Atrophy*
Cerebral Atrophy
Cortical Atrophy *USE Cerebral Atrophy*
Muscular Atrophy
Atropine
Attachment Behavior
Reactive Attachment Disorder
USE Failure to Thrive
Attack Behavior
Heart Attacks *USE Heart Disorders*
Attainment (Achievement)
USE Achievement
Attempted Suicide
School Attendance
Attendants (Institutions)
Flight Attendants *USE Aerospace Personnel*
Hospital Attendants *USE Attendants (Institutions)*
Residential Care Attendants *USE Attendants (Institutions)*
Attention
Attention Deficit Disorder
Attention Span
Divided Attention
Selective Attention
Stimulus Attenuation
Attitude Change
Attitude Formation
Attitude Measurement
Attitude Measures
Attitude Similarity
Minnesota Teacher Attitude Inventory
Opinion Attitude and Interest Survey
Parent Attitude Research Instrument
Attitudes
Adolescent Attitudes
Adult Attitudes
Aged (Attitudes Toward)
Aging (Attitudes Toward)
Alcohol Drinking Attitudes
Birth Control Attitudes *USE Family Planning Attitudes*
Child Attitudes
Childrearing Attitudes
Client Attitudes
Community Attitudes
Computer Attitudes
Consumer Attitudes
Counselor Attitudes
Death Attitudes
Drug Usage Attitudes
Eating Attitudes
Employee Attitudes
Employer Attitudes
Environmental Attitudes
Family Planning Attitudes
Handicapped (Attitudes Toward)
Health Attitudes

Health Personnel Attitudes
Homosexuality (Attitudes Toward)
Job Applicant Attitudes
Lower Class Attitudes
Marriage Attitudes
Mental Illness (Attitudes Toward)
Mental Retardation (Attit Toward)
Middle Class Attitudes
Occupational Attitudes
Parental Attitudes
Patient Attitudes *USE Client Attitudes*
Physical Handicaps (Attit Toward)
Physical Illness (Attitudes Toward)
Political Attitudes
Psychologist Attitudes
Psychotherapist Attitudes
Public Attitudes *USE Public Opinion*
Race Attitudes *USE Racial and Ethnic Attitudes*
Racial and Ethnic Attitudes
Sensory Handicaps (Attit Toward)
Sex Role Attitudes
Sexual Attitudes
Social Class Attitudes
USE Socioeconomic Class Attitudes
Socioeconomic Class Attitudes
Stereotyped Attitudes
Student Attitudes
Teacher Attitudes
Therapist Attitudes
Upper Class Attitudes
Work (Attitudes Toward)
Attorneys
Interpersonal Attraction
Physical Attractiveness
Attribution
Experimental Attrition
Student Attrition
Atypical Paranoid Disorder
USE Paranoia (Psychosis)
Atypical Somatoform Disorder
USE Dysmorphophobia
Audiences
Audiogenic Seizures
Audiology
Audiometers
Audiometry
Bone Conduction Audiometry
Audiotapes
Audiovisual Communications Media
Audiovisual Instruction
Educational Audiovisual Aids
Auditory Acuity
Auditory Cortex
Auditory Discrimination
Auditory Displays
Auditory Evoked Potentials
Auditory Feedback
Auditory Hallucinations
Auditory Localization
Auditory Masking
Auditory Nerve *USE Acoustic Nerve*
Auditory Neurons
Auditory Perception
Auditory Stimulation
Auditory Thresholds
Delayed Auditory Feedback
Wepman Test of Auditory Discrim
Augmentative Communication
Aura
Intra Aural Muscle Reflex *USE Acoustic Reflex*
Aurally Handicapped
Heart Auricles
Australia
Austria
Authoritarianism
Authoritarianism (Parental)
USE Parental Permissiveness
Authoritarianism Rebellion Scale

Parental **Authoritarianism**
   USE Parental Permissiveness
Authority
Authors *USE Writers*
Autism
Early Infantile **Autism**
Autistic Children
Autistic Psychopathy
   USE Aspergers Syndrome
Autistic Thinking
Autobiographical Memory
Autobiography
Autoeroticism *USE Masturbation*
Autogenic Training
Autohypnosis
Autoimmune Disorders
   USE Immunologic Disorders
Autokinetic Illusion
Automated Information Coding
Automated Information Processing
Automated Information Retrieval
Automated Information Storage
Automated Speech Recognition
Automatic Speaker Recognition
   USE Automated Speech Recognition
Automation
Automatism
Automobile Accidents
   USE Motor Traffic Accidents
Automobile Safety *USE Highway Safety*
Automobiles
Autonomic Ganglia
Autonomic Nervous System
Autonomic Nervous System Disorders
Postganglionic Autonomic Fibers *USE Autonomic Ganglia*
Preganglionic Autonomic Fibers *USE Autonomic Ganglia*
Autonomy (Government)
Autonomy (Personality)
   USE Independence (Personality)
Autopsy
Psychological **Autopsy**
Autoregulation *USE Homeostasis*
Autoshaping
Autosome Disorders
Autosomes
Autotomy *USE Self Mutilation*
Gradepoint Average *USE Academic Achievement*
Aversion
Aversion Conditioning
Aversion Therapy
Odor Aversion Conditioning
   USE Aversion Conditioning
Taste Aversion Conditioning
   USE Aversion Conditioning
Aversive Stimulation
Aviation
Aviation Personnel
   USE Aerospace Personnel
Aviation Safety
Aviators *USE Aircraft Pilots*
Avoidance
Avoidance Conditioning
Active Avoidance *USE Avoidance Conditioning*
Passive Avoidance *USE Avoidance Conditioning*
Avoidant Personality
Awareness
Body **Awareness**
Axons
Azidothymidine *USE Zidovudine*
AZT *USE Zidovudine*
Babbling *USE Infant Vocalization*
Babies *USE Infants*
Bush Babies *USE Lemurs*
Test Tube Babies *USE Reproductive Technology*
Babinski Reflex
Baboons
Babysitting *USE Child Care*
Back (Anatomy)
Back Pain

Educational **Background**
Family **Background**
Parent Educational **Background**
Backward Masking *USE Masking*
Baclofen
Bacteria *USE Microorganisms*
Bacterial Disorders
Bacterial Meningitis
Bahama Islands
Balance (Motor Processes)
   USE Equilibrium
Ballet *USE Dance*
Head **Banging**
Bangladesh
Bannister Repertory Grid
Barbados
Barbital
Barbiturate Poisoning
Barbiturates
Bargaining
Barium
Barometric Pressure
   USE Atmospheric Conditions
Baroreceptors
Epstein **Barr** Viral Disorder
Barrett Lennard Relationship Invent
Blood Brain **Barrier**
Barron Welsh Art Scale
Basal Ganglia
Basal Metabolism
Basal Readers *USE Reading Materials*
Basal Skin Resistance
Nucleus **Basalis** Magnocellularis
Baseball
Curriculum **Based** Assessment
Knowledge Based Systems *USE Expert Systems*
Basic Skills Testing
   USE Minimum Competency Tests
Iowa Tests of **Basic** Skills
Basketball
Bass (Fish)
Bats
Battered Child Syndrome
Battered Females
General Aptitude Test **Battery**
Halstead Reitan Neuropsych **Battery**
Kaufman Assessment **Battery** Children
Luria Nebraska Neuropsych **Battery**
Woodcock Johnson Psychoed **Battery**
Bayes Theorem *USE Statistical Probability*
Bayley Scales of Infant Development
Beavers
Beck Depression Inventory
Bedwetting *USE Urinary Incontinence*
Beer
Bees
Beetles
Fund Interper Rela Orientat **Beh** Ques
Behavior
Behavior Analysis
   USE Behavioral Assessment
Behavior Change
Behavior Contracting
Behavior Disorders
Behavior Modification
Behavior Problems
Behavior Therapy
Adaptive **Behavior**
Adjunctive **Behavior**
Aggressive **Behavior**
Agonistic Behavior *USE Aggressive Behavior*
Animal Behavior *USE Animal Ethology*
Animal Aggressive **Behavior**
Animal Courtship **Behavior**
Animal Defensive **Behavior**
Animal Drinking **Behavior**
Animal Escape **Behavior**
Animal Exploratory **Behavior**
Animal Feeding **Behavior**

Animal Foraging **Behavior**
Animal Grooming **Behavior**
Animal Hoarding **Behavior**
Animal Innate Behavior *USE Instinctive Behavior*
Animal Licking Behavior *USE Licking*
Animal Maternal **Behavior**
Animal Mating **Behavior**
Animal Nocturnal **Behavior**
Animal Open Field **Behavior**
Animal Parental **Behavior**
Animal Paternal **Behavior**
Animal Predatory **Behavior**
Animal Sexual **Behavior**
Animal Social **Behavior**
Antisocial **Behavior**
Assistance (Social **Behavior)**
Attachment **Behavior**
Attack **Behavior**
Charitable **Behavior**
Child **Behavior** Checklist
Childhood Play **Behavior**
Choice **Behavior**
Classroom **Behavior**
Classroom **Behavior** Modification
Cognitive Behavior Therapy *USE Cognitive Therapy*
Collective **Behavior**
Conservation (Ecological **Behavior)**
Consumer **Behavior**
Coping **Behavior**
Coronary Prone **Behavior**
Deviant Behavior *USE Antisocial Behavior*
Disruptive Behavior *USE Behavior Problems*
Drinking **Behavior**
Driving **Behavior**
Exploratory **Behavior**
Health **Behavior**
Help Seeking **Behavior**
Helping Behavior
   USE Assistance (Social Behavior)
Illness **Behavior**
Instinctive **Behavior**
Maternal Behavior (Human)
   USE Mother Child Relations
Migratory **Behavior** (Animal)
Modeling Behavior *USE Imitation (Learning)*
Organizational **Behavior**
Prosocial **Behavior**
Psychosexual **Behavior**
Rotational **Behavior**
Runaway **Behavior**
Self Defeating **Behavior**
Self Destructive **Behavior**
Sexual Behavior *USE Psychosexual Behavior*
Sharing (Social **Behavior)**
Social **Behavior**
Stereotyped **Behavior**
Trust (Social **Behavior)**
Voting **Behavior**
Wandering **Behavior**
Behavioral Assessment
Behavioral Contrast
Behavioral Genetics
Behavioral Health
   USE Health Care Psychology
Behavioral Medicine
   USE Health Care Psychology
Behavioral Sciences *USE Social Sciences*
Behaviorism
Well **Being**
Belgium
Beliefs (Nonreligious) *USE Attitudes*
Irrational **Beliefs**
Religious **Beliefs**
Belize
Wechsler **Bellevue** Intelligence Scale
Safety **Belts**
Seat Belts *USE Safety Belts*
Bem Sex Role Inventory
Bemegride

Benactyzine
Benadryl *USE Diphenhydramine*
Bender Gestalt Test
Employee **Benefits**
Employee Leave **Benefits**
Vacation Benefits *USE Employee Leave Benefits*
Benign Neoplasms
Benin
Benton Revised Visual Retention Test
Benzedrine *USE Amphetamine*
Benzodiazepine Agonists
Benzodiazepine Antagonists
Benzodiazepines
Bereavement *USE Grief*
Bermuda
Beta Blockers
   USE Adrenergic Blocking Drugs
Between Groups Design
White **Betz** A B Scale
Beverages (Nonalcoholic)
Alcoholic **Beverages**
Cultural Test **Bias**
Experimenter **Bias**
Item Bias *USE Test Bias*
Response **Bias**
Test **Bias**
Biased Sampling
Bible
Bibliography
Bibliotherapy
Bicuculline
Spina **Bifida**
Bile
Bilingual Education
Bilingualism
Double **Bind** Interaction
Receptor **Binding**
Stanford **Binet** Intelligence Scale
Binge Eating
Binocular Vision
Binomial Distribution
Bioavailability
Biochemical Markers
   USE Biological Markers
Biochemistry
Bioequivalence *USE Bioavailability*
Biofeedback
Biofeedback Training
Biographical Data
Biographical Inventories
Biography
Biological Family
Biological Markers
Biological Psychiatry
Biological Rhythms
Biological Symbiosis
Animal **Biological** Rhythms
Daily Biological Rhythms (Animal)
   USE Animal Circadian Rhythms
Human **Biological** Rhythms
Biology
Cells **(Biology)**
Hybrids **(Biology)**
Biopsy
Biopsychosocial Approach
Biopsychosocial Model
   USE Biopsychosocial Approach
Biosynthesis
Bipolar Depression
   USE Manic Depression
Birds
Birth
Birth Control
Birth Control Attitudes
   USE Family Planning Attitudes
Birth Injuries
Birth Order
Birth Parents *USE Biological Family*
Birth Rate

ROTATED ALPHABETICAL TERMS SECTION

Birth Rites
Birth Trauma
Birth Weight
Diaphragms **(Birth** Control)
Home Birth *USE Midwifery*
Low Birth Weight *USE Birth Weight*
Premature **Birth**
Multiple **Births**
Point **Biserial** Correlation
Bisexuality
Nail **Biting**
Bitterness *USE Taste Perception*
Black Power Movement
Blackbirds
Blacks
Blacky Pictures Test
Bladder
Blame
Rotter Incomplete Sentences **Blank**
Strong Vocational Interest **Blank**
Blind
Deaf **Blind**
Color **Blindness**
Hysterical Blindness
        USE Hysterical Vision Disturbances
Word Blindness *USE Alexia*
Blink Reflex *USE Eyeblink Reflex*
Kohs **Block** Design Test
Beta Blockers *USE Adrenergic Blocking Drugs*
Calcium Channel Blockers *USE Channel Blockers*
Channel **Blockers**
Adrenergic **Blocking** Drugs
Cholinergic **Blocking** Drugs
Ganglion **Blocking** Drugs
Neuromuscular Blocking Drugs
        USE Muscle Relaxing Drugs
Blood
Blood Alcohol Concentration
Blood and Lymphatic Disorders
Blood Brain Barrier
Blood Cells
Blood Circulation
Blood Coagulation
Blood Donation *USE Tissue Donation*
Blood Flow
Blood Glucose *USE Blood Sugar*
Blood Groups
Blood Plasma
Blood Platelets
Blood Pressure
Blood Pressure Disorders
Blood Proteins
Blood Serum
Blood Sugar
Blood Transfusion
Blood Vessels
Blood Volume
Cerebral **Blood** Flow
Red Blood Cells *USE Erythrocytes*
White Blood Cells *USE Leucocytes*
Blue Collar Workers
State Board Examinations
        USE Professional Examinations
Boarding Schools
Boards of Education
Geniculate **Bodies** (Thalamus)
Mammillary Bodies (Hypothalamic)
        USE Hypothalamus
Body Awareness
Body Fluids
Body Height
Body Image
Body Image Disturbances
Body Language
Body Rocking
Body Rotation *USE Rotational Behavior*
Body Size
Body Sway Testing
Body Temperature

Body Types *USE Somatotypes*
Body Weight
Amygdaloid **Body**
Mind Body *USE Dualism*
Out of **Body** Experiences
Pineal **Body**
Thermoregulation **(Body)**
Tissues **(Body)**
Bolivia
Bombesin
Bonding (Emotional)
        USE Attachment Behavior
Bone Conduction Audiometry
Bone Disorders
Bone Marrow
Bones
Bonuses
Book
Books
Borderline Mental Retardation
Borderline Mentally Retarded
        USE Slow Learners
Borderline States
Boredom
Botany
Botswana
Bottle Feeding
Outward Bound *USE Wilderness Experience*
Upward **Bound**
Sexual **Boundary** Violations
        USE Professional Client Sexual Relations
Bourgeois *USE Middle Class*
Bowel Disorders *USE Colon Disorders*
Irritable **Bowel** Syndrome
Shuttle **Box** Grids
Shuttle **Box** Hurdles
Shuttle **Boxes**
Skinner **Boxes**
Boys *USE Human Males*
Brachial Plexus *USE Spinal Nerves*
Bradycardia
Braille
Braille Instruction
Brain
Brain Concussion
Brain Damage
Brain Damaged
Brain Disorders
Brain Injuries *USE Brain Damage*
Brain Lesions
Brain Maps *USE Stereotaxic Atlas*
Brain Metabolism *USE Neurochemistry*
Brain Neoplasms
Brain Self Stimulation
Brain Size
Brain Stem
Brain Stimulation
Brain Weight
Blood **Brain** Barrier
Chemical **Brain** Stimulation
Decortication **(Brain)**
Electrical **Brain** Stimulation
Left **Brain**
Minimal **Brain** Disorders
Minimally **Brain** Damaged
Monoamines (Brain) *USE Catecholamines*
Organic **Brain** Syndromes
Right **Brain**
Split Brain *USE Commissurotomy*
Brainstorming
Brainwashing
Brand Names
Brand Preferences
Bravery *USE Courage*
Brazil
Nervous Breakdown *USE Mental Disorders*
Psychotherapeutic **Breakthrough**
Breast

Breast Examination
USE Self Examination (Medical)
Breast Feeding
Breast Neoplasms
Breathing *USE Respiration*
Animal **Breeding**
Selective **Breeding**
Brief Psychotherapy
Brief Reactive Psychosis
USE Acute Psychosis
Myers **Briggs** Type Indicator
Bright Light Therapy *USE Phototherapy*
Brightness Constancy
Brightness Contrast
Brightness Perception
Great **Britain**
Watson (John **Broadus)**
Lithium **Bromide**
Bromides
Bromocriptine
Bronchi
Bronchial Disorders
Brothers
Spearman **Brown** Test
Bruxism
Buddhism
Zen **Buddhism**
Budgerigars
Budgets *USE Costs and Cost Analysis*
Taste **Buds**
Bufotenine
Nest **Building**
Religious **Buildings**
Olfactory **Bulb**
Bulgaria
Bulimia
Bulls *USE Cattle*
Medial Forebrain **Bundle**
Bupropion
Caregiver **Burden**
Burma
Burnout *USE Occupational Stress*
Burns
Skinner **(Burrhus** Frederic)
Buses *USE Motor Vehicles*
Bush Babies *USE Lemurs*
Business
Business and Industrial Personnel
Business Education
Business Management
Business Organizations
Business Students
Buspirone
Butterflies
Butyrylperazine
Buying *USE Consumer Behavior*
Vitamin C *USE Ascorbic Acid*
Cadres *USE Social Groups*
Caffeine
Cage Apparatus
Calcium
Calcium Channel Blockers
USE Channel Blockers
Calcium Ions
Calculators *USE Digital Computers*
Calculus *USE Mathematics*
California F Scale
California Psychological Inventory
California Test of Mental Maturity
California Test of Personality
Corpus **Callosum**
Animal Distress **Calls**
Calories
Cambodia
Cameras
Cameroon
Political **Campaigns**
Camping
Concentration **Camps**

Recreational Day Camps *USE Summer Camps (Recreation)*
Summer **Camps** (Recreation)
Therapeutic **Camps**
Campuses
Canada
Ear Canal *USE External Ear*
Semicircular **Canals**
Canaries
Terminal **Cancer**
Cancers *USE Neoplasms*
Political **Candidates**
Cannabinoids
Cannabis
Canonical Correlation
USE Multivariate Analysis
Human Channel **Capacity**
Capgras Syndrome
Capillaries (Anatomy)
Capital Punishment
Capitalism
Capsaicin
Captivity (Animal) *USE Animal Captivity*
Animal **Captivity**
Captopril
Carbachol
Carbamazepine
Carbidopa
Carbohydrate Metabolism
Carbohydrates
Carbon
Carbon Dioxide
Carbon Monoxide
Carbon Monoxide Poisoning
Lithium **Carbonate**
Carbonic Anhydrase
Carboxyhemoglobinemia
USE Carbon Monoxide Poisoning
Carcinogens
Carcinomas *USE Neoplasms*
Wisconsin **Card** Sorting Test
Cardiac Disorders *USE Heart Disorders*
Cardiac Rate *USE Heart Rate*
Cardiography
Cardiology
Cardiotonic Drugs
Cardiovascular Disorders
Cardiovascular Reactivity
Cardiovascular System
Ambulatory Care *USE Outpatient Treatment*
Child **Care**
Child **Care** Workers
Child Day **Care**
Child Self **Care**
Day **Care** Centers
Day Care (Treatment)
USE Partial Hospitalization
Elder **Care**
Foster **Care**
Health **Care** Costs
Health **Care** Delivery
Health **Care** Policy
Health Care Professionals *USE Health Personnel*
Health **Care** Psychology
Health **Care** Services
Health **Care** Utilization
Home **Care**
Intensive **Care**
Long Term **Care**
Managed **Care**
Medical Care Costs *USE Health Care Costs*
Mental Health Care Costs *USE Health Care Costs*
Mental Health Care Policy *USE Health Care Policy*
Palliative **Care**
Prenatal **Care**
Primary Health **Care**
Quality of **Care**
Residential Care Attendants
USE Attendants (Institutions)
Residential **Care** Institutions

251

Respite **Care**
Self **Care** Skills
Career Aspirations
　USE Occupational Aspirations
Career Change
Career Choice *USE Occupational Choice*
Career Counseling
　USE Occupational Guidance
Career Development
Career Education
Career Exploration *USE Career Education*
Career Goals
　USE Occupational Aspirations
Career Guidance
　USE Occupational Guidance
Career Maturity *USE Vocational Maturity*
Career Preference
　USE Occupational Preference
Career Transitions
　USE Career Development
Careers *USE Occupations*
Dual **Careers**
Nontraditional **Careers**
Caregiver Burden
Caregivers
Family **Caregivers** *USE Caregivers*
Jung **(Carl)**
Rogers **(Carl)**
Carotid Arteries
Carp
Cartoons (Humor)
Case History *USE Patient History*
Case Law
Case Management
Case Report
Social **Casework**
Caseworkers *USE Social Workers*
Social **Caseworkers** *USE Social Workers*
Caste System
Castration
Castration Anxiety
Male **Castration**
Cat Learning
CAT Scan *USE Tomography*
Crying **Cat** Syndrome
Catabolism
Catabolites *USE Metabolites*
Catalepsy
Catamnesis *USE Posttreatment Followup*
Cataplexy
Cataracts
Catatonia
Catatonic Schizophrenia
Catecholamines
Categorizing
　USE Classification (Cognitive Process)
Catharsis
Catheterization
Cathexis
Cathode Ray Tubes
　USE Video Display Units
Roman **Catholicism**
Cats
Cattell Culture Fair Intell Test
　USE Culture Fair Intelligence Test
Cattell Infant Intelligence Scale
　USE Infant Intelligence Scale
Cattle
Caucasians *USE Whites*
Cauda Equina *USE Spinal Nerves*
Caudate Nucleus
Causal Analysis
Celiac Plexus *USE Autonomic Ganglia*
Celibacy *USE Sexual Abstinence*
Cell Nucleus
Sickle **Cell** Disease
Single **Cell** Organisms *USE Microorganisms*
Cells (Biology)
Blood **Cells**

Connective Tissue **Cells**
Epithelial **Cells**
Ganglion **Cells** (Retina)
Nerve **Cells** *USE Neurons*
Purkinje **Cells**
Red Blood **Cells** *USE Erythrocytes*
White Blood **Cells** *USE Leucocytes*
Censorship
Client **Centered** Therapy
Centering
Assessment **Centers**
Community Mental Health **Centers**
Day Care **Centers**
Growth **Centers** *USE Human Potential Movement*
Learning **Centers** (Educational)
Rehabilitation **Centers**
Shopping **Centers**
Suicide Prevention **Centers**
Central America
Central Nervous System
Central Nervous System Disorders
Central Nervous System Drugs
　USE CNS Affecting Drugs
Central Tendency Measures
Central Vision *USE Foveal Vision*
CER (Conditioning)
　USE Conditioned Emotional Responses
Cerebellopontile Angle *USE Cerebellum*
Cerebellum
Cerebral Aqueduct
　USE Cerebral Ventricles
Cerebral Arteriosclerosis
Cerebral Atrophy
Cerebral Blood Flow
Cerebral Cortex
Cerebral Dominance
Cerebral Hemorrhage
Cerebral Ischemia
Cerebral Lesions *USE Brain Lesions*
Cerebral Palsy
Cerebral Vascular Disorders
　USE Cerebrovascular Disorders
Cerebral Ventricles
Atrophy **(Cerebral)** *USE Cerebral Atrophy*
Trigonum **Cerebrale** *USE Fornix*
Cerebrospinal Fluid
Cerebrovascular Accidents
Cerebrovascular Disorders
Stroke **(Cerebrum)**
　USE Cerebrovascular Accidents
Certification Examinations
　USE Professional Examinations
Professional **Certification**
Locus **Ceruleus**
Cervical Plexus *USE Spinal Nerves*
Cervix
Smoking **Cessation**
Markov **Chains**
Chance (Fortune)
Attitude **Change**
Behavior **Change**
Career **Change**
Culture **Change**
Job **Change** *USE Career Change*
Life **Change** *USE Life Experiences*
Opinion **Change** *USE Attitude Change*
Organizational **Change**
Personality **Change**
Sex **Change**
Social **Change**
Stimulus **Change**
Channel Blockers
Calcium **Channel** Blockers *USE Channel Blockers*
Human **Channel** Capacity
Chaplains
Character *USE Personality*
Client **Characteristics**
Counselor **Characteristics**
Demographic **Characteristics**

ROTATED ALPHABETICAL TERMS SECTION

Employee **Characteristics**
Job **Characteristics**
Parental **Characteristics**
Patient Characteristics *USE Client Characteristics*
Population Characteristics
    USE Demographic Characteristics
Speech **Characteristics**
Student **Characteristics**
Teacher **Characteristics**
Therapist **Characteristics**
Charisma
Charitable Behavior
Cri du Chat Syndrome
    USE Crying Cat Syndrome
Cheating
Gough Adjective **Check** List
Learys Interpersonal **Check** List
Mooney Problem **Check** List
Child Behavior **Checklist**
Symptom **Checklists**
Chemical Brain Stimulation
Chemical Elements
Chemicals
Chemistry
Chemoreceptors
Chemotherapy *USE Drug Therapy*
Chess
Chest *USE Thorax*
Chewing Tobacco
    USE Smokeless Tobacco
Chi Square Test
Optic **Chiasm**
Chicanos *USE Mexican Americans*
Chickens
Child Abuse
Child Advocacy *USE Advocacy*
Child Attitudes
Child Behavior Checklist
Child Care
Child Care Workers
Child Custody
Child Day Care
Child Discipline
Child Guidance Clinics
Child Neglect
Child Psychiatric Clinics
    USE Child Guidance Clinics
Child Psychiatry
Child Psychology
Child Psychotherapy
Child Self Care
Child Support
Child Visitation
Child Welfare
Adoption **(Child)**
Battered **Child** Syndrome
Father **Child** Communication
Father **Child** Relations
Mother **Child** Communication
Mother **Child** Relations
Parent **Child** Communication
Parent **Child** Relations
Slosson Intelligence Test for **Child**
Childbirth *USE Birth*
Childbirth Training
Labor **(Childbirth)**
Natural **Childbirth**
Childhood
Childhood Development
Childhood Memories *USE Early Memories*
Childhood Neurosis
Childhood Play Behavior
Childhood Play Development
Childhood Psychosis
Childhood Schizophrenia
Early Childhood *USE Preschool Age Children*
Early **Childhood** Development
Childlessness
Childrearing Attitudes

Childrearing Practices
Children
Adopted **Children**
Adult Children *USE Adult Offspring*
Autistic **Children**
Exceptional Children (Gifted) *USE Gifted*
Exceptional Children (Handicapped) *USE Handicapped*
Foster **Children**
Grown Children *USE Adult Offspring*
Illegitimate **Children**
Kaufman Assessment Battery **Children**
Latchkey Children *USE Child Self Care*
Only **Children**
Preschool Age **Children**
School Age **Children**
Wechsler Intelligence Scale **Children**
Childrens Apperception Test
Childrens Manifest Anxiety Scale
Childrens Personality Questionnaire
Childrens Recreational Games
Chile
Chimpanzees
China *USE Peoples Republic of China*
Peoples Republic of **China**
Chinchillas
Chinese Americans *USE Asians*
Chloral Hydrate
Chloralose
Chlordiazepoxide
Chloride Ions
Chlorimipramine
Chlorisondamine
Chloroform
Chlorophenylpiperazine *USE Piperazines*
Chlorpromazine
Chlorprothixene
Choice Behavior
Choice Shift
Career Choice *USE Occupational Choice*
Forced **Choice** (Testing Method)
Multiple **Choice** (Testing Method)
Occupational **Choice**
Vocational Choice *USE Occupational Choice*
Cholecystokinin
Cholesterol
Choline
Cholinergic Blocking Drugs
Cholinergic Drugs
Cholinergic Nerves
Cholinesterase
Cholinesterase Inhibitors
Cholinolytic Drugs
    USE Cholinergic Blocking Drugs
Cholinomimetic Drugs
Chorda Tympani Nerve *USE Facial Nerve*
Chorea
Huntingtons **Chorea**
Choroid *USE Eye (Anatomy)*
Choroid Plexus *USE Cerebral Ventricles*
Christianity
Chromosome Disorders
Deletion **(Chromosome)**
Sex **Chromosome** Disorders
Translocation **(Chromosome)**
Chromosomes
Sex **Chromosomes**
Chronic Alcoholic Intoxication
Chronic Illness
Chronic Pain
Chronic Psychosis
Chronic Schizophrenia
    USE Schizophrenia
Chronicity (Disorders)
Churches *USE Religious Buildings*
Cichlids
Cigarette Smoking *USE Tobacco Smoking*
Cimetidine
Gyrus **Cinguli**

253

Circadian Rhythms (Human)
  USE Human Biological Rhythms
Animal **Circadian** Rhythms
Quality Circles *USE Participative Management*
Closed **Circuit** Television
Blood **Circulation**
Circulatory Disorders
  USE Cardiovascular Disorders
Circumcision *USE Birth Rites AND Surgery*
Cirrhosis (Liver)
Cities *USE Urban Environments*
Senior Citizens *USE Aged*
Citizenship
Inner City *USE Urban Environments*
Civil Law
Civil Rights
Civil Rights Movement
Civil Servants *USE Government Personnel*
Volunteer **Civilian** Personnel
Clairvoyance
Lower **Class**
Lower **Class** Attitudes
Middle **Class**
Middle **Class** Attitudes
Social **Class**
Social Class Attitudes
  USE Socioeconomic Class Attitudes
Socioeconomic **Class** Attitudes
Upper **Class**
Upper **Class** Attitudes
Form **Classes** (Language)
Words (Form Classes) *USE Form Classes (Language)*
Classical Conditioning
Classification (Cognitive Process)
Classification Systems *USE Taxonomies*
Army General **Classification** Test
Psychiatric Classifications (Taxon)
  USE Psychodiagnostic Typologies
Classmates
Classroom Behavior
Classroom Behavior Modification
Classroom Discipline
Classroom Environment
Classroom Instruction *USE Teaching*
Open **Classroom** Method
Classrooms
Claustrophobia
Cleft Palate
Clergy
Clerical Personnel
Clerical Secretarial Skills
Client Abuse *USE Patient Abuse*
Client Attitudes
Client Centered Therapy
Client Characteristics
Client Counselor Interaction
  USE Psychotherapeutic Processes
Client Education
Client Rights
Client Satisfaction
Client Violence *USE Patient Violence*
Counselor Client Interaction
  USE Psychotherapeutic Processes
Professional **Client** Sexual Relations
Clients
Climacteric Depression
  USE Involutional Depression
Climacteric Paranoia
  USE Involutional Paranoid Psychosis
Climate (Meteorological)
  USE Atmospheric Conditions
Organizational **Climate**
Climax (Sexual) *USE Orgasm*
Clinical Judgment (Med Diagnosis)
  USE Medical Diagnosis
Clinical Judgment (Not Diagnosis)
Clinical Judgment (Psychodiagnosis)
  USE Psychodiagnosis
Clinical Markers *USE Biological Markers*

Clinical Methods Training
Clinical Psychologists
Clinical Psychology
Clinical Psychology Grad Training
Clinical Psychology Internship
Clinical Supervision
  USE Professional Supervision
Millon **Clinical** Multiaxial Inventory
Clinicians
Clinics
Child Guidance **Clinics**
Child Psychiatric Clinics *USE Child Guidance Clinics*
Outpatient Psychiatric Clinics *USE Psychiatric Clinics*
Psychiatric **Clinics**
Walk In **Clinics**
Cliques *USE Social Groups*
Clomipramine *USE Chlorimipramine*
Clonazepam
Clonidine
Closed Circuit Television
Closedmindedness *USE Openmindedness*
Perceptual **Closure**
Clothing
Clozapine
Cloze Testing
School **Club** Membership
Clubs (Social Organizations)
Therapeutic Social **Clubs**
Cluster Analysis
CNS Affecting Drugs
CNS Depressant Drugs
CNS Stimulating Drugs
Stimulants of CNS *USE CNS Stimulating Drugs*
Coaches
Blood **Coagulation**
Coalition Formation
Coast Guard Personnel
Ivory **Coast**
Cobalt
Cocaine
Cochlea
Cochlear Implants
Cochran Q Test
Cockroaches
Code Switching
Codeine
Codependency
Automated Information **Coding**
Coeducation
Pearson Prod Moment Correl Coeff *USE Statistical Correlation*
Phi **Coefficient**
Coercion
Coffee *USE Beverages (Nonalcoholic)*
Cognition
Cognition Enhancing Drugs
  USE Nootropic Drugs
Social **Cognition**
Sorting (Cognition)
  USE Classification (Cognitive Process)
Transposition **(Cognition)**
Cognitions
Cognitive Ability
Cognitive Behavior Therapy
  USE Cognitive Therapy
Cognitive Complexity
Cognitive Contiguity
Cognitive Development
Cognitive Discrimination
Cognitive Dissonance
Cognitive Functioning
  USE Cognitive Ability
Cognitive Generalization
Cognitive Hypothesis Testing
Cognitive Load
  USE Human Channel Capacity
Cognitive Maps
Cognitive Mediation
Cognitive Processes
Cognitive Psychology

254

Cognitive Rehabilitation
Cognitive Restructuring
Cognitive Style
Cognitive Techniques
Cognitive Therapy
Classification **(Cognitive** Process)
Cohabitation
Group **Cohesion**
Cohort Analysis
Coitus *USE Sexual Intercourse (Human)*
Coitus (Animal)
    USE Animal Mating Behavior
Cold Effects
Colitis
Ulcerative **Colitis**
Collaboration *USE Cooperation*
Blue **Collar** Workers
White **Collar** Workers
Data **Collection**
Collective Behavior
College Academic Achievement
College Athletes
College Degrees
    USE Educational Degrees
College Dropouts
College Education
    USE Undergraduate Education
Coll Ent Exam Bd Scholastic Apt Test
College Environment
College Graduates
College Major
    USE Academic Specialization
College Students
College Teachers
Community **College** Students
Junior **College** Students
School and **College** Ability Test
Colleges
Community **Colleges**
Junior Colleges *USE Colleges*
Inferior **Colliculus**
Superior **Colliculus**
Colombia
Colon Disorders
Color
Color Blindness
Color Constancy
Color Contrast
Color Perception
Color Pyramid Test
Achromatic **Color**
Eye **Color**
Stroop **Color** Word Test
Animal **Coloration**
Colostomy
Raven **Coloured** Progressive Matrices
Columbia Mental Maturity Scale
Spinal **Column**
Coma
Combat Experience
Physical **Comfort**
Commerce *USE Business*
Commissioned Officers
Hippocampal Commissure *USE Fornix*
Commissurotomy
Commitment
Commitment (Outpatient)
    USE Outpatient Commitment
Commitment (Psychiatric)
Organizational **Commitment**
Outpatient **Commitment**
Communes
Communicable Diseases
    USE Infectious Disorders
Communication
Communication Apprehension
    USE Speech Anxiety
Communication Disorders

Communication (Professional)
    USE Scientific Communication
Communication Skills
Communication Skills Training
Communication Systems
Communication Theory
Animal **Communication**
Augmentative **Communication**
Facilitated Communication
    USE Augmentative Communication
Father Child **Communication**
Interpersonal **Communication**
Manual **Communication**
Mother Child **Communication**
Nonverbal **Communication**
Oral **Communication**
Parent Child **Communication**
Persuasive **Communication**
Privileged **Communication**
Professional Communication
    USE Scientific Communication
Scientific **Communication**
Verbal **Communication**
Written **Communication**
Communications Media
Audiovisual **Communications** Media
Printed **Communications** Media
Communicative Competence
    USE Communication Skills
Communism
Communities
Community Attitudes
Community College Students
Community Colleges
Community Facilities
Community Mental Health
Community Mental Health Centers
Community Mental Health Services
Community Mental Health Training
Community Psychiatry
Community Psychology
Community Services
Community Welfare Services
Therapeutic **Community**
Commuting (Travel)
Comorbidity
Companies *USE Business Organizations*
Comparative Psychiatry
    USE Transcultural Psychiatry
Comparative Psychology
Social **Comparison**
Interpersonal **Compatibility**
Compensation (Defense Mechanism)
Workmens **Compensation** Insurance
Compensatory Education
Competence
Competence (Social) *USE Social Skills*
Communicative Competence *USE Communication Skills*
Competency to Stand Trial
Minimum **Competency** Tests
Competition
Franck Drawing **Completion** Test
Sentence **Completion** Tests
Electra **Complex**
Oedipal **Complex**
Cognitive **Complexity**
Stimulus **Complexity**
Task **Complexity**
Compliance
Medical Regimen Compliance *USE Treatment Compliance*
Treatment **Compliance**
Obstetrical **Complications**
Postsurgical **Complications**
Surgical Complications
    USE Postsurgical Complications
Comprehension
Comprehension Tests
Listening **Comprehension**
Number **Comprehension**

Reading **Comprehension**
Sentence **Comprehension**
Verbal **Comprehension**
Compressed Speech
Compulsions
Compulsive Gambling
    USE Pathological Gambling
Compulsive Neurosis
    USE Obsessive Compulsive Neurosis
Compulsive Personality Disorder
    USE Obsessive Compulsive Personality
Compulsive Repetition
Obsessive Compulsive Disorder
    USE Obsessive Compulsive Neurosis
Obsessive **Compulsive** Neurosis
Obsessive **Compulsive** Personality
Computer Applications
Computer Assisted Diagnosis
Computer Assisted Instruction
Computer Assisted Testing
Computer Attitudes
Computer Games
Computer Literacy
Computer Peripheral Devices
Computer Programing
Computer Programing Languages
Computer Programs
    USE Computer Software
Computer Searching
Computer Simulation
Computer Software
Computer Training
Programing (Computer) *USE Computer Programing*
Computerized Databases *USE Databases*
Computers
Analog **Computers**
Digital **Computers**
Personal Computers *USE Microcomputers*
Concentration
Concentration Camps
Blood Alcohol **Concentration**
Concept Formation
Concept Learning
    USE Concept Formation
Concept Validity *USE Construct Validity*
Conservation **(Concept)**
Self **Concept**
Temporal Spatial **Concept** Scale
Tennessee Self **Concept** Scale
Concepts
God **Concepts**
Mathematics **(Concepts)**
Conceptual Imagery
Conceptual Tempo
Conceptualization
    USE Concept Formation
Concurrent Reinforcement Schedules
Concurrent Validity
Brain **Concussion**
Conditioned Emotional Responses
Conditioned Inhibition
    USE Conditioned Suppression
Conditioned Place Preference
    USE Place Conditioning
Conditioned Reflex
    USE Conditioned Responses
Conditioned Responses
Conditioned Stimulus
Conditioned Suppression
Conditioning
Conditioning (Verbal) *USE Verbal Learning*
Aversion **Conditioning**
Avoidance **Conditioning**
CER (Conditioning)
    USE Conditioned Emotional Responses
Classical **Conditioning**
Escape **Conditioning**
Eyelid **Conditioning**
Fading **(Conditioning)**

Instrumental Conditioning *USE Operant Conditioning*
Odor Aversion Conditioning *USE Aversion Conditioning*
Operant **Conditioning**
Pavlovian Conditioning *USE Classical Conditioning*
Place **Conditioning**
Respondent Conditioning *USE Classical Conditioning*
Taste Aversion Conditioning *USE Aversion Conditioning*
Verbal Conditioning *USE Verbal Learning*
Atmospheric **Conditions**
Working **Conditions**
Condoms
Conduct Disorder
Bone **Conduction** Audiometry
Skin Conduction *USE Skin Resistance*
Cones (Eye)
Confabulation
Conference Proceedings
    USE Professional Meetings and
        Symposia
Confession (Religion)
Confidence Limits (Statistics)
Confidence (Self) *USE Self Confidence*
Self **Confidence**
Confidentiality of Information
    USE Privileged Communication
Confirmatory Factor Analysis
    USE Factor Analysis
Conflict
Conflict Resolution
Marital **Conflict**
Role **Conflicts**
Conformity (Personality)
Mental **Confusion**
Congenital Disorders
Drug Induced **Congenital** Disorders
Congenitally Handicapped
Congo
Self **Congruence**
Conjoint Measurement
Conjoint Therapy
Connectionism
Connective Tissue Cells
Connective Tissues
Connotations
Consanguineous Marriage
Conscience
Conscious (Personality Factor)
Consciousness Disturbances
Consciousness Raising Groups
Consciousness States
Self Consciousness *USE Self Perception*
Informed **Consent**
Conservation (Concept)
Conservation (Ecological Behavior)
Conservatism
Political **Conservatism**
Wilson Patterson **Conservatism** Scale
Conservatorship *USE Guardianship*
Consistency (Measurement)
Internal Consistency *USE Test Reliability*
Response Consistency *USE Response Variability*
Consonants
Brightness **Constancy**
Color **Constancy**
Perceptual **Constancy**
Size **Constancy**
Constipation
Construct Validity
Laborers (Construct and Indust)
    USE Blue Collar Workers
Personal Construct Theory *USE Personality Theory*
Test **Construction**
Constructionism *USE Constructivism*
Constructivism
Consultation Liaison Psychiatry
Mental Health Consultation
    USE Professional Consultation
Professional **Consultation**
Consumer Attitudes

Consumer Behavior
Consumer Fraud *USE Fraud*
Consumer Protection
Consumer Psychology
Consumer Research
Consumer Satisfaction
Consumer Surveys
Contact Lenses
Eye **Contact**
Physical **Contact**
Contagion
Cost **Containment**
Content Analysis
Content Analysis (Test)
Dream **Content**
Emotional **Content**
Item **Content** (Test)
Thought Content *USE Cognitions*
Contextual Associations
Cognitive **Contiguity**
Contingency Management
Contingent Negative Variation
Continuing Education
Continuous Reinforcement
    USE Reinforcement Schedules
Contour *USE Form and Shape Perception*
Contraception *USE Birth Control*
Contraceptive Devices
Oral **Contraceptives**
Behavior **Contracting**
Muscle **Contraction** Headache
Muscle **Contractions**
Behavioral **Contrast**
Brightness **Contrast**
Color **Contrast**
Successive Contrast *USE Afterimage*
Visual **Contrast**
Control Groups *USE Experiment Controls*
Air Traffic **Control**
Birth **Control**
Birth Control Attitudes
    USE Family Planning Attitudes
Diaphragms (Birth **Control)**
Emotional **Control**
Gun **Control** Laws
Health Locus of Control *USE Health Attitudes*
Internal External Locus of **Control**
Population Control *USE Birth Control*
Quality **Control**
Rotter Intern Extern Locus **Cont** Scal
Self **Control**
Social **Control**
Stimulus **Control**
Thought Control *USE Brainwashing*
Weight **Control**
Experiment **Controls**
Instrument **Controls**
Eye **Convergence**
Convergent Thinking
    USE Inductive Deductive Reasoning
Conversation
Conversion Hysteria
    USE Conversion Neurosis
Conversion Neurosis
Criminal **Conviction**
Convulsions
Cooperating Teachers
Cooperation
Cooperative Education
Cooperative Learning
Cooperative Therapy *USE Cotherapy*
Motor **Coordination**
Perceptual Motor **Coordination**
Coping Behavior
Copper
Copulation
    USE Sexual Intercourse (Human)
Copulation (Animal)
    USE Animal Mating Behavior

Cranial Spinal **Cord**
Lumbar Spinal **Cord**
Spinal **Cord**
Spinal **Cord** Injuries
Vocal **Cords**
Cornea
Coronary Disorders
    USE Cardiovascular Disorders
Coronary Heart Disease
    USE Heart Disorders
Coronary Prone Behavior
Coronary Thromboses
Coronary Vessels *USE Arteries (Anatomy)*
Corporal Punishment *USE Punishment*
Corporations *USE Business Organizations*
Job **Corps**
Peace **Corps**
Corpus Callosum
Corpus Striatum *USE Basal Ganglia*
Correctional Institutions
Pearson Prod Moment Correl Coeff *USE Statistical Correlation*
Personality **Correlates**
Physiological **Correlates**
Psychological Correlates *USE Psychodynamics*
Canonical Correlation *USE Multivariate Analysis*
Point Biserial **Correlation**
Rank Difference **Correlation**
Rank Order **Correlation**
Statistical **Correlation**
Tetrachoric **Correlation**
Adrenal **Cortex** Hormones
Adrenal Cortex Steroids *USE Corticosteroids*
Auditory **Cortex**
Cerebral **Cortex**
Motor **Cortex**
Prefrontal **Cortex**
Somatosensory **Cortex**
Striate Cortex *USE Visual Cortex*
Visual **Cortex**
Organ of Corti *USE Cochlea*
Cortical Atrophy *USE Cerebral Atrophy*
Cortical Evoked Potentials
Corticoids *USE Corticosteroids*
Corticosteroids
Corticosterone
Corticotropin
Corticotropin Releasing Factor
Cortisol *USE Hydrocortisone*
Cortisone
Cost Containment
Cost Effectiveness
    USE Costs and Cost Analysis
Costs and **Cost** Analysis
Costa Rica
Costs and Cost Analysis
Health Care **Costs**
Medical Care Costs *USE Health Care Costs*
Mental Health Care Costs *USE Health Care Costs*
Cotherapy
Counselees *USE Clients*
Counseling
Counseling Psychologists
Counseling Psychology
Career Counseling *USE Occupational Guidance*
Educational **Counseling**
Family Counseling *USE Family Therapy*
Genetic **Counseling**
Group **Counseling**
Guidance Counseling *USE School Counseling*
Individual Counseling *USE Individual Psychotherapy*
Marriage **Counseling**
Pastoral **Counseling**
Peer **Counseling**
Premarital **Counseling**
Psychotherapeutic **Counseling**
Rehabilitation **Counseling**
School **Counseling**
Vocational Counseling *USE Occupational Guidance*
Counselor Attitudes

257

Counselor Characteristics
Counselor Client Interaction
   USE Psychotherapeutic Processes
Counselor Education
Counselor Effectiveness
   USE Counselor Characteristics
Counselor Personality
   USE Counselor Characteristics
Counselor Role
Counselor Trainees
Client Counselor Interaction
   USE Psychotherapeutic Processes
Counselors
Rehabilitation **Counselors**
School **Counselors**
Vocational **Counselors**
Over The Counter Drugs
   USE Nonprescription Drugs
Counterconditioning
Countertransference
Countries
Developed **Countries**
Developing **Countries**
Third World Countries *USE Developing Countries*
Underdeveloped Countries *USE Developing Countries*
Couples
Couples Therapy
Married Couples *USE Spouses*
Courage
Course Evaluation
Course Objectives
   USE Educational Objectives
Disease **Course**
Disorder Course *USE Disease Course*
Court Ordered Treatment
   USE Court Referrals
Court Referrals
Juvenile Court *USE Adjudication*
Courts *USE Adjudication*
Animal **Courtship** Behavior
Animal **Courtship** Displays
Human **Courtship**
Cousins
Analysis of **Covariance**
Covert Sensitization
Least Preferred **Coworker** Scale
Cows *USE Cattle*
Crabs
Crafts
Cramps (Muscle) *USE Muscular Disorders*
Muscle Cramps *USE Muscular Disorders*
Cranial Nerves
Cranial Spinal Cord
Crayfish
Creative Arts Therapy
Creative Writing
Writing (Creative) *USE Creative Writing*
Creativity
Creativity Measurement
Credibility
Creutzfeldt Jakob Syndrome
Aircraft Crew *USE Aerospace Personnel*
Cri du Chat Syndrome
   USE Crying Cat Syndrome
Crib Death *USE Sudden Infant Death*
Crime
Crime Prevention
Crime Victims
Criminal Conviction
Criminal Justice
Criminal Law
Criminal Responsibility
Criminally Insane
   USE Mentally Ill Offenders
Criminals
Female **Criminals**
Male **Criminals**
Criminology
Crippled *USE Physically Handicapped*

Crises
Family **Crises**
Organizational **Crises**
Crisis Intervention
Crisis Intervention Services
Crisis (Reactions to)
   USE Stress Reactions
Identity **Crisis**
Research Diagnostic **Criteria**
Student Admission **Criteria**
Criterion Referenced Tests
Critical Flicker Fusion Threshold
Critical Period
Critical Scores *USE Cutting Scores*
Criticism
Professional **Criticism**
Professional **Criticism** Reply
Crocodilians
Cross Cultural Differences
Cross Cultural Treatment
Cross Disciplinary Research
   USE Interdisciplinary Research
Crossed Eyes *USE Strabismus*
Crowding
Marlowe **Crowne** Soc Desirabil Scale
CRT *USE Video Display Units*
Cruelty
Crustacea
Crying
Crying Cat Syndrome
Cuba
Cuban Americans *USE Hispanics*
Cued Recall
Cues
Cultism
Cultural Assimilation
Cultural Deprivation
Cultural Familial Mental Retardation
   USE Psychosocial Mental Retardation
Cultural Psychiatry
   USE Transcultural Psychiatry
Cultural Sensitivity
Cultural Test Bias
Cross **Cultural** Differences
Cross **Cultural** Treatment
Culturally Disadvantaged
   USE Cultural Deprivation
Culture (Anthropological)
Culture Change
Culture Fair Intelligence Test
Culture Shock
Cattell Culture Fair Intell Test
   USE Culture Fair Intelligence Test
Curare
Curiosity
Curricular Field Experience
Curriculum
Curriculum Based Assessment
Curriculum Development
Cursive Writing
Cushings Syndrome
Child **Custody**
Joint **Custody**
Cutaneous Receptive Fields
Cutaneous Sense
Cutting Scores
Cybernetics
Lunar Synodic **Cycle**
Menstrual **Cycle**
Sleep Wake **Cycle**
Work Rest **Cycles**
Cyclic Adenosine Monophosphate
Cycloheximide
Cyclothymic Disorder
   USE Cyclothymic Personality
Cyclothymic Personality
Cynicism
Cyprus
Cysteine

Cystic Fibrosis	Isolation **(Defense** Mechanism)
Cytochrome Oxidase	Projection **(Defense** Mechanism)
Cytology	Regression **(Defense** Mechanism)
Cytoplasm	Repression **(Defense** Mechanism)
Czechoslovakia	Self **Defense**
Daily Activities	Suppression **(Defense** Mechanism)
Daily Biological Rhythms (Animal)	Withdrawal **(Defense** Mechanism)
USE Animal Circadian Rhythms	Animal **Defensive** Behavior
Activities of **Daily** Living	**Defensiveness**
Brain **Damage**	Nutritional **Deficiencies**
Brain **Damaged**	Acquired Immune **Deficiency** Syndrome
Minimally Brain **Damaged**	Mental Deficiency *USE Mental Retardation*
Dance	Protein **Deficiency** Disorders
Dance Therapy	Vitamin **Deficiency** Disorders
Dangerousness	Attention **Deficit** Disorder
Dark Adaptation	Deformity *USE Physical Disfigurement*
Darwinism	College Degrees *USE Educational Degrees*
Data Collection	Educational **Degrees**
Data Processing	Graduate Degrees *USE Educational Degrees*
Biographical **Data**	Undergraduate Degrees *USE Educational Degrees*
Statistical **Data**	**Dehydration**
Databases	Lactate **Dehydrogenase**
Computerized Databases *USE Databases*	**Dehydrogenases**
Online Databases *USE Databases*	Alcohol **Dehydrogenases**
Date Rape *USE Acquaintance Rape*	**Deinstitutionalization**
Social **Dating**	Deja Vu *USE Consciousness States*
Daughters	**Delay** of Gratification
Day Care Centers	Language **Delay**
Day Care (Treatment)	Reinforcement **Delay**
USE Partial Hospitalization	**Delayed** Alternation
Day Hospital *USE Partial Hospitalization*	**Delayed** Auditory Feedback
Child **Day** Care	**Delayed** Development
Recreational Day Camps	**Delayed** Feedback
USE Summer Camps (Recreation)	**Delayed** Parenthood
Daydreaming	Delayed Speech
Guided Daydreams *USE Directed Reverie Therapy*	*USE Retarded Speech Development*
DDT (Insecticide)	**Deletion** (Chromosome)
Deaf	Juvenile **Delinquency**
Deaf Blind	Sexual Delinquency *USE Promiscuity*
Word Deafness *USE Aphasia*	Female **Delinquents**
Deanol	Juvenile **Delinquents**
Death and Dying	Male **Delinquents**
Death Anxiety	**Delirium**
Death Attitudes	**Delirium** Tremens
Death Education	Health Care **Delivery**
Death Instinct	**Delta** Rhythm
Death Penalty *USE Capital Punishment*	**Delusions**
Death Rate *USE Mortality Rate*	**Dementia**
Death Rites	Dementia (Multi Infarct)
Crib Death *USE Sudden Infant Death*	*USE Multi Infarct Dementia*
Near **Death** Experiences	Dementia Paralytica *USE General Paresis*
Sudden Infant **Death**	Dementia Praecox *USE Schizophrenia*
Debriefing (Experimental)	Multi Infarct **Dementia**
Decarboxylase Inhibitors	Presenile **Dementia**
Decarboxylases	Senile **Dementia**
Memory **Decay**	**Democracy**
Decentralization	Democratic Party *USE Political Parties*
Deception	East German Democratic Republic *USE East Germany*
Decerebration	**Demographic** Characteristics
Decision Making	Social **Demonstrations**
Group **Decision** Making	**Dendrites**
Lexical **Decision**	**Denial**
Management **Decision** Making	**Denmark**
Legal **Decisions**	Social **Density**
Decoding	**Dental** Education
USE Human Information Storage	**Dental** Students
Decompression Effects	**Dental** Surgery
Decortication (Brain)	**Dental** Treatment
Inductive **Deductive** Reasoning	Dentist Patient Interaction
Deer	*USE Therapeutic Processes*
Self **Defeating** Behavior	**Dentistry**
Defecation	**Dentists**
Defendants	**Deoxycorticosterone**
Defense Mechanisms	**Deoxyglucose**
Compensation **(Defense** Mechanism)	**Deoxyribonucleic** Acid
Displacement **(Defense** Mechanism)	DNA (Deoxyribonucleic Acid)
Fantasy **(Defense** Mechanism)	*USE Deoxyribonucleic Acid*
Identification **(Defense** Mechanism)	Field **Dependence**
Insanity **Defense**	**Dependency** (Personality)

Drug **Dependency**
Dependent Personality
Dependent Variables
State **Dependent** Learning
Depersonalization
CNS **Depressant** Drugs
Appetite **Depressing** Drugs
Depression (Emotion)
Agitated Depression *USE Major Depression*
Anaclitic **Depression**
Beck **Depression** Inventory
Bipolar Depression *USE Manic Depression*
Climacteric Depression *USE Involutional Depression*
Endogenous **Depression**
Involutional **Depression**
Major **Depression**
Manic **Depression**
Postpartum **Depression**
Reactive **Depression**
Recurrent **Depression**
Spreading **Depression**
Treatment Resistant **Depression**
Tricyclic Resistant Depression
USE Treatment Resistant Depression
Unipolar Depression *USE Major Depression*
Winter Depression
USE Seasonal Affective Disorder
Zungs Self Rating **Depression** Scale
Manic Depressive Psychosis
USE Manic Depression
Neurotic **Depressive** Reaction
Psychotic Depressive Reaction
USE Major Depression
Deprivation
Animal Maternal **Deprivation**
Cultural **Deprivation**
Food **Deprivation**
REM Dream **Deprivation**
Sensory **Deprivation**
Sleep **Deprivation**
Social **Deprivation**
Stimulus **Deprivation**
Water **Deprivation**
Depth Perception
Depth Psychology
Ergot **Derivatives**
Opium Derivatives *USE Opiates*
Phenothiazine **Derivatives**
Dermatitis
Dermatomes
USE Cutaneous Receptive Fields
Desegregation *USE Social Integration*
Systematic **Desensitization** Therapy
Between Groups **Design**
Environmental Design *USE Environmental Planning*
Experimental **Design**
Interior **Design**
Kohs Block **Design** Test
Man Machine Systems **Design**
Research Design *USE Experimental Design*
Within Subjects Design *USE Repeated Measures*
Memory for **Designs** Test
Desipramine
Edwards Social **Desirability** Scale
Marlowe Crowne Soc **Desirabil** Scale
Social **Desirability**
Desires *USE Motivation*
Self **Destructive** Behavior
Anatomically **Detailed** Dolls
Signal **Detection** (Perception)
Legal **Detention**
Self **Determination**
Threshold **Determination**
Verdict Determination *USE Adjudication*
Detoxification
Kupfer **Detre** Self Rating Scale
Folie A **Deux**
Developed Countries
Developing Countries

Development
Adolescent **Development**
Adult **Development**
Animal **Development**
Bayley Scales of Infant **Development**
Career **Development**
Childhood **Development**
Childhood Play **Development**
Cognitive **Development**
Curriculum **Development**
Delayed **Development**
Early Childhood **Development**
Ego **Development**
Emotional **Development**
Frostig **Development** Test Vis Percept
Human **Development**
Infant **Development**
Intellectual **Development**
Language **Development**
Management Development *USE Career Development*
Moral **Development**
Motor **Development**
Neonatal **Development**
Neural **Development**
Organizational **Development**
Perceptual **Development**
Perceptual Motor **Development**
Personality **Development**
Personnel Development *USE Personnel Training*
Physical **Development**
Precocious **Development**
Prenatal **Development**
Professional **Development**
Program **Development**
Psychological Development *USE Psychogenesis*
Psychomotor **Development**
Psychosexual **Development**
Psychosocial **Development**
Retarded Speech **Development**
Sensorimotor Development
USE Perceptual Motor Development
Sexual **Development**
Social Development
USE Psychosocial Development
Speech **Development**
Developmental Age Groups
Developmental Differences
USE Age Differences
Developmental Disabilities
Developmental Measures
Developmental Psychology
Developmental Stages
Prenatal **Developmental** Stages
Sex Linked **Developmental** Differences
Deviant Behavior *USE Antisocial Behavior*
Deviation IQ *USE Standard Scores*
Standard **Deviation**
Sexual **Deviations**
Devices (Experimental) *USE Apparatus*
Computer Peripheral **Devices**
Contraceptive **Devices**
Intrauterine **Devices**
Medical Therapeutic **Devices**
Safety **Devices**
Dexamethasone
Dexamethasone Suppression Test
Dexedrine *USE Dextroamphetamine*
Physical **Dexterity**
Dextroamphetamine
Diabetes
Diabetes Insipidus
Diabetes Mellitus
Diacetylmorphine *USE Heroin*
Diagnosis
Diagnosis Related Groups
Diagnosis) *USE Medical Diagnosis*
Clinical Judgment (Med Diagnosis) *USE Medical Diagnosis*
Clinical Judgment (Not **Diagnosis)**
Computer Assisted **Diagnosis**
Differential **Diagnosis**

Dual **Diagnosis**
Educational **Diagnosis**
Medical **Diagnosis**
Prenatal **Diagnosis**
X Ray Diagnosis *USE Roentgenography*
Diagnostic and Statistical Manual
Diagnostic Interview Schedule
Research **Diagnostic** Criteria
Dialect
Dialectics
Dialysis
Diaphragm (Anatomy)
Diaphragms (Birth Control)
Diarrhea
Diastolic Pressure
Diazepam
Dichoptic Stimulation
Dichotic Stimulation
Dictionary
Dieldrin
Diencephalon
Dietary Restraint
Lysergic Acid **Diethylamide**
Diets
Rank **Difference** Correlation
Age **Differences**
Animal Sex **Differences**
Animal Strain **Differences**
Cross Cultural **Differences**
Developmental Differences *USE Age Differences*
Gender Differences *USE Human Sex Differences*
Human Sex **Differences**
Individual **Differences**
Racial and Ethnic **Differences**
Sex Linked Developmental **Differences**
Species **Differences**
Differential Aptitude Tests
Differential Diagnosis
Differential Limen *USE Thresholds*
Differential Personality Inventory
Differential Reinforcement
Semantic **Differential**
Sex Differentiation Disorders
　　　USE Genital Disorders
Difficulty Level (Test)
Task Difficulty *USE Task Complexity*
Test Difficulty *USE Difficulty Level (Test)*
Digestion
Digestive System
Digestive System Disorders
Digit Span Testing
Digital Computers
Digits (Mathematics)
　　　USE Numbers (Numerals)
Dihydroergotamine
Dihydroxyphenylacetic Acid
Dihydroxytryptamine
Dilantin *USE Diphenylhydantoin*
Pupil **Dilation**
Prisoners **Dilemma** Game
Dimethylaminoethanol *USE Deanol*
Carbon **Dioxide**
Diphenhydramine
Diphenylhydantoin
High School Diplomas *USE Educational Degrees*
Diptera
Directed Discussion Method
Directed Reverie Therapy
Self Directed Learning
　　　USE Individualized Instruction
Advance **Directives**
Developmental **Disabilities**
Learning **Disabilities**
Reading **Disabilities**
Disability Evaluation
Disability Laws
Disability Management
Disadvantaged
Culturally Disadvantaged *USE Cultural Deprivation*

Economically Disadvantaged *USE Disadvantaged*
Socially Disadvantaged *USE Disadvantaged*
Disappointment
Disasters
Natural **Disasters**
Discharge Planning
Facility **Discharge**
Hospital **Discharge**
Psychiatric Hospital **Discharge**
Cross Disciplinary Research
　　　USE Interdisciplinary Research
Child **Discipline**
Classroom **Discipline**
Disclosure (Experimental)
　　　USE Debriefing (Experimental)
Self **Disclosure**
Discovery Teaching Method
Discrimination
Discrimination Learning
Age **Discrimination**
Auditory **Discrimination**
Cognitive **Discrimination**
Distance Discrimination *USE Distance Perception*
Drug **Discrimination**
Employment **Discrimination**
Ethnic Discrimination
　　　USE Race and Ethnic Discrimination
Figure Ground **Discrimination**
Job Discrimination
　　　USE Employment Discrimination
Loudness **Discrimination**
Minority Group Discrimination
　　　USE Race and Ethnic Discrimination
Odor **Discrimination**
Pattern **Discrimination**
Perceptual **Discrimination**
Pitch **Discrimination**
Race and Ethnic **Discrimination**
Racial Discrimination
　　　USE Race and Ethnic Discrimination
Sex **Discrimination**
Size **Discrimination**
Social **Discrimination**
Spatial Discrimination *USE Spatial Perception*
Stimulus **Discrimination**
Tactual Discrimination *USE Tactual Perception*
Taste Discrimination *USE Taste Perception*
Visual **Discrimination**
Wepman Test of Auditory **Discrim**
Discriminative Stimulus
　　　USE Conditioned Stimulus
Directed **Discussion** Method
Group **Discussion**
Nondirected **Discussion** Method
Disease Course
Addisons **Disease**
Alzheimers **Disease**
Coronary Heart Disease *USE Heart Disorders*
Duchennes Disease *USE Muscular Disorders*
Menieres **Disease**
Parkinsons **Disease**
Picks **Disease**
Raynauds Disease *USE Cardiovascular Disorders*
Sickle Cell **Disease**
Tay Sachs Disease *USE Amaurotic Familial Idiocy*
Diseases *USE Disorders*
Communicable Diseases *USE Infectious Disorders*
Kidney **Diseases**
Sexually Transmitted Diseases *USE Venereal Diseases*
Venereal **Diseases**
Physical **Disfigurement**
Disgust
Dishonesty
Dislike *USE Aversion*
Disorder Course *USE Disease Course*
Acute Paranoid Disorder *USE Paranoia (Psychosis)*
Attention Deficit **Disorder**
Atypical Paranoid Disorder *USE Paranoia (Psychosis)*
Atypical Somatoform Disorder *USE Dysmorphophobia*

Compulsive Personality Disorder
        USE Obsessive Compulsive Personality
Conduct **Disorder**
Cyclothymic Disorder *USE Cyclothymic Personality*
Dysthymic **Disorder**
Epstein Barr Viral **Disorder**
Generalized Anxiety Disorder *USE Anxiety Neurosis*
Gilles de la Tourette **Disorder**
Histrionic Personality Disorder *USE Hysterical Personality*
Obsessive Compulsive Disorder
        USE Obsessive Compulsive Neurosis
Panic **Disorder**
Paranoid Disorder *USE Paranoia (Psychosis)*
PKU (Hereditary Disorder) *USE Phenylketonuria*
Posttraumatic Stress **Disorder**
Reactive Attachment Disorder *USE Failure to Thrive*
Schizoaffective **Disorder**
Schizophreniform **Disorder**
Seasonal Affective **Disorder**
Shared Paranoid Disorder *USE Folie A Deux*
Somatization Disorder *USE Psychosomatic Disorders*
        Disorders
Adjustment **Disorders**
Adrenal Gland **Disorders**
Affective Disorders *USE Affective Disturbances*
Allergic **Disorders**
Allergic Skin **Disorders**
Anxiety Disorders *USE Anxiety Neurosis*
Appetite **Disorders**
Articulation **Disorders**
Autoimmune Disorders *USE Immunologic Disorders*
Autonomic Nervous System **Disorders**
Autosome **Disorders**
Bacterial **Disorders**
Behavior **Disorders**
Blood and Lymphatic **Disorders**
Blood Pressure **Disorders**
Bone **Disorders**
Bowel Disorders *USE Colon Disorders*
Brain **Disorders**
Bronchial **Disorders**
Cardiac Disorders *USE Heart Disorders*
Cardiovascular **Disorders**
Central Nervous System **Disorders**
Cerebral Vascular Disorders *USE Cerebrovascular Disorders*
Cerebrovascular **Disorders**
Chromosome **Disorders**
Chronicity **(Disorders)**
Circulatory Disorders *USE Cardiovascular Disorders*
Colon **Disorders**
Communication **Disorders**
Congenital **Disorders**
Coronary Disorders *USE Cardiovascular Disorders*
Digestive System **Disorders**
Drug Induced Congenital **Disorders**
Ear **Disorders**
Eating Disorders *USE Appetite Disorders*
Endocrine **Disorders**
Endocrine Sexual **Disorders**
Ethnic Disorders *USE Ethnospecific Disorders*
Ethnospecific **Disorders**
Eye **Disorders**
Factitious **Disorders**
Gastrointestinal **Disorders**
Genetic **Disorders**
Genital **Disorders**
Gynecological **Disorders**
Hearing **Disorders**
Heart **Disorders**
Hematologic Disorders
        USE Blood and Lymphatic Disorders
Hepatic Disorders *USE Liver Disorders*
Hereditary Disorders *USE Genetic Disorders*
Hypophysis Disorders *USE Pituitary Disorders*
Immunologic **Disorders**
Infectious **Disorders**
Joint **Disorders**
Karyotype Disorders *USE Chromosome Disorders*
Labyrinth **Disorders**

Language **Disorders**
Laryngeal **Disorders**
Learning **Disorders**
Lipid Metabolism **Disorders**
Liver **Disorders**
Lung **Disorders**
Male Genital **Disorders**
Memory **Disorders**
Menstrual **Disorders**
Mental **Disorders**
Metabolism **Disorders**
Minimal Brain **Disorders**
Motor Disorders *USE Nervous System Disorders*
Movement **Disorders**
Muscular **Disorders**
Musculoskeletal **Disorders**
Neonatal **Disorders**
Nervous System **Disorders**
Neurological Disorders *USE Nervous System Disorders*
Neuromuscular **Disorders**
Onset **(Disorders)**
Ovary Disorders
        USE Endocrine Sexual Disorders
Parasitic **Disorders**
Parathyroid **Disorders**
Peripheral Nerve **Disorders**
Personality **Disorders**
Pharyngeal **Disorders**
Pituitary **Disorders**
Protein Deficiency **Disorders**
Psychiatric Disorders *USE Mental Disorders*
Psychophysiologic Disorders *USE Psychosomatic Disorders*
Psychosomatic **Disorders**
Recovery **(Disorders)**
Relapse **(Disorders)**
Remission **(Disorders)**
Respiratory Tract **Disorders**
Scalp Disorders *USE Skin Disorders*
Sense Organ **Disorders**
Severity **(Disorders)**
Sex Chromosome **Disorders**
Sex Differentiation Disorders *USE Genital Disorders*
Sex Linked Hereditary **Disorders**
Sexual Disorders (Physiological)
        USE Genital Disorders
Skeletomuscular Disorders *USE Musculoskeletal Disorders*
Skin **Disorders**
Sleep **Disorders**
Speech **Disorders**
Susceptibility **(Disorders)**
Testes Disorders
        USE Endocrine Sexual Disorders
Thyroid **Disorders**
Toxic **Disorders**
Treatment Resistant **Disorders**
Urinary Function **Disorders**
Urogenital **Disorders**
Vascular Disorders *USE Cardiovascular Disorders*
Viral **Disorders**
Vision **Disorders**
Vitamin Deficiency **Disorders**
Voice Disorders *USE Dysphonia*
Schizophrenia (Disorganized Type)
        USE Hebephrenic Schizophrenia
Place **Disorientation**
Time **Disorientation**
Displacement (Defense Mechanism)
Video Display Terminals
        USE Video Display Units
Video **Display** Units
        Displays
Animal Courtship **Displays**
Auditory **Displays**
Graphical **Displays**
Tactual **Displays**
Visual **Displays**
Disposition *USE Personality*
Disruptive Behavior
        USE Behavior Problems

Dissatisfaction
Drug **Dissociation**
    USE State Dependent Learning
Hysterical Neurosis (Dissociation) *USE Dissociative Neurosis*
Dissociative Neurosis
Dissociative Patterns
Cognitive **Dissonance**
Distance Discrimination
    USE Distance Perception
Distance Perception
Apparent **Distance**
Interpersonal Distance *USE Personal Space*
Perceptual **Distortion**
Spatial **Distortion**
Distractibility
Distraction
Distress
Animal **Distress** Calls
Respiratory **Distress**
Distributed Practice
Binomial **Distribution**
Frequency **Distribution**
Normal **Distribution**
Poisson Distribution *USE Skewed Distribution*
Skewed **Distribution**
Distributive Justice *USE Justice*
Distrust *USE Suspicion*
Affective **Disturbances**
Body Image **Disturbances**
Consciousness **Disturbances**
Fantasies (Thought **Disturbances)**
Hysterical Vision **Disturbances**
Judgment **Disturbances**
Perceptual **Disturbances**
Sexual Function **Disturbances**
Thought **Disturbances**
Emotionally **Disturbed**
Disulfiram
Diuresis
Diuretics
Diurnal Variations
    USE Human Biological Rhythms
Divergent Thinking
Divided Attention
Division of Labor
Animal **Division** of Labor
Physical Divisions (Geographic) *USE Geography*
Political Divisions (Geographic) *USE Geography*
Divorce
Divorced Persons
Dizygotic Twins *USE Heterozygotic Twins*
Dizziness *USE Vertigo*
DNA (Deoxyribonucleic Acid)
    USE Deoxyribonucleic Acid
Doctors *USE Physicians*
Dogmatism
Rokeach **Dogmatism** Scale
Dogs
Seeing Eye Dogs *USE Mobility Aids*
Doll Play
Anatomically Detailed **Dolls**
Tic Doloureux *USE Trigeminal Neuralgia*
Dolphins
Domestic Service Personnel
Domestic Violence *USE Family Violence*
Animal **Domestication**
Dominance
Dominance Hierarchy
Animal **Dominance**
Cerebral **Dominance**
Eye Dominance *USE Ocular Dominance*
Genetic **Dominance**
Lateral **Dominance**
Ocular **Dominance**
Domination *USE Authoritarianism*
Dominican Republic
Blood Donation *USE Tissue Donation*
Organ Donation *USE Tissue Donation*
Sperm Donation *USE Tissue Donation*

Tissue **Donation**
DOPA
L Dopa *USE Levodopa*
DOPAC *USE Dihydroxyphenylacetic Acid*
Dopamine
Dopamine Agonists
Dopamine Antagonists
Dopamine Metabolites
Dormitories
Dorsal Horns
Dorsal Roots
Drug **Dosages**
Double Bind Interaction
Doubt
Doves
Downs Syndrome
Doxepin
Draftees
Drama
Draw A Man Test
    USE Human Figures Drawing
Goodenough Harris Draw A Person Test
Drawing
Franck **Drawing** Completion Test
Human Figures **Drawing**
Dream Analysis
Dream Content
Dream Interpretation *USE Dream Analysis*
Dream Recall
REM **Dream** Deprivation
Dreaming
Lucid **Dreaming**
Rapid Eye Movement Dreams *USE REM Dreams*
REM **Dreams**
DRGs *USE Diagnosis Related Groups*
Drinking Behavior
Alcohol **Drinking** Attitudes
Alcohol **Drinking** Patterns
Animal **Drinking** Behavior
Problem Drinking *USE Alcohol Abuse*
Social **Drinking**
Drive *USE Motivation*
Sex **Drive**
Driver Education
Driver Safety *USE Highway Safety*
Drivers
Driving Behavior
Driving Under The Influence
Drunk Driving *USE Driving Under The Influence*
Dropouts
College **Dropouts**
Potential **Dropouts**
Research Dropouts *USE Experimental Attrition*
School **Dropouts**
Treatment **Dropouts**
Drosophila
Drowsiness *USE Sleep Onset*
Drug Abstinence
Drug Abuse
Drug Abuse Liability
Drug Abuse Prevention
Drug Addiction
Drug Administration Methods
Drug Adverse Reactions
    USE Side Effects (Drug)
Drug Allergies
Drug Dependency
Drug Discrimination
Drug Dissociation
    USE State Dependent Learning
Drug Dosages
Drug Education
Drug Effects *USE Drugs*
Drug Induced Congenital Disorders
Drug Induced Hallucinations
Drug Interactions
Drug Laws
Drug Overdoses
Drug Potentiation *USE Drug Interactions*

ROTATED ALPHABETICAL TERMS SECTION

Drug **Rehabilitation**
Drug **Sensitivity**
Drug Synergism *USE Drug Interactions*
Drug Testing *USE Drug Usage Screening*
Drug **Therapy**
Drug **Tolerance**
Drug **Usage**
Drug **Usage Attitudes**
Drug **Usage Screening**
Drug **Withdrawal**
Ecstasy (Drug)
   USE Methylenedioxymethamphetamine
Intravenous **Drug** Usage
IV Drug Usage *USE Intravenous Drug Usage*
LSD (Drug) *USE Lysergic Acid Diethylamide*
Side Effects **(Drug)**
Tobacco (Drug) *USE Nicotine*
Drugs
Abstinence (Drugs) *USE Drug Abstinence*
Abuse Potential (Drugs) *USE Drug Abuse Liability*
Adrenergic **Drugs**
Adrenergic Blocking **Drugs**
Adrenolytic **Drugs**
Analeptic **Drugs**
Analgesic **Drugs**
Anesthetic **Drugs**
Anorexigenic Drugs *USE Appetite Depressing Drugs*
Anti Inflammatory **Drugs**
Antianxiety Drugs *USE Tranquilizing Drugs*
Anticholinergic Drugs *USE Cholinergic Blocking Drugs*
Anticholinesterase Drugs *USE Cholinesterase Inhibitors*
Anticoagulant **Drugs**
Anticonvulsive **Drugs**
Antidepressant **Drugs**
Antiemetic **Drugs**
Antiepileptic Drugs *USE Anticonvulsive Drugs*
Antihistaminic **Drugs**
Antihypertensive **Drugs**
Antinauseant Drugs *USE Antiemetic Drugs*
Antineoplastic **Drugs**
Antiparkinsonian Drugs *USE Antitremor Drugs*
Antipsychotic Drugs *USE Neuroleptic Drugs*
Antipyretic Drugs *USE Anti Inflammatory Drugs*
Antischizophrenic Drugs *USE Neuroleptic Drugs*
Antispasmodic **Drugs**
Antitremor **Drugs**
Antitubercular **Drugs**
Antiviral **Drugs**
Anxiety Reducing Drugs *USE Tranquilizing Drugs*
Anxiolytic Drugs *USE Tranquilizing Drugs*
Appetite Depressing **Drugs**
Ataractic Drugs *USE Tranquilizing Drugs*
Ataraxic Drugs *USE Tranquilizing Drugs*
Cardiotonic **Drugs**
Central Nervous System Drugs *USE CNS Affecting Drugs*
Cholinergic **Drugs**
Cholinergic Blocking **Drugs**
Cholinolytic Drugs *USE Cholinergic Blocking Drugs*
Cholinomimetic **Drugs**
CNS Affecting **Drugs**
CNS Depressant **Drugs**
CNS Stimulating **Drugs**
Cognition Enhancing Drugs *USE Nootropic Drugs*
Emetic **Drugs**
Ganglion Blocking **Drugs**
Hallucinogenic **Drugs**
Heart Rate Affecting **Drugs**
Hypnotic **Drugs**
Memory Enhancing Drugs *USE Nootropic Drugs*
Muscarinic Drugs *USE Cholinergic Drugs*
Muscle Relaxing **Drugs**
Narcoanalytic **Drugs**
Narcotic **Drugs**
Neuroleptic **Drugs**
Neuromuscular Blocking Drugs *USE Muscle Relaxing Drugs*
Nonprescription **Drugs**
Nootropic **Drugs**
Over The Counter Drugs *USE Nonprescription Drugs*
Pain Relieving Drugs *USE Analgesic Drugs*

Parasympatholytic Drugs *USE Cholinergic Blocking Drugs*
Parasympathomimetic Drugs *USE Cholinomimetic Drugs*
Prescribing **(Drugs)**
Prescription **Drugs**
Pressors (Drugs) *USE Vasoconstrictor Drugs*
Psychedelic **Drugs**
Psychoactive Drugs *USE Drugs*
Psychotomimetic **Drugs**
Psychotropic Drugs *USE Drugs*
Respiration Stimulating **Drugs**
Sleep Inducing Drugs *USE Hypnotic Drugs*
Sympatholytic **Drugs**
Sympathomimetic **Drugs**
Thymoleptic Drugs *USE Tranquilizing Drugs*
Tranquilizing **Drugs**
Vasoconstrictor **Drugs**
Vasodilator **Drugs**
Vasopressor Drugs *USE Vasoconstrictor Drugs*
Vomit Inducing Drugs *USE Emetic Drugs*
Drunk **Driving**
   USE Driving Under The Influence
Drunkenness *USE Alcohol Intoxication*
DSM
   USE Diagnostic and Statistical Manual
Cri du Chat Syndrome
   USE Crying Cat Syndrome
Dual **Careers**
Dual **Diagnosis**
Dualism
Duchennes Disease
   USE Muscular Disorders
Ducks
Duodenum *USE Intestines*
Response **Duration**
Stimulus **Duration**
Treatment **Duration**
Pituitary Dwarfism *USE Hypopituitarism*
Dyads
Dying Patients *USE Terminally Ill Patients*
Death and **Dying**
Group **Dynamics**
Intergroup **Dynamics**
Dynorphins
Dysarthria
Dyscalculia *USE Acalculia*
Dysfunctional Family
Dyskinesia
Tardive **Dyskinesia**
Dyslexia
Dysmenorrhea
Dysmetria *USE Ataxia*
Dysmorphophobia
Dyspareunia
Dysphasia
Dysphonia
Dysphoria *USE Major Depression*
Postnatal Dysphoria *USE Postpartum Depression*
Dyspnea
Dyspraxia *USE Movement Disorders*
Dysthymia *USE Dysthymic Disorder*
Dysthymic Disorder
Dystonia *USE Muscular Disorders*
Muscular **Dystrophy**
Eagerness *USE Enthusiasm*
Ear **(Anatomy)**
Ear Canal *USE External Ear*
Ear **Disorders**
Ear Ossicles *USE Middle Ear*
External **Ear**
Inner Ear *USE Labyrinth (Anatomy)*
Middle **Ear**
Early **Childhood**
   USE Preschool Age Children
Early **Childhood Development**
Early **Experience**
Early **Infantile Autism**
Early **Intervention**
Early **Memories**
Earthworms

East Africa
East German Democratic Republic
  USE East Germany
East Germany
Middle **East**
Eastern Europe
Eating
Eating Attitudes
Eating Disorders *USE Appetite Disorders*
Binge **Eating**
Retinal **Eccentricity**
Echinodermata
Echoencephalography
Echolalia
Echolocation
Eclectic Psychology
  USE Theoretical Orientation
Eclectic Psychotherapy
Ecological Factors
Ecological Psychology
Conservation **(Ecological** Behavior)
Ecology
Income **(Economic)**
Political **Economic** Systems
Economically Disadvantaged
  USE Disadvantaged
Economics
Home **Economics**
Economy
Token **Economy** Programs
ECS Therapy
  USE Electroconvulsive Shock Therapy
Ecstasy (Drug)
  USE Methylenedioxymethamphetamine
ECT (Therapy)
  USE Electroconvulsive Shock Therapy
Ecuador
Eczema
Educable Mentally Retarded
Education
Education Students
Accreditation **(Education** Personnel)
Adult **Education**
Affective **Education**
Alcohol Education *USE Drug Education*
Art **Education**
Bilingual **Education**
Boards of **Education**
Business **Education**
Career **Education**
Client **Education**
College Education *USE Undergraduate Education*
Compensatory **Education**
Continuing **Education**
Cooperative **Education**
Counselor **Education**
Death **Education**
Dental **Education**
Driver **Education**
Drug **Education**
Elementary **Education**
Environmental **Education**
Equal **Education**
Foreign Language **Education**
Graduate **Education**
Graduate Psychology **Education**
Health **Education**
Higher **Education**
Humanistic Education *USE Affective Education*
Industrial Arts Education *USE Vocational Education*
Inservice Teacher **Education**
Language Arts **Education**
Mathematics **Education**
Medical **Education**
Middle School **Education**
Multicultural **Education**
Music **Education**
Nontraditional **Education**
Nursing **Education**

Paraprofessional **Education**
Parochial School Education *USE Private School Education*
Patient Education *USE Client Education*
Physical **Education**
Preschool **Education**
Private School **Education**
Psychology **Education**
Public School **Education**
Reading **Education**
Religious **Education**
Remedial **Education**
Science **Education**
Second Language Education
  USE Foreign Language Education
Secondary **Education**
Sex **Education**
Social Studies **Education**
Social Work **Education**
Special **Education**
Special **Education** Students
Special **Education** Teachers
Teacher **Education**
Technical Education Teachers
  USE Vocational Education Teachers
Theories of **Education**
Undergraduate **Education**
Vocational **Education**
Vocational **Education** Teachers
Educational Administration
Educational Administrators
  USE School Administrators
Educational Aspirations
Educational Audiovisual Aids
Educational Background
Educational Counseling
Educational Degrees
Educational Diagnosis
Educational Field Trips
Educational Financial Assistance
Educational Guidance
  USE Educational Counseling
Educational Incentives
Educational Inequality
  USE Equal Education
Educational Laboratories
Educational Measurement
Educational Objectives
Educational Personnel
Educational Placement
Educational Process *USE Education*
Educational Program Accreditation
Educational Program Evaluation
Educational Program Planning
Educational Programs
Educational Psychologists
Educational Psychology
Educational Supervision
  USE Professional Supervision
Educational Television
Educational Therapy
  USE School Counseling
Educational Toys
Accreditation (Educational Programs)
  USE Educational Program Accreditation
Field Work (Educational)
  USE Curricular Field Experience
Grading **(Educational)**
Guidance (Educational) *USE Educational Counseling*
Learning Centers **(Educational)**
Mainstreaming **(Educational)**
Motion Pictures **(Educational)**
Parent **Educational** Background
Edwards Personal Preference Schedule
Edwards Personality Inventory
Edwards Social Desirability Scale
EEG (Electrophysiology)
  USE Electroencephalography
Effect Size (Statistical)
Generation **Effect** (Learning)

265

Halo **Effect**
Isolation **Effect**
Magnitude of Effect (Statistical)
    USE Effect Size (Statistical)
Primacy **Effect**
Recency **Effect**
Serial Position **Effect**
Stroop **Effect**
Cost Effectiveness
    USE Costs and Cost Analysis
Counselor Effectiveness
    USE Counselor Characteristics
Organizational **Effectiveness**
Parent Effectiveness Training
    USE Parent Training
Teacher Effectiveness
    USE Teacher Characteristics
Teacher **Effectiveness** Evaluation
Therapist Effectiveness
    USE Therapist Characteristics
Treatment **Effectiveness** Evaluation
Acceleration **Effects**
Altitude **Effects**
Cold **Effects**
Decompression **Effects**
Drug Effects *USE Drugs*
Environmental **Effects**
Gravitational **Effects**
Heat **Effects**
Iatrogenic Effects *USE Side Effects (Treatment)*
Noise **Effects**
Side **Effects** (Drug)
Side **Effects** (Treatment)
Temperature **Effects**
Underwater **Effects**
Efferent Pathways
Efficacy Expectations *USE Self Efficacy*
Self **Efficacy**
Employee **Efficiency**
Effort *USE Energy Expenditure*
Egalitarianism
Ego
Ego Development
Ego Identity
Egocentrism
Egotism
Egypt
Eidetic Imagery
Ejaculation *USE Male Orgasm*
Premature **Ejaculation**
EKG (Electrophysiology)
    USE Electrocardiography
El Salvador
Elavil *USE Amitriptyline*
Elbow (Anatomy)
Elder Abuse
Elder Care
Elected Government Officials
    USE Government Personnel
Political **Elections**
Elective Abortion *USE Induced Abortion*
Elective Mutism
Electra Complex
Electric Fishes
Electrical Activity
Electrical Brain Stimulation
Electrical Injuries
Electrical Stimulation
Skin **Electrical** Properties
Electro Oculography
Electrocardiography
Electroconvulsive Shock
Electroconvulsive Shock Therapy
Electrodermal Response
    USE Galvanic Skin Response
Electrodes
Electroencephalography
Electrolytes
Electromyography

Electronystagmography
Electrophysiology
EEG (Electrophysiology)
    USE Electroencephalography
EKG (Electrophysiology)
    USE Electrocardiography
EMG (Electrophysiology)
    USE Electromyography
EOG (Electrophysiology)
    USE Electro Oculography
GSR (Electrophysiology)
    USE Galvanic Skin Response
Electroplethysmography
Electroretinography
Electroshock Therapy
    USE Electroconvulsive Shock Therapy
Electrosleep Treatment
Elementarism *USE Reductionism*
Elementary Education
Elementary School Students
Elementary School Teachers
Elementary Schools
Chemical **Elements**
Metallic **Elements**
Nonmetallic **Elements**
Elephants
Ellis (Albert)
Embarrassment
Embedded Figures Testing
Embolisms
Embryo
Emergency Services
Emetic Drugs
EMG (Electrophysiology)
    USE Electromyography
Nocturnal **Emission**
Positron Emission Tomography *USE Tomography*
Depression **(Emotion)**
Expressed **Emotion**
Emotional Abuse
Emotional Adjustment
Emotional Content
Emotional Control
Emotional Development
Emotional Expressiveness
    USE Emotionality (Personality)
Emotional Immaturity
Emotional Inferiority
Emotional Insecurity
    USE Emotional Security
Emotional Instability
Emotional Maladjustment
    USE Emotional Adjustment
Emotional Maturity
Emotional Responses
Emotional Restraint
    USE Emotional Control
Emotional Security
Emotional Stability
Emotional States
Emotional Superiority
Emotional Trauma
Bonding (Emotional) *USE Attachment Behavior*
Conditioned **Emotional** Responses
Emotionality (Personality)
Animal **Emotionality**
Emotionally Disturbed
Emotions
Rational **Emotive** Therapy
Empathy
Pulmonary **Emphysema**
Empirical Methods
Employability
Employee Absenteeism
Employee Assistance Programs
Employee Attitudes
Employee Benefits
Employee Characteristics
Employee Efficiency

Employee Health Insurance
Employee Interaction
Employee Leave Benefits
Employee Motivation
Employee Pension Plans
Employee Productivity
Employee Selection
    USE Personnel Selection
Employee Skills
Employee Termination
    USE Personnel Termination
Employee Turnover
Employees *USE Personnel*
Employer Attitudes
Employment *USE Employment Status*
Employment Discrimination
Employment History
Employment Interviews
    USE Job Applicant Interviews
Employment Processes
    USE Personnel Recruitment
Employment Status
Employment Tests
Self **Employment**
Supported **Employment**
Empowerment
Empty Nest
Encephalitis
Encephalography
Encephalography (Air)
    USE Pneumoencephalography
Air Encephalography
    USE Pneumoencephalography
Encephalomyelitis
Encephalopathies
Toxic **Encephalopathies**
Encoding
    USE Human Information Storage
Encopresis *USE Fecal Incontinence*
Encounter Group Therapy
Encouragement
Nerve **Endings**
Endocrine Disorders
Endocrine Gland Secretion
Endocrine Gland Surgery
Endocrine Glands
Endocrine Neoplasms
Endocrine Sexual Disorders
Endocrine System
Endocrinology
Endogamous Marriage
Endogenous Depression
Endogenous Opiates
Endorphins
Endurance
Physical **Endurance**
Psychological **Endurance**
Energy Expenditure
Law **Enforcement**
Law **Enforcement** Personnel
Engineering Psychology
Genetic **Engineering**
Human Factors **Engineering**
Engineers
England
Limited English Proficiency
    USE Language Proficiency
Nonstandard **English**
Fertility **Enhancement**
Cognition Enhancing Drugs *USE Nootropic Drugs*
Memory Enhancing Drugs *USE Nootropic Drugs*
Enjoyment *USE Pleasure*
Enkephalins
Enlisted Military Personnel
Military **Enlistment**
Job **Enrichment**
School **Enrollment**
Enteropeptidase *USE Kinases*
Motion Pictures **(Entertainment)**

Enthusiasm
Entrance Examinations
Coll **Ent** Exam Bd Scholastic Apt Test
Entrapment Games
Entrepreneurship
Enuresis *USE Urinary Incontinence*
Environment
Academic **Environment**
Classroom **Environment**
College **Environment**
Facility **Environment**
Home **Environment**
Hospital **Environment**
Office Environment *USE Working Conditions*
Person **Environment** Fit
School **Environment**
Zoo Environment *USE Animal Captivity*
Environmental Adaptation
Environmental Attitudes
Environmental Design
    USE Environmental Planning
Environmental Education
Environmental Effects
Environmental Planning
Environmental Psychology
Environmental Stress
Environmental Therapy
    USE Milieu Therapy
Restricted Environmental Stimulation
    USE Stimulus Deprivation
Animal **Environments**
Factory Environments *USE Working Conditions*
Rural **Environments**
Social **Environments**
Suburban **Environments**
Urban **Environments**
Work Environments *USE Working Conditions*
Envy *USE Jealousy*
Penis **Envy**
Enzyme Inhibitors
Enzymes
EOG (Electrophysiology)
    USE Electro Oculography
Ependyma *USE Cerebral Ventricles*
Ephedrine
Epidemiology
Epilepsy
Experimental **Epilepsy**
Grand Mal **Epilepsy**
Petit Mal **Epilepsy**
Epileptic Seizures
Epinephrine
Acute Psychotic Episode *USE Acute Psychosis*
Psychotic Episode (Acute) *USE Acute Psychosis*
Episodic Memory
Epistemology
Epithelial Cells
Epithelium *USE Skin (Anatomy)*
Epstein Barr Viral Disorder
Equal Education
Social **Equality**
Score **Equating**
Test Equating *USE Score Equating*
Structural **Equation** Modeling
Equilibrium
Equimax Rotation
Cauda Equina *USE Spinal Nerves*
Equipment *USE Apparatus*
Equity (Payment)
Equity (Social)
High School Equivalency *USE Adult Education*
Erection (Penis)
Ergonomics
    USE Human Factors Engineering
Ergot Derivatives
Erikson **(Erik)**
Erikson (Erik)
Eroticism
Errata

Error Analysis
Error of Measurement
Error Variance *USE Error of Measurement*
Standard Error of Measurement
    USE Error of Measurement
Trial and Error Learning
Errors
Prediction Errors
Refraction Errors
Type I Errors
Type II Errors
Erythroblastosis Fetalis
    USE Rh Incompatibility
Erythrocytes
Escape *USE Avoidance*
Escape Conditioning
Animal Escape Behavior
Eserine *USE Physostigmine*
Eskimos
Esophagus
ESP (Parapsychology)
    USE Extrasensory Perception
Essay Testing
Essential Hypertension
Self Esteem
Esterases
Estimation
Magnitude Estimation
Parameter Estimation *USE Statistical Estimation*
Statistical Estimation
Time Estimation
Estradiol
Estrogen Antagonists *USE Antiestrogens*
Estrogen Replacement Therapy
    USE Hormone Therapy
Estrogens
Estrone
Estrus
Ethanal *USE Acetaldehyde*
Ethanol
Ether (Anesthetic)
Work Ethic *USE Work (Attitudes Toward)*
Ethics
Experimental Ethics
Professional Ethics
Ethiopia
Ethnic Discrimination
    USE Race and Ethnic Discrimination
Ethnic Disorders
    USE Ethnospecific Disorders
Ethnic Groups
Ethnic Identity
Ethnic Sensitivity *USE Cultural Sensitivity*
Ethnic Values
Race and Ethnic Discrimination
Racial and Ethnic Attitudes
Racial and Ethnic Differences
Racial and Ethnic Relations
Ethnocentrism
Ethnography
Ethnolinguistics
Ethnology
Ethnospecific Disorders
Animal Ethology
Ethyl Alcohol *USE Ethanol*
Ethylaldehyde *USE Acetaldehyde*
Etiology
Etymology
Eugenics
Euphoria
Europe
Eastern Europe
Western Europe
Eustachian Tube *USE Middle Ear*
Euthanasia
Evaluation
Course Evaluation
Disability Evaluation
Educational Program Evaluation

Forensic Evaluation
Mental Health Program Evaluation
Peer Evaluation
Personnel Evaluation
Program Evaluation
Self Evaluation
Teacher Effectiveness Evaluation
Treatment Effectiveness Evaluation
Vocational Evaluation
Evangelists
Anniversary Events
Experiences (Events)
Evidence (Legal) *USE Legal Evidence*
Legal Evidence
Evoked Potentials
Auditory Evoked Potentials
Cortical Evoked Potentials
Motor Evoked Potentials
    USE Somatosensory Evoked Potentials
Olfactory Evoked Potentials
Somatosensory Evoked Potentials
Visual Evoked Potentials
Theory of Evolution
Breast Examination
    USE Self Examination (Medical)
Coll Ent Exam Bd Scholastic Apt Test
Eye Examination
    USE Ophthalmologic Examination
Graduate Record Examination
Mini Mental State Examination
Ophthalmologic Examination
Physical Examination
Self Examination (Medical)
Certification Examinations
    USE Professional Examinations
Entrance Examinations
Licensure Examinations
    USE Professional Examinations
Professional Examinations
State Board Examinations
    USE Professional Examinations
Exceptional Children (Gifted) *USE Gifted*
Exceptional Children (Handicapped)
    USE Handicapped
Information Exchange
Excretion
Executives *USE Top Level Managers*
Exercise
Aerobic Exercise
Exhaustion *USE Fatigue*
Exhibitionism
Existential Therapy
Existentialism
Exogamous Marriage
Life Expectancy
Expectant Fathers
Expectant Mothers
Expectant Parents
Expectations
Efficacy Expectations *USE Self Efficacy*
Experimenter Expectations
Role Expectations
Teacher Expectations
Energy Expenditure
Experience Level
Experience (Practice) *USE Practice*
Combat Experience
Curricular Field Experience
Early Experience
Job Experience Level
Therapist Experience *USE Therapist Characteristics*
Wilderness Experience
Experiences (Events)
Life Experiences
Near Death Experiences
Out of Body Experiences
Psychedelic Experiences
Vicarious Experiences
Experiential Psychotherapy

Experiment Controls
Experiment Volunteers
Experimental Apparatus USE Apparatus
Experimental Attrition
Experimental Design
Experimental Epilepsy
Experimental Ethics
Experimental Instructions
Experimental Laboratories
Experimental Methods
Experimental Neurosis
Experimental Psychologists
Experimental Psychology
Experimental Psychosis
Experimental Replication
Experimental Subjects
Debriefing (Experimental)
Devices (Experimental) USE Apparatus
Disclosure (Experimental)
  USE Debriefing (Experimental)
Sampling (Experimental)
Experimentation
Experimenter Bias
Experimenter Expectations
Experimenters
Expert Systems
Expert Testimony
Expertise USE Experience Level
Career Exploration USE Career Education
Exploratory Behavior
Animal Exploratory Behavior
Explosive Personality
Intermittent Explosive Personality
  USE Explosive Personality
Exposure Time (Stimulus)
  USE Stimulus Duration
Occupational Exposure
Prenatal Exposure
Expressed Emotion
Facial Expressions
Expressive Psychotherapy
Emotional Expressiveness
  USE Emotionality (Personality)
School Expulsion
Extended Family
Agricultural Extension Workers
External Ear
External Rewards
Internal External Locus of Control
Rotter Intern Extern Locus Cont Scal
Externalization
Extinction (Learning)
Thyroid Extract
Extracurricular Activities
Extradimensional Shift Learning
  USE Nonreversal Shift Learning
Extramarital Intercourse
Extrapyramidal Symptoms
Extrapyramidal Tracts
Extrasensory Perception
Extraversion
Extrinsic Motivation
Extrinsic Rewards USE External Rewards
Eye (Anatomy)
Eye Color
Eye Contact
Eye Convergence
Eye Disorders
Eye Dominance USE Ocular Dominance
Eye Examination
  USE Ophthalmologic Examination
Eye Fixation
Eye Movements
Cones (Eye)
Iris (Eye)
Lens (Eye)
Nonrapid Eye Movement Sleep USE NREM Sleep
Pupil (Eye)
Rapid Eye Movement

Rapid Eye Movement Dreams
  USE REM Dreams
Rapid Eye Movement Sleep USE REM Sleep
Rods (Eye)
Saccadic Eye Movements USE Eye Movements
Seeing Eye Dogs USE Mobility Aids
Eyeblink Reflex
Eyelid Conditioning
Crossed Eyes USE Strabismus
Eyewitnesses USE Witnesses
Eysenck Personality Inventory
F Test
California F Scale
Face (Anatomy)
Face Perception
Face Recognition USE Face Perception
Lips (Face)
Facial Expressions
Facial Features
Facial Muscles
Facial Nerve
Facilitated Communication
  USE Augmentative Communication
Social Facilitation
Community Facilities
Maximum Security Facilities
School Facilities
Treatment Facilities
Facility Admission
Facility Discharge
Facility Environment
Facility Readmission
  USE Facility Admission
Factitious Disorders
Factor Analysis
Factor Structure
ACTH Releasing Factor USE Corticotropin Releasing Factor
Confirmatory Factor Analysis USE Factor Analysis
Conscious (Personality Factor)
Corticotropin Releasing Factor
Nerve Growth Factor
Unconscious (Personality Factor)
Factorial Validity
Ecological Factors
Human Factors Engineering
Personality Factors USE Personality Traits
Psychoanalytic Personality Factors
Psychosocial Factors
Sixteen Personality Factors Question
Sociocultural Factors
Thermal Factors USE Temperature Effects
Factory Environments
  USE Working Conditions
Faculty USE Educational Personnel
Fading (Conditioning)
Fads and Fashions
Failure
Failure to Thrive
Academic Failure
Fainting USE Syncope
Cattell Culture Fair Intell Test
  USE Culture Fair Intelligence Test
Culture Fair Intelligence Test
Fairy Tales USE Folklore
Faith Healing
Faking
False Pregnancy USE Pseudocyesis
Fame
Amaurotic Familial Idiocy
Cultural Familial Mental Retardation
  USE Psychosocial Mental Retardation
Familiarity
Family
Family Background
Family Caregivers USE Caregivers
Family Counseling USE Family Therapy
Family Crises
Family Life USE Family Relations
Family Medicine

269

Family Members
Family of Origin
Family Physicians
Family Planning
Family Planning Attitudes
Family Relations
Family Resemblance
Family Size
Family Socioeconomic Level
Family Structure
Family Therapy
Family Violence
Biological Family
Dysfunctional Family
Extended Family
Interethnic Family
Interracial Family
Natural Family USE Biological Family
Nuclear Family
Schizophrenogenic Family
Fantasies (Thought Disturbances)
Fantasy USE Imagination
Fantasy (Defense Mechanism)
Guided Fantasy USE Directed Reverie Therapy
Laborers (Farm) USE Agricultural Workers
Migrant Farm Workers
Farmers USE Agricultural Workers
Fascism
Fads and Fashions
Fat Metabolism USE Lipid Metabolism
Fatalism
Father Absence
Father Child Communication
Father Child Relations
Fathers
Adolescent Fathers
Expectant Fathers
Single Fathers
Teenage Fathers USE Adolescent Fathers
Fatigue
Fatty Acids
Fear
Fear of Public Speaking
USE Speech Anxiety
Fear of Strangers
USE Stranger Reactions
Fear of Success
Fear Survey Schedule
Facial Features
Fecal Incontinence
School Federal Aid
USE Educational Financial Assistance
West German Federal Republic USE West Germany
Fee for Service
Feedback
Auditory Feedback
Delayed Feedback
Delayed Auditory Feedback
Sensory Feedback
Visual Feedback
Feeding Practices
Animal Feeding Behavior
Bottle Feeding
Breast Feeding
Anesthesia (Feeling)
Feelings USE Emotions
Professional Fees
Feet (Anatomy)
Felonies USE Crime
Female Animals
Female Criminals
Female Delinquents
Female Genitalia
Female Orgasm
Male Female Relations
Battered Females
Human Females
Femininity
Feminism

Feminist Therapy
Testicular Feminization Syndrome
Femoral Nerve USE Spinal Nerves
Fenfluramine
Fentanyl
Fertility
Fertility Enhancement
Fertilization
In Vitro Fertilization
USE Reproductive Technology
Fetal Alcohol Syndrome
Erythroblastosis Fetalis USE Rh Incompatibility
Fetishism
Fetus
Fever USE Hyperthermia
Hay Fever
Rheumatic Fever
Postganglionic Autonomic Fibers USE Autonomic Ganglia
Preganglionic Autonomic Fibers USE Autonomic Ganglia
Fibrillation (Heart)
Fibromyalgia Syndrome
USE Muscular Disorders
Cystic Fibrosis
Fiction USE Literature
Field Dependence
Field Instruction
USE Curricular Field Experience
Field Work (Educational)
USE Curricular Field Experience
Animal Open Field Behavior
Curricular Field Experience
Educational Field Trips
Visual Field
Cutaneous Receptive Fields
Receptive Fields
Visual Receptive Fields
Fire Fighters
Fighting USE Aggressive Behavior
Figurative Language
Figure Ground Discrimination
Welsh Figure Preference Test
Figures of Speech
USE Figurative Language
Embedded Figures Testing
Hidden Figures Test
Human Figures Drawing
Fiji
Perceptual Fill USE Perceptual Closure
Film Strips
Filtered Noise
Filtered Speech
Educational Financial Assistance
Fine Motor Skill Learning
Finger Tapping
Fingers (Anatomy)
Fingerspelling
Finland
Fire Fighters
Fire Prevention
Firearms USE Weapons
Firesetting USE Arson
FIRO-B
USE Fund Interper Rela Orientat Beh
Ques
Bass (Fish)
Fishes
Electric Fishes
Goodness of Fit
Person Environment Fit
Physical Fitness
Eye Fixation
Ocular Fixation USE Eye Fixation
Visual Fixation USE Eye Fixation
Fixed Interval Reinforcement
Fixed Ratio Reinforcement
Flashbacks USE Hallucinations
Flexibility (Personality)
USE Adaptability (Personality)
Flexion Reflex

Flextime *USE Work Scheduling*
Critical **Flicker** Fusion Threshold
Flies *USE Diptera*
Flight Attendants
    USE Aerospace Personnel
Flight Instrumentation
Flight Simulation
Flooding Therapy *USE Implosive Therapy*
Blood **Flow**
Cerebral Blood **Flow**
Verbal **Fluency**
Fluid Intake
Amniotic **Fluid**
Cerebrospinal **Fluid**
Spinal Fluid *USE Cerebrospinal Fluid*
Body **Fluids**
Fluoxetine
Fluphenazine
Flurazepam
Fluvoxamine
Fruit Fly *USE Drosophila*
Focusing (Visual)
    USE Ocular Accommodation
Folic Acid
Folie A Deux
Folk Medicine
Folklore
Follicle Stimulating Hormone
Project **Follow** Through
Followup Studies
Posttreatment **Followup**
Food
Food Additives
Food Allergies
Food Deprivation
Food Intake
Food Preferences
Football
Animal **Foraging** Behavior
Air **Force** Personnel
Forced Choice (Testing Method)
Forebrain
Medial **Forebrain** Bundle
Foreign Language Education
Foreign Language Learning
Foreign Language Translation
Foreign Languages
Foreign Nationals
Foreign Organizations
Foreign Policy Making
Foreign Students
Foreign Study
Foreign Workers
Industrial **Foremen**
Forensic Evaluation
Forensic Psychiatry
Forensic Psychology
Forgetting
Forgiveness
Form and Shape Perception
Form Classes (Language)
Words (Form Classes)
    USE Form Classes (Language)
Attitude **Formation**
Coalition **Formation**
Concept **Formation**
Impression **Formation**
Reaction **Formation**
Reticular **Formation**
Test **Forms**
Theory **Formulation**
Fornix
FORTRAN
    USE Computer Programing Languages
Chance **(Fortune)**
Forward Masking *USE Masking*
Foster Care
Foster Children
Foster Homes *USE Foster Care*

Foster Parents
Fovea
Foveal Vision
Fowl *USE Birds*
Foxes
Fragile X Syndrome
Fragmentation (Schizophrenia)
Frail *USE Health Impaired*
Rod and **Frame** Test
France
Franck Drawing Completion Test
Frankness *USE Honesty*
Fraternity Membership
Fraud
Consumer Fraud *USE Fraud*
Skinner (Burrhus **Frederic)**
Free Association
Free Recall
Free Will *USE Volition*
Association (Free) *USE Free Association*
Freedom
Frequency Distribution
Pitch **(Frequency)**
Response **Frequency**
Spatial **Frequency**
Stimulus **Frequency**
Temporal **Frequency**
Tone (Frequency) *USE Pitch (Frequency)*
Word **Frequency**
Freud (Sigmund)
Freudian Psychoanalytic School
Friendship
Frigidity
Frogs
Frontal Lobe
Frostig Development Test Vis Percept
Fruit Fly *USE Drosophila*
Frustration
Rosenzweig Picture **Frustration** Study
Fugue Reaction
Fulfillment *USE Satisfaction*
Sexual **Function** Disturbances
Urinary **Function** Disorders
Functionalism
Cognitive Functioning *USE Cognitive Ability*
Intellectual Functioning *USE Cognitive Ability*
Fund Interper Rela Orientat Beh Ques
Fundamentalism
Funding
Funerals *USE Death Rites*
Furniture
Critical Flicker **Fusion** Threshold
Future
Fuzzy Set Theory
Galanthamine
Galvanic Skin Response
Gambling
Compulsive Gambling *USE Pathological Gambling*
Pathological **Gambling**
Game Theory
Prisoners Dilemma **Game**
Games
Childrens Recreational **Games**
Computer **Games**
Entrapment **Games**
Non Zero Sum **Games**
Simulation **Games**
Video Games *USE Computer Games*
Gamma Aminobutyric Acid
Gamma Aminobutyric Acid Agonists
Gamma Aminobutyric Acid Antagonists
Gamma Globulin
Ganglia
Autonomic **Ganglia**
Basal **Ganglia**
Spinal **Ganglia**
Ganglion Blocking Drugs
Ganglion Cells (Retina)
Stellate Ganglion *USE Autonomic Ganglia*

Juvenile **Gangs**
Ganser Syndrome
  USE Factitious Disorders
Generation **Gap**
Gastrointestinal Disorders
Gastrointestinal System
Gastrointestinal Ulcers
Gastropods *USE Mollusca*
Gates MacGinitie Reading Tests
Gating (Sensory) *USE Sensory Gating*
Sensory **Gating**
Gay Liberation Movement
  USE Homosexual Liberation Movement
Gay Males *USE Male Homosexuality*
Gay Parents *USE Homosexual Parents*
Gazing *USE Eye Fixation*
Geese
Gender Differences
  USE Human Sex Differences
Gender Identity
General Anesthetics
General Aptitude Test Battery
General Health Questionnaire
General Paresis
General Practitioners
Army **General** Classification Test
Medical Treatment **(General)**
Typologies (General) *USE Taxonomies*
Generalization (Learning)
Cognitive **Generalization**
Response **Generalization**
Semantic **Generalization**
Stimulus **Generalization**
Generalized Anxiety Disorder
  USE Anxiety Neurosis
Generation Effect (Learning)
Generation Gap
Transformational **Generative** Grammar
Generators (Apparatus)
Genes
Genetic Counseling
Genetic Disorders
Genetic Dominance
Genetic Engineering
Genetic Linkage
Genetic Recessiveness
Genetics
Behavioral **Genetics**
Population **Genetics**
Geniculate Bodies (Thalamus)
Genital Disorders
Genital Herpes *USE Herpes Genitalis*
Male **Genital** Disorders
Female **Genitalia**
Male **Genitalia**
Herpes **Genitalis**
Geniuses *USE Gifted*
Genocide
Genotypes
Genuineness *USE Sincerity*
Geographic Regions *USE Geography*
Physical Divisions (Geographic) *USE Geography*
Political Divisions (Geographic) *USE Geography*
Geographical Mobility
Geography
Geomagnetism *USE Magnetism*
Geometry *USE Mathematics*
Gerbils
Geriatric Patients
Geriatric Psychotherapy
Geriatrics
German Measles *USE Rubella*
East German Democratic Republic
  USE East Germany
West German Federal Republic
  USE West Germany
Germany
East **Germany**
West **Germany**

Gerontology
Gestalt Psychology
Gestalt Therapy
Bender **Gestalt** Test
Gestation *USE Pregnancy*
Gestures
Ghana
Ghettoes
Gifted
Exceptional Children (Gifted) *USE Gifted*
Gilles de la Tourette Disorder
Girls *USE Human Females*
Adrenal **Gland** Disorders
Adrenal **Gland** Secretion
Endocrine **Gland** Secretion
Endocrine **Gland** Surgery
Pituitary **Gland**
Pituitary Gland Surgery *USE Hypophysectomy*
Secretion **(Gland)**
Thyroid **Gland**
Glands
Adrenal **Glands**
Endocrine **Glands**
Mammary **Glands**
Parathyroid **Glands**
Salivary **Glands**
Glaucoma
Gamma **Globulin**
Globulins
Globus Pallidus
Glossary
Glossolalia
Glossopharyngeal Nerve
  USE Cranial Nerves
Glucagon
Glucocorticoids
Glucose
Glucose Metabolism
Blood Glucose *USE Blood Sugar*
Glue Sniffing
Glutamic Acid
Glutamine
Glutethimide
Glycine
Glycogen
Glycoproteins *USE Globulins*
Goals
Career Goals *USE Occupational Aspirations*
Organizational Goals *USE Organizational Objectives*
Goats
God Concepts
Goiters
Goldfish
Goldstein Scheerer Object Sort Test
Gonadotropic Hormones
Gonads
Gonorrhea
Goodenough Harris Draw A Person Test
Goodness of Fit
Gorillas
Gossip
Gough Adjective Check List
Government
Government Agencies
Government Personnel
Government Policy Making
Government Programs
Autonomy **(Government)**
Elected Government Officials
  USE Government Personnel
Law **(Government)**
Welfare Services **(Government)**
Grade Level
Academic Grade Level *USE Grade Level*
Gradepoint Average
  USE Academic Achievement
Grading (Educational)
Graduate Degrees
  USE Educational Degrees

Graduate Education
Graduate Psychology Education
Graduate Record Examination
Graduate Schools
Graduate Students
Clinical Psychology **Grad** Training
College **Graduates**
High School **Graduates**
Graduation (School)
    USE School Graduation
School **Graduation**
Grammar
Grammar Schools
    USE Elementary Schools
Transformational Generative **Grammar**
Grand Mal Epilepsy
Grandchildren
Grandiosity
Grandparents
Great Grandparents *USE Ancestors*
Graphical Displays
Graphology *USE Handwriting*
Grasshoppers
Delay of **Gratification**
Myasthenia **Gravis**
Gravitational Effects
Periaqueductal **Gray**
Great Britain
Great Grandparents *USE Ancestors*
Greece
Gregariousness
Bannister Repertory **Grid**
Shuttle Box **Grids**
Grief
Grimaces
Nocturnal Teeth **Grinding**
Teeth Grinding *USE Bruxism*
Animal **Grooming** Behavior
Gross Motor Skill Learning
Ground Transportation
Figure **Ground** Discrimination
Group Cohesion
Group Counseling
Group Decision Making
Group Discussion
Group Dynamics
Group Health Plans
    USE Health Maintenance Organizations
Group Homes
Group Instruction
Group Participation
Group Performance
Group Problem Solving
Group Psychotherapy
Group Size
Group Structure
Group Testing
Group Therapy
    USE Group Psychotherapy
Encounter **Group** Therapy
Marathon **Group** Therapy
Minority Group Discrimination
    USE Race and Ethnic Discrimination
Ability **Grouping**
Agencies (Groups) *USE Organizations*
Between **Groups** Design
Blood **Groups**
Consciousness Raising **Groups**
Control Groups *USE Experiment Controls*
Developmental Age **Groups**
Diagnosis Related **Groups**
Ethnic **Groups**
Minority **Groups**
Reference **Groups**
Social **Groups**
Support **Groups**
T Groups *USE Human Relations Training*
Grown Children *USE Adult Offspring*
Growth *USE Development*

Growth Centers
    USE Human Potential Movement
Growth Hormone *USE Somatotropin*
Growth Hormone Inhibitor
    USE Somatostatin
Nerve **Growth** Factor
Personal Growth Techniques
    USE Human Potential Movement
Physical Growth *USE Physical Development*
GSR (Electrophysiology)
    USE Galvanic Skin Response
Guanethidine
Guanosine
Coast **Guard** Personnel
Guardianship
National **Guardsmen**
Guatemala
Guessing
Guest Workers *USE Foreign Workers*
Guidance Counseling
    USE School Counseling
Guidance (Educational)
    USE Educational Counseling
Career Guidance *USE Occupational Guidance*
Child **Guidance** Clinics
Educational Guidance *USE Educational Counseling*
Occupational **Guidance**
School Guidance *USE School Counseling*
Vocational Guidance *USE Occupational Guidance*
Guided Daydreams
    USE Directed Reverie Therapy
Guided Fantasy
    USE Directed Reverie Therapy
Guilford Zimmerman Temperament Surv
Guilt
Guinea
Guinea Pigs
Papua New **Guinea**
Sea **Gulls**
Gun Control Laws
Gustatory Perception
    USE Taste Perception
Guyana
Gymnastic Therapy
    USE Recreation Therapy
Gynecological Disorders
Gynecologists
Gynecology
Gypsies
Gyrus Cinguli
Habilitation
Habitat Selection *USE Territoriality*
Habits
Study **Habits**
Habituation
Hair
Hair Loss *USE Alopecia*
Hair Pulling
Haiti
Halfway Houses
Residence Halls *USE Dormitories*
Hallucinations
Auditory **Hallucinations**
Drug Induced **Hallucinations**
Hypnagogic **Hallucinations**
Visual **Hallucinations**
Hallucinogenic Drugs
Hallucinosis
Alcoholic **Hallucinosis**
Halo Effect
Haloperidol
Halstead Reitan Neuropsych Battery
Hamsters
Hand (Anatomy)
Handedness
Handicapped
Handicapped (Attitudes Toward)
Adventitiously **Handicapped**
Aurally **Handicapped**

Congenitally **Handicapped**
Exceptional Children (Handicapped) *USE Handicapped*
Multiply **Handicapped**
Orthopedically Handicapped *USE Physically Handicapped*
Physically **Handicapped**
Sensorially **Handicapped**
Speech **Handicapped**
Visually **Handicapped**
Self **Handicapping** Strategy
Language Handicaps *USE Language Disorders*
Physical **Handicaps** (Attit Toward)
Sensory **Handicaps** (Attit Toward)
Handicrafts *USE Crafts*
Handwriting
Handwriting Legibility
Printing **(Handwriting)**
Happiness
Haptic Perception *USE Cutaneous Sense*
Sexual **Harassment**
Hardiness *USE Psychological Endurance*
Maslow (Abraham **Harold)**
Goodenough **Harris** Draw A Person Test
Hashish
Hate
Hawaii
Hay Fever
Hazardous Materials
Hazards
Head (Anatomy)
Head Banging
Head Injuries
Project **Head** Start
Headache
Migraine **Headache**
Muscle Contraction **Headache**
Tension Headache
    USE Muscle Contraction Headache
Faith **Healing**
Health
Health Attitudes
Health Behavior
Health Care Costs
Health Care Delivery
Health Care Policy
Health Care Professionals
    USE Health Personnel
Health Care Psychology
Health Care Services
Health Care Utilization
Health Education
Health Impaired
Health Insurance
Health Knowledge
Health Locus of Control
    USE Health Attitudes
Health Maintenance Organizations
Health Personnel
Health Personnel Attitudes
Health Promotion
Health Screening
    USE Physical Examination
Health Service Utilization
    USE Health Care Utilization
Behavioral Health *USE Health Care Psychology*
Community Mental **Health**
Community Mental **Health** Centers
Community Mental **Health** Services
Community Mental **Health** Training
Employee **Health** Insurance
General **Health** Questionnaire
Group Health Plans
    USE Health Maintenance Organizations
Holistic **Health**
Mental **Health**
Mental Health Care Costs
    USE Health Care Costs
Mental Health Care Policy
    USE Health Care Policy

Mental Health Consultation
    USE Professional Consultation
Mental **Health** Inservice Training
Mental **Health** Personnel
Mental **Health** Personnel Supply
Mental **Health** Program Evaluation
Mental **Health** Programs
Mental **Health** Services
Primary **Health** Care
Primary Mental **Health** Prevention
Public **Health**
Public **Health** Service Nurses
Public **Health** Services
Wholistic Health *USE Holistic Health*
Hearing Acuity *USE Auditory Acuity*
Hearing Aids
Hearing Disorders
Partially **Hearing** Impaired
Sensorineural Hearing Loss *USE Hearing Disorders*
Speech and **Hearing** Measures
Heart
Heart Attacks *USE Heart Disorders*
Heart Auricles
Heart Disorders
Heart Rate
Heart Rate Affecting Drugs
Heart Surgery
Heart Transplants
    USE Organ Transplantation
Heart Valves
Heart Ventricles
Arrhythmias **(Heart)**
Atria (Heart) *USE Heart Auricles*
Coronary Heart Disease *USE Heart Disorders*
Fibrillation **(Heart)**
Heartbeat *USE Heart Rate*
Heat Effects
Hebephrenic Schizophrenia
Hedonism
Heels (Anatomy) *USE Feet (Anatomy)*
Body **Height**
Helicopters
Helium
Help Seeking Behavior
Self **Help** Techniques
Helping Behavior
    USE Assistance (Social Behavior)
Learned **Helplessness**
Hematologic Disorders
    USE Blood and Lymphatic Disorders
Hematoma
Hemianopia
Hemiopia *USE Hemianopia*
Hemiplegia
Hemispherectomy
Hemispheric Specialization
    USE Lateral Dominance
Hemodialysis
Hemoglobin
Hemophilia
Hemorrhage
Cerebral **Hemorrhage**
Henmon Nelson Tests Mental Ability
Heparin
Hepatic Disorders *USE Liver Disorders*
Hepatitis
Toxic **Hepatitis**
Hereditary Disorders
    USE Genetic Disorders
PKU (Hereditary Disorder)
    USE Phenylketonuria
Sex Linked **Hereditary** Disorders
Heredity *USE Genetics*
Hermaphroditism
Hermeneutics
Heroin
Heroin Addiction
Herpes Genitalis
Herpes Simplex

Genital Herpes *USE Herpes Genitalis*
Heterogeneity of Variance
  USE Variance Homogeneity
Heterosexual Interaction
  USE Male Female Relations
Heterosexuality
Heterozygotic Twins
Heuristic Modeling
Hexamethonium
Hexobarbital
Hibernation
Hidden Figures Test
Dominance **Hierarchy**
High Risk Populations
  USE At Risk Populations
High Sch Personality Questionnaire
High School Diplomas
  USE Educational Degrees
High School Equivalency
  USE Adult Education
High School Graduates
High School Students
High School Teachers
High Schools
Junior **High** School Students
Junior **High** School Teachers
Junior **High** Schools
Higher Education
Highway Safety
Hinduism
Hippies *USE Subculture (Anthropological)*
Hippocampal Commissure *USE Fornix*
Hippocampus
Hips
Hiring *USE Personnel Selection*
Hispanics
Hispaniola
Histamine
Histidine
Histology
History
History of Psychology
Case History *USE Patient History*
Employment **History**
Medical History *USE Patient History*
Patient **History**
Psychiatric **History** *USE Patient History*
Histrionic Personality Disorder
  USE Hysterical Personality
HIV *USE Human Immunodeficiency Virus*
HMO
  USE Health Maintenance Organizations
Animal **Hoarding** Behavior
Hobbies
Hoffmanns Reflex
Holidays
Holistic Health
Holocaust
Holocaust Survivors
Holtzman Inkblot Technique
Homatropine
Home Accidents
Home Birth *USE Midwifery*
Home Care
Home Economics
Home Environment
Home Reared Mentally Retarded
Home Schooling
Home Visiting Programs
Return to Home *USE Empty Nest*
Homebound
Homeless
Homemaking
  USE Household Management
Homeostasis
Foster Homes *USE Foster Care*
Group **Homes**
Nursing **Homes**
Homesickness

Homework
Homicide
Homing (Animal) *USE Animal Homing*
Animal **Homing**
Variance **Homogeneity**
Homographs
Homonyms
Homophobia
  USE Homosexuality (Attitudes Toward)
Homosexual Liberation Movement
Homosexual Parents
Homosexuality
Homosexuality (Attitudes Toward)
Male **Homosexuality**
Homovanillic Acid
Honduras
Honesty
Hong Kong
Hope
Hopelessness
Hormone Therapy
ACTH (Hormone) *USE Corticotropin*
Follicle Stimulating **Hormone**
Growth Hormone *USE Somatotropin*
Growth Hormone Inhibitor *USE Somatostatin*
Luteinizing **Hormone**
Melanocyte Stimulating **Hormone**
Parathyroid **Hormone**
Thyroid Stimulating Hormone *USE Thyrotropin*
Thyrotropic Hormone *USE Thyrotropin*
Hormones
Adrenal Cortex **Hormones**
Adrenal Medulla **Hormones**
Gonadotropic **Hormones**
Pituitary **Hormones**
Progestational **Hormones**
Sex **Hormones**
Thyroid **Hormones**
Dorsal **Horns**
Horses
Hospice
Hospital Accreditation
Hospital Administration
Hospital Admission
Hospital Attendants
  USE Attendants (Institutions)
Hospital Discharge
Hospital Environment
Hospital Programs
Hospital Psychiatric Units
  USE Psychiatric Units
Hospital Staff *USE Medical Personnel*
Day Hospital *USE Partial Hospitalization*
Psychiatric **Hospital** Admission
Psychiatric **Hospital** Discharge
Psychiatric **Hospital** Programs
Psychiatric **Hospital** Readmission
Psychiatric **Hospital** Staff
Readmission (Hospital) *USE Hospital Admission*
Hospitalization
Partial **Hospitalization**
Psychiatric **Hospitalization**
Hospitalized Patients
Hospitals
Mental Hospitals *USE Psychiatric Hospitals*
Psychiatric **Hospitals**
State Hospitals *USE Psychiatric Hospitals*
Hostages
Hostility
Hot Line Services
Telephone Hot Lines *USE Hot Line Services*
Household Management
Household Structure
  USE Living Arrangements
Halfway **Houses**
Housewives
Housework *USE Household Management*
Housing
Hue

275

Human Animal Interaction
  USE *Interspecies Interaction*
Human Biological Rhythms
Human Channel Capacity
Human Courtship
Human Development
Human Factors Engineering
Human Females
Human Figures Drawing
Human Immunodeficiency Virus
Human Information Processes
  USE *Cognitive Processes*
Human Information Storage
Human Males
Human Mate Selection
Human Migration
Human Potential Movement
Human Relations Training
Human Resources
  USE *Personnel Management*
Human Rights
Human Sex Differences
Animal **Human** Interaction
  USE *Interspecies Interaction*
Circadian Rhythms (Human) USE *Human Biological Rhythms*
Maternal Behavior (Human) USE *Mother Child Relations*
Sexual Intercourse **(Human)**
Humanism
Humanistic Education
  USE *Affective Education*
Humanistic Psychology
Mates (Humans) USE *Spouses*
Surrogate Parents **(Humans)**
Humor
Cartoons **(Humor)**
Hungary
Hunger
Huntingtons Chorea
Shuttle Box **Hurdles**
Husbands
Hybrids (Biology)
Hydralazine
Chloral **Hydrate**
Hydrocephaly
Hydrocortisone
Hydrogen
Hydroxydopamine (6-)
Hydroxyindoleacetic Acid (5-)
Hydroxylamine
Hydroxylase Inhibitors
Hydroxylases
Hydroxytryptamine (5-) USE *Serotonin*
Hydroxytryptophan (5-)
Hydroxyzine
Hygiene
Hyoscine USE *Scopolamine*
Hyoscyamine (dl-) USE *Atropine*
Hyperactivity USE *Hyperkinesis*
Hypercholesterolemia
  USE *Metabolism Disorders*
Hyperglycemia
Hyperkinesis
Hyperparathyroidism
  USE *Parathyroid Disorders*
Hyperphagia
Hypersexuality
Hypersomnia
Hypertension
Essential **Hypertension**
Hyperthermia
Hyperthyroidism
Hyperventilation
Hypnagogic Hallucinations
Hypnoanalysis USE *Hypnotherapy*
Hypnosis
Self Hypnosis USE *Autohypnosis*
Hypnotherapists
Hypnotherapy
Hypnotic Drugs

Hypnotic Susceptibility
Age Regression **(Hypnotic)**
Hypnotists
Hypochondriasis
Hypogastric Plexus
  USE *Autonomic Ganglia*
Hypoglossal Nerve USE *Cranial Nerves*
Hypoglycemia
Hypogonadism
Hypomania
Hypoparathyroidism
  USE *Parathyroid Disorders*
Hypothalamo **Hypophyseal** System
Hypophysectomy
Hypophysis Disorders
  USE *Pituitary Disorders*
Hypopituitarism
Hypotension
Mammillary Bodies (Hypothalamic) USE *Hypothalamus*
Hypothalamo Hypophyseal System
Hypothalamus
Hypothalamus Lesions
Hypothermia
Hypothesis Testing
Cognitive **Hypothesis** Testing
Null **Hypothesis** Testing
Hypothyroidism
Hypoxia USE *Anoxia*
Hysterectomy
Hysteria
Conversion Hysteria USE *Conversion Neurosis*
Mass **Hysteria**
Hysterical Anesthesia
Hysterical Blindness
  USE *Hysterical Vision Disturbances*
Hysterical Neurosis (Dissociation)
  USE *Dissociative Neurosis*
Hysterical Paralysis
Hysterical Personality
Hysterical Vision Disturbances
Iatrogenic Effects
  USE *Side Effects (Treatment)*
Ibotenic Acid
Iceland
Iconic Memory
Id
Ideal Self USE *Self Concept*
Idealism
Ideation
Suicidal **Ideation**
Identical Twins USE *Monozygotic Twins*
Identification (Defense Mechanism)
Projective **Identification**
Identity Crisis
Identity (Personal) USE *Self Concept*
Identity (Professional)
  USE *Professional Identity*
Ego **Identity**
Ethnic **Identity**
Gender **Identity**
Professional **Identity**
Social **Identity**
Amaurotic Familial **Idiocy**
Idiot Savants
Ileum USE *Intestines*
Mentally **Ill** Offenders
Terminally **Ill** Patients
Illegitimate Children
Illinois Test Psycholinguist Abil
Illiteracy USE *Literacy*
Illness Behavior
Chronic **Illness**
Mental Illness USE *Mental Disorders*
Mental **Illness** (Attitudes Toward)
Physical Illness USE *Disorders*
Physical **Illness** (Attitudes Toward)
Work Related **Illnesses**
Illumination
Illumination Therapy USE *Phototherapy*

Autokinetic **Illusion**
Mueller Lyer **Illusion**
Illusions (Perception)
Optical Illusions *USE Illusions (Perception)*
Body **Image**
Body **Image** Disturbances
Mirror **Image**
Retinal **Image**
Self Image *USE Self Concept*
Imagery
Conceptual **Imagery**
Eidetic **Imagery**
Spatial **Imagery**
Onomatopoeia and **Images** Test
Imagination
Magnetic Resonance **Imaging**
Imipramine
Imitation (Learning)
Emotional **Immaturity**
Immersion Programs
USE Foreign Language Education
Immigrants *USE Immigration*
Immigration
Social Immobility *USE Social Mobility*
Tonic **Immobility**
Acquired **Immune** Deficiency Syndrome
Immunization
Human **Immunodeficiency** Virus
Immunogens *USE Antigens*
Immunoglobulins
Immunologic Disorders
Immunology
Immunopathology *USE Immunology*
Immunoreactivity
Impaired Professionals
Health **Impaired**
Partially Hearing **Impaired**
Cochlear **Implants**
Implosive Therapy
Impotence
Impression Formation
Impression Management
Imprinting
Impulsiveness
Inadequate Personality
Incarceration
Incentives
Educational **Incentives**
Monetary **Incentives**
Incest
Incidental Learning
Income (Economic)
Income Level
Lower **Income** Level
Middle **Income** Level
Upper **Income** Level
Rh **Incompatibility**
Incomplete Man Test
Rotter **Incomplete** Sentences Blank
Fecal **Incontinence**
Urinary **Incontinence**
Incubators (Apparatus)
Independence (Personality)
Independent Living *USE Self Care Skills*
Independent Living Programs
Independent Party (Political)
USE Political Parties
Independent Study
USE Individualized Instruction
Independent Variables
India
American **Indians**
Myers Briggs Type **Indicator**
West **Indies**
Indifference *USE Apathy*
Individual Counseling
USE Individual Psychotherapy
Individual Differences
Individual Psychology

Individual Psychotherapy
Individual Testing
Individual Therapy
USE Individual Psychotherapy
Individualism *USE Individuality*
Individuality
Individualized Instruction
Separation **Individuation**
Indonesia
Induced Abortion
Drug **Induced** Congenital Disorders
Drug **Induced** Hallucinations
Sleep Inducing Drugs *USE Hypnotic Drugs*
Vomit Inducing Drugs *USE Emetic Drugs*
Inductive Deductive Reasoning
Laborers (Construct and Indust) *USE Blue Collar Workers*
Industrial Accidents
Industrial Arts Education
USE Vocational Education
Industrial Foremen
Industrial Psychologists
Industrial Psychology
Industrial Safety *USE Occupational Safety*
Business and **Industrial** Personnel
Skilled **Industrial** Workers
Unskilled **Industrial** Workers
Industrialization
Industry *USE Business*
Educational Inequality *USE Equal Education*
Infant Development
Infant Intelligence Scale
Infant Vocalization
Bayley Scales of **Infant** Development
Cattell Infant Intelligence Scale
USE Infant Intelligence Scale
Sudden **Infant** Death
Infanticide
Infantile Neurosis
USE Childhood Neurosis
Infantile Paralysis *USE Poliomyelitis*
Infantile Psychosis
USE Childhood Psychosis
Early **Infantile** Autism
Paralysis (Infantile) *USE Poliomyelitis*
Symbiotic **Infantile** Psychosis
Infantilism
Infants
Infants (Animal)
Newborn Infants *USE Neonates*
Dementia (Multi Infarct) *USE Multi Infarct Dementia*
Multi **Infarct** Dementia
Myocardial **Infarctions**
Infectious Disorders
Inference
Inferior Colliculus
Emotional **Inferiority**
Infertility
Infirmaries *USE Hospitals*
Anti **Inflammatory** Drugs
Inflection
Self **Inflicted** Wounds
Driving Under The **Influence**
Parental Influence *USE Parent Child Relations*
Interpersonal **Influences**
Social **Influences**
Influenza
Informants
Information
Information Exchange
Information (Messages) *USE Messages*
Information Seeking
Information Services
Information Specialists
Information Systems
Information Theory
Automated **Information** Coding
Automated **Information** Processing
Automated **Information** Retrieval
Automated **Information** Storage

Confidentiality of Information
    USE Privileged Communication
Human Information Processes
    USE Cognitive Processes
Human **Information** Storage
Management Information Systems
    USE Information Systems
Informed Consent
Ingratiation *USE Impression Management*
Inhalant Abuse
Inhibition (Personality)
Conditioned Inhibition *USE Conditioned Suppression*
Proactive **Inhibition**
Reciprocal **Inhibition** Therapy
Retroactive **Inhibition**
Growth Hormone Inhibitor *USE Somatostatin*
Amine Oxidase **Inhibitors**
Cholinesterase **Inhibitors**
Decarboxylase **Inhibitors**
Enzyme **Inhibitors**
Hydroxylase **Inhibitors**
Monoamine Oxidase **Inhibitors**
Initial Teaching Alphabet
Initiation Rites
Initiative
Injections
Intramuscular **Injections**
Intraperitoneal **Injections**
Intravenous **Injections**
Subcutaneous **Injections**
Injuries
Birth **Injuries**
Brain Injuries *USE Brain Damage*
Electrical **Injuries**
Head **Injuries**
Spinal Cord **Injuries**
Holtzman **Inkblot** Technique
Inmates (Prison) *USE Prisoners*
Animal Innate Behavior *USE Instinctive Behavior*
Inner City *USE Urban Environments*
Inner Ear *USE Labyrinth (Anatomy)*
Inner Speech *USE Self Talk*
Innovativeness *USE Creativity*
Inquisitiveness *USE Curiosity*
Criminally Insane *USE Mentally Ill Offenders*
Insanity *USE Mental Disorders*
Insanity Defense
DDT **(Insecticide)**
Insecticides
Insects
Emotional Insecurity *USE Emotional Security*
Artificial Insemination
    USE Reproductive Technology
Insensitivity (Personality)
    USE Sensitivity (Personality)
Inservice Teacher Education
Inservice Training
Mental Health **Inservice** Training
Insight
Insight (Psychotherapeutic Process)
Insight Therapy
Diabetes **Insipidus**
Insomnia
Emotional **Instability**
Death **Instinct**
Instinctive Behavior
Institution Visitation
Institutional Release
Institutional Schools
Institutionalization
Institutionalized Mentally Retarded
Attendants **(Institutions)**
Correctional **Institutions**
Residential Care **Institutions**
Instruction *USE Teaching*
Audiovisual **Instruction**
Braille **Instruction**
Classroom Instruction *USE Teaching*
Computer Assisted **Instruction**

Field Instruction
    USE Curricular Field Experience
Group **Instruction**
Individualized **Instruction**
Programed **Instruction**
Self Instruction *USE Individualized Instruction*
Televised **Instruction**
Videotape **Instruction**
Instructional Media
Instructional Objectives
    USE Educational Objectives
Self **Instructional** Training
Experimental **Instructions**
Instructors *USE Teachers*
Instrument Controls
Parent Attitude Research **Instrument**
Instrumental Conditioning
    USE Operant Conditioning
Instrumental Learning
    USE Operant Conditioning
Instrumentality
Flight **Instrumentation**
Musical **Instruments**
Insulin
Insulin Shock Therapy
Insurance
Insurance Agents *USE Sales Personnel*
Employee Health **Insurance**
Health **Insurance**
Life **Insurance**
Workmens Compensation **Insurance**
Intake Interview
Fluid **Intake**
Food **Intake**
Water **Intake**
Intersensory Integration *USE Sensory Integration*
Racial Integration *USE Social Integration*
School **Integration**
Sensory **Integration**
Social **Integration**
Cattell Culture Fair Intell Test
    USE Culture Fair Intelligence Test
Intellectual Development
Intellectual Functioning
    USE Cognitive Ability
Intellectualism
Intellectualization
Intelligence
Intelligence Age *USE Mental Age*
Intelligence Measures
Intelligence Quotient
Artificial **Intelligence**
Cattell Infant Intelligence Scale
    USE Infant Intelligence Scale
Culture Fair **Intelligence** Test
Infant **Intelligence** Scale
Leiter Adult **Intelligence** Scale
Lorge Thorndike **Intelligence** Test
Slosson **Intelligence** Test for Child
Stanford Binet **Intelligence** Scale
Wechsler **Intelligence** Scale Children
Wechsler Adult **Intelligence** Scale
Wechsler Bellevue **Intelligence** Scale
Signal Intensity *USE Stimulus Intensity*
Stimulus **Intensity**
Intensive Care
Intention
Intentional Learning
Interaction Analysis (Statistics)
Interaction Variance
Animal Human Interaction *USE Interspecies Interaction*
Client Counselor Interaction
    USE Psychotherapeutic Processes
Counselor Client Interaction
    USE Psychotherapeutic Processes
Dentist Patient Interaction *USE Therapeutic Processes*
Double Bind **Interaction**
Employee **Interaction**
Heterosexual Interaction *USE Male Female Relations*

Human Animal Interaction *USE Interspecies Interaction*
Interhemispheric **Interaction**
Interpersonal **Interaction**
Interspecies **Interaction**
Nurse Patient Interaction *USE Therapeutic Processes*
Patient Therapist Interaction
    USE Psychotherapeutic Processes
Physician Patient Interaction *USE Therapeutic Processes*
Social **Interaction**
Teacher Student **Interaction**
Therapist Patient Interaction
    USE Psychotherapeutic Processes
Symbolic **Interactionism**
Drug **Interactions**
Extramarital **Intercourse**
Premarital **Intercourse**
Sexual **Intercourse** (Human)
Interdisciplinary Research
Interdisciplinary Treatment Approach
Interest Inventories
Kuder Occupational **Interest** Survey
Occupational **Interest** Measures
Opinion Attitude and **Interest** Survey
Strong Vocational **Interest** Blank
Interests
Occupational **Interests**
Vocational Interests *USE Occupational Interests*
Interethnic Family
Interethnic Marriage
    USE Exogamous Marriage
Interfaith Marriage
Interference (Learning)
Interferons
Intergenerational Relations
Intergroup Dynamics
Interhemispheric Interaction
Interhemispheric Transfer
    USE Interhemispheric Interaction
Interior Design
Interleukins
Intermarriage *USE Exogamous Marriage*
Intermediate School Students
Intermittent Explosive Personality
    USE Explosive Personality
Intermittent Reinforcement
    USE Reinforcement Schedules
Internal Consistency *USE Test Reliability*
Internal External Locus of Control
Internal Rewards
Rotter **Intern** Extern Locus Cont Scal
International Organizations
International Relations
Internists
Clinical Psychology **Internship**
Medical **Internship**
Teaching Internship *USE Student Teaching*
Interobserver Reliability
    USE Interrater Reliability
Interocular Transfer
Interpersonal Attraction
Interpersonal Communication
Interpersonal Compatibility
Interpersonal Distance
    USE Personal Space
Interpersonal Influences
Interpersonal Interaction
Interpersonal Perception
    USE Social Perception
Fund **Interper** Rela Orientat Beh Ques
Learys **Interpersonal** Check List
Dream Interpretation *USE Dream Analysis*
Psychoanalytic **Interpretation**
Psychological Interpretation
    USE Theoretical Interpretation
Test **Interpretation**
Theoretical **Interpretation**
Interracial Adoption
Interracial Family
Interracial Marriage

Interracial Offspring
Interrater Reliability
Interresponse Time
Legal **Interrogation**
Police Interrogation *USE Legal Interrogation*
Intersensory Integration
    USE Sensory Integration
Intersensory Processes
Interspecies Interaction
Interstimulus Interval
Intertrial Interval
Interval Reinforcement
    USE Fixed Interval Reinforcement OR
          Variable Interval Reinforcement
Fixed **Interval** Reinforcement
Interstimulus **Interval**
Intertrial **Interval**
Variable **Interval** Reinforcement
Stimulus **Intervals**
Crisis **Intervention**
Crisis **Intervention** Services
Early **Intervention**
Diagnostic **Interview** Schedule
Intake **Interview**
Psychodiagnostic **Interview**
Interviewers
Interviewing
Interviews
Employment Interviews *USE Job Applicant Interviews*
Job Applicant **Interviews**
Intestines
Intimacy
Acute Alcoholic **Intoxication**
Alcohol **Intoxication**
Chronic Alcoholic **Intoxication**
Intra Aural Muscle Reflex
    USE Acoustic Reflex
Intracranial Self Stimulation
    USE Brain Self Stimulation
Intramuscular Injections
Intraperitoneal Injections
Intrauterine Devices
Intravenous Drug Usage
Intravenous Injections
Intrinsic Motivation
Intrinsic Rewards *USE Internal Rewards*
Introjection
Introspection
Introversion
Intuition
Minn Multiphasic Personality **Inven**
Inventories
Biographical **Inventories**
Interest **Inventories**
Barrett Lennard Relationship **Invent**
Beck Depression **Inventory**
Bem Sex Role **Inventory**
California Psychological **Inventory**
Differential Personality **Inventory**
Edwards Personality **Inventory**
Eysenck Personality **Inventory**
Maudsley Personality **Inventory**
Millon Clinical Multiaxial **Inventory**
Minnesota Teacher Attitude **Inventory**
Omnibus Personality **Inventory**
Personal Orientation **Inventory**
Psychological Screening **Inventory**
State Trait Anxiety **Inventory**
Invertebrates
Investigation *USE Experimentation*
Involuntary Treatment
Involutional Depression
Involutional Paranoid Psychosis
Involvement
Job **Involvement**
Ions *USE Electrolytes*
Calcium **Ions**
Chloride **Ions**
Magnesium **Ions**

Potassium **Ions**
Sodium **Ions**
Iowa Tests of Basic Skills
Iproniazid
Deviation IQ *USE Standard Scores*
Iran
Iraq
Ireland
Northern **Ireland**
Iris (Eye)
Iron
Irradiation *USE Radiation*
Laser **Irradiation**
Irrational Beliefs
Irritability
Irritable Bowel Syndrome
Ischemia
Cerebral **Ischemia**
Islam
Bahama **Islands**
Pacific **Islands**
Virgin **Islands**
Isocarboxazid
Isoenzymes *USE Isozymes*
Isolation (Defense Mechanism)
Isolation Effect
Social **Isolation**
Isoniazid
Isoproterenol
Isozymes
Israel
Political **Issues**
Social **Issues**
Italy
Itching *USE Pruritus*
Item Analysis (Statistical)
Item Analysis (Test)
Item Bias *USE Test Bias*
Item Content (Test)
Item Response Theory
Test **Items**
IV Drug Usage
   USE Intravenous Drug Usage
Pavlov **(Ivan)**
Ivory Coast
Jails *USE Prisons*
Creutzfeldt **Jakob** Syndrome
Jamaica
James (William)
Japan
Japanese Americans *USE Asians*
Jaundice
Jaw
Jealousy
Piaget **(Jean)**
Jews *USE Judaism*
Job Analysis
Job Applicant Attitudes
Job Applicant Interviews
Job Applicant Screening
Job Applicants
Job Change *USE Career Change*
Job Characteristics
Job Corps
Job Discrimination
   USE Employment Discrimination
Job Enrichment
Job Experience Level
Job Involvement
Job Mobility *USE Occupational Mobility*
Job Performance
Job Promotion *USE Personnel Promotion*
Job Reentry *USE Reemployment*
Job Satisfaction
Job Search
Job Security
Job Selection *USE Occupational Choice*
Job Status *USE Occupational Status*
Job Training *USE Personnel Training*

On the **Job** Training
Jobs *USE Occupations*
Watson **(John** Broadus)
Woodcock **Johnson** Psychoed Battery
Joint Custody
Joint Disorders
Temporomandibular Joint Syndrome
   USE Musculoskeletal Disorders
Joints (Anatomy)
Jokes
Jordan
Journalists
Joy *USE Happiness*
Judaism
Judges
Judgment
Judgment Disturbances
Clinical **Judgment** (Med Diagnosis)
   USE Medical Diagnosis
Clinical **Judgment** (Not Diagnosis)
Clinical Judgment (Psychodiagnosis)
   USE Psychodiagnosis
Probability **Judgment**
Judo
Jumping
Jung (Carl)
Jungian Psychology
Junior College Students
Junior Colleges *USE Colleges*
Junior High School Students
Junior High School Teachers
Junior High Schools
Juries
Jury Selection
Justice
Criminal **Justice**
Distributive Justice *USE Justice*
Juvenile Court *USE Adjudication*
Juvenile Delinquency
Juvenile Delinquents
Juvenile Gangs
Offenders (Juvenile) *USE Juvenile Delinquents*
Kainic Acid
Kangaroos
Karate *USE Martial Arts*
Karyotype Disorders
   USE Chromosome Disorders
Kaufman Assessment Battery Children
Medical Records **Keeping**
Kenya
Keyboards
Kibbutz
Kidnapping
Kidney Diseases
Kidney Transplants
   USE Organ Transplantation
Kidneys
Mercy Killing *USE Euthanasia*
Mouse Killing *USE Muricide*
Kinases
Kindergarten Students
Vane **Kindergarten** Test
Kindergartens
Kindling
Kinesthetic Perception
United **Kingdom**
Kinship
Kinship Recognition
Kinship Structure
Kleptomania
Klinefelters Syndrome
Knee
Knowledge Based Systems
   USE Expert Systems
Knowledge Level
Knowledge of Results
Health **Knowledge**
Kohlberg (Lawrence)
Kohs Block Design Test

Kolmogorov Smirnov Test
Hong **Kong**
Korea
North **Korea**
South **Korea**
Koro
Korsakoffs Psychosis
Kuder Occupational Interest Survey
Kuder Preference Record
Kupfer Detre Self Rating Scale
Kuwait
Kwashiorkor
L Dopa *USE Levodopa*
Labeling
Labor (Childbirth)
Labor Management Relations
Labor Union Members
Labor Unions
Animal Division of **Labor**
Division of **Labor**
Educational **Laboratories**
Experimental **Laboratories**
Language **Laboratories**
Laborers (Construct and Indust)
    USE Blue Collar Workers
Laborers (Farm) *USE Agricultural Workers*
Labyrinth (Anatomy)
Labyrinth (Apparatus) *USE Mazes*
Labyrinth Disorders
Lactate Dehydrogenase
Sodium Lactate *USE Lactic Acid*
Lactation
Lactic Acid
Response Lag *USE Reaction Time*
Landscapes *USE Topography*
Language
Language Alternation
    USE Code Switching
Language Arts Education
Language Delay
Language Development
Language Disorders
Language Handicaps
    USE Language Disorders
Language Laboratories
Language Proficiency
Body **Language**
Figurative **Language**
Foreign **Language** Education
Foreign **Language** Learning
Foreign **Language** Translation
Form Classes **(Language)**
Modern **Language** Aptitude Test
Morphology **(Language)**
Second Language Education
    USE Foreign Language Education
Sign **Language**
Written **Language**
Computer Programing **Languages**
Foreign **Languages**
Sri **Lanka**
Laos
Larvae
Laryngeal Disorders
Larynx
Laser Irradiation
Latchkey Children *USE Child Self Care*
Response **Latency**
Latent Learning
Latent Trait Theory
    USE Item Response Theory
Lateral Dominance
Latin America
Latinos *USE Hispanics*
Laughter
Law Enforcement
Law Enforcement Personnel
Law (Government)
Law Students

Case **Law**
Civil **Law**
Criminal **Law**
Kohlberg **(Lawrence)**
Laws
Abortion **Laws**
Disability **Laws**
Drug **Laws**
Gun Control **Laws**
Marihuana **Laws**
Lawyers *USE Attorneys*
Lay Religious Personnel
Lead (Metal)
Lead Poisoning
Leadership
Leadership Style
Learned Helplessness
Slow **Learners**
Learning
Learning Ability
Learning Centers (Educational)
Learning Disabilities
Learning Disorders
Learning Rate
Learning Schedules
Learning Strategies
Learning Style *USE Cognitive Style*
Learning Theory
Cat **Learning**
Concept Learning *USE Concept Formation*
Cooperative **Learning**
Discrimination **Learning**
Extinction **(Learning)**
Extradimensional Shift Learning *USE Nonreversal Shift Learning*
Fine Motor Skill **Learning**
Foreign Language **Learning**
Generalization **(Learning)**
Generation Effect **(Learning)**
Gross Motor Skill **Learning**
Imitation **(Learning)**
Incidental **Learning**
Instrumental Learning *USE Operant Conditioning*
Intentional **Learning**
Interference **(Learning)**
Latent **Learning**
Mastery **Learning**
Maze **Learning**
Mnemonic **Learning**
Motor Skill Learning *USE Perceptual Motor Learning*
Nonreversal Shift **Learning**
Nonsense Syllable **Learning**
Nonverbal **Learning**
Observational **Learning**
Paired Associate **Learning**
Perceptual Motor **Learning**
Probability **Learning**
Rat **Learning**
Recall **(Learning)**
Recognition **(Learning)**
Reconstruction **(Learning)**
Reversal Shift **Learning**
Rote **Learning**
Rule Learning
    USE Cognitive Hypothesis Testing
School **Learning**
Self Directed Learning *USE Individualized Instruction*
Sequential **Learning**
Serial **Learning**
Serial Anticipation **(Learning)**
Skill **Learning**
Social **Learning**
Spatial **Learning**
Spontaneous Recovery **(Learning)**
State Dependent **Learning**
Strategies (Learning) *USE Learning Strategies*
Transfer **(Learning)**
Trial and Error **Learning**
Verbal **Learning**
Learys Interpersonal Check List

Least Preferred Coworker Scale
Least Squares
Annual Leave *USE Employee Leave Benefits*
Employee **Leave** Benefits
Sick Leave *USE Employee Leave Benefits*
School **Leavers**
Lebanon
Lecithin
Lecture Method
Left Brain
Leg (Anatomy)
Legal Arrest
Legal Decisions
Legal Detention
Legal Evidence
Legal Interrogation
Legal Personnel
Legal Processes
Legal Psychology
    USE Forensic Psychology
Legal Testimony
Evidence (Legal) *USE Legal Evidence*
Marihuana **Legalization**
Legibility
Handwriting **Legibility**
Legislative Processes
Leisure Time
Leiter Adult Intelligence Scale
Lemniscal System
Lemurs
Work Week **Length**
Barrett **Lennard** Relationship Invent
Lens (Eye)
Contact **Lenses**
Sierra **Leone**
Lesbian Parents
    USE Homosexual Parents
Lesbianism
Sectioning (Lesion) *USE Lesions*
Lesions
Brain **Lesions**
Cerebral Lesions *USE Brain Lesions*
Hypothalamus **Lesions**
Neural **Lesions**
Subcortical Lesions *USE Brain Lesions*
Lesson Plans
Letters (Alphabet)
Leucine
Leucocytes
Leukemias
Leukotomy *USE Psychosurgery*
Vygotsky **(Lev)**
Ability **Level**
Academic Grade Level *USE Grade Level*
Activity **Level**
Aspiration **Level**
Difficulty **Level** (Test)
Experience **Level**
Family Socioeconomic **Level**
Grade **Level**
Income **Level**
Job Experience **Level**
Knowledge **Level**
Lower Income **Level**
Middle **Level** Managers
Middle Income **Level**
Sound Pressure Level *USE Loudness*
Top **Level** Managers
Upper Income **Level**
Noise **Levels** (Work Areas)
Levodopa
Lexical Access
Lexical Decision
Drug Abuse **Liability**
Professional **Liability**
Consultation **Liaison** Psychiatry
Liberalism
Political **Liberalism**

Gay Liberation Movement
    USE Homosexual Liberation Movement
Homosexual **Liberation** Movement
Womens **Liberation** Movement
Liberia
Libido
Librarians
Libraries
School **Libraries**
Librium *USE Chlordiazepoxide*
Libya
Professional **Licensing**
Licensure Examinations
    USE Professional Examinations
Licking
Animal Licking Behavior *USE Licking*
Lidocaine
Liechtenstein
Life Change *USE Life Experiences*
Life Expectancy
Life Experiences
Life Insurance
Life Review
Life Satisfaction
Life Span *USE Life Expectancy*
Family Life *USE Family Relations*
Philosophy of Life *USE World View*
Quality of **Life**
Quality of Work **Life**
Lifesaving *USE Artificial Respiration*
Lifestyle
Tubal **Ligation**
Light *USE Illumination*
Light Adaptation
Light Refraction
Bright **Light** Therapy *USE Phototherapy*
Likability
Maximum **Likelihood**
Likert Scales
Liking *USE Affection*
Limbic System
Artificial Limbs *USE Prostheses*
Phantom **Limbs**
Limen *USE Thresholds*
Differential Limen *USE Thresholds*
Limited English Proficiency
    USE Language Proficiency
Time Limited Psychotherapy
    USE Brief Psychotherapy
Confidence **Limits** (Statistics)
Allport Vernon **Lindzey** Study Values
Hot **Line** Services
Linear Perspective
Linear Regression
Telephone Hot Lines *USE Hot Line Services*
Linguistics
Linkage Analysis *USE Genetic Linkage*
Genetic **Linkage**
Sex **Linked** Developmental Differences
Sex **Linked** Hereditary Disorders
Lipid Metabolism
Lipid Metabolism Disorders
Lipids
Lipoproteins
Lipreading
Lips (Face)
Liquor
Gough Adjective Check **List**
Learys Interpersonal Check **List**
Mooney Problem Check **List**
Listening *USE Auditory Perception*
Listening Comprehension
Literacy
Computer **Literacy**
Literature
Literature Review
Religious **Literature**
Lithium
Lithium Bromide

282

Lithium Carbonate
Litter Size
Liver
Liver Disorders
Cirrhosis **(Liver)**
Living Alone
Living Arrangements
Living Wills *USE Advance Directives*
Activities of Daily **Living**
Independent Living *USE Self Care Skills*
Independent **Living** Programs
Lizards
Cognitive Load *USE Human Channel Capacity*
Mental Load *USE Human Channel Capacity*
Work **Load**
Frontal **Lobe**
Occipital **Lobe**
Optic **Lobe**
Parietal **Lobe**
Temporal **Lobe**
Lobotomy *USE Psychosurgery*
Local Anesthetics
Auditory **Localization**
Perceptual **Localization**
Sound Localization *USE Auditory Localization*
Animal **Locomotion**
Locus Ceruleus
Health Locus of Control *USE Health Attitudes*
Internal External **Locus** of Control
Rotter Intern Extern **Locus** Cont Scal
Logic (Philosophy)
Logical Thinking
Logistic Models
    USE Item Response Theory
Logotherapy
Loneliness
Long Term Care
Long Term Memory
Long Term Potentiation
    USE Postactivation Potentials
Longevity *USE Life Expectancy*
Longitudinal Studies
Loosening of Associations
    USE Fragmentation (Schizophrenia)
Lorazepam
Lordosis (Animal)
    USE Animal Sexual Receptivity
Lorge Thorndike Intelligence Test
Hair Loss *USE Alopecia*
Sensorineural Hearing Loss *USE Hearing Disorders*
Loudness
Loudness Discrimination
Loudness Perception
Love
Low Birth Weight *USE Birth Weight*
Lowenfeld Mosaic Test
Lower Class
Lower Class Attitudes
Lower Income Level
Loxapine
Loyalty
LSD (Drug)
    USE Lysergic Acid Diethylamide
Saint **Lucia**
Lucid Dreaming
Luck *USE Chance (Fortune)*
Lumbar Spinal Cord
Lumbrosacral Plexus *USE Spinal Nerves*
Luminance
Luminance Threshold
    USE Brightness Perception AND Visual
        Thresholds
Lunar Synodic Cycle
Lung
Lung Disorders
Lupus
Luria Nebraska Neuropsych Battery
Luteinizing Hormone
Mueller **Lyer** Illusion

Lying *USE Deception*
Blood and **Lymphatic** Disorders
Lymphocytes
Lysergic Acid Diethylamide
Gates **MacGinitie** Reading Tests
Machiavellianism
Man **Machine** Systems
Man **Machine** Systems Design
Teaching **Machines**
Madagascar
Magazines
Magical Thinking
Magnesium
Magnesium Ions
Magnet Schools
    USE Nontraditional Education
Magnetic Resonance Imaging
Magnetism
Magnetoencephalography
Magnitude Estimation
Magnitude of Effect (Statistical)
    USE Effect Size (Statistical)
Nucleus Basalis **Magnocellularis**
Maids *USE Domestic Service Personnel*
Mail Surveys
Mainstreaming
Mainstreaming (Educational)
Health **Maintenance** Organizations
Methadone **Maintenance**
Major Depression
Major Tranquilizers
    USE Neuroleptic Drugs
College Major *USE Academic Specialization*
Decision **Making**
Foreign Policy **Making**
Government Policy **Making**
Group Decision **Making**
Management Decision **Making**
Policy **Making**
Grand **Mal** Epilepsy
Petit **Mal** Epilepsy
Emotional Maladjustment *USE Emotional Adjustment*
Social Maladjustment *USE Social Adjustment*
Malaria
Malawi
Malaysia
Male Animals
Male Castration
Male Criminals
Male Delinquents
Male Female Relations
Male Genital Disorders
Male Genitalia
Male Homosexuality
Male Orgasm
Gay Males *USE Male Homosexuality*
Human **Males**
Mali
Malignant Neoplasms *USE Neoplasms*
Neuroleptic **Malignant** Syndrome
Malingering
Malnutrition *USE Nutritional Deficiencies*
Malpractice *USE Professional Liability*
Mammals
Mammary Glands
Mammary Neoplasms
    USE Breast Neoplasms
Mammillary Bodies (Hypothalamic)
    USE Hypothalamus
Mammography
Man Machine Systems
Man Machine Systems Design
Draw A **Man** Test *USE Human Figures Drawing*
Incomplete **Man** Test
Managed Care
Management
Management Decision Making
Management Development
    USE Career Development

283

Management Information Systems
    USE Information Systems
Management Methods
Management Personnel
Management Planning
Management Training
Business **Management**
Case **Management**
Contingency **Management**
Disability **Management**
Household **Management**
Impression **Management**
Labor **Management** Relations
Pain **Management**
Participative **Management**
Personnel **Management**
Self **Management**
Stress **Management**
Time **Management**
Middle Level **Managers**
Top Level **Managers**
Mandibula *USE Jaw*
Mania
Manic Depression
Manic Depressive Psychosis
    USE Manic Depression
Childrens **Manifest** Anxiety Scale
Taylor **Manifest** Anxiety Scale
Mann Whitney U Test
Mannerisms *USE Habits*
Manpower *USE Personnel Supply*
Mantis
Praying Mantis *USE Mantis*
Manual Communication
Diagnostic and Statistical **Manual**
Manufacturing *USE Business*
Maprotiline
Brain Maps *USE Stereotaxic Atlas*
Cognitive **Maps**
Tactual Maps *USE Mobility Aids*
Marathon Group Therapy
Marihuana
Marihuana Laws
Marihuana Legalization
Marihuana Usage
Marine Personnel
Marital Adjustment *USE Marital Relations*
Marital Conflict
Marital Relations
Marital Satisfaction
Marital Separation
Marital Status
Marital Therapy *USE Marriage Counseling*
Biochemical Markers *USE Biological Markers*
Biological **Markers**
Clinical Markers *USE Biological Markers*
Marketing
Animal Scent **Marking**
Markov Chains
Marlowe Crowne Soc Desirabil Scale
Marriage
Marriage Attitudes
Marriage Counseling
Marriage Rites
Consanguineous **Marriage**
Endogamous **Marriage**
Exogamous **Marriage**
Interethnic Marriage *USE Exogamous Marriage*
Interfaith **Marriage**
Interracial **Marriage**
Miscegenous Marriage *USE Interracial Marriage*
Married Couples *USE Spouses*
Never **Married**
Bone **Marrow**
Marsupials
Martial Arts
Marxism *USE Communism*
Masculinity
Masking

Auditory **Masking**
Backward Masking *USE Masking*
Forward Masking *USE Masking*
Visual **Masking**
Maslow (Abraham Harold)
Masochism
Sexual **Masochism**
Masochistic Personality
Mass Hysteria
Mass Media
Massed Practice
Mastectomy
Mastery Learning
Mastery Tests
    USE Criterion Referenced Tests
Masticatory Muscles
Masturbation
Matching Test *USE Matching to Sample*
Matching to Sample
Mate Selection
    USE Animal Mate Selection OR Human
        Mate Selection
Mate Swapping
    USE Extramarital Intercourse
Animal **Mate** Selection
Human **Mate** Selection
Materialism
Hazardous **Materials**
Reading **Materials**
Maternal Behavior (Human)
    USE Mother Child Relations
Animal **Maternal** Behavior
Animal **Maternal** Deprivation
Mates (Humans) *USE Spouses*
Mathematical Ability
Mathematical Modeling
Mathematical Psychology
Mathematicians
Mathematics
Mathematics Achievement
Mathematics Anxiety
Mathematics (Concepts)
Mathematics Education
Digits (Mathematics) *USE Numbers (Numerals)*
Animal **Mating** Behavior
Assortative **Mating**
Assortive Mating *USE Assortative Mating*
Matriarchy
Raven Coloured Progressive **Matrices**
Raven Progressive **Matrices**
Matriculation *USE School Enrollment*
Maturation *USE Human Development*
California Test of Mental **Maturity**
Career Maturity *USE Vocational Maturity*
Columbia Mental **Maturity** Scale
Emotional **Maturity**
Physical **Maturity**
Vineland Social **Maturity** Scale
Vocational **Maturity**
Maudsley Personality Inventory
Mauritius
Maxilla *USE Jaw*
Maximum Likelihood
Maximum Security Facilities
Maze Learning
Maze Pathways
Porteus **Maze** Test
Runways (Maze) *USE Maze Pathways*
Mazes
T **Mazes**
MCPP *USE Piperazines*
MDMA
    USE Methylenedioxymethamphetamine
Mealtimes *USE Feeding Practices*
Mean
Meaning
Nonverbal **Meaning**
Verbal **Meaning**
Word **Meaning**

Meaningfulness
Measles
German Measles *USE Rubella*
Measurement
Attitude **Measurement**
Conjoint **Measurement**
Consistency **(Measurement)**
Creativity **Measurement**
Educational **Measurement**
Error of **Measurement**
Predictability **(Measurement)**
Profiles **(Measurement)**
Psychophysical **Measurement**
Standard Error of Measurement *USE Error of Measurement*
Statistical **Measurement**
Variability **Measurement**
Achievement **Measures**
Aptitude **Measures**
Attitude **Measures**
Central Tendency **Measures**
Developmental **Measures**
Intelligence **Measures**
Nonprojective Personality **Measures**
Occupational Interest **Measures**
Perceptual **Measures**
Perceptual Motor Measures *USE Sensorimotor Measures*
Personality **Measures**
Preference **Measures**
Projective Personality **Measures**
Reading **Measures**
Repeated **Measures**
Retention **Measures**
Sensorimotor **Measures**
Speech and Hearing **Measures**
Mecamylamine
Mechanical Aptitude
Speech Processing **(Mechanical)**
Compensation (Defense **Mechanism)**
Displacement (Defense **Mechanism)**
Fantasy (Defense **Mechanism)**
Identification (Defense **Mechanism)**
Isolation (Defense **Mechanism)**
Projection (Defense **Mechanism)**
Regression (Defense **Mechanism)**
Repression (Defense **Mechanism)**
Suppression (Defense **Mechanism)**
Withdrawal (Defense **Mechanism)**
Defense **Mechanisms**
Mechanoreceptors
Clinical Judgment (Med Diagnosis) *USE Medical Diagnosis*
Audiovisual Communications **Media**
Communications **Media**
Instructional **Media**
Mass **Media**
Printed Communications **Media**
Telecommunications **Media**
Medial Forebrain Bundle
Median
Median Nerve *USE Spinal Nerves*
Mediated Responses
Mediation
Cognitive **Mediation**
Medicaid
Medical Care Costs
    USE Health Care Costs
Medical Diagnosis
Medical Education
Medical History *USE Patient History*
Medical Internship
Medical Model
Medical Patients
Medical Personnel
Medical Personnel Supply
Medical Psychology
Medical Records Keeping
Medical Regimen Compliance
    USE Treatment Compliance
Medical Residency
Medical Sciences

Medical Students
Medical Therapeutic Devices
Medical Treatment (General)
Military **Medical** Personnel
Self Examination **(Medical)**
Medicare
Medication *USE Drug Therapy*
Self **Medication**
Medicine (Science of)
    USE Medical Sciences
Behavioral Medicine *USE Health Care Psychology*
Family **Medicine**
Folk **Medicine**
Preventive **Medicine**
Psychosomatic **Medicine**
Veterinary **Medicine**
Medics
Meditation
Medulla Oblongata
Adrenal **Medulla** Hormones
Professional **Meetings** and Symposia
Melancholia *USE Major Depression*
Melancholy *USE Sadness*
Melanin
Melanocyte Stimulating Hormone
Melanotropin
    USE Melanocyte Stimulating Hormone
Melatonin
Mellaril *USE Thioridazine*
Diabetes **Mellitus**
Family **Members**
Labor Union **Members**
Fraternity **Membership**
School Club **Membership**
Sorority **Membership**
Nictitating **Membrane**
Tympanic Membrane *USE Middle Ear*
Membranes
Childhood Memories *USE Early Memories*
Early **Memories**
Memory
Memory Decay
Memory Disorders
Memory Enhancing Drugs
    USE Nootropic Drugs
Memory for Designs Test
Memory Trace
Memory Training
Autobiographical **Memory**
Episodic **Memory**
Iconic **Memory**
Long Term **Memory**
Photographic Memory *USE Eidetic Imagery*
Semantic **Memory**
Short Term **Memory**
Spatial **Memory**
Verbal **Memory**
Visual **Memory**
Wechsler **Memory** Scale
Working Memory *USE Short Term Memory*
Men *USE Human Males*
Menarche
Menieres Disease
Meninges
Meningitis
Bacterial **Meningitis**
Meningomyelocele *USE Spina Bifida*
Menopause
Menstrual Cycle
Menstrual Disorders
Menstruation
Mental Age
Mental Confusion
Mental Deficiency
    USE Mental Retardation
Mental Disorders
Mental Health
Mental Health Care Costs
    USE Health Care Costs

Mental Health Care Policy
   USE Health Care Policy
Mental Health Consultation
   USE Professional Consultation
Mental Health Inservice Training
Mental Health Personnel
Mental Health Personnel Supply
Mental Health Program Evaluation
Mental Health Programs
Mental Health Services
Mental Hospitals
   USE Psychiatric Hospitals
Mental Illness *USE Mental Disorders*
Mental Illness (Attitudes Toward)
Mental Load
   USE Human Channel Capacity
Mental Retardation
Mental Retardation (Attit Toward)
Mental Rotation
Borderline **Mental** Retardation
California Test of **Mental** Maturity
Columbia **Mental** Maturity Scale
Community **Mental** Health
Community **Mental** Health Centers
Community **Mental** Health Services
Community **Mental** Health Training
Cultural Familial Mental Retardation
   USE Psychosocial Mental Retardation
Henmon Nelson Tests **Mental** Ability
Mini **Mental** State Examination
Primary **Mental** Health Prevention
Psychosocial **Mental** Retardation
Mentally Ill Offenders
Mentally Retarded
Borderline Mentally Retarded *USE Slow Learners*
Educable **Mentally** Retarded
Home Reared **Mentally** Retarded
Institutionalized **Mentally** Retarded
Mildly Mentally Retarded
   USE Educable Mentally Retarded
Moderately Mentally Retarded
   USE Trainable Mentally Retarded
Profoundly **Mentally** Retarded
Severely **Mentally** Retarded
Trainable **Mentally** Retarded
Mentor
Meperidine
Mephenesin
Meprobamate
Mercury (Metal)
Mercury Poisoning
Mercy Killing *USE Euthanasia*
Organizational **Merger**
Mescaline
Mesencephalon
Mesoridazine
Messages
Information (Messages) *USE Messages*
Meta Analysis
Metabolic Rates
Metabolism
Metabolism Disorders
Basal **Metabolism**
Brain Metabolism *USE Neurochemistry*
Carbohydrate **Metabolism**
Fat Metabolism *USE Lipid Metabolism*
Glucose **Metabolism**
Lipid **Metabolism**
Lipid **Metabolism** Disorders
Protein **Metabolism**
Metabolites
Dopamine **Metabolites**
Norepinephrine **Metabolites**
Serotonin **Metabolites**
Metacognition
Lead **(Metal)**
Mercury **(Metal)**
Metalinguistics
Metallic Elements

Metals
Metamemory *USE Metacognition*
Metaphor
Metaphysics
Metapsychology
Climate (Meteorological)
   USE Atmospheric Conditions
Volt **Meters**
Methadone
Methadone Maintenance
Methamphetamine
Methanol
Methaqualone
Methedrine *USE Methamphetamine*
Methionine
Directed Discussion **Method**
Discovery Teaching **Method**
Forced Choice (Testing **Method)**
Lecture **Method**
Montessori **Method**
Multiple Choice (Testing **Method)**
Nondirected Discussion **Method**
Open Classroom **Method**
Rhythm **Method**
Team Teaching **Method**
Methodology
Clinical **Methods** Training
Drug Administration **Methods**
Empirical **Methods**
Experimental **Methods**
Management **Methods**
Observation **Methods**
Physical Treatment **Methods**
Research Methods *USE Methodology*
Scientific Methods *USE Experimental Methods*
Stimulus Presentation **Methods**
Teaching **Methods**
Testing **Methods**
Methohexital
Methoxamine
Methoxyhydroxyphenylglycol (3,4)
Methyl Alcohol *USE Methanol*
Methylatropine *USE Atropine*
Methyldopa
Methylenedioxymethamphetamine
Methylmorphine *USE Codeine*
Alpha **Methylparatyrosine**
Methylphenidate
Methylphenyltetrahydropyridine
Methysergide *USE Serotonin Antagonists*
Metrazole *USE Pentylenetetrazol*
Metronomes
Metropolitan Readiness Tests
Mexican Americans
Mexico
MHPG
   USE Methoxyhydroxyphenylglycol (3,4)
Mianserin
Mice
Microcephaly
Microcomputers
Microcounseling
Microorganisms
Microscopes
Micturition *USE Urination*
Midazolam
Midbrain *USE Mesencephalon*
Middle Aged
Middle Class
Middle Class Attitudes
Middle Ear
Middle East
Middle Income Level
Middle Level Managers
Middle School Education
Middle School Students
Midwifery
Migraine Headache
Migrant Farm Workers

Human **Migration**
Migratory Behavior (Animal)
Mildly Mentally Retarded
   USE Educable Mentally Retarded
Milieu Therapy
Militancy
Military Enlistment
Military Medical Personnel
Military Officers
   USE Commissioned Officers
Military Personnel
Military Psychology
Military Recruitment
Military Schools
Military Training
Military Veterans
Enlisted **Military** Personnel
Volunteer **Military** Personnel
Miller Analogies Test
Millon Clinical Multiaxial Inventory
Mind
Mind Body *USE Dualism*
Mini Mental State Examination
Minimal Brain Disorders
Minimally Brain Damaged
Minimum Competency Tests
Ministers (Religion)
Minks
Minn Multiphasic Personality Inven
Minnesota Teacher Attitude Inventory
Minor Tranquilizers
Minority Group Discrimination
   USE Race and Ethnic Discrimination
Minority Groups
Mirror Image
Misanthropy
Misbehavior *USE Behavior Problems*
Miscarriage *USE Spontaneous Abortion*
Miscegenous Marriage
   USE Interracial Marriage
Misconduct *USE Behavior Problems*
Misdemeanors *USE Crime*
Misogyny *USE Misanthropy*
Missionaries
Mistakes *USE Errors*
Mnemonic Learning
Mobility Aids
Geographical **Mobility**
Job Mobility *USE Occupational Mobility*
Occupational **Mobility**
Physical **Mobility**
Social **Mobility**
Vocational Mobility *USE Occupational Mobility*
Biopsychosocial Model *USE Biopsychosocial Approach*
Medical **Model**
Rasch Model *USE Item Response Theory*
Modeling *USE Simulation*
Modeling Behavior
   USE Imitation (Learning)
Heuristic **Modeling**
Mathematical **Modeling**
Stochastic **Modeling**
Structural Equation **Modeling**
Models
Animal **Models**
Logistic Models *USE Item Response Theory*
Role **Models**
Moderately Mentally Retarded
   USE Trainable Mentally Retarded
Modern Language Aptitude Test
Behavior **Modification**
Classroom Behavior **Modification**
Molindone
Mollusca
Pearson Prod Moment Correl Coeff
   USE Statistical Correlation
Monetary Incentives
Monetary Rewards
Money

Mongolism *USE Downs Syndrome*
Monitoring
Self **Monitoring**
Self **Monitoring** (Personality)
Monkeys
Monoamine Oxidase Inhibitors
Monoamine Oxidases
Monoamines (Brain) *USE Catecholamines*
Monocular Vision
Monolingualism
Cyclic Adenosine **Monophosphate**
Monotony
Carbon **Monoxide**
Carbon **Monoxide** Poisoning
Monozygotic Twins
Montessori Method
Moodiness
Moods *USE Emotional States*
Mooney Problem Check List
Moral Development
Morale
Morality
Morals *USE Morality*
Mores *USE Values*
Morita Therapy
Morocco
Morphemes
Morphine
Morphology
Morphology (Language)
Mortality *USE Death and Dying*
Mortality Rate
Lowenfeld **Mosaic** Test
Mosaicism *USE Chromosome Disorders*
Moslems *USE Islam*
Mother Absence
Mother Child Communication
Mother Child Relations
Mothers
Adolescent **Mothers**
Expectant **Mothers**
Schizophrenogenic **Mothers**
Single **Mothers**
Teenage Mothers *USE Adolescent Mothers*
Unwed **Mothers**
Moths
Motion Perception
Motion Pictures
Motion Pictures (Educational)
Motion Pictures (Entertainment)
Motion Sickness
Motivation
Motivation Training
Academic Achievement **Motivation**
Achievement **Motivation**
Affiliation **Motivation**
Animal **Motivation**
Employee **Motivation**
Extrinsic **Motivation**
Intrinsic **Motivation**
Motor Coordination
Motor Cortex
Motor Development
Motor Disorders
   USE Nervous System Disorders
Motor Evoked Potentials
   USE Somatosensory Evoked Potentials
Motor Neurons
Motor Pathways *USE Efferent Pathways*
Motor Performance
Motor Processes
Motor Skill Learning
   USE Perceptual Motor Learning
Motor Skills
Motor Traffic Accidents
Motor Vehicles
Balance (Motor Processes) *USE Equilibrium*
Fine **Motor** Skill Learning
Gross **Motor** Skill Learning

Perceptual **Motor** Coordination
Perceptual **Motor** Development
Perceptual **Motor** Learning
Perceptual **Motor** Measures
          USE Sensorimotor Measures
Perceptual **Motor** Processes
Purdue Perceptual **Motor** Survey
Motorcycles *USE Motor Vehicles*
Mourning *USE Grief*
Mouse Killing *USE Muricide*
Mouth (Anatomy)
Movement Disorders
Movement Perception
          USE Motion Perception
Apparent **Movement**
Black Power **Movement**
Civil Rights **Movement**
Gay Liberation Movement
          USE Homosexual Liberation Movement
Homosexual Liberation **Movement**
Human Potential **Movement**
Nonrapid Eye Movement Sleep *USE NREM Sleep*
Rapid Eye **Movement**
Rapid Eye Movement Dreams *USE REM Dreams*
Rapid Eye Movement Sleep *USE REM Sleep*
Stroboscopic Movement *USE Apparent Movement*
Womens Liberation **Movement**
Activist **Movements**
Eye **Movements**
Radical **Movements**
Saccadic Eye Movements *USE Eye Movements*
Social **Movements**
Vergence Movements *USE Eye Convergence*
Movies
          USE Motion Pictures (Entertainment)
Mozambique
MPTP
          USE Methylphenyltetrahydropyridine
MRI *USE Magnetic Resonance Imaging*
Nasal **Mucosa**
Olfactory **Mucosa**
Mucus
Mueller Lyer Illusion
Multi Infarct Dementia
Dementia (Multi Infarct) *USE Multi Infarct Dementia*
Millon Clinical **Multiaxial** Inventory
Multicultural Education
Multidimensional Scaling
Multidisciplinary Research
          USE Interdisciplinary Research
Multidisciplinary Treatment Approach
          USE Interdisciplinary Treatment
          Approach
Multidrug Abuse *USE Polydrug Abuse*
Multilingualism
Multimodal Treatment Approach
Minn **Multiphasic** Personality Inven
Multiple Births
Multiple Choice (Testing Method)
Multiple Personality
Multiple Regression
Multiple Sclerosis
Multiple Therapy *USE Cotherapy*
Multiply Handicapped
Multivariate Analysis
Munchausen Syndrome
Murder *USE Homicide*
Muricide
Muscarinic Drugs *USE Cholinergic Drugs*
Muscimol
Muscle Contraction Headache
Muscle Contractions
Muscle Cramps *USE Muscular Disorders*
Muscle Relaxation
Muscle Relaxation Therapy
          USE Relaxation Therapy
Muscle Relaxing Drugs
Muscle Spasms
Muscle Tone

Cramps (Muscle) *USE Muscular Disorders*
Intra Aural Muscle Reflex *USE Acoustic Reflex*
Muscles
Facial **Muscles**
Masticatory **Muscles**
Oculomotor **Muscles**
Rigidity (Muscles) *USE Muscle Contractions*
Muscular Atrophy
Muscular Disorders
Muscular Dystrophy
Musculocutaneous Nerve
          USE Spinal Nerves
Musculoskeletal Disorders
Musculoskeletal System
Music
Music Education
Music Therapy
Rock **Music**
Musical Ability
Musical Instruments
Musicians
Muslims *USE Islam*
Mutations
Self **Mutilation**
Mutism
Elective **Mutism**
Mutual Storytelling Technique
Myasthenia
Myasthenia Gravis
Myelin Sheath
Myelitis
Myelomeningocele *USE Spina Bifida*
Myenteric Plexus *USE Autonomic Ganglia*
Myers Briggs Type Indicator
Myocardial Infarctions
Myocardium
Myoclonia
Myofascial Pain
Myopia
Myotonia
Mysticism
Myths
Myxedema *USE Hypothyroidism*
Nabilone *USE Cannabinoids*
NAch *USE Achievement Motivation*
Nail Biting
Nalorphine
Naloxone
Naltrexone
Names
Brand **Names**
Naming
Napping
Narcissism
Narcissistic Personality
Narcoanalysis
Narcoanalytic Drugs
Narcolepsy
Narcosis
Narcotic Agonists
Narcotic Antagonists
Narcotic Drugs
Nasal Mucosa
National Guardsmen
Nationalism
Foreign **Nationals**
Native Americans *USE American Indians*
Natural Childbirth
Natural Disasters
Natural Family *USE Biological Family*
Nature Nurture
Nausea
Animal Navigation
          USE Migratory Behavior (Animal)
Navigators (Aircraft)
          USE Aerospace Personnel
Navy Personnel
Nazism *USE Fascism*
Near Death Experiences

Nearsightedness *USE Myopia*
Luria **Nebraska** Neuropsych Battery
Neck (Anatomy)
Need Achievement *USE Achievement Motivation*
Need for Affiliation *USE Affiliation Motivation*
Need Satisfaction
Needle Sharing
Needs
Needs Assessment
Special **Needs**
Negative Reinforcement
Negative Transfer
Contingent **Negative** Variation
Negativism
Child **Neglect**
Perceptual **Neglect** *USE Sensory Neglect*
Sensory **Neglect**
Spatial **Neglect** *USE Sensory Neglect*
Visual **Neglect** *USE Sensory Neglect*
Negotiation
Negroes *USE Blacks*
Neighborhoods
Henmon **Nelson** Tests Mental Ability
Nembutal *USE Pentobarbital*
NeoFreudian School
  USE Neopsychoanalytic School
Neologisms
Neonatal Development
Neonatal Disorders
Neonates
Neonates (Animal) *USE Infants (Animal)*
Neonaticide *USE Infanticide*
Neophobia
Neoplasms
Benign **Neoplasms**
Brain **Neoplasms**
Breast **Neoplasms**
Endocrine **Neoplasms**
Malignant Neoplasms *USE Neoplasms*
Mammary Neoplasms *USE Breast Neoplasms*
Nervous System **Neoplasms**
Neopsychoanalytic School
Neostigmine
Nepal
Nerve Cells *USE Neurons*
Nerve Endings
Nerve Growth Factor
Nerve Tissues
Abducens **Nerve**
Accessory Nerve *USE Cranial Nerves*
Acoustic **Nerve**
Auditory Nerve *USE Acoustic Nerve*
Chorda Tympani Nerve *USE Facial Nerve*
Facial **Nerve**
Femoral Nerve *USE Spinal Nerves*
Glossopharyngeal Nerve *USE Cranial Nerves*
Hypoglossal Nerve *USE Cranial Nerves*
Median Nerve *USE Spinal Nerves*
Musculocutaneous Nerve *USE Spinal Nerves*
Obturator Nerve *USE Spinal Nerves*
Oculomotor Nerve *USE Cranial Nerves*
Olfactory **Nerve**
Optic **Nerve**
Peripheral **Nerve** Disorders
Phrenic Nerve *USE Spinal Nerves*
Radial Nerve *USE Spinal Nerves*
Sciatic Nerve *USE Spinal Nerves*
Trigeminal **Nerve**
Trochlear Nerve *USE Cranial Nerves*
Ulnar Nerve *USE Spinal Nerves*
Vagus **Nerve**
Adrenergic **Nerves**
Cholinergic **Nerves**
Cranial **Nerves**
Spinal **Nerves**
Thoracic Nerves *USE Spinal Nerves*
Anorexia **Nervosa**
Nervous Breakdown
  USE Mental Disorders

Nervous System
Nervous System Disorders
Nervous System Neoplasms
Nervous System Plasticity
  USE Neural Plasticity
Autonomic **Nervous** System
Autonomic **Nervous** System Disorders
Central **Nervous** System
Central **Nervous** System Disorders
Central Nervous System Drugs
  USE CNS Affecting Drugs
Parasympathetic **Nervous** System
Peripheral **Nervous** System
Sclerosis **(Nervous** System)
Sympathetic **Nervous** System
Nervousness
Nest Building
Empty **Nest**
Netherlands
Netherlands Antilles
Networks (Social)
  USE Social Networks
Neural **Networks**
Social **Networks**
Social Support **Networks**
Neural Analyzers
Neural Development
Neural Lesions
Neural Networks
Neural Pathways
Neural Plasticity
Neural Receptors
Neural Regeneration
  USE Neural Development
Neural Transplantation
Neuralgia
Trigeminal **Neuralgia**
Neurasthenic Neurosis
Neuroanatomy
Neurobiology
Neurochemistry
Neurodermatitis
Neuroendocrinology
Neuroinfections
  USE Infectious Disorders AND Nervous
    System Disorders
Neuroleptic Drugs
Neuroleptic Malignant Syndrome
Neurolinguistic Programing
Neurolinguistics
Neurological Disorders
  USE Nervous System Disorders
Neurologists
Neurology
Neuromuscular Blocking Drugs
  USE Muscle Relaxing Drugs
Neuromuscular Disorders
Neurons
Auditory **Neurons**
Motor **Neurons**
Sensory **Neurons**
Neuropathologists *USE Neurologists*
Neuropathology
Neuropathy
  USE Nervous System Disorders
Neuropeptides *USE Peptides*
Neurophysiology
Halstead Reitan **Neuropsych** Battery
Luria Nebraska **Neuropsych** Battery
Neuropsychiatrists *USE Psychiatrists*
Neuropsychiatry
Neuropsychological Assessment
Neuropsychology
Neurosciences
Neurosis
Anxiety **Neurosis**
Childhood **Neurosis**
Compulsive Neurosis
  USE Obsessive Compulsive Neurosis

Conversion **Neurosis**
Dissociative **Neurosis**
Experimental **Neurosis**
Hysterical Neurosis (Dissociation)
    USE Dissociative Neurosis
Infantile Neurosis *USE Childhood Neurosis*
Neurasthenic **Neurosis**
Obsessive Neurosis
    USE Obsessive Compulsive Neurosis
Obsessive Compulsive **Neurosis**
Occupational **Neurosis**
Phobic Neurosis *USE Phobias*
Traumatic **Neurosis**
Neurosurgeons *USE Surgeons*
Neurosurgery
Neurosyphilis
Neurotensin
Neurotic Depressive Reaction
Neuroticism
Neurotoxins
Neurotransmitters
Never Married
New Zealand
Papua **New** Guinea
Newborn Infants *USE Neonates*
Professional Newsletters
    USE Scientific Communication
Newspapers
Niacin *USE Nicotinic Acid*
Niacinamide *USE Nicotinamide*
Nialamide
Nicaragua
Nicotinamide
Nicotine
Nicotinic Acid
Nicotinic Acid Amide *USE Nicotinamide*
Nictitating Membrane
Niger
Nigeria
Night Terrors *USE Sleep Disorders*
Nightmares
Substantia **Nigra**
Nihilism
Nitrazepam
Nitrogen
NMDA *USE N-Methyl-D-Aspartate*
N-Methyl-D-Aspartate
Nociception *USE Pain Perception*
Nociceptors
Nocturnal Emission
Nocturnal Teeth Grinding
Animal **Nocturnal** Behavior
Noise Effects
Noise Levels (Work Areas)
Noise (Sound) *USE Auditory Stimulation*
Filtered **Noise**
White **Noise**
Nomenclature (Psychological)
    USE Psychological Terminology
Nomifensine
Non Zero Sum Games
Beverages **(Nonalcoholic)**
Noncommissioned Officers
Nonconformity (Personality)
Noncontingent Reinforcement
Nondirected Discussion Method
Nondirective Therapy
    USE Client Centered Therapy
Nongraded Schools
Primates **(Nonhuman)**
Nonlinear Regression
Nonmetallic Elements
Nonparametric Statistical Tests
Nonprescription Drugs
Nonprofessional Personnel
Nonprofit Organizations
Nonprojective Personality Measures
Nonrapid Eye Movement Sleep
    USE NREM Sleep

Beliefs (Nonreligious) *USE Attitudes*
Rites **(Nonreligious)**
Rituals (Nonreligious) *USE Rites (Nonreligious)*
NonREM Sleep *USE NREM Sleep*
Nonreversal Shift Learning
Nonsense Syllable Learning
Nonstandard English
Nontraditional Careers
Nontraditional Education
Nonverbal Ability
Nonverbal Communication
Nonverbal Learning
Nonverbal Meaning
Nonverbal Reinforcement
Nonviolence
Nootropic Drugs
Noradrenaline *USE Norepinephrine*
Norepinephrine
Norepinephrine Metabolites
Normal Distribution
Test Normalization *USE Test Standardization*
Social **Norms**
Statistical **Norms**
Test **Norms**
North America
North Korea
North Vietnam *USE Vietnam*
Northern Ireland
Nortriptyline
Norway
Norway Rats
Nose
Note Taking
Nouns
Novelty Seeking *USE Sensation Seeking*
Stimulus **Novelty**
Novocaine *USE Procaine*
NREM Sleep
Nuclear Family
Nuclear Technology
Nuclear War
Raphe **Nuclei**
Septal **Nuclei**
Thalamic **Nuclei**
Nucleic Acids
Nucleotides
Nucleus Accumbens
Nucleus Basalis Magnocellularis
Caudate **Nucleus**
Cell **Nucleus**
Red Nucleus *USE Mesencephalon*
Nudity
Null Hypothesis Testing
Number Comprehension
Number Systems
Numbers (Numerals)
Numbers **(Numerals)**
Numerical Ability *USE Mathematical Ability*
Numerosity Perception
Nuns
Nurse Patient Interaction
    USE Therapeutic Processes
Nursery School Students
Nursery Schools
Nurses
Psychiatric **Nurses**
Public Health Service **Nurses**
School **Nurses**
Nursing
Nursing Education
Nursing Homes
Nursing Students
Nurturance
Nature **Nurture**
Nutrition
Nutritional Deficiencies
Nymphomania *USE Hypersexuality*
Nystagmus
Optokinetic Nystagmus *USE Nystagmus*

Vestibular Nystagmus *USE Nystagmus*
Obedience
Obesity
Obituary
Object Permanence
Object Relations
Goldstein Scheerer **Object** Sort Test
Objective Referenced Tests
USE Criterion Referenced Tests
Objectives *USE Goals*
Course Objectives *USE Educational Objectives*
Educational **Objectives**
Instructional Objectives *USE Educational Objectives*
Organizational **Objectives**
Objectivity
Transitional **Objects**
Oblique Rotation
Medulla **Oblongata**
Obscenity
Observation Methods
Self Observation *USE Self Monitoring*
Observational Learning
Observers
Obsessions
Obsessive Compulsive Disorder
USE Obsessive Compulsive Neurosis
Obsessive Compulsive Neurosis
Obsessive Compulsive Personality
Obsessive Neurosis
USE Obsessive Compulsive Neurosis
Obstetrical Complications
Obstetricians
Obstetrics
Obturator Nerve *USE Spinal Nerves*
Occipital Lobe
Occultism
Parental **Occupation**
Occupational Adjustment
Occupational Aspirations
Occupational Attitudes
Occupational Choice
Occupational Exposure
Occupational Guidance
Occupational Interest Measures
Occupational Interests
Occupational Mobility
Occupational Neurosis
Occupational Preference
Occupational Safety
Occupational Status
Occupational Stress
Occupational Success
Occupational Success Prediction
Occupational Tenure
Occupational Therapists
Occupational Therapy
Kuder **Occupational** Interest Survey
Prestige (Occupational) *USE Occupational Status*
Occupations
Religious Occupations *USE Religious Personnel*
Octopus
Ocular Accommodation
Ocular Dominance
Ocular Fixation *USE Eye Fixation*
Electro **Oculography**
Oculomotor Muscles
Oculomotor Nerve *USE Cranial Nerves*
Oculomotor Response
USE Eye Movements
Odor Aversion Conditioning
USE Aversion Conditioning
Odor Discrimination
Oedipal Complex
Offenders (Adult) *USE Criminals*
Offenders (Juvenile)
USE Juvenile Delinquents
Mentally Ill **Offenders**
Sex **Offenses**

Office Environment
USE Working Conditions
Commissioned **Officers**
Military Officers *USE Commissioned Officers*
Noncommissioned **Officers**
Parole **Officers**
Probation **Officers**
Elected Government Officials *USE Government Personnel*
Stimulus **Offset**
Offspring
Adult **Offspring**
Interracial **Offspring**
Old Age *USE Aged*
Very **Old**
Olfactory Bulb
Olfactory Evoked Potentials
Olfactory Mucosa
Olfactory Nerve
Olfactory Perception
Olfactory Stimulation
Olfactory Thresholds
Oligophrenia *USE Mental Retardation*
Oligophrenia (Phenylpyruvic)
USE Phenylketonuria
Omission Training
Omnibus Personality Inventory
Omnipotence
On the Job Training
Time **On** Task
Online Databases *USE Databases*
Online Searching
USE Computer Searching
Only Children
Onomatopoeia and Images Test
Onset (Disorders)
Sleep **Onset**
Stimulus **Onset**
Ontogeny *USE Development*
Open Classroom Method
Open Universities
USE Nontraditional Education
Animal **Open** Field Behavior
Openmindedness
Operant Conditioning
Operation (Surgery) *USE Surgery*
Ophidiophobia
Ophthalmologic Examination
Ophthalmology
Opiate Agonists *USE Narcotic Agonists*
Opiate Antagonists
USE Narcotic Antagonists
Opiates
Endogenous **Opiates**
Opinion Attitude and Interest Survey
Opinion Change *USE Attitude Change*
Opinion Questionnaires
USE Attitude Measures
Opinion Surveys *USE Attitude Measures*
Public **Opinion**
Opinions *USE Attitudes*
Opioids *USE Opiates*
Opium Alkaloids
USE Alkaloids AND Opiates
Opium Derivatives *USE Opiates*
Opossums
Optic Chiasm
Optic Lobe
Optic Nerve
Optic Tract
Optical Aids
Optical Illusions *USE Illusions (Perception)*
Optimism
Optokinetic Nystagmus *USE Nystagmus*
Optometrists
Optometry
Oral Communication
Oral Contraceptives
Oral Reading
Birth **Order**

Pecking Order *USE Animal Dominance*
Rank **Order** Correlation
Court Ordered Treatment *USE Court Referrals*
Organ Donation *USE Tissue Donation*
Organ of Corti *USE Cochlea*
Organ Transplantation
Sense **Organ** Disorders
Organic Brain Syndromes
Organic Therapies
Single Cell Organisms *USE Microorganisms*
School Organization
    USE Educational Administration
Spatial **Organization**
Organizational Behavior
Organizational Change
Organizational Climate
Organizational Commitment
Organizational Crises
Organizational Development
Organizational Effectiveness
Organizational Goals
    USE Organizational Objectives
Organizational Merger
Organizational Objectives
Organizational Performance
    USE Organizational Effectiveness
Organizational Psychology
    USE Industrial Psychology
Organizational Structure
Organizations
Business **Organizations**
Clubs (Social **Organizations)**
Foreign **Organizations**
Health Maintenance **Organizations**
International **Organizations**
Nonprofit **Organizations**
Professional **Organizations**
Religious **Organizations**
Advance **Organizers**
Sense **Organs**
Orgasm
Female **Orgasm**
Male **Orgasm**
Orientals *USE Asians*
Fund Interper Rela **Orientat** Beh Ques
Perceptual **Orientation**
Personal **Orientation** Inventory
Professional Orientation *USE Theoretical Orientation*
Spatial **Orientation** (Perception)
Theoretical **Orientation**
Orienting Reflex
Orienting Responses
Family of **Origin**
Originality *USE Creativity*
Word Origins *USE Etymology*
Orphanages
Orphans
Orphenadrine
Orthogonal Rotation
Orthography
Orthopedically Handicapped
    USE Physically Handicapped
Orthopsychiatry
Oscilloscopes
Ear Ossicles *USE Middle Ear*
Osteoporosis
Significant **Others**
Otosclerosis
Out of Body Experiences
Acting **Out**
Time **Out**
Psychotherapeutic **Outcomes**
Therapeutic Outcomes *USE Treatment Outcomes*
Treatment **Outcomes**
Outpatient Commitment
Outpatient Psychiatric Clinics
    USE Psychiatric Clinics
Outpatient Treatment
Commitment (Outpatient) *USE Outpatient Commitment*

Outpatients
Outward Bound
    USE Wilderness Experience
Ovariectomy
Ovaries
Ovary Disorders
    USE Endocrine Sexual Disorders
Over The Counter Drugs
    USE Nonprescription Drugs
Academic **Overachievement**
Overcorrection
Drug **Overdoses**
Overlearning
Overpopulation
Structured Overview *USE Advance Organizers*
Overweight *USE Obesity*
Ovulation
Ownership
Oxazepam
Amine **Oxidase** Inhibitors
Cytochrome **Oxidase**
Monoamine **Oxidase** Inhibitors
Oxidases
Monoamine **Oxidases**
Oxilapine *USE Loxapine*
Oxygen
Oxygenation
Oxytocin
Substance **P**
Artificial **Pacemakers**
Pacific Islands
South **Pacific**
Pacifism
Pain
Pain Management
Pain Perception
Pain Receptors *USE Nociceptors*
Pain Relieving Drugs
    USE Analgesic Drugs
Pain Thresholds
Back **Pain**
Chronic **Pain**
Myofascial **Pain**
Psychogenic **Pain**
Painting (Art)
Paired Associate Learning
Pakistan
Cleft **Palate**
Palestinians *USE Arabs*
Palliative Care
Globus **Pallidus**
Palm (Anatomy)
Palsy *USE Paralysis*
Cerebral **Palsy**
Panama
Pancreas
Pancreozymin *USE Cholecystokinin*
Panic
Panic Disorder
Pantherine *USE Muscimol*
Papaverine
Papua New Guinea
Parachlorophenylalanine
Paradigmatic Techniques
    USE Paradoxical Techniques
Paradoxical Sleep *USE REM Sleep*
Paradoxical Techniques
Paragraphs
Paraguay
Paraldehyde
Paralegal Personnel *USE Legal Personnel*
Paralysis
Paralysis Agitans
    USE Parkinsons Disease
Paralysis (Infantile) *USE Poliomyelitis*
Hysterical **Paralysis**
Infantile Paralysis *USE Poliomyelitis*
Dementia Paralytica *USE General Paresis*
Paramedical Personnel

Paramedical Sciences
Parameter Estimation
    USE Statistical Estimation
Response **Parameters**
Statistical Sample **Parameters**
Stimulus **Parameters**
Parametric Statistical Tests
Paranoia
Paranoia (Psychosis)
Climacteric Paranoia
    USE Involutional Paranoid Psychosis
Paranoid Disorder
    USE Paranoia (Psychosis)
Paranoid Personality
Paranoid Schizophrenia
Acute Paranoid Disorder
    USE Paranoia (Psychosis)
Atypical Paranoid Disorder
    USE Paranoia (Psychosis)
Involutional **Paranoid** Psychosis
Shared Paranoid Disorder *USE Folie A Deux*
Paraphilias *USE Sexual Deviations*
Paraplegia
Paraprofessional Education
Paraprofessional Personnel
Parapsychological Phenomena
Parapsychology
ESP (Parapsychology)
    USE Extrasensory Perception
Parasitic Disorders
Parasitism *USE Biological Symbiosis*
Parasuicide *USE Attempted Suicide*
Parasympathetic Nervous System
Parasympatholytic Drugs
    USE Cholinergic Blocking Drugs
Parasympathomimetic Drugs
    USE Cholinomimetic Drugs
Parathion
Parathyroid Disorders
Parathyroid Glands
Parathyroid Hormone
Parent Attitude Research Instrument
Parent Child Communication
Parent Child Relations
Parent Educational Background
Parent Effectiveness Training
    USE Parent Training
Parent School Relationship
Parent Training
Parental Absence
Parental Attitudes
Parental Authoritarianism
    USE Parental Permissiveness
Parental Characteristics
Parental Influence
    USE Parent Child Relations
Parental Occupation
Parental Permissiveness
Parental Role
Animal **Parental** Behavior
Authoritarianism (Parental) *USE Parental Permissiveness*
Parenthood Status
Delayed **Parenthood**
Parents
Adoptive **Parents**
Birth Parents *USE Biological Family*
Expectant **Parents**
Foster **Parents**
Gay Parents *USE Homosexual Parents*
Homosexual **Parents**
Lesbian Parents *USE Homosexual Parents*
Single **Parents**
Surrogate **Parents** (Humans)
General **Paresis**
Pargyline
Parietal Lobe
Parkinsonism
Parkinsons Disease

Parks (Recreational)
    USE Recreation Areas
Parochial School Education
    USE Private School Education
Parole
Parole Officers
Parolees *USE Parole*
Paroxetine
Partial Hospitalization
Partial Reinforcement
    USE Reinforcement Schedules
Partially Hearing Impaired
Partially Sighted
Participation
Athletic **Participation**
Group **Participation**
Political **Participation**
Participative Management
Political **Parties**
Partner Abuse
Parturition *USE Birth*
Democratic Party *USE Political Parties*
Independent Party (Political) *USE Political Parties*
Republican Party *USE Political Parties*
Rites of **Passage**
Passive Aggressive Personality
Passive Avoidance
    USE Avoidance Conditioning
Passiveness
Pastoral Counseling
Pastors *USE Ministers (Religion)*
Animal **Paternal** Behavior
Path Analysis
Pathogenesis *USE Etiology*
Pathological Gambling
Pathologists
Pathology
Afferent **Pathways**
Efferent **Pathways**
Maze **Pathways**
Motor Pathways *USE Efferent Pathways*
Neural **Pathways**
Sensory Pathways *USE Afferent Pathways*
Patient Abuse
Patient Attitudes *USE Client Attitudes*
Patient Characteristics
    USE Client Characteristics
Patient Education *USE Client Education*
Patient History
Patient Rights *USE Client Rights*
Patient Satisfaction
    USE Client Satisfaction
Patient Seclusion
Patient Therapist Interaction
    USE Psychotherapeutic Processes
Patient Therapist Sexual Relations
    USE Professional Client Sexual Relations
Patient Violence
Dentist Patient Interaction
    USE Therapeutic Processes
Nurse Patient Interaction
    USE Therapeutic Processes
Physician Patient Interaction
    USE Therapeutic Processes
Seclusion (Patient) *USE Patient Seclusion*
Therapist Patient Interaction
    USE Psychotherapeutic Processes
Therapist Patient Sexual Relations
    USE Professional Client Sexual Relations
Patients
Dying Patients *USE Terminally Ill Patients*
Geriatric **Patients**
Hospitalized **Patients**
Medical **Patients**
Psychiatric **Patients**
Surgical **Patients**
Terminally Ill **Patients**
Patriarchy
Pattern Discrimination

Personality Assessment
USE Personality Measures
Personality Change
Personality Correlates
Personality Development
Personality Disorders
Personality Factors
USE Personality Traits
Personality Measures
Personality Processes
Personality Theory
Personality Traits
Adaptability **(Personality)**
Antisocial **Personality**
Asthenic **Personality**
Autonomy (Personality)
USE Independence (Personality)
Avoidant **Personality**
California Test of **Personality**
Childrens **Personality** Questionnaire
Compulsive Personality Disorder
USE Obsessive Compulsive Personality
Conformity **(Personality)**
Conscious **(Personality** Factor)
Counselor Personality *USE Counselor Characteristics*
Cyclothymic **Personality**
Dependency **(Personality)**
Dependent **Personality**
Differential **Personality** Inventory
Edwards **Personality** Inventory
Emotionality **(Personality)**
Explosive **Personality**
Eysenck **Personality** Inventory
Flexibility (Personality) *USE Adaptability (Personality)*
High Sch **Personality** Questionnaire
Histrionic Personality Disorder
USE Hysterical Personality
Hysterical **Personality**
Inadequate **Personality**
Independence **(Personality)**
Inhibition **(Personality)**
Insensitivity (Personality) *USE Sensitivity (Personality)*
Intermittent Explosive Personality *USE Explosive Personality*
Masochistic **Personality**
Maudsley **Personality** Inventory
Minn Multiphasic **Personality** Inven
Multiple **Personality**
Narcissistic **Personality**
Nonconformity **(Personality)**
Nonprojective **Personality** Measures
Obsessive Compulsive **Personality**
Omnibus **Personality** Inventory
Paranoid **Personality**
Passive Aggressive **Personality**
Perceptiveness **(Personality)**
Projective **Personality** Measures
Psychoanalytic **Personality** Factors
Rigidity **(Personality)**
Sadomasochistic **Personality**
Schizoid **Personality**
Schizotypal **Personality**
Self Monitoring **(Personality)**
Sensitivity **(Personality)**
Sixteen **Personality** Factors Question
Split Personality *USE Multiple Personality*
Stimulation Seeking (Personality) *USE Sensation Seeking*
Teacher **Personality**
Therapist Personality *USE Therapist Characteristics*
Type A Personality *USE Coronary Prone Behavior*
Type B Personality *USE Coronary Prone Behavior*
Unconscious **(Personality** Factor)
Personnel
Personnel Development
USE Personnel Training
Personnel Evaluation
Personnel Management
Personnel Placement
Personnel Promotion
Personnel Recruitment

Personnel Selection
Personnel Supply
Personnel Termination
Personnel Training
Accreditation (Education **Personnel)**
Aerospace **Personnel**
Air Force **Personnel**
Army **Personnel**
Aviation Personnel *USE Aerospace Personnel*
Business and Industrial **Personnel**
Clerical **Personnel**
Coast Guard **Personnel**
Domestic Service **Personnel**
Educational **Personnel**
Enlisted Military **Personnel**
Government **Personnel**
Health **Personnel**
Health **Personnel** Attitudes
Law Enforcement **Personnel**
Lay Religious **Personnel**
Legal **Personnel**
Management **Personnel**
Marine **Personnel**
Medical **Personnel**
Medical **Personnel** Supply
Mental Health **Personnel**
Mental Health **Personnel** Supply
Military **Personnel**
Military Medical **Personnel**
Navy **Personnel**
Nonprofessional **Personnel**
Paralegal Personnel *USE Legal Personnel*
Paramedical **Personnel**
Paraprofessional **Personnel**
Police **Personnel**
Prison **Personnel**
Professional **Personnel**
Religious **Personnel**
Sales **Personnel**
Secretarial **Personnel**
Service **Personnel**
Student **Personnel** Services
Technical **Personnel**
Technical Service **Personnel**
Volunteer **Personnel**
Volunteer Civilian **Personnel**
Volunteer Military **Personnel**
Divorced **Persons**
Single **Persons**
Perspective Taking *USE Role Taking*
Linear **Perspective**
Time **Perspective**
Visual Perspective *USE Linear Perspective*
Perspiration *USE Sweat*
Persuasion Therapy
Persuasive Communication
Peru
Pessimism
Pesticides *USE Insecticides*
Pet Therapy
USE Animal Assisted Therapy
Petit Mal Epilepsy
Pets
Petting
Peyote
Phantom Limbs
Pharmacists
Pharmacology
Pharmacotherapy *USE Drug Therapy*
Pharyngeal Disorders
Pharynx
Phenaglycodol
Phencyclidine
Phenelzine
Phenethylamines
Pheniprazine
Phenmetrazine
Phenobarbital
Parapsychological **Phenomena**

295

Phenomenology
Phenothiazine Derivatives
Phenotypes
Phenoxybenzamine
Phenylalanine
Phenylketonuria
Oligophrenia (Phenylpyruvic) *USE Phenylketonuria*
Phenytoin *USE Diphenylhydantoin*
Pheromones
Phi Coefficient
Philippines
Philosophies
Philosophy of Life *USE World View*
Logic **(Philosophy)**
Realism **(Philosophy)**
School **Phobia**
Snake Phobia *USE Ophidiophobia*
Social **Phobia**
Spider Phobia *USE Phobias*
Phobias
Phobic Neurosis *USE Phobias*
Phonemes
Words **(Phonetic** Units)
Phonetics
Phonics
Phonology
Phosphatases
Phosphatides
Phospholipids *USE Phosphatides*
Phosphorus
Phosphorylases
Photic Threshold
   USE Illumination AND Visual Thresholds
Photographic Art
Photographic Memory
   USE Eidetic Imagery
Photographs
Photopic Stimulation
Photoreceptors
Phototherapy
Phrases
Phrenic Nerve *USE Spinal Nerves*
Phylogenesis
Physical Abuse
Physical Agility
Physical Appearance
Physical Attractiveness
Physical Comfort
Physical Contact
Physical Development
Physical Dexterity
Physical Disfigurement
Physical Divisions (Geographic)
   USE Geography
Physical Education
Physical Endurance
Physical Examination
Physical Fitness
Physical Growth
   USE Physical Development
Physical Handicaps (Attit Toward)
Physical Illness *USE Disorders*
Physical Illness (Attitudes Toward)
Physical Maturity
Physical Mobility
Physical Restraint
Physical Strength
Physical Therapists
Physical Therapy
Physical Trauma *USE Injuries*
Physical Treatment Methods
Physically Handicapped
Physician Patient Interaction
   USE Therapeutic Processes
Physicians
Family **Physicians**
Physicists
Physics
Physiological Aging

Physiological Arousal
Physiological Correlates
Physiological Psychology
Physiological Stress
Absorption **(Physiological)**
Sexual Disorders (Physiological) *USE Genital Disorders*
Physiology
Physiotherapy *USE Physical Therapy*
Physique
Physostigmine
Piaget (Jean)
Piagetian Tasks
Piano *USE Musical Instruments*
Pica
Picketing *USE Social Demonstrations*
Picks Disease
Picrotoxin
Pictorial Stimuli
Peabody **Picture** Vocabulary Test
Rosenzweig **Picture** Frustration Study
Blacky **Pictures** Test
Motion **Pictures**
Motion **Pictures** (Educational)
Motion **Pictures** (Entertainment)
Pigeons
Pigments
Pigs
Guinea **Pigs**
Pilocarpine
Aircraft **Pilots**
Pimozide
Pineal Body
Pinealectomy
Piperazines
Pipradrol
Piracetam
Pitch Discrimination
Pitch (Frequency)
Pitch Perception
Speech **Pitch**
Pituitary Disorders
Pituitary Dwarfism *USE Hypopituitarism*
Pituitary Gland
Pituitary Gland Surgery
   USE Hypophysectomy
Pituitary Hormones
PKU (Hereditary Disorder)
   USE Phenylketonuria
Place Conditioning
Place Disorientation
Conditioned Place Preference *USE Place Conditioning*
Placebo
Educational **Placement**
Personnel **Placement**
Placenta
Planarians
Discharge **Planning**
Educational Program **Planning**
Environmental **Planning**
Family **Planning**
Family **Planning** Attitudes
Management **Planning**
Program Planning *USE Program Development*
Urban **Planning**
Employee Pension **Plans**
Group Health Plans
   USE Health Maintenance Organizations
Lesson **Plans**
Blood **Plasma**
Plastic Surgery
Nervous System Plasticity *USE Neural Plasticity*
Neural **Plasticity**
Blood **Platelets**
Play *USE Recreation*
Play Therapy
Animal **Play**
Childhood **Play** Behavior
Childhood **Play** Development
Doll **Play**

Playgrounds
Role **Playing**
Stage Plays *USE Theatre*
Pleasure
Plethysmography
Brachial Plexus *USE Spinal Nerves*
Celiac Plexus *USE Autonomic Ganglia*
Cervical Plexus *USE Spinal Nerves*
Choroid Plexus *USE Cerebral Ventricles*
Hypogastric Plexus *USE Autonomic Ganglia*
Lumbrosacral Plexus *USE Spinal Nerves*
Myenteric Plexus *USE Autonomic Ganglia*
Submucous Plexus *USE Autonomic Ganglia*
PMS *USE Premenstrual Tension*
Pneumoencephalography
Pneumonia
Poetry
Poetry Therapy
Point Biserial Correlation
Poisoning *USE Toxic Disorders*
Barbiturate **Poisoning**
Carbon Monoxide **Poisoning**
Lead **Poisoning**
Mercury **Poisoning**
Poisons
Poisson Distribution
USE Skewed Distribution
Poland
Police Interrogation
USE Legal Interrogation
Police Personnel
Policy Making
Foreign **Policy** Making
Government **Policy** Making
Health Care **Policy**
Mental Health Care Policy *USE Health Care Policy*
Public Policy *USE Government Policy Making*
Poliomyelitis
Political Assassination
Political Attitudes
Political Campaigns
Political Candidates
Political Conservatism
Political Divisions (Geographic)
USE Geography
Political Economic Systems
Political Elections
Political Issues
Political Liberalism
Political Participation
Political Parties
Political Processes
Political Radicalism
Political Refugees *USE Refugees*
Political Revolution
Political Socialization
Independent Party (Political) *USE Political Parties*
Politicians
Politics
Pollution
Polydipsia
Polydrug Abuse
Polygamy
Polygraphs
Pons
Popularity
Population
Population Characteristics
USE Demographic Characteristics
Population Control *USE Birth Control*
Population Genetics
Population (Statistics)
At Risk **Populations**
High Risk Populations *USE At Risk Populations*
Pornography
Porphyria
Porpoises
Porteus Maze Test
Portugal

Serial **Position** Effect
Positive Reinforcement
Positive Transfer
Positivism
Positron Emission Tomography
USE Tomography
Possession *USE Ownership*
Postactivation Potentials
Postganglionic Autonomic Fibers
USE Autonomic Ganglia
Postgraduate Students
Postgraduate Training
Posthypnotic Suggestions
Postnatal Dysphoria
USE Postpartum Depression
Postnatal Period
Postpartum Depression
Postpartum Psychosis
USE Postpartum Depression
Postsurgical Complications
Posttesting
Posttraumatic Stress Disorder
Posttreatment Followup
Posture
Threat **Postures**
Potassium
Potassium Ions
Potential Dropouts
Abuse Potential (Drugs)
USE Drug Abuse Liability
Achievement **Potential**
Human **Potential** Movement
Skin **Potential**
Auditory Evoked **Potentials**
Cortical Evoked **Potentials**
Evoked **Potentials**
Motor Evoked Potentials
USE Somatosensory Evoked Potentials
Olfactory Evoked **Potentials**
Postactivation **Potentials**
Somatosensory Evoked **Potentials**
Visual Evoked **Potentials**
Drug Potentiation *USE Drug Interactions*
Long Term Potentiation *USE Postactivation Potentials*
Short Term Potentiation *USE Postactivation Potentials*
Poverty
Poverty Areas
Power
Black **Power** Movement
Statistical **Power**
Practice
Distributed **Practice**
Experience (Practice) *USE Practice*
Massed **Practice**
Private **Practice**
Childrearing **Practices**
Feeding **Practices**
Religious **Practices**
Practicum Supervision
General **Practitioners**
Prader Willi Syndrome
Dementia Praecox *USE Schizophrenia*
Pragmatics
Pragmatism
Praise
Prayer
Praying Mantis *USE Mantis*
Preadolescents
Precocious Development
Precognition
Preconditioning
Sensory Preconditioning *USE Preconditioning*
Serotonin **Precursors**
Animal **Predatory** Behavior
Predelinquent Youth
Predictability (Measurement)
Prediction
Prediction Errors
Academic Achievement **Prediction**

297

Occupational Success **Prediction**
Predictive Validity
Predisposition
Prednisolone
Preference Measures
Career Preference *USE Occupational Preference*
Conditioned Place Preference *USE Place Conditioning*
Edwards Personal **Preference** Schedule
Kuder **Preference** Record
Occupational **Preference**
Vocational Preference *USE Occupational Preference*
Welsh Figure **Preference** Test
Preferences
Aesthetic **Preferences**
Brand **Preferences**
Food **Preferences**
Preferred Rewards
Least **Preferred** Coworker Scale
Prefrontal Cortex
Preganglionic Autonomic Fibers
USE Autonomic Ganglia
Pregnancy
Adolescent **Pregnancy**
False Pregnancy *USE Pseudocyesis*
Teenage Pregnancy *USE Adolescent Pregnancy*
Prejudice
Religious **Prejudices**
Preliminary Scholastic Aptitude Test
USE Coll Ent Exam Bd Scholastic Apt
Test
Premarital Counseling
Premarital Intercourse
Premature Birth
Premature Ejaculation
Premenstrual Syndrome
USE Premenstrual Tension
Premenstrual Tension
Premorbidity
Prenatal Care
Prenatal Development
Prenatal Developmental Stages
Prenatal Diagnosis
Prenatal Exposure
Preoptic Area
Preschool Age Children
Preschool Education
Preschool Students
Preschool Teachers
Wechsler **Preschool** Primary Scale
Prescribing (Drugs)
Prescription Drugs
Symptom Prescription *USE Paradoxical Techniques*
Presenile Dementia
Stereoscopic **Presentation**
Stimulus **Presentation** Methods
Tachistoscopic **Presentation**
Preservice Teachers
Pressoreceptors *USE Baroreceptors*
Pressors (Drugs)
USE Vasoconstrictor Drugs
Pressure Sensation
Barometric Pressure *USE Atmospheric Conditions*
Blood **Pressure**
Blood **Pressure** Disorders
Diastolic **Pressure**
Peer **Pressure**
Sound Pressure Level *USE Loudness*
Systolic **Pressure**
Prestige (Occupational)
USE Occupational Status
Pretesting
Pretraining (Therapy)
USE Client Education
Prevention
Accident **Prevention**
AIDS **Prevention**
Crime **Prevention**
Drug Abuse **Prevention**
Fire **Prevention**

Primary Mental Health **Prevention**
Relapse **Prevention**
Substance Abuse Prevention *USE Drug Abuse Prevention*
Suicide **Prevention**
Suicide **Prevention** Centers
Preventive Medicine
Price *USE Costs and Cost Analysis*
Pride
Priests
Primacy Effect
Primal Therapy
Primary Health Care
Primary Mental Health Prevention
Primary Reinforcement
Primary School Students
Primary Schools *USE Elementary Schools*
Wechsler Preschool **Primary** Scale
Primates (Nonhuman)
Primidone
Priming
Semantic **Priming**
School **Principals**
Printed Communications Media
Printing (Handwriting)
Prismatic Stimulation
Prison Personnel
Inmates (Prison) *USE Prisoners*
Prisoners
Prisoners Dilemma Game
Prisoners of War
Prisons
Privacy
Private Practice
Private School Education
Private Sector
Privileged Communication
Proactive Inhibition
Probability
Probability Judgment
Probability Learning
Response **Probability**
Statistical **Probability**
Probation
Probation Officers
Probenecid
Problem Drinking *USE Alcohol Abuse*
Problem Solving
Anagram **Problem** Solving
Group **Problem** Solving
Mooney **Problem** Check List
Behavior **Problems**
Social Problems *USE Social Issues*
Procaine
Conference Proceedings
USE Professional Meetings and
Symposia
Process Psychosis
Process Schizophrenia
USE Process Psychosis AND
Schizophrenia
Classification (Cognitive **Process)**
Educational Process *USE Education*
Insight (Psychotherapeutic **Process)**
Associative **Processes**
Balance (Motor Processes) *USE Equilibrium*
Cognitive **Processes**
Employment Processes *USE Personnel Recruitment*
Human Information Processes *USE Cognitive Processes*
Intersensory **Processes**
Legal **Processes**
Legislative **Processes**
Motor **Processes**
Perceptual Motor **Processes**
Personality **Processes**
Political **Processes**
Psychomotor Processes
USE Perceptual Motor Processes
Psychotherapeutic **Processes**

Sensorimotor **Processes**
    USE Perceptual Motor Processes
Social **Processes**
Therapeutic **Processes**
Automated Information **Processing**
Data **Processing**
Speech **Processing** (Mechanical)
Word **Processing**
Prochlorperazine
Procrastination
Pearson **Prod** Moment Correl Coeff
    USE Statistical Correlation
Employee **Productivity**
Profanity
Professional Certification
Professional Client Sexual Relations
Professional Communication
    USE Scientific Communication
Professional Consultation
Professional Criticism
Professional Criticism Reply
Professional Development
Professional Ethics
Professional Examinations
Professional Fees
Professional Identity
Professional Liability
Professional Licensing
Professional Meetings and Symposia
Professional Newsletters
    USE Scientific Communication
Professional Organizations
Professional Orientation
    USE Theoretical Orientation
Professional Personnel
Professional Referral
Professional Specialization
Professional Standards
Professional Supervision
Assistance Seeking (Professional) *USE Health Care Utilization*
Communication (Professional)
    USE Scientific Communication
Identity (Professional) *USE Professional Identity*
Specialization (Professional)
    USE Professional Specialization
Health Care Professionals *USE Health Personnel*
Impaired **Professionals**
Professors *USE College Teachers*
Language **Proficiency**
Limited English Proficiency *USE Language Proficiency*
Profiles (Measurement)
Profoundly Mentally Retarded
Progestational Hormones
Progesterone
Progestins *USE Progestational Hormones*
Prognosis
Program Development
Program Evaluation
Program Planning
    USE Program Development
Educational **Program** Accreditation
Educational **Program** Evaluation
Educational **Program** Planning
Mental Health **Program** Evaluation
Programed Instruction
Programed Textbooks
Programing (Computer)
    USE Computer Programing
Computer **Programing**
Computer **Programing** Languages
Neurolinguistic **Programing**
Accreditation (Educational Programs)
    USE Educational Program Accreditation
Computer Programs *USE Computer Software*
Educational **Programs**
Employee Assistance **Programs**
Government **Programs**
Home Visiting **Programs**
Hospital **Programs**

Immersion Programs
    USE Foreign Language Education
Independent Living **Programs**
Mental Health **Programs**
Psychiatric Hospital **Programs**
Social **Programs**
Token Economy **Programs**
Work Study Programs *USE Educational Programs*
Progressive Relaxation Therapy
Raven **Progressive** Matrices
Raven Coloured **Progressive** Matrices
Project Follow Through
Project Head Start
Projection (Defense Mechanism)
Projective Identification
Projective Personality Measures
Projective Techniques
Projective Testing Technique
Prolactin
Proline
Prolixin *USE Fluphenazine*
Promazine
Promethazine
Promiscuity
Health **Promotion**
Job Promotion *USE Personnel Promotion*
Personnel **Promotion**
Coronary **Prone** Behavior
Accident **Proneness**
Pronouns
Pronunciation
Proofreading
Propaganda
Skin Electrical **Properties**
Property *USE Ownership*
Propranolol
Proprioceptors
Prose
Prosencephalon *USE Forebrain*
Proserine *USE Neostigmine*
Prosocial Behavior
Prosody
Prosopagnosia
Prostaglandins
Prostate
Prostheses
Prostitution
Consumer **Protection**
Protein Deficiency Disorders
Protein Metabolism
Protein Sensitization
    USE Anaphylactic Shock
Sensitization (Protein) *USE Anaphylactic Shock*
Proteinases
Proteins
Blood **Proteins**
Protest (Student) *USE Student Activism*
Student Protest *USE Student Activism*
Protestantism
Protozoa
Prozac *USE Fluoxetine*
Pruritus
Pseudocyesis
Pseudodementia
Pseudopregnancy *USE Pseudocyesis*
Pseudopsychopathic Schizophrenia
    USE Schizophrenia
Psilocybin
Psychedelic Drugs
Psychedelic Experiences
Psychiatric Aides
Psychiatric Classifications (Taxon)
    USE Psychodiagnostic Typologies
Psychiatric Clinics
Psychiatric Disorders
    USE Mental Disorders
Psychiatric History *USE Patient History*
Psychiatric Hospital Admission
Psychiatric Hospital Discharge

Psychiatric Hospital Programs
Psychiatric Hospital Readmission
Psychiatric Hospital Staff
Psychiatric Hospitalization
Psychiatric Hospitals
Psychiatric Nurses
Psychiatric Patients
Psychiatric Report
   USE Psychological Report
Psychiatric Residency
   USE Medical Residency AND Psychiatric
   Training
Psychiatric Social Workers
Psychiatric Training
Psychiatric Units
Child Psychiatric Clinics
   USE Child Guidance Clinics
Commitment **(Psychiatric)**
Hospital Psychiatric Units *USE Psychiatric Units*
Outpatient Psychiatric Clinics *USE Psychiatric Clinics*
Psychiatrists
Psychiatry
Adolescent **Psychiatry**
Biological **Psychiatry**
Child **Psychiatry**
Community **Psychiatry**
Comparative Psychiatry *USE Transcultural Psychiatry*
Consultation Liaison **Psychiatry**
Cultural Psychiatry *USE Transcultural Psychiatry*
Forensic **Psychiatry**
Social **Psychiatry**
Transcultural **Psychiatry**
Psychoactive Drugs *USE Drugs*
Psychoanalysis
Psychoanalysts
Psychoanalytic Interpretation
Psychoanalytic Personality Factors
Psychoanalytic Theory
Psychoanalytic Therapy
   USE Psychoanalysis
Psychoanalytic Training
Freudian **Psychoanalytic** School
Psychobiology
Psychodiagnosis
Clinical Judgment (Psychodiagnosis) *USE Psychodiagnosis*
Psychodiagnostic Interview
Psychodiagnostic Typologies
Psychodrama
Psychodynamics
Woodcock Johnson **Psychoed** Battery
Psychoeducation
Psychogenesis
Psychogenic Pain
Psychohistory
Psychoimmunology
   USE Psychoneuroimmunology
Psychokinesis
Illinois Test **Psycholinguist** Abil
Psycholinguistics
Psychological Abuse
   USE Emotional Abuse
Psychological Adjustment
   USE Emotional Adjustment
Psychological Autopsy
Psychological Correlates
   USE Psychodynamics
Psychological Development
   USE Psychogenesis
Psychological Endurance
Psychological Interpretation
   USE Theoretical Interpretation
Psychological Reactance
Psychological Report
Psychological Screening Inventory
Psychological Stress
Psychological Terminology
Psychological Testing *USE Psychometrics*
California **Psychological** Inventory

Nomenclature (Psychological)
   USE Psychological Terminology
Psychologist Attitudes
Psychologists
Clinical **Psychologists**
Counseling **Psychologists**
Educational **Psychologists**
Experimental **Psychologists**
Industrial **Psychologists**
School **Psychologists**
Social **Psychologists**
Psychology
Psychology Education
Adolescent **Psychology**
Analytic Psychology *USE Jungian Psychology*
Applied **Psychology**
Child **Psychology**
Clinical **Psychology**
Clinical **Psychology** Grad Training
Clinical **Psychology** Internship
Cognitive **Psychology**
Community **Psychology**
Comparative **Psychology**
Consumer **Psychology**
Counseling **Psychology**
Depth **Psychology**
Developmental **Psychology**
Eclectic Psychology *USE Theoretical Orientation*
Ecological **Psychology**
Educational **Psychology**
Engineering **Psychology**
Environmental **Psychology**
Experimental **Psychology**
Forensic **Psychology**
Gestalt **Psychology**
Graduate **Psychology** Education
Health Care **Psychology**
History of **Psychology**
Humanistic **Psychology**
Individual **Psychology**
Industrial **Psychology**
Jungian **Psychology**
Legal Psychology *USE Forensic Psychology*
Mathematical **Psychology**
Medical **Psychology**
Military **Psychology**
Organizational Psychology *USE Industrial Psychology*
Physiological **Psychology**
School **Psychology**
Self **Psychology**
Social **Psychology**
Sport **Psychology**
Transpersonal **Psychology**
Psychometrics
Psychomotor Development
Psychomotor Processes
   USE Perceptual Motor Processes
Psychoneuroimmunology
Psychoneurosis *USE Neurosis*
Psychopath *USE Antisocial Personality*
Psychopathology
Psychopathy
Autistic Psychopathy *USE Aspergers Syndrome*
Psychopharmacology
Psychophysical Measurement
Psychophysics
Psychophysiologic Disorders
   USE Psychosomatic Disorders
Psychophysiology
Toxic **Psychoses**
Psychosexual Behavior
Psychosexual Development
Psychosis
Acute **Psychosis**
Affective **Psychosis**
Alcoholic **Psychosis**
Brief Reactive Psychosis *USE Acute Psychosis*
Childhood **Psychosis**
Chronic **Psychosis**

ROTATED ALPHABETICAL TERMS SECTION

Experimental **Psychosis**
Infantile Psychosis *USE Childhood Psychosis*
Involutional Paranoid **Psychosis**
Korsakoffs **Psychosis**
Manic Depressive Psychosis *USE Manic Depression*
Paranoia **(Psychosis)**
Postpartum Psychosis *USE Postpartum Depression*
Process **Psychosis**
Reactive **Psychosis**
Senile **Psychosis**
Symbiotic Infantile **Psychosis**
Traumatic Psychosis *USE Reactive Psychosis*
Psychosocial Development
Psychosocial Factors
Psychosocial Mental Retardation
Psychosocial Readjustment
Psychosocial Rehabilitation
Psychosocial Resocialization
    USE Psychosocial Readjustment
Psychosomatic Disorders
Psychosomatic Medicine
Psychosurgery
Psychotherapeutic Breakthrough
Psychotherapeutic Counseling
Psychotherapeutic Outcomes
Psychotherapeutic Processes
Psychotherapeutic Resistance
Psychotherapeutic Techniques
Psychotherapeutic Transference
Insight **(Psychotherapeutic** Process)
Psychotherapist Attitudes
Psychotherapist Trainees
    USE Therapist Trainees
Psychotherapists
Psychotherapy
Psychotherapy Training
Adlerian Psychotherapy
    USE Individual Psychotherapy
Adolescent **Psychotherapy**
Analytical **Psychotherapy**
Brief **Psychotherapy**
Child **Psychotherapy**
Eclectic **Psychotherapy**
Experiential **Psychotherapy**
Expressive **Psychotherapy**
Geriatric **Psychotherapy**
Group **Psychotherapy**
Individual **Psychotherapy**
Reconstructive Psychotherapy *USE Psychotherapy*
Short Term Psychotherapy *USE Brief Psychotherapy*
Supportive Psychotherapy *USE Psychotherapy*
Time Limited Psychotherapy *USE Brief Psychotherapy*
Psychotic Depressive Reaction
    USE Major Depression
Psychotic Episode (Acute)
    USE Acute Psychosis
Acute Psychotic Episode *USE Acute Psychosis*
Psychoticism
Psychotomimetic Drugs
Psychotropic Drugs *USE Drugs*
PTA *USE Parent School Relationship*
Puberty
Pubescence *USE Sexual Development*
Public Attitudes *USE Public Opinion*
Public Health
Public Health Service Nurses
Public Health Services
Public Opinion
Public Policy
    USE Government Policy Making
Public Relations
Public School Education
Public Sector
Public Speaking
Public Transportation
Public Welfare Services
    USE Community Welfare Services
Fear of Public Speaking *USE Speech Anxiety*
Retraction of **Publication**

Puerto Rican Americans *USE Hispanics*
Puerto Rico
Hair **Pulling**
Pulmonary Emphysema
Pulmonary Tuberculosis
Arterial **Pulse**
Punishment
Capital **Punishment**
Corporal Punishment *USE Punishment*
Pupil Dilation
Pupil (Eye)
Purdue Perceptual Motor Survey
Purkinje Cells
Puromycin
Rotary **Pursuit**
Putamen
Color **Pyramid** Test
Pyramidal Tracts
Pyramidotomy
Pyromania
Q Sort Testing Technique
Cochran **Q** Test
Quadriplegia
Quails
Quality Circles
    USE Participative Management
Quality Control
Quality of Care
Quality of Life
Quality of Work Life
Quartimax Rotation
Fund Interper Rela Orientat Beh **Ques**
Sixteen Personality Factors **Question**
Questioning
Childrens Personality **Questionnaire**
General Health **Questionnaire**
High Sch Personality **Questionnaire**
Questionnaires
Opinion Questionnaires *USE Attitude Measures*
Quinidine
Quinine
Quinpirole
Intelligence **Quotient**
Rabbis
Rabbits
Race and Ethnic Discrimination
Race (Anthropological)
Race Attitudes
    USE Racial and Ethnic Attitudes
Race Relations
    USE Racial and Ethnic Relations
Racial and Ethnic Attitudes
Racial and Ethnic Differences
Racial and Ethnic Relations
Racial Discrimination
    USE Race and Ethnic Discrimination
Racial Integration *USE Social Integration*
Racial Segregation (Schools)
    USE School Integration
Segregation (Racial) *USE Social Integration*
Racism
Radial Nerve *USE Spinal Nerves*
Radiation
Radiation Therapy
Radical Movements
Political **Radicalism**
Radio
Radiography *USE Roentgenography*
Radiology
Rage *USE Anger*
Railroad Trains
Consciousness **Raising** Groups
Random Sampling
Wide **Range** Achievement Test
Rank Difference Correlation
Rank Order Correlation
Wilcoxon Sign **Rank** Test
Rape
Acquaintance **Rape**

301

Date Rape *USE Acquaintance Rape*
Raphe Nuclei
Rapid Eye Movement
Rapid Eye Movement Dreams
   USE REM Dreams
Rapid Eye Movement Sleep
   USE REM Sleep
Rapport *USE Interpersonal Interaction*
Rasch Model *USE Item Response Theory*
Rat Learning
Birth **Rate**
Cardiac Rate *USE Heart Rate*
Death Rate *USE Mortality Rate*
Heart **Rate**
Heart **Rate** Affecting Drugs
Learning **Rate**
Mortality **Rate**
Response Rate *USE Response Frequency*
Speech **Rate**
Metabolic **Rates**
Rating
Rating Scales
Kupfer Detre Self **Rating** Scale
Zungs Self **Rating** Depression Scale
Ratio Reinforcement
   USE Fixed Ratio Reinforcement OR
      Variable Ratio Reinforcement
Fixed **Ratio** Reinforcement
Variable **Ratio** Reinforcement
Ratiocination *USE Logical Thinking*
Rational Emotive Therapy
Rationalization
Rats
Norway **Rats**
Rauwolfia
Raven Coloured Progressive Matrices
Raven Progressive Matrices
Cathode Ray Tubes *USE Video Display Units*
X Ray Diagnosis *USE Roentgenography*
X Ray Therapy *USE Radiation Therapy*
Raynauds Disease
   USE Cardiovascular Disorders
RDC *USE Research Diagnostic Criteria*
Psychological **Reactance**
Reaction Formation
Reaction Time
Fugue **Reaction**
Neurotic Depressive **Reaction**
Psychotic Depressive Reaction *USE Major Depression*
Anniversary Reactions *USE Anniversary Events*
Crisis (Reactions to) *USE Stress Reactions*
Drug Adverse Reactions *USE Side Effects (Drug)*
Stranger **Reactions**
Stress **Reactions**
Reactive Attachment Disorder
   USE Failure to Thrive
Reactive Depression
Reactive Psychosis
Reactive Schizophrenia
   USE Reactive Psychosis AND
      Schizophrenia
Brief Reactive Psychosis *USE Acute Psychosis*
Cardiovascular **Reactivity**
Readability
Readaptation *USE Adaptation*
Basal Readers *USE Reading Materials*
Metropolitan **Readiness** Tests
Reading **Readiness**
School **Readiness**
Reading
Reading Ability
Reading Achievement
Reading Comprehension
Reading Disabilities
Reading Education
Reading Materials
Reading Measures
Reading Readiness
Reading Skills

Reading Speed
Gates MacGinitie **Reading** Tests
Oral **Reading**
Remedial **Reading**
Silent **Reading**
Selected **Readings**
Psychosocial **Readjustment**
Readmission (Hospital)
   USE Hospital Admission
Facility Readmission *USE Facility Admission*
Psychiatric Hospital **Readmission**
Realism (Philosophy)
Reality
Reality Testing
Reality Therapy
Self Realization *USE Self Actualization*
Home **Reared** Mentally Retarded
Animal **Rearing**
Reasoning
Inductive Deductive **Reasoning**
Syllogistic Reasoning
   USE Inductive Deductive Reasoning
Sexual Reassignment *USE Sex Change*
Authoritarianism **Rebellion** Scale
Rebuttal *USE Professional Criticism Reply*
Recall (Learning)
Cued **Recall**
Dream **Recall**
Free **Recall**
Serial **Recall**
Recency Effect
Receptive Fields
Cutaneous **Receptive** Fields
Visual **Receptive** Fields
Animal Sexual **Receptivity**
Receptor Binding
Neural **Receptors**
Pain Receptors *USE Nociceptors*
Genetic **Recessiveness**
Recidivism
Reciprocal Inhibition Therapy
Reciprocity
Recognition (Learning)
Automated Speech **Recognition**
Automatic Speaker Recognition
   USE Automated Speech Recognition
Face Recognition *USE Face Perception*
Kinship **Recognition**
Species **Recognition**
Word **Recognition**
Reconstruction (Learning)
Reconstructive Psychotherapy
   USE Psychotherapy
Graduate **Record** Examination
Kuder Preference **Record**
Tape **Recorders**
Videotape **Recorders**
Academic Records *USE Student Records*
Medical **Records** Keeping
Student **Records**
Recovery (Disorders)
Spontaneous **Recovery** (Learning)
Recreation
Recreation Areas
Recreation Therapy
Summer Camps **(Recreation)**
Recreational Day Camps
   USE Summer Camps (Recreation)
Childrens **Recreational** Games
Parks (Recreational) *USE Recreation Areas*
Military **Recruitment**
Personnel **Recruitment**
Teacher **Recruitment**
Recurrent Depression
Red Blood Cells *USE Erythrocytes*
Red Nucleus *USE Mesencephalon*
Anxiety Reducing Drugs *USE Tranquilizing Drugs*
Reductionism
Reemployment

Reentry Students
Job Reentry *USE Reemployment*
Reference Groups
Self **Reference**
Criterion **Referenced** Tests
Objective Referenced Tests
    USE Criterion Referenced Tests
Referral (Self) *USE Self Referral*
Professional **Referral**
Self **Referral**
Court **Referrals**
Reflectiveness *USE Impulsiveness*
Achilles Tendon **Reflex**
Acoustic **Reflex**
Babinski **Reflex**
Blink Reflex *USE Eyeblink Reflex*
Conditioned Reflex *USE Conditioned Responses*
Eyeblink **Reflex**
Flexion **Reflex**
Hoffmanns **Reflex**
Intra Aural Muscle Reflex *USE Acoustic Reflex*
Orienting **Reflex**
Stapedius Reflex *USE Acoustic Reflex*
Startle **Reflex**
Unconditioned Reflex *USE Unconditioned Responses*
Reflexes
Reformatories
Refraction Errors
Light **Refraction**
Reframing *USE Paradoxical Techniques*
Refugees
Political Refugees *USE Refugees*
Refusal (Treatment)
    USE Treatment Refusal
School **Refusal**
Treatment **Refusal**
Neural Regeneration *USE Neural Development*
Medical Regimen Compliance
    USE Treatment Compliance
Arctic **Regions**
Geographic Regions *USE Geography*
Regression Analysis
    USE Statistical Regression
Regression (Defense Mechanism)
Age **Regression** (Hypnotic)
Linear **Regression**
Multiple **Regression**
Nonlinear **Regression**
Statistical **Regression**
Rehabilitation
Rehabilitation Centers
Rehabilitation Counseling
Rehabilitation Counselors
Alcohol **Rehabilitation**
Cognitive **Rehabilitation**
Drug **Rehabilitation**
Psychosocial **Rehabilitation**
Vocational **Rehabilitation**
Rehearsal *USE Practice*
Reinforcement
Reinforcement Amounts
Reinforcement Delay
Reinforcement Schedules
Reinforcement (Vicarious)
    USE Vicarious Experiences
Concurrent **Reinforcement** Schedules
Continuous Reinforcement
    USE Reinforcement Schedules
Differential **Reinforcement**
Fixed Interval **Reinforcement**
Fixed Ratio **Reinforcement**
Intermittent Reinforcement
    USE Reinforcement Schedules
Interval Reinforcement
    USE Fixed Interval Reinforcement OR
    Variable Interval Reinforcement
Negative **Reinforcement**
Noncontingent **Reinforcement**
Nonverbal **Reinforcement**

Partial Reinforcement
    USE Reinforcement Schedules
Positive **Reinforcement**
Primary **Reinforcement**
Ratio Reinforcement
    USE Fixed Ratio Reinforcement OR
    Variable Ratio Reinforcement
Secondary **Reinforcement**
Self **Reinforcement**
Social **Reinforcement**
Token Reinforcement
    USE Secondary Reinforcement
Variable Interval **Reinforcement**
Variable Ratio **Reinforcement**
Verbal **Reinforcement**
Vicarious Reinforcement *USE Vicarious Experiences*
Reinnervation *USE Neural Development*
Halstead **Reitan** Neuropsych Battery
Rejection (Social) *USE Social Acceptance*
Social Rejection *USE Social Acceptance*
Relapse (Disorders)
Relapse Prevention
Diagnosis **Related** Groups
Work **Related** Illnesses
Family **Relations**
Father Child **Relations**
Fund Interper **Rela** Orientat Beh Ques
Human **Relations** Training
Intergenerational **Relations**
International **Relations**
Labor Management **Relations**
Male Female **Relations**
Marital **Relations**
Mother Child **Relations**
Object **Relations**
Parent Child **Relations**
Patient Therapist Sexual Relations
    USE Professional Client Sexual Relations
Peer **Relations**
Professional Client Sexual **Relations**
Public **Relations**
Race Relations *USE Racial and Ethnic Relations*
Racial and Ethnic **Relations**
Sibling **Relations**
Therapist Patient Sexual Relations
    USE Professional Client Sexual Relations
Relationship Therapy
Barrett Lennard **Relationship** Invent
Parent School **Relationship**
Relaxation
Relaxation Therapy
Muscle **Relaxation**
Muscle Relaxation Therapy
    USE Relaxation Therapy
Progressive **Relaxation** Therapy
Muscle **Relaxing** Drugs
Relearning
Institutional **Release**
ACTH Releasing Factor
    USE Corticotropin Releasing Factor
Corticotropin **Releasing** Factor
Interobserver Reliability *USE Interrater Reliability*
Interrater **Reliability**
Statistical **Reliability**
Test **Reliability**
Pain Relieving Drugs *USE Analgesic Drugs*
Religion
Confession **(Religion)**
Ministers **(Religion)**
Rites (Religion) *USE Religious Practices*
Rituals (Religion) *USE Religious Practices*
Religiosity
Religious Affiliation
Religious Beliefs
Religious Buildings
Religious Education
Religious Literature
Religious Occupations
    USE Religious Personnel

Religious Organizations
Religious Personnel
Religious Practices
Religious Prejudices
Lay **Religious** Personnel
REM *USE Rapid Eye Movement*
REM Dream Deprivation
REM Dreams
REM Sleep
Remarriage
Remedial Education
Remedial Reading
Remembering *USE Retention*
Reminiscence
Remission (Disorders)
Spontaneous **Remission**
Symptom **Remission**
Remote Associates Test
Repairmen *USE Technical Service Personnel*
Repeated Measures
Bannister **Repertory** Grid
Compulsive **Repetition**
Estrogen Replacement Therapy
    USE Hormone Therapy
Experimental **Replication**
Professional Criticism **Reply**
Annual **Report**
Case **Report**
Psychiatric Report *USE Psychological Report*
Psychological **Report**
Self **Report**
Repression (Defense Mechanism)
Repression Sensitization
Repression Sensitization Scale
Sexual **Reproduction**
Reproductive Technology
Reptiles
Dominican **Republic**
East German Democratic Republic *USE East Germany*
Peoples **Republic** of China
United Arab Republic *USE Egypt*
West German Federal Republic *USE West Germany*
Republican Party *USE Political Parties*
Union of Soviet Socialist **Republics**
Research *USE Experimentation*
Research Design
    USE Experimental Design
Research Diagnostic Criteria
Research Dropouts
    USE Experimental Attrition
Research Methods *USE Methodology*
Research Subjects
    USE Experimental Subjects
Consumer **Research**
Cross Disciplinary Research *USE Interdisciplinary Research*
Interdisciplinary **Research**
Multidisciplinary Research *USE Interdisciplinary Research*
Parent Attitude **Research** Instrument
Family **Resemblance**
Resentment *USE Hostility*
Reserpine
Residence Halls *USE Dormitories*
Medical **Residency**
Psychiatric Residency
    USE Medical Residency AND Psychiatric
      Training
Residential Care Attendants
    USE Attendants (Institutions)
Residential Care Institutions
Schizophrenia (Residual Type) *USE Schizophrenia*
Basal Skin **Resistance**
Psychotherapeutic **Resistance**
Skin **Resistance**
Treatment **Resistant** Depression
Treatment **Resistant** Disorders
Tricyclic Resistant Depression
    USE Treatment Resistant Depression
Psychosocial Resocialization
    USE Psychosocial Readjustment

Conflict **Resolution**
Resonance *USE Vibration*
Magnetic **Resonance** Imaging
Resource Teachers
Human Resources *USE Personnel Management*
Self Respect *USE Self Esteem*
Respiration
Respiration Stimulating Drugs
Artificial **Respiration**
Respiratory Distress
Respiratory System
Respiratory Tract Disorders
Respite Care
Respondent Conditioning
    USE Classical Conditioning
Response Amplitude
Response Bias
Response Consistency
    USE Response Variability
Response Duration
Response Frequency
Response Generalization
Response Lag *USE Reaction Time*
Response Latency
Response Parameters
Response Probability
Response Rate *USE Response Frequency*
Response Set
Response Speed *USE Reaction Time*
Response Time *USE Reaction Time*
Response Variability
Electrodermal Response *USE Galvanic Skin Response*
Galvanic Skin **Response**
Item **Response** Theory
Oculomotor Response *USE Eye Movements*
RT (Response) *USE Reaction Time*
Responses
Alarm **Responses**
Conditioned **Responses**
Conditioned Emotional **Responses**
Emotional **Responses**
Mediated **Responses**
Orienting **Responses**
Unconditioned **Responses**
Responsibility
Criminal **Responsibility**
Work **Rest** Cycles
Restlessness
Dietary **Restraint**
Emotional Restraint *USE Emotional Control*
Physical **Restraint**
Restricted Environmental Stimulation
    USE Stimulus Deprivation
Cognitive **Restructuring**
Knowledge of **Results**
Retail Stores *USE Retailing*
Retailing
Retaliation
Borderline Mental **Retardation**
Cultural Familial Mental Retardation
    USE Psychosocial Mental Retardation
Mental **Retardation**
Mental **Retardation** (Attit Toward)
Psychosocial Mental **Retardation**
Retarded Speech Development
Borderline Mentally Retarded *USE Slow Learners*
Educable Mentally **Retarded**
Home Reared Mentally **Retarded**
Institutionalized Mentally **Retarded**
Mentally **Retarded**
Mildly Mentally Retarded
    USE Educable Mentally Retarded
Moderately Mentally Retarded
    USE Trainable Mentally Retarded
Profoundly Mentally **Retarded**
Severely Mentally **Retarded**
Trainable Mentally **Retarded**
Retention
Retention Measures

Retention (School) *USE School Retention*
Benton Revised Visual **Retention** Test
School **Retention**
Reticular Formation
Retina
Ganglion Cells **(Retina)**
Retinal Eccentricity
Retinal Image
Retinal Vessels *USE Arteries (Anatomy)*
Retirement
Retraction of Publication
Automated Information **Retrieval**
Retroactive Inhibition
Rett Syndrome
Return to Home *USE Empty Nest*
Return to Work *USE Reemployment*
Revenge *USE Retaliation*
Directed **Reverie** Therapy
Reversal Shift Learning
Life **Review**
Literature **Review**
Peer Review *USE Peer Evaluation*
Benton **Revised** Visual Retention Test
Political **Revolution**
Reward Allocation
Rewards
External **Rewards**
Extrinsic Rewards *USE External Rewards*
Internal **Rewards**
Intrinsic Rewards *USE Internal Rewards*
Monetary **Rewards**
Preferred **Rewards**
Rh Incompatibility
Rheoencephalography
Rhetoric
Rheumatic Fever
Rheumatism *USE Arthritis*
Rheumatoid Arthritis
Spearman Rho *USE Rank Difference Correlation*
Rhodopsin
Rhythm
Rhythm Method
Alpha **Rhythm**
Delta **Rhythm**
Speech **Rhythm**
Theta **Rhythm**
Animal Biological **Rhythms**
Animal Circadian **Rhythms**
Biological **Rhythms**
Circadian Rhythms (Human)
    USE Human Biological Rhythms
Daily Biological Rhythms (Animal)
    USE Animal Circadian Rhythms
Human Biological **Rhythms**
Ribonucleic Acid
RNA (Ribonucleic Acid) *USE Ribonucleic Acid*
Costa **Rica**
Puerto **Rican** Americans *USE Hispanics*
Puerto **Rico**
Right Brain
Civil **Rights**
Civil **Rights** Movement
Client **Rights**
Human **Rights**
Patient Rights *USE Client Rights*
Visitation Rights *USE Child Visitation*
Rigidity (Muscles)
    USE Muscle Contractions
Rigidity (Personality)
Riots
Risk Analysis
Risk Taking
At **Risk** Populations
High Risk Populations *USE At Risk Populations*
Risky Shift *USE Choice Shift*
Ritalin *USE Methylphenidate*
Rites (Nonreligious)
Rites of Passage
Rites (Religion) *USE Religious Practices*

Birth **Rites**
Death **Rites**
Initiation **Rites**
Marriage **Rites**
Rituals (Nonreligious)
    USE Rites (Nonreligious)
Rituals (Religion) *USE Religious Practices*
Rivalry
RNA (Ribonucleic Acid)
    USE Ribonucleic Acid
Robbery *USE Theft*
Robins
Robotics
Rock Music
Body **Rocking**
Rod and Frame Test
Rodents
Rods (Eye)
Roentgenography
Rogers (Carl)
Rokeach Dogmatism Scale
Role Conflicts
Role Expectations
Role Models
Role Perception
Role Playing
Role Satisfaction
Role Strain *USE Role Conflicts*
Role Taking
Bem Sex **Role** Inventory
Counselor **Role**
Parental **Role**
Sex **Role** Attitudes
Therapist **Role**
Roles
Sex **Roles**
Roman Catholicism
Romania
Roommates
Dorsal **Roots**
Ventral **Roots**
Rorschach Test
Rosenzweig Picture Frustration Study
Rotary Pursuit
Body Rotation *USE Rotational Behavior*
Equimax **Rotation**
Mental **Rotation**
Oblique **Rotation**
Orthogonal **Rotation**
Quartimax **Rotation**
Statistical **Rotation**
Varimax **Rotation**
Rotational Behavior
ROTC Students
Rote Learning
Rotter Incomplete Sentences Blank
Rotter Intern Extern Locus Cont Scal
RT (Response) *USE Reaction Time*
Rubella
Rule Learning
    USE Cognitive Hypothesis Testing
Rumors *USE Gossip*
Runaway Behavior
Running
Runways (Maze) *USE Maze Pathways*
Rural Environments
Rwanda
Saccadic Eye Movements
    USE Eye Movements
Saccharin
Tay Sachs Disease
    USE Amaurotic Familial Idiocy
SAD *USE Seasonal Affective Disorder*
Sadism
Sexual **Sadism**
Sadness
Sadomasochism
Sadomasochistic Personality
Safety

Safety Belts	**Scaling** (Testing)
Safety Devices	Multidimensional **Scaling**
Automobile **Safety** *USE Highway Safety*	**Scalp** (Anatomy)
Aviation **Safety**	Scalp Disorders *USE Skin Disorders*
Driver **Safety** *USE Highway Safety*	CAT Scan *USE Tomography*
Highway **Safety**	**Scandinavia**
Industrial **Safety** *USE Occupational Safety*	Animal **Scent** Marking
Occupational **Safety**	Diagnostic Interview **Schedule**
Water **Safety**	Edwards Personal Preference **Schedule**
Saint Lucia	Fear Survey **Schedule**
Saint Vincent	Concurrent Reinforcement **Schedules**
Salamanders	Learning **Schedules**
Salaries	Reinforcement **Schedules**
Sales Personnel	Work **Scheduling**
Stimulus **Salience**	Goldstein **Scheerer** Object Sort Test
Saliva	**Schema**
Salivary Glands	**Schizoaffective** Disorder
Salivation	**Schizoid** Personality
Salmon	**Schizophrenia**
Saltiness *USE Taste Perception*	Schizophrenia (Disorganized Type)
El **Salvador**	*USE Hebephrenic Schizophrenia*
American **Samoa**	Schizophrenia (Residual Type)
Western **Samoa**	*USE Schizophrenia*
Matching to **Sample**	Acute **Schizophrenia**
Statistical **Sample** Parameters	Catatonic **Schizophrenia**
Statistical **Samples**	Childhood **Schizophrenia**
Sampling (Experimental)	Chronic Schizophrenia *USE Schizophrenia*
Biased **Sampling**	Fragmentation **(Schizophrenia)**
Random **Sampling**	Hebephrenic **Schizophrenia**
Sanatoriums	Paranoid **Schizophrenia**
Sarcomas *USE Neoplasms*	Process Schizophrenia
SAT	*USE Process Psychosis AND*
USE Coll Ent Exam Bd Scholastic Apt	*Schizophrenia*
Test	Pseudopsychopathic Schizophrenia *USE Schizophrenia*
Satiation	Reactive Schizophrenia
Satisfaction	*USE Reactive Psychosis AND*
Client **Satisfaction**	*Schizophrenia*
Consumer **Satisfaction**	Simple Schizophrenia *USE Schizophrenia*
Job **Satisfaction**	Undifferentiated **Schizophrenia**
Life **Satisfaction**	**Schizophreniform** Disorder
Marital **Satisfaction**	**Schizophrenogenic** Family
Need **Satisfaction**	**Schizophrenogenic** Mothers
Patient Satisfaction *USE Client Satisfaction*	**Schizotypal** Personality
Role **Satisfaction**	Scholarships
Sexual **Satisfaction**	*USE Educational Financial Assistance*
Saudi Arabia	Scholastic Achievement
Idiot **Savants**	*USE Academic Achievement*
Authoritarianism Rebellion **Scale**	Scholastic Aptitude
Barron Welsh Art **Scale**	*USE Academic Aptitude*
California F **Scale**	Scholastic Aptitude Test
Cattell Infant Intelligence Scale *USE Infant Intelligence Scale*	*USE Coll Ent Exam Bd Scholastic Apt*
Childrens Manifest Anxiety **Scale**	*Test*
Columbia Mental Maturity **Scale**	Coll Ent Exam Bd **Scholastic** Apt Test
Edwards Social Desirability **Scale**	Preliminary Scholastic Aptitude Test
Infant Intelligence **Scale**	*USE Coll Ent Exam Bd Scholastic Apt*
Kupfer Detre Self Rating **Scale**	*Test*
Least Preferred Coworker **Scale**	School Accreditation
Leiter Adult Intelligence **Scale**	*USE Educational Program Accreditation*
Marlowe Crowne Soc Desirabil **Scale**	School Achievement
Repression Sensitization **Scale**	*USE Academic Achievement*
Rokeach Dogmatism **Scale**	**School** Adjustment
Rotter Intern Extern Locus Cont **Scal**	School Administration
Sensation Seeking **Scale**	*USE Educational Administration*
Stanford Binet Intelligence **Scale**	**School** Administrators
Taylor Manifest Anxiety **Scale**	**School** Age Children
Temporal Spatial Concept **Scale**	**School** and College Ability Test
Tennessee Self Concept **Scale**	**School** Attendance
Vineland Social Maturity **Scale**	**School** Club Membership
Wechsler Adult Intelligence **Scale**	**School** Counseling
Wechsler Bellevue Intelligence **Scale**	**School** Counselors
Wechsler Intelligence **Scale** Children	**School** Dropouts
Wechsler Memory **Scale**	**School** Enrollment
Wechsler Preschool Primary **Scale**	**School** Environment
White Betz A B **Scale**	**School** Expulsion
Wilson Patterson Conservatism **Scale**	**School** Facilities
Zungs Self Rating Depression **Scale**	School Federal Aid
Bayley **Scales** of Infant Development	*USE Educational Financial Assistance*
Likert **Scales**	**School** Graduation
Rating **Scales**	School Guidance *USE School Counseling*

School Integration
School Learning
School Leavers
School Libraries
School Nurses
School Organization *USE Educational Administration*
School Phobia
School Principals
School Psychologists
School Psychology
School Readiness
School Refusal
School Retention
School Superintendents
School Suspension
School to Work Transition
School Truancy
Elementary School Students
Elementary School Teachers
Freudian Psychoanalytic School
Graduation (School) *USE School Graduation*
High School Diplomas *USE Educational Degrees*
High School Equivalency *USE Adult Education*
High School Graduates
High Sch Personality Questionnaire
High School Students
High School Teachers
Intermediate School Students
Junior High School Students
Junior High School Teachers
Middle School Education
Middle School Students
NeoFreudian School *USE Neopsychoanalytic School*
Neopsychoanalytic School
Nursery School Students
Parent School Relationship
Parochial School Education
   USE Private School Education
Primary School Students
Private School Education
Public School Education
Retention (School) *USE School Retention*
Vocational School Students
Home Schooling
Schools
Alternative Schools *USE Nontraditional Education*
Boarding Schools
Elementary Schools
Graduate Schools
Grammar Schools *USE Elementary Schools*
High Schools
Institutional Schools
Junior High Schools
Magnet Schools *USE Nontraditional Education*
Military Schools
Nongraded Schools
Nursery Schools
Primary Schools *USE Elementary Schools*
Racial Segregation (Schools) *USE School Integration*
Technical Schools
Vocational Schools *USE Technical Schools*
Sciatic Nerve *USE Spinal Nerves*
Science Education
Medicine (Science of) *USE Medical Sciences*
Sciences
Behavioral Sciences *USE Social Sciences*
Medical Sciences
Paramedical Sciences
Social Sciences
Scientific Communication
Scientific Methods *USE Experimental Methods*
Scientists
Sclera *USE Eye (Anatomy)*
Sclerosis (Nervous System)
Multiple Sclerosis
Scopolamine
Score Equating
Critical Scores *USE Cutting Scores*
Cutting Scores

Standard Scores
Test Scores
Z Scores *USE Standard Scores*
Scoring (Testing)
Scotland
Scotopic Stimulation
Scratching
Screening
Screening Tests
Drug Usage Screening
Health Screening *USE Physical Examination*
Job Applicant Screening
Psychological Screening Inventory
Scripts *USE Schema*
Sculpturing
Sea Gulls
Seals (Animal)
Job Search
Visual Search
Computer Searching
Online Searching *USE Computer Searching*
Seasonal Affective Disorder
Seasonal Variations
Seat Belts *USE Safety Belts*
Seclusion (Patient) *USE Patient Seclusion*
Patient Seclusion
Secobarbital
Seconal *USE Secobarbital*
Second Language Education
   USE Foreign Language Education
Secondary Education
Secondary Reinforcement
Secrecy
Secretarial Personnel
Clerical Secretarial Skills
Secretion (Gland)
Adrenal Gland Secretion
Endocrine Gland Secretion
Sectioning (Lesion) *USE Lesions*
Private Sector
Public Sector
Emotional Security
Job Security
Maximum Security Facilities
Social Security
Sedatives
Seduction
Seeing Eye Dogs *USE Mobility Aids*
Assistance Seeking (Professional)
   USE Health Care Utilization
Help Seeking Behavior
Information Seeking
Novelty Seeking *USE Sensation Seeking*
Sensation Seeking
Sensation Seeking Scale
Stimulation Seeking (Personality)
   USE Sensation Seeking
Segregation (Racial)
   USE Social Integration
Racial Segregation (Schools)
   USE School Integration
Seizures *USE Convulsions*
Audiogenic Seizures
Epileptic Seizures
Selected Readings
Selection Tests
Selection (Therapist)
   USE Therapist Selection
Animal Mate Selection
Employee Selection *USE Personnel Selection*
Habitat Selection *USE Territoriality*
Human Mate Selection
Job Selection *USE Occupational Choice*
Jury Selection
Mate Selection
   USE Animal Mate Selection OR Human
   Mate Selection
Personnel Selection
Therapist Selection

307

Toy **Selection**
Selective Attention
Selective Breeding
Self Acceptance *USE Self Perception*
Self Actualization
Self Analysis
Self Assessment *USE Self Evaluation*
Self Care Skills
Self Concept
Self Confidence
Self Congruence
Self Consciousness *USE Self Perception*
Self Control
Self Defeating Behavior
Self Defense
Self Destructive Behavior
Self Determination
Self Directed Learning
   USE Individualized Instruction
Self Disclosure
Self Efficacy
Self Employment
Self Esteem
Self Evaluation
Self Examination (Medical)
Self Handicapping Strategy
Self Help Techniques
Self Hypnosis *USE Autohypnosis*
Self Image *USE Self Concept*
Self Instruction
   USE Individualized Instruction
Self Instructional Training
Self Management
Self Medication
Self Monitoring
Self Monitoring (Personality)
Self Mutilation
Self Observation *USE Self Monitoring*
Self Perception
Self Psychology
Self Realization *USE Self Actualization*
Self Reference
Self Referral
Self Reinforcement
Self Report
Self Respect *USE Self Esteem*
Self Stimulation
Self Talk
Brain **Self** Stimulation
Child **Self** Care
Confidence (Self) *USE Self Confidence*
Ideal Self *USE Self Concept*
Intracranial Self Stimulation
   USE Brain Self Stimulation
Kupfer Detre **Self** Rating Scale
Referral (Self) *USE Self Referral*
Tennessee **Self** Concept Scale
Zungs **Self** Rating Depression Scale
Selfishness
Semantic Differential
Semantic Generalization
Semantic Memory
Semantic Priming
Semantics
Semicircular Canals
Seminarians
Seminaries
Semiotics
Senegal
Senescence *USE Aged*
Senile Dementia
Senile Psychosis
Senior Citizens *USE Aged*
Sensation *USE Perception*
Sensation Seeking
Sensation Seeking Scale
Pressure **Sensation**
Sense Organ Disorders

Sense Organs
Cutaneous **Sense**
Vomeronasal **Sense**
Sensitivity (Personality)
Sensitivity Training
Cultural **Sensitivity**
Drug **Sensitivity**
Ethnic Sensitivity *USE Cultural Sensitivity*
Spectral Sensitivity *USE Color Perception*
Sensitization (Protein)
   USE Anaphylactic Shock
Covert **Sensitization**
Protein Sensitization *USE Anaphylactic Shock*
Repression **Sensitization**
Repression **Sensitization** Scale
Sensorially Handicapped
Sensorimotor Development
   USE Perceptual Motor Development
Sensorimotor Measures
Sensorimotor Processes
   USE Perceptual Motor Processes
Sensorineural Hearing Loss
   USE Hearing Disorders
Sensory Adaptation
Sensory Deprivation
Sensory Feedback
Sensory Gating
Sensory Handicaps (Attit Toward)
Sensory Integration
Sensory Neglect
Sensory Neurons
Sensory Pathways
   USE Afferent Pathways
Sensory Preconditioning
   USE Preconditioning
Gating (Sensory) *USE Sensory Gating*
Sentence Completion Tests
Sentence Comprehension
Sentence Structure
Sentences
Rotter Incomplete **Sentences** Blank
Sentencing *USE Adjudication*
Separation Anxiety
Separation Individuation
Marital **Separation**
Septal Nuclei
Septum *USE Septal Nuclei*
Sequential Learning
Serial Anticipation (Learning)
Serial Learning
Serial Position Effect
Serial Recall
Time **Series**
Seriousness
Serotonin
Serotonin Agonists
Serotonin Antagonists
Serotonin Metabolites
Serotonin Precursors
Serpasil *USE Reserpine*
Serum Albumin
Blood **Serum**
Civil Servants *USE Government Personnel*
Service Personnel
Domestic **Service** Personnel
Fee for **Service**
Health Service Utilization
   USE Health Care Utilization
Public Health **Service** Nurses
Technical **Service** Personnel
Volunteers in **Service** to America
Servicemen *USE Military Personnel*
Community **Services**
Community Mental Health **Services**
Community Welfare **Services**
Crisis Intervention **Services**
Emergency **Services**
Health Care **Services**
Hot Line **Services**

Information **Services**
Mental Health **Services**
Public Health **Services**
Public Welfare Services
    USE Community Welfare Services
Social **Services**
Student Personnel **Services**
Welfare **Services** (Government)
Fuzzy **Set** Theory
Response **Set**
Severely Mentally Retarded
Severity (Disorders)
Sex
Sex Change
Sex Chromosome Disorders
Sex Chromosomes
Sex Differentiation Disorders
    USE Genital Disorders
Sex Discrimination
Sex Drive
Sex Education
Sex Hormones
Sex Linked Developmental Differences
Sex Linked Hereditary Disorders
Sex Offenses
Sex Role Attitudes
Sex Roles
Sex Therapy
Animal **Sex** Differences
Bem **Sex** Role Inventory
Human **Sex** Differences
Sterilization **(Sex)**
Sexism
Sexual Abstinence
Sexual Abuse
Sexual Arousal
Sexual Attitudes
Sexual Behavior
    USE Psychosexual Behavior
Sexual Boundary Violations
    USE Professional Client Sexual Relations
Sexual Delinquency *USE Promiscuity*
Sexual Development
Sexual Deviations
Sexual Disorders (Physiological)
    USE Genital Disorders
Sexual Function Disturbances
Sexual Harassment
Sexual Intercourse (Human)
Sexual Masochism
Sexual Reassignment *USE Sex Change*
Sexual Reproduction
Sexual Sadism
Sexual Satisfaction
Animal **Sexual** Behavior
Animal **Sexual** Receptivity
Climax (Sexual) *USE Orgasm*
Endocrine **Sexual** Disorders
Patient Therapist Sexual Relations
    USE Professional Client Sexual Relations
Professional Client **Sexual** Relations
Therapist Patient Sexual Relations
    USE Professional Client Sexual Relations
Sexuality
Sexually Transmitted Diseases
    USE Venereal Diseases
Shamanism
Shame
Form and **Shape** Perception
Shared Paranoid Disorder
    USE Folie A Deux
Sharing (Social Behavior)
Needle **Sharing**
Myelin **Sheath**
Sheep
Sheltered Workshops
Shelters
Choice **Shift**

Extradimensional Shift Learning
    USE Nonreversal Shift Learning
Nonreversal **Shift** Learning
Reversal **Shift** Learning
Risky Shift *USE Choice Shift*
Workday **Shifts**
Shock
Shock Therapy
Shock Units
Anaphylactic **Shock**
Culture **Shock**
Electroconvulsive **Shock**
Electroconvulsive **Shock** Therapy
Insulin **Shock** Therapy
Shoplifting
Shopping *USE Consumer Behavior*
Shopping Centers
Short Term Memory
Short Term Potentiation
    USE Postactivation Potentials
Short Term Psychotherapy
    USE Brief Psychotherapy
Shoulder (Anatomy)
Shuttle Box Grids
Shuttle Box Hurdles
Shuttle Boxes
Shyness *USE Timidity*
Siamese Twins
Sibling Relations
Siblings
Sick Leave *USE Employee Leave Benefits*
Sickle Cell Disease
Motion **Sickness**
Side Effects (Drug)
Side Effects (Treatment)
Sierra Leone
Sight Vocabulary
Partially **Sighted**
Freud **(Sigmund)**
Sign Language
Sign Test
Wilcoxon **Sign** Rank Test
Signal Detection (Perception)
Signal Intensity *USE Stimulus Intensity*
Statistical **Significance**
Significant Others
Silent Reading
Attitude **Similarity**
Stimulus **Similarity**
Simile *USE Figurative Language*
Simple Schizophrenia *USE Schizophrenia*
Herpes **Simplex**
Simulation
Simulation Games
Computer **Simulation**
Flight **Simulation**
Simulators *USE Simulation*
Sin
Sincerity
Singapore
Single Cell Organisms
    USE Microorganisms
Single Fathers
Single Mothers
Single Parents
Single Persons
Sisters
Sixteen Personality Factors Question
Size
Size Constancy
Size Discrimination
Apparent **Size**
Body **Size**
Brain **Size**
Effect **Size** (Statistical)
Family **Size**
Group **Size**
Litter **Size**

Skeletomuscular Disorders
  USE Musculoskeletal Disorders
Skewed Distribution
Skill Learning
Fine Motor **Skill** Learning
Gross Motor **Skill** Learning
Motor Skill Learning
  USE Perceptual Motor Learning
Skilled Industrial Workers
Skills *USE Ability*
Basic Skills Testing
  USE Minimum Competency Tests
Clerical Secretarial **Skills**
Communication **Skills**
Communication **Skills** Training
Employee **Skills**
Iowa Tests of Basic **Skills**
Motor **Skills**
Reading **Skills**
Self Care **Skills**
Social **Skills**
Social **Skills** Training
Study Skills *USE Study Habits*
Writing **Skills**
Skin (Anatomy)
Skin Conduction *USE Skin Resistance*
Skin Disorders
Skin Electrical Properties
Skin Potential
Skin Resistance
Skin Temperature
Allergic **Skin** Disorders
Basal **Skin** Resistance
Galvanic **Skin** Response
Skinner Boxes
Skinner (Burrhus Frederic)
Skull
Slang
Sleep
Sleep Apnea
Sleep Deprivation
Sleep Disorders
Sleep Inducing Drugs
  USE Hypnotic Drugs
Sleep Onset
Sleep Talking
Sleep Treatment
Sleep Wake Cycle
Nonrapid Eye Movement Sleep *USE NREM Sleep*
NonREM Sleep *USE NREM Sleep*
NREM **Sleep**
Paradoxical Sleep *USE REM Sleep*
Rapid Eye Movement Sleep *USE REM Sleep*
REM **Sleep**
Slow Wave Sleep *USE NREM Sleep*
Sleepwalking
Slosson Intelligence Test for Child
Slow Learners
Slow Wave Sleep *USE NREM Sleep*
Slums *USE Poverty Areas*
Smell Perception
  USE Olfactory Perception
Smiles
Kolmogorov **Smirnov** Test
Smokeless Tobacco
Tobacco (Smokeless) *USE Smokeless Tobacco*
Smoking Cessation
Cigarette Smoking *USE Tobacco Smoking*
Tobacco **Smoking**
Snails
Snake Phobia *USE Ophidiophobia*
Snakes
Glue **Sniffing**
Snuff *USE Smokeless Tobacco*
Sobriety
Soccer
Sociability
Social Acceptance
Social Adaptation *USE Social Adjustment*

Social Adjustment
Social Anxiety
Social Approval
Social Behavior
Social Casework
Social Caseworkers *USE Social Workers*
Social Change
Social Class
Social Class Attitudes
  USE Socioeconomic Class Attitudes
Social Cognition
Social Comparison
Social Control
Social Dating
Social Demonstrations
Social Density
Social Deprivation
Social Desirability
Social Development
  USE Psychosocial Development
Social Discrimination
Social Drinking
Social Environments
Social Equality
Social Facilitation
Social Groups
Social Identity
Social Immobility *USE Social Mobility*
Social Influences
Social Integration
Social Interaction
Social Isolation
Social Issues
Social Learning
Social Maladjustment
  USE Social Adjustment
Social Mobility
Social Movements
Social Networks
Social Norms
Social Perception
Social Phobia
Social Problems *USE Social Issues*
Social Processes
Social Programs
Social Psychiatry
Social Psychologists
Social Psychology
Social Reinforcement
Social Rejection *USE Social Acceptance*
Social Sciences
Social Security
Social Services
Social Skills
Social Skills Training
Social Stigma *USE Stigma*
Social Stress
Social Structure
Social Studies Education
Social Support Networks
Social Values
Social Work *USE Social Casework*
Social Work Education
Social Workers
Animal **Social** Behavior
Assistance (**Social** Behavior)
Clubs (**Social** Organizations)
Competence (Social) *USE Social Skills*
Edwards **Social** Desirability Scale
Equity (**Social**)
Marlowe Crowne **Soc** Desirabil Scale
Networks (Social) *USE Social Networks*
Psychiatric **Social** Workers
Rejection (Social) *USE Social Acceptance*
Sharing (**Social** Behavior)
Therapeutic **Social** Clubs
Trust (**Social** Behavior)
Vineland **Social** Maturity Scale
Socialism

Union of Soviet **Socialist** Republics
Socialization
Political **Socialization**
Socially Disadvantaged
   USE Disadvantaged
Society
Sociobiology
Sociocultural Factors
Socioeconomic Class Attitudes
Socioeconomic Status
Family **Socioeconomic** Level
Socioenvironmental Therapy
   USE Milieu Therapy
Sociograms
Sociolinguistics
Sociologists
Sociology
Sociometric Tests
Sociometry
Sociopath *USE Antisocial Personality*
Sociopathology *USE Antisocial Behavior*
Sociotherapy
Sodium
Sodium Ions
Sodium Lactate *USE Lactic Acid*
Sodium Pentobarbital *USE Pentobarbital*
Computer **Software**
Solvent Abuse *USE Inhalant Abuse*
Solvents
Anagram Problem **Solving**
Group Problem **Solving**
Problem **Solving**
Somalia
Somatization
Somatization Disorder
   USE Psychosomatic Disorders
Atypical Somatoform Disorder
   USE Dysmorphophobia
Somatosensory Cortex
Somatosensory Evoked Potentials
Somatostatin
Somatotropin
Somatotypes
Somesthetic Perception
Somesthetic Stimulation
Somnambulism *USE Sleepwalking*
Sonar
Sons
Sorority Membership
Goldstein Scheerer Object **Sort** Test
Q **Sort** Testing Technique
Sorting (Cognition)
   USE Classification (Cognitive Process)
Wisconsin Card **Sorting** Test
Sound *USE Auditory Stimulation*
Sound Localization
   USE Auditory Localization
Sound Pressure Level *USE Loudness*
Noise (Sound) *USE Auditory Stimulation*
Sourness *USE Taste Perception*
South Africa
South America
South Korea
South Pacific
South Vietnam *USE Vietnam*
Southeast Asia
Union of **Soviet** Socialist Republics
Personal **Space**
Working **Space**
Spacecraft
Spaceflight
Spain
Attention **Span**
Digit **Span** Testing
Life Span *USE Life Expectancy*
Spanish Americans *USE Hispanics*
Spasms
Muscle **Spasms**
Spatial Ability

Spatial Discrimination
   USE Spatial Perception
Spatial Distortion
Spatial Frequency
Spatial Imagery
Spatial Learning
Spatial Memory
Spatial Neglect *USE Sensory Neglect*
Spatial Organization
Spatial Orientation (Perception)
Spatial Perception
Temporal **Spatial** Concept Scale
Automatic Speaker Recognition
   USE Automated Speech Recognition
Fear of Public Speaking *USE Speech Anxiety*
Public **Speaking**
Spearman Brown Test
Spearman Rho
   USE Rank Difference Correlation
Special Education
Special Education Students
Special Education Teachers
Special Needs
Information **Specialists**
Specialization (Professional)
   USE Professional Specialization
Academic **Specialization**
Hemispheric Specialization *USE Lateral Dominance*
Professional **Specialization**
Species Differences
Species Recognition
Spectral Sensitivity *USE Color Perception*
Speech *USE Oral Communication*
Speech and Hearing Measures
Speech Anxiety
Speech Characteristics
Speech Development
Speech Disorders
Speech Handicapped
Speech Pauses
Speech Perception
Speech Pitch
Speech Processing (Mechanical)
Speech Rate
Speech Rhythm
Speech Therapists
Speech Therapy
Accelerated Speech *USE Speech Rate*
Articulation **(Speech)**
Automated **Speech** Recognition
Compressed **Speech**
Delayed Speech
   USE Retarded Speech Development
Figures of Speech *USE Figurative Language*
Filtered **Speech**
Inner Speech *USE Self Talk*
Retarded **Speech** Development
Synthetic **Speech**
Speechreading *USE Lipreading*
Speed *USE Velocity*
Reading **Speed**
Response Speed *USE Reaction Time*
Spelling
Sperm
Sperm Donation *USE Tissue Donation*
Spider Phobia *USE Phobias*
Spiders *USE Arachnida*
Spina Bifida
Spinal Column
Spinal Cord
Spinal Cord Injuries
Spinal Fluid *USE Cerebrospinal Fluid*
Spinal Ganglia
Spinal Nerves
Cranial **Spinal** Cord
Lumbar **Spinal** Cord
Spinothalamic Tracts
Spiperone *USE Spiroperidol*
Spirituality

311

Spiroperidol
Spleen
Split Brain *USE Commissurotomy*
Split Personality *USE Multiple Personality*
Spontaneous Abortion
Spontaneous Alternation
Spontaneous Recovery (Learning)
Spontaneous Remission
Sport Performance
   USE Athletic Performance
Sport Psychology
Sport Training *USE Athletic Training*
Sports
Spouse Abuse *USE Partner Abuse*
Spouses
Spreading Depression
Chi Square Test
Least Squares
Squirrels
Sri Lanka
Emotional Stability
Hospital Staff *USE Medical Personnel*
Psychiatric Hospital Staff
Stage Plays *USE Theatre*
Developmental Stages
Prenatal Developmental Stages
Stammering *USE Stuttering*
Competency to Stand Trial
Standard Deviation
Standard Error of Measurement
   USE Error of Measurement
Standard Scores
Test Standardization
Standardized Tests
Professional Standards
Stanford Achievement Test
Stanford Binet Intelligence Scale
Stanines *USE Standard Scores*
Stapedius Reflex *USE Acoustic Reflex*
Starfish *USE Echinodermata*
Project Head Start
Startle Reflex
Starvation
State Board Examinations
   USE Professional Examinations
State Dependent Learning
State Hospitals *USE Psychiatric Hospitals*
State Trait Anxiety Inventory
Mini Mental State Examination
Borderline States
Consciousness States
Emotional States
United States
Statistical Analysis
Statistical Correlation
Statistical Data
Statistical Estimation
Statistical Measurement
Statistical Norms
Statistical Power
Statistical Probability
Statistical Regression
Statistical Reliability
Statistical Rotation
Statistical Sample Parameters
Statistical Samples
Statistical Significance
Statistical Tables
Statistical Tests
Statistical Validity
Statistical Variables
Statistical Weighting
Diagnostic and Statistical Manual
Effect Size (Statistical)
Item Analysis (Statistical)
Magnitude of Effect (Statistical) *USE Effect Size (Statistical)*
Nonparametric Statistical Tests
Parametric Statistical Tests
Statistics

ANOVA (Statistics) *USE Analysis of Variance*
Confidence Limits (Statistics)
Interaction Analysis (Statistics)
Population (Statistics)
Status
Employment Status
Job Status *USE Occupational Status*
Marital Status
Occupational Status
Parenthood Status
Socioeconomic Status
Stealing *USE Theft*
Stelazine *USE Trifluoperazine*
Stellate Ganglion *USE Autonomic Ganglia*
Brain Stem
Stepchildren
Stepfamily
Stepparents
Stereopsis *USE Stereoscopic Vision*
Stereoscopic Presentation
Stereoscopic Vision
Stereotaxic Atlas
Stereotaxic Techniques
Stereotyped Attitudes
Stereotyped Behavior
Sterility
Sterilization (Sex)
Steroids
Adrenal Cortex Steroids *USE Corticosteroids*
Sticklebacks
Stigma
Social Stigma *USE Stigma*
Stimulants of CNS
   USE CNS Stimulating Drugs
CNS Stimulating Drugs
Follicle Stimulating Hormone
Melanocyte Stimulating Hormone
Respiration Stimulating Drugs
Thyroid Stimulating Hormone *USE Thyrotropin*
Stimulation
Stimulation Seeking (Personality)
   USE Sensation Seeking
Afferent Stimulation
Auditory Stimulation
Aversive Stimulation
Brain Stimulation
Brain Self Stimulation
Chemical Brain Stimulation
Dichoptic Stimulation
Dichotic Stimulation
Electrical Stimulation
Electrical Brain Stimulation
Intracranial Self Stimulation *USE Brain Self Stimulation*
Olfactory Stimulation
Perceptual Stimulation
Photopic Stimulation
Prismatic Stimulation
Restricted Environmental Stimulation *USE Stimulus Deprivation*
Scotopic Stimulation
Self Stimulation
Somesthetic Stimulation
Subliminal Stimulation
Tactual Stimulation
Taste Stimulation
Vestibular Stimulation *USE Somesthetic Stimulation*
Visual Stimulation
Stimulators (Apparatus)
Acoustic Stimuli *USE Auditory Stimulation*
Pictorial Stimuli
Verbal Stimuli
Stimulus Ambiguity
Stimulus Attenuation
Stimulus Change
Stimulus Complexity
Stimulus Control
Stimulus Deprivation
Stimulus Discrimination
Stimulus Duration
Stimulus Frequency

Stimulus Generalization
Stimulus Intensity
Stimulus Intervals
Stimulus Novelty
Stimulus Offset
Stimulus Onset
Stimulus Parameters
Stimulus Pattern *USE Stimulus Variability*
Stimulus Presentation Methods
Stimulus Salience
Stimulus Similarity
Stimulus Variability
Conditioned Stimulus
Discriminative Stimulus *USE Conditioned Stimulus*
Exposure Time (Stimulus) *USE Stimulus Duration*
Unconditioned Stimulus
Stipends
    USE Educational Financial Assistance
Stochastic Modeling
Stomach
Automated Information Storage
Human Information Storage
Retail Stores *USE Retailing*
Storytelling
Mutual Storytelling Technique
Strabismus
Animal Strain Differences
Role Strain *USE Role Conflicts*
Stranger Reactions
Fear of Strangers *USE Stranger Reactions*
Strategies
Strategies (Learning)
    USE Learning Strategies
Learning Strategies
Self Handicapping Strategy
Physical Strength
Stress
Stress Management
Stress Reactions
Environmental Stress
Occupational Stress
Physiological Stress
Posttraumatic Stress Disorder
Psychological Stress
Social Stress
Striate Cortex *USE Visual Cortex*
Corpus Striatum *USE Basal Ganglia*
Strikes
Film Strips
Stroboscopic Movement
    USE Apparent Movement
Stroke (Cerebrum)
    USE Cerebrovascular Accidents
Strong Vocational Interest Blank
Stroop Color Word Test
Stroop Effect
Structural Equation Modeling
Structuralism
Factor Structure
Family Structure
Group Structure
Household Structure *USE Living Arrangements*
Kinship Structure
Organizational Structure
Sentence Structure
Social Structure
Text Structure
Structured Overview
    USE Advance Organizers
Strychnine
Student Activism
Student Admission Criteria
Student Attitudes
Student Attrition
Student Characteristics
Student Personnel Services
Student Protest *USE Student Activism*
Student Records
Student Teachers

Student Teaching
Protest (Student) *USE Student Activism*
Teacher Student Interaction
Students
Business Students
College Students
Community College Students
Dental Students
Education Students
Elementary School Students
Foreign Students
Graduate Students
High School Students
Intermediate School Students
Junior College Students
Junior High School Students
Kindergarten Students
Law Students
Medical Students
Middle School Students
Nursery School Students
Nursing Students
Postgraduate Students
Preschool Students
Primary School Students
Reentry Students
ROTC Students
Special Education Students
Transfer Students
Vocational School Students
Followup Studies
Longitudinal Studies
Social Studies Education
Study Habits
Study Skills *USE Study Habits*
Allport Vernon Lindzey Study Values
Foreign Study
Independent Study *USE Individualized Instruction*
Rosenzweig Picture Frustration Study
Work Study Programs
    USE Educational Programs
Stuttering
Cognitive Style
Leadership Style
Learning Style *USE Cognitive Style*
Perceptual Style
Subconscious
Subcortical Lesions *USE Brain Lesions*
Subculture (Anthropological)
Subcutaneous Injections
Subjectivity
Experimental Subjects
Research Subjects *USE Experimental Subjects*
Within Subjects Design *USE Repeated Measures*
Sublimation
Subliminal Perception
Subliminal Stimulation
Submarines
Submissiveness *USE Obedience*
Submucous Plexus
    USE Autonomic Ganglia
Substance Abuse *USE Drug Abuse*
Substance Abuse Prevention
    USE Drug Abuse Prevention
Substance P
Substantia Nigra
Subtests
Suburban Environments
Subvocalization
Success *USE Achievement*
Fear of Success
Occupational Success
Occupational Success Prediction
Successive Contrast *USE Afterimage*
Succinylcholine
Sucking
Sudan
Sudden Infant Death
Suffering

313

Blood **Sugar**
Sugars
Suggestibility
Posthypnotic **Suggestions**
Suicidal Ideation
Suicide
Suicide Prevention
Suicide Prevention Centers
Attempted **Suicide**
Sulpiride
Non Zero **Sum** Games
Summer Camps (Recreation)
Superego
School **Superintendents**
Superior Colliculus
Emotional **Superiority**
Superstitions
Supervising Teachers
USE Cooperating Teachers
Clinical **Supervision** *USE Professional Supervision*
Educational **Supervision** *USE Professional Supervision*
Practicum **Supervision**
Professional **Supervision**
Supervisors *USE Management Personnel*
Medical Personnel **Supply**
Mental Health Personnel **Supply**
Personnel **Supply**
Support Groups
Child **Support**
Social **Support** Networks
Supported Employment
Supportive Psychotherapy
USE Psychotherapy
Suppression (Defense Mechanism)
Conditioned **Suppression**
Dexamethasone **Suppression** Test
Surgeons
Surgery
Dental **Surgery**
Endocrine Gland **Surgery**
Heart **Surgery**
Operation (Surgery) *USE Surgery*
Pituitary Gland Surgery *USE Hypophysectomy*
Plastic **Surgery**
Surgical Complications
USE Postsurgical Complications
Surgical Patients
Surinam
Surrogate Parents (Humans)
Fear **Survey** Schedule
Guilford Zimmerman
Temperament **Surv**
Kuder Occupational Interest **Survey**
Opinion Attitude and Interest **Survey**
Purdue Perceptual Motor **Survey**
Surveys
Consumer **Surveys**
Mail **Surveys**
Opinion Surveys *USE Attitude Measures*
Telephone **Surveys**
Survivors
Holocaust **Survivors**
Susceptibility (Disorders)
Hypnotic **Susceptibility**
School **Suspension**
Suspicion
Swallowing
Mate Swapping *USE Extramarital Intercourse*
Body **Sway** Testing
Swaziland
Sweat
Sweating
Sweden
Sweetness *USE Taste Perception*
Swimming
Code **Switching**
Switzerland
Nonsense **Syllable** Learning
Syllables

Syllogistic Reasoning
USE Inductive Deductive Reasoning
Biological **Symbiosis**
Symbiotic Infantile Psychosis
Symbolic Interactionism
Symbolism
Sympathectomy
Sympathetic Nervous System
Sympatholytic Drugs
Sympathomimetic Amines
Sympathomimetic Drugs
Sympathy
Professional Meetings and **Symposia**
Symptom Checklists
Symptom Prescription
USE Paradoxical Techniques
Symptom Remission
Symptoms
Extrapyramidal **Symptoms**
Synapses
Syncope
Acquired Immune Deficiency **Syndrome**
Aspergers **Syndrome**
Battered Child **Syndrome**
Capgras **Syndrome**
Creutzfeldt Jakob **Syndrome**
Cri du Chat Syndrome *USE Crying Cat Syndrome*
Crying Cat **Syndrome**
Cushings **Syndrome**
Downs **Syndrome**
Fetal Alcohol **Syndrome**
Fibromyalgia Syndrome *USE Muscular Disorders*
Fragile X **Syndrome**
Ganser Syndrome *USE Factitious Disorders*
Irritable Bowel **Syndrome**
Klinefelters **Syndrome**
Munchausen **Syndrome**
Neuroleptic Malignant **Syndrome**
Prader Willi **Syndrome**
Premenstrual Syndrome *USE Premenstrual Tension*
Rett **Syndrome**
Temporomandibular Joint Syndrome *USE Musculoskeletal Disorders*
Testicular Feminization **Syndrome**
Turners **Syndrome**
Wernickes **Syndrome**
Syndromes
Organic Brain **Syndromes**
Drug Synergism *USE Drug Interactions*
Lunar **Synodic** Cycle
Synonyms
Syntax
Synthetic Speech
Syphilis
Syria
Autonomic Nervous **System**
Autonomic Nervous **System** Disorders
Cardiovascular **System**
Caste **System**
Central Nervous **System**
Central Nervous **System** Disorders
Central Nervous System Drugs *USE CNS Affecting Drugs*
Digestive **System**
Digestive **System** Disorders
Endocrine **System**
Gastrointestinal **System**
Hypothalamo Hypophyseal **System**
Lemniscal **System**
Limbic **System**
Musculoskeletal **System**
Nervous **System**
Nervous **System** Disorders
Nervous **System** Neoplasms
Nervous System Plasticity *USE Neural Plasticity*
Parasympathetic Nervous **System**
Peripheral Nervous **System**
Respiratory **System**
Sclerosis (Nervous **System)**
Sympathetic Nervous **System**
Urogenital **System**

Systematic Desensitization Therapy
Systems
Systems Analysis
Systems Theory
Anatomical **Systems**
Classification Systems *USE Taxonomies*
Communication **Systems**
Expert **Systems**
Information **Systems**
Knowledge Based Systems *USE Expert Systems*
Man Machine **Systems**
Man Machine **Systems** Design
Management Information Systems *USE Information Systems*
Number **Systems**
Political Economic **Systems**
Telephone **Systems**
Systolic Pressure
Szondi Test
T Groups *USE Human Relations Training*
T Mazes
T Test
Statistical **Tables**
Taboos
Tachistoscopes
Tachistoscopic Presentation
Tachycardia
Tactual Discrimination
    USE Tactual Perception
Tactual Displays
Tactual Maps *USE Mobility Aids*
Tactual Perception
Tactual Stimulation
Tailored Testing *USE Adaptive Testing*
Taiwan
Note **Taking**
Perspective Taking *USE Role Taking*
Risk **Taking**
Role **Taking**
Test **Taking**
Talent *USE Ability*
Talented *USE Gifted*
Fairy Tales *USE Folklore*
Self **Talk**
Sleep **Talking**
Tantrums
Tanzania
Tape Recorders
Finger **Tapping**
Tardive Dyskinesia
Task Analysis
Task Complexity
Task Difficulty *USE Task Complexity*
Time On **Task**
Piagetian **Tasks**
Taste Aversion Conditioning
    USE Aversion Conditioning
Taste Buds
Taste Discrimination
    USE Taste Perception
Taste Perception
Taste Stimulation
Taurine
Taxation
Psychiatric Classifications (Taxon) *USE Psychodiagnostic Typologies*
Taxonomies
Tay Sachs Disease
    USE Amaurotic Familial Idiocy
Taylor Manifest Anxiety Scale
Tea *USE Beverages (Nonalcoholic)*
Teacher Accreditation
    USE Accreditation (Education Personnel)
Teacher Aides
Teacher Attitudes
Teacher Characteristics
Teacher Education
Teacher Effectiveness
    USE Teacher Characteristics
Teacher Effectiveness Evaluation
Teacher Expectations

Teacher Personality
Teacher Recruitment
Teacher Student Interaction
Teacher Tenure
Teacher Training *USE Teacher Education*
Inservice **Teacher** Education
Minnesota **Teacher** Attitude Inventory
Teachers
College **Teachers**
Cooperating **Teachers**
Elementary School **Teachers**
High School **Teachers**
Junior High School **Teachers**
Preschool **Teachers**
Preservice **Teachers**
Resource **Teachers**
Special Education **Teachers**
Student **Teachers**
Supervising Teachers *USE Cooperating Teachers*
Technical Education Teachers
    USE Vocational Education Teachers
Vocational Education **Teachers**
Teaching
Teaching Internship
    USE Student Teaching
Teaching Machines
Teaching Methods
Discovery **Teaching** Method
Initial **Teaching** Alphabet
Student **Teaching**
Team **Teaching** Method
Team Teaching Method
Teams
Technical Education Teachers
    USE Vocational Education Teachers
Technical Personnel
Technical Schools
Technical Service Personnel
Holtzman Inkblot **Technique**
Mutual Storytelling **Technique**
Projective Testing **Technique**
Q Sort Testing **Technique**
Cognitive **Techniques**
Paradigmatic Techniques *USE Paradoxical Techniques*
Paradoxical **Techniques**
Personal Growth Techniques
    USE Human Potential Movement
Projective **Techniques**
Psychotherapeutic **Techniques**
Self Help **Techniques**
Stereotaxic **Techniques**
Technology
Nuclear **Technology**
Reproductive **Technology**
Teenage Fathers *USE Adolescent Fathers*
Teenage Mothers
    USE Adolescent Mothers
Teenage Pregnancy
    USE Adolescent Pregnancy
Teenagers *USE Adolescents*
Teeth (Anatomy)
Teeth Grinding *USE Bruxism*
Nocturnal **Teeth** Grinding
Ventral Tegmental Area *USE Tegmentum*
Tegmentum
Telecommunications Media
Telekinesis *USE Psychokinesis*
Telemetry
Telencephalon
Telepathy
Telephone Hot Lines
    USE Hot Line Services
Telephone Surveys
Telephone Systems
Televised Instruction
Television
Television Advertising
Television Viewing
Closed Circuit **Television**

Reality **Testing**
Scaling **(Testing)**
Scoring **(Testing)**
Tailored Testing *USE Adaptive Testing*
Testosterone
Tests *USE Measurement*
Ability Tests *USE Aptitude Measures*
Comprehension **Tests**
Criterion Referenced **Tests**
Differential Aptitude **Tests**
Employment **Tests**
Gates MacGinitie Reading **Tests**
Henmon Nelson **Tests** Mental Ability
Iowa **Tests** of Basic Skills
Mastery Tests *USE Criterion Referenced Tests*
Metropolitan Readiness **Tests**
Minimum Competency **Tests**
Nonparametric Statistical **Tests**
Objective Referenced Tests *USE Criterion Referenced Tests*
Parametric Statistical **Tests**
Performance **Tests**
Screening **Tests**
Selection **Tests**
Sentence Completion **Tests**
Sociometric **Tests**
Standardized **Tests**
Statistical **Tests**
Verbal **Tests**
Testwiseness
Tetrabenazine
Tetrachoric Correlation
Tetrahydrocannabinol
Text Structure
Textbooks
Programed **Textbooks**
Texture Perception
Thailand
Thalamic Nuclei
Thalamotomy
Thalamus
Geniculate Bodies **(Thalamus)**
Thalidomide
Thanatology *USE Death Education*
Thanatos *USE Death Instinct*
Theatre
Theft
Thematic Apperception Test
Theology *USE Religion*
Theophylline
Bayes Theorem *USE Statistical Probability*
Theoretical Interpretation
Theoretical Orientation
Theories
Theories of Education
Theory Formulation
Theory of Evolution
Theory Verification
Communication **Theory**
Fuzzy Set **Theory**
Game **Theory**
Information **Theory**
Item Response **Theory**
Latent Trait Theory *USE Item Response Theory*
Learning **Theory**
Personal Construct Theory *USE Personality Theory*
Personality **Theory**
Psychoanalytic **Theory**
Systems **Theory**
Therapeutic Abortion
    USE Induced Abortion
Therapeutic Alliance
Therapeutic Camps
Therapeutic Community
Therapeutic Outcomes
    USE Treatment Outcomes
Therapeutic Processes
Therapeutic Social Clubs
Medical **Therapeutic** Devices
Organic **Therapies**

Therapist Attitudes
Therapist Characteristics
Therapist Effectiveness
    USE Therapist Characteristics
Therapist Experience
    USE Therapist Characteristics
Therapist Patient Interaction
    USE Psychotherapeutic Processes
Therapist Patient Sexual Relations
    USE Professional Client Sexual Relations
Therapist Personality
    USE Therapist Characteristics
Therapist Role
Therapist Selection
Therapist Trainees
Patient Therapist Interaction
    USE Psychotherapeutic Processes
Patient Therapist Sexual Relations
    USE Professional Client Sexual Relations
Selection (Therapist) *USE Therapist Selection*
Therapists
Occupational **Therapists**
Physical **Therapists**
Speech **Therapists**
Therapy *USE Treatment*
Activity Therapy *USE Recreation Therapy*
Animal Assisted **Therapy**
Art **Therapy**
Aversion **Therapy**
Behavior **Therapy**
Bright Light Therapy *USE Phototherapy*
Client Centered **Therapy**
Cognitive **Therapy**
Cognitive Behavior Therapy *USE Cognitive Therapy*
Conjoint **Therapy**
Cooperative Therapy *USE Cotherapy*
Couples **Therapy**
Creative Arts **Therapy**
Dance **Therapy**
Directed Reverie **Therapy**
Drug **Therapy**
ECS Therapy
    USE Electroconvulsive Shock Therapy
ECT (Therapy)
    USE Electroconvulsive Shock Therapy
Educational Therapy *USE School Counseling*
Electroconvulsive Shock **Therapy**
Electroshock Therapy
    USE Electroconvulsive Shock Therapy
Encounter Group **Therapy**
Environmental Therapy *USE Milieu Therapy*
Estrogen Replacement Therapy *USE Hormone Therapy*
Existential **Therapy**
Family **Therapy**
Feminist **Therapy**
Flooding Therapy *USE Implosive Therapy*
Gestalt **Therapy**
Group Therapy *USE Group Psychotherapy*
Gymnastic Therapy *USE Recreation Therapy*
Hormone **Therapy**
Illumination Therapy *USE Phototherapy*
Implosive **Therapy**
Individual Therapy *USE Individual Psychotherapy*
Insight **Therapy**
Insulin Shock **Therapy**
Marathon Group **Therapy**
Marital Therapy *USE Marriage Counseling*
Milieu **Therapy**
Morita **Therapy**
Multiple Therapy *USE Cotherapy*
Muscle Relaxation Therapy *USE Relaxation Therapy*
Music **Therapy**
Nondirective Therapy *USE Client Centered Therapy*
Occupational **Therapy**
Personal **Therapy**
Persuasion **Therapy**
Pet Therapy *USE Animal Assisted Therapy*
Physical **Therapy**
Play **Therapy**

Poetry **Therapy**
Pretraining (Therapy) *USE Client Education*
Primal **Therapy**
Progressive Relaxation **Therapy**
Psychoanalytic Therapy *USE Psychoanalysis*
Radiation **Therapy**
Rational Emotive **Therapy**
Reality **Therapy**
Reciprocal Inhibition **Therapy**
Recreation **Therapy**
Relationship **Therapy**
Relaxation **Therapy**
Sex **Therapy**
Shock **Therapy**
Socioenvironmental Therapy *USE Milieu Therapy*
Speech **Therapy**
Systematic Desensitization **Therapy**
Triadic Therapy *USE Conjoint Therapy*
Vitamin **Therapy**
X Ray Therapy *USE Radiation Therapy*
Thermal Acclimatization
Thermal Factors *USE Temperature Effects*
Thermoreceptors
Thermoregulation (Body)
Theta Rhythm
Thigh
Thinking
Autistic **Thinking**
Convergent Thinking
USE Inductive Deductive Reasoning
Divergent **Thinking**
Logical **Thinking**
Magical **Thinking**
Thiopental
Thioridazine
Thiothixene
Third World Countries
USE Developing Countries
Thirst
Thoracic Nerves *USE Spinal Nerves*
Thorax
Thorazine *USE Chlorpromazine*
Lorge **Thorndike** Intelligence Test
Thought Content *USE Cognitions*
Thought Control *USE Brainwashing*
Thought Disturbances
Fantasies **(Thought** Disturbances)
Threat
Threat Postures
Threshold Determination
Critical Flicker Fusion **Threshold**
Luminance Threshold
USE Brightness Perception AND Visual
Thresholds
Photic Threshold
USE Illumination AND Visual Thresholds
Thresholds
Auditory **Thresholds**
Olfactory **Thresholds**
Pain **Thresholds**
Vibrotactile **Thresholds**
Visual **Thresholds**
Failure to **Thrive**
Thromboses
Coronary **Thromboses**
Project Follow **Through**
Thumb
Thumbsucking
Thymoleptic Drugs
USE Tranquilizing Drugs
Thyroid Disorders
Thyroid Extract
Thyroid Gland
Thyroid Hormones
Thyroid Stimulating Hormone
USE Thyrotropin
Thyroidectomy
Thyrotoxicosis
Thyrotropic Hormone *USE Thyrotropin*

Thyrotropin
Thyroxine
Tibet
Tic Doloureux *USE Trigeminal Neuralgia*
Tics
Time
Time Disorientation
Time Estimation
Time Limited Psychotherapy
USE Brief Psychotherapy
Time Management
Time On Task
Time Out
Time Perception
Time Perspective
Time Series
Exposure Time (Stimulus) *USE Stimulus Duration*
Interresponse **Time**
Leisure **Time**
Reaction **Time**
Response Time *USE Reaction Time*
Timers (Apparatus)
Timidity
Tinnitus
Tiredness *USE Fatigue*
Tissue Donation
Connective **Tissue** Cells
Tissues (Body)
Connective **Tissues**
Nerve **Tissues**
Toads
Tobacco (Drug) *USE Nicotine*
Tobacco (Smokeless)
USE Smokeless Tobacco
Tobacco Smoking
Chewing Tobacco *USE Smokeless Tobacco*
Smokeless **Tobacco**
Trinidad and **Tobago**
Toes (Anatomy) *USE Feet (Anatomy)*
Tofranil *USE Imipramine*
Toilet Training
Token Economy Programs
Token Reinforcement
USE Secondary Reinforcement
Tolerance
Tolerance for Ambiguity
Drug **Tolerance**
Toluene
Tomography
Positron Emission Tomography *USE Tomography*
Tone (Frequency) *USE Pitch (Frequency)*
Muscle **Tone**
Tonga
Tongue
Tonic Immobility
Tool Use
Animal Tool Use *USE Tool Use*
Top Level Managers
Topography
Torticollis
Tortoises *USE Turtles*
Torture
Totalitarianism
Touch *USE Tactual Perception*
Touching *USE Physical Contact*
Gilles de la **Tourette** Disorder
Towns
Toxic Disorders
Toxic Encephalopathies
Toxic Hepatitis
Toxic Psychoses
Toxic Waste *USE Hazardous Materials*
Toxicity
Toxicomania
Toxins *USE Poisons*
Toy Selection
Toys
Educational **Toys**
Memory **Trace**

Trachea
Tracking
Visual **Tracking**
Optic **Tract**
Respiratory **Tract** Disorders
Tractotomy
Extrapyramidal **Tracts**
Pyramidal **Tracts**
Spinothalamic **Tracts**
Traditionalism *USE Conservatism*
Air **Traffic** Accidents
Air **Traffic** Control
Motor **Traffic** Accidents
Trainable Mentally Retarded
Counselor **Trainees**
Psychotherapist Trainees *USE Therapist Trainees*
Therapist **Trainees**
Training *USE Education*
Training (Athletic) *USE Athletic Training*
Assertiveness **Training**
Athletic **Training**
Autogenic **Training**
Biofeedback **Training**
Childbirth **Training**
Clinical Methods **Training**
Clinical Psychology Grad **Training**
Communication Skills **Training**
Community Mental Health **Training**
Computer **Training**
Human Relations **Training**
Inservice **Training**
Job Training *USE Personnel Training*
Management **Training**
Memory **Training**
Mental Health Inservice **Training**
Military **Training**
Motivation **Training**
Omission **Training**
On the Job **Training**
Parent **Training**
Parent Effectiveness Training *USE Parent Training*
Personnel **Training**
Postgraduate **Training**
Psychiatric **Training**
Psychoanalytic **Training**
Psychotherapy **Training**
Self Instructional **Training**
Sensitivity **Training**
Social Skills **Training**
Sport Training *USE Athletic Training*
Teacher Training *USE Teacher Education*
Toilet **Training**
Work Adjustment **Training**
Railroad **Trains**
Latent Trait Theory *USE Item Response Theory*
State Trait Anxiety Inventory
Personality **Traits**
Major Tranquilizers *USE Neuroleptic Drugs*
Minor **Tranquilizers**
Tranquilizing Drugs
Transactional Analysis
Transaminases
Transcultural Psychiatry
Transducers
Transfer (Learning)
Transfer Students
Interhemispheric Transfer *USE Interhemispheric Interaction*
Interocular **Transfer**
Negative **Transfer**
Positive **Transfer**
Transferases
Psychotherapeutic **Transference**
Transformational Generative Grammar
Blood **Transfusion**
Transgenerational Patterns
Transistors (Apparatus)
School to Work **Transition**
Transitional Objects
Career Transitions *USE Career Development*

Foreign Language **Translation**
Translocation (Chromosome)
Sexually Transmitted Diseases
USE Venereal Diseases
Transpersonal Psychology
Neural **Transplantation**
Organ **Transplantation**
Heart Transplants *USE Organ Transplantation*
Kidney Transplants *USE Organ Transplantation*
Transportation
Transportation Accidents
Air **Transportation**
Ground **Transportation**
Public **Transportation**
Water **Transportation**
Transposition (Cognition)
Transracial Adoption
USE Interracial Adoption
Transsexualism
Transvestism
Tranylcypromine
Birth **Trauma**
Emotional **Trauma**
Physical Trauma *USE Injuries*
Traumatic Neurosis
Traumatic Psychosis
USE Reactive Psychosis
Commuting **(Travel)**
Traveling
Trazodone
Treatment
Treatment Compliance
Treatment Dropouts
Treatment Duration
Treatment Effectiveness Evaluation
Treatment Facilities
Treatment Outcomes
Treatment Refusal
Treatment Resistant Depression
Treatment Resistant Disorders
Treatment Termination
Treatment Withholding
Court Ordered Treatment *USE Court Referrals*
Cross Cultural **Treatment**
Day Care (Treatment) *USE Partial Hospitalization*
Dental **Treatment**
Electrosleep **Treatment**
Interdisciplinary **Treatment** Approach
Involuntary **Treatment**
Medical **Treatment** (General)
Multidisciplinary Treatment Approach
USE Interdisciplinary Treatment Approach
Multimodal **Treatment** Approach
Outpatient **Treatment**
Physical **Treatment** Methods
Refusal (Treatment) *USE Treatment Refusal*
Side Effects **(Treatment)**
Sleep **Treatment**
Delirium **Tremens**
Tremor
Trends
Triadic Therapy *USE Conjoint Therapy*
Trial and Error Learning
Competency to Stand Trial
Triazolam
Tribes
Trichotillomania *USE Hair Pulling*
Tricyclic Resistant Depression
USE Treatment Resistant Depression
Trifluoperazine
Triflupromazine
Trigeminal Nerve
Trigeminal Neuralgia
Trigonum Cerebrale *USE Fornix*
Trihexyphenidyl
Triiodothyronine
Trinidad and Tobago
Triplets

Educational Field **Trips**
Trisomy
Trisomy 21
Trochlear Nerve *USE Cranial Nerves*
Truancy
School **Truancy**
Trucks *USE Motor Vehicles*
Trust (Social Behavior)
Tryptamine
Tryptophan
Tubal Ligation
Eustachian **Tube** *USE Middle Ear*
Test **Tube** Babies
USE Reproductive Technology
Tuberculosis
Pulmonary **Tuberculosis**
Cathode Ray **Tubes** *USE Video Display Units*
Tubocurarine
Tumors *USE Neoplasms*
Tunisia
Tunnel Vision
Turkey
Turners Syndrome
Employee **Turnover**
Turtles
Tutoring
Peer **Tutoring**
Tutors *USE Teachers*
Twins
Dizygotic **Twins** *USE Heterozygotic Twins*
Heterozygotic **Twins**
Identical **Twins** *USE Monozygotic Twins*
Monozygotic **Twins**
Siamese **Twins**
Chorda **Tympani** Nerve *USE Facial Nerve*
Tympanic Membrane *USE Middle Ear*
Type A Personality
USE Coronary Prone Behavior
Type B Personality
USE Coronary Prone Behavior
Type I Errors
Type II Errors
Myers Briggs **Type** Indicator
Schizophrenia (Disorganized **Type**) *USE Hebephrenic Schizophrenia*
Schizophrenia (Residual **Type**) *USE Schizophrenia*
Body **Types** *USE Somatotypes*
Typing
Typists *USE Clerical Personnel*
Typologies (General) *USE Taxonomies*
Psychodiagnostic **Typologies**
Tyramine
Tyrosine
Mann Whitney **U** Test
Uganda
Ulcerative Colitis
Gastrointestinal **Ulcers**
Peptic **Ulcers** *USE Gastrointestinal Ulcers*
Ulnar Nerve *USE Spinal Nerves*
Ultrasound
Uncertainty
Unconditioned Reflex
USE Unconditioned Responses
Unconditioned Responses
Unconditioned Stimulus
Unconscious (Personality Factor)
Driving **Under** The Influence
Academic **Underachievement**
Underdeveloped Countries
USE Developing Countries
Undergraduate Degrees
USE Educational Degrees
Undergraduate Education
Undergraduates *USE College Students*
Underprivileged *USE Disadvantaged*
Understanding *USE Comprehension*
Underwater Effects
Underweight
Undifferentiated Schizophrenia
Unemployment

Union of Soviet Socialist Republics
Labor **Union** Members
Labor **Unions**
Unipolar Depression
USE Major Depression
United Arab Republic *USE Egypt*
United Kingdom
United States
Hospital Psychiatric **Units** *USE Psychiatric Units*
Psychiatric **Units**
Shock **Units**
Video Display **Units**
Words (Phonetic **Units**)
Universities *USE Colleges*
Open **Universities** *USE Nontraditional Education*
Unskilled Industrial Workers
Unwed Mothers
Upper Class
Upper Class Attitudes
Upper Income Level
Upward Bound
Urban Environments
Urban Planning
Urbanization
Uric Acid
Urinalysis
Urinary Function Disorders
Urinary Incontinence
Urination
Urine
Urogenital Disorders
Urogenital System
Uruguay
Drug **Usage**
Drug **Usage** Attitudes
Drug **Usage** Screening
Intravenous Drug **Usage**
IV Drug **Usage** *USE Intravenous Drug Usage*
Marihuana **Usage**
Animal Tool **Use** *USE Tool Use*
Tool **Use**
Uterus
Health Care **Utilization**
Health Service **Utilization** *USE Health Care Utilization*
Vacation Benefits
USE Employee Leave Benefits
Vacationing
Vaccination *USE Immunization*
Vagina
Vaginismus
Vagotomy
Vagus Nerve
Concept **Validity** *USE Construct Validity*
Concurrent **Validity**
Construct **Validity**
Factorial **Validity**
Predictive **Validity**
Statistical **Validity**
Test **Validity**
Valium *USE Diazepam*
Valproic Acid
Values
Allport Vernon Lindzey Study **Values**
Ethnic **Values**
Personal **Values**
Social **Values**
Heart **Valves**
Vandalism
Vane Kindergarten Test
Variability Measurement
Response **Variability**
Stimulus **Variability**
Variable Interval Reinforcement
Variable Ratio Reinforcement
Dependent **Variables**
Independent **Variables**
Statistical **Variables**
Variance Homogeneity
Analysis of **Variance**

320

Error Variance *USE Error of Measurement*
Heterogeneity of Variance *USE Variance Homogeneity*
Interaction **Variance**
Contingent Negative **Variation**
Diurnal Variations *USE Human Biological Rhythms*
Seasonal **Variations**
Varimax Rotation
Vascular Disorders
    USE Cardiovascular Disorders
Cerebral Vascular Disorders
    USE Cerebrovascular Disorders
Vasectomy
Vasoconstriction
Vasoconstrictor Drugs
Vasodilation
Vasodilator Drugs
Vasopressin
Vasopressor Drugs
    USE Vasoconstrictor Drugs
Motor **Vehicles**
Veins (Anatomy)
Velocity
Venereal Diseases
Venezuela
Ventral Roots
Ventral Tegmental Area *USE Tegmentum*
Cerebral **Ventricles**
Heart **Ventricles**
Verapamil
Verbal Ability
Verbal Communication
Verbal Comprehension
Verbal Conditioning *USE Verbal Learning*
Verbal Fluency
Verbal Learning
Verbal Meaning
Verbal Memory
Verbal Reinforcement
Verbal Stimuli
Verbal Tests
Conditioning (Verbal) *USE Verbal Learning*
Verbalization *USE Oral Communication*
Verbs
Verdict Determination *USE Adjudication*
Vergence Movements
    USE Eye Convergence
Theory **Verification**
Vernier Acuity *USE Visual Acuity*
Allport **Vernon** Lindzey Study Values
Vertebrates
Vertigo
Very Old
Blood **Vessels**
Coronary Vessels *USE Arteries (Anatomy)*
Retinal Vessels *USE Arteries (Anatomy)*
Vestibular Apparatus
Vestibular Nystagmus *USE Nystagmus*
Vestibular Stimulation
    USE Somesthetic Stimulation
Military **Veterans**
Veterinary Medicine
Vibration
Vibrators (Apparatus)
Vibrotactile Thresholds
Vicarious Experiences
Vicarious Reinforcement
    USE Vicarious Experiences
Reinforcement (Vicarious) *USE Vicarious Experiences*
Victimization
Crime **Victims**
Video Display Terminals
    USE Video Display Units
Video Display Units
Video Games *USE Computer Games*
Videotape Instruction
Videotape Recorders
Videotapes
Vietnam
North Vietnam *USE Vietnam*

South Vietnam *USE Vietnam*
World **View**
Television **Viewing**
Vigilance
Saint **Vincent**
Vineland Social Maturity Scale
Sexual Boundary Violations
    USE Professional Client Sexual Relations
Violence
Client Violence *USE Patient Violence*
Domestic Violence *USE Family Violence*
Family **Violence**
Patient **Violence**
Viral Disorders
Epstein Barr **Viral** Disorder
Virgin Islands
Virginity
Human Immunodeficiency **Virus**
Vision
Vision Disorders
Binocular **Vision**
Central Vision *USE Foveal Vision*
Foveal **Vision**
Hysterical **Vision** Disturbances
Monocular **Vision**
Peripheral **Vision**
Stereoscopic **Vision**
Tunnel **Vision**
Visitation Rights *USE Child Visitation*
Child **Visitation**
Institution **Visitation**
Home **Visiting** Programs
VISTA Volunteers
    USE Volunteers in Service to America
Visual Acuity
Visual Contrast
Visual Cortex
Visual Discrimination
Visual Displays
Visual Evoked Potentials
Visual Feedback
Visual Field
Visual Fixation *USE Eye Fixation*
Visual Hallucinations
Visual Masking
Visual Memory
Visual Neglect *USE Sensory Neglect*
Visual Perception
Visual Perspective
    USE Linear Perspective
Visual Receptive Fields
Visual Search
Visual Stimulation
Visual Thresholds
Visual Tracking
Benton Revised **Visual** Retention Test
Focusing (Visual) *USE Ocular Accommodation*
Frostig Development Test **Vis** Percept
Visualization *USE Imagery*
Visually Handicapped
Vitamin C *USE Ascorbic Acid*
Vitamin Deficiency Disorders
Vitamin Therapy
Vitamins
In Vitro Fertilization
    USE Reproductive Technology
Vocabulary
Peabody Picture **Vocabulary** Test
Sight **Vocabulary**
Words (Vocabulary) *USE Vocabulary*
Vocal Cords
Vocalization
Infant **Vocalization**
Animal **Vocalizations**
Vocational Adjustment
    USE Occupational Adjustment
Vocational Aspirations
    USE Occupational Aspirations

Vocational Choice
   USE Occupational Choice
Vocational Counseling
   USE Occupational Guidance
Vocational Counselors
Vocational Education
Vocational Education Teachers
Vocational Evaluation
Vocational Guidance
   USE Occupational Guidance
Vocational Interests
   USE Occupational Interests
Vocational Maturity
Vocational Mobility
   USE Occupational Mobility
Vocational Preference
   USE Occupational Preference
Vocational Rehabilitation
Vocational School Students
Vocational Schools
   USE Technical Schools
Strong **Vocational** Interest Blank
Vocations *USE Occupations*
Voice
Voice Disorders *USE Dysphonia*
Voles *USE Rodents*
Volition
Volt Meters
Blood **Volume**
Volunteer Civilian Personnel
Volunteer Military Personnel
Volunteer Personnel
Volunteers in Service to America
Experiment **Volunteers**
VISTA Volunteers
   USE Volunteers in Service to America
Vomeronasal Sense
Vomit Inducing Drugs *USE Emetic Drugs*
Vomiting
Voting Behavior
Vowels
Voyeurism
Deja Vu *USE Consciousness States*
Vygotsky (Lev)
Wages *USE Salaries*
Sleep **Wake** Cycle
Wakefulness
Wales
Walk In Clinics
Walking
Abdominal **Wall**
Wandering Behavior
War
Nuclear **War**
Prisoners of **War**
Wasps
Toxic Waste *USE Hazardous Materials*
Water Deprivation
Water Intake
Water Safety
Water Transportation
Watson (John Broadus)
Slow Wave Sleep *USE NREM Sleep*
Weaning
Weapons
Weather *USE Atmospheric Conditions*
Wechsler Adult Intelligence Scale
Wechsler Bellevue Intelligence Scale
Wechsler Intelligence Scale Children
Wechsler Memory Scale
Wechsler Preschool Primary Scale
Work **Week** Length
Weight Control
Weight Perception
Birth **Weight**
Body **Weight**
Brain **Weight**
Low Birth Weight *USE Birth Weight*
Statistical **Weighting**

Weightlessness
Weightlifting
Welfare Services (Government)
Animal **Welfare**
Child **Welfare**
Community **Welfare** Services
Public Welfare Services
   USE Community Welfare Services
Well Being
Wellness *USE Health*
Welsh Figure Preference Test
Barron **Welsh** Art Scale
Wepman Test of Auditory Discrim
Wernickes Syndrome
West Africa
West German Federal Republic
   USE West Germany
West Germany
West Indies
Western Europe
Western Samoa
Whales
Wheelchairs *USE Mobility Aids*
Whistleblowing *USE Informants*
White Betz A B Scale
White Blood Cells *USE Leucocytes*
White Collar Workers
White Noise
Whites
Mann **Whitney** U Test
Wholistic Health *USE Holistic Health*
Wide Range Achievement Test
Widowers
Widows
Wilcoxon Sign Rank Test
Wilderness Experience
Free Will *USE Volition*
Prader **Willi** Syndrome
James **(William)**
Willpower *USE Self Control*
Living Wills *USE Advance Directives*
Wilson Patterson Conservatism Scale
Wine
Winter Depression
   USE Seasonal Affective Disorder
Wisconsin Card Sorting Test
Wisdom
Witchcraft
Withdrawal (Defense Mechanism)
Alcohol **Withdrawal**
Drug **Withdrawal**
Treatment **Withholding**
Within Subjects Design
   USE Repeated Measures
Witnesses
Wives
Wolves
Women *USE Human Females*
Working **Women**
Womens Liberation Movement
Woodcock Johnson Psychoed Battery
Word Associations
Word Blindness *USE Alexia*
Word Deafness *USE Aphasia*
Word Frequency
Word Meaning
Word Origins *USE Etymology*
Word Processing
Word Recognition
Stroop Color **Word** Test
Words (Form Classes)
   USE Form Classes (Language)
Words (Phonetic Units)
Words (Vocabulary) *USE Vocabulary*
Work Adjustment Training
Work (Attitudes Toward)
Work Environments
   USE Working Conditions
Work Ethic *USE Work (Attitudes Toward)*

Work Load
Work Related Illnesses
Work Rest Cycles
Work Scheduling
Work Study Programs
    USE Educational Programs
Work Week Length
Field Work (Educational)
    USE Curricular Field Experience
Noise Levels (Work Areas)
Quality of Work Life
Return to Work *USE Reemployment*
School to Work Transition
Social Work *USE Social Casework*
Social Work Education
Workday Shifts
Workers *USE Personnel*
Agricultural Workers
Agricultural Extension Workers
Blue Collar Workers
Child Care Workers
Foreign Workers
Guest Workers *USE Foreign Workers*
Migrant Farm Workers
Psychiatric Social Workers
Skilled Industrial Workers
Social Workers
Unskilled Industrial Workers
White Collar Workers
Working Alliance
    USE Therapeutic Alliance
Working Conditions
Working Memory
    USE Short Term Memory
Working Space
Working Women
Workmens Compensation Insurance
Sheltered Workshops
World View
Third World Countries
    USE Developing Countries
Worms
Worry *USE Anxiety*
Worship *USE Religious Practices*
Wounds
Self Inflicted Wounds
Wrist
Writers
Writing (Creative) *USE Creative Writing*
Writing Skills
Creative Writing
Cursive Writing
Written Communication
Written Language
Wryneck *USE Torticollis*
X Ray Diagnosis *USE Roentgenography*
X Ray Therapy *USE Radiation Therapy*
Fragile X Syndrome
Xylocaine *USE Lidocaine*
Yawning
Yemen
Yoga
Yohimbine
Young Adults
Predelinquent Youth
Yugoslavia
Z Scores *USE Standard Scores*
Zulliger Z Test
Zaire
Zambia
New Zealand
Zen Buddhism
Non Zero Sum Games
Zidovudine
Zimbabwe
Zimeldine
Guilford Zimmerman Temperament Surv
Zinc
Zoo Environment *USE Animal Captivity*

Zoology
Zulliger Z Test
Zungs Self Rating Depression Scale

Alphabetical Clusters and Subclusters

Disorders Cluster

Antisocial Behavior & Behavior Disorders
Diagnosis
Disorder Characteristics
Learning Disorders & Mental Retardation
Physical & Psychosomatic Disorders
Psychological Disorders
Speech & Language Disorders
Symptomatology

Educational Cluster

Academic Learning & Achievement
Curricula
Educational Personnel & Administration
Educational Testing & Counseling
Schools & Institutions
Special Education
Student Characteristics & Academic
    Environment
Student Populations
Teaching & Teaching Methods

Geographic Cluster

Africa
Antarctica
Asia
Central America
Europe
Latin America
North America
Pacific Islands
South America
West Indies

Legal Cluster

Adjudication
Criminal Groups
Criminal Offenses
Criminal Rehabilitation
Laws
Legal Issues
Legal Personnel
Legal Processes

Neuropsychology & Neurology Cluster

Assessment & Diagnosis
Electrophysiology
Neuroanatomy
Neurological Disorders
Neurological Intervention
Neurosciences
Neurotransmitters & Neuroregulators

Occupational & Employment Cluster

Career Areas
Employee, Occupational & Job Characteristics
Management & Professional Personnel Issues
Occupational Groups
Organizations & Organizational Behavior
Personnel Management

Statistical Cluster

Design, Analysis & Interpretation
Statistical Reliability & Validity
Statistical Theory & Experimentation

Tests & Testing Cluster

Academic Achievement & Aptitude Measures
Attitude & Interest Measures
Intelligence Measures
Nonprojective Personality Measures
Perceptual Measures
Projective Personality Measures
Testing
Testing Methods

Treatment Cluster

Alternative Therapies
Behavior Modification
Counseling
Hospitalization & Institutionalization
Medical & Physical Treatment
Psychotherapy
Rehabilitation
Treatment (General)
Treatment Facilities

DISORDERS CLUSTER

- Antisocial Behavior & Behavior Disorders
- Diagnosis
- Disorder Characteristics
- Learning Disorders & Mental Retardation
- Physical & Psychosomatic Disorders
- Psychological Disorders
- Speech & Language Disorders
- Symptomatology

Antisocial Behavior & Behavior Disorders

Acquaintance Rape
Acute Alcoholic Intoxication
Addiction
Alcohol Abuse
Alcoholism
Antisocial Behavior
Antisocial Personality
Arson
Attempted Suicide
Battered Child Syndrome
Battered Females
Behavior Disorders
Behavior Problems
Child Abuse
Child Neglect
Chronic Alcoholic Intoxication
Conduct Disorder
Crime
Criminals
Driving Under The Influence
Drug Abuse
Drug Addiction
Drug Dependency
Elder Abuse
Emotional Abuse
Exhibitionism
Family Violence
Female Criminals
Female Delinquents
Fetishism
Genocide
Glue Sniffing
Heroin Addiction
Homicide
Incest
Infanticide
Inhalant Abuse
Intravenous Drug Usage
Juvenile Delinquency
Juvenile Delinquents
Juvenile Gangs
Kidnapping
Kleptomania
Male Criminals
Male Delinquents
Masochistic Personality

Partner Abuse
Pathological Gambling
Patient Abuse
Patient Violence
Pedophilia
Perpetrators
Physical Abuse
Polydrug Abuse
Pyromania
Rape
Sadomasochism
Sadomasochistic Personality
School Phobia
Sex Offenses
Sexual Abuse
Sexual Deviations
Sexual Masochism
Sexual Sadism
Shoplifting
Suicidal Ideation
Suicide
Theft
Transvestism
Truancy
Vandalism
Violence
Voyeurism

Diagnosis

Anatomically Detailed Dolls
Angiography
Biological Markers
Biopsy
Cardiography
Clinical Judgment (Not Diagnosis)
Comorbidity
Computer Assisted Diagnosis
Dexamethasone Suppression Test
Diagnosis
Diagnosis Related Groups
Diagnostic and Statistical Manual
Diagnostic Interview Schedule
Differential Diagnosis
Drug Usage Screening
Dual Diagnosis
Echoencephalography
Electro Oculography
Electrocardiography
Electroencephalography
Electromyography
Electronystagmography
Electroplethysmography
Electroretinography
Encephalography
Magnetic Resonance Imaging
Mammography
Medical Diagnosis
Medical Model
Neuropsychological Assessment
Ophthalmologic Examination
Physical Examination

Plethysmography
Pneumoencephalography
Prenatal Diagnosis
Prognosis
Psychodiagnosis
Psychodiagnostic Interview
Psychodiagnostic Typologies
Research Diagnostic Criteria
Rheoencephalography
Roentgenography
Screening
Symptom Checklists
Urinalysis

Disorder Characteristics

At Risk Populations
Chronicity (Disorders)
Client Attitudes
Client Characteristics
Comorbidity
Disease Course
Dual Diagnosis
Epidemiology
Ethnospecific Disorders
Etiology
Illness Behavior
Mortality Rate
Onset (Disorders)
Patient History
Predisposition
Premorbidity
Recovery (Disorders)
Relapse (Disorders)
Remission (Disorders)
Seasonal Variations
Severity (Disorders)
Spontaneous Remission
Susceptibility (Disorders)
Symptom Remission
Symptoms
Syndromes
Treatment Resistant Disorders

Learning Disorders & Mental Retardation

Acalculia
Alexia
Amaurotic Familial Idiocy
Anencephaly
Attention Deficit Disorder
Autism
Borderline Mental Retardation
Crying Cat Syndrome
Downs Syndrome
Dyslexia
Educable Mentally Retarded
Home Reared Mentally Retarded
Hyperkinesis
Idiot Savants
Institutionalized Mentally Retarded
Learning Disabilities

Consult Relationship Section for more information

Learning Disorders & Mental Retardation — (cont'd)

Learning Disorders
Mental Retardation
Mentally Retarded
Microcephaly
Profoundly Mentally Retarded
Psychosocial Mental Retardation
Reading Disabilities
Rett Syndrome
Severely Mentally Retarded
Trainable Mentally Retarded
Trisomy
Trisomy 21

Physical & Psychosomatic Disorders

Acquired Immune Deficiency Syndrome
Addisons Disease
Adrenal Gland Disorders
Adventitiously Handicapped
Agnosia
Agraphia
Allergic Disorders
Allergic Skin Disorders
Alopecia
Alzheimers Disease
Amblyopia
Amenorrhea
Amputees
Anaphylactic Shock
Anemia
Anencephaly
Aneurysms
Angina Pectoris
Anomie
Anorexia Nervosa
Anosmia
Anosognosia
Aphagia
Aphasia
Apnea
Appetite Disorders
Apraxia
Arrhythmias (Heart)
Arteriosclerosis
Asthenia
Asthma
Ataxia
Atherosclerosis
Athetosis
Audiogenic Seizures
Aurally Handicapped
Autonomic Nervous System Disorders
Autosome Disorders
Bacterial Disorders
Bacterial Meningitis
Barbiturate Poisoning
Benign Neoplasms
Birth Injuries

Blind
Blood and Lymphatic Disorders
Blood Pressure Disorders
Bone Disorders
Bradycardia
Brain Concussion
Brain Damage
Brain Damaged
Brain Disorders
Brain Neoplasms
Breast Neoplasms
Bronchial Disorders
Bulimia
Burns
Carbon Monoxide Poisoning
Cardiovascular Disorders
Catabolism
Catalepsy
Cataplexy
Cataracts
Central Nervous System Disorders
Cerebral Arteriosclerosis
Cerebral Hemorrhage
Cerebral Ischemia
Cerebral Palsy
Cerebrovascular Accidents
Cerebrovascular Disorders
Chorea
Chromosome Disorders
Chronic Pain
Cirrhosis (Liver)
Cleft Palate
Colitis
Colon Disorders
Color Blindness
Congenital Disorders
Congenitally Handicapped
Constipation
Coronary Prone Behavior
Coronary Thromboses
Creutzfeldt Jakob Syndrome
Crying Cat Syndrome
Cushings Syndrome
Cystic Fibrosis
Deaf
Deaf Blind
Dementia
Dermatitis
Developmental Disabilities
Diabetes
Diabetes Insipidus
Diabetes Mellitus
Diarrhea
Digestive System Disorders
Disorders
Drug Induced Congenital Disorders
Drug Induced Hallucinations
Dysarthria
Dyskinesia
Dysmenorrhea
Dysmorphophobia

Dyspareunia
Dyspnea
Ear Disorders
Eczema
Electrical Injuries
Embolisms
Encephalitis
Encephalomyelitis
Encephalopathies
Endocrine Disorders
Endocrine Neoplasms
Endocrine Sexual Disorders
Epilepsy
Epileptic Seizures
Epstein Barr Viral Disorder
Essential Hypertension
Ethnospecific Disorders
Eye Disorders
Failure to Thrive
Fecal Incontinence
Fetal Alcohol Syndrome
Fibrillation (Heart)
Food Allergies
Fragile X Syndrome
Frigidity
Gastrointestinal Disorders
Gastrointestinal Ulcers
General Paresis
Genetic Disorders
Genital Disorders
Gilles de la Tourette Disorder
Glaucoma
Goiters
Gonorrhea
Grand Mal Epilepsy
Gynecological Disorders
Handicapped
Hay Fever
Head Injuries
Headache
Health Impaired
Hearing Disorders
Heart Disorders
Hematoma
Hemianopia
Hemiplegia
Hemophilia
Hemorrhage
Hepatitis
Hermaphroditism
Herpes Genitalis
Herpes Simplex
Human Immunodeficiency Virus
Huntingtons Chorea
Hydrocephaly
Hyperglycemia
Hyperkinesis
Hyperphagia
Hypersexuality
Hypersomnia
Hyperthyroidism

Consult Relationship Section for more information

Physical & Psychosomatic Disorders — (cont'd)

Hypochondriasis
Hypoglycemia
Hypogonadism
Hypopituitarism
Hypotension
Hypothyroidism
Immunologic Disorders
Impotence
Infectious Disorders
Infertility
Influenza
Injuries
Insomnia
Irritable Bowel Syndrome
Ischemia
Jaundice
Joint Disorders
Kidney Diseases
Klinefelters Syndrome
Labyrinth Disorders
Laryngeal Disorders
Lead Poisoning
Leukemias
Lipid Metabolism Disorders
Liver Disorders
Lung Disorders
Lupus
Malaria
Male Genital Disorders
Measles
Memory Decay
Memory Disorders
Menieres Disease
Meningitis
Menstrual Disorders
Mercury Poisoning
Metabolism Disorders
Microcephaly
Migraine Headache
Minimal Brain Disorders
Minimally Brain Damaged
Motion Sickness
Movement Disorders
Multi Infarct Dementia
Multiple Sclerosis
Multiply Handicapped
Munchausen Syndrome
Muscle Contraction Headache
Muscle Spasms
Muscular Atrophy
Muscular Disorders
Muscular Dystrophy
Musculoskeletal Disorders
Myasthenia
Myasthenia Gravis
Myelitis
Myocardial Infarctions
Myoclonia
Myopia

Myotonia
Nail Biting
Narcolepsy
Narcosis
Neonatal Disorders
Neoplasms
Nervous System Disorders
Nervous System Neoplasms
Neuralgia
Neurasthenic Neurosis
Neurodermatitis
Neuromuscular Disorders
Neurosis
Neurosyphilis
Nocturnal Teeth Grinding
Nutritional Deficiencies
Nystagmus
Obesity
Obstetrical Complications
Organic Brain Syndromes
Osteoporosis
Otosclerosis
Paralysis
Paraplegia
Parasitic Disorders
Parathyroid Disorders
Parkinsons Disease
Partially Hearing Impaired
Partially Sighted
Pellagra
Perceptual Disturbances
Peripheral Nerve Disorders
Petit Mal Epilepsy
Phantom Limbs
Pharyngeal Disorders
Phenylketonuria
Physical Disfigurement
Physically Handicapped
Pica
Picks Disease
Pituitary Disorders
Pneumonia
Poliomyelitis
Porphyria
Prader Willi Syndrome
Premature Ejaculation
Premenstrual Tension
Presenile Dementia
Prosopagnosia
Protein Deficiency Disorders
Pruritus
Pseudodementia
Psychogenic Pain
Psychosomatic Disorders
Pulmonary Emphysema
Pulmonary Tuberculosis
Quadriplegia
Respiratory Distress
Respiratory Tract Disorders
Rett Syndrome
Rheumatic Fever

Rheumatoid Arthritis
Rubella
Sclerosis (Nervous System)
Self Inflicted Wounds
Senile Dementia
Senile Psychosis
Sense Organ Disorders
Sensorially Handicapped
Sex Chromosome Disorders
Sex Linked Hereditary Disorders
Sexual Function Disturbances
Sickle Cell Disease
Skin Disorders
Sleep Apnea
Sleep Disorders
Spina Bifida
Spinal Cord Injuries
Sterility
Sudden Infant Death
Syncope
Syndromes
Syphilis
Tachycardia
Terminal Cancer
Terminally Ill Patients
Testicular Feminization Syndrome
Thromboses
Thyroid Disorders
Thyrotoxicosis
Tinnitus
Torticollis
Toxic Disorders
Toxic Encephalopathies
Toxic Hepatitis
Toxic Psychoses
Toxicomania
Trigeminal Neuralgia
Tuberculosis
Tunnel Vision
Turners Syndrome
Ulcerative Colitis
Urinary Function Disorders
Urinary Incontinence
Urogenital Disorders
Vaginismus
Venereal Diseases
Viral Disorders
Vision Disorders
Visually Handicapped
Vitamin Deficiency Disorders
Wernickes Syndrome
Work Related Illnesses
Wounds

Psychological Disorders

Acrophobia
Acute Psychosis
Acute Schizophrenia
Adjustment Disorders
Affective Disturbances
Affective Psychosis

Consult Relationship Section for more information

Psychological Disorders — (cont'd)

Agoraphobia
Alcoholic Hallucinosis
Alcoholic Psychosis
Alexithymia
Amnesia
Anaclitic Depression
Anorexia Nervosa
Anxiety Neurosis
Aspergers Syndrome
Asthenic Personality
Auditory Hallucinations
Autism
Autistic Children
Avoidant Personality
Body Image Disturbances
Borderline States
Bulimia
Capgras Syndrome
Castration Anxiety
Catatonic Schizophrenia
Childhood Neurosis
Childhood Psychosis
Childhood Schizophrenia
Chronic Psychosis
Claustrophobia
Compulsive Repetition
Confabulation
Consciousness Disturbances
Conversion Neurosis
Cyclothymic Personality
Delirium Tremens
Delusions
Dementia
Dependent Personality
Depersonalization
Depression (Emotion)
Dissociative Neurosis
Dissociative Patterns
Dysfunctional Family
Dysmorphophobia
Dysthymic Disorder
Early Infantile Autism
Elective Mutism
Electra Complex
Emotionally Disturbed
Endogenous Depression
Explosive Personality
Factitious Disorders
Fantasies (Thought Disturbances)
Fetal Alcohol Syndrome
Folie A Deux
Fragmentation (Schizophrenia)
Fugue Reaction
Hallucinations
Hallucinosis
Hebephrenic Schizophrenia
Hypnagogic Hallucinations
Hypomania
Hysteria
Hysterical Anesthesia

Hysterical Paralysis
Hysterical Personality
Hysterical Vision Disturbances
Inadequate Personality
Infantilism
Involutional Depression
Involutional Paranoid Psychosis
Judgment Disturbances
Koro
Korsakoffs Psychosis
Major Depression
Malingering
Mania
Manic Depression
Mental Disorders
Mentally Ill Offenders
Multiple Personality
Munchausen Syndrome
Narcissistic Personality
Neuroleptic Malignant Syndrome
Neurosis
Neurotic Depressive Reaction
Obsessive Compulsive Neurosis
Obsessive Compulsive Personality
Occupational Neurosis
Oedipal Complex
Ophidiophobia
Organic Brain Syndromes
Panic Disorder
Paranoia (Psychosis)
Paranoid Personality
Paranoid Schizophrenia
Passive Aggressive Personality
Personality Disorders
Phobias
Postpartum Depression
Posttraumatic Stress Disorder
Presenile Dementia
Process Psychosis
Pseudocyesis
Pseudodementia
Psychogenic Pain
Psychopathology
Psychopathy
Psychosis
Reactive Depression
Reactive Psychosis
Recurrent Depression
Schizoaffective Disorder
Schizoid Personality
Schizophrenia
Schizophreniform Disorder
Schizophrenogenic Family
Schizophrenogenic Mothers
Schizotypal Personality
School Phobia
Seasonal Affective Disorder
Self Defeating Behavior
Self Destructive Behavior
Self Mutilation
Senile Dementia

Senile Psychosis
Separation Anxiety
Social Phobia
Speech Anxiety
Spreading Depression
Stress Reactions
Symbiotic Infantile Psychosis
Syndromes
Tardive Dyskinesia
Thought Disturbances
Toxic Psychoses
Traumatic Neurosis
Treatment Resistant Depression
Undifferentiated Schizophrenia
Visual Hallucinations
Work Related Illnesses

Speech & Language Disorders

Alexia
Aphasia
Articulation Disorders
Communication Disorders
Dysarthria
Dysphasia
Dysphonia
Echolalia
Glossolalia
Language Delay
Language Disorders
Mutism
Retarded Speech Development
Speech Disorders
Speech Handicapped
Stuttering

Symptomatology

Acting Out
Agitation
Akathisia
Amnesia
Anhedonia
Anoxia
Aphagia
Apnea
Apraxia
Asthenia
Ataxia
Athetosis
Automatism
Back Pain
Behavior Change
Binge Eating
Body Rocking
Bruxism
Catalepsy
Catatonia
Chronic Pain
Coma
Convulsions
Delirium
Diarrhea

Consult Relationship Section for more information

Symptomatology — (cont'd)

Extrapyramidal Symptoms
Fatigue
Hair Pulling
Head Banging
Headache
Hematoma
Hemorrhage
Hypersomnia
Hyperthermia
Hyperventilation
Hypothermia
Insomnia
Mental Confusion
Nail Biting
Nausea
Pain
Parkinsonism
Pruritus
Respiratory Distress
Restlessness
Scratching
Shock
Somatization
Spasms
Symptom Checklists
Symptom Remission
Symptoms
Syncope
Tics
Tremor
Vertigo
Vomiting
Wandering Behavior

EDUCATIONAL CLUSTER

- Academic Learning & Achievement
- Curricula
- Educational Personnel & Administration
- Educational Testing & Counseling
- Schools & Institutions
- Special Education
- Student Characteristics & Academic Environment
- Student Populations
- Teaching & Teaching Methods

Academic Learning & Achievement

Academic Achievement
Academic Achievement Motivation
Academic Achievement Prediction
Academic Aptitude
Academic Failure
Academic Overachievement
Academic Specialization
Academic Underachievement
College Academic Achievement

Cooperative Learning
Discrimination Learning
Foreign Language Learning
Generalization (Learning)
Incidental Learning
Intentional Learning
Interference (Learning)
Latent Learning
Learning
Learning Ability
Learning Rate
Learning Schedules
Learning Strategies
Learning Theory
Mastery Learning
Mathematics Achievement
Metacognition
Nonsense Syllable Learning
Nonverbal Learning
Note Taking
Observational Learning
Overlearning
Paired Associate Learning
Perceptual Motor Learning
Probability Learning
Reading Achievement
Reading Readiness
Reading Skills
Reading Speed
Recall (Learning)
Recognition (Learning)
Reconstruction (Learning)
Relearning
Retention
Rote Learning
School Graduation
School Learning
Sequential Learning
Serial Anticipation (Learning)
Serial Learning
Skill Learning
Social Learning
State Dependent Learning
Time On Task
Transfer (Learning)
Trial and Error Learning
Verbal Learning

Curricula

Adult Education
Affective Education
Art Education
Bilingual Education
Business Education
Career Education
Clinical Methods Training
Clinical Psychology Grad Training
Clinical Psychology Internship
Compensatory Education
Computer Training
Continuing Education

Cooperative Education
Counselor Education
Curriculum
Curriculum Development
Death Education
Dental Education
Driver Education
Drug Education
Education
Educational Program Accreditation
Educational Program Planning
Educational Programs
Elementary Education
Environmental Education
Equal Education
Extracurricular Activities
Foreign Language Education
Foreign Study
Graduate Education
Graduate Psychology Education
Health Education
Higher Education
Home Schooling
Inservice Teacher Education
Language Arts Education
Mathematics Education
Medical Education
Middle School Education
Multicultural Education
Music Education
Nonstandard English
Nontraditional Education
Nursing Education
Paraprofessional Education
Phonics
Physical Education
Postgraduate Training
Preschool Education
Private School Education
Project Follow Through
Project Head Start
Psychology Education
Psychotherapy Training
Public School Education
Reading Education
Religious Education
Remedial Education
Remedial Reading
Science Education
Secondary Education
Sex Education
Social Studies Education
Social Work Education
Special Education
Spelling
Sports
Teacher Education
Undergraduate Education
Upward Bound
Vocational Education

Consult Relationship Section for more information

Educational Personnel & Administration

Accreditation (Education Personnel)
Boards of Education
College Teachers
Cooperating Teachers
Educational Administration
Educational Personnel
Educational Program Accreditation
Educational Psychologists
Elementary School Teachers
High School Teachers
Junior High School Teachers
Parent School Relationship
Preschool Teachers
Preservice Teachers
Resource Teachers
School Administrators
School Counselors
School Nurses
School Principals
School Psychologists
School Superintendents
Special Education Teachers
Student Teachers
Teacher Aides
Teacher Attitudes
Teacher Characteristics
Teacher Education
Teacher Effectiveness Evaluation
Teacher Expectations
Teacher Personality
Teacher Recruitment
Teacher Student Interaction
Teacher Tenure
Teachers
Vocational Counselors
Vocational Education Teachers

Educational Testing & Counseling

Adaptive Testing
Coll Ent Exam Bd Scholastic Apt Test
Computer Assisted Testing
Course Evaluation
Cultural Test Bias
Curriculum Based Assessment
Educational Counseling
Educational Diagnosis
Educational Financial Assistance
Educational Measurement
Educational Placement
Educational Program Evaluation
Educational Psychology
Entrance Examinations
Essay Testing
Grading (Educational)
Graduate Record Examination
Group Testing
Minimum Competency Tests
Posttesting

Pretesting
School Counseling
School Psychology
Student Admission Criteria
Student Personnel Services
Student Records
Teacher Effectiveness Evaluation
Test Taking
Testing Methods
Testwiseness

Schools & Institutions

Boarding Schools
Campuses
Colleges
Community Colleges
Dormitories
Elementary Schools
Graduate Schools
High Schools
Institutional Schools
Junior High Schools
Kindergartens
Learning Centers (Educational)
Military Schools
Nongraded Schools
Nursery Schools
School Facilities
School Libraries
Schools
Technical Schools

Special Education

Acalculia
Agnosia
Agraphia
Alexia
Amaurotic Familial Idiocy
Anencephaly
Aphasia
Apraxia
Articulation Disorders
Ataxia
Attention Deficit Disorder
Aurally Handicapped
Autism
Autistic Children
Behavior Disorders
Behavior Problems
Borderline Mental Retardation
Braille Instruction
Cleft Palate
Communication Disorders
Compensatory Education
Crying Cat Syndrome
Deaf
Delayed Development
Developmental Disabilities
Downs Syndrome
Dysarthria
Dyskinesia

Dyslexia
Dysphasia
Dysphonia
Ear Disorders
Early Infantile Autism
Echolalia
Educable Mentally Retarded
Emotionally Disturbed
Gifted
Hearing Disorders
Home Reared Mentally Retarded
Hyperkinesis
Idiot Savants
Institutionalized Mentally Retarded
Language Disorders
Learning Disabilities
Learning Disorders
Mainstreaming (Educational)
Memory Disorders
Mental Retardation
Mentally Retarded
Microcephaly
Minimal Brain Disorders
Minimally Brain Damaged
Mutism
Partially Hearing Impaired
Perceptual Disturbances
Profoundly Mentally Retarded
Psychosocial Mental Retardation
Reading Disabilities
Remedial Education
Remedial Reading
Retarded Speech Development
Severely Mentally Retarded
Slow Learners
Special Education
Special Education Students
Speech Disorders
Speech Handicapped
Stuttering
Trainable Mentally Retarded

Student Characteristics & Academic Environment

Ability Level
Academic Achievement
Academic Achievement Motivation
Academic Aptitude
Academic Environment
Academic Failure
Academic Overachievement
Academic Specialization
Academic Underachievement
Artistic Ability
Athletic Participation
Classroom Behavior
Classroom Environment
Classrooms
Coeducation
Cognitive Ability
College Academic Achievement

Consult Relationship Section for more information

Student Characteristics & Academic Environment — (cont'd)

College Environment
Computer Literacy
Educational Aspirations
Educational Background
Educational Degrees
Educational Incentives
Educational Objectives
Fraternity Membership
Grade Level
Learning Ability
Literacy
Mathematics Anxiety
Musical Ability
Nonverbal Ability
Performance Anxiety
Reading Ability
Reading Comprehension
Reading Skills
School Adjustment
School Attendance
School Club Membership
School Enrollment
School Environment
School Expulsion
School Graduation
School Integration
School Phobia
School Readiness
School Refusal
School Retention
School Suspension
School to Work Transition
School Truancy
Sorority Membership
Special Needs
Student Activism
Student Attitudes
Student Attrition
Student Characteristics
Student Records
Study Habits
Teacher Student Interaction
Truancy
Verbal Ability
Writing Skills

Student Populations

Business Students
Classmates
College Athletes
College Dropouts
College Graduates
College Students
College Students
Community College Students
Dental Students
Dropouts

Education Students
Elementary School Students
Foreign Students
Gifted
Graduate Students
High School Graduates
High School Students
Intermediate School Students
Junior College Students
Junior High School Students
Kindergarten Students
Law Students
Medical Students
Middle School Students
Nursery School Students
Nursing Students
Postgraduate Students
Potential Dropouts
Preschool Students
Primary School Students
Reentry Students
ROTC Students
School Dropouts
School Leavers
Special Education Students
Students
Transfer Students
Vocational School Students

Teaching & Teaching Methods

Ability Grouping
Advance Organizers
Audiovisual Instruction
Braille Instruction
Classroom Behavior Modification
Classroom Discipline
Computer Assisted Instruction
Cooperative Learning
Curricular Field Experience
Directed Discussion Method
Discovery Teaching Method
Education
Educational Audiovisual Aids
Educational Field Trips
Educational Incentives
Educational Laboratories
Educational Objectives
Educational Television
Educational Toys
Feedback
Film Strips
Group Discussion
Group Instruction
Home Schooling
Homework
Individualized Instruction
Initial Teaching Alphabet
Instructional Media
Language Laboratories
Lecture Method
Lesson Plans

Montessori Method
Motion Pictures (Educational)
Nondirected Discussion Method
Open Classroom Method
Peer Tutoring
Programed Instruction
Programed Textbooks
Psychoeducation
Remedial Reading
Selected Readings
Self Instructional Training
Sight Vocabulary
Silent Reading
Student Teaching
Teaching
Teaching Machines
Teaching Methods
Team Teaching Method
Televised Instruction
Textbooks
Theories of Education
Tutoring
Videotape Instruction

GEOGRAPHIC CLUSTER

- Africa
- Arctic Regions
- Asia
- Central America
- Europe
- Latin America
- North America
- Pacific Islands
- South America
- West Indies

Africa

Africa
Algeria
Angola
Benin
Botswana
Cameroon
Congo
East Africa
Egypt
Ethiopia
Ghana
Guinea
Ivory Coast
Kenya
Liberia
Libya
Madagascar
Malawi
Mali
Morocco
Mozambique
Niger
Nigeria

Consult Relationship Section for more information

Africa — (cont'd)
Rwanda
Senegal
Somalia
South Africa
Sudan
Tanzania
Tunisia
Uganda
West Africa
Zaire
Zambia
Zimbabwe

Arctic Regions
Alaska
Antarctica
Canada
Union of Soviet Socialist Republics

Asia
Afghanistan
Asia
Bangladesh
Burma
Cambodia
Hong Kong
India
Indonesia
Iran
Iraq
Israel
Japan
Jordan
Korea
Kuwait
Laos
Lebanon
Malaysia
Mauritius
Middle East
Nepal
North Korea
Pacific Islands
Pakistan
Peoples Republic of China
Philippines
Saudi Arabia
Singapore
South Korea
South Pacific
Southeast Asia
Sri Lanka
Syria
Taiwan
Thailand
Tibet
Turkey

Union of Soviet Socialist Republics
Vietnam
Yemen

Central America
Belize
Central America
Costa Rica
El Salvador
Guatemala
Honduras
Nicaragua
Panama

Europe
Austria
Belgium
Bulgaria
Cyprus
Czechoslovakia
Denmark
East Germany
Eastern Europe
England
Europe
Finland
France
Germany
Great Britain
Greece
Hungary
Iceland
Ireland
Italy
Liechtenstein
Northern Ireland
Norway
Poland
Portugal
Romania
Scandinavia
Scotland
Spain
Sweden
Switzerland
Turkey
Union of Soviet Socialist Republics
United Kingdom
Wales
West Germany
Western Europe
Yugoslavia

Latin America
Latin America

North America
Alaska
Appalachia
Bermuda

Canada
Mexico
North America
United States

Pacific Islands
American Samoa
Australia
Fiji
Hawaii
New Zealand
Pacific Islands
Papua New Guinea
South Pacific
Tonga
Western Samoa

South America
Argentina
Bolivia
Brazil
Chile
Colombia
Ecuador
Guyana
Paraguay
Peru
South America
Surinam
Uruguay
Venezuela

West Indies
Bahama Islands
Barbados
Cuba
Haiti
Hispaniola
Jamaica
Puerto Rico
Saint Lucia
Trinidad and Tobago
Virgin Islands
West Indies

LEGAL CLUSTER
- Adjudication
- Criminal Groups
- Criminal Offenses
- Criminal Rehabilitation
- Laws
- Legal Issues
- Legal Personnel
- Legal Processes

Adjudication
Adjudication
Capital Punishment
Commitment (Psychiatric)

Consult Relationship Section for more information

Adjudication — (cont'd)

Competency to Stand Trial
Court Referrals
Crime Victims
Criminal Conviction
Criminal Justice
Criminal Responsibility
Defendants
Expert Testimony
Informants
Informed Consent
Insanity Defense
Juries
Jury Selection
Justice
Law Enforcement
Legal Arrest
Legal Decisions
Legal Detention
Legal Evidence
Legal Interrogation
Legal Processes
Legal Testimony
Parole
Polygraphs
Probation
Witnesses

Criminal Groups

Criminals
Defendants
Female Criminals
Female Delinquents
Juvenile Delinquency
Juvenile Delinquents
Juvenile Gangs
Male Criminals
Male Delinquents
Mentally Ill Offenders
Perpetrators
Predelinquent Youth
Prisoners

Criminal Offenses

Acquaintance Rape
Arson
Battered Child Syndrome
Battered Females
Child Abuse
Child Neglect
Crime
Driving Under The Influence
Elder Abuse
Family Violence
Fraud
Gambling
Genocide
Homicide
Incest
Infanticide

Kidnapping
Kleptomania
Obscenity
Pathological Gambling
Pedophilia
Persecution
Political Assassination
Pornography
Prostitution
Rape
Runaway Behavior
Sex Offenses
Sexual Abuse
Sexual Deviations
Sexual Harassment
Sexual Sadism
Shoplifting
Social Discrimination
Terrorism
Theft
Torture
Vandalism
Victimization
Voyeurism

Criminal Rehabilitation

Correctional Institutions
Criminology
Forensic Psychiatry
Forensic Psychology
Incarceration
Institutional Release
Institutional Schools
Institutionalization
Maximum Security Facilities
Parole
Penology
Prisons
Probation
Recidivism
Reformatories

Laws

Abortion Laws
Affirmative Action
Case Law
Civil Law
Criminal Law
Disability Laws
Drug Laws
Equal Education
Government Policy Making
Gun Control Laws
Health Care Policy
Law (Government)
Laws
Legal Decisions
Legislative Processes
Marihuana Laws
Medicare

Social Security
Social Security
Taxation

Legal Issues

Affirmative Action
Age Discrimination
Capital Punishment
Censorship
Child Care
Civil Rights
Cohabitation
Crime Prevention
Criminal Justice
Criminal Responsibility
Dangerousness
Drug Usage Screening
Employment Discrimination
Equal Education
Eugenics
Euthanasia
Human Rights
Illegitimate Children
Informed Consent
Marihuana Legalization
Morality
Political Revolution
Privileged Communication
Professional Liability
Race and Ethnic Discrimination
Refugees
Riots
Safety Belts
Safety Devices
School Integration
School Truancy
Self Defense
Sex Discrimination
Social Discrimination
Social Equality
Social Integration
Surrogate Parents (Humans)
Treatment Withholding
Victimization

Legal Personnel

Attorneys
Judges
Juries
Law Enforcement Personnel
Law Students
Legal Personnel
Parole Officers
Police Personnel
Prison Personnel
Probation Officers

Legal Processes

Adoption (Child)
Advance Directives
Advocacy

Consult Relationship Section for more information

Legal Processes — (cont'd)

Autopsy
Censorship
Child Custody
Child Support
Child Visitation
Child Welfare
Citizenship
Civil Rights
Client Rights
Commitment (Psychiatric)
Conflict Resolution
Consumer Protection
Court Referrals
Crime Prevention
Criminology
Divorce
Forensic Evaluation
Forensic Psychiatry
Forensic Psychology
Foster Care
Guardianship
Immigration
Interracial Adoption
Involuntary Treatment
Joint Custody
Labor Management Relations
Labor Union Members
Labor Unions
Legal Processes
Marihuana Legalization
Marital Separation
Mediation
Organizational Merger
Outpatient Commitment
Professional Licensing
Social Integration
Strikes

NEUROPSYCHOLOGY & NEUROLOGY CLUSTER

- Assessment & Diagnosis
- Electrophysiology
- Neuroanatomy
- Neurological Disorders
- Neurological Intervention
- Neurosciences
- Neurotransmitters & Neuroregulators

Assessment & Diagnosis

Bender Gestalt Test
Echoencephalography
Electroencephalography
Halstead Reitan Neuropsych Battery
Luria Nebraska Neuropsych Battery
Magnetic Resonance Imaging
Magnetoencephalography
Memory for Designs Test
Mini Mental State Examination

Neuropsychological Assessment
Pneumoencephalography
Rheoencephalography
Wechsler Memory Scale
Wisconsin Card Sorting Test

Electrophysiology

Alpha Rhythm
Auditory Evoked Potentials
Contingent Negative Variation
Cortical Evoked Potentials
Delta Rhythm
Electrical Activity
Electroencephalography
Electrophysiology
Evoked Potentials
Kindling
Magnetoencephalography
Olfactory Evoked Potentials
Postactivation Potentials
Somatosensory Evoked Potentials
Theta Rhythm
Visual Evoked Potentials

Neuroanatomy

Abducens Nerve
Acoustic Nerve
Adrenergic Nerves
Afferent Pathways
Amygdaloid Body
Auditory Cortex
Auditory Neurons
Autonomic Ganglia
Autonomic Nervous System
Axons
Baroreceptors
Basal Ganglia
Blood Brain Barrier
Brain
Brain Size
Brain Stem
Brain Weight
Caudate Nucleus
Central Nervous System
Cerebellum
Cerebral Blood Flow
Cerebral Cortex
Cerebral Dominance
Cerebral Ventricles
Cerebrospinal Fluid
Chemoreceptors
Cholinergic Nerves
Cones (Eye)
Cranial Spinal Cord
Cutaneous Receptive Fields
Cutaneous Sense
Dendrites
Diencephalon
Dorsal Horns
Dorsal Roots
Efferent Pathways

Extrapyramidal Tracts
Facial Nerve
Forebrain
Fornix
Fovea
Frontal Lobe
Ganglia
Ganglion Cells (Retina)
Geniculate Bodies (Thalamus)
Globus Pallidus
Gyrus Cinguli
Hippocampus
Hypothalamo Hypophyseal System
Hypothalamus
Inferior Colliculus
Interhemispheric Interaction
Lateral Dominance
Left Brain
Lemniscal System
Limbic System
Locus Ceruleus
Lumbar Spinal Cord
Mechanoreceptors
Medial Forebrain Bundle
Medulla Oblongata
Meninges
Mesencephalon
Motor Cortex
Motor Neurons
Myelin Sheath
Nerve Endings
Nerve Growth Factor
Nerve Tissues
Nervous System
Neural Analyzers
Neural Development
Neural Pathways
Neural Plasticity
Neural Receptors
Neurons
Nociceptors
Nucleus Basalis Magnocellularis
Occipital Lobe
Ocular Dominance
Olfactory Bulb
Olfactory Nerve
Optic Chiasm
Optic Lobe
Optic Nerve
Optic Tract
Parasympathetic Nervous System
Parietal Lobe
Periaqueductal Gray
Peripheral Nervous System
Photoreceptors
Pons
Preoptic Area
Proprioceptors
Purkinje Cells
Pyramidal Tracts
Raphe Nuclei

Consult Relationship Section for more information

Neuroanatomy — (cont'd)

Receptive Fields
Receptor Binding
Reticular Formation
Retina
Right Brain
Rods (Eye)
Sense Organs
Sensory Neurons
Septal Nuclei
Somatosensory Cortex
Spinal Ganglia
Substantia Nigra

Neurological Disorders

Acalculia
Agnosia
Agraphia
Alcoholic Hallucinosis
Alcoholic Psychosis
Alexia
Alzheimers Disease
Anencephaly
Anoxia
Aphasia
Apraxia
Ataxia
Athetosis
Audiogenic Seizures
Autonomic Nervous System Disorders
Back Pain
Bacterial Meningitis
Brain Concussion
Brain Damage
Brain Damaged
Brain Disorders
Brain Neoplasms
Catalepsy
Cataplexy
Central Nervous System Disorders
Cerebral Arteriosclerosis
Cerebral Atrophy
Cerebral Hemorrhage
Cerebral Ischemia
Cerebral Palsy
Cerebrovascular Accidents
Cerebrovascular Disorders
Chorea
Chronic Pain
Coma
Convulsions
Creutzfeldt Jakob Syndrome
Delirium Tremens
Dementia
Dysarthria
Dyskinesia
Dyslexia
Dysphasia
Dysphonia
Encephalitis

Encephalomyelitis
Encephalopathies
Epilepsy
Epileptic Seizures
Extrapyramidal Symptoms
General Paresis
Gilles de la Tourette Disorder
Grand Mal Epilepsy
Head Injuries
Headache
Hemianopia
Hemiplegia
Huntingtons Chorea
Hydrocephaly
Hyperkinesis
Korsakoffs Psychosis
Memory Disorders
Meningitis
Microcephaly
Migraine Headache
Minimal Brain Disorders
Minimally Brain Damaged
Movement Disorders
Multi Infarct Dementia
Multiple Sclerosis
Muscle Contraction Headache
Muscular Dystrophy
Myasthenia Gravis
Myelitis
Myoclonia
Myofascial Pain
Narcolepsy
Nervous System Disorders
Nervous System Neoplasms
Neuralgia
Neuroleptic Malignant Syndrome
Neuromuscular Disorders
Neuropathology
Neurosyphilis
Organic Brain Syndromes
Pain
Paralysis
Paraplegia
Parkinsons Disease
Peripheral Nerve Disorders
Petit Mal Epilepsy
Picks Disease
Poliomyelitis
Presenile Dementia
Quadriplegia
Sclerosis (Nervous System)
Senile Dementia
Senile Psychosis
Spasms
Spinal Cord Injuries
Tardive Dyskinesia
Tics
Torticollis
Toxic Encephalopathies

Tremor
Trigeminal Neuralgia
Wernickes Syndrome

Neurological Intervention

Afferent Stimulation
Brain Lesions
Brain Self Stimulation
Brain Stimulation
Chemical Brain Stimulation
Commissurotomy
Decerebration
Decortication (Brain)
Electrical Brain Stimulation
Hemispherectomy
Hypothalamus Lesions
Kindling
Neural Lesions
Neural Transplantation
Neurosurgery
Psychosurgery
Pyramidotomy
Stereotaxic Techniques
Sympathectomy
Thalamotomy
Tractotomy
Vagotomy

Neurosciences

Neural Networks
Neural Transplantation
Neuroanatomy
Neurobiology
Neurochemistry
Neuroendocrinology
Neurolinguistics
Neurology
Neuropathology
Neurophysiology
Neuropsychiatry
Neuropsychology
Neurosciences
Neurosurgery
Psychoneuroimmunology
Psychopharmacology
Psychosurgery

Neurotransmitters & Neuroregulators

Acetylcholine
Acetylcholinesterase
Adenosine
Alanines
Angiotensin
Aspartic Acid
Bombesin
Catecholamines
Cholecystokinin
Choline
Cholinesterase

Consult Relationship Section for more information

Neurotransmitters & Neuroregulators — (cont'd)

Dihydroxyphenylacetic Acid
Dihydroxytryptamine
Dopamine
Dopamine Metabolites
Dynorphins
Endogenous Opiates
Endorphins
Enkephalins
Epinephrine
Gamma Aminobutyric Acid
Glutamic Acid
Glycine
Histamine
Homovanillic Acid
Hydroxydopamine (6-)
Hydroxyindoleacetic Acid (5-)
Ibotenic Acid
Kainic Acid
Melanocyte Stimulating Hormone
Methoxyhydroxyphenylglycol (3,4)
Monoamine Oxidases
Neurotensin
Neurotoxins
Neurotransmitters
Norepinephrine
Norepinephrine Metabolites
Oxytocin
Peptides
Phenethylamines
Serotonin
Serotonin Metabolites
Somatostatin
Substance P
Taurine
Tryptamine
Tyramine

OCCUPATIONAL & EMPLOYMENT CLUSTER

- Career Areas
- Employee, Occupational & Job Characteristics
- Management & Professional Personnel Issues
- Occupational Groups
- Organizations & Organizational Behavior
- Personnel Management

Career Areas

Advertising
Air Traffic Control
Business
Business Management
Child Care
Child Day Care
Community Psychology

Computer Programing
Consultation Liaison Psychiatry
Data Processing
Educational Administration
Educational Psychology
Entrepreneurship
Experimental Psychology
Forensic Psychiatry
Forensic Psychology
Gynecology
Health Promotion
Human Factors Engineering
Hypnotherapy
Industrial Psychology
Job Corps
Law Enforcement
Nontraditional Careers
Obstetrics
Occupational Therapy
Optometry
Paramedical Sciences
Pastoral Counseling
Pathology
Peace Corps
Pediatrics
Physical Therapy
Physics
Politics
Psychiatry
Psychology
Psychotherapy
Public Relations
Rehabilitation
Rehabilitation Counseling
Retailing
School Psychology
Self Employment
Social Casework
Social Psychology
Sociology
Speech Therapy
Sport Psychology
Sports
Surgery
Veterinary Medicine
Vocational Rehabilitation
Word Processing
Zoology

Employee, Occupational & Job Characteristics

Career Change
Clerical Secretarial Skills
Division of Labor
Dual Careers
Employability
Employee Absenteeism
Employee Attitudes
Employee Characteristics
Employee Efficiency
Employee Interaction

Employee Motivation
Employee Productivity
Employee Skills
Employee Turnover
Employer Attitudes
Employment History
Employment Status
Health Personnel Attitudes
Impaired Professionals
Income Level
Industrial Accidents
Job Applicant Attitudes
Job Characteristics
Job Enrichment
Job Experience Level
Job Involvement
Job Performance
Job Satisfaction
Job Search
Job Security
Labor Union Members
Mentor
Noise Levels (Work Areas)
Occupational Adjustment
Occupational Aspirations
Occupational Attitudes
Occupational Choice
Occupational Exposure
Occupational Interests
Occupational Mobility
Occupational Neurosis
Occupational Preference
Occupational Safety
Occupational Status
Occupational Stress
Occupational Success
Occupational Tenure
Organizational Commitment
Private Practice
Professional Identity
Professional Specialization
Quality of Work Life
Reemployment
Retirement
Salaries
School to Work Transition
Typing
Unemployment
Vocational Maturity
Work (Attitudes Toward)
Work Adjustment Training
Work Load
Work Related Illnesses
Work Rest Cycles
Work Scheduling
Work Week Length
Workday Shifts
Working Conditions
Working Space
Working Women

Consult Relationship Section for more information

Management & Professional Personnel Issues

Affirmative Action
Career Development
Entrepreneurship
Labor Management Relations
Leadership
Leadership Style
Management
Management Decision Making
Management Methods
Management Personnel
Management Planning
Management Training
Middle Level Managers
Participative Management
Policy Making
Private Practice
Professional Certification
Professional Consultation
Professional Development
Professional Ethics
Professional Examinations
Professional Fees
Professional Identity
Professional Liability
Professional Licensing
Professional Referral
Professional Specialization
Professional Standards
Professional Supervision
Quality Control
Stress Management
Strikes
Top Level Managers

Occupational Groups

Accountants
Aerospace Personnel
Agricultural Extension Workers
Agricultural Workers
Air Force Personnel
Aircraft Pilots
Anthropologists
Apprenticeship
Architects
Army Personnel
Artists
Astronauts
Athletes
Attendants (Institutions)
Attorneys
Blue Collar Workers
Business and Industrial Personnel
Chaplains
Child Care Workers
Clergy
Clerical Personnel
Clinical Psychologists
Clinicians

Coaches
Coast Guard Personnel
College Teachers
Commissioned Officers
Cooperating Teachers
Counseling Psychologists
Counselor Trainees
Counselors
Dentistry
Dentists
Domestic Service Personnel
Draftees
Educational Personnel
Educational Psychologists
Elementary School Teachers
Engineers
Enlisted Military Personnel
Evangelists
Experimental Psychologists
Family Physicians
Fire Fighters
Foreign Workers
General Practitioners
Government Personnel
Gynecologists
Health Personnel
High School Teachers
Hypnotherapists
Hypnotists
Industrial Foremen
Industrial Psychologists
Informants
Information Specialists
Internists
Interviewers
Job Applicants
Journalists
Judges
Junior High School Teachers
Labor Union Members
Law Enforcement Personnel
Lay Religious Personnel
Legal Personnel
Librarians
Management Personnel
Marine Personnel
Mathematicians
Medical Personnel
Medics
Mental Health Personnel
Middle Level Managers
Migrant Farm Workers
Military Medical Personnel
Military Personnel
Ministers (Religion)
Missionaries
Musicians
National Guardsmen
Navy Personnel
Neurologists
Noncommissioned Officers

Nonprofessional Personnel
Nuns
Nurses
Obstetricians
Occupational Therapists
Occupations
Optometrists
Paramedical Personnel
Paraprofessional Personnel
Parole Officers
Pathologists
Pediatricians
Personnel
Pharmacists
Physical Therapists
Physicians
Physicists
Police Personnel
Politicians
Preschool Teachers
Preservice Teachers
Priests
Prison Personnel
Probation Officers
Professional Personnel
Psychiatric Aides
Psychiatric Hospital Staff
Psychiatric Nurses
Psychiatric Social Workers
Psychiatrists
Psychoanalysts
Psychologists
Psychotherapists
Public Health Service Nurses
Rabbis
Rehabilitation Counselors
Religious Personnel
Resource Teachers
Sales Personnel
School Administrators
School Counselors
School Nurses
School Principals
School Psychologists
School Superintendents
Scientists
Secretarial Personnel
Seminarians
Service Personnel
Skilled Industrial Workers
Social Psychologists
Social Workers
Sociologists
Special Education Teachers
Speech Therapists
Student Teachers
Surgeons
Teacher Aides
Teachers
Technical Personnel
Technical Service Personnel

Consult Relationship Section for more information

Occupational Groups — (cont'd)

Therapist Trainees
Therapists
Top Level Managers
Unskilled Industrial Workers
Vocational Counselors
Vocational Education Teachers
Volunteer Civilian Personnel
Volunteer Military Personnel
Volunteer Personnel
Volunteers in Service to America
White Collar Workers
Working Women
Writers

Organizations & Organizational Behavior

Business Organizations
Choice Shift
Decentralization
Division of Labor
Entrepreneurship
Foreign Organizations
Government Agencies
International Organizations
Labor Unions
Nonprofit Organizations
Organizational Behavior
Organizational Change
Organizational Climate
Organizational Commitment
Organizational Crises
Organizational Development
Organizational Effectiveness
Organizational Merger
Organizational Objectives
Organizational Structure
Organizations
Professional Organizations
Religious Organizations
Teams

Personnel Management

Affirmative Action
Age Discrimination
Assessment Centers
Bonuses
Career Development
Career Education
Conflict Resolution
Disability Evaluation
Disability Management
Employee Assistance Programs
Employee Benefits
Employee Health Insurance
Employee Leave Benefits
Employee Pension Plans
Employee Turnover
Employer Attitudes
Employment Discrimination

Employment Tests
Inservice Training
Job Analysis
Job Applicant Interviews
Job Applicant Screening
Job Search
Labor Management Relations
Management Training
Mediation
Medical Personnel Supply
Mental Health Inservice Training
Mental Health Personnel Supply
Military Recruitment
Military Training
Occupational Guidance
Occupational Success Prediction
On the Job Training
Personnel Evaluation
Personnel Management
Personnel Placement
Personnel Promotion
Personnel Recruitment
Personnel Selection
Personnel Supply
Personnel Termination
Personnel Training
Policy Making
Quality Control
Race and Ethnic Discrimination
Reemployment
Salaries
Sex Discrimination
Sexual Harassment
Social Security
Stress Management
Strikes
Supported Employment
Teacher Recruitment
Unemployment
Vocational Evaluation
Workmens Compensation Insurance

STATISTICAL CLUSTER

- Design, Analysis & Interpretation
- Statistical Reliability & Validity
- Statistical Theory & Experimentation

Design, Analysis & Interpretation

Algorithms
Analysis of Covariance
Analysis of Variance
Between Groups Design
Causal Analysis
Central Tendency Measures
Chi Square Test
Cluster Analysis
Cochran Q Test
Cohort Analysis
Content Analysis
Content Analysis (Test)

Equimax Rotation
Error Analysis
Error of Measurement
Experimental Design
F Test
Factor Analysis
Factor Analysis
Factor Structure
Fuzzy Set Theory
Goodness of Fit
Heuristic Modeling
Interaction Analysis (Statistics)
Interaction Variance
Item Analysis (Statistical)
Item Analysis (Test)
Item Response Theory
Kolmogorov Smirnov Test
Least Squares
Linear Regression
Mann Whitney U Test
Markov Chains
Mathematical Modeling
Maximum Likelihood
Mean
Median
Meta Analysis
Multidimensional Scaling
Multiple Regression
Multivariate Analysis
Nonlinear Regression
Nonparametric Statistical Tests
Oblique Rotation
Orthogonal Rotation
Parametric Statistical Tests
Path Analysis
Phi Coefficient
Point Biserial Correlation
Probability
Q Sort Testing Technique
Quartimax Rotation
Rank Difference Correlation
Rank Order Correlation
Repeated Measures
Scaling (Testing)
Score Equating
Sign Test
Spearman Brown Test
Standard Deviation
Standard Scores
Statistical Analysis
Statistical Correlation
Statistical Data
Statistical Estimation
Statistical Measurement
Statistical Norms
Statistical Probability
Statistical Regression
Statistical Rotation
Statistical Tables
Statistical Tests
Statistical Weighting

Consult Relationship Section for more information

Design, Analysis & Interpretation — (cont'd)

Stochastic Modeling
Structural Equation Modeling
T Test
Tetrachoric Correlation
Time Series
Variability Measurement
Variance Homogeneity
Varimax Rotation
Wilcoxon Sign Rank Test
Zulliger Z Test

Statistical Reliability & Validity

Concurrent Validity
Construct Validity
Content Analysis
Content Analysis (Test)
Error Analysis
Error of Measurement
Factorial Validity
Interrater Reliability
Item Analysis (Statistical)
Item Content (Test)
Predictive Validity
Statistical Power
Statistical Reliability
Statistical Validity
Test Reliability
Test Validity

Statistical Theory & Experimentation

Biased Sampling
Binomial Distribution
Confidence Limits (Statistics)
Conjoint Measurement
Consistency (Measurement)
Cutting Scores
Data Collection
Data Processing
Dependent Variables
Double Bind Interaction
Effect Size (Statistical)
Empirical Methods
Experiment Controls
Experimental Design
Experimental Replication
Experimental Subjects
Experimentation
Experimenter Bias
Frequency Distribution
Fuzzy Set Theory
Halo Effect
Independent Variables
Knowledge of Results
Mathematical Psychology
Maximum Likelihood
Methodology
Normal Distribution

Null Hypothesis Testing
Population (Statistics)
Prediction Errors
Random Sampling
Sampling (Experimental)
Skewed Distribution
Statistical Data
Statistical Sample Parameters
Statistical Samples
Statistical Significance
Statistical Tables
Statistical Variables
Statistics
Type I Errors
Type II Errors

TESTS & TESTING CLUSTER

- Academic Achievement & Aptitude Measures
- Attitude & Interest Measures
- Developmental Measures
- Intelligence Measures
- Neuropsychological Measures
- Nonprojective Personality Measures
- Perceptual Measures
- Projective Personality Measures
- Testing
- Testing Methods

Academic Achievement & Aptitude Measures

Achievement Measures
Aptitude Measures
Coll Ent Exam Bd Scholastic Apt Test
Comprehension Tests
Differential Aptitude Tests
Educational Measurement
Entrance Examinations
Gates MacGinitie Reading Tests
General Aptitude Test Battery
Graduate Record Examination
Iowa Tests of Basic Skills
Metropolitan Readiness Tests
Minimum Competency Tests
Modern Language Aptitude Test
Professional Examinations
Reading Measures
Retention Measures
School and College Ability Test
Stanford Achievement Test
Verbal Tests
Wide Range Achievement Test
Woodcock Johnson Psychoed Battery

Attitude & Interest Measures

Attitude Measurement
Attitude Measures
Consumer Surveys
Interest Inventories

Kuder Occupational Interest Survey
Kuder Preference Record
Least Preferred Coworker Scale
Minnesota Teacher Attitude Inventory
Occupational Interest Measures
Opinion Attitude and Interest Survey
Parent Attitude Research Instrument
Preference Measures
Strong Vocational Interest Blank
Wilson Patterson Conservatism Scale

Developmental Measures

Bayley Scales of Infant Development

Intelligence Measures

Army General Classification Test
Benton Revised Visual Retention Test
California Test of Mental Maturity
Columbia Mental Maturity Scale
Creativity Measurement
Culture Fair Intelligence Test
Frostig Development Test Vis Percept
Goodenough Harris Draw A Person Test
Henmon Nelson Tests Mental Ability
Hidden Figures Test
Illinois Test Psycholinguist Abil
Infant Intelligence Scale
Intelligence Measures
Kaufman Assessment Battery Children
Kohs Block Design Test
Leiter Adult Intelligence Scale
Lorge Thorndike Intelligence Test
Lowenfeld Mosaic Test
Miller Anaiogies Test
Peabody Picture Vocabulary Test
Porteus Maze Test
Raven Coloured Progressive Matrices
Raven Progressive Matrices
Remote Associates Test
Slosson Intelligence Test for Child
Stanford Binet Intelligence Scale
Temporal Spatial Concept Scale
Vane Kindergarten Test
Verbal Tests
Wechsler Adult Intelligence Scale
Wechsler Bellevue Intelligence Scale
Wechsler Intelligence Scale Children
Wechsler Memory Scale
Wechsler Preschool Primary Scale

Neuropsychological Measures

Bender Gestalt Test
Halstead Reitan Neuropsych Battery
Luria Nebraska Neuropsych Battery
Mini Mental State Examination
Wechsler Memory Scale
Wisconsin Card Sorting Test

Consult Relationship Section for more information

Nonprojective Personality Measures

Allport Vernon Lindzey Study Values
Authoritarianism Rebellion Scale
Bannister Repertory Grid
Barrett Lennard Relationship Invent
Barron Welsh Art Scale
Beck Depression Inventory
Bem Sex Role Inventory
California F Scale
California Psychological Inventory
California Test of Personality
Child Behavior Checklist
Childrens Manifest Anxiety Scale
Childrens Personality Questionnaire
Differential Personality Inventory
Edwards Personal Preference
    Schedule
Edwards Personality Inventory
Edwards Social Desirability Scale
Embedded Figures Testing
Eysenck Personality Inventory
Fear Survey Schedule
Fund Interper Rela Orientat Beh Ques
General Health Questionnaire
Goldstein Scheerer Object Sort Test
Gough Adjective Check List
Guilford Zimmerman Temperament
    Surv
High Sch Personality Questionnaire
Kupfer Detre Self Rating Scale
Learys Interpersonal Check List
Marlowe Crowne Soc Desirabil Scale
Maudsley Personality Inventory
Memory for Designs Test
Millon Clinical Multiaxial Inventory
Minn Multiphasic Personality Inven
Mooney Problem Check List
Myers Briggs Type Indicator
Nonprojective Personality Measures
Omnibus Personality Inventory
Personal Orientation Inventory
Personality Measures
Psychological Screening Inventory
Repression Sensitization Scale
Rod and Frame Test
Rokeach Dogmatism Scale
Rotter Intern Extern Locus Cont Scal
Sensation Seeking Scale
Sixteen Personality Factors Question
State Trait Anxiety Inventory
Taylor Manifest Anxiety Scale
Tennessee Self Concept Scale
Vineland Social Maturity Scale
Welsh Figure Preference Test
White Betz A B Scale
Zungs Self Rating Depression Scale

Perceptual Measures

Perceptual Measures
Psychophysical Measurement
Purdue Perceptual Motor Survey
Sensorimotor Measures
Speech and Hearing Measures
Stroop Color Word Test
Wepman Test of Auditory Discrim

Projective Personality Measures

Bender Gestalt Test
Blacky Pictures Test
Childrens Apperception Test
Color Pyramid Test
Franck Drawing Completion Test
Holtzman Inkblot Technique
Human Figures Drawing
Incomplete Man Test
Onomatopoeia and Images Test
Personality Measures
Projective Personality Measures
Projective Techniques
Projective Testing Technique
Rorschach Test
Rosenzweig Picture Frustration Study
Rotter Incomplete Sentences Blank
Sentence Completion Tests
Szondi Test
Thematic Apperception Test
Zulliger Z Test

Testing

Concurrent Validity
Consistency (Measurement)
Construct Validity
Content Analysis (Test)
Cultural Test Bias
Cutting Scores
Difficulty Level (Test)
Employment Tests
Factor Analysis
Factor Structure
Factorial Validity
Foreign Language Translation
Inventories
Item Analysis (Test)
Item Content (Test)
Item Response Theory
Measurement
Performance Tests
Piagetian Tasks
Predictive Validity
Profiles (Measurement)
Psychometrics
Rating Scales
Score Equating
Scoring (Testing)
Screening Tests
Selection Tests
Semantic Differential

Sociometric Tests
Sociometry
Standard Scores
Standardized Tests
Statistical Weighting
Subtests
Test Administration
Test Anxiety
Test Bias
Test Construction
Test Forms
Test Interpretation
Test Items
Test Norms
Test Reliability
Test Scores
Test Standardization
Test Taking
Test Validity
Testing
Testwiseness

Testing Methods

Adaptive Testing
Behavioral Assessment
Biographical Inventories
Body Sway Testing
Cloze Testing
Computer Assisted Testing
Criterion Referenced Tests
Digit Span Testing
Essay Testing
Forced Choice (Testing Method)
Group Testing
Individual Testing
Inventories
Likert Scales
Matching to Sample
Multiple Choice (Testing Method)
Neuropsychological Assessment
Posttesting
Pretesting
Q Sort Testing Technique
Questionnaires
Rating Scales
Scaling (Testing)
Surveys
Testing Methods

TREATMENT CLUSTER

- Alternative Therapies
- Behavior Modification & Therapy
- Counseling
- Hospitalization & Institutionalization
- Medical & Physical Treatment
- Psychotherapy
- Rehabilitation
- Treatment (General)
- Treatment Facilities

Consult Relationship Section for more information

Alternative Therapies

Acupuncture
Aerobic Exercise
Animal Assisted Therapy
Art Therapy
Autohypnosis
Communication Skills Training
Consciousness Raising Groups
Creative Arts Therapy
Dance Therapy
Encounter Group Therapy
Faith Healing
Folk Medicine
Holistic Health
Home Care
Home Visiting Programs
Hospice
Human Relations Training
Hypnosis
Hypnotherapy
Imagery
Meditation
Milieu Therapy
Morita Therapy
Motivation Training
Music Therapy
Outpatient Treatment
Pain Management
Partial Hospitalization
Phototherapy
Poetry Therapy
Primal Therapy
Recreation Therapy
Role Playing
Self Medication
Sensitivity Training
Sex Therapy
Sleep Treatment
Social Skills Training
Sociotherapy
Stress Management
Support Groups
Therapeutic Camps
Therapeutic Community
Therapeutic Social Clubs
Wilderness Experience

Behavior Modification & Therapy

Assertiveness Training
Aversion Therapy
Behavior Contracting
Behavior Modification
Behavior Therapy
Biofeedback Training
Contingency Management
Counterconditioning
Covert Sensitization
Fading (Conditioning)
Implosive Therapy
Omission Training

Overcorrection
Progressive Relaxation Therapy
Reciprocal Inhibition Therapy
Relaxation Therapy
Self Help Techniques
Self Management
Systematic Desensitization Therapy
Time Out
Token Economy Programs

Counseling

AIDS Prevention
Counseling
Counseling Psychology
Couples Therapy
Crisis Intervention
Crisis Intervention Services
Drug Abuse Prevention
Family Planning
Feminist Therapy
Genetic Counseling
Group Counseling
Health Promotion
Hot Line Services
Marriage Counseling
Pastoral Counseling
Peer Counseling
Premarital Counseling
Psychotherapeutic Counseling
Rehabilitation Counseling
Social Casework
Suicide Prevention
Suicide Prevention Centers

Hospitalization & Institutionalization

Deinstitutionalization
Discharge Planning
Emergency Services
Hospital Administration
Hospital Admission
Hospital Discharge
Hospital Environment
Hospital Programs
Hospitalization
Hospitalized Patients
Hospitals
Institution Visitation
Institutional Release
Institutionalization
Intensive Care
Nursing
Outpatient Treatment
Partial Hospitalization
Patient Seclusion
Psychiatric Hospital Admission
Psychiatric Hospital Discharge
Psychiatric Hospital Programs
Psychiatric Hospital Readmission

Psychiatric Hospitalization
Psychiatric Units
Therapeutic Community

Medical & Physical Treatment

Acupuncture
Adrenalectomy
Amputation
Artificial Pacemakers
Artificial Respiration
Biopsy
Blood Transfusion
Castration
Catheterization
Cochlear Implants
Colostomy
Commissurotomy
Dental Surgery
Dental Treatment
Dialysis
Diuresis
Drug Therapy
Electroconvulsive Shock Therapy
Electrosleep Treatment
Endocrine Gland Surgery
Family Medicine
Fertility Enhancement
Health Care Services
Health Maintenance Organizations
Heart Surgery
Hemispherectomy
Hemodialysis
Hormone Therapy
Hypophysectomy
Hysterectomy
Immunization
Induced Abortion
Insulin Shock Therapy
Intensive Care
Laser Irradiation
Male Castration
Mastectomy
Medical Therapeutic Devices
Medical Treatment (General)
Mobility Aids
Neural Transplantation
Neurosurgery
Organ Transplantation
Organic Therapies
Outpatient Treatment
Ovariectomy
Pain Management
Phototherapy
Physical Therapy
Physical Treatment Methods
Pinealectomy
Plastic Surgery
Postsurgical Complications
Prenatal Care
Preventive Medicine
Primary Health Care

Consult Relationship Section for more information

Medical & Physical Treatment — (cont'd)

Prostheses
Psychosomatic Medicine
Psychosurgery
Public Health Services
Pyramidotomy
Radiation Therapy
Self Medication
Sex Change
Shock Therapy
Sleep Treatment
Stereotaxic Techniques
Surgery
Sympathectomy
Thalamotomy
Thyroidectomy
Tractotomy
Tubal Ligation
Vagotomy
Vasectomy
Vitamin Therapy

Psychotherapy

Adolescent Psychotherapy
Age Regression (Hypnotic)
Analytical Psychotherapy
Autogenic Training
Bibliotherapy
Brief Psychotherapy
Centering
Child Psychotherapy
Client Centered Therapy
Cognitive Restructuring
Cognitive Techniques
Cognitive Therapy
Conjoint Therapy
Consultation Liaison Psychiatry
Cotherapy
Countertransference
Couples Therapy
Crisis Intervention
Directed Reverie Therapy
Dream Analysis
Eclectic Psychotherapy
Existential Therapy
Experiential Psychotherapy
Expressive Psychotherapy
Family Therapy
Feminist Therapy
Geriatric Psychotherapy
Gestalt Therapy
Group Psychotherapy
Hypnotherapy
Individual Psychotherapy
Insight (Psychotherapeutic Process)
Insight Therapy
Logotherapy
Marathon Group Therapy
Marriage Counseling

Morita Therapy
Mutual Storytelling Technique
Outpatient Treatment
Paradoxical Techniques
Personal Therapy
Persuasion Therapy
Play Therapy
Primal Therapy
Psychoanalysis
Psychodrama
Psychotherapeutic Breakthrough
Psychotherapeutic Counseling
Psychotherapeutic Outcomes
Psychotherapeutic Processes
Psychotherapeutic Resistance
Psychotherapeutic Techniques
Psychotherapeutic Transference
Psychotherapy
Rational Emotive Therapy
Reality Therapy
Relationship Therapy
Self Analysis
Self Help Techniques
Social Casework
Therapeutic Community
Transactional Analysis

Rehabilitation

Activities of Daily Living
Adaptive Behavior
Alcohol Rehabilitation
Alcoholics Anonymous
Augmentative Communication
Cochlear Implants
Cognitive Rehabilitation
Detoxification
Disability Management
Drug Rehabilitation
Habilitation
Halfway Houses
Mainstreaming
Memory Training
Methadone Maintenance
Occupational Therapy
Physical Therapy
Prostheses
Psychosocial Rehabilitation
Rehabilitation
Rehabilitation Centers
Rehabilitation Counseling
Sheltered Workshops
Smoking Cessation
Speech Therapy
Therapeutic Social Clubs
Vocational Evaluation
Vocational Rehabilitation
Work Adjustment Training

Treatment (General)

Advance Directives
Aftercare

AIDS Prevention
Autopsy
Biological Psychiatry
Biopsychosocial Approach
Caregiver Burden
Caregivers
Child Psychiatry
Child Psychology
Childbirth Training
Client Education
Clinical Psychology
Community Mental Health
Cost Containment
Cross Cultural Treatment
Discharge Planning
Drug Abuse Prevention
Drug Education
Early Intervention
Fee for Service
Health Care Costs
Health Care Delivery
Health Care Policy
Health Care Psychology
Health Care Services
Health Care Utilization
Health Education
Health Insurance
Health Promotion
Help Seeking Behavior
Holistic Health
Informed Consent
Intake Interview
Interdisciplinary Treatment Approach
Involuntary Treatment
Long Term Care
Managed Care
Medicaid
Medical Patients
Medical Psychology
Medical Records Keeping
Medical Treatment (General)
Medicare
Multimodal Treatment Approach
Needs Assessment
Nonprescription Drugs
Optical Aids
Outpatient Commitment
Palliative Care
Patient Abuse
Patient History
Patient Seclusion
Physical Examination
Posttreatment Followup
Prescribing (Drugs)
Prescription Drugs
Primary Mental Health Prevention
Private Practice
Professional Client Sexual Relations
Psychiatric Patients
Psychoeducation
Psychotherapeutic Processes

Consult Relationship Section for more information

Treatment (General) — (cont'd)

Quality of Care
Relapse Prevention
Respite Care
Self Examination (Medical)
Self Medication
Self Referral
Sex Education
Side Effects (Treatment)
Social Psychiatry
Social Services
Surgical Patients
Therapeutic Alliance
Therapeutic Processes
Therapist Selection
Treatment

Treatment Compliance
Treatment Dropouts
Treatment Duration
Treatment Effectiveness Evaluation
Treatment Outcomes
Treatment Refusal
Treatment Termination
Treatment Withholding

Treatment Facilities

Child Guidance Clinics
Clinics
Community Facilities
Community Mental Health Centers
Community Mental Health Services
Day Care Centers
Health Maintenance Organizations

Hospitals
Mental Health Programs
Mental Health Services
Nursing Homes
Orphanages
Psychiatric Clinics
Psychiatric Hospitals
Psychiatric Units
Public Health Services
Rehabilitation Centers
Residential Care Institutions
Sanatoriums
Social Services
Suicide Prevention Centers
Therapeutic Community
Treatment Facilities
Walk In Clinics

Consult Relationship Section for more information